Published in the series:
1. *Supranational Criminal Law: a System Sui Generis*, ROELOF HAVEMAN, OLGA KAVRAN and JULIAN NICHOLS (eds.)
2. *Double Jeopardy Without Parameters: Re-characterization in International Criminal Law*, OLAOLUWA OLUSANYA
3. *Harmonization of Criminal Law in Europe*, ERLING JOHANNES HUSABØ and ASBJØRN STRANDBAKKEN (eds.)
4. *Sentencing and Sanctioning in Supranational Criminal Law*, ROELOF HAVEMAN and OLAOLUWA OLUSANYA (eds.)
5. *Application of International Humanitarian and Human Rights Law to the Armed Conflicts of the Sudan: Complementary or Mutually Exclusive Regimes?*, MOHAMED ABDELSALAM BABIKER
6. *Supranational Criminology: Towards a Criminology of International Crimes*, ALETTE SMEULERS and ROELOF HAVEMAN (eds.)
7. *Individual Criminal Liability for the International Crime of Aggression*, GERHARD KEMP
8. *Collective Violence and International Criminal Justice – An Interdisciplinary Approach*, ALETTE SMEULERS (ed.)
9. *International Criminal Law from a Swedish Perspective*, IAIN CAMERON, MALIN THUNBERG SCHUNKE, KARIN PÅLE BARTES, CHRISTOFFER WONG and PETTER ASP
10. *The Implementation of the European Arrest Warrant in the European Union: Law, Policy and Practice*, MASSIMO FICHERA
11. *The Principle of Mutual Recognition in Cooperation in Criminal Matters*, ANNIKA SUOMINEN
12. *The European Public Prosecutor's Office*, MARTIJN WILLEM ZWIERS

Editors:
Dr. Roelof H. Haveman (editor in chief)
Dr. Paul J.A. De Hert (European Law)
Dr. Alette L. Smeulers (Criminology)

VICTIMOLOGICAL APPROACHES TO INTERNATIONAL CRIMES: AFRICA

Edited by

Rianne LETSCHERT
Roelof HAVEMAN
Anne-Marie DE BROUWER
Antony PEMBERTON

intersentia

Cambridge – Antwerp – Portland

Intersentia Ltd
Trinity House | Cambridge Business Park | Cowley Road
Cambridge | CB4 0WZ | United Kingdom
mail@intersentia.co.uk

Distribution for the UK:
Hart Publishing Ltd.
16C Worcester Place
Oxford OX1 2JW
UK
Tel.: +44 1865 51 75 30
Email: mail@hartpub.co.uk

Distribution for the USA and Canada:
International Specialized Book Services
920 NE 58th Ave. Suite 300
Portland, OR 97213
USA
Tel.: +1 800 944 6190 (toll free)
Email: info@isbs.com

Distribution for Austria:
Neuer Wissenschaftlicher Verlag
Argentinierstraße 42/6
1040 Wien
Austria
Tel.: +43 1 535 61 03 24
Email: office@nwv.at

Distribution for other countries:
Intersentia Publishers
Groenstraat 31
2640 Mortsel
Belgium
Tel.: +32 3 680 15 50
Email: mail@intersentia.be

Victimological Approaches to International Crimes: Africa
Rianne Letschert, Roelof Haveman, Anne-Marie de Brouwer and Antony
Pemberton (eds.)

© 2011 Intersentia
Cambridge – Antwerp – Portland
www.intersentia.com | www.intersentia.co.uk

Cover illustration: Francisco de Goya (1746-1828), Etching, Plate 15 from The
Disparates

ISBN 978-94-000-0090-2
NUR 828

British Library Cataloguing in Publication Data. A catalogue record for this
book is available from the British Library.

WORDS OF APPRECIATION

We would like to express some special words of appreciation. First, we wish to thank the director of TAI/GLR, Alphonse Muleefu, who was instrumental in organising the conference and inviting local stakeholders from Rwanda and other African countries. Secondly, we thank Tim van den Meijdenberg, student assistant at the department of Criminal Law of Tilburg Law School, who was responsible for compiling the bibliography list. Finally, a special word of thank you goes to Tilburg Law School, whose ambition to encourage international and interdisciplinary projects and facilitate networking seminars enabled us to pursue this project by covering for the expenses made.

CONTENTS

INTRODUCTION: VICTIMOLOGICAL APPROACHES TO INTERNATIONAL CRIMES

In 2009, the International Victimology Institute Tilburg (INTERVICT/Tilburg University, the Netherlands), in collaboration with Together Against Impunity in the Great Lakes Region (TAI/GLR) (a Rwandan NGO focusing on victims' rights), The Legal Aid Forum (a platform with member organisations engaged in the provision of legal aid services to indigent and vulnerable groups in Rwanda) and Ibuka (the umbrella organization for genocide survivors organizations in Rwanda), organized a five days international conference in Kigali, Rwanda, on developing victimological approaches applied to international crimes – genocide, crimes against humanity and war crimes – with a focus on Africa. A mix of academics and practitioners participated in the conference, composed of a combination of insiders describing the processes they helped establish and guide outsiders with more theoretical expert knowledge on these processes. The speakers came from different academic disciplines and from all over the world. Moreover, several speakers of Rwandan NGOs, universities and governmental organizations were invited who shared their experiences coming from a country in which genocide took place so recently. The valuable input from representatives of NGOs enabled to combine the academic perspective with reflections from people working on the ground. In addition, the visits to various genocide memorials left an unforgettable impression on the participants and enriched our understanding of the complexities at hand. This book contains the results of the conference in four clusters, which reflect the conference themes.[1]

The wide range of topics addressed was instrumental in guaranteeing in-depth and constructive discussions on developing victimological approaches

---

[1] Some participants in the conference did not contribute to this book, but did participate actively in the conference for which we would like to thank them. They concern, in random order: Jeanne Marie Ntete (psychologist, National University of Rwanda, Rwanda); Charles Ntare (FACT and The Legal Aid Forum, Rwanda); Justice Elizabeth Nahamya (High Court, Uganda); Annelies Hellemans (researcher Katholieke Universiteit Leuven/Leuven Institute of Criminology, Belgium); Francesca Capone (PhD researcher, Scuola Superiore Sant'Anna, Italy); Theodore Simburudari, Immaculée Mukankubito and Benoit Kaboyi (Ibuka, Rwanda); Pastor Antoine Rutayisire and Oswald Rutimburana (National Unity and Reconciliation Commission, Rwanda); Albert Nzamukwereka (Radio La Benevolencija, Rwanda); Eric Kabera (Rwanda Cinema Centre); and Alphonse Sebazungu (Deputy Attorney General, Ministry of Justice) who opened the conference.

to international crimes. Correcting the unsettling observation that one stands a better chance of being tried and judged for killing one human being than for killing 100,000 has been a driving force behind the (international) criminal justice initiatives focusing on international crimes. The establishment of the International Criminal Tribunal for the former Yugoslavia (ICTY) in 1993, followed a year later by a sister institution for Rwanda (ICTR), signalled the first steps of the global community in addressing these crimes. The move was later replicated in the form of internationalized tribunals, such as those for Sierra Leone, Cambodia, East Timor and Lebanon. Since all these tribunals are *ad hoc* in nature, the establishment of a permanent International Criminal Court (ICC) in 1998 is considered to be a milestone in the development of a legal response to the aforementioned atrocities. The ICC became operational in 2002. In its first years, the ICC has focused on Africa trying crimes committed in the Central African Republic (CAR), the Democratic Republic of the Congo (DRC), Northern Uganda, Darfur in Sudan, Kenya and Libya. There are several other countries in Africa and elsewhere which might fall under the ICC's jurisdiction and might call for the ICC's involvement in the future.

These international criminal legal approaches have considerable shortcomings in dealing with victims of genocide, war crimes and crimes against humanity. Much focus has been on punishment of a small group of the main responsible offenders and on retribution. Victims' suffering and needs have hardly been a priority. Formal criminal justice mechanisms have generally overlooked the fact that, while the damage caused to society and humanity at large is real, the sufferance incurred by the direct victims is, at least, as great and deserves much more attention than has been the case so far (Drumbl 2007)·.

The notion that the needs and views of victims and survivors of international crimes are insufficiently represented in the formal criminal justice response is one of the main impetuses behind the development of other forms of providing redress to victims of international crimes, such as for instance tradition-based responses and truth commissions. Here the emphasis is not (only) on the punishment of offenders, but on unravelling the narrative of the international crimes committed, simultaneously offering victims an opportunity to voice their experiences and receive acknowledgement of the wrongs committed against them. However, where the formal criminal justice response may lay too much emphasis on punishing the offenders of crimes, the experience with truth commissions suggests that here, also from the victims point of view, there is too little emphasis on retribution. Also, the implementation of recommendations made by truth commissions aiming to provide reparation to victims has been largely unsatisfactory. This implies that from a societal and academic point of view, one of the most vexing questions confronting the development of transitional justice is how to balance and maybe combine the strengths of truth commissions with an (international) criminal justice response (Roht-Arriazza & Mariezcurrena 2006).

The legal response is thus neither the only nor necessarily the most important aspect of meeting victims' needs in the aftermath of genocide, crimes against humanity and war crimes. Many victims of such crimes deal with a full-scale disruption of their entire lives. They may have suffered (extreme) physical and psychological damage, for which medical and psychological assistance is often necessary. They regularly have an urgent need for compensation for their financial losses and may have additional material needs, for example relating to housing or employment. The problems faced by individual victims are compounded by the fact that most international crimes lead to mass victimization in situations of large scale conflicts. The massive number of victims and offenders poses challenges to societal recovery. Individual and collective victimization; the resulting trauma but also the sometimes changing roles between victims and offenders are some of the challenges to post-conflict recovery. Furthermore, the inescapable reality of the victims who have to live together with their offenders after the conflict is an enormous challenge for the efforts to assist victims to come to terms with their experiences.

The peculiar situation of victims of international crimes calls for a comprehensive approach that links various relevant fields such as traumatic stress, the social psychology of group conflict and resolution and the psychology and sociology of legal processes. The latter is important in its own right, but also for the ongoing efforts in transitional and international criminal justice, as it can provide the empirical underpinning of the choices and developments in these fields. Transcending the disciplinary divisions in the study of victims of international crimes is the main focus of this volume of victimological essays. Focusing on Africa, the stage for most of the international crimes committed in recent years, scholars and experts from different disciplines will reflect on a variety of ways to address the intricacies of victimization by international crimes. This endeavour transcends academic interest, as an approach of this kind is essential to mend societies ravaged by genocide, crimes against humanity and/or war crimes.

The first part provides the first general impetus to devising a victimological framework applied to international crimes. It draws, among other things, from existing victimological notions and theories developed in mainstream victimology. Contributors argue that the demand to advance the cause of victims recognizing them as autonomous stakeholders with particular rights has implications for the criminal justice model, especially at the international level (Groenhuijsen & Pemberton; Chouliaras). Part I shows the importance of including survivors' voices and the historical context in any analysis, since often in conflict-torn societies, gross victimizations are linked to historical victimizations and how they are perceived in the collective memory (Ruvebana). Another topic addressed in this part relates to the erosion of the myth of pure evil which depicts the world in two absolutes in which evil and guilty perpetrators attack good and innocent victims. This discussion demonstrates the difficulties in conceptualising victimhood in war torn societies. Although it would be appealing to consider victims and perpetrators as two mutually exclusive groups, this does not always reflect reality (Smeulers; Erez & Meroz-Aharoni).

The second part deals with various aspects of reparative justice. Reparative justice in the context of international crimes can be loosely defined as the total of initiatives and measures seeking to ensure that all persons victimized are offered an adequate level of protection under the law. Contributors discuss the challenges in finding an adequate balance between the needs of individual victims and the collective when designing and implementing reparative measures (Wemmers; Letschert & Van Boven; Correa). Part II also demonstrates the need to devise a comprehensive framework of reparative justice, aiming to overcome the severe trauma victims have suffered during a period of mass atrocities (Danieli).

The third part focuses on a variety of non-criminal approaches to international crimes. The times that a criminal approach to mass atrocities was considered the one and only approach fitting each and every situation of mass atrocities is since long gone. Even the times that other approaches were seen as 'alternatives' to the criminal one has silently passed. No one can ignore any longer the existence of other approaches, such as providing amnesty, truth and reconciliation mechanisms and tradition-inspired mechanisms. The effect and impact of granting amnesties to perpetrators of international crimes to justice and reconciliation is the focus of two chapters (Haldemann; Van Wijk). Further, the difficulties in reaching some form of reconciliation (be it on the interpersonal, community, international, political, or social level) is addressed, drawing from the experience of the South-African Truth and Reconciliation Commission (Peacock) and by referring to empirical studies carried out in Bosnia (Parmentier & Sullo). Three chapters present examples of how tradition-inspired mechanisms aim to provide redress to victims of international crimes (Schotsmans; Kaitesi & Haveman; Ndahinda) Also, the important role of civil society in addressing the needs of victims is stressed (Muleefu).

The fourth part of the book mainly deals with international and national legal and policy approaches. Despite its relatively short existence, the ICC has already been instrumental in creating and expanding on victims' rights, such as the right to participate in trial proceedings and to request reparation. However, to effectively organize in practice the participation of victims during the proceedings remains a difficult task (McGronigle Leyh). This pertains even more to victims of sexual violence (Mesters & Adeboyejo; Chu, De Brouwer & Römkens); crimes which the international community are increasingly paying heed to and for which preventive measures are slowly being put into place (Chu,

De Brouwer & Römkens). With regard to children, the international tribunals have only slowly recognized the importance of child participation and testimony in trial proceedings, despite the large-scale impact conflict has had on children (Grossman). In general, given their limited mandate, the international criminal tribunals will only be capable of pursuing a handful of cases, with a focus on those most responsible. The exercise by states of universal jurisdiction is therefore important in establishing accountability for international crimes, and ensuring that there are no 'safe havens'. The territorial state, however, should still be the primary state responsible for prosecuting international crimes, be it through the classical state penal system or – more contested – through tradition-inspired mechanisms (Ferstman & Schurr; Ndahinda).

The book ends with a chapter elaborating on the different elements needed to devise comprehensive victimological approaches applied to international crimes. It also provides a tentative agenda for future studies. The bibliography in this book provides an overview of the wealth of literature from various disciplines that can be used when studying the victimology of international crimes.

In 2012, a follow-up conference will be organized in Cambodia, where we will continue studying these themes and simultaneously review the Asian context. This will not only further enrich the already gathered material, but will also enable us to analyse potential regional and/or cultural differences as well as similarities concerning victimological approaches to international crimes.

Editors, June 2011

PART I
VICTIMS OF
INTERNATIONAL CRIMES

I. GENOCIDE, CRIMES AGAINST HUMANITY AND WAR CRIMES

A Victimological Perspective on International Criminal Justice

Marc S. GROENHUIJSEN and Antony PEMBERTON

1. INTRODUCTION

Violence is a human universal.[1] It is of all times. This relativist truism should not cloud our awareness of the fact that during the past century interpersonal violence has acquired a new dimension. The 20th century has demonstrated mass violence on a scale and with an intensity hitherto unknown to mankind (e.g. Glover 2001; Mazower 2002). To name but a few sobering examples: there were the two World Wars, the horrors of the Stalinist era and the cultural revolution in China, the killing fields in Cambodia, the atrocities in the Balkans, and quite a few so-called regional conflicts on the African continent (see e.g. Power 2003; Mann 2005; Prunier 2009). The atrocities involved hundreds of millions of casualties.[2] Like never before, the lethal combination of human flaws and modern technology and weaponry created an opportunity to inflict suffering beyond comprehension.

There has been another shift worth noticing. During previous centuries, mass violence was closely connected to warfare, while the latter was primarily an affair between the armies of sovereign nations. Hence the individuals who used to pay the ultimate price for these conflicts were predominantly professional soldiers. In the course of the 20th century this has gradually changed. In the First World War, a significant majority of casualties still came from military ranks. The Second World War reduced this proportion to some 50%, with the other half taken from the civilian population. During the Vietnam War, some 70% of

---

[1]   See for instance Baumeister 2005.
[2]   The exact figure is unclear but according to the figures reported in McNamara & Blight (2001) 160 million people died in wars, while Rummel (1994) mentions a similar figure for '20th century democide'. Accounting for some overlap the total sum should be estimated to be somewhere between 250 million and 300 million deaths.

ordinary civilians accounted for the total loss of life. In subsequent armed conflicts, this percentage further increased (Valentino 2005). In a macabre sense there is evidence of an unmistakable 'civilization of warfare' (see e.g. Chesterman 2001).

These developments necessitated the definition of new concepts of crime. Mass violence, often committed in the name of the State, called for its own labels to capture the essence of this new level of injustice (see Lemkin 1947; Bassiouni 1992; Power 2003). The abuse of sovereign power inherent in these atrocities led to the development of the so-called international crimes: crimes against humanity, war crimes and the crime of genocide.

Besides new categories of perpetrators, the conflicts of the 20th century also established a new kind of victims: victims of mass violence. It is noteworthy to review how the academic community dealt with this topic. We contend that academia's response has been rather paradoxical. On the one hand, it can be argued that the horrors of the Second World War form part of the roots of the academic field of study called 'victimology' (van Dijk, Groenhuijsen & Winkel 2007, 10). After all, it was Hans von Hentig, supposedly one of the founders of this discipline, who mused in his military hospital bed in Jerusalem at the end of the war:

> *Why in history has everyone always focused on the guy with the big stick, the hero, the activist, to the neglect of the poor slob who is at the end of the stick, the victim, the passivist – or maybe, the poor slob (in bandages) isn't all that much of a passive victim – maybe he asked for it?* (quoted in Mueller & Adler 2005).

Hence the suffering brought about by the Nazi-regime is a main source of inspiration for the systematic study of causes and effects of victimization.

Yet on the other hand it cannot be denied that over the course of the following decades the new branch of research was largely preoccupied with victims of ordinary crime. Similar to criminology[3] and with a few notable exceptions,[4] mainstream victimology has concentrated on small scale crime. It is only after the atrocities in Rwanda and the former Yugoslavia and the subsequent developments in international criminal law (the Tribunals for Yugoslavia and Rwanda and the International Criminal Court) that criminologists recognised the need to develop a specialised criminology of international crimes (Smeulers & Haveman 2008). In its slipstream victimology has now rediscovered victims of international crimes as a special target group for academic research.

This chapter is structured as follows. First we will outline some of the features that distinguish the international crimes from criminal behaviour in the

---

[3]   See e.g. Smeulers & Haveman (2008); Hagan & Rymond-Richmond (2009) for a discussion of criminology's neglect of international crimes.

[4]   Such as Yael Danieli, Irene Mellup, and other representatives of the World Society of Victimology who insisted on including victims of abuse of power in the UN Declaration.

domestic sphere (section 2). In the subsequent sections these features will be examined in more detail (sections 3–5). We will reflect on these special features and use our reflections to develop a victimological framework concerning international criminal justice (concluding section 6).

From the above it follows that our observations cover a lot of ground. This chapter provides a general frame of reference for the rest of the volume, by identifying some of the basic problems and by providing an account of what directions the search for solutions might take. In quite a few instances, we leave the more in depth analyses to our colleagues.

2. SPECIAL FEATURES OF GENOCIDE, WAR CRIMES AND CRIMES AGAINST HUMANITY

In what way are the international crimes under consideration defined? For present purposes, it is not necessary to trace the historical roots of this branch of criminal law.[5] Suffice it to say that they originated in instruments of international law.[6] We will rely on the wording in the Rome Statute, since this represents the current state of the art (likewise: Haveman & Smeulers 2008, 15).

The most serious crime, then, is genocide.[7] Article 6 of the ICC Statute conceives of it as acts such as murder or measures to prevent births when committed with the intent to destroy, in whole or in part, a national, ethnical, racial or religious group, as such.

War crimes are delineated in Article 8 of the ICC Statute. These amount to grave breaches and other serious violations of the law of the war, in particular when committed as part of a plan or policy or as a part of a large scale commission of such crimes.[8]

Article 7 of the ICC Statute concerns crimes against humanity. These are described as acts such as[9] murder, deportation and rape, if and when committed

---

[5] See Bassiouni 1992.
[6] For genocide: the UN Convention on the Prevention and Punishment of the Crime of Genocide, Res. 260 A (III) 1948. For war crimes (grave breaches and other serious violations of the laws or customs of war), reference should be made to the 1949 Geneva Conventions and 1977 Additional Protocols. For crimes against humanity: the Neuremberg Charter, the Tokyo Charter and the Statutes of the ICTY, the ICTR and the ICC.
[7] In academic literature this is often referred to as 'the crime of crimes', or similar designations. De Brouwer 2005, 83 argues for an amended definition of genocide that includes genocidal rape and gender as a group.
[8] We are forced to give a general summary: Article 8 consists of 50 different subparagraphs.
[9] 'Such as' meaning that the list of concrete acts in Article 7 is enumerative rather than exhaustive. This is also evidenced by Article 7(1)(k), reading: "other inhumane acts of a similar character intentionally causing great suffering, or serious injury to body or to mental or physical health."

as part of a widespread or systematic attack directed against any civilian population, with knowledge of the attack.

Comparing the definitions of the major international crimes, they appear to have at least three features in common (see also Kauzlarich, Matthews & Miller 2001) which – taken together – distinguish them from domestic crimes. First, government agencies are complicit in the behaviour that is criminalized.[10] The State participates in or at least condones the commission of these crimes and the direct or indirect involvement of government officials is conspicuous. As Luban (2005) calls it, these are situations of 'politics gone cancerous'.

Secondly, the definitions consistently point to instances of mass victimisation. In the case of genocide it is a 'group' which lacked adequate protection; in the wording of war crimes reference is made to 'a plan or a policy' or 'large scale commission of crimes'; and crimes against humanity are only possible when there is a 'widespread or systematic attack' against a 'civilian *population*'. All of these phrases only apply to a multitude of victims, quite often even a vast number of victims when compared to conventional crime.

The third feature of these international crimes is not so much evident by their definition in the ICC Statute, but becomes clear when one looks beyond the legal wording to the underlying reality. It concerns the relationship between the victims of these international crimes and their perpetrators. In fact, it is not so much a relationship as well as a perception of a complete absence of 'normal' human relationships. To be more precise: the relevant international crimes are usually committed by perpetrators who conceive of the victims as perpetrators of crime or even atrocity themselves (e.g. Mann 2005; Staub 1992; Waller 2007). And with this comes the connotation of 'enemies', of 'other' people who are dangerous. It is obvious that this special feature of the crimes under consideration usually is implicitly or explicitly invoked by those guilty of the acts to justify their deeds, but it also has consequences for the preferred way of reacting to injustice from the victims' perspective.

Each of the special features has victimological significance. In the following sections we will discuss each of them in turn and summarize their implications in terms of victimological theories.

---

[10] Technically the crime of genocide may be perpetrated by individuals. The crime of genocide, unlike the crimes against humanity and war crimes is defined by the collective nature of the *victim population*, which is targeted for extermination, rather than that of the perpetrators (Luban 2005). Indeed close inspection of the definition reveals that as long as there is *intent* to destroy a group, a single instance of violence may fulfill the definition. However, there is no instance of genocide of which we are aware that did not involve collective perpetration. Indeed as will be discussed in more detail in section 5, the perpetration of genocide normally involves a complex social process that includes many people in a variety of roles (e.g. Waller 2007).

3. VICTIMS OF CRIME COMMITTED OR CONDONED BY THE STATE

Genocide, crimes against humanity and war crimes are usually committed under the cover of state authority. This fact alone accounts in large part for the so-called culture of impunity (e.g. Akhavan 2001; Crocker 1998; McSherry & Molina Mejia 1992). Former UN High Commissioner for Human Rights Lasso has stated that "a person stands a better chance of being tried and judged for killing one human being than for killing 100,000", which has been repeatedly confirmed by research and experience (e.g. Opotow 2001). Some insights in this phenomenon are necessary for the development of our victimological perspective. Hence the following reflections.

3.1. THE CULTURE OF IMPUNITY AS THE ULTIMATE PERVERSION OF THE RULE OF LAW

Let us briefly dwell on the foundations of a legal order. In essence, every legal system is aimed at the protection of its citizens. This is hard to capture in just a couple of well phrased sentences, but at its core this constitutes the vital difference between the *rule of law* and the *rule of men*. Legal subjects, ordinary people, citizens of the State should not only be protected by the system against fellow citizens and against enemies from the outside world, but above all against the potential enemy from within: i.e. against those persons within the jurisdiction who possess the definitional power, the power to determine the difference between right and wrong (e.g. Arendt 1970).

The most precious spot – and at the same time the most vulnerable one – of any legal order can be identified as the place where the content is defined of which types of behaviour shall be acknowledged as crime and which acts shall be considered as justified. In the well know vocabulary of H.L.A. Hart: in the end, every jurisdiction is based on an *ultimate rule of recognition* (Hart 1961). This rule of recognition has a formal nature. The point of concern here is that we have individuals and bodies operating the system who are charged with the institutional power to determine the way in which the 'rule of recognition' shall be substantively applied. In a democracy this is the majority (usually the majority of the parliament). In other societies it can be a more limited number of people, or even just one man. Those who are possessed with this definitional power bear a huge responsibility. Those who abuse the definitional power, the power to distinguish right from wrong, manoeuvre the people, the population, the citizens of society, into a defenceless position. Completely defenceless even, because the whole machinery of the State is geared towards enforcement of the validly proclaimed obtaining laws and its procedures rest on the truth of the claims to knowledge that are inherent in these laws. It logically follows that abusing the definitional power just referred to, constitutes the most fundamental perversion of the rule of law that can be conceived of within any legal order. Taking the argument one step further, the same applies to abusing the State monopoly on the use of physical force.

This is the core essence of many genocides, crimes against humanity and war crimes. Either formally or materially, the exact same power that was established in order to *protect* the citizens is then employed to *harm* them or even to *kill* a substantial number of them.[11] For the individual citizens involved, there is no defence available within the confines of that legal order. The severe damage wreaked by the international crimes is further compounded by the apparent support by society and even legality of these instances of extreme cruelty.

3.2. REINSTATING THE RULE OF LAW: BACKWARD AND FORWARD LOOKING ASPECTS

Now that we have gained some insight in the nature of the extreme injustices created by the international crimes, the next question is what this means in terms of considering a legitimate reaction. The answers to the ultimate perversion of the rule of law do not necessarily have to be limited to the same measures we deem adequate for responding to 'ordinary' violations of – or threats to – the legal order.[12]

As Teitel (2002) shows, reinstating the rule of law has 'backward' and 'forward-looking' aspects.[13] It should be backward-looking by offering a legal reaction to the mass atrocities committed under the previous regime. In a manner keeping with both its purpose (i.e. the protection of citizens versus arbitrary treatment; e.g. Radin 1989) and main features (presumption of innocence for the suspect and the like, see Aukerman 2002), the rule of law is formally reinstated as a reaction to criminal wrongdoing.

The forward-looking function relates to the rule of law in a material sense. Both legal scholars (e.g. Fallon 2005) and social scientists (e.g. Tyler 2003) confirm that perceived legitimacy of government and legal authorities are essential for the rule of law to take root. Inhabitants of countries where the rule of law has broken down and/or has been perverted, have evidently good reason

---

[11] Not all genocidal regimes have extended the perversion of the *formal* legal framework to the extremes of Nazi-Germany, re the well-known debate at the Wannsee conference concerning the legal framework of the Holocaust. See for an overview Mann 2005.

[12] Indeed Aukerman (2002) concludes that the analogy of ordinary crime to the situation of international crimes is sometimes surprisingly ill-fitting.

[13] The reader should take care to refrain from confusing these backward and forward looking functions with the retributive (indeed reactive) and preventative (forward-looking) functions of criminal justice procedures in the domestic context.

to withhold this perception of legitimacy. In our view, this means that, more so than at the national level, the legal reaction to international crimes should affirm 'the value of law, strengthen social solidarity and incubate moral consensus among the public' (Drumbl 2007, 17), or in other words the expressivist function of criminal justice (Feinberg 1970). Expressivism here concerns the messaging effect of the reaction to crime (e.g. Drumbl 2007).[14]

3.3. REACTING TO ATROCITIES: ADAPTING CRIMINAL JUSTICE

It strikes us that international criminal justice has until now primarily focused on the backward-looking aspects of reinstating the rule of law. Indeed the adaptation of criminal justice principles to the situation of international crimes is mainly related to this backward looking function.

In an attempt to halt the culture of impunity, to make trials for the crimes committed under the rogue regime an attainable objective, international criminal justice violates principles of criminal law and criminal procedure which are in normal circumstances regarded as valuable, even as virtually sacrosanct. Extraordinary remedies form part and parcel of the reaction to international crimes. A prime example of this is the criminalisation ex post facto. This occurred in the wake of the Second World War, both in domestic jurisdictions and in connection with the tribunals set up in Nuremberg and Tokyo. The exception made to the fundamental principle of *nullum crimen, nulla poena sine praevia lege poenali* was deliberately accepted as the price to be paid to make justice possible.[15] In a similar vein the penalties for crimes included in criminal codes were made more severe at a point in time when the illegal acts had already been committed.

A third example of an extraordinary remedy is the situation where an amnesty law that was adopted by the government guilty of large scale violations of human rights is subsequently nullified by the succeeding government. During the past decades this has happened several times (e.g. Snyder & Vinjamuri 2004). Usually, the justification for this drastic measure has been found in principles of international customary law.

Finally, we point to the maxim *male captus, bene detentus* and the doctrine of universal jurisdiction. The maxim, a procedural declaration, holds that when someone is apprehended by authorities exceeding their legal powers, the State

---

[14] In fact we use expressivism in a slightly more expansive way than Drumbl (2007) does. He conceives it to be the purpose of trials, punishment and verdicts, see also Amann (2001), while we consider it can be applied to other elements of the reaction to crime as well.

[15] See generally the well-known debate of Hart and Fuller (both 1958), Bassiouni 1996, Boot 2001 and for a full overview and rebuttal of arguments against the charge of retro-activity, Quint 2000.

shall nevertheless be considered competent to try and convict that person (Paulussen 2010). The most prominent example of this is the abduction of Eichman by Israeli authorities – in direct violation of the rights of the sovereign State of Argentina – which did not prevent them from staging a trial and procuring a conviction. The doctrine of universal jurisdiction removes the territorial limits of the competence of national courts (Bassiouni 2001; see also Ferstmann & Schurr, this volume). Where this competence normally only relates to events within the states borders, matters with direct implications for the states affairs or involving the states' inhabitants, universal jurisdiction means that, for the relevant international crimes, none of these restrictions apply.

3.4. SOME UNRESOLVED QUESTIONS IN INTERNATIONAL CRIMINAL JUSTICE

However, other principles of criminal law have not been adapted, even though there is reason to question their applicability in situations of international crime. A full discussion of these differences is beyond the scope of our current endeavour, nor do we intend to pass judgement on the preferred way of dealing with these tensions, but the following issues are important:

- The complexities of establishing individual guilt for crimes committed as a collective and/ or in the name of a collective (e.g. Drumbl 2005; Levinson 2003; Osiel 2005); in other words the discrepancy between collective responsibility for the crimes committed and individual guilt;[16]
- The uncertain line between culpable and inculpable parties (Osiel 2000), including the role of bystanders (Drumbl 2007; Fletcher 2005; Staub 1996);
- The abundance of evidence of collective evil, coupled with a lack of proof of individual wrongdoing;
- The difficulty of finding a remedy suitable to the enormity of the crimes committed (Osiel 2000; 2005);
- And coupled with the previous points the diminished likelihood of reaching 'traditional' goals of criminal justice like retribution and general or special prevention (Aukerman 2002).

---

[16]   The definition of international crimes in terms of collective perpetration, sits somewhat uneasily with the attempts to place the blame exclusively on individuals (see also Luban 2005). Indeed one can question the almost religious insistence on strict liberal legalism (see already a convincing critique in Shklar 1964) by many human rights scholars. Even a remote departure from this philosophy is attacked and ridiculed (e.g. viewing Joint Criminal Enterprise to be synonymous to 'Just Convict Everybody'), without any empirical support (see Aukerman 2002).

International criminal justice is wrestling with some of these issues (e.g. the debate concerning command responsibility and joint criminal enterprise; see Danner & Martinez 2005; Osiel 2005), has not paid much attention to others (clearly articulating (the limits of) its goals and aims) and may in fact just not be suitable to some. Indeed there appears to be an imbalance between the overtly optimistic and triumphant rhetoric surrounding international criminal justice and the extent to which it can or should be expected to deliver justice in the aftermath of international crimes (e.g. Drumbl 2005; 2007).

3.5. A RUPTURE BETWEEN BACKWARD AND FORWARD-LOOKING FUNCTIONS OF ICJ

The point we want to stress here is that the difficulties mentioned put pressure on the presumed link between the backward-looking and forward-looking aspects of reinstating the rule of law. Where many scholars and human rights advocates assert that holding trials for previous atrocities will automatically contribute to rebuilding the rule of law (e.g. Orentlicher 1991; Landsman 1996), there is good reason and evidence to think otherwise (e.g. Drumbl 2007, Fletcher & Weinstein 2002; Snyder & Vinjamuri 2004; Vinjamuri & Snyder 2004). The theoretical underpinning of this automatism rests to a greater degree on good faith than good science. The notion that a norm cascade (see Finnemore and Sikkink 1998) will lead the ravaged societies to replicate the good example of international criminal justice in their own domestic legal system is not confirmed by the evidence (Snyder & Vinjamuri 2004). As Snyder and Vinjamuri (2004, 6) succinctly state: "Justice does not lead; it follows". Even the inevitable first step in this line of reasoning – that international criminal proceedings will succeed in delivering a sense of justice – is suspect. The extent to which this is likely to be the case is hampered both by the experience of these crimes in itself[17] and the awkward relationship between individualized criminal justice and collective perpetration. This is further compounded by at least three other problems, which all feed on each other.

In the first place international criminal justice in the aftermath of atrocities is necessarily selective. Only a minority of perpetrators will be tried for their crimes and although the aim will be to try the 'Big Fish', it is in fact likely that the difficulties in establishing individual culpability for the leaders of the

---

[17]   We have noted that the experience of the breakdown of the rule of law will inevitably limit the trust that a victimized population will have in the legitimacy of law and authorities. In addition the negative impact of victimisation in terms of psychological consequences will also have a detrimental effect on victims' perception of justice. Victims suffering from PTSD are less likely to see the trial as having a fair outcome (Phom *et al.* 2004; Orth *et al.* 2006) and recent research show similar effects concerning victims with extreme feelings of anger (Murphy & Tyler 2008).

atrocities will mean that relatively low level officials, the 'Small Fry', will bear the brunt of the criminal law reaction (Goldstone 1996).[18] This leads to a discrepancy between (perceived) wrongdoing and punishment, which is not helped by the fact that the punishment meted out by institutions of international criminal justice is *lower* rather than higher than the punishment for severe crime in the domestic sphere and that punishment practices within international criminal justice suffer from good deal of incoherence.[19] Both the poor coverage rate and insufficiently proportional punishment practices sit uneasily with the need for justice in societies which have experienced international crimes.

It is unlikely that this will be remedied by emphasizing procedural requirements of criminal law. In the domestic sphere, the legitimacy of the process and the authorities may cushion the experience of negative outcomes (Tyler 2003; Wemmers 1996).[20] However, within international criminal law, it is apparent that those affected by international crimes will not automatically perceive the organisations holding the trials as legitimate bearers of justice. Of course this is the case for those who belong to the same collective as the perpetrators of these crimes – the perception of victor's justice may be reduced, not overcome – but applies to the victimized population as well. Indeed, the failure of the international community to do anything while the atrocities took place in former Yugoslavia and Rwanda does not bode well for the acceptance of the same international community to address justice violations, which they could and should have prevented (see Minow 1998). As Aukerman (2002) notes: "If the international community sits by and watches while atrocities occur, demanding prosecution only after the violence stopped, arguments about deterrence will ring hollow".[21]

Finally international criminal justice follows domestic criminal justice in its independence. An independent and neutral administration of justice is, it goes without saying, crucial to its realisation. In individual trials judges should under no circumstance be swayed by any other considerations than the facts of the case before them. However an excessive level of independence is not necessary for the institution of international criminal law as whole. Commentators have correctly

---

[18] This may also be due to the political reality. Trying previous leaders may result in renewed bloodshed (e.g. Snyder & Vinjamuri 2004).

[19] Unfortunately we can expand "a person stands a better chance of being tried and judged for killing one human being than for killing 100,000" with "(…) and his punishment will be more severe as well". See Drumbl 2007.

[20] An important caveat is that also in the domestic situation the pre-eminence of procedural justice for severe crimes is highly questionable, see Rock 1998; Armour 2007; and Pemberton 2009.

[21] In addition the wisdom of removing the trials from the communities that experienced them, is often questioned. The site of the trials is often far away from where the crimes were committed. The persons undertaking them are members of the international rather than the afflicted community. The probable goal is to prevent perceptions of victors' justice, although this perception persists, while the removal of trials may negatively affect the perception of justice in afflicted communities (Drumbl 2007; Fletcher & Weinstein 2002).

criticized the divorce of international criminal proceedings from other, simultaneous, domestic attempts to try atrocities and to reinstate the rule of law and rebuild ravaged societies;[22] the shortcomings of an enforcement of one-size-fits-all-justice that trumps domestic traditions,[23] and the reluctance to acknowledge the importance of political realism and the subsequent absence of a principled manner to balance power considerations and human rights (e.g. Licklider 2008; Snyder & Vinjamuri 2004).

The principled difficulties and shortcomings in implementation suggest that international criminal justice is not yet reaching its full potential. Indeed the results from research into the perceptions of inhabitants of former Yugoslavia and Rwanda reveal a lack of information about and a diminished sense of satisfaction with the results of the respective tribunals and a good measure of scepticism concerning the large investment needed for their functioning (see Longman, Pham & Weinstein 2004; Meernik 2005; Lutz 2006).

3.6. BASIC PREMISES OF A VICTIMOLOGICAL PERSPECTIVE

Both backward and forward looking aspects of reinstating the rule of law are of great importance to victims who suffered atrocities. In turn, their acceptance of the rule of law is crucial for its working. Victims of international crimes are a main, maybe *the* main, constituency in the reinstatement of the rule of law.[24] It is their assessment of the reaction to the atrocities that provides its link with the restitution of an effective rule of law. This does not imply that their need for justice will automatically trump other considerations. The prevention of further bloodshed and/ or an assessment of the political reality will also factor in victim's perceptions.[25] Insufficient attention to the perception of victims, however, may result in enduring violence and political instability, when the erstwhile victims retaliate and become perpetrators themselves (see e.g. Mani 2005).

Moving from a mere legal reaction to one that incubates a sense of justice is therefore paramount in establishing the link between the backward and forward-

---

[22]   Drumbl calls this the neglect of vertical and horizontal integration respectively. See Drumbl 2007.

[23]   This is the main shortcoming that Fletcher and Weinstein seek to remedy in their ecological model of social repair: see Fletcher & Weinstein 2002.

[24]   It may be argued that crime is in the first place a breach of an abstract legal order rather than a wrong committed against an actual victim (see e.g. Ashworth 2002).This would suggest that the victimized population is of no more concern than the rest of the world's citizens. We however view this perspective as outmoded. In the past thirty years it has been increasingly recognized that a criminal event is in fact both. Accordingly victims should be awarded more consideration in their cases than non-victims (see also Groenhuijsen 1999; Pemberton 2010c).

[25]   See for instance Gibson's (2004) results concerning South Africa.

looking aspects of reinstating the rule of law. In the first place this means that the legal reaction should be adapted, as much as possible, in an attempt to meet the realities and needs of the victimized population. Legal practices and principles, even those that may be sacrosanct in the domestic sphere, need to be rethought and recast in the arena of international criminal justice. We will suggest a number of concrete victim oriented reforms, related to the general characteristics of victims of international crimes, throughout the remainder of this chapter. In addition the reaction should be sensitive to the differences between situations. Both the notion of vertical integration – establishing a clear connection between the domestic and international criminal reaction (Drumbl 2007) – and the ecological model of social repair (the extent to which the legal reaction meshes with cultural and political realities (Fletcher & Weinstein 2002)) are of great importance in this respect.

In the second place the limits of international criminal law should be clearly acknowledged. International criminal justice is partial justice, at best (see also Roberts 2003). The issues of collective responsibility versus individual guilt, the role of bystanders and the selectivity of international criminal justice are not likely to be resolved within the criminal justice setting, at least not without discarding most of its main features. Nor should we hold high expectations for the extent to which international criminal justice will deter future wrongdoing or serve as sufficient retribution, not in the least because sufficient retribution for genocide is not a likely outcome in any case.[26] Acknowledging these limitations opens up the possibilities for linking international criminal justice, to other measures which may contribute to the sense of justice (what Drumbl calls horizontal integration), like truth commissions, reparations programs and other means to hold perpetrators, or collectives of perpetrators accountable and in addition, to programmes of broader social repair and reconstruction. It allows reflection on the use and the purpose of international criminal justice in the aftermath of atrocities and its place vis-à-vis other available options.

3.7. CONSEQUENCES OF STATE CRIME FOR A VICTIMOLOGICAL PERSPECTIVE

As noted, considering extraordinary remedies in the case of international crimes is in line with the peculiar character of these crimes and the legal reaction to

---

[26] An additional limitation that may be self-evident is the inherently pragmatic nature of international criminal justice. Establishing criminal justice processes at the international level that can challenge vested power interests seems – at least for now – a bridge too far. That means that expectations of any international-preventative effect of international criminal justice should be greatly reduced. Like in the past perpetrators of gross human rights violations have every reason to expect impunity as long as their standing with Security Council members is in the latter's interest (see also Sands 2006).

them. That is to say: remedies which are at odds with principles that in normal times must prevail. In any event, the level of consideration of the interests of victims of crime should be higher, and under no circumstances be lower than in instances of conventional crime. To be more specific, we envisage several areas where additional protection can be awarded.

First, one could conceive of robust measures to protect the physical safety of victims of international crimes. We have to bear in mind that – as a consequence of government involvement in these crimes – it can be extremely dangerous for victims to testify as witnesses in subsequent proceedings. Hence it appears to be realistic to provide for precautions in connection with their physical safety which exceed the levels of these provisions in ordinary criminal trials. In trials where conventional crimes are at stake, most jurisdictions employ methods like screens, CCTV and questioning in a room separate from the courtroom, in order to avoid face to face confrontations between defendant and victim/witness. In the case of international crimes, complete anonymity should be an option for victims/ witness to provide testimony. This instrument should be explicitly provided for in protocols on international criminal proceedings, and where such explicit provisions are lacking – like in the Rome Statute, the prevailing Articles should be interpreted in such a way as to come as close to anonymity as is possible (see for a full overview of pros and cons Garkawe 2003).

The second area where 'normal' standards should be adapted to extraordinary circumstances is reparation.[27] The standard of proof in connection to individual claims for damages needs to be reconsidered. In warlike circumstances it is virtually impossible for victims to collect the kind of material evidence that can normally be expected in cases of conventional crime. This is indeed the main reason for the difficulties in succeeding to convict the main perpetrators. It only seems fair to take this basic fact into account when assessing the merits of a claim for damages in cases of international crimes.

There is another way in which reparation in these cases merits different decision criteria. When conventional crime has been committed, it is good practice to order reparation to be paid on the basis on the individual guilt of the perpetrator. However, considering the number of victims involved, the individual perpetrator in international crimes is unlikely to be in a position to compensate each of his victims. Moreover the meagre conviction rate of perpetrators implies that following the domestic order will lead to many victims not receiving compensation.

The solution should lie in the administration of compensation invoking notions of collective responsibility. The qualms with notions of collective perpetration when it comes to punishment do not apply with equal force to compensation issues (see e.g. Drumbl 2007). Where collective responsibility may

---

[27] 'Reparation' is referred to here in the classical sense of a transfer of payment to the victim. In paragraph 5 we will examine a broader meaning of the concept of reparation.

not be a suitable concept in punishment, it is in settling compensation matters. We will return to this matter in section 4.

4. LARGE NUMBERS OF VICTIMS

Conventional crime usually is targeted against only one person, or at most against a small group of individuals. These victims are awarded procedural rights in a subsequent criminal trial. In most domestic jurisdictions, it is rare that the system has to deal with a much larger group of victims (see for a more extensive discussion Letschert & Ammerlaan 2010). These exceptions do occur, for instance, in some notorious cases of financial or economic crime (e.g. 'pyramid-schemes'). When a situation like that presents itself, the most common response is to suspend the rights of the victims to play their normal role. Many jurisdictions have special provisions preventing victim involvement from disturbing the ordinary course of a criminal trial; in others 'force majeure' is invoked to dissuade the victims from playing their normal part.[28]

In the case of international crimes, the exception and the rule are reversed. Genocide, crimes against humanity and war crimes are almost by definition targeted against large numbers of victims. The overviews of death tolls in Rummel (1994) and Harff (2003) are telling. The crimes at stake in the trial of individual suspects in international criminal justice proceedings will normally involve many victims. Invoking a 'force majeure' in these cases is therefore tantamount to denying victim involvement in these cases.

The model of the Rome Statute[29] is superior to the procedural rules governing the operation of the ICTY and ICTR in the sense that it awards victims the right to participation and the right to reparation. The model may be hailed as 'state of the art' from a victimological point of view, although it suffers from severe shortcomings and one may have grave doubts about its operation in the face of access by large numbers of victims (Groenhuijsen 2009). Three main issues can be identified in this respect: the difficulties in achieving victim status, the possibility that large numbers of victims will access procedural rights and the implementation of reparation measures. We will discuss these issues and reflect on both good practice and shortcomings of this ICC-model to further our understanding of international criminal justice.

---

[28]   In Dutch case-law, for instance, the Supreme Court sustained a ruling by a Court of Appeals which held that a number of 302 victims is in and of itself prohibitive for dealing with their claim for damages in a criminal trial. HR 18 April 2006, NJ 2007, 295 with comments by M.S. Groenhuijsen.

[29]   Including its accompanying RPE and Regulations of the Court.

4.1. THE PRESUMPTION OF VICTIMHOOD

The RPE of the ICC provides for a strict definition of a 'victim'. Rule 85(a) reads: "'Victims' means natural persons who have suffered harm as a result of the commission of any crime within the jurisdiction of the Court". A victim is not automatically accepted in that capacity by his claim that he meets the standards of Rule 85(a). Instead, an application procedure has been devised as a sort of entrance gate into the ICC-system. And the gate is built to deter all but those with the most stamina. A person who wishes to receive the status of 'victim' in a situation or in a case must complete an application form (17 and 19 pages long, respectively). The length of the forms and the details required in order to complete the forms is troublesome for many victims (De Brouwer & Groenhuijsen 2009). Two specifics might suffice to indicate how unsatisfactory the operation of the model has been up to now. Many victims who have submitted an application years ago, are still waiting for a decision of the Chamber today. And secondly: those applicants who did receive a decision, were in an overwhelming majority denied the status of victim.[30] This must be devastating for the confidence of victimised populations in the entire ICC-model. It surely cannot be seriously argued that victims should find justice in a system that repeatedly does nothing to prevent atrocities from occurring; subsequently fails to punish all but a small minority of perpetrators and then informs them after a few years wait that they, in the eyes of the international community, are not considered to be victims after all.

The procedure of the ICC in determining victimhood is an unfortunate departure from domestic practice. Here, when a person reports a crime and claims he is the victim of it, police and subsequent other authorities handling the case will automatically treat the person in the capacity of 'victim', until the moment when either law enforcement officials or a court determines that there was no crime or that the person did not suffer as a result of the crime committed.[31] Seeing that it is extremely unlikely that the ICC will decide the former – the question at stake is normally not whether a crime was committed, but rather whether the suspect can be deemed sufficiently culpable for its perpetration – and is most often not in a position to determine the latter, the only reason for the excessive procedure to grant someone victim status must lie in the ICC's need to establish a barrier against access by large numbers of victims. As noted, this comes with a high price; too high indeed, for this mode of operation is likely to defeat any expected benefit of victim participation.

---

[30] For a recent breakdown see www.icc-cpi.int/iccdocs/asp_docs/RC2010/Stocktaking/ Victims%20Factsheet.pdf (last visited: 6 October 2010).

[31] See Brienen & Hoegen 2000, 30.

4.2. PROCEDURAL RIGHTS

In the *Lubanga* case the trial decision of 18 January 2008 made it clear that there are at least five modalities of victim participation under the ICC rules:

- access to the public record;[32]
- to tender and examine evidence, and to challenge the admissibility or relevance of evidence when the victims' interests are concerned;
- access to hearings, status conferences and trial proceedings & to file written submissions;
- to make opening and closing statements;
- to initiate special proceedings.

It is obvious that these are far-reaching interventions. The participation of victims in these ways could have a considerable impact on the course of the proceedings (Zappala 2010). It can significantly affect the procedural battle between the prosecution and the defence. Since it involves numerous modalities, it could also impact an orderly and expeditious course of the trial. The main problem, of course, would be if many victims present themselves in order to give essentially the same input. It would be clearly impractical if, say, 25 victims exercise their right to make an opening statement, rehearsing the very same facts many times over.

Can this problem be tackled without denying the victims the kind of involvement they are entitled to? The key to the question lies in the concept of common legal representation (Rule 90 and Regulation 79). The ICC has the power to "request" the victims or a particular group of victims "to choose a common legal representative or representatives for the purposes of ensuring the effectiveness of the proceedings". The application of Rule 90 seems to be more difficult than may have been foreseen (De Brouwer & Groenhuijsen 2009). First, early case law appears to indicate that victims can decline the 'request' by the Court and still retain their standing in the proceedings (Zegveld 2009). This interpretation is self-defeating and does not serve victims' interests in the long run (Groenhuijsen 2009). A second problem that remains is that victimized populations are not homogenous. They will differ on many demographic characteristics, the exact nature of the crime suffered and will not necessarily hold the same opinions about the best way to proceed with the criminal trial (see more extensively Pemberton 2009). In those cases a solution could be to organise subgroups and provide each one of them with separate common legal representation (De Brouwer & Groenhuijsen 2009).

---

[32]   Only in exceptional circumstances access to confidential filings is allowed.

4.3. REPARATION

As a starting point, it has to be recalled that in domestic jurisdictions reparation has consistently proved to be the single most difficult aspect of legal reform on behalf of crime victims. On the international stage, reparation to individual victims has played no role at all after the second World War and only a theoretical role at the ICTY and ICTR (Van Boven 1999). The reparation regime under the ICC[33] is clearly a novelty in international criminal law (De Brouwer & Groenhuijsen 2009). Three elements are of particular relevance.

First, Rule 97 opens the possibility to order reparation on an individualised basis or, where it deems it appropriate, on a collective basis, or both. The power to award reparation on a collective basis can simultaneously reduce the necessity for individual proof (see section 3) and provide for a more efficient way to handle the reparation needs of large groups of victims. In this way an entire group of victims may be awarded a symbolically significant sum of money and at the same time be granted recognition of their suffering.

The second innovation is that the Court is supposed to establish principles relating to reparations, including restitution, compensation and rehabilitation (Article 75 Statute). The preparatory documents leading up to the Rome Statute clearly indicate that the principles for reparation should be inspired by the so-called Van Boven/Bassiouni Principles. This means that the classical vocabulary used in victimology is abandoned. Victimologists used to speak of reparation and restitution as interchangeable concepts, meaning: forced payment of money by the offender to the victim, based on liability for the damages caused by the crime. By contrast, the concept of compensation was used to refer to the mechanism of a payment by the State to the victim, based on the idea of social solidarity. The Van Boven/Bassiouni principles have enriched and improved this conceptual framework. According to these principles, reparation includes the following forms: restitution (restoration of liberty, return to one's place of residence, return of property), compensation (economically assessable damage (material damages and loss of earnings, moral damage), rehabilitation (medical and psychological care, legal and social services), satisfaction (verification of the facts, public apology, commemorations and tributes to the victims), and guarantees of non-repetition. We feel that this wide range of mechanisms to achieve reparation could and should be used in a creative way to best meet the circumstances of every single case and are convinced that dogmatic or doctrinal objections to linking this kind of reparation to more general projects of humanitarian assistance, like projects of the World Bank, are misguided.[34]

---

[33] Articles 75 and 79 of the Statute and Rules 94–99 RPE.
[34] Even though these kinds of joint ventures were explicitly rejected by those negotiating the Rome Statute.

Finally, the reparation regime under the ICC is innovative because it has introduced the Trust Fund for Victims. In a way this fund can be regarded as the international equivalent of a State compensation scheme, but it also has additional meaning. The mission of the Trust Fund is "to support *programs* which address the harm resulting from the crimes under the jurisdiction of the ICC by assisting the victims to return to a dignified and contributory life within their communities." The Fund has a dual mandate:

- to implement reparations awards from the Court, and
- to provide assistance to victims in general through the use of "other resources".

In January 2008 the Trust Fund notified the Court that it had identified two 'situations' (the DRC and Northern Uganda) where projects assisting victims should be proposed. Examples of projects in the DRC include (De Brouwer & Groenhuijsen 2009): 'rehabilitation reinsertion of victims' and 'socio-economic reintegration' as projects aiming for physical rehabilitation; 'healing of memories' and 'support to victims of sexual violence' as projects aiming for psychological rehabilitation; and finally 'holistic community rehabilitation', 'non-formal education' and 'taking care of each other' as projects aiming materially to support victims.[35]

4.4. NOTIONS FROM A VICTIMOLOGICAL PERSPECTIVE

As stated in the introduction of this section, the ICC model is the state of the art in victim-oriented handling of international criminal justice cases. It offers a wider range of participation options for victims of international crimes, which, as we shall further show in section 5, may be of great importance in handling of international crimes. The reparation programme has been significantly adapted to the situation of victims of international crimes. The possibilities for collective reparation may relieve a number of the problems discussed in section 3. Finally the use of the Van Boven/Bassiouni principles allow for increased flexibility in the manner of providing redress and the Trust Fund has the potential to advance on being an International Compensation Scheme.

---

[35] The most inspiring concrete example we have found so far is the Secretariat of the Trust Fund's gesture to provide a group of widows in the DRC with 200 chickens on loan for a year. After eight months, the chickens were returned as the animals had sufficiently multiplied and had enabled the women to buy cattle to generate an even better income. For an overview of recent projects, see www.trustfundforvictims.org/.

So far, so good. However the barrier erected before victims may be recognized as such already negates the benefits of these improvements for most applicants, as they will not be afforded victim status.[36] In fact this is more than a denial of benefits, as rejecting victim status, in particular considering the laborious and time-consuming application process, amounts to secondary victimization. Even for those able to pass this 'victim exam', problems remain. Instead of a clear endorsement of the connection to reparation measures external to the ICC, the Rome statute explicitly rejects these links. Seeing our arguments for horizontal integration in the previous section, we find this a regrettable and unnecessary shortcoming. The Trust Fund may be imbued with generally well-chosen principles, but the Fund's funding remains an issue (see Garkawe 2003). The merits of individual participation may run foul of the overall collective objective of a swift and expeditious trial of the perpetrators, while overtly repetitive use of procedural rights may diminish much of the worth of participating for each individual participant.

On a more general level we find that, like in the domestic sphere, the benefits of victim participation are as much related to practice as principle (see Groenhuijsen & Pemberton 2009). Victims' rights will only benefit victims, when their implementation in practice is secured. The notion that anything is better than nothing when it comes to victims procedural rights has been repeatedly refuted by research (e.g. Herman 2003). Allowing victims to participate and then disrespecting them or flagrantly failing to meet their expectations will lead to secondary victimisation (Orth 2002). One of us has extensively argued that a bedrock principle of victims' procedural rights is 'do no further harm' (Groenhuijsen 1999; Groenhuijsen & Kwakman 2002).

The same may be said concerning the provision of victims' rights that lack coherence. In the case of the ICC the rather extensive procedural rights for some victims lead to the necessity of denying many others any acknowledgement of their victimisation. Indeed, seeing the characteristics of victimisation by international crimes, the latter issue – some formal recognition of victimisation – may be of far greater value than the former. Furthermore, it seems fair to question the necessity of applying the same application procedures to victims who do not seek the far-reaching forms of individual participation. If the domestic experience is anything to go by, a majority of victims will find acknowledgement, some information and maybe compensation and collective participation to be sufficient (see e.g. Pemberton 2010a).

---

[36]   This specifically applies to the Chamber, rather than the Trust Fund.

5. VICTIMS ARE PERCEIVED AS ENEMIES AND AS PERPETRATORS

The final defining feature of international crimes is the way the crimes against victims and survivors of mass killing and genocide are perpetrated. Contrary to popular perception these atrocities are not mainly the work of handful of demonic perpetrators, but are committed by ordinary people (see Baumeister 1997; Chirot & McCauley 2006; Staub 2000; Waller 2007; Zimbardo 2007). As Baumeister has convincingly shown, 'pure evil' is most often a myth.

The consequences are no less severe, though. Apart from the multitude of fatalities, survivors are faced with an immense damage to their personal and social life (see for an overview Danieli 2009 and Danieli in this volume). Their health may be severely impaired, their houses destroyed, their jobs gone. They may have lost their families, have suffered and/or witnessed horrific events, and their psychological and social functioning may be tremendously impaired as a consequence. The experience of extreme and severe crime and its psychological consequences are also important for the way victims may view justice. Both the severity of crime (see Robinson & Darley 2007) and traumatization (see Orth, Montada & Maercker 2006; Lens, Pemberton & Groenhuijsen 2010) are connected with a desire for revenge and retribution.

5.1. THE SOCIAL DEATH OF VICTIMS

The features of the experience of genocide and mass killing have other implications for the way victims view justice. James Waller (2007) shows that, although there is variation in the exact circumstances of the perpetration of genocide, three constructions converge interactively to impact individual behaviour in situations of collective violence.

In the first place there is the *cultural construction of worldview*. Perpetrator groups may often be defined by a combination of collectivistic values, a strong adherence to authority and a high need for social dominance.[37] In the second place there is the *social construction of cruelty*. This concerns the influence of professional socialization, group identification and other group processes in

---

[37] Collectivistic cultures, focus on the group over the individual, with preeminent values like obedience, conformity, tradition, safety (e.g. Brewer & Chen 2007). Here group-based identity is an integral and defining characteristic of one's own identity, and group goals are often indistinguishable from individual goals. Authority orientation refers to a cultural model that orders the social world and relates to people according to their position and power in social hierarchies (see e.g. Haidt 2007). Social dominance orientation refers to the degree to which people want their own group to dominate other groups. People high on SDO are more often racist, patriotic and against equal rights for minorities and women (e.g. Sidanius & Pratto 1999).

creating an immediate social context in which perpetrators initiate, sustain and cope with their cruelty.[38]

For our current purpose Waller's *psychological construction of the 'other'* is the most important. In essence justice does not apply to victims anymore. Their suffering and the cruelty visited upon them falls beyond the scope of justice (see also Clayton and Opotow 2003). Victims of genocide and mass killing become simply 'objects' of perpetrators' actions through the processes of us-them thinking, moral disengagement and blaming the victims, which together leads to their 'social death': victims become excluded from the perpetrator's moral community.

1. *Us-them thinking.* Research has shown from Sherif *et al.* (1954) onwards, the tendency to define the world into us and them is one of the true human universals, while collectives may differ in the extent to which this is reproduced in their shared culture. Both ethnocentrism and xenophobia are innate realities of human life, when viewed through their least normative definitions.[39] Tapping into a severely escalated form of us-them thinking is essential to the perpetration of mass killing.

2. *Moral disengagement.* Singer (1981) discusses the notion of a moral circle, that embraces those worthy of our moral consideration. The process of civilisation can be tied to an expansion of this circle from our closest kin to all of mankind (as in the Universal Declaration of Human Rights). However this circle can contract rapidly in times of fear, hatred and scarcity of resources. This moral disengagement, in which victims are defined as being outside the perpetrator's universe of moral obligation, is a necessary, although not sufficient condition for genocide and mass killing. Moral disengagement contains three processes through which perpetrators make their reprehensible conduct acceptable and to distance themselves from the conduct of their actions: moral justification, dehumanization of the victims and euphemistic labelling of evil actions.

   In *moral justification* the mass-murder of the victims is justified by its portrayal as serving a worthwhile cause in either social or moral terms. This may reach the level a moral imperative; where the violence is an essential means of self-defence (see also Mann 2005). This may have some factual base; victimized populations may be more likely to commit mass political violence than populations without such a history (Staub 2000). But it may also be 'a self-justifying mental gymnastic', a component of an ideology that breathes

---

38   See Darley 1999; Baumeister 1997.
39   Ethnocentrism is then the technical name for the view of things in which one own's group is the centre of everything, and all others are scaled and rated with reference to it. Xenophobia relates to the fear of outsiders and strangers.

hate into populations, by convincing them that they are under continuous threat from the out-group (Waller 2007).

Dehumanization involves casting an out-group as subhuman creatures (animals) or negatively evaluated unhuman creatures (monsters) (e.g. Haslam 2006). This often proceeds through processes of infra-humanization, in which out-group members 'lose' secondary, more human, emotions, like jealousy, love, shame etc. and become defined in primary emotions, like anger and fear (Leyens *et al.* 2004)[40] and involves derogatory linguistics (for instance the use of 'cockroaches' in the case of Rwanda). Kelman and Hamilton (1989) show that this leads to the dual deprivations of being placed outside the realm of humanity, but also losing individuality.

The euphemistic labelling of evil actions refers to the fact that genocides are rarely named as such. For instance the Nazi's named the extermination of Jews the Final Solution. Other genocidal campaigns have used similar linguistic devices. In addition genocides and mass killing are commonly discussed in agentless, passive style, conveying a sense that they happen by a force of nature rather than by conscious evil-doing (Bandura 1999).

3. *Blaming the victims.* Lerner's just world theory concerns the fundamental delusion that people have a fundamental need to believe that good things happen to good people and bad things to bad people (Lerner 1980; Hafer & Begue 2005) and subsequently that those suffering misfortune and injustice are in some way deserving of this fate. The need to believe in a just world leads to the rationalization of genocide due to the blameworthiness of the victims. In the commission of genocide and mass killing victim-blaming transcends mere self-protective use (Waller 2007). Blaming the victims here provides perpetrators with self-esteem. The fact that the victims are suffering due to their own shortcomings, reinforces both the cultural and moral superiority of the group to which the perpetrator belongs.

5.2. THE CHARACTERISTICS OF PERPETRATION OF GENOCIDE AND A VICTIMOLOGICAL PERSPECTIVE

What does this analysis have to teach us about the development of a victimological perspective on justice procedures after genocide? We find justice procedures should strive to act as a countervailing force to the processes mentioned under the psychological construction of the other (us-them thinking, moral justification, dehumanizing, euphemistic labelling of evil actions and

---

[40] The stereotype of the angry Muslim in many Western media outlets is a clear case in point. By shedding secondary emotions the out-group becomes more similar (i.e. all Muslims are angry) while gaining a sense of collective and negative purpose (i.e. all Muslims are angry at us). See Pemberton, 2010b.

blaming the victims). Thus justice should involve re-humanizing victims, communicating their membership of the moral sphere and reducing victim blame. In addition it should take into account the dynamics of perpetration of mass atrocity, and in particular the somewhat unsettling observation that ordinary people are the perpetrators of these crimes, as well as viewing the potential impact of criminal justice processes in lieu of the enormity of the consequences. This leads us to the following reflections.

In the first place the positive impact of criminal justice processes on participating victims is highly limited. Criminal justice procedures should not be expected to overcome the deep-seated causes of genocide, nor the fundamental human processes of which it may be the extreme outcome. Fletcher has correctly noted that the expectations of a large therapeutic impact of these processes have no actual base in fact and reflect an understanding of psychology that has been outmoded for a very long time (Fletcher 2005). Recovering from extreme trauma is a process: not one cathartic moment.

Nevertheless including victims in justice procedures after genocide is of great importance. In genocide and mass killing victims have been placed outside the scope of morality and justice. A justice procedure dealing with genocide should attempt to communicate to victims that they are part of a moral community, in the very least by acknowledging their victimization. That may in fact be a more important component, than more far-reaching rights. A justice procedure that does not do so or treats victims in a disrespectful manner is likely to reinforce the experience of exclusion from the moral sphere that the genocide was already viciously inflicted on victims.

Similarly the acknowledgement of victim status, may contribute to a reduction of victim blame. Blaming the victims is not only endemic among perpetrators of genocide, but among victims as well. Many suffer from PTSD, of which self-blame is often an integral part (see Foa & Rothbaum 1998; Janoff-Bulman 1985; Staub et al. 2005). Clear allocation of responsibility and communication of this responsibility may serve to reduce this victim blame after mass victimisation, although a justice procedure should not be expected to achieve this feat alone. Indeed the complexities of assigning responsibility, for instance in the case of bystanders, who may not be deemed criminally culpable, but are a necessary component in the commission of international crimes (e.g. Staub 2000), entail the implementation of additional measures.

One of those measures may be a truth commission of some form. A major benefit of such a commission from a victimological perspective may be its value in re-humanizing victims; allowing them to voice their individual perspective and combatting euphemistic language. In Truth Commissions victims may act as individuals, rather than as a member of a victimized group. In addition they allow more personal language use, than formal criminal justice procedures. Like criminal justice procedures, one should, however, not expect a Truth Commission to be a highly effective therapeutic method. There is no evidence of 'healing' impacts of these measures and even evidence of counterproductive functioning (e.g. Brouneus 2008, 2010; see also Mendeloff 2009; Brahm 2006).

Finally one can wonder what version of the truth may be most beneficial to victimized populations. Unfortunately the real truth of genocide is that ordinary people are capable of unspeakable acts and that many, many others will do nothing to prevent perpetration of these acts. That does not seem reassuring, but the alternative: reviewing individual atrocities outside of their social context will merely reinforce the Myth of Pure Evil (Baumeister 1997; Smeulers, this volume). It may make sense then to supplement the accounts of the perpetrators with interventions that strive to help victims understand the causes of genocide. In the work of Ervin Staub and his colleagues in Rwanda this combination has proved beneficial, both for victims and perpetrators (Staub *et al.* 2005; Staub 2006).

6. A VICTIMOLOGICAL FRAMEWORK FOR REVIEWING INTERNATIONAL CRIMINAL JUSTICE

International criminal justice is an integral part of the international community's attempt to remedy some of the most heinous acts committed by man. It seeks to combat the culture of impunity for crimes committed in jurisdictions where the rule of law has collapsed and also to rebuild the rule of law in these areas. These are the backward and forward looking aspects of reinstating the rule of law.

These two aims are separate. Where many advocates of international criminal justice seem to suggest a smooth link between holding trials for perpetrators of international crimes and rebuilding a sense of justice in brutalized countries, we find this connection to be more problematic. Indeed, in its current state, there is good reason to doubt what, if anything, international criminal justice is contributing to the resurrection of the rule of law in these cases.

In our opinion improving this link rests to a great deal on the extent to which the position of victimized populations can be improved. The framework for doing so rests on three principles.

In the first place the criminal legal reaction should be adapted to the needs of the victimized population. We have argued for a review of principles in the domestic sphere of criminal justice to see the extent to which they are appropriate at the international level. This should acknowledge the specific situation of victimized populations. We have noted the importance of mere acknowledgement of victims in international criminal justice, in the sense that this welcomes victims back into the moral sphere from which they were excluded by the genocide. In similar vein the reaction to atrocities should attempt to re-humanize victims and reduce the extent of victim-blame, although this in large part may be beyond the remit of criminal proceedings. The conversion from the domestic to the international sphere should also acknowledge cultural and political realities. Societies' perspectives on doing justice may differ, the measures needed for social repair may differ and indeed the political playing field may do so as well. The positive impact of international criminal justice is then likely to depend on its link with domestic justice procedures and its ecological appropriateness.

In the second place we should acknowledge the limits of international criminal justice. Trials are not magical vessels of catharsis, nor should they be expected to be. Both the impact of international criminal justice as a means of retribution or of deterrence is likely to be very slight. Future atrocities are not likely to be prevented and the enormity of evil in these cases explodes the limits of sufficient retribution. This implies that the expressive function of criminal justice is its most important one. The contribution of international criminal justice, concerns the extent to which justice is *seen* to be done. Moreover international criminal justice is partial justice. It will not be feasible to successfully try all perpetrators or indeed all those people who were necessary for the atrocities to come about. Acknowledging these limits also allows international criminal justice to cooperate with other legal and quasi-legal measures that seek to provide justice, redress and reparations for victimized populations. This horizontal integration makes more sense than debating which solution – Trials, Truth Commissions, Amnesties – is the best (see for similar reflections Roht-Arriaza 2006).

Finally the structure of victim-oriented measures needs to be internally coherent and to be complemented by adequate implementation. As in the domestic sphere the proof of the pudding of providing victim benefits in the criminal justice system is in the eating, more so than in its guiding principles. A main component of both principle and implementation should be the prevention of secondary victimisation. Do no further harm. Respectful treatment in practice and more extensive protection rights both share this aim. Acknowledgement and formal recognition of victimisation may be the most important features of participating in international criminal justice. Providing more extensive procedural rights for some victims should not stand in the way of this acknowledgement for many others. Finally where one can consider the notion of collective responsibility to be an empirical fact in genocide, it is at odds with the individualized base through which criminal justice determines punishment. We would not argue that criminal justice should override this principle, but do consider a collective responsibility approach to be advisable in compensation matters.

The 20th century saw the human predisposition for violence taken to new extremes. We have not much hope that humanity will be able to avoid similar massive atrocities in the 21st century, irrespective of the advances international criminal justice will or will not make. The best we can hope for is a legal reaction that does some good and no additional harm to the victims of future atrocities. Pursuing the lines of thought we have outlined in this chapter, hopefully will contribute to this modest, but nevertheless important, goal.

II. THE VICTIMOLOGICAL CONCERN AS THE DRIVING FORCE IN THE QUEST FOR JUSTICE FOR STATE-SPONSORED INTERNATIONAL CRIMES

Athanasios Chouliaras*

1. INTRODUCTION

Since the publication of Gustave Le Bon's study on crowd psychology (1895) there has been a growing acknowledgement of the idea that mass or collective violence is essentially different from individual violence (Grimshaw 1970; Summers & Markusen 1999; Barkan & Snowden 2001; Tilly 2003). Horrific incidents, like those occurred during the decade of 1990 in the former Yugoslavia and Rwanda, renewed academia's interest in the most extreme forms of organized and systematic manifestations of collective violence (Ceretti 2009; Smeulers 2010). This brute reality fuelled the development of a new paradigm in criminal sciences, encapsulated in the unprecedented development of the branch of international criminal law (Bassiouni 2003; Cassese 2003; Werle 2009) and the criminology of international crimes (Smeulers & Haveman 2008). Genocide, crimes against humanity, war crimes and aggression, termed nowadays as *core international crimes*,[1] offer the common ground of these two disciplines.

Although both disciplines converge on the centrality of the collective dimension of core international crimes, they diverge crucially in the way they address it: international criminal law seeks to develop concepts, categories and theories of liability apposite to determine individual criminal responsibility in

---

* I would like to express my gratitude to the Max Planck Institute for Foreign and International Criminal Law (Freiburg/Germany) for granting a scholarship for the first two months of my research visit to the Institute, making possible the writing of this chapter.

[1] Bassiouni has identified 28 categories of international crimes, which are considered as the *ratione materiae* of the discipline of international criminal law (2003, 116–117). Most authors adopt a narrower sense of international criminal law, focusing on the international crimes derived from the legacy of Nuremberg ('core international crimes'), the commission of which entails direct individual criminal responsibility under international law and falls within the jurisdiction of the International Criminal Court (Broomhall 2003, 9–10; Werle 2009, 29–30; Damgaard 2008, 56–71).

the context of collective violence with systemic traits, whereas criminology urges for an ethically and legally appropriate allocation of responsibility to different kinds of actors (individual, state and state-like) with respect to different kinds of offending conducts. In other words, whereas international criminal law analyses core international crimes mainly as instances of individual deviance, criminology analyses them as instances of organizational deviance (Chouliaras 2010c).

Another central issue is the consideration of state involvement in the commission of core international crimes. International criminal law scholars have characterized them as characteristic instances of "abuse of state power" (Bergsmo & Triffterer 2008, 8), given that they "presume a context of systemic or large-scale use of force (…) typically a state" (Werle 2009, 32). In the same vein Schabas posits that "these are generally crimes of State, in that they involve the participation or the acquiescence of a government, with the consequence that the justice system of the country concerned is unlikely to address the issue" (2010, 40). On the other hand, criminology examines core international crimes as emblematic instances of state crime, which subsume to the broader category of "abuse of power" (Friedrichs 2007, 116, 118). According to the criminological perspective, the commission of core international crimes is conceivable only at the behest of or in furtherance of the state (Mullins & Rothe 2008; Chouliaras 2010a).

It is obvious that the criminological concept of state crime is not synonymous with the legal concept of core international crimes. State crime is broader in the sense that it includes forms of crimes not qualified as core international crimes. On the other hand, core international crimes are not exclusively committed by states, but by other collective entities as well (e.g. rebel armies) (Haveman & Smeulers 2008, 7). Accordingly, whereas for international criminal law state involvement offers the wider context within which individual contributions to a criminal result is calibrated, for criminology it is the establishment of state involvement that constitutes the primary objective.[2]

In this context, both disciplines have highlighted the collective and international dimension of core international crimes (Smeulers 2010; Van der Wilt & Nollkaemper 2009) as well as their organizational and political nature (Smeulers & Haveman 2008), justifying their qualification from a phenomenological point of view as acts of "extraordinary international criminality" (Drumbl 2007, 4) or "mass atrocity" (Osiel 2009). Such an acknowledgment produces a twofold result: it differentiates them radically from ordinary domestic crimes, raising axiomatically concern over the most adequate way to deal with them. It goes

---

[2]   It should be underlined that for various scholars the involvement of a state is a prerequisite for the commission of a core international crime, which also explains the impunity that accompany them: "We do not, by and large, have the same problem of impunity with respect to non-State actors. Most States are both willing and able to prosecute the terrorist groups, rebels, mafias, motorcycle gangs, and serial killers who operate within their own borders." (Schabas 2008, 974).

without saying that there are different approaches to this vexing issue, largely shaped by the objectives to be sought and the interests to be promoted. In other words, justice for victims, fairness for offenders and truth for the public or all the implicated parties prove to cut to the core of the discussion on the best way to tackle state-sponsored international crimes, meaning core international crimes committed at the behest of or in furtherance of the state.

Adopting a victims' perspective, this chapter asserts that the driving force behind the development of diverse models of justice for state-sponsored international crimes is primarily composed of victimological concern. In particular, the point will be made that it is the need to create adequate frameworks for addressing the plight of victims of abuse of state power that lies at the heart of both the criminal justice model, which is grounded in the institution of trials, and the restorative justice model, epitomized by the establishment of truth and reconciliation commissions (TRCs) (Llewellyn 2007). In a nutshell, it will be argued that the demand to advance the cause of victims recognizing them as autonomous stakeholders with particular rights has implications for the criminal justice model, especially at international level, and offers the groundwork for the emergence of alternative forums in the perspective of the establishment of the whole truth – and not only the procedural truth – and the delivering of substantial justice. A brief overview of the discipline of victimology with special focus on the victims of state crime proves to be indispensable in order to circumscribe the discussion.

2. CONSTRUCTING THE VICTIM

The objective of this part is to offer an account of the way the figure of the victim has been analysed and constructed. After a brief overview of the basic objectives of the victimological enterprise, the subject matter is restricted to the victims of state crime by resorting to the criminological concept of state crime. Such an approach will facilitate a qualitative analysis of the resulting victimization and will offer the ground for the evaluation of the form in which victims of state-sponsored crimes have been recognized at international law.

2.1. FROM POSITIVIST TO CRITICAL VICTIMOLOGY AND TO SOCIOLOGY OF HARM

If the need to develop a critical analysis of the criminal phenomenon became an imperative during the decades of 1960 and 1970 giving rise to a new critical paradigm in criminology (Taylor, Walton & Young 1975; Lynch & Michalowski 2006; Van Swaaningen 1997), then the prospect of adopting a victim perspective was equally advanced as a major breakthrough. This is due to the fact that the victim was not considered as an important element in the traditional criminal justice discourse (Viano 1976; Falandysz 1982; Fattah 1992). The above claim does not necessarily mean that the basic distinction produced within criminology between a critical and a positivist stance did not find its way in the victimological research agenda as well. On the contrary, it is the critique articulated by the former towards the latter that paved the way for the emergence of the major issues that lie at the heart of the struggle for justice for victims of state crimes. In what follows, after reporting the priorities of positivist victimology, I focus on its critique as articulated by critical victimology as well as on the building blocks of this latter current. Finally, I perceive and describe the emerging discipline of the sociology of harm as a reflective evaluation of critical criminology inspired by the victimological enterprise.

In general terms positivist victimology, sharing *mutatis mutandis* the same objectives with positivist criminology, seeks to measure the amount of victimization, construct victim typologies, explain why some people are more prone to victimization than others and how the victim participates in its own victimization and precipitates crime (Miers 1989). It goes without saying that the victimological study is limited to the victims of conventional crime – such as street crime – entailing in many cases interpersonal violence (Walklate 1990, 26). The major shortcoming of such an enterprise is double-faceted: it is limited to a micro-analysis and takes for granted an existing consensus on which situations produce personal and social harm, excluding others (e.g. harms produced by corporations and nation states). In other words, the produced images of victimhood are unacceptably narrow, resulting either from the criminal law or from the self-evident nature of the victim's suffering. This assumption conceals an inherently static and functionalist view of society, focusing on consensus and stability; it offers minor indicia of the ways in which the law or the state contributes to the social construction of the victim, or of the processes of criminal victimisation or processes of social change that may be unforeseen (Walklate 1992).

On the other hand, the critical trend refuses to confine its research agenda to the definitions of victimhood produced by the criminal justice system and strives to portray the social reality of victimization amply. Critical victimology, by adding meso- and macro-level analyses to the traditional micro-focus and by conceiving the categories of crime and victim as the result of an interaction among the factors of cultural production, ideological construction and political economy, engages in a twofold task: to cast light on the institutions and structural relations that favour specific images of victimization at the expense of others (contextualization); and to draw attention to situations that, despite producing serious victimization, are not designated as such (Walklate 1990; Mawby & Walklate 1994, 18–21).

The first line of critical inquiry has led, among other things, to the identification of the "ideal victim", that is "a person or a category of individuals who – when hit by crime – most readily are given the complete and legitimate status of being a victim" (Christie 1986a, 18). Simply put, the 'ideal victim', embodying the official narrative on victimhood, shapes public perceptions of a victim and contributes to the reproduction of the status quo. It is forged as a reflection of the "suitable enemy" that has provided the key elements of the formal version of criminality (Christie 1986b). Its mystifying effect is revealed when compared to the real victim: "the real victims are so to say the negation of those who are most frequently represented" (Christie 1986a, 27). Consequently, the identification and projection of the real victim constitutes the second major line of critical victimology.

The starting point of this endeavour is the assumption that "'the victim' is a social construction" (Quinney 1972, 321; Miers 1990), a statement that acquires its full meaning when considered in the framework of labelling and conflict theory. The deriving proposal of such a context alerts us to the fact that victimhood does not constitute an intrinsic quality of some individuals but simply a designation resulting from a complex process of social interaction (Watson 1976; Becker 1962), while at the same it politicizes the whole issue by declaring that the range of the concept of victimization is determined by a concrete system of power relations. In other words, provided the political nature of criminal law, this should not be conceived narrowly as a static system of norms but broadly as a dynamic system of functions reflecting the interests of the powerful (class, elite, etc.). It is the means in the hands of those who hold the power of definition to shape the notions of crime and victimhood. In this sense, the current concept of victimization is the product of a selection process in which some socially harmful situations are designated as crimes producing victims and some others are not (Vold 1958; Turk 1972; Quinney 1974; Chambliss 1993).[3] Simultaneously, it is important to bear in mind that, in sharp contrast with the notions of crime and criminal, the acknowledgment of the status of victim equates to the ascription of a positive social role that legitimizes expectations on the part of the victim, i.e. establishes moral rights awaiting to be converted into legal rights, which will involve concrete responsibilities on the side of the state and civil society.

In this context, critical victimology aspires to be an analytic social science that by posing its own standards determines certain patterns of victimization and therefore indicates 'who is the victim'. This is a prerequisite in order to

---

[3]   Although the original application of these theories took place in the area of crime, their basic tenets can be analogically transferred and applied to that of victim as well. For example, Quinney (1972) extended his interpretation of crime as a construct to the understanding of victimization and Freidrichs (1983, 288) urged to develop a radical concept of victimization that would enable victimologists to "work out more fully the differences between victimization linked with purely personal attributes and victimization linked with class position."

formulate later on normative claims, leading to the official recognition of a victim, given that "the question of what is leads inevitably to the question of what ought to be" (Birkbeck 1983, 274).

There seems to be unanimity among scholars that the primary element of victimhood is the presence of harm or injury (Fattah 2010, 54–55). Accordingly, it has been argued that harm is what distinguishes victim from other social categories (Birkbeck 1983, 272) and that its cause should not be restricted to a criminal act nor to an individual actor (Burt 1983, 262).

It is also worth mentioning that the notion of harm has been employed in criminal law theory and criminology. In the former, the harm principle constitutes a means to rationalize criminalization, as it provides both a negative constraint and a positive claim (Feinberg 1984, 1988). In the latter, harm, demarcated by reference to the historically determined rights of individuals, offers a powerful alternative to the traditional legal definition of crime, that could be used as a bedrock for the development of a dynamic social definition of what constitutes 'crime' (Schwendingers 1970).

The growing criminological literature on 'crimes of the powerful', encompassing white-collar crime, corporate crime, state crime, etc. brought to the surface a huge area of socially harmful activities systematically ignored or downplayed by the criminal justice system. This alternative reality imposed the need to develop a radical concept of victimization (Friedrichs 1983), apposite to include "the victims of police force, the victims of war, the victims of 'correctional' system, the victims of state violence, the victims of oppression of any sort" (Quinney 1972, 321). A series of studies highlighted the institutional and systemic nature of these neglected forms of victimization, promoting the idea to appeal to supranational standards and institutions in order to recognize these social harms and oblige some form of action (Johnson 1973, 1974; Dardian 1974; de Cataldo Neuberger 1985; Gullota 1985; Harff & Gurr 1989). International human rights standards were proposed as an alternative and broader framework that would supply victimology with an objective measure of actual victimization (Elias 1985, 1986).

Recently an agenda has been set to establish a discipline with central object of focus the study of social harm. According to its proponents,

> *the principal aim of a social harm approach is to move beyond the narrow confines of criminology with its focus on harms defined by whether or not they constitute a crime, to a focus on all the different types of harms, which people experience from the cradle to the grave.* (Hillyard, Pantazis, Tombs & Gordon 2004, 1)

Given that the notion of social harm suffers from inherent broadness, one of the primary endeavours was to delimit it. Under this scope, Hillyard and Tombs identify four main categories: *physical harms*, such as premature deaths, exposures to various environmental pollutants, lack of adequate food and shelter, torture and brutality by state officials, etc.; *financial/economic harm*, including poverty, unemployment, cash loss incurred through fraud, increased prises for goods and services due to cartelisation and price-fixing, etc.; *emotional and psychological harm* as well as social harm resulting from threats to *cultural safety*, that encompass notions of autonomy, development and growth, access to cultural resources, etc. (2004, 19–20). The various chapters in this volume elaborate further on some of these forms of social harm, illustrating that the notion is partially constituted by its operationalization. Nevertheless, what remains a plain fact is that the new approach is concerned with a wide range of harms. Yet, this should be perceived more as an advantage rather than as a disadvantage, since the social harm perspective includes "the potential to have a much grater degree of ontological reality than is possible with the notion of crime" (Hillyard *et al.* 2004, 272).

The picture becomes even clearer when one considers that this new perspective, although sprang from a "'critical' critique to criminology" (Hillyard & Tombs 2004, 11–18), goes actually 'beyond criminology'. This is due to the fact that a comparative analysis of harm, rather than that of crime carried out through criminal statistics, may offer a more accurate account of the chronic conditions – and not only of instant acts – that affect people in their everyday living throughout their life cycle. Moreover such an approach represents the first step to overcome the atomized thinking concerning the causes of harm, which in extent turns to be the main precondition for the emancipation from the narrow individualistic notion of liability and for the consideration of organizational responsibility and accountability. This seems also to be the unique way to address seriously the issue of mass harms resulting from state and corporate activity, which cannot be scrutinized through the traditional individualistic legal notions of action, omission and intention harm. What is more, the final objective is not narrowly defined, consisting in some form of retribution or punishment, but broadly, comprising the development of policies that would deal with every source of harm at the level of its manifestation with the view to reduce it (Hillyard & Tombs 2004, 21–24). All in all, the abandonment of any reference to crime, law and criminal justice, which compose the terrain of criminology, and the adoption of a multi-disciplinary approach are presented as the departure point for the development of a novel and effective form of prevention and not simply of redress of harm (Hillyard *et al.* 2004, 270, 275; Pemberton 2007).

Any objection with respect to the comprehensiveness of this approach and consequently whether it could be called victimology (or better 'zemiology'?)[4]

---

[4]   Zemiology gets its name from the Greek word 'zemia' (meaning harm) and consists in the study of social harms. It originated as a critique of criminology and the notion of crime in the mid 1990's within the context of the annual conference of the European Group for the Study of Deviance and Social Control. Although the use of the term zemiology is gradually extending, serious concerns remain with respect to its appropriateness (Hillyard *et al.* 2004, 1, note 1).

should take into consideration that one of the 'founding fathers' of victimology, Beniamin Mendelshon, envisioned it as the science that would study all victims (1974).

2.2. THE VICTIMS OF STATE: DELIMITATION THROUGH THE CONCEPT OF STATE CRIMES

It is a truism that the lack of delimitation of the exact bounds within which research should be conducted does not jeopardize the scientific validity of victimology – method offers the crucial criterion. However, it is also a truism, that the adoption of a definitional framework with respect to harmful state activity potentially offering a case before an international criminal tribunal or other normative bodies is essential in order to outline the qualitative traits of the victimization that it entails. In this respect, the notion of social harm is restricted by reference to the criminological concept of state crime. The above said does not mean that criminological theory offers a single definition of state crime. On the contrary, one could identify two major lines: one driven by the social harm perspective, although more restricted, and another that is law directed (Matthews & Kauzlarich 2007).

According to the former, state crime is defined as "state organizational deviance involving the violation of human rights" (Green & Ward 2004, 2). Two crucial elements should be analysed here: the concept of human rights and of deviance. As far as the former is concerned, Green and Ward, following essentially the tradition of the Schwendingers (1970), reject a strict approach that would engage them into a legalistic interpretation of various international instruments, like the one provided by international courts, and opt for a more creative and radical approach, based on the "fundamental premises underlying human rights law" (2004, 7). At the same time, bearing in mind that the genuine universalism of human rights involves an inherent danger for their ideological use by global hegemony, they appeal directly to the *raison d'être* of the human rights movement: the promotion and satisfaction of all human needs that are necessary preconditions for persons to exert and develop their capacities as purposeful agents. In this sense, human rights equate to moral rights, understood as morally valid claims that anyone can make simply by virtue of being human (Green & Ward 2000a, 103–104; 2004, 7–8).[5]

The full potential of this normative option is revealed when combined with the inherent dynamic that the concept of deviance encapsulates. The latter is employed every time a social audience considers that an act contravenes a widely

---

5   Sen's theory of human rights could offer the philosophical foundation of this approach. Sen defines human rights as "primarily ethical demands' that relate 'to the significance of the freedoms that form the subject matter of these rights" (2004, 319, 320 ff.).

accepted social rule, to which it is also willing to impose a significant sanction. The function of the concept is essentially analogous to that of an open system, provided that it permits a smooth input of information with respect to the crucial framework (rule), the evaluator (audience), the relevant actor and the eventual consequence (sanction). So, in the case of state crimes, a broad normative arsenal, ranging from national law to international collective conscience, can be employed by a variety of audiences, including international organizations, states, national and global civil society, in order to evaluate an act performed by an governmental organization or a state and potentially impose formal or informal sanctions, i.e. legal punishment, banishment, censure, and shame. The flexibility of the concept of deviance allows for its use also 'from below' in labelling a state practice as crime (Green & Ward 2000a, 104–108; 2004, 4–5). The above mentioned definition of state crimes, based on a restrictively constructed notion of social harm (violation of human rights), should not be confused with the broader concept of state harms. The latter includes any harm caused by normal (meaning not deviant) state functioning: "'state harm' is an invasion by a state agency of any person's welfare interests, whether such invasion is justified or not" (Ward 2004, 86).[6]

On the other hand, some scholars opt for a narrower, somehow 'legalistic' definition of state crime (Matthews & Kauzlarich 2007, 45). Their determination to sketch autonomously the confines of the criminological enterprise stimulates them to reject the traditional legalistic concept of crime, consisting of acts included in domestic criminal codes, and to construct a dynamic one, which, however, presupposes the violation of some form of law. Especially in the case of state crime, given the reluctance of states to criminalize their own wrongdoing, it is necessary to appeal to external standards, like those provided by international law, and apply them accordingly, even when there is no equivalent precedent (Molina 1995; Kauzlarich 1995; Kauzlarich & Kramer 1998; Mullins & Rothe 1998). Kramer, Michalowski and Rothe conceive international law as an evolving branch of law that crystallizes "multilateral reasoning, debating and treaty" that offer a specific indicator on how the "world community has decided should regulate state practices" (2005, 54). In the same vein, Kauzlarich posits that the use of international law for incriminating harmful actions of states not only "advances a humanistic perspective on crime and criminality", but contributes to the legitimacy of the study of state crime both within the discipline of criminology and toward the general public (1995, 40).

Which of the above two approaches frames the study of state crime will impact the types of harm studied, determining consequently the cycle of victims

---

6   Developing a political economy of state harm, Ward distinguishes between weak states, 'strong' states in crisis, and state socialism (or state capitalism). What is more, state harms are divided into three categories: acknowledged harms, contested harms, and putatively legitimate harms (Ward 2004, 91 ff.).

and permitting further classification. The broader the definition, the broader the number of people defined as victims of some harmful state activity. Needless to reiterate that from a victimological point of view nobody could exclude the venture to study the victims of all state harms; but such an option would equate with an endeavour 'beyond criminology'.

In the framework of the legalistic approach, Kauzlarich, Matthews and Miller have identified victims of state crime in the following way: "Individuals or groups of individuals who have experienced economic, cultural, or physical harm, pain, exclusion, or exploitation because of tacit or explicit state actions or policies which violate law or generally defined human rights" (2001, 176). Departing from this general definition, the authors differentiate between victims of domestic and international state crime, depending on whether state activity undermines the rights of its own citizens or citizens of other countries. A further classification takes additionally into account the branch of law that has been violated: domestic law, international law, or human rights standards (Kauzlarich, Matthews & Miller 2001, 177–183).

2.3. A QUALITATIVE ANALYSIS OF STATE CRIME VICTIMIZATION

Although state crime takes a variety of forms, limiting our analysis to its most solemn version also typified in international criminal law ('core international crimes'), it is possible to trace some intrinsic characteristics that differentiate them substantially from ordinary domestic crimes: they posses a *collective and international dimension*, as well as an *organizational and political nature*. The analysis of these qualitative traits offer the guidelines in an attempt to highlight the mechanics of state crime victimization, comprising a *collective, systemic, structural, institutional, organizational and political element*.

It is now a widely shared belief that the *collective or group element* is a constant feature of core international crimes, vindicating their study under the rubric of collective and not individual violence (Ceretti 2009; Smeulers 2010). In sharp contrast to the bulk of ordinary domestic crimes, "most of the time these [core] crimes do not result from the criminal propensity of single individuals but constitute manifestations of collective criminality: the crimes are often carried out by groups of individuals acting in pursuance of a common criminal design" (Tadić Case 1999, para. 191). This position does not imply that interpersonal violence is absent in the context of collective violence, but only draws attention to the fact that the latter has structural roots and a significantly different dynamic and impact (Barkan & Snowden 2001). More particularly, what appears to be crucial is

the instrumental use of violence by people who identify themselves as members of a group – whether this group is transitory or has a more permanent identity – against

*another group or set of individuals, in order to achieve political, economic or social
objectives.* (Zwi, Garfield & Loretti 2002, 215)

In a similar vein, Tilly analyses collective violence as a form of contentious
politics. Such an approach rests on a twofold basis: collective violence results
from collective claim-making that affects the interests of participants and of
course their relations to government, representing a struggle for power. This is
why the shape and intensity of collective violence depends notably on each
regime's governmental capacity – relating to the control of resources, activities,
and population within a territory – and democracy – referring to the existence of
broad and equal relations of communication and control between the population
and the state (Tilly 2003).

The significance of this element is both theoretical and practical, reflecting
on the very subject matter of international criminal law. Slowly but steadily,
international criminal justice theory has taken conscience of the fact that the
enforcement of international criminal law should be focused on instances of
collective violence that present an additional *systemic dimension* (Van der Wilt &
Nollkaemper 2009). It is submitted here that collective violence should also
display an *institutional aspect*, in the sense that it is exercised in the context of
some institution of legitimate governance. The addition of this requirement will
entail the exclusion of forms of violence that, although collective in nature, are
not endowed with this crucial aspect (e.g. riots, cults, hate groups, gangs,
criminal organizations, etc.). From this standpoint, a helpful tool proves to be
Galtung's concept of structural violence, i.e. violence built into the social and
power structure, which usually serves as the breeding ground for direct violence
as well (Galtung 1969).

In this framework, criminological theory becomes a valuable instrument,
provided that it scrutinizes and defines state crime as instance of *organizational
deviance*. One of the proposed definitions conceptualizes state crime as "an
illegal or injurious act of omission or commission by an individual or group of
individuals in an institution of legitimate governance which is executed for the
consummation of the operational goals of that institution of governance"
(Kauzlarich 1995, 39). The analytic value of this definition consists in the
provision that the act is committed by state officials on behalf of the state,
through the use of resources of the state, while its commission reflects norms
and values that have been developed within the state (Kauzlarich & Friedrichs
2003). This latter condition echoes one of the basic positions of organisation
theory, that organisations, of which states are an example, develop policies for
the achievement of goals that frame individual actions (Mohr 1972; Georgiou
1973). One should also be mindful of the distinction between official, meaning
declared, and operative goals, which are embedded in the daily decisions of the
personnel. It is firstly and foremost these operative goals that should be traced

and evaluated in order to reveal the exact and real content of state policies (Perrot 1961).

Immediate corollary of the abovementioned is the principle that 'structure' and 'agency' should constitute different units of analysis that stand in a relation of dialectical interplay. The state, as an organization providing collective resources and mechanisms, transforms individual actions into corporate agency. In this sense, it should be approached from two angles: from within the organization, where the organization influences the behaviour of individuals, and from the outside, where the organization is analyzed as an autonomous actor within the broader socio-economical and political milieu (Gross 1980). If the former approach corresponds to a micro and the latter to a macro perspective, then the development of a meso-level analysis, touching on organizational settings, has been proposed as a crucial step with the view to bringing to light the factors that act as catalysts in the shaping of individual decisions and actions (Vaughan 2002, 2007). Therefore, it comes as no surprise that the most recent criminological studies tend to analyse international criminality in terms of conformity instead of deviancy (Drumbl 2007). Individual crimes committed within this organizational context are considered 'crimes of obedience' to the authority, being essentially its expression and contributing to its furtherance and consolidation (Kelman & Hamilton 1989).

As it has been already stated, the reality of organizations is the presence and pursuit of goals. This tenet will be further illustrated and specified in the case of the state, if this is analysed as the regulatory idea of *governmental rationality*. Foucault posits that the state should be conceived both as a principle of intelligibility of the existing reality and as a strategic objective. The former implies that the state provides the general scheme through which it is possible from the 17th century and onwards to reflect systematically on public affairs, taking into account the totality of the elements, practices and institutions that compose it (sovereign, territory, law, population, etc.). The latter suggests that the state constitute at the same time the final outcome of this new way of reflection. It can be visualized as the tangible result of this intellectual activity or "the end of the operation of rationalization of the art of government" (Foucault 2004a, 295–296). Therefore, the government according to the reason of state can be defined as a finalist multifaceted activity ensuring that the state will be rendered solid, permanent and of course mighty vis-à-vis every threat and enemy, internal or external (Foucault 2004b, 6). The central point of this approach is that, despite the incessant effort to limit and regulate this mode of governance through the cultivation of the 'judicial reason' (social contract theory, positivation of human rights, rule of law, etc.), it will always remain a latent element of modern state policy in the pursuit of the legitimate goal of national security (Chouliaras 2010b).

This last remark, highlighting the *political dimension* of state crime, leads to the identification of another element of core crimes: their *international dimension* that relies on a double acknowledgment. First, core crimes endanger legally protected values of the international community as a whole, meaning "the peace, security and well-being of the world" (Preamble (3) of the Rome Statute). This wide-ranging impact is inherent to the special conditions within which core international crimes occur: crimes against humanity take place during a widespread or a systematic attack against a civilian population (Article 7 (1) Rome Statute); genocide presupposes that an assault against a protected group must be made with an intention to destroy it in whole or in part (Article 6 Rome Statute); war crimes occur in the course of an armed conflict (Article 8 Rome Statute), whereas the crime of aggression is considered as a straightforward breach of international peace (Werle 2009). On the other hand, core crimes are also perceived as a direct offence to the dignity of humanity, composed of "the individuality of each human being, not reducible to membership in a group, and the equal membership of each in the human community as a whole" (Delmas-Marty 2009, 13). Consequently, their occurrence "shock[s] the conscience of humanity" (Preamble (2) of Rome Statute). However, what is usually not said, although implied, is that core crimes incorporate an international aspect for the additional reason that they are committed by states, meaning legitimate institutions of governance, which are supposed to be the guardians of the domestic rule of law and, in any case, they do not stand any more above the international rule of law. In this line, every incidence of core crime should be additionally conceived as a breach by states of their most fundamental obligation, not to commit crimes against their citizens or to prevent their occurrence.

The above brief analysis sets the tone concerning the identification of the key aspects of state crime victimization. My intention here is not to engage in a detailed presentation, but just to show how the qualitative elements of state crimes reflect on the side of victims, composing at the end a unique pattern of victimization. Starting from the *collective element*, it has been observed that it is not an exclusive trait of the victimizer but it can be traced on the part of victim as well. The term *'collective victims'* refers to "groups or groupings of individuals linked by special bonds, considerations, factors or circumstances which, for these very reasons make them the target or object of victimization" (Bassiouni 1988a, 183). Distinguished examples of this category are the victims of 'politicide' and genocide. The basic feature of such episodes lies in the systematic persecution of a political or communal group through the state apparatus. Whereas political groups are defined "in terms of their hierarchical position or political opposition to the regime and dominant groups", communal groups are perceived in terms of their communal characteristics (Harff & Gurr 1989, 24). In the case of crimes against humanity, the object of attack must be 'any civilian population', which not only implies the collective nature of crimes but also that the victims are not randomly selected (Article 7(1) Rome Statute). Specific acts are typified as war crimes when committed in the context of an international or non-international armed conflict and against specific categories of victims (combatants or civilians) (Article 8 Rome Statute).

In other words, the victim is identified with a group of persons and not with a concrete individual. What lies essentially beneath this pattern of victimization is a process of de-individuation of victims, where "individuals are not seen or paid attention to as individuals" (Festinger, Pepitone & Newcomb 1952, 382). The organizational nature of state crimes proves to be the catalyst in this process. Within this context it is submitted that collective victims should be conceived as *organizational victims* too. Such a qualification is based on the observation that their victimhood results from the mobilization of a bureaucratic apparatus endowed with a high division of labour and directed to the achievement of specific goals. The de-individuation process works both ways: deadening the inner restraints of victimizers and increasing the vulnerability of victims. State officials, the physical perpetrators of core crimes who materialize a state policy, are ordinary employees who have accepted the normality of the organizational routine within which they live and work. Their acts, even if illegal or immoral, form part of the role they have to perform and usually constitute a necessary means to the achievement of positive ends (state security, common good, etc.). Victims, on the other hand, are nothing more than the personification of a threat to the national security or an impediment to the attainment to a national objective (e.g. ethnic purity). Names are not important, only roles are (threat, evil, etc.); there is no distinguishable person, only an abstracted victim.

A *structural and a functional element* appears to be an inherent characteristic of state crime victimization. Heinous core crimes do not occur out of the blue. They do not constitute simply the violent expression of ephemeral passions, but the culmination of long-lasting societal conflicts. It is for this reason that they involve an enduring victimization rooted in society's values, stratification, institutions and power relations (Fattah 1991). On the other hand, the functional element springs from the very fact that state crime victimization serves the maintenance and the reproduction of the dominant system, challenged through group conflict. However, it can be functional the other way round: as a means to radical structural change within the system – e.g. convert an ethnically heterogeneous society into homogeneous by committing genocide (Dadrian 1974).

All the above indicate that we are dealing with a form of *massive victimization* producing multifaceted impact. The large scale and organised manner of commission of core crimes entails a vast number of victims that may range from a specific group to the whole society. It is needless to reiterate specific types of harms resulting form state criminality, shocking numbers of combatants or civilians killed during armed conflicts, astonishing numbers of refugees, of individuals raped, tortured, etc. Several empirical studies substantiate all our fears and the worst of scenarios concerning the lethal capacity of state apparatus (Turković 2002; Kiza 2006; Bijleveld & Morssinkhof 2006; Kiza, Rathgeber & Rohne 2006). Further sophisticated distinctions between direct and indirect victims, first-generation and second-generation victims, direct and indirect consequences, etc. are indications of a laborious effort to capture the amount of harm, injury and suffering provoked by state criminality. The exact determination of harm in quantitative terms is important for at least one reason: it corroborates the remarks made above on the qualitative elements of state criminality and victimization (Bijleveld 2008).

The collective, systemic, structural, institutional, organizational and political nature of state crime victimization supports the research lines drawn by critical criminologists. In particular, the identification of a positive connection between the unequal distribution of power and the level and frequency of state crime reflects the collective and structural dimension of state crime victimization. In other words, powerlessness proves to be a precondition for being a victim of state crime, both at national and international levels. The organizational dimension of victimization does not only correspond to the tenet that state crime results from organizational pressure to achieve organizational goals, but also explains why the phenomenon persists, being irrelevant whether we are dealing with a democratic regime or not (of course this may reflect on the intensity and the specific form of state crime). The institutional dimension entails that victims of state crimes are usually targets of repeated victimization, facing the additional difficulty of being obliged to rely as a rule on the victimizer or civil society movements for redress (Kauzlarich, Matthews & Miller 2001; Kauzlarich 2008).

What also proves to be a constant feature of state crime victimization is the denial of its acknowledgment. Cohen (2001) has offered a powerful and pioneering analysis of its potential manifestations. In particular he identifies three types of denial: literal, where the fact or knowledge of the fact is denied; interpretive, where the raw facts are not denied but only given a different meaning; and implicatory, where the denial refers not to the fact or its meaning but to its psychological, political or moral implications, leading more or less to its justification (see Haldemann, this volume). As far as the organization is concerned, denial can be personal, cultural or official. It is this latter pattern that is most relevant here, given that it is "initiated, structured and sustained by the massive resources of the modern state" (Cohen 2001, 10). State denial fuels the international dimension of state crime victimization, in the sense that it compels victims to search for recognition and justice at the international level.

2.4. RECOGNITION OF STATE-SPONSORED CRIME VICTIMS AT INTERNATIONAL LEVEL

The preceding analysis, bringing to light the patterns and circumstances of state-sponsored criminality, has established that its victims are 'real' although not 'ideal', at least from the criminal state's viewpoint. What rests to be seen is whether they are also 'official', meaning whether the victim status has been afforded to them at the international level, to what extent and with what limitations (Burt 1983). If someone accepts the view that victimization implies, in addition to the conditions mentioned above, "an imbalance of strength and a disequilibrium in the positions of power" (Fattah 1991, 4), then the struggle for recognition of the status of victims of state-sponsored crime represents the first step in the quest for redress.

The First and Second World War imposed the general acknowledgment of the fact that the commission of gross human rights violations or heinous crimes is strictly linked to state action or inaction, intentional or negligent. Thus, it became crystal clear that there was a vital need to expand the traditional list of rights and obligations provided in the case of interpersonal relations so as to cover all the possible forms of manifestation of the relationship between victim-victimizer. The development of international human rights law responds to this fundamental need. Two instruments are of major importance in concrete: the *Declaration of Basic Principles of Justice for Victims of Crime and Abuse of Power* (hereinafter, 1985 Declaration of Basic Principles) and the *Basic Principles and Guidelines on the Right to a Remedy and Reparation for Victims of Gross Violations of International Human Rights Law and Serious Violations of International Humanitarian Law* (hereinafter, 2005 Basic Principles and Guidelines).[7] These two instruments, focusing respectively on victims of domestic crimes and on victims of international crimes, reaffirm the current legal status of victims or call for its extension and encapsulate their rights to access to justice and obtain reparation for their harm (Bassiouni 2006).

At the international level, the identification of a positive connection between power and victimization was articulated broadly in terms of abuse of power. Granted the complexity of the phenomenon, suffice it to say that it refers generally to the use of legitimate or illegitimate means for the achievement of unlawful ends or to the employment of illegitimate means for the attainment of legitimate and laudable objectives (Fattah 1989). More specially, the drafters of the 1985 Declaration of Basic Principles addressed the phenomenon of abuse of power in a double sense: as "non-enforcement abuse of power", referring to conduct that although proscribed by national criminal law is not enforced because of the political and economic power of the perpetrators, and as

---

[7]   Both adopted by the UN General Assembly in its Resolutions 40/34 of 29 November 1985 and 60/147 of 21 March 2005, respectively.

"immoral abuse of power", touching on conduct which, even if not typified as conventional crime, contravenes a universally acceptable moral standard (Lamborn 1988).

In this framework, the UN General Assembly declared that it was "cognizant that millions of people throughout the world suffer harm as a result of crime and the abuse of power and that the rights of these victims have not been adequately recognized". In order to overcome this situation, the 1985 Declaration of Basic Principles, next to the classical figure of individual victims (Articles 1 and 2), recognizes the victims of power abuse defined as

> *persons who, individually or collectively, have suffered harm, including physical or mental injury, emotional suffering, economic loss or substantial impairment of their fundamental rights, through acts or omissions that do not yet constitute violations of national criminal laws but of internationally recognized norms relating to human rights.* (Article 18)

It is a positive development that the above instrument distinguishes between victimization deriving from actions in breach of national criminal law committed by private actors or the state and those resulting from abuse of power by the state. By doing so, the 1985 Declaration of Basic Principles not only recognizes the existence and the gravity of the latter situation, but also calls on states to incorporate into national criminal law "norms proscribing abuses of power and providing remedies to victims of such abuses" (Article 19). It is important to notice that this instrument is non-binding on states and therefore does not confer rights, but only recognizes and affirms rights that already exist or should exist (Bassiouni 1988b). In this line, it urges states to criminalize conducts that violate internationally recognized norms relating to human rights and to enact legislation providing for victims of abuse of power the same rights as those conferred upon victims of conventional crimes, namely access to justice, fair treatment, restitution, compensation and assistance. The additional fact that the above instrument is composed of 21 provisions out of which only four refer to victims of abuse of power substantiates the allegation that we are dealing with an important but timorous development concerning policy implication.

On the other hand, the 2005 Basic Principles and Guidelines further provides that:

> *Where appropriate, and in accordance with domestic law, the term "victim" also includes the immediate family or dependants of the direct victim and persons who have suffered harm in intervening to assist victims in distress or to prevent victimization.* (Article 8)

The quoted definition broadens the concept of victim by including, next to individuals or collectivities that directly suffer harm, their families and other persons who are injured while trying to intervene on behalf of the victims. These victims have a right to access to justice as individuals or as groups both at national and international levels (Articles 12–14), a right to have the harm suffered repaired thought restitution, compensation, rehabilitation, satisfaction and guarantees of non-repetition (Articles 15–23), and a right to truth (Article 24). Again, as it is emphasized in the Preamble, the 2005 Basic Principles and Guidelines "do not entail new international or domestic legal obligations".

The above developments support the conclusion that victims of state-sponsored crime, national or international, are officially recognized as such. The said recognition does not entail the acknowledgment of a corresponding state responsibility. As it will be further showed below, individuals are provided with both a right to access to justice and a right to an effective remedy. However, these rights should not be confused with and do not amount to a right to bring claims against states before an international tribunal under general international law (it can only be founded on national law or specific treaty regimes). Such a right is only conferred to the state of nationality of harmed individuals, which can espouse their claims on a discretionary basis (institution of diplomatic protection) (Tomuschat 1999). This is due to the fact that, according to the International Law Commission's *Draft Articles on State Responsibility* (2001), the concept of *injured state* is central to the invocation of state responsibility. The injured state can be defined individually or collectively (plurality of states), depending on the nature of the violated international norm and the consequences produced by the wrongful act (Articles 40–48) (Crawford 2002, 254–280). That means that an individual or a non-state actor cannot figure as a party in the legal relationship brought into being by a breach of a rule of international law. Bassiouni eloquently observes that "governments did not want to assume any responsibility, even for the acts of their own agents, preferring to limit victims' rights to the commission of crimes committed by non-State actors". (2006, 247)

3. DEALING WITH STATE-SPONSORED CRIMES AND ADDRESSING THE PLIGHT OF ITS VICTIMS

The main purpose of this section is to systematize the rationale and techniques of two different methods of reckoning with state-sponsored crimes, that is the institution of criminal trials and the promotion of alternative strategies, like TRCs. The contextualization of this vexing issue through the allusion to some basic policy aspirations offers the common ground of these outwardly incompatible methods.

3.1. CONTEXTUALISATION AND POLICY CONSIDERATIONS

How to confront core international crimes? The question invites a wide range of disciplines to submit their particular perspective, which does not necessarily mean that each one will set forth a uniform proposal. Limiting the discussion to the normative domain, one could generally identify two major trends: one consisting in the prevailing paradigm of punishment of perpetrators of core crimes after the establishment of their personal guilt though formalized criminal trials; and another based on more flexible mediated procedures, where the priority is the production of an inclusive narrative through the identification of the originating causes of the social conflict and the description of what really happened in its course (Kritz 1996).

In the former case, justice is narrowly constructed in terms of trials, criminal statutes and punishment. In this context, accountability equates to individual criminal liability and impunity to the *de facto* or *de jure* inertia (immunity, extremely brief statutory limitations, defence of superior orders or due obedience, sweeping amnesty laws, pardon) of the criminal justice system. Contrary, in the latter case, justice is broadly envisaged in order to include non-judicial bodies, whose procedures and discourse have a great value for a post-conflict society in the perspective of healing and reconciliation (Botberg & Thompson 2000). Thus, here accountability consists primarily in truth telling, and impunity results from the absence of any response to mass human rights violations, whether in criminal, civil, administrative, disciplinary and generally restorative measures.[8]

Which of the two strategies will be promoted is chiefly a political choice conditioned by the political reality and societal needs of a particular nation (Nino 1991; Huyse 1995; Landsman 1996). In any case, both approaches share the elementary objectives to prevent the repetition of past abuses and to repair the damage caused, even though only by addressing their originating factors and recognising their multifaceted consequences. In this context, there seems to be an agreement that any legitimate policy of reckoning with mass atrocities should meet some minimum standards: a) the ultimate goal is the establishment of the truth, which must be officially sanctioned and publicly disclosed. That means that individual knowledge about what actually happened should be incorporated and reconstructed into a public acknowledgement of the existence and

---

8   "'Impunity' means the impossibility, de jure or de facto, of bringing the perpetrators of human rights violations to account – whether in criminal, civil, administrative or disciplinary proceedings – since they are not subject to any inquiry that might lead to their being accused, arrested, tried and, if found guilty, sentenced to appropriate penalties, and to making reparations to their victims." *Question of the impunity of perpetrators of human rights violations (civil and political).* Revised final report prepared by Mr. Joinet pursuant to Sub-Commission decision 1996/119, (E/CN.4/Sub.2/1997/20/Rev.1), 2 October 1997. See also Joinet 2002.

implementation of an abusive state policy; b) the policy should be bottom-up driven, which involves that it should echo the popular will, expressed either explicitly through a referendum or implicitly through the public support of governmental choices; c) the policy should not contravene state obligations stemming from international human rights law. For instance, criminal trials should be conducted along the lines of general principles of criminal law and fair trial requirements (Zalaquett 1990). On the other hand, although there is no regulatory framework for truth and reconciliation commissions (TRCs), the experience of the past permits the articulation of some minimal standards, the satisfaction of which would contribute to their prestige and success (Hayner 1996; Abrams & Hayner 2002).

In what follows I will briefly present the rationale of the above-mentioned strategies assuming a victimological standpoint. Suffice it to mention that the analysis touches on abstract models of justice with a view to highlighting their general distinctive traits and does not ender into a case study. The fact that specific remarks potentially do not fit particular cases does not affect the validity of the argument. It should also be stressed that the institution of criminal trials and the use of TRCs are not by definition mutually exclusive. On the contrary, as it will be showed, the appearance and growth of the latter practice sprang form the inherent limitations of the former in dealing with state-sponsored criminality. Consequently, these two strategies are considered here as potentially complementary and not as inevitably alternative (Roht-Arriaza 2006; Sebba 2006; Villa-Vicencio 2006; Orentlicher 2007). In any case, it should be reminded that both criminal trials and TRCs do not constitute ends in themselves but only means to ends. Their value depends on the extent that they achieve to establish the truth, provide public platform to victims, promote accountability, comply with the rule of law, recommend reparations for victims and institutional reform, advance reconciliation, and stimulate public deliberation (Crocker 1999).

3.2. (INTERNATIONAL) CRIMINAL TRIALS

State monopoly on violence is considered the most adequate way to restrain individual vengeance (vendetta) and to guarantee the peaceful regulation of social conflicts (Weber 2002, 43–44). This principle generates a double effect: individuals should abstain from the violent settlement of their differences otherwise the state is authorized to intervene through the institution of punishment. In a liberal system of criminal justice the idea of human rights is central and reflects on both aspects: individual violence entails the harm of a legally protected individual and/or social interest, which opens the door for the penal intervention of the state. Granted that the latter also implies the breach of the rights of the offender, it should be strictly regulated in order not to become violations of human rights. This is realized through the exhaustive provision in advance of the occasions on which state penal intervention is legitimized, the determination of the procedure that has to be followed, and the guarantees that have to be observed.[9]

State crime consists in the illegitimate exercise of state violence accompanied in principle with impunity. Under the first quality, it violates gravely the collective conscience of a society, composed of the most fundamental sentiments that comprise the psychological link between their members (human dignity, solidarity, etc.) (Durkheim 1893), bringing additionally into question its most basic institutions guaranteeing its peaceful continuity (justice, rule of law, etc.). The total lack of penal intervention, or more broadly the inept or corrupt state response – impunity in this context – corroborates the organizational, political, structural and institutional dimension of the phenomenon. In this sense, impunity should not be conceived strictly in its legal dimension, i.e. as the lack of attribution of criminal liability to perpetrators of acts constituting core international crimes, but broadly as denial of the reality as such; as a manifestation of an abusive conception of power that becomes synonymous to arbitrariness. Thus, impunity entails both the lack of recognition of the occurrence of a violation and the denial of attribution to someone of the quality of victim. If the former is defined as victimization, then the latter can be considered as a further, secondary victimization (see also Haldemann and Van Wijk, both this volume).

Behind the demand to combat impunity and bring perpetrators to criminal justice lies always a retributive or 'just desert' rationale (see also Wemmers, this volume). Although other justifications of punishment, like incapacitation, deterrence and rehabilitation, have also been invoked, retribution proves to be the predominant objective in the case of punishment of perpetrators of mass human right violations both at national and international levels (Drumbl 2007, 60–61, 150). Retribution in its pure form is a backward looking theory based on the Kantian categorical imperative to punish every violation of law, being irrelevant whether punishment will prevent future crime or rehabilitate the offender. In this framework, crime is perceived as an offence to a specific society as a whole and in the case of core international crimes to the international society as well. It is the seriousness of the crime that determines the perpetrator's guilt, which depends on and is proportionate to his moral culpability (Moore 2009). Seen through this prism, criminal trials represent a legitimate means to channel the reasonable demands of vengeance and to break with the cycle of personal revenge.

---

[9] International institutions, like the international courts, are also assigned to control the potential violation of these conditions. For example, within the system of the Council of Europe, the European Court of Human Rights has jurisdiction to rule on individual applications alleging violations of the civil and political rights set out in the European Convention on Human Rights (ECHR). In this framework, Article 6 of the ECHR secures the right to fair trial, while Article 7 stipulates the principle *nullum crimen nulla poena sine lege*.

On the other hand, it should be underscored that there is a systematic effort to found the need of criminal trials on more forward-looking theories that take into account the demands of victims and the symbolic value of punishment especially for a post-conflict society (Zalaquett 1990; Malamud-Goti 1990; Orentlicher 1991). In this framework, prosecutions are presented as a *moral duty* of the state, as a *state obligation stemming from international law*, and as a *victim's right*.

Under the light of the first approach – prosecutions as a moral duty – prosecutions are evaluated as the most effective means in the process of reaffirmation of the centrality of individual rights and dignity and (re) establishment of the rule of law in a society (Malamud-Goti 1990; Orentlicher 1991). The trial offers a forum where all parties implicated into a conflict have the chance to express their subjective versions of reality following specific rules. Trial results into a judgment that objectifies these usually divergent accounts. As the same word implies, a verdict is the declaration on the truth, an authoritative statement on the facts. The ritual followed does not only bring about the systematization of detached individual experiences in one official narrative, but primarily transforms individual knowledge into public acknowledgment. None of the implicated parties can challenge the factual findings, which acquire the quality of the historical fact. So, the creation of an accurate historical record about what happened as well as the reestablishment and reaffirmation of some basic values constitute the ulterior objective that is usually linked with the educational function of criminal law. The expressive dimension of punishment facilitates the restoration of a rudimentary common sense or moral universe, indispensable for the rebuilt of social solidarity (Joyce 2004; Nimanga 2007; Drumbl 2007, 173 ff.).

The very holding of trials represents a radical change or a sign of normalization. So, if impunity for crimes committed at the behest of the state offer the general setting, the mobilization of the criminal justice system is tangible proof that something is changing. It signifies the abolition of a dual system of justice that permitted the punishment of perpetrators of conventional crimes and crimes against the state and guaranteed the immunity of perpetrators of state crimes. In this sense, trials represent a clear rupture with respect to the past, putting an end to anomie. At the same time, they symbolize the beginning of a new era, promoting the general confidence on the rule of law and on the equality of all citizens. In a nutshell, they fulfil the double function of the epilogue to a violent past and of the prologue to a peaceful and law-governed future. What is more, a criminal process against state criminals is a signal of institutional reform, the success of which requires also broader changes at the organizational and structural levels and can only be estimated in the long term (Malamud-Goti 1990; Cohen 1995).

A question arises at this point on whether criminal prosecutions constitute a legal obligation under international law. An affirmative answer presupposes the detection of specific human rights violations that the state is obliged to criminalize under international law or that are originally defined as crimes at the international level. The commission of such crimes entails a responsibility on the part of the state to conduct investigations and to punish the wrongdoers. A thorough examination of the various international and regional legal instruments as well as international customary law support the conclusion that states bear the non-derogable obligation towards the international community as a whole to translate the most serious human rights violations into crimes, and prosecute and punish them (or alternative to extradite the offenders in order to be prosecuted elsewhere – *aut dedere aut judicare*). The most serious human rights violations concern the right to life and physical integrity, which are always impinged in the context of commission of core international crimes. It is also true that limitations on prosecutions, focusing for instance on the gravest crimes and/or the 'most responsible' offenders are compatible with the aforementioned obligation (Roht-Arriaza 1990; Orentlicher 1991; Bassiouni 1996a, 2008).

Given that criminal trials seek to calibrate individual guilt in order to ascribe criminal liability, it is natural that the offender is the central figure of the whole process. If the need to avert excessive state intervention into individual freedoms offered the foundation for the extensive stipulation of the rights of the accused in international human rights law, then it was the demand to fight impunity for serious violations of human rights that imposed the necessity to improve the position and role of the victim. The neglect of the victim, who actually suffered the criminal harm, is the by-product of the substitution of the disorganized system of personal revenge for a centralised criminal justice system. Crime is considered primarily an offence against the state or the society and secondarily as an offence against the victim. This situation led to the position that the state has a right and an obligation to prosecute, whereas victims have only a legitimate expectation. Nevertheless, the situation is changing. Recent developments in international human rights law support the assertion that the victim is acknowledged as the most directly harmed party by a crime, which justifies a more active standing in the criminal process. The development of what Aldana-Pindell calls "victim-focused prosecution norms" seem to substantiate the emergence of a victim's justifiable right to prosecution for serious human rights violations, which coexists with and complements the relevant state's duty to prosecute (2002, 2004).

The aforementioned right is the final outcome of the conjunctive judicial interpretation by e.g. the European Court of Human Rights of two other rights recognized to victims: to have access to justice (Article 6(1) ECHR) and to obtain an effective remedy (Article 13 ECHR). The underlying rationale consists in the ruling that states should abstain from any measure that would curtail or impede the scrutiny of a case and additionally ought to organize and conduct a thorough and effective investigation capable of leading to the identification and punishment of those responsible. In this context, the payment of compensation to the victim, although desired where appropriate and when granted, is not sufficient. Prosecutions are considered an essential element of the remedy states should guarantee to victims of certain grave crimes. The strengthening of victims' participatory rights in criminal process is the other side of the same coin, provided that it facilitates the monitor of state actions. So, victims should have the possibility to provoke the review of prosecutor's decisions not to institute criminal proceedings in a case, access to investigation and court documents, access to witness statements, etc. (Aldana-Pindell 2002, 2004).

Even though the duty to mount prosecutions for state-sponsored crimes rests principally on states, the international community has justly envisaged the possibility that the latter may be unwilling or unable to do so. The creation of *ad hoc* international criminal tribunals and most importantly the establishment of the permanent International Criminal Court (ICC) for the direct application of international criminal law validate the existence of some minimum universal standards and the rudimentary belief that the commission of national and international crimes cannot be justified on the grounds of alleged higher interests of states. The creation of an international criminal jurisdiction transforms the criminal justice model into a universal paradigm on how to reckon with state-sponsored crimes and corroborates the contention that the protection of human rights cannot be considered as another internal national issue (Bassiouni 2002). In this vein, the Preamble of the Rome Statute declares that "unimaginable atrocities that deeply shock the conscience of humanity" and "threaten the peace, security and well-being of the world" must not go unpunished. After recalling that it is "the duty of every State to exercise its criminal jurisdiction over those responsible for international crimes", it affirms that the establishment of the ICC aspires "to put an end to impunity for the perpetrators of these crimes and thus to contribute to the prevention of such crimes".

Although the Rome Statute does not grant victims complete autonomy neither with respect to the initiation of an investigation nor during proceedings, it is true that it contains the most comprehensive and specific list of victim's rights – further detailed in the *Rules of Procedure and Evidence* (Section III, 'Victims and witnesses', Rules 85–99), echoing its emerging right to prosecutions. In particular, it is the first time that it is provided for victims' access to all the organs of the ICC, namely the Registry, Pre-Trial Chamber, Trial and Appeals Chambers and the Office of the Prosecutor. It is also stipulated that victims' views and concerns must be taken into account by the appropriate officials responsible for the decisions and that victims must be kept informed of the proceedings. For instance, Article 68(3) of the Rome Statute provides that "where the personal interests of the victims are affected, the Court shall permit their views and concerns to be presented and considered at all stages of the proceedings". Victims are also permitted to have legal representatives in order to make their presentations during the various stages of proceedings and to have their interests and rights better served. So, even though victims are not formally a party in the proceedings and a lot of issues await resolution, various 'victims-friendly' provisions guarantee a more active role for victims, substantiating the contention that victims' interests are relevant for international criminal justice (Garkawe 2001; Jorda & De Hemptinne 2002; McDonald 2006; McGonigle Leyh, this volume).

The above developments offer a positive testimony to the influence of the victimological concern on the (international) criminal justice enterprise, proving that the two disciplines are moving closer together. In this line, critical analysis of the Rome Statute provisions on victims standing in the proceedings seek to highlight its shortcomings and to promote specific amendments and general reforms. By way of illustration, it has been argued that victims' participation is more symbolic than real, which enhances the danger of 'victims objectification' through their instrumental use as witnesses for exclusively condemnatory purposes (Garkawe 2001; Henham 2004; Halsam 2004; McGonigle Leyh, this volume). On the other hand, the victimological ideal of the empowerment of victims and communities in the trial process is put forward through the proposal of structural reforms based on the communitarian process model, which will also contribute substantially to the general legitimacy of the ICC (Findlay & Henham 2005, 2010; Findlay 2009).

3.3. NON-CRIMINAL JUSTICE STRATEGIES: THE CASE OF TRUTH AND RECONCILIATION COMMISSIONS AS RESTORATIVE JUSTICE MECHANISMS

Although state-sponsored crimes are radically different in comparison to ordinary crimes both in terms of pattern of commission and resultant victimization, they nevertheless trigger the same normative reaction. Drumbl asserts that "despite the proclaimed extraordinary nature of atrocity crime, its modality of punishment, theory of sentencing, and process of determining guilt or innocence, each remain disappointingly, although perhaps reassuringly, ordinary" (2007, 6). In other words, the targeted actors, the method, the means and the outcomes remain surprisingly identical, which is explained by the fact that transposition without contextualization seems to be the leading principle ("legal mimicry", Drumbl 2007, 123). The situation becomes worse if one considers that serious reservations have been articulated in relation to the capacity of criminal law to cope with the atrocious nature of state-sponsored criminality: the evil is so radical that no punishment is enough; it simply "explode[s] the limits of the law" (Arendt, quoted in Osiel 2000, 128).

Non-criminal strategies offer a completely different path and are usually described as the 'second-best' option for dealing with state-sponsored crimes, at least in the context of western legal culture. However, it is important to understand that the establishment of a TRC in the wake of collective violence serves a totally different approach dictated essentially by the need to overcome the inherent and intractable limitations of highly formalized criminal procedures (Nikolic-Rstanovic 2006; Wemmers, this volume).[10]

The starting point of this different philosophy lies in the realization that a comprehensive scrutiny of the root causes of mass atrocities cannot be fully achieved through the individualistic, adversarial, dichotomist and reductionist reasoning of criminal law. Individualism posits that all social facts must be explained exhaustively in terms of the actions, beliefs, and desires of individual human beings. In other words, collectivities and structures lack an autonomous reality. The adversarial method of criminal trials is not based on truthful dialogue but on litigation: one party strives to prove what usually the other party denies. This is due to a certain extent to the fact that criminal law is built on dichotomies: right or wrong, legal or illegal, guilty or innocent; there is no middle position. What is more, the guilt can only be personalized; there is no such a thing like 'system-guilt'. Not all facts are relevant, but only those that can back up the particular claim of a criminal case. Testifying and cross-examination are technical ordeals that restrict the flow of information. Thus, reality and more specifically the extremely compound reality of mass atrocities is deconstructed and reconstructed in very concrete legal terms. What is redundant is aborted. The final product is but a narrow and simplistic version of reality. The concept of 'judicial truth' indicates that the result consists more in a technical finding, reached through a sophisticated process, than in the genuine and complete truth about past crimes. Finally, despite the appeal to alternative rationales, the essence of penal process in practice remains the delivery of pain to the offender, not appeasement and reconciliation, despite its official goals. Besides, the concept of secondary victimization was originally coined in order to describe the additional harm inflicted to the victim through the criminal trial (Hulsman 1986, 1991; Christie 2001, 2007; Ewald 2008).

TRCs offer a distinctive pathway. In general terms, they are official bodies created by the government, the legislature or inter-governmental organizations for a limited period of time with the purpose to investigate a concrete period of human rights abuses committed usually within a single country and to report

---

[10] "Truth and Reconciliation Commissions (TRCs) are official, typically non-judicial inquiries into past periods of repression, conflict, atrocity or human rights abuse that seek to establish an accurate historical record of events and otherwise take non-penal steps to address the legacies of those events." (Cockayne 2009, 543).

publicly on their findings. The central aim of these commissions is the conservation of the circumstantial, documentary and material evidence of the acts committed, the collection of victims' and witnesses' testimonies and the creation of a comprehensive record that would shed light on the patterns of state-sponsored criminality. This aim is better conceived if it is moreover compared to the one sought by NGOs. whereas the latter produce reports with the purpose to denounce ongoing human rights violations and mobilize public opinion, truth commissions seek to establish the truth over the past in an official way, which will generate the political and moral responsibility of the state, its obligation to provide reparations to victims, to investigate and tackle the perpetrators of mass atrocities, etc. (Mattarollo 2002).

The victim figures as the central concern of truth commissions. This is natural, since their aim is not to determine the responsibility of an individual but to yield accounts of entire regimes giving public voice to victims. Their method of work consists in offering the possibility to the victims to recount their calamities in their own words, liberated from the strict rules of a legal process and the terminology of the specialists. The biggest challenge does not lay in the reconstruction of the gruesomeness of mass atrocity in legal terms, but simply in the description of the reality as faithfully as possible. It should be noted that there is both a quantitative and qualitative concern underlying this process, given that the compilation of numerous testimonies is combined with an effort to relate individual and group cases. By doing so, it is possible to identify individual and collective victims. This is presented as the best way to illustrate the pervasiveness, systemic nature and ubiquity of state terror.

It should be stressed that the importance of this enterprise consists both in the process and in the final outcome. Giving testimonials has a significant therapeutic value for individuals and for the whole nation (Minow 2000; Danieli 2006). Victims, witnesses and the community are given the possibility to express their feelings, their fears, their agonies and their desires in public. The break of silence is driven by a simple rule: what is important to the parties is relevant to the process. In this context, TRCs become "a forum for expression of sorrow and blame, but without decisions on the delivery of pain attached" (Christie 2007, 367). In a similar vein, Minow posits that "the language of healing casts the consequences of collective violence in terms of trauma; the paradigm is health, rather than justice. Justice reappears in the idea that its pursuit is to heal victims of violence and to reconcile opposing groups" (1998, 63). A traumatized nation is a nation in mourning. The exposure of its wounds is the first step for their healing: the trauma becomes part of the past, as its treatment marks the present and frames the future (Danieli 2009). Psychological restoration and healing from 'extreme traumatisation' require that victims will be heard in a safe environment. Truth commissions may offer such a space (Hamber 2001), notwithstanding the fact that recent empirical studies raise reasonable doubts (Mendeloff 2009; Brounéus 2010).

The final report of the commission is an authoritative overall statement on the truth, not only a decision confirming or rejecting certain accusations. It is the delivery of the truth of the victims, witnesses and offenders to the wider public unaffected by technical rules and the interests of victors. It is a holistic truth that can address the role played not only by individuals but also by structures, institutions, ideologies, and policies. It is a detailed description of harms suffered, including those qualified as marginal, unimportant or unrepresentative in a trial process. In this sense, it is an official acknowledgement of widely known, but systematically denied truths, which simply cannot enter in the rigid form of a judgment. It is a full account on the historical, social and political context that triggered the conflict, on the deficits of institutions and procedures, on the democracy that proved extremely fragile or inexistent. In a nutshell, it is history written in terms of victimhood and accountability (Hayner 1994, 2001).It is exactly this multifaceted and wide-ranging version of truth that opens the door for appeasement and reconciliation (Du Toit 2000; Boraine 2000; Froestad & Shearing 2007). It should be noted that in the context of TRCs reconciliation is primarily promoted on national and political level. It is connected with the creation of democratic public sphere, where former opponents relate on the basis of a common version of the past. Reconciliation on individual level is a far more complex process that depends on direct communication between victim and offender, mediated or not (also Haldemann, this volume). But usually the former facilitates the latter (Aertsen *et al.* 2008).

What is more, TRCs are in the position to make recommendations that will smooth the progress of reconciliation, advance the democratization of the state and guarantee the long-term development, averting essentially the probability of repetition of collective conflicts. The identification of the structural causes that triggered the social conflict permit commissions as independent bodies with an overall picture of the situation to recommend changes that will take into account all levels of analysis, i.e., micro, meso, and macro. That may include reforms of the law and of the basic state institutions (judiciary, police, military, government, etc.), enforcement of welfare state, creation of more economic opportunities for the lower strata, etc. Commissions, offering a platform to victims and their families, are in the position to know at first hand their situation and needs, which enable them to contribute to the design of adequate reparations policy (Correa, Guillerot & Magarrell 2009). Only through such initiatives can accountability be complete and justice pluralized (Bassiouni 1996b).

Flexibility in functioning and procedure may be considered strategic options in pursuit of the establishment of a more inclusive truth about state-sponsored crimes than the one produced by criminal courts, but at the same time they constitute sources of criticism with respect to the objectivity and the perceived value of the work of a commission. The development of some basic guidelines touching on the composition of the commission, the extent and length of its mandate, its powers of investigation, the rules of procedure and evidence that should be followed, etc. seek to overcome some of the problems that have aroused in practice offering the ground for justified critiques (Hayner 1996; Abrams & Hayner 2002; Mattarollo 2002).

In the same vein, the idea has been launched to establish a permanent international truth commission (Scharf 1997). The creation of a body endowed with stable personnel and infrastructure would offer the following benefits: a superior sufficiency of resources, such as funding, staff and expertise, which are essential for a commission to carry out its work in an uninterrupted and effective way; enhanced guarantees of neutrality, which is a precondition for its findings not to be contested by none of the implicated parties; greater autonomy towards domestic influences, which is important for the reveal of the whole truth; and greater speed in launching and concluding investigations, which is necessary for the safeguard of the evidence and the respect of the right to expedite trial. An international commission could investigate more effectively the potential role of international actors, the possible complicity of bystanders and the probable inaction of international community. What is more, a permanent structure could resolve easier the vexing question of whether to name perpetrators by incorporating due process norms and thus giving to the latter the possibility to present their version and confront their accusers personally or through a representative (Scharf 1997).

The above analysis illustrate that TRCs can function as mechanisms of restorative justice in the wake of mass atrocities, given that they permit victims to gain a sense of ownership over the facts and centrality in a process, aspiring to the establishment of truth and to the promotion of accountability, reconciliation and reparations (Weitekamp *et al.* 2006; Van Ness 2007; Parmentier, Vanspauwen & Weitekamp 2008).

4. A TENTATIVE CONCLUSION: PLURALISING JUSTICE AS VICTIMS' NEED, VICTIMIZED SOCIETIES' DEMAND AND (INTERNATIONAL) LAW'S WAGER

The mechanics and patterns of state-sponsored criminality impose the duty to develop normative frameworks that can adequately address their complex reality. This venture should not be perceived and approached as an end in itself, but as a means to deliver justice to those directly affected by state-sponsored crime. The demand for international justice has not only brought to the fore the abused party, the victims, but has also revealed their suffering and their typology:

individual and collective victims, direct and indirect victims, communities, nations, and the whole international community.

The classical criminal justice model falls short of this task for the elementary reason that it declares the state as the victim in criminal cases (Barnett 1977, 287; Wemmers, this volume), constraining the real victims to a merely instrumental role, like that of witness or civil party etc. The positive steps made at national and international levels in the direction of advancing a more active participation of the victim have doubtless augmented its stake in the criminal process. This progress has been interpreted as a sign of shift from a purely retributive to a more restorative model of justice. TRCs, on the other hand, are one of the most innovative responses to the post-conflict justice puzzle. Inspired by the principles of restorative justice, they constitute genuine "answers to deficits in modernity" (Christie 2007). The above analysis substantiates the assertion that they offer a sophisticated mechanism indispensable for addressing the collective, organizational, international and political dimension of state-sponsored crimes. Of course, such an acknowledgment should not be interpreted as a disregard of the shortcomings of this institution and of the need to take further steps for its evolution.

It is safe to argue that initiatives in both fields are driven by the ideas of engagement and empowerment. Engagement is considered a precondition for the production of an official acknowledgment of past human right violations that shapes collective memory; collective memory offers the raw material for the construction of a shared identity, which functions as a guarantee of a nations' unity. Empowerment should not be conceived only as a power to participate but also as an entitlement to determine the content of a process. In other words, the process of justice should seek to restore the power to the victim in a double sense: providing him/her with a sense of ownership over the facts and reparation for the abuse of state power (Sawin & Zehr 2007; Havel 2002). In this second line, Hulsman posits that "the most fundamental right of a victim is that his definition of the event and his expressed needs are taking as the starting point for the consideration of an intervention in the public sphere" (1989, 31).

In this framework, the wager for academia and for law is to find the most rational way to ensure a functional relationship between the ICC and the institution of TRCs (Villa-Vicencio 2000; Dugard 2002; Seibert-Fohr 2003; Stahn 2005; Sunga 2009). The keywords of this venture should be synthesis and synergy, given that "only by interweaving, sequencing and accommodating multiple pathways to justice could some kind of larger justice in fact emerge" (Roht-Arriaza 2006, 8). In my understanding, such an endeavour may represent a need for victims and a demand of victimized communities.

III. ERODING THE MYTH OF PURE EVIL

When Victims become Perpetrators and Perpetrators Victims

Alette SMEULERS

1. INTRODUCTION

The myth of pure evil defines the way we look at extreme atrocities (Baumeister 1999). It portrays the perpetrators thereof as bad and evil and the victims as good and innocent and thus classifies the victims and the perpetrators in two extremes, namely two mutually exclusive groups: the good and the bad. One may wonder, however, whether this is always fair. The distinction between perpetrators and victims might be clear cut when looking at a single event, for example a woman who kills her husband with a knife. Yet, if we look at the context, the distinction between perpetrator and victim might not be so clear cut when – to use the same example – it turns out that the wife has been abused, mistreated and sexually exploited by her husband for years and that he was about to attack her again. This could be no different for perpetrators of international crimes. The international legal framework has qualified perpetrators of international crimes as *hostes humani generis*; enemies of all humankind and thus seems to endorse the myth of pure evil. Yet, one may wonder if this classification is always adequate. In order to answer this we need to take the person who committed the crimes into account as well as the context in which the crime has been committed. The aim of this chapter is to do this and test whether the myth of pure evil in which the two groups are mutually exclusive is an adequate representation of reality or whether we need to take a more nuanced view.

In the following sections I will focus on perpetrators of international crimes and discuss to what extent perpetrators can also be victims and victims can become perpetrators. In the sections 2 to 4 three types of situations are distinguished. In section 2, perpetrators who are driven by an ideology in which they themselves are depicted as the victims are considered. In section 3, the focus is on victims who, as a means of self-defence, commit atrocities and thus become perpetrators themselves. In section 4, the focus will be on various situations of enforced compliance and cooperation in which individuals or even whole groups are pressured and forced by others to go along. Section 5 discusses three case studies in which victims come to cooperate with the oppressor and commit atrocities. I will focus on Ans van Dijk, a Jewish woman who, during the Second World War, betrayed more than one hundred fellow Jews causing their deportation to a death camp; Joe Mamasela, a black South African *askari* who started to work for the white apartheid state and became involved in 44 killings; and Ishmael Beah, a child soldier from Sierra Leone who committed atrocities. These extreme cases show more than anything else that the distinction between victims and perpetrators can become blurred and that ultimately victims can become perpetrators. It shows in other words that people can be victims and perpetrators at the same time. These sad and tragic cases have led and still lead to all kind of difficult moral, ethical and legal dilemmas which will be discussed in section 6.

2. THE ROLE OF PAST VICTIMHOOD IN GENOCIDAL AND OTHER VIOLENT IDEOLOGIES

Genocide, crimes against humanity and war crimes are by definition committed in a period of collective violence in which political ideologies usually play a crucial role (Cf. Fein 1993; Staub 2003; Alvarez 2008). Ideologies provide the motivation, rationalization and justification for the violence used and thus serve as catalysts for action. Ideologies often rely on the myth of pure evil and portray battles as good versus evil. Von Clausewitz, one of the most prominent scholars on war, concluded that: "War is inconceivable without a clearly defined image of the enemy". To depict the enemy as evil helps to "create an obligation and an incentive to fight. If the enemy is clearly evil, then it is right to hate him and it is appropriate to do one's part to defeat and destroy him" (cited in Baumeister 1999, 84). If the other is pure evil, this would justify the use of whatever means available.

The myth of pure evil, however, is not only used in war but also figures in the ideologies of states that use one-sided (genocidal) violence against a certain group of people. The myth is usually based on past victimization. Together with a perceived threat past victimization, just like alleged past victimization, is one of the most powerful motivating factors. Many perpetrators of international crimes have been motivated by their aim to avenge crimes committed against them or their people in the past and to thus set the record straight. The fact that past victimhood is such a powerful motivating factor has often been abused by political entrepreneurs, as shown by several examples in history. Especially when a state faces difficult life conditions it is appealing and psychologically comforting to blame someone else rather than oneself for the misfortune (Staub 1989). Hitler's rise to power was to a large extent based on the 'stab in the back legend' in which the Jews were blamed for Germany's disgraceful loss in the First World War. In addition, the Jews were blamed for many other misfortunes, such as the economic crisis which, according to the Nazi ideology, was caused by Jewish greed. However, to blame a privileged minority for the misfortune of others is not a unique feature of Nazi ideology. Many political power holders have used this type of political propaganda as a means to justify their violence. Stalin, for example, justified his oppressive policies by asserting that a group of political saboteurs conspired to bring down the Soviet State and caused his five year plans to fail. By arbitrarily arresting people, by sending them to work camps for hard labour, by torturing them and forcing them to admit to their "guilt" in show trials, Stalin tried to depict his political opponents as terrorists who needed to be treated harshly, and the Soviet population as the victims in need of protection. Political rhetoric in which past victimhood is combined with an alleged new threat is particularly effective to motivate people, as we have seen in 1994 during the Rwanda genocide. While it is still debated who killed President Habyarimana of Rwanda by bringing down his plane in the evening of the 6th of April, the Tutsi were immediately blamed for his death. Rumours were started that the Tutsi were about to commit genocide against the Hutu, thus motivating a large number of Hutu to sincerely believe that they were doing good and merely protecting themselves, while in reality they were the aggressors and were committing genocide.[1]

Genocidal and other violent ideologies do not only rely on the myth of pure evil, they also refer to past victimhood to mobilize the masses and to politically justify the violence. Baumeister (1999, 95) concluded:

> *The myth of pure evil encourages people to believe that they are good and will remain good no matter what, even if they perpetrate severe harm on their opponents. Thus, the myth of pure evil confers a kind of moral immunity in people who believe in it. (...) It allows evil to masquerade as good.*

In conclusion, we can say that many perpetrators use violence because they feel entitled to do so (cf. Foster *et al.* 2005) and this entitlement is likely based on past victimhood. In other words: many perpetrators see themselves as victims (cf. Baumeister 1999, 47–48) and whether this perception is based on true facts or fabricated does not make a difference to the perpetrator once he sincerely believes in it.[2] To us it shows that whether someone perceives him- or herself as a victim or a perpetrator can be biased.

---

[1] Obviously this is not the only explanation for the genocide as many other factors played a role as well. See, for example, Straus 2006; Fuij 2009; Smeulers & Hoex 2010.

[2] See the famous quote by Thomas & Thomas (1929, 572): "if men define situations as real, they are real in their consequences."

3. COMMITTING CRIMES WHILE ASSERTING THE RIGHT TO SELF DEFENCE

Within many violent political conflicts, victims fight back as a means of self-defence. Self-defence is both morally and legally considered a legitimate reason to use violence. The Charter of the United Nations provides the right to self-defence in case a state is attacked (see Article 51 UN Charter). However, even when an oppressed group uses its legitimate right to strike back and the outside world acknowledges this right, this group can still come to commit crimes especially when its struggle is considered illegitimate by the political power holders it fights. An example thereof is the African National Congress (ANC) which at first tried to fight the apartheid regime with peaceful means. But after the Sharpeville massacre in which 69 people were shot, the ANC decided to take up arms. In their struggle against the brutal apartheid regime, they themselves, however, also committed atrocities. Not only against the white oppressor, but also against alleged traitors amongst their own people.[3] In its report the South African Truth and Reconciliation Commission (TRC) mentions widespread excesses, abuses and gross human rights violations by supporters and members affiliated to the anti-apartheids movements. A particularly infamous method used by young activists was neck lacing: a method whereby a tire filled with gasoline is forced around the neck of a victim and set on fire resulting in a brutal and painful death. Most violence was however obviously directed against the white oppressor. As a final conclusion, the TRC noted that it

> *fully endorsed the international law position that apartheid was a crime against humanity. It also recognised that both the African National Congress (ANC) and the Pan African Congress (PAC) were internationally recognised liberation movements that conducted a legitimate struggle against the former South African governments and its policy of Apartheid.*[4]

It, however, also stressed that it was important to draw a distinction between the conduct of a 'just war' and the question of 'just means' and concluded: "(…) whilst its struggle was just, the ANC had, in the course of the conflict, contravened the Geneva Protocols and was responsible for the commission of gross human rights violations". The TRC thus took a fair and nuanced view on the blameworthiness of the various groups who committed crimes (see also Peacock, this volume).

The openness of the ANC in this respect is, however, rather unique. Most victim groups do not like to be questioned on crimes they themselves might have

---

[3] Truth and Reconciliation Commission of South Africa, *Report*, 1998, Vol. 6, section 3, Chapter 3, p. 655.

[4] *Idem*, p. 642.

committed. In Rwanda, in 1994, the Hutu committed genocide on the Tutsi and were thus responsible for the most atrocious crimes. It is, however, equally true that the RPF/RPA (Rwandan Patriotic Front/Rwandan Patriotic Army), the mainly Tutsi rebel force which tried to stop the genocide and gain political control over Rwanda, committed atrocities as well. Unfortunately, the current regime, dominated by the RPF and led by Paul Kagame, the former commander of the RPF in 1994, is not very open for any allegation on this point, as was noticed by Carla del Ponte when she, acting in her position as prosecutor of the ICTR, wanted to investigate alleged crimes (Del Ponte 2008). Apart from a number of trials in Rwanda itself most crimes have not been investigated. Post-conflict justice is usually victor's justice. The Allies never wanted to accept that the bombing of several German cities and the dropping of two atomic bombs on Hiroshima and Nagasaki killing many thousands of people while there was no absolute military necessity to do so, might be considered a war crime as well. These examples all show that, even in a perfectly legitimized struggle in which we can identify a perpetrator/aggressor and a victim/saviour, the latter can commit crimes. These examples yet again teach us that the world is not as black and white as we like to perceive it.

The most extreme examples in which victims become perpetrators is when their compliance and cooperation is enforced by – sometimes extreme – pressure. These cases will be discussed in the following section.

4. ENFORCED COMPLIANCE AND COOPERATION

Repressive states often use a system of enforced compliance and cooperation to make sure that people go along with their policies. There are many forms and examples of enforced compliance, and when discussing them we should clearly distinguish between these forms. Huge differences exist in the amount and form of pressure used but also, and maybe even more importantly, in the vulnerability of the person put under pressure. Enforced compliance can furthermore lead to several types of cooperation, such as people who are forced to play a minor role, to people who are forced to actually torture or kill someone else. All oppressive states who systematically commit international crimes use a certain degree of enforced compliance. Most middle and low-ranking perpetrators themselves experience at least a certain degree of pressure to comply. They are usually members of a militarized unit and within these units obedience, compliance and loyalty are highly valued virtues. All militarized units are hierarchically structured and members of such units are usually under a military and legal obligation to obey orders from their superiors and thus a certain amount of pressure and force is inherent to the system. Disobedience and non-compliance will often lead to disciplinary sanctions or criminal prosecution. They carry heavy sanctions especially in war time; desertion may often even result in the death penalty as disobedience and desertion can be considered high treason which is a severe crime in many countries. Such pressure leads to a situation in which many recruits do as they are told, even if they do not agree with the orders. In some cases, such pressure becomes extreme as is the case in the documented study on the training of the military recruits of the ESA under the Greek colonels regime. The study by Gibson and Haritos-Fatouras (1986) and later by Haritos-Fatouras (2003) clearly shows that these recruits were trained in an extremely coercive environment in which they lived in constant fear and were continuously humiliated, threatened and abused themselves and thus had few options but to comply. After studying these coercive training methods, Gibson and Haritos-Fatouras (1986, 50) concluded that there is a cruel method to train people how to torture: "almost everyone can learn it". The recruits from this Greek torture school were for a prolonged period of time put under extreme duress and as a consequence thereof were successfully transformed into torturers who committed horrendous crimes.

Next to coercive training, people are sometimes forced to comply and cooperate and commit a certain crime by using a more direct threat. During the Rwandan genocide, for example, many Hutu had to prove their loyalty by raping, mutilating or killing Tutsi. The penalty for not doing so often was that they themselves were raped, mutilated or killed. Testimonial evidence shows that many Hutu who did not comply with such orders were killed and many testified that they were more afraid of their fellow Hutu than they were afraid of the Tutsi. A direct death threat is a very effective means to enforce compliance and many perpetrators have experienced such pressure. Erdemovic, who stood trial before the ICTY, said that after he complained about the order to shoot all Muslim men who were brought to their units by bus, he was given the choice to join the ranks of the shooters or to stand in line with the victims and be shot together with them.[5] Pressure, force and threats appear in all kind of forms and, depending on the situation, can be effective or not. From the outside it is difficult to judge if the threat is perceived as a serious threat by the person who is put under pressure.

Coercion and threats are often used against people who are vulnerable and thus more likely to give in. There are many ways in which people can be vulnerable. They can be very old or very young, female in a male's world, physically weak or mentally unstable but they can also be vulnerable because of their affiliations with the targeted group. In Rwanda, for example, Hutu who did not agree with the genocidal policy or were married to a Tutsi, who had Tutsi friends or family members, were all extremely vulnerable. They felt pressured to

---

[5] *Prosecutor versus Erdemovic*, Case no. IT-96–22-A, Judgment, 7 October 1997.

prove their loyalty to the Hutu cause and by doing so hoped to save their beloved ones:

> *I joined a group of killers from the Interahamwe. They were already trained. I needed to go with them; otherwise I would be killed myself.* (Personal interview)[6]

> *They were saying we were also Tutsi – people coming from other parts of the country said we were Tutsi. Then a relative who was a soldier took me and gave me a gun to protect my family (…) Another soldier came and ordered me to kill people who were in the church and I killed them. (…) I only wanted to protect my family.* (Personal interview)[7]

The most extreme and also most tragic form of enforced cooperation is when perpetrators force members from the targeted victim group to cooperate with them and play a role in the discrimination and destruction of their own people. Unfortunately, several dictatorial and oppressive regimes have successfully relied on this method. In some cases victims are forced to cooperate at gunpoint whereas other perpetrators have used more refined methods in which they compromised victims into cooperation. In some cases this enforced cooperation is so successful that those pressured into cooperation become real perpetrators themselves. While people who commit crimes at gunpoint are rarely considered perpetrators, those who fully adapt to their new enforced identities as perpetrators generally receive little sympathy. The emphasis on the remainder of this chapter is on the latter group as this group shows that there are cases in which we can consider certain people as victims and perpetrators at the same time.

These extreme cases have been deliberately picked because they are the best and most illustrative examples of why and how the myth of pure evil is eroded.

5. CASE STUDIES

The three case studies which are presented in this section show victims who were forced to cooperate with the perpetrator, gave in and became active participants in atrocities themselves. The first case study is of Ans van Dijk, a Jewish woman who during the Second World War betrayed hundreds of fellow Jews. She was one of the many victims of the Nazi system which used forced compliance and cooperation extensively. The second case study is from South Africa in which the white oppressor managed a very successful *askari*-system in which black people were used and abused by the white oppressor to fight the resistance movement

---

[6]   This is a quote from an interview with a prisoner from central prison in Kigali who was suspected of genocide, which I have conducted together with Lotte Hoex in May 2009.

[7]   *Ibidem.*

(see also Peacock, this volume). The story of Joe Mamasela, one of the best known *askaris*, will illustrate how the system worked. The last subsection will focus on Ishmael Beah, a former child soldier from Sierra Leone, exposing the enforced compliance and cooperation of child soldiers and the effects thereof. Like Ans van Dijk and Joe Mamasela, Beah too ended up committing atrocities.

5.1. THE ROLE OF THE JEWS IN THE HOLOCAUST

The Nazis were extremely successful in enforcing compliance and cooperation of the Jews in the occupied territories during the Second World War. They installed Jewish Councils which performed the duties of spokes organs and which had to meet with the Germans on a regular basis. They were thus compromised into cooperation. The members of the Jewish Councils were given some privileges but in the meantime were requested to compile lists of Jews to be deported. They faced a devils choice: by cooperating they actually played a role in the deportation and destruction of their own people but by cooperating they could at least save their own lives for the time being and make sure that at least some human considerations were taken into account when selecting people and organizing the means of selection (cf. Arendt 1964; Somers 2010). The use of Jewish Councils was, however, certainly not the only means the Nazis used to enforce compliance and cooperation. Even within the concentration and death camps, inmates themselves played an important role in organizing the daily routine of the camps. Some inmates, usually former convicts or political prisoners, became Kapo, and had a privileged status and a position of power over other inmates. The Nazis used this method to keep a tight control on the inmates. Jewish inmates were often forced to work. Some had to assist Mengele and the other Nazi doctors in conducting cruel medical experiments on the human body and others were forced to play a role in the extermination of their fellow inmates. They helped with the selection; they were forced to make sure that the extermination process would run smoothly by comforting and deceiving the people who were destined to die, in making them believe that they would merely take a shower. Members of the so-called *Sonderkommandos* were Jewish inmates who were responsible for the disposal and burning of the bodies of the inmates who had just been killed and exterminated in the gas chambers.

The most effective and damaging means of enforced compliance and cooperation within occupied territories was, however, achieved by giving arrested Jews the choice to either be immediately deported or to save their lives by cooperating with the Germans and by providing names of other Jews who went into hiding. Although we do not know any exact figures on how many Jews accepted the offer, we know that at least some did. Amongst them Ans van Dijk. Koos Groen (1994) wrote a book about her life.

Ans van Dijk was born in the Netherlands in 1905. She was a Jewish businesswoman who owned her own shop. After the Nazis occupied the Netherlands and forbade Jews to have their own businesses, her shop was taken by the Germans. Shortly thereafter Ans van Dijk started to work for the resistance movement. As such, she helped Jews by providing them with money, false identity cards and shelter and even helped people to escape from the Netherlands and thus from a certain death at the hands of the German oppressor. Van Dijk had not registered as a Jew and thus could escape arrest herself until she was betrayed and arrested by Schaap on the 26th of April 1943. Schaap was a Dutch policeman who worked for the department of Jewish affairs, a specialized section of the German Security forces (the SD or *Sicherheitsdienst*). The extra money (*Kopgeld*) which could be earned for each Jew they arrested became an incentive for a number of people amongst whom Dutch policemen to organize a Jew hunt. Schaap's unit which became infamous for its violence and ruthlessness was one of these units which started to show a particular zeal in arresting and deporting Jews. They used refined methods of compromising their victims into cooperation as Ans van Dijk would soon come to experience. When Schaap arrested Ans van Dijk, he offered her a deal: she could save her life by revealing the whereabouts of other Jews or be deported to a death camp straight away. In his testimony after the war, Schaap explained that all Jews were offered such deals and that many of them accepted the deal. People who had accepted such deals however did not get off the hook by betraying only a few others, they – contrary to their own initial expectation – often had to continuously prove themselves by betraying more and more people.

Ans van Dijk, accepted the deal and revealed the whereabouts of a number of Jews. After her initial cooperation she was however put under further pressure to keep working for Schaap and to thus keep herself safe. She was set free and was ordered to stay in touch with the resistance movement and the Jews in Amsterdam who tried to hide from the police and the Nazis and she had to reveal their whereabouts. Sometimes she had to check whether Jews were present at the addresses provided to her by the policemen. On other occasions, she was put in a cell together with other Jews pretending she too was arrested in order to gain their trust and find out about other hiding Jews. By doing so, she could keep her freedom and prevent to being sent off to Auschwitz or another death camp in Nazi Germany herself.

Sadly enough Ans van Dijk did her job very well and was particularly effective. Schaap, who had forced at least 9 other Jews to work for him, described her as his best employee (Groen 1994, 83). She became the leader of a small group of Jews who tried to save their lives this way and worked closely together with the Dutch police. The group was formed on the initiative of Schaap and consisted mainly of other Jews who had been offered similar deals. The group became extremely efficient in their betrayal and at some point were even financially rewarded for this by the Dutch police. Groen (1994, 124) calculated that 145 people were betrayed by Ans van Dijk and her group. 107 Jews of whom at least 80 died, and 38 non-Jews of whom at least 4 died. Amongst the ones she betrayed were her own brother and his family and the families of her friends and business partners (Groen 1994, 9). Ans van Dijk continued her work until the end of the war

On the 20th of June 1945, only a few weeks after the official end of the Second World War, Ans van Dijk was arrested and prosecuted for the betrayal of Jews. At her trial she stated that she had been terrified: Schaap knew about her illegal activities within the resistance movement prior to her arrest and she was in danger of being deported to a death camp any time. She said she had no choice but to cooperate (Groen 1994). Schaap on the other hand tried to convince the judges that all their employees worked on the basis of their own free will (Groen 1994, 149 & 151). Schaap tried to diminish his own role and stated that Ans van Dijk was very willing to help them. He even declared that he did not have to force van Dijk. But he also admitted that if she would not help him, she would have been send to Poland towards an almost certain death in one of the extermination camps. During the entire trial, Ans van Dijk was reproached by the public, prosecutors and judges who all ignored the difficult position she had faced. No real attention was given to the fact that she was Jewish and that her life was in peril (Cf. Groen 1994). Her being Jewish was seen as an aggravating rather than a mitigating circumstance (Groen 1994, 240). Ans van Dijk was described as cowardly and egoistic. Ans van Dijk was also homosexual and during her trial this was used against her. Her homosexuality was described as sexual perversion which could indicate abnormalcy (Groen 1994, 181). All odds were against her and despite the difficult situation she had faced and despite the undeniable fact that Ans van Dijk was a victim and only started to betray fellow Jews after she was betrayed and arrested herself and in danger of being instantly deported to a death camp, she was convicted to the death penalty. The fact that she did show remorse did not help her. Ans van Dijk was executed on the 13th of January 1948.

Groen (1994) found little answers to the question as to why she became such an effective traitor. He, however, points out that it is very remarkable that a Jewish woman, whose fate would have been deportation to a death camp had she not cooperated with the Nazis, was convicted to the death penalty and executed. He wondered whether the fact that she was Jewish, a woman and a known homosexual, might have played a role. There are clear incidents in her life in which she herself was discriminated precisely for these three reasons. It is, however, impossible to give definite answers. We merely know that in a written statement Ans van Dijk stated: "I admit that I played an awful role. But I did not do this out of my own accord but because I was afraid of Schaap. He continuously threatened to kill me if I did not betray more Jews. I did not have a regular salary but was given some money every now and then" (Groen 1994, 149, translation

AS). In another statement in which the judge asked her to explain why she betrayed so many people, she said: "I was completely insane. I was terrified of the SD. They had threatened me. I could not go into hiding" (Groen 1994, 164, translation AS). The weeks before her execution she started to embrace the Catholic religion and had long talks with one of the nuns. She said that she felt guilty and felt remorse. Her victims appeared in her dreams. She saw them standing before a firing squad and still felt terrified (Groen 1994, 205).

Within the Netherlands the name of Ans van Dijk became a symbol: she became the personification of treason and betrayal. She committed crimes by betraying over one hundred fellow Jews, including direct family members. There is no way of ignoring the fact that she was a victim too: the threat of being sent to a death camp herself would have been an always present and imminent threat in her life. She, at some point however must have accepted her fate and adapted to her role and unfortunately became a very good and efficient tool in the hands of greedy and ruthless Dutch policemen. By doing so she saved her own life but she did so at great expense of others. Ans van Dijk can therefore be considered a victim and a perpetrator at the same time.

The Nazis were not the only ones to coerce the targeted victims into cooperation. In the following section we will see how, in South Africa, black people were coerced to work for the white oppressor.

5.2. THE SOUTH AFRICAN ASKARIS

When the South African National Party gained political power in South Africa in the 1940s, it installed a system of racial segregation better known as Apartheid, in which the privileged white minority suppressed the underprivileged black majority. Until 1960, the black majority organized peaceful protests, but after the police had violently crushed a demonstration and killed 69 people at Sharpeville on the 21st of March 1960, the ANC announced it would take up weapons against the white oppressors. ANC's military wing, *Umkhonto we Sizwe* (MK), took the lead in the guerrilla warfare. But even peaceful black protests were forcefully crushed, leading to another massacre in 1976 in Soweto when 170 people, amongst whom more than 100 schoolchildren, were killed. In 1977, then Prime Minister Vorster launched his "Total Strategy" in which almost any means to suppress the black population as well as all other political opposition was considered acceptable and legitimate. This policy led to mass arrests, political killings and systematic torture. The South African Police, and particularly the security police, had a fearsome reputation for interrogation and torture (Pauw 1991, 63; see also Foster *et al.* 1987). Many prisoners died at the hands of their torturers.

Within the country, several death squads such as Vlakplaas and the Northern Transvaal Security Branch became operational. In addition to being a death squad, the purpose of Vlakplaas was to serve as 'a place to rehabilitate turned terrorists'.[8] When Dirk Coetzee was appointed as the first commander of Vlakplaas in 1980, there were 17 so-called *askaris*. *Askari* is a Swahili word for black soldiers who were "former members of the liberation movements. The aim was to transform these *askaris* into spies who came to work for the Security Branch, providing information, and identifying and tracing former comrades".[9] The practice had successfully been used by *Koevoet* (which means Doe's foot), an elite corps which operated in the Rhodesian war and which systematically tried to 'turn' captured guerrillas into *askaris*: traitors who helped them by telling on their former comrades as a means of counter-insurgency. In some cases, former members of the liberation movement defected on their own accord but many more were forced to work for the security forces after they were arrested, abducted or otherwise captured. The 'turning processes' included extensive torture and those who did not accept the deal were "brutally killed and often buried in secret locations or in unnamed graves in cemeteries".[10]

After their transformation, the *askaris* at Vlakplaas had to infiltrate the mass movements and pose themselves as MK operatives and identify military trainees of the MK. They had to tell on others, lure them into ambushes or personally kill them. At some point, *askaris* were given bounty money for people they informed on; later they received a regular salary. *Askaris* however could never be safe. They were carefully monitored and there were strict disciplinary rules and all those whose loyalty was questioned or who were considered a threat or 'weak link' in the chain were killed.[11] In its final report, the South African Truth and Reconciliation Commission (TRC) concluded that the practice of abducting, torturing and transforming former guerrillas into *askaris* was extremely effective.[12] According to Pauw (1997, 172), more than a hundred *askaris* were deployed by the security forces. Joe Mamasela was one of them. His story was reconstructed by Pauw (1991 & 1997) and a couple of others (Cf. Krog 1999).

Joe Mamasela worked for Vlakplaas and later for the Northern Transvaal Security Branch and as such became involved in at least 44 murders amongst which the well documented murder of Mxenge (Pauw 1991, 15; Bell 2003, 15). Joe Mamasela was an active member of the student's movement and worked for the ANC in 1977 as an undercover agent. One day he was (allegedly) arrested by the security forces for theft and brutally tortured for 48 hours before he broke down and agreed to start working for the security forces (Krog 1999, 263; Pauw 1997,

---

8   Truth and Reconciliation Commission of South Africa, *Report*, 1998, Vol. 2, Chapter 3, p. 317.
9   *Idem*, Vol. 6, section 3, Chapter 1, p. 217.
10   *Idem*, Vol. 2, Chapter 6, p. 545.
11   No one was spared. One of the first main tasks of Eugene de Kock when he became a leader of Vlakplaas was to kill his predecessor Dirk Coetzee. A mail bomb addressed to kill Coetzee ended up in the hands of his lawyer killing him instead of Coetzee.
12   Truth and Reconciliation Commission of South Africa, *Report*, 1998, Vol. 6, section 3, Chapter 1, p. 218.

170). Mamasela explains that he was tortured by a man he described as 'diabolic and satanic' and who forced him to undress and poured ice cold water over him:

> They put electronic apparatus all over my genitals, my entire body, underneath my toes and all that. But the worst thing that this man did was to take something like an electronic stick that they use to prod cattle with, he stuck it in my anus and that was the most excruciating pain I have experienced in my life. I lost consciousness for a long, long time and when I woke up; I found that every part of my body was bleeding. My nostrils, ears, mouth, my genitals were bleeding. This man kept on repeating this sadistic way of torturing me (…). There was no way I could resist further, they left no doubt in my mind that they can, and will, and are eager to kill me. So I said no, I will help you, what do you want me to do? (Pauw 1997, 172–173)

After he agreed to cooperate Mamasela infiltrated in groups and lured young activists to death by promising them to bring them to ANC training camps (Pauw 1997, 176). In some cases, he killed his victims (all black activists) by strangulation but made it look like a neck lace murder in order to implicate other black activists (Pauw 1997, 187). Mamasela was involved in many brutal operations and many killings. He abducted young men, drugged them and burned them to death (Bell 2003, 344). Mamasela was known for his cruelty and effectiveness to which he admitted himself: "My role was to choke them, to strangle them. Just to keep them quiet" (Pauw 1997, 178). He sometimes used unnecessary cruelty by making fun of his victims and ordering them to recite prayers (Pauw 1991, 34).

Just like Ans van Dijk, Mamasela turned out to be very good at his job and somehow accepted and adapted into his new role. Dirk Coetzee, the first commander of Vlakplaas, said: "He was ruthless and had the killer instinct. He was a born killer" (Pauw 1997, 171). Coetzee admitted that "in a way he was forced into killing. But he never objected and was always willing to do the job. He was an outstanding criminal and a cruel man". Several other former white policemen who had worked with Mamasela confirmed that he was a cruel man who had a talent for killing and was very useful to them (Pauw 1997, 176). "If you wanted it quick and clean, you sent Mamasela," one of them said (Krog 1999, 265). His white colleagues however also offered an alternative explanation of why Mamasela cooperated with them: "Mamasela hated the ANC as much as we did. He was waging his own war against them" (Pauw 1997, 171). And: "Mamasela shared our sentiments about the ANC. He hated the ANC and was taking revenge for the neck lacing of his brother" (Pauw 1997, 176). Allegedly, Mamasela, together with his brother, was arrested by the ANC after he had started to work as a traitor and his cover blew. While Mamasela himself managed to flee, his brother was killed and Mamasela vowed that he would not rest until he had avenged his brother's life.

After Coetzee had been fired and revealed the existence of death squads such as Vlakplaas in South Africa in the late 1980s, a huge cover-up was organized. Mamasela received a large amount of money for his services and in order to make sure that he would keep his mouth shut. Several of his former commanders such as Van Vuuren and De Kock said that Mamasela always wanted money (Pauw 1997, 176). He wanted money for the killings and, according to De Kock, excessive amounts to keep his mouth shut (Pauw 1997, 179). Pauw himself noted that Mamasela was always talking about money. Mamasela financially gained from his role in South Africa's Apartheid state and he is known to live an expensive life style in the nineties (Cf. Pauw 1997 and Krog 1998).

After the TRC was installed and investigated the crimes of the Apartheid state, Mamasela refused to apply for amnesty because he regarded himself a victim of the Apartheid system rather than a perpetrator (Pauw 1997, 170). In 1997, he explained in court: "I'm a black person. I was born and brought up in this country. Every black person is a victim of the oppressive regime of the South African police, of the South African government in the past, and that's a fact" (Pauw 1997, 171). In his statements before the Truth and Reconciliation Commission, Mamasela explained that he had to follow the orders and that he would have been killed if he would not have done so. In an interview with Antjie Krog, he stated: "I had to fight for my own survival. I was a political hostage, a dog of war" (Krog 1999, 265).

Mamasela became a well known figure especially when testifying for the TRC as a state witness. As a consequence of his confessions and the people he implicated, many of them came forward. Yet people doubt whether Mamasela told the truth. It was suggested that he was not arrested for illegal political activities but for common crimes. Pauw (1997, 172) suggests that Mamasela, in order to avoid a jail sentence for his common crimes, might have falsely told the police that he was an ANC member and offered his help. Although the systematic and exploitative use of *askaris* by the security police is undeniable, Mamasela's story of his extreme torture was never corroborated while other possible motives for his crimes like revenge, material gain (money) and the urge to indulge his sadism emerged. Unlike many *askaris* who never returned to live an ordinary live as they were rejected by their communities (Pauw 1997, 69), Mamasela seemed, at least the last time Pauw saw him, to live a fairly good and wealthy life.

One might wonder whether Mamasela indeed took advantage of the situation or whether we do not do him any justice by shedding doubt on his story because we feel a lack of sympathy for this man who became involved in so many murders. Mamasela was a perpetrator, there is no doubt about that, he was also a member of the targeted group and functioned in a known system of enforced compliance and cooperation. His story and the possible (unsympathetic) ulterior motives show how difficult it is to reconcile the fact that he still is, besides a perpetrator, also a victim.

5.3. CHILD SOLDIERS

War used to be a battle fought between two professional national armies in a deserted area. Worldwide, the nature of warfare has, however, changed. Only a few international conflicts exist nowadays. Most wars are internal wars fought within populated areas in which not just soldiers but also many civilians are involved and targeted. The ranks of the fighting parties are no longer filled exclusively with grown males but many children are amongst the armed forces, sometimes joining the ranks of the adults, sometimes having their own units. It is estimated that there are 300,000 child soldiers world-wide.[13] The use of children has many advantages: they are cheap because they are unlike adults rarely paid and more easily conditioned into using violence (Singer 2006, 55; Wessels 2006, 2 & 37). Children furthermore sometimes lack a sense of both fear and morality which makes them ideal soldiers. Singer (2006) and Wessels (2006) concluded that since many children around the world have to live in poor conditions, it is not a surprise that "the overwhelming majority of child soldiers are drawn from the poorest, least educated, and most marginalized sections of society" (Singer 2006, 44). A new type of weapons which are light and easy to use further contributed to the usefulness of child soldiers (Wessels 2006, 18). Most child soldiers are between 13 and 18 years old but some are as young as seven (Wessels 2006, 7 and x.).

Some children join the armed forces voluntarily because they are "simply fascinated by the prestige and thrill of serving in a unit and having a gun" (Singer 2006, 66, according to whom this is about 15%) or because they want to obtain power, wealth, education or a meaning in life (Wessels 2006, 45). Children "may see violence as an acceptable way to replace the existing social order with one offering social justice and positive economic and political opportunities" (Wessels 2006, 3). Yet, others are forced by the circumstances: they conclude that they are better off in the armed forces or by joining the rebels than by not doing so (Wessels 2006, 22). They are alone and lost and join the armed forces in search for food and shelter or they are out for revenge (Wessels 2006, 22). Others join the forces because they are abducted and forced to join the armed forces (Singer 2006, 58; Wessels 2006, 37). Once within the army or rebel forces, children are often brutally trained and quickly initiated in committing violence. In some cases, they have to torture or kill their parents and other relatives, which has a tremendous impact and makes it impossible for them to return home. Life within a military unit always includes resocialization (cf. Wessels 2006, 57). Children are disciplined and have to subdue themselves to the hierarchy within the unit. Merely aiming to survive, children will gradually start to adapt to the new social

---

[13]   Machel, G., *Impact of Armed Conflict on Children, Report of the Expert of the Secretary-General, Ms. Graça Machel*, Submitted pursuant to General Assembly Resolution 48/157 26th August 1996, www.unicef.org/graca/a51–306_en.pdf (last visited: March 2010).

norms and values in which violence is considered normal and justified. Moreover, the children are often given alcohol and drugs such as cocaine or heroine. Recruits are not free to leave. Those who try to escape are usually recaptured and often killed in order to set an example for the others.

Children react differently to their recruitment. Wessels (2006, 74) concluded that some children "fight reluctantly, kill only when necessary, and constantly look for escape opportunities, whereas others learn to enjoy combat and redefine their identities as soldiers". Child soldiers can become very efficient and fearless fighters. Singer (2006, x.) for instance concludes: "These new soldiers are not simply children; they can also be callous killers capable of the most terrible acts of cruelty and brutality" (Singer 2006, x; Wessels 2006, 79). Child soldiers units can be particularly vicious. Singer (2006, 106) quotes a UNICEF worker who states: "Boys will do things that grown men can't stomach. Kids make more brutal fighters because they haven't developed a sense of judgment". These differences teach us that children despite their young age are not passive automatons. They usually show a strong sense of adaptation, resilience and they purposefully take up new identities.

Sierra Leone is one of the countries in which the use of child soldiers was particularly widespread. The civil war lasted from 1991–2001 and apparently as many as 50%-80% of the soldiers in the Revolutionary United Front (RUF) were aged between seven and fourteen years old (Singer 2006, 15, quotes a report by Save the Children on the highest estimate and Wessels 2006, 13, talks about 50%). The so-called small boys units which consisted of boys less than 12 years of age were infamous for their ruthlessness and cruel behaviour (cf. Wessels 2006, 7).[14] Ishmael Beah was a child soldier in Sierra Leone who wrote down his story in a book entitled *A long way gone* (Beah 2007).

When Ishmael Beah was 12 years old, the war reached his part of the country. He was separated from his family and tried to flee from the violence with several of his friends. During their flight they were captured several times; once by the rebels who wanted to recruit them but they managed to escape. A few other times Ishmael and his friends were captured by ordinary civilians who thought they were child soldiers. "People were terrified of boys our age", Ishmael states (Beah 2007, 37). At some point, he gets lost and separated from his friends and lives alone in a forest for a while. He manages to survive and finds another group of boys who accompany him in his flight. During his flight he sees a lot of atrocities and is told that his parents and brothers have been killed. One day, the group is captured by soldiers from the regular army and taken to their base. Here they do ordinary jobs but at some point the war comes close and the commander asks all boys to help to defend the village. "This is your time to revenge the deaths of your families and to make sure more children do not lose their families," the commander said. The men and boys were left with the choice to either help

---

14   Also: Human Rights Watch, *Sowing terror. Atrocities against civilians in Sierra Leone*, 1998.

defend the village or to disappear. The next morning, two bodies were shown to the crowd. They were dead and soaked in blood allegedly killed by the rebels after they had left the base. The commander continued talking about the rebels: "They have lost everything that makes them human. They do not deserve to live. That is why we must kill every single one of them. Think of it as destroying a great evil. It is the highest service you can perform for your country" (Beah 2007, 108).

Ishmael, just like the others, had little choice. If he wanted to stay with the soldiers, he had to join them in their fight, otherwise he had to flee again and would be in danger of being captured by the rebels who would have forced him to fight or kill him straight away. There were about thirty boys, mainly between 13 and 16 years old, who joined the forces. They were given clothes, shoes and guns and were taught how to handle their weapons and fight. During the training, the commander kept on telling them. "Visualize the enemy, the rebels who killed your parents, your family, and those who are responsible for everything that has happened to you" (Beah 2007, 112). Then they were given drugs.

Ishmael recounts that he had never been so afraid in his whole life as on that first day in which he had to fight. At first he is unable to shoot and feels like being in some sort of nightmare. People die around him, spattering blood in his face. Then he discovers that two of his friends have been killed in the fight:

> *I turned toward the swamp, where there were gunmen running, trying to cross over. My face, my hands, my shirt and gun were covered with blood. I raised my gun and pulled the trigger, and I killed a man. Suddenly, as if someone was shooting them inside my brain, all the massacres I had seen since the day I was touched by war began flashing in my head. Every time I stopped shooting to change magazines and saw my two young lifeless friends, I angrily pointed my gun into the swamp and killed more people. I shot everything that moved, until we were ordered to retreat (…). (Beah 2007, 119)*

During that first night he has nightmares and shoots his own gun in the middle of the night but he gets used to it and ultimately Ishmael becomes a ruthless soldier. He used drugs, watched violent movies and went out to kill. During this period, Ishmael Beah and his fellow child soldiers commit many atrocities. They raid rebel camps, attack villages and capture new recruits. They made a group of prisoners bury their own graves, they stabbed them in the legs with their bayonets and they buried them alive while they were making jokes. One day Ishmael got shot in his foot which put him in terrible pain. He took revenge by lining up a group of prisoners and shooting all of them in the foot. He explains:

> *I am not sure if one of the captives was the shooter, but any captive would do at that time. So they were all lined up, six of them, with their hands tied. I shot them on their feet and watched them suffer all day before finally shooting them in the head so that*

they would stop crying. Before I shot each man, I looked at him and saw how his eyes gave up hope and steadied before I pulled the trigger. I found their sombre eyes irritating. (Beah 2007, 159)

At some point, killing contests are organized. The young soldiers had to slice the throats of captured prisoners and the person whose prisoner died first would win the contest (Beah 2007, 124). Ishmael was one of the soldiers picked for the contest and he remembers: "I didn't feel a thing for him, didn't think that much about what I was doing. I just waited for the corporal's order. The prisoner was simply another rebel who was responsible for the death of my family, as I had come to truly believe" (Beah 2007, 124). Ishmael won the contest and was promoted to the rank of junior lieutenant and became the leader of a small unit which he celebrated with more drugs and more war movies.

Together with a number of other child soldiers, Ishmael was at some point captured by UN soldiers and sent to a rehabilitation centre. In the beginning, he had difficulty to adapt and his group got into a fight with other former child soldiers who had fought for the rebels.

I stabbed him in his foot. The bayonet stuck, so I pulled it out with force. He fell and I began kicking him in the face (...). Alhaji had stabbed him in the back. He pulled the knife out, and we continued kicking the boy until he stopped moving. I wasn't sure whether he was unconscious or dead. I didn't care. (Beah 2007, 135)

In this fight between two groups of former child soldiers at the UN rehabilitation centre, six former child soldiers were killed. Ishmael remembers that he was angry and missed his squad and the excitement of fighting. He had trouble sleeping and when he slept he had frequent nightmares. But Ishmael finally adapted to peace and was rehabilitated. He now lives in the United States. He has devoted his life to make people aware that wars are not heroic and devastate the life of the victims, and child soldiers in particular. In a television interview, Ishmael states that he can never forget what he has seen and done but that he has learned to live with it.[15]

5.4. PARALLELS AND DIFFERENCES

The stories of Ans van Dijk, Joe Mamasela and Ishmael Beah have a few things in common. All three belonged to a vulnerable group; Ans van Dijk and Joe Mamasela belonged to the targeted group and Ishmael Beah was just a kid who lost his family and tried to escape the war. All three fell prey to a system of abuse: the use of traitors by the Nazis, the use of *askaris* by the South African Security

---

[15] See the interview with Ismael Beah on Youtube: www.youtube.com/watch?v=5K4yhPSQEzo.

Branch and the (forced) recruitment of child soldiers in Sierra Leone. All three had a choice but the choice seemed to be between cooperating (and saving ones life) or almost certain death. All three choose to save their lives and complied. Ishmael Beah by joining the ranks of the military, Ans van Dijk by working with the oppressor and Joe Mamasela by joining a death squad. All three can be seen as victims but all three also committed crimes. Ishmael Beah committed war time atrocities by his unnecessary and cruel behaviour, Joe Mamasela betrayed, tortured and killed people and Ans van Dijk betrayed fellow Jews who were as a consequence thereof sent to death camps in which many of them died.

Unlike many others who were in a similar position, the three individuals we studied were special: Ishmael Beah became a ruthless soldier while Joe Mamasela and Ans van Dijk were particularly efficient in their 'jobs'. While some of Joe Mamasela's fellow *askaris* were indeed killed many others also worked for the death squad but were less efficient and not as good at their job as Mamasela. The same is true for Ans van Dijk. In general it is difficult to tell what the fate of other Jews who were offered a similar deal was. Some will have said no and will have been deported, others probably cooperated but no one reached the level of efficiency as Ans van Dijk did. One thus may wonder what made these victims become such efficient perpetrators. From research on perpetrators it is known that perpetrators slowly but gradually adapt to their role: they get brutalized, the violence normalizes, and perpetrators sooth their conscience by rationalizing and justifying their actions (see for the complete transformation process Smeulers 2004). It is likely that the same happens to victims who get involved in the discrimination or even extermination of their own group. They adapt to the situations and take up new roles which for whatever reason suit them. Yet, it is also true that ulterior motives might have played a role. Both Ishmael Beah and Joe Mamasela were at least partially driven by revenge. Mamasela and Van Dijk both materially profited from their work and, lastly, Mamasela was described by his colleagues as bloodthirsty and a born killer which might indicate that he had a violent nature or sadistic impulses. Although some doubt was shed on whether or not Mamasela was indeed severely tortured, it is equally true that all three fell prey to a system in which the perpetrators deliberately abused the vulnerability of members of certain groups and deliberately forced them to cooperate. These three case studies show more than anything else that victims and perpetrators are not always two distinguishable and mutually exclusive categories but that victims can become perpetrators and perpetrators can become victims.

This finding raises an intriguing question, namely how to deal with victims who become particularly effective perpetrators. There were probably many victims who only cooperated with their oppressor when a loaded gun pointed at their head. These victims can hardly be considered perpetrators, but what about those at the other end of the scale, like Mamasela, Van Dijk and Beah who started to accept and adapt to their role and become real perpetrators. In the following section, I will compare what happened to Ans van Dijk, Joe Mamasela and Ishmael Beah after they committed their crimes and will see to what extent current international criminal law has found an adequate means to deal with this type of perpetrator.

6. THE AFTERMATH

After the war Ans van Dijk was arrested, prosecuted and executed. Ten people within the Netherlands were executed Ans van Dijk was the only Jew and the only woman amongst them. The fact that she was Jewish was considered an aggravating rather than a mitigating circumstance. While Ans van Dijk was executed, the two leading Nazis, Aus der Fünten and Lages, were spared. They were both given the death penalty but their penalty was reversed into a life sentence. Lages was released from prison in 1966 because of poor health and died in 1971. Aus der Fünten was released from prison in 1990 and died one year later.

Joe Mamasela was never punished for his crimes. He testified before the Truth and Reconciliation Commission in South Africa but merely as a witness, not in order to ask amnesty. He simply said that he too had been a victim and despite the fact that his story was never corroborated he was not called to justice. The South African TRC had trouble dealing with the *askaris* and concluded in its final report that it is a "thorny question of whether perpetrators may also be viewed as victims".[16] The TRC finally stated that:

> To understand these potential grey areas involve being drawn into a position of some sympathy with the perpetrator. The dangers of this are twofold: first to forget and ignore the suffering of victims of abuse, and second, to exonerate the doer of violent deeds. From the third perspective of the Commission, difficulties are once again manifest. Two statements may be fruitful. First, it is important to recognize that perpetrators may in part be victims. Second, recognition of the grey areas should not be regarded as absolving perpetrators of responsibility for their deeds.[17]

While the South African TRC clearly struggled with the dilemma of perpetrators being victims at the same time, the Dutch court after the Second World War did not take this mitigating circumstance into account and considered Ans van Dijk a perpetrator. The conviction and execution of Ans van Dijk seems to have been met with broad acceptance at the time but strikes us now – many years later – as unfair and too harsh, while the lack of prosecution of Joe Mamasela who committed so many crimes equally strikes us as unjust. According to the current

---

[16]   Truth and Reconciliation Commission of South Africa, *Report*, 1998, Vol. 5, Chapter 7, p. 274.
[17]   *Ibidem.*

state of the law one would expect that both would nowadays be prosecuted for their crimes but that duress would be the obvious line of defence. Duress is the pressure or threat an individual experiences and because of which he or she commits a crime. In the Erdemovic case, the ICTY decided that while duress cannot be a complete defence in relation to international crimes, it can be taken into account as a mitigating factor.[18] It will thus never completely dissolve the perpetrator of his blame but these factors will be taken into account in the sentencing phase. The ICC, however, takes a different stance in Article 31 (1)d Rome Statute. According to the Rome Statute a person can be absolved from criminal responsibility but only under strict conditions. In his book Cassese (2003, 242) enumerates these conditions as follows: (1) the act charged is done under an immediate threat of severe and irreparable harm to life or limb; (2) there is no adequate means of averting such evil; (3) the crime committed is not disproportionate to the evil threatened (the contrary would, for example, occur in case of killing in order to avert a sexual assault). In other words, to be proportionate, the crime committed under duress or necessity must, on balance, be the lesser of two evils or an evil as serious as the one to be averted; (4) the situation leading to duress or necessity must not have been voluntarily brought about by the person coerced.[19] It seems that neither Van Dijk nor Mamasela could rely on duress as a complete defence. In both cases duress will however be likely to be accepted as a mitigating factor. It however remains to be seen how current international criminal law will strike the balance in judging these perpetrators who both fell prey to a system of abuse and who can be considered victims and perpetrators at the same time.

Ishmael Beah on the other hand, like many other child soldiers, was never held accountable for the crimes he committed in Sierra Leone. Although the Special Court for Sierra Leone (SCSL) had jurisdiction over child soldiers as of the age of 15, it became a widespread and general policy not to prosecute child soldiers. The SCSL thus seems to absolve child soldiers of any blame and responsibility for their actions. Article 49 (c) SCSL, however, lists "conscripting or enlisting children under the age of 15 into armed forces or groups or using them to participate actively in hostilities" as a crime. There have been four cases before the SCSL in which charges related to the recruitment of child soldiers played a role. In the so-called AFRC-case, the Trial Chamber stated that enlistment of child soldiers is a crime even if the child consents.[20] The SCSL thus prosecuted those who abused the vulnerability of others rather than those whose vulnerability was abused.[21]

---

[18] *Prosecutor v. Erdemovic*, Case No. IT-96-22-A, Judgment, 7 October 1997.

[19] See also Article 31(1)(d) of the Rome Statute in which similar criteria are mentioned.

[20] *Prosecutor v. Brima, Kamara, and Kanu*, Case No. SCSL-04-16-T, T. Ch. SCSL, 20 June 2007, par. 735.

[21] See also some of the other charges against Katanga and Chui (DRC), Ntaganda (DRC) and Kony (Uganda).

The lack of accountability of child soldiers can however be criticized. Drumbl (2010b) for instance argues that it is not a good development to completely exonerate children of any criminal responsibility because children are not hapless individuals who lack agency and free will. Drumbl contends that the discourse which depicts them as innocent is too absolute. They are victims but perpetrators at the same time as they can commit gruesome acts, and international criminal law needs to take that into account. Olusanya (2006, 88) also argues that immunity from prosecution is "unworkable in the supranational criminal law system". According to Olusanya immunity might lead to deliberate abuse.

The ICC nevertheless followed this line. According to Article 26 of the Rome Statute, it has no jurisdiction over any person under the age of 18. It does however hold child recruiters who abuse the vulnerability of children responsible. According to Article 8(2)(b) (xxvi) and Article 8(2)(e)(vii) of the Rome Statute, conscription or enlistment of children under the age of 15 is a war crime in national and international armed conflicts.

The prosecution of Domenic Ongwen by the ICC might shed some light on how the ICC will deal with child soldiers and child recruitment in the future.[22] The case of Domenic Ongwen is intriguing because he has been forcefully recruited into the army as a ten year old kid, was socialized into killing at a very young age and was thus transformed into a particularly vicious perpetrator who has committed tremendous crimes (Baines 2009). Ongwen is indicted by the ICC but he is only prosecuted for the crimes committed after he turned 18 and remarkably enough – considering his life story – he is accused of forcefully recruiting child soldiers. The law thus seems to suggest that Ongwen turned from a victim into a perpetrator at 18. It remains to be seen how the Court will deal with this paradoxal case: how it will strike the balance between the clear duress used against him when he was young and the horrendous crimes he committed thereafter. It remains to be seen to what extent the ICC will consider him a victim as well as a perpetrator.

7. CONCLUSION

The aim of this chapter was to erode the myth of pure evil which depicts the world in two absolutes in which evil and guilty perpetrators attack good and innocent victims. Although it would be appealing to consider victims and perpetrators as two mutually exclusive groups, this does not always reflect reality. Firstly, many perpetrators are motivated by past victimhood; whether this victimhood is real or alleged does not really make a difference to the perpetrator.

---

[22] See the arrest warrant issued by the ICC on Domenic Ongwen and the case *Prosecutor v. Joseph Kony, Vincent Otti, Okot Odhiambo and Dominic Ongwen.*

This unfortunately leads to many crimes which are committed in order to avenge other crimes (real or alleged). Furthermore, perpetrators often legitimize their crimes as being a defence against a real or alleged threat. Thirdly we have seen that victims in a legitimate struggle against an oppressor can also come to commit crimes and become perpetrators. Most attention in this chapter was, however, given to a fourth situation, notably in which victims became perpetrators due to an efficient system of enforced compliance and cooperation by the oppressor. In order to clearly show that people can be victims and perpetrators at the same time three extreme cases of victims who became very efficient perpetrators have been discussed in more detail. In cases in which people are forced to commit crimes with a loaded gun pointed at their heads, the victims of such pressure cannot be considered perpetrators. This is different in the three cases described. The case studies show that some people who are victimized by a deliberate and abusive system which enforces compliance and cooperation adapt to their situations and become real perpetrators thus eroding the myth of pure evil. The lesson we can draw from this is that we sometimes have to take a more nuanced view towards perpetrators and victims alike and accept that victims and perpetrators are not always two mutually exclusive groups. Strange as it may seem sometimes people are victims and perpetrators at the same time.

IV. VICTIMS OF THE GENOCIDE AGAINST THE TUTSI IN RWANDA

Etienne RUVEBANA

1. HISTORICAL BACKGROUND OF THE GENOCIDE AGAINST THE TUTSI

To understand what happened in Rwanda, it is worth mentioning briefly something about the Rwandan history in as far as the preparation of the genocide and its execution are concerned. Before 1994, Rwanda, which is situated immediately south of the Equator, bordering the Democratic Republic of Congo, Uganda, Tanzania, and Burundi, was the most densely populated African country with more than 7 million inhabitants on only 26,338 square kilometres of land. As written by Melvern, the pre-colonial period was largely a mystery for that its history was recalled only in poems and myths. By that time, Rwanda being a Kingdom, the King owned everything: the land, the cattle and the people (Melvern 2004, 7). After the Berlin conference of 1885, in which the main European powers divided the African continent and Rwanda was given to Germany, Rwanda continued to have its monarchy, which was one of the impressing Kingdoms among other African ones (Des Forges *et al.* 1999, 47). Germany ruled through that monarchy since the time it installed itself in Rwanda in 1897. In 1917, the League of Nations gave Belgium the mandate to administer Rwanda. In its summary of Rwandan history, the International Criminal Tribunal for Rwanda (ICTR) mentioned that Rwanda was a complex and advanced monarchy. The monarch ruled the country through his official representatives drawn from the Tutsi nobility. Thus, a highly sophisticated political culture emerged which enabled the king to communicate with the people.[1]

Both German and Belgian colonial authorities, if only at the outset as far as the latter are concerned, relied on an elite essentially composed of people who referred to themselves as Tutsi, a choice which, according to Des Forges, was

---

[1]   *Prosecutor v. Akayesu Jean Paul*, Case No. ICTR-96–4-T, Judgment, 02 September 1998, para. 80.

born of racial or even racist considerations.[2] In the minds of the colonizers, the Tutsi looked more like them, because of their height and colour, and were, therefore, more intelligent and better equipped to govern.[3] Unlike Germany's policy of indirect rule, Belgium's policy became direct rule, which eroded the power of the King. In November 1931 the King, Mwami Musinga, who was against colonization, was deposed by the Belgian administration with little objection from the League of Nations (Melvern 2004, 10). His son, Mutara Rudahigwa, replaced him. The Belgian rule was harsh on Hutu and, as Belgian rule consolidated, hundreds of thousands of Hutu peasants fled the country to neighbouring Uganda to become migrant labourers (Melvern 2004, 10).

During this period, Belgian authorities introduced a permanent distinction by defining the three main groups as ethnic groups, with the Hutu representing about 84% of the population, while the Tutsi (about 15%) and Twa (about 1%) accounted for the rest.[4] Yet, before the colonization, being Hutu, Tutsi or Twa did not determine a fixed identity (Gaudin 2002, 3). The people shared the same language and culture and even though intermarriage was not that frequent, it was not impossible in some cases.

Thus, these categories were reflecting the social status rather than the ethnic group as such since it was even possible to change categories. But in the 1930s, Belgian colonizers quickly referred to the notion of race as this was much easier and familiar to them.[5] In line with this division, it became mandatory for every Rwandan to carry an identity card mentioning his or her ethnicity.[6]

From the late 1940s, at the dawn of the decolonization process, the Tutsi became aware of the benefits they could derive from the privileged status conferred to them by the Belgian colonizers and the Catholic Church. They then attempted to free themselves somehow from Belgian political stewardship and to emancipate Rwandan society from the grip of the Catholic Church. The desire for independence shown by the Tutsi elite certainly caused both the Belgians and the Catholic Church to shift their alliances from the Tutsi to the Hutu, a shift rendered more radical by the change in the church's philosophy after the second world war, with the arrival of young priests from a more democratic and egalitarian trend of Christianity, who sought to develop political awareness among the Tutsi-dominated Hutu majority.[7] In fact, even if some Tutsi families had been privileged (especially the chiefs' families and others close to the King) they were not satisfied as the powers of the King and his chiefs were quasi-inexistent from the beginning of the colonisation. The King could no longer determine the outcome of important issues as was the case before

---

2   *Idem*, para. 82.
3   *Ibidem*.
4   *Idem*, para. 83.
5   *Ibidem*.
6   *Ibidem*.
7   *Idem*, para. 85.

colonisation. Furthermore, the anger among the royal family about the deportation of King Musinga had not disappeared either. One of the signs of his disapproval of Belgian colonisation, King Mutara III Rudahigwa, whose father had been deported, was his attempt to join the African nationalism campaign hoping that this would increase sympathy from the international community, as a step towards decolonisation (Lugan 1997, 355). Among other things, this angered Belgian colonizers who thought that it was better to support and emancipate Hutu with a strong belief that they would be more cooperative.

From that moment, Belgian colonizers offered more opportunities to Hutu. But the Tutsi continued to seek for independence which further inflamed the colonizers. While the Tutsi were pushing for the end of Belgian domination, the Hutu elites, for tactical reasons, were favouring the continuation of the domination, hoping to make the Hutu masses aware of their political weight in Rwanda, in a bid to arrive at independence, which was unavoidable, at least on the basis of equality with the Tutsi. Belgium particularly appreciated this attitude as it gave them reason to believe that with the Hutu, independence would not spell a severance of the ties between Belgium and Rwanda.[8] They could not expect this from the Tutsi, because according to their analysis, after independence, the Tutsi would not accept and tolerate the Belgians in Rwanda anymore.

That is why in the same period – the 1950s – they continued to raise Hutu awareness of their majority status which would allow them to win elections forever in Rwanda. They then helped them to create political parties. In 1956, in accordance with the directives of the United Nations Trusteeship Council, Belgium organized elections on the basis of universal suffrage in order to choose new members of local organs, such as the grassroots representative Councils.[9] With the electorate voting on strictly ethnic lines, the Hutu of course obtained an overwhelming majority and thereby became aware of their political strength. The Tutsi, who were hoping to achieve independence while still holding the reins of power, came to the realization that universal suffrage meant the end of their supremacy; hence, confrontation with the Hutu became inevitable.[10] This was followed by the creation of the first political parties in 1957.

In 1959, after the death of King Mutara Rudahigwa in Burundi, the so-called Social Revolution of 1959 started, as a result of which 150,000 Tutsi were either killed or forced to flee to neighbouring Uganda, Burundi, Democratic Republic of Congo (then called Zaire) and Tanzania (Percival & Homer-Dixon 1995). This was the first slaughter of the Tutsi population. The new Tutsi King, Kigeli V, left Rwanda as well, never to return. The Belgians described the violence as a race problem between Hutu and Tutsi, and on 1 November 1959, Belgium placed Rwanda under military rule, its fortunes entrusted to the Belgian colonel Guy

---

[8]   *Idem*, para. 83.
[9]   *Idem*, para. 87.
[10]   *Ibidem*.

Logiest, who immediately began to replace Tutsi chiefs with Hutu, and announced to the Belgian administration that in the future the Hutu would be favoured within the administration (Melvern 2004, 14).

One year after the independence, which was declared on July 1st, 1962, when Gregoire Kayibanda (a Hutu) became the President of the first Republic (whose government was composed of Hutu), some Tutsi in exile tried to make incursions to Rwanda from neighbouring countries, mainly Burundi. This led to another horrible slaughter of the remaining Tutsi population in Rwanda as retaliation (Lugan 1997, 434). It is difficult to estimate the exact number of victims of this slaughter due to small number of neutral individuals on the ground by then. However, in the province of Gikongoro alone estimates run as high as 8,000 to 12,000 fatalities (Lugan 1997, 435). The consequences of this slaughter for the Tutsi population in the whole country were enormous (Lugan 1997, 435–438).

Some individuals had the courage to denounce the killings of 1963–1964 but this did not improve the situation. For example, a Swiss Professor in the University of Rwanda, Denis Vuillemin, condemned the genocide and publicly castigated Belgium. He contributed a piece for a newspaper under the headline *L'extermination des Tutsis*, stating that Belgium was responsible for complicity to genocide, and that he resigned from his job because he refused to represent such a country (Melvern 2004, 18). Apart from the Tutsi who survived the slaughters of 1959 and 1963–1964 and fled the country, others remained in Rwanda and often intermarried with Hutu and continued to live together in Rwandan society despite what had happened to them. They believed that by intermarrying, they would get protection from Hutu if a slaughter against them was to happen again.

In 1973, a putsch initiated by the Chief of Staff of the national army at the time, Major General Juvenal Habyarimana, took place and President Kayibanda was overthrown from power and killed. He was accused by Habyarimana, supported by a group of senior officers in the army originating from the Northern Rwanda, of favouring people from the southern region known as 'Nduga' at the expense of Northern people. Although this had nothing to do with the Tutsi, it was followed by massacres against the Tutsi and again many of them were forced to flee the country, in large part to the four neighbouring countries Burundi, Zaire, Tanzania and Uganda.

In 1982, the Tutsi who had fled to Uganda were harshly forced to return home by Obote, then President of Uganda. However, they were denied entry to Rwanda by the Habyarimana regime arguing that Rwanda was like a glass full of water and there was no space for more people. The few who persisted and refused to go back to Uganda were taken to Nasho in Akagera National Park where they were mistreated. Many died and others went to Tanzania never to return during the Habyarimana regime. Many young refugees joined the Ugandan rebel movement led by Museveni, which came into power in 1986.

In 1987, the Tutsi in exile created a political movement in Uganda, the Rwandan Patriotic Front (RPF). In October 1990, with its military wing, the RPA (Rwandan Patriotic Army), the RPF launched an attack from Uganda into Eastern Rwanda. This rebel movement was mainly composed of the children of the 1959 refugees.

Hutu extremists feared loss of power due to the consistent threat of invasion by the RPF. Rather than directing this fear at the RPF itself, it was generalized to the Tutsi as an ethnic group (Bijleveld *et al.* 2009). That is the reason why in some targeted places like Kibilira and Bigogwe in the North and Bugesera in the East, thousands of Tutsi were cruelly slaughtered. It was continually stressed that there was a "Tutsi threat". The genocide was thus a result of the Hutu elite propaganda campaign against the Tutsi and this genocide would not have been as fast as it has been, if the Hutu community had not been mobilized in advance.

Despite the cease-fire and power-sharing accords between the RPF and the Rwandan government that were concluded and signed in 1993 in Arusha, the *Interahamwe* – bands of Hutu militias – continued to be trained, and weapons were continuously imported. Also, in 1993 the propaganda against Tutsi increased by *Radio-television Libre des Mille Collines* (RTLM) whose shareholders included President Habyarimana himself. With this generalized propaganda for many years, the real genocide started in April 1994, preceded by the death of President Juvenal Habyarimana on April 6, 1994, who returned from Arusha, Tanzania to sign the peace accord.

Interahamwe, backed by the government and the army, roamed the towns and the countryside, killing, raping and looting the Tutsi (Bijleveld *et al.* 2009). In one hundred days of genocide, an estimated 800.000 Tutsi and moderate Hutu were slaughtered in every part of Rwanda. The killers resorted to various barbarous practices and means aiming at the destruction of the Tutsi ethnic group. This put the country in the darkest situation ever. The next section will discuss the perpetration of the genocide, its victims and means and practices used to kill the victims.

2. THE PERPETRATORS AND VICTIMS OF THE RWANDAN GENOCIDE

2.1. THE PERPETRATORS OF THE GENOCIDE AND THEIR TECHNIQUES/MEANS

Before discussing the perpetrators of the genocide it is important to first recall the definition of the crime of genocide. According to Article II of the Genocide Convention, genocide means:

any of the following acts committed with the intent to destroy, in whole or in part, a national, ethnic, racial or religious group as such:

(a) *Killing members of the group;*
(b) *Causing serious bodily or mental harm to members of the group;*
(c) *Deliberately inflicting on the group conditions of life calculated to bring about its physical destruction in whole or in part;*
(d) *Imposing measures intended to prevent births within the group;*
(e) *Forcibly transferring children of the group to another group.*[11]

The crime of genocide involves a wide range of actions, the deprivation of life but also actions considerably endangering life and health. All these actions are subordinated to the criminal intent to destroy a human group. The acts are selected for the destruction of people only because they belong to one of these groups (Heidenrich 2001, 3). So, genocide means the destruction of a particular group of people, in whole or in part.

In the case of the genocide against the ethnic Tutsi, most of the acts mentioned in Article II of the Genocide Convention were committed; the responsibility for killing almost the entire Tutsi population of Rwanda falls on the perpetrators. These include Hutu extremists who planned, prepared, instigated and incited the commission of genocide. It also includes other Hutu extremists who, even though they did not physically participate in the genocide, had designed the plan to annihilate the Tutsi.

Although the techniques used in the Holocaust by Nazi against Jews were not executed in the same length of period as in the case of the genocide in Rwanda, some are very similar to those used in the genocide against the Tutsi. For instance, in both the Holocaust and the genocide against the Tutsi, the attacks against the targeted groups were systematic and organized. In the genocide against the Tutsi though, the techniques aimed specifically at exterminating the entire Tutsi population in as short a period as possible.

Interahamwe militia had been trained for this purpose and their trainings aimed to kill one thousand Tutsi in twenty minutes. For them it was a matter of pride to kill as many Tutsi as possible as quickly as possible whatever the means used. All techniques and/or means were accepted, as long as their end-result was the annihilation of the Tutsi population.

In this regard, it must be emphasized that for genocide to be possible, the killers focused on some specific areas, including the political, social, economic, biological, physical, moral and religious ones (Lemkin 1944, 82–89). Due to a limitation of space, this section only discusses the political, economic, religious and physical areas.

---

[11] Convention on the Prevention and Punishment of the Crime of Genocide, adopted by resolution 260 (III) A of the UN General Assembly on 9 December 1948.

Starting with the political field, the killers in Rwanda knew that some political parties would oppose the genocide. Those political parties were mainly the *Mouvement Democratique Rwandais* (MDR), the *Parti Libéral* (PL), and the *Parti Socialiste pour la Democratie* (PSD). The Government started by dividing these political parties. Indeed, in the MDR the so-called *MDR power* was formed. This had the same ideology – to wipe out all the Tutsi – to the extremist Hutu parties MRND and CDR. Likewise, the PL was divided. Here a *PL power*-faction was created with the same hate ideology. Those who did not belong to the extremist branches were considered to be traitors; many of the key persons within these political parties were immediately killed in the days following the downing of the presidential airplane in the evening of April 6th 1994. For instance, the Hutu Prime Minister Mme Agathe Uwiringiyimana was assassinated the day after the crash of the Presidential aircraft. She was known to oppose any discrimination and was preparing a speech on the national radio, calling for calm. Others were Landoald Ndasingwa, first vice-president of the PL (Lugan 2004, 163) who was killed at approximately 300 meters from the UNAMIR Headquarters while he was on the phone seeking assistance of Colonel Luc Marchal of the UNAMIR; Kavaruganda Joseph and Nzamurambaho Frederic, respectively President of the Constitutional Court and the President of the PSD (and Minister of Agriculture); and Ngango Felicien, first vice-president of the PSD, all three Hutu but opponents of genocide. Likewise, Ngurinzira Boniface, former Minister of Foreign Affairs, accused of having been the first Hutu to accept the negotiations with the RPF, was assassinated in the early days of the genocide (Lugan 2004, 163). Similar to what happened to the German resistance movement against Hitler's plan to murder all European Jews (Triffterer 2001), the above mentioned Hutu paid with their lives for their opposition to the plan to wipe out the Tutsi population.

As far as the economic field is concerned, it is worth mentioning that during the genocide the Tutsi were deprived of their properties. Their houses and cars were burnt or demolished and their cattle killed or taken from them by the Hutu. Their money was stolen by the perpetrators and many Tutsi were no longer able to provide the basic means of existence for themselves and their families until eventually they were murdered.

Concerning the religious sphere, most Rwandans were religious, predominantly Christians, in majority Catholics. The role of the religion was important in daily life, and the population respected the religious leaders. Therefore any important message could successfully be implemented if it was announced through the Church. In this regard, not only were many of the masterminds of the genocide Christians themselves but they used Church leaders and churches to kill as many Tutsi as possible. Many church leaders actively participated in the leadership of political parties and were involved in decision making. Some were used to convince their fellow Christians that the churches were the best places to seek refuge, and a huge number of Tutsi (children, men, women, old people) gathered in different churches like Sainte Famille and Saint Paul in Kigali, Catholic churches of Nyamata and Ntarama in Bugesera, Kibeho in former Gikongoro (now Southern province), Nyarubuye in former Kibungo (now Eastern Province), Cyahinda in Nyakizu Commune, Butare Prefecture (now district of Nyaruguru in Southern Province), and were defencelessly slaughtered in a ferocious way. One of the most heinous examples of the role of church leaders in the elimination of the Tutsi is the participation of Priest Seromba Athanase in the destruction of the church in Nyange Parish killing 1,500 Tutsi refugees sheltering inside.[12]

As for the physical field, the plan was the total physical destruction of the whole Tutsi population. To make it possible, the media which had been used ever since the RPF had invaded Rwanda, became harsher against the Tutsi. The popular "Hutu Ten Commandments" were read out loud on radio RTLM, aiming at convincing all Hutu that the Tutsi were evil and that they deserved to be physically destroyed. The Nazis used similar methods against the Jews, as Nazi anti-Semitic doctrine was disseminated through *Der Stuermer* and other publications, as well as in the speeches and public declarations of the Nazi leaders broadcasted on the radio (France *et al.* 1996). For instance, in a September 1938 diatribe in *Der Stuermer*, editor Julius Streicher described the Jew "as a germ and a pest, not a human being, but a parasite, an enemy, an evil-doer, a disseminator of diseases who must be destroyed in the interest of mankind" (France *et al.* 1996). In May 1939 an article was published in *Der Stuermer* that:

> *A punitive expedition must come against the Jews in Russia. A punitive expedition which will provide the same fate for them that every murderer and criminal must expect: Death sentence and execution. The Jews in Russia must be killed. They must be exterminated root and branch.* (France *et al.* 1996)

For the Tutsi the same means was used. That is the dehumanization of them. They were not only said to be arrogant, proud and deceivers but they also and especially were qualified as snakes, cockroaches and enemies which put all of them in a category of people who deserved to be destroyed in order to preserve Hutu from any problem that the Tutsi could cause to them. Dehumanizing the Tutsi was a way to make their extermination easier since killers could kill as many as possible without feeling any remorse.

To this end, all means leading to the total extermination of the Tutsi were welcome. Fire weapons, grenades, and traditional arms were used, the latter in all parts of the country since at least every person could afford to obtain a machete, spear, knife or any other traditional weapon. Although these traditional arms are not considered to be weapons of mass destruction, one might say that

---

12   *Prosecutor v. Seromba Athanase*, ICTR-01-66-A, Appeal chamber, ICTR, 12 March 2008, para. 206.

in the Rwandan genocide, this was the case, as it was possible to use them to kill hundreds of thousands of Tutsi in a very short period. For hundred days, the majority group of Hutu extremists massacred the minority ethnic group, in the aim to solve the so-called 'Tutsi problem' once and for all. This caused unimaginable human suffering, although it is not possible to exhaustively describe the full hardship victims experienced. The next paragraph discusses some cases revealing the horrible experience of the Tutsi during the genocide.

2.2. VICTIMS DURING THE GENOCIDE

When talking about victims of the genocide, it is important to mention that the same as for other crimes, there are direct victims who suffered the damage caused in violation of their rights and indirect victims who have suffered because of the damage caused to a person who is directly linked to them.

The UN General Assembly offered a broad definition of victim by stating that 'victims' means persons who, individually or collectively, have suffered harm, including physical or mental injury, emotional suffering, economic loss or substantial impairment of their fundamental rights, through acts or omissions that are in violation of criminal laws operative within Member States, including those laws proscribing criminal abuse of power.[13] The same UN declaration continues that a person may be considered a victim, under this Declaration, regardless of whether the perpetrator is identified, apprehended, prosecuted or convicted and regardless of the familial relationship between the perpetrator and the victim. The term 'victim' also includes, where appropriate, the immediate family or dependants of the direct victim and persons who have suffered harm in intervening to assist victims in distress or to prevent victimization.[14]

Considering this definition it can be said that in the context of the genocide against the Tutsi in Rwanda, direct victims were both those who perished in that genocide and those who were directly wounded by it. And the indirect victims are those who, even though they were neither killed nor were they directly physically wounded, suffered and/or still suffer the consequences of the genocide because of the relationship between them and the direct victims. However, since the discussion on knowing the victim of the genocide can be immense, it is not the purpose of this sub-paragraph to go in deep with this notion of victim. The purpose is rather to show with some examples the hardship of the victims of the genocide during the time of the genocide.

Even though it is always difficult for survivors to reiterate their horrific experience mainly because of the profound pains it brings back by recalling the

---

13   UN GA, *Declaration of Basic Principles of Justice for Victims of Crimes and Abuse of Power*: Resolution adopted by the General Assembly, 29 November 1985, A/RES/40/34.
14   *Ibidem.*

losses of their beloved ones and the terrible memory of hardship they went through, in the interviews I conducted for this chapter, some survivors shared their sad experience in the genocide and expressly accepted that this would be published.

Kantarama Donatha is a young girl survivor of the genocide who was born in 1985 in Nyakizu, Butare Prefecture (now Southern province). At the age of nine, she lost her parents, brothers and sisters and of the whole family of fourteen persons, only four survived.[15]

> *I never forget how my father was butchered. I perpetually see in my mind how I saw him suffering after he was cut by Interahamwe who deliberately left him before he died. They wanted him to suffer, and this was achieved because he really suffered before he died many hours after he was butchered. I never stop from thinking and dreaming about this. It was so horrible.*

In her long testimonial, Donatha explained how the members of her family were killed with terrible ferocity. Here is the summary of her testimonial:

> *After the death of the then president, I heard screaming voices in different hills surrounding our place. I saw many people running, and I was told that they were being hunted by Hutu extremists. I was still young and it was even hard for me to know to distinguish Hutu from Tutsi. I could see many people coming at our house and they said they were running away from the Hutu who wanted to kill them just because they belonged to the Tutsi ethnic group. It did not take long for some Hutu to come to our house. They surrounded our house and some entered into it. It was early in the morning, around 6.00 a.m. When they started to kill members of my family, my elder brother took me to hide with him in the ceiling of our house. By then, my father had been cut by machete and we thought he was already dead, but he was not yet dead. Some of my elder sisters had just also been killed with machete. And unlike my father, they were already dead. Those who tried to run away were followed by Interahamwe and were killed nearby our house. Those Hutu said that they were leaving but that they would come back in the evening to see if my father was still alive and in the affirmative, they would end up his life. They also wanted to burn our house the same evening. When my brother with whom I was hiding heard about that, he probably was afraid and he quitted that place and went down and he was immediately killed there. It really pains me. I think he wanted to see how my father was suffering and see if there was a way he could help him. I always think that my brother was no longer able to think well because of what was happening to my father and other members of my family. He probably*

---

15 Interview with Kantarama Donatha, August 20, 2009 in the Village of Kiberinka, Nyamirambo Sector, District of Nyarugenge, Kigali. She lives in a grouped settlement called *Nimudusange* literally meaning: 'come to us'. This grouped settlement (commonly called *Umudugudu* in Rwanda) is made of 10 houses which, at the date of the interview were occupied by 72 persons divided in 23 families, each family living in one room whatever the number and sex of the members of that family.

could not control his emotions anymore. He was immediately killed by those Hutu. I remember him all the time. I loved him and he loved me. I wish he never left me in the ceiling, because probably those Interahamwe would not have known that we were there and may be he would not have been killed. And we could have may be survived together, without all this big and deep scars on my head, neck and everywhere.

Later on, I heard and recognized the voices of some two Hutu men that I knew (although I did not know before that they were Hutu). These were our neighbours Andre and Bizimana. They were saying that they wanted to put an end to the life of my father. Like my brother, I could not take this, and I screamed and when they heard my voice, they asked me to go down myself and they promised that they would not kill me. But as I arrived down, they told me that my father had just been killed. In my mind I could secretly thank God that I did not watch them killing him. They remorselessly showed me the body of my father, my three sisters and my brother with whom I was on the ceiling as well as my cousins and many other relatives. There were many dead bodies of Tutsi. I asked the two guys to forgive me and not to kill me. They told me that it was not worth killing me because even staying alone was equivalent to death. They said they would not kill me and I naively believed in them. They forced me to come with them wherever they were going. And they were only killing people all along their way. I could watch everything and this memory comes to my mind all the time up to know. I never forget those women, men, and children that I saw being killed. It still hurts me and I think it will always hurt me. It was terrible and it is still fresh in my mind, even now after fifteen years.

After four days with them, some soldiers came to them to supply some machetes and grenades. They gave them a clear instruction that no single Tutsi should survive. After this, the two men asked me if I wanted to be killed or not. Although I was extremely tired, hungry thirsty and I had lost my family, I still had the desire to live! I don't know why but that is how I was feeling. My answer to them was a 'yes' and I therefore asked them again to forgive me. They took me to my home and there I could see how our house was burnt. I also still remember that very bad day because I saw the bodies of my beloved ones which had started to deteriorate. They asked me to say goodbye to the dead bodies of my farther, my three sisters and my brother because I was also going to be killed and I would never have the chance to see them again. Bizimana immediately hit me with a big nailed club on my head and when I fell down he cut me with the machete on my head as you can see these big scars at the back of my head and above the ear. Others also hit me on my head and they left me there. They thought I was dead already. However, even though I was dying, I was not dead as they thought. I was near the river and it was on the road and everyone was making fun about beating me, a Tutsi as I could hardly hear them saying. One Hutu lady, whose name is Félicité, took me and brought me near dead persons. I don't know if she did it to protect me or if she thought I was dead and wanted me to be with other corpses. When the two men who tried to kill me found me at a different place, they said that I was still alive and they hit me again in my joints and on my head and since I was very weak, I was no longer able to move because I was almost dead, they became convinced that I was dead and they left again.

The following day was dedicated to burying all those bodies including mine. They dug a communal grave and they started to throw each corpse in this grave. When it was my turn to be thrown in the grave, they realized that I was not yet dead and the head of the militia group whose name is Kinyange opposed the idea to burry me alive. He said that I was in a critical situation and that I would die later and then be buried after.

Surprisingly, on the fifth day from the day I was cut, the same Kinyange came and took me from there and put me near the road to Burundi. He said that I could be taken by Tutsi and may be they would take care of me. I don't know what pushed him to do so, because I wonder how he would have had the 'heart' to save me while he was the head of the Interahamwe group which had already killed a huge number of Tutsi. There, I saw one Tutsi man with his wife and child hiding in the bush near the road. When they saw me, they sympathized with me, but they were also hiding and I could not expect anything big from them. Immediately later, they saw a small truck coming and the Tutsi man tried to stop it and the driver asked why he was stopping him. The driver was a Hutu, but we could not know that he was also one of the killers. And the Tutsi man begged him to take us and bring us to the border with Burundi. The driver accepted but said he could only do that if they paid him money, which they did. I remember that the Tutsi man insisted to the driver who was refusing to take me because he said I was dead but the Tutsi said that even though I was dead, they still wanted to take me with them because I was their child. They loaded me as objects and we were put in the car with machetes and other arms then we came to know that he was using the car to supply those traditional arms to Interahamwe here and there. On our way, we were stopped at a roadblock of Interahamwe. They checked the car and took the three Tutsi with whom I was. They took the child and hit his head on the road pavement, her mother strongly screamed saying "banyiciye umwana!!!" which means they have killed my child. I never stop from hearing how the child cried when he was taken from his mother before he was hit to the pavement. The voice of the mother when she screamed over the killing of her child also comes always to my mind! It is a bad memory ever! It is a suffering that none can never imagine! But the mother was not even given the chance to mourn her child even for one minute. They took her and killed her as well. The father was also immediately killed. I can't know which arms were used to kill them because what I could hear was only the screaming, they were begging them for forgiveness, which they never got. Yet they were innocent. But the killers had no 'heart' to forgive. They might have used machetes because I did not hear the sound of gun. I never understand how a human being can have such a deep hatred and kill such a young child that way. It was horrible. They opted to kill the child first, yet he was not the dangerous one!!! They just wanted to make their parents suffer more! As for me, I was taken out from the car and thrown on the road with uncountable blows. They thought I was already dead.

I am very thankful to Burundian soldiers who later crossed the border and forcibly saved us. They shot on Interahamwe and even burnt the car which was supplying arms to them (the one which brought us). I, with some other few Tutsi, was taken to the hospital in Kayanza. I was treated there for a long time. And then, even though I had seen the corpses of my father, my three sisters and my brother, I still did not know what happened to my mother and other brothers and sisters. I was convinced that everybody was killed.

In 2000, two years after I came back to Rwanda, through a soldier who used to be our neighbour before the genocide, I got to know that there were my two young sisters who had survived and who were in Kibungo at the time. The two sisters had been brought back by the UNHCR from Congo where they might have gone in the crowd of people fleeing to there. They were so young during the genocide. They were with my mother in Nshili, where my mother had taken refuge in a Hutu family. They do not know how they separated with my mother nor do they even remember her. They also did not know how they went to Congo. So, up to now, I do not know how my mother was killed, the person who killed her and the place she was buried or thrown. The only thing I am sure of is that she was killed. Because it is now fifteen years, and she was among the hunted people. I wish I can ever get someone to tell me about her death. It does not matter how horrible it might have been for her. I need it and I think this can relieve me somehow. Of course if I get to know that she was just killed without being raped by Hutu extremists I would feel better. But I doubt if I will ever know about her sufferings and death. She was a good mother, and she really did not deserve what happened to her. It is hard for me to accept that. I still have some hope to see her some time, but not on this earth because I know she is not alive. I will always miss her love that I lost at an earlier age. She can never be replaced. I go through difficult times and I think this would never happen to me if my mother was alive.

Later on, I also came to know that there was another young sister who had fled to Burundi. So in the family of fourteen members, nine of them perished in the genocide and one brother died in the army (after the genocide). I wish the whole world could know all these unimaginable things that happened to us, and then maybe, it could prevent it from happening again. And although I don't know how to explain it, but I feel like I can feel somehow relieved if the world gets to know this tragedy and the long journey of hardship and sorrow we went and still go through.

Francois Xavier Ndagijimana, is another survivor of the genocide. He was born in 1982 in Kivu commune (now Nyaruguru District in the Southern Province). Before the genocide, his family had eleven members. He was the ninth child, the youngest. Only three of them survived. Below, he explains what happened to him and his family:[16]

In my childhood, I used to watch where Tutsi were hunted; their properties had always been either burnt or taken from them by Hutu extremists. But I had never thought this would amount to what I saw in 1994. The situation became worse when the genocide started from the 7th April 1994. I could see many people fleeing their neighbourhoods, and they were escaping the killings directed against the Tutsi.

In the morning of April 11, a Monday, we saw many Interahamwe coming towards us. My mother sent me to my father who was grazing our cows in the farm. She asked me to go and take care of our cows and tell to my farther to come home because she needed him. At that time I could not know what she wanted but now I think she probably wanted to ask him what to do with what was happening. May be she wanted that we flee as well and wanted to know how we could do that. I went there and did all she had asked me.

---

[16]   Interview with Francois Xavier Ndagijimana, a young survivor of genocide. He has worked very hard to make sure he goes to school and at the time of the interview, he was a student of the Kigali Independent University where this interview was conducted on August 27, 2009.

After a few minutes, they came to pick me up and we immediately fled to a hill called Kabilizi. It was a hill predominantly inhabited by Tutsi. And there were many Tutsi from different places, and they were trying to find a way to defend themselves instead of just dying passively. Since the militias could not manage to kill all of us, the army and the 'gendarmerie' attacked us and killed many people. Those who did survive from this attack fled to a catholic church in Muganza, in the same Kivu commune. People naively thought that none could dare following them in the church and kill them there. They believed that the church was a holy place and none could ever commit such a horrible sin in the church. But that was not the case during those days. Biniga, who was the Deputy provincial prefet (Sous-prefet of Munini) organized a meeting with other leaders. The aim of the meeting was to improve the way to kill so that all the Tutsi in that area could be annihilated in a short time. They asked the gendarmerie to kill us.

In the night of that very same day, A Hutu seminarist whose name I can't remember and who just came from that meeting, came to us and disclosed to us what was being planned against us. He advised us to leave the place early the morning. In the morning, we started the long and hard journey, and the Hutu seminarist came with us to show us the way. I think he was a person with a "heart". We were going to Kibeho in a big crowd. I don't know exactly the number, but I think we were around 8,000. On our way, we met with a few Tutsi survivors from Kibeho, the place we were going to. We could not continue that way and there was no other option but to go in the Parish of Cyahinda where we found thousands of other Tutsi refugees. All along our way, we were stopped by Interahamwe militia, and many of our people were killed, but other continued their walk up to the Parish of Cyahinda. The Hutu seminarist was still accompanying us. In the church, Interahamwe launched several attacks to us but Tutsi men tried to defend us until elements of the army and gendarmerie came and used guns to kill us. My father who had watched several killings on our way was already traumatized, and he was no longer able to stand by himself. He was leaning on my sister who never tried to run away from that attack because she did not want to leave my father alone. She died with him. Although I would have wished my sister to survive as I did, I am very grateful to her for what she has been for our beloved father. She had a genuine love to our father. They were butchered with machetes together. I ran away and hardly escaped from them. I and other survivors from that attack went to a hill called Gasasa, not far from the parish of Cyahinda though. I think it was April 18, and we arrived at that hill around 3.00 p.m. A Tutsi whose name was Sagatarama and who was very brave put us together and suggested that we leave the place to flee to Burundi. He divided us in two groups which had to pass in two different ways in the direction to Burundi. But it rained right after the meeting and we were unable to leave immediately. It was a heavy rain that I had never seen before. After the rain we started another hardship. The whole night none could claim to get a rest because we wanted at least to be near to Burundi by the next day. We walked and passed by a place called Nshili which was not the nearest way, but we thought it was a bit safer. But it was really not. Many people were killed by Interahamwe on our way. When we arrived to a centre called Mugisenyi in Nshili commune around 09.00 a.m, we got stopped by an attack of Interahamwe and policemen led by the then "Bourgmestre" (mayor) of Nshili commune. His name was Kadogi. Some of them had traditional arms but others had guns and they started shooting on us. When they first shot in our crowd, my elder brother who was holding me by his arm, jumped over a channel of water by fear and he tried to run. When I tried to do the same I fell in that channel of water but I could still watch how the very same brother was butchered there with machete. Other brothers were also killed there. I later found my mother hanging in that channel of water. It always comes back in my mind. I saw things that I had never thought about before. In the evening, I crawled like an animal and managed to hide in a bush nearby that place. I thought killers had gone but they had not. They saw me and came to kill me. With fear and sufferings, I asked them to forgive me, but they had no "heart" to forgive. They cut me with machetes. As you can see me, they cut me on the neck, on my head, in my face, under my eye and under my ear. I became unconscious and I think they left me there thinking I was dead. After some time or some days (I don't know since I was unconscious), I regained my consciousness and it was raining. I think the rain helped me to recover some energy. I woke up but I was still bleeding and I took my head with my two arms to keep it at its place because I thought there was a risk that it could fall down since as it can be seen on my big scar on my neck, I had a very big wound there.

With the consciousness that I regained, I still could think that I had to continue my way to Burundi. Yet I did not know the way and I was alone. On my way I met with Interahamwe but they refused to kill me and I heard them saying that they wanted to let me suffer. They said that killing me was equivalent to helping me, which they did not want to do. I met with an old Hutu woman who was with a small Tutsi baby boy that she had taken from Tutsi corpses including his mother's. She had found that baby sucking at his mother's breast after her death. The baby was also seriously injured in his face. She took us and helped us to cross the border to Burundi. There, she managed to get some milk for us. We were so hungry and thirsty. She also managed to get some food for us. I did not know her, and she did not know us either, but she really saved us. At that time I did not ask her to tell me her name. I was still so young to think about that. And I was really suffering from all the wounds I had. My wounds had started to stink and there was still no hope for treatment. But I was taken later to a hospital in Kayanza in Burundi where I spent a couple of months. I was saved by the Hutu old woman. I did not know she was a Hutu, because I believed all the Hutu were evils, but there are some who could have a 'heart'. She saved me and I owe her a lot. I am glad that I finally got to be able to go to look for her in 2004. It was not easy since I did not know her name. The only reference I had was that she is an old woman who saved a young baby and me. She was mostly known for the baby she saved and I then got to meet her. Her name is Nyirakamana.

Hutu extremists did terrible things to us. I cannot see any punishment that can be proportionate to what they did to us. Even if the capital punishment had not been abolished, it still would not be equivalent to what they did. No, they caused us profound sufferings, it shocks our conscience. They vandalized our hearts. Nothing can make me happy. The only two more survivors in the whole family of eleven persons have become disabled. I cannot even ask them any advice.

Mukagihana Annonciata is another survivor of the genocide. She was born in Taba commune (now Kamonyi) and she still lives there. Her mother was killed during the genocide and thrown in the Nyabarongo river which flows to the Akagera and Nile rivers. When the genocide started, she was married and had four children. In her testimonial, she described the sexual slavery she endured during the genocide:[17]

> *When the genocide started, killers took my husband by buses from Kabwayi to Gisenyi [in the north-west of Rwanda] with some of his brothers, cousins as well as many other Tutsi. When I got news about them later, I heard that they were all burned alive in Ngororero. In burning them, killers used tyres and I was told that it took long for them to completely die. They really suffered. They were burned until they became ashes.*
>
> *As for me, I saw many people fleeing but I could not flee because I was sick at that time and was still under treatment. My toe had just been imputed at Remera Rukoma Hospital. But I could not stay at my home either. I had no other option but to go to my neighbour's house. This neighbour not only was a Hutu but she also had a brother who was Interahamwe. There were other Tutsi though who were hiding there. But her brother got to know that there were Tutsi there and he came with other Interahamwe to kill us that very same night. In the big crowd trying to run away to escape them, I went in a bush near that house and stayed there for two days. I was not able to walk long because my wound was causing me pains. Since I could no longer take any medicine, the wound started not only to stink but also to expand. I got so thirsty and hungry; I had not eaten since a couple of days ago. I later decided to go to another Hutu neighbour's house to see if I could get at least some water to drink. I had never been before as thirsty as I was that time. I was still naïve; I was thinking that they were still our friends. But things had changed. Before I arrived there, I was surprised to be stopped by a big group of Hutu, led by the man of the house of whom I was going to ask some water to drink. They took me and I could not understand how this was done by my neighbour who I used to consider as a good friend. That was really a betrayal.*
>
> *Before killing me, they first discussed about where they would throw my body. Some were suggesting in Nyabarongo River whereas others were suggesting in the toilette. But, as if killing me was not enough, others said they would rape me before to kill me. They said that it was their first chance to discover how Tutsi sex was tasteful. They took me with them to a roadblock where I was repeatedly raped by different Hutu young men who used to work for us in our farms and who really looked homeless. They were dirty, ugly and were smelling very bad. This smell always comes back in my nose. I do not know how many Hutu raped me. They were so many and they were replacing each other. I saw three other Tutsi women there and they suffered the same fate as me. But for these three other women, killers were not very sure that they were Tutsi. They took them in their villages to ask their neighbours, and I later got to know that they were killed there after one week of torture by being raped.*
>
> *I was later on taken by soldiers of the FAR to their barracks. And there, I was raped again and again. I do not know how many times. There were so many Tutsi women there, and all were being raped. I stayed there for 3 days before being given to another Hutu originating from Ndusu in Ruhengeri. This Hutu took me and raped me also. But from then, he said I was becoming his wife because he had given money to the head of*

---

17   Interview with Mukagihana Annonciate, August 27, 2009 in Kigali at the office of AVEGA Agahozo which is an Association of women widowed by the genocide against Tutsi. She regularly comes there for treatment and sometimes for any other assistance.

sector who, after having taken me from the barracks, decided to give me to that Hutu. The Hutu he gave me to was among those who used to work for us. I knew him before, and he had left his home in the north to come at our commune because of poverty. Yet, I was forced to become his wife. But it was not really to become a normal wife. No, I was a wife for just satisfying his sexual desires. He could rape me anywhere he would feel that desire. And on our way; he said he was taking me to his commune of origin (Ndusu). And there, he said he would protect me as his wife. When we arrived in Ndusu, I was told that all Tutsi who inhabited there before had been exterminated. I was not safe either. But I was lucky that it did not take time before the RPF soldiers took control of that commune. This Hutu fled to Congo and he wanted to take me with him there, but I escaped from him and went to seek protection from the RPF soldiers. But I was already pregnant as a result of the rape. I was carrying a Hutu child as a result of rape and torture. I could not know who made me pregnant since I had been raped by many men during the same period. I only got to know his father when I gave birth to the child in 1995. He resembled to the last rapist. So, I then became sure that he was the father of that child who was never liked by my other children nor was he liked by other survivors in my neighbourhood. None of them like him. Let alone them, even for me it was difficult to feed him. I fed him only for six months. I was always having nightmares, always seeing in my dreams, killers coming to kill or rape me. Then it reached a point when I could not continue to feed that child because in feeding him I was like seeing his father and was thinking of all the sufferings that he caused to me. I abandoned that child and my brother took care of him. I became like mentally ill and I was taken to Ndera Hospital, but I was not crazy as people think that all people who are treated in Ndera Hospital are crazy. I was just disturbed by the bad memories. After three months of treatment in Ndera Hospital, I came back home. But still, I could not feel any mother love towards him. I was looking at him all the time and I was seeing him as a memory of all hardship that I went through. But on the other hand, I was remembering that I was his mother, and he deserved my love. He was innocent and I could see this even in his eyes. He was calling me his mother like my other children. I knew that all children are innocent, but I could not prevent myself from seeing him as a result of a cruelty against me and my people.

It is difficult to say, but this child has been a heavy burden to me. Yet, he is my child! When he does good things, I tend to love him like my other children but when he makes a mistake, even a simple one, I remember who he is and where he comes from. And then I feel all the pains again. It is difficult.

Living on this earth after what happened to me during the genocide is a hell. I do not know the words to use which can express exactly what happened to us during the genocide. We were mothers but were not respected for that, and we were raped several times by whoever wanted to do so even those who really looked homeless. And now some of them are in prison, just in prison!! This is not enough compared to sufferings they inflicted to us. But on the other hand, I cannot think of any punishment to them that will ever make me regain my joy. No, whatever can happen to them, I will still live with the consequences of the genocide. But I am not saying they should be released though. I think they should not, because I always think that they can repeat it again.

As I came to know that many women who were raped during the genocide have been infected by HIV, I decided also to be tested. I found out that I was HIV positive as well. This is a hell, really a hell. That is why I always come here at AVEGA to get some medicine to treat the HIV.

Mukacyaka Gloriose is another survivor of the genocide. She was born in 1984 in Nyakizu commune in Butare (now Nyaruguru district in Southern province). Her family consisted of five people. She is the oldest sibling, followed by another girl and a boy. She lost her father, mother and brother. She and her sister Kanzayire survived. With deep sorrow, she describes her memories of what happened to her family and herself:[18]

In our village, the genocide started on April, 15, 1994. Killers started to burn houses and to kill people and we fled to the Parish of Cyahinda. Killers attacked us and started shooting on us. Many were killed immediately there. Those who were not yet killed, run towards a hill called Gasasa. From there, we run in a crowd towards Nshili, in the direction to Burundi. I separated with my parents and my sister and brother from there. I was only with the cousin of my mother called Mukamana. I had never seen a dead person before, nor had I seen that a person kills another.

The mayor of Nshili commune whose name is Kadogi was given instructions to kill all Tutsi. They killed many people there but some Tutsi managed to escape and I was among those who escaped, and then we went to a place called Mugisenyi, where a large number of Tutsi perished. I do not know how we managed to escape from that mass killing in Mugisenyi. I do not remember a lot of things, because not only I was still so young, but also we saw things that are difficult to explain. My cousin never left me behind. She took me with her up to Burundi. I never saw my father again, nor did I see my mother or my brother again. I only got to know that my young sister whose name is Kanzayire Marie Claire survived. During the Genocide, she was nearly four years old and she was with my mother. When I saw her for the first time in 1997, I asked her about my mother. She said she thought my mother was still alive because some men just went with her. She was too young to know what happened. She had been taken by a Hutu lady called Immaculee who fled to Congo with her. I think she did it out of pity or sympathy because I do not know any other reason. Kanzayire never believed that my mother was not alive until 2005 when some Hutu who killed her confessed in Gacaca. They said that they used machetes to kill her but that she did not die immediately until she was buried after three days. She really suffered. I wish they killed her with a gun or any other means that can kill immediately. She suffered in the three days, and as if this was not bad enough, they buried her before she was completely dead. That is enormous animosity. Although I

---

18   Interview with Mukacyaka Gloriose in Kigali on August 25, 2009. At the time of interview, she was in Year I Management at the Kigali Independent University. She is known for having raised her voice to speak loud on the life of sixty-four orphans in Huye (southern province) then living in one small house. Together with other orphans, she was interviewed by Geoffrey Mutagoma, a journalist of BBC and she explained the conditions in which they were then living.

cannot thank these Hutu for having revealed my mother's whereabouts, I know how much it helped us at least to be sure that she was dead and not expect to see her anymore. And by this information, we got also to know where she was buried. Knowing this was extremely important since from then, my sister and I became sure that our mother was not alive as my sister used to believe and try to make me believe. But for my father and brother, we have never heard about them. And although we know they were killed, we wish at least we can also know about their death as we got to know about our mother's. But I think we will never know that because even Gacaca in which some information about some victims of genocide is sometimes obtained, is finishing soon.

3. THE CONSEQUENCES AND NEEDS OF VICTIMS POST-GENOCIDE

Due to the magnitude of the genocide and to the huge consequences of it on victims, this section does not purport to state all the consequences for survivors. The testimonials exemplify the situation of other survivors of genocide. In this section, I will restrict the discussion to show some of the consequences for victims of genocide, such as the disabilities and incurable diseases, the consequences for widows and orphaned children including the psychological trauma.

3.1. DISABILITIES AND INCURABLE DISEASES

The consequences of the genocide on its survivors are immense. Some of them did not only lose their loved ones but were also disabled by the genocide and now, not only mostly lack the means for elementary subsistence but also perpetually live with pains left by beatings and/or shootings. Kantarama Donatha[19] explains her situation:

When they took me in Kayanza hospital during the genocide, I was treated there but my wounds were so deep and had deteriorated that it was difficult for me to recover. I never recovered up to now. I still have pains in my head and these have become perpetual. Yet, I have been operated four times, in the National University Hospital for the first time, then in Kabgayi by a white medical doctor called Le Grand and two times in CHUK. Le Grand made an operation both on my head and ear. Both had never stopped to swell and it had always been aching. I never have long hairs like other young girls because at the hospital they ask me to always remove my hairs because of the permanent headache. I do not know if this really helps much since I never stop from having headache. In CHUK, I got an operation of my belly, because I have got many

---

19   See footnote above on the interview with Kantarama Donatha.

beatings on it and the wounds never healed. But even after all those operations, I still suffer up to now, and the only remaining hospital I have not gone to so far is the King Faysal Hospital. But there too, I have an appointment with a doctor today to seek if something can be done for my head. However, although it is always advised to have trust in medical doctors when they treat you, a trust that I do have, but considering how my wounds and other beatings were so deep and severe to the extent that they have always caused me harsh pains and sufferings, I do not expect to ever get better. But I still have to go there and I will not stop.

In addition to these disabilities, there are incurable diseases caused by the killers during the genocide. Among those diseases, a large number of women were infected with HIV as rape and sexual torture were used as one of the means to exterminate the Tutsi (also Kaitesi & Haveman, this volume). This was a result of the successful propaganda by Hutu power through the notorious "Hutu Ten Commandments". The first three of these "commandments" made a caricature of Tutsi women as subversive temptresses who should be avoided at all costs.[20] In this propaganda, Tutsi women were considered likely to be transformed into pistols that their brothers could use to conquer Rwanda. So for Hutu to be safe, no Tutsi woman should be allowed to live.[21] This led to unspeakable cruelty where Tutsi women were not only raped but also in many cases, the rapists used objects, to destroy their vaginas after repeated rapes. It was extreme barbarity and most Tutsi women were killed after all those brutal acts against them. Even those who escaped from death could not escape from the consequences of those cruel, humiliating and degrading atrocities. Some of those who survived were spared death not because of sympathy or pity of the killers but only to be used for sexual purposes, as was the case for Mukagihana Annonciata[22] who was made a sex slave during the genocide.

As recognized by the International Panel of Eminent Personalities which investigated the genocide against the Tutsi and its surrounding events, during the genocide, rape was routinely used as an instrument of war by the *genocidaires* to destroy women's psyches, to isolate them from their family or community ties and to humiliate their families and husbands.[23] And even now, although they were innocent, the women who survived rape during the genocide are still filled with shame,[24] humiliation, stigmatization, while many suffer from HIV/AIDS inflicted on them by their rapists. The United Nations General Assembly

---

[20] Organization of African Unity/African Union, *Rwanda: The Preventable Genocide*, Report of the International Panel of Eminent Personalities to Investigate the 1994 Genocide in Rwanda and the Surrounding Events, 7th July 2000, Addis Ababa, Ethiopia, para. 16.2.

[21] *Idem*, para. 16.3.

[22] See footnote above on the interview with Mukagihana Annonciata.

[23] Organization of African Unity/African Union, *Rwanda: The Preventable Genocide*, Report of the International Panel of Eminent Personalities to Investigate the 1994 Genocide in Rwanda and the Surrounding Events, 7th July 2000, Addis Ababa, Ethiopia, para. 16.18.

[24] See footnote above on the interview with Mukagihana Annonciata.

recognized in 2004 that survivors of sexual violence and sexual torture are among those who face the greatest hardship in post-conflict Rwanda.[25] Mukagihana Annonciata[26] explains the consequences for her:

> *My health is precarious because of the rape I endured during the genocide and because of the HIV/AIDS I was infected with then. I have never had the child I got from this rape tested. I do not know if he is also infected or not. We live in extreme poverty because due to my state of health, I am unable to dig the soil (...). I do not have life, really no life, because I feel like I can die any time. And if I die, I do not know what will be the fate of my children. I live with a deep sorrow and I never prevent myself from thinking about the disease I got from rape. Nothing can ever make me happy in my life, nothing, nothing. I do not know where this can ever come from. Because, when your body is suffering, your heart is remembering the cruel atrocities ever, then I do not see where the joy can come from.*

3.2. WIDOWS AND WIDOWERS

As for those widows and widowers whose children and relatives were killed, they suffer tremendously. They have noone to take care of them, to show them love and compassion. They live in abject poverty, with no possibility of improving their situation. A widow interviewed[27] in Kigali did not want her name to be disclosed because as she said, she did not want the killers to know how bad her life was and was she still afraid they might kill her. In strong words full of sorrow, she shows how she has suffered from the loss of her husband and her five children. Not only did she receive intensive beatings on her leg and belly which have left her in chronic pain, she also has noone to help her to receive medical treatment nor does she have any person to take care of her in everyday life. Since she does not enjoy life, she tried to commit suicide various times but failed or was prevented from doing so. This led to chronic trauma and she is treated as a crazy woman by her neighbours. This is just one example of many similar cases.

---

[23]   UN GA, Resolution 59/137 of 10 December 2004 on Assistance of the 1994 genocide in Rwanda, particularly orphans, widows and victims of sexual violence, A/RES/59/137,2004, cited by De Brouwer and Chu 2009, 11.

[26]   See footnote above on the interview with Mukagihana Annonciata.

[27]   This woman lives in one of the grouped settlements in the suburbs of Kigali. She lives in an extreme poverty and this cannot only be known from what she says but also and especially seen from the conditions in which she lives. In an interview with her, she shows a deep sorrow and she seems to have no hope in her future. She however commends the efforts of the President of the Republic of Rwanda who brought peace in the country but she says that this peace never gets into her heart and mind. And she cannot enjoy the peace that cannot give the peace in her.

3.3. PLIGHT OF CHILDREN

As far as children are concerned, it is worth mentioning that in Rwandan society children traditionally occupied a key position. The child was seen as the hope and future of the family[28] and this is commonly known in Kinyarwanda as *Rwanda rw'ejo* which literally means 'the Rwanda of tomorrow'. Thus, in Rwandan custom, children were supposed to enjoy love, care and the protection of the family and the community.[29] But the genocide turned these values completely upside down by not only killing a very large number of children during the genocide, but also 'killing' the hope of the future of the children who survived. Many children who survived found themselves alone, without parents, brothers, sisters or relatives. And not only did they lose the love and care of their parents but also did they loose even the little hope of a better future.

Some of the surviving children found themselves in refugee camps in Zaire (now DR-Congo). After their separation from or loss of their families, they followed the mass exodus of the Hutu population to Zaire and other neighbouring countries. Those who were not killed by diseases there could be returned to Rwanda by the UNHCR and other organizations. That is what happened to the two sisters of Kantarama Donatha. They were brought back by the UNHCR from DR-Congo. They were too young during the genocide to know how they went there, or even to know how they were separated from their mother, who might have been killed in Nshili, where she had taken refuge in a Hutu family.[30] The three sisters now live together in a small room in a settlement built in Nyamirambo in Kigali. With laudable efforts of Ibuka and AOCM (*Association des Orphelins Chefs des Ménages,* an organisation of children heading households) this settlement of 10 houses was built to at least offer these children a place to stay, but due to limited resources of the two organisations the orphans still live in difficult conditions. For instance, the room for the three sisters not only serves as a bedroom but also as a stock for their belongings. And as if this room is not already too small to serve as a full house, they host two surviving cousins during the holidays because they have nowhere else to live after the orphanage in which they used to stay in Nyanza has closed. Since they have no income, they have to turn to charity for their basic means of existence. An example is *Radio Contact F.M.,* which in 2009 mobilized people to give some food supplies; the Radio collected and brought this food to them. But this aid is not structural, so they cannot rely solely on this. They have to struggle for their survival and they try to fend for themselves. Some children do not go to school,

---

28 Organization of African Unity/African Union, *Rwanda: The Preventable Genocide*, Report of the International Panel of Eminent Personalities to Investigate the 1994 Genocide in Rwanda and the Surrounding Events, 7th July 2000, Addis Ababa, Ethiopia, para. 16.54.

29 *Ibidem.*

30 See footnote above on the interview with Kantarama Donatha.

especially those who head the households, because not only can they sometimes not afford the school fees, but they also have to struggle to obtain food and they have to take on any kind of job that can offer the possibility of food and other very basic amenities.

In a moving interview with orphans living in Huye (Sourthern province) conducted by BBC journalist Geoffrey Mutagoma in April 2007,[31] the orphans narrated the difficulties they were still going through. They described the conditions of their lives. In a house of only three rooms, these children explained that they were sixty-four (boys and girls together), sharing one small kitchen and one toilet.

In another interview with one of these children, Mukacyaka Gloriose,[32] conducted by myself, she explains her life before and after going to this house. This young girl lost her father, mother and brother, with only her younger sister surviving. After the genocide she stayed with Mukamana, who is a cousin of her mother, in her home village in a house of a Hutu neighbour who had fled, since their own houses had been destroyed during the genocide. But later on, Mukamana got married and Gloriose could not follow her. She stayed with her younger sister Kanzayire and two other children and thus became head of the household. They had to dig the soil since they had no other means of livelihood. Subsequently she suspended her education because not only did she have chronic headache but she also had to work for her survival as well as her sister's (despite the permanent headache). However, after one year she decided to send her sister to Mukamana's home and she herself went back to school in Huye, but she had nowhere to go for holidays. At school she found other students in the same situation and they decided to submit their problem to the representative of FARG in Huye, who contacted 'Page Rwanda', an association of Rwandans living in Canada, which bought three houses in Huye for the children by then numbering forty-five. When they were visited by the BBC in 2007 there were sixty-four, all living in one house since the other two houses were under reconstruction.

At the time of my interview with her there were fifty-two, as some left to get married or for other reasons. She recognized how the BBC interview positively impacted their life. After the time this journalist revealed their fate, some of the children got the chance to get people to pay school fees for them at the University. But still, many of them are still there, without hope for their future. She concluded by saying that whatever might be done, these children will lack still something, which is love.

---

[31] This interview was broadcasted in Kinyarwanda by the BBC Kinyarwanda-Kirundi Section. This made this journalist get an award later from them for having revealed their fate. Geoffrey was honoured later by these children organized in club Urumuli, at the occasion of launching two new big houses built by the administration after their fate was revealed on the BBC.

[32] See footnote above on the interview with Mukacyaka Gloriose.

We lost our families at a very young age and consequently some of us grew up in orphanages or in different families which not only did not care much about our education but also did not show us love. That is something very important that we lack and miss. We need to be loved or at least to be understood. We are children and like other children who have families, we can make mistakes, some misconduct, but when we do, no one corrects us, people don't care, and in that case, we feel abandoned by the world. People would just sit and say: he/she did this or that because he/she lacks education, yet their children also can do wrong things. I don't know what they say when their own children misbehave. Furthermore, we should not be seen as people who will remain perpetually with problems. I think in the future we could be better. And although nothing can ever fill our hearts with the love we lost, we feel relieved when people come to us and show us their sympathy. Our hearts need that, but some people think that they cannot come to us when they have no money or food to give us. No, we need to be loved more than we need to be fed. When I do well at school, I need to be given compliments, and when I don't do well, I need someone to show me that he/she is not happy with that, and then I can do better for the next semester.

The experience of children who survived the genocide is so sad, not only because of what they had to endure during the genocide but also because of what they had to endure afterwards. Francois Xavier Ndagijimana explains his experience from the end of the genocide until the time of interview.[33]

Only one sister, one brother and I survived of our entire family of eleven persons. But this sister became chronically traumatized, and my young brother became a street boy. He had none to take care of him. As for me, I was taken to an orphanage in Burundi and later in another one in Butare. But for me I later got the chance to go to school through the assistance of FARG and with that, I managed to finish my secondary school. But I did not score the required grade for FARG to continue to sponsor me at the University. And I could not easily get a job that could pay me a salary that I could use for University studies. I got a job that I would never do in a normal situation. I was employed as a sentry at SOLACE Ministries [a survivor-run organization for survivors of the genocide]. I did my job very well, and although it was a bit shameful for someone who had completed his secondary school to do such a job, I had no choice. I wanted to get something just as elementary and basic means for existence. My traumatized sister was no longer able to take care of my niece who survived during the genocide. She is a daughter of one of my elder brothers, and she survived while she was only eight months old. I had to at least take her from my sister and stay with her. I could never do it without means to do so. But since my salary was so tiny, I had to work several months to be able to pay just the monthly house rent.

I used to tell some people there at SOLACE Ministries that I had completed my secondary school and that I failed to continue my studies due to lack of financial means. After some time, Mr. Dan Miller came to SOLACE Ministries and he wanted to pay for ten students at University. I was then offered this opportunity and he paid university fees for me up to now that I am almost finishing my Bachelor studies. In the meantime,

---

33   See footnote above on the interview with Ndagijimana Francois Xavier.

as Dan Miller was only providing school fees, I had to continue my struggle to be able to stay with my niece and now I am with her.

Another category of children also merits attention. The children who were conceived during the genocide through rape. These children do not fit the term survivor in a real sense, but since they are a current consequence of the genocide and are part of the life of survivors, it is worth mentioning how their mothers and their community view them and what this implies for their lives.

In a recent interview by Jean Claude Mwambutsa, a BBC journalist, with some of the women who were raped during the genocide and were impregnated by their rapists, these women revealed how it feels to have a child of this kind and how their children suffered and still suffer.[34] As these women are always ashamed to have been raped, they are ashamed to have products of that rape and living with them. In a sorrowful voice, one of the interviewed women said:

I was under anaesthetic when I was giving birth to the child and when I got out from it, I screamed saying I had given birth to an animal and I did not want that animal. I hated him, and I never stopped to beat him.

And another woman testified in a crying voice:

I have been always saying that I do not want that child next to me, but as I received some training and as I could see some other women who had passed through the same experience as me, I tried to learn how to show love to my child.

The third interviewed woman said:

I never gave peace to my child, I never showed him love and I could always beat him for nothing, and now my child never gets good results at school, but I am sure it is because of me, but on the other hand it is not my fault either, it is because of the sad experience, najye sinjye ni iminsi.[35]

The children of this category were born in 1995, and they are now 15 years old. But many of them did not go to school, not only due to lack of care and love by their mothers but also due to a lack of means. And although there has not been a survey of the exact number of children fitting this category, the estimated number of 250,000–500,000 women raped during the genocide implies that their number is not negligible.

---

[34] Interview of Jean Claude Mwambutsa of the BBC, with women raped during the genocide. Broadcasted by the Kinyarwanda-Kirundi Section of the BBC on November 20, 2009 in the news of 06.30 p.m.

[35] Literally meaning 'it is not me but because of days'. This means that she should not be blamed for that because in normal situation she could never do that, but because of what happened, everything can happen.

3.4. TRAUMA

All the problems mentioned above amount to another frequent and extreme consequence of the genocide which is trauma. Although this problem will be treated more particularly later in this volume, it is worth mentioning that in all the categories of vulnerable people mentioned above, a large number of them was traumatized,[36] although at different levels.

On the issue of trauma, Musoni Donatien[37], who is one of the heads of child-headed households, explained how he has been traumatized at several times. He is only one of two survivors in his family of seven persons. Having watched terrible things during the genocide and having experienced a difficult life after the genocide, he gets traumatized regularly. Not only has he himself experienced many physical beatings (e.g. with a nailed club), but he also witnessed *Interahamwe* killing his brother in a place where Tutsi were asked to dig their own grave before being killed. Through all these memories and the recollection of eighty women whom he saw being killed near a place where he was hiding, Musoni Donatien has never stopped to suffer from different kinds of trauma. He lost trust in other people and always preferred to stay alone. For him life was nothing, having the feeling of hating everybody, and he was unable to enjoy life with people he hated. He later had recurring nightmares, always dreaming about people killing him with a machete, bleeding and dying. It reached a point he could not speak anymore, because of a permanent and profound sorrow (known in Kinyarwanda as *ikiniga*) which led him to be brought to Ndera Mental Hospital where he spent several months. But the hospital did not help him much. As he explains:

> In Ndera Hospital, I was treated as a crazy person, yet I was not. The medicine I was treated with was not appropriate to my case. I resisted this, but since I could not speak, they probably thought it was the resistance that most crazy persons have and they forced me to have that treatment. This increased my trauma. And later when they got to know that I was not crazy but traumatized, they changed the way to treat me. They could talk to me about my experience because it is believed that it is one of the therapies for traumatized people, but this did not apply to me. I did not want to hear about that anymore.

Trauma is the logical consequence of what the survivors have seen. They always think of what they saw during the genocide, for instance that members of their

---

[36]   See example of statistics on trauma by Dr. Paul Mahoro, who together with Dr. Naasson Munyandamutsa, conducted the research; results showed that out of the 1,000 Rwandans that were taken as a sample group, 28.54% suffer from Post-Traumatic Stress Disorder (PTSD). See http://allafrica.com/stories/201004050746.html (last visited: 5 November 2010).

[37]   Interview with Musoni Donatien on August 18, 2009 in Kigali. He lives in the same *umudugudu* as Kantarama Donatha (see note on the interview with her). He is the head of the *umudugudu*.

families as well as other people were killed, either with a machete or any other weapon, injured, raped, buried alive, or children being taken from the wombs of their mothers.

And all this is compounded by the feeling that their future is uncertain, because not only did they witness terrible cruelty and lost their beloved ones but also because they lost everything that could help them to live. So, it is not difficult to know what their needs are, what is difficult is to get what they need. Indeed, they simply need what they do not have, the basic necessities for a person to live. There are of course a lot of things they can never recover, nor will they recover their lost families and friends, but the basic needs for at least a normal life are of the utmost importance for their survival.

Finally, it should be said that the consequences of genocide on survivors are immense, too immense to be exhaustively treated in one book, or indeed in only one section of one chapter (although the few cases presented above mirror the situation of other survivors). Books cannot do justice to this immensity. That only becomes visible by the lived experience on the ground.

4. CONCLUSION

As shown in this chapter, the enormous consequences of the genocide against the Tutsi are the logical results of a carefully planned and successfully executed genocide. And this carefully planning led to the loss of more than one million lives. It has been the fastest and most vicious genocide yet recorded in human history.

However, due to methodological limitations and the countless number of problems due to the genocide, this chapter did not purport to deal with all its consequences, but instead explored and discussed some instances to understand the concrete situation of victims of the genocide.

In this regard though, an important part would be missing if the chapter omitted to give the background of the genocide. Indeed, the historical background in the first section revealed its genesis. Likewise, in the second section on the preparation and perpetration of genocide as well as the means used, the hardship through which victims passed was discussed. In fact, it would be an ommission to try to understand the life of victims today without knowledge of their background. In this respect and by using the testimonials of survivors, the section explained the suffering of victims during the genocide, which in most cases created permanent damage either by incurable diseases or disabilities as well as trauma. The latter consequences are the subject of the third section, which examined the life and needs of victims of genocide. The section considered the life of categories of victims such as those disabled or infected with an incurable disease, widows, orphans and children born as result of rape, and those suffering psychological trauma. With testimonials, this section showed how terrible the life of many people in these categories is ever since they lost their families or were disabled or HIV/aids infected.

One of the biggest challenges is the lack of sufficient means to deal with the tremendous consequences of the genocide. But where to find means to support all survivors? Who has the obligation and is able and willing to provide them with proper means to improve the lives of survivors? This requires a separate study.

Finally, it must be said that survivors of genocide need special attention by whoever is responsible, able and willing. Yes, I agree with Raphael Lemkin who asserted that "(...) It is then too late for remedies, for after liberation such populations can at best obtain only reparation of damages but never restoration of those values which have been destroyed which cannot be restored, such as human life, treasures and historical archives" (Lemkin 1944, 95), but since they survived, they now exist, they therefore need to live and not die of the consequences of the genocide, and they cannot achieve this on their own because they lost everything during the genocide.

V. PRIMARY AND SECONDARY VICTIMS AND VICTIMIZATION DURING PROTRACTED CONFLICT

National Trauma through Literary Lens in Jerusalem and Kigali

Edna Erez and Tikva Meroz-Aharoni*

> *I am a woman from Rwanda.*
> *I did not learn to write my ideas in books.*
> *I lived in the spoken world.*
> *But I met an author and he will tell my story.*
> Yolande Mukagasana**

1. INTRODUCTION

Over the last decades, with landmark international crimes such as the genocides in Bosnia and Rwanda, war crimes in Liberia, the former Yugoslavia, Sderot, Israel and Gaza, the Palestinian territories, and crimes against humanity in Darfur (Sudan), Eastern DR-Congo, Uganda and Sierra Leone, there has been increased awareness of victims and victimization in the context of international crime. Unlike the effects of conventional criminality, which involves a relatively small number of victims, international crimes result in mass victimization. Furthermore, the scope of its resulting victimization is broader, as international crimes tend to encompass several circles of victims and incorporate aspects of victimization that are not merely additive but multiplicative in their impact.

Whereas the issue of responsibility for international crimes and blameworthiness of individual perpetrators has been the subject of much discussion and scholarly attention, victims of international crimes have for a long time remained invisible and the extent and types of their injuries have not received the same level of consideration. Although the establishment of

---

*   Names of authors appear alphabetical. Both contributed equally to the chapter.
** Explaining in her book *La Mort Ne Veut Pas de Moi*, (1997) why she needed a ghost writer to describe her horrific experiences during the 1994 genocide.

international criminal tribunals to address the crimes committed in the former Yugoslavia and Rwanda, and the creation of the International Criminal Court, have provided initial opportunities to study victims of international crimes, there are still gaps in our understanding of the variety of victims and extent of victimization in the context of protracted conflict.

In this chapter, we explore the reflection of victimization in the context of international crime through the lens of writers who experienced or witnessed the crimes. Specifically, we compare how national trauma is narrated by Israeli and Rwandan writers, both of whom have written against a backdrop of genocide and holocaust. We first present the socio-political background of Israel and Rwanda, their similarities and divergence, making the case for the comparative analysis. We then provide a framework for conceptualizing victimization in an international context, extrapolating from conventional to international crimes. We address aspects of victimization related to international crimes that have been ignored in mainstream victimological research and discourse – the ways in which victimization and national trauma of innocent civil society is presented in its literature.

2. BETWEEN KIGALI AND JERUSALEM

There are numerous differences between Rwanda and Israel, historically, politically, culturally and socially. Yet, there are sufficient similarities in the victimization experienced by the two peoples, rendering our comparative analysis worthwhile. In particular, the place of genocide in the collective memory and national identity of the respective societies and its impact on the literature they produce are of prime comparative significance.

Both the Jewish and Rwandese Tutsi people had been subjected to lengthy and extensive disparate treatment in the societies they lived in. They were described as the diabolical "Other" that should be avoided, excommunicated or outright killed. Despite significant contributions to their respective countries,[1] both were considered inferior creatures, vicious, exploitative, and lacking humanity, depicted with monstrous traits and features. The long list of stigmas incessantly used to describe these people created stereotypical images that permitted humiliation, separation and eventually physical destruction of the groups.

There are parallels between the dehumanization of Jews in Europe and that of the Tutsi. The latter were demonized, being presented as cockroaches, snakes, and as foreign elements in the country, presumably of Ethiopian origin. Like

---

[1]   We refer mostly to countries in Europe where Jews resided and were persecuted prior to the establishment of Israel. Jews were also persecuted in countries in Asia, the Arab world etc.

Jews in Europe, the Tutsi were viewed as a minority group contaminating the race of its majority host.

Yet, there are some differences between the two groups. The genocide of the Jews, the Holocaust, occurred on the land to which they allegedly did not belong, and in which they were presumably outsiders. Following the genocide of the Jews at the hands of the Nazis, Israel was established as a Jewish homeland. This new home allowed the Jews to leave behind the horrific reminders of what they lost in terms of human (as well as cultural and material) harm, and the ability to maintain physical distance from their communal gravesites.

Rwandans, on the other hand, could not detach themselves from their past by moving away. Despite the allegations made by the Hutu about the presumed foreign roots of the Tutsi, Rwanda has long been the home of the two groups involved, becoming the site of the genocide. In the aftermath of the crimes, the Tutsi could not segregate themselves from the Hutu, and instead had to continue living side by side with their killers.

After moving to Israel, Jews have shared other experiences with countries that have experienced protracted war and violent clashes. The history of the conflict between Jews and Arabs in Israel, the new Jewish homeland, points to similarities in the source of the hostilities that characterized the two adversaries in Rwanda. The colonial British mandate in Palestine that began in 1918 (which included parts of Israel pre-1948 and the Palestinian territories) inflamed the local clash between Arabs and Jews, adhering to the time-honoured policy of divide and rule. An external intervention, the partition decision reached by the League of Nations (the predecessor of the UN) in 1947, facilitated the establishment of the State of Israel as the Jewish homeland. It led to the 1948 Israel Independence War declared by Israel's neighbouring Arab countries. This conflict, which began in the 1921 pogroms of Jews in Palestine, has exacerbated with the establishment of the State of Israel, and has resulted in six wars and the two Palestinian *Intifadas* (uprisings).

The Belgian colonial regime in Rwanda had likewise created a chasm between Rwanda's two main ethnic groups, the Hutu and the Tutsi (see Ruvebana, this volume). The Belgians used the Tutsi to rule and oppress their fellow Hutu countrymen, creating a backdrop for hostilities between groups that led to the Rwandan genocide. By creating artificial measures to distinguish between presumably different races or social groups, the idea of inferiority of one group and the superiority of the other was planted and internalized by their members, resulting in numerous outbursts of violence and bloodshed perpetrated by one group against the other.

In sum, despite the differences in time, place, political circumstances or ethnic composition between Israel and Rwanda, the pitting by a foreign ruler of one group against another has been a major factor at the root of the hostilities, leading to the violence and killings in both countries. The claim of each group to the land, the view that the other group comprises a foreign element that does not belong, and the resulting self-attribution of victimhood by both parties (e.g. Erez 2006) has likewise been a common political feature of the two societies and countries.

3. SECONDARY VICTIMIZATION AND VICTIMS – A CONCEPTUAL FRAMEWORK

Extant research on conventional crimes differentiates between primary, secondary, and tertiary victims and as well as primary and secondary victimization. In the following section, we make a conceptual distinction between various types/circles of victims and levels of victimization.

Victims are commonly divided into three circles: Primary victims – those who are affected directly by the criminal event and suffer physical, emotional or financial harm. In the context of international crime, primary victims are those who are killed, injured, sexually assaulted and enslaved, displaced, kidnapped, tortured, used as human shields, humiliated, or deprived of human dignity. Their houses may be demolished, their property destroyed, or they are forced to live in exile.

Secondary victims, the second circle of victims, are those who are related to the primary victims through family, friendship, or professional ties. They experience harm by observing, listening, living with, taking care of, or responding to the needs to primary victims. International legal instruments often include first responders in this category (for instance, the 1985 UN *Declaration of Basic Principles of Justice for Victims of Crime and Abuse of Power*).

The nature of the relationship with the victim may determine the extent of the harm secondary victims sustain – the closer the relationship, the more intensive is their harm. Thus, women who take care of injured intimate partners, or of their children, experience a daily extensive harm as secondary victims, compared to more distant relatives or friends who may not have daily contact with them. The impact of primary injury on secondary victims is a function of the society or community's character, and social-familial relationships within it – the more homogenous and closer, the more intensive is the impact of harm on secondary victims.

Tertiary victims are the largest category of individuals.[2] This third circle of victims includes individuals affected by the harm due to cultural proximity to, or shared national, ethnic or religious identity with primary and secondary

---

[2]   The US Department of Justice has included in the definition of secondary and tertiary victims affected by the Oklahoma bombing of 1995 the following: 'Secondary' and 'tertiary' victims include social service and mental health professionals; volunteers; fire, police, and other

victims. Tertiary victims suffer harm through second hand experience, including listening to or observing media reports about the crime and its aftermath, or reading documentation and literature about these events. We submit that in a contemporary, technological era, with intensive coverage of international crimes through mass media and versatile forms of communication, the circle of those who become tertiary victims is expanding, and may include individuals who are geographically remote or dispersed around the globe. We also submit that literary works may play the same role as mass communication, by bringing the atrocities to readers around the globe. By reading literary works written about horrific events and their victims, readers can relive the trauma and deeply identify with the victims.

In the context of international crimes, the distinctions between primary, secondary, and tertiary victims often become blurred; individuals may simultaneously occupy more than one circle, for instance, when they and their family members sustain harm. Because some international crimes receive heightened coverage that extends throughout the protracted conflict, the harm of primary or secondary victims may be exacerbated as these victims watch the presentation of atrocities in the media, thereby adding tertiary elements of harm.[3] Literary work on the topic may have similar effects. Indeed, literary works immortalizing wars and describing traumatic events has preceded the reporting of national trauma through mass communication.

Victimization, on the other hand, is the process of becoming a victim, and includes negative victim experiences due to institutional responses to the harm caused by the crime. The responses to victimization include the various stages and arenas of vindicating the victims: psychologically, medically, legally, or financially. Primary victimization is the direct experience of harm inflicted by the criminal event. Secondary victimization is the harm that results from the response of agencies responsible for addressing the crime, whether it is law enforcement's response to the violation and bringing the offender to justice, or medical and social service providers responding to the physical and psychological trauma sustained by victims. As previously stated, in the context of international crime, first responders have been recently added to the list of those who sustain secondary victimization.

---

emergency response-and-rescue personnel; colleagues and friends; attorneys who worked with witnesses and sifted evidence; medical personnel; victim advocates; clergy who consoled victims and officiated at many funerals; schoolteachers; and children whose belief in a safe future was shattered. The circle of those affected also includes jurors, dentists with identification responsibilities, bomb technicians, morgue workers, technical investigators, National Guard members, reporters, photographers, construction workers, and the larger community of Oklahoma City. From June 1, 1995, to February 29, 1998, an unduplicated count of 8,869 persons received counseling, support group, or crisis intervention services. www.ojp.usdoj.gov/ovc/publications/infores/.../chap5.html.

3   For the impact of showing clips of the Rwanda genocide on Rwandans, see http://allafrica. com/stories/201004130775.html.

4. LITERATURE AS CONSTITUTIVE AND EXPRESSIVE OF SECONDARY VICTIMIZATION

Literary writers act as agents of awareness and consciousness-raising when their works address traumatic events such as wars, terrorism, or genocide. Whether they have experienced harm from the protracted conflict as primary, secondary or tertiary victims, their writings reflect and commemorate the victimization. We focus on this literary expression of victimization as we consider literature to have a durable impact on its readers, one that historically precedes other mass communication modes, such as television, movies, or popular music.

The structure of news reporting is comprised of a certain pattern of staging that can be found in any presentation of traumatic events. It includes pictures of the scene, the destruction that took place, the individuals killed and wounded, and reactions of their families, friends, or neighbours. In some cases funerals are also shown. The standard reporting of current news does not usually cover subsequent time periods and does not examine the long term impact of the horrific events on victims or their significant others. The most recent news soon replaces the old news, creating a "Marathon of disasters" (Liebes & Kamph 2005). One tends to forget the details of the horrific loss of life, damage or injuries as soon as another trauma producing event takes place. Further, this Marathon may lead observers become desensitized to the enormity of the trauma involved, and to develop a self-protective distance from the horrors they learn about.[4]

The effects of television and mass media presentation are immediate and their impact is commonly short lived. During protracted conflict, another traumatic event always comes into focus. When one watches a succession of horrific events taking place in a distant, unfamiliar milieu, one is likely to experience minimal emotional involvement (Liebes & Kamph 2005). But one is likely to relate to a victim's story, even in the midst of endless victimization stories.

Movies and non-documentary film are commonly based on actions and dialogues by the protagonists, which often maintain the traumatic event in the background. But films, by their nature, focus on the plot as they provide visual presentations of feelings. They often do not allow for detailed description of the protagonists' inner world, feelings, thoughts and wishes. In contrast, literary works, through the use of metaphoric language, have the capability of describing lengthy and complex processes of the traumatic event and its aftermath. Novels are able to portray psychological, emotional and cognitive processes that victims experience, the changes they undergo as a result of the victimization,

---

[4]   In Israel, famous examples of desensitized reactions occurred during the assault of Yom Kippur war in Sinai, where those who worked in military communication and had to listen to the numerous alarming calls for help; when the soldiers in the trenches saw the Egyptian army approaching them, they started to ignore the call or even imitate the callers.

any post-traumatic stress they may suffer, and the long term effects of the events at hand.

Literature, by definition, is preoccupied by the spiritual experience of humankind, which created a language that preserves its victories and defeats, dreams and desperations (Shipley 1970). Ezra Pound has been quoted to note that great literature is simple language charged with meaning to the utmost possible degree (Kolber 1997). Plot consists of a sequence of interrelated events that form the outcome of a central episode, with a beginning, middle, and end. This definition also suits the realistic novel that sees causality at the core of events. At the centre of the plot there are characters, who, due to differences in their backgrounds, present different outlooks, world views and experiences.

We argue that literature is an effective medium to express and address traumatic national experiences. Literary authors – those agents mentioned in the opening statement to this chapter – provide the materials through which individuals may become tertiary victims. Their works provide a detailed description of events, including the psychological processes that the protagonist experiences during the events and their aftermaths.

Literature preserves and immortalizes the memory of those who were killed, injured, or violated. Each novel describes an individual victim, who represents a group of victims. This individual protagonist represents the many other victims who perished in the same manner; describing one victim, however, is a more manageable way to convey the horrors of terror.

The language of literature demands from the reader a profound examination of the events described in the text, and in return, the reader is provided with a comprehensive understanding of the era, the conflict, the motivations of the characters and their responses to the trauma. Literature is best suited to express what it is like to be a primary victim, but reading novels describing primary victimization may transform readers to tertiary victims. Literature, we suggest, has long lasting impact, as the act of reading a novel demands that the reader analyses, constructs, imagines and reproduces the literary text rather than rely on a producer to do it for him or her.

Over the years, literary works have immortalized historically painful events, reaching out to a large audience, far greater than any historical documentation could ever achieve. Literature commonly reflects, through the perspective of the character, what statistics and research data show about a phenomenon.

Literature is structured to appeal to the informed general public, independent of place and time. Common examples of influential commemoration of traumatic historical events are presented in works such as: *War and Peace* (1869) by Leo Tolstoy, which describes Napoleon's defeat in Russia and the enormous loss of life in these wars; *For Whom the Bell Tolls* (1940) by Ernest Hemingway, which describes the horrors of the 1936 civil war in Spain; and *All Quiet on the Western Front* (1929) by Erich Maria Remarque, which describes the experiences of a

German soldier during the First World War.[5] Novels that depict crimes of genocide include Franz Werfel's *Forty Days of Musa Dagh* (1933), which describes the massacre of the Armenians by the Turks, and two books on the Holocaust – Elie Wiesel's *Night* (first published in Yiddish in 1955 and in English in 1960) and Primo Levi's *Se Questo E Un Homo* (1947) published in the U.S. as *Survival in Auschwitz* (1958). The latter describes Levy's personal journey through the horrific genocide of the Jews by the Nazis.

To analyse literary expressions of national trauma resulting from mass victimization in Israel and Rwanda, we present the written works published in the two countries on their respective victimizations. We begin with juxtaposing the content of novels written by Israeli authors before or during the first *Intifada* (prior to 1993) with those written following the second *Intifada* (2000), noting the impact of threat of extermination via terrorism on Israeli literature. We then present works about the Rwandan genocide written by Rwandans and non-Rwandan authors. We conclude with reflections on the manner in which mass victimization affects literary expression of national trauma.

5. SECONDARY VICTIMIZATION, TERTIARY VICTIMS

5.1. LITERARY WORK WRITTEN BY ISRAELI AUTHORS DURING PERIODS OF MASS VICTIMIZATION

In the novels written during the two *Intifadas,* like the novels of other traumatic world events, there are two components: first, the way individuals cope with events, and second, the inner struggle of the protagonist. Thus, in such novels the private experiences of the protagonists, together with the historical backdrop, make up the content of the literary work. In the literature of the two *Intifadas,* it is possible to examine the Jewish destiny according to what is likely to happen, based on the past. The literature written during the first *Intifada* embodies well-known Israeli poet, Hayim Guri's comments about the Eichmann trial in Israel:

> *the offspring of the generation that witnessed the gas chambers have remembered the lessons of the past. They have begun to take seriously the 1967 call for the Jews, made by Muhamad Shukera, to learn how to swim, as they will all have to do it when they are pushed into the Mediterranean Sea.*

Guri, like other writers of his time, expressed the prevailing feelings of the time that "we are in a pre-Holocaust period" (Guri 2008, 17)

---

5   Remarque's anti-war message prompted in Germany book burnings of his novel during the Nazi rise to power.

The sense of fear Israelis experienced during the siege that preceded the Six Day War of 1967 was soon replaced, following the swift victory achieved in this short war, with a sense of guilt toward the Palestinian people. In the minds of many Israelis, the Palestinians have gradually transformed from being a threat to Israel into victims of the Israeli occupation. This ambivalence toward the war and its aftermath has been well reflected in the literature that followed; post 1967 authors have expressed fears of becoming an occupying force in the Palestinian territories (e.g. Tamuz 1974). However, with the increased murder of innocent civilians due to horrific suicide missions by Palestinian, Israeli fears of imminent extermination returned, viewing terrorist attacks as genocide by instalments.

The first Palestinian *Intifada* began in 1987 and continued until 1993, when the Oslo agreement was signed. This *Intifada* was characterized by demonstrations, civic disorder, strikes, boycotts of Israeli products, refusal to pay taxes, graffiti and barricades, and other forms of popular protest and resistance. It also involved violent outbursts, in the form of stone throwing, but also use of Molotov cocktails, hand grenades and assaults with guns or explosives. The number of Israelis killed was less than 200, and the number of Palestinians killed was estimated to be about 1100. In addition, almost the same number of Palestinians were killed by other Palestinians for actual or suspected collaboration with Israel.

In contrast, the onset of the second *Intifada* in September of 2000 led to unprecedented victimization in the form of frequent and intense terrorist[6] attacks that resulted in large number of fatalities and injuries. In military terms, the situation had been defined as 'low intensity combat' ('LIC'). Although the two sides still disagree about the reasons for its eruption,[7] there is no disagreement that the second *Intifada* marks a new era in mass victimization involving personal, social,[8] and economic harm.

---

[6]   The word *terror* (or *terrorism*) itself is contested by many Palestinians, who refer to terrorist activities perpetrated by fellow Palestinians as violence and not terrorism. Palestinians commonly label terror as what Israelis perceive as defensive acts of the Israeli government and its military.

[7]   The Palestinians attribute the onset of the *Intifada* to Ariel Sharon's 'provocative' visit to Mount Temple (in Arabic Haram-a-Sharif, meaning the site of the respected holiness). Israelis have argued that the Sharon visit was merely an excuse and the *Intifada* was in the making for a while, with the background of the reluctance of Yasar Arafat to accept the offer of peace for land presented by Barak under the auspices of President Clinton in August 2000. This was confirmed by the former Palestinian Authority Minister of Communications, Immad Al-Faluji in a speech he made in Lebanon in March 2001: "Whoever thinks that the *Intifada* broke out because of the despised Sharon's visit to the Al-Aqsa Mosque, is wrong, even if this visit was the straw that broke the back of the Palestinian people. This *Intifada* was planned in advance, ever since President Arafat's return from the Camp David negotiations, where he turned the table upside down on President Clinton. [Arafat] remained steadfast and challenged [Clinton]. He rejected the American terms and he did it in the heart of the US." (Al Safir, Lebanon, March 3, 2001).

[8]   One important social cost in the context of the *Intifada*, which has not been addressed in this article, is the impact of the protracted war and terrorism on the relations between the Israeli

During the second *Intifada,* Israelis were subjected to over 24,400 attempted or completed terrorist incidents,[9] including suicide bombings, knife attacks, shootings, bombings, being run over with cars, lynching, car bombs, mortar bombs, rocket attacks and home intrusions. Civilians of all ages, of every ethnic group and religious affiliation, have been killed or injured. Toward the end of the second *Intifada* (the end of 2004), almost a thousand Israelis were killed, and almost 7000 were injured, many disabled for life.[10]

Most attacks have been perpetrated against Jewish targets, although mixed Arab-Jewish enterprises and areas have not been spared.[11] Incidents have occurred primarily in the large cities, although attacks have also occurred in smaller communities, villages, towns, and on the roads. Attacks have taken place on buses, at bus stops and train stations, in shops and markets, in places of entertainment and celebration, in private homes or hotels, and other places where people congregate. The attacks have occurred during morning and evening rush hours, when people are going to work or school, and throughout the day into the late hours of the night. There has been a general sense among Israelis that there is no pattern to the attacks, and neither time nor place can be predicted (Gidron, Kaplan, Vent & Shalem 2004).

Daily life has often been disrupted, as people avoid places perceived as possible targets. Extra security measures have been taken to thwart terrorism, including security guards at entrances to public buildings, entertainment

---

Arab and Jewish communities. Arab Israelis have been conflicted in the current political situation, feeling loyalty to both the state of Israel and to their fellow Palestinians in the West Bank and Gaza. The few cases in which Arab Israelis have been found to collaborate with or aid terrorists led to increased suspicion and distrust between the two communities in Israel, with some Israeli Jews questioning of the loyalty of Arab Israeli citizens to the state of Israel. On the other hand, there have been numerous instances in which Arab Israelis have helped in a variety of ways in combating terrorism, in addition to being victims of the terror themselves. Israeli Arabs make up 20% of the Israeli population (7.3 million), and are totally enmeshed in Israel's society, culture, economy and security. While almost all of them empathize with the Palestinian cause, they are in no way monolithically 'pro-Palestinian' or 'anti-Israeli'. As in any society, there are extremists on both sides, and a broad majority of those in the middle. On the one hand, there is a minority of Israeli Arabs involved in active terror and terror support, as well as Arabs (not just the Bedouins and Druze) who serve in the Israel Defense Forces (the IDF, the Israeli military), police, Shabak and Mossad. There are Arab members of Knesset (Israeli parliament), and government department and agency heads, numerous Arabs in the Israeli diplomatic corp (including ambassadors), Arab newscasters, editors and producers in the mainstream media, department heads in the top hospitals, wealthy businessmen, actors, etc. Many of the Magen David Adom (the Israeli counterpart of the Red Cross) first responders to terrorist acts around the country are Israeli Arab medics and doctors.

9   These numbers do not include numerous plans and efforts to perpetrate attacks that were thwarted by pre-emptive strikes of the military.

10   Most of the victims were civilians and less than a third were security personnel. Considering that the population of Israel at the time was about 6 million, the number of victims injured and killed as a result of terrorist attacks amount to mass victimization. In terms of the psychological impact, the rate of victimization is far greater, as discussed later in the article.

11   The terrorist attack on the Maxim restaurant in Haifa in the summer of 2003.

establishments, eating places, shopping malls and schools. It has become difficult to adhere to a time schedule, whether for work, school, or leisure activities – lengthy traffic jams resulting from road checks or the closing of areas were common experiences. Newspaper articles have described cases in which, due to delays at a checkpoint, security checks or a roadblock, a couple was two hours late to their own wedding, a surgery could not be performed as scheduled, and a woman gave birth in a car on her way to the hospital.

The result of the protracted war was a pervasive sense of anxiety and uncertainty; no one has felt safe or secure (Dekel 2004). There also was widespread mistrust and suspicion of anyone who seemed "out of place" or might be a potential terrorist, who would previously have seemed benign. Perpetrators of terrorism have appeared in soldiers' uniforms, impersonated orthodox rabbinical (*Yeshiva*) students, or dressed as young punks when mingling in crowds to perform their killing mission.

The physical and psychological signs of the protracted war were visible as well as invisible. The visible ranged from security pits at every street corner used to dispose or hold suspicious items, to signs calling for awareness of unusual objects or people, barricades erected in front of public buildings, and security checkpoints at every gathering place.

Specialized rituals, language, laws and social institutions were created to address the victimization resulting from the protracted war. Routines and practices regarding every aspect of daily life in Israel have been re-evaluated due to the constant security threats. Discourse has developed recently that centres on stress and post-traumatic stress disorder, referred to by Israelis as *hamatzav*, in Hebrew 'the situation' (Adelman 2003).

In comparison to victims of crime or other ill fortune, victims of the political conflict in Israel are placed higher on the moral hierarchy of victimhood, often triggering police investigations to ascertain whether victimization resulted from criminal or 'nationalistic' motives. While Israel does not have reparation laws or compensation programs for crime victims, it has a special law and elaborate rules providing reparations to victims of acts of war or hostile actions, including terrorism (The Law for the Rehabilitation of Victims of Hostility Acts, 1974).

The "emergency routine" (Beilin 1992), of which Israelis have long been accustomed to, has recently taken over all areas of Israeli social life. "The situation" has been used not only as a reason to postpone serious discussion of critical social problems,[12] but also for delays in needed communal, economic or

---

[12]   Yael Dayan, an Israeli Parliament (Knessett) member, has stated, in the Knessett and in speeches addressing recent increases in woman killing (femicide) in Israel, that the war with the Palestinians should not take precedence over the war in the home, meaning domestic violence.

legal reforms[13] and intervention in citizens' lives, which amount to civil rights violations in some cases (Al-Haj & Ben Eliezer 2003).

The financial burden of the increase in security expenses has resulted in substantial cuts in social security and welfare services and delays in paying local government wages, which adversely affects the financial status of most sectors of Israeli society. Changes in investments and capital flight have been associated with the conflict (Fielding 2004). Although some state assistance to businesses that have suffered economic harm as a result of the protracted war has been initiated (e.g. reduced taxes or incentives to continue business as usual), the overall economic growth had declined.

Victimization resulting from protracted war includes three circles of being a victim, denoted by proximity to the direct victim: primary or first order victims, those who suffer harm directly, whether it is injury, loss or death; secondary or second order victims, family members, relatives or friends of primary victims; this category also includes those who in the context of their work respond to victimization, such as first responders; and tertiary or third order victims – those who observe the victimization, are exposed to it through television, or radio coverage of the victimization (Sprang 2001; Omer, Buchbinder, Peled-Avram & Ben-Yizhack 2004).[14] Research has documented the powerful anxiety-inducing effect of the media when showing terror (Slone 2000). With reminders[15] of the war and its victims abounding, the impact of the terror is amplified. For many people, some or all of the three dimensions overlap.

The omnipresent fear of victimization associated with terrorism has led to Israelis' preoccupation with concerns for physical protection, emotional protection of significant others, and the creation of normality and routine (Strous & Kotler 2004; Dekel 2004). Mothers, in particular, have been seriously concerned with what will happen to their children if they are killed in a terrorist attack (Dekel 2004). These concerns about safety have had a substantial impact on Israelis' willingness to go out. The frequency of the terrorist attacks, more than their severity, has resulted in a substantial decrease in tourism (Pizam & Fleischer 2002), which is a major part of the nation's economy. Reduction in both

---

13   The needed change in the Israeli legal situation, which since the establishment of the state in 1948 has been officially defined as 'emergency condition', has recently been noted by the Israeli High Court of Justice. The relevant 1948 definition includes regulations that provide for administrative detentions, and other problematic legal scenarios. The High Court has given the Israeli legislature a six month period to complete the task of changing the legal situation (see *Haaretz*, September 10, 2004).

14   In the Oklahoma bombing trial, fire fighters who rescued victims were allowed to provide victim impact statements at the trial of Timothy McVey, thereby officially being recognized as victims.

15   Reminders in the form of memorials to casualties of war and terror can be found in every public or private and semi-private places in Israel. Pictures and names of victims can be found in the schools they attended, the universities they enrolled or graduated from, in their workplace or in public buildings of cities, towns and villages they lived in and on the roads where they were killed.

domestic and overseas tourism has, in turn, led to businesses closing and, therefore, an increase in poverty and unemployment. There is also evidence that the atmosphere of political violence has led to an increase in violence by Israelis against each other, particularly in violence against women (Adelman 2003). Property crime has also risen due to the higher level of poverty and unemployment (Israeli Police Crime Statistics 2005).

There is no one in Israel who has not been touched by the terror, directly or indirectly. Studies of Israel (Bleich, Gelkopf, Solomon 2003; Gidron, Kaplan, Velt & Shalem 2004) found that almost one-fifth (16%) of a national sample had been directly exposed to a terrorist attack and over one-third (37%) had a family member or friend who had been exposed. The Bleich *et al.* study also reported that of those who responded to questions about emotional harm, over three quarters (77%) had at least some traumatic stress symptoms and almost one-tenth (9.4%) had acute stress, with over half (59%) reporting feelings of depression (Bleich, Gelkopf, Solomon 2003). The reduced sense of safety was related to the perceived unpredictability of the terrorism (Gidron, Kaplan, Velt & Shalem 2004).[16]

The protracted conflict, and the traumatic events, carnage and destruction associated with the second *Intifada*, serve as the backdrop for the novels we analyse below. As we show, unlike the writings that preceded it, the enormity of the trauma associated with the protracted conflict and carnage of the second *Intifada* has caused Israeli authors' attention to shift from relating to the suffering of both sides, to focusing instead on the trauma experienced by Israelis alone, as described in the next sections.

5.2. HISTORICAL BACKGROUND: ARAB-JEWISH/ISRAELI RELATIONS IN THE LENS OF LITERATURE

Literary works on Arab-Jewish relations and co-existence in Israel have been written since the early waves of immigration of Jews to Palestine, around the first half of the 20th century. Jewish Israeli writers who escaped the pogroms of southern Russia in 1888 and immigrated to Palestine/Eretz Yisrael (the land of Israel), began to develop literary centres and writing that were characterized by support for co-existence with the Arab population (Shaked 1983, 72). Major writers in this period include Shmuel Yosef Agnon, a Noble prize winner, who well understood the complexity of co-existence. Another significant writer who favoured good neighbourly relations with the Arab population in Palestine was Yossef Chayim Brenner. Despite his strong beliefs in and support for co-existence,

---

16 The Palestinians have also suffered many casualties, estimated at over 5000 casualties. The large number of military and civil fatalities was caused by Israeli defensive tactics and preventive military actions against those responsible for the attacks on Israel.

Brenner was murdered in 1921 by Arab gangs, and his funeral became a protest against indiscriminate killing of Jews.

In the spirit of a famous Hebrew adage that states, "When the cannons blast, the muses become silent," we submit that when the cannons stop blasting, the muses are awakened, and function to immortalize the human loss resulting from the hostilities. In the section below we compare the literary reactions to, and expressions of, the national trauma as expressed in writings that preceded the second *Intifada* and those written following this protracted conflict.

5.3. COMPARISON OF LITERARY WORKS WRITTEN BEFORE AND AFTER THE SECOND INTIFADA

Comparison of the literature written before and following the second *Intifada* (September of 2000–2005) shows that the most striking difference between them is the salience of Arab victimization in these literary works. In the novels published before the first *Intifada*, such as David Grossman's *The Smile of the Lamb* (1983), and continued with writings of the first *Intifada*, such as Smadar Hertzfeld's *Inti Omri* (1994) (in Arabic, 'you are my life'), Ronit Matalon's *Sarah, Sarah* (2000), and Yael Medini's *Ballad to Terror* (2000), attention is given to multiple social and political aspects of the Israeli-Arab conflict, with a view that provides equal consideration to the Israeli and Arab perspectives. Great emphasis is placed upon the fact that there are victims on both sides, and these novels illustrate how political entanglement produces harm and pain for both parties to the conflict.

The 1983 novel by Grossman examines the relationship between a sensitive young man who, as a soldier, has to confront the evils of occupation. He is captured by an old Arab man, who, through old Arabic legends, reveals to him the importance of honesty and freedom. Through these legends, the soldier discovers a world of contradictions, which not only contain side by side hostilities and fears, but also intimacy, friendship, and trust. At the same time, the developmentally disabled son of this friendly old Arab is selected by a terrorist organization to execute a terrorist attack. The old father is torn between his love for his son and the disdain toward those who plan to exploit his son's disability by recruiting him and training him to become a murderous terrorist.

In her book *Sarah, Sarah*, Ronit Matalon describes how a married Jewish woman, the mother of a young boy, is active in a civil rights organization. In the course of her civil rights activities, she falls madly in love with an Arab actor and pursues him. This love is portrayed as the result of her identification with the suffering of the Arab population. The Arab actor, however, does not reciprocate and abandons her after their short affair, which caused the woman to separate from her husband. Another protagonist in the book is a Jewish Moroccan woman who travels to a family funeral in France, and participates in family discussions on Israeli-Arab relations. Her relatives in France, who claim they have experience living with the Arab population in their birthplace of Morocco, explained that they avoided moving to Israel as they were certain that there would always be problems in trying to co-exist with the Arabs.

Inta Omri by Hertzfeld describes a love story between a young Jewish woman and a young Arab man who are both students at the Hebrew University of Jerusalem. The man works as a waiter to support his studies, and he lives in one of the villages that surround the city of Jerusalem. He feels both an oppressive inability to express to his Arab family and neighbours his admiration of the Israeli accomplishments, including the level of personal and social freedom Israelis enjoy. At the same time, he experiences suspicion and distrust by his Jewish friends and colleagues. The young woman also experiences pressure to terminate her relations with the young Arab man. The message conveyed by the plot is that in the complex political situation between the Arabs and the Jews in Israel, such a love story, as fervent and passionate it may be, is bound to fail. Both protagonists come out of this short lived love story deeply wounded.

Another representative book of this era, Medini's novel *A Ballad to the Terror*, describes a young Israeli man who falls in love with a young Arab woman, who is married to her cousin.[17] The cousin/husband works for an Israeli contractor and is involved in terrorist activities. The wife and her mother are refugees of an Arab village, whose residents fled during the 1948 Israeli Independence War. These two women return to the area they left years ago, moving to a Jewish village and making a living in its agricultural enterprise. The Israeli man, whose father was killed in a terrorist act, is highly sensitive to the plight of the Arab 'Other'. The husband/cousin of the young woman suspects that the Israeli man feels affectionate toward his wife and pressures his wife to exploit his interest in her to facilitate a massive terrorist attack. She complies and in the process the Israeli young man is killed. The young Arab woman grieves his death, particularly since she is pregnant with his child. Once the baby is born, both the Arab and Jewish grandmothers raise him, while his mother has to earn a living.

These books of the pre-second *Intifada* point to willingness of Israeli authors, reflecting the general mood of the country, to build and carry on integrated lives and co-existence with their Arab neighbours. As discussed below, these views and wishes are sparse in the literature that emerges in the period of the second *Intifada,* due to the traumatic imprint it has left on the Israelis.

The literature written in response to the second *Intifada* is silent about the victimization of the Arab 'Other', focusing on the harm sustained by the Israelis. Examination of four representative books (prose) written during this era – A.B. Yehoshua's *A Woman in Jerusalem* (2004), Naomi Regen's *The Covenant* (2004),

---

17 This detail is relevant in the story for various reasons: first, marrying cousins is a common practice in Arab society. Also, the fact that the couple is first cousins makes divorce a difficult option as it may bring about cleavage within families.

Shifra Oren's *Hymn to Joy* (2004), and Sarah Shilo's *No Gnomes will Appear* (2005), confirm their preoccupation with Israeli suffering. Three of the books take place in Jerusalem, where the majority of the terror, including suicide bombings, occurred during the second *Intifada*. Jerusalem, the capital of Israel and a city considered holy by three major religions – Judaism, Christianity, and Islam – is a city in which Jews and Arabs live in close proximity. The absence of any physical barriers between them makes it relatively easy to carry out terrorist attacks against Israelis.

In the period prior to the second *Intifada,* an internationally recognized Israeli writer, A.B. Yehoshua, devoted much attention to the rights of Palestinians to live on Israeli land in both his novels and political essays; he continuously stressed the importance of making concessions in an attempt to resolve the conflict and establish co-existence. However, following the second *Intifada*, Yehoshua published *A Woman in Jerusalem,* a significant novel, which focuses on the impact of incessant terrorist attacks on everyday life in Jerusalem. The story is based on a horrific terrorist act – a bombing in the cafeteria of the Hebrew University of Jerusalem, which took the lives of 21 students and faculty at Hebrew University's Mount Scopus campus. The perpetrator was an Arab contractor from one of the nearby Arab villages, who had unrestricted access to the University campus because of his work assignment.

The plot of the story revolves around a woman in her forties, who was seriously injured in a terrorist attack in the Jerusalem market. She eventually dies of her wounds and lies anonymously in the city morgue, without any documentation that can shed light on her identity or family ties. After a lengthy search, it is discovered that she is a Russian woman, an engineer by profession, who followed her Jewish lover to Jerusalem. Her lover had returned to Russia because he could not find suitable work, while she, mesmerized by the spirituality of Jerusalem, did everything in her power to stay in the city she so loved. To support herself, she took a job as a cleaning lady in a bakery. Once it is discovered that she is a gentile woman from Russia, without any family relatives in Israel, her body is transferred to Russia for burial. As the body reaches her home town in Russia, her elderly mother insists that her daughter should be buried at the place she loved so much and wanted to live in. The body is then carried back to Jerusalem, accompanied by her mother and son.

Another example of a novel that focuses only on Israeli victims is *Hymn to Joy* by Shifra Horn (2004). It describes a horrendous terrorist attack on a public transportation bus full of children and adults which travels from the city's centre to the major hospital in Jerusalem. The protagonist, a woman driving behind the bus, witnesses the explosion, and the event completely transforms her life. Her trauma as a secondary victim, causes her to examine her priorities, and change her future plans regarding her personal and professional lives. This woman, like many Israelis, is a second generation Holocaust survivor, accustomed to endure, adapt, and carry on with life. The horrific national trauma experienced first-hand by her father, told and retold to her as she grew up, equipped her with the tools to overcome personal loss, pain, and trauma, and cling to life in Israel, as she believes there is no other country for the Jews.

Naomi Regen's novel, *The Covenant*, describes how a physician working in the main hospital in Jerusalem is kidnapped, together with his daughter, by terrorists. Both the father and daughter come from a family that immigrated to Israel from the U.S. Immediately following the kidnapping, the doctor's mother-in-law, a holocaust survivor, begins to mobilize worldwide resources to release the doctor and his daughter. Meanwhile, a pro-Palestinian, British Jewish journalist, whose reporting about the Arab-Israel conflict was considered by Israelis as one-sided and biased, is injured in a suicide bombing in Jerusalem. As she becomes a direct victim, she realizes that the tactics taken by the Arabs are unacceptable. The mother-in-law receives information about the location of the kidnapped son-in-law and her granddaughter. With the help of an Arab woman, who was a patient of the kidnapped doctor, the daughter is rescued while her father, the doctor, is killed in the rescue attempt.

It is important to note that the author of this novel, Naomi Regen, was a victim of a terrorist attack during Passover in the Park Hotel in Netanya, where 32 people celebrating the holiday were killed. Her personal experience became the trigger for the novel's lengthy plot, which reflects elements of various terrorist attacks that took place during this time. The failed attempt to rescue the doctor parallels an attempt by Israel to release a kidnapped soldier whose parents were personal friends of the author. The novel ends with newspaper clips documenting the terrorist event appearing in the plot.

The fourth book in this group, Sarah Shilo's *No Gnomes Will Appear* (2005), describes everyday life of residents of a northern border town near Lebanon, most of whom are Jewish refugees from various Arab countries. The residents, who live within the Green zone – the agreed upon borders of Israel as determined by the UN partition – nonetheless live under fear of daily terror attacks. The book provides detailed analyses of the psychological and economic toll associated with living under threat of terrorist attacks. *No Gnomes Will Appear* revolves around one family which loses their father to illness. The wife who cares for her four children finds out that she is also going to have twins when the husband passes away. The novel's focus on the children allows the reader to appreciate how children at different ages understand and respond to the fear of unpredictable missiles, hostile bombings, and shootings. Day and night spent in dark shelters becomes the norm, and the intolerable conditions of the crowded and uncomfortable shelters underground comprise the bulk of the book.

These books reflect the personal trauma of the authors, who experienced harm as primary or secondary victims. The novels are anchored in reality, and the plots document real events that become the basis for the text. The works comprise the vehicle by which the authors express long lasting effects of the harms sustained as a result of the violence. The protagonist represents a larger group of similarly situated individuals who have sustained harm, making the individual's story accessible to readers.

5.4. THE RWANDAN LITERARY PRESENTATION OF PERSONAL AND NATIONAL TRAUMA

The Rwandan works addressing the genocide focus on the extent and horrors involved in the 1994 genocide, paying little attention to the historical background of the conflict or to previous outbursts of violence between the two groups involved. The enormity of the genocide, it seems, cause writers to focus on the genocide they experienced as primary or secondary victim, or as outsiders who were horrified by the events.

The books written about the genocide can be divided into two groups: the first, documentaries or testimonials written by native Rwandans who have been either primary or secondary victims. Testimonial literature, by its nature, tends to focus on the victim and his or her family. The second group includes both documentaries and fictions authored by non-Rwandans who address the genocide and its aftermath. Attention is sometimes given in both groups to the silence of the world in the face of the atrocities perpetrated against the Tutsi and their supporters.

A major work in the first group is Yolande Mukagasana's (1997) *La Mort Ne Veut Pas de Moi*. In the preface to her book, she notes the oral tradition of Rwanda's literature, which explains why she needed a writer to put together and tell her story. She narrates as a primary victim – a Tutsi woman who survived the 1994 genocide in Rwanda. According to Mukagasana, since the genocide, she has had only one friend, her testimony, although she still hopes to one day have friends again. Despite her personal tragedy, she is capable of engraving nature's beauty into the horrifying descriptions of the genocide, using nature as a metonymy for the human condition. In this book, Mukagasana – a well-respected professional nurse who built a health centre for the poor in Kigali and was admired by her community for her activism and personality – suggests that her position earmarked her for priority killing. In the RTLM radio program inciting the killing of Tutsi, among other false accusations, she was described as the person charged with overseeing the plan to infect the Hutu with HIV. In the night between April 6 and 7, 1994, a few hours after the plane crash of the Rwandan president, the killings started. The Tutsi, who over the years suffered from periodical pogroms, demonization and prejudice, continuously feared genocide. During the next 100 days, every Tutsi was hunted, as the old social fabric of good neighbourly relationships and friendships was shattered. The Hutu did not rush into killing; anxiety and fear were core elements in the systematic extermination and torture of the Tutsi. Those Tutsi who could not withstand the anxiety turned themselves in to the guards who staffed road intersections throughout the country. In these locations, teams of Hutu demanded that everyone produces Identification Cards, and those who were identified as Tutsi were killed on the spot. The author tells how just before the genocide, she and her husband discussed sending their three children to Uganda to protect them from the anticipated harm. Her husband, whose parents were murdered in the 1954 pogrom of the Tutsi and grew up without his parents, opposed the idea as he did not want his children to be raised by others. Feeling guilty about not protecting his children, he turned himself in to the guards at the crossroads, hoping that while they will be engaged in killing him, his children and wife will have an opportunity to escape. As Mukagasana notes, the distance between her family and death was only three hours of driving. Mukagasana pleaded for help from everyone she thought could help her family to escape – the UN representatives, the Belgian Red Cross, the Parliament where the Arusha agreements were signed – but to no avail. One of her neighbours, whose wife was treated by Mukagasana, told her that he was ordered to set the surrounding fields on fire so that she and her family would be burnt and suggested that she seek shelter somewhere else. She sent her children to her Hutu niece, and she found refuge in a closet, under the sink of her Hutu friend's house. The killers reached the apartment of her niece, forced everyone to take their clothes off and marched them to a ditch they dug and killed them with machetes. She subsequently learnt that her son, Christian, marched at the head of the procession, chanting and praying. Her daughter died of machete striking and her youngest frightened daughter jumped into the ditch, calling her mother's name. She eventually suffocated in the ditch. All these events took place while Mukagasana was hiding one hundred meters away. Mukagasana then ran away and was hiding at the house of a Hutu colonel, who was one of the leaders of the genocide. While hiding in his place, he tried to rape her. She eventually managed to escape and was evacuated from the *Hotel des Mille Collines* in Kigali, where she found refuge.[18] Mukagasana critiques the Europeans governments that pretend as if there is orderly government in Kigali, when in fact chaos, violence, and cruelty reigned. The Christian world, according to Mukagasana, focuses on the suffering of Jesus, but ignored the killing and torture of thousands of Rwandans. She comments on the hypocrisy of many religious leaders who were instrumental in the killing of so many people that sought refuge in churches. She also ridicules Western intellectuals who talk about the importance of forgiveness but ignore human destruction and genocide. She particularly criticizes the English newspapers that present the genocide as a tribal war, and ignore the colonialist background of the conflict. According to Mukagasana, a Rwandan corpse would never weigh as a Belgian corpse. She

---

18   Mukagasana emphasizes the importance of knowing one's persecutors so that future genocide can be avoided, a motif found also in Primo Levy's writing.

distinguishes between European and Rwandan morality, as she states that to cut off children's arms with machetes and rape pregnant women before they violently extract their babies out of the womb is undoubtedly savage. The West, according to Mukagasana, is more refined and allows people to starve before killing them. The Final Solution of the Jews, she adds, is as barbaric as the savagery of the Africans.

Immaculee Ilibagiza's *Left to Tell: Discovering God Amidst the Rwandan Holocaust* (2007), is also a non-fiction book written by a Rwandan native who was a primary victim of the genocide. Ilibagiza came home from college to celebrate Easter with her family. During her visit, the three month slaughter of nearly one million ethnic Tutsi began. She survived by hiding in a Hutu pastor's bathroom with seven other women for 91 days. She subsisted on scraps of food and went from 115 to 65 pounds. All around her she could hear the *Interahamwe* militia massacring her neighbours, friends, and family. Her first-hand account describes both the evil she encountered, including the vicious murders of her family members, and how her faith gave her the strength to cope with such traumatic experiences. Ilibagiza's book is able to both describe the brutality of genocide through her personal experience while demonstrating how she used her deep faith to forgive the genocides perpetrators and begin the road to recovery.

Mary K. Blewitt's *You Alone May Live* (2010), is also a non-fiction book. It describes the lifelong persecution experience of Mary Blewitt, a native Rwandan who incorporates the genocide's impact on her life as a Tutsi woman and a secondary victim. Blewitt was out of the country during the genocide, but came home to chaos and had to begin picking up the pieces. Fifty of Blewitts's family members were among the Tutsi murdered by Hutu militias. Upon returning to Rwanda, Blewitt painstakingly looked for the bodies of her massacred family members to lay them to rest. The title of the book originates from a narrative of a woman who was raped in front of her family, and then forced to watch as members of her family members were murdered. She was told by the militiamen, "you alone may live so that you will die in sadness". Blewitt discusses how many female survivors echoed such experiences. The book begins with Blewitt's childhood in exile in Burundi, Tanzania and Uganda, continues with her coping with the immense loss of her family during the Rwandan Genocide, and ends with her personal pain to reach out to others affected by the Rwandan Genocide and the establishment of the Survivors Fund (SURF), an organization dedicated to helping Rwandan survivors. Once the killings ended, she travelled around Rwanda in order to gain a better understanding of the events that tore her life apart. She believed that she survived the atrocity in order to help others and ensure that their stories were told. Blewitt is able to both describe her personal experience and broaden the scope to carry out her mission of sharing the Rwandan's stories of horror, tragedy, and survival.

In the second group of written work we find Gil Courtemanche's *A Sunday at the Pool in Kigali* (2004). The book is a fictional love story set against the backdrop of the Rwandan Genocide. Courtemanche, a Canadian Journalist, was in Rwanda in 1994, making a film about AIDS in Rwanda when the massacre began. He states that all the characters are real; however, he used fiction to create a personal depiction of the atrocity, while making it more accessible to a wider audience. Footnotes throughout the book provide historical context and explanations. The main character, Valcourt, a Canadian Journalist, spends much of his time at the pool of the *Hotel des Mille Collines*. The pool represents a microcosm of Rwandan society. At the pool there are diplomats, journalists, aid workers, middle-class Rwandans, and prostitutes. Here, the Canadian journalist observes the corrupt interactions of diplomats, politicians, and military leaders, and the exploitation of the AIDS epidemic by Rwandan leaders. Valcourt describes the corrupt climate that precipitated the genocide. At the pool, Valcourt falls in love with Gentille, a young Hutu woman who looks like a Tutsi. Valcourt focuses his attention on Gentille's physical attributes, which infuses his book with an adolescent preoccupation with sex. The love story is juxtaposed with the horror and sadness that is occurring around them. Valcourt reports the carnage and brutality he witnesses around him with special attention to the female victims of the Rwandan Genocide. He explains how the Rwandan's exploitation of women's sexuality laid the foundation for the horror women endured during the conflict. Once the massacres begin, Valcourt describes in heart-breaking detail, the rapes, torture, and violence experienced by Rwandan women. The book is realistic in describing the inhumanity that engulfed Rwanda, and does not try to 'soften the story' by offering a happy ending. Gentille is mutilated by militiamen and refuses to be seen by Valcourt after she is disfigured.

A second book in this group is the book by French journalist Jean Hatzfeld, *The Antelope's Strategy* (2009). The book chronicles the victimization experience of those involved in the genocide and its aftermath, including the subsequent legal processing of the crime. This book joins Hatzfeld's two previous works on the Rwandan genocide. In the first one, *Life Laid Bare (2006)*, Hatzfeld interviews Tutsi survivors of the Rwandan genocide; in the second, *Machete Season (2005)*, he interviews Hutu perpetrators in prison. *The Antelope's Strategy* chronicles the experiences of both Tutsi survivors and Hutu perpetrators six years after Hutu militia are released from prison. In 2003, following a presidential decree, more than 40,000 Hutu perpetrators of the genocide were released from prison and returned to their old neighbourhoods, to live side by side with the Tutsi survivors. Hatzfeld offers a diverse representation of Rwandan perspectives from oral narratives that depict distrust, grief, nightmares, flashbacks of running away from militia, and victims' inability to forgive a Tutsi woman who married a Hutu man who played a role in the murder of her family. He also captures the feelings of relief expressed by the Hutu released from prison, granting them freedom.

Forced into reconciliation by the country's politicians, the two ethnic groups appear to apprehensively and suspiciously coexist.

A third book by non-Rwandans is Phillip Gourevitch's (1998) *We Wish to Inform You That Tomorrow We Will be Killed With Our Families*. Gourevitch – a staff writer for *The New Yorker* – covered the genocide for the magazine and later returned to the country to try to make sense of the events that unfolded. The stories told in this book are both the author's description of his visit to this country and his interviews with Rwandans. His interviews include a Tutsi doctor who witnessed his family's murder, a hotel manager who saved hundreds of Tutsi by hiding them, and a bishop implicated in killing Tutsi school children. The book title originates from one of these interviews: A Tutsi pastor describes how he wrote a pleading letter to his Hutu church president, and in response received the message: "We wish to inform you that tomorrow we will be killed with our families". Along with sharing the oral histories of Rwandans, Gourevitch extends responsibility for the genocide to the international community. He criticizes the French for supporting the Hutu, and condemns the United Nations, the international relief agencies, the surrounding countries that exploited the conflict in the region, and the international community that stood back and did nothing to prevent the horrors perpetrated during the 100 days of the genocide or alleviate the suffering that ensued.

In *Shake Hands with the Devil,* Lt.-Gen. Roméo Dallaire, also a non-Rwandan, uses his first-hand experience to describe the atrocities that occurred in Rwanda. Dallaire, of the Canadian Army, served as a UN force commander in Rwanda between 1993 and 1994. During the election period, he requested 5,000 UN troops for Rwanda to monitor its procedures and to return refugees. He received far less than what he asked for, weakening the UN's ability to prevent the massacre and causing Dallaire himself to leave the army as a damaged person with PTSD. Dallaire details the failing of the UN to secure peace in the region from diary entrees he wrote during his service in Rwanda. He blames the member countries, especially the U.S. and the Security Council, for lack of support and courage in enforcing peace. According to Dallaire, the Rwandan genocide was entirely preventable had the conflict been addressed in the beginning stages, and if enough troops were deployed to prevent the bloody escalation. The book records the chaos in Rwanda while chronicling Dallaire's transformation from a strong, confident warrior to a broken man.

Another book written by a non-Rwandan author is *Baking Cakes in Kigali: A Novel* (2009) by Galile Parkin. The novel describes an enthusiastic Tanzanian woman, Angel Tungaraza, who has recently moved to Rwanda from her native Tanzania. Angel, a professional cake-baker and amateur matchmaker, offers her clients a listening ear and a shoulder to cry on. With her husband Pius, and the five orphaned children of their late son and daughter, she is busy from sunset to sundown. Menopausal and putting on weight, she is an enthusiastic baker of delicious, brightly-iced cakes, which she sells to friends and neighbors. The story takes place six years after Rwanda's genocide of 1994.

The novel is divided into 14 sections, each of which comprises an occasion for which Angel bakes a cake. But over each celebration and the sign of life it symbolizes, hangs the shadow of the terrible past. The book structure, which is based on 14 different stories rather than one plot, facilitates the description of a wide range of Rwandans experiences during the genocide. It includes celebrations of marriage, baptism and clitorectomy. For instance, a wedding cake marks the union of the shopkeeper Leocadie, whose mother has been imprisoned as a *génocidaire*, with the security guard Modeste, whose whole family was slaughtered. Their marriage is an example of Rwanda's efforts at reconciliation. Despite the humor and hope that resonate in the stories, the underlining message is that reconciliation is difficult to accomplish, both on the personal and national levels.

The work by Anne-Marie de Brouwer and Sandra Ka Hon Chu *The Men Who Killed Me: Rwandan Survivors of Sexual Violence* (2009), the authors, both non-Rwandans, provide a composition of personal testimonies of 16 female and one male survivors of sexual violence during the Rwandan genocide. De Brouwer, an international criminal law associate professor in the Netherlands, and Chu, a lawyer and senior policy analyst for the Canadian HIV/AIDS legal network, worked together in the Hague and decided to collect the underreported stories of sexual violence that occurred during the conflict. From 2007 to 2008, they travelled to Rwanda and visited Solace Ministries, a grassroots organization in Kigali providing aid to widows and orphans of the Rwandan Genocide. At Solace Ministries, they met with the survivors and collected their stories. This collection describes how sexual violence was used as a weapon, sparing few women from sexual abuse. De Brouwer and Chu chronicle the stories of girls abducted from their families and taken into sexual slavery, mothers and grandmothers raped in front of their children and grandchildren, fathers forced to have sex with their daughters. The vast majority of female survivors were sexually victimized and an overwhelming majority of them became HIV-positive. This book brings sexual violence to the forefront of the Rwandan genocide and exposes the brutal use of sexual violence as a weapon to enhance the ethnic cleansing of the Tutsi.

6. SUMMARY AND CONCLUSION

This chapter has examined the expression of victimization in the context of international crime through a literary lens in Israel and Rwanda. We noted the relative size of literary work addressing national trauma resulting from victimization as well as the salience of works by noted writers in Israel compared to Rwanda. Israel has witnessed a fairly large number of literary works by well-regarded authors in a relatively short period following the fierce terrorist attacks of the second *Intifada*. On the other hand in Rwanda, with its oral tradition, written works were sparse and a significant portion of them was written by non-Rwandan. The paucity of literary work in Rwanda, however, can be attributed to its lack of tradition of written words or the absence of literary agents. As Nigerian author, Chimamanda Naguzi Adichia, in a January 30, 2009 interview to the Israeli newspaper *Haaretz*, has noted:

> *The tragedies of Africa have failed to attract international attention to the same degree that tragedies such as the Holocaust had done in the West. This failure is not because the African tragedies are less horrific but rather because the tragedies of the West have had better agents that helped in bringing them to the attention of the international public.*

Granted the differences between the two people and countries, the analysis shows that traumatic events lead to a proliferation of literary writings documenting and expressing national trauma. Following the genocide, Rwanda's literary expression that is traditionally oral, has produced written works that chronicle the victimization and national trauma via the story of individual primary or secondary victims. Israeli literature, following the trauma associated with the events of the second *Intifada*, had also taken a turn in focus and approach – it no longer included the pain of the other party to the conflict as it has previously done. The outburst of writings on the topic also subsided once the horrific victimization diminished. While Rwandan primary or secondary victims-turned-authors have documented the atrocities in written works, Israeli as well as non-Rwandan authors, by and large, have described victimization through fictional works based on real events.

The horrific events of the genocide in Rwanda and the incessant terrorist attacks in Israel produce fears that the very existence of the respective peoples is threatened. To Israelis, whose collective memory carries the burden of the Holocaust, the gruesome terror was perceived as a slow but deliberate attempt to annihilate them. The speed with which the works related to the second *Intifada* works were published is also an indication of the depth of the trauma. For Rwandans, the genocide marked a clear message that they are targeted for annihilation. The enormity of the trauma may have also caused a shift from the traditional oral expression of experiences to written ones.

The prospects of annihilation also affected the attention that writers gave to the 'Other' in the conflict. As the atrocities associated with the second *Intifada* began, Israeli authors no longer expressed compassion for the suffering of the Palestinians, as their previous works have shown. Rwandan authors on the other hand, in their focus on the horrific events of the genocide, tend to be silent about the historical background that caused the Hutu to loathe the Tutsi or, in the case of Mukagasana, confined their grievances to the colonialist regimes that exacerbated the ethnic conflict or turned a blind eye to the massacre.

Our article has introduced the idea that mass victimization and national trauma related to international crime may be studied through literary lens. The paucity of literary works in Rwanda may make our conclusion tentative. Future victimological research may further explore the notion that literature may reflect aspects of victimization not found in social science research, or alternatively confirm social science findings. Regardless of the outcome, the field of victimology will be enriched by such explorations.

PART II
REPARATIVE JUSTICE

VI. VICTIMS' NEED FOR JUSTICE
Individual versus Collective Justice

Jo-Anne WEMMERS

1. INTRODUCTION

Victimologists have traditionally studied the needs of crime victims at the individual level. In contrast, the collective needs of victims following mass victimizations such as genocide have, until recent years, received little attention in the field of victimology. Mass victimization affects the entire community and the trauma is experienced collectively (Josse & Dubois 2009). When there is intergroup conflict, the victim is affected not only as an individual but also as a group member. Hence, Hamber (2009) argues that in order to transform war-torn societies we cannot follow a solely individualistic approach. Based on his experience with victims of political violence, Hamber argues that there cannot be a medical solution to political trauma. This requires an understanding of the collective needs of victims. Drawing on social psychological theory and research, this chapter examines victims' need for justice. Justice is one of the key issues for victims in transitional societies both at the individual and group levels (Wemmers 1996; Herman 2003; Hamber 2009; Nader & Shnable 2008). When justice is not done, this can negatively impact both the individual victims' recovery as well as that of the society (Josse & Dubois 2009). In particular, the absence of justice can affect intergroup relations and consequently reconciliation (Nadler & Shnable 2008). In this chapter, I examine the meaning of justice for victims at the individual and group levels.

2. JUSTICE AT THE LEVEL OF THE INDIVIDUAL

The notion of justice has received considerable attention from social psychologists since the early 1960s. Early theorists focused on outcomes or *distributive justice* (Homans 1961; Adams 1965; Deutsch 1975; Walster, Walster & Berschied 1973). However, since the 1970s, psychologists have emphasized that in addition to outcomes, *procedural justice* is also important (Thibaut & Walker 1975). More recently some psychologists have argued that in addition to procedural justice, one must also consider *interactional justice* (Colquitt 2001). In the following these notions will be explained.

2.1. PROCEDURAL AND INTERACTIONAL JUSTICE

Procedural justice refers to the perceived fairness of procedures. Lind and Tyler (1989; 1992) present two models of procedural justice: the instrumental model and the group-value model. According to the instrumental model fair procedures are important because they maximize the probability of a positive outcome. In the group-value model, fair procedures are important because they recognize or reinforce the status of the individual as a worthy group member. Hegtvegt (2006) argues that the two models are essentially quite similar. They both focus on maximizing outcomes, however, where the instrumental model focuses on tangible, material outcomes, the group-value model focuses on intangible, infinite social well-being. Research with crime victims finds overall support for the group-value model versus the instrumental model: fair procedures are important in and of themselves, regardless of whether or not they impact sentencing (Wemmers 1996).

When are procedures fair? In the early studies on procedural justice, Thibaut and Walker (1975) identified two determinants of procedural justice: process control and decision control. Process control refers to whether and to what extent parties are able to present information throughout the decision-making procedure. Later, this was referred to as 'voice' (Folger 1977) and since then, 'voice' has been identified as one of the most stable findings in procedural justice research (Van den Bos 1996). Decision control refers to whether or not parties have control over the outcome. In other words, do they have the power to accept or refuse decisions made by a third-party (veto power)?

In their group-value model, Tyler and Lind (1992) specify three determinants of procedural justice: trust, standing and neutrality. Trust is directed at the individual's concern about an authority's intentions (e.g. is the authority trying to do right?). Standing is defined in terms of being treated with dignity and respect and showing respect for the rights of the individual. When people are treated with dignity and respect, they feel like valued members of society and feel good about themselves. Neutrality refers to honesty, the absence of bias, and making informed decisions based on the facts of the case. People want authorities, such as the police and judges, to be impartial and free from any bias.

In my research with victims of crime (Wemmers 1996), I did not find evidence of Tyler and Lind's three-factor model of procedural justice. Instead, I found evidence of a two-factor model: respect and neutrality. Neutrality is based on victims' perceptions that authorities were impartial, honest and made informed decisions based on the facts of the case. Respect refers to the quality of the interpersonal treatment of crime victims by criminal justice authorities. It includes whether or not victims were treated in a friendly manner, whether they were given an opportunity to express themselves (voice), whether or not authorities showed an interest in the victims and took their concerns into consideration. These findings suggest that the quality of the interaction between victims and criminal justice authorities is essential for victims' procedural justice judgements.

More recently, Tyler (2003) has argued that fair procedures are made up of two factors: the quality of the treatment and the quality of the decision-making. The quality of decision-making reflects the neutrality of the decision-maker (absence of bias, neutrality). The second determinant, quality of the treatment, is essentially whether the individual was treated with dignity and respect. However, others argue (Bies & Moag 1986; Colquitt 2001) that procedural justice is about formal rules and procedures. In their view, the quality of the treatment is a separate variable and they refer to it as *interactional* justice.

Regardless of whether it is considered a part of procedural justice or a separate variable, how people are treated affects their justice judgements (Lind & Tyler 1989; Tyler & Lind 1992; Wemmers 1996; Wemmers & Cyr 2006; Colquitt 2001). This may be particularly salient for victims who are often unaware of the formal legal rules and procedures and therefore rely heavily on their personal experiences. Research shows that when forming justice judgements, people use the information that is available to them (Van den Bos & Lind 2002; Van den Bos, Lind & Wilke 2001). The typical victim is not a legal expert and will not have access to information about formal rules and procedures on which they can base their justice judgements.

2.2. DISTRIBUTIVE JUSTICE

Distributive justice refers to people's moral evaluation in response to the allocation of rewards and punishments (Austin & Tobias 1984). It is promoted when outcomes are consistent with certain implicit norms for the allocation or distribution of resources, such as equality (everyone gets the same) or need (the most needy receive the most). With respect to crime victims, distributive justice is often discussed in the context of equity theory (Walster *et al.* 1973). Equity theory specifies that justice is achieved when the input (costs) and outcomes (benefits) for both parties are in balance. In other words, victims' fairness judgements are based on the outcomes or sentences imposed upon offenders relative to the victim's losses. The idea of proportionality is an old notion in justice. *Lex talion* – or an eye for an eye – is a basic legal notion which dates back to pre-Christian societies. However, perceptions of loss as well as gain are subjective and some losses cannot be calculated.

Just deserts theorists (Von Hirsch 1985; Ashworth & Von Hirsch 1998) deal with this problem by focussing on objective losses and gains. Just deserts emphasizes fairness in terms of proportionality and equality in sentencing and has fuelled the public discourse on punishments (Garland 2001). However, just deserts theorists, such as Ashworth (1993, 2000), exclude victim participation in criminal justice procedures because inclusion of the victim and their subjective experiences risks introducing ambiguity into sentencing and therefore threatens the delicate balance between crime and punishment. While just deserts emphasizes the harm caused to the victim and society, it focuses on objective rather than subjective harm. The inclusion of victims in the criminal justice system feeds concerns among some legal experts that they will upset the balance of justice and their desire for revenge will lead to harsher punishments (Roach 1999; Ashworth 2000).

However, research with crime victims shows that victims' satisfaction with the outcome means more than just the severity of sentencing (Erez 1999). Orth reaches a similar conclusion based on a study in which he examined the punishment goals of 174 victims of rape and non-sexual assault (Orth 2003). Orth examined a variety of goals including just deserts and found that victims pursue diverse punishment goals. Victims gave the highest support to instrumental goals namely deterrence of the offender and the security of the victim and society. Just deserts and revenge received less support from the victims in this study. These results suggest that victims are not only interested in retaliation.

Punishment is, however, not the only way in which equity can be restored, there is also reparation. Whereas punishment imposes losses on the offender in an effort to restore justice, reparation attempts to restore equity by reducing the losses suffered by the victim or the community. This is referred to as reparation or restorative justice. Examples of reparation include the restitution of goods, financial compensation for losses, as well as recognizing and apologizing for any wrong-doing.

3. JUSTICE AT THE LEVEL OF THE GROUP

In their work on justice, Lillie and Janoff-Bulman (2007) distinguish between justice at the micro level and the macro level. According to the authors, micro level justice focuses on the needs of the individual victim and concerns the relationships among individuals. In contrast, macro level justice focuses on the needs of the society as whole. It concerns the structure and development of the social order. More specifically, it is about the needs of the social group.

A social group is two or more people who share the same social identity (Hogg 2006). The social group is particularly salient with respect to genocide and crimes against humanity, where specific social groups may be targeted. When people share the same social identity, they identify and evaluate themselves in the same way and have the same definition of who they are, what attributes they have, and how they relate to and differ from people who are not in their group or who are in particular out-groups (Tajfel & Turner 1979; Hogg 2006). In contrast, personal identity is construed by the individual and is made up of personality traits or characteristics that are not shared with their group and are considered unique to them as an individual (Hogg 2006). People have as many social and personal identities as there are groups they belong to and personal relationships they are involved in.

How does this help to understand perceptions of fairness at the group level? Lillie and Janoff-Bulman (2007, 223) state that macro justice does not readily map onto past typological distinctions drawn in the justice literature such as procedural and distributive justice. However, because of group membership, social identity theory is linked with social justice theory and can help explain how group processes impact group members. Social identity is motivated by two processes: self-enhancement and uncertainty reduction (Hogg 2006) and both of these processes are also pertinent for justice judgements. The normative or group value model of procedural justice is based on the notion that people seek information about their social standing (Tyler & Lind 1992). Belonging to a group that is evaluated positively makes us feel good about ourselves. Uncertainty motivates social identity as well as fairness judgements. When people are confronted with uncertainty in their environment they turn to impressions of fair treatment to help them decide how to react (Lind & Van den Bos 2002; Van den Bos & Lind 2002). Social identity helps by letting us know what to expect. Taken together, this suggests that procedural justice could be the linking pin between the individual and the group In the following this notion will be examined in further detail.

3.1. PROCEDURAL JUSTICE

Procedural justice judgements link social cognitions with individual behaviour. As was mentioned earlier, in their Group Value Model of procedural justice, Tyler and Lind (1992) identify standing to be a determinant of procedural justice judgements. Standing is about people's social identity and being treated with respect. Procedures, they argue, send people a message about their value in the group. When people are treated with dignity and respect, they feel that they are valued and respected members of the group.

However, in addition to sending a message about their value to the group, respect also sends a message about the value of their group. Janoff-Bulman and Werther (2008) distinguish between contingent and categorical respect. Categorical respect is based on one's membership in a group. The notion of innate and inalienable human rights is an example of rights recognized due to membership in the group 'human beings'. Similarly, civil rights recognize membership in a nation or state. Janoff-Bulman and Werther argue that categorical respect confers the right to participate and grants people a voice. They are recognized and not ignored or silenced. Categorical respect is not something that is earned but something that is acquired automatically with membership in the group. Janoff-Bulman and Werther equate categorical respect with rights, voice and fair treatment, arguing that they all imply in-group inclusion and participation. In other words, categorical respect is associated with procedural justice at the group level.

Contingent respect provides status or standing *within* the group (Tyler & Lind 1992; Blader &Tyler 2003). Like achieved status, contingent respect is earned. Once earned, it provides the individual with influence and power within the group. Janoff-Bulman and Werther (2008) indicated that a person granted contingent respect is necessarily also granted categorical respect within the group, with the rights and voice accorded to in-group members.

The absence of categorical respect is a major source of frustration for victims who seek acknowledgement of the injustice done (Ferstman 2005). Emphasizing the importance of the group, Stover (2005) finds that victims testifying at the International Criminal Tribunal for the former Yugoslavia always wanted to talk about impact on the group and not just on how they themselves were affected. Similar experiences were reported by professionals working at the International Criminal Court (Wemmers 2009). In other words, victims seemed to seek recognition for their group as well as recognition of them individually.

3.2. DISTRIBUTIVE JUSTICE

What is collective distributive justice? At the level of the individual distributive justice is based on outcomes such as punishment or reparation. Similarly at the group level, distributive justice should be outcome oriented, however, the outcomes should be measured in terms of gains for the group rather than personal gains.

In a series of experiments, Lillie and Janoff-Bulman (2007) examined the impact of evoking collective needs versus individual needs. The researchers found that when respondents focus on collective needs they are less punitive in sentencing than those who focus on the needs of the individual victim. Specifically, respondents who were prompted to focus on collective needs judged the South African Truth and Reconciliation Commission to be fairer than respondents who were cued to focus on the needs of individual victims. However, this study was experimental and used psychology students rather than actual victims, which makes it difficult to generalize the findings.

Van Der Merwe (2008), however, studied victims' perceptions of justice following mass victimization. Specifically, Van der Merwe used a random sample of transcripts from the South African Truth and Reconciliation Commission (TRC), in order to study what victims said about justice. He found that victims' perceptions of justice focussed on two main themes: retributive and restorative justice.

Restorative justice focuses on healing the harm done by the crime and this includes both the harm done to the individual as well as harm done to society or the community (Zehr 2002). However, Van der Merwe points out that in the context of political violence, conventional definitions of restorative justice may not be adequate. In the case of collective victimization, where the individual crime takes place within a context of underlying political divisions, he argues that restoration may take on another meaning. Van der Merwe prefers the term accountability to restorative justice, thus emphasizing the link with transitional justice, which studies justice in the context of political change (Teitel 2003). However, the author also says that survivors' responses were largely about finding answers in order to understand why the crime occurred. This is a common finding in victimology and many victims enter into restorative justice programs because they want to ask their offender why he did what he did (Wemmers & Canuto 2002). Thus, these victims' perceptions of justice appear to correspond with a form of restorative justice. In all, 37% of the survivors' in Van der Merwe's study supported this form of justice and another 13% expressed a need for both restorative and retributive justice (see also Peacock, this volume).

Retribution, or punishment, was the goal of half of the apartheid survivors in Van der Merwe's study. They felt that the offenders should be made to pay for what they did. In the context of the TRC, which promised amnesty to those who came forward and admitted their crimes, this is an interesting finding. It underscores the claims of many human rights organisations namely that impunity is harmful to victims and must be stopped (also Van Wijk, this volume). The creation of the International Criminal Court (ICC) by the international community was indeed meant to put an end to impunity and to "bring justice to victims" (Kofi Anan 2002). However, the victimological literature has made it very clear that victims are often very dissatisfied with classical criminal (retributive) justice (Shapland, Wilmore & Duff 1985; Baril 1984; Wemmers 2003). Thus attention to the process or procedural justice is also important.

In criminology, punishment is believed to have a deterrent effect: at the level of the individual it is believed to prevent the individual offender from committing new crimes in the future and at the level of society it is believed to prevent others from committing similar crimes. Prevention is also an important goal for victims (Orth 2002). In the context of mass victimization, prison may prevent individual offenders from regaining power and committing further violence, however, it does not guarantee the cessation of violence in general. At the group level, prevention can mean rule of law. A key aspect of transitional justice is the introduction of rule of law in order to prevent abuses of power and gross violations of human rights in the future. Although the victims in Van der Merwe's study did not explicitly discuss prevention, this may be because at the time of the TRC, political changes had already been put into place. With the rule of law established, it was perhaps not necessary for survivors to further elaborate on that.

In the case of inter-group conflict, which underlies crimes like genocide, crimes against humanity and war crimes, prevention can also mean reconciliation between groups. Pratto and Glasford (2008) argue that when a group has been harmed by another group, key issues that need to be addressed in order to facilitate intergroup reconciliation are the restoration of collective self-esteem and collective integrity. It is important to note the overlap between these notions and categorical respect, as discussed above. If, by giving victims voice, one promotes collective self-esteem and integrity, one would in effect be promoting reconciliation between groups. Thus, victim participation, because of its importance in terms of categorical respect, could enhance the probability that inter-group violence would cease.

4. CONCLUDING REMARKS

Justice is a concept that touches both individual victims as well as their social groups. In this chapter I examined the meaning of justice at both the individual and the group levels. Mass victimisations, especially those that target specific social groups, such as genocide, social identity is particularly salient as well as perceptions of justice at the level of the group. When people focus on the collective needs of their social group they are less punitive than when they focus on their individual needs. However, procedural justice is important for both individual and group perceptions of fairness. Victims seek recognition and validation in procedures. When crimes have been committed against a social group, it is important that the victimized group be recognized through, for example, the participation of its members in justice procedures such as Truth Commissions, criminal courts or reparation programs. If their group is not recognized, this will frustrate victims and undermine their self-esteem as a member of the group. This in turn can fuel animosity between social groups. Hence procedural justice, and the categorical respect that it provides victims, is important as a means to promote peace and the restoration of justice.

VII. PROVIDING REPARATION IN SITUATIONS OF MASS VICTIMIZATION
Key Challenges Involved

Rianne LETSCHERT and Theo VAN BOVEN

1. SETTING A TREND TOWARDS REPARATIVE JUSTICE

Over the past century, millions of civilians have fallen victim to acts of violence during conflict. The scale of violence against civilians has been far greater in the previous century than ever before. This has not only led to a dramatic increase in the numbers of civilian casualties of war during the 20th century, but also to a likewise dramatic increase in the proportion of civilian casualties as opposed to military casualties: From about 14% in World War I over 67% in World War II, to 90% by the end of the last century (Levi & Sider 1997). Civilians, notably women and children, are increasingly targeted. Conflicts involving child soldiers, widespread attacks on civilian populations, destruction and looting of civilian residences and institutions, abductions, the use of rape as an instrument of warfare, and massive deportations and ethnic cleansing have become common practices.

According to the UNHCR's annual 'Global Trends' report of June 2010, at the end of 2009, the number of people forcibly uprooted by conflict and persecution worldwide stood at 43.3 million, the highest number since the mid-nineties.[1] The total includes 15.2 million refugees and asylum seekers and 27.1 million internally displaced people uprooted within their own countries.[2]

One particular aspect of addressing the terrible consequences of mass victimization is found in providing reparation to victims. Mass atrocities cause large scale sufferings inflicted on individual human persons, collectivities and entire populations. More often than not victims of mass atrocities are ignored.

---

[1]   Www.unhcr.org/4c11f0be9.html.
[2]   Even though the first Human Security Report of 2005, the Human Security Brief of 2007, and the latest Human Security Report of 2009 all document a dramatic, but largely unknown decline in the number of wars, genocides and human rights abuses over the past decade.

Many societies do not have a genuine interest in the fate of victims; there is great reluctance to face and acknowledge cruelties that occurred and a sense prevails of irreparable harm anyway. In addition, societies trying to overcome a period of conflict show several profound shortcomings, both in the legal and social order that also affect proper reparation afterwards. Tomuschat singles out four main general areas (Tomuschat 2008, 54). First, inadequate laws, restrictions in legal scope and content relating to the committed crimes, impediments in getting access to justice and restrictive attitudes of courts are some of the *legal obstacles*. Second, often societies face *political obstacles* mainly from authorities and certain groups in society unwilling to recognise that wrongs were committed. Third, *severe economic consequences* as a result of a shortage or unjust distribution of resources further preclude easy recovery. Especially in those countries that already belonged to the developing countries, ensuring economic recovery is extra difficult. In addition, most conflicts lead to an enormous number of victims, putting stress on any proposed reparation regime. Prioritizing the allocation of resources thus poses vexing questions (Duthie 2009). Fourth, *under-empowerment* of victims themselves should be mentioned, mainly because of a lack of knowledge and capacity to present and pursue their claims. The last aspect is compounded by the vulnerability of groups of victimized persons, notably women, children, and members of specific racial, ethnic or religious groups. In addition, most contemporary conflicts are intra-state in nature, posing additional pressure and difficulties for reparation processes (Garfield & Neugut 1997; Fletcher & Weinstein 2002).[3]

It is undeniable that law and society for a long time were not victim oriented. In international law, reparations were for long not to the benefit of human beings. States were the main subjects of law and reparations were a matter of inter-State relations and obligations. Only in recent times, reflecting a process of "humanization of international law" (Meron 2006), victims' rights are receiving wider international recognition, as evident in international human rights instruments and in opinions of international human rights adjudicators, notably the European and Inter-American Courts of Human Rights. Similarly, the Statute of the International Criminal Court (ICC) opened up ways and means for victims to participate in the proceedings before the Court and to be afforded reparations. Along the same line victims' rights were in recent decades explicitly recognized in transitional justice processes, particularly in Latin America and in Africa, in serious efforts to come to terms with a legacy of large-scale human rights abuses. In the light of these developments attempts were made to further spell out and create mechanisms and tools for combating impunity and strengthening the normative basis of reparative justice. Thus, the

---

3   Fletcher & Weinstein (2002, 576–577) refer in particular to the human suffering on a communal level which is a shared feature in many contemporary conflicts, where neighbour-on-neighbour violence is characteristic of this form of aggression.

United Nations General Assembly adopted in 2005 after a lengthy process of preparations and negotiations the *Basic Principles and Guidelines on the Right to a Remedy and Reparation for Victims of Gross Violations of International Human Rights Law and Serious Violations of International Humanitarian Law* (hereafter Reparation Principles).[4] In the same year the United Nations Commission on Human Rights endorsed an *Updated Set of Principles for the Protection and Promotion of Human Rights through Action to Combat Impunity* (Impunity Principles).[5]

International lawyers continue the discussions on reparative principles. As an expression of strong interest and commitment on the part of international civil society, women's rights groups and activists adopted in 2007 the *Nairobi Declaration on Women's and Girls' Rights to a Remedy and Reparation.*[6] More recently, the International Law Association discussed a Draft Declaration containing principles for reparation for victims of armed conflict at its annual meeting in August 2010.

While the legal and judicial approach to victims' entitlement to redress and reparation largely focused on the rights of individual victims, the acknowledgement of mass abuses and gross violations made the principle of reparative justice a subject of legitimate international concern. In response, the United Nations developed special procedures of investigation and retribution as a political and moral commitment to deal with consistent patterns of mass atrocities and gross violations of human rights. The initial focus was on apartheid and colonialism with progressive extension to many other situations of large-scale repression and conflict entailing mass crimes. In a parallel fashion, at domestic levels in the wake of mass atrocities, mechanisms and processes of transitional justice were developed, often in combination, such as criminal prosecutions, truth and reconciliation commissions, reparation schemes, and institutional reform. Thus, a complex arsenal of domestic mechanisms and processes came into being with differing levels of international involvement.[7]

---

4   The guidelines were adopted and proclaimed by the UN General Assembly on 16 December 2005 (resolution 60/147), after a 15-year period of negotiations. Note that the Preamble mentions that the principles and guidelines do not "entail new international or domestic legal obligations, but identify mechanisms, modalities, procedures and methods for the implementation of existing legal obligations under international human rights law and international humanitarian law which are complementary though different as to their norms."

5   UNCHR, *Updated Set of Principles for the Prosecution and Promotion of Human Rights through Action to Combat Impunity*, UN doc. E/CN.4/2005/102/Add. 1.

6   Http://womensrightscoalition.org/reparation.

7   UN, *The Rule of Law and Transitional Justice in Conflict and Post-Conflict Societies.* Report of the Secretary General, S2004/616, Geneva: UN, 23th August 2004, para. 8.

2. OUTLINE CHAPTER

An abundance of scholarly literature exists on reparation theories and legal procedures or administrative programmes set up to provide reparation to victims of mass atrocities or international crimes, often also referred to as gross violations of human rights and humanitarian law. This chapter aims to provide an analysis of what we consider to be the main challenges to carefully consider when devising and implementing reparative justice measures, whereby the focus is on victims of international crimes leading to mass victimization. In all regions and countries violations of human rights and fundamental freedoms occur and victims should be entitled to redress and reparation. However, in the context of this book not incidental or sporadic violations are the subject of close attention. The focus is on situations involving gross and massive violations of human rights, often amounting to crimes under international law as defined in the Statute of the ICC.

A first challenge is how to conceptualize victimhood in post-conflict situations. As noted by Mani "conflict or repression is often so widespread and traumatising that the entire society is victimised, and there is a need to redefine victims as the entire society" (Mani 2005, 68). The conception on who should be considered victims in societies in transition poses several complexities that will be further reflected upon.

The second challenge is how to adapt the existing judicial right to an effective *individual* remedy to the context of mass victimization where it is often claimed that *collective* reparations might be better suited to provide reparative justice (Roht-Arriaza 2003–2004; Van Boven 1995). Implementing a collective perspective may also result in including general goals of development aid in reparative measures. The third challenge will reflect upon this, by some contested, inclusion of development strategies in reparation programmes (De Greiff & Duthie 2009; Saris & Lofts 2009). In order to present arguments on how to balance this individual versus collective perspective and the inclusion of development goals, we will draw from victimological studies into the needs of victims and notions presented by the human security concept.

We realize that providing reparative justice to victims of international crimes requires tailor-made solutions in which the specific (historical, cultural and economic) context of the country should be taken into account. That being said, we do believe that the challenges discussed in this chapter apply in general to situations of mass victimization.

3. PARAMETERS OF REPARATIVE JUSTICE

The processes by which a state seeks to redress violations of a past regime are often labelled under the heading of 'transitional justice' initiatives (Fletcher &

Weinstein 2002, 574). Following Mani (2005, 55), transitional justice focuses on

> *how to address the legitimate claims for justice of victims and survivors of horrific abuses in a way that treads the delicate balance between averting a relapse into conflict or crisis on the one hand, and on the other hand consolidating long-term peace based on equity, respect and inclusion – which often requires considerable institutional reform and systematic change.*

Where transitional justice is referred to, it often includes truth commissions and trials, and institutional reform, for instance in the justice or security sector (Mani 2005, 55).

3.1. RIGHT TO KNOW, RIGHT TO JUSTICE, RIGHT TO REPARATION

Restoring the rule of law in societies that have been struck by serious violations of basic norms of humanity requires the building of basic domestic justice capacities. Reparation to victims, in its various modalities and in individual and collective dimensions, is to be devised and materialized within the broader setting of transitional justice. In this connection the Impunity Principles, referred to above, provide important guidance in mapping out (i) *The Right to Know,* (ii) *The Right to Justice* and (iii) *The Right to Reparation,* which, together with Guarantees of Non-Recurrence, are basic premises to serve the plight of victims.

The Right to Know as an inalienable right of people and as a right of victims and their families includes the right to know the truth about heinous crimes committed and circumstances and reasons leading thereto as well as what happened to victims, individually and collectively.[8] Article 24 of the Reparation Principles mentions that victims are entitled to seek and obtain information on the causes leading to their victimization, and to learn the truth with regard to these violations. The right to learn the truth is not incorporated so prominently in other international victims' rights instruments.[9] For victims of international crimes, this is an important aspect that needs to be addressed when guaranteeing the right to information. It goes beyond existing regulations about providing

---

[8]   See in detail Impunity Principles 2–5.

[9]   It is also included in the International Convention for the Protection of All Persons from Enforced Disappearances, entered into force on 23 December 2010, which states in Article 24.2 that each victim has the right to know the truth. This Convention is strongly influenced by the Reparation Principles.

information on important developments in a possible criminal procedure or the availability of services.[10]

The Right to Justice involves the duty of states to carry out prompt and impartial investigations of violations of human rights and international humanitarian law and bring to justice those responsible for serious crimes under international law.[11] Multigenerational research findings suggest that the process of redress and the attainment of justice can be critical to the healing for individual victims, as well as their families, societies and nations (see also Danieli, this volume).

The Right to Reparation completes this trilogy of basic justice. It is a victim oriented right implying a duty on the part of the state to provide reparation and the possibility for victims to seek redress from the perpetrator.[12] The Right to Reparation is also the main thrust of the Reparation Principles. The overarching principle on reparations is contained in Part IX, para 18. It notes that

> *in accordance with domestic and international law, and taking account of individual circumstances, victims of gross violations of international human rights law and serious violations of international humanitarian law should, as appropriate and proportional to the gravity of the violation and the circumstances of each case, be provided with full and effective reparation (...).*[13]

It should be noted that the right to a remedy entails two elements; the *procedural* right of access to justice and the *substantive* right to redress for injury suffered. The procedural dimension is reflected in the concept of the duty to provide "effective domestic remedies" as included in almost all human rights instruments. The substantive part relates to the duty to provide redress for harm suffered in the form of restitution, compensation, rehabilitation, satisfaction and – by way of institutional reforms and enhancing respect for the rule of law – guarantees of non-repetition and prevention of violations.[14] In our discussion we focus on these five forms of providing reparation.[15]

Restitution refers to restoring the victim to the original situation before the violation took place, including, among other things, restoration of liberty, enjoyment of human rights, identity, family life and citizenship, return to one's

---

[10] For more information on the Reparation Principles and reparation in general, see Shelton 2005, 11–32.

[11] See Impunity Principles 19 ff.

[12] See Impunity Principles 31 ff.

[13] Previous drafts used headings such as 'victims' rights to reparations'; the current heading is reparation for harm suffered. Also previous drafts used the word 'shall' instead of should.

[14] Although the two concepts are often confused, the terms 'remedy' and 'reparation' are therefore not synonyms. The definition of 'remedy' includes the right to equal and effective access to justice, the admission to relevant information concerning violations and redress mechanisms, and the right to prompt and adequate reparation.

[15] See Reparation Principles 19–23.

place of residence, restoration of employment and return of property. This reflects the original meaning of the principle of *restitutio in integrum*.

Compensation is defined as providing for any economically assessable damage, listing the following items: physical or mental harm, lost opportunities, including employment, education and social benefits, material damages and loss of earnings, including loss of earning potential, moral damage, and costs required for legal or expert assistance, medicine and medical services, and psychological and social services. International mechanisms such as the Inter-American Court and the European Court of Human Rights appear to agree on the following interpretation of fair and adequate compensation: "The ideal behind reparations is 'full restitution' (restitutio in integrum), that is the restoration of the *status quo ante*". (De Greiff 2006, 455) In cases where this is not possible, for example when death has occurred, compensation is required. Case law of international and regional bodies has further elaborated this principle. See, for instance, the extensive case law of the Inter-American Court of Human Rights, which has also defined crucial concepts such as moral damage, damage to a life plan, and has interpreted the right to receive reparations taking into account the peculiarities of groups or communities (such as indigenous groups) which could serve as an exemplary model.

Rehabilitation includes medical and psychological care as well as legal and social services (Section IX, Article 21).[16] Article 22 elaborates the different forms of *satisfaction,* including, where applicable, any or all of the following: (a) Effective measures aimed at the cessation of continuing violations; (b) Verification of the facts and full and public disclosure of the truth to the extent that such disclosure does not cause further harm or threaten the safety and interests of the victim, the victim's relatives, witnesses, or persons who have intervened to assist the victim or prevent the occurrence of further violations; (c) The search for the whereabouts of the disappeared, for the identities of the children abducted, and for the bodies of those killed, and assistance in the recovery, identification and reburial of the bodies in accordance with the expressed or presumed wish of the victims, or the cultural practices of the families and communities; (d) An official declaration or a judicial decision restoring the dignity, the reputation and the rights of the victim and of persons closely connected with the victim; (e) Public apology, including acknowledgment of the facts and acceptance of responsibility; (f) Judicial and administrative sanctions against persons liable for the violations; (g) Commemorations and tributes to the victims;[17] (h) Inclusion of an accurate account of the violations

---

16 Special legislation for victims of terrorism often stipulates that social rehabilitation is one of the goals to achieve.

17 The setting up of commemorations is not always easy. Note, for instance, the discussions between the victims' families of 9/11 and the business developers regarding the reconstruction of the site of the World Trade Center. See for more information, Issacharoff & Mansfield 2006, 307 ff.

that occurred in international human rights law and international humanitarian law training and in educational material at all levels (Section IX, Article 22 a-h). Finally, States should take measures for the *guarantees of non-repetition*, which will also contribute to prevention (Section IX, Article 23).

The Reparation Principles have furthermore incorporated some of the general victims of crime rights, such as Article 10 relating to the treatment of victims (ensuring that victims should be treated with humanity and respect for their dignity, ensure their safety, physical and psychological well-being and privacy, and the prevention of secondary victimization). Another example of a classical victims' right is the right to information (Article 24), urging states to develop means of informing the general public and, in particular, victims of gross violations, of the rights and remedies contained in the Basic Principles, and of all available legal, medical, psychological, social, administrative and all other services to which victims may be entitled.

3.2. REPARATION-AS-RIGHT, AS-SYMBOL, AS-PROCESS

Before taking up the challenges of mass victimization and of affording reparative justice in those situations, it may be instructive to distinguish between three conceptual frameworks of reparations: *reparation-as-right, reparation-as-symbol,* and *reparation-as-process* (Saris & Lofts 2009, 86–87). Reparation-as-right as discussed in section 3.1 involves the victim's right to remedies, notably access to justice; adequate, effective and prompt reparations for harm suffered; access to relevant information concerning violations and reparation mechanisms.[18] Reparation-as-right is viewed from the perspective of the individual victim and often assessed and measured in terms of monetary compensation for the harm suffered in proportion to the gravity of the violation. This rests on the principle that the violation of an individual's rights creates a corresponding individual right to a remedy, and is thus consistent with the classic juridical understanding of the consequences proceeding from a violation of international law (Saris & Lofts 2009, 86). The law on State responsibility further prescribes that the breach of an international obligation by a state entails the duty of the state to make reparations.[19]

Reparation-as-symbol marks the symbolic meaning of certain forms of reparation and goes beyond individual victims' rights and interests. It represents strong social and community values. Reparation-as-symbol provides recognition to victims not only as victims but also as citizens and as rights holders more

---

[18]   See Reparation Principles, sections VII, VIII, IX, X.
[19]   *Factory at Chorzow*, Judgment No. 8, 1927, P.C.I.J., Series A, no. 17, at 29. Article 1 of the Draft Articles on Responsibility of States for Internationally Wrongful Acts, adopted by the International Law Commission at its 53rd Session 2001.

generally.[20] It falls in the category of satisfaction and may include official declarations to restore the dignity, the reputation and the rights of victims, public apologies, commemorations and tributes, rededication of places of detention and torture, as well as inclusion of an accurate account of past wrongs in educational and training materials.

Finally, reparation-as-process establishes a link of the past with the future. It gives prominence to participation and empowerment, in particular with respect to victimized persons and groups. Its ultimate aim is reconciliation and a fair and equitable share in reconstruction efforts.

The 2005 Reparation Principles include these different conceptual perspectives on reparation. The Basic Principles acknowledge that

> *the judicial approach serves here as a means to activate non-judicial schemes and programmes for the benefit of large numbers of victims affected by gross and consisted violations of human rights. Both the judicial and the non-judicial approach should interrelate and interact in a complementary fashion for the reparation and other assistance to victims.* (Van Boven 2005, vii)

4. FIRST CHALLENGE – CONCEPTUALIZATION OF VICTIMHOOD

The conceptualization of victimhood in societies in transition poses several complexities. Important scholarly work within victimology has been done in conceptualizing victimhood by categorizing groups in primary, secondary and tertiary (or vicarious) victims. This part will analyse whether such categorization can offer useful tools in the conceptualization of victimhood in the context of international crimes (Letschert *et al.* 2010). At first let us explain how some of the existing international victims' rights instruments define who is entitled to victim protection. The 1985 UN *Declaration of Basic Principles of Justice for Victims of Crime and Abuse of Power* contains the following definition in Articles 1 and 2:

> *1. 'Victims' means persons who, individually or collectively, have suffered harm, including physical or mental injury, emotional suffering, economic loss or substantial impairment of their fundamental rights, through acts or omissions that are in violation of criminal laws operative within Member States, including those laws proscribing criminal abuse of power".*

---

[20]   UNHCHR, *Rule-of-Law Tools for Post-Conflict States; Reparations Programmes*, HR/PUB/08/1, 2008, p. 23.

"2. [...] The term 'victim' also includes, where appropriate, the immediate family or dependants of the direct victim and persons who have suffered harm in intervening to assist victims in distress or to prevent victimisation. (emphasis added)

The Reparation principles in Article V.8 use the same definition. Legal persons are not entitled to protection under these two documents, contrary to the scope of protection offered by the Rules of Procedure and Evidence for the purpose of the Statute of the ICC. Rule 85 notes that the notion of victims may also include

organizations or institutions that have sustained direct harm to any of their property, which is dedicated to religion, education, art or science or charitable purposes, and to their historic monuments, hospitals and other places and objects for humanitarian purposes.[21]

The reference in the UN definitions to individual *and* collective victims' suffering of various kinds of harm gives room for a broad interpretation of the concept of victimhood. The second paragraph, however, limits the protection by referring to the *direct* victim, thereby implying that the category under paragraph 1 should be directly victimized by the act. Broadening the scope of victim protection and thereby offering all the different victims' rights included in these documents to all categories (direct and indirect) of victims would make the implementation of these provisions unrealistic. Therefore, following an analysis that was made with regard to defining categories of victims of terrorism (Letschert *et al.* 2010), a distinction could be made between the following categories of victims:

- Primary victims: those persons who suffered harm, including physical or mental injury, emotional suffering or economic loss directly caused by the act.
- Secondary victims: consisting of dependants or relatives of the deceased and first responders to acts of terrorism (see also the definition in the UN Declaration and the Reparation principles).
- Tertiary victims: All others not listed under primary and secondary victims could be considered tertiary victims.[22]

---

[21]   The Rules of Procedure and Evidence set out general principles and clear descriptions of specific procedures underpinning and supplementing the provisions of the Statute. They are subordinate to the provisions of the Statute.

[22]   This third category includes each and every person that feels victimized by the event, whether actually present during the conflict or a so-called 'outsider'. Research conducted after 9/11 revealed for instance levels of PTSD with persons who watched the plane fly into the World Trade Towers at the television. See also Schmid (2003) who refers, among others, to the constituency/society at large, or others who have reason to fear that they might be the next targets (referring to terrorism).

The distinction discussed before relating to reparation-as-right, as symbol or as process, could be an appropriate framework through which to address the entitlements and needs of these three victim categories. As to reparation-as-right, in several cases it was argued that compensation or reparation should be granted to other individuals as the direct victim as well. As Hofmann indicated in his commentary to the 2010 ILA Declaration (2010, 10)

> *harm can be suffered not only by the individual whose rights have been violated but also by third persons. As an example, the killing of a person may cause mental injury (e.g. posttraumatic stress disorder) to members of his or her family or persons present at the scene. There is precedence in State practice that such persons should have a right to reparation as well.*

The Inter-American Court of Human Rights acknowledged for example in the *Aloeboetoe* case that under limited conditions, third parties might file a claim for compensatory damages.[23] The UN Compensation Commission (Holtzmann & Kristjánsdóttir 2007, 59),[24] the European Court of Human Rights[25] as well as the Human Rights Committee have taken similar approaches. The Human Rights Committee goes even further by stating that

> *it is the suffering of harm which qualifies these third persons as victims. It sees no compelling reason to a priori restrict this group of third persons to members of the 'immediate family', 'dependants' or 'persons who have suffered harm in intervening to assist victims in distress or to prevent victimization' as done in the Basic Principles.[26]*

As to connecting the harm to the violation the Committee suggests that two considerations guide the choice of the appropriate criterion to apply: "first, the need to exclude harm that is too remote (such as e.g. unrelated persons far removed from the conflict who are emotionally affected by news of the suffering); and second, the need not to unduly limit the number of victims. The two aspects should be balanced carefully" (UN Human Rights Committee Communication

---

[23] *Aloeboetoe et al. v. Suriname*, Reparations (Article 63 (1) American Convention on Human Rights), Judgement of September 10, 1993, Inter-AmCtHR (Ser.C) No.15 (1994), paras 67, 76. See also *Loayza Tamayo v. Peru*, Judgement of November 27, 1998, Inter-AmCtHR (Ser.C) No.42; and *Blake v. Guatemala*, Judgement of January 22, 1999, Inter-AmCtHR (Ser.C) No.48. For further reference see Schönsteiner 2008, 133 ff.

[24] According to decision S/AC.26/1991/3, Nr. 3 (c) of the Governing Council of the UN Compensation Commission, October 18, 1991, a spouse, child or parent of the individual who suffered death may claim compensation for pecuniary losses resulting from mental pain and anguish.

[25] See e.g. *Velikova v. Bulgaria*, Application No. 41488/98, Judgement of May 18, 2000 and *Kurt v. Turkey*, Application No. 15/1997/799/1002, Judgement of 25 May 1998.

[26] See e.g. *Mr. S. Jegatheeswara Sarma v. Sri Lanka*, Communication No. 950/2000, U.N. Doc. CCPR/C/78/D/950/2000 (2003).

2000, 11). Also the 2008 UN Report[27] argues that setting the bar too high will leave out many victims.

> *The requirements for qualifying as a beneficiary should be sensitive not just to the needs of victims (...), but also to their possibilities. The more demanding the evidentiary requirements, the more false claims will be excluded; but so will perfectly legitimate claims, preventing the programme from achieving completeness.*

Taking these observations into account, from a purely legal point of view it seems reasonable to include both primary and secondary victims under the reparation-as-right formula. However, in situations of mass victimization this might be too ambitious and in the end raise false expectations by victims.

When providing reparation-as-symbol, or as process, the entitlements and the needs of communities affected by mass violence can be addressed, thereby including all three victim categories and depending on the form of reparation, also the community at large. Many conflicts are characterized by, as Roht-Arriaza calls it, shades of grey (2006, 4), whereby in the aftermath society (often through trials) tries to divide the population into a small group of guilty parties and an innocent majority, which was thereby cleansed of wrongdoing. Rama Mani (2005, 69) argued that

> *by ignoring (...) vast categories of society but creating deep and often fallacious and misleading distinctions between people defined solely in terms of victims and perpetrators, transitional justice as currently practiced divides and alienates. What is needed in the aftermath of conflict and political crisis for a peaceful and just transition is a more inclusive notion that encompasses all parts of society whatever their past role/s during the conflict or crisis. It is a notion based on all individuals within society defined collectively as "survivors" rather than victims, perpetrators or beneficiaries and bystanders.*

Rombouts for her part describes the differences in approach between the South-African and Rwandan reparation regime. The conception of victim in South-Africa is evidence of a holistic conflict approach, where in Rwanda a more segmental conflict approach is adopted (2004, 360). According to Fletcher and Weinstein (2002, 581)

> *there is a collective nature to mass violence that challenges the validity of the construct of the innocent bystander. The literature on social psychology suggests that individual action or inaction is influenced profoundly by social context, particularly in situations of conflict. This leads up to the question whether the consequences of collective violence*

---

[27]   UNHCHR, *Rule-of-Law Tools for Post-Conflict States; Reparations Programmes*, HR/PUB/08/1, 2008, p. 17, relating to evidentiary requirements.

can be effectively addressed without attending to the collective as a unit of analysis. In addition, at 605, they assert that *we find evidence to support the proposition that there is communal engagement with mass violence and this dimension is not addressed by individualized criminal trials. Work of social psychologists forces us to rethink the question of collective responsibility.*

Another important aspect to take into account is that within the course of the same conflict groups and individuals may switch roles over time: a victim one day might turn perpetrator the next in a perceived struggle for survival (see also Smeulers, this volume):

> *As the OAU eminent panel documented, in Rwanda many ordinary dutiful Hutus were galvanised to slaughter their Tutsi neighbours by propaganda urging them to exterminate the Tutsi enemy before they were exterminated themselves. Children forced to commit atrocities in war, as in Sierra Leone and Uganda, are as much victims as perpetrators. In such situations to draw a categorical dividing line between victims and survivors is often both erroneous and divisive.* (Rama Mani 2005, 67)

Devising reparation measures in these contexts is therefore a difficult if not sometimes impossible task, especially if it entails categorizing individuals or groups in beneficiaries or victimized groups. Reparative measures in these contexts should therefore aim to be as inclusive as possible, thereby recognizing the tremendous harm suffered by different individuals and groups in society.[28]

5. SECOND CHALLENGE – INDIVIDUAL VERSUS COLLECTIVE REPARATIONS

As already mentioned and as situations of repression, conflict and abuse dramatically bear out, mass victimization poses great challenges to societies so as to repair the harm inflicted on people. Harm is understood in a material and immaterial sense and people comprise individual human beings and collectivities. In such situations different and seemingly opposing considerations and factors may play a role, such as on the one hand the legal and moral consideration to make reparations complete and inclusive with respect to all victims, and on the other hand the policy factor where to draw lines of

---

[28] See in this regard also: UNHCHR, *Rule-of-Law Tools for Post-Conflict States; Reparations Programmes*, HR/PUB/08/1, 2008, where a further elaboration is given of the notions of inclusiveness and completeness. See a recent report of the International Center of Transitional Justice in which the regulations governing the distribution of reparations to victims of the apartheid era in the form of medical and educational benefits is criticized (at http://ictj.org/news/south-africa-new-reparations-plan-embitters-many-victims?utm_source=Internationa l+Center+for+Transitional+Justice+Newsletter&utm_campaign=739f317712-World_Report_ Issue_1_June_20116_8_2011&utm_medium=email, May 2011.

demarcation in view of the large number of victims. Approaches to afford adequate, fair and rightful reparation to victims may differ. In the reparation-as-right formula legal and judicial means prevail, as reflected in the Reparation Principles and the Impunity Principles. However, the reparation-as-right approach in no way rules out non-judicial schemes and programmes offering redress and reparation for the benefit of large numbers of victims. The reparation-as-symbol approach is, generally speaking, not geared towards legal action but inspired by considerations of morality and compassion. Thus, a broad scala of reparation programmes may be introduced and made operative as transitional justice processes and mechanisms (see also Correa, this volume).

5.1. INDIVIDUAL (LEGAL) APPROACH TO REPARATIONS

In order to grasp the individual perspective in the reparation debate, some words on its historic origin seem appropriate. Considering the number of books and articles written on this topic, we shall be brief and only highlight the most important issues relevant for our argumentation.

As the result of an international normative process, the legal basis for a right to a remedy and reparation became firmly anchored in the elaborate framework of international human rights' instruments, now widely ratified by States (Van Boven 2009, 21; Shelton 2008, 12).[29] Traditionally, under international law, States were held accountable only for what they did directly or through an agent, rendering acts of purely private individuals outside the scope of state responsibility (see Articles 1 and 2 of the ILC Draft Articles on State Responsibility). Articles 31–34 prescribe the content of reparations (see for a commentary Kerbrat, in Crawford *et al.* 2010, 573 ff). Article 31 notes that:

1. The responsible State is under an obligation to make full reparation for the injury caused by the internationally wrongful act.
2. Injury includes any damage, whether material or moral, caused by the internationally wrongful act of a State.

Article 34 lists the various forms of reparation, namely restitution, compensation and satisfaction, either singly or in combination. More recently, the concept of

---

[29] See specifically Article 8 of the Universal Declaration of Human Rights, Articles 2(3), 9(5) and 14(6) of the International Covenant on Civil and Political Rights, Article 39 of the Convention on the Rights of a Child., Article 14 of the Convention against Torture and Other Cruel, Inhuman or Degrading Treatment or Punishment, Articles 5(5), 13 and 41 of the European Convention for the Protection of Human Rights and Fundamental Freedoms, and Articles 25, 68 and 63(1) of the Inter-American Convention on Human Rights as well as Article 21(2) of the African Charter on Human and People's Rights.

state responsibility has expanded. Nowadays, obligations assumed by a State under international human rights and humanitarian law entail legal consequences not only vis-à-vis other States but also with respect to individuals and groups of persons who are under the jurisdiction of the State. The understanding of state responsibility for the acts of private actors, even though clearly developed in international human rights law, is not as such reflected in international public law in general. This is also evidenced from the work of the International Law Commission that drafted the Articles on State Responsibility. During the Articles' long development process, much of the action in international law in the field of determining state responsibilities shifted to specialized regimes, such as regional human rights bodies. Many have by now their own *lex specialis* on responsibility. This increasing specialization and fragmentation of international law will influence the ILC project of elaborating a general law of state responsibility (Bodansky & Crook 2002).

In international academic fora, intensive debates are being held whether individuals have a legal right to claim individual reparation under international law. Seibert-Fohr (2009, 246) notes that

> *although recent developments under the international human rights treaties and the provisions on reparations for victims in the Rome Statute (Article 75) all provide evidence that there are emerging principles, in the absence of further State practice it is too early to speak of a rule of general international law providing the individual with a right to claim compensation for human rights violations.*

On the other hand, Hofmann, rapporteur of the ILA Committee on Reparations for Victims of Armed Conflicts[30] notes that

> *in view of the relevant state practice and taking note of a strong majority among scholars, the Committee came to the conclusion that, until most recently, international law did not provide for any right to reparation for victims of armed conflicts. The Committee submits, however, that the situation is changing: There are increasing examples of international bodies proposing, or even recognising, the existence of, or the need to establish, such a right.*

In this situation, the ILA Committee on Reparations to Victims of Armed Conflicts decided to draft a Declaration which is reflecting international law as it is progressively developing. The Reparation Principles, the Impunity Principles and the Chicago Principles on Post-Conflict Justice (Principle 3) are further evidence of such development. A right to reparation has also emerged in international criminal law (De Brouwer & Heikkilä 2012, forthcoming). Article 75 of the Rome Statute stipulates that the court may award reparation while

---

[30] International Law Association, *The Hague Conference, Reparation for Victims of Armed Conflict*, 2010, at 2; available through www.ila-hq.org/en/committees/index.cfm/cid/1018.

taking into account the scope and extent of any damage, injury and loss occurred (Zegveld 2010).

Nevertheless, there are still considerable difficulties for victims of international crimes to access effective and enforceable remedies and reparations for the harm they suffered (Falk in De Greiff, 491). Only few reparations have actually been paid in the aftermath of mass atrocities (Roht-Arriaza 2003–2004). Mere codification of this general overarching right in various national and international instruments is just a first step. A process of consistent implementation of and compliance with the various rights embodied under this general principle is one of the biggest challenges of the future (Tomuschat 1999, 161). So far, analytical strength did not find a response in operational strategies (Van Boven 1995). Whereas States are willing to ratify international or regional instruments, it appears more complex when it comes to truly granting remedies to the victims of a breach of an international obligation. The 2010 ILA Declaration added a provision on obligations for States aiming to strengthen the rights of victims in that regard. Article 11 notes:

1. Responsible parties shall make every effort to give effect to the rights of victims to reparation.
2. They shall establish programmes and maintain institutions to facilitate access to reparation, including possible programmes addressed to persons affected by armed conflicts other than the victims defined in this Declaration.

As the commentary to this provision notes "taking account of the dissociation of rights and enforcement mechanisms in international law, this provision represents a necessary complement to the victims' rights to reparation (…)".

Scholars and international lawyers question whether such a rule of general international law would be desirable in every case. Quoting Seibert-Fohr again (2009, 244),

> especially in case of past large-scale human rights abuses, the reconstruction of a democratic government can be jeopardized if there is a right of every victim to claim adequate compensation. Such a right would give rise to an extensive financial burden for the new government.

The UN report on implementing guidelines of reparation seems to acknowledge this by noting that

> while, under international law, gross violations of human rights and serious violations of international humanitarian law give rise to a right to reparation for victims, implying a duty on the State to make reparations, implementing this right and corresponding duty is in essence a matter of domestic law and policy. In this respect, national Governments possess a good deal of discretion and flexibility. (…) The Basic

Principles and Guidelines are to serve as a source of inspiration, as an incentive, and as a tool for victim-oriented policies and practices.[31]

Indeed, we would say, the limits of the juridical individual approach become clear if we take into account the magnitude of harm done, especially when directed at a large class of victims and in societies in the setting of transitions to democracy, and also taking into account the difficulties in conceptualizing victimhood as discussed in section 4. This makes it impractical to evaluate individual claims on a case-by-case basis in most instances, and therefore might not be consistent with the international law approach based on the individual that is embedded in human rights law (Falk 2006, 495). With regard to international crimes, this is in many cases unrealistic. A scarcity of resources often makes it unfeasible to satisfy the claims of all victims. As put by De Greiff, "the capacity of the State to redress victims on a case-by-case basis is overtaken when the violations cease to be the exception and become frequent" (2006, 454). On the other hand, we should not forget that

> *international law has also contributed to a generalized atmosphere of support, a reparations ethos, for compensating victims as part of its overall dedication to global justice and the enforcement of claims, and thus lends support to the domestic willingness to provide reparations when contextual factors are favourable.* (Falk 2006, 497)

The question thus poses itself whether in situations where mass atrocities have occurred reparative justice may be better served by collective measures rather than by litigation and decisions on individual claims. The rationale is twofold; the number of victims is often so high which, combined with a lack of resources, makes a collective approach more realistic. In addition, the communal aspect of violence is important to underscore in any reparation programme. The overall social context of gross and systematic violations is different compared to cases of individual human rights violations because often the entire population is victimized (see also Shelton 2008, 389 ff; Saris & Lofts 2009, 84). The work of Fletcher and Weinstein (2002) also suggests that communal actions may require communal responses (at 612), also when implementing reparations programmes when the aim is to achieve social repair.

5.2. COLLECTIVE REPARATION; LATITUDES AND LIMITS

On the other hand, from an individual human rights perspective a purely collective approach may be problematic. Much depends on how concrete

---

[31]   UNHCHR, *Rule-of-Law Tools for Post-Conflict States; Reparations Programmes*, HR/PUB/08/1, 2008, p. 14.

meaning is given to "adequate, effective and prompt reparation for harm suffered".[32] As generally assumed in connection with the Reparation Principles, there are no 'one size fits all' solutions to reparative justice. The Reparation Principles provide a good deal of latitude in affording reparations, as is implied in such terms as "taking into account of individual circumstances" and "as appropriate".[33] While perceptions and policies of reparation are mostly discussed and understood in monetary terms, the importance of non-monetary forms of reparation, referred to above as 'symbolic reparations', must be appreciated as forms of rendering satisfaction. Acknowledgement of harm inflicted and suffered and attribution of responsibility for grave abuses are important steps on the path of reparative justice but cannot be considered a mere substitute for restitutional measures and compensatory schemes. Further, any margins or latitudes in shaping reparative policies and programmes may never ignore the principle of non-discrimination and non-exclusion as stipulated in the Reparation Principles.[34] Another basic consideration is the principle of equal and effective access to justice as a right of victims. The most vulnerable segments among victimized groups and persons often lack the knowledge and the means and encounter many obstacles depriving them of access to reparation to which they are entitled (Van Boven 2007).

Social psychologists have also reflected on the "competing and often diverging psychological needs of the individual and the society with regards to making reparations" (Hamber 1998c, 1). In a paper with Wilson (1999), Hamber warns that psychologising the nation is problematic. The authors caution against the subordination of individual needs to the exigencies of national unity and reconciliation, and suggest that there may be many divergences between individual psychological processes and national processes such as truth commissions. At the same time, they recognise that the two are in some ways closely bound, as evidenced by the psychological importance for some of speaking in public at the TRC hearings (See further also Haldemann and Peacock, both this volume).

5.3. COLLECTIVE REPARATION; AFFIRMATION AND ASSERTION

In situations where gross and massive violations of human rights have occurred and the abuses constituted crimes under international law, adequate and effective reparation may well imply and require a resort to collective redress and collective means of reparation. Already in the early stages of the preparation of the

---

[32] Reparation Principles, principle 11 (b).
[33] Reparation Principles, principle 18.
[34] Reparation Principles, principle 25.

Reparation Principles attention was paid to individuals and collectivities as victims and it was submitted that, in addition to individual means of reparation, adequate provision be made to entitle groups of victims or victimized communities to present collective claims and to receive collective reparation accordingly. In this connection it was mentioned that the coincidence of individual and collective aspects is particularly manifest with regard to the rights of indigenous peoples.[35] While in the drafting process and negotiations of the Reparation Principles, the notion of collective reparation was contested as at variance with the premise that the right to reparation was *per se* a right of individual victims, this view did not prevail. Thus, the Reparation Principles refer, in addition to individual access to justice, to groups of victims to present claims and receive reparation.[36] The acknowledgement of the victimological notion of collective victimhood makes this instrument conceptually truly innovative. The Preamble explicitly notes that "contemporary forms of victimization, while essentially directed against persons, may nevertheless also be directed against groups of persons who are targeted collectively".

In a similar vein, the Impunity Principles refer to individuals and communities to whom reparations programmes may be addressed.[37] However, neither the Reparation Principles nor the Impunity Principles spell out the meaning of collective reparations. In this regard the 2008 United Nations publication on Reparations Programmes, published in the series of Rule of Law Tools for Post-Conflict States, is lucid and informative. It argues that the term 'collective' applies to reparative measures and types of goods and services made available by way of reparations but may also aim at a victimized group or community as the beneficiary of reparations. Symbolic reparations, such as public apology and setting up memorials, are collective forms of satisfaction extended to victimized groups or communities. But also the provision of material goods and services so as to restore decent living conditions, and to secure health and educational facilities, may serve as a mode of collective reparation.[38]

Besides their inclusion in the Reparation and Impunity Principles, the concept of collective reparation has been less explored compared to individuals' claims for reparation. Still, there are some developments that indicate that international law endorses collective reparation (Rosenfeld 2010; Dubinsky 2004; Roht-Arriaza 2004; Lapante 2007). In the 2010 ILA commentary to the Draft

---

[35] Theo van Boven, Special Rapporteur, Final Report, *Study concerning the right to restitution, compensation and rehabilitation for victims of gross violations of human rights and fundamental freedoms*, UN doc. E/CN.4/Sub.2/1993/8, paras. 14–15.

[36] Reparation Principles, principle 13.

[37] Impunity Principles, principle 32.

[38] A notable example is provided in the *Case of Aloeboetoe et al. v. Suriname*, where the Inter-American Court of Human Rights ordered the Government of Suriname to reopen and staff a school and to make a medical unit operational as an act of reparation for the deadly attack on twenty members of the indigenous Saramaka tribe (Judgement of 10 September 1993, Ser. C. No. 15).

Declaration on Reparation to Victims of Armed conflicts,[39] several references can be found to case law of the Inter-American Court of Human Rights where collective reparations were awarded (Hofmann 2010, 19). In *Moiwana v. Suriname* the Court held the following:

> *Given that the victims of the present case are members of the N'duka culture, this Tribunal considers that the individual reparations to be awarded must be supplemented by communal measures; said reparations will be granted to the community as a whole.*[40]

The ILA Commentary also refers to recommendations from several Truth Commissions. Examples include the recommendations of the truth commissions for Peru,[41] Guatemala,[42] Sierra Leona,[43] and Timor-Leste.[44] Collective reparations are also endorsed by the Rules of Procedure and Evidence of the ICC which stipulate that the Court may order reparation "on a collective basis" and that, where appropriate, a "collective award" can be made through the Trust Fund (Articles 75 and 79.1).

The ILA report[45] claims that there is considerable State practice supporting the view that the non-performance of the obligation to make full reparation might be justified in immediate post-conflict situations. The Ethiopia Eritrea Claims Commission, for example, held:

> *[T]he Commission could not disregard the possibility that large damages awards might exceed the capacity of the responsible State to pay or result in serious injury to its population if such damages were paid. It thus considered whether it was necessary to limit its compensation awards in some manner to ensure that the ultimate financial burden imposed on a Party would not be so excessive, given its economic condition and its capacity to pay, as to compromise its ability to meet its people's basic needs.*

---

[39] International Law Association, *The Hague Conference, Reparation for Victims of Armed Conflict, including a Draft Declaration of International Law Principles on Reparation for Victims of Armed Conflict*, 2010; available through www.ila-hq.org/en/committees/index. cfm/cid/1018.

[40] IACtHR, *Case of the Moiwana Community v. Suriname*, Judgement of June 15, 2005 (Preliminary Objections, Merits, Reparations and Costs), para. 194.

[41] Peruvian Truth and Reconciliation Commission, Plan of Integral Reparations (PIR), June 2003, para. 3.6, available at: www.cverdad.org.pe/.

[42] Guatemala, Memory of Silence, Report of the Commission for Historical Clarification, Conclusions and Recommendations, III, para. 10, available at: http://shr.aaas.org/guatemala/ceh/report/english/toc.html.

[43] Final Report of the Truth & Reconciliation Commission of Sierra Leone, Vol. 2, Chapter 4, Reparations, para. 27, available at:http://trcsierraleone.org/.

[44] Chegal, Report of the Commission for Reception, Truth and Reconciliation in Timor-Leste (CAVR), available at: www.cavrtimorleste.org/en/chegaReport.htm.

[45] International Law Association, *The Hague Conference, Reparation for Victims of Armed Conflict, including a Draft Declaration of International Law Principles on Reparation for Victims of Armed Conflict*, 2010, at 20; available through www.ila-hq.org/en/committees/index.cfm/cid/1018.

In support of this approach, it pointed at human rights considerations as well as the function of reparation, emphasizing that reparation has a remedial and not a punitive function.

Considering the collective nature of international crimes, or in some cases human rights violations in general, several Governments have set up specific reparation programmes providing forms of redress to victims. It is beyond the scope of this contribution to go into a detailed discussion of the specifics of these programmes (see further Correa, this volume). The Handbook edited by Pablo de Greiff (2006) provides an excellent resource with case studies on several programmes. It suffices to say that they vary as to what kind of measures they take (individual or collective) and who takes responsibility for the design. History shows examples where Truth and Reconciliation Commissions recommend what kind of measures should be taken and who the beneficiaries are (think of South-Africa, Guatemala), whereas in other cases government institutions or self-standing reparations committees or procedures were set up (Brazil, Germany, Malawi, Morocco).

6. THIRD CHALLENGE – LINKING REPARATIVE JUSTICE TO DEVELOPMENT AID

6.1. HUMAN SECURITY AND REPARATIVE JUSTICE

For some time now, discussions are held whether transitional or reparative justice initiatives should include also specific development aims that target not only the victimized groups but the community at large. We have seen that individual reparative measures can include providing housing, social services or other socio-economic benefits (think of pensions). Until recently, collective reparative measures mostly entailed symbolic reparation such as a public apology or organizing commemorations. The ICC Trust Fund has recently awarded collective reparations to victims' group that benefit the larger community as well.[46]

What becomes clear also from closely reading the Reparation Principles is that the focus is not merely on justice mechanisms. Especially measures relating to satisfaction and guarantees of non-repetition have a wide scope and will involve substantial resources. The idea behind it is to offer as much as possible a comprehensive approach in offering redress to victims. This ties in closely with the promoted concept of human security. Human security, as argued by one of its apostles, former Canadian Minister of Foreign Affairs Lloyd Axworthy, is "in essence, an effort to construct a global society where the safety of the individual

---

[46] For an update on their projects, see www.trustfundforvictims.org/.

is at the centre of international priorities and a motivating force for international action".[47] Three main reports form the basis for the human security concept as it stands today: the *Human Development Report* issued by the UN Development Programme (1994), *Human Security Now* (2003) drafted by the Independent Commission on Human Security (initiated by Japan), and *Human Security Report, War and Peace in the 21st Century* by the Human Security Centre of the University of British Columbia in Canada (2005).[48] Whereas its predecessor, the concept of human development, exclusively focused on the right to a long and healthy life, education and access to health care, human security adds the right to live free of violations of human rights, criminal acts and political violence. It highlights the interrelationships between the threats of global crimes and other security risks such as those of extreme poverty or health. The human security concept thus tries to complement other related notions. For example, many of the existing human rights, such as the right to food and the right to education, are part of the holistic approach the human security concept aims to promote.[49] Other notions which the human security concept aims to combine are those of national security, the previous mentioned concept of human development and humanitarian intervention such as the concept of 'responsibility to protect.'[50] Human security aims to overcome the compartmentalization of these other notions (Letschert 2010; Bodelier 2010).[51]

The concept aims to systematically and coherently address the various threats[52] to the security of human beings. It is a concept that comprehensively

---

[47]   Lloyd Axworthy talks to *Canada World View*. www.dfait-maeci.gc.ca/canada-magazine/special/se1t3-en.asp.

[48]   Commission on Human Security, *Human Security Now, Final Report*, New York, 2003, p. 4. As the forward of the report makes it clear (pages iv-v), the said commission was inspired by the 2000 UN Millennium Summit; funded by Japan under UN facilitation. UNDP, 'New dimensions of human security', *Human Development Report 1994*. Human Security Centre (HSC), *Human Security Report 2005: War and Peace in the 21st Century*, University of British Columbia, Canada, New York/Oxford, Oxford University Press, 2005.

[49]   In addition, the often proclaimed specific characteristics of human rights, being universal, interdependent and interrelated, are also reflected upon in the human security debate. The 1994 Human Development Report, for instance, notes that human security is a universal concern, of which the components are interdependent. UNDP, *Human Development Report*, 1994, New Dimensions of Human Security, New York, Oxford University Press, p. 22.

[50]   For a description of the similarities and differences between these notions, see Tadjbakhsh & Chenoy 2007.

[51]   There is still discussion how wide the scope of human security should be. The narrow approach limits it to violent threats to individuals from internal violence (an approach promoted by Canada), while the broad approach also includes threats like hunger, disease and natural disaster (as promoted in the UNDP Human Development Report of 1994 or by the Government of Japan). The wide approach of the human security concept aims to include under its scope each and every individual living in each and every country; everyone means the women who survived the multiple rapes in Rwanda, but also the single mother living in a dangerous neighbourhood in New York, or the business man residing in Tokyo.

[52]   Note that the meaning of the word 'threat' also includes helping countries to recover from conflicts. See also Human Security Now. Protecting and Empowering People. Commission

addresses both 'freedom from fear' and 'freedom from want'. It aims to deal with the capacity to identify threats and the underlying interdependencies, prevent them when possible and mitigate their effects when they do occur. In order to do so, a wide range of actors as potential providers of security and protection need to be involved, multiplying the opportunities for coordinated, international responses within a normative framework as well as for new institutional arrangements.[53]

Its relevance to the field of victimology and reparative justice is that human security claims to be people-oriented, thereby moving away from the State-centred approach that we see in traditional security debates (Tadjbakhsh & Chenoy 2007, 238). The individual human being is not only defined in terms of vulnerabilities, but also as someone who is capable of affecting change, that is, of empowering him or herself. Both elements of protection and empowerment play an important role.[54] Emphasis is therefore placed on a bottom-up approach: on communication, consultation, dialogue and partnership with the local population in order to improve early warning, intelligence gathering, the mobilization of local support, implementation and sustainability.[55] The emphasis is thus on the strength of individuals, particularly relevant to the human security debate in the sense that it prioritizes people above institutions. This actor-oriented approach forms a sharp contrast to established approaches in the national security domain that often present people as passive victims of violence or merely recipients of emergency relief.

By conceptualizing reparation or reparative justice not only as an individual right but also as a symbol or process (see section 3), emphasis is put on the role that reparations play in the complex transition out of a period of mass crimes and human rights violations, for individuals and society. In facilitating this process, reparations should aim to be both participatory and empowering (see also Saris & Lofts 2009).[56] Next to the participatory aspect, providing a comprehensive set of reparative measures is just as important. As Fletcher and Weinstein (2002, 623) describe

one of the consequences of mass violence is that the social fabric of a society is torn apart. Despite the fact that the prior social arrangements may not have guaranteed adequate respect and protection of human rights, there was a measure of stability. Yet

---

on Human Security. Washington 2003: "cease-fire agreements and peace-settlements mark the end of violent conflict, but they do not ensure peace and human security", p. 57.

[53]   For critical remarks regarding the concept, see Letschert 2010; Paris 2001.

[54]   See also the Barcelona Report of the Study Group on Europe's Security Capabilities,' A Human Security Doctrine for Europe, Barcelona, 15 September 2004, executive summary.

[55]   "A key consideration must also be how, if and where possible, to involve the individual in the promotion of his/her own human security after all; individual empowerment is both a means as well as an objective of human security." Tadjbakhsh & Chenoy 2007, 238.

[56]   See also UNHCHR, *Rule-of-Law Tools for Post-Conflict States; Reparations Programmes*, HR/PUB/08/1, 2008, 15.

the destabilization brought about by mass violence is so profound that the old ways are no longer viable options. Thus, social and institutional arrangements in this new era may not necessarily duplicate those prevailing during the pre-conflict period. Rather than reconstruction, peace and stability require construction of new societal structures and relationships.

Following their analysis, this process of social reconstruction should consist of multiple approaches, consisting of the following elements: 1. justice initiatives; 2. democracy; 3. economic prosperity and transformation and 4. reconciliation. Fletscher and Weinstein's ecological model of responses to social breakdown demonstrates the different elements that need to be addressed in order for any reparation measure to have lasting effects. Such a comprehensive approach to address threats is also encouraged by the human security concept (see also on the different elements in providing reparative justice Danieli 2009).

Some prioritization is of course necessary. Already in 1968, Maslow developed his pyramid of needs. Taking a closer look at these needs, we can argue that he was not far away from promoting a human security concept (Maslows' needs theory was also applied to victims of international crimes by Wemmers & De Brouwer 2010). According to Maslow, people first have to satisfy their basic needs such as food and shelter as well as medical care. Often victims have lost their house, their family and are unable to work due to injuries suffered as a result of the victimization. These victims will, in the first place, need urgent medical care for their injuries as well as food and a place to stay. In addition, immediate trauma counselling is of utmost importance. However, Becker *et al.* argue that "victims know that individual therapeutic intervention is not enough. They need to know that their society as a whole acknowledges what has happened to them" (1990, 174).

The second level of needs identified by Maslow is safety. People need to feel safe and secure. The third and fourth levels of needs are a feeling of belonging or affection and self-esteem. Informal support can provide victims with a sense of feeling loved and accepted which in a conflict setting is often difficult to realise because of the many casualties within families and communities. The fifth need of self-actualization is the last stage, and according to Maslow only achievable if all the other needs are satisfied. While Maslow's hierarchy of needs was developed independent of both human security and victimology, it is important to note the convergence between the needs identified by Maslow and those of victims of international crimes (Wemmers & De Brouwer 2010; Letschert 2010). Both Amartya Sen and Martha Nussbaum, two prominent human security scholars, closely touch upon Maslow's ideas with their capabilities theory (Nussbaum & Sen 1993). Lastly, also Fletcher and Weinstein argued, referring to Maslow's theory, that *reconciliation – which requires empathy, forgiveness, and altruism – draws on higher order manifestations of need that cannot be addressed until the more basic needs are satisfied. An ecological model addresses this dynamic by assuring that attention is paid to these multiple levels of unsatisfied need both at an individual and community level.* (2002, 625)

6.2. LINKING REPARATIVE JUSTICE AND DEVELOPMENT GOALS

Several academics argued that transitional justice without a focus on socio-economic development would not achieve the goals it aims for (Miller 2008; Carranza 2008). Miller wrote that the separation of development strategies from transitional justice "allows a myth to be formed that the origins of conflict are political or ethnic rather than economic or resource based" (Miller 2008, 267–268). Others argued that even without a specific focus on social and economic development, transitional justice initiatives will undoubtedly also affect such development by creating conditions that may facilitate development. Duthie noted that

such measures as individual and collective reparations, property restitution, rehabilitation, and reintegrating victims and perpetrators (...) may alleviate marginalization, exclusion, and vulnerability by bringing people and groups into the economy, recognizing and empowering them as citizens, and perhaps generating economic activity. (Duthie 2009, 20)

While in societies that have been struck by gross and massive violations of human rights, collective reparations focusing also on development aid can be considered a possible and effective means to achieve a fair degree of reparative justice, such an approach is not without perils. One such problem is that what is being offered by way of reparation, for instance basic social services is to be provided anyway to all citizens as an entitlement under general human rights law (Rombouts, Sardaro & Vandeginste 2005). Reparations are a means to achieve justice for the benefit of individual and collective victims by redressing harm done to them but they are no substitute for meeting targets that are pursued on other grounds. This also poses the question of the relationship between reparation programmes and development programmes. Both 'developing' and 'developed' countries may prefer for expeditious policy reasons to avoid honouring obligations arising from the duty to afford reparations. 'Developing' countries facing demands for reparations are inclined to argue that development *is* reparation. Similarly, 'developed' countries that are called upon to repair historical wrongs (slavery and colonialism), argue that compensatory measures are not the appropriate means for redressing historical injustice, but that instead greater development efforts are needed to achieve a more just and equitable distribution of wealth and resources, in particular vis-à-vis disadvantaged, deprived and systematically injured groups.[57] It is enticing indeed to make a shift from reparation to development. Complex and agonizing issues of accountability are being avoided as well as troublesome classifications of people, as victims and as perpetrators. Such expeditious policy considerations appear to be attractive but they fail to recognize the essential notion of reparation as constituting part of a process towards peace, justice and reconciliation. They also fail to acknowledge a victim-oriented perspective that keeps faith with the plight of victims and survivors (Saris & Loft 2009, 90).[58] Quite significantly the Nairobi *Declaration on Women's and Girls' Right to a Remedy and Reparation* distances itself from development as a substitute for reparation. It urges the retention of reparation programmes but as an integral part of reconstruction and development programmes. The relevant section of the Nairobi Declaration reads:

> *Governments should not undertake development instead of reparation. All post-conflict societies need both reconstruction and development, of which reparation programmes are an integral part. Victims, especially women and girls, face particular obstacles in seizing the opportunities provided by development, thus risking their continued exclusion. In reparation, reconstruction and development programmes, affirmative action measures are necessary to respond to the needs and experiences of those women and girls.[59]*

7. VICTIMS' PERSPECTIVES ON REPARATIONS

Several surveys conducted in the last decade have analysed victims' perspectives on reparations. The Human Rights Centre of Berkeley University analysed victims' perspectives on different forms of reparations. Surveys were, for instance, carried out in DR-Congo, Cambodia and Northern Uganda. In the Northern Uganda survey (Pham, Vingh, Stover 2007) respondents were asked "what should be done for victims". Direct compensation to individuals was the

---

[57]   Netherlands Advisory Council on International Affairs, *The World Conference against Racism and the Right to Reparation*, Report No. 22, June 2001.

[58]   Also UNHCHR, *Rule-of-Law Tools for Post-Conflict States; Reparations Programmes*, HR/PUB/08/1, 2008, p. 26.

[59]   See also Brooks 1999, 89: "Japan's approach to monetary redress in fact turned out to be controversial. The Government set up the 'Asian Women's' Fund' which is funded by donations from private individuals and organisations and does not pay compensation to individual survivors but rather is used to improve the conditions of all the women. This attempt at a community rehabilitative approach has been severely criticised by survivors. They have argued that it is a welfare-type system based on socio-economic need rather than on moral restitution, and thus fails to take responsibility for the wrongs committed."

most common answer, including financial compensation (52%), food (9%), and livestock/cattle (8%). Equal numbers (7%) mentioned counselling and education for children. Apologies, justice, or reconciliation were mentioned by 10 percent of respondents. Ninety-five percent of respondents said they wanted memorials to be established to remember what happened in Northern Uganda during the war (2007, 10 and 33). The Congo survey revealed that victims mostly wanted

> *material compensation, including money (40%), housing (28%), food (28%), and other material compensation (40%). Most respondents said such reparations should be provided to both individuals and the community as a whole (43%); 35 percent said it should be for individuals only, and 22 percent for the community only. One out of five considered that punishing those responsible should be done for the victims, and 17 percent indicated that an official recognition of the victims' suffering would also be important.* (Vinck et al. 2008, 52)

In March 2011, a Report of the Panel on Remedies and Reparations for Victims of Sexual Violence in the DRC was submitted to the UN High Commissioner for Human Rights.[60] Victims foremost expressed their need for health care and education, focussing on socio-economic reintegration programmes. Also, the need for recognition and acknowledgment of the enormous suffering was repeatedly expressed, for instance through public apologies, monuments and other forms of tribute. Some information on collective reparations is provided in the report. The panel noted that some of the victims who obtained court judgments expressed concern that collective reparations will benefit everyone, and not particularly those who were victimized.[61] The Panel gave as main reason the toll that their individual cases have taken on them.

In Cambodia, the ECCC judges have the authority to rule that only reparations of a collective, symbolic, and moral – but not financial – nature be provided to certain groups of victims (i.e., civil parties) (see further De Brouwer & Heikkilä 2012, forthcoming). Such reparations could include building statues, memorials, renaming public facilities, establishing days of remembrance, expunging criminal records, issuing declarations of death, exhuming bodies, and conducting reburials. Following a survey conducted in 2009,

> *the vast majority of our respondents (88%) said reparations should be provided to victims of the Khmer Rouge, and that they should be provided to the community as a whole (68%). Over half (53%) said reparations should be in a form that affects the daily lives of Cambodians, including social services (20%), infrastructure development (15%), economic development programs (12%), housing and land (5%), and provision of livestock, food, and agriculture tools (1%).*

---

[60]   UNHCHR, *Report of the Panel on Remedies and Reparations for Victims of Sexual Violence in the Democratic Republic of Congo to the High Commissioner for Human Rights*, 2011.

[61]   *Idem*, p. 50.

Based on these results, it was recommended to

> recognize that the vast majority of Cambodians view themselves as direct or indirect
> victims of the Khmer Rouge and desire some form of collective and symbolic reparations.
> Why this is a pressing issue for the ECCC is reflected in the finding that most
> respondents said it was more important for the country to focus on problems
> Cambodians face in their daily lives than the crimes committed by the Khmer Rouge.
> This suggests that the ECCC must find ways to ground its activities in the current
> concerns and needs of the population. Providing reparations – especially those aimed
> at providing social services and infrastructure development – could help meet this need.
> (Pham et al. 2009, 4, 6)

Research on the perspectives of victims of the South-African Apartheid regime
towards reparations also demonstrated the difficulty of establishing what victims
need in terms of reparations because victims' perspectives change over time (the
surveys were carried out by the Centre for the Study of Violence and
Reconciliation). One of the tasks of the South African Truth and Reconciliation
Committee (TRC) was to implement measures aimed at the granting of
reparation to, and the rehabilitation and restoration of the dignity of, victims of
violation, and to this end, a Reparations and Rehabilitation Committee was
established (see further Peacock, this volume). In 1998 a first survey was
conducted. The report found

> that a majority of participants regarded reconciliation and reparation as integrally
> linked, and that there would be no resolution without some form of reparation. Also of
> concern were the ongoing psychological problems of survivors and the lack of
> mechanisms for their continuing support. Participants generally were in favour of
> symbolic reparation to help do away with the legacy of the past.[62]

The second CSVR paper (2000) analyses the views of survivors on reparation two
years after the TRC final report. Here the authors note a shift in perceptions:

> at the time of the first study, people thought about reparation primarily in terms of
> their immediate needs arising from the traumas suffered, for example medical
> treatment, reburial of bodies or erecting of tombstones. The idea of restitution was
> seldom expressed, and the authors suggest that it was beyond the belief of most that the
> damage could be repaired or that they could be returned to the financial position they
> had lost. Feelings of entitlement to restitution or demands for large sums of money were
> not usually expressed. However, according to the second piece of research, the passage
> of time, combined with the treatment of both victims and perpetrators, led to a change
> in victims' attitudes toward and expectations of reparation. In particular, seeing the
> granting of amnesties and legal assistance to perpetrators while most victims had no

---

[62]   Quoted in Redress, *Torture Survivors' Perceptions of Reparations. Preliminary Survey*, 2001,
45, www.redress.org/downloads/publications/TSPR.pdf.

assistance with their statements to the TRC, or with challenging its findings, led to a certain bitterness.[63]

The authors conclude that these factors have led to a situation where "victims now understand that it is only through reparations that there could be any sort of equity and justice resulting from the TRC process" (p. 2). Victims, it seems, are still waiting for a "fair deal" and are increasingly likely to regard reparation as the only route that may yield this.

The third piece of research relating to South-Africa is Simpson's (1998) evaluation of the TRC process. He found that the needs of victims were complex and changed over time, particularly when it came to the issue of reparation. For some, principal desire was for information; for others it was for widespread public acknowledgement of what had happened to them. Some rejected the TRC process entirely, including any form of reparation, as an inadequate substitute for punishment, and demanded "full justice"; others wanted direct confrontation with the perpetrator(s). Simpson found that the needs of some survivors were personal and private, whereas for others the goal was community-based or political vindication. He also found that needs changed over time for the same individual.[64]

8. CONCLUDING REMARKS

Whereas the three challenges discussed in this chapter are likely to be applicable to all post-conflict situations, providing general answers on how to address them in different contexts becomes more difficult. We stated already before that the need for contextualization of reparative justice processes is increasingly acknowledged. Orentlichter notes that "given the extraordinary range of national experiences and cultures, how could anyone imagine there to be a universally relevant formula for transitional justice" (2007, 18). Or "is it helpful for international law to mandate particular responses to past atrocities and thereby narrow the scope of local variation in responding to similar atrocities? Or, instead, is the best response invariably particular to each society?" (2007, 11) We would argue that the latter is the case. Increasingly, scholars argue that transitional justice initiatives should be established 'bottom down', 'from the grass root level', 'including local ownership'; an understanding also encouraged by the human security concept or the ecological model of Fletcher and Weinstein as discussed in the previous sections. This also fits into the notion of reparation-

---

[63] *Idem*, p. 46.

[64] *Ibidem.* See also Picker, R., *Victims' Perspectives about the Human Rights Violation Hearings*, Research Report Written for the Centre for the Study of Violence and Reconciliation, 2005; www.csvr.org.za/docs/humanrights/victimsperspectivshearings.pdf (last visited: 12 February 2010).

as-process where concepts such as participation and empowerment of victims take a prominent role. The brief review of victims' perceptions on reparations in the previous section also demonstrates the importance of including victims' voices in the design of reparative measures.

The idea of local ownership reflects also the increasing tendency to give due regard to tradition-based or tradition-inspired conceptions of providing justice. The chapter by Schotsman in this volume illustrates the variety of different tradition-inspired mechanisms used in countries such as Sierra Leone, Uganda and Rwanda to deal with the atrocities of the past. Differences in culture and tradition may impact upon processes of community repair that may be very different from previous applied models in other countries (Fletscher & Weinstein 2002, 633). Also relating to the inclusion of development aims similar observations are made. Higonett notes that

> post-atrocity legal structures must incorporate elements of local justice and culture or, at the very least, be sensitive to realities and norms on the ground. A useful parallel to draw here is the near universal consensus in development philosophy that local involvement is critical to sustainable long-term development. (2006, 360)

The UN Secretary-General also acknowledged that "we must learn as well to eschew one-size-fits-all formulas and the importation of foreign models, and, instead, base our support on national assessments, national participation and national needs and aspirations".[65] How, and if, such local traditions correspond to international norms merits further research (see for some research done already, Viaene & Brems 2010).

That being said, various studies reveal that it is still exceptional that transitional justice efforts, including reparative measures, are based on perceptions of future beneficiaries (Redress 2001; Pham *et al.* 2009). In addition, the impact of interventions, be it tradition-based or internationally influenced, or mixtures of both, is hardly consistently evaluated. This makes it difficult to give far-fledged or evidence-based statements regarding the short or long term effects of such measures on individual or collective groups of victims or society at large.

What appears from international (quasi) legal instruments is the need to find a balance between individual and collective and judicial and non-judicial forms of reparation. While the judicial approach to reparation characterizes the Reparation and Impunity Principles, non-judicial schemes and programmes offering redress and reparation do also contribute to reparative justice for the benefit of large number of victims. The Reparation principles also reflect this by combining individual measures intended to implement the right to reparation

---

[65]   UN SG, *The Rule of Law and Transitional Justice in Conflict and Post-Conflict Societies.* Report of the Secretary General, S2004/616, 23th August 2004.

(restitution, compensation and rehabilitation) as well as a strong focus on collective measures of satisfaction and guarantees of non-repetition.

Providing reparations to victims of international crimes is a fundamental requirement of law and morality, most directly for relieving the suffering of and affording justice to victims individually and collectively but also for the sake of healing a society whose integrity may be profoundly affected. There is a close link between the right to reparation and the right to know the truth. Verification of the facts and full and public disclosure of the truth are an important means to provide satisfaction to victims.[66] At the same time the process of linking reparations to revealing the truth forms part of the deployment of efforts to create safeguards against recurrence of violations. Guarantees of non-repetition imply a combination of looking backward and looking forward. As the UN Secretary-General stated in a report to the Security Council on transitional justice, looking backward and looking forward are inherent in processes of transitional justice in "a society's attempts to come to terms with a legacy of large-scale past abuses, in order to ensure accountability, serve justice and achieve reconciliation".[67] Reparation is imperative in situations of gross, consistent and massive violations. Consequently, the *opinio iuris* is shaping steadily and progressively towards the abolition of legal prescriptions that foster a culture of impunity and for that matter impede or adversely affect policies and programmes of reparation. Developments in that direction are encouraging, but they do not as yet represent a general *acquis*. At any rate, the requirement of squarely facing the past, opening up the truth, repairing harm done, restoring the rule of law and preventing the recurrence of abuses must be a standing assignment in implementing domestic and global reparative justice agendas.

In this chapter we discussed three main challenges which illustrate the complexities in providing reparative justice in post-conflict societies. In section 3 we presented the conceptual framework of reparation as right, as symbol and as process. Analysing reparation through such an analytical lense helps addressing the three challenges discussed in this chapter. We first discussed the difficulties in conceptualizing victimhood in post-conflict situations (challenge 1), where the demarcation between victim and perpetrator groups is not always clear-cut and which poses several complexities; not only with regard to determining who is considered eligible to reparative measures, but also with regard to assessing the possible negative impact of reparative measures on wider societal concerns such as encouraging reconciliation and (re)-constructing the socio-economic infrastructure of post-conflict societies. A distinction was made between three different groups of victims, consisting of direct victims, indirect victims such as family members, and society at large. The first two categories

---

[66]   Reparation Principles, principle 22 (b).
[67]   UNCHR, *Updated Set of Principles for the Prosecution and Promotion of Human Rights through Action to Combat Impunity*, UN doc. E/CN.4/2005/102/Add. 1, para. 8.

should be entitled to individual reparative measures. We also acknowledged, however, that implementing this right in situations with huge numbers of victims will not be realistic. The impediments mentioned in the introduction of which the economic consequences of conflicts are most apparent, will often hinder governments in guaranteeing individual reparation. Also, having individual perpetrators actually pay for reparative measures is highly unrealistic. For this reason, providing collective reparations might be a more realistic solution. We have presented arguments against and in favour of collective reparations (challenge 2). Especially the provision of symbolic reparations, such as public apology and setting up memorials, are collective forms of satisfaction which extend to victimized groups or communities. But also the provision of material goods and services so as to restore decent living conditions, and to secure health and educational facilities (thereby also including development objectives in reparative justice measures which was discussed under challenge 3), may serve as a mode of collective reparation which will not only benefit victimized communities but also has the potential to benefit society at large. Such latter measures may never stand alone; various victimological studies reveal that denying specific acknowledgment and recognition of a person's individual victimization can have negative effects on victim's recovery.

What seems to be the biggest challenge for the future therefore is how to find an appropriate balance between satisfying individual victims' needs and collective needs, not only of victim groups, but also society at large. This requires more research, whereby insights from relevant fields such as international law, development studies, traumatic stress studies, the social psychology of group conflict and resolution, and the psychology and sociology of national and international legal processes should be closely integrated.

VIII. REPARATIONS FOR VICTIMS OF MASSIVE CRIMES

Making Concrete a Message of Inclusion

Cristian CORREA*

1. INTRODUCTION

Responding to victims of massive human rights violations, violations of humanitarian law or international (criminal) law poses many challenges that require approaching the subject with a different perspective than the one used in dealing with individual or a limited number of crimes. Often the number of victims, the dimensions of the harm suffered and the challenges that accompany a transition to democracy or the end of a conflict make it impractical for a society to take an individual approach to reparations. The overall challenges of a post-conflict society in an impoverished country, such as Rwanda, require that most of the attention and efforts be focused on development and poverty alleviation. However, the needs and demands of victims must by necessity be addressed if a society is to successfully move forward. Responding to those demands are not necessarily opposed to improving the socioeconomic condition of the general population. Although no past effort can ever stand as a perfect measure for the future, especially given the diversity of contexts and conflicts, many useful lessons may nonetheless be drawn from the experiences of countries that have attempted to repair victims in contexts of transitional justice or post-conflict. This article provides some concrete examples on how to define and implement reparations for victims, not relying on judicial decisions or standards, but on policy and administrative mechanisms that work to address the most fundamental needs of victims. The examples also demonstrate the advantages of comprehensive transitional justice policies, which include establishing the crimes committed and what made them possible to happen; making a serious effort to investigate and try the most severe crimes; and reforming institutions in order to avoid repetition of such crimes. Such an approach can both provide coherence to

* The author would like to thank the substantial contribution of Elena Naughton, ICTJ fellow, in helping writing this chapter.

the reparations effort, and also demonstrates the sincerity of the state to implement them.

Reparations usually come in the form of a judicial decision, where a court or other authority recognizes the claim of a victim to receive some form of compensation from the one who caused the injury or harm. Court-based reparations require formal proffers of evidence by a claimant, establishing the harm suffered and the responsibility of the defendant. Individually-based, they require a committed claimant with enough resources to set in motion the judicial machinery and with the requisite resolve and stamina to provide the evidence required and to sustain a long battle in court. Ultimately, judicial reparations entail an individual assessment of the consequences that a particular crime had for a particular victim, and are generally understood to be complete, covering the full scope of damages and restoring the victim as nearly as possible to the *status quo ante*. Criminal justice can have an important reparatory effect even for victims not included in the incident being investigated, but since it is impossible to try and establish responsibility for every single crime committed, reparations should not depend on the success of court decisions, as will be argued later. The conditions for reaching a successful verdict hardly, if ever, exist for the massive numbers of victims of human rights violations or gross breaches of humanitarian law.

Furthermore, court-based solutions are usually inadequate. Poorer victims often face additional difficulties, accessing a court or finding the evidence required to prove harm and to establish the guilt of those responsible. Many victims are reluctant or even afraid to take on a public role as advocate of their rights; many more are wary of revisiting traumatic events, especially when they continue to suffer ongoing trauma or stigma, as is so often the case in the wake of, for instance, episodes of sexual violence. Many don't have the resources to challenge a state, a former head of state or somebody with power and influence. Still, victims have the right to receive reparations and addressing this right is an important condition to any attempt of re-building a society after conflict.

In the wake of massive crimes, societies need to address the suffering of victims, examining the policy choices available in a way that recognizes the extraordinary nature and scale of the events and harm suffered. Massive crimes, which have severely disrupted the political life of a society, cannot be fully addressed by institutional mechanisms that were designed to respond to ordinary crimes. Widespread violence warrants extraordinary policies to address its consequences. States need to take the initiative and approach all victims in a reparatory effort, translating victims' often disparate needs and harms into a coherent reparations program that can be implemented as state policy.

Individual court-based reparations most often operate within a circumscribed legal and political framework, grounded in criminal justice and tort law. Massive human rights violations, however, implicate broader societal norms and rights, linking social justice to claims of human dignity, the need for societal approbation and such long-term imperatives as preventing a reoccurrence of criminal wrongdoing; claims with perhaps a greater political and moral claim on the State and society at large. Given these realities, massive reparations programs implicate objectives distinct from those governing individual claims or even claims involving groups of claimants. Individual approaches rarely achieve the level of public discourse needed. Only a broad societal dialogue, sensitive to the actual situation of victims, can ensure that any reparations initiative is seen not merely as a compensatory pay-out, but instead bears an appropriate message of inclusion and recognition. Different design imperatives are required to achieve these goals while responding to the complex questions about who to include and how to address the different needs of a broad number of victims. Effective tools for implementing the program are equally important, given the complexities involved in registering and delivering one or more reparative measures, sometimes over a long period of time to large numbers of victims.

One fundamental aspect of administrative reparations programs is guaranteeing accessibility. Even in those cases where hybrid systems, based on court decisions, have been created to provide for justice and reparations to victims, the problem of accessibility still remains. Simplified systems of justice and of weighing evidence in regards to reparations claims, as in the cases of the *gacaca* courts in Rwanda and the Peace and Justice Law in Colombia, have been unsuccessful in responding to the demands of hundreds of thousands of victims registered by them. In both cases funds have been created to allow victims to effectively receive reparations (such as the *Fonds d'Indemnization* (FIND)). In both cases, only a few decisions granting reparations have been made by the courts, compared with the number of victims, and only a handful of victims have actually received what has been decided in their favour, as reported by Rombouts and Vandeginste (2005) in the Rwandan case, and by Díaz and Bernal (2009) in regards to Colombia.

This chapter will offer ideas about what principles and objectives should guide the process in situations of mass criminal wrongdoing, distinguishing it from the legal theories that traditionally underlie the right to reparations (see further Letschert & Van Boven, this volume), and offering ideas about the definition of such programs, the registration of victims and the implementation of reparations on a mass scale.

2. AIMS OF A REPARATIONS PROGRAM FOR MASSIVE CRIMES

The traditional approach to reparations derives from the notion of *restitutio in integrum*, which is the base of the legal theory for individual reparations derived from Roman law. Under this notion, reparations should restitute the victim to the previous situation or compensate him in those aspects in which he cannot be restituted, which is also translated into the concept of *restitutio to the status quo ante*. Reparations are intended to make the harm economically neutral: the victim should not be made either poorer or richer as result of the harm. While this approach makes sense in the context of material harm, it is obviously more difficult when the harm is immaterial, which is the case of victims of violence. In too many instances, there is no adequate form for restoring the victim to the previous situation, for compensating those left behind for the loss of a loved one or for remedying the suffering endured during torture. Still, moral damages are paid to victims in attempts to compensate these forms of suffering, although very different standards often apply in different jurisdictions.

In the case of massive human rights violations, the notion of *restitutio to the status quo ante* becomes even less helpful as a guiding principle for reparations. Defining the goal of a reparations program to restitute all victims to the situation before the crimes were committed is unrealistic in these cases. Defining such an impossible goal does not help to set standards of fairness for a reparations program that are achievable. On the contrary, it contributes to creating expectations among victims that will not be satisfied, thus generating even more frustration.

In addition, restituting all victims to their previous situation requires the effort of establishing such situation for each victim, which is an impossible task when there may be thousands or tens of thousands of victims. Making an economic assessment of every type of harm suffered is not only costly, but such an effort could actually cause more harm to victims, subjecting them to different forms of re-victimization. For example, the reparations program established by Germany for the victims of the Holocaust as result of the Federal Restitution Law (BEG) Final Law of 1965, in its attempt to establish individual harm, subjected victims to complex processes of examination, especially in regards to non-material claims (harm to the body or health). Such examinations were perceived by some victims as new forms of victimization, as explained by Pross (1998) and by Colonomos and Armstrong (2006).

Moreover, as explained by De Greiff (2006b), a case-by-case approach may send victims the message that lives of people have different value, which might not be a problem for a court deciding individually case by case, but will be problematic for a national policy that tries to address a legacy of violence and exclusion. Such an individualized effort would furthermore require huge administrative costs. It is also unclear which standards could be used to assess moral damages in such cases. Even if individual assessments could be made, the costs of implementing full restitution and compensation would likely be insurmountable as was also established by De Greiff in regards to the exercise done by the Peruvian Truth Commission in projecting the amounts given by the

Inter American Court of Human Rights to every one of the estimated 69,000 victims of killings and disappearances of the internal armed conflict it investigated.

Given that the notion of *restitutio to the status quo ante* is only minimally useful as a reference point in situations of massive violence, other more relevant terms of reference need to be considered and defined to ensure that reparations programs are fair, are attuned to the realities in developing or undeveloped countries, and are not based on unrealistic expectations or approaches derived solely from the First World. By paying greater attention to the objectives of reparations programs for massive human rights violations, societies can help establish parameters that are both consistent with society's obligations to victims and administratively workable.

Rombouts (2004, 49) reaches a similar conclusion, suggesting that reparations should aim for "seeking a new balance". She argues for future-oriented reparations that do not deny the violations, as might be the case with *restitutio to the status quo ante* and its pretence that the harm did not happen, but to integrate what happened through a perspective influenced by psychological approaches to trauma. In her search for a definition of the standards of such new balance, she concludes that it is not possible to provide answers regarding the content of reparations measures. Instead, she recommends a process approach that emphasizes the role of victims in the definition of reparations.

However, without denying the importance of the process and of participation in defining and implementing these programs, there are valuable lessons from concrete experiences about the mechanisms that could provide redress to victims. Those experiences can help define some criteria that could guide the process of determining the standards of what is fair in different cases. Having common standards and expectation might help in the negotiation and participatory process that will be required to define a reparations program. Guillerot and Magarrell (2006) report how having some common standards and clear expectations helped during the dialogue and negotiations between victims' and groups, civil society organizations and the Peruvian truth commission in defining the reparations program finally recommended by the later.

Suffering a violent crime, such as being subjected to torture or rape, having your house or your village razed and destroyed, or experiencing the kidnapping and disappearance of one or more members of a person's family, can have devastating effects. These crimes, and the cruelty with which they are committed, represent a total disregard for the victim's dignity. Often they carry an implicit, or sometimes even explicit, underlying message. Victims are told in no uncertain terms that they are worthless and are not entitled to the treatment they deserve as fellow humans.

When these crimes are committed on a communal level, affecting not only the individual but his or her whole family and extended community, the message of exclusion is stronger yet, signalling that the whole group doesn't deserve to be considered human. This message of exclusion is only reinforced when society and its institutions are unable to protect victims, or remain openly indifferent to or even complicit in the atrocities.

This is particularly true if the crimes were committed by state agents who supposedly were acting to protect society from a perceived threat and thus bear society's mantle of legitimacy with its implicit grant of impunity. In these cases, it is not just the direct perpetrators that send a message of exclusion and that deny basic human rights. State institutions, such as the police, the judiciary, or even the press or the legal profession, who were created to protect citizens from crimes and to provide defence and legal remedies, may have renounced to their obligations to protect victims or even have aligned themselves with the wrongdoers themselves, only strengthening the sense of marginalization and alienation that victims suffer. The crime, the lack of respect to their human condition and the lack of usual institutional safeguards for protecting a community and its members stand as a stark message to victims that they are not worthy of being treated as members of the political community and are not seen as humans.

Social exclusion can also be increased by the sense of isolation victims face as result of the crimes suffered. Trauma can render victims incapable of functioning socially, or even communicating intimately. For many reasons, survivors of torture or other serious crimes don't talk about their experiences even with their loved ones. Sometimes, they hope to shield others from suffering or merely hope to avoid remembering themselves. Whatever the form, this conspiracy of silence, a concept described by Danieli (2009), increases the degree of isolation and magnifies the perverse consequences of these crimes in the life of victims and their immediate families. This phenomenon was also reported by the National Commission on Political Imprisonment and Torture of Chile.[1]

This sense of exclusion is not attributable, however, only to the crime itself. The state and its actors sometimes multiply the wrong and the attendant harm, by not investigating the crimes, by denying their occurrence, or by having accused victims of being terrorists or of having provoked what may at the time have been considered to be a deserved reaction from the security forces. Later on, victims may be black listed, leaving them with few economic or professional options and the burden of guilt or resentment that comes from not being able to provide for their families as they had once expected. Situations such as these increase poverty and marginalization and the degree of isolation felt by victims, especially where available social networks have been dismantled or poisoned by distrust.

---

[1] Comisión Nacional sobre Prisión Política y Tortura, *Informe de la Comisión Nacional sobre Prisión Política y Tortura*, Santiago, 2004, 503; www.comisionvalech.gov.cl/informeValech/ (last visited: 21 June 2010).

Reparations should reverse this message of exclusion and worthlessness. A reparations program for massive crimes should be capable of communicating to victims that they are valued members of the society that once excluded them; it should express, in concrete terms, that the harm done to victims was wrong and acknowledge that the rest of society cares about the consequences. In sum, reparations should recognize the dignity of victims and reaffirm their sense of belonging.

This message should be communicated concretely. It is not just a discourse, but a discourse accompanied by concrete action. Since systemic crimes themselves combine both symbolic and physical components, and so often communicate a meaning of exclusion, reparations should express an opposite message of inclusion, both symbolically and materially. As it is said in the theory of communications, it is impossible not to communicate; every action or omission communicates something. Some measures may be more symbolic, while others may be more material, but all carry a message, and that message should be a coherent one.

This sense of belonging needs to be translated into a concrete offer that gives victims the opportunity to live in conditions similar to their fellow citizens. From this perspective, reparations should facilitate the reintegration of victims into the life of the community, to be part of it and to re-establish trust in it. In political terms, this means that reparations programs need to create conditions for re-establishing civic trust and a confidence that the institutions that rule the political life of the community will treat victims going forward with fairness and according to pre-established rules, as De Greiff (2006b) proposes.

3. THE COHERENCE OF THE MESSAGE OF ACKNOWLEDGMENT AND INCLUSION

To effectively recognize the dignity of victims and restore their sense of belonging in society, a reparations program must be part of a broader process of accountability. Transitional justice mechanisms have great synergistic potential and should be managed in ways that are mindful of those compatibilities. As argued by De Greiff (2006a), reparations must be accompanied by efforts to learn the truth, to establish responsibility and to prevent the reoccurrence of the crimes, if they are to achieve the kind of external coherence that is required.

Victims will not perceive that society truly acknowledges the seriousness of the crimes committed against them if they are not investigated or if significant segments of the population still deny them. Victims need to know that society is listening, that it hears them, and shares their stories of suffering. Reparations delivered in the absence of a sincere effort to investigate the truth will not carry an effective message of acknowledgment and sorrow. On the contrary, participation in a truth seeking effort can be a reparatory experience for many victims, if they are listened to and treated with respect. An overwhelmingly majority of witnesses who gave statements at the Sierra Leone Truth and Reconciliation Commission reported later that they "felt very good about having given testimony," despite the bad memories, headaches and stomach pain suffered immediately after the hearings. Many of them "said they felt listened too" as a result of the sympathy expressed by the commissioners and the public and the, although limited, counselling offered, as reported by Schotsmans (2005, 111). This is also consistent with what has been reported by several truth commissions, as mentioned in the reports of the National Commission on Political Imprisonment and Torture of Chile,[2] the Commission of Reception, Truth and Reconciliation of Timor-Leste,[3] and the Truth and Reconciliation Commission of Peru.[4]

Investigating and acknowledging the events, through non-criminal processes offers the possibility of unravelling a broader truth than the one referred to by single crimes. The work of truth commissions can allow victims to feel recognized and listened, as well as to provide a broad account of the policies that led to the crimes, as well as to establish the political responsibilities of those who designed or tolerated those policies (see Peacock, this volume).

In addition to this broad truth, criminal investigations allow another opportunity for society to acknowledge the gravity of the crimes committed. Judging and sentencing those responsible affirms the inappropriateness of the crimes, while reaffirming the dignity of victims, even when those repaired are a partial, and not complete, number of victims. In the absence of a criminal investigation, reparations may be understood as buying the victims' consciences or exchanging their rights for money. It sends the message that the suffering and harm caused was more akin to something uncontrollable that just happened, such as a natural disaster, where nobody can be adjudged responsible. As Schotsmans (2005, 114) describes, based on her work with victims in Chad, Rwanda, and Sierra Leone, "victims want confirmation of the fact that what happened to them was not normal, that it was a breach of the social contract of norms and values, that the acts were fundamentally wrong". And when such fundamentally wrong acts are committed, society promises (has the obligation) to investigate them and judge those responsible.

---

2   Comisión Nacional sobre Prisión Política y Tortura, *Informe de la Comisión Nacional sobre Prisión Política y Tortura*, Santiago, 2004, 40; www.comisionvalech.gov.cl/informeValech/ (last visited: 21 June 2010).

3   Commission of Reception, Truth and Reconciliation, *"Chega!" Report of the Commission of Reception, Truth and Reconciliation of Timor-Leste*, Dili, Timor-Leste, 2005, Chapter 10, p. 18.

4   Comisión de Verdad y Reconciliación, *Informe Final de la Comisión de Verdad y Reconciliación*, Lima, 2003, Vol. 1, p. 59.

When massive crimes are committed it might be impossible to prosecute every perpetrator, but at least there must be in place the possibility of investigating and judging the crimes committed. Such possibility should not be just theoretical, but demonstrated by more than a handful of rulings. In this way, the possibility for prosecutions must counter the impression that the crimes committed were not serious or that victims do not matter, and must reinforce one of the key objectives of reparations: to affirm that society cares for victims and that they are valued members of it. In that way, justice for individual victims can support the effort to provide reparations to all of them.

Finally, if the message of acknowledgment and belonging is to be truly effective, it is important that society undertakes a process to guarantee that the crimes will not be repeated. Reform may take many forms, but it is vital that the repressive institutions that did and could threaten victims are identified and dismantled, and that general efforts to promote transparency, accountability, and a system of institutional checks and balances are undertaken. This could be done by establishing institutions for the protection and promotion of human rights; guaranteeing that perpetrators do not keep their positions of power, and addressing the historical, cultural and normative factors in society and inside the institutions that implemented the repressive policies or failed to provide the protection deserved. Many victims' organizations rally for the ratification of international human rights conventions in their countries, or for the creation of national institutions for the protection of human rights, inspired by the model of the Ombudsman and defined by the 1991 Paris Principles for National Institutions of Human Rights. Moreover, some organizations, such as the Argentinean *Madres de Plaza de Mayo*, were active participants in the discussions that led to the creation of the International Convention against Enforced Disappearances.

Pairing reparations with other transitional justice mechanisms creates a multiplier effect. Victims perceive reparations not as mere efforts to buy their silence or conscience, but as part of a broader and sincere attempt at accountability. As argued by Hamber (2005, 139–140), "reparations cannot be seen as simply a substitute for truth and justice". Victims demand "vindication", which

> *can come from punishment or the sentencing of the perpetrator, but can also be brought about or forwarded by the recognition of injury, offering support to the victim, giving guarantees of non-repetition, making structural and social changes that gave rise to the violations, affording space for victims to tell their stories, making reparations and granting compensation, and establishing the truth about past atrocities.*

The challenge, he continues, "is to consider how different strategies and approaches interact and deliver holistically".

Conversely, reparations conceived of as a quick, one-off solution may be seen as an empty gesture, especially when they are limited to material benefits, as concluded by Espinoza, Ortiz and Rojas (2003), in a study that included interviews of 60 victims of Argentina, Chile, El Salvador, Guatemala and South Africa. The victims expressed frustration for only material reparations and limited truth-seeking efforts, as was the case in Argentina and Chile, and expressed fear that violence might recur. They demanded moral, symbolic and comprehensive reparations, including ceremonies of recognition, memorials and guaranteeing that society had learned the lesson and is committed to avoid a recurrence, as well as criminal investigations. Hamber (2005) reaches a similar conclusion based on his research with victims in South Africa.

A negative perception about a reparations program may be heightened in the context of a massive reparations program that does not have the ability to restore victims to the *status quo ante* or to provide compensation in proportion to the suffering. However, the emptiness of the gesture could be perceived even in a situation where the amounts given are significant, as was the case of reparations given in Argentina by the same government that pardoned those military officers responsible for the crimes (Guembe 2006).

Affirming the inclusion of victims also implies avoiding any form of victim stigmatization, or the creation of such differences that could contribute to the creation of more resentment against them. This is a significant risk in impoverished countries where reparations could create differences with the rest of the population, when victims receive as reparations what their neighbours perceive that they are also entitled to. This can happen especially in regards to reparations provided in the forms of social services, such as access to free health care through the public health care network, when the rest of the population does not have the same degree of accessibility. In such cases, victims could be labelled as the beneficiaries of unfair advantages, as has been reported in Rwanda, where the *Fonds National d' Assistance aux victimes les plus nécessiteuses du génocide et des massacres,* known as *Fond pour les Rescapés du Génocide* (FARG) is called the "Tutsi fund" (Rombouts & Vandeginste 2005, 334). It is interesting to note that the full name includes the notion of victim, not *rescapés*, and includes also massacres. Addressing this issue requires defining the notion of victims and beneficiaries in an objective way, as well as in a way that does not deny all victims their particular suffering.

4. ELEMENTS OF A REPARATIONS PROGRAM

Given that reparations policy cannot be adequately defined with reference to concepts of *restitutio to the status quo ante*, nor by applying some statistical standard of compensation for economically assessable damages, different terms of reference need to be established in cases involving massive criminal wrongdoing. Broader notions relating to restoring human dignity and providing conditions for social inclusion should serve as baseline concepts whenever reparations are conceptualized, designed and ultimately implemented. The specific measures should be defined according to the general type of harm and suffering caused to victims.

Even though the condition of victims varies in different scenarios (depending on the nature of the conflict, culture and country involved), victims are usually impoverished as result of the crimes suffered. Frequently, they are unable to sustain themselves economically or suffer severe hardships, often through a combination of general conditions of poverty and oppression, some of which have roots previous to the conflict and are shared by their neighbours, as well as by a direct result of the harm suffered. Often victims of enforced disappearance, killings, political imprisonment or torture were and are the main breadwinners in a household. Their long absence, the trauma and physical deterioration that affect them when released or the chronic unemployment they often face upon being blacklisted, have serious impact on the ability of the family to meet its economic needs, as reported by the Chilean Commission on Political Imprisonment and Torture. Women are subjected also to a double form of suffering, as direct victims as well as relatives and often dependants of the direct victims. The search for the disappeared, the struggle to obtain justice or the support for those imprisoned may compete with the need to provide sources of income for the rest of the family members, in addition to the psychological effects of the loss. It is common that children are not able to continue their education, perpetuating the economic harm to the next generation. The psychological impact of the suffering often has somatic expressions, contributing to the development of physical symptoms and disease.

Massive conflicts that affect a high portion of the population of a certain region can have an even more devastating effect on the socioeconomic conditions of victims, as is the case in Rwanda, Northern Uganda or East Congo. For example, in a survey of people living in Northern Uganda in 2007 (Pham *et al.* 2007, 27), 95% of respondents said that they were direct victims of the conflict, and 76% reported having had a family member killed, which reflects the impact of the violence in the general population. The survey concluded that:

> general economic consequences of the violence were frequently reported [by respondents from all] eight districts [included in the survey]: 86 percent reported losing income, 86 percent had their house destroyed, 85 percent had productive assets such as cattle taken away, and 87 percent had other assets taken away. Very few respondents remained untouched by the direct or indirect economic consequences of the conflict.

In order to restore dignity and allow victims to live lives as full members of society, reparations should address the consequences of the crimes. Reparations should provide the means by which victims can attain an income that can sustain their life, provide measures for the education of children or grandchildren that could reverse the trans-generational impoverishing effect, and have access to physical and mental health adequate to their needs. This is consistent with the opinions reported by Makhalemele (2009) of survivors from the Apartheid regime living in the Vaal townships, who manifested their frustration for having received only a lump sum instead of more comprehensive support in a package of services that could provide long term sustainability. The same conclusion was arrived at by a study of the more than 7,000 statements presented to the Truth and Reconciliation Commission of Sierra Leone, mentioned by Schabas (2005, 299), which reported that "the most important forms of assistance and redress for victims were homes and shelter (49%), schools and education (41%), and hospitals and medical care (27%), followed, in fourth place, by cash (18%)". The recommendations made by the Sierra Leonean Commission were consistent with the opinions expressed by the victims. Their focus was "on the rehabilitation of victims through the distribution of a service packages and symbolic measures which acknowledge the past and the harm to victims, and give them the opportunity to move on".[5]

The survey done in Northern Uganda reached a similar conclusion. Victims listed as their top priorities "health (45%), peace (44%), education (31%), and livelihood concerns, including food (43%), land (37%), [and] money (35%)" (Pham *et al.* 2007, 22). When asked about what should be done for victims, "direct compensation to individuals was frequently proposed, including financial compensation (52%), food (9%), and livestock/cattle (8%). Equal numbers (7%) mentioned counselling and education for children. Ten percent mentioned apologies, justice, or reconciliation" (Pham *et al.* 2007, 32). These results are similar to the ones obtained in a similar survey two years earlier, before the Lord's Resistance Army had withdrawn from the area (Pham *et al.* 2005).

4.1. GUARANTEEING INCOME

To affirm the dignity of victims, the state has an obligation, at least, to provide them and their direct family with some form of a permanent source of income to guarantee a decent livelihood. This approach differs substantially from the logic of restitution and compensation that is often debated when defining reparations and is often not the alternative preferred by victims. It differs also from the commonly adopted method of providing a one-time payment or a lump-sum paid over a few instalments. The idea that society should provide victims with a

---

5 Sierra Leone Truth and Reconciliation Commission, *Witness to Truth: Report of the Sierra Leone Truth and Reconciliation Commission*, 2004, vol. II, p. 232; http://reliefweb.int/rw/rwb. nsf/db900sid/EVOD-73HJHY/$File/full_report.pdf.

livelihood emanates from a logic different than that traditionally applied to reparations.

The approach suggested here is rather different. It is victim-centred and impact-driven and is based on certain indispensible objectives of reparations: how to have more impact in improving the life of victims, especially the poorest and most vulnerable; how to redress the long term consequences of the crimes; and how to minimize unwanted negative effects. Living in poverty is a form of denial of socio-economic rights and a form of denial of people's dignity and sense of citizenship. One of the aims of a reparations program, thus, should be to avoid that victims, as result of the crimes they suffered, live in poverty.

Although different countries may adopt different approaches to suit the context, one approach seems ready-made for each situation: the provision of lifetime pensions to some categories of victims. Pensions are flexible policy mechanisms. They can include a range of survivors and beneficiaries, covering an array of crimes and resultant harms that severely impact the life of victims and their families, as is the case of torture, rape and other forms of abuse, as sexual slavery, forced labour or detention in humiliating conditions.

Pensions can effectively reduce the socio-economic effects caused by these crimes, while doubling as a tangible signal to victims that society cares for them. They can have a significant impact in the well-being of the victims and their families, especially in the long term.

Pensions can also reduce the likelihood of creating the pernicious effects that have been reported in some cases when significant amounts of money are given to only those identified as victims in a community that has a more collective understanding of the suffering and of life in general, as Schotsmans (2005) warns. Similar effects have been reported regarding payments delivered to victims of the Canadian Indian Residential Schools by the Aboriginal Healing Foundation,[6] and in regards to payments delivered by the Guatemalan National Program for Redress.[7]

In the case of Chile, where pensions and an initial lump sum were paid to the relatives of the disappeared and killed, there have been fewer reports of family or community conflicts created by them. Durán, Bacic and Pérez (1998) reported these types of conflict when studying the effects of reparations in indigenous communities. It is interesting to note, however, that the testimonies quoted in the study, portray divisions between the children of victims on how they took care of the aging mother, who was the recipient of the reparations pension, but in any case and for which ever reasons, the aging mothers were able to get some care. A regular payment of an amount that equals a family income is less likely to create family or community conflicts about the use of the money or resentment

---

[6]   Aboriginal Healing Foundation, *Lump Sum Compensation Payment Research Project: The Circle Rechecks Itself*, Ottawa: Aboriginal Healing Foundation, 2007.

[7]   Conversation with Rosalina Tuyuc, then President of the Program, July 2007.

by those not favoured by the measure than a more substantial one-time payment. Such form of individual reparations should be accompanied by other forms of reparations, in health care or education, in addition to community reparations in case they are applicable.

Contrary to a common practice, where pensions are granted only to those victims that are disabled, the provision of pensions as reparations shouldn't be conditioned on disability. A reparatory measure, with symbolic and material meaning, should not be confused with an insurance or social security policy. In addition, by subjecting victims to an evaluation of their degree of capacity or incapacity for work, disability pensions might be perceived as a dismissal of the consequences that the crimes have on the victims, and favouring mostly those with physical disabilities. As a result, a high proportion of victims might be excluded, especially women, who are frequently more exposed to forms of violence that not always create lasting physical impairment, especially common forms of sexual violence. Instead, given the seriousness of the crimes and the patterns of how they affect victims in general, the severe harm in victims should be presumed. In the case of those victims who do not think they need this form of reparations, the mere act of waiving benefits may serve to affirm their dignity, and they should be allowed to reject them or donate them as they choose. In the context of scarcity that characterizes Sierra Leone, the Truth and Reconciliation Commission recommended the evaluation of disability only in the case of war wounded, exempting from such evaluation amputees and victims of sexual violence.[8]

A form of lifetime economic support may also be given to widows, widowers, parents and handicapped children, as well as to certain underage children until they reach some age. Children who were raised by the victim or in some cases other relatives who depended on the victim, and were very close to them, are often seriously affected by a death or disappearance and could be exceptionally included. The concept of 'family' should be defined according to the customs of the victims, recognizing permanent relationships that go beyond strict definitions of marriage or consanguinity, and without excluding same sex partnerships.

The amount of a pension should be defined with an eye toward context. A country's specific socio-economic condition and other realities on the ground may need to be considered when evaluating the income needs of victims and the type and level of benefits that will provided so as to attain some degree of dignity. In some cases, such as Sierra Leone, the Truth and Reconciliation Commission recommended that the amount of the pension "should consider the standard of living, the amount provided to ex-combatants on a monthly basis under the National Commission for Disarmament, Demobilization and Reintegration

---

8   Sierra Leone Truth and Reconciliation Commission, *Witness to Truth: Report of the Sierra Leone Truth and Reconciliation Commission*, 2004, vol. II, p. 259; http://reliefweb.int/rw/rwb. nsf/db900sid/EVOD-73HJHY/$File/full_report.pdf.

programme, and the amount that the war-wounded Sierra Leone Army soldiers received from the government".[9] However, none of this has been implemented, and victims recently received a one-time payment equivalent to USD $80 as an interim payment, through a program funded by the United Nations Peace Building Fund.[10] The standards defined for veterans or demobilized militias usually reflect an amount that is considered appropriate for each country, as defined in the Veterans Law of Timor–Leste or in the policy implemented by the Peruvian government for the members of the militias assisted by the Army during the internal conflict. Those amounts could serve also to define the amount required to express recognition and dignity of victims.

In the case of Argentina, a pension equivalent to the minimum pension for civil servants was paid to the relatives of the disappeared. This included their children (until age 21, later extended to age 25, or for life if disabled), the surviving spouse, parents or siblings disabled or who have no source of income, and orphan siblings that lived with the victims. Later, in addition to these pensions, victims received a very substantial payment in the form of bonds of consolidation of public debt, which is the most renowned aspect of the Argentinean reparations policy (Guembe 2006).

In Chile, a similar pension scheme was used for repairing the relatives of those disappeared or killed. The quantity of the pension was based on a specific reference amount, equivalent to the medium family income, to calculate the amounts to be granted to every relative. The spouse received 40% of the reference amount; each child (no matter how many) received 15%; and the mother (and in her absence, the father) 30%. The amounts were not reduced if the number of beneficiaries (several children, the existence of a mother of extramarital children in addition to the spouse, etc.) made the total family amount exceed 100% of the reference amount. Twelve years later the pensions were increased by 50%, given the socio-economic changes experienced by the country and the relatively low amounts of the original ones. In the case of survivors of torture, the pension established was equivalent to the minimum wage, which was considered insufficient by the victims. Later, this pension was extended to the widows of the survivors of torture, equivalent to 60% of the one the direct victims were entitled to; a substantial reduction of an already insufficient amount.

The periodicity of the payments should also correspond to the local context. In urban settings, where people are used to receiving salaries or pensions monthly, or every one or two weeks, those periods should be used for delivering the payments. In rural settings, where income is more irregular and is received

---

9   *Ibidem.*

10   Correa, C. & Suma, M., *Report and Proposals for the Implementation of Reparations in Sierra Leone*, International Center for Transitional Justice, 2009, www.ictj.org/static/Africa/ SierraLeone/ICTJ_SL_ReparationsRpt_Dec2009.pdf.

in longer periods, payments should be made monthly, or according to context. This could also make travelling to the small cities to receive the payments easier.

One aspect difficult to define is how many differences among victims should be established. Should all victims, the relatives of the killed and disappeared, the victims of torture, those who were raped or subjected to sexual violence, those who were detained, receive the same? How many distinctions should be made, without making the process too complex, requiring evidence difficult to find and making differentiations between types of crime and suffering that are difficult to fairly evaluate in abstract? On the other hand, if the objective of the reparation policy is to generally transmit to all victims their dignity, and the amounts to be established are going to be based on some socio-economic standard of what is needed to live in dignity in a certain society, making these distinctions may not be needed or making them may be inconsistent with such an objective. Making them could even be contradictory to the guarantee of some degree of income that could keep victims out of poverty. To be consistent with the objective of the pension representing a common sense of dignity, it might be advisable that the pension received by the widow or widower of a victim of disappearance or killing be equivalent to the one received by a survivor of torture, rape or other forms of sexual violence equivalent in severity. The same could be said for children born from rape, given also the severity of such condition.

In the case of survivors of political imprisonment in Chile, no distinctions were made and all received the same pension. According to the context and the conditions of imprisonment, it was presumed that they were subjected to torture, which also made the process of verification easier, having to rely only on determining the politically motivated detention. Argentina, on the contrary, provided reparations to political prisoners according to the time they were detained, without addressing torture, and giving substantial and symbolically defined amounts to victims (the equivalent of the daily salary of the highest civil servant per each day of detention). However, the form of payment, through bonds of consolidation of public debt and a financial crisis, reduced the real value of the amounts paid.

By virtue of their long-term and continuing nature, pensions provide a permanent message of acknowledgment, reinforcing monthly the fact that the state recognizes its responsibility and is providing for the livelihood of the victims. Its repetition, especially once ceremonies or other symbolic measures have faded away in memory, can keep alive the message of inclusion. As concluded by Danieli (2005, 60), "the monthly check in some ways weakens the trauma. When it becomes routine, it transforms into something permanent that somehow enables overcoming survivor guilt". By guaranteeing some level of income, society promises to take care of victims, at least in their basic needs.

Over the years, the amounts granted by a pension may not be so different from the awards obtained in a settlement or a judicial decision.

However, sometimes pensions have a very limited symbolic effect at first. They often do not have a significant impact on the life of victims and may even be perceived as a cheap response. To strengthen the immediate symbolic effect of such a measure, it can be accompanied by a more significant first payment. For instance, the reparations pensions paid in Chile were accompanied by a larger initial payment (equivalent to one year of the pension), that served to compensate for the administrative delays of setting up the payment process and of individualizing the beneficiaries.

In the case of children of victims of enforced disappearance and killing that are not handicapped, a pension could be granted until they attain an age at which it could be presumed that they can sustain themselves. The exact age may vary by country, but generally it is not advisable to set it too low. In the case of Chile and in a revised version of the Argentinean law, the relevant age was set at 25 years old, since that is the age children enrolled in higher education are covered by the health care insurance provided by their parents. However, in several cases, because of their age, many children who lost their mother or father will not receive a significant amount over time, or they could be over the maximum age when reparations are granted. This is a common problem when years have passed since the death or the disappearance of the victims. These types of inequities were addressed in Chile by establishing a minimum amount that children might receive in total, equivalent to the sum they were eligible to receive over several years of the pension.

Nonetheless, it is possible that victims who are distrustful of the state might prefer to receive a more substantial amount, instead of a doubtful commitment to receive a pension for life. That was the result of the consultations made by the Truth Commission of Ecuador.[11] Such distrust reflects a serious problem for the credibility of the institutions. In such a situation, the lack of credibility should also be addressed in the policies of institutional reform, as part of a comprehensive reparations policy.

Pension measures can carry both an immediate, as well as permanent, message of recognition if established in a way and under conditions that guarantees their fulfilment. Such long-term obligations need to be established by law, so they are not susceptible to easy alternation by a new administration or by a unilateral presidential decision. Their funding must be guaranteed, and not be limited by the total amount of a fund created for that purpose, by assets eventually recovered from perpetrators or by other states or donor contributions. They should be the responsibility of the state and should be included in its permanent budget.

---

11   Comisión de la Verdad, *Sin Verdad no Hay Justicia: Informe de la Comisión de la Verdad*, Quito, 201, 446.

A form of medium-to-long-term economic support through a one-time payment has been employed in Rwanda, where 2000 cows have been distributed to genocide survivors so far. The program has been recently implemented and it is too early to fully evaluate its impact. Distributing livestock makes the process of delivery easier, compared to regular payments. However, it has some inherent risks and it is difficult to foresee the impact such measure will have on the wellbeing of victims.

4.2. PROVIDING HEALTH CARE AND PSYCHOSOCIAL SUPPORT

Despite the possible positive effects attributable to pensions, or to any financial form of reparations, limiting reparations to a sum of money will rarely address the personal dimension of suffering. In addition, a one-size-fits-all measure that doesn't distinguish among different forms and degrees of suffering can likewise have a limited effect in addressing the particular needs of victims. Physical health care programs and psychosocial support can complement the impersonal and cold effect of pensions or other form of financial reparations.

A reparations policy that deals with the physical and psychological consequences of the harm suffered, by direct victims and by their relatives, helps personalize the reparatory meaning and the message of dignity and inclusion that the policy is intended to provide. Although victims may share some relatively common sets of symptoms, each victim ultimately manifests trauma and suffering differently, exhibiting a diverse range of conditions or illnesses that need to be treated individually and in-person, after direct consultation with the victims.

Dealing with the body or psyche is a personal matter, addressed best within the context of a personal and ongoing relationship that gives the practitioner time to know the victim, and win their trust. Practitioners and victims need to be able to tailor treatment, varying the emphasis and orientation of the approach, to respond to the different needs and situations of the victim. In this way, they may be more effective and may more often provide the kind of attentive, responsive, face-to-face contact that victims seek. Victims value that such personal services are provided by professionals who are sensitive to their needs, as reported by Baristain (2009, 286 & 309). Furthermore, it is not enough to have the capacity to correctly diagnose the symptoms that a victim is suffering; to define a treatment it is essential to understand that those symptoms are a result of having experienced extreme suffering caused by violence. An ICTJ project working with communities affected by violence in rural Peru links work on mental health to working with the community's memory about the conflict. The project, assisted by mental health experts of REDINFA, an NGO, seeks ways to provide support to those affected by recognizing their suffering, as well as through community resources that have been used throughout their history.

These services should be flexible enough to cover any type of condition suffered by those who are eligible. Categories of harm or lists of eligible disorders should not be limited to only those conditions that are conventionally considered to be the demonstrable consequences of the crimes suffered, nor should they be limited even to conditions associated with similar types or categories of abuse. Such restrictions could prove contradictory to the purpose of the reparations policy, and require costly examinations of evidence to prove a link between the violation and the condition. This is especially true considering that it is almost impossible to rule out a link between a condition and severe trauma, especially after years of social marginalization and lack of treatment. In fact, victims will more often than not associate any severe condition with the brutal harm to which they were subjected (Baristain 2009, 292–293). A better approach may be to provide victims with universal health care, without imposing the requirement of demonstrating a provable link to the crimes suffered and the current condition, an exercise fraught with uncertainty and that could lead to secondary victimization and distrust. Universal health care obviates the need for time-consuming battles over proof, provides the requisite care, and accomplishes the objectives of a reparations policy to provide recognition and dignity to victims.

Mental health care should vary according to the culture of the victims and the availability of resources. This does not necessarily mean creating a network of psychiatric services, which is impossible in most countries, but exploring ways of providing support in ways appropriate to the victims' culture through "interdisciplinary and intercultural teams", involving "local or indigenous expertise" (Lykes & Mersky 2006, 610). Victim support groups, organized and led by trained monitors or professionals, are often easier to implement and more effective, increasing their sense of agency, as they take on the role of point person for fellow victims. Victims support groups create peer networks, consisting of victims like them, who understand and sympathize with their struggle, and are often close at hand. Trained victims may even participate as monitors, paid and supervised within the program, expanding the coverage of these measures, while ensuring that those in need of professional help are still referred out when necessary and linking their work with a broader network of services, depending on what is available in the country. The use of monitors for early diagnosis, accompany the sick, helping them get their medicine, and referring them to secondary or tertiary health care centres could also be part of a physical health care program.

In the context of violence suffered by rural communities, mental health services require implementation at the community level, not only at the individual level. Strategies in mental health care at the community level have been successfully implemented in several cases as result of a decision of the Inter

American Court of Human Rights (Beristain 2009, 299–301), and several lessons can be draw from those experiences. They include

(1) the need to include community leaders and community organizations structure in the implementation of the program, not only the health care services;
(2) obtaining an agreement with the community;
(3) integration of regular services to guarantee continuity;
(4) cultural sensitivity in the way the community understands life, death, health, sickness, healing, etc.;
(5) simple registration, information and evaluation systems that can help integrate the services with general health care policies;
(6) inclusion of a health care prevention strategy, as is frequently done in any public health policy; and
(7) staff recruitment and training that guarantees not only knowledge about health care, but the inclusion of skills in effective communication with the members of the community.

In the case of Guatemala, where the violations affected mostly Mayan communities, a psychosocial community approach should involve also a multicultural component, as has been argued by Gonzalez-Rey (2007) and by Velasquez (2007).

In the case of physical health a similar model can be adopted. In the Chilean Comprehensive Reparations and Health Care Program (PRAIS), small teams consisting of a social worker, a psychologist and general physician were employed in cities and associated with hospitals, which provided basic support to victims and, most importantly, a friendly face from a sensitive and trained team. These types of professional, hands-on services are especially important to help prevent the onset of ancillary conditions and ensure that victims who are suffering from disease receive more specialized services when required. Disease itself makes people feel vulnerable, so being taken care of in a sensitive way can have a very strong symbolic effect, reinforcing their sense as valued members of society. The Chilean program grants access to all medical services provided by the public network and it does not require determining a direct link between the health problem and the type of crime suffered.

Many countries that have been affected by massive crimes do not have a public network of health care services for their population, particularly for those poor or living in rural areas. It might be impossible for them to set up a reparations network of services for victims if there is no current health care program in operation or if it is insufficient to respond to all the population needs. This could lead to a lack of implementation of programs recommended, as was the case so far of Sierra Leone, as Schotsmans (2005) long ago warned. In such a context, implementing reparations is usually portrayed as competing with the need of providing development and services to all the poor people of the country.

Rather than seeing reparations as a zero sum game, the needs of victims could be presented as an additional motivation for designing and implementing a program for improving the health care network for the whole population. In this way, responding to the past crimes could reinforce policies of guaranteeing economic and social rights of the whole population (also Letschert & Van Boven, this volume). A policy for improving the coverage and services of health care throughout the country could be complemented by adding the capacity for responding to the traumatized population and to victims. For instance by providing special training for practitioners in how to deal and listen to victims, as well as to include services that are appropriate to, and are most frequently used by victims but are not exclusively granted to them, such as forms of psychosocial support, prosthetic and physical therapy services and other measures recommended by the Truth and Reconciliation Commission of Sierra Leone. Donors and development agencies might be interested in supporting such a program that tries to address both needs.

A very interesting experience of improving the health care network through monitors has been implemented in Rwanda with *animateurs de santé*. The initiative, implemented by the Ministry of Health with support from the organization Partners in Health, consists of providing trained community counsellors to provide home-based care and psychosocial support to patients. The counsellors act as a link between the patient and the health centre, carry our active case findings and educate the community on a variety of health topics. With adequate supervision, training and a modest salary, the *animateurs* have the capacity to expand the reach and coverage of the health care system.[12] This strategy could serve as inspiration for other countries and for providing basic services for victims, including psychosocial support.

4.3. GUARANTEEING ACCESS TO EDUCATION

Education is a powerful tool for improving people's lives and for diminishing the likelihood that they will be relegated to an underclass of the poor. Education expands a person's capacity to earn an income, not only by providing specific training, but also by improving the ability to communicate, plan and build social capital. It often increases the self-esteem of victims, encouraging learning, personal development and a sense of self-fulfilment. Providing education to victims and their children is the best way to guarantee the sustainability of a

---

[12] Global Health Delivery Project, 2008; www.ghdonline.org/adherence/discussion/community-health-workers-in-rwanda/ (last visited: 9 August 2010).

reparations program, reinforcing the impact of the measures related to income and health care.

From a restitution perspective, educational reparations are important, because they allow victims the opportunity to continue the educational process they couldn't finish. However, care must be taken to ensure that educational benefits are not defined too narrowly, limited, for instance, in scope (e.g. to the completion of specific courses that were interrupted) or by age (open only to those children currently of a school age). These kinds of conditions can create obstacles for the very individuals whose lives and educations were interrupted, making both them and the program largely irrelevant. In addition, providing educational benefits beyond direct victims, to the children of victims, or eventually to their grandchildren, could help diminish the trans-generational impact that the crimes have on the families of victims, mitigating some of the poverty associated with them.

Considering reparations as a way to affirm the dignity and sense of belonging of victims opens the possibility of using education in a broader way, in both a reparatory and a transformative sense. Educational benefits to all kinds of victims, no matter their age or if they have completed certain levels of formal education or not, could provide victims with the opportunity to embark on a second career, to study a second language, or to, generally, improve their abilities. This can have an enormous potential for dignifying people.

When broadly defined, programs of education especially directed to those who are no longer of school age, that include literacy programs or skill training, can provide a form to repair those adult victims who, due to the conflict, or the general socio-economic conditions, weren't able to study when young. Such comprehensive approach was followed by the Peruvian Truth Commission, which defined that reparations through education should "give facilities and offer new or better opportunities of access for people who, as a result of the internal armed conflict, missed out on the chance of receiving suitable education or finishing their studies".[13] The same definition was later incorporated in the decree that detailed the content of the reparations plan. This includes exemptions for tuition and exam fees for university studies, housing and meal stipends for university students in qualified cases, adult education and literacy programs, free access to primary and secondary education, and access to vocational training. These measures are defined to benefit the children of direct victims, those who were forcefully recruited and all those victims who were forced to interrupt their studies. However, in the more than four years that have passed since the decree was issued, the measures have not been implemented, and the registration of victims has not been finished.

---

[13]   Comisión de Verdad y Reconciliación, *Informe Final de la Comisión de Verdad y Reconciliación*, Lima, 2003, Vol. IX, 156.

A similar approach has been implemented in Rwanda, where the FARG provides scholarships and stipends for transportation, and school materials have been given to victims. FARG recently announced that 17,209 genocide survivors were able to graduate from university in the last 12 years, and 39,000 students in upper secondary are receiving support. However, the disbursement of the transportation and materials stipends has been problematic, requiring each student to open a bank account, according to a news report.

From the transformative perspective, broad educational programs that include literacy and adult education to all victims offer the possibility to reduce the marginalization of victims, particularly in situations where women suffer from limited access to education. By guaranteeing or promoting the education of all victims and their closer relatives, it can also help reverse different forms of historical marginalization in regards to access to education, as it happens frequently to women or members of indigenous communities. In this way, educational programs may address the general consequences that the conflict had on an entire generation that lost out on an education because of the conflict and thereby having a transformative effect.

By necessity, educational programs must differ depending on the general conditions of the victims and the capabilities of the country. However, they should all be designed to respond to the different reasons why victims were and are unable to study. In some cases, for instance, the programs may be limited to providing free tuition to students. In other cases, study allowances that help pay for books, transportation or other expenses might be the best approach. In some instances, additional incentives might be required, allowing for conditional payments to families, conditioned on school attendance.

However, it is important to attach some conditions for the renewal of these benefits to guarantee that they are used properly and that the recipient will finalize the course or career, especially when the program includes university scholarships. Performance and attendance requirements should be attached to the benefits. Some of the benefits could even be subjected to a process of application and not just granted to any program at the beneficiary's choice. The programs should be subjected to quality control before public funds are issued. Finally, recipients may also receive some form of counselling for making good educational decisions or for solving problems.

As in the case of health care, educational programs could be linked to broader policies for increasing the coverage and the quality of regular education and adult education. A reparations program in education could be used as a way to develop expertise and a network for a future broader educational policy. It could also be developed as part of a general policy to increase educational coverage and to strengthen or guarantee attendance of all children to school, or for specific groups that have lower coverage or low attendance rates, which is often the case with girls.

4.4. HOUSING AND OTHER FORMS OF SUPPORT

Depending on the circumstances, other forms of support and subsidies can help dignify victims. They could be part of a special policy of providing material benefits through one-time payments, subsidies or goods.

Housing is an additional benchmark that may be considered in assessing the quality of life of the families affected by massive crimes. Home improvement subsidies could especially benefit those families that are in poverty, and serve as a redistributive policy. In addition to providing a regular income, a subsidy that could allow victims to obtain a house or improve his or her house could provide a form of support with long-term effects. The measures and the exact mechanisms should vary depending on the context. This could include also special programs for regularizing the property in which the victim's family lives.

In Rwanda, a housing program for genocide survivors (*rescapés*) has been implemented by the FARG (see Muleefu, this volume). According to a news report, as of August 2010, 38,657 vulnerable families of genocide survivors had received housing since the Fund was created in 1998. There are 173,663 who still need assistance. However, there have been accusations of mismanagement and corruption in the program and a senatorial investigation is ongoing. One of the problems that have led to mismanagement is the lack of a list of victims that could provide transparency in housing allocation.

4.5. COLLECTIVE REPARATIONS

In cases of widespread devastation or conflicts that affected whole regions or especially rural areas, reparations policy needs to address the collective harm caused. This is of particular importance in places where violence marked communities of people or where the affected people identified with or were part of a strong community. In these instances, the damages are no longer only individual, but become collective.

In some contexts, collective reparations are understood as community reparations, meaning reparations focused to certain communities affected by a conflict. The Peruvian law that creates the Comprehensive Reparations Plan identifies the following factors for defining indigenous or rural communities entitled to collective reparations: Concentration of crimes that affected individuals, levelling, forced displacement, destruction or serious disruption of communal institutions, and loss of family or communal infrastructure.

In other cases, when repressive policies have targeted specific regions of a country, collective reparations should also address the consequences of such policies. That is the case of the program being implemented by Morocco, which includes a development and infrastructure policy focused on the 11 regions that were affected by the years of political repression and policy of exclusion and marginalization. The program also funds community projects presented by organizations located in those regions.

In the two examples mentioned, collective reparations include the participation of the victims and of the inhabitants of the regions or communities affected. Although the types of activities and works funded may not differ substantially from development projects, they need to reflect the vision that the victims have about their past and the future they envision. Thus, collective reparations are seen as an effort from the state to change the relationship of historical marginalization or repression, and as a first sign of their inclusion to the development of the rest of society.

Another form of collective reparations is the one being implemented in Sierra Leone that takes on a decidedly symbolic form. This initiative was inspired by the work done by an NGO, the Forum of Conscience, and is named *Fambul Tok* or 'Family Talk', drawing on the tradition of discussing and resolving issues within the security of a family circle. It combines official ceremonies of remembrance and apology, community dialogue about the conflict and the erection of a monument or planting a tree to symbolize reconciliation (see Schotsmans, this volume). This program was part of the reparations policy implemented in Sierra Leone during 2009, reaching several chiefdoms, and is expected to expand its reach in 2010.

It can also be discussed that reparations in health care or in education are of collective nature. They are if they target regions or communities affected by the conflict, or if by improving the health care and educational services the general damages suffered by people are addressed. However, a general approach of providing these services to the whole population that does not link adequately reparations, harm and acknowledgment of responsibility could be easily confused with the general obligation of the state to provide services and to guarantee social and economic rights to all. The improvement of the network and infrastructure to provide services to the whole population could serve a reparations purpose, though, when such infrastructure is also used to provide special services to victims or victims are granted special accessibility to them, as was argued before. Those special services are individual in nature, benefiting those listed as individual victims. But it could be hardly argued that providing these services to all, without making any distinction that could address the specific harms suffered by victims or their additional obstacles to access these services, could be a form of reparations to them. Building the infrastructure could also be used to recognize victims, as a form of symbolic reparations, by naming them in honour of certain victims and dedicating them in ceremonies where victims are recognized.

Precisely, collective reparation programs can fall short when they are not accompanied by individual forms of reparations or do not include a clear acknowledgment of the crimes committed and the responsibility of the state. This is partly the case of the Peruvian program on collective reparations. In a survey done in an early stage of the implementation of the program, 30% of the people living in communities affected by violence where collective reparations projects were being implemented did not know about the project or did not know about its reparative nature. On the contrary, many of them believed that the benefits they have received were just regular development projects, and were unaware of their reparatory intent.[14] Reparations should not be merely a re-classified form of the social and economic assistance that the state is already obliged to provide. Reparations in name, but not in fact, are not reparations. In addition, they should never do harm, for instance, by forcing a sense of community reconciliation or by pushing victims to express forgiveness or renounce their rights to pursue justice. They should strive to be inclusive, reflecting the interests of women and other disempowered members of the community. To guard against these risks and to make certain that collective reparations are used correctly, careful planning and monitoring is required, complete with opportunities for victim participation and feedback.

5. FINANCING REPARATIONS

One of the most difficult issues for defining and implementing reparations is estimating their cost and identifying sources for financing them. Policymakers will almost always raise other competing needs, the lack of funding or the costs associated with the implementation of reparations measures as an excuse for not engaging in discussions about reparations or for dismissing any attempt to implement them. These concerns are understandable. All societies and governments need to prioritize between different public policies and, sometimes contradictory, needs, especially in contexts of reconstruction. These priorities are often defined by matters of urgency, but also by how close the leadership feels to victims and how much they care for them. By approaching reparations as a policy to provide support to victims in the context of a message of acknowledgment and inclusion, policymakers may help define forms of reparations that have a smaller impact on the national budget and are more consistent with other development or social security policies.

---

[14] Asociación Pro Derechos Humanos & International Center for Transitional Justice, *Escuchando las Voces de las Comunidades: Reporte Nacional de Vigilancia del Programa de Reparaciones Colectivas*, Lima, 2008; http://ictj.org/node/4515. More efforts had been done in communicating the reparatory intent of the program in subsequent stages of its implementation, especially during the ceremonies of finalizing the works. However, in many cases what is stressed is the recognition of the fight against subversive groups, and not the suffering of victims caused by those groups, as well as the armed forces. In those ceremonies little attention is paid to the responsibility of the state in the whole conflict.

It is not possible to commit to an expensive program if its costs are not established, at least, in broad terms. Fiscal responsibility demands a serious assessment of costs; it also requires flexibility. Categories of victims and the scope of reparations measures need to be defined, and efforts need to be undertaken to estimate the number of beneficiaries, usually through a process of victim registration. While a full registration effort is not essential for establishing a clear estimation of the overall cost and budget of the reparations program, some dedicated effort is vital to obtain a solid figure. Registration can also be helpful in identifying some of the difficulties that the program might need to overcome to deliver the reparations to the beneficiaries. Given the number of victims and the extent of the suffering of victims of genocide in Rwanda, the government allocated 5% of the national budget to the FARG. There is no other case of such a significant fiscal commitment to pay reparations that respond to the unique conditions created by the genocide and the nature of the Rwandan Patriotic Front (RPF) government.

As with any other expense, policymakers are always tempted to find extraordinary sources of funding so that the reparations policy does not affect the national budget. Strong calls for international support, based sometimes on the establishment of the responsibility of other countries or of an undefined international community, are frequently made, with or without sufficient bases. However, even in cases of clear responsibility of some states or the UN, especially for failing to provide protection, as in the case of Rwanda, those efforts have been futile. The most states are willing to commit is to provide forms of relief or assistance, but never to acknowledging responsibility and contributing to reparations, as in the case of the Belgian Senate resolution on recommending the creation of a fund to support victims of the Rwandan genocide (Rombout & Vandeginste 2005, 327). States are also reluctant to demand the responsibility of another state when they cherish their aid and good relations, as in the case of Timor-Leste towards Indonesia, or Rwanda towards Belgium or France.

In regards to contributions to reparations by the international community, even in the case of countries with low levels of development, and substantial international support for international or national prosecutions, or for the establishment of a truth commission, there are no precedents of a substantial contribution of the international community to implement reparations. The United Nations Peace Building Fund granted USD 3 million to Sierra Leone for the implementation of a reparations program in 2009, which helped to register almost 30,000 victims. However, the program fell short in responding to victims' needs and in meeting the recommendations of the Truth and Reconciliation Commission. Once the funds were exhausted, the program was not continued by the Sierra Leonean government. There are other cases where specific reparations policies have been financed by donors or through grants of international aid, but those refer mostly to the establishment of a program to be later continued by the state or to discrete actions. The Peruvian Reparations Council has received grants from international donors to help with efforts of registering victims, and there are numerous cases of international aid given for processes of consultation with victims or technical assistance in drafting a law or implementing certain policies. Nevertheless, there is no precedent for international aid as the primary funder for reparations to victims, especially if such aid includes continued services or payments that involve long-term financial commitment. The closest one can come to an example of such a commitment is in the context of disarmament, demobilization and reintegration programs, which are often limited to a few years. Such efforts, unfortunately, often receive more political attention than reparations, because they are more directly perceived as being important strategic policies for guaranteeing peace.

In addition, if reparations are about expressing the inclusion of victims to society, it seems contradictory that society refuses to provide funding for them, and resorts to international aid. Even in cases where other countries were significantly involved in the conflict and in the perpetration of massive crimes, domestic national responsibility should not be diminished. A reparations program should be owned by the society that seeks to integrate its victims, and thus the program should be funded primarily by that society.

Nevertheless, an important form of contribution to financing reparations from the international community is debt relief. This could free significant resources to a heavily indebted country, but still allows for national ownership of the process. In some cases where the external debt was incurred by the repressive regime responsible for human rights violations, debtor countries may own up to the role they played supporting it. This was used in Ghana, where the government agreed on a Multilateral Debt Relief Initiative with major creditor countries and international financial institutions. Part of the funds relieved from servicing the debt were allocated for financing reparations from the national budget, and were used to pay lump sums to victims (Oduro 2008).

One commonly-used mechanism for financing reparations is the establishment of a reparations fund. This type of fund could receive contributions from the government, as well as from other institutions held responsible or through voluntary contributions. Some funds are the result of settlements among states, private companies or organizations and victims' organizations, as is the case of the Foundation Remembrance, Responsibility and Future of Germany established to pay compensation to slave workers and forced labour of the Nazi Germany, or the General Settlement Fund of Austria. Others funds, for instance in the case of the South African President's Fund or the Victims' Trust Fund of Sierra Leone, were established by the national authorities to provide reparations and to channel voluntary contributions. By asking for voluntary contributions, these funds offer the possibility of attracting states that are not willing to accept responsibility for the violations, but in some way intend to express solidarity and support for victims. Even though this could be regarded as a cynical position, many victims would still welcome it, if the contribution provides some relief to their situation. However, very often these funds do not receive substantial contributions, as the case of Sierra Leone demonstrates. In the case of the South African fund, after a one-time payment was disbursed, which was far below what was recommended by its truth commissions, no other measure has been implemented.

Even if contributions for these funds are guaranteed, as is the case of the settlements, funds can only implement reparations policies consisting of one-time payments. It is not possible for them to finance such permanent or long-term payments – as pensions – and they have limited capacity to fund such other long-term activities as health care services for victims. Moreover, even when financing lump-sum payments, they can fall short, as the number of beneficiaries or the amount of the claims could exceed the fund. In both the cases of Germany and Austria, the amounts given to some categories of victims or in response to certain claims had to be reduced, making the payments even more reduced and symbolic than they were originally intended to be. Claimants demanding compensation for property loss at the Austrian Fund had to go through a complex process of determining the value of the loss, but ended up receiving 15% to 10% of the value that was established.

On the whole, a reparations program that includes a series of measures that require implementation over several years is better allocated at the national budget. Greater flexibility is provided if the number of victims increases, due to large-than-expected registrations, or decreases, due to recipient deaths. The establishment of the type and amount of benefits by law provides victims certainty and a system for demanding them.

Reparation policies that are implemented over time also help to ease the burden on a particular fiscal year. The costs of pensions, scholarships and health are distributed over time, in contrast with lump-sum payments or housing subsidies. Thus, by not putting all the finance pressure into a certain fiscal year, those policies could provide for substantial benefits to victims over their duration.

In some cases, lump-sum payments have been distributed in several instalments. The Truth and Reconciliation Commission of South Africa recommended a grant based on the median annual household income (the exact amount for each victim varied according to different factors), to be paid each semester over six years. However, the government finally paid a more reduced amount in one instalment.

Another strategy used to ease the financial pressure in a fiscal year was adopted in Argentina, through the issuance of public debt consolidation bonds. These bonds matured in 16 years, allowing people to exchange them in the bonds market at a lower value or to wait until their maturity. The bonds' holders began receiving interest and monthly payments 6 years after issuance. While perhaps an attractive budgeting approach, this policy failed to convey an unambiguous message of inclusion. It was essentially a promise deferred; passing the obligation to pay onto the next government, without requiring shared sacrifice today. It did not generate much satisfaction on the part of victims, despite the amounts nominally granted, partly because of the form the mechanism took, but also because it was implemented in the context of continuing impunity of perpetrators, where presidential pardons were granted even to the few who were convicted. In such context, some organizations of victims even rejected receiving reparations (Guembe 2006). It is not clear how much of the opposition that this reparation policy suffered was because of the use of this deferral mechanism. However, it seems very obvious that postponing payments might have affected the sincerity of the message of inclusion.

Debates over reparations funding also offer a possibility for a debate about the allocation of resources of the state budget. Debating the national budget is one of the most important aspects of political debate in a democratic society, but so often it falls to experts and legislators who work behind closed doors. If resources are to be allocated appropriately and if priorities are to be defined in a way that acknowledges victims, a transparent debate is important. In analysing reparations in South Africa, Hamber and Rasmussen (2000) offer an interesting comparative chart of the cost of the reparations program proposed by the Truth and Reconciliation Commission and several indicators, including the total government expenditure and the national defence budget. Talking in comparative figures helps having a perspective of the priorities set by governments and parliaments in regards to expenditure. However, these comparisons can also be used by those arguing against reparations, usually comparing the costs of a reparations program with other social programs, such as building schools or hospitals, or the number of children whose education could be paid. When debating reparations, the national budget as a whole should be considered, including all significant expenditures, such as the defence budget in the comparison, so that the debate is not merely one between the relative cost of social expenditures, but about the relative costs of all of the government's priorities. Transparent information and public debate can counter arguments used for denying reparations based on the scarcity of resources, by demonstrating that funding depends on political will and not on the unavailability of funds. The debate could lead to a redistribution of expenditures or to the creation of new taxes that could help finance the effort, if that is needed and prioritized.

Finally, understanding that public expenditure is the main source for funding reparations, the recovery of assets from perpetrators could have an important symbolic effect. It links the direct responsibility of the crimes with the reparations effort. However, making reparations dependent on the recovery of assets can have serious problems, as it is uncertain how much and when the assets will be recovered. After several years of implementing a novel process that tries to combine demobilization of former combatants, justice, revealing the truth about crimes, and reparations – through what was called a Peace and Justice Law –, Colombia's government realized in 2008 that, in addition, they needed to implement an administrative reparations program. The Peace and Justice process established reduced sentences for demobilized commanders of paramilitary units conditioned on full disclosure of the crimes committed in judicial hearings, and to seizing all their assets to pay reparations for the victims of those crimes. The design of the process shows a great deal of legal creativity, including the possibility of victims who cannot identify the perpetrators of the crimes they suffer to also apply for reparations. The reparations fund receives contributions not only from the assets recovered from the demobilized former paramilitaries, but also from the state. However, the process ended up being too complicated and long, and even after several years, the more than 230,000 victims registered by the special prosecutors have not received reparations. The government realized that it needed to implement, in parallel, an administrative reparations process for all victims of non-state actors (including the demobilized paramilitaries and guerrillas, but also those guerrillas not yet demobilized), as Díaz and Sánchez (2009) reported. There are serious objections to the administrative process, but it proves the need of not relying absolutely or even in a significant part on a judicial process or on the recovery of assets for providing reparations for massive number of victims. In a context where a massive number of perpetrators has no assets, victims cannot be left without any form of redress. That explains the creation of a fund to provide reparations for victims even if the perpetrators found guilty of their crimes are poor, as it is in the case of the FIND. In sum, assets recovered from perpetrators can be important contributions for a reparations program and they add a significant symbolic value, but they should not become an obstacle or create delay in reparations processes that need to be implemented promptly and without making too many distinctions between victims.

6. IMPLEMENTING REPARATIONS

The design of reparations programs that include all types of victims and comprehensive policies are not rare. Interesting recommendations were made by different truth commissions in the last 20 years that include this type of programs.[15] Unfortunately, the gap between recommendations and concrete implementation is immense. Few policies have been executed in experience.

---

[15]   Among them are the reports of the Truth and Reconciliation Commission of Chile, in 1991; of the Truth and Reconciliation Commission of South Africa, in 1998; of the Commission of Historical Clarification of Guatemala, in 1998; of the Truth and Reconciliation Commission

Why the gap? The implementation of reparations programs faces several challenges after they had been recommended by an independent body, even in case those recommendations include concrete provisions and can be used as bases for the design of those programs. Among the difficulties it is possible to identify the following: (1) defining victims and beneficiaries; (2) transforming the recommendations into law; (3) defining and creating implementing institutions; (4) registering victims; (5) providing services and goods; and (6) communicating with victims.

6.1. DEFINING VICTIMS AND BENEFICIARIES

The definition of victims entitled to reparations is a complex political task. It requires creating an objective definition of 'victim' that will include people who suffered crimes from any side in the conflict, or from a specific side of it. It also includes defining which are the crimes to be included – if all of them, or if some form of prioritization should be made. Finally, it also involves including, or not, some form of additional priority in terms of needs or vulnerability of those entitled to reparations. All these choices are very sensitive matters that will affect not only the capacity to implement reparations, but also how they will be perceived by the victims and by the general population, a crucial issue if reparations are understood as a message of inclusion.

The question about including victims of all sides of the conflict is probably the most political one. It defines the role played by the different actors during the conflict, especially by current authorities. Different reparations programs, some based on the work of truth commissions and some not, have been defined to include only victims of one side of the conflict, excluding those associated with whoever is understood as 'the enemy' or the main violator. The Argentinean National Commission for the Disappeared, by defining the scope of its truth seeking effort to that crime, limited itself to crimes committed by the dictatorship. This was consistent with the fierce opposition that the Argentinean human rights organizations made against what was called 'the theory of the two demons', or the attempt to equalize the crimes committed by the insurgency with the crimes committed by the state. Later, reparations were paid to the relatives of the disappeared, as well as to other categories of victims of the state security forces.

Colombia's situation is different, as it is implementing reparations efforts through the Peace and Justice Law and through a humanitarian assistance law, refereed only to victims of the guerrillas or the demobilized paramilitaries that

---

of Peru, in 2003; of the Truth and Reconciliation Commission of Sierra Leone, in 2004; of the National Commission of Political Imprisonment and Torture of Chile, in 2004; and of the Commission on Reception, Truth and Reconciliation of Timor-Leste, in 2005.

fight them, but that do not include victims of the state. The government has refused to accept responsibility for the crimes committed by its agents, and bases reparations efforts on solidarity and not on its failed obligation to protect victims. Victims of state agents need to resort to the judiciary to obtain compensation.

In other cases of truth commissions which have led to reparations programs, as in Chile, Guatemala, Peru, Timor-Leste, Sierra Leone or South Africa, both victims of state agents and insurgents have been included. In all these cases, except for Peru and Sierra Leone, the proportion of victims of state agents is considerably higher than that of insurgent groups (in Chile, only 2% of the killings are attributed to opposition groups, and no disappearances; in Guatemala, 4% of the killings and disappearances are attributed to the guerrillas). Despite these figures, the truth seeking and reparations efforts were defined as comprehensive efforts towards reconciliation, rejecting the crimes and acknowledging the suffering of victims, no matter which side their perpetrators were representing.

In the cases of Peru and Sierra Leone, which suffered crimes committed by different actors, reparations have been recommended for victims of all sides. Peru has recognized its direct responsibility in the crimes committed by its agents (37% of the total estimation of crimes, according to the Truth and Reconciliation Commission). It has also accepted responsibility for not providing protection to victims of the Shining Path guerrillas (54%) and the Tupac Amaru Revolutionary Movement (3%). The reparations law excludes members of both subversive groups, but it is still not clear how this membership will be established, if by a definitive judicial decision or by less strict mechanisms.

A different example is offered by the Chilean Commission on Political Imprisonment and Torture. The Commission was created to establish the victims of state agents, and cases of political kidnapping by subversive groups (three in total) were not covered by its mandate. What is interesting for this debate is that the commission recognized as victims also those who, after being tortured, became themselves state agents or collaborators, participating in the torture of their former comrades. The reasoning of the Commission was that it was created to establish the victims of such state sponsored crimes, and not to qualify other aspects of their historical behaviour. The Commission also rejected excluding victims for having committed serious crimes, considering that in those cases they should have been put on trial, but not tortured.

The same reasoning might be applied to other cases were the same person is both a victim and a perpetrator. However, as the exclusion mentioned in Peru shows, it might be unpopular to grant reparations to someone responsible for mass atrocities. Peruvian authorities have recently argued that reparations granted by the Inter American Court of Human Rights to members of subversive groups should be compensated with what those victims owe the state as result of the crimes for which they are responsible. The argument might be correct for those cases where a judicial decision has established the victims' responsibility to pay damages to the state for certain crimes they committed. However, and in the context of the tens of thousands of victims waiting reparations in Peru, such argument is mere manipulation. Compensating debts will not include, obviously, the forms of symbolic reparations ordered by the Court to the State. Finally, even though it is also controversial, it is generally accepted that child soldiers should be considered victims, since they were forcefully recruited. However, this should not exempt them for their responsibilities for crimes committed once they reached a certain age, according to the national laws and the Convention on the Rights of the Child (see also Grossman, Smeulers, this volume).

Usually the exclusion of certain categories of victims, when it exists, is based on a definition of the crimes covered, which makes it look like an objective definition, not based on the side of the perpetrator or the victims during the conflict. That is the case in Argentina, where only crimes committed by state agents were defined as part of the truth seeking and reparations efforts. This might be technically correct, as it would be incorrect to label the kidnapping or political assassinations of entrepreneurs or security agents in Argentina as enforced disappearances. The use of a concept of victim entitled to reparations that excludes other categories of victims that suffered from massive crimes during the same conflict has also been used in Rwanda. Employing the notion of *rescapés du génocide* for defining the people entitled to reparations under the FARG excludes or makes it extremely difficult for Hutu to be recognized as victims. The notion involves having survived from the persecution of the *génocidaires*. The notion excludes any victim of the RPF, but also makes it difficult for Hutu who were persecuted during the genocide for protecting Tutsi or for being moderate. They will find more obstacles for proving that they were persecuted, a situation that could be presumed in the case of a Tutsi (Rombouts & Vandeginste 2005).

Both cases reflect forms of discrimination of certain categories of victims based on what seems to be objective criteria. In the case of Argentina, crimes committed by the state apparatus, as part of a repressive policy, are more serious in nature and that is why they constitute gross violations of human rights. It would also be technically incorrect to name as victims of genocide those victims of the RPF. They are victims of war crimes, not genocide. These options could be considered reasonable, based on the strong rejection that genocide or a state policy of disappearance deserves. However, as has been showed by the examples of other countries, these are not the only options available. On the contrary, accepting responsibilities for their own crimes, even when they represent a minimal portion of the crimes committed, does not necessarily undermine the responsibility of the main perpetrator or the legitimacy of those who defeated them. Moreover, rejecting all crimes committed, but also making the necessary distinctions between them, has the potential of signalling the rejection of all crimes and value that human rights has for the transitional government. This is especially important for the perception of legitimacy of a reparations program, given that for each victim, the loss of a loved one has a serious impact on his or her life, no matter who committed the crime.

Defining who the victims who deserve reparations are includes also deciding if they should be defined as victims of all the crimes committed, or some of them. Not all reparations programs have had a comprehensive focus on all crimes. As mentioned, the first measures of reparations in Argentina were given to the relatives of the disappeared. Later, substantial amounts were also given to certain political prisoners. That led to the inclusion of other groups of political prisoners and later to the relatives of the disappeared and children removed from their disappeared mother and raised with different identities. In Chile, only the victims of the executed and disappeared were initially included in the truth seeking and reparations efforts. Later, those dismissed from civil service and public companies received reparations, and only after 13 years were the survivors of torture recognized and scheduled for reparations.

Examples of comprehensive reparations programs, which include victims of killings, disappearance, torture, kidnapping, amputation or disability, and sexual violence are found in the recommendations of truth commissions or laws of Peru, Guatemala, Timor-Leste and Sierra Leone. However, few of them have been implemented.

Finally, the recommendations of the truth commissions of Timor-Leste and Sierra Leone included some provisions to prioritize the most vulnerable victims. A similar notion is found in the Rwandan FARG, which defines beneficiaries as those victims in most need. In Peru, the current discussion about individual reparations includes starting the disbursement of money and health care services to the eldest. These could be legitimate options consistent with the need for reaching those most vulnerable. They are also consistent with the notion of establishing a reparations standard that could, at least, guarantee a minimal level of survival with dignity, as is being proposed in this chapter.

6.2. TRANSFORMING RECOMMENDATIONS INTO LAW

Usually truth commissions, even when formed by independent and well-respected persons, do not have the authority to pass mandatory provisions. This is understandable, because according to traditional constitutionalism, the state organs with authority to create mandatory general provisions (laws) is the legislative branch, and the ones with authority to regulate the exercise of rights and duties established by law reside in the executive branch. In addition, national budgets are defined by law in negotiations that also include the executive branch of government. All of them derive their legitimacy in the popular election of their members, as representatives of the people. However, even in cases where the mandate of a truth commission is passed into law, and its recommendations become mandatory, political will is still required to effectively implement what is most commonly a complex set of policies. To make this happen, the policies should reflect a broad agreement among the political representatives of the people. The provision of resources from the state budget, the appointment of qualified people to coordinate or directly implement the reparations program, the commitment of state services to join the implementation effort require political will. The recommendations of a commission that dissolves after delivering its report does not necessarily convince authorities that might have been absent from the commission's deliberations. Governing authorities need to assume the recommendations as their own, holding public debates that could translate recommendations into a full-fledged policy decision to implement, whether fully or partially, the recommendations.

The end of the mandate of a truth commission affects the possibilities of transforming its recommendations into law or effective policy. Even when political debate does occur, the opinions and experiences of the truth commissioners may not be included. The Commission in Peru tried a different approach, extending the mandate of the commissioners for several months after the report was delivered, so they could guarantee that it was debated. This included a plan for conferences, as well as debate at the National Congress. However, this plan was not implemented and that crucial stage of the commission work was abandoned. Nevertheless, part of the reparations program recommended by the Peruvian commission was passed into law two years after delivering its report. This was done partly as result of the strong civil society participation during the debates inside the commission about reparations. The inclusion of civil society and victims organizations in drafting the recommendations of reparations increased the number of stakeholders, beside the commissioners, who felt that the recommendations reflected their interests. Those organizations mobilized their influence to push for a debate about reparations in the National Congress agenda; and, through their active lobby, the National Congress was able to pass a law that created a comprehensive reparations program, followed by a presidential decree that helped define its content (Correa, Guillerot & Magarrell 2009). Despite this, the actual implementation of the law has been slow. The recent election of Álan García, in whose first presidency the commission to investigate repressive policies and massacres occurred,[16] has created an additional obstacle for implementing the recommendations of the Commission. During his current presidency, the implementation of reparations has been limited to collective reparations and delayed by the government's refusal to provide enough

---

[16] Álan García was president of Peru from 1985 to 1990. Under his presidency, 8,173 persons were killed or disappeared, 30% of which corresponds to actions of the state security forces.

funding for the registration of victims. A slow progress, but even that would have been impossible, under the political circumstances, if there had not been a program approved by law and a strong civil society pushing for its implementation.

In the case of Rwanda, despite the early announcements of a reparations policy and the creation of the FARG and the FIND, delays and continuous changes in different drafts demonstrate a lack of clear commitment. Establishing reparations by law implies defining the beneficiaries objectively, defining the benefits to which they are entitled, guaranteeing the funding, and defining the implementing institution. All of this means transforming an aspiration, based on international or national principles and commitments, into an obligation, whose fulfilment can be demanded by victims. It means passing from the rhetoric of supporting and expressing solidarity with victims to recognizing them as right-holders against the state, a step that in many cases is not an easy one.

6.3. DEFINING AND ESTABLISHING IMPLEMENTING INSTITUTIONS

The definition of an implementing institution is usually part of the political debate of approving a reparations law. In some cases, the reparations law creates a new institution. In other instances the role is assigned to an existing one.[17] New institutions are created based on the need of having independent bodies that could offer credibility to the society as a whole, instead of assigning the role purely to government institutions. The National Corporation of Reparations and Reconciliation of Chile was governed by a board, whose president was appointed by the President of the Republic and whose remaining six members were appointed by agreement of the Senate and the President of the Republic. The Council of Registry of Peru is governed by a Board of seven members selected by

---

[17] As in the case of Chile, where Law 19,123 of 1992, which established a reparations program for the victims of killing and disappearances of the 1973–1990 dictatorship, created the National Corporation of Reparation and Reconciliation. Law 28,592 of 2005, of Peru, established the Comprehensive Reparations Program for victims of the 1980–2000 internal armed conflict, creating the Council of Registry. The law assigns the coordination role of the program to an existing commission of representatives of different ministries and of members of civil society created previously for the coordination of all peace and reparations policies. In Timor-Leste a law for the creation of a follow up institution for the implementation of the recommendations of the Commission on Truth Reception and Reconciliation and of the Commission on Truth and Friendship is being discussed. In Morocco, the reparations recommended by the Equity and Reconciliation Commission are being implemented by the Advisory Council of Human Rights, a pre-existing institution modelled under the 1991 Paris Principles of National Institutions of Human Rights.

the President of the Republic and includes a balanced number of retired officers of the armed forces and civil society representatives.

In addition to the Reparations Council in charge of registering victims, a government-led commission was created to coordinate all aspect of the implementation of reparations. It is the High Level Multisector Commission to provide follow-up on actions and state policies regarding peace, collective reparations, and national coordination (known as CMAN, by the Spanish acronym of the first four words of this long name), and includes representatives of all the different ministries involved, as well as four civil society representatives. The Commission is chaired by the President of the Ministry Council, a kind of *primus inter pares* in the cabinet, and its executive secretary has taken the role of directly implementing the collective reparations program.

Other examples of institutional creation come from the cases of multiparty settlement that bring life to reparations programs, as is the case of the Foundation Remembrance, Responsibility and Future of Germany. In the case of Austria, the General Settlement Fund is implemented by the existing National Fund of the Republic of Austria for Victims of National Socialism, also created by law.[18] All these institutions are governed by an autonomous board of trustees, established in the law.

In other cases implementation has been left to a government agency or ministry, as in the case of Argentina, where the task of receiving and evaluating the applications of potential beneficiaries was left to different ministries defined by the laws.[19] Reparations not established by law have been implemented by existing government agencies in charge of the implementation of social policies, as in the case of the National Commission of Social Action of Sierra Leone, or the Ministry of Justice and Attorney General, in the case of Ghana.

The diversity of alternatives reflects the need to respond to different contexts. However, in defining the implementation body it might be important to consider a delicate balance between autonomy and authority. On the one hand, such institution needs legitimacy, in the eyes of victims and society in general, which could mean establishing some degree of autonomy from the government. On the other hand, it might need to effectively coordinate policies that are going to be implemented by government agencies. Some aspects of the implementation might require more autonomy, for instance relating to the registration of victims,

---

[18] Created by Law 432 of 1995, which also established a reparations program previous to the 2000 Washington Agreement that resulted in the General Settlement and of additional reparations policies.

[19] Law 23,466 of 1987, which established a pension for the relatives of the disappeared, assigned the review of applications to the Ministry of Health and Social Action. Laws 24,043 of 1992 and 24,411 of 1994assigned that task to the Ministry of Interior, once it was created a Directorship of Human Rights. The Directorship was later upgraded to an Undersecretary of Human and Social Rights, and later to a Secretariat of Human Rights under the Ministry of Justice, Security and Human Rights.

and others might require a closer relationship with government agencies, as in the case of the coordination or supervision of the implementation of public policies on health care or others as part of the reparations program.

6.4. REGISTERING VICTIMS

Identifying victims through a process of registration is one of the main challenges that a reparations program faces. Insufficient or erroneous registration that leads to the exclusion of some victims or the delivery of reparations to people that are not victims will diminish the legitimacy of the reparations effort. Victims excluded will feel resentful and the general population will perceive that the program is not more than a corrupt effort to reward supporters. Some of the criticism and accusations of corruption in the implementation of the housing program by FARG, in Rwanda, could have been prevented with a better system of registration that firmly established the identity of those entitled to housing.

When a reparations program derives from the work of a truth commission, the commission is usually able to register some victims, not all of them, due to their time limits and other competing responsibilities. Usually not all victims are reached in the short life of a truth commission, or not all the information needed to implement a reparations program is requested, as in the case of the registration of the relatives entitled to reparations. Frequently a new effort of registration is needed to complete the list of victims and beneficiaries or to update it for the implementation of reparations.

Some truth commissions, in Argentina, Chile and Morocco for example, registered most of the victims of the crimes they were investigating. That allowed policymakers to define the reparations programs without having to perform an additional registration process. Reparations were implemented simultaneously to the additional registration required to finish the list of victims, which resulted in no more delays. In addition, subsequent registration efforts did not increase considerably the number of victims, or created a serious budgetary problem. However, it is interesting to note that in these cases, despite the comprehensive efforts to register victims early on, additional registration processes were implemented several years after.[20] In addition, when beneficiaries are the relatives

---

[20]   In Argentina the different process of registration of victims done by the Ministry of Interior had been reopened several times, to include people that weren't registered previously. Likewise, in Chile law 20,405 of 2009 created a new commission to identify victims of both previous truth seeking and registration efforts, after registration for victims of killings and disappearances was completed in 1996 and registration of victims of political imprisonment and torture was completed in 2005. This decision, though, was motivated especially by the need to extend what was evaluated as a very short process of registration of victims of political imprisonment and torture, which lasted only six months.

of the victims, a registration process is also required, but does not necessarily constitute a precondition for defining the reparations measures.

Unlike Argentina, Chile and Morocco where the numbers of victims were more limited, commissions involving broader and more massive conflicts, have not been able to individualize victims and have resorted to estimations for reaching their conclusions. Such was the case in Peru, Sierra Leone and Timor-Leste. Despite the effort to reach and register victims here, the members of these commissions understood that a massive follow-up registration process would be needed. In these cases, it is more difficult to define the reparations measures without a more precise estimate of the total number of victims.

Victim registration should not merely be a bureaucratic necessity. When done well, it offers an additional opportunity to listen to victims and acknowledge the responsibility of the state for the crimes suffered. Officers of the state, acting in the name of the state, are given the chance to meet victims in an official setting, to listen and to acknowledge. This alone can have a very important reparatory effect for victims. Although these interviews need to be carefully conducted to avoid any perception that victims are being forced to describe in detail things they rather not discuss, such opportunities should not be forsaken. Some victims might need to describe in detail what happened to them, while others might need to remain in silence and only say what is essential for the process of verification. The interview process should be conducted in a way that is flexible and responsive to different victim's needs. In addition, it should be conducted so as to avoid opening wounds or sparking psychological responses that cannot be closed in the interview.

However, in many cases, victims have registered by using individual applications forms and submitting documentary evidence for evaluation. That was the process employed in Argentina and in the case of the slave workers and forced labour reparations program implemented by the Foundation Remembrance, Responsibility and Future of Germany. Other massive processes of registration, such as the ones being implemented in Peru by the Council of Registration or by the National Commission of Social Action of Sierra Leone, can leave little space for active listening and engagement with victims. Even if listening and receiving the victims is defined as part of the objectives of the interviews, as is the case of the two truth commissions in Chile and the current new process of registration, practicalities may intrude: time constraints and conflicting objectives, such as an obligation to evaluate the accuracy of the testimonies being received, may make it difficult to actively listen to victims. One statement taken by a state representative at the current *Comisión Asesora para la calificación de Detenidos Desaparecidos, Ejecutados Políticos y Víctimas de Prisión Política y Tortura* formally expresses, in the name of the state, how sorry she is for the suffering caused to the person interviewed. However, this is left to the staff initiative rather than being part of an official policy of the Commission. A more intentioned policy for providing support to victims and for having a victim-centred approach during the process of statement taking was implemented by the Commission of Reception (*Acolhimento*), Truth and Reconciliation of Timor-Leste. It included special training for statement takers to allow them to be alert to the victims needs of further support, as well as the official policy of understanding that the "statement taking was the first step in the healing process the Commission was promoting," as stated in the Commission report.[21]

An important aspect of a registration process is defining its duration. As with truth commission mandates, registration efforts are usually defined to last several months or, at most, a few years. They are seen as extraordinary efforts that need to have a limited life and to produce quick and concrete results, especially when identifying victims is part of the process of defining a reparations policy. Often the effort is concentrated in a specific term, after which implementation of reparations soon follows. However, time restraints inevitably lead to exclusions. Insufficient outreach may exclude some victims. Others may be reluctant to present their testimonies out of a lack of confidence in the process caused by years of denial of the crimes committed, a frustration with the legacy of the human rights violations themselves, a lack of confidence about the confidential use of the records, political disagreement with the reparations policies or the profound trauma caused by the crimes. Some victims may have difficulty even recognizing themselves as victims or may feel psychologically unready to talk about their suffering, after many years trying to suppress or even erase the horrible memories. Past experiences bear out these patterns of behaviour.

In many cases where registration efforts were of limited duration, new processes of registrations had to be re-opened. Argentina and Chile provide two cases on point. In Chile, a review of the cases received during a second registration process currently being implemented shows that many victims knew about the previous registration process, but did not feel prepared to give their testimonies or did not trust it. Apparently, only after several years and the implementation of concrete measures of reparations, did they feel safe enough and prepared to declare. Nevertheless, subsequent processes of registration run the risk of being used by people attempting to present false claims, attracted by the possibility of receiving benefits.

In other cases the registration process remained open indefinitely, an approach more consistent with the principle that no statute of limitations should limit the right to reparations of human rights violations. Actually, limiting registration to a term makes it difficult to justify the exclusion of victims for not having applied on time. However, even an open-ended approach presents

---

[21] Commission of Reception, Truth and Reconciliation, *"Chega!" Report of the Commission of Reception, Truth and Reconciliation of Timor-Leste*, Dili, Timor-Leste, 2005, Chapter 10, p. 18.

challenges. Administrators must find a way of building the necessary sense of bureaucratic urgency into a permanent process. Otherwise, all or most victims may not be reached promptly, outreach efforts could falter and the range of geographic coverage, especially in outlying cities and rural areas, as well as among victims living in the diasporas, may be circumscribed.

Confidentiality is another important component of any victim registration process, and must apply not only within the context of the process itself, but must also protect the confidentiality of information gathered during the process. This is particularly important in the case of humiliating crimes or crimes that can affect the prestige or inclusion of the victims in their communities, as is often the case with crimes of sexual violence. Although some victims assume a vocal position in the process, using it to make their stories known, most victims are not able to take such a public attitude. Confidentiality must be protected unless the victim says the contrary.

In some cases, statement takers should be the same sex as the victim, or be of certain age, to show respect and to know what the interview is about. Officials in Sierra Leone in 2009 tried to respond to these kinds of issues. They conducted their registration of interviews with women victims of sexual violence inside an office, while general registration was done outside. However, unfortunately, this approach had some unintended consequences. In small communities where everybody knows everybody, victims were labelled victims just by allowing them to be interviewed inside an office.

The assurance of confidentiality also involves the access to the statements after the process of verification has finished, as well as the information included in the list of victims entitled to reparations. Two extreme examples of confidentiality are the sealing for 50 years of the files of the Commission of Historical Clarification of Guatemala, imposed by the United Nations, and a similar measure established by law in regards to the files of the Commission on Political Imprisonment and Torture of Chile. Under the need of confidentiality, even the victims themselves cannot demand to receive a copy of their files, nor can the courts access them for criminal investigations. Even though, in the case of the Chilean commission, the files do not have much information useful for establishing the criminal responsibility of perpetrators – the purpose of the commission was to establish the detention of victims, not who was the perpetrator, and the files do not include much information about it –, it seems a reasonable demand that victims could obtain a copy of their files, once cleaned from references to the names of other victims.

There is also room for controversy in regards to how the list of victims is used. The list of victims needs to be accessible to the implementing institutions. Some information such as address or profile information is also necessary for implementation purposes. Additionally, given the need for transparency whenever benefits are disbursed to individuals, it might be advisable that the list of names be public, especially in the case of financial reparations. However, transparency does not require full disclosure. A general list of recipients may suffice and should not identify and link specific victims to specific crimes. Lists of beneficiaries might be organized in broad benefit categories rather than by crime or even specific harm, to avoid disclosing any information that could affect the victims' reputation.

Finally, it is necessary to verify the accuracy of victims' testimonies when registering them, either for determining if the situation they suffered is covered under the scope of crimes included in the reparations program or for determining its veracity. As argued before, a massive process should not comply with the same standards as a judicial investigation. Massive reparations programs are premised on a general acknowledgment that massive crimes were committed and thus can rely on historical information about the events. Especially in cases of massive crimes committed in rural areas or under circumstances of widespread violence and little possibilities for registration or filing complaints, it can be presumed that people of a certain profile living in those areas at that time presenting their application to the registry and tell a coherent history, were victims of some crimes. In some cases, laws or regulations explicitly reverse the burden of proof in favour of victims, as occurred in Peru (Article V of the Preliminary Title). In other cases the process of verification is left to the discretion of the commissioners. In the case of the Commission of Political Imprisonment and Torture of Chile, close to 40% of the testimonies were unsupported by documentation and were not in official records. Each of them was evaluated on their own merit according to the general coherence of the testimony and the circumstances of the event. For those crimes committed during the early years of the dictatorship, human rights organizations were just starting their job of advocacy and registering. And for those committed in rural areas, the lack of documents or registration was considered not essential for verification purposes. The evidentiary bar was set higher in urban cases that occurred in the later years, when an independent media and a more active human rights movement existed and was actively covering claims of human rights violations.

As for verification of torture after several years, the same commission did not demand medical evaluations, but found that it was enough if convincing evidence existed showing that the victims were detained based on repressive laws. Given the massive number of reports of torture, contained in 94% of the testimonies received, the commission presumed that torture happened. The definition of the commission mandate did not require distinguishing cases of political imprisonment where torture occurred from those where it did not happen, and the commission recommended one general category of victim, which helped the process of identification and of the implementation of reparations.

However, the different evidentiary standards that can be based on legitimate distinctions about what can be presumed in different places and circumstances cannot result in the discrimination of certain categories of victims. That is the case with establishing higher standards of evidence for *rescapés du génocide* who are Hutu, in Rwanda. Even though such a requirement could respond to the additional difficulty in determining that a Hutu was persecuted as part of the genocide directed against the Tutsi, the main problem lays in the use of the notion of *rescapés du génocide*, as argued previously.

Another aspect to be defined is how centralized or decentralized the effort should be. Centralization offers the advantage of having a more consistent criterion for verification of who should be registered. On the other hand, a decentralized effort could use the help of local resources and knowledge for outreach and verification. However, decentralization may result in problems with regard to objectivity; for example, registering cronies of those in charge of the verification process, not guaranteeing confidentiality of the stories told by victims and acceptance or rejection based on criteria not relevant for the reparations process, all of which could lead to the exclusion of victims based on animosity. Another problem with a decentralized process is the disparity of the criteria used to verify the condition of victim, where local teams or organizations might hold different standards.

A final challenge in registering beneficiaries is establishing familial relationships with the direct victims in the context of massive numbers of undocumented people. Strict documentation requirements of familial relationships or even of the existence of someone disappeared can pose a significant obstacle for registering victims, especially those who are more poor or marginal. This difficulty is increased in cases of large massacres or displacements, in which the possibility of finding witnesses of the crimes, as well as relationships to victims, is severely diminished.

6.5. PROVIDING SERVICES AND GOODS

The actual delivery of reparations requires the coordination of a network of services that are both efficient and able to transmit the symbolic content. This is a vital part of reparations policy. As discussed in the section about the different types of implementing bodies, although it is not easy to combine these two goals, it is relevant to achieve the objectives of this policy.

In some cases, existing public services may participate directly using their operational networks to reach people, as well as local authorities spread throughout the national territory. When disbursing payments, authorities, for instance, may use the same facilities as are used to pay public servants in rural areas as an inexpensive alternative. Although some adaptation might be required to avoid cumbersome requirements to poor or illiterate victims, such as the opening of banking accounts, by using existing services, governments can avoid duplicative institutional structures, save costs and time, and ensure efficiency in the delivery. However, these benefits will naturally depend on the quality of the services in place and their effective capacity to reach people with the profile of the victims.

For services of a more personal nature, governmental efforts may be complemented by NGOs, community organizations or victims' organizations. Such partnerships can bring confidence and trust to the process, as well as some expertise needed, for example, in regards to psychosocial support. Nevertheless, the exact equation will also depend on the quality of the organizations, their willingness to participate and the needs of victims.

As been argued, for delivering a consistent message of inclusion and recognition, the way that the services and goods are delivered are as important as the goods and services itself. Working with motivated people, who understand the needs of victims and that can be sympathetic with them is crucial. This also translates in the need of consulting victims and of defining with them methods of delivery, as is being discussed below.

6.6. VICTIMS' PARTICIPATION AND COMMUNICATION EFFORTS

The ability of the program to communicate with victims, and to include them and their organizations in the implementation effort, will be fundamental to the success of the program. Participation of victims is important to reinforce the message that the state cares about them and their opinions. It can also improve the effectiveness of the program and to respond to cultural sensitivities. It will allow a more correct diagnosis of the priorities of victims and of their preferences regarding how the program should be implemented.

However, participation is not always easy and selecting the victims who should have a voice in the different stages of implementation is also difficult. One organization cannot be expected to represent all victims, and usually those living in rural areas do not have communication lines with the main organizations, even if they formally belong to them. Competition among victims' organizations is frequent and difficult to avoid. Nevertheless, these difficulties do not diminish the importance of participation and its benefits for achieving the goals of a reparations program.

Based on the experiences of reparations programs designed by several truth commissions, Correa, Guillerot and Magarrell (2009) identify the main advantages and challenges of participation. They identify three stages in which participation is crucial: defining the framework of the truth commission and, consequentially, of the reparations program; defining the reparations policy; and implementing it. They highlight how frequently and easily victims are forgotten in these three stages. Forgetting victims does not necessarily mean not working with victims' organizations, but in relying on a limited number of them. A common mistake lays in understanding that non-governmental organizations express the voice of victims, without engaging directly with victims groups and with unorganized victims. Also, some umbrella organizations do not represent a wide range of victims.

One contentious aspect is defining the role of victims' organizations in the process of registration. These organizations can provide invaluable support in reaching victims who have no information or confidence in a registration process, as well as information that could help with the process of verification. Such was the case with the support provided by organizations at the district level in the registration implemented in Sierra Leone, as well as in reaching women.[22] However, relying exclusively on victims' organizations can create incentives for corruption and manipulation. Problems of such nature have been identified in different registration and implementation efforts, where those registered are only members of certain organizations and unorganized victims are left behind. Complaints about this had been raised by some organizations in Guatemala, where the National Program for Redress is working primarily with one umbrella organization. The commission on torture of Chile faced the same problem when relying exclusively on testimonies of victims' organizations and used additional means of verification during its registry process.

7.   CONCLUSIONS

In much of the literature discussing transitional justice mechanisms, reparations are consistently accorded special stature as the most victim-centred of transitional justice mechanisms. They often represent society's best, and sometimes only, chance to touch victims in their daily lives and needs, and convey a message of inclusion and dignity after a time of severe disaffection and violence. As such, victims and their needs must provide the central reference point in every reparations initiative. Every facet of that effort should be marked by and oriented toward communicating a consistent message that victims are worthy members of the community who have been wronged and deserve assistance. Using past reparations efforts as guides, this chapter has sought to highlight an approach for doing so that is based not on the notion of *restitutio in integrum* or *restitution to the status quo ante*, a concept of minimal use in situations of mass-victimization, but instead is grounded on pragmatic concerns about what will work best for victims while imparting an unequivocal message of inclusion, recognition and acknowledgment.

---

[22]   Correa, C. & Suma, M., *Report and Proposals for the Implementation of Reparations in Sierra Leone*, International Center for Transitional Justice, 2009, www.ictj.org/static/Africa/ SierraLeone/ICTJ_SL_ReparationsRpt_Dec2009.pdf.

Given the complex realities of governance with its budgeting, funding and capacity-building concerns, it is not surprising that reparations efforts often struggle to meet the needs of victims while also maintaining an appropriate balance between the consideration of the past and the challenges of the present and future. It is also not surprising that governments struggle and, at times, fail to achieve an adequate balance between symbolic and material measures, leaving victims dissatisfied and untreated. However, many of these difficulties may be overcome by understanding that there is a symbolic and a material component in every action done, and that reparations initiatives speak to victims. What they say about victims and their place in society matters. Reparations programs need to maintain a consistent orientation toward victims, reaffirming their dignity and worth as citizens and humans.

As had been argued, this message should be expressed in concrete terms, through actions, goods and services, combined with speeches and ceremonies. Victims need to be guaranteed a level of well-being, above poverty, if any true sense of dignity and belonging is to be affirmed. Specific policy choices will inevitably either enhance or undermine this message, and thus decisions need to be made with an eye toward privileging measures that generate a bigger impact in the permanent and future well-being of victims, and overcome, in some degree, the trans-generational consequences of the crimes.

This approach argues for replacing, as contextually unworkable, the notion of restitution to *the status quo ante* or of compensation of all the economically assessable damages. Instead, reparations efforts following mass violence need to focus on more relevant terms of reference, applying a clearer standard of what is fair and appropriate in such situations, and to maintain at all times an overriding objective for policymaking, the need to affirm the dignity and sense of belonging of victims, without disregarding the particularities of each society. This approach does not impose an insurmountable burden on states, but bases its standards on the realities of each country. At every stage in the reparations process, serious discussions and negotiations provide an opportunity at the national level for states to assess, according to national socio-economic standards, what should be done to guarantee dignity and a sense of inclusion.

This approach places reparations not in contradiction with social or development policy, but in symbiosis with it. By highlighting the objective of guaranteeing the well-being of victims, reparations policy is oriented to the present and future and can reinforce and work in parallel with the social policy. Both policies share some features or can be implemented, in a significant form, by the same public services or programs if the reparations measures contain an additional component that makes them different enough that they are perceived by victims as value added measures. A reparations policy can also help set the standard for future social policies or create a network of services that could help in the future to broaden coverage for all. This is especially the case when improvements are made to such areas of the public health care network, as mental health or trauma services.

Although the types of reparations programs discussed may generate more impact in low income families than in middle class ones, who are above the poverty line and have access to private health care, reparations can be designed to have a wider impact. University-level educational scholarships for instance, may be seen by middle class families as something of material value. The same holds true for pensions, because of the symbolic nature of a periodic payment. A reparations program that consists of different services that complement each other and that produces symbolic and material effects can more easily respond to the diverse needs of the victims, attending to each of them where they need the most and creating some degree of satisfaction. Moreover, this potentially redistributive effect of the measures mentioned can be seen as a policy focused on those more vulnerable. That is precisely the orientation of the recommendations of the truth commissions of Timor-Leste and Sierra Leone, and also of the Rwandan FARG, which understand reparations in a context of massive victimization and within the challenges of national reconstruction.

This understanding of reparations also helps define the way reparations should be implemented. Reparations work best when they are delivered expeditiously and when supported by a coordinating body that guarantees the efficacy of the policy, that encourages personal contact and that transmits a coherent message when actual delivering services. This approach prioritizes all these components of good implementation policy. Finally, by emphasizing a victim-focused approach, it seeks to address head-on the different obstacles that victims might face to actually benefit from the reparations policies, particularly in regards to people living in rural areas, or to women who are discriminated against by legal provisions or by traditional practices for administering their own resources, signing contracts or dealing with financial services.

Finally, reparations that involve long-term services require particularized funding. They demand a long-term financial commitment that cannot be addressed through a fund, by voluntary contributions or by resources obtained in a one-time settlement. They require a budgetary commitment spanning perhaps many years. However, while reducing the impact on a specific fiscal year, reparations also cushion the impact over many years, allowing societies to move forward without having to incur debt, use financial reserves or privatize public assets. Moreover, reparations offer an opportunity to rethink priorities and entertain the possibility of getting the country accustomed to a higher public expense in social services that eventually could become part of a permanent policy of social protection and poverty alleviation.

Nevertheless, the challenges facing the implementation of reparations policies are immense. Registering victims and working with almost inexistent networks of social services, especially in the areas of education and health care, pose enormous challenges to poor countries, such as Sierra Leone, Rwanda and Timor-Leste. However, low-cost strategies used in other social services, such as the *animateurs du santé* in Rwanda, can provide ingenious solutions to some of these challenges. Other challenges are common to most countries in a post conflict situation, such as the manipulation of the discourse of human rights violations and the exclusion of broad categories of victims of massive crimes.

Reparations can be seen, then, as an opportunity for the country to come to terms with a tragic past. They can address the consequences of decisions and policies implemented by the country in the past, and they may influence other decisions and policies that may be implemented in the future. Most significantly, however, they can and should oppose the message of exclusion and denial of the human dignity of victims, that took on concrete forms through killings, disappearances, torture and rape. Reparations can and should communicate the opposite message unqualifiedly that all the inhabitants of the country have the same dignity and that victims are valued members of society, delivered by concrete measures that guarantee such dignity. By doing so, they can help set up the foundations of a society which puts the dignity of its people at the centre.

IX. MASSIVE TRAUMA AND THE HEALING ROLE OF REPARATIVE JUSTICE

Yael DANIELI

1. INTRODUCTION

Emphasising the need for a multi-dimensional, multi-disciplinary, integrative framework for understanding massive trauma and its aftermath, this chapter examines victims/survivors' experiences primarily from the psychological perspective. It describes how victims are affected by mass atrocities, their reactions, concerns and needs. Delineating necessary elements in the recovery processes from the victims' point of view, the chapter will focus in particular on those elements of healing that are related to justice processes and victims' experiences of such processes. *Reparative justice* insists that every step throughout the justice experience – from the first moment of encounter of the Court with a potential witness through the follow-up of witnesses after their return home to the aftermath of the completion of the case – presents an opportunity for redress and healing, a risk of missing or neglecting the opportunity for healing victims and reintegrating them into their communities and societies, or, worse, causing (re)victimization and (re)traumatization. While restitution, rehabilitation or compensation may only come after the process has concluded, there are still opportunities along the way. Although not sufficient in itself, *reparative justice* is nonetheless an important, if not necessary, dynamic component among the healing processes. Missed opportunities and negative experiences will be examined as a means to better understand the critical junctures of the trial and victims' role within the process that can, if conducted optimally, lead to opportunities for healing. In what follows I therefore discuss why it is essential to devote resources to *all* elements of justice. In line with the focus of this volume, the chapter will cite related experiences in Africa.

2. CONSPIRACY OF SILENCE

It was in the context of studying the phenomenology of hope in the late 1960s that I interviewed survivors of the Nazi Holocaust. To my profound anguish and outrage, *all* of those interviewed asserted that no one, including mental health professionals, listened to them or believed them when they attempted to share their Holocaust experiences and their continuing suffering. They, and later their children, concluded that people who had not gone through the same experiences could not understand and/or did not care. With bitterness, many thus opted for silence about the Holocaust and its aftermath in their interactions with non-survivors. The resulting *conspiracy of silence* between Holocaust survivors and society (Danieli 1981a; 1982) including mental health, justice and other professionals (Danieli 1981a; 1984) has proven detrimental to the survivors' familial and socio-cultural reintegration by intensifying their already profound sense of isolation, loneliness, and mistrust of society. This has further impeded the possibility of their intrapsychic integration and healing, and made mourning their massive losses impossible.

This imposed silence proved particularly painful to those who had survived the war determined to bear witness. Keilson (1992) similarly demonstrated that a poor post-war environment ("third traumatic sequence") could intensify the preceding traumatic events and, conversely, a good environment might mitigate some of the traumatic effects (Op den Velde 1998).

Because the conspiracy of silence most often follows the trauma, it is the most prevalent and effective mechanism for the transmission of trauma on all dimensions. Both intrapsychically and interpersonally protective, silence is profoundly destructive, for it attests to the person's, family's, society's, community's, and nation's inability to integrate (and constructively respond to) the trauma. They can find no words to narrate the trauma story and create a meaningful dialogue around it. This prevalence of a conspiracy of silence stands in sharp contrast to the widespread research finding that social support is the most important factor in coping with traumatic stress. This applies as well to justice processes. When done optimally, these processes can lead whole societies to begin to dissipate the detrimental effects of the conspiracy of silence.

Nagata (1998) reported that more than twice as many Sansei (children of Japanese-Americans interned by the U.S. Government) whose fathers were in camps, died before the age of 60 compared to Sansei whose fathers were not interned.[1] Nagata speculated that there may be a link between their early deaths and their general reluctance to discuss the internment. Pennebaker and others' (1989) research suggests that avoidance of discussing one's traumatic experience may negatively affect physical health, and Nagata in the present study reported

---

[1] See, also, on the survivors of the Nazi Holocaust, Eitinger 1980. On the fathers of the disappeared in Argentina, see Edelman *et al.* 1992.

that the Sansei's fathers were much less likely to bring up the topic of internment than were their mothers.

The conspiracy of silence is also used *as a defence* for trying to prevent total collapse and breakout of intrusive traumatic memories and emotions. Like paper, it is a very thin and flimsy protection that rips easily. Children of survivors' conflicting attempts to both know and to defend against such knowledge (Auerhahn & Laub 1998) is ubiquitous as well. Aarts (1998) concluded that the conspiracy of silence often is at the core of dynamics that may lead to symptomatology in the second generation. Op den Velde (1998) demonstrated that when offspring of Dutch WWII sailors and resistance fighters observed the "family secret", separation and identification problems arose. Bernstein (1998) chronicled the isolation and emotional distance created when U.S. WWII Prisoners of War avoided close emotional relationships with their spouse and children. In studies of Israel, West Germany and the former GDR, Rosenthal and Volter (1998) found that collective silence had endured, despite the recent emergence of a more open social dialogue about the Holocaust. Their case analyses clearly showed that silence, family secrets, and myths are effective mechanisms that ensure the traumata's continued impact on subsequent generations. As Hannaham (1996, 24) states, "What's left in posterity [is] what Parks,[2] in her drama *The America Play* (1992, 1994) on African American experience calls 'the Great Hole of History'." As Bettelheim (1984, 166) observed, "What cannot be talked about can also not be put to rest; and if it is not, the wounds continue to fester from generation to generation".

My own work in the African context with, for example, victim/survivors in South Africa, Rwanda and Uganda has borne full resemblance to the aforementioned examples. Not astonishingly, Rwanda's President Paul Kagame opened his 10th anniversary speech recognizing that,

> there are people in Rwanda that haven't spoken of the genocide to this day (...). Ten years on, the survivors of these gruesome crimes still suffer in silence. There has been dual survival. Survival of the ordeal and survival of the aftermath of the genocide. A decade has done little to alleviate the anguish.[3]

Victims of dictatorships in Africa as well as elsewhere have suffered silence as an integral part of their trauma, and it is the silence of others that contributed to preventable genocides. There is no wonder that Priscilla Hayner (2001) named her noted book on truth commissions, *Unspeakable Truths*. Oupa Makhalemele (2009) named her analysis of South Africa's survivors' experiences of the process of receiving financial reparations from their government, *Still not Talking*.

---

2   Parks, S-L. (1995). "The America Play (1992, 1994)," in S-L Parks *The America Play and other works*. New York: Theatre Communications Group, at pp. 157–199.

3   Excerpts: Kagame marks genocide http://news.bbc.co.uk/2/hi/africa/3609001.stm.

Though descriptions of what is now understood as post-traumatic stress have appeared throughout recorded history, the development of the field of traumatic stress, or traumatology, has been episodic, marked by interest and denial, and plagued with errors in diagnostic and treatment practices (Herman 1992; Solomon 1995). Indeed, one of the most prevalent and consistent themes during the 20th century has been the denial of psychic trauma and its consequences (Lifton 1979), particularly in the myriad deadly conflicts that find their multigenerational origins in history, the non-resolution of which ensures their perpetuation. One can only marvel at the international dimensions of the conspiracy of silence, as shown by the slowness of the world community to acknowledge and act on the terrible events in the Former Yugoslavia, Rwanda, Burundi and the Sudan.

3. THE NEED FOR A MULTIDIMENSIONAL, MULTIDISCIPLINARY INTEGRATIVE FRAMEWORK

Massive trauma causes such diverse and complex destruction that only a multidimensional, multi-disciplinary integrative framework is adequate to describe it (Danieli 1998). An individual's identity involves a complex interplay of multiple spheres or systems. Among these are the biological and intrapsychic; the interpersonal – familial, social, communal; the ethnic, cultural, ethical, religious, spiritual, natural; the educational/ professional/ occupational; the material/ economic, legal, environmental, political, national and international. Each dimension may be in the domain of one or more disciplines, which may overlap and interact, such as biology, psychology, sociology, economics, law, anthropology, religious studies, and philosophy. Each discipline has its own views of human nature and it is those that inform what the professional thinks and does. These systems dynamically coexist along the time dimension to create a continuous conception of life from past through present to the future. Ideally, the individual should simultaneously have free psychological access to and movement within all these identity dimensions.

Exposure to trauma causes a *rupture*, a possible regression, and a state of being 'stuck' in this free flow, which I have called *fixity*. The time, duration, extent and meaning of the trauma for the individual, the survival mechanisms/ strategies utilised to adapt to it (Danieli 1985), as well as post-victimisation traumata, especially the *conspiracy of silence* elaborated upon above, will determine the elements and degree of rupture, the disruption, disorganisation and disorientation, and the severity of the fixity. The fixity may render the individual vulnerable, particularly to further trauma/ ruptures, throughout the life cycle. It also may render immediate reactions to trauma (e.g. acute stress disorder) *chronic*, and, in the extreme, become life-long *post-trauma/victimisation adaptational styles* (Danieli 1985), when survival strategies generalise to a way of life and become an integral part of one's personality, repertoire of defence, or character armour.

These effects may also become intergenerational in that they affect families and succeeding generations (Danieli 1985; 1998). In addition, they may affect groups, communities, societies and nations. Thus, it is not only what the victim has experienced and suffered during the trauma, be it genocide, crimes against humanity, or war crimes. It is what happens *after* the trauma that crucially affects the long-term, including multigenerational, legacies of the trauma (Keilson 1992).

Multigenerational findings uniformly suggest that the process of redress and the attainment of justice are critical to the healing for individual victims, as well as their families, societies and nations. Klain (1998) underscores its importance for succeeding generations, "to break the chain of intergenerational transmission of hatred, rage, revenge and guilt".

This framework allows evaluation of each system's degree of rupture or resilience, and thus informs the choice and development of optimal multilevel intervention. Repairing the rupture and thereby freeing the flow rarely means, 'going back to normal'. Clinging to the possibility of 'returning to normal' may indicate denial of the survivors' experiences and thereby fixity. The same holds true for expecting testifying in court or any other single measure in the posttraumatic period, to 'make it all OK'. Justice processes, when done optimally, might contribute to lessening the feeling of being stuck for both the survivors and their societies. When they are not, they may exacerbate the fixity by participating in the conspiracy of silence.

In response to some trends in the literature to pathologise, overgeneralise and/or stigmatise survivors' and children of survivors' Holocaust-related phenomena, as well as differences emerging between the clinical and the research literature, I (Danieli 1981) have emphasised the *heterogeneity* of adaptation among survivors' families. Studies by Rich (1982), Klein (1987) and Sigal and Weinfeld (1989) have empirically validated my descriptions of at least four differing post-war "adaptational styles" of survivors' families: the *Victim* families, *Fighter* families, *Numb* families, and families of *'Those who made it'*. This family typology illustrates life-long and intergenerational transmission of Holocaust traumata, the conspiracy of silence, and their effects. Findings by Klein-Parker (1988), Kahana, Harel and Kahana (1989) Kaminer and Lavie (1991) and Helmreich (1992) confirm an *heterogeneity* of *adaptation* and *quality of adjustment* to the Holocaust and post-Holocaust life experiences. This heterogeneity is noted by numerous experts working with other massively traumatised populations. These adaptational styles shape the way survivors view the world and interact with it, including the justice system.

Common sense dictates that it is inevitable for the massive traumata experienced by victims of mass atrocities to have had immediate and possibly long-term effects on them and even on their offspring. Nevertheless, the vast literature on these consequences reveals an arduous struggle in law (Kestenberg 1982), but even more so in psychiatry (Eitinger & Krell 1985), to prove the existence of these effects. Only in 1980 did the evolving descriptions and definitions of the "survivor syndrome" in the psychiatric literature win their way into the *Diagnostic and Statistical Manual of Mental Disorders* as a separate, valid category of 'mental disorder' – 309.81 Post-traumatic Stress Disorder.[4]

4. POST-TRAUMATIC STRESS DISORDER (PTSD) AND OTHER DIAGNOSTIC CONDITIONS

Victims respond to trauma in rather predictable ways. They suffer shock and helplessness, and experience difficulty concentrating, sleeping and bodily tensions of all kinds; guilt and shame, anger and profound grief. They re-experience the events of the victimisation that many of them dedicate their whole lives to avoiding. They also exhibit sometimes striking resilience.

The psychological effects in the most seriously affected individuals are defined narrowly in both of the world's primary nosologies (reference sources), ICD-10[5] and DSM-IV.[6] The most directly relevant syndromes include acute stress disorder (ASD) in the short, and post-traumatic stress disorder (PTSD) in the longer term. PTSD is characterised by intrusive recollections, avoidance reactions, and symptoms of increased arousal. PTSD has been found to be associated with stable neurobiological alterations in both the central and autonomic nervous systems.[7]

Table A, taken from Fabri (2007) provides comparative examples of the frequency of PTSD diagnoses across several massive trauma situations. Her work with colleagues on the prevalence and predictors of PTSD and depression in HIV-infected and at-risk Rwandan women in particular demonstrated high prevalence of PTSD and depressive symptoms among them, with "four of five HIV-infected women had depressive symptoms, with highest rates among women with CD4 cell counts <200" (Cohen *et al.* 2009, 1783).

---

4   American Psychiatric Association, *Diagnostic and Statistical Manual of Mental Disorders* (1980).

5   World Health Organization (WHO), *International Classification of Diseases* (10th revision 1992).

6   American Psychiatric Association, *Diagnostic and Statistical Manual of Mental Disorders* (4th ed., 1994).

7   Neuropharmacologic and neuroendocrine abnormalities have been detected in the noradrenergic, hypothalamic-pituitary-adrenocortical, and endogenous opioid systems. These data are reviewed extensively elsewhere. See Friedman *et al.* 1995.

Table A. Frequency of PTSD Diagnoses

Study Population	PTSD Dx	Comments
Cambodian Refugees, 2005	62%	Composite International Diagnostic Interview
Bosnian Refugees, 1999	26.2%	IITQ Diagnostic Algorithm
Post-Conflict, Settings, 2001	Algeria – 37.4% Cambodia – 28.4% Ethiopia – 17.8% Gaza – 17.8%	Composite International Diagnostic Interview
South Africa, HIV+, 2005	14.8%	MINI International Neuropsychiatric Interview
USA, HIV+ Women, 2002	42%	PTSD Checklist – Civilian Version
Rwanda Communities, 2004	24.8%	PTSD Checklist – Civilian Version

Additional disorders that frequently occur after exposure to trauma include depression, other anxiety disorders, and substance abuse. Conversion and somatisation disorders (expressing emotional reactions via the body) may also occur, and may be more likely to be observed in non-Western cultures (Engdahl *et al.* 1999). Complicated bereavement (Horowitz 1976) and traumatic grief (Prigerson & Jacobs 2001) have been noted as additional potential effects. Shear and colleagues (2001) define "traumatic grief" as a constellation of symptoms, including preoccupation with the deceased, longing, yearning, disbelief and inability to accept the death, bitterness or anger about the death, and avoidance of reminders of the loss. Research shows that traumatic events that are man-made and intentional, unexpected, sudden and violent have a greater adverse impact than natural disasters (Norris 2002).

Indeed, perhaps the most important challenge confronting victims, especially of the massive crimes we are deliberating, is the impossibility of mourning the loss and destruction rendered by such crimes. Isabella Leitner, a Holocaust survivor, expressed it thus:

> *The sun made a desperate effort to shine on the last day of May in 1944. The sun is warm in May. It heals. But even the heavens were helpless on that day. A force so evil ruled heaven and earth that it altered the natural order of the universe, and the heart of my mother was floating in the smoke-filled sky of Auschwitz. I have tried to rub the smoke out of my vision for forty years now, but my eyes are still burning, Mother.* (Leitner 1985, vii)

Later, writing in America, she adds,

> *I search the sky (...) in desperate sorrow but can discern no human form (...) There is not a trace. No grave. Nothing. Absolutely nothing. My mother lived for just a while –*

Potyo for less than fourteen years. In a way they did not really die. They simply became smoke. How does one bury smoke? How does one place headstones in the sky? How does one bring flowers to the clouds? Mother, Potyo (...) I am trying to say good-bye to you. I am trying to say good-bye. (Leitner 1985)

I have read her words in many presentations across the world – In South Africa, Rwanda, Bosnia, Australia, Israel, the Americas – and have been uniformly told by listeners that they have experienced her words as comforting and transforming. For example, my reading them to Dr. Neil Cohen, then Commissioner of Health and Mental Health of the City of New York on 11 September 2001 to ensure that the families of victims of 9/11 received some remnant of Ground Zero, led to Mayor Rudy Giulianni's decision to give each family an urn containing ashes from the World Trade Center site.

5. SURVIVOR'S SHAME AND GUILT

In the Rwandan context,

[m]any survivors decided to be silent because they felt guilty, ashamed, or afraid. The paradoxical guilt experienced by many of the other survivors around Esther Mujawayo resulted from the fact that they – and not the others – survived, that they could not save their loved ones, or that they could not find their loved ones' bones. (...) [T]he shame (...) is often linked with the violence, especially sexual violence, that they underwent. Even though eighty percent of the women who survived were raped, the reality of this specific violence is still a taboo... According to representatives of the Association of Genocide Widows (AVEGA) (...), '[T]he rape, you bear it silently, in such a shame that no one could even imagine. But you, you always feel like a stink inside your body and a grime that itches your skin'. (Brudholm & Rosoux 2009, 43)

And this shame and constant humiliation is reinforced by the stigmatisation.

In a memorial for a survivor friend, Elie Wiesel (1985) said that the hearts of the survivors have served as the graveyards for the known and the nameless dead of the Holocaust who were turned into ashes, and for whom no graves exist. Many children of survivors also share this sentiment. Elsewhere (Danieli 1981a), I stated my belief that much of the unhedonia (constant suffering) and the holding on to the guilt, shame, and pain of the past had to do with these internally carried graveyards. Survivors fear that successful mourning may lead to letting go and thereby to forgetting the dead and committing them to oblivion – which for many of them amounts to perpetuating Nazi crimes. Thus, guilt also serves a commemorative function and as a vehicle of loyalty to the dead, keeping survivors and succeeding generations engaged in relationships with those who perished, and maintaining a semblance of familial and communal continuity.[8] It also leads to what some call chronic collective mourning or 'depression' in communities, groups and nations.

One of the most powerful functions of 'survivor's guilt' is to serve as a defence against existential helplessness. Being totally passive and helpless in the face of mass atrocities is perhaps the most devastating experience for victim survivors, one that was existentially intolerable and necessitated psychological defence. Elsewhere (Danieli 1981a; also 1982b) I have speculated that much of what has been termed 'survivor's guilt' (Niederland 1964) may be an unconscious attempt to deny or undo this helplessness. Guilt presupposes the presence of choice and the power, the ability, and the possibility to exercise it. It states, "I chose wrong. I *could* have done something (to prevent what happened) and I didn't;" or, "There is something I *can* do, and if I only tried hard enough I will find what it is". Guilt as a defence against utter helplessness links both the survivors and their children's generations to the trauma: The children, in their turn, are helpless in their mission to undo the Holocaust both for their parents and for themselves. This sense of failure often generalises to "No matter what I do or how far I go, nothing will be good enough" (Danieli 1984). Guilt was one of the most potent means of control in these victim families, keeping many adult children from questioning parents about their war experience, expressing anger toward them, or 'burdening' them with their own pain.

Justice as well as transitional justice mechanisms, including truth and reconciliation commissions, can help victims feel vindicated of some portion of this often crippling guilt.

Exposure to trauma may also prompt review and re-evaluation of one's self-perception, beliefs about the world, and values. Although changes in self-perception, beliefs, and values can be negative, varying percentages of trauma-exposed people report positive changes as a result of coping with the aftermath of trauma (Tedeschi & Calhoun 1996). Survivors have described an increased appreciation for life, a reorganisation of their priorities, and a realisation that they are stronger than they thought. This is related to my recognition of competence vs. helplessness in coping with the aftermath of trauma (Danieli 1994). Competence (through one's own strength and/or the support of others), coupled with an awareness of options, can provide the basis of hope in recovery from traumatisation.

Of course, the symptoms described above would affect the victims' behaviour as witnesses in courts. Not less importantly, they would affect the listeners. All will need psychosocial protection before, during and after their involvement in the process of justice so the victims are not retraumatised (which the criminal justice system has done for years) and the listeners are not vicariously traumatised. Studies of psychotherapists working with victims of massive trauma

---

8   For additional functions of guilt, see Danieli 1984.

have shown how, while attempting to protect themselves against their own vicarious victimisation, they too participate in the *conspiracy of silence* (Danieli 1982; Figley 1995). Justice professionals have responded similarly. Indeed, the field of traumatology has recognised the necessity for specialised training to protect all involved in these horrific experiences and in bearing witness to them.

6. THE HEALING PROCESS

Cognitive recovery involves the ability to develop a realistic perspective of what happened, by whom, to whom, and accepting the reality that it had happened the way it did. For example, what was and was not under the victim's control, what could not be, and why. Accepting the impersonality of the events also removes the need to attribute personal causality and consequently guilt and false responsibility. An educated and contained image of the events of victimisation is potentially freeing from constructing one's view of oneself and of humanity solely on the basis of those events. For example, having been helpless does not mean that one is a helpless person; having witnessed or experienced evil does not mean that the world as a whole is evil; having been betrayed does not mean that betrayal is an overriding human behaviour; having been victimised does not necessarily mean that one has to live one's life in constant readiness for its re-enactment; having been treated as dispensable vermin does not mean that one is worthless; and, taking the painful risk of bearing witness does not mean that the world will listen, learn, change, and become a better place (Danieli 1988).

The Latin American Institute of Mental Health and Human Rights in Santiago, Chile stated that

> [t]he victims know that individual therapeutic intervention is not enough. They need to know that their society as a whole acknowledges what has happened to them...Truth means the end of denial and silence...Truth will be achieved only when literally everyone knows and acknowledges what happened during the military regime. (...) [They concluded:] Social reparation is thus (...) simultaneously a sociopolitical and a psychological process. It aims to establish the truth of political repression and demands justice for the victims (...) both through the judicial process and through the availability of health and mental health services...The new democracy that now offers the possibility of reparation will deteriorate into a frail bureaucratic system if the process of social mourning is not realized fully. (Becker et al. 1990, 147–148)[9]

These concerns might well apply to any of the new democracies in Africa.

---

[9]   For related programmes see Kordon *et al.* 1988 and I. Genefke, *The Most Effective Weapon against Democracy: Torture – It Concerns Us All*, Testimony to the Subcommittee on Foreign Operations, Export Financing and Related Expenses for the Rehabilitation Centre for Torture Victims, Copenhagen, 1st May 1992.

Thus, you need to heal the sociopolitical context for the full healing of the individuals and their families, as you need to heal the individuals to heal the sociopolitical context. This is a mutually reinforcing context of shared mourning, shared memory, a sense that the memory is preserved, that the nation transformed it into a part of its global consciousness. The nation shares the horrible pain. The survivors are not lonely in their pain. Reparative justice is fundamental to this dimension of healing.

Integration of the trauma must take place in *all* of life's relevant dimensions or systems and cannot be accomplished by the individual alone. Systems can change and recover independently of other systems. Rupture repair may be needed in all systems of the survivor, in his or her community and nation, and in their place in the international community (Danieli 1998). Reparative justice is a necessary but not sufficient part of this process. To fulfil the reparative and preventive goals of trauma recovery, perspective, and integration through awareness and containment must be established so that one's sense of continuity and belongingness is restored. To be healing and even self-actualising, the integration of traumatic experiences must be examined from the perspective of the *totality* of the trauma survivor's family and community members' lives.

7. NECESSARY ELEMENTS OF HEALING (SUMMARY)

The following summarizes what victims/survivors consider to be necessary components for healing in the wake of massive trauma. They emerged from interviews with survivors of the Nazi Holocaust, Japanese and Armenian Americans, victims from Argentina and Chile, and professionals working with them, both in and outside their countries (Danieli 1992). Presented as goals and recommendations, these elements are organised from the (A) individual, (B) societal, (C) national, and (D) international, perspectives, as follows:

A. *Reestablishment of the victims' equality of value, power, esteem (dignity), the basis of reparation in the society or nation.* This is accomplished by, a. compensation, both real and symbolic; b. restitution; c. rehabilitation; d. commemoration.

B. *Relieving the victim's stigmatisation and separation from society.* This is accomplished by, a. commemoration; b. memorials to heroism; c. empowerment; d. education.

C. *Repairing the nations' ability to provide and maintain equal value under law and the provisions of justice.* This is accomplished by, a. prosecution; b. apology; c. securing public records; d. education; e. creating national mechanisms for monitoring, conflict resolution and preventive interventions.

D. *Asserting the commitment of the international community to combat impunity and provide and maintain equal value under law and the provisions of justice and redress.* This is accomplished by, a. creating ad hoc and permanent mechanisms for prosecution (e.g. *ad hoc* Tribunals and an International Criminal Court); b. securing public records; c. education; d. creating international mechanisms for monitoring, conflict resolution and preventive interventions.

It is important to emphasise that this comprehensive framework, rather than presenting *alternative* means of reparation, sets out necessary *cumulative complementary* elements, *all* of which are needed to be applied in different weights, in different situations, cultures and contexts. It is also crucial that victims/survivors participate in the choice of the reparation measures adopted for them.[10] While justice is crucially one of the healing agents, it does not replace the other psychological and social elements necessary for recovery. It is thus a necessary, but not a sufficient condition for healing.

Some of the elements summarized earlier had already been recognised among the measures recommended in the United Nations Declaration of Basic Principles of Justice for Victims of Crime and Abuse of Power,[11] the Magna Carta for victims. These include, at the international and regional levels, improving access to justice and fair treatment, restitution, compensation and necessary material, medical, psychological, and social assistance and support for such victims. Adopted in 1985 by the UN General Assembly, although it was conceived and drafted in what was then the UN Crime Branch, the Declaration was listed as well by the UN Commission on Human Rights as a human rights instrument – one of very few such documents.

The above framework partly informed the Basic Principles and Guidelines on the Right to a Remedy and Reparation for Victims of Gross Violations of International Human Rights Law and Serious Violations of International Humanitarian Law[12] which were adopted on 16 December 2005.[13] Earlier in that year, the United Nations Human Rights Commission also took note, with appreciation, of the recently revised Set of Principles for the Protection and Promotion of Human Rights through Action to Combat Impunity, updated by Professor Diane Orentlicher.[14] This set of principles includes the right to

---

[10]   "A constant under all these approaches is the need to involve the victims and their organizations in discussions about what reparations, like other post-conflict strategies, should look like." Roht-Arriaza (2004).

[11]   G. A. res. 40/34, U.N. GAOR, 40th Sess., Supp. No. 53, at 213, U.N. Doc. A/40/53 (1986).

[12]   Commission on Human Rights Res. E/CN.4/2005/L.48 (2005).

[13]   G.A. res. 60/147.

[14]   U.N. Doc. E/CN.4/2005/102/Add.1 (2005).

know, the right to justice, and the right to reparation/guarantees of non-recurrence[15] (see Letschert & Van Boven, this volume).

8. IMPUNITY – A SOCIETAL INSTANCE OF THE CONSPIRACY OF SILENCE

Impunity, by definition, is the opposite of justice (Roht-Arriaza 1995). Why, then, would it be embraced? One reason – in parts of Latin America and South Africa – is that it was required by military dictatorships or the racial minority government for relinquishing power or negotiating a peace settlement (Shriver 1995). A second reason for accepting impunity is the belief that 'forgive and forget' is the route to follow in order to heal societies torn apart by conflict. This was the route chosen, for example, by Spain following its civil war. However, the critical question remains: what does it do for a society if individuals' and groups' claims to justice are set aside in the name of what is purported to be the greater good?

Victims and their offspring who have been wronged by a government or society find it considerably more difficult to begin the healing process if the responsible individuals cannot be identified and punished for their crimes (Raphael *et al.* 1998; also Duran *et al.* 1998; Gagne 1998; Cross 1998). The attempted genocide of the Armenians stands as one of the most grievous instances of injustice in the last century, one in which none of the necessary steps for resolution of the trauma have been taken by the perpetrators, the Turks (Kupelian 1998). Not only does the current generation of Turks refuse to acknowledge, apologise and compensate for the genocide, its ongoing campaign of denial, de legitimisation, and disinformation affects the Armenians as a psychological continuation of persecution.

The creation of 'truth commissions' would seem to be an integral tool of justice. In many cases, however, such commissions have not identified those responsible and have been accompanied by amnesty laws or pardons that enshrine impunity (see the Guatemalan Commission on Clarification of the Past). In South Africa's Truth and Reconciliation Commission, pardons were granted for any actions taken during the *Apartheid* years if they were for political reasons and there is full disclosure (see Peacock, this volume). Simpson (1998) scathingly criticises it, calling this "flight into reconciliation" an imposed conspiracy of silence that fails to deal with the multigenerational effects of trauma, and states that this process is a poor substitute for justice for individual or groups of victims. For the victims, according to Edelman and

---

15   See also: The Administration of Justice and The Human Rights of Detainees, Revised Final Report Prepared by Mr. Joinet pursuant to Sub-Commission decision 1996/119, U.N. Doc. E/CN.4/Sub.2/1997/20/Rev.1 (1997).

others (1998), impunity has become "a new traumatic factor" so detrimental that it renders closure impossible. For their societies, moreover, impunity may contribute to a loss of respect for law and government, and to a subsequent increase in crime.

Emboldened by the world's indifference to the Armenian genocide, Hitler proceeded with the systematic attempt to annihilate the Jewish people. Much preventable pain is likely to occur in the future if atrocities are not stopped, and justice done in the present. The struggle for victims and the generations that follow them is to defy the dominance of evil and find a way to restore a sense of justice and compassion to the world. Victim/survivors of trauma feel a need to bear witness to their own and their people's losses, to speak the truth, to urge the world to ensure that such injustices never happen again. But some cannot say "never again" because it has happened again – in Cambodia, Rwanda, Bosnia, Sudan, and elsewhere (Danieli 1998).

International justice has acknowledged this. One significant trend countering such amnesties and pardons is found in the creation by the United Nations of several *ad hoc* international criminal tribunals and of the permanent International Criminal Court (ICC).

The opening statements of legal representatives for victims in the *Lubanga* trial,[16] articulated the importance of justice to Africans in particular:

This trial is an opportunity for the victims to learn the truth and to have right – a right to justice. The truth about the real motives that caused them to be torn from their families and sent to fight and to die for the cause of defending their community. (...) [T] he trial which opens today will one day come to a close, but the war which these children have been through will never end. They will relive it each day, each time they wake from a nightmare at night. They will relive it at the sound of gunfire, at the sight of any military uniform, and they are reliving it still through this trial. That is to say if they have the good fortune that someone lets them watch it on television. That is to say if they are not sent packing because they have become outcasts, because they have sunk into alcoholism, become addicted to the drugs that used to be put in their food to make them aggressive and numb to danger. (Lubanga Trial at 47–49)

(...) I wish through this Court to address those who are listening to us in Bunia and in Ituri, listening to transistor radios or looking at computer screens, be they Hema, Lendu, Alur, or other. Today is a day of hope, not only for the International Criminal Court which hereby opens its first trial but also...for the thousands of victims of the Congolese conflict which seems to be without end, for these former child soldiers who are attempting to rehabilitate and rebuild their lives, for their families, and finally for those who today are still somewhere in the bush, filthy, exhausted, anxious, hungry, suffering aches and pains, crying themselves to sleep thinking of their old friends and their old school, and with just a bit of hemp to console them (...). (International) justice

---

[16] Www.icc-cpi.int/iccdocs/doc/doc623638.pdf, (*Lubanga* Trial) pp. 47–49; 67–68.

offers an alternative to stigmatisation of whole communities as being guilty. (*Lubanga* Trial at 67–68)

In an interview in 1995, Judge Richard Goldstone stated:[17]

I have no doubt that you cannot get peace without justice (…). If there is not justice, there is no hope of reconciliation or forgiveness because these people do not know who to forgive [and they] end up taking the law into their own hands, and that is the beginning of the next cycle of violence (…). I don't think that justice depends on peace, but I think peace depends on justice.

The panel on Peace and Justice, Stocktaking of International Criminal Justice during the Review Conference of the Rome Statute of the ICC held in Kampala, Uganda 21 June 2010 addressed a wide range of challenges related to this seeming dilemma of peace and justice, particularly that now, after the establishment of the ICC, impunity was no longer available for the most serious crimes. Many of the suggested solutions recognized sequencing and widening the complex notion of peace as guiding principles. It was acknowledged that victims' views tend to shift over time, with an immediate goal for peace followed by a quest for justice that does not abate over time.[18]

Hurinet's statement to the review conference corroborates the above conclusion:[19]

We acknowledge the challenge of delivering justice in the context of an ongoing conflict, there is always the temptation to sacrifice justice at the altar of peace, it is noteworthy that peace and justice are not mutually exclusive but could be pursued reasonably without neglecting either. This is vindicated by the situation in Northern Uganda – at the height of the conflict, victims and affected communities, because of inadequate protection, demanded (…) peace. Today, because the situation is relatively peaceful, the demands for justice have come to the fore.

9. THE REPARATIVE ASPECTS OF VICTIMS' PARTICIPATION IN THE JUSTICE PROCESS

Although the study on the necessary elements of healing summarized above focused on the meanings of reparation to victims and not on reparative justice generally, it clearly hints at some aspects of what victims consider healing or

---

[17]   Interview with Judge Richard Goldstone, *Transnational Law & Contemporary Problems* 5 (1995), 374–385, at 376.
[18]   Www.icc-cpi.int/iccdocs/asp_docs/RC2010/RC-ST-PJ-1-Rev.1-ENG.pdf.
[19]   Www.icc-cpi.int/iccdocs/asp_docs/RC2010/Statements/ICC-RC-gendeba-HURINET-ENG.pdf.

reparative in the justice process as a whole. Indeed, many of the aforementioned healing elements that victims identified can, and optimally *should*, be fulfilled through the justice processes. As acknowledged by Supreme Court Justice Albie Sachs of South Africa, "Justice is also in the process, not only in the outcome".[20] I refer here in particular to *reparative justice* processes, in which reparation *per se* is neither the sole component nor the only ultimate goal for the victims. Every step throughout the justice experience as a whole – from the first moment of encounter of the Court with a potential witness through the follow-up of witnesses after their return home to the aftermath of the completion of the case – presents an opportunity for redress and healing. Conversely, every step throughout the justice experience might exacerbate the conspiracy of silence by missing or neglecting the opportunity for healing victims and reintegrating them into their communities and societies, or worse, by (re)victimising and (re) traumatising victims, or compounding their victimisation. Thus, what follows addresses what it is about both courts' processes and outcomes that might miss opportunities but, when done optimally, might help victims. An overarching psychological concern must be to remain sensitive to who the survivor is, what is her or his pre-trauma history, and where she or he is along the posttraumatic healing time-line: At what point in time do you meet him or her? Is it when the victim/survivor is still in shock and acutely symptomatic? Where the survivor is: In a DP camp? (With or without a refugee status?) Already somewhat settled? At home? Years later? And tailor your approach accordingly.

9.1. (MISSED) OPPORTUNITIES AND FURTHER VICTIMISATION

Tragically, as with all-too-many other legacies mentioned above, the continuing attempted denial of both the Armenian genocide and the Nazi Holocaust, and the legacy of the Nuremberg trials with regard to Holocaust victims, foreshadowed ongoing problems. Consider also, the distance in time from the genocide in Cambodia in the mid-1970s to the creation of the Extraordinary Chambers in the Courts of Cambodia to prosecute its perpetrators. Africa too waited long for official apologies for participation in slave trade and slavery, for reflection on the long-term effects of colonialism, and for admissions of allowing preventable genocides to take place.

---

[20] A. Sachs, *The Raul Wallenberg Memorial Lecture at the International Human Rights Symposium to educate leaders of tomorrow*, Osgoode Hall Law School, York University, Toronto, 17th January 2005.

9.2. REMOTE, EXCLUSIONARY, AND PARTIAL JUSTICE: JUSTICE FOR THE WORLD VS. JUSTICE FOR VICTIMS

At Nuremberg, the decision to rely primarily on documentary evidence minimised the role of victims/survivors in the trials. Moreover, by focusing mostly on war crimes, the trials failed to comprehend the full scope of the Jewish tragedy of the Holocaust. While aiming at the best judicial methodology, the Nuremberg trials have thus, either by design or unwittingly, nonetheless participated in the conspiracy of silence, particularly about the *nature* and *meaning* of the survivors' Holocaust experiences. In that, the trials did not differ from the ubiquitous behaviour of the post-Holocaust world. As a result, the trials not only missed a healing opportunity of welcoming demoralised survivors to a world with justice, but they added little meaning to the survivors and their re-emerging communities. Not until the end of the 1990s did various European countries officially begin observing Holocaust Memorial Day. Not until 27 January 2006 did the United Nations observe the first International Day of Commemoration in Memory of the Victims of the Holocaust.

Frederick Terna, a survivor of various concentration camps, among them Ghetto Theresienstadt, Auschwitz, and Kaufering (a sub-camp of Dachau), remembers:

> *I was hospitalized in Bavaria and then in Prague when the trials started in 1945–46. Recovering from the physical effects of the camps after liberation absorbed a good deal of attention. Then followed the need to get the basic necessities: food, shelter, clothes, in an environment that was less than supportive. Attempts to recover property or possessions were rebuffed at every turn. An official's comment to me [summed up the general attitude], 'You must have been some scoundrel to have survived concentration camps.' There were but few survivors of the Prague Jewish community. Communication was minimal and focused on day-to-day problems.[21]*

His comments presage the immediate aftermath of so many other massive traumata. For example, consider the lives of victims in Northern Uganda right now. They too are just trying to survive. Abducted and sexually enslaved girls, now back in their communities, are rejected from their families, begging in the streets, becoming prostitutes and, in some cases, forced to marry their perpetrators so that they have a livelihood and can support their babies.

Terna continues:

> *We wanted to know whether the commanders and troops of the SS of the camps where we had been inmates were captured and brought to trial. What we knew did not raise our hopes for justice. Even collaborators among the Czech officials who during the war helped rounding up Jews were often employed in their former positions. Generally, I*

---

[21] Interview with Frederick Terna (31 October 2005).

was aware that the trials were going on (...). [But] justice was a far-away concept. It certainly was not available on a personal or local level. The Nuremberg trials were a distant happening, important for the abstract concept of international law, but did not touch us personally then.[22]

Despite the generally purposeful attention paid to rape victims both by the Truth and Reconciliation Commission and by the Special Court for Sierra Leone (Nowrojee 2005a), a recent example of a missed opportunity by deliberate exclusion is the *Civil Defence Force (CDF)* case in the Special Court for Sierra Leone (SCSL) (Kendall & Staggs 2005). The case considered wide-spread killing and offences against the person, but excluded charges of sexual violence. As women called to testify invariably spoke of the sexual violence and systematic rape they suffered, the Prosecution decided to stop calling female witnesses. The judges refused to have the indictment amended even though the trial had not yet begun. At the time, this was in stark contrast to the *Akayesu* case before the International Criminal Tribunal for Rwanda (ICTR). There, the trial was temporarily suspended to allow the prosecutor to investigate. Subsequently, the indictment was amended 5 months into trial to include cases of sexual violence (Wise *et al.* 2004). The Judgment resulting from this case has been called "the most ground-breaking decision advancing gender jurisprudence worldwide". Yet, despite this landmark jurisprudence that recognized rape as a crime against humanity and an instrument of genocide, subsequent cases largely or wholly failed to adequately address gender crimes (Askin 2004). Alas, as Nowrojee (2005b, 5) summarizes:

Rwandan women express deep concern that the ICTR is not fully and properly prosecuting the crimes that occurred against them: that the court is not acknowledging their pain, not telling their story, not enshrining their experience of the genocide (...). They want the ICTR to say loudly and in no uncertain terms that what was done to women was a crime of genocide, and that as rape survivors they did not willingly collaborate with those who committed genocide, who kept them alive to rape.

When asked about her thoughts on justice and the ICTR, a young mother with HIV began to cry and said:

For those of us on the road to death, this justice will be too slow. We will be dead and no one will know our story. Our families have been killed and our remaining children are too young to know. What happened to us will be buried with us (...). We will be dead before we see any justice. Nowrojee (2005b, 5)

---

[22]   *Ibidem.*

For rape victims, the breaking of the silence that surrounds the sexual violence directed at them is all the more important because of the stigma and shame attached to rape.

The documenting of historical truth is another important function of justice, because history is not simply what happened in the past, but rather the scribe's interpretation of events. In this case, the ICTR serves not only as an arbiter of justice, but also as a documenter of the narrative of the Rwandan genocide. Implicit in the mandate to prosecute persons responsible for serious violations of international humanitarian law in Rwanda is the need to establish an accurate public record of the events of 1994. The court's interpretation of those events, through its judgements, will colour how generations to come will view what happened in Rwanda and who bears responsibility. If the current trend continues, when the doors of the ICTR close, the judgements from this court will not tell the full story of what happened during the Rwandan genocide. They will not correctly reflect responsibility for the shocking rapes, sexual slavery and sexual mutilations that tens of thousands of Rwandan women suffered.

The jurisprudence as it now stands – with a growing string of acquittals for rape – will, in fact, do the opposite. The record of this tribunal in history will not only minimize responsibility for the crimes against women, but will actually deny that these crimes occurred. A reader of the ICTR jurisprudence will be left mistakenly believing that the mass rapes had little or nothing to do with the genocidal policies of their leaders. This is indeed a serious miscarriage of justice. Askin (2008) summarizes both the failures and successes of the ICTR:

> *In short, the failure to investigate or indict for rape crimes, dropped sex crime charges, and excessive acquittals for sex crimes when there is sufficient evidence to support the crimes, distorts the history of what happened during the genocide, further victimizes the survivors, and sends a message to the victims and perpetrators that the court doesn't take sex crimes very seriously (…). [W]hile there have been many missed opportunities and some downright negligent actions or inactions, the gender justice accomplishments of the ICTR are major and they are enduring. We cannot overestimate the jurisprudential legacy of the Akayesu case.*

In the *Thomas Lubanga* case before the ICC, the prosecution is focusing on the undoubtedly important use of child soldiers but is not pursuing the equally important issues of sexual violence. Some observers wonder whether this is another case of exclusion, and an unduly narrow focus for the Court's first case (Ferstman & Goetz 2009).

Victims/survivors themselves have also chosen exclusion as a statement of protest (refusing to testify in response to the ICTR case of the laughing judges below) or refusal of reparation as "blood" or "dirty" money, such as some of the Holocaust and Argentine survivors (Danieli 2009a).

The remote justice of the International Criminal Tribunal for the former Yugoslavia (ICTY), ICTR and ICC, has faced the similar consequent challenges to Nuremberg of (potential) irrelevance to and neglect of the realities and concerns of millions of victims and the societal and cultural contexts in which they live.[23] Research conducted in the former Yugoslav federation and in Rwanda between 1999 and 2002 suggests that while informants generally supported trials as a means of punishing the guilty, they viewed the ad hoc international tribunals as distant institutions that had little to do with their lives. Eighty-seven percent of 2,091 Rwandans surveyed in 2002 were either 'not well informed' or 'not informed at all' about the work of the international tribunal in Arusha. Similarly, in their survey of 1,624 residents of Croatia and Bosnia, a significant number of Serbs and Croats expressed strong resentment toward the Hague tribunal largely – biased against their national group (Stover & Weinstein 2004). Each of the tribunals and the ICC have undertaken progressively outreach activities to attempt to avert these dangers and meet the challenges. The ICC strategies for informative outreach and access should be regularly monitored and evaluated to ensure that they realise the spirit of the Rome Statute for victims' participation and reparation. Data should be regularly and systematically collected from the outset on victims' attitudes and feelings about every aspect of testifying, and of their satisfaction with the justice process. When these strategies are successful, the victims' traumatogenic sense of having been forgotten in a world where the *conspiracy of silence* rules without solidarity and compassion, might lessen, and their sense of empowerment, efficacy and control, and of belongingness to their own community and the community of humanity would augment their healing and hope for a future free of atrocities.

Pursuing justice and truth nationally as well as internationally should reduce both the sense of irrelevance of remote justice alone, and the witnesses' estrangement and possibly threat from their communities after testifying.

9.3. BEING TREATED WITH DIGNITY AND RESPECT

In one particularly egregious example of judicial insensitivity, at the ICTR *Butare* trial, the judges guffawed during the testimony of a rape victim. They suddenly burst out laughing while witness TA, a victim of multiple rapes during the genocide, was being cross-examined by a defence lawyer.

---

23 See also Stover 2005, 144: "This is regrettable, as it has deprived the people of the former Yugoslavia of an independent focal point for analyzing the past war devoid of nationalist distortions."

As lawyer Mwanyumba ineptly and insensitively questioned the witness at length about the rape, the judges burst out laughing twice at the lawyer while witness TA described in detail the lead-up to the rape. Witness TA had undergone a day and a half of questioning by the prosecutor, before being put through a week of cross-examination by the counsel of the six defendants. One of the more offensive questions put by defence lawyer Mwanyumba included reference to the fact that the witness had not taken a bath, and the implication that she could not have been raped because she smelled. Other questions asked were, "Did you touch the accused's penis?", "How was it introduced into your vagina?" and "Were you injured in the process of being raped by nine men?" To which witness TA responded, "If you were raped by nine people, you would not be intact.[24]

The three judges – William Sekule (Tanzania), Winston Maqutu (Lesotho) and Arlette Ramaroson (Madagascar) – never apologised to the rape victim on the stand, nor were they reprimanded in any way for their behaviour.

She said that originally she had agreed to testify when she was asked because she thought that if she refused the strangers (the ICTR investigators), they would 'think I had lied and nothing would happen to those in jail'. Witness TA lost her whole family during the genocide. She said: My parents, my brother and my sister were killed. I'm all alone. My relatives were killed in a horrible fashion. But I survived – to answer the strange questions that were asked by the ICTR. If you say you were raped, that is something understandable. How many times do you need to say it? When the judges laughed, they laughed like they could not stop laughing. I was angry and nervous. When I returned, everyone knew I had testified. My fiancé refused to marry me once he knew I had been raped. He said, you went to Arusha and told everyone that you were raped. Today I would not accept to testify, to be traumatized for a second time. No one apologized to me.

Only Gregory Townsend [the ICTR prosecuting lawyer] congratulated me after the testimony for my courage. When you return you get threatened. My house was attacked. My fiancé has left me. In any case, I'm already dead. (Nowrojee 2005b, 24)

In a society such as Rwanda, where women are valued highly for their roles as wives and mothers, witness TA's reintegration into society was very much predicated on her 'marriageability.' The exposure of TA's status as a rape victim following the publicity that surrounded the incident resulted in her fiancé breaking off their relationship. A split second of careless laughter by the ICTR judges destroyed this woman's best chance to rebuild her life.[25]

Stover adds,

---

[24]   See, "UN Judges Laugh at Rape Victim," available at: www.globalpolicy.org/intljustice/tribunals/2001/0512rwa.htm. See also Nowrojee 2005, 24.

[25]   See also (then President) Judge Pillay's cautious statement about the incident, ICTR/INFO-9-3-07.EN Arusha, 14 December 2001 available at: http://69.94.11.53/ENGLISH/PRESSREL/2001/9-3-07.htm.

On leaving the courtroom, witnesses are generally anxious to receive some form of appreciation from their prosecutors, but often the lawyers, for some reason or another, are not available to debrief or even thank them. Witnesses may also feel that the court did not 'respect' them, especially if they had to endure an intense cross-examination or were not given extra time to say what they wanted at the end of their testimony. And, in a few cases, witnesses may even travel to The Hague but end up not testifying for trial-related reasons.

The key here is to ensure that victim-witnesses, especially those who have suffered rape or torture or witnessed the death of family members, testify in an environment that is, to the greatest extent possible, predictable and controlled. Judges must be proactive in the courtroom and intervene if a prosecutor or defense counsel begins to insult, badger, or manipulate a witness. (Stover 2005, 129–130)

ICTY Witnesses were embittered by what they viewed as extremely short prison sentences. Still others said that their 'work as a witness' would only be complete once they had testified against *local* war criminals whom they held directly responsible for the deaths of family members and neighbours.

Both Dembour and Haslam's (2004) and Stover's (2005) analyses of ICTY trial transcripts present ample evidence of insensitivity and inappropriate, un-empathic behaviour by judges toward victim-witnesses. Dembour and Haslam go as far as to recommend creating "a space for the victims to tell their stories in non-legal arenas [that] would be at least as, if not more, beneficial to them than their participation in the ICTY" (2004, 117). Mollica (2006, 231) goes as far as to suggest that the human rights and humanitarian fields must shift their focus away from strict legal definitions, link their work to the healing process and extend a commitment to providing universal medical and mental health care to all victims of violence. "[It] must ask: 'How are my projects and policies affecting the health and well-being of survivors? Are these projects promoting the self-healing of the communities and persons being served?'."

Even under optimal conditions, in a society mindful of victims' rights, individual rape victim/survivors have mixed reactions to participation in legal processes. A 1999 Canadian study of rape victims who had pursued compensation through civil suits and quasi-judicial remedies (Feldthusen 2000) found testifying "completely anti-therapeutic" and reported some negative emotional consequences" from their participation in the judicial process (not just from testifying), including depression, suicidal tendencies, frustration, and anger. Despite these stresses, a plurality (48 percent) reported that the overall effect of the experience had been positive, giving them a "sense of closure, validation, empowerment, or relief.

Indeed, my own ongoing psychosocial project in Bosnia and Herzegovina which I had, in uninspired prose, named *Promoting a Dialogue*, was renamed by its participants, *Democracy Cannot be Built with the Hands of Broken Souls*.

9.4. BEING AFFORDED SUPPORT, ASSISTANCE AND PROTECTION

Justice loses its meaning for the victims when it does not provide full – both physical and psychosocial – protection, support and assistance while using the victims as witnesses. There are ample examples from both the ICTY and ICTR of the negative impact of the absence of these crucial measures.[26] These problems were prevalent particularly in the early stages. Later, mechanisms were put in place.

In 2002, the Coalition for Women's Human Rights in Conflict Situations prepared a comprehensive set of recommendations for policies and procedures for respecting the needs and effectively involving women in the ICTR process.[27] The recommendations deal with procedures before, during and after the trial designed to protect the witnesses' right to life and identity and their psychological integrity. Goetz (2006) elaborates:

> *The issue of medical care for victims testifying before the Tribunal has been seriously criticised by victim groups in Rwanda (AVEGA and IBUKA being the leading critics). Overwhelmingly, victims testifying for rape offences are HIV positive and need medical assistance. The ICTR was committed to providing medical assistance to all witnesses under the Tribunal's Witness and Victims Support Section (WVSS), however this did not extend to long-term needs when witnesses returned to Rwanda after testifying. Women's rights groups in Rwanda were appalled and launched an international petition against the Tribunal and the UN advocating against cooperation with the process (resulting in diminishing numbers of testimonies for gender violence). They claimed that the Tribunal operated a double standard: the male perpetrators in the custody were provided with anti-retroviral treatment, while they, the female victims were denied the vital treatment. The UN held that the Tribunal was not a humanitarian agency, and other UN agencies located in Rwanda, such as UNDP and UNICEF were better placed to ensure the long-term provision of medical care to all victims of the genocide.*

However, the ICTY and ICTR as well as the SCSL, none of which have a mandate to award compensation to victims, could not provide for their long-term needs

---

[26]   Www.womensrightscoalition.org/advocacyDossiers/rwanda/witnessProtection/report_ en.php and www.womensrightscoalition.org/advocacyDossiers/rwanda/witnessProtection/ protectionofwitnesses_en.php.

[27]   *The Protection of Women as Witnesses and the ICTR* (prepared by Eva Gazurek and Anne Saris) found at www.womensrightscoalition.org/advocacyDossiers/rwanda/witnesses.

as a form of reparation within the framework of reparative justice. Victims were left to seek reparation, if any, within the national framework. Compensation was to be claimed through national courts under Rules 105 and 106 of the Composite International Diagnostic Interview Rules of Procedure and Evidence (see also Nowrojee 2005b).

Victim and Witness Units should therefore make periodic assessments of the most vulnerable witnesses and monitor their situation. They should also, in consultation with the prosecutor's offices, conduct pre-trial assessments in communities where it is likely that cases will increase inter-group tensions and animosities, and try to devise appropriate protective and conflict resolution mechanisms.

In her article *Trauma and isolation await many witnesses of UN court at home*,[28] Isabelle Wesselingh reports that "Many war crimes victims who testify at the UN court for the former Yugoslavia return home traumatized after a psychologically demanding court appearance and often feel isolated". Wesselingh elaborates:

> *In stark contrast to their crucial role in the legal process, the victims that testify in The Hague find themselves alone upon their return home.[29] There is no follow-up counseling or material help for the witnesses who often come back to a country facing economic hardship. 'They are proud to have testified but post-traumatic stress is heavier after they leave The Hague because they had to recount very difficult events,' said Dubranka Dizdarevic, a Sarajevo psychologist who has worked with torture victims that testified in The Hague.*

Some witnesses are shunned by their community because they gave evidence about crimes committed by fellow villagers. "One of my colleagues at the hospital, a Bosnian Serb nurse, fell into a depression for almost a year after she went to The Hague. For lots of people around her, the people who work with the tribunal are traitors," Miodrag Milanovic, a psychiatrist from Prijedor in northwestern Bosnia, said.

The dire economic situation and the sense of insecurity, especially for victims living in areas where nationalists still hold power, take a heavy toll on those who testify. "Witnesses are telling us they need material goods. Sometimes the witnesses feel used, they have expectations that the court cannot fulfill," said Wendy Lobwein, Deputy Head, Victims and Witnesses section of the ICTY and a trauma counsellor.[30]

---

[28]   Agence France-Presse, 16 January 2004.

[29]   Stover also reports that the few ICTY witnesses he interviewed who experienced cathartic feelings immediately or soon after testifying in The Hague found that "the glow quickly faded once they returned to their shattered villages and towns." (2005, 131).

[30]   Interview with Wendy Lobwein (7 March 2008).

"To soften the blow for returning witnesses, the victims and witnesses section of the tribunal [decided to] set up a health and welfare network in Bosnia-Hercegovina where 59 percent of the tribunal's 2,330 witnesses who testified since 1998 reside".[31]

In December 2003, in a conference paid for by the European Union, 24 psychologists, psychiatrists and social workers from Bosnia – Bosnian Serbs, Bosnian Croats and Bosnian Muslims – met at the tribunal. The goal of the conference was to exchange experiences and discuss a protocol for follow-up services when witnesses return home, especially in regard to issues of confidentiality.

"The professionals who work with victims feel very isolated in Bosnia. It is very positive to be able to meet each other here in The Hague and see that all the victims are equal and have the same problems," Tuzla psychiatrist Alija Sutovic, who works with survivors of the Srebrenica massacre, told AFP.

According to Lobwein, this conference was followed by others convening health care specialists from Serbia and Montenegro, Croatia and Kosovo. Support group members were brought to The Hague to learn in vivo the workings of the Court to enable them to provide meaningful support to victim/witnesses before, during and after testifying. This led to the establishment of a support network in place in every state. A final conference brought 60 select members of these groups to Sarajevo, together with 20 judges and prosecutors from each state or province, to apply the knowledge they had accumulated in The Hague and from their own experiences to future collaboration and exchange of witnesses. Lobwein concluded, "It worked, because 18 months later three states signed a collaborative agreement. It was a dream come true".[32]

It behoves the ICC to continue to learn from the earlier tribunals' flaws and attempted solutions and to find optimal ways to support victims prior to, during and following giving testimony.

10. CONCLUSION

Emphasising the need for a multi-dimensional, multi-disciplinary, integrative framework for understanding massive trauma and its aftermath, particularly the *conspiracy of silence*, this chapter has examined victims/survivors' experiences from the psychological perspective. It has delineated victim/survivors' needs and concerns as they apply to reparative justice, in which reparation *per se* is neither the sole component nor the only ultimate goal for the victims. Rather, reparative justice insists that every step throughout the justice experience as a whole – from the first moment of encounter of the Court with a potential witness through the

---

31   *Ibidem.*
32   *Ibidem.*

follow-up of witnesses after their return home to the aftermath of the completion of the case – presents an opportunity for redress and healing. Conversely, every step throughout the justice experience might exacerbate the conspiracy of silence by missing or neglecting the opportunity for healing victims and reintegrating them into their communities and societies, or worse, by (re)victimising and (re)traumatising them, or compounding their victimisation. While restitution, rehabilitation or compensation may only come after the process has concluded, the process may nonetheless provide numerous forms of satisfaction along the way, particularly if all professionals interfacing with victims act in an empathic, dignified and respectful manner, mindfully protecting victims from further trauma and from unnecessary bureaucracies, and facilitating opportunities to contribute to a collective record and shared memory. If potential witnesses come to regard their treatment as demeaning, unfair, too remote, or unconcerned with their rights and interests, this neglect may hinder the future cooperation of the very people we are trying to serve.

This requires ongoing training of all professionals, be it judges, prosecutors, lawyers, interpreters, on all aspects of the courts' mandates related to victims, including their particular cultures and traditions as they pertain to both justice and to trauma. This training should as well include continued attention to self-care to counteract vicarious victimisation (Danieli 2002; Danieli 1994b). Much of the substance of this chapter should be also taken as an invitation for sorely needed systematic empirical research and curricula development. The task may be immense, but in the long run the results will be an invaluable building block in the edifice of international law.

Regarding funds, which all-too-often are insufficient, I concur with Stover that in the final analysis it seems hypocritical to create an international court with a wide array of witness protections and support services on paper, and fail to provide its staff with adequate resources to fulfil their duties and obligations as set forth in courts' Statute and Rules.

Witnesses in Stover's ICTY study gave the highest marks to prosecutors and investigators, who treated them with respect, informed them of their entitlements, apprised them of development in their case, prepared them to testify, and debriefed them after they left the stand. According to them, good pre-trial preparation included informing witnesses of their trial date well in advance; apprising them of available protective measures; maintaining contact during the pre-trial phase, especially concerning delays in trial dates; orienting them to the physical layout of the court; and briefing them on the adversarial nature of the trial proceedings. Above all, he suggests, prosecutors and investigators should be required during their first encounter with all potential witnesses to inform them of their rights and entitlements. The prosecutor's office should also develop a procedure, in consultation with the witness section, for following up with prosecution witnesses should an appellate chamber overturn a guilty verdict in cases in which they testified (Stover 2005, 152). I agree wholeheartedly with these recommendations.

Judges can play an extremely important role in ensuring that witnesses are treated with dignity. In particular, they should be vigilant of and more quickly to end any abusive or disrespectful behaviour on the part of both defence counsel and prosecutors during cross-examination; provide witnesses with an opportunity to make a statement at the conclusion of their testimony; conduct periodic assessments of the effectiveness of the court's protection measures and issue recommendations for improving these procedures (Stover 2005, 153).

One of the obstacles to mourning experienced by survivors is *survivors' guilt*. The act of public witnessing and giving testimony, and the judgment by the Court, give the victims vindication for their survivor's guilt. Also, every victim has only his or her own story of rupture. By generating records, courts help the victims not only to create a coherent narrative of what they themselves have gone through, and a sense of what relatives whose fate they have no knowledge of have suffered, but also to comprehend the global context for their suffering.

PART III
AMNESTY, TRUTH, RECONCILIATION AND TRADITION

X. DRAWING THE LINE: AMNESTY, TRUTH COMMISSIONS AND COLLECTIVE DENIAL

Frank HALDEMANN

1. INTRODUCTION

Turning a blind eye, looking the other way, averting your gaze, wearing blinkers, living a lie, burying your head in the sand, putting a gloss on the truth. These are some of the expressions and phrases that are commonly used to describe the concept of denial.[1] As individuals, we can be said to 'live in denial' when we avoid focusing our attention on information that is too disturbing, unsettling or shameful to be faced and openly acknowledged. The political echoes of these states of mind may be found in official defence mechanisms ('It didn't happen', 'What happened is not what it looks like', 'It was an isolated incident', 'We had no idea that this was happening', 'They brought it on themselves really', 'Anyway it was justified') through which entire societies try to conceal, suppress or dissociate themselves from a record of past atrocities. If such denials of past horrors are initiated by the state, or built into its ideological façade, few would doubt that something wrong is being done. This sort of official denial is immoral, because it involves treating the victims of those wrongs as if they simply did not matter, as if they were politically and morally negligible – an attitude that is disrespectful in its very essence.[2]

The opposite of denial is acknowledgement. To deny that something once happened is to fail to acknowledge that it did happen. This distinction between denial and acknowledgement may look simple enough, but it becomes blurred when one considers the varieties of denial or gradations of acknowledgment (half-truth, evasions, legalistic sophistries and so on) that may appear in official discourse in the aftermath of collective violence. So what exactly does it mean

---

[1] For an impressive account of the phenomenon, see Cohen 2001.
[2] Drawing on Harry Frankfurt (1997, 12), we might say that this way of treating the victims of massive human rights abuses is disrespectful because "it conveys a refusal to acknowledge the truth about them" – because they are dealt with as though they are not what they actually are. See also Govier 2003, 84.

for a society to 'acknowledge' its record of public and political atrocities? And how can this acknowledgement be transformed into action? Part of the answer to these questions will depend on "the nature of the previous regime, its residual power, how the transition happened, and the character of the new society" (Cohen 2001, 222). In other words, local conditions have a crucial bearing on how the relevant facts may be transformed into acknowledgement in particular political contexts. It is, however, essential to be clear on the full range of moral issues that arise when societies emerging from mass atrocity decide what, if anything, they should do about past violations of human rights (Crocker 2003, 58).

In some parts of the world, for example in South Africa, collective acknowledgement has taken the form of truth commissions – temporary bodies officially authorized by the state to investigate into a pattern of human rights abuses.[3] By far the most troubling issue about creating truth commissions as a response to mass atrocity is the place of amnesty, whether the amnesty is generalized or particularized. In some cases, amnesty – the protection from liability (criminal, civil, or both) – may be the only viable option, especially when transitional regimes face the threat of a military coup or civil unrest. But is the granting of amnesty for gross human rights abuses morally acceptable? How can we accept the spectacle of torturers and state-sponsored killers getting off 'scot-free'? Shouldn't we reject amnesty as a form of impunity and official denial? *More generally: Where do we draw the line separating amnesty from collective denial?* (see also Van Wijk, this volume)

In addressing these issues, I use the concept of recognition (or, interchangeably, acknowledgement) to offer a moral framework for integrating the victims' point of view into public and politic discourses about what has now been termed as 'transitional justice'.[4] Drawing on the ideas of critical thinkers such as Axel Honneth and Avishai Margalit, I propose to construe transitional justice as a moral, political and legal project of 'overcoming denial' that puts victims and their legitimate feelings of indignation and resentment at its centre. When do the victimized have moral *reasons* to feel humiliated, ignored, abandoned, *mis*recognized as a result of the policies and attitudes adopted in the aftermath of atrocity? The aim of this paper is to construe the concept of denial in terms of such negative moral phenomena, and in particular to reflect on how the victims' legitimate sense of resentment and grief may be converted into vocabularies of acknowledgement. My interest, then, is more in the *moral*

---

3   For a more complete definition, see Hayner 2002, 14.

4   The terms 'Transitional Justice' is increasingly employed to describe the process by which societies confront legacies of widespread or systematic human rights abuses as they move from repression or civil war to a more just, democratic and non-violent order. Transitional Justice as a field of academic and policy interest has grown tremendously over the last 15 years or so. Classic conceptualizations include, to name just a few, Kritz 1995; McAdams 1997; Minow 1998; Teitel 2000.

consequences of the public's selective concern about past atrocities and suffering than in the psychic causes of states of denial.[5]

My discussion proceeds in five parts. In the first section, I elucidate the concept of collective denial and explore the ways in which it may be related to practices of total or conditional amnesty. Then, in the second and third section, I reflect on the significance of recognition for overcoming institutionalized patterns of collective denial in the aftermath of mass atrocities. In the forth section, I go on to describe the basic features of the amnesty process employed by the South African Truth and Reconciliation Commission (TRC), a process often portrayed as a model for future truth commissions. Finally, in the fifth section, I critically examine this process in the light of the proposed account of recognition.

2. BLOCKING OUT THE PAST

As individuals and groups, we are often unwilling to acknowledge our errors, shortcomings, and failings. There are many ways of denying or deceiving ourselves about what we would prefer to forget, or continue to ignore. Self-deceptive mechanisms of many kinds enable people to avoid focusing on the events, or at least on their shameful features. Similarly, societies can be said to 'live in denial' when their institutions, or those who run and support these institutions, are engaged in misrepresenting or concealing unwelcome truths about past wrongs.

This is especially true with regard to legacies of widespread and systematic human rights abuses. As Stanley Cohen (1996) points out in his analysis of government responses to human rights reports, the discourse of denial is one of the 'classic' strategies adopted by 'perpetrator' states that plan, permit or condone atrocities. Cohen (1996, 517–543) usefully distinguishes three forms of denial that appear in the discourse of official responses to allegations about human rights violations: literal denial ('nothing happened'); interpretive denial ('what happened is really something else'), and implicatory denial ('what happened is justified').

But similar forms of official denial might also be used by societies making a transition from authoritarianism or civil war to a more just, democratic, or peaceful order (Cohen 2001, 101–116). As Timothy Garton Ash (1998, 35) observes, there is some historical evidence that "the advocates of forgetting are numerous and weighty". For example, French post-World War II democracy was constructed on a foundation of suppressing the painful memory of the Vichy collaboration, emphasising Charles de Gaulle's unifying myth of French resistance. In West Germany, Konrad Adenauer's democratic government also

---

5   On the psychology of denial, see Cohen 2001, 21–50.

showed little interest in investigating individuals accused of crimes related to National Socialist rule; a vast purge process (denazification) was set in motion, but turned de facto into a "machine for political rehabilitation" (Frei 2002, 38). Think, too, of Spain after 1975, where no efforts were made to confront General Francisco Franco's legacy of human rights abuses. The major justification that has been offered for such a policy of historical amnesia is the claim that forgetting facilitates the institutionalisation of democratic structures and the rule of law. Along these lines, one might argue that in countries such as Spain, or more recently Poland, a policy of drawing a 'clean slate' was successful, if success is measured exclusively in terms of democracy and stability.

Yet there are important moral objections to this sort of amnesia. Forced silence might create what Paul Ricœur (2000, 455) once called "imaginary unity" (*unité imaginaire*) – a kind of artificial stability fostered by communal rites and ceremonies. But the moral price is high. The result is a peace built upon the public suppression of memory. The past is thus erased from official discourse, debate, and narratives, turning the victims into nameless, faceless abstractions. The victimised are then treated as though they simply do not matter – as though their suffering and needs, and indeed their dignity and moral status as equal human beings, do not need to be taken into account. With this message of moral insignificance the initial experience of insult and humiliation is likely to develop into "a second wound of silence", a deep sense of hurt stemming from the feeling that "people condone the wrongs and do not care about the baneful results" (Govier 2003, 85).

To be sure, there are many ways of collectively denying atrocities and suffering, and some are more complex than others. Collective denial, in its crudest form, can be a matter of obvious lying – as when the entire rhetoric of government is used to deliberately misrepresent, cover up, explain away the information about atrocities or public wrongdoing. A different, more complex form of collective denial is selective social attention – the deliberate choice of people and societies not to expose themselves to such unwelcome truths of their histories. In such cases, 'denial' refers to collective modes of switching off or blocking out certain unpalatable information. Sometimes, though, there seem to be states of collective denial, in which 'knowledge' about atrocities is not wholly clear. When confronted with information that is literally unthinkable or unbearable, the psyche tends to set up "a barrier which prevents the thought from reaching conscious knowledge" (Cohen 2001, 5). Yet, as Trudy Govier (2006, 51) notes, "to *ignore* something we must first have some *awareness* of it". Govier's example of a householder who ignores cobwebs in a high corner of the room is telling here. To ignore the presence of the cobwebs, the householder must "first notice them and then decide to put them out of her mind – not think about them" (Govier 2006, 51). Thus a conscious choice is made, "a choice that requires a moment of knowing what it is that one decides to ignore" (Govier 2006, 51).

These remarks on the phenomenon of selective attention seem particularly significant when we move from the psychic to the political realm. Political denials of the past – the deliberate cover-up, the rewriting of history through official state policy – are best seen as collective modes of concerted or strategic *ignorance* constructed to avoid information that seems too disturbing, threatening, and shameful to be openly and collectively acknowledged (Cohen 2001, 6). This is the zone of what Govier (2006) terms "culpable ignoring". While selective attention may at times be unavoidable – if not necessary – in human life, it is something that cannot be condoned in the face of publicly known atrocities and mass suffering. As Govier perceptively observes, ignoring those who suffer in the aftermath of public wrongs is morally objectionable

> *because it allows us to deny any obligations to damaged people. It allows us to hold back from asking whether we share responsibility for the acts and policies that caused this harm and suffering. It enables us to avoid asking whether we should take on some responsibility for responding to the damage that has been done. Ignoring the suffering of others, we may avoid knowing whether we are in any sense responsible for that suffering; we have ignored evidence that could have led us to knowledge.* (Govier 2006, 52–53)

Denial, so understood, can be contrasted with acknowledgement: the opposite of denying past horrors is to *acknowledge* what happened. To acknowledge that such wrongs were committed means, in effect, avowing one's knowledge of them and rendering that knowledge explicit. To overcome and break through collective denials of the past, acknowledgement must be public and officially organized by the state. While some people may know what happened and keep this information intact in private memory, this information now has to enter public discourse and be converted into official truth (Cohen 2001, 225). Acknowledgement, in this sense, is "what happens and can only happen to knowledge when it is officially sanctioned, when it is made part of the public cognitive scene".[6]

This kind of acknowledgement communicates a collective *recognition* of those who have been wronged. It entails recalling and reaffirming their very moral dignity and worth as human beings and fellow citizens. Thus, such calls for acknowledgement are expressive of a public commitment to equality and civility, and this is perhaps the most important rationale for granting collective acknowledgement to the victims of mass violence. But what exactly does it mean to 'recognize' the victims of past atrocities? Which vocabularies of recognition are appropriate after mass violence and genocide? When do survivors and victims have moral reasons for feeling humiliated, indeed 'misrecognized', by the public and political discourse about the past? How to transform the experience of socially approved injustice and humiliation into an increased sense

---

[6]   To use an expression coined by Thomas Nagel (quoted in Weschler 1990, at 4).

of recognition and social approval? These and related questions are the main focus of the next section.

3. COLLECTIVE DENIAL AS MISRECOGNITION

In exploring what exactly it could mean for a political community to 'recognize' the aggrieved and their experience of injustice, it is crucial to bear in mind the *symbolic* dimension of serious wrongdoing. One reason why we deeply resent serious wrongdoings is not simply that they threaten or produce physical harm or a loss of value; it is because they express a lack of concern and respect. As Jeffrie Murphy (1988) observes, such injuries are also messages or symbolic communications. "They are ways", he writes, "a wrongdoer has of saying to us, 'I count but you do not', 'I can use you for my purpose', or 'I am here up and you are there below'". (Murphy 1988, 25) Thus, intentional wrongdoing, unlike damage produced by accident or natural forces, involves a kind of moral injury that results from the experience of being insulted and degraded. I will use the word 'misrecognition' to denote this sort of symbolic depreciation – treating others as inferior, minor, negligible, or simply invisible. Human beings are vulnerable to such moral injuries, which attack us – our sense of self-worth – in profound and deeply threatening ways.[7]

In contexts of mass suffering and public atrocities, those wronged against suffer an additional injustice of misrecognition – that of being ignored, silenced, smothered, suppressed from the *public* eye. When an entire community or group – such as a state or government – plans, permits or condones acts that are terribly unjust and humiliating, it sends a message to the individual victim; she is told that her presence, indeed her life, counts for nothing in the society's scheme of things. One consequence of this sort of collective evil, which creates collective victims, is the victim's disappearance from the public and political domain. As Rajeev Bhargava (2000, 47) helpfully suggests, the act of collective violence conveys to its victims

> *that their views on the common good – on matters of public significance – do not count, that their side of the argument has no worth and will not be heard, that they will not be recognized as participants in any debate, and, finally, that to negotiate, or even to reach a compromise with them, is worthless.*

---

[7]   Charles Taylor (1995, 225) makes this point eloquently when he writes: "The thesis is that our identity is partly shaped by recognition or its absence, often by the *mis*recognition of others, and so a person or group of people can suffer real damage, real distortion, if the people or society around them mirror back to them a confining or demeaning or contemptible picture of themselves."

But misrecognition, as a matter of turning a blind eye on victims and their suffering, may even occur in the aftermath of mass atrocity. And this is the crucial issue for what has come to be known as 'transitional justice'. In periods of transition, marked by radical transformations of the surrounding societies, there is always a strong impulse to put the past aside and move on to normal life. As suggested above, there is more than one way of denying collectively past atrocities, and thus more than one mode of hiding mass suffering from the public gaze (disinformation, lying, cover-up, collusion, normalization and so on). But there is, it seems to me, one element that is common to all types of collective denial: the suppression of the victims' point of view from the public record. In other words, we may think of collective denials as ways a community has to make those who have been wronged *socially invisible*. As Axel Honneth (2001, 111) explains, social invisibility is "a form of being made invisible, of being made to disappear, that evidently involves not a *physical* non-presence, but rather non-existence in a social sense". It is a matter of being "looked through" by others, of being denied "the status of a full partner in social interaction" (Fraser 2001, 27).

To *misrecognize* the victims of collective wrongdoing means, on this account, to treat them (institutionally) as though they had no reality – as though they are not what they actually *are* (human beings and citizens who have suffered severe violence and persecution at the hand of the community). It is a matter of depriving these people of the basic recognition of who they are, of intentionally failing to respond to the realities of their condition. Thus, this kind of mistreatment, which is disrespectful in its very essence (Frankfurt 1997, 12), can be been seen as a fundamental assault upon the victims' personal reality, locking them into a distorted and false mode of being.[8]

In times of political transition, newly democratic regimes can 'look through' – and thus (institutionally) misrecognize – the victims of collective wrongdoing in more than one way. Misrecognition is direct when a new regime has an official policy of trying to cover up or deny past wrongs. It is indirect when the regime fails to properly respond to, act in the light of, the humiliating subordination, rejection or exclusion inherent in collectively perpetrated wrongs. This is obviously the case when a society and its institutions do nothing in response to the harms suffered. But even when something is done in response, it may fail to give *adequate* attention to those who have been injured. This occurs, for instance, when an individual's experience of harm and injury is made to look 'normal', little, unimportant, or even banal. But, as I have argued elsewhere (2008, 696), the victims can also suffer (indirect) misrecognition as a result of what I call, for want of a better expression, 'negative symbolism' – the sort of symbolic depreciation which is intimately tied up with what the black American political thinker W.E.B. Du Bois described as "this sense of always looking at one's self

---

[8]   These terms are from Charles Taylor's (1995, 225) description of misrecognition or non-recognition.

through the eyes of others, of measuring one's soul *by the tape of a world that looks on in amused contempt and pity"*.[9]

Before proceeding any further, let me note that I am concerned here with a normative rather than a psychological sense of the injury called 'misrecognition'. Some people may regard a certain treatment as insulting without having sound reasons for feeling this way or they may have sound reasons for feeling insulted without actually feeling insulted; for a person to be injured in a normative sense, however, there must be a *sound reason* for that person to think he has experienced treatment which is not sufficiently respectful of his moral worth as a human being and citizen. Now, there is nothing metaphorical in the mental pain that is involved in the type of misrecognition that I have sought to describe above. When recognition is denied, the victims of collective violence can justifiably be said to suffer moral injury – the injury of being ignored, of being rendered passive, powerless, voiceless, or simply invisible in matters that deeply affect them (as human beings, as citizens, and as victims). And if, as Avishai Margalit (1996, 88) correctly asserts, the essence of morality is the aim of eliminating cruelty (including mental cruelty), then this way of mistreating people is clearly morally relevant.

4. VOCABULARIES OF RECOGNITION

Having outlined a broad (admittedly cursory) phenomenology of what it means for the victims of collective wrongdoing to be 'misrecognized', let me now look at the reverse side of the phenomenon: what is to grant public recognition to those who have been wronged? If, as we saw above, misrecognition is a matter of 'looking through' and rendering socially invisible the victimized, then the remedy required to redress this injustice of misrecognition will become sort of 'social visibility'. But what, exactly, does it mean to render visible the victims and their sense of injustice? And by what means can this be achieved?

As Axel Honneth (2001) explains, our identity as full and 'visible' members in social life depends crucially on forms of direct and interpersonal communication that are grounded in, expressive of, the approval or validation of others. On this account, we experience social recognition through "a multitude of finely nuanced, expressive responses" – responses which "are supposed to make publicly clear to the person in question that she has been accorded social approval or possesses social validity, in the role of a specific social type" (Honneth 2001, 119). There exists, Honneth contends, "a symbolic relation to the expressive gestures that in direct communication ensure that a human being attains social visibility" (Honneth 2001, 119).

---

[9]   Quoted in Lukes 1997, 46; the emphasis is mine.

It is this line of thought that I want to extend by applying it to the specific context of transitional justice and the victims' demands for recognition. At this stage, the following working definition of 'recognition' may be proposed: granting recognition to the victims of public atrocities means manifesting an affirmative attitude *to* them, in response to their *special* situation. As I see it, there are two distinct levels at which the proposed concept of recognition may operate. While the first level focuses on an understanding of crime as interpersonal conflict, the second level concerns the inherently political nature of large-scale instances of evil. Far from being at odds with one another, these levels are complementary, or so shall I argue. In what follows, I shall sketch these two approaches to recognition and show how each of them operates.[10]

4.1. INTERPERSONAL RECOGNITION

Let me begin by proposing an analysis of recognition that focuses on individuals and their personal responsibility. In proposing to assess recognition claims from the standpoint of particular persons, I shall suggest that we think of recognition quite generally in terms of what Thomas Nagel (1979, 67) once called, in reference to restrictions in warfare, "the maintenance of a direct interpersonal response to the persons one deals with". My claim is that this formulation serves to ground an interpersonal account of recognition that belongs in the lexicon of societal responses to mass violence. Central, here, is the idea (common to restorative justice models) that criminal behaviour is first and foremost a conflict between individuals, rather than a violation of the state.[11] As this mode of recognition is rooted in and expressive of a fundamentally individualizing view of wrongdoers and their deeds, I shall henceforth refer to it as 'interpersonal recognition'.

The underlying assumption, here, is that hostility or aggression is primarily a conflict between persons. As Nagel (1979, 68) has argued, persuasively, "to treat someone else horribly puts you in a special relation to him, which may have to be defended in terms of other features of your relation to him". Serious wrongdoing, in this view, requires a response that can be offered *to* that person as a subject and received by him as a true response to his personal needs and claims. Drawing on this idea, I shall argue that to recognize the victims of public crimes means, among other things, to provide them with "a direct interpersonal response" (to borrow Nagel's phrase). As such, three points are in order.

First, recognition requires a proper *response* to serious wrongdoing (criterion of responsiveness). Responding to something means, in the first instance, manifesting our awareness of some antecedent state of affairs. It entails *acknowledging* the truth about some aspects of the world – articulating to

---

10   For a more detailed account see Haldemann 2008.
11   See e.g. Galaway & Hudson 1996, 2.

ourselves and to others what we *know*. Thus, to recognize my wrongdoing (and to respond to it) is to face up to what I have done and address the factors or motives that let me commit the wrong. I admit and avow my past wrongdoing and take responsibility for it. I acknowledge as mine that harmful action and choose words to describe it adequately. Crucial here is the communicative nature of the process of responding. By retelling the wrong and admitting to the knowledge of it, I manifest a certain attitude towards the person who suffered because of *me*: your pain and suffering is real and I accept responsibility for it.

Second, the kind of recognition that is an adequate response to crime should come from the offender and be presented *directly* to the victim (criterion of directness). While others might criticize him for what he did, or might provide material help or sympathetic support to the victim, only the offender can accept or assume responsibility by admitting that there is no way of justifying to the victim what was done to him. Furthermore, the wrongdoer's recognition must be offered to the victim specifically, rather than just to the world at large. If recognition is to occur, the culpable offender's reaction has to be such that it can be offered to the victim and received by him as a direct response to his specific situation and needs.

Third, the response offered by the perpetrator should take the form of an *interpersonal* reaction that is offered to the victim as a response to the wrongdoer's special relation to him or her (criterion of personal interaction). To raise the relationship he jeopardized to the level of true dialogue, the offender must engage in a process of addressing and facing the victim as the particular *person* at whom the initial wrong was directed. One might think here of recognition as a form of personal confrontation: the perpetrator is required to come forward and explain his actions *to* the victim who, in turn, is enabled to confront him directly and explicitly. Perhaps, this kind of exchange reveals itself most clearly in face-to-face interaction. We might indeed say, with reference to Emmanuel Lévinas (1969, 50), that the very sense of moral responsibility, in its original form of response and recognition, manifests itself most urgently in the encounter with "the face of the other" (*le visage d'autrui*).

When viewed under this aspect, recognition appears as a speech act in which the speaker expresses that he morally regrets doing what he did. In recognizing his wrongdoing, the offender takes the side of the victim, accepts responsibility, and admits the absence of good *reasons* for his harmful acts.[12] However, the success of the project of (interpersonal) recognition, as I understand it, does not depend on emotional or internal states such as repentance or remorse. These and

---

[12] This approach to recognition is linked to an understanding of politics that focuses more on action and civil behaviour than on particular sentiments and attitudes. For such an understanding, see Digeser 2001, 17. As I have it, this does not mean that legitimate feelings (of distress, discomfort etc.) produced by human *action*, or omission, should be excluded from moral consideration, quite the contrary. It does mean, however, that the deepest aspects of people's attitudes and convictions are not the proper concern of an acceptably liberal state.

other subjective elements are not part of the model of recognition proposed here. Rather, it involves the *performance* of a behaviour that can be reasonably interpreted as expressing moral regret, regardless of whether the actor is really motivated by sentiments of guilt, or remorse, or shame.[13]

Given its focus on the direct exchanges between particular wrongdoers and their victims, the proposed model of interpersonal recognition appears to be wholly individual, personal and private – confined to the dyadic ('micro-level') relationship between the offender and the offended. That immediately raises the question of its application to the public realm. How can this account be transposed to ('macro-level') relations among and within political communities? Does it make any sense to speak of interpersonal recognition in the context of public institutions and activities? Is 'authentic' interpersonal recognition restricted to only one mode of speech whose meaning resides within the individual?

I do not think so. Although I cannot make the full argument here, my contention is that interpersonal recognition can take on public significance through the intervention of a third party: the State as the representative of the society. What I have in mind, roughly, is a *process of triadic interaction* in which the state or 'Collective Other' emerges as a kind of moral stand-in, or authority figure, whose role consists in initiating and monitoring the appropriate behavioural procedures that are conducive to recognizing the victim's moral injuries.[14] As I conceive it, this process involves some formalized ritual devised in a way that expresses publicly the offender's recognition of the wrong he has done. As such, it requires the offender's compliance with externals, but not internal commitment. This is to say that the offender is asked to perform certain

---

13 Therefore it is not necessary for the offender, in order to complete the process, to be emotionally engaged with it; although it might be better in various ways (better for the victims; better for the goal of reconciliation) if he or she is sincerely repentant, it is the mere doing of certain 'performative' acts or rituals that brings about recognition. What matters, in other words, is that the ritual of recognition be appropriately performed, regardless of whether the actor is really motivated by sentiments of guilt, remorse, or shame. Now, it might be objected that the very act of recognition risks being superficial and meaningless, or even insulting, if it is not sincere. While this objection seems particularly relevant in private – and especially intimate – contexts, I doubt that it has real force when we look at less intimate, public relationships (such as our dealings with our fellow citizens). But whether or not I am right on this point, I think there is a more fundamental reason why we should not inquire into the offender's internal or emotional states. If we take liberal values such as privacy and autonomy seriously, then we should assume an understanding of recognition – and of politics, for that matter – that focuses on civil behaviour rather than people's feelings and motivations. This is, it seems to me, the price to be paid for an acceptably liberal – as distinct from intrusive, tyrannical – order. I owe this way of stating my position to Duff (2001, especially 109–110) and Bennett (2006).

14 The model of recognition developed here has something in common with Nicholas Tavuchis's (1991, 55–64) account of collective apology as a process of triadic interaction. I have also been inspired by some of the formulations in Duff's (2001) communicative theory of punishment and the ritualistic view of restorative justice as elaborated by Christopher Bennett (2006).

rituals (for instance, making an apology, making amends etc.) whose sincerity may be uncertain or doubtful but that, *qua* performance, send a message to the victim acknowledging her loss and reaffirming her dignity. What becomes of paramount importance in this context is the presence of the third parties, as authoritative spokespersons for the collectivity, which allows for a kind of officially validated testimony and serves to demonstrate the community's solidarity with the victim.

This process has some kinship with that of an ordinary trial. Most obviously, a criminal trial involves a censorial judgment about guilt and responsibility. By calling a citizen to answer a charge of wrongdoing, it provides an interpretation of his conduct as a public wrong and can thus play a crucial role in showing that society at large recognizes and takes seriously the victim's condition *as* a victim. Similarly, a truth commission, established to search for the historical truth about past atrocities (but with no linkage to the implementation of judicial punishment), can provide a public space for recognition that serves to recall and reaffirm the victim's civic worth (I shall return to this point shortly).

4.2. COLLECTIVE RECOGNITION

A purely individual-based approach, focused on the personal responsibility of individual agents, can hardly capture the moral complexity of collective and public atrocities. Characteristically, episodes of massive evils, such as massacres and genocide, are rooted in ideology – in some collective conviction, however misguided, about how a society should be shaped or transformed. Collective wrongdoing, as a social and political fact, represents more than just an aggregation of violent acts. It symbolizes a society's sheer lack of respect and contempt for some individuals or groups of individuals. There is a sense, here, in which society as a whole is complicit in the crime. It seems, then, that there is a need for *collective* shifts in our thinking about recognition and its role in transitional justice. If, as noted, acts of widespread violence tend to be political in nature, then we may speak of an institution or collective as recognizing past wrongs.[15]

In contrast to unmediated or mediated interpersonal relations of recognition, where the analytical focus is upon interaction between particular wrongdoers

---

[15]　To be sure, the kind of collective recognition envisaged here presupposes that collective entities, such as governments or states, can be *responsible* for wrongdoing. Although I cannot discuss this point further, I think that Peter French's (1984) concept of 'corporate intentionality' helps us to make sense of the notion of collective responsibility. According to the International Law Commission's Draft Articles on State Responsibility for Internationally Wrongfull Acts, States can be held accountable for breaches of international obligations. See Article 2 which holds that "there is an internationally wrongful act of a State when conduct consisting of an action or omission: (a) is attributable to the State under international law; and (b) constitutes a breach of an international obligation of the State."

and their victims, the kind of discourse of recognition that concerns us shifts the moral burden onto the political community by taking up the perspective of 'collective' victims – individuals or groups within the society who were (in effect and by design) persistently or systematically excluded from the rights and benefits of the community. Although the form collective recognition takes will depend on the nature of the previous regime, I propose to briefly outline five distinctive characteristics that give this kind of recognition its particular timbre.

1. To provide recognition of collective evildoing, a society must disclose and publicly disseminate the facts so that the truth[16] may be known and made part of its history. The events need to be authoritatively established and officially recounted by the state, for this is the only way for the society at large to show that it acknowledges that something morally unacceptable has been committed by – or in the name of – the collective.

2. A collective recognition, publicly uttered in response to socially organized cruelty, can be performed successfully only by an individual (or several individuals) possessing the authority to speak on behalf of the collectivity. That is to say, it is the speaker's status as an authorized representative that makes his or her positions and statements official, binding, and collective.

3. Granting recognition to victims of collective violence requires lending them a restored political and juridical standing. This involves, in particular, setting the record 'straight' on prior false allegations of political criminality and removing the stigma of social defamation.

4. The offering of collective recognition is quintessentially a public event – one that puts things on 'record' and cultivates a sense of shared collective interest. As a particular form of social intercourse, it speaks to a society at large – its institutional context and history – and entails public representation of the collectivity's moral position in a broader social web.

5. We are dealing here with a form of moral discourse that bespeaks a collective commitment to correcting past wrongs and ensuring that similar acts will not be repeated in the future. In this sense, it is a transformative project, expressly designed to remedy the kinds of exclusion that in the past denied some people the status of full members of the polity. To be sure, promoting democratic consolidation and equitable socioeconomic development is an important part of that project.

---

[16] Some 'postmodernist' critics may object that the very idea of an official truth is deeply flawed. I cannot address this issue here other than by suggesting that historical events can be authoritatively established and officially recounted. This does not mean, however, that we can ever claim to have found 'the Truth' – with a capital T – about history. But what it does mean is that official narratives can provide some sort of 'historical justice' by unmasking the mass of lies, deceits, misrepresentations, distortions, and half-truths that often, far too often, dominate public discourse. See Maier 2000.

To actualize these purposes of collective recognition, societies emerging from mass atrocity may employ various tools or practical measures. Although I cannot discuss them in detail here, the following modes of collective recognition should be considered: truth-telling, compensation, public apology, disqualification (lustration), commemoration and memorialisation, institutional reform and reconstruction (creating the conditions for democracy and legality), education and prevention.[17] These methods and means, which can be used in many different combinations, may serve as a useful framework when particular societies deliberate about how to transform images of public atrocities and mass suffering into collective acknowledgement and consequential social actions.

This completes my analysis of the two levels at which recognition, as conceived of here, may operate. In my view, there are good reasons to argue for a comprehensive approach to transitional justice that embodies both aspects of recognition. The point is that, in the context of public and collective atrocities, the wrongs committed have a dual character. On the one hand, they have an inherently social and political dimension that is captured by the idea of collective recognition. On the other hand, these crimes are, first and foremost, planned and performed by individuals against individuals and thus remain rooted in perceptions of interpersonal meaning – that is why interpersonal recognition is important. From this perspective, it is only in the combination of these two levels that the discourse of recognition can reach its full potential.

5. SOUTH AFRICA'S SEARCH FOR TRUTH AND RECONCILIATION

As widely known, in South Africa the chosen route from apartheid to a democratic form of government has been by way of a Truth and Reconciliation Commission (TRC) (see also Peacock, this volume). The decision to opt for such a commission was the result of a political compromise; it came about, as Charles Villa-Vincencio (2003, 236) notes, "through negotiation, not through victory on the field of battle or through the collapse of the old regime". In the negotiation process between the former apartheid National Party and the black majority African National Congress (ANC), the TRC was presented as an alternative to two options open to the negotiators of the new political order. The first option was that of full or blanket amnesty. This option, strongly urged by proponents of the former apartheid government, was clearly untenable for the ANC, representing the majority of those who had suffered under apartheid rule. Then there was the option of trials and prosecutions, which was strongly supported by many within the ANC and other liberation movements. But political factors

---

[17]   Some of these methods for granting recognition are discussed in Haldemann 2008, 724–732.

made this choice impossible, particularly since senior generals of the security threatened to make a peaceful election totally impossible if they had to face compulsory trials and prosecutions following the elections.[18] Thabo Mbeki, then Deputy President of South Africa, put it this way:

> *Within the ANC the cry was to 'catch the bastards and hang them' but we realised that you could not simultaneously prepare for a peaceful transition. If we had not taken that route I do not know where the country would be today. Had there been a threat of Nuremberg-style trials over members of the apartheid security establishment we would never have undergone peaceful change.* (quoted in Boraine 2000, 143)

Thus, the political option that finally gained the majority was the TRC as a "third way" (Boraine 2000, 143), "a *via media* (a middle way) between blanket amnesty and the sledgehammer of retributive justice of the criminal courts" (Ntsebeza 2000, 165). In late 1993, the National Party government agreed to relinquish power on the basis of an *Interim Constitution* which committed post-apartheid South Africa to a policy of reconciliation and reconstruction. In pursuance of this goal it provided that "amnesty shall be granted in respect of acts, omissions and offences associated with political objectives and committed in the course of the conflicts of the past". Only later, when South Africa's first democratically elected Parliament enacted the Promotion of the National Unity and Reconciliation Act 34 of 1995 (*Reconciliation Act*), this amnesty was linked to the creation of a Truth and Reconciliation Commission of seventeen members, appointed by the President in consultation with the Cabinet. The Act provided for three committees that primarily constituted the TRC: the Committee on Amnesty (CA), which processed and decided individual applications for amnesty; the Human Rights Violations Committee (HRVC), which was responsible for collecting the public testimony of victims of gross human rights violations; and the Committee on Reparation and Rehabilitation (CRR), which had to make recommendations to the president for appropriate reparations to victims by the state. Thus, three areas of concern were in the centre of the TRC's work: amnesty, victim testimony, and reparations. It is appropriate here to consider them in more detail:

1. One of the major innovations of the TRC was an amnesty procedure that had as its purpose the revelation of truth. In this sense, the process was not a blanket or total grant. Rather, it made amnesty conditional on full disclosure of offenders' crimes. Amnesty – as a protection from criminal and civil

---

[18]   As pointed out by Martin Meredith (2005, 654), Mandela once remarked privately, that if he were to announce a series of criminal trials, he could well wake up the following morning to find his home ringed by tanks. See also Lodge 2003, 176 (arguing that an agreement on amnesty 'was an indispensable condition for a peaceful transition to democracy in South Africa').

liability – was only available to individuals who personally applied for it and who testified fully about the facts of misdeeds that could fairly be characterized as serving political ends.

More precisely, the Committee of Amnesty could grant amnesty only to those who made "full disclosure"[19] of their deeds and showed them to be "associated with a political objective".[20] The legal criteria for deciding whether an act was politically motivated were drawn from the principles generally used in extradition law (Norgaard Principles of Extradition) to define and apply the 'political offence' exception. These criteria included, among other things, the object and context of the act (or omission); the factual nature and the gravity of the act; whether the act was executed in response to an order from, with the approval of, a political organization; and, particularly, whether there was 'proportionality' between the act and the political objective pursued.[21] Crimes committed for personal gain or out of personal malice, ill-will or spite, were not eligible for amnesty.[22]

When granted, amnesty exempted individuals from both criminal and civil liability.[23] It thus allowed those who had committed gross violations of human rights to walk free, without taking any legal responsibility. Further, amnesty did not exclude agents of the apartheid state from public office (Villa-Vicencio 2003, 238); further still, it indemnified the state from any liability that might result from the acts applied for.[24] Conversely, prosecutions and civil suits were potential options that remained open against any perpetrators who did not apply for amnesty or whose applications were denied. In that sense, the amnesty process "constituted a delicate balance between the 'carrot' of absolving perpetrators from criminal and civil liability and the 'stick' of the prosecution of perpetrators in the criminal courts" (Ntsebeza 2000, 165).

2. The main role of the Committee on Human Rights Violations was to provide a process for the testimony of victims. It took testimony from more than 22,000 victims and witnesses, of whom more than 2,000 appeared in public hearings. As they received extensive coverage through radio, television and print media, these hearings became highly public events available to the entire nation.[25] In stark contrast to ordinary trials, the TRC Human Rights Violations Committee hearings were intended to be more informal and to give victims the chance to tell their stories before sympathetic listeners,

---

19   *Reconciliation Act,* Section 20(1)(c).
20   Section 20(1)(b).
21   See Section 20(3).
22   Section 20(3)(f).
23   Section 20(7)(a).
24   Section 20(7)(a). See Hayner 2002, 99.
25   For a harrowing and haunting account of the victims' hearings, see Krog 1999.

without the threat of cross-examination.[26] Crucial, here, was an effort to restore 'the human and civil dignity' of the victimized by providing them with a public space within which they could feel heard and respected.[27]

In addition to holding hearings where individuals could tell their stories, the Committee for Human Rights Violations invited the representatives of various sectors of South Africa's society to participate in special and institutional hearings. As part of an effort to establish "as complete a picture as possible of the nature, cause and extent of gross human rights violations",[28] these hearings were not limited to the armed forces and state institutions, but also inquired into the roles of political parties, the media, the health sector, business, the churches, and the legal profession.[29] Although the hearings were a mixed success – with the legal and the political parties hearings thwarted by the refusal of the judiciary and some political parties to cooperate – they nevertheless prompted a national debate about collective responsibility and enabled the TRC to make extensive recommendations for reform of these sectors of society.

3. The primary function of the third TRC committee, the Committee on Reparation and Rehabilitation, was to formulate a reparation and rehabilitation policy to restore 'the human and civil dignity of victims'.[30] In drafting such a policy, the CRR could only make recommendations to the government; it did have no authority, infrastructure or resources to assist victims directly.[31] As laid out in volume five of the TRC's Report, the proposed reparation and rehabilitation policy had five components: urgent interim reparation (assistance for people in urgent need); individual reparation (a financial grant paid to each victim of a gross human rights violation); symbolic reparation/legal and administrative measures (identifying a national day of remembrance and reconciliation, erection of memorials and monuments, the development of museums, assisting individuals to obtain death certificates, expedite outstanding legal matters and expunge criminal records); community rehabilitation measures (the establishment of community-based services and activities, aimed at

---

[26] However, while the victims' hearings were intended to encourage survivors to tell their stories without being limited by formal rules of evidence and subjected to cross-examination by defense lawyers, the legal situation changed after the ruling of the Supreme Court of Appeal in *Du Preez v Truth and Reconciliation Commission*. Drawing on Section 30 of the Reconciliation Act, the Court obliged the TRC to give prior notice to alleged perpetrators likely to be named in a public hearing, as well as to provide the implicated persons with enough information to enable them to make representations to the Commission.

[27] See *Reconciliation Act* Section 3(1)(c).

[28] Section 3(1)(a).

[29] For a detailed and fascinating account of these hearings, see Boraine 2000, 145–187. Also Peacock, this volume.

[30] *Reconciliation Act* Section 4(f)(i).

[31] For a critical discussion of these constraints, see Orr 2000, 239–249.

promoting the recovery of communities affected by human rights violations); institutional reform (including legal, administrative and institutional measures designed to prevent the recurrence of human rights abuses) (Boraine 2000, 336–337).

So much for a very general overview of the three fields of concern – amnesty, victim testimony, reparation and rehabilitation – that were placed at the centre of the TRC's aims and activities. At this stage, it would be interesting to assess the success and shortcomings of what has become the main reference point for all future commissions. This, however, is not the place for a full exposition of the alleged benefits and the problems of the TRC process,[32] nor of the new moral vocabularies – such as 'restorative justice', 'reconciliation' and 'truth' – that are expressive of the commission's moral ambition.[33] My aim here is more modest – it is to critically examine South Africa's amnesty provisions in light of our previous discussion of recognition. Specifically, I intend to address the question of whether the TRC created a level of accountability appropriate to the victims' legitimate demands for recognition.

6. TRUTH, AMNESTY AND DENIAL

The TRC process, with its focus on victims and their sense of injustice, has obvious similarities with the model of *interpersonal recognition* developed above. The point of the process consisted precisely in enabling the victims of gross human rights violations 'to tell their own story', in the presence of respectful third parties – the commissioners as the official representatives of the state. The TRC's Committee on Human Rights Violations provided a public forum for victims to share their experiences of injustice and have them acknowledged officially. With the aim of placing the victims at the centre of its work, it adopted a repertoire of special norms and practices by which to honour the dignity of former victims of oppression – including a commitment to allow survivors to tell, fully, their own story, without interruption; the creation of an informal, compassionate setting, marked by the presence of sympathetic witnesses; the performance of acts and rituals of symbolic acknowledgement (such as the ritual of commissioners rising when victims entered to give testimony); the provision of assistance to victim-witnesses before and after their testimony. Crucial, here, was an effort to "render vivid and palpable the human faces of suffering, and survival" (Minow 1998, 84) – to enable individual victims to articulate the lived, emotional meanings of their traumatic experiences. The TRC represented, in sum, a public commitment to the recognition of the moral agency of those

---

[32] See e.g. Garkawe 2003.
[33] See e.g. the contributions in Rotberg & Thompson 2000.

previously excluded, by encouraging them to tell their stories to someone who listened seriously and who validated them with official acknowledgement.[34]

Further, it is important to bear in mind that those seeking amnesty for gross human rights violations were required to participate in an amnesty hearing where they had to publicly answer questions from the committee members and, in most cases, from victims, victims' families, and their representatives. Through such hearings, the perpetrators were required to provide full testimony about their involvement in past crimes and to accept responsibility for their misdeeds. For their part, victims had a right to confront their perpetrators, engaging them in serious discourse about what they had done. These features of the TRC – especially the focus on interpersonal (face to face) interactions and 'narrative truths' – can be related in a very direct way to the model of interpersonal recognition I have offered.

At the same time, the TRC process afforded an institutional framework for providing *collective recognition* of the victims' suffering and loss. One of the most remarkable features of the TRC was that it had as its primary purpose the detailed *public disclosure* of past crimes. In taking testimonies directly from the principals (victims, perpetrators, and representatives of leading institutions), the TRC played a crucial role in publicly disseminating the truth about past atrocities and in establishing a reasonably full picture of who did what to whom and under whose orders. The TRC also contributed directly to what I have termed 'positive symbolism' – as a matter of recreating the criminal past through *symbols* of public rituals. South Africa's effort to uncover the truth and restore the victims' civic dignity marked, symbolically, a break with the past and the establishment of a new moral framework, in which victims could receive validation of their humanity and acknowledgement of the utter wrongness of its violation.[35] Furthermore, the TRC's Committee on Reparation and Rehabilitation made detailed recommendations for a reparation policy, which (as I have argued earlier) is another avenue for granting collective recognition to the victims and their experience of injustice. However, the CRR's lack of power to implement its recommendations was a point of considerable frustration and disappointment for many victims, as South Africa's governments failed to respond to these recommendations in a timely and adequate manner (Simpson 2002, 242–243).

All of this suggests that the TRC process provided potentially powerful ways of bringing *recognition* to the experiences of survivors of atrocity, and their families. It remains an open question, however, whether a truth commission like the South African TRC created a level of accountability appropriate to victims and their need for recognition. Certainly, the South African truth commission furthered some degree of accountability by making amnesty conditional on full

---

[34]   For such an argument, see Allen 1999, 315.

[35]   For an illuminating discussion of the role of symbolic action in marking a new moral order, see Bhargava 2000, 57.

disclosure of offenders' crimes. Being required to make public statements of guilt or responsibility is an experience that, presumably, only few perpetrators of offences wanted to undergo – in this sense, we may think of the process as "a disruption of the freedom to pursue the satisfaction of one's desires".[36] Thus, the TRC endeavour can be qualified as a process of punitive communication, intended to be painful or burdensome not for its own sake but as a matter of conveying a moral message – a message aimed at expressing the community's refusal to tolerate the bad example established by the crime.

We may say, then, that the South African amnesty process furthered some form of accountability, at least in a 'weak' sense. Even so, the question remains whether the kind of public acknowledgement provided by the TRC process was sufficient as a response to the humiliating aspects of collective crime. After all, the trade of truth for amnesty did allow those who committed gross human rights violations to walk free without being required to take any legal responsibility for the consequences of what they had done. One may argue, not implausibly, that society fails to fully respect the victims if there is no punishment for the most egregious crimes. Truth-telling, however crucial, may simply be insufficient. Some harms, it seems, go so deep that something more is owed to the victim – something that will recognize and address the seriousness of the wrong that she or he has suffered.[37] To think that the torturer or mass murderer could just testify, and then return to normal life, would be to minimize and trivialize the victim's trauma and loss of trust in the social order. What we owe the victim, we may say, is truthful testimony *plus* some further and separate measures – measures that exclude the offender from participation in the ordinary life of the community (e.g. imprisonment) or that are burdensome in other ways (e.g. restitution, fines, compulsory community services), independently of their censorial meaning.

Let me elaborate. As we saw earlier, serious wrongdoing consists in assuming a certain sort of illegitimate superiority with respect to others. Drawing on Jean Hampton's analysis of retribution, we might argue that punishment "is not so much the infliction of pain as it the infliction of a *defeat* that annuls the wrongdoer's claim of superiority" (Hampton 1988, 143, her emphasis). Punishment, for Hampton, is needed to make clear that society will not tolerate the insult and degradation inherent in such crimes; it is, therefore, an expression of how *valuable* society takes the victim to be. The point of retribution, so understood, is to correct the perpetrator's implied message that it is really quite all right for his victim to be treated in this way. After wrongdoing, the truth of the victim's value must be publicly reasserted, and punishment is an especially powerful way of communicating that reassertion. In the absence of punitive actions, the response to crime risks seeming superficial or meaningless. This is

---

[36]   To use Jean Hampton's formulation, quoted in Allen 1999, 327.
[37]   This way of putting the argument is due to Duff 2001, 94–96.

what Jaime Malmud Goti (2002, 504) has in mind when he writes: "Only public admission by authoritative institutions that we were wronged will legitimize us in our own eyes, and punishment of the violators of our rights is the clearest and strongest statement". Consequently, South Africa's truth commission, like any other process that sacrifices the rights of victims to receive their due, carries a heavy moral burden. As Raquel Aldana (2006, 108) remarks, the trade of truth for amnesty is likely to undermine "the condemnatory message that states must send to perpetrators and the public about the nature of the crimes, thereby disparaging the victims' plight".

From this perspective, closing down the pursuit of justice through criminal and civil action seems a very high price to ask victims to pay. It might be argued, however, that this was the price that South Africa had to pay for democracy and stability. All considered, the TRC process – with its emphasis on truth-gathering and victim testimony – can be seen as an acceptable compromise between the demands of making peace and the victims' moral claims for recognition. Still, it remains an open question whether the compromise was greater than what was needed. Although I cannot offer anything close to a full analysis to this important issue, I want to suggest that there are at least three aspects of the South African TRC that could be criticized from the standpoint of victim-centred recognition.

First, one might wonder whether the goal of promoting peace and democracy justified sacrificing the justice provided by civil liability. While exemptions from criminal prosecution were defensible to ensure relative lasting peace and to deflect other great social harms, one can reasonably disagree, I think, about the necessity to foreclose the possibility of victims receiving compensation via the civil courts. In my view there was a strong case for some form of moderate civil liability, making offenders vulnerable up to a percentage of their assets or income. As Kent Greenawalt (2000, 202) argues, this form of redress of victims would probably not have discouraged offenders from admitting their guilt, since they could have earned immunity from criminal prosecution and a partial civil immunity (preventing them from being excessively impoverished by having to pay damages).

Second, as I have already noted, the South African governments may be criticized for its slowness to act on the matter of reparation (also Letschert & Van Boven, this volume). While perpetrators felt the benefit of a positive amnesty decision at once, victims would wait for years to receive reparations from the state. Since the CRR had no authority and no budget to implement its own recommendations, the blame for the slow progress on providing reparations to victims must lie less with the TRC and more with the South African government. Perhaps the most significant problem was that the legislation governing the question of reparations did not set any clear rules about the time limits for responding to reparation recommendations and the procedure to be followed (Garkawe 2003, 377).

Third and finally, it may be a concern that the TRC actively encouraged forgiveness as opposed to negative emotions such as bitterness, anger and resentment. While neither an apology nor any sign of remorse was necessary to be granted amnesty, the TRC routinely urged the victims after their testimony to forgive their perpetrators. The idea of forgiveness, emotional healing and cathartic transformation became indeed an integral part of the TRC's discourse and practices. Desmond Tutu, the chairperson of the TRC, publicly praised forgiveness and reconciliation as "the only truly viable alternatives to revenge, retribution, and reprisal" (quoted in Brudholm 2008, 29). In this picture, the only alternative to forgiveness is vengeance or hatred as something profoundly immoral, demeaning or irrational – something that needs to be transcended, overcome and abandoned. However, we might object to this discourse of either forgiveness or revenge that it does not appropriately take into account the situation of the unforgiving victim – the resentment and the indignation he or she may feel and have reasons to feel. To talk as if these feelings of anger were illegitimate sentiments, denies the victimized the basic *recognition* of who they are and of what they have suffered. As Thomas Brudholm (2008, 30) explains, this seems wrong "not only because it misrepresents what unforgiving victims may feel or desire, but also because it might push people to forgive when they are not ready to do so".

7. CONCLUDING REMARKS

As I have argued throughout this chapter, due recognition is something we owe the victims of mass atrocities, and when it is lacking they have *moral* reasons for feeling insulted or humiliated. To be sure, the personal and collective recognition of wrongdoing was an important aspect of South Africa's Truth and Reconciliation Commission. The quest for truth through investigations, open hearings (including institutional hearings) and public testimonies contributed significantly to public debates that encouraged a society-wide acknowledgement of collective injustices. As a public space devoted to documenting the crimes committed under apartheid and locating the victims' experiences of injustice in a larger political context, the TRC has become one of the most resonant symbols for the acknowledging of past atrocities and the overcoming of collective denials, lies, cover-ups and evasions.

But there is another side to the story. Our analysis is seriously incomplete if it does not come to terms with the moral costs related to South Africa's amnesty policy, even while recognizing that it was a precondition for a peaceful transition to democracy. After all, the trade of amnesty for testimony obliterated the prospect for criminal and civil actions, allowing many people to get away with deeds of torture and illegal killing. Thus, victims and relatives may reasonably perceive that some significant part of justice was sacrificed to the goal of social unity and democratisation. Nkosinathi Biko (2000, 198), the eldest son of the murdered anti-apartheid activist Steve Biko, brings out vividly why their righteous resentment or indignation occasioned by the original offences and the amnesty policy should not be ignored:

> *Those who have suffered have acted generously. Yet the privileged classes in South Africa lack the wisdom to acknowledge the shamefulness of our past and their part in it. Yet mere words are not enough; there must be a willingness to ensure that those at the bottom of the pit are high on the national agenda. Until this willingness takes place, national reconciliation (including the Reconstruction and Development Program, employment equity and economic empowerment) will be crushed under the weight of the 'huge denial'.*

This is precisely why so much effort has to be devoted to *acknowledging* the amnesty policy's moral costs for the survivors of past horrors. Social institutions, policy strategies and even a new language should be visibly in place to validate the victims' related emotions or attitudes – outrage, anger, consternation, horror, fear, distrust, shame, and the like. Otherwise, the rhetoric of 'national reconciliation', especially if coupled with the demand for forgiveness, will dangerously look like a strategy to evade accountability and perpetuate historical denial.

XI. SHOULD WE EVER SAY NEVER?
Arguments against Granting Amnesty Tested

Joris van Wijk

1. INTRODUCTION

Over the past decades the idea that serious perpetrators of international crimes – genocide, crimes against humanity and war crimes – can be amnestied has been severely challenged. According to Cherif Bassiouni (2002, 3): "The realpolitik of reaching political settlements without regard to a post-conflict justice component is no longer acceptable". In its early peace-building efforts the United Nations has generally felt free of legal or moral constraints in endorsing amnesty-for-peace deals. In many of these cases such amnesties were accompanied by the parallel establishment of truth commissions, such as in El Salvador (1991), Haiti (1994), South Africa (1995) and Guatemala (1996) (Stahn 2002, 192–195). Over the last decades the United Nations and many other actors have shifted to a more rigid doctrine that serious perpetrators of international crimes should always be prosecuted, no matter what accompanying activities are organised. It has led to the establishment of new (international) forums and mechanisms to prosecute perpetrators of international crimes. The United Nations argues that "carefully crafted amnesties" can help in the return and reintegration of displaced civilians and former fighters, but that "these can never be permitted to excuse genocide, war crimes, crimes against humanity or gross violations of human rights".[1] Likewise, other policy makers, scholars and international NGOs have taken a firm position opposing the granting of amnesties to any serious perpetrators of international crimes.

The consequences of this shifting position are not abstract. They are very real. It has for example led to the establishment of the International Criminal Court (ICC) with a Prosecutor's Office that can independently decide on the

---

1 UN SG, *The Rule of Law and Transitional Justice in Conflict and Post-Conflict Societies*. Report of the Secretary General, S2004/616, 23th August 2004.

prosecution of the most serious suspects of international crimes. Once this office has issued an arrest warrant, there is no turning back. Recent history has taught the prosecutor's inflexible position regarding amnesties. After two years of serious negotiations between the Ugandan government and the rebels of the Lord's Resistance Army (LRA), LRA leader Joseph Kony considered making use of the government's offer for amnesty (Mukasa 2008). He however wanted existing ICC arrest warrants against the LRA leadership lifted before demobilising. The Chief Prosecutor of the ICC refused to meet the rebels' demands and stated that "arrest warrants issued by the court (…) remain in effect and have to be executed".[2] Discussions on whether Kony should be prosecuted by the ICC or a special Ugandan Court are currently taking place. No peace agreement has yet been signed, LRA rebels have left Uganda, but continue to kill civilians in the north-east of DR-Congo, Sudan and the Central African Republic.[3]

In this chapter I will explore why advocates of criminal prosecution deem granting amnesty to serious perpetrators of international crimes no longer acceptable. What arguments do (often legal) scholars, NGOs, journalists and policy makers use to substantiate their claims? And how convincing are these arguments? I will firstly identify the various arguments that are most often used. Secondly, I will assess to what extent it is possible to test whether these arguments hold true. I will illustrate this by analysing the effects of amnesties granted in Mozambique, Angola and Uganda. It leads me to the conclusion that certain assumed negative effects of amnesties cannot be observed in these three countries. Either because no indicators of the assumed negative effects in the countries exist, or because no indicators can be found resulting from a paucity of reliable data. And when indicators of the assumed effects are found, it proves impossible to establish a causal relation between certain observed indicators and the granting of amnesty.

---

[2]   BBC, 5 March 2008, *ICC rejects Uganda rebel overture*. Already November 2007 the Prosecutor's Office had ruled out cancelling the arrest warrants, saying the rebel leaders and not the warrants were an obstacle to peace. The Deputy Prosecutor said in a statement that people like Joseph Kony committed "unspeakable atrocities" which are a "stumbling block to lasting peace and security". She continued "ICC is not an impediment to peace (…). I think the warrants that have been issued by the ICC have contributed tremendously to making the perpetrators of these crimes come to, even negotiate with the government (…). This idea of 'because we are talking peace therefore justice should be thrown out of the window' is not the correct position that has to be taken" (Agence France Presse 2007).

[3]   Human Rights Watch, *Trail of Death; LRA Atrocities in Northeastern Congo*, 2010. Clingendael, *The Lord's Resistance Army; in Search for a New Approach*, Expert Meeting Report, Conflict Research Unit, The Hague, 25th June 2010, available at www.clingendael.nl/publications/2010/20100629_cru_report_jhemmer.pdf.

2. ARGUMENTS AGAINST GRANTING AMNESTY

A variety of actors, ranging from politicians, journalists, NGOs, IGOs and academics actively participate in what can be labelled as the 'doing justice' versus 'granting amnesty' debate (e.g. Freeman 2009; Scharf 2007; Snyder & Vinjamuri 2004). Those who promote 'doing justice' often take a rigid stance and argue that prosecution of the most serious perpetrators of international crimes should *always* take place. Those who criticize 'doing justice' do not necessarily embrace granting amnesty as a 'better' option in *all* situations, but do not rule out the possibility that it is the case in *particular* situations. 'Doing justice' and 'granting amnesty' are vague terms. Doing justice could be defined as

> *an ideal of accountability and fairness in the protection and vindication of rights and the prevention and punishment of wrongs (...). It is a concept rooted in all national cultures and traditions and, while its administration usually implies formal judicial mechanisms, traditional dispute resolution mechanisms are equally relevant.*[4]

The most radical interpretation of justice and accountability is criminal prosecution.

Granting amnesty could be defined as a promise not to prosecute perpetrators of certain crimes. Amnesties can be limited to certain persons, and/or be of a conditional nature, whereby a perpetrator must admit to the crime before being excluded from prosecution. The most radical form is an unconditional blanket amnesty where no conditions are set and no type of prosecution whatsoever takes place. In this chapter I will focus on the two most radical positions in the spectrum: 'doing justice' is regarded as – and limited to – (inter)national criminal prosecution of serious perpetrators of international crimes, while 'granting amnesty' is regarded as – and limited to – an unconditional blanket amnesty.

Disentangling the foundations of the various arguments that are used to promote doing justice is not straightforward. As Snyder and Vinjamuri (2004, 8) note, the strategies adopted by political actors inevitably include a mix of arguments: "Human rights 'norms entrepreneurs' argue not only that following their prescriptions is morally right; they also claim that these principles are grounded in a correct empirical theory of the causes of behaviour and will therefore lead to desirable outcomes". When analysing the various arguments used against the granting of amnesty – and consequently favouring doing justice – it is indeed necessary to differentiate between *dogmatic*[5] considerations on

---

[4]   UN SG, *The Rule of Law and Transitional Justice in Conflict and Post-Conflict Societies*. Report of the Secretary General, S2004/616, 23th August 2004, at 4.

[5]   Others might refer to these as 'deontological', 'legalist', or 'Kantian' arguments. For more information regarding these concepts, see Singer 2000.

the one hand and *pragmatic*[6] ones on the other. Someone who uses dogmatic arguments argues that amnestying perpetrators of international crimes is intrinsically and ethically wrong. Someone who uses pragmatic arguments claims that amnestying perpetrators of international crimes leads to certain negative consequences.

2.1. DOGMATIC ARGUMENTS

A first line of argumentation to 'do justice' – hence against amnesty – is dogmatic in nature. It is argued that the international community has a moral obligation to prosecute perpetrators of international crimes and that victims of such crimes have a moral right that their perpetrators are prosecuted.

2.1.1. International community's moral obligation

The German philosopher Immanuel Kant once stated that "justice must be done even should the heavens fall" (Kant 1991/1785, 141). The meaning of justice has over the past decades evolved in such a way, that it entails a general obligation to prosecute perpetrators of international crimes. The United Nations, often regarded as the embodiment of the international community, considers it to be a fundamental responsibility of States to prevent and end impunity for genocide, crimes against humanity, and war crimes.[7]

Why has international criminal law evolved this way? The international community – as representative of humankind, i.e. all of us – deems it necessary that perpetrators of international crimes are sanctioned, because 'we' are shocked, offended and angry. Retribution should take place "duly expressing the outrage of the international community" at the crimes committed, as the International Criminal Tribunal for the former Yugoslavia's (ICTY) Trial Chamber has argued in *Prosecutor v. Oric*.[8] The underlying normative argumentation why international criminal law has evolved in this way is that these crimes are "violations of rules intended to protect values considered important by the whole international community" (Cassese 2003, 23). International crimes "shock the conscience of humanity" (Bassiouni 1996, 69) and perpetrators of these crimes are regarded *hostes humani generis* – enemies of all humankind. As such, it has become a moral imperative to rigorously pursue perpetrators (Meron 1993, 123). The norm to prosecute is well established by treaty and custom and can be regarded as a *jus cogens* norm that is non-derogable

---

[6]   Others might refer to these as 'empirical', 'consequentialist', 'realist', or 'utilitarian' arguments. For more information regarding these concepts, see Singer 2000.

[7]   UN SC, *On the Role of the Security Council in the Prevention of Armed Conflicts*, United Nations Security Council Res. 1366, UN Document S/RES/1366, 30th August 2001.

[8]   Case N. IT 03–68, Judgement, 30 July 2006, paras. 718–722, referring to previous case law.

in nature (Bassiouni 2000). The legal obligation which arises from the higher status of international crimes includes the *obligatio erga omnes* – the duty of all – to prosecute (Bassiouni 1996, 63). This obligation is stipulated in various sources of international law such as customary international law, the Geneva Conventions, the Torture Convention, the Genocide Convention, general Human Rights Conventions, and, most recently, in the Rome Statute that established the ICC, which states: "The most serious crimes of concern to the international community as a whole must not go unpunished". To summarize: the international community is shocked because of the gravity of the acts and therefore demands criminal justice to be done.

2.1.2. Victims' rights

Prosecuting the perpetrator is not only regarded a moral obligation of the international community, it is also regarded a fundamental right of the victims. The preamble of the Basic Principles and Guidelines on the Right to a Remedy and Reparation for Victims of Gross Violations of International Human Rights Law and Serious Violations of International Humanitarian Law (2005) recognizes that "in honouring the victims' right to benefit from remedies and reparation, the international community keeps faith with the plight of victims, survivors and future human generations and reaffirms international law in the field". The international law that is referred to encompasses the duty to prosecute. Illustrative that this victim's right is referred to in order to argue against granting amnesties is the statement given by the United Nations Assistance Mission in Afghanistan in response to the proposal to grant amnesty to (former) war lords: "No one has the right to forgive those responsible for human rights violations other than the victims themselves" (Gall 2007). Another example regards the proposed amnesty law in Algeria in 2006. Amnesty International, Human Rights Watch, the International Center for Transitional Justice, and the International Federation for Human Rights called on the Algerian government in an open letter "to uphold the right of all victims of serious human rights abuses to truth, justice, and full reparation".[9]

2.2. PRAGMATIC ARGUMENTS

Commentators also use a number of pragmatic arguments against granting amnesty to perpetrators of international crimes. The dogmatic arguments differ from pragmatic arguments in the sense that they do not need further 'proof'. Dogmatic arguments are true, as long as their proponent considers them to be

---

[9]   Www.hrw.org/en/news/2006/02/28/algeria-new-amnesty-law-will-ensure-atrocities-go-unpunished (last visited: October 2009).

valid. Where the dogmatic arguments largely speak for themselves, pragmatic arguments envisage a causal relationship between the grant of amnesty and certain negative effects. Pragmatic arguments can therefore be distinguished from dogmatic arguments in the sense that they can in principle be empirically tested. As long as such empirical substantiation does not exist the argument is merely a theoretical assumption. In this regard it is striking to note that some authoritative commentators argue without much empirical support that 'doing justice' is likely to lead to certain positive effects, while granting amnesty is argued to cause certain negative effects. And in case authors do refer to any empirical data, they often use concrete cases as illustrations to substantiate their general argument, rather than basing their general argument on a solid analysis of empirical data. In the following paragraph I will list the seven most often used pragmatic arguments against granting amnesty and present some illustrations of the empirical support referred to (or not).

2.2.1. Granting amnesty leads to impunity

Some authors criticize granting amnesty because it creates impunity. Amnesty International for example, issued a statement in 2005 in which it criticized a planned amnesty in Macedonia because the "proposed amnesty leads to impunity".[10] This is indisputable when Amnesty International refers to a narrow definition of impunity of for example the United Nations Commission on Human Rights: as the impossibility of bringing perpetrators of violations to account since they are not subject to any inquiry that might lead to their being accused, arrested, tried and, if found guilty, sentenced to appropriate penalties.[11] In this case amnesty – again, by which I mean blanket amnesty – actually does not *lead* to impunity, it *is* impunity. Although presented as an argument against granting amnesty, it would then be not more than a factual statement on the meaning of the concepts involved. In case Amnesty International refers to a broader definition of 'impunity' it is unclear what definition is used and how the proposed amnesty could lead to the (assumed) negative effect of that more broadly defined concept of impunity.

2.2.2. Granting amnesty creates a culture of impunity

Other authors allege that granting amnesty leads to negative consequences because it would create a *culture* of impunity. This culture – it is argued – might embolden perpetrators to continue committing crimes. Sadat (2007, 227) for

---

[10] Amnesty International, *Macedonia: proposed amnesty leads to impunity*, public statement, 24 January 2005.
[11] This is a summarized version of the definition of impunity given by the UNCHR in *Updated Set of Principles for the Prosecution and Promotion of Human Rights through Action to Combat Impunity*, UN doc. E/CN.4/2005/102/Add. 1.

example takes the position that "evidence suggests" that "warlords and political leaders capable of committing human rights atrocities are not deterred by the amnesties obtained, but emboldened". The evidence referred to are the cases of Sierra Leone, the former Yugoslavia and Haiti, where amnesties – according to Sadat – "at best created a temporary lull in the fighting" (2007, 227). Except for these illustrations, no other evidence is presented or evaluated, nor does she discuss the effects of amnesty for others than warlords and political leaders.

A second potentially negative effect of the culture of impunity sometimes mentioned is that it might encourage other regimes or perpetrators to commit international crimes. This is for example what Richard Goldstone, the former Prosecutor of the ICTY, suggested:

> *The failure of the international community to prosecute Pol Pot, Idi Amin, Saddam Hussein and Mohammed Aidid, among others, encouraged the Serbs to launch their policy of ethnic cleansing in the former Yugoslavia with the expectation that they would not be held accountable for their international crimes.* (in: Scharf 2007, 252)

This suggests that there was some causal relation between the ethnic cleansing by the Serbs and the lack of accountability for the mentioned *de facto* amnestied perpetrators. Goldstone, however, does not present proof that the Serbian leadership was indeed encouraged by that lack of accountability or earlier mentioned perpetrators.

A third potentially negative effect of the culture of impunity sometimes mentioned, is that this leads to a (more) crime prone society. The empirical substantiation of authors who use this argument is not always satisfying. Wilson (2001, 228) for example, explicitly links the lack of respect for state institutions and rising crime rates in South Africa to the lack of legal accountability. In this regard he makes a rather bold statement based on a rather limited analysis. Wilson states: "There is evidence enough in the crime statistics and the wild justice in places like Sharpeville to assert that criminality has been exacerbated by the lack of full accountability for human rights offenders". That the level of crime has "exacerbated by the lack of accountability" and not by other factors is however not substantiated. Scharf and Rodley (2002, 90) refer to the same negative effects of amnesty when they state that "fact finding reports on Chile and El Salvador indicate that the granting of amnesty or 'de facto' impunity has led to an increase in abuses in those countries". The report on Chile, however, does not conclude anything about the effects of amnesty, but only that impunity as such has caused and encouraged violations during the dictatorship.[12] The

---

[12]   UN, Report Prepared by the Special Rapporteur on the Situation of Human Rights in Chile in Accordance with Paragraph 11 of the Commission of Human Rights Resolution 1983/38, March, UN Document A/38/385. In paragraph 341 the Special Rapporteur states that impunity enjoyed by the Chilean security organs "is the cause, and an undoubted encouragement in the commission, of multiple violations of fundamental rights."

question whether impunity of members of a sitting regime encourages them to continue with their violations differs from the question whether amnestying former regime encourages future violations (by others). Sadat (2007, 230) concludes that "what longitudinal case studies we have suggest that our intuitions about amnesties are correct – they promote a culture of impunity in which violence remains the norm rather than the exception". Sadat, however, does not refer to any of such longitudinal case studies.

2.2.3. Granting amnesty does not take the victims' wishes into account

Victims' wishes and feelings are – in particular by NGOs – regularly used as an argument that amnesties should not be granted. The Swiss NGO TRIAL for example knows that "Impunity is an insult to the victims".[13] It does not refer to any surveys or data that support this argument. Journalist Dieng (2009, 24) tells us that "the majority of the Congolese people said that the amnesty [granted in 2002, JvW] was impunity in the name of reconciliation" and that "many Congolese believed that reconciliation through justice and truth was crucial". Finding out what 'the majority' of people in a certain country say or believe is very challenging indeed, especially in a country as vast and chaotic as Congo. The author does not mention any surveys or research. Academics and commentators also refer to victims' wishes and perceptions. Lambourne (2004, 5) and Francis (2000, 364) for example agree that power sharing with criminals and amnesties for their crimes is perceived by the victims or survivors as an "unjust peace". Again, they do not refer to any surveys. Although the above mentioned commentators imply they can speak on behalf of 'the victims' and suggest that they know what kind of transitional justice victims want, it is in reality very challenging to establish what victims want. Whom to ask? Only directly affected, or also indirectly affected victims? When to ask? During a conflict or dictatorship, directly after such conflict or dictatorship has ended, or several years afterwards? And how to ask? Should one merely ask whether victims want suspects of international crimes to be criminally prosecuted, or (also) whether they are willing to grant amnesty if this might increase the chances for peace?

2.2.4. Granting amnesty increases victim traumatisation

There are many studies that indicate that granting amnesty might lead to victim traumatisation. The outcome of such studies are sometimes used to call for accountability. Danieli (2009, 351) for example concludes in an analysis of the experiences of victims of massive human rights violations that "although not sufficient in itself, reparative justice is a necessary component among the healing

---

[13]   Www.trial-ch.org/en/about-us.html (last visited: October 2009).

processes". Based on in-depth interviews with 180 survivors of the Nazi Holocaust, Japanese and Armenian Americans, and victims from Argentina and Chile, Danieli (2009, 354) recommends that the international community should be committed to combat impunity. Referring to victims of the Argentinean junta, Kordon *et al.* (1998, 43/44) contend: "Impunity generates feelings of defenselessness and abandonment, accompanied by symptoms such as nightmares, depression, insomnia, and somatizations". Bringing perpetrators to justice is in this respect seen as an essential component for a victim's recovery and psychological healing (Shuman & McCall 2000; Kaminer *et al.* 2001). De Jong *et al.* (2000, 2068) refer specifically to the situation in Sierra Leone: "The presence in Freetown streets of former [amnestied, JvW] perpetrators of human rights abuses is a continuous trigger of traumatic memories for those trying to overcome the horrific experiences".

The existing body of empirical research substantiating this argument is much stronger than the earlier mentioned arguments. Some scholars, however, challenge the idea that lack of justice increases victim traumatisation. Based on a recent and extensive assessment of the psychological and emotional effects of post-conflict justice Mendeloff (2009, 616) for example concludes that the limited existing empirical record offers little support for claims of either salutary or harmful effects of post-conflict justice. The assessment of the available evidence therefore "calls into question the claim that victims require justice and truth in order to heal from psychological trauma or to mitigate desire for vengeance". He continues: "In short, victims' psychological suffering is likely more of an individual and public health issue, rather than an issue of conflict prevention and war" (Mendeloff 2009, 618).

2.2.5. *Granting amnesty leads to vigilante justice by the victims*

It is furthermore regularly assumed that victims will settle the scores themselves if perpetrators are not otherwise held accountable for their acts. Mostly this is presented as a potential (theoretical) risk, without referring to empirical data. Othman (2005, 254) for example theorizes that the positive effect of doing justice is that "proving justice minimizes the possibility of resort to 'summary' justice". Kritz (1996, 127) theorizes that: "[t]he assumption that individuals or groups who have been victims of hideous atrocities will simply forget about them or expunge their feelings without some form of accounting, some semblance of justice, is to leave in place the seeds of future conflict". UN Secretary General Kofi Anan warned that: "[i]mpunity gives rise to frustrations and anguish, which may result in renewed cycles of violence".[14] Scharf & Rodley (2002, 90) warn

---

[14] UN, *Situation of Human rights in East Timor, Note by the Secretary General*, Report of the Joint Mission to East Timor of the UN Special Rapporteurs, UN Document A/54/660, par. 64, 10th December 1999.

that prosecuting members of a former regime that committed atrocities can "prevent private acts of revenge by those who, in the absence of justice, would take it into their own hands". Positive in this respect is that Scharf (2007, ftn. 38) supports his argument by referring to one example. In Haiti citizens committed acts of violence against the former members of the brutal military regime who were given amnesty for their abuses. Dieng (2009, 23/25) also presents an example to support that a desire for vengeance after a lack of accountability fuels "repetitive cycles of 'revenge'". It is mentioned that the history of the Great Lakes Region shows this, particularly in Burundi and Rwanda.

2.2.6. Granting amnesty hinders truth-seeking

Another argument that is sometimes used to underline the importance of excluding blanket amnesties is that amnesties might encourage perpetrators to 'reinvent' the truth. Scharf and Rodley (2002, 90) argue that there is no better means for establishing the truth than a formal justice setting. "While there are various means to achieve a full accounting of the truth, the most authoritative rendering of truth is possible only through the crucible of a trial that accords full due process". This would in other words imply that when amnesty is granted this "most authoritative rendering of the truth" will not be possible. It is however questionable whether granting amnesty does indeed hinder authoritative truth-seeking. Osiel (1999, 279) for example, believes that a criminal trial is not well-designed for establishing society-wide consensus over the interpretation of tremendously controversial events. In courts conflicts emerge about the appropriate interpretation of events, with one interpretation being propagated by the defence and one by the prosecution (Osiel 1999, 283–284). Trials create or might suggest a one-dimensional victor's truth. The Nuremberg trials never addressed the massive extent of rape of German women by the Russian troops or the extraordinary gruesome bombings of Dresden. Though the processes were complicated, examples in other countries demonstrate that it is in fact possible to establish sound truth-seeking initiatives in parallel, or following the granting of blanket amnesties. Truth commissions were for example set up in Argentina and Chile, directly after the self-proclaimed amnesties of the military juntas (Hayner 2002; see also Haldemann and Peacock, both this volume).

Figure 1. Arguments why amnesty should not be granted

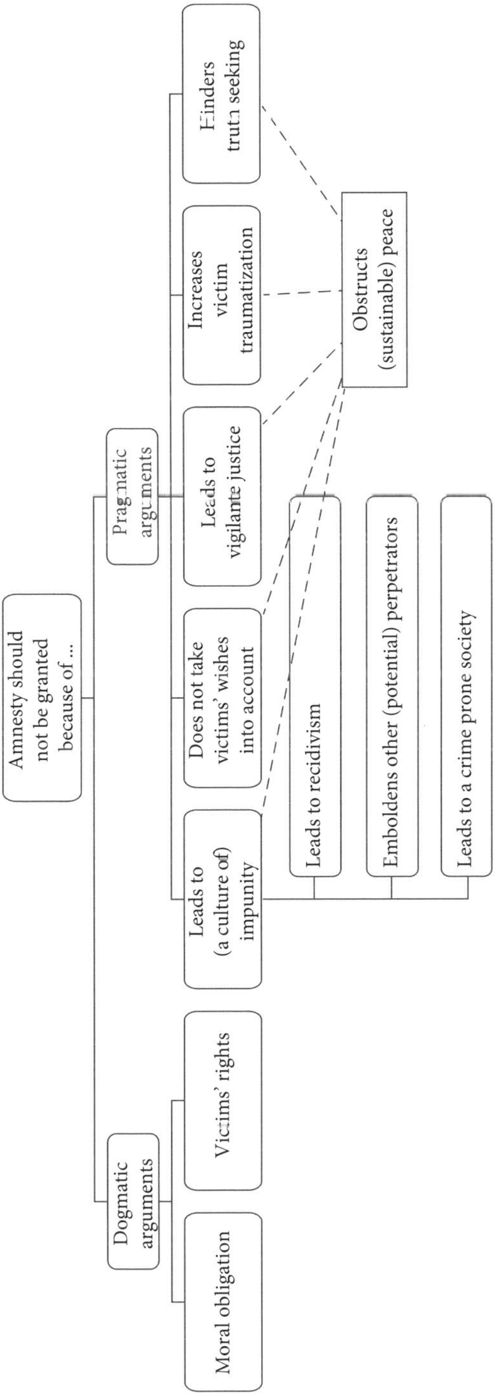

2.2.7. Granting amnesty obstructs (sustainable/lasting) peace

The most fundamental critique against granting amnesty is that it frustrates post-conflict states to establish sustainable or lasting peace. This argument is in fact the culmination of the other pragmatic arguments mentioned above. Some actors assert without any references that amnesty will obstruct the achievement of sustainable peace. An NGO like Amnesty International, for example, claims without referring to any studies that "there can be no reconciliation, and therefore no lasting peace, without both truth and justice".[15] It is not defined what is meant by 'reconciliation', 'truth', 'justice' or – in the context of this paragraph most important – 'lasting peace'. But also legal scholar Cherif Bassiouni (2002, 54) states without referring to any solid empirical data or without clear definitions that: "[a]ccountability and victim redress are fundamental to post-conflict justice, as the re-establishment of a fair and functioning criminal justice system in the aftermath of conflicts is the *only means* [italic JvW] to avoid impunity and ensure a lasting peace". Legal scholar Sadat (2007, 230) claims that "only South Africa can be evoked as an example of a successful transition to democratic and peaceful rule accompanied by the grant of amnesties". She refrains from defining what is meant by a "transition to democratic and peaceful rule", yet her statement suggests that countries like Spain, Argentina and Cambodia at least have not known such transitions after amnesties were proclaimed.

The figure on the previous page summarizes the various dogmatic and pragmatic arguments distinguished in this paragraph.

3. THE EFFECTS OF AMNESTIES IN MOZAMBIQUE, ANGOLA AND UGANDA

The above demonstrates that some commentators argue without much empirical support that doing justice is likely to lead to certain positive effects, while granting amnesty is believed to cause certain negative effects. Some use concrete cases as illustrations to substantiate their general argument, rather than basing their general argument on a solid analysis of empirical data. None of the authors refer to case studies of countries where all of the above mentioned pragmatic arguments were tested.

In the following paragraph I will test whether I can find any evidence for indicators of the assumed negative effects of granting amnesty in three countries

---

[15]   Www.amnesty.org.ru/library/Index/ENGAFR120022002?open&of=ENG-AGO (last visited: October 2009).

where amnesties were granted: Mozambique, Angola and Uganda.[16] As these case studies will illustrate, it is in actual practice very difficult to conclude that granting amnesty leads to any of the assumed negative effects. The analysis shows that the assumed negative effects cannot be found in these three countries. Either because there are no indicators of the assumed effects present in any of the countries, or because of a paucity of reliable data. Another reason why the assumed effects cannot be found is because it proves difficult to find a causal relation between the observed indicators and the granting of amnesty. Based on the analysis it can often merely be concluded that there is a correlation.[17]

Please note that one can study the indicators of the assumed negative effects only in absolute terms. It is for example possible to establish if there is *any* recidivism of perpetrators as an indicator for the negative effects of the culture of impunity. Similarly it is possible to establish if there are *any* attacks on former perpetrators as an indicator of vigilante justice. In order to establish if amnesty leads to *more* recidivism or attacks than doing justice – which is the (implicit) thesis of many of the doing justice-advocates – one actually has to define the indicators in relative terms. In order to establish whether granting amnesty leads to more negative effects than doing justice, one has to put the findings in perspective and compare these to other *exactly similar* situations where justice has been done. For reliable results one should, for example, answer the question: Is there more recidivism of former perpetrators in post-conflict Angola after the grant of a blanket amnesty than in another post-conflict country where justice was done, where the war was fought during the same time-frame, because of the same motives, with the same number of warring parties, with the same number of rebels, in the same political, cultural, social and economic context, (etc. etc. etc.) as in Angola? As history is not a science lab, such comparable conditions do never exist and such an analysis is virtually impossible to make. Ascertaining that any negative effects would not be witnessed if only justice would have been done requires devil's proof. To what extent amnesties are likely to lead to *more* or *less* negative effects than doing justice will therefore always remain open to debate and is not analysed in this contribution. The present contribution merely studies whether *any* negative effects of granting amnesty can be witnessed.

---

16   I will not test the argument whether amnesty leads to impunity, since – as stated in paragraph 2.2.1 – I take it that this is merely a factual statement.

17   A *causal* relation implies that A causes B (such as smoking causes lung cancer), while a *correlation* merely describes that there is a relation between A and B (such as smoking is correlated with alcoholism). Just because smoking and alcoholism occur together does not mean that one causes the other. Likewise, a correlation between amnesty and the resumption of fighting does for example not necessarily imply that there is also a *causal* relation between the two variables.

3.1. THREE COUNTRIES

The three countries were selected because they share a number of characteristics. The amnesties granted were unconditional and blanket. Not a single perpetrator was exempted from the amnesty,[18] not a single perpetrator had to fulfil any additional requirements.[19] No criminal prosecution was organized in any of the three countries, no official truth-finding efforts were made, no reparation was offered to victims, neither were there any serious nationally coordinated activities organized that focused on reconciliation. The activities that come closest to some type of transitional justice were *ad hoc* such as locally organized healing ceremonies that were not officially supported by the national governments. The amnesties were granted in the context of a civil war between government troops and rebels (albeit with strong international ramifications) and the countries are – apart from Uganda – rarely discussed in the context of the 'doing justice' versus 'granting amnesty' debate.

The information for the empirical analysis concerning Angola and Mozambique is obtained through a literature study and three interviews with experts in the field of Lusophone Africa. The information regarding Uganda is based on a literature study and a two-week field visit to Northern Uganda, where 25 interviews were taken with key informants such as peace negotiators, journalists, traditional leaders, psychologists, lawyers, government officials, politicians and representatives of NGOs. Whenever I refer to 'respondents', I refer to either the experts on Lusophone Africa or the interviewees in Uganda.

In Mozambique, Uganda and Angola amnesty laws were issued respectively in 1992, 2000 and 2002. In Mozambique and Angola they marked the end of long and intensive conflicts. In Uganda it was issued during a conflict that is still ongoing. During the conflicts international crimes were not only committed by rebels, but also by government troops. In all the three countries the amnesty was offered by the government to members of the rebelling factions. In that same process all three governments also produced a self-proclaimed amnesty. While acknowledging that government troops have also violated international criminal law in the course of conflict, I will in the context of this chapter only focus on crimes committed by – and the effects of the amnesty granted to – the rebels.

3.1.1. Mozambique[20]

The war in Mozambique started in the early 1980s, after several years of lower-scale violence caused by a group called *Africa Livre*, later adopted and supported

---

[18] In Uganda this has changed over time. See the country description in this paragraph for details.

[19] Other than standard conditions such as for example demobilisation and disarmament.

[20] For extensive recordings of the history of the Mozambican conflict and peace process, see: Vines (1991), Igreja (2007), Cobban (2007) and Van den Bergh (2009).

by the secret service of neighbouring Rhodesia (today's Zimbabwe) under the name *Renamo* (*Resistência Nacional Moçambicana*) and by sporadic military incursions by the Rhodesian Armed Forces. Apart from the international players, the main protagonists were the Government of Mozambique, led by *Frelimo* (*Frente de Libertação de Moçambique*) that had won Mozambique's independence from Portugal in 1975, and the *Renamo* rebel group. It leaves no doubt that especially *Renamo*, which turned the country's rural areas increasingly into zones of insecurity and fear, has committed international crimes in the course of the conflict. The definition of war crimes in an internal armed conflict in common Article 3 to the four Geneva Conventions of 12 August 1949 includes for example "violence to life and person, in particular murder of all kinds, mutilation, cruel treatment and torture". Indeed, there are sufficient indications that such crimes have been committed in Mozambique by *Renamo* "as part of a plan or large-scale commission", as common Article 3 prescribes. There is ample evidence that murder, kidnapping, hostage taking and summary executions have taken place on a large-scale. Hundreds of thousands of civilians died as a result of the war and by 1989 about five million people were internally displaced.

After more than a decade of fighting, the government concluded that it was incapable of imposing a military solution to the conflict. In the peace negotiations that followed *Frelimo* asked *Renamo* to acknowledge its crimes as a condition for peace, while *Renamo* responded by saying that *Frelimo* also had to acknowledge its own past crimes. The outcome of the negotiations was a policy of reconciliation. This was interpreted as forgiveness for crimes committed and taken to imply a general amnesty. In 1992, after two years of direct peace talks, both parties signed the General Peace Accord (GPA) in Rome. In the years after the GPA the Mozambican government did not adopt any additional transitional justice mechanisms. In the four subsequent parliamentary and presidential elections *Frelimo* has consistently renewed its democratic mandate, while *Renamo* is the main opposition party.

3.1.2. Angola[21]

Since its independence from Portugal in 1975 until 2002, the government troops of the MPLA (*Movimento Popular de Libertação de Angola*) backed by a large Cuban expeditionary force, fought the rebels of UNITA (*União Nacional para a Independência Total de Angola*), who occasionally received support from South African and Zairian (now DRC) troops. All these years UNITA was led by its charismatic founder Jonas Savimbi, while the MPLA was headed by the technocrat President José Eduardo dos Santos for most of the period. During the conflict the stakes changed from political influence in the 1980s to the control of

---

[21] For extensive recordings of the history of the Angolan conflict and peace process, see: Hodges (2001), Pearce (2005), Comerford (2005) and Malaquias (2007).

natural resources in the 1990s. In 1991–92 and 1994 two peace agreements failed; the first one after Savimbi rejected the results of parliamentary and presidential elections bringing the country back to war.

There is little doubt that during the Angolan conflict international crimes were committed, especially in the periods 1992–1994 and 1998–2002 (Doria 2004, 34). There is abundant proof that UNITA burnt down villages and killed and abducted villagers, while the MPLA-government has been accused of ruthlessly applying a scorched-earth tactic in its hunt for Savimbi after 1998. In the course of the conflict hundreds of thousands of civilians died and millions were displaced.

In February 2002 Jonas Savimbi was killed in combat by government troops. At that moment UNITA consisted of 85,000 fighters. During the following weeks peace negotiations between the remaining UNITA commanders and the Angolan government commenced. In April 2002, the National Assembly approved a general amnesty law for all infractions of military discipline and crimes against the state security forces committed during the conflict.[22] That same month the Luena Memorandum of Understanding was signed. The Memorandum granted a blanket amnesty concerning all crimes committed during the conflict. Paragraph 2.1 reads:

> *The Government guarantees, in the interest of peace and national reconciliation, the approval and publication, by the competent organs and institutions of the State of the Republic of Angola, of an Amnesty Law for all crimes committed within the framework of the armed conflict between the UNITA military forces and the Government.*[23]

No further provisions were made regarding complementing methods to promote reconciliation. The granting of amnesty itself – according to the government – encompassed the process of reconciliation. This can be deduced from the fact that the amnesty law was the sole paragraph in the Memorandum under the heading 'Issues of National Reconciliation'. No official efforts to reflect on the causes of the conflict were initiated, nor was a truth commission installed, nor were any other organized mechanisms introduced to bring former warring parties together. Such issues, as Malaquias (2007, 167) puts it, "had been buried with Savimbi". In September 2008 parliamentary elections were held. The MPLA government won with 81% share of the votes.[24]

---

[22] Www.hrw.org/wr2k3/pdf/angola.pdf (last visited: October 2009).
[23] Www.c-r.org/our-work/accord/angola/memorandum-of-understanding.php (last visited: October 2009).
[24] Http://news.bbc.co.uk/2/hi/africa/7605454.stm (last visited: June 2009).

3.1.3. Uganda[25]

Since 1987 Northern Uganda has been the scene of a civil war between Joseph Kony's Lord's Resistance Army (LRA) and the central government, led by Yoweri Museveni. The LRA initially drew its support mainly from the Acholi people in Northern Uganda, who felt marginalized by Museveni's government. Though the LRA had some popular support in its early days, it lost this support by using indiscriminate violence against the civilian population, including their 'own' Acholi people. The LRA was and still is accused of international crimes such as widespread and systematic murder, rape, enslavement, mutilation and recruitment of child soldiers. A particular feature of the conflict in Northern Uganda is that many of the LRA rebels were abducted as children and integrated by force into the rebel army (Eichstaedt 2009). In total the group is estimated to have killed 65,000 civilians, to have abducted as many as 40,000 children and to have destroyed hundreds of villages in Uganda, southern Sudan and the DRC. As a result, hundreds of thousands of civilians were forced to live in enclosed camps guarded – or protected, depending on the perspective – by government troops.

By the end of the 1990s the Ugandan government concluded that a military option alone would not suffice to defeat the LRA. In January 2000 an Amnesty Act was passed which stated that "all Ugandans who engaged in a war of armed rebellion against the government since the 26th of January 1986" could apply for amnesty on the conditions that they would report to a local authority, renounce and abandon the rebellion and surrender all weapons in their possession. Any rebel could opt for amnesty, no matter whether (s)he was arrested by government troops or had defected.

In 2002 the military presence in the conflict region increased. In December 2003 the Ugandan government asked the prosecutor of the ICC to investigate the situation in Northern Uganda. By mid-2004 over 5,000 adult former LRA fighters had surrendered and applied for amnesty. Among them were some 30 high ranking commanders who were not indicted by the ICC. There is little doubt that they have been engaged in organising and committing war crimes such as recruiting child soldiers and killing large numbers of civilians. According to a representative of the Amnesty Commision in Gulu all these applicants were granted amnesty.

In October 2005, the ICC unsealed the arrest warrants for five senior leaders of the LRA, including Kony. A year later, negotiations between the LRA and the Ugandan government started. In 2006, Museveni pledged to grant Kony total amnesty if he gave up fighting, while the Ugandan government simultaneously requested the ICC to drop the indictments issued in 2005. The ICC refused to do so. After long deliberations Kony decided in April 2008 to refuse signing the

---

[25] For extensive recordings of the history of the conflict in Northern Uganda and the peace process, see: Allen (2006), Amoru & Lawino (2009), Eichstaedt (2009) and Dolan (2009).

peace agreement if it did not guarantee his immunity from international criminal prosecution. By December 2008, the total number of LRA fighters that was granted amnesty had risen to approximately 17,000. Currently, Kony and his group are at large in the inaccessible jungle in neighbouring DRC, Southern Sudan or the Central African Republic, where they continue to kill civilians and abduct children. One indicted top leader has died in combat, while four others are still active and wanted by the ICC.[26] A representative of the Amnesty Commission in Gulu estimated the LRA in 2009 consisted of almost 3,000 people, including women and children. Latest reports, however, estimate the number of fighters to have decreased to about 200 (Mukasa 2010).

3.2. PRAGMATIC ARGUMENTS REINTERPRETED

After this brief introduction to the amnesty processes in Mozambique, Angola and Uganda, we now come to the point of evaluating what empirical data is available to substantiate if the blanket amnesties in these countries have led to the assumed negative effects.

3.2.1. Does granting amnesty create a culture of impunity?

In paragraph 2.2.2 I described that the assumed negative effects of a culture of impunity are that perpetrators repeat their offences, that other (potential) perpetrators are encouraged, and that it causes a crime prone society.

There is little to no quantitative information available on recidivism of former perpetrators in any of the three countries. The only information available is of an anecdotal and qualitative nature. With regard to Mozambique, this information does not suggest that former rebel leaders have since the amnesty process been engaged in new rebel activities. *Renamo* has not been engaged in new rebel activities after 1992. The most notable former rebel leaders are rather well known public figures working as politicians or businessmen. Coelho (2003) has compared the level of criminal activities of lower ranking ex-combatants to other civilians in Mozambique. He concludes that there is no evidence that ex combatants evolve a stronger propensity in engaging in criminal activities on street level than other social groups (2003, 221). Based on the qualitative information regarding Angola, there are also no indications that new rebel forces consisting of former UNITA members have come into existence over the past few years. Most high ranking UNITA members are doing relatively well, working as businessmen or senior civil servants. Lower ranking UNITA members mainly returned to their villages and work as farmers or in small business.[27] A limited

---

[26] Www.icc-cpi.int/Menus/ICC/Situations+and+Cases/Situations/Situation+ICC+0204/ (last visited: 30 June 2010).

[27] See paragraph 2.5.4 for more information on the whereabouts of former UNITA commanders.

number has been incorporated in the national police and the armed forces.[28] According to my Ugandan respondents most amnestied former LRA commanders in Uganda exist as businessmen and live a normal life: some study, others preach, or work for the Ugandan military. There is, however, also evidence that some ex-rebels have returned to crime. The amnestied former LRA chief of operations for example has – together with nine other former rebels – recently been convicted for aggravated robbery (Amoru & Lawino 2009). I could not find any empirical evidence available whether former lower ranking rebels in Uganda engage more often than other citizens in (new) rebel activities. According to Ugandan respondents many of them get by as *boda boda* – motorcycle taxi driver – while others returned to their villages where they 'dig', as the Ugandans refer to farming. This, however, obviously does not exclude the possibility that some might reengage in rebel activities.

Have the amnesties in Mozambique, Angola and Uganda 'encouraged' regimes or rebels abroad to commit international crimes? To empirically assess this is virtually impossible. One has to test if indeed perpetrators in for example Sudan, Afghanistan or the Central African Republic have come to their acts *because* amnesty was granted earlier in Mozambique, Angola and Uganda. This is in fact not feasible. One would need some sort of 'Armenian quote'[29] from a perpetrator who claims to have committed international crimes knowing that he would get away with it, *because* perpetrators in Mozambique, Angola or Uganda could. Neither are there any indications that the amnesties in any of the three countries have led to new domestic rebel groups. In Angola no new rebel forces have for example emerged after the amnesties were granted in 1991, 1994 and 2002, respectively. In Mozambique no new rebel forces have emerged after the 1992 amnesty. In Uganda, there are indications that certain new rebel groups have emerged since the Amnesty Act of 2000 (Kato 2009),[30] yet there is no indication that these groups were emboldened or encouraged by the amnesty law.

As discussed above some authors argue that granting amnesty leads to a (more) crime-prone society. It has proven impossible to empirically test whether the societies of Angola, Mozambique and Uganda have become more insecure or crime-prone because of the amnesty process. First of all, it is impossible to obtain reliable crime statistics concerning the periods before and after the amnesties

---

[28]   Human Rights Watch, *World Report; Events of 2002*, 2003.

[29]   Adolf Hitler allegedly made his (in)famous reference to the Armenian genocide in a 1939 speech to his reluctant General Staff in order to ensure them that they could get away with committing systematic crimes. Referring to the international amnesty given to the Turkish officials responsible for the massacre of an estimated 1 million Armenians during WWI he is said to have stated: "Who after all speaks today of the annihilation of the Armenians?"

[30]   Whether these are truly rebel groups opposing the government is, however, uncertain. Some respondents claim that government itself – and the military in particular – has a political interest in suggesting that there still is rebel activity. This only strengthens their mandate. Reported attacks by new 'rebel groups' might therefore just as well have been carried out by government troops pretending to be new rebels.

were granted. There is only some anecdotal information that crime levels in the capitals of Mozambique and Angola crime have risen.[31] However, there is no evidence that this potential rise occurred because of the amnesties or some other factor. Higher crime levels could be caused by a multitude of factors, such as decreased military presence, a higher level of relative deprivation, a stronger willingness by victims to report or better investigation activities.

3.2.2. Does granting amnesty not take victims' wishes into account?

The three case studies demonstrate that it is difficult, yet possible to establish in actual reality what victims think about an amnesty. For Angola no surveys about victims' wishes during or after the conflict are available. Regarding Mozambique there is some quantitative data available on the perspective of victims ten years after the amnesty. Igreja (2007) interviewed 293 survivors in the war-affected Gorongosa region in 2002. 38% of the interviewees indicated positively that criminal justice for the former perpetrators would be the best way to deal with the legacies of the war, whereas 50% was negative about the idea of retributive justice. 12% was indifferent (Igreja 2007, 200).[32] Cobban (2007) and Van den Bergh (2009) performed qualitative research by interviewing victims. They report mixed results; some victims believe granting amnesty was a good idea, while others would have preferred criminal prosecution.

Uganda is one of the few places in the world where several large-scale surveys were conducted during the conflict. The outcome demonstrates that victims do not simply support or disapprove an amnesty. In 2007 three large-scale surveys were carried out among civilians and so-called internally displaced persons (IDPs) in Northern Uganda. The studies concluded that the reactions of the respondents on the question whether (and if so, how) justice should be done were either "greatly mixed",[33] "complex",[34] or "contradictory" (Pham *et al.* 2007, 4). The survey by the University of California concluded that 66% of IDPs wanted to see the LRA-rebels punished, while at the same time 65% answered that they supported the amnesty process. 76% of the respondents said that those responsible for abuses should be held accountable for their actions, but when respondents were asked whether they would accept amnesty if it were the only road to peace, 71% said yes (Pham *et al.* 2005). In summary: the majority of the

---

31 With regard to Northern Uganda respondents only mentioned the situation has become safer over the last years.

32 The data provided by Igreja (2007, 200) are inconsistent. Igreja states to have questioned a total number of 392 people, though he presents figures that only count up to 293. I have therefore chosen to recalculate the percentages, based on the absolute data that Igreja presents.

33 UNHCHR, *Making Peace Our Own; Victims' Perspectives of Accountability, Reconciliation and Transitional Justice in Northern Uganda*, 2007, at 2.

34 Oxfam, The Building Blocks of Sustainable Peace; the Views of Internally Displaced People in Northern Uganda, Oxfam Briefing Paper 106, 2007, 16.

respondents wanted LRA commanders punished, but they were willing to surrender this desire if that would prevent ongoing civil war. The interpretation of the figures is best expressed by a consultant in peace building that I interviewed who said: "I do not think any sane Ugandan would want responsible commanders to return with impunity. But the line of thinking is: 'if it would end this mess, it's worth it'". The results of the surveys in Uganda demonstrate that it is under certain conditions quite possible to assess 'what victims want', but that their position might in actual reality be rather nuanced.[35]

3.2.3. Does granting amnesty increase the risk of victim traumatisation?

As far as I could find there is no detailed information available whether the amnesties in the three case studies have led to increased traumatisation of the victims. Scant qualitative academic research that is available on Angola and Mozambique, however, does suggest that criminal prosecution might in these regions have certain negative effects. Criminal prosecution by definition implies that witness statements have to be taken and that victims have to talk about their past experiences. Research by psychologist Honwana (2005)[36] indicates that many people in Angola and Mozambique believe that talking about the past (the trauma) can be equivalent to opening the door for the malevolent human beings or spiritual forces to intervene again. "Hence, forgetting about the past may be one way of coping with it" (Honwana 2005, 87). Her expert opinion therefore is that talking about the past does not necessarily constitute a positive effect. "On the contrary, talking about what happened can in some cases complicate and set back processes of dealing with trauma" (2005, 98). Honwana's view at least challenges the notion that criminal prosecution in Angola and Mozambique would have been more beneficial for victims' dealing with trauma than granting amnesty. But again; this does not provide insight whether the granted amnesties have led to increased or decreased traumatisation of victims. Such information in the three regions is as far as I could find not available.

3.2.4. Does granting amnesty lead to vigilante justice by victims?

In Mozambique, there are no indications that retributive violence directed at former leading perpetrators has taken place. The 'most responsible' perpetrator – the former commander in chief and still leader of *Renamo* Afonso Dhlakama – currently is a Member of the National Assembly. He or any other high-ranking *Renamo* members and former fighters have not yet been victimized as a result of

---

35 In this regard it is striking that the Dutch Ambassador to Uganda in 2009 simplified the wishes of the Ugandan victims by stating that "there is need to ensure that those who committed atrocities against innocent civilians don't go unpunished. The victims of this war do not want impunity" (Ocowun 2009, 3).

36 For her research Honwana interviewed civilians in Angola and Mozambique.

vigilante justice. There are also no indications that less responsible and less powerful former rebel fighters are threatened by former victims. Igreja (2007, 250) noted a general absence of revenge and a willingness to move on in the local communities he studied. The Mozambican psychotherapist Inglês told Cobban (2007, 165) that she has not witnessed any "cycles of violence" resulting from the war.

Also in Angola few indications exist that retributive violence is directed at former perpetrators. Former military commanders of UNITA – including the highest ranking – are known by name and whereabouts. Very few UNITA militants emigrated. Instead, they are currently well-known public figures in Angola and still members of the political wing of UNITA. Most of them nowadays hold political, military, or business positions. Following the peace agreement – and in some cases even long before that – UNITA officials were *inter alia* appointed to ministerial posts, including the Ministers of Commerce, of Hotels and Tourism, of Health, and of Geology and Mines. In some provinces, high-ranking authorities are (ex)-UNITA members.[37] Former UNITA militants publicly talk and write about their past. Samuel Chiwale, a 64 year old ex-commander of UNITA, in August 2008 presented his autobiography *Cruzei-me com a historia* (I crossed with history).[38] The former General Commander of UNITA Abreu Muengo 'Kamorteiro', currently holds the position of second vice General Commander of the National Angolan Army (FAA).[39] He is no exception; some thirty generals and other former high-ranking UNITA officers officially joined the Angolan army.[40] In June 2003 – this is just over a year after the peace agreement – UNITA held its 9th Party Congress in Luanda without any incidents. UNHCR observed that a few protection issues relating to the harassment of former UNITA fighters by individuals within resident communities have been reported. "Such problems have however remained isolated and do not appear to indicate any trend". Interviews that UNHCR has conducted with former UNITA soldiers have been illustrative of an overall positive environment of reconciliation.[41]

In Northern Uganda, some examples of vigilante justice are known. A member of the local amnesty commission in Gulu stated that resentment will always exist. "They [the perpetrators, JvW] can easily provoke others". He referred for example to an ex-rebel who started bragging in a bar on what crimes he had committed and that he was the 'big guy'. He was beaten up and had to be rescued by the police. When a defected LRA commander, described by the

---

37   Www.unhcr.org/refworld/pdfid/4020db6c4.pdf (last visited: October 2009).
38   Http://dn.sapo.pt/2008/08/10/internacional/autobiografia_samuel_chiwale_quer_re.html (last visited: October 2009).
39   Www.angonoticias.com/full_headlines.php?id=4691<b (last visited: October 2009).
40   Http://news.bbc.co.uk/2/hi/africa/2168871.stm (last visited: October 2009).
41   UNHCR, *UNHCR Position on Return of Rejected Asylum Seekers to Angola*, 10 January 2004, available at www.unhcr.org/refworld/docid/4020db6c4.html (last visited: 21 June 2011).

Ugandan army as "the main military and technical brain behind the rebellion",[42] started building a house in his native village, it was made clear that he was not welcome. His arrival caused aggression and threats since his former unit was suspected of having killed, chopped to pieces, boiled and even having forced others to eat villagers. He decided not to continue building and currently lives in the provincial capital of Gulu. Just like many other former LRA commanders, he is known by name and appearance and it is a public secret where he lives and works. So far, aggression towards him has remained at the level of threats.

3.2.5. Does granting amnesty hinder truth seeking?

Although a limited number of individuals or organizations have called for truth-seeking activities in Mozambique, Angola and Uganda, no serious activities in this respect have started yet. In the context of this chapter, the main question to be answered is if the granting of the amnesty can be blamed for this. Although difficult to assess, this is not necessarily the case. Granting amnesty does not automatically exclude truth-seeking activities. Amnesty can also be regarded as a window of opportunity to come to truth-seeking activities. The reasons why the governments in Mozambique, Angola and Uganda were, and still are, not that keen on installing truth commissions are unknown but could be manifold.

3.2.6. Does granting amnesty obstruct (sustainable/lasting) peace?

Up to this day a common UN definition of 'peace' is non-existent. As highlighted above, this does not withhold some authors and NGOs from making bold and sweeping statements about the perceived impossibility of achieving 'lasting' or 'sustainable' peace when no criminal prosecution has taken place.

If we want to find out whether the three countries have reached any level of peace, Galtung's (1969) distinction between "negative peace" and "positive peace" might be a good starting point. Negative peace should be understood as a situation where there is an end of direct physical or personal violence. There are various sources of information at our disposal that describe the level of negative peace. The Institute of Economics and Peace (IEP) for example publishes the authoritative Global Peace Index which defines peace as "the absence of violence".[43] Out of the 149 countries ranked in the 2010 report Mozambique ranks 47, Angola 86 and Uganda 100.[44] These relative figures tell us something about the position of the three nations, but do not yet answer whether or not

---

[42] Human Rights Watch, *Uprooted and Forgotten; Impunity and Human Rights Abuses in Northern Uganda*, vol. 17, no. 12(a), 2005, at 38.

[43] Institute for Economics and Peace, *2010 Methodology, Results and Findings; Global Peace Index*, 2010; www.visionofhumanity.org/wp-content/uploads/PDF/2010/2010%20GPI%20Results%20Report.pdf.

[44] Ranking 1 means a high level of negative peace, 149 a low level.

negative peace is actually reached. In order to do so, we need absolute data. There are strong indications that in Angola and Mozambique fighting has largely stopped. The report 'Global burden of armed violence' of the Geneva Declaration (2008), for example states that no conflict-related deaths are known in the period 2004–2007 in Angola and Mozambique. There are no reports available suggesting that the situation in both countries has from 2007 onwards changed for the worse. The conflict in Northern Uganda is still smouldering. The number of conflict-related deaths dropped from 1,649 in 2004 to 111 in 2007 (Geneva Convention 2008). From 2007 onwards LRA rebel activities have stalled in Uganda itself. Currently, the LRA is still active in the neighbouring Democratic Republic of Congo, Sudan and the Central African Republic.[45] Based on the above, it can be concluded that currently negative peace has largely been achieved within the borders of the three studied countries.

Positive peace can be described as a situation where there is an end of indirect structural and cultural violence that threatens economic, cultural and social wellbeing (Galtung 1969). Testing whether a situation of positive peace is reached is – again – difficult. Indexes that measure indicators such as the rule of law or political terror give some idea. The *Ibrahim Index*[46] on the Rule of Law, Transparency and Corruption for example shows that out of 48 Sub-Saharan countries Uganda ranks 20, Mozambique 27 and Angola 41. A second example of an indicator that to some extent informs us on the level of positive peace is the *Political Terror Scale.*[47] This instrument measures levels of political violence and terror that a country experiences based on a 5-level 'terror scale'. Angola and Mozambique both have a level of 3, while Uganda a level between 3 and 4. Such figures may for a variety of contexts be useful, they do however not clarify whether any of the three countries currently knows a situation of positive peace. They only depict the relative position of countries, instead of answering the question whether or not positive peace is reached.

It is even more challenging to establish if, and to what extent sustainable peace has been reached in any of the three countries. Since the transition from peace to justice is by definition a long-term process, it is difficult to pinpoint the precise moment when to assess if peace has proven to be sustainable. Testing if the granting of amnesty has frustrated sustainable peace is therefore virtually impossible. This is the more difficult because a correlation between amnesty and the resumption of fighting does not necessarily mean that there is also a causal relation between the two variables. A statement by Amnesty International in

---

[45]   Human Rights Watch, *Trail of Death; LRA Atrocities in Northeastern Congo*, 2010.

[46]   Ranking 1 means a relatively established rule of law, a transparent government and a low level of corruption. Ranking 48 means a relatively poor established rule of law, a non-transparent government and high level of corruption. See: http://site.moibrahimfoundation.org/the-index.asp (last visited: October 2009).

[47]   A level of 5 means a high level of terror, while 1 means a low level. See: www.politicalterrorscale.org (last visited: October 2009).

2002 may serve as an illustration how tricky differentiating the two can be. Days after the Luena Memorandum of Peace in Angola had been signed, Amnesty International issued the following statement in a press release: "While acknowledging the difficulties in reaching a cease-fire agreement, Amnesty International maintains that there can be no reconciliation, and therefore no lasting peace, without both truth and justice".[48] The organization suggested that "a main reason for the break-down of the Angolan peace agreements of 1991 and 1994 was the failure to end impunity and to protect human rights". There are, however, no indications that resumed fighting after 1991 and 1994 was a consequence of the granted amnesty. Rather, technical and political failures in the implementation of the peace agreements proved to be the key problem (Venâncio 1992; Vines 1998a; Ali, Matthews & Spears 2004; Messiant 2004; Malaquias 2007). The most prominent flaws of the 1991 Bicesse Accord were firstly that the two parties had equal custodianship; because a third and independent party was absent, animosity and distrust made collaboration virtually impossible. Secondly, rivalry was exacerbated by the prospect of the upcoming 'winner take-all' elections. Thirdly, as part of the race for parliament both MPLA and UNITA bolstered their electoral support through the use of aggressive anti-propaganda. In a sense, democracy had come too soon (Venâncio 2004, 34). In the words of Africa Confidential, the pre-election campaign "shunned the peace process ideal of national reconciliation in favour of blatant intimidation" (Venâncio 2004, 34). A fourth element was that the timetable for demobilization and reintegration of troops turned out to be overly ambitious. The Lusaka Protocol of 1994 essentially committed the government and UNITA to implement the 1991 Bicesse Accords (Malaquias 2007, 164) and was therefore destined to fail for roughly the same reasons (Messiant 2004).

4. CONCLUSION

Granting amnesty after large scale atrocities has over the last decades regularly been used as a last resort to broker peace deals. The case studies of Angola, Mozambique and Uganda may serve as illustrations. Advocates of 'doing justice' lobby to change this practice. Some contend that blanket amnesties for perpetrators of war crimes, crimes against humanity and genocide should *never* be granted. Not only because this 'ought' not to happen (dogmatic arguments), but also because the absence of prosecutions (may) lead(s) to certain negative effects (pragmatic arguments). Those who claim that amnesties lead to certain negative effects have a much stronger case if they can substantiate this claim with

---

[48]   Amnesty International, *Angola – a new ceasefire – a new opportunity for human rights*, press release 5 April 2002.

empirical data. As long as such empirical substantiation lacks, these pragmatic arguments remain theoretical assumptions.

In this chapter I presented some examples of authoritative policy makers, journalists, (I)NGO's and scholars who use pragmatic arguments, without referring to convincing empirical support. Subsequently, I made an attempt to test if it is possible to assess whether granting amnesty in three countries has led to the assumed negative effects. With regard to Mozambique, Angola and Uganda, I conclude that the assumed negative effects cannot be found. Either because there are no indicators of the assumed effects in any of the countries, or because of a paucity of reliable data. Sound statistics are not available and clear definitions are lacking. And when indicators of the assumed effects are found, it proves impossible to establish a causal relation between the observed indicators of these effects and the granting of amnesty.

Please note that it is *not* argued that amnesties in these countries 'work' or have been effective. Neither is it argued that prosecution in these countries would not have worked or would have been ineffective. Rather, the research presented in this chapter demonstrates that there is no sufficient or reliable empirical data to conclude that the pragmatic arguments against granting amnesties in these three countries hold true. While some case studies might suggest that granting amnesty leads to certain identifiable negative effects, the three country studies presented in this analysis illustrate that this is not always the case.

This leads me to the conclusion that the most often used pragmatic arguments against granting amnesty do not indisputably hold true. Until future research leads to accurate and convincing factual information that amnesties in the majority of cases leads to the assumed negative effects, the pragmatic arguments discussed in this text are therefore not more than theoretical assumptions. And I would argue that theoretical assumptions alone do not suffice to under all circumstances repudiate the option to grant blanket amnesties. In the context of war and tyranny one should not rigorously exclude a potential solution on the basis of theory.

Although the above questions the validity of the most often used pragmatic arguments, it does not question the weight of the dogmatic line of argumentation; we – the 'international community' – might still be shocked by the gravity of certain acts committed and *therefore* demand that criminal prosecution takes place. No matter what potential solutions to war and tyranny may be missed. However, the fundamental question we need to answer is if this dogmatic line of argumentation is sufficient to take the inflexible and rigid position that perpetrators of international crimes should *never* be granted amnesty? Is this argumentation sufficient, *even* if the most directly affected victims might want to make use of the slightest chance that amnesty may help to end the conflict? To make it concrete: is it sufficient to explain to Sudanese and Congolese villagers who currently fall prey to the attacks of Kony's LRA that Kony should never be granted amnesty, *only* because the 'international community' is shocked?

XII. THE SOUTH AFRICAN TRUTH AND RECONCILIATION COMMISSION

Challenges in Contributing to Reconciliation

Robert PEACOCK

1. INTRODUCTION

South Africa is a country that emerged from the most inhumane racial oppression orchestrated by the apartheid regime. Apartheid sought to dehumanise South Africans and the Truth and Reconciliation Commission (TRC) forced a country to redefine itself through the accounts of its victims and perpetrators, or as Krog (2002, 293) asserted "we have to become each other, or for ever lose the spine of being". The TRC is the most visible vehicle that made this redefinition possible but for a new democratic and reconciled order whose future relies on emerging and transcending an atrocious past, reconciliation had to become part of a much broader process. The following discussion will focus on various challenges associated with reconciliation, but for purposes of contextualising the challenges of a transitional society, it is first necessary to briefly discuss the institution of apartheid as well as key elements pertaining to the nature and functioning of the TRC.

2. BRIEF OVERVIEW OF APARTHEID

In South Africa the roots of apartheid can be traced back to its colonial era. In 1652, Jan van Riebeeck from the Dutch East India Trading Company founded a permanent settlement in the Cape of Good Hope. In 1795 the Cape colony was seized by the British, recovered by the Dutch and seized again by the British in 1806. Since its first colonisation and regardless of its colonial powers, and with the aid of slavery, a long history was established of white dominance over Africans in this region (Elian 2003; Loomba 2005). Despite such prolonged period of white dominance, the term *apartheid* (from the Afrikaans word 'apartness') only emerged as a political slogan of the National Party in the early 1940s (Oomen 2005). Subsequently, when the Afrikaner Nationalists came into power in 1948, the white supremacist policy of racial domination and segregation was further institutionalised through a plethora of laws:

- The Population Registration Act (Act No 30 of 1950) that formalised racial classification can be referred to as the first 'grand' apartheid law that classified all South Africans into one of four racial categories: Bantu (black African), white, 'Coloured' (of mixed race) and Asian (Indians and Pakistanis). This classification led to the creation of a national register in which every person's race was recorded. A Race Classification Board took the final decision on what a person's race was in 'disputed' cases.
- The Group Areas Act (Act 41 of 1950) enforced the physical separation between races by creating different residential areas for different races. This lead to the forced removals of individuals and communities who were living in 'wrong' areas, for example, those individuals from mixed racial descent, i.e 'Coloureds' living in District Six in Cape Town.
- Apartheid laws (Natives Laws Amendment Act 54 of 1952, Natives Act 67 of 1952 –also known as the Pass Laws – and the Influx Control Act 68 of 1986) further restricted movement of Africans in so-called 'white only' areas and together with the already limited rights of black Africans to own land, entrenched the white minority's control of over 80 percent of South African land.
- The Prohibition of Mixed Marriages Act No 55 of 1949 and the Immorality Amendment Act 21 of 1950 prohibited most social contacts between the races. In addition, to enforce the segregation of public facilities (public buildings, amenities and public transport), the Reservation of Separate Amenities Act 49 of 1953 was passed with signs 'Europeans Only' and 'Non-Europeans Only' displayed in public spaces, reserving also parks, beaches, churches, schools, universities and hospitals for the use of whites only. This act stated that facilities provided for different races need not be equal.
- Various laws prescribed the separation of educational standards for different race groups (Bantu Education Act No 47 of 1953), created race-specific job categories, restricted the powers of non-white unions and curbed non-white participation in government (Bantu Building Workers Act No 27 of 1951; Separate Representation of Voters Act No 46 of 1951; Bantu Authorities Act No 68 of 1951).
- Further laws were aimed at repressing resistance to the apartheid regime, for instance, communism was outlawed and defined so broadly that it encompassed any call for major change in South Africa. Communists (real or alleged) could have been banned from participating in political organisations, or from residing in particular residential areas (Suppression of Communism Act No 44 of 1950).

From the above it is evident that apartheid legislation had as aim to permeate, control and distort all facets of live in South Africa. At the heart of the massive violations of human rights within apartheid lied the need for a cheap and a readily available supply of labour to ensure the continued exploitation of the country's great mineral wealth by the white elite. Hendrik Verwoerd, the architect of apartheid, said in 1953 in parliament *(whites only)*: "When I have control over native education, I will reform it so that natives will be taught from childhood that equality with Europeans is not for them". He continues in 1955: "There is no place for the Bantu in the European community above the level of certain forms of labour" (Peacock 1989, 61).

It took a number of decades before the international community was ready to openly condemn the apartheid regime. On 30 November 1973, the United Nations General Assembly opened for signature and ratification of the International Convention on the Suppression and Punishment of the Crime of Apartheid (ICSPCA). It defined the crime of apartheid as "inhuman acts committed for the purpose of establishing and maintaining domination by one racial group of persons over any other racial group of persons and systematically oppressing them".[1]

Although the enforcement of apartheid was accompanied by tremendous suppression of opposition,[2] resistance to apartheid continued to grow within South Africa. Since the 1950s the youth wing of the African National Congress (ANC) initiated a series of strikes, boycotts and civil disobedience actions that lead to violent clashes with the police force. The Sharpeville massacre took place on 21 March 1960 when a group – disenchanted ANC members who formed the Pan Africanist Congress (PAC) – was protesting against the Natives Act of 1952 (also known as the Pass Laws) that required African people to carry on their person identification cards at all times in order to restrict their movement in so-called 'white only' urban areas. Sixty nine people were killed and numerously injured when the South African police force opened fire on the approximately 300 demonstrators. Subsequently, the regime declared a State of Emergency and more than 18 000 people were arrested and detained, including leaders of the ANC and PAC. Both organisations were banned and the resistance movement went underground. The ANC formed a military wing, *Umkhonto we Sizwe* (MK)

---

[1]   The crime of apartheid is also defined by the 2002 Rome Statute of the International Criminal Court as inhumane acts of a character similar to other crimes against humanity "committed in the context of an institutionalized regime of systematic oppression and domination by one racial group over any other racial group or groups and committed with the intention of maintaining that regime."

[2]   The research of Peacock (1991), Shaw (1996) and Slabbert (1980) showed that during this time of racial oppression the main aim of the criminal justice system was to enforce apartheid rather than curbing crime. South Africa had the highest prison population per capita in the world, of which 80% were short-term prisoners – most of them incarcerated under the pass laws.

which would perform acts of sabotage on tactical state structures. The *Azanian People's Liberation Army* (APLA) became the military wing of the PAC.

Attempts to reform apartheid in the 1980s failed due to continued opposition (both internally and internationally), and in 1990, the leader of the National Party, De Klerk, engaged in negotiations to end apartheid, culminating in 1994 in the first free and non-racial elections. This was duly won by the ANC and Nelson Mandela became the first democratically elected president of the Republic of South Africa.

3. LEGISLATIVE FRAMEWORK AND NATURE OF THE SOUTH AFRICAN TRUTH AND RECONCILIATION COMMISSION

With the release of Nelson Mandela from prison in the beginning of 1990 together with the unbanning of the African National Congress, an Interim Constitution (Act No 200 of 1993) was negotiated to prepare the way for South Africa's first democratic elections. The past dictated the future and to make elections possible, the final clause in the Interim Constitution provided amnesty for all offences committed with political motives, requiring that the applicant fully disclosed all relevant facts in respect to the act, or omission for which amnesty was sought (Sections 20(1)(b) and 20(1)(c)). The Promotion of National Unity and Reconciliation Act (Act No 34 of 1995) provided the TRC with a mandate to establish as complete as possible the causes, nature and extent of gross human rights violations committed under apartheid from March 1960 to December 1993, later amended to May 1994. This was to be achieved through investigations and the holding of public hearings. Also, the Commission was to restore the human and civil dignity of victims, formulate recommendations for reparations, and to compile a written report including measures to prevent future violations of human rights. The seventeen member Commission was appointed through a transparent process after a panel considered 299 nominations from different stakeholders comprising of members of both civil society and government. On 29 November 1995, the first democratically elected president of the Republic of South Africa, President Nelson Mandela appointed 17 commissioners from a shortlist of 25 candidates (Emmanuel 2007).

The TRC was duly established and comprised of three committees. The first was the *Human Rights Violation Committee* tasked with assessing the accounts of victims through hearings and investigations. The Human Rights Violations Committee gathered 21 296 statements during the course of its work.[3] The second committee, namely the *Amnesty Committee* had to evaluate amnesty applications.

---

3   Truth and Reconciliation Commission of South Africa, *Report*, 1998.

It was steered by five members, three of which were independent judges. Amongst others, this committee was bound by the *Norgaard principles* to determine the granting of amnesty (Elian 2003).[4] These principles stated:

i)   if the motivation for acts was political,
ii) if the target was governmental or military,
iii) if the act took place within a framework of 'due obedience' and
iv) if full disclosure took place, then amnesty could be granted.

None of the decisions of the *Amnesty Committee* could have been overruled by the Commission itself. Of the 7,115 amnesty applications received, 1,146 (about 16%) were granted amnesty and 5,504 (77.3%) were declined (TRC 1998).[5]

The third committee was the *Reparation and Rehabilitation Committee* tasked to formulate a reparation policy to restore and rehabilitate survivors of human rights violations. The Commission was finally assisted by a Research Unit and an Investigative Unit and had the powers to subpoena individuals.[6]

4.   TRUTH AND RECONCILIATION

The idea of achieving reconciliation resonates with the African philosophy of *Ubuntu*. The ancient philosophy of *Ubuntu* can be described as emphasising communality and interdependence where the life and dignity of another is considered as valuable as one's own. *Umuntu ngumuntu ngabantu* means to be human is to affirm one's humanity of others in its infinite variety of context and form. We therefore gain our own sense of humanity from the humanity we share with others (Louw 2006; Bohler-Muller 2008). *Ubuntu,* furthermore, inspires individuals to expose their feelings and thoughts to others thereby also evoking differences in humanness so as to inform, extend and enrich ones' own sense of humanity. Moreover, *Ubuntu* seeks to redress imbalances and the restoration of relationships through agreement and a basic respect and compassion for others (Louw 2006).[7] The spirit of *Ubuntu* is enshrined in the Promotion of National Unity and Reconciliation Act (No 34 of 1995, section 3(1)(c)) and reads as follows:

> *Establishing or making known the fate or whereabouts of victims and by restoring the human and civil dignity of such victims by granting them an opportunity to relate their own accounts of the violations of which they are the victims, and by recommending reparation measures in respect of them.*

---

4   *Ibidem.*
5   *Ibidem.*
6   *Ibidem.*
7   *White Paper of the Department of Social Welfare* (1997), Pretoria: Government Printer.

The epilogue of the Interim Constitution (Republic of South Africa 1994) also emphasised at the dawn of a new democratic order for South Africa, the "need for understanding but not vengeance, a need for reparation but not for retaliation, a need for *Ubuntu* but not for victimisation".

Memory relates to identity, and it may therefore not be feasible to achieve societal reconciliation on the basis of a divided, repressed or incomplete memory and historical identity. An imperative for reconciliation and nation building would thus be to place key aspects of a divided nation's historical and ethical past on the public record, and in such a manner that the past cannot be denied. Also Boraine *et al.* (1994) are of the opinion that without truth, reconciliation is not possible. However, the specific definition of truth is also important (Williams 2000). In this regard, the TRC conceptualised five kinds of truth:[8]

i)   factual or forensic truth (using science to elucidate factual truth),
ii) corroborated evidence to obtain reliable information through impartial and objective procedures,
iii) personal or narrative truth entailing accounts from both victims and perpetrators,
iv) social or dialogue truth as viewed as the truth of experience established through interaction, discussion and debate, and
v)   healing or restorative truths by placing facts in the context of interpersonal relationships between citizens and also between citizens and the state.

The section below will further examine in what way the TRC was successful in contributing to any of these forms of truth.

It is important to highlight first that the TRC could be criticized for adopting a too narrow definition of gross violations of human rights abuses of the apartheid regime.[9] Within a very specific time frame – from March 1960 to May 1994 – the focus of the TRC was mainly on the cruel and brutal activities of the apartheid security police force. Mamdani (2000) argues that the TRC obscured the truth because it did not consider, amongst others, the forced removals of the apartheid regime, its Pass laws and racialised poverty and racialised wealth that were all at the centre of gross human rights violations. Moreover, denying equal educational opportunities to race groups other than whites formed the corner stone of the apartheid policies and was perhaps one of the most pronounced forms of human rights abuses perpetrated by the apartheid state.

The quasi-judicial nature of the amnesty process focused on facts that related to particular incidents and to a large extend excluded dimensions that could

---

8   Truth and Reconciliation Commission of South Africa, *Report*, 1998.
9   See also the mandate of the TRC as mentioned above under the Interim Constitution of the Republic of South Africa (1994) and the Promotion of National Unity and Reconciliation Act 34 of 1995.

account for the motives and perspectives of those responsible for past violations (Emmanuel 2007). In other words, while primarily assigning guilt to individuals who were *directly* involved with human rights abuses, the wider social system that provided incentives and justifications – as discussed above – did not receive adequate attention when attempts were made to uncover the truth about South Africa's racist and brutal past. This also influenced the impact on contributing to in particular the fifth conceptualisation of truth as referred to above.

Various researchers (Emmanuel 2007; Lerche 2000; Posel & Simpson 2002) are furthermore of the opinion that for the most part, the truthfulness of the TRC testimonies was not corroborated. This is problematic as victims and perpetrators with possible reparations and amnesty in mind could have disclosed their testimonies with varying degrees of honesty. Also, with a lapse of time since the incidents took place, false memories, fractured and selective truths may have made it increasingly difficult to distinguish between emotional and subjective versions of the truth and what actually occurred (Alison 2005; Pakes & Pakes 2009).

Despite this criticism against the truth as presented by the TRC, the TRC was nevertheless crucial in breaking the tyranny of silence, a silence imposed not only by state censorship, but also by clandestine activities of the state security forces such as the abductions, torture, murder and detention without trial of political opponents (Foster *et al.* 1987).[10] The following discussion will elaborate on different accounts of the truth provided by politicians, the media and church, business and community members.

4.1. POLITICIANS

Maybe the greatest test *and* success concerning the credibility of the TRC was that none of the political role players were satisfied with its findings. Both the African National Congress (ANC) and ruling National Party sought court interdicts to prevent certain information to be published in the final TRC report. De Klerk from the National Party was successful in removing the sole half-page concerning himself from the final report. This was the president who repeatedly claimed he was unaware of the political atrocities perpetrated by his security forces.[11] The ANC objected to the notion of being accused of utilising – as also in

---

10   Truth and Reconciliation Commission of South Africa, *Report*, 1998.
11   Although in terms of international humanitarian law and the Geneva Conventions (see www.genevaconventions.org/), the State is held strictly responsible for the conduct of its agents who commit gross violations of human rights, and that State responsibility may be invoked even where the identity of the agent is unknown, the TRC remains a commission of enquiry and therefore, the findings of the TRC are not bound by the same rules of evidence as a court of law. Its conclusions cannot be interpreted as judicial findings of guilt but rather as findings of responsibility within the context of its enabling Promotion of National Unity and Reconciliation Act No. 34 of 1995.

the case of the Pan African Africanist Congress (PAC) – 'unjust means' to fight a 'just war'. 'Unjust means' would constitute gross human rights violations. Inkatha Freedom Party (IFP) leader Mangosuthu Buthelezi compared the Commission to the McCarthy Commission and Spanish Inquisition. According to a statement submitted, the IFP (in alliance with the apartheid regime) was (is) of the opinion that the combination of amnesty, compensation and truth-finding was a recipe for great evil. It was further alleged that the ANC killed more IFP members than the apartheid rulers ever did. Eugene Terblanche, the deceased leader of the far right wing Afrikaner Weerstandsbeweging (AWB), refused to participate in the TRC, believing it would absorb him and his people into one of the most "bizarre" democracies in the world, where the unemployed will take charge of those who are economically productive (Coleridge 2000; Emmanuel 2007; Krog 2002).

Despite the mentioned political dissatisfaction with the findings of the TRC, it should be noted that it was extremely difficult for the TRC to attribute direct political responsibility for many of the violations.[12] During the 1990s in particular when political conflict gained intensity, more gross violations were perpetrated by members of the South African society than by both the state security forces and guerrilla organisations such as MK. Such activists were acting in pursuit of what they believed to be a political ideal rather than executing the express orders from a political party. According to the report of the TRC:[13]

> Both the state security services and guerrilla organisations such as MK aimed to supply such social actors (activists) with the means to achieve their aims – including weapons, information, trained personnel, and, in the case of the state, funding. It was therefore difficult to attribute direct responsibility for many violations, such as the lynchings or necklacings carried out by crowds loosely aligned to the ANC/UDF in the 1980s, and attacks carried out by social groups such as the 'witdoeke' in Crossroads, encouraged and endorsed by state security forces.

4.2. MEDIA

By its very nature the media should reflect images of society and prevailing concerns, thereby also influencing and shaping the contours of social debate (Williams 2000). The TRC's investigation into the media took place from 15 to 17 September 1997 to establish the role the media played during apartheid and to determine whether the media was directly or indirectly responsible for gross human rights violations. The mainstream Afrikaans press openly opposed the TRC and criticised it constantly (sometimes in sarcastic language and tone),

---

[12] Truth and Reconciliation Commission of South Africa, *Report*, 1998.
[13] *Idem*, Vol. 2, Chapter 1, p. 12.

referred to it as a failure prior to completing its work, and refused furthermore to present submissions to the TRC. It also requested for the TRC to be abolished (De Beer & Fouche 2000). Elements in the English press stated that it would be inappropriate for the TRC to investigate the media as the TRC was a state-sponsored body. However, the media group *Independent Newspapers* became the first to admit historical shortcomings and apologised for past failures.[14] The Black press detailed its position during apartheid but was also outspoken against the English press (the latter was generally considered to be more involved with the liberation struggle than the Afrikaans press). Issues mostly raised by the black journalists during the media hearings related to spies operating in the newsrooms, separate toilet facilities and cafeterias for blacks and whites and the impossibility of promotions in the English organisations.

The TRC concluded that the English media enforced self-censorship by not publishing accounts of the brutality of the security forces and practiced apartheid in its own newsrooms, that the Afrikaans press supported apartheid and activities of the security forces, imposed gender and racial discrimination in the workplace, and that the National Television Broadcaster (SABC) was a "direct servant" of the apartheid regime. Overall it was found that the mainstream media failed to report adequately on the gross human rights violations perpetrated by the apartheid state, thereby sustaining and prolonging its existence (De Beer & Fouche 2000; Williams 2000).

4.3. BUSINESS

The TRC undertook special hearings into the role of large business in South Africa's apartheid past. At first prominent business leaders denied their involvement, alleging that they did not benefit from apartheid, with some even stating that apartheid prevented them from realising their full potential. However, according to Krog (2002), the indignant big companies realised quickly that their insistent pleas of innocence amounted to bad public relations. Within three days all admitted that they had indeed benefited and offered apologies concerning their profits. The TRC found that some sectors of business were more involved with the apartheid regime than others, but for the most, businesses were culpable simply by virtue of having benefited from operating in a racially structured environment with its perpetuation of a super-exploitative cheap labour system (Nattrast 1999).

---

14   M. Morris, Press group regrets its human rights failings, *Sunday Independent,* 23 February.

4.4. CHURCH

Although predominantly Christian, South Africa is a country with diverse religions. In total 41 faith-based communities made submissions to the TRC. For the most part Afrikaans churches however refrained from testifying before the commission, seemingly afraid of a so-called "witch hunt" by the Commission. Furthermore, the Afrikaans' churches considered "Confession and forgiveness" to be "a religious act, how can it be done in a secular way?" (Krog 2002, 164). Apart from the issue of criminal, political, moral and metaphysical guilt, Afrikaans churches also have a pastoral function and could have supported amnesty applicants, victims and communities alike during the TRC hearings in their areas. An act of commission refers to providing a theological argument for the justification of apartheid and the racist policies of separate development of the apartheid regime. Not condoning apartheid constituted an act of omission. According to TRC findings,[15] acts of commission took the following forms:

i)   Participating in state structures (not only Afrikaans churches but Anglican, Methodist, Presbyterian, Baptist, Apostolic Faith Mission and Roman Catholic churches appointed chaplains in the apartheid military),

vi) Suppressing and censuring dissidents (not only failing to provide support to anti-apartheid activists but branding them as 'heretics' i.e. Beyers Naude),

vii) Internalising racism ('whites only' churches but discrimination was also prevalent in the non-Christian faith communities with for example, ethno-class and theological distinctions between Indian and Malay Muslims),

viii) Propagating 'state theology' where the powerful was blessed and the poor to be reduced to passivity, obedience and apathy.

But different faith groups also suffered the wrath of the apartheid regime. For instance, as the result of directs attacks, *Khotso House*, the headquarters of the South African Council of Churches was bombed by the security forces. Six weeks later the headquarters of the South African Catholic Bishops' Conference was destroyed by arsonists and its General Secretary detained and tortured; and Father Micahael Lapsley lost both his arms and an eye in a parcel bomb attack, two months *after* the unbanning of liberation movements. According to the TRC (1998) faith communities were furthermore affected by the closing of buildings and schools, and repression of religious and cultural values with the apartheid state viewing itself as a guardian of 'Christian civilisation'.[16]

---

[15]   Truth and Reconciliation Commission of South Africa, *Report*, 1998.
[16]   *Ibidem*.

4.5. INDIVIDUAL VICTIMS

The Commission received 21,296 statements regarding gross violations of human rights. Besides the structural human rights abuses as reflected upon under section 4 (racialised poverty and exclusion from the educational system), the Commission received various statements on brutal incidents of mental or physical abuses. The chapter on children and youth in the TRC report describes in particular the devastating effects of apartheid on young people in South Africa.[17] It also pays tribute to the extraordinary heroism of the youth who risked their education and lives for a just South Africa. However, many did not live beyond their teens and became victims of the very system against which they struggled. On 16 June 1976 (now commemorated as *Youth Day* in South Africa) students protested in the streets of Soweto against the inferior Bantu education system and forced tuition in Afrikaans. The police force then opened fire on what was supposed to be a peaceful demonstration. According to official reports, 23 students were killed but some news agencies estimated the casualties rather to be closer to 600 with an additional count of 4,000 students that sustained injuries. When a State of Emergency was declared in June 1986, (giving the police and military forces wide ranging powers to suppress the political unrest), 173,000 children and juveniles were detained under security legislation in prison or police cells for extended periods, without trial or legal representation (Foster *et al.* 1987; Langa 1987). These figures do not include the detention of children in the then so-called 'independent homelands'. It also does not refer to children dealt with by unofficial vigilante forces allied with and often directed by the apartheid regime. According to the Detainees' Parents' Support Committee 30–40% of all people killed, wounded, arrested or detained in police or prison cells were children and juveniles.[18]

A submission from medical practitioners to the TRC detailed a 94% incidence of either physical or mental abuse that was experienced in a study among former detainees.[19] Half of the sample was exhibiting physical symptoms of abuse during the time of examination and forty eight percent was found to be psychologically 'dysfunctional'. The Commission established that deaths in detention were commonplace, usually as a direct or indirect result (suicide) of torture. Torture techniques that were identified ranged from assault to various forms of suffocation (including the 'wet bag' or 'tubing' method), enforced posture, electric shocks, sexual torture, psychological torture and solitary confinement. The Commission found that the South African government condoned the use of torture as official practice. Despite the common occurrence of torture and

---

17   *Ibidem.*
18   Detainees' Parents' Support Committee, *Abantwana Bazabalaza: A Memorandum on Children under Repression,* Johannesburg: University of the Witwatersrand, 1987.
19   Truth and Reconciliation Commission of South Africa, *Report,* 1998.

maltreatment of those held in custody under security legislation (detention without trial), only 20 amnesty applications were received for torture.[20]

According to the research of Picker,[21] a mere fraction (about 8%) of the above-mentioned 21,296 cases were selected for the public Human Rights Violation hearings due to practical constraints such as limited time. The Commission selected participants to be "representative of the broadest political spectrum". The studies of Hamber *et al.* (1998) and Van der Merwe[22] show that communities were not always consulted when the TRC prioritised cases for hearings or for further investigation. Community members were especially concerned when local events were not taken seriously by the TRC when an incident still had important repercussions in the present. Amongst the eight percent that was eventually selected, the TRC accepted that some subsets ("victim groupings") were poorly represented.[23] For instance, a lack of participation was noted of combatants who might have been reluctant to be perceived as victims as opposed to liberation heroes that fought for a moral and just cause. Cases of detention without trial and violations experienced *other* than torture during the course of incarceration were also under-represented. As a final example of a lack of representation, the Commission noted it did not receive a single Human Rights Violation statement from any of the Rivonia trialists.[24]

Despite their small numbers, the Commission provided a space to a select group of survivors to share their own accounts of the violations they experienced. It can be said that truth should be a requirement before one is to engage in a reconciliation process; how is one to reconcile if not knowing who to forgive or for what forgiveness is sought? But when survivors in the qualitative and explorative study of Hamber, Nagen and O'Malley (2000) reflected on the value of the truth before and after testifying in front of the Commission, it was felt that the truth was not enough to lead to reconciliation on an individual level. They did not, in other words, assume that truth alone would replace justice and contribute to reconciliation. Nevertheless, as in the study of Picker,[25] the

---

20 *Ibidem.*
21 Picker, R., *Victims' Perspectives about the Human Rights Violation Hearings*, Research Report Written for the Centre for the Study of Violence and Reconciliation, 2005; www.csvr.org.za/docs/humanrights/victimsperspectivshearings.pdf (last visited: 12 February 2010).
22 Van der Merwe, H., *National Narrative versus Local Truths: The Truth and Reconciliation Commission's Engagement with Duduza*, 2000; www.csvr.org.za/docs/trc/nationalnarrative.pdf (last visited: 12 February 2010).
23 Truth and Reconciliation Commission of South Africa, *Report*, 1998.
24 *Ibidem.* The Rivonia Trial took place during the years 1963 and 1964 when sixteen leaders of the ANC were tried for 221 acts of sabotage to "ferment violent revolution" and who spent decades in prison on Robben Island. See www.guardian.co.uk/world/2001/feb/11/nelsonmandela.southafrica2 for the historical background to Nelson Mandela's final public speech for 27 years.
25 Picker, R., *Victims' Perspectives about the Human Rights Violation Hearings*, Research Report Written for the Centre for the Study of Violence and Reconciliation, 2005; www.csvr.org.za/docs/humanrights/victimsperspectivshearings.pdf (last visited: 12 February 2010).

research participants highlighted that the success of the TRC was largely on a national level in that revelations of the truth were essential for the common good rather than for individual benefits. They participated in the hearings to also contribute their "part of the truth" to history. It does not surprise that these survivors and families of victims began to experience a range of psychological problems after their testimony, as "going public makes you vulnerable" particularly in the absence of debriefing and counselling services after testifying (Bohler-Muller 2008; Nomoyi 2001).[26] Feelings of vulnerability do not refer only to the re-enactment of traumatic experiences, but translate also into fears surrounding the loss of anonymity, the fear of retaliation and the fear of continued conflicts within one's community.

A number of survivors in the study of Picker complained about how they were treated by the TRC in comparison to the perpetrators.[27] It was felt that while the perpetrators did not "pay for their deeds" their lives as victims did not improve. They still lived in poverty exacerbated by the violations. A similar sentiment was expressed by the participants in the research of Kayser[28] and Nomoyi (2001) who felt economic restitution was the key to reconciliation. Likewise, the slogan 'No reconciliation without reparation' was expressed in the workshops of Hamber *et al.* (1998). Some community members in the explorative study of Colvin supported a more holistic approach to reconciliation, acknowledging in addition to economic needs, the needs for psychological healing, repentance of the perpetrator, compromise and conciliation.[29] The qualitative study of Heylen, Parmentier and Weitekamp (2008) supports the notion that deficient accommodation of basic needs is a major impediment toward reconciliation but in order to generalise, this finding needs to be tested with a randomised sample/s.

Finally, very few statements were received from victims outside the borders of South Africa whilst it has been argued that the majority of the gross violations of human rights were indeed committed *outside* the borders of the country. Cross border raids of the South African Defense Force (SANDF) into

---

[26] *Ibidem.*
[27] *Ibidem.*
[28] Kayser, U., *Interventions after the TRC – Reconciliation, Advocacy and Healing*, 2001; www.csvr.org.za/wits/papers/papkays3.htm (last visited: 25 May 2010).
[29] All of the research subjects in the mentioned studies participated in the TRC hearings except for the participants in the study of Colvin who formed part of a post–TRC space (Cape Town's Trauma Centre for Survivors of Violence and Torture, the Torture Project and the Khulumani Support Group) in order to engage with personal memories and the apartheid past. See C.J. Colvin, '*We Are Still Struggling*': Storytelling, Reparations and Reconciliation after the TRC, 2000; Research Report of the Centre for the Study of Violence and Reconciliation in collaboration with Khulumani (Western Cape) Victims Support Group and the Cape Town Trauma Centre for Survivors of Violence and Torture, *Survivors' Perceptions of the Truth and Reconciliation Commission and Suggestions for the Final Report*, Johannesburg, 1998; available at www.csvr.org.za/docs/trc/wearestillstruggling.pdf.

neighbouring states such as Angola were rather commonplace[30] and evidence before the TRC[31] suggested that conflicts in southern African states, particularly in Mozambique, Namibia and Angola, were inextricably linked to the struggle for control of the South African state. Evidence before the Commission also showed that members of the ANC and PAC in exile were involved in the commission of gross violations of human rights, particularly within their own ranks.[32]

5. ASSESSING THE TRC'S CONTRIBUTION TO TRUTH AND RECONCILIATION

In recovering the spirit of *Ubuntu* after the onslaught of apartheid, the TRC had as a major objective to restore broken relationships in South Africa, and in specific, to restore the human and civil dignity of victims and survivors through reparations and by providing to them the opportunity to voice their own victimisation experiences. However, it is somewhat problematic to assess on an individual level the effectiveness of this objective when referring to the small fraction of survivors who experienced direct interaction with the Commission. The experiences of the small subset (8%) of the mere 21,296 cases selected for public human rights hearings, cannot be described as representative of the experiences of all victims/survivors of gross violations of human rights in South Africa under the apartheid regime (see 4.5).

Moreover, despite the availability of a sampling frame that contains an exhausted list of all of the elements in the total *universum* or *population* that did participate in the TRC hearings – albeit small numbers – empirical studies alluding to the successes/failures of the Commission in achieving reconciliation relied in addition to the concern expressed above, mostly on small and non-representative samples (see for instance, Hamber 2000; Hamber, Maepa, Mofokeng & Van der Merwe 1998; Nomoyi 2001).[33] Within a predominantly

---

30   For instance, more than 600 people were killed in one day at Kassinga by the SANDF. According to the then South African government, Kassinga in Angola was a guerrilla base and thus a legitimate military target but other accounts refer to the victims of the massacre as unnamed refugees (TRC 1998).

31   Truth and Reconciliation Commission of South Africa, *Report*, 1998.

32   *Ibidem.*

33   See also Picker, R., *Victims' Perspectives about the Human Rights Violation Hearings*, Research Report Written for the Centre for the Study of Violence and Reconciliation, 2005; www.csvr. org.za/docs/humanrights/victimsperspectivshearings.pdf (last visited: 12 February 2010). Kayser, U., *Creating a Space for Encounter and Remembrance: The Healing of Memories Process*, 2000; www.csvr.org.za/wits/papers/paphom.htm (last visited: 25 May 2010). Kayser, U., *Interventions after the TRC – Reconciliation, Advocacy and Healing*, 2001; www.csvr.org. za/wits/papers/papkays3.htm (last visited: 25 May 2010). T. Abrahamsen & H. van der Merwe, *Reconciliation through Amnesty? Amnesty Applicants' Views of the South African Truth and Reconciliation Commission*, 2005, available at www.csvr.org.za/docs/trc/

qualitative framework and in the absence of control groups, such findings provide little value other than what applies to the non-random samples (Babbie 1990). This lack of external validity (generalizability) of numerous studies should be born in mind when attempts are made to assess the effectiveness of the TRC in achieving reconciliation.

In assessing perceptions whether truth leads to reconciliation, the quantitative research of Gibson (2004) provided also for the views of South Africans who were not necessarily participants in the TRC hearings. By utilising a rigorous and systematic research methodology, Gibson (2004) employed a large stratified probability sample that represented a subset of the South African population (eighteen years and older), referring here also to gender, race, urban and rural contexts. A high level of participation was achieved with an over-all response rate of 87%. However, a sizable subset of his sample has never experienced apartheid directly as adults with one third of the African respondents less than sixteen years old and 42.1 percent eighteen years old or younger when it became defunct.

According to the findings of Gibson (2004) the TRC did not engage in a "witch hunt" as was alleged by some extreme political fractions. All South Africans were victimised by apartheid and unilateral blame for the atrocities of the past was not likely to produce reconciliation. Gibson (2004) could not however establish a clear cause and effect relationship that the TRC process was indeed responsible for shaping attitudes towards the rule of law. Almost all the participants were nevertheless aggrieved by the lack of fairness of the amnesty process – most opposed the granting of amnesty to those who committed gross human rights violations during the struggle against apartheid – thereby neutralising racial differences in fairness assessments. The respondents in the study viewed justice to entail more than mere compensation but more research is required to fully understand the role of public apology as the analysis provided by Gibson (2004) referred mainly to perceptions of ordinary South Africans, not specifically those who were victimised under apartheid. According to Gibson (2004) it is almost impossible to answer the question how much reconciliation is necessary for the consolidation of democracy in South Africa. The research focuses though on individual-level reconciliation, ignoring macro-level processes (political and institutional factors) that could further shape reconciliation in South Africa.

---

reconciliationthroughamnesty.pdf; and C.J. Colvin, 'We Are Still Struggling': Storytelling, Reparations and Reconciliation after the TRC, 2000; Research Report of the Centre for the Study of Violence and Reconciliation in collaboration with Khulumani (Western Cape) Victims Support Group and the Cape Town Trauma Centre for Survivors of Violence and Torture, Survivors' Perceptions of the Truth and Reconciliation Commission and Suggestions for the Final Report, Johannesburg, 1998; available at www.csvr.org.za/docs/trc/wearestillstruggling.pdf.

When attempts are made to assess the contributions of the TRC in establishing truth and reconciliation, a methodological issue would refer to the absence of pre-test data in general. Typically of cross-sectional research (see for instance Gibson, 2004) is that different variables are measured at the same time rendering it difficult (if not impossible) to control for rival hypotheses when attempts are made to establish cause and effect relationships. Studies such as those of Kagee (2006) seeking to assess relationships between participation in the South African TRC and the psychological distress and healing of victims, are of little value in the absence of pre-test data. An independent measure of the psychological well-being of the participants should have been obtained *prior* to their participation in the hearings if scientific attempts were to be made in establishing a clear cause and effect relationship between participation (the independent variable) and psychologically well-being (the dependent variable). Pre-test data could have isolated the mediating or 'contaminating' effect of background or 'noise' variables on the research. On the other hand, the study of Hamber, Nageng and O'Malley (2000) focused on survivor perspectives of the TRC *before* and *after* testifying, but once again, in the absence of randomisation, the qualitative findings apply only to their sample and cannot be generalised (Bless & Higson-Smith 1995; Mouton & Marais 1988).

With the afore-mentioned in mind, empirical evidence suggests the need for more research on the following aspects of the TRC and reconciliation:

The differences in hierarchy of needs of the survivors that were recorded in the various explorative studies highlight the functional imperative of an operationalized and standardised definition of reconciliation from the South African experience that is as holistic as possible, for both purposes of research as well as for potential TRCs elsewhere. It is excepted that the multitude of individual and material needs of survivors can never be addressed through a TRC, or any organisation, body or institution for that matter, but Hamber, Nageng and O'Malley (2000) are of the opinion that in South Africa, this situation was made even more problematic when the concepts of truth, justice and reparation were treated by the TRC as separate issues due to sheer pragmatism or expediency. For the non-random subset of survivors in their study, truth, justice and reparation were inter-linked, or in other words, justice is reparation and without truth and reparation, there is no justice.

A more general experience of the TRC that requires further inquiry refers to the amnesty process: With the granting of amnesty to former state operatives, the state removed automatically the victims' rights to civil claims by indemnifying itself. Certain reciprocity in the balancing acts of reparations and amnesty granted by the Commission should have been established. With the state that took responsibility for reparations, all that was required from the amnesty applicants was to convince the Amnesty Committee that the acts were indeed associated with a political motive and that full disclosure was made, but it was not necessary to express remorse or ask for forgiveness in order to receive amnesty (see section 3). According to Abrahamsen and Van der Merwe, this lack of a formal apology remains one of the most controversial aspects of the South African amnesty process.[34] Such negation of acknowledgement, repentance and inter-communal understanding certainly distracts from the healing potential of the spirit of *Ubuntu*, and therefore, also on achieving reconciliation at inter-personal level.

In the absence of baseline studies prior to embarking on the TRC process in South Africa (Emmanuel 2007), more experimental research is required to evaluate the effectiveness of the TRC as a transitional tool of justice. Experimental research can dissect and disassemble various components of the quandary which would be invaluable for determining the very nature and impact of societal structures and processes on truth and reconciliation. Within the context of a transitional society, a range of socio-economic and political variables may be at play, influencing effective transformation and delivery of programs that should under ideal circumstances contribute to an environment for sustainable reconciliation. Heylen, Parmentier and Weitekamp (2008) refer to the concept of "holistic reconciliation" as a type of transitional justice process, in which all levels and dynamics are addressed in one singular and well-coordinated approach. According to Brocklehurst *et al.* (2000), the concept of transition needs to be understood in the context of policy making. Simpson, Hamber and Stott concur by highlighting the need for policies that are deliverable, not just about vision but to set and act on a future agenda.[35] The success of a Truth and Reconciliation Commission (not only in South Africa but elsewhere as well) must therefore not only be evaluated by its own work but also by the adoption and execution of its proposals and recommendations, in particular relating to providing reparations, by the government. In this regard the South African TRC[36] expressed the hope that its work would be ongoing, seeking to promote the course of national unity and justice.

Although a number of lessons can be learned from the South African TRC experience – such as the need to establish a relevant domestic framework given uniqueness of context, and the need for political will – Emmanuel (2007) raises the concern that other regions tend to adopt the South African model with little regard to the actual achievement or non-achievement of its stated goals. In South Africa the criminal justice system was used to enforce apartheid, and subsequently became tainted with a lack of legitimacy, and therefore not the

---

34   T. Abrahamsen & H. van der Merwe, *Reconciliation through Amnesty? Amnesty Applicants' Views of the South African Truth and Reconciliation Commission*, 2005, available at www.csvr. org.za/docs/trc/reconciliationthroughamnesty.pdf.

35   Simpson, G., Hamber, B., & Stott, N., *Future Challenges to Policy-Making in Countries in Transition*, 2001; available at: www.csvr.org.za/ (last visited: 11 May 2010).

36   Truth and Reconciliation Commission of South Africa, *Report*, 1998.

most appropriate vehicle to deal with the atrocities of the past. Due to similar circumstances, and/or a lack of capacity to deal with mass victimisations, the non-judicial road may also be the preferred route for other regions, but from the South African experience the spirit of *Ubuntu* needs to move from the peripheral to centre stage if reconciliation is to be realised. Secondary victimisation of the survivors as in the case of formal judicial proceedings (Davis & Snyman 2005) was presented as a salient theme throughout this discussion. For preventative measures more research is required, but also in terms of the principle of proportionality during reparations, how does one arrive at a quantum value of human suffering, referring for instance to the death of a breadwinner or a poor education?

6. THE FALSE VICTIM – OFFENDER DICHOTOMY

In addition to first conducting baseline studies prior to embarking on TRC processes elsewhere in order to enable analyses of its effectiveness and for a TRC to be more representative, cognisance also needs to be taken of another short-coming of the South African TRC, namely that the South African TRC did not solve the complexities relating to the inter-changeability of victim and offender roles by largely excluding ex-combatants as victims during its human rights violation hearings (see 4.5).

When confronted with the cruel acts committed by fellow humans, it is often human nature to attempt to distance oneself from the perpetrators of such acts. But it would be misguided to believe that perpetrators are fundamentally different from law-abiding citizens, or victims (Fattah 1997). Positivist criminology attempted to pathologise and 'over-pathologise' offenders and offending behaviour with its focus on their supposedly abnormal personalities, deviant behaviour, or cognitive distortions whereas on the contrary, individuals suffering from mental illnesses are in fact less likely to commit criminal offences in comparison to general populations (Bartol & Bartol 2005). In support, Fattah (2006) refers to empirical evidence (experiments of Milgram and Zimbardo) to demonstrate that anyone placed in certain situations, under certain conditions, and subjected to certain pressures and constraints is capable of committing horrendous acts of extreme atrocity, cruelty, genocide and cupidity.

However, according to Emmanuel (2007), the distinction between victims and perpetrators is alive and should be emphasised in the South African context and possibly in various other comparable situations. The author nevertheless concedes that this so-called 'dichotomy' is far more complex and intricate than generally assumed. However, if we take perpetrators own history of victimisation into account, for instance the *askaris* – former liberation movement operatives recruited by the apartheid security forces (see also Smeulers, this volume) – it is obvious that the proposed victim-offender dichotomy is a false dichotomy. Conversely, some former victims may also perpetrate criminal acts, the clearest example being Winnie Madikizela Mandela who was linked to murder and kidnapping by the findings of the TRC.[37] By atomising the victim and by ignoring the dynamics of violent behaviour and rapidly changing nature of potentially violent situations, the popular victim-offender dichotomy is created, ignoring that offender and victim populations are not necessarily mutually exclusive, but indeed overlapping (Fattah 2006). This may have implications for the true understanding of conflict, reparations and reconciliation during TRC hearings.

7. CONCLUSION

As a bridge-building process, a central component of the TRC's reconciliation agenda was to develop and promote a common understanding of the atrocities of South Africa's apartheid past. But a society cannot reconcile itself on the grounds of a divided or repressed memory, particularly if narrow and inadequate definitions of representation, truth and reconciliation are adopted. Apart from the gross human rights violations under the apartheid regime, truth and reconciliation also need to refer to the transformation of unjust inequalities, to address successfully the dehumanising effects of poverty induced by the structural violence of the apartheid state; and as social justice, to commit to the full development of a person, his/her community, society and a nation. But the politics of reconciliation, the rhetoric of unity and reconciliation may not reflect the experiences of ordinary citizens in post-apartheid South Africa where societal imbalances continue to prevail. From silence and forgetfulness, memory and identity need to complete the past, providing the foundations of justice for future generations.

---

[37]   *Ibidem.*

XIII. VOICES FROM THE FIELD

Empirical Data on Reconciliation in Post-War Bosnia and Their Relevance for Africa

Stephan PARMENTIER and Pietro SULLO*

1. INTRODUCTION

'Reconciliation' has become one of the buzz words of the last decade. Rooted in the work of the South African Truth and Reconciliation Commission (hereafter: TRC), it has rapidly conquered the world of international politics and international law. The 2003 Brahimi Report included "conflict resolution and reconciliation techniques" in the set of peace-building tools,[1] and the Utstein Study indicated that reconciliation is one of the strongest post-conflict sectors in attracting western donors' funding (on this point see Smith 2004). According to former UN Secretary General Kofi Annan in his 2004 report on the rule of law and transitional justice in conflict and post-conflict societies, reconciliation is one of the proclaimed transitional justice goals.[2] The United Nations declared 2009 to be the 'international year of reconciliation', recognising

> that reconciliation processes are particularly necessary and urgent in countries and regions of the world which have suffered or are suffering situations of conflict that have affected and divided societies in their various internal, national and international facets.[3]

In other words, there is a growing awareness that a lack of focus on the legacy of the past violence will undermine democracy consolidation.

---

* The authors like to express their sincere gratitude to Marc Groenhuijsen and Rianne Letschert from Intervict, Tilburg University, for providing the ideal working environment to finish this chapter in good standing.

1 See UN, *Report of the Panel on United Nations Peace Operations*, UN doc. A/55/305-S/2000/809, 21 August 2003, p. 3.

2 UN SG, *The rule of law and transitional justice in conflict and post-conflict societies*, Report of the Secretary-General to the Security Council, 23 August 2004, S/2004/616, para. 8.

3 UN General Assembly Resolution on the International Year of Reconciliation 2009, adopted on 23 January 2007, A/RES/61/17.

Indeed, the notion of reconciliation has gained momentum during and after times of political transitions, when societies are moving away from an autocratic regime to more democratic forms of government. At that time, the new elites are openly confronted with the fundamental question on how to address the heavy burden of their dark past and if they aim at organising a period of 'transitional justice'. The latter is defined in older writings as "the study of the choices made and the quality of justice rendered when states are replacing authoritarian regimes by democratic state institutions" (Siegel 1998), and has expanded more recently to include "the full range of processes and mechanisms associated with a society's attempts to come to terms with a legacy of large-scale past abuses, in order to ensure accountability, serve justice and achieve reconciliation".[4]

Despite this international recognition, the very concept of reconciliation is far from clear and encompasses many different meanings and many different realities. Furthermore, what does reconciliation mean to victims, offenders and society? The answers to these questions are particularly troublesome when looking at the level of individual countries that have adopted an official discourse of reconciliation. Hence the major objective of this chapter is to bring some more clarity in relation to reconciliation and its impact, first by reporting on our own empirical research conducted in post-war Bosnia and second by sketching the potential relevance for African countries in a post-conflict situation.

2. RECONCILIATION: WHAT IS IN A NAME?

The current-day notion of reconciliation is closely connected to the work of the South African Truth and Reconciliation Commission that operated between 1995 and 1998 to investigate more than three decades of serious crimes committed under the Apartheid regime. The TRC has attracted an enormous amount of attention from many observers world wide, including activists, policy-makers, academics, the press, and ordinary citizens (see Peacock, this volume). While the vast majority of the comments and the debates have centred around the notion of truth, far less attention has been paid to the second key notion in the Commission's name, that of "promoting national unity and reconciliation" (according to the Promotion of National Unity and Reconciliation Act No 34 (the Act) of 19 July 1995).[5]

The importance attached to reconciliation in the South African TRC, and later in other truth and reconciliation commissions, does not mean that reconciliation had no earlier traces. On the contrary, the notion already figures in the Statute of the International Criminal Tribunal for Rwanda (ICTR) of 1994,

---

[4]   UN SG, *The rule of law and transitional justice in conflict and post-conflict societies*, Report of the Secretary-General to the Security Council, 23 August 2004, S/2004/616, para. 4.

[5]   Truth and Reconciliation Commission of South Africa, *Report*, 1998, Vol. 1, p. 48 ff.

stating that the work of the tribunal should be seen as "to contribute to the process of national reconciliation and to the restoration and maintenance of peace".[6] And of course, a couple of years earlier reconciliation was the central concept of the 1991 Act in Australia to establish a special council for dealing with the relations between indigenous and non-indigenous people and giving rise to the politics of "practical reconciliation" (Pratt 2005). But it is fair to say that none of the above examples has received the kind of attention that the South African TRC was able to attract.

Despite the multiple use of the notion of reconciliation over the last decade – in policy, practice and academia – it is not without many problems. Here we just list the most salient ones.

First, the TRC Report of 1998 itself has recognised that reconciliation is not a singular concept but may be seen to operate at various levels:[7]

(1) the individual level of coming to terms with a painful truth, e.g. after exhumations and reburials of beloved ones;
(2) the interpersonal level of specific victims and their perpetrators;
(3) the community level, when addressing the internal conflicts inside and between local communities; and
(4) the national level, by focusing on the role of the state and non-state institutions.

This distinction in levels is of course merely a formal one and does not give substance to the notion of reconciliation on each of these levels. Moreover, it does not address the question how these levels relate to one another, and whether reconciliation at one level is required before reconciliation at another level can be envisaged. The TRC Report is limited to simple references about the "restoring civil and human dignity" for all South Africans.[8]

A second confusion surrounding reconciliation stems again from the South African experience. It has to do with the strong emphasis on forgiveness for the crimes of the past, to originate with the victims who suffered the consequences of the crime of Apartheid in its many forms. Bishop Tutu himself has been one of the strongest advocates of forgiveness, witness his bold statement that there can be "no future without forgiveness" (Tutu 1999). This link between reconciliation and forgiveness has traced the former concept back to its theological roots, and in particular to its Judeo-Christian origins (Czarnota 2007). It could be argued that both aspects, the pressure on victims as well as the close links with Christianity, have actually weakened the concept and the reality of reconciliation and its potential for expansion to the whole world.

---

6   UN Document S/RES/955 (8 November 1994).
7   Truth and Reconciliation Commission of South Africa, *Report*, 1998, Vol. 1, p. 106–110.
8   *Idem*, Vol. 1, p. 125–131.

Another problem is of an ideological nature. Many advocates of reconciliation suggest that it is important to restore the individual and social balance of the past disrupted by violent conflicts. In such context, re-conciliation would imply to go back to that past and to revive the relationships, individual and social, that existed before (as much as restorative justice is aimed at restoring the relationships between victims and offenders of crimes). But in the context of violent conflicts, it can be argued that going back to the past and restoring the balance between offenders and victims, often anonymous to one another, is simply impossible. Even more, if re-conciliation were to go back to the harmony in the past it could mean another means of duplicating the inequalities and the cleavages in society. And even if reconciliation is thought of as forward-looking in order to create "trust and understanding between former enemies" in the future (Bloomfield 2003), it is unclear how such orientation is capable of transforming the many social and political problems in a given society.

In view of the many problems that surround reconciliation, practice and theory have often opted for a maximalist notion that amalgamates the various dimensions into one mega concept: reconciliation in such concept would embody several levels (from the individual to the state or the interstate level); it would also include several fields, the interpersonal field, the social field and the political field; it would be both backward-looking in dealing with the past and forward-looking in preparing the future; and it would be both a process that is undertaken on a continuous basis, as well as an outcome of such process. However, by turning it into an all-encompassing concept, we argue that reconciliation becomes void of concrete sense. It is increasingly depicted as the overarching objective of transitional justice processes, a rhetorically stated goal that is as popular as evanescent, a must-be in the post-conflict and peace-building realm whose definition (and consequent practice implications) often force scholars into a conundrum. Also Galtung "admits the defeat" of researchers in defining reconciliation, affirming that "[r]econciliation is a theme with deep psychological, sociological, theological, philosophical, and profoundly human roots – and nobody really knows how to successfully achieve it" (Galtung 2001). And Bloomfield (2007) tellingly highlights the doubts and uncertainties surrounding the concept of reconciliation by elaborating on the main features of the debate surrounding it and clarifies that it can be conceived as both a process and an outcome:

> *Is reconciliation a national, societal, even political, process? Is it an individual, psychological, even 'theological', process? Is it a process at all, or does it describe a state of relationships at the end of a process? (...) It can be all these and more; but that it is critical to try to separate at least some of these complex strands, if only for the very pragmatic reason that different types, levels and facets of reconciliation demand very different approaches, mechanisms and contexts.*

It should be clear that the term 'reconciliation' is very difficult to define and to come to grips with. For this reason, we like to have a closer look at how people in post-conflict situations themselves conceive of reconciliation and what it may entail. This approach very well fits into the general theoretical framework of transitional justice "from below" as coined by McEvoy and McGregor (2008). For this purpose, we will draw on our own empirical research in post-war Bosnia aimed at obtaining a better understanding of reconciliation, after which we highlight the relevance of collecting voices from the field for African countries and situations.

3. BOSNIA AND POST-WAR RECONCILIATION

In early 1992, following the breakup of Yugoslavia, Bosnia and Herzegovina[9] plunged into a devastating war that would last for almost four years and would take an enormous toll on its population, infrastructure and cultural heritage. Estimates point to around 100,000 deaths and 2.2 million displaced people. Atrocities such as mass murders, extrajudicial executions, torture, rape, illegal detention, forced displacement, looting and destruction of religious and cultural sites are fairly well documented though responsibilities for them continue to be contested. It would take until December 1995 before the Dayton Peace Agreements would be signed, officially ending the war in Bosnia. The Agreements created a complex political and territorial structure in order to respond to the parties' demands, dividing the country into two entities: the Federation of Bosnia and Herzegovina, inhabited predominantly by a Bosniak and Bosnian Croat population, and the Republika Srpska, inhabited predominantly by Bosnian Serbs. The Agreements also provided for a far-reaching intervention of the international community in both civilian and military affairs in post-war Bosnia. The involvement of the international community in transitional justice issues began even before the end of the war, with the creation in 1993 of the International Criminal Tribunal for the former Yugoslavia (ICTY) by Resolution 827 of the United Nations Security Council, and has continued well after the war with reforms of various key sectors, including criminal justice (Aitcheson 2011). The complexity surrounding the causes and nature of the war as well as the involvement of a multiplicity of internal and external actors in the war and the post-war period complicate the Bosnian transitional justice context. This complexity necessarily adds interesting albeit difficult challenges to those who engage in research in Bosnia.

As mentioned before, reconciliation may take place at various levels – from an individual or inter-personal, to the community and to the national level –,

---

[9] For reasons of simplification we will use hereafter Bosnia (or BiH) to refer to the country Bosnia and Herzegovina.

and in the case of Bosnia, even to the regional level of the neighbouring countries involved in the war. Reconciliation has been a highly controversial term and concept in Bosnia since the end of the violent conflict in 1995. It has been more often than not regarded as a threat to criminal accountability and for that reason encountered strong resistance, both from individuals and organisations, national and international. A minimalist approach to reconciliation has been defended by some, at best, but this raises of course the issue of representativity. To overcome this problem it is arguably important to focus on people's opinions in Bosnia in relation to issues of post-conflict justice, including the important issue of reconciliation. The objective should be to understand both inter-personal processes of reconciliation and factors at the macro level that have been fostering or hampering the process of reconciliation in Bosnia.

In the following paragraphs we report on some major findings of our own empirical research conducted in Bosnia in 2006 by means of a self-administered quantitative survey carried out through written questionnaires. The aim of this survey was to inquire about the attitudes and opinions of individuals about the process of dealing with the past in Bosnia, with a particular focus on the opportunities for and the potential of a restorative approach to such process (Parmentier & Weitekamp, forthcoming in 2011). As general framework we used the TARR model developed by Parmentier over the last years (Parmentier 2003; Parmentier & Weitekamp 2007). The model is composed by four building blocks that correspond to four key issues in the process of dealing with the past by new regimes, namely: to search for truth about the past (T), to ensure accountability of the offenders (A), to provide some form of reparation for the victims (R), and to promote reconciliation between former enemies (R). It provides a useful framework to analyse the various relations between two or more of its building blocks, it allows us to examine specific institutions and mechanisms of dealing with the past in relation to each of these issues, and finally it suggests that transitional justice approaches will result from the interplay between these four building blocks (Weitekamp et al. 2006). The exact methodology of the survey comprised four key steps presented elsewhere (Parmentier, Valiñas & Weitekamp 2009): (a) creating a written questionnaire for data gathering; (b) selecting an adequate group of respondents through a 'quota sampling method',[10] amounting to 855 valid responses; (c) collecting the data; and (d) analysing the data.

---

[10]   Unlike in stratified random sampling (a probability method), in quota sampling (a non-probability method) "the sampling of individuals is not carried out randomly, since the final selection of people is left to the interviewer." See Bryman 2008, 102.

3.1. RECONCILIATION AND TRUST

Reconciliation has been a highly controversial term and concept in Bosnia since the end of the war. It has been more often than not regarded as a threat to criminal accountability and for that reason it has encountered strong resistance, both from individuals and both national and international organisations. A minimalist approach to reconciliation has at best been defended by some. One of the observations from the face-to-face interviews conducted during the exploratory phase of our field research was that in the discourse on dealing with the past 'trust' was much better accepted than 'reconciliation'. While reconciliation seemed to entail for our interlocutors some form of impunity or an acceptance that the two sides had become involved in conflict in the same way and with the same degree of responsibility, rebuilding trust suggested that social relationships had been broken and now needed to be mended.

A first set of questions concerned the relation between reconciliation and trust. When asked whether they thought that it is possible for people in Bosnia to trust each other again or to reconcile with each other, the respondents' reactions did differ but not in the way we had expected. The respondents seemed to believe that reconciliation was more likely (40%) than rebuilding trust (30%). Also, whereas in the question on trust most respondents said that it is *not* possible for Bosnians to trust each other again (38%), in the question on reconciliation most respondents said that it is possible for Bosnians to reconcile with each other (40%). In fact, it is interesting that roughly the same number of respondents who believe it is possible to reconcile, also say that it is not possible for Bosnians to trust each other again.

Table 1. Chances for Trust

	n	%
No	321	38
I don't know	266	32
Yes	256	30

Missing cases: 1,4%.

Question: Do you think it is possible for people of Bosnia and Herzegovina to trust each other again?

Table 2. Chances for Reconciliation

	n	%
Yes	339	40
I don't know	266	31
No	245	29

Missing cases: 1%.
Question: Do you think it is possible for people of Bosnia and Herzegovina to reconcile with each other?

These findings could be due to a minimalist understanding of reconciliation mentioned before. In other words, respondents may have understood reconciliation as simply living side by side, or the absence of inter-ethnic violence. In this sense, rebuilding trust implies much more: the readiness to interact, to have mutual respect, to work together and to even develop friendships. The understanding that respondents have of reconciliation is very important to fully understand these responses. An open question was included in the survey on what reconciliation meant to each respondent (see below).

In both questions it is important to note the high number of respondents – about 1/3 – who answered 'I don't know': 32% on the question about trust and 31% on the question about reconciliation. In both cases these percentages were higher than one of the two 'extreme options' given (yes/no). These are very significant numbers of respondents who have mixed opinions, doubts, and uncertainties. It might seem at first that only around 40% and 30% believed that reconciliation and trust, respectively, are possible. However, there is a critical number of people who could tend to optimism in the future relations between the conflicting parties or, on the contrary, to pessimism.

3.2. INTER-PERSONAL RECONCILIATION

When the question was formulated in more personal terms, and respondents were asked whether they themselves would be able to reconcile with the persons who caused the victimisation they described, the percentage of those answering 'no' rose to more than half (53%). There were still a considerable number of respondents who answered 'I don't know' (30%) and only a minority answered 'yes' (17%). Indeed, taking into consideration the views that are mostly widespread in the public discourse in Bosnia, one would have expected that a higher percentage of people would have answered categorically 'no' to this question.

Table 3. Chances for Individual Reconciliation with Perpetrator

	n	%
No	437	53
I don't know	247	30
Yes	138	17

Missing cases: 4%.
Question: Would you be able to reconcile with the persons that did to you the things described in question nr. 8 [i.e. that victimized you]?

Given the importance of the religious dimension in the conflict in Bosnia we wanted to know if the previous answers would vary according to religious affiliation. There was a greater tendency among Catholics to reconcile, in comparison to Muslims and Orthodox. However, even among Catholics, a majority said they would not be able to reconcile. Orthodox were the least ready to reconcile: the higher percentage of those who were not ready to reconcile are Orthodox, and these were also the ones who have fewer doubts.

Table 4. Crosstabulation between Reconciliation with Perpetrator and Religious Affiliation

	Catholic	Muslim	Orthodox
Yes	25	12	13
No	41	58	60
I don't know	34	30	27

Values shown are for% within religious affiliation. Pearson Chi-square 33.601 [8 cells (44.4%) have expected count less than 5. The minimum expected count is.34.].
Question: Would you be able to reconcile with the people who 'victimised' you?

3.3. THE MACRO LEVEL OF RECONCILIATION AND TRUST

In order to introduce the question of which factors had been helping or hampering the process of rebuilding trust and of reconciliation in Bosnia, we wanted to know where this process stood in the eyes of the respondents. When asked to what extent trust has already been rebuilt a majority of the respondents said trust among the people of Bosnia has *not* yet been rebuilt (65%), about a quarter said they did not know (26%), and only 10% said it had already been rebuilt. The comparison between these results and those presented in other surveys on the level of inter-ethnic relations or coexistence is interesting and once again highlights the difference between what has been called the 'normalisation of relations' and rebuilding trust.[11]

Table 5. Is trust rebuilt?

	n	%
No	554	65
I don't know	214	25
Yes	81	10

Missing cases: 1%.
Question: Has this trust [among the people of Bosnia and Herzegovina] already been rebuilt?

This suggests that in the respondents' view there was still much to be done for this trust to be rebuilt. That is why it is relevant to understand which factors at the macro level, in their perspective, have been fostering or hampering the process of rebuilding trust and reconciliation. A vast majority of the respondents said the major obstacle in this process have been the attitudes and strategies of politicians (72%), the second major obstacle seems to be the trauma that individuals still suffer from the war (67%), followed by the media (51%). In terms of what has been helping more, 65% of the respondents pointed to the positive memories people have from the times before the war, 59% to the role of non-governmental organisations, and 58% said the time that passed since the end of the war was a factor that was helping this process. The presence and role of the international community was seen by 53% of the respondents as a positive factor. Half of the respondents said prosecution in national courts was a positive factor, and almost the same amount saw prosecutions at the ICTY as a positive factor in this process. Other factors which were seen by more respondents as positive rather than negative were: the acknowledgement of each others' suffering (48%) and the role of the schools (46%). The answers given concerning schools indicated mixed opinions: while 46% said they regarded the school as a factor fostering the process of rebuilding trust, 44% regarded it as hampering that same process.

---

[11]   In the 2005 Survey on Truth and Justice carried out by the UNDP, 71,3% of the respondents said that "Tolerance between different ethnic groups in [their] area" was "good or acceptable and no urgent steps are needed". UNDP, *Early Warning System Special Edition 'Justice and Truth in Bosnia and Herzegovina: Public Perceptions'*, 2005.

Table 6. Factors Promoting the Reconciliation Process

	Not helping at all	Not helping	Helping	Helping very much	Don't know
The attitudes and strategies of politicians	59	13	10	10	8
The schools	26	18	21	25	10
Media	32	19	20	22	7
The role of non-governmental organisations	17	14	23	36	11
The presence and role of the international community	25	12	21	32	10
The positive memories people have from the times before the war	16	11	20	45	8
The acknowledgement of each other's suffering	25	14	19	29	13
The time that has already passed since the war ended	18	16	21	36	8
The trauma that individuals still suffer from the war	54	13	9	10	14
Criminal prosecutions at the International Criminal Tribunal for the former Yugoslavia	29	11	18	31	12
Criminal prosecutions at the national courts	26	12	18	32	12

Missing cases: Politicians 14,5%; Schools 13,9%; Media 14,2%; NGOs 13,3%; IC 12,2%; Memories 12%; Acknowledgement 15%; Time 12,3%; Trauma 15,1%; ICTY 13,6%; National courts 14,4%.
Question: What do you think has been helping in rebuilding this trust?

Contrary to what we had anticipated, there were no significant differences in the answers given to the question on the influence of these factors in rebuilding trust and to the question on the influence of the same factors in the process of reconciliation. This may mean two things, either the respondents could not give any different answers to the two questions, or that they could not distinguish the two notions of reconciliation and trust in the first place. Further research would be needed to probe these conceptual issues more.

3.4. THE MEANING OF RECONCILIATION

In order to fully understand the answers on the readiness for reconciliation and the factors which have been fostering or hampering reconciliation we found it essential to ask respondents about their interpretation of the term 'reconciliation'. We opted to use the open-question method ('what does reconciliation mean to you') to ensure we were not limiting or inducing the answers given, and thus combined qualitative (coding) and quantitative (statistical) methods of analysis.

The concepts most often expressed by the respondents were 'peaceful coexistence' (24%) and 'forgiveness' (21%). These were followed by 'forgetting the past' (10%), returning to the 'status ante' (10%) and by 'respect' (9%). A considerable percentage said that reconciliation was either 'impossible' (8%) or that it meant 'nothing' to them (7%). Here we were counting together the times when the respondent only referred to forgiveness as well as when the respondent referred to forgiveness and something else.

Taking a look at all the different possible answers separately, it can be noted that the order in which the concepts were most often mentioned remained the same, except for 'forgetting the past'. This means that 'forgetting the past' was mostly combined with other concepts and was not as much referred to on its own as the other concepts – peaceful coexistence and forgiveness – were. 'Forgetting the past' was combined with concepts such as 'forgiveness', 'trust', 'status quo ante', 'encounter', 'peaceful existence'. Some of these answers – for example, 'forgetting the past and trust' – were not statistically significant because they were given by only one or two respondents.

From a qualitative point of view it was interesting to understand which concepts were put together by respondents. The most frequent combination was 'forgive and forgetting the past' (3% of the respondents who answered this question), followed by 'peaceful coexistence and respect' (2%) and by 'peaceful coexistence and better living conditions' (2%). While 'forgiving' ranked high not only on its own but also in combination with other concepts, 'forgetting' did not rank as high on its own, but came in third place when taking into consideration the times when each concept was mentioned, including in combination with others. This means that when someone said that reconciliation means – or implies – forgetting what happened, or moving on, they found it important to mention something else in addition. When combined with concepts such as 'forgiveness', 'trust', 'status quo ante', 'encounter' or 'peaceful existence', forgetting did not seem to imply pure amnesia. With all this in mind, it seems that those who referred to 'forgetting' did so on a rather forward-looking note.

Table 7. The Meaning of Reconciliation

	N	Valid %
Peaceful coexistence	127	24
Forgive	110	21
Forget	53	10
Status ante	51	10
Respect	49	9
Impossible	43	8
Nothing	35	7
Trust	31	6
One united Bosnia	23	4
Ethnic separation	9	2
Better living conditions	19	4
No nationalism	10	2
Respect for human rights	22	4
Justice	4	.8
Reparation/compensation	4	.8
Encounter	5	1
Security	2	.4
Prosecution	19	4
Remembrance	6	1
Dialogue	2	.4
Good governance	5	1
Acceptance of responsibility	16	3
Truth	18	3
Victim assistance	1	.2

Question: What does reconciliation mean for you?

Finally, when looking at the distribution of the answers given in the seven most frequent meanings of reconciliation according to religious affiliation, there were some differences worth noting. Catholics, once again, seemed to give considerably more importance to forgiveness than Muslims and Orthodox and they were also the ones who believed the most that reconciliation implies respect. As was to be expected both Catholics and Muslims liked things to go back to the way they were before the war (and thus keep positive memories of that time); there were much fewer Orthodox that thought the same. In fact, for most Orthodox who at the time lived in Republika Srpska, the status ante meant being in a united Bosnia rather than the current division of the country in two entities. It was also among Serbs that the opinion of reconciliation being impossible was stronger.

3.5. INTERIM CONCLUSION ON BOSNIA

Having reviewed some aspects on reconciliation in Bosnia, it is worthwhile to draw some concise conclusions. It should be clear that these are not based on an extensive, let alone an exhaustive, review of the literature, but only on a specific survey on post-conflict justice issues conducted by ourselves and focusing on truth, accountability, reparation and reconciliation.

There is no doubt that the issues of forgiveness, trust and reconciliation were, if not the most, among the most controversial ones discussed in our survey. This can easily be illustrated by the fact that none of the optional answers gathered a broad consensus and that considerable numbers of respondents opted for the 'I don't know' answer category. Indeed, we consider it important to take into consideration the group of respondents whose opinions are mixed or uncertain (i.e. those who opted for 'I don't know') because it refers to a large group of people whose opinions may be more easily influenced towards a more optimistic or pessimistic attitude. Opinions on these topics, particularly on reconciliation, seem to change when questions are formulated at a more abstract or at a more personal level.

As to how reconciliation is seen by the respondents, it seems to receive a negative connotation because of its trivialisation in the public discourse. Probably because it is regarded through minimalist lenses, reconciliation is still seen as more likely to become a reality than the rebuilding of trust among Bosnians. Moreover, in the process of rebuilding trust in Bosnia there seems to be consensus about the negative role played by politicians, trauma and the media.

4. THE RELEVANCE OF EMPIRICAL STUDIES FOR AFRICA

The previous part has made clear that a lot is to be gained from listening to voices from the field, as they tend to provide very interesting information about people's perceptions, attitudes, expectations and opinions in relation to post-conflict justice in general and reconciliation in particular. In the following paragraphs, we briefly want to sketch how in our view such empirical research could be relevant for African countries that emerge out of war or other forms of violent conflict and are trying to deal with the legacy of the past while at the same time reconstructing society in all its components. We will first give two illustrations of empirical researches that have already been conducted in Africa and then list some problems when undertaking such type of research.

4.1. EXAMPLE OF EMPIRICAL STUDIES ON POST-CONFLICT JUSTICE IN AFRICA

One of the reports most often referred to when it comes to understanding what people think about issues of post-conflict societies is called *Forgotten Voices* (Pham *et al.* 2005), a population-based survey on attitudes about peace and justice in Northern Uganda. The region has been prone to two decades of violent conflict with the Lord's Resistance Army (LRA) fighting against the Ugandan government and applying extreme brutality against the people of the region. Countless civilians were mutilated and tens of thousands of children and adults were abducted to serve as soldiers and sex slaves for the commanders. Unable to beat the LRA in a military way or even to bring it to the negotiation table, the Ugandan government in December 2003 decided to refer the situation in Northern Uganda to the International Criminal Court (ICC) in order to conduct investigations and to issue indictments against LRA commanders. This decision, and the ensuing indictments by the Court, sparked huge and at times fierce debates in Uganda, both in the circles of the state institutions and with civil society, as well as within the international community. The empirical research was aimed at measuring the exposure to violence and the opinions and attitudes of the population about specific transitional justice mechanisms, as well as to understand these opinions in more depth and to assess the needs of the population. For this purpose the authors held interviews with more than 2,500 respondents from four districts in Northern Uganda, using random sampling methods to obtain a representative overview of the situation. The face-to-face interviews were conducted by a wide number of teams of trained interviewers in April and May 2005, using a structured questionnaire.

The survey concluded that people in Northern Uganda had been exposed to extreme levels of violence, with 40% of the respondents having been abducted by the LRA, 45% having witnessed the killing of a family member and 23% having been mutilated physically (Pham *et al.* 2005). When it came to assessing the various mechanisms for post-conflict justice, accountability for crimes committed by all sides was seen as a priority. A two-third majority preferred punishment for the perpetrators (i.e. trials and imprisonment, and even killing), while 22% favoured forgiveness, reconciliation and reintegration of the offenders into society. 65% of the respondents supported the amnesty process for LRA combatants but the vast majority of respondents found that amnesty could not be granted unconditionally and without some form of acknowledgement. The respondents were also asked to give their views on broad notions as 'human rights', 'peace', 'justice' and 'reconciliation'. As to the latter, a little more than half associated it with forgiveness and one quarter believed it entailed confessions. Overall, the respondents did not view peace and justice as mutually exclusive, but they saw the complex relationship and listed several conditions to move forward in both fields. On the basis of their findings the researchers issued various recommendations, including an appeal to the Ugandan government for making the amnesty process more inclusive and thus meeting the victims' expectations better, as well as an appeal to the international community for facilitating meetings with all shareholders concerned to develop a comprehensive strategy for peace and justice.

In late 2005 the situation dramatically changed in Northern Uganda with the withdrawal of the LRA forces from Uganda into other countries of the Central African region and peace talks between the LRA and the government started in the summer of 2006. They led to a joint agreement in June 2007 on how to deal with accountability and reconciliation. For these reasons, more or less the same research team decided to conduct a follow-up study using a similar survey as the 2005 one and supplemented by in-depth qualitative interviews (Pham *et al.* 2007). A roughly equal number of around 70% of the respondents indicated that those responsible for the crimes should be held accountable. Also similar to the earlier survey, about two-thirds of the respondents said that whomever would receive amnesty should apologise before returning to the community. However, a much higher number than in the previous survey (54% vs. 22%) preferred forgiveness, reconciliation and reintegration, thus suggesting "a willingness to compromise for the sake of peace" (Pham *et al.* 2007, 4). Also much more emphasis than before was put on mechanisms for truth-seeking about the crimes of the past and on reparations to victims. The combination of these new findings led the researchers to recommend to the government and the international community to promote the national dialogue for truth-seeking in Northern Uganda and to set up a reparations programme for victims, and to the negotiators of the Juba Peace Talks to continue working towards an integrated approach to accountability and reconciliation.

4.2. PROBLEMS OF DOING EMPIRICAL RESEARCH ABOUT RECONCILIATION AND POST-CONFLICT JUSTICE

Despite the fact that the last ten to fifteen years has witnessed between twenty and thirty empirical researches in relation to transitional justice the total body of knowledge is still very limited. This is particularly problematic when it comes to trying to assess the effects of transitional justice mechanisms in reality or to get an overview of people's perceptions and attitudes. In a 2008 report Canadian researchers have provided a summary of empirical research findings and have discussed the implications for analysts and for practitioners (Thoms *et al.* 2008). Their conclusions are quite sobering to read after two decades of intensive research on transitional justice issues and mechanisms. First, they argue that there is little evidence for some of the major claims that abound in the transitional justice literature, namely that the mechanisms would contribute to reconciliation and healing, that they would foster respect for human rights and the rule of law, or that they would help in establishing the conditions for countries being run in a peaceful and democratic way. The researchers indicate their surprise about the fact that many commentators have expressed very strong positions about the effects of transitional justice with so little empirical evidence around. A second major conclusion calls for more research that is carefully crafted, of a comparative nature and can be sustained over time. This is the only way to move from "faith-based" to "fact-based" discussions on transitional justice and to produce more reliable findings, the authors maintain (Thoms *et al.* 2008, 5; compare Van Wijk, this volume, regarding amnesty). Finally, they wonder whether better research necessarily leads to better policy making, but at least indicate that an increase in the knowledge base can increase the possibilities for evidence-based policy in the field of transitional justice. In attachment to the report, the authors provide a very good overview of the existing empirical studies, each with their strengths and weaknesses. In the case of Africa, they list country surveys on South Africa, Rwanda and Uganda.

Although Pham *et al* (2005; 2007) in their study on Uganda are strong supporters of empirical studies to bring the voices from the field to the surface, they are far from blind for the problems that may arise. Both reports list a number of limitations that the researchers encountered while conducting the survey and they can be generalised into more generic problems of doing research in conflict zones and in post-conflict situations (also Smyth & Robinson 2001).

One area of problems concerns the context within which surveys or other forms of empirical studies take place. For as long as violent conflicts are ongoing researchers face many security concerns when going to places and talking to people to collect data. Even when hostilities have come to an end many security concerns may be persisting. Furthermore, empirical research in the field requires a lot of time and resources but every study is necessarily limited in both. Connected is the issue of the representativity of the data, because doing some interviews with some people will always be suspicious if no efforts are made to cover as widely as possible a country, its various regions and its various groups.

A second set of problems relates to the condition of the interviewees or the respondents in general. Their recollection of the facts of the past could be contaminated, both by the lapse of time and by the degree of traumatisation they have incurred after having been the subjects of long-standing and extreme violence. As a result of the foregoing, or even independently from it, respondents may be prone to prefer socially desirable answers over what they really think or feel. Such attitude may be part of a general culture of pleasing the other party, it may be associated with the expectations of receiving benefits from the interviewer or it may even be linked to the fear for reprisals. Furthermore, interviewers have to be careful when asking specific questions about recent or ongoing events because situations of violent conflict or post-conflict are often volatile and change very quickly, thus leading to rapidly outdated information.

These are just some of the problems that may occur when empirical studies in or about conflict and post-conflict situations are conducted and for which researchers need to be very sensitive. Many of these issues will also apply to research in Africa.

5. CONCLUSION

The notion of reconciliation has become very popular over the last two decades, and particularly through the work of the South African Truth and Reconciliation Commission in the 1990s. Despite its multiple use, however, it is not without many problems. In this chapter, we have tried to highlight some of these problems by looking at a specific case.

Our analysis of the Bosnian case was based on a quantitative population survey following a theoretical framework consisting of four key issues: truth, accountability, reparation and reconciliation (TARR). It became clear that the issues of reconciliation and trust building were amongst the most problematic ones, leading to lots of different interpretations but also to a great deal of uncertainty as illustrated by the large percentage of 'I don't know' replies. Reconciliation in Bosnia obviously means different things to different people and it can take place at different levels. The deeper reasons for these divergences should be investigated further: they may have to do with the absence of any real 'restorative justice' approach in the country, be the result of the official use of reconciliation measures by government institutions, or even be lined to the continuing tensions in the complex patchwork that Bosnia represents.

Next we have tried to sketch the relevance of empirical studies for other regions of the world, and particularly for Africa. Some limited examples have illustrated how empirical research can contribute to a better understanding of people's attitudes and opinions and how it can have an impact on policy making in relation to transitional justice strategies and mechanisms. Such type of research is never easy, it consumes lots of time, energy and funds and it is likely to encounter many other methodological problems as well. However, if the debates about transitional justice in Africa are to move from 'faith-based' to 'fact-based' they will have to include the results of empirical studies that are complying with the highest scientific standards and are maintained over time.

XIV. JUSTICE AT THE DOORSTEP

Victims of International Crimes in Formal Versus Tradition-Based Justice Mechanisms in Sierra Leone, Rwanda and Uganda*

Martien Schotsmans**

1. INTRODUCTION

Sierra Leone, Rwanda and Uganda are only three out of so many countries in Sub-Saharan Africa that suffered from violent conflict during the past two decades. What is particular to all three countries is that many or even most crimes during the conflict targeted civilians. In addition, civilians often joined the armed forces in committing these crimes, after forceful or voluntary conscription or as a result of hate campaigns. This means that victims and perpetrators, even if they did not know each other directly, were often from the same village or region and have to live together after the conflict ends. This chapter focuses on coexistence between victims and perpetrators and therefore on the micro-level of dealing with the consequences of armed conflict, even though this level is closely inter-related with the intergroup- and national level. The micro-level does not only include the individual relation between victim and perpetrator, but also the community to which they belong.

The assumption explored in this chapter is that in post-conflict situations where victims and perpetrators live together, especially in areas where tradition is often still part of daily life, tradition-based justice pays more consideration to the victims' rights and needs, compared to formal justice. This chapter assesses the actual consideration of victims' needs in the three countries by both formal and tradition-based mechanisms. Interestingly, each of the three countries has

---

* The title is borrowed from a respondent in: Redress & African Rights, *Survivors and Post-genocide Justice in Rwanda. Their Experiences, Perspectives and Hopes*, 2008, 32.

** The author wishes to acknowledge the funding of the Aftralaw research project by the Belgian Government, Belgian Science Policy Office (BELSPO). She also wants to thank Prof. Eva Brems and the editors of the volume for their valuable constructive comments on the chapter, as well as all interviewees and those who shared documents and other information.

developed a different relationship between formal and tradition-based justice mechanisms in the framework of transitional justice, allowing comparison between the ways victims' rights and needs have been addressed in those varying mechanisms.

The chapter is based on three types of information: (1) existing academic research and grey literature; (2) 209 semi-structured interviews I conducted in Sierra Leone, Rwanda and Uganda in April, July and August 2009 and in July 2010, with international donors and organisations, as well as state actors, civil society organisations, traditional authorities, academics and participants in tradition-based justice activities; (3) my previous professional experience in Rwanda with genocide trials at the level of national courts in the years 1998 to 2000 and as a consultant for various organisations in the following years, and in Sierra Leone with the Truth and Reconciliation Commission in 2003.

A word of caution is in place: the limited frame of this chapter does not allow in depth description and analyses, nor does it allow the presentation of all nuances to which the described processes are entitled. In addition, the focus being on victims, the representation of their views does not imply an overall assessment of the process by other stakeholders or observers. More detailed analyses are offered by authors referred to in the chapter. By no means I want to pretend presenting the final assessment of the transitional justice processes in the three countries.

2. BACKGROUND TO THE CONFLICTS

A brief description of the background and nature of the conflict in each country will help to understand some of the transitional justice choices they made.

Sierra Leone experienced a violent conflict between 1991 and 2002. This opposed, on the one hand, the rebels of the Revolutionary United Front (RUF) supported by Liberia, later joined by the military of the Armed Forces Revolutionary Council (AFRC) who overthrew the government in 1997 – and on the other hand the government army (SLA) and local Civil Defence Forces (CDF). Many war crimes and crimes against humanity were committed by all armed factions, be it not to the same extent: the abduction and forceful conscription of children, large scale sexual violence, mutilation (cutting off ears and lips) and amputations are but the most notorious ones. After the invasion of Freetown on 6 January 1999 and international armed intervention, the Lomé peace agreement was signed on 7 July 1999, providing for a blanket amnesty, disarmament, power sharing and new elections. However, violence resumed in May 2000 and the war was not declared over until 18 January 2002. During the conflict, over 2 million persons have been displaced, an estimated 50,000 to 75,000 people were killed, tens of thousands of women and girls have been victims of sexual violence, about 10,000 children have participated in the fighting and about 4,000 persons are victim of amputation (Dougherty 2004a).[1] Bad governance, large-scale corruption, regional discrimination and political polarisation were identified as the causes of the conflict, and not diamonds and other natural resources as often portrayed.[2] Sierra Leone has since known various democratic elections, as well as a peaceful regime change.

In Rwanda, crimes of genocide against the Tutsi had been committed and remained unpunished at various times since 1959, causing the exile of many Tutsi. The civil war, which lasted from 1 October 1990 to 4 July 1994, was initiated by a movement, the Rwandan Patriotic Front (RPF), mainly composed of Tutsi refugees from neighbouring countries wanting to return home. The war exacerbated the number and intensity of genocide crimes, culminating in the 100 days of genocide of the Tutsi from 6 April to 4 July 1994. The killings were committed according to a plan developed and implemented by Hutu extremists in the government, who did not agree with the power sharing deals negotiated in Arusha under international pressure. It involved trained militia's called *Interahamwe* as well as large numbers of ordinary citizens, incited by hate campaigns broadcasted over *Radio Télévision Libre des Mille Collines*-RTLM-radio. The genocide allegedly caused the death of 800,000 to 1,000,000 victims, including victims of crimes against humanity committed against moderate Hutu, and in addition to victims of war crimes committed by the RPF (Des Forges 1999). In a survey conducted in 2000, 36% of respondents claimed to have lost family members due to the genocide and 23% due to massacres (Gasibirige 2002, 48).[3] The war ended by a victory of the RPF, which transformed into a political party that still dominates the political landscape today, following several elections.

In Northern Uganda (mainly the districts of Gulu, Kitgum and Pader) the conflict between Joseph Kony's Lord's Resistance Army (LRA) and the Ugandan army (UPDF) supported by Local Defence Units (LDUs) dates from 1986. It has to be understood both in the context of internal politics, including discrimination of the Northern region of Uganda, and the regional conflict, since the government of Sudan was supporting the LRA until the Comprehensive Peace Agreement (CPA) ended the conflict between North and South Sudan in 2005, while Uganda was supporting the South–Sudanese secession movement (Latigo 2007). The LRA has used extreme violence and committed many crimes against the

---

1   Also C. Correa & M. Suma, *Report and Proposals for the Implementation of Reparations in Sierra Leone*, International Center for Transitional Justice, 2009, www.ictj.org/static/Africa/ SierraLeone/ICTJ_SL_ReparationsRpt_Dec2009.pdf. International Crisis Group, *Sierra Leone: Time for a New Military and Political Strategy*, ICG Africa Report No. 28, 2001.

2   Truth and Reconciliation Commission, *Witness to truth, Report of the Sierra Leone Truth and Reconciliation Commission*, Sierra Leone, 2004, Vol. 2 and 3A.

3   The survey does not mention whether those crimes were committed in 1994 or before (or after), nor wether there is a possible overlap between both categories.

population, the most notorious being the abduction and use of children in the hostilities, estimated between 30,000 and 50,000,[4] in addition to sexual violence and other attacks against the civilian population. In order to secure the region, the Ugandan government decided to regroup about 80% of the population, over 1,700,000 persons, in internally displacement-camps (IDP-camps), where they have spent over 20 years and suffered from many crimes, including violations committed by the UPDF. There are no exact numbers of persons killed, but my respondents estimated they mount up to 15,000. Although a relative security has been established in Northern Uganda,[5] and many people have started to leave the IDP-camps, the conflict with the LRA has not officially ended and many people still fear a new outbreak of violence and the return (or even spiritual omnipresence) of Joseph Kony.

3. FORMAL V. TRADITION-BASED JUSTICE

This section will define the concepts of formal and traditional justice, then compare some of their features and finally consider the current use and creation of tradition-based justice mechanisms in post-conflict situations.

3.1. FORMAL JUSTICE

Formal justice in this chapter refers to (supra-)state-organised justice based on the court model, i.e. justice mechanisms established by UN resolutions, international conventions, the Constitution or by state laws as part of a national justice system. As we will see, such existing or *ad hoc* created formal criminal justice mechanisms deal with mass crimes related to the conflict in all three countries. Huyse (2008, 5) defines formal justice as initiated, organised and controlled by national or international state institutions and having formal and rational-legalistic procedures, of which criminal court proceedings are the prototype.

---

[4]   Human Rights Watch, *Stolen Children: Abduction and Recruitment in Northern Uganda* 15, no. 7(a), 2003, 5.

[5]   Meanwhile the LRA has moved to Southern Sudan, the Democratic Republic of Congo and the Central African Republic, committing similar atrocities there. See for instance: Human Rights Watch, CAR/DR-Congo: LRA Conducts Massive Abduction Campaign, Press release, 11 August 2010. International Crisis Group, *LRA: a regional strategy beyond killing Kony*, Africa Report n° 157, 28 April 2010.

3.2. TRADITIONAL JUSTICE

The concept of traditional justice is a much contested one and often used interchangeably, though not necessarily correctly, with informal, non-state, indigenous, native or customary justice. According to Huyse (2008, 8) traditional justice mechanisms are community-initiated and community-organised and have informal and ritualistic-communal procedures. The definition of Penal Reform International defining traditional justice as "non-state justice systems which have existed, although not without change, since pre-colonial times and are generally found in rural areas",[6] is more relevant in the context of this chapter, since it refers both to the pre-existence of the mechanism in relation to the armed conflict and to its evolving nature

Before colonial times, all three countries – like many others in Africa[7] – had a system of traditional ruling by chiefs or kings. These chiefs or kings also provided for conflict resolution in varying ways. Sierra Leone had various systems, depending on each of the 17 ethnic groups, but in most groups the king was not autocratic, since he ruled together with a council and with the secret society (traditional associations of people who have been initiated together), delegating parts of his power to chiefs and sub-chiefs. The secret societies also played a very important role in settling disputes (Alie 1990). In the more centralised Rwandan kingdom conflicts were traditionally settled at the level of the chief of the household (*urugo*), then at the family level (*inzu*), the clan level (*umuryango*) and finally at the level of the *mwami* or king, who could also delegate his power to a lower chief. The prime goal was the restoration of social harmony. For capital crimes, however, this required the killing of a person of the killer's family of equal value as the victim, although settlement by gifts or giving a girl for marriage would also be possible and became more common over time (Ingelaere 2008, 33).[8] The Acholi in Northern Uganda did not have a central king, but were ruled by chiefs or *rwodi* at the level of the chieftaincies, assisted by the council of elders, also for dispute settlement. The elders in turn composed the Grand Council, who would settle disputes among clans (Latigo 2008, 102). It is important to note that traditional chiefs have continued to be officially recognized though highly politicized in Sierra Leone (Keen 2003, 71), while in Rwanda they have been abolished in 1961 (Reyntjens 1985, 272–273) and in Uganda they have been abolished but reinstated in 1993, whit limited ceremonial and cultural functions (Beke 2004, 156–7).

---

[6] Penal Reform International, *Access to Justice in Sub-Saharan Africa. The Role of Traditional and Informal Justice Systems*, 2000, 11.

[7] *Ibidem.*

[8] Nations Unies, Haut Commissariat aux Droits de l'Homme, *Gacaca. Le Droit Coutumier au Rwanda,* Rapport Final de la Première Phase d'Enquête sur le Terrain, Kigali, 31/01/1996; Rapport de la Deuxième Phase d'Enquêtes sur le Terrain, Kigali, 30/06/1996, 16.

Colonial rule gradually replaced these systems by more or less formalized native or customary courts, composed of laypersons which were often appointed by the colonial authorities. They would deal with civil matters and minor crimes among natives, applying customary law, while more serious crimes had to be dealt with by formal courts applying colonial legislation (John-Nambo 2002). All three countries still have this legal pluralism today, or have reinstated it, in which case semi-formalised customary courts co-exist with formal justice.[9] This level of semi-formal justice is benefitting from a revived level of attention in recent years, mainly in view of increasing access to justice for the poor (Corradi 2010).[10]

This chapter does not deal with such semi-formalised mechanisms of colonial or post-colonial origins, since they generally have no jurisdiction over serious crimes. Under the surface of formal and semi-formal justice, informal mechanisms have remained operational throughout colonial times and since independence. Although not legally recognized, traditional or other local leaders have continued to settle disputes, sometimes even related to serious crimes which officially fall under the jurisdiction of the formal courts.[11] Some of these mechanisms have recently become a source of inspiration to create new tradition-based mechanisms, adjusting aspects of tradition to the need of dealing with serious crimes committed during a conflict. Before looking into such tradition-based mechanisms – which are the focus of this chapter – I will compare some relevant features commonly used to distinguish traditional and formal justice.

3.3. SOME DIFFERENCES AND SOME NUANCES

Penal Reform International has identified a number of salient features of traditional justice as opposed to formal justice, among which: the fact that the problem is viewed as belonging to the whole community or group; the emphasis on reconciliation and restoring social harmony; the fact that the traditional arbitrators are appointed from within the community on the basis of status or lineage; a high degree of public participation; the voluntary nature of the process and the enforcement of decisions through social pressure; the fact that decisions

---

9   Sierra Leone, Local Courts Act, 1963; Uganda, Local Council Courts Act, 2006; the more recently established conciliation committees of Abunzi in Rwanda, Organic law N° 31/2006 of 14/08/2006.

10   Penal Reform International, *Access to Justice in Sub-Saharan Africa. The Role of Traditional and Informal Justice Systems*, 2000; Department for International Development (DFID), *Safety, Security and Accessible Justice. Putting Policy into Practic*, 2002; UNDP, *Doing Justice: How Informal Justice Systems Can Contribute*, 2006.

11   Nabudere, D. W., *Ubuntu Philosophy. Memory and Reconciliation*, 2002, 25; http://repositories. lib.utexas.edu/bitstream/handle/2152/4521/3621.pdf?sequence=1 (last visited: 26 November 2010). Penal Reform International, *Access to Justice in Sub-Saharan Africa. The Role of Traditional and Informal Justice Systems*, 2000, 20.

are only partially based on rules, while like cases need not be treated alike; and finally, the fact that the decision is confirmed through rituals aiming at reintegration.[12] In addition to these, Huyse (2008, 13–16) mentions proximity and consensus-building. None of these features specifically refers to the position of the individual victim.

The communal aspect is not entirely absent in formal justice, since in both formal and traditional justice a crime is not considered to be just a violation of the victim's rights, but also and firstly a breach of societal norm. Therefore, in both mechanisms, social harmony needs to be restored and norms to be confirmed. However, the way in which this is achieved seems very different, although less than sometimes assumed.

First, procedure wise, in formal justice the violation of common values is denounced by the public prosecutor and confirmed by the fact that decisions are taken by a judge or a jury on behalf of the state. In traditional justice, community participation is much more direct: either all members of the community, including the victim(s), are present and can intervene during each phase of the proceeding, or mediation takes place between traditional leaders, clan or family elders, with the public event rather being the confirmation of the outcome of the process.[13] Such proximity and direct participation create a sense of ownership and support, which is merely absent in the formal justice system in many African countries, where geographical, cultural and often linguistic barriers are numerous.

Second, the high degree of public participation reflects a different view on the attribution of responsibility for the breach of norms. In formal justice only the perpetrator's accountability is at stake, and any sanction will be inflicted on this individual. But in a traditional setting the community, clan or family is responsible for not having controlled the perpetrator, whose acts caused a violation of social balance. Therefore, the family or clan will play an important role in solving the conflict with the help of traditional leaders or other intermediaries. This also includes a collective responsibility to repair the harm done, considering the lack of conceptual distinction between punitive sanctions and civil compensation in traditional justice. In formal justice, compensation is clearly distinguished from penalties, and will be imposed on the individual perpetrator only, even though in some cases there is a shared civil liability (e.g. in case of complicity, or under certain conditions parents for their minor children, employers for their employees, a state for its civil servants).

---

[12]   Penal Reform International, *Access to Justice in Sub-Saharan Africa. The Role of Traditional and Informal Justice Systems*, 2000, 22.

[13]   External observers sometimes mistake such public events or concluding rituals to be the entire process, ignoring the complexity of the preceding steps. See for instance: Human Rights Watch, Benchmarks for Assessing Possible National Alternatives to International Criminal Court Cases Against LRA Leaders. Human Rights Watch's First Memorandum on Justice Issues and the Juba Talks. May 2007, p. 7.

Thirdly, while the focus of traditional justice is on reintegration in society through reconciliation, this does not prohibit individual sanctions, such as afflicting corporal punishment, ostracizing the perpetrator or killing the perpetrator or a relative.[14] Likewise, formal justice is not always merely punitive, as sanctions can be mitigated in exchange for confessions, commuted in community service, replaced by victim-offender mediation or accompanied by reintegration programmes. Depending on the gravity of the crime, reintegration in or (temporary) exclusion of the perpetrator from society are responses of both traditional and formal justice to a varying extent. Both types of responses aim at the restoration of social harmony, be it not necessarily to the benefit of the individuals involved. Thus, the often stated dichotomy between traditional justice as restorative (see below) and formal justice as retributive and punitive justice is too simplistic (Vanspauwen & Savage 2008, 404).

Fourth, while formal justice has coercive powers to force the individual perpetrator to subject himself to the system and to establish guilt in an adversarial procedure based on forensic evidence, traditional justice seems to be based on voluntary participation and confessions only. This too is a simplification. In Sierra Leone (Zack-Williams 2006, 126; Stark 2006, 210) and Northern Uganda,[15] the perpetrator of a homicide will be haunted by the spirit of the killed person and by the ancestors. This will lead to nightmares, flash-backs, psycho-somatic illness, etc., which social science might label as Post-Traumatic Stress Disorder (PTSD). The victim's relatives too might be haunted if the culprit is not found and the harm not restored. This reality will bring perpetrators and survivors to submit their problem to family or clan elders, who will turn to traditional leaders. In cases where the perpetrator does not confess, traditional ceremonies such as oath taking or swearing will be used: if the perpetrator lies, illness, bad harvest, poverty or other calamities will come over him, his family, his clan, his village (Alie 1990, 25; Alie 2008, 136–137). Likewise, in formal justice, witnesses – not accused – have or had to swear on the Bible or the Koran. These tools can be very effective in the truth finding process, but only if spiritual beliefs are still present in a community.[16]

---

14   For Sierra Leone: Manifesto '99, *Traditional Methods of Conflict Management/Resolution of Possible Complementary Value to the Proposed Sierra Leone Truth and Reconciliation Commission,* 2002. For Rwanda: Nations Unies, Haut Commissariat aux Droits de l'Homme, *Gacaca. Le Droit Coutumier au Rwanda,* Rapport Final de la Première Phase d'Enquête sur le Terrain, Kigali, 31/01/1996; Rapport de la Deuxième Phase d'Enquêtes sur le Terrain, Kigali, 30/06/1996, 16. For Uganda: *Beyond Juba, Tradition in Transition,* Working Paper no. 1; Transitional Justice Project of the Faculty of Law, Makerere University, The Refugee Law Project and the Human Rights & Peace Centre, 2009, 19; Penal Reform International, *Access to Justice in Sub-Saharan Africa. The Role of Traditional and Informal Justice Systems,* 2000, 22–23.

15   Caritus Gulu Archdiocese, *Traditional ways of coping in Acholi. Cultural provisions for reconciliation and healing from war,* 2006, 59.

16   Manifesto '99, *Traditional Methods of Conflict Management/Resolution of Possible Complementary Value to the Proposed Sierra Leone Truth and Reconciliation Commission,*

Fifth, in formal justice the range of beneficiaries of compensation is limited to direct victims, and in absence of the latter the immediate family members. In traditional justice, as providing reparation is typically the family's or clan's responsibility, it is not necessarily the individual victim who is entitled to compensation either. Indeed, he or she is not the only one affected by the crime, but the entire family or clan is. While in general compensation is due to this family or clan, the husband or the father will often be the beneficiary in cases of sexual assault (called 'women damage' in some parts of Sierra Leone).[17] Likewise, saving the family's honour takes priority over the individual victim's needs or wishes in cases of rape of a young girl, where the rapist will be held to marry his victim.[18] Reparations for homicide too are rather focusing on restoring the bereaved family (by providing a girl to produce new family members or cattle to pay the dowry for a bride to join the family for the same purpose)[19] rather than alleviating the grief of the widow or children. Social pressure on victims to accept the solution agreed upon by the community can be enormous, if not even the victim's consent is merely assumed or irrelevant as soon as his family or clan agrees.

Thus, even though it is correct that traditional justice is more focused on consensus, this consensus is achieved rather at the communal level, among clans or families, than among the individuals concerned. Looking through the lens of international standards, consensus is sometimes reached at the expense of the both victims' and offenders' individual rights, while the treatment of the parties involved will depend on power relations.[20] This often means that the opinion of women or youth – victims of many violations during armed conflict – will not be considered. This apparent lack of interest for the rights of the individual victim is to be understood in view of the traditional cosmovision, which is communal in essence: the idea of intertwined humanity (Skelton 2007, 232) or *ubuntu* in Southern Africa, means that one can be a person only through others (Zartman 2000, 170) and that after harm dignity and joint humanity need to be restored (Tschudi 2008, 49). In traditional societies, people have multiplex relationships: they are economically and socially interdependent, beyond the conflict to resolve.[21] This cosmovision can explain why the restoration of social

---

2002, 21–23.

[17]   Manifesto '99, *Traditional Methods of Conflict Management/Resolution of Possible Complementary Value to the Proposed Sierra Leone Truth and Reconciliation Commission*, 2002.

[18]   Caritus Gulu Archdiocese, *Traditional ways of coping in Acholi. Cultural provisions for reconciliation and healing from war*, 2006, 80.

[19]   *Ibidem.*

[20]   Nabudere, D. W., *Ubuntu Philosophy. Memory and Reconciliation*, 2002, 8; http://repositories. lib.utexas.edu/bitstream/handle/2152/4521/3621.pdf?sequence=1 (last visited: 26 November 2010). UNDP, *Doing Justice: How Informal Justice Systems Can Contribute*, 2006, 20–23.

[21]   Penal Reform International, *Access to Justice in Sub-Saharan Africa. The Role of Traditional and Informal Justice Systems*, 2000, 22.

harmony can take priority over immediate individual needs and still be beneficial to and supported by those individuals concerned. As Nabudere states:[22]

> *Reconciliation is about the transformation of the conflict into a non-conflictual situation for the good of the larger humanity (...). Both parties must define the stakes involved and relativise these stakes for the sake of the wider community as well as for the future of the unborn.*

As we will see, even when traditional mechanisms are modernized to include individual victims' rights, this will not prohibit the agency of empowered victims in deciding to accept solutions which benefit more to the community then to themselves.

This leads to the recent use of hybridized tradition-based mechanisms after mass conflict and the position of the victim therein.

3.4. FROM TRADITIONAL TO TRADITION-BASED TO HYBRID

In transitional justice discourse, the debate has shifted in recent years from the top-down application and the import of one-size-fits-all models towards a variety of mechanisms and tools – from international courts to truth commissions, reparation programs, vetting procedures and institutional reform – which are supposed to complement each other (Huyse 2008; Orentlicher 2007; Roht-Arriaza & Mariezcurrena 2006; Kritz 2002). In this landscape, more attention is brought to local mechanisms used to deal with past crimes. These may include traditional conflict resolution mechanisms.[23]

As Huyse explains (2008, 182–193) any post-conflict context presents important challenges to the potential use of traditional justice. Firstly, serious crimes have been committed at a large scale, across ethnic boundaries, by groups of perpetrators against groups of victims, sometimes even with interchanging roles. In addition, the social context may have been disrupted: people have been displaced or lived in camps for many years, traditional leaders have not always been neutral in the conflict, many generation-conflicts occur between the elders and the youth, and poverty is so overwhelming that a perpetrator, even if severely

---

[22] Nabudere, D. W., *Ubuntu Philosophy. Memory and Reconciliation*, 2002, 17; http://repositories. lib.utexas.edu/bitstream/handle/2152/4521/3621.pdf?sequence=1 (last visited: 26 November 2010).

[23] UN SG, The Rule of Law and transitional justice in conflict and post-conflict societies, Report of the Secretary General, 23 August 2004, S/2004/616. UN SG. Guidance Note of the Secretary-General. United Nations Approach to Transitional Justice, March 2010. Nuremberg Declaration on Peace and Justice, transmitted to the Secretary-General of the United Nations by letter of 13 June 2008, A/62/885.

haunted by his victims' spirit, may decide to remain silent in order not to impose the burden of compensation on his family.

Not surprisingly, as traditional justice mechanisms are not static but flexible and dynamic,[24] post-conflict societies adjust traditional mechanisms to this reality and create new tradition-based mechanisms, inspired one the one hand by the underlying traditional justice and reconciliation values, on the other hand by modern human rights standards. This can be done by either civil society organisations, or national authorities, or by joint efforts of both. The *Fambul Tok* project in Sierra Leone is such a tradition-based mechanism, initiated by civil society. Tradition-based mechanisms can also become real hybrids, mixing many aspects of modern, formal justice with a few elements of traditional justice, as in the *gacaca* justice developed by the Rwandan government, which combines formal proceedings and penalties with community participation, among others (see Ndahinda and Kaitesi & Haveman, both this volume).

Whether such mechanisms are traditional *per se* or invented is in fact a false debate: the important issue is that they are inspired by existing values regarding appropriate responses of a society or community to crime. It is not because a specific mechanism has not constantly been practiced for a certain time and is not as such known by the younger generations, that the underlying values have disappeared from people's cosmovision. These underlying values are expressed and confirmed in evolving ways over time, through mechanisms which are not static but dynamic. They can adjust to the needs of today's reality and integrate external influences, especially if these resonate with existing values. Looking for inspiration in the community's (former) traditional practices can have the advantage of calling upon an existing normative framework. In such cases, tradition-based hybrid mechanisms may have better chances for popular ownership and support than international courts or tribunals, which are alien to the society concerned.

This recent tendency to create hybrid mechanisms (Clark 2007), trying to marry international standards and local practices, will become more important in the future and presents important challenges. One of the main challenges is finding the balance between the community's goal of restoring social equilibrium and the respect of individual rights of both perpetrator and victim, of which people even in remote areas have become increasingly aware. The question here is to assess whether such tradition-based or hybrid mechanisms, adjusting traditional justice and reconciliation to post-conflict needs, better succeed in responding to victims' needs than formal justice.

---

[24]   Nabudere, D. W., *Ubuntu Philosophy. Memory and Reconciliation*, 2002, 33; http://repositories. lib.utexas.edu/bitstream/handle/2152/4521/3621.pdf?sequence=1 (last visited: 26 November 2010).

4. RIGHTS AND NEEDS OF VICTIMS

Whereas the needs and expectations of victims of mass crime obviously depend on each specific context, international instruments and available research allow to identify some common features. The relative importance of each of these will differ from situation to situation and will evolve over time.

4.1. INTERNATIONAL INSTRUMENTS

At the international level, attention for victims' rights and needs has increased in the last two decades. While provisions regarding victims' rights were limited to protection in the statute of the International Criminal Tribunal for Rwanda, recently adopted non-binding instruments emphasize the right of the victims to be consulted, the right to reparation or redress, the right to protection (mainly for victims acting as witnesses), the right to be treated with humanity and respect, the right to know the truth, the right to justice, the right to participate in proceedings.[25]

Only some of the acknowledged needs – mainly access to justice, protection and reparation – are part of positive law, through conventions adopted in the three countries, such as the International Covenant on Civil and Political Rights and the Convention against Torture, among others (Shelton 2005, 13).

The Rome Statute, ratified by both Sierra Leone and Uganda but not by Rwanda, provides for a right for protection (for both witnesses and participating victims) and participation (Article 68) as well as for reparation (Article 75), and for the possibility to receive interim assistance by the Trust Fund for Victims (Article79). The recently adopted legislation implementing the Rome Statute in Uganda does not include these rights in Uganda's national legislation and only makes provisions regarding requests of the ICC for assistance in victims' protection and the enforcement of reparation orders.[26] Sierra Leone has not yet

---

[25]   Among others: UN SG. Guidance Note of the Secretary-General. United Nations Approach to Transitional Justice, March 2010. UN SG, The Rule of Law and transitional justice in conflict and post-conflict societies, Report of the Secretary General, 23 August 2004, S/2004/616. UN, The Basic Principles and Guidelines on the Right to a Remedy and Reparation for Victims of Gross Violations of International Human Rights Law and Serious Violations of International Humanitarian Law, adopted by the General Assembly of the United Nations on 24 October 2005, A/C.3/60/L.24. UNEcoSoC, Report of the independent expert to update the Set of principles to combat impunity, Diane Orentlicher, Addendum: Updated Set of principles for the protection and promotion of human rights through action to combat impunity, 8 February 2005, E/CN.4/2005/102/Add.1 Nuremberg Declaration (2008), Nuremberg Declaration on Peace and Justice, transmitted to the Secretary-General of the United Nations by letter of 13 June 2008, A/62/885.

[26]   Article 58 resp. 64, The International Criminal Court Act 2010, Act 11, Acts Supplement n° 6 to the Uganda Gazette n° 39 Volume CIII, 25 June 2010.

enacted an ICC implementation law. Clearly, international positive law mainly focuses on victims' rights in the framework of retributive justice.

4.2. RESTORATIVE JUSTICE

As mentioned, some researchers claim that tradition-based justice is more restorative than retributive (Clark 2007, 63; Baines 2007, 96). Restorative justice is typically an inclusive, participatory and deliberately problem-solving process, balancing the needs of victim, perpetrator and community by actively involving them as main stakeholders, focusing on responsibility and repairing (Aertsen 2008). Restorative justice in the West is preferably used to settle minor crimes, in cases where the facts are already established and acknowledged, where victim and perpetrator are identified and participate voluntarily. This model[27] will clearly not be applicable to the most serious crimes committed during an armed conflict, but Aertsen finds that restorative objectives can guide both formal and traditional responses to large-scale violent conflict. These objectives are: providing support to victims, give a voice to victims and enable their participation, repair damaged relations in a consensual way, denounce crime as unacceptable and reaffirm community values, encourage all parties to take responsibility, focus on restorative, forward-looking outcomes, reduce recidivism by reintegrating the perpetrator and changing his behaviour, and identify causes of the crimes and inform the authorities.

Comparing restorative justice elements in formal versus informal justice mechanisms, Aertsen concludes that although more of these can be found in informal than in formal mechanisms, informal mechanisms are not per se restorative justice. They can create a high level of relational restoration only if they comprise mediation, bring parties together, provide inter-group dialogue facilitation and comprise the acknowledgment of guilt, a request for forgiveness, a promise not to repeat the past and rituals of purification. Many of these features are confirmed by research on what victims want after mass conflict, as will be further elaborated below.

4.3. IN COUNTRY RESEARCH

Considering victims' opinion regarding justice and reconciliation after mass conflict has only come to the forefront in recent years. Allowing victims to be stakeholders in the peace negations or at least in the development of the

---

[27] UN EcoSoC Basic principles on the use of restorative justice programmes in criminal matters, E/cn.15/2002/L.2/Rev.1, 18 April 2002; Council of Europe recommendation n° R(99)19 regarding mediation in penal matters.

transitional justice framework is even more recent. Hence, research on the topic – be it quantitative or qualitative – is still limited. What Pham and Vinck (2007) call "formative evaluation" with the purpose of collecting data in view of conceptualisation and planning of transitional justice mechanisms was rare before 2000. While some "process monitoring and evaluation" during the implementation phase has been conducted since, "outcome monitoring and evaluation", i.e. assessing the impact, is even more exceptional.

This is reflected in the three case studies. In Rwanda, where the conflict ended in 1994, the population's opinion on how the crimes of the past should be dealt with or on what the concepts of accountability, justice, reconciliation, etc. mean to them was never asked. In contrast, consultations and research on people's opinion regarding mechanisms already operational or planned for, mainly regarding the *gacaca* jurisdictions, is available (Karekezi, Nshimiyimana & Mutamba 2004; Longman, Pham & Weinstein 2004; Longman & Rutagengwa 2004; Stover & Weinstein 2004; Gasibirege 2002).[28] As Longman *et al.* point out (2004, 206), such top-down planning without consultation of the population is not unique to Rwanda.

In Sierra Leone, civil society (not necessarily victims' representatives) had some input during the peace negotiations in 1999 (Hayner 2007). With the exception of a quantitative research regarding sexual violence[29] popular surveys only occurred later on[30] together with some qualitative research either on particular mechanisms such as the Special Court or the TRC (Sawyer & Kelsall 2007; Shaw 2007; Kelsall 2005; Dougherty 2004a & 2004b) or on the reintegration of ex-combatants and reconciliation (Boersch-Supan 2009; Stovel 2010; Stovel 2008; Humphreys & Weinstein 2007). For these two countries, research mainly concerns the general population's and sometimes the victims' post factum opinion.

Since the peace negotiations regarding Northern Uganda are more recent, the current trend to consider victims as stakeholders and agents is reflected in a number of popular surveys (Pham, Vinck *et al.* 2007; Pham *et al.* 2005)[31] and in qualitative research mainly on the controversy between the ICC and traditional

---

[28] See also Republic of Rwanda, Ministry of Justice, *Seventh Periodic Report of Rwanda to the African Human and People's Rights 1999–2002*, DOC/OS/(XXXVI) 373b, February 2003.

[29] Physicians for Human Rights, *War-Related Sexual Violence in Sierra Leone. A Population-Based Assessment*, 2002.

[30] BBC World Service Trust, International Center for Transitional Justice & Search for Common Ground, *Peace, Justice and Reconciliation in Sierra Leone: A Survey of Knowledge and Attitudes Towards Transitional Institutions in Post-Conflict Sierra Leone*, 2008, available at www.communicatingjustice.org/files/content/file/Surveys/Sierra%20Leone%20primo%20 PDF%20version.pdf.

[31] UNHCHR, *Making Peace Our Own; Victims' Perspectives of Accountability, Reconciliation and Transitional Justice in Northern Uganda*, 2007.

justice (Quinn 2009; Baines 2007; Allen 2006).[32] The surveys did not only ask the population questions about specific mechanisms, but also about what they consider to be conditions for peace, and more in particular their understanding of justice, reconciliation, forgiveness, etc. Whereas some of this research distinguishes among various categories within the population (victims, prisoners, the families of prisoners, the general population), others consider the victimisation of the population in general.

As a consequence, comparing the outcome of such a variety of research on people's opinion brings along various complexities.[33] However, some common needs can be identified in the available materials on the three countries, even though expressed in different ways and at different times in the transitional justice process: the need to know the truth (although not necessarily in detail), the need for perpetrators to accept their wrong-doing or at least be held accountable, the hope for sincere apologies offered to the victim directly, the opportunity for victims to decide on the acceptance of apologies (as opposed to pressure to forgive and to amnesty or lenient sentences granted by the state) and last but not least for reparation. In addition, in Uganda and Sierra Leone people clearly see different levels of accountability between commanders and low level perpetrators: while they prefer prosecutions for the commanders, acknowledgement, apologies, and compensation might do for the others. Another common finding is that peaceful cohabitation of perpetrators and victims can hide patterns of distrust, rejection and discrimination in the absence of any type of acknowledgement or accountability.

4.4. CONCLUDING ON VICTIMS' RIGHTS AND NEEDS

My previous field experience in working with victims of mass crime in various countries brought me to distinguish between the following needs and expectations of victims: the need for security as a preliminary condition to any type of dealing with the past, the need to see their victimization acknowledged, the need to establish the accountability of the perpetrator, through confessions (active accountability) or a verdict of a court (passive accountability), the need to know the truth and the need for reparations (Schotsmans 2005).

---

[32]   Also *Beyond Juba, Tradition in Transition*, Working Paper no. 1; Transitional Justice Project of the Faculty of Law, Makerere University, The Refugee Law Project and the Human Rights & Peace Centre, 2009; Justice and reconciliation Project, Gulu District NGO Forum and Liu Institute for Global Issues, '*The cooling of hearts'. Community truth-telling in Acholi-land*, Special report, 2007; Refugee Law Project, *Whose Justice? Perceptions of Uganda's Amnesty Act 2000: The Potential for Conflict Resolution and Long-Term Reconciliation*, Working Paper No. 15, 2005.

[33]   For a critical analyses of surveys and other tools used to verify people's opinion on transitional justice, see Thoms *et al.* 2008.

Considering the above mentioned research as well as my recent research in the three countries studied here, I argue that additional attention needs to go to the interaction between victim and perpetrator. This is particularly so for victims of proximity crimes, i.e. when victim and perpetrator know each other, lived in each other's neighbourhood before the crime or have to live together after the crime. A qualitative, although limited, research I conducted among survivors in Rwanda in 2000 (Schotsmans 2000, 42) confirmed the idea that victims – if given the choice – would prefer not to live with the perpetrators again, because they "do not want to see them". However, when people realise that they will have no choice but to live together, they seem to become more pragmatic and attach more importance to the restoration of social harmony and good neighbourhood. This requires an occasion for encounter and dialogue, for the expression of war-related and even older grievances, for a process of social or restorative truth finding, for acknowledgment of wrongdoing, sincere apologies and the possibility for the victims to accept (or not) such apologies, and finally the mutual engagement to leave the past behind (also: Stovel 2010, 45; Parmentier, Vanspauwen & Weitekamp 2008; Ingelaere 2008, 50; Daly & Sarkin 2007, 162). Some research even shows that victims attach more importance to these aspects than to punishment (Longman & Rutagengwa 2004, 173), although this obviously is a generalisation, since victims in any given country are not a monolithic group and may have conflicting expectations. Some victims will continue to insist on prosecution and punishment of all perpetrators and on compensation, while others claim they have already forgiven the perpetrators, even without confessions or reparation.

In the following section, I will compare formal and tradition-based justice in the three countries, focusing on the need for accountability, truth finding, participation, reparation and encounter (including dialogue, apologies and closing rituals).

5. VICTIMS IN THE THREE COUNTRIES

The three countries present a different landscape of transitional justice mechanisms and the combination thereof. They have two common aspects: the prosecution of those who bear the greatest responsibility for the most serious crimes on the one hand (which will not be considered here) and the goal of reconciliation on the other hand.

Although all three countries have experienced mass violence targeting the civilian population and all three have to reconstruct their society considering the proximity between perpetrators and victims, they each have a different approach on how to deal with rank and file perpetrators: Rwanda decided to prosecute all perpetrators, while Sierra Leone granted a blanket amnesty and prosecuted virtually no perpetrators not falling under the amnesty regulation, and Uganda granted amnesty to those applying for it, focusing on traditional mechanisms as a complement.

5.1. SIERRA LEONE: FORMAL JUSTICE AND NON-OFFICIAL USE OF TRADITION

The Lomé Peace Agreement[34] granted a blanket amnesty for all crimes committed prior to 6 June 1999 and provided for the establishment of a Truth and Reconciliation Commission (TRC). After a new outbreak of violence in 2000, the United Nations and the government of Sierra Leone established the Special Court for Sierra Leone (SCSL) to prosecute those who bear the greatest responsibility for serious violations of international humanitarian law committed in Sierra Leone since 30 November 1996.[35] It has effectively prosecuted nine persons, eight of whom are now serving their sentences in Rwanda, while the trial against Charles Taylor is ongoing.[36] Both at the Special Court and at national courts victims can only intervene as witnesses and are not entitled to reparations. At the national level, two trials have taken place convicting 17 low level perpetrators for relatively minor crimes committed after the Lomé Peace agreement (Horovitz 2009, 26–30).

The TRC operated from 2002 to 2004 and issued a report, providing a historical record of the conflict, identifying the causes of the conflict and recommending institutional reform, more reconciliation activities and reparations, among others. The TRC heard witnesses in each district during only one week and did not have the possibility to organise hearings at the lowest administrative levels. Following the TRC's recommendations, the reparations programme has only started to be implemented since September 2008, with funding from the United Nations Peace Building Fund.[37]

The use of tradition-based mechanisms was not part of the official transitional justice policy, although traditional reconciliation and cleansing ceremonies have been used by both demobilisation programmes and the TRC. Further initiatives have mainly been left with religious and civil society organisations. One of such

---

34 Peace Agreement between the Government of Sierra Leone and the Revolutionary United Front of Sierra Leone, 7 July 1999, transmitted to the Security Council on 12 July 1999 (S/1999/777).

35 Agreement between the United Nations and the Government of Sierra Leone on the establishment of a Special Court for Sierra Leone, 16 January 2002. Statute of the Special Court for Sierra Leone, Article1.1.

36 For more details see the website of the Special Court www.sc-sl.org.

37 C. Correa & M. Suma, *Report and Proposals for the Implementation of Reparations in Sierra Leone*, International Center for Transitional Justice, 2009, www.ictj.org/static/Africa/SierraLeone/ICTJ_SL_ReparationsRpt_Dec2009.pdf.

initiatives is the *Fambul Tok* project of the Sierra Leonean NGO Forum of Conscience (Hoffman 2008).[38]

Fambul Tok[39] is a tradition-based mechanism, which uses traditional methods and values, although adjusting them to some extent. The methodology involves several steps, starting with consultations and training (on traditional reconciliation values, mediation, PTSD and human rights), preliminary mediation of cases presented by either victim or perpetrator to a Reconciliation Committee, concluded by a reconciliation ceremony. The latter comprises a bonfire in the evening where victims and perpetrators share their experiences, perpetrators apologize and ask for forgiveness and are being embraced by victims and community leaders. The following day traditional ceremonies are performed to achieve reconciliation between perpetrator and victim; between perpetrator and community and between community and ancestors. Rituals to appease the ancestors may include prayers, sacrifices, the pouring of libation or purification and cleansing.[40] Although many of my respondents viewed reparations as a condition to reconciliation, reality forces victims to accept apologies anyhow, since most perpetrators lack the necessary means. Both victims and ex-combatants I interviewed several weeks after the ceremony said that they had been living peacefully together before, but that there was a lot of mutual distrust, lack of communication and lack of collaboration. (also: Boersch-Supan 2009) They emphasized they felt much better since the *Fambul Tok* activities and said that reconciliation was easier, although it would take time. Sometime after my visit, they started a joined project of communal farming (Schotsmans 2010). Being a civil society initiative, *Fambul Tok* has conducted over 60 reconciliation ceremonies and established 30 projects of community farming since it started in 2008,[41] and thus remains a small scale civil society project.

The *Fambul Tok* project uses the setting of traditional conflict resolution – the African palaver –, the traditional values of mediation and the restoration of relationships and concludes with a traditional ritual of reconciliation with the community and the ancestors. Meanwhile, it integrates modern values: victims, ex-combatants, women and youths participate in the decision and implementation phase, the traditional practices of swearing and oath-taking are replaced by mediation and voluntary confessions and discrimination against women and children is countered by human rights training provided by Forum of Conscience.

---

[38]   Fambul Tok International, *Community Healing in Sierra Leone. Our First Year*, 2009, www. fambultok.org/wp-content/uploads/FTAnnualReport2009.pdf; *Our Second Year*, 2010, www. fambultok.org/wp-content/uploads/FTIAnnualReport2010.pdf.

[39]   Krio for Family Talk, referring to the traditional way of conflict resolution through palaver.

[40]   Manifesto '99, *Traditional Methods of Conflict Management/Resolution of Possible Complementary Value to the Proposed Sierra Leone Truth and Reconciliation Commission*, 2002, 20–23.

[41]   Fambul Tok International, *Community Healing in Sierra Leone. Our Second Year*, 2010, www. fambultok.org/wp-content/uploads/FTIAnnualReport2010.pdf.

In sum, since this analysis is limited to the needs of victims regarding those perpetrators they have to live with after the conflict, it is clear that formal justice did not provide for any accountability, victim participation, reparation or encounter at that level. Meanwhile, the other formal mechanism, the TRC – while granting extensive participation to victims – only provided a minimal number of occasions for acknowledgment of wrongdoing, encounter and apologies at the district level, leaving the issue of reparation to the implementation of its recommendations by the government. While private projects such as *Fambul Tok*, although limited in scope and space, seem to achieve better results with regards to accountability, participation, truth seeking and encounter, they have not been able the fill the need for reparation either, as illustrated above.

5.2. RWANDA: FORMAL JUSTICE AND OFFICIAL HYBRIDIZATION OF TRADITION

Immediately after the genocide, Rwanda opted for criminal prosecutions of all those suspected of having committed the crime of genocide and related crimes against humanity. The idea of a blanket amnesty was outright rejected.[42] Criminal prosecutions took place at several levels. The United Nations created the International Criminal Tribunal for Rwanda (ICTR),[43] which has tried 48 persons so far.[44] Regarding reparations, the ICTR did not provide any possibility for reparations to victims (except for restitution, Article 23 Statute), who could only participate in the trials as witnesses (Rombouts & Vandeginste 2005).

In addition to the ICTR and to some trials in third countries using universal jurisdiction powers (Ferstman & Schurr, this volume),[45] Rwanda prosecuted about 10,000 accused at the domestic level (Schabas 2008, 218; Des Forges & Longman 2004, 59; Ndahinda, this volume). Since Rwanda's justice system is based on the Belgian civil law system, victims can participate in the trials as *partie civile*, i.e. intervene as full parties in the proceeding regarding the establishment of the perpetrator's guilt, present evidence and witnesses, file appeal and claim compensation. The 1996 Organic Law[46] provided for reduced sentences in exchange for confessions, which led to almost 30% of accused confessing and offering apologies.[47] However, the geographical distance to the

---

[42] Republic of Rwanda, Office of the President, *Recommendations of the Conference Held in Kigali from November 1st to 5th, 1995, on Genocide, Impunity and Accountability: Dialogue for a National and International Response*, 1995.

[43] UN Resolution S/RES/955.

[44] Www.ictr.org Status of detainees consulted on 19 April 2010.

[45] Redress & African Rights, *Extraditing Genocide Suspects from Europe to Rwanda, Issues and Challenges*, Report of a Conference Organised by Redress and African Rights at the Belgian Parliament on 1 July 2008.

[46] Organic Law n° 8/96 of 30 August 1996,Offical Gazette n° 17 of 01 September 1996.

[47] Avocats Sans Frontières, *Justice pour Tous au Rwanda*, Rapport Annuel, 1999, 38–39.

courts, the lack of transport and the numerous postponement of cases, among others, often withheld victims from intervening. The law also provided for reparations by both the perpetrator and the Rwandan state, in addition to a Victims' Compensation Fund (see Ndahinda and Muleefu, both this volume). Although the tribunals often granted compensation to the victims and established joint State liability for the damages caused by the previous regime, to my knowledge none of these judgments have ever been implemented (Rombouts & Vandeginste 2005). Meanwhile, a Fund[48] provides assistance (housing, medical care, school fees) to survivors. This assistance is based on the needs of indigent survivors only, instead of repairing the damages of all victims. Victims feel FARG cannot be a substitute to the promised compensation fund.[49] Furthermore, 35 cases of crimes 'of revenge' committed by RPF soldiers have been prosecuted by the military courts at the domestic level,[50] which is generally felt to be disproportionate.

Considering the huge numbers of detainees[51] and the limited capacity of the formal justice system, a new, hybrid *gacaca* justice system was created in 2001,[52] involving a mixture of traditional *gacaca* and modern retributive trials. In contrast to traditional *gacaca*, *gacaca* justice or *inkiko gacaca* is a formalised, state-organised justice mechanism, officially part of the country's transitional justice policy. *Gacaca* jurisdictions – following several modifications – deal with almost all crimes of genocide and related crimes against humanity, except for the crime of organising or planning the genocide at the national or prefecture level. War crimes, such as those committed by RPF military, do not fall under the jurisdiction of *gacaca* justice, nor do revenge crimes committed by either military or survivors. By the end of April 2009 1,138,860 cases had been tried by *gacaca*

---

48 Fond d'Assistance aux Rescapés du Génocide.

49 African Rights and Redress, *Survivors and post-genocide justice in Rwanda, Their Experiences, Perspectives and Hopes*, November 2008, 105.

50 Ministry of Defense, Military Prosecution, RPA soldiers who committed crimes of revenge during and after 1994 genocide and were prosecuted before Rwandan military courts, April 2007.

51 112,000 in 2000 according to Avocats Sans Frontières, *Justice pour Tous au Rwanda, Rapport d'Activités*, 2000.

52 Organic Law N° 40/2000 of 26 January 2001 setting up 'Gacaca Jurisdictions' and Organizing Prosecutions for Offences Constituting the Crime of Genocide or Crimes against Humanity Committed between October 1, 1990 and December 31, 1994, Official Gazette, No. 6 of 15 March 2000, (hereinafter the 2001 *Gacaca* law). Modified by Organic Law N° 16/2004 of 16 June 2004 establishing the Organisation, Competence and Functioning of Gacaca Courts Charged with Prosecuting and Trying the Perpetrators of the Crime of Genocide and other Crimes against Humanity, Committed between October 1, 1990 and December 31, 1994, Official Gazette, No. Special of 19 June 2004 (hereinafter the 2004 *Gacaca* law), adding the need to try the accused with promptitude. Modified by Organic Law N° 28/2006 of 27 June 2006, Official Gazette, No. Special of 12 July 2006; Organic Law N° 10/2007 of 1 March 2007, Official Gazette N° 5 of 1 March 2007 and Organic Law N° 13/2008 of 19 May 2008, Official Gazette N° 11 of 1 June 2008 (hereafter the 2006, 2007 and 2008 *Gacaca* laws).

justice.[53] In July 2010, the process had largely ended, with the exception of some appeal and revision cases.

Gacaca justice has been extensively described, analysed and assessed (Clark 2010; Ingelaere 2008; Haveman 2008; Clark 2007; Waldorf 2006; Ndahinda, this volume; Kaitesi & Haveman, this volume; and many others), which allows me to mention only those features related to the subject of this chapter.

Gacaca justice has been severely criticized for not respecting fair trial standards and leading to many abuses. Even though all agreed that there had been false accusations (rather made by non-survivors than by survivors in recent years), complots of silence (*ceceka*), buying of the hill (*kugura agasozi*: someone takes the blame on him, in exchange for support to the family) and corruption of both judges and witnesses, many of my respondents felt *gacaca* justice had to a large extent achieved its goal of accountability. Survivors even found that the process of establishing individual guilt made it more comfortable for them to interact with those not accused or convicted, since they would previously suspect all Hutu to be guilty.[54] Even if they already knew the truth – which is not automatically the case, since survivors were often in hiding – they were still relieved if the perpetrator acknowledged his role and responsibility.

Surprisingly, many of the survivors I interviewed felt the goal of truth finding was most achieved by *gacaca* justice (in contrast to: Shaw & Waldorf 2010, 18; Ingelaere 2008, 55): many thought *gacaca* justice had been able to reveal much more of the truth than formal justice would ever have. This was mainly attributed to the possibility of reduced sentences and community service, not to any per se willingness of perpetrators to confess. Clearly, they referred to the factual truth regarding the physical acts of killing and the location of bodies, even though the exact role of each perpetrator was not necessarily established correctly, following the practices mentioned above. Factual truth was typically also the only type of truth established by the ordinary courts in Rwanda, in contrast to the ICTR which also examined the historical truth of the genocide (Schabas 2008, 211). Accordingly, those survivors who did not found out the location of their relatives' bodies are very frustrated and cannot find closure, even if the perpetrators are convicted or if compensation for stolen property is granted. Finally, the truth about RPF crimes could not be told in *gacaca* justice, which created a sense of victor's justice (Ingelaere 2008, 55). During my interviews, several relatives of RPF victims, some of which are genocide survivors as well, spontaneously mentioned the need to deal with those cases too.

---

[53]   Information from the National Service of Gacaca Jurisdictions, received in July 2009.

[54]   Penal Reform International (PRI), *The Contribution of the Gacaca Jurisdictions to Resolving Cases Arising from the Genocide. Contributions, Limitations and Expectations of the Post-Gacaca Phase*, 2010, 27. Institut de Recherche et de Dialogue pour la Paix, *Analyse du processus gacaca et de son impact sur la réconciliation et la cohésion sociale au Rwanda. Note de discussion.* Kigali, Mai 2008, 21.

Popular participation was a decisive motive for the government to introduce *gacaca* justice: since the genocide had been committed at the community level, all citizens were supposed to participate and contribute to the truth finding process, which in turn would have an educational outcome.[55] The law (Article 29, 2004 Organic Law) makes it compulsory to all Rwandans to participate and to provide testimony on what they know. In addition, victims can make statements, ask questions and file appeal if the decision does not satisfy them. Nevertheless, the actual popular participation, i.e. beyond mere physical presence, has been one of the most criticized aspects of *gacaca* justice (Shaw & Waldorf 2010; Clark 2010; Ingelaere 2008, 55; Clark 2008, 317).[56] In addition, a number of killings of victims, witnesses and *Inyangamugayo* (*gacaca* judges) instilled some fear to participate (Ingelaere 2009). Some survivors I interviewed also mentioned that they did not feel being taken seriously when they spoke, that the population mocked them, called them deranged etc., thus discouraging them from testifying. Others claimed they had been able to speak freely and to ask questions. Much would depend on the proportion of survivors in the community and in the *gacaca* process, as the presence of only a few victims would allow the community to disregard them more easily (Ingelaere 2009).

While *gacaca* legislation abolished the possibility to claim compensation from the State, the long promised Victims' Fund was finally established on paper in 2008, but has not become operational yet.[57] Only *gacaca* jurisdictions dealing with property crimes can decide on restitution or compensation for the victims. The implementation of such compensation orders has become an important concern to many, considering the amounts granted and the poverty of the convicts. Broadly, survivors present three attitudes: they are willing to negotiate with those convicted persons who have confessed and apologised – assisted by local organisations or the authorities – on the amount, on instalments, or on alternate labour; with others they will either proceed to forced implementation with the help of a bailiff, with the risk of causing even more resent, or simply abandon the hope to ever receive anything. In addition to these compensation orders several memorials and commemoration activities of the genocide take place in Rwanda each year in April. While commemoration is also a form of

---

[55]   Republic of Rwanda, Office of the President, *Report on the reflection meetings held in the office of the President of the Republic from May 1998 to March 1999*, Kigali, August 1999, 57 (hereafter: Urugwiro).

[56]   See also Penal Reform International (PRI), *The Contribution of the Gacaca Jurisdictions to Resolving Cases Arising from the Genocide. Contributions, Limitations and Expectations of the Post-Gacaca Phase*, 2010, 17–18. Avocats Sans Frontières, *Monitoring des Juridictions Gacaca. Phase de Jugement*, Rapport Analytique, no. 2, 2006, Brussels, 21–22.

[57]   Law N° 69/2008 of 30/12/2008 Relating of the Establishment of the Fund for the Support and Assistance to the Survivors of the Genocide against the Tutsi and Other Crimes against Humanity Committed between 1st October 1990 And 31st December 1994, and Determining its Organisation, Competence and Functioning, No. Special of 15 April 2009 (hereinafter 2008 FARG law).

reparation, Sebarenzi (2009, 226), a survivor himself feels that it is counterproductive to reconciliation and rather serves political purposes.

Although in a country where about 15,000 jurisdictions have been operating simultaneously one can certainly not generalize, what seems to have been lacking in many *gacaca* trials is exactly the feature of traditional justice often promoted for its restorative value: encounter or dialogue.[58] As one of my respondents stated: "*Dans gacaca on parle, mais on ne se parle pas,*" meaning "in *gacaca* we talk, but we do not talk with each other". Accused, survivors and other community members take turns in providing testimony, asking questions or giving statements, but do not enter into a genuine dialogue. In previous years, survivors I interviewed often expressed their frustration about the fact that during *gacaca* hearings apologies were offered to "God, the State and the victims", expressed as a legal requirement for reduced sentences, but not addressed to them and that released prisoners did not even make an effort to come and visit them.[59]

According to a report of the National Commission on Unity and Reconciliation (NURC) based on a survey conducted in 2008, the lack of reparations, absence of apologies after *gacaca*, testimonies during *gacaca* and the pressure of government to reconcile are among the main reasons for persisting distrust between survivors and their neighbours.[60] Based on field visits some years before, Buckely-Zistel (2008, 141) found a "shocking absence of projects dedicated to bringing the former parties to the conflict together".

As *gacaca* proceedings are not concluded by consensus, the ritual celebration of the agreement to leave the past behind is equally lacking. Even in a country where traditional rites have disappeared from the public landscape, simple rituals such as sharing a beer or a meal, are often mentioned as signs of reconciliation. But after a *gacaca* hearing everyone just returns home. In other words, there is no closure of the process, and therefore no new beginning. For this reason, many observers I interviewed in 2009 were looking forward to what would come after *gacaca* – the post-*gacaca* – hoping it would bring healing and start a process of reconciliation through sincere dialogue (Ingelaere 2008, 54).[61]

---

[58] Penal Reform International (PRI), *The Contribution of the Gacaca Jurisdictions to Resolving Cases Arising from the Genocide. Contributions, Limitations and Expectations of the Post-Gacaca Phase*, 2010, 16. Institut de Recherche et de Dialogue pour la Paix, *Analyse du processus gacaca et de son impact sur la réconciliation et la cohésion sociale au Rwanda. Note de discussion*. Kigali, Mai 2008, 23–26.

[59] Penal Reform International (PRI), *The Contribution of the Gacaca Jurisdictions to Resolving Cases Arising from the Genocide. Contributions, Limitations and Expectations of the Post-Gacaca Phase*, 2010, 36–39.

[60] 77,6% of survivors distrust their neighbours, compared to 37% of released prisoners and 53,3% of the general population. Republic of Rwanda, National Unity and Reconciliation Commission, *Social Cohesion in Rwanda. An Opinion Survey, 2005–2008*, 2009, 37–38.

[61] Also Penal Reform International (PRI), *The Contribution of the Gacaca Jurisdictions to Resolving Cases Arising from the Genocide. Contributions, Limitations and Expectations of the*

More recent information I gathered shows efforts are being made in this regard. Many survivors I talked to mentioned that the perpetrator, once released and returned to the hills (and probably encouraged by the official discourse on reconciliation), had come to see them, offered apologies directly and negotiated about compensation, at least those convicted to pay any. These survivors mostly said they had accepted the apologies, some with relief, others expressing their lack of choice. Few survivors said they had refused and did not feel ready (yet). Those who had accepted felt the visit was a first step in living together again and developing normal day-to-day relationships.

In addition, in various sectors of the districts of Huye and Rwamagana I visited, projects and associations have been set up in recent years – some by NURC volunteers, others by local organisations or the communities themselves – bringing together survivors with former detainees, relatives of detainees and the 'righteous' (i.e. those who saved people during the genocide) to discuss common problems and set up joint economic projects. Several participants expressed their satisfaction with these initiatives and emphasized how talking with each other and working together had improved relationships among the various categories. Local observers emphasize both the importance of creating space where unity and reconciliation can grow steadily and the genuine intentions of the participants. Nevertheless, they fear that social and political pressure might false the process, in a sense that reconciliation might remain superficial, while people keep many problems in their heart. Indeed, a lot of mistrust remains, regardless of positive signs such as working together in projects, sharing drinks, paying each other visits, participating in marriages and funerals, helping out with transport to the hospital, even mixed marriages and the symbolically very important gift of a cow. With regards to perpetrators who did not confess and remain in prison, but will be released one day, mistrust is even undisputed.[62] Or as one survivor quoted by Hatzfeld (2007, 107) expressed it: "If we talk together, one cannot be sure they will not start (killing) again. But if we don't talk, one can be sure they will try to".[63] Meanwhile, post-*gacaca* initiatives seem to provide occasions for the start of a process of encounter and dialogue, which will certainly take many years.

Summarizing, considering the difficult context and conditions, both the formal and the hybrid tradition-based justice seem to have performed relatively well in view of accountability, truth finding and victim participation. However, the proximity, the testimonies of many community members, the number of jurisdictions and the offer of reduced sentences allowed *gacaca* justice to perform much better in this regard. As to reparations, *gacaca* justice provided for

---

Post-Gacaca Phase, 2010, 47. Republic of Rwanda, National Unity and Reconciliation Commission, *Social Cohesion in Rwanda. An Opinion Survey, 2005–2008*, 2009, 58.

[62] Not only between survivors and perpetrators, but also between those in prison and those outside who have accused them.

[63] Author's translation.

restitution or compensation in cases of property crimes, but not for cases of murder or other injuries. Finally, the possibility for a genuine dialogue between victim and perpetrator was merely absent in both processes. The question is whether encounter as an objective of restorative justice is a realistic expectation for a hybrid mechanism like *gacaca* justice, being a formal procedure guided by the law and by political guidelines of conduct for participants. Perhaps truth finding and accountability through *gacaca* justice – partial as they may be – were preliminary conditions in a long process towards genuine dialogue, of which one can catch a cautious glimpse in Rwanda nowadays.

5.3. UGANDA: OFFICIAL COMPLEMENTARITY

In Northern Uganda, the transitional justice framework is still being developed. Peace negotiations regarding the conflict have been ongoing for many years (Latigo 2008). In 2000, at the request of the Acholi population (the ethnic group of Kony and many of his abductees) an Amnesty law was adopted, granting a blanket amnesty for crimes since 1986 to those who renounce affiliation to a rebel group. This was successful: by August 2009, a total of 23.521 ex-combatants had reported to the Amnesty Commission, of which 53,75% of the LRA, the majority of which was below the age of 18.[64]

In December 2003, president Museveni referred the situation to the International Criminal Court (ICC), which has issued arrest warrants against Kony and his commanders in 2005. The intervention of the ICC concurred with renewed peace negotiations in 2006 which resulted in – among others – an Agreement on Accountability and Reconciliation and the Annexure to the Agreement on Accountability and Reconciliation. These were signed in 2007 and 2008 respectively, by the Ugandan government and an LRA representative, but not by Joseph Kony, who requested in vein that the ICC arrest warrants be withdrawn first.

The agreements provide three transitional justice mechanisms: the establishment of a War Crimes Division at the High Court of Kampala to deal with "serious crimes or human rights violations", but not with "state actors"; the establishment of a truth commission; and the "adoption and recognition of complementary alternative justice mechanisms" to promote reconciliation, including "traditional justice processes". Although the agreements have not been signed by Kony, the government has engaged to implement them. The War Crimes Division has been established in 2008. Only one former LRA commander, Thomas Kwoyelo, has been accused so far. The other two mechanisms provided in the Agreement have not been established yet. Issues of jurisdiction, double jeopardy and complementarity have yet to be dealt with.

---

[64]   Amnesty Commission Kampala, 20 August 2009.

The national courts in Uganda do not have provisions for participation of victims or reparation in criminal trials. It is unclear to date whether the War Crimes Division will have such provisions, since its rules still need to be developed. Although the Agreement mentions the effective and meaningful participation of victims in accountability and reconciliation proceedings, collective as well as individual reparations, its implementation is still awaited for.

Thus, after a yearlong vibrant debate among traditional leaders, the Uganda government, Ugandan and international NGOs, as well as scholars on ICC versus traditional justice (Baines 2007; Allan 2006; among others),[65] both formal and traditional mechanisms have been officially accepted as part of the transitional justice policy. Considering the context, the traditional mechanisms will have to be adjusted to deal with mass crimes, and the debate on such adjustments and the creation of one or more hybrids is ongoing.[66]

In Acholi tradition, many ritual procedures exist for solving various conflict situations, while other ethnic groups have other rituals mentioned in the peace agreement.[67] Extensive use has been made of traditional cleansing and welcoming home rituals, such as *nyono tong gweno* (stepping on the egg on a special stick called *layibi*). In addition, now that people are leaving the IDP-camps (internally displaced persons) and returning home, ceremonies to clean the land of the bad spirits of people killed there are being performed (*tumo cere* or *tumu kir*). The main objective of such rituals, mainly applied to formerly abducted children and adults, seems to be purification and reintegration, not accountability. For this reason, victims in Northern Uganda expressed dissatisfaction with the fact that some LRA commanders had been granted amnesty and even benefits from the government after a cleansing ceremony, without even acknowledging what they did or offering sincere apologies. To many people, amnesty for high and mid-level commanders should be conditioned by truth telling and compensation, which can be achieved through local practices such as *mato oput*.[68] *Mato oput*, a term sometimes wrongly used to indicate any type of traditional reconciliation[69] seems to be the only accountability

---

[65] Also Refugee Law Project, *Whose Justice? Perceptions of Uganda's Amnesty Act 2000: The Potential for Conflict Resolution and Long-Term Reconciliation*, Working Paper No. 15, 2005.

[66] *Beyond Juba, Tradition in Transition*, Working Paper no. 1; Transitional Justice Project of the Faculty of Law, Makerere University, The Refugee Law Project and the Human Rights & Peace Centre, 2009.

[67] Caritus Gulu Archdiocese, *Traditional ways of coping in Acholi. Cultural provisions for reconciliation and healing from war*, 2006.

[68] UNHCHR, *Making Peace Our Own; Victims' Perspectives of Accountability, Reconciliation and Transitional Justice in Northern Uganda*, 2007, 54. Conciliation Resources, *Choosing to Return. Challenges Faced by the Lord's Resistance Army's Middle-Ranking Commander*, London, October 2010, 14.

[69] Caritus Gulu Archdiocese, *Traditional ways of coping in Acholi. Cultural provisions for reconciliation and healing from war*, 2006, 79.

mechanism for homicide in Acholi culture. It comprises the following steps: the perpetrator, haunted by *cen* (bad spirit), or his family contacts the clan elders and reveals what has happened. He will then be confined to his house and not be allowed to share any meals or drinks with others, since the spirit of the killed person may also affect the community. The same applies to the families and clans of victim and killer, thus preventing the conflict from escalating. Elders, representing the chief or *rwot*, will start mediation between the clans of victim and perpetrator to decide on the compensation to be paid. When an agreement is reached and implemented, which can even take years, the families will come together and a ceremony will be performed, including spiritual prayers, ritual sacrifices of animals, the drinking of *mato oput* (the juice of the bitter root of a specific tree) and finally the sharing of drinks and a meal. It is important to note that the ceremonies, which can sometimes be observed by external persons, are only the climax of a lengthy procedure which involves several previous steps, during which accountability is being established. The rituals confirm the reconciliation between the families and with the ancestors.

Obviously *mato oput* will not always be possible for LRA crimes, since many ex-combatants do not know whom they have killed. When an individual is haunted by the spirit of such a person, whose identity he does not know, another ceremony can be performed: *lakere ket* (or: *moyo kom*). This ritual, however, is merely a ceremony to cleans an individual from spiritual impurity and does not seem to include an element of accountability or compensation. It involves the killing of several animals, traditional dances and purification rites with water and fire.[70]

In reality, *mato oput* has not been applied to LRA crimes, or only to a very limited extent, while it is currently used for non-war related killings, even when a person returns after having served a prison sentence (Baines 2007, 110; Allan 2006, 165).[71] Indeed, ex-combatants have only returned from the LRA recently and are still afraid to talk, while many do not know their victims and have benefited from blanket amnesty without any threat of prosecution. In addition, a huge compensation needs to be paid by the clan of the offender (which sometimes is also the clan of the victim) for which no money is available.[72] These high rates

---

[70]   Interviews traditional chief, Caritas Gulu and one beneficiary of lakere ket ceremony, Gulu, August 2009. Caritus Gulu Archdiocese, *Traditional ways of coping in Acholi. Cultural provisions for reconciliation and healing from war*, 2006.

[71]   Also *Beyond Juba, Tradition in Transition*, Working Paper no. 1; Transitional Justice Project of the Faculty of Law, Makerere University, The Refugee Law Project and the Human Rights & Peace Centre, 2009, 27. Caritus Gulu Archdiocese, *Traditional ways of coping in Acholi. Cultural provisions for reconciliation and healing from war*, 2006, 90.

[72]   The Ker Kwaro Acholi, the cultural institution of the Acholi traditional leaders, issued a Law to declare the Acholi Customary Law, 19 June 2001, which provides the payment of 35 herds of cattle and 3 goats for killing another person, in addition to lodging fees to the traditional leaders, as well animals and other items to perform the ceremony.

might either lead to the non-use of *mato oput*[73] or to the fact that victims accept the absence of compensation, as in other countries. However, since many LRA combatants had formerly been abducted and the Government is blamed for not protecting the communities, the idea that the Government should provide reparations is widespread.[74] In general, the idea is that people need to return to their home villages first, settle all the upcoming land disputes, benefit from programmes focusing on economic revival and feel secure, before they will start talking.

While it is early days to compare the yet non-operational transitional justice mechanisms in Uganda, clearly the War Crimes Division will not allow for accountability, truth telling or victim participation regarding low level perpetrators, nor regarding UPDF crimes. Whether ordinary courts will play a role in this regard is unlikely, considering the amnesty. With a cautious note on the challenges caused by the generation long displacement of the population, the dire poverty and others, traditional mechanisms such as *mato oput* seem to have the potential of providing more accountability, truth finding, victim participation and dialogue. Compensation might be problematic once again. It remains to be seen if the process of hybridization of these traditional mechanisms will allow them to safeguard this potential while finding answers to the many challenges.

6.   PRELIMINARY ASSESSMENT

Comparing the consideration of victims' rights and needs in formal and tradition-based justice after mass conflict comes down to using the benchmark of a non-existent ideal to assess two imperfect types of responses. In the three countries, international, mixed or national courts rightly prosecute those who bear the greatest responsibility for the gravest crimes committed. Thus, they contribute to accountability and truth finding for high-level commanders, but hardly to the victims' need for participation, reparation or encounter. In none of the three countries formal, classical justice has been able to deal with all low-level perpetrators with whom victims will have to live again at the community level. Only in Rwanda the formal courts made a serious effort to provide accountability at this level, but the country was soon confronted with the limits of the system. Thus, the formal criminal prosecution model leaves an important accountability and truth finding gap at the level of mid- and low-level perpetrators, while the victims' need for (even non-criminal) accountability has

---

[73]   Caritus Gulu Archdiocese, *Traditional ways of coping in Acholi. Cultural provisions for reconciliation and healing from war*, 2006, 90.

[74]   *Beyond Juba, Tradition in Transition*, Working Paper no. 1; Transitional Justice Project of the Faculty of Law, Makerere University, The Refugee Law Project and the Human Rights & Peace Centre, 2009, 38.

been identified in all three countries. National policy makers or at least civil society have tried to fill this gap, using traditional justice as a source of inspiration to create new tradition-based mechanisms.

Whereas international lawyers do not seem to have a problem with tradition-based mechanisms used for reintegration or reconciliation purposes, they often oppose their use as an alternative to criminal prosecution, since they consider it a contradiction with the prohibition of amnesty for international crimes. This view is based on the equation of the need for justice and accountability with a need for criminal prosecution and sanctions (Orentlicher 2007; Allen 2006). However, the criticism ignores traditional concepts of accountability of which acknowledgement, truth telling, apologies and reparation are important elements. Tradition-based mechanisms have the potential to provide such accountability in the absence or as an alternative to formal prosecution at the lower level.

Indeed, tradition-based mechanisms are not to be considered as mere second-best solutions. Compared to formal justice, their advantage lays in the fact that they are based on local accountability values and on proximity, which allows popular – including victim – participation and ownership.

In reality however, as the examples of the three countries show, the tradition-based alternatives are also imperfect and limited: nor in Sierra Leone, nor in Uganda (as yet) have they been able to deal with large numbers of perpetrators. In Rwanda, *gacaca* justice did, using a highly formalised and highly contested tradition-based hybrid. In neither country, these mechanisms have been able to provide proper compensation to victims. And their outcome highly depends on power relations and the presence of spiritual belief systems.

Spiritual beliefs and social pressure encourage the perpetrator to come forward and acknowledge his wrongdoing *vis-à-vis* the victim in *mato oput* and *Fambul Tok*. In Rwanda, where ancient spiritual beliefs seem to have disappeared, the incentive to confess is offered by the possibility of reduced penalties, one of the formal justice aspects of the *gacaca* legislation. This leads only to a partial factual truth, which victims nevertheless seem to appreciate, since they believe even less truth is revealed in formal trials. It remains to be seen, however, if tradition-based mechanisms can be successful in this regard, when neither pressure inspired by strong spiritual beliefs, social pressure or official sanctions are available.

Tradition-based mechanisms have the advantage that they are community-based processes, although not always community driven, as the example of Rwanda shows. Their proximity to the location of the facts allows for a more important physical participation of the population in the process. Not only can victims attend and listen to what the perpetrator has to say, in addition, the nature of the process provides them with an opportunity to speak out, and even to share their feelings and opinions if they want to. Whether this can be done in person or only through (family) representatives, during preliminary mediation by traditional or other leaders, or also during public sessions and ceremonies depends on each mechanism. Such participation, through the expression of their views, is an acknowledgement as such of their victimhood and the harm caused to them. Whether those victims who would want to participate actually use the opportunity depends not only on proximity, but also on how enabling the social setting is. Here, the physical security of participating victims, the respect for victims' dignity and suffering, the position of the victims in the context of local power relations and community priorities are important. As survivors in Rwanda mentioned, *gacaca* justice does not automatically perform well in this regard, as the way victims are treated often depends on their proportional presence in a given community. Participation is also legally possible – although not always feasible – in formal justice trials in the civil law system, as in Rwanda, but not in trials in the adversary system, where they are only questioned as witnesses. More in general, reflecting existing social values, vulnerable persons, such as women and youth, will not always be able to participate in the same way or to the same extent as adult men in both formal and tradition-based justice.

As mentioned above, tradition-based mechanisms do not offer better chances for effective compensation by the perpetrators than formal trials, even if granted. Compensation for property crimes leads to many discussions in Rwanda – which authorities and local organisations try to solve through negotiation – while survivors remain frustrated over the lack of compensation for capital crimes, promised by the State for many years. In Sierra Leone, victims seemed to have accepted that nothing will come from the perpetrators. In Uganda too, it remains to be seen if tradition-based mechanisms based on *mato oput* or others will be able to provide any compensation. Poverty seems to be the main obstacle here, even though symbolic gestures of reparation, such as providing labour or a token compensation, seem rare too. Often, apologies seem the only type of reparation offered to victims.

As mentioned above, in post-conflict situations where victims have no choice but to live together with the perpetrators they often feel the need for dialogue or encounter. Such encounter is an integral part of the restorative justice process – generally used for minor crimes. Considering proximity and the possibility of participation, tradition-based justice has the potential to provide a better occasion for interaction between victim and perpetrator, for encounter and dialogue, than formal justice. If the perpetrator reveals what happened, allows the victim to question him, takes responsibility for the victim's suffering, offers his apologies and commits to not repeating the past, and the victim has the possibility to accept (or not) such apologies (which is not the same as forgiving) social harmony can be restored. This would require the opening of a setting or space, where victim and perpetrator supported by clan leaders or other community representatives can interact freely. However, tradition-based justice does not necessarily fulfil this expectation. In Rwanda, with exceptions, many feel the *gacaca* proceedings did not offer an occasion for encounter, nor did they bring any closure. The more formalised procedural setting of *gacaca* did probably not allow a real encounter, even though the process of exchanging versions of the truth and listening to each other is important in itself and can create the conditions for future dialogue and encounter. Similar observations have been noted regarding the dissatisfaction of victims who attended public events during which former LRA commanders were cleansed, granted amnesty and reintegrated, while offering apologies only in a very general way (which is different from *mato oput*). Small scale, mainly informal projects like *Fambul Tok,* where rituals are performed after preliminary mediation, seem to provide better opportunities in this regard, for as long as victims are not hastened into accepting apologies. Clearly, formal justice offers even fewer chances for encounter: even when victims are full *parties civiles*, as in Rwanda, and are not discouraged from participation by long distances or lengthy procedures, such trials do not allow a real interaction with the accused. If the latter confesses, he might offer apologies to the victim, probably using a general phrase, as was often the case in the *gacaca* jurisdictions. This can bring some relief, but is not a dialogue.

As mentioned above, the community's interest to restore social balance, reaffirm societal norms and reintegrate the perpetrators so that they can contribute to rebuilding the country is often more important than the individual victim's needs. The community might feel that the victims need to move on with life and to settle with what is available: a certain level of acknowledgment, a certain level of truth telling, a certain level of apologies, a certain level of reparations, or none at all. This traditional precedence of collective goals over individual interests is being countered by the emphasis on the individual in the human rights and transitional justice debate. This does not imply that any transitional justice mechanism should be merely victim-centred. In post-conflict justice victims, perpetrators and the community (both the local and the global) are equally important. Tradition-based justice mechanisms seek to combine traditional justice goals, i.e. the restoration of social harmony, with the rights and needs of individual victims (and perpetrators), inspired by the human rights debate. Following, they try to balance both dimensions and should not be assessed through the individual rights' lens only.

Many victims in the three countries realise all too well that they depend on their family, community and fellow-citizens for survival and support. The communal cosmovision is still a reality, even in war-torn societies. At the same time, civil society organisations provide victims with information on their rights and with support to claim them, which changes their social value system. However, victims are not just passive beneficiaries of rights, they have agency and make choices, as individuals and as part of their community. Such choices may involve claiming or not claiming one's rights, prioritizing certain over others or trading off some against others. They may be the expression of powerlessness or disillusion, but can also be deliberate, realistic choices, considering the options and the communal interest of restoring social balance and achieving sustainable peace. When victims accept that no compensation will come from the perpetrator, this might be inspired by a lack of power to claim any (Stovel 2010, 259), but can also be an expression of commitment to building a new common future considering limited resources (Minow 1998, 106) or of the victim's preference for acknowledgment, sincere apologies and a promise not to reoffend (Hamber 2006, 567). In cases where perpetrators have previously been abducted and forced to kill, as in Uganda and Sierra Leone, not claiming compensation can also be an acknowledgment of this reality. Likewise, social pressure on victims to forgive the perpetrator and to accept him back into the community can be enormous, as in Rwanda, which doesn't mean such forgiveness and acceptance cannot be a deliberate choice of victims. Allowing a victim to withhold forgiveness is part of his empowerment (Minow 1998, 17). Thus, the victim's agency as a community member may include that he accepts the importance of restoring social balance over enforcing a particular individual right, while at the same time pursuing another one for his personal well-being. The future is as important as the past and it is both individual and collective.

7. CONCLUSION

It is time to become realistic and to acknowledge both the limited potential of formal justice after mass conflict and the added value of even imperfect tradition-based accountability solutions. In the three countries studied, victims who have to live with their perpetrators at the community level, express a need for accountability, truth finding, reparations, participation and encounter. These needs are not fully met by either mechanism.

At this lower community level, tradition-based justice mechanisms, building on the society's value system, offer more opportunities for accountability, truth telling and victim participation than formal justice. However, these outcomes are conditioned by the presence of spiritual beliefs and existing power relations. Encounter and sincere dialogue seem to be facilitated by rather informal and small scale settings. Balancing societal goals and individual needs, future tradition-based mechanisms will need to counter power imbalances by integrating human rights, to create the conditions for a genuine encounter between victims, perpetrators and the community, and to insist on a type of reparation meaningful to victims.

Formal and tradition-based mechanisms can coexist, alternate and complement each other. Both systems need to improve their consideration of victims' rights and needs, with an empowering respect for victims' agency as individuals and as community members.

XV. PROSECUTION OF GENOCIDAL RAPE AND SEXUAL TORTURE BEFORE THE GACACA TRIBUNALS IN RWANDA

Usta KAITESI and Roelof HAVEMAN

1. INTRODUCTION

The genocide that hit Rwanda in 1994 has been the topic of many publications, academic and journalistic alike. From the start, a specific focus was put on sexual violence committed during the genocide. Many are the stories of women and men being the victims of rape and sexual torture. By including rape and sexual torture in the list of crimes to be tried, first by state courts, later shifted to the *gacaca* tribunals, these crimes have officially been acknowledged as acts of genocide within the Rwandan judicial system.

Rape and sexual torture were among the last crimes to be tried by the *gacaca* tribunals. Starting mid-2008 and running to mid-2009, about 7,000 cases of rape and sexual torture were tried by 17,000 *gacaca* judges (*Inyangamugayo*) in 1,900 *gacaca* tribunals. Although it is extremely difficult to distinguish between bad and worse acts during genocide, rape and sexual torture may be considered among the worst. Trying genocide cases in general is not an easy task, but it may easily be assumed that trying sexual torture cases are amongst the most difficult; for the judges, and even more so for the victims involved, who have to narrate and relive the most intimate details of acts committed to them.

It is therefore that early 2008 it was decided that the *Inyangamugayo* should receive at least some training about how to deal with rape and sexual torture cases. Because of the language and the very specific experiences, it was decided that the experts/trainers should be Rwandans. Two trainers were identified: a lawyer for the legal issues (the first author of this chapter) and a psychologist for the psychological part of the training (Jeanne Marie Ntete). However, as it would have been impossible for two expert trainers to train all 17,000 *Inyangamugayo* within a reasonable time, it was decided to train a group of about 250 trainers, forming teams of a lawyer and a trauma counsellor, who together would train all *Inyangamugayo* during a three month period. This chapter describes sexual violence during the 1994 genocide on the Tutsi in Rwanda, and the way the *Inyangamugayo* were trained to handle these cases in the *gacaca* tribunals.

2. SEXUAL VIOLENCE DURING THE GENOCIDE

One of the most difficult exercises to perform is probably to quantify the occurrence of sexual violence during the genocide. Many of the victims may have been killed afterwards; some were already dead when being violated (sexual mutilation of corpses); victims who survived have not always been willing to speak about it; witnesses – if still alive – have sometimes been reluctant to testify. Often the response to this problem is that 'every rape is one rape too many', that it makes no difference whether the number of victims is 100,000 or 200,000, both numbers being huge, and similar statements. This may all be true, but the fact that every author again tries to make estimations shows that there is a need to quantify. In the case of genocide it becomes particularly important to know the number, as it is one of the factors to conclude whether the sexual violence and sexual torture was used as a tool to commit genocide, i.e. as a tool to destroy in whole or in part a group on the basis of ethnicity. Bijleveld *et al.* mention various other reasons why quantification indeed is important, of which we would like to highlight one in particular, notably regarding the impact of the sexual violence:

> *Though the large-scale murders that occurred during the genocide uncontestedly destroyed Rwandan society, rape contributed to the destruction in its own way. Rape served to break the resistance, to humiliate victims, as the spoils of war, as revenge, and ultimately to destroy also those who survived rape itself and break up their societies by bestowing them with these victims and their mostly unwanted offspring, and often also with HIV infections. As such, reliable estimates of rape prevalence are necessary to evaluate comprehensively the quantitative impact of the genocide.* (Bijleveld *et al.* 2009, 211)

When trying to quantify sexual violence and sexual torture, the statement of the UN Special Rapporteur for Rwanda, René Degni Séqui,[1] is often quoted, noting that "Rape was the rule and its absence the exception".[2] But without further explanation this does not say that much. Bijleveld *et al.* are the first to make a well-informed estimation of the occurrence of sexual violence during the Rwandan genocide. Based upon the few existing numbers of the genocide (those

---

[1]   UN EcoSoC, *Report on the Situation of Human Rights in Rwanda*, René Degni-Ségui, E/CN.4/1996/68, 1996, 7.

[2]   He made a very rough estimation – between 250,000 and 500,000 – based upon the number of pregnancies resulting from rape.

being killed, survivors, birth rate etc) and an attempt to quantify statements such as the one quoted from Degni-Ségui, they

> *arrive at a total number of 354,440 women who were raped during the genocide in Rwanda in 1994 (...) or somewhat less than half the number of people killed. Based on an estimated population of approximately 7,7 million (...), of whom just less than 4 million were female, more than 350,000 women were raped. This translates to approximately 8,972 rapes per 100,000 women.*

> *Thus, our calculations show that in the 100 days of the genocide, the risk for a Rwandan female to be raped at least once was about 1 in 11, or about 9%. Obviously, the risk for Tutsi women was much higher, being more than 80%.* (Bijleveld *et al.* 2009, 219)

While all these numbers may not represent an accurate figure of victims of rape and sexual torture during the genocide, all writers confirm that the number of gender and sexual crimes committed during the Tutsi genocide was enormous. However, it is not only the number that may give an indication that rape and sexual torture were used as a tool in the genocide, hence become genocidal sexual violence. It is also the intent that counts. Mullins defines genocidal rape

> *as a systematically organized military tactic of terror and genocide (...) used to generate fear in subdued populations, humiliate the population (both men and women), derogate women (through spoilage of identity), and create a cohort of mixed ethnic children to maintain the humiliation/spoilage/domination. Such a use of sexual assault is an orchestrated tactic of warfare or genocide.* (Mullins 2009, 18)

Based upon an analysis of the sexual violence cases prosecuted before the ICTR, he concludes that there was a clear involvement of state agencies and state actors, "more than lenient commanders and over-stimulated men", in rape and sexual torture, used as one of many tools to eliminate the Tutsi population.

> *It was not merely an ad hoc tactic used spontaneously by men during the broader homicidal violence. It was specifically modelled and encouraged by leaders on the ground during the genocide.* (Mullins 2009, 30)

3. GACACA

Gacaca is a formalised form of a traditional way to resolve conflicts. *Gacaca*, previously existing in Rwanda as customary law, refers to a soft kind of grass/ herb – *umucaca* – on which traditionally a community – that is, the men – came together to discuss conflicts within or between families or inhabitants on a certain hill, and sometimes conflicts with 'strangers'. (Reyntjens 1990; Ntaganda 2003). The traditional *gacaca* served as a basis when working out the new *gacaca*, 'adapted to the period in which Rwandans are living', that is: adapted to the specific circumstances of a post-genocide society. The new *gacaca* are bouncing between the customary version and classical state justice, having drifted too far away from the ancient *gacaca* to be called customary *strictu sensu*, but bearing too many customary law characteristics to be considered part of the classical (penal) system (Haveman 2011).

The procedures as well as the crimes to be tried by the new *gacaca* tribunals have been laid down in the law. The preamble of the law is clear on what moved the government of Rwanda to create *gacaca* tribunals:

> *Considering the necessity to eradicate for ever the culture of impunity in order to achieve justice and reconciliation in Rwanda, and thus to adopt provisions enabling rapid prosecutions and trials of perpetrators and accomplices of genocide, not only with the aim of providing punishment, but also reconstructing the Rwandan Society that had been destroyed by bad leaders who incited the population into exterminating part of the Society.*[3]

This law was amended several times, to adapt to problems arising during trials, and to adapt to new and changing realities.

3.1. GENOCIDE AND CRIMES AGAINST HUMANITY

The crimes covered by the *gacaca*-law are crimes against humanity and acts of genocide committed between October 1st 1990 and December 31st 1994, that is starting the day the RPA/RPF invaded Rwanda and the war started. The overarching assumption in the law is that the acts were committed as part of a widespread or systematic attack or with the intent to destroy, in whole or in part, a racial or ethnical group, and therefore constitute crimes against humanity and acts of genocide.

---

[3] This consideration did not appear in the 2001-version of the law. It is an often heard sentence: with the *gacaca* Rwanda shows the world that it can handle its problems itself. Various laws subsequently regulated the *gacaca*: Organic Law N° 40/2000 of 26 January 2001 setting up 'Gacaca Jurisdictions' and Organizing Prosecutions for Offences Constituting the Crime of Genocide or Crimes against Humanity Committed between October 1, 1990 and December 31, 1994, Official Gazette, No. 6 of 15 March 2000 (hereinafter the 2001 *Gacaca* law). Organic Law N° 16/2004 of 16 June 2004 establishing the Organisation, Competence and Functioning of Gacaca Courts Charged with Prosecuting and Trying the Perpetrators of the Crime of Genocide and other Crimes against Humanity, Committed between October 1, 1990 and December 31, 1994, Official Gazette, No. Special of 19 June 2004 (hereinafter the 2004 *Gacaca* law). Modifications and complements can be found in: Organic Law N° 28/2006 of 27 June 2006, Official Gazette, No. Special of 12 July 2006; Organic Law N° 10/2007 of 1 March 2007, Official Gazette N° 5 of 1 March 2007 and Organic Law N° 13/2008 of 19 May 2008, Official Gazette N° 11 of 1 June 2008 (hereinafter the 2006, 2007 and 2008 *Gacaca* laws).

The crimes have been grouped in three categories.[4] The *first category* is formed by those who planned and organised the genocide, those who committed crimes as high ranking officials within religious or state institutions or in militia, or incited to commit crimes, supervised and led others in executing the genocide. Those who committed rape and sexual torture also fall within this category; they stand out as a group for the gravity of the act they committed (or aided and abetted) rather than reflecting its role in influencing others. This category comprises an estimate 10,000 suspects of whom 7,000 were suspected of sexual torture and rape and have been tried accordingly.[5]

The *second category* comprises those who distinguished themselves by the zealousness or excessive wickedness with which they took part in the genocide, the torturers – except the sexual torturers falling in the first category –, violators of corpses, those who 'just' killed someone else, and those who acted with the intention to kill however did not succeed, and other criminal acts against persons without the intention to kill. Within this category about 400,000 cases have been tried.

The *third category* is formed by those who committed acts against property. Also this category numbers up to an approximate 400,000 cases. Although traditionally speaking acts against property do not fall under the definitions of genocide and sexual torture, genocide laws in Rwanda have included this category especially because the destruction was based on the same reasons as the haunting and killing of the owners. The properties were both symbols – for example cows – and sources of livelihood for those persons destined for destruction – like housing –, hence targets for destruction too.

All these crimes include the accomplice, i.e. the person who has, "by any means, provided assistance to commit offences with persons" who committed the said acts themselves.[6] Superiors are criminally responsible for the acts of their subordinates "if he or she knew or could have known that his or her subordinate was getting ready to commit this act or had done it, and that the superior has not taken necessary and reasonable measures to punish the authors or prevent that the mentioned act be not committed when he or she had means".[7]

---

[4]   Article 11 of the 2007 *Gacaca* law. Initially (Article 51 of the 2001 *Gacaca* law) there were four categories. These four categories have been refined and, broadly speaking, by combining the initial 2nd and 3rd category, been brought back to three categories.

[5]   Until the 2007 *Gacaca* law was adopted, the 1st category entailed also those who distinguished themselves by the zealousness or excessive wickedness with which they took part in the genocide, and violators of corpses. As at the end of the information phase of the *gacaca* this category turned out to be too big – about 70–80.000 suspects – to be tried by the regular courts within a reasonable time (as 1st category cases are), the 1st category has been diminished, and these two groups have been shifted to the 2nd category.

[6]   Article 53 of the 2004 *Gacaca* law.

[7]   *Ibidem.*

The law provides for general punishments per category: prison – in custody and suspended[8] –, community service,[9] and the payment of damages. Initially also the death penalty was possible. In 1998, a total of 22 people have been brought to death in public execution ceremonies. Since then, more than 500 1st category offenders have been sentenced to death, but no one has been executed. The death penalty has been abolished in Rwanda in 2007.

Regarding rape and sexual torture – first category – the applicable penalties are life imprisonment or a prison sentence of up to 30 years. An important determining factor is whether the suspect/offender has confessed, pleaded guilty, repented and apologised: in that case the punishment is substantially diminished in order to encourage confessions. Offenders of rape and sexual torture who confessed and repented face a prison sentence between 20 and 30 years.[10] Community service is not possible. Apart from prison, offenders who were 18 years and older when they committed the crimes "are liable to"[11] the withdrawal of civil rights, perpetual or for the duration of the sentence, i.e. the right to be elected, to become leaders, to serve in the armed forces, to serve in the National Police and other security organs, and to be a teacher, a medical staff, a magistrate, a public prosecutor and a judicial council.[12] The rights to be withdrawn and the duration depend on the category and whether the offender has confessed.

3.2. THE PROCEDURE

A small part of the first category accused persons are tried before regular criminal courts, namely the planners and organisers of the genocide. The main part, among who those accused of rape and sexual torture, as well as all second and third category accused persons – the vast majority of all persons accused of genocide and crimes against humanity – are tried by the *gacaca* tribunals. There are three different levels of *gacaca*: the *gacaca* tribunals of the cell (which is the lowest administrative level), the *gacaca* tribunals of the sector and the *gacaca*

---

8   The 2007 *Gacaca* law introduced the suspended sentence; the reason behind it is that the number of persons convicted to prison is expected to be too high to harbour all of them in the prisons.

9   Article 13 of the 2007 *Gacaca* law.

10   Within the group of confessors a distinction has been made according to the moment the confession has been made: before the name was included on the list of perpetrators drawn up by the cell gacaca: 20 to 24 years, and after that moment, when the suspect already appears on that list: 25 to 30 years. This distinction already existed for 2nd category cases, but has been introduced with regards to 1st category offenders by the 2007 *Gacaca* law.

11   We understand that "are liable to" (in the French text: "*encourent*") means: rights may be withdrawn but not necessarily are.

12   Article 15 of the 2007 Gacaca law. In the previous law, art 76, also the right to vote was withdrawn.

tribunals of appeal.[13] Each *gacaca* tribunal is made up of a General Assembly, a Bench and a Coordination Committee.[14]

The general assembly on the lowest level, that of the cell, consists of all the cell's residents of 18 years and older, at least 200 persons.[15] The general assembly for the sector is composed of all judges of the cell *gacaca* in that sector, together with the sector judges and the judges of the appeals *gacaca*.[16] Each bench consists of seven, judges, 'persons of integrity' – the so-called *Inyangamugayo* – and 2 substitutes. They are the lay judges to try the cases before the *gacaca* tribunals. The members of the bench elect out of their midst the coordination committee, that serves as some sort of a daily management team.

Three phases can be distinguished in the activities of the *gacaca* tribunals. The first phase, in particular for the cell *gacaca,* has been the making of a list of persons who reside in the cell, who resided in the cell before the genocide (and locations they kept shifting to and routes they took), who were killed in the cell of residence or outside, who were victimized[17] and whose property was damaged, and the alleged authors of the offences. This can be done on the basis of confessions, guilty pleas, files forwarded by the public prosecutor, material evidence and testimonies, and other information. The second phase for the cell *gacaca* has been to categorize the suspects in one of the three categories of crimes as mentioned above. On the basis of this categorisation suspects were subsequently tried during the third phase.[18] In order to fulfil these tasks the *gacaca* tribunals have various competences, such as to summon any person to appear in a trial, to order and carry out a search, to take temporary protective measure against the property of an accused, and to issue summons to the alleged authors of crimes and order detention or release on parole.[19]

Gacaca tribunals take place once a week, if the quorum is present – that is: five of the seven members of the bench and 100 members of the general assembly – and are public except when decided differently.[20] Decisions are made in consensus and if this turns out to be impossible with an "absolute majority" of its

---

[13] Articles 3 and 4 of the 2004 *Gacaca* law as amended by Articles 1 and 2 of the 2006 *Gacaca* law.

[14] Article 5 of the 2004 *Gacaca* law.

[15] Article 6 of the 2004 *Gacaca* law as amended by Article 3 of the 2006 *Gacaca* law; if the number of 200 persons for the general assembly is not met, this *gacaca* tribunal of the cell has to be merged with another neighbouring *gacaca* tribunal.

[16] Article 7 of the 2004 *Gacaca* law.

[17] A victim is defined as "anybody killed, hunted to be killed but survived, suffered acts of torture against his or her sexual parts, suffered rape, injured or victim of any other form of harassment, plundered, and whose house and property were destroyed because of his or her ethnic background or opinion against the genocide ideology"; Article 34 of the 2004 *Gacaca* law.

[18] See the activities as enumerated in Articles 33 and 34 of the 2004 *Gacaca* law 2004.

[19] Article 39 of the 2004 *Gacaca* law.

[20] Article 17 and further of the 2004 *Gacaca* law, Article 23 amended by Article 5 of the 2006 *Gacaca* law.

members.[21] Decisions and deliberations of judges are made in secret and judgements must be motivated,[22] but proceedings are public, except in cases of rape and sexual torture. Acts of rape and sexual torture – first category acts – cannot be confessed in public; confession will take place behind closed doors. A victim of these acts (or in case of death or incapacity an interested party) chooses one or more members of the seat to submit her complaint, either in words or in writing, or, in case she does not trust the members of the seat for whatever reason, to the public prosecution.[23]

3.3. HEARING AND JUDGEMENT

The steps to be taken during the proceedings before the *gacaca* tribunals have been laid down in the law, separate for the cell *gacaca* and the sector and appeals *gacaca*. For the sector and appeals *gacaca* they are in broad lines as follows (we leave the cell gacaca out, as they are only dealing with property crimes). The sector and appeals *gacaca* start, in case of a confession, with the identification of the defendants and the plaintiff. All charges against the defendant are read out loud as well as the minutes of the defendant's confession. Each defendant may comment on the accusation. Then

> any interested person takes the floor to testify in favour or against the defendant and responds to questions put to him or her. Every person taking the floor to testify on which he or she knows or witnessed, takes oath to tell the truth by raising his or her right arm, saying: 'I take God as my witness to tell the truth'.

The plaintiff describes all the offences suffered and how they were committed, upon which the defendant responds. Then the bench of the *gacaca* tribunal establishes a list of the victims and the offences each of them suffered, upon which the defendant can respond. The minutes of the hearing are read out loud, and when all agree, the parties to the trial, all who took the floor, and the bench put their signatures or fingerprints on the statement of the hearing. Finally, the hearing is closed, or postponed if deemed necessary to obtain further information.[24] When there was no preceding confession the defendant gets the opportunity to confess during the hearing.[25]

Confession, guilty plea, repentance and apology play an important role in the *gacaca* proceedings: a special procedure has been introduced in the law, to which every person who has committed one of the three category crimes has recourse.

---

[21] Article 24 of the 2004 *Gacaca* law.
[22] *Idem*, Articles 21 and 25.
[23] *Idem*, Article 38.
[24] *Idem*, Article 64.
[25] *Idem*, Article 65; see Article 66 in case of a trial *in absentia*.

To be accepted as confessions, guilty plea, repentance and apology, the law determines that the defendant must:

1. give a detailed description of the confessed crime, how (s)he carried it out, where and when, witnesses to the fact, the persons victimized, where (s)he threw their dead bodies and the damage caused;
2. reveal the co-authors, accomplices and any other information useful to the exercise of the public action;
3. apologise for the offences that (s)he committed.[26]

The confession, guilty plea, repentance and apology have to be done before the bench of the *gacaca* tribunal, the judicial police officer or the public prosecution officer in charge of investigating the case. It shall be done orally during the *gacaca* session or in the form of a written statement (bearing his or her signature or fingerprint). An apology however "shall be made publicly to the victims in case they are still alive and to the Rwandan Society".[27]

Offenders who confessed, pleaded guilty, repented and apologised enjoy a substantive reduction of their sentence. First category offenders, however, only benefit from it when they confessed before the moment the cell *gacaca* made up the list of offenders at the end of the information phase, nor does it benefit offenders who confess only during the appeals proceedings.[28]

The judgement contains, apart from information on the proceedings and identity of parties, the charges against the defendant, the facts presented by the parties, the motives of the judgement, the offence of which the defendant is found guilty and the penalties pronounced. The judgement is given at the same day of the final hearing or at the subsequent hearing, in public, the date and time of which all present in the hearing are informed.[29]

3.4. PARTICIPATIVE LAY JUSTICE

The *gacaca* is a form of participative justice. Every citizen is obliged to take part in the *gacaca*.[30] This is less strange than it seems at first glance when read in conjunction with the duty to testify. In the preamble to the law establishing the *gacaca* it is made clear that every Rwandan citizen is obliged to testify on what he or she has seen or knows. The first substantive consideration reads that the crimes were

---

26   *Idem*, Article 54.
27   *Idem*, Articles 59–63.
28   *Idem*, Articles 55–58, art 58 amended by Article 12 of the 2006 *Gacaca* law.
29   Articles 67, 69–70, 83 of the 2004 *Gacaca* law.
30   *Idem*, Article 29; the previous 2001 *Gacaca* law did not contain such a provision.

publicly committed in the eyes of the population, which thus must recount the facts, disclose the truth and participate in prosecuting and trying the alleged perpetrators.

The second one is of the same character:

Considering that testifying on what happened is the obligation of every Rwandan patriotic citizen and that nobody is allowed to refrain from such an obligation whatever reasons it may be.[31]

The message is clear: every citizen is obliged to the take part in the *gacaca*, as all having been witnesses to the crimes. Persons who omit or refuse to testify on what they have seen or know, as well as persons who make a slanderous denunciation, face a prison sentence of three to six months.[32] A similar fate face those who exercise pressure[33] or attempt to do so or threaten[34] witnesses or members of the bench: 3 months to 1 year imprisonment.[35]

The participative aspect of *gacaca* is also demonstrated by the number of persons involved in the *gacaca* as 'judges'. In October 2001, more than 254.000 *Inyangamugayo*, the *gacaca* judges, were elected by the population to fill the benches of about 11.000 *gacaca* tribunals.[36] This means that, together with the suspects, about 1,250,000 persons take part in the *gacaca* in an 'official' capacity, leaving aside the victims and witnesses as well as the population in general who attend the *gacaca* sessions.

The *Inyangamugayo* are ordinary people from the villages: a report for instance revealed that 92% of the *Inyangamugayo* are farmers of whom 81% earn less than 5,000 RWF (appr. € 7) per month, which is a reflection of the general situation in Rwanda. *Gacaca* therefore is also a form of lay justice. This is not uncommon for Rwanda: before 1994 only about 5% of the judges were lawyers.[37]

---

31   The preamble of the 2001 *Gacaca* law reads: "Considering that the duty to testify is a moral obligation, nobody having the right to get out of it for whatever reason it may be".

32   Article 29 of the 2004 *Gacaca* law, doubled in case of a repeated offence. The previous 2001 *Gacaca* law did contain a similar provision in Article 32, with a prison sentence of 1 to 3 years maximum.

33   "Anything aiming at coercing the Seat into doping against its will, translated into actions, words or behaviour threatening the Seat, and clearly meaning that if the latter fails to comply with, some of its members or the entire Seat may face dangerous consequences".

34   "Words or actions clearly meant to threaten the witnesses or the Seat members for a *gacaca* tribunal, aiming at winning acceptance for his or her wish".

35   Articles 30–32 of the 2004 *Gacaca* law.

36   See e.g. Presidential Order N° 12/01 of 26/6/2001 Establishing Modalities for Organizing Elections of Members of Gacaca Jurisdictions' Organs.

37   Compare: in 2006, 95% of the judges are lawyers, not surprisingly all very young. To compare furthermore: before the genocide there was only one faculty of law, producing about 25 lawyers per two year. Moreover, judges were rather marginalised; the main power within the judiciary was with the prosecution and police.

The *Inyangamugayo* have to swear an oath before exercising their duties, including that they work for the consolidation of national unity, without any discrimination whatsoever.[38] They cannot judge in a case in which (s)he is one way or another involved, e.g. when the case concerns relatives, good friends or sworn enemies.[39]

According to the law, *Inyangamugayo* are persons who have not participated in the genocide, are "free of the spirit of sectarianism" and from genocide ideology,[40] are of high morals and conduct, truthful, honest, and characterised by a "spirit of speech sharing". Government officials, politicians, soldiers, policemen and magistrates cannot be elected as *Inyangamugayo*.[41]

Inyangamugayo can be replaced when, for instance, they are absent from the sessions of the *gacaca* for three consecutive times without good reason, having been convicted to imprisonment for at least six months, prompting "sectarianism" or genocide ideology, or doing "any act incompatible with the quality of a person of integrity". Also the bench as a whole can be dissolved, when is it taking "sentimental decisions", lacks "consensus spirit", is incompetent or behaves incompatible with *gacaca* tribunals activities.[42] Involvement in genocide has been an important reason for replacement of *Inyangamugayo*. An alleged 40% of them turned out to having been involved in genocidal activities in 1994 themselves.[43]

4. SPECIFIC RULES REGARDING RAPE AND SEXUAL TORTURE

When the *gacaca* tribunals were first established, they lacked competence to try any of the category one offences including rape and sexual torture. The

---

[38] Article 9 of the 2004 *Gacaca* law.

[39] *Idem*, Article 10.

[40] "(…) an aggregate of thoughts characterized by conduct, speeches, documents and other acts aiming at exterminating or inciting others to exterminate people basing on ethnic group, origin, nationality, region, color, physical appearance, sex, language, religion or political opinion, committed in normal periods or during war."; Article 2 of Law N° 18/2008 of 23/07/2008 Relating to the Punishment of the Crime of Genocide Ideology. See also Articles 3, 5–13.

[41] Articles 14 and 15 of the 2004 *Gacaca* law as amended by Article 3 and 4 of the 2007 *Gacaca* law.

[42] Article 16 of the 2004 *Gacaca* law as amended by Article 4 of the 2007 *Gacaca* law; Instructions N° 06/2005 of 20/7/2005 of the executive secretary of the national service of gacaca tribunals on dismissal of the judge Inyangamugayo from the gacaca tribunal bench, dissolution of a gacaca tribunal bench and replacement of the judges Inyangamugayo.

[43] See e.g. The New Times, 21/22 December 2005: *28.000 leaders implicated in genocide*. This article mentions that since the information gathering started March 2005, the number of 'leaders' being suspected of involvement in the genocide has increased from 688 to 28.477 in December. If understood correctly, over 90% of them are *Inyangamugayo*.

prosecution and trial of rape and sexual torture cases were done by the national public prosecution authority before regular state courts, as all other first category cases. Nonetheless, the *gacaca* tribunals of the cell charged with information gathering had competence in the information phase to hear information about rape and sexual torture. This led to a situation where persons publicly testified about rape and sexual torture and in some cases perpetrators pleaded guilty for these offences. The pilot phase report in 2004 revealed that the public nature of the information gathering and guilty pleas exposed victims of sexual torture to further victimisation, resulting in social and cultural stigma related to the offence, if victims were willing to testify at all.

In response, in 2004 a new law was adopted to address loopholes identified during the pilot phase.[44] Under this law, rules governing guilty pleas and information relating to rape were altered removing the public nature and allowing anybody with such information to report to one *Inyangamugayo* in whom they confided, who in turn would report the case to the public prosecution authority for further investigation.

Since cases of rape and sexual torture remained within the jurisdiction of ordinary courts despite their clear ineffectiveness in prosecuting and judging genocide, this meant in practice that victims and perpetrators of rape and sexual torture did not have the chance to access justice without undue delay.

It is only since 2008 that the *gacaca* tribunals have been given the competence to try some category one offenders,[45] among who those accused of acts of sexual violence: "any person who committed the offence of rape or sexual torture, together with his or her accomplice".[46] The same law introduced new rules of procedure to be followed in adjudicating cases of rape and sexual torture, for instance regarding lodging an accusation for the first time and the role of victims; the closed session trials and the professional secrecy thereto required, including serious punishments in case of breach; and matters of the impact of guilty plea and confessions and sentencing.

With regard to lodging a complaint relating to rape and sexual torture, the law provides that cases arising from the information gathering phase and those already at the prosecution office and ordinary courts are transferred to the competent *gacaca* tribunals. For new claims, the law provides that only the victim has the right to lodge it. Only in case the victim is dead or is incapable of lodging a claim, the law allows any other concerned party to lodge it. All claims are lodged secretly.[47]

---

44   The 2004 *Gacaca* law.
45   Article 6 of the 2008 *Gacaca* law. Most of the 1st category cases were moved to the *gacaca*; a small number of "leaders" were left to the competence of the regular courts.
46   Article 9 para. 5 of the 2008 *Gacaca* law; Articles 1 and 7 establish the powers to adjudicate rape and sexual torture committed during the genocide.
47   Article 6 of the 2008 *Gacaca* law.

The same law prohibits any confession for rape and sexual torture in public.[48] In all the other cases it is required that guilty pleas be made in public and in cases where they have been recorded be read to the public; the rule on acts of rape and sexual torture alters this general rule, it instead establishes a closed session confession. The law requires that also the trials must be in closed session (*in camera* trial) where the general public is excluded except for the persons that the law allows to attend in order to safeguard the smooth running of the trial. These include the participation of trauma counsellors, security officers and a delegate of the *National Service of Gacaca Jurisdictions* (SNJG).[49] As a safeguard for basic human rights, the judgment is pronounced publicly.

This publicity maintains basic protection for the victim but only limited to unveiling the details of the violence. Since the victims are the principle accusers their names are mentioned in the pronouncement of the judgment.

In cases where the accused committed several offences including rape and sexual torture on the same person, the whole trial shall be conducted in closed session; if the victim of rape and sexual torture is different from the other offences, trials will be conducted separately for rape and sexual torture in closed sessions and for the other offences in public.[50]

Penalties were introduced for the *Inyangamugayo* who would breach the secrecy of the *in camera* trial; such breach of confidentiality is not only a reason to be removed as an *Inyangamugayo* but is an offence that is punishable with a prison sentence ranging from one to three years.[51]

The *in camera* trial, prohibition of a guilty plea and confession in public, and the decisive role given to victims in cases of rape and sexual torture to lodge a claim is to ensure that the trial itself does not further victimise the victim or her family. Although it is unusual – and highly disputed – for the victim in a criminal case to determine whether the case should be tried or not, in the case of rape and sexual torture before *gacaca*, this choice was made based on the nature of the crime and with restorative justice as the purpose. Ordinary criminal justice traditionally does not reflect on the needs of the victim and often may do justice at the expense of victims. Restorative justice allows all stakeholders to participate not only in the court but also in the decision to either enter into the criminal process or not. The power given to the victim in cases of rape and sexual

---

48   *Ibidem.*
49   In Rwanda usually the French abbreviation for this service is used: SNJG or *Service National de Jurisdictions Gacaca*. It was established by Law n° 08/2004 of 28 April 2004 on the establishment, organisation, duties and functioning of the National Service in charge of follow-up, supervision and coordination of the activities of Gacaca Jurisdictions.
50   (Instructions of Executive Secretary of the SNJG) Amabwiriza n° 16/2008 yo ku 05/06/2008 y'Umunyamabanga Nshingwabikorwa w'Urwego rw'Igihugu rushinzwe Inkiko gacaca arebana n'imanza z'abaregwa ibyaha bya jenoside n'ibindi byaha byibasiye inyokomuntu byo mu rwego rwa mbere, imanza za jenoside zizava mu nkiko zisanzwe n'iza gisirikare no gusubiramo imanza mu nkiko gacaca Articles 4,5,8.
51   Article 5 of the 2008 *Gacaca* law.

torture allows her to calculate the impact of a criminal trial in advancing or preventing secondary victimisation. An important reason for giving the victim a decisive role in the question of either or not to lodge a claim is the fact that some accusations were lodged maliciously by others in order to expose and further attack the victims, especially given the social context, where victims of these crimes are stigmatised by their families whenever they learn that one is a victim of rape or sexual torture.

In terms of punishment, it should be observed that persons convicted of rape and sexual torture serve only prison sentences and do not benefit from suspended sentences and community service as alternative sentences. Offenders also loose all their civic rights for life.

5. TRAINING THE INYANGAMUGAYO

Shortly before the official publishing of the law moving the majority of the 1st category cases including all rape and sexual torture cases from the regular courts to the *gacaca* tribunals, the idea came up to organise a special training for the *Inyangamugayo* on the specific aspects of these rape and sexual torture cases. In response to the sensitive nature and new procedures, the *National Service of Gacaca Jurisdictions*-SNJG together with the post graduate training institute for the justice sector in Rwanda (ILPD)[52] organised an expert training for persons who in turn would train the *Inyangamugayo* in order to minimize shortcomings during the trial phase of cases relating to rape and sexual torture.[53] The interdisciplinary training covered both legal and psychological aspects of the law and judicial process.

5.1. BACKGROUND TO THE TRAINING

Since it was impossible for the two expert trainers to train the high number of *Inyangamugayo*, a training of trainers was instead conducted after which the trainees eventually conducted the training of the *Inyangamugayo*. The purpose of the training was to give the trainees and consequently the *Inyangamugayo* the

---

[52]   The ILPD-Institute of Legal Practice and Development is the post graduate training institute for the justice sector in Rwanda. The ILPD organises an initial training programme for judges, prosecutors and advocates, as well as continuing legal education for the entire justice sector. The second author was the vice rector academic affairs and research of the ILPD during the time of the training.

[53]   The training was funded by the embassy of the Netherlands in Kigali. The ILPD also approached a human rights organisation active in Rwanda to take part in the training, but they refused, apparently unwilling to get involved in an activity they might want to criticise later.

skills to handle cases of rape and sexual torture, and to facilitate them to realize and feel themselves the sensitive nature of having to testify about such a crime affecting the most intimate aspects of a person's life.

In previous years, the *Inyangamugayo* had dealt with genocide cases involving especially second degree victims, where either the case concerned their relatives or their property. Only in a few cases did they have immediate contacts with the real victim.

Cases of rape and sexual torture were regarded unique in different dimensions. The nature of the offence itself required special attention. The violent nature of the crime left a lot of physical, psychological and social stigma not only to the surviving victim but also to their families and within their communities. Socially and traditionally sexual purity of women is highly expected. Sexual language is uncommonly used and often not personalised when it must be spoken. When information revealing the sexual abuse of especially a member of a family becomes public it creates stigma resulting from the shame attached to the absence of sexual purity.

The fact that in some of these cases a confrontation between the victim and the offender would take place required better management of the trial in order to minimise further victimisation. Sexual language is rarely spoken and heard in the Rwandan public and is often regarded immoral and inappropriate in the public domain. Considering this context, it was required to prepare the *Inyangamugayo* to be ready to hear and encourage the parties to speak about their experiences and sexual ordeal in order to serve justice in a more effective manner. It was also intended to help the *Inyangamugayo* to understand the difficulties involved in speaking about such intimate and violent abuse of a person.

The training manual that was developed had two major components: firstly the legal part relating to the new procedures and rules governing the trial of rape and sexual torture before *gacaca* tribunals and, secondly, the psychological impact of the trials. From the legal point of view, the training concerned rules governing the filing of an accusation, the *in camera* procedure, breach of confidentiality and matters relating to guilty pleas and sentencing. With regard to the psychological aspects participants were trained on understanding sexual violence; the state of the victim; how to assist the victims, *Inyangamugayo* and others involved in order to prevent secondary trauma; and the importance of *gacaca* tribunals in dealing with rape and sexual torture.

The manual as well as the training were prepared and implemented by a team of the first author based on her expertise on *gacaca* tribunals, gender, genocide and the Rwandan criminal justice system, together with a colleague from the department of Clinical Psychology, Faculty of Medicine of the National University of Rwanda, a Rwandan herself, whose research on the psychological impact of *gacaca* tribunals on the perpetrators and victims made her exceptionally competent for the job. Third on the team were different lawyers of the *gacaca* service according to the region they were in charge of.

5.2. HARMONISING THE TRAINING MANUAL

As a matter of procedure, we agreed that the three team members would meet to harmonise the training manual. This meeting turned out to be much more challenging than expected, considering that all of us had been deeply involved with the subject matter for years. The meeting instead turned out to be an eye opener and a turning point in our understanding of rape and sexual torture committed during the Tutsi genocide. Our experience, however rich, could not effectively grasp the complexity of genocidal sexual violence nor the challenges involved in addressing such a complex reality. This was in particular felt after some of the *gacaca* lawyers had shared some challenging cases within their jurisdiction.

Each new case proved extremely complex, different, horrifying, and challenging in terms of facts but also in terms of redress. We specifically remember a case from the western province relating to a detained suspect who had pleaded guilty for having raped a lady who had fortunately survived the genocide. The shock in this case was not only the painful details of the plea but mainly the fact that the alleged victim vehemently denounced the plea, claiming that she had never been raped. In such a situation one wonders what and to whom should justice be done. One wonders whether any legal system has the potential to prove or disprove such a case especially in such a tradition where oral testimony forms the most available and in many cases the only information. At first glance, one assumes the suspect is probably out of mind, especially in legal systems where guilty pleas are discouraged to avoid self-incrimination. On the other hand, to avoid immediate and blunt conclusions it is necessary to take the contextual aspect of the case into account. The perpetrator probably wishes to come to terms with himself, with the community and with God, especially since the role of community and religion in making guilty pleas has proved to be an effective tool. From another angle maybe, the denying victim might indeed be correct in stating that she was never abused, and the pleading suspect is instead trying to destroy her social networks since he is aware of the social stigma and orchestration attached to being a victim of rape and sexual torture. Given the context, it could also be true that he indeed raped her, but that she has decided to go on with her life and therefore keeps that part of reality as a secret to avoid any further stigma and pain. Should in that case her wish be honoured and the prosecution be stopped? And what if her son, who witnessed and even was forced to take part in the torture, demands prosecution?

Another case concerned a woman who, at the time of the genocide, was raped and forced to cohabit with a man, and later continued to stay with that man and live as husband and wife. Her relatives had reported him as her rapist. The supposed victim had come to the *gacaca* lawyers in the area expressing that the man now is her husband and that she loves him and resists those accusing him as malicious and ill intending. How could the *Inyangamugayo* be prepared to face and handle such a case? The victim has created a new life with her previous captor although the reason of her choice is not self-explanatory. Is she still his captive and is she speaking from her own choice? But what if her choice is now deliberate; does this guarantee no prosecution for her now beloved husband? Doesn't she instead seem to obstruct justice? How does this balance with the desire to eradicate impunity and establish the truth?

Furthermore, the *gacaca* lawyers revealed that in some areas, especially in the southern and western provinces, a number of victims will never see justice before the *gacaca* tribunals or any other criminal justice system yet they desperately want it. The reason is that in some parts of the country the genocide was executed very effectively by a high participation of the then government soldiers, and, in some cases, foreign soldiers as revealed by the Mucyo commission,[54] especially for the victims in the *zone turquoise*.[55] In these cases victims will not be able to recognise the perpetrators because they were unknown to them, being deployed soldiers and foreigners.

When the lawyers raised these kinds of cases they seemed to seek an expertise approach from us, only to realize that we were first of all not capable of resolving cases at that level but also that we were unable to grasp the magnitude of a topic whose complexity depended on each and every individual case, yet massive in numbers. Genocide is a very shocking crime, yet the real shock of the cruelty of the Tutsi genocide can better be revealed by the details of the trends that rape and sexual torture took. Every case reveals that any legal framework is poorly equipped to capture the character, cruelty and impact of the offence. As experts on matters relating to the law, we realised that the absence of details on sexual offences under Rwandan law was in itself a limitation; the Rwandan penal code only criminalises rape and indecent assault. Having to fit what had been done in these legal boxes would be too demeaning, yet they represent the legal lines from which redress could effectively follow. Indeed so much heinous violent acts were

---

54   The *Commission Nationale Indépendante chargée de Ressembler les preuves montrant l'implication du l'État Français dans les génocide perpétré sur Rwanda en 1994*, established by Organic Law nr. 05/2005 of 14 April 2005; generally referred to as the Mucyo commission after its President, Jean de Dieu Mucyo. Its report was published 17 November 2007.

55   *Opération Turquoise* is the code name, generally used, to indicate the intervention of France during the genocide, 'securing' the south western part of the country – *zone Turquoise* – from the approaching RPF/RPA in favour of the old regime; in this part of the country the genocide continued when the rest of the country already had been overtaken by the RPF. The Security Council allowed France to intervene in Rwanda under Chapter VII: SC Resolution 929 of 22 June 1994. For some of those cases see the Report of the Mucyo Commission, pp. 90, 102, 262 and 268.

committed that both ordinary and legal language just lacked words to express and grasp its magnitude.

From sharing knowledge and experiences with the *gacaca* lawyers, we realized that our task and duty was yet one of becoming partners in the process of grasping the manner and nature of rape and sexual torture during the genocide and in the process of applying the law created to address these crimes. However frustrating the meetings with the *gacaca* lawyers could be, working hand in hand with them was most assuring, especially because of their familiarity with the process of seeking for solutions. The head of the team of lawyers argued with his colleagues to not despair, reminding them that for any case that would prove difficult they would have to return to the 'garage', the name given to their meeting room in order to study and seek for means to resolve the problem within the limits of the law. They expressed commitment to finding legal solutions to any arising case, and expressed that they would deal with each case as it came up instead of seeking for a generalized solution. He advised that in some cases it would be important to speak to the parties involved to understand their positions in order to give the right advice, and where this would not work out, the lawyers had to return to the 'garage'.

5.3. THE TRAINING

The training was organized in order to prepare the 17,000 selected *Inyangamugayo* in 1,900 *gacaca* benches that had the duty to try cases of rape and sexual torture. Given the number of *Inyangamugayo* and the need to expedite the long awaited justice, this specific training targeted persons who were yet to train the *Inyangamugayo*. It aimed at training a total of 240 trainers composed of 120 *gacaca* District Coordinators and 120 trauma counsellors, who subsequently would train the 17,000 *Inyangamugayo*. The *gacaca* District Coordinators, most of whom were lawyers, and the trauma counsellors from IBUKA, an umbrella organization of Survivors' organizations,[56] were chosen because of their knowledge of the functioning of the *gacaca* tribunals and their familiarity with the experiences of the victims of the genocide in general and those of rape and sexual torture in particular.

From a logistical point of view, the training of the *Inyangamugayo* had to start as soon as the trainers had been trained. The SNJG-*National Service of Gacaca Jurisdictions* agreed with the ILPD-*Institute of Legal Practice and Development* that because of the importance the training would carry, no trials relating to rape and sexual torture would begin than after the concerned

---

[56] The trauma counsellors are partly professional counsellors, partly genocide survivors themselves who got a short training some years ago in order to be able to counsel other survivors.

Inyangamugayo had been trained. Hence, the training was organized in a manner that whenever the trainers finished their training, they would immediately begin their training of *Inyangamugayo,* often in about two days. Subsequently, procedures to try the rape and sexual torture cases began as soon as a bench of *Inyangamugayo* had been trained, in order to minimize the delays in trials. The southern province was trained first because of the number of cases in the province, which, as revealed by the SNJG, was more than half of the entire gender violence case load nation-wide. Twelve 'train the trainers' groups were formed, each consisting of maximum 20 trainees (10 lawyers, 10 trauma counsellors), resulting in ten teams of a lawyer and a counsellor per group. This resulted in a total of 120 teams of a lawyer and a trauma counsellor, that subsequently trained the *Inyangamugayo* in groups of 27 persons each (= 3 benches of *Inyangamugayo* per training). The 'training of trainers' took about 8 weeks (3 days each group); the training of *Inyangamugayo* about nine weeks (2 days each group). Hence the total training programme took about ten weeks, with the training of the first *Inyangamugayo* starting the second week, as soon as the first trainers had been trained. For logistical purposes the trainings were conducted in the nearest possible training centres in the district from where the trainees came.

The training had to be interactive and small in number to facilitate full participation of those trained in order to better equip them for the training that they would conduct with the *Inyangamugayo*. Whereas the training on the legal part could have been done in bigger groups, for the skills part of the training it was essential that it would be exercised in small groups, in order to let each and every trainee individually experience the difficulty of speaking about sexual violence and subsequently obtain skills to work with persons who face this ordeal.

Methodologically, the training of the trainers ran for three days. At the beginning of each training, the purpose and intention of the training was stressed. Trainees were reminded that even though the *Inyangamugayo* they would train have been serving as such for a while, they deserved special training. Firstly because of the new legal procedures especially based on the nature and consequences of sexual violence. Secondly, they were reminded that a fundamental difference with previous genocide cases tried would be the fact that in many of these sexual violence cases primary victims will face their abusers, different from those of category two and three offenses in which trials focused mainly on victims who had been killed or property that had been destroyed. It meant remembering and telling about what happened to oneself rather than remembering and talking about what happened to others. Victims were invited to relive their own ordeal before the tribunal. Neither the victim nor the accused were expected to go through such trial without personal effects. Thirdly, and equally important, was the fact that, even though none of the information about genocide has ever been easy to hear and understand, the nature and forms of rape and sexual torture victims suffered were yet to shock the conscious of the *Inyangamugayo*. Hence the training was to prepare them, however minimal it would be, for the task ahead. In these trials, words almost never heard in public were bound to be heard; cases of a complexity hardly imaginable had to be managed, in particular the manner in which the victims, perpetrators and *Inyangamugayo* could afford justice on matters deemed so secretive in Rwandan society.

After an introduction of the participants, the trainers and the programme, the training than started with aspects of the law with emphasis on the procedures and their application. On the second day trainers discussed the psychological aspects of the training and its purpose. In this regard the trainer involved the trainees to trying to understand all the persons involved in the trial ranging from the victim, perpetrator, *Inyangamugayo* and others allowed to participate in the trial. Trainees were divided in groups to elaborate in detail on the psychological state of the victim and the perpetrator before trial, during trial and after the *gacaca* trial. At all times both the counsellors and District Coordinators participated together.

On the third day, one that we would consider the most interesting one, participants, through a role play, played the *gacaca* trial. In the following paragraphs, we will discuss in more detail issues discussed during the 36 days training project and their implication to justice.

5.4. SHARING EXPERIENCES: BREAKING THE ICE

Just like during the preparatory meeting with the lawyers of the SNJG, the most difficult moments concerned the particularity of the cases rather than the process. Starting from the southern part of the country made the task even harder because statistically speaking this province registered more than half of all sexual violence cases that *gacaca* tribunals were to handle. Thus, the trauma was equally big. Other than the legal issues we often introduced for an hour into our discussion, participants were initially invited to speak about a very intimate experience, which many choose not to do, as well as to speak about a sexual violence case that they knew about. As the first trainer for all groups, the burden of having them start talking about this was solely mine.[57] This was not only important for the individual trainee but for every one, because it would often reveal the context in which gender violence was committed in that specific region and the level at which the genocide was executed. Often, when trainees remained silent, I shared a case of sexual violence which I call 'breaking the ice'. Although the initial reaction was always "we all understand what happened" and "must we

---

[57] This paragraph describes the experience of the first author of this chapter during the training.

speak of such evil?", often the ice was broken when I shared the story of my friend, a survivor of genocidal sexual violence.

Nana's story, like most of the stories heard during the training, is one of pain and suffering. She was fourteen years when the genocide begun, the seventh born and second last of a family of four brothers and two sisters. Her dreams and those of her family turned into a nightmare from the 7th April 1994 when two of her brothers and her mother were killed in cold blood. She and the rest of the family ran for refuge in different places; in search of her refuge, she moved during the night and hide in the day for three days from Ruyenzi, her home village, to Nyamirambo, hoping that reaching the home of her elder sister married to a Hutu would save her. Nana's life was shattered on the second day at her sister's house when her brother in law gave her to a group of *Interahamwe*[58] as a ransom for the protection of his wife and children who were not accepted as purely Hutu due to their mother's blood. The *Interahamwe* took her to a seemingly abandoned house from which sounds of screaming and groaning came. Upon entering the house, Nana was stripped naked and violently raped; she remembers she lost her consciousness when the seventh man raped her. Most of her abusers forced her to also drink their sperm from the condoms they had used.

After narrating Nana's story I insisted that participants should share related stories familiar to them. For purposes of clarity I will reproduce some of the cases that our trainees narrated. I should observe that each case was difficult and that the first hour of each new group of trainees was intimidating because I would hear what I assumed was the worst, until the worst could not seem worse enough in the next group. Nevertheless, during the training I realised that this difficult information is what victims want to be known of their pain. It was even harder because most trainees spoke of cases of persons they knew. relatives, mothers, sisters, children or neighbours.

The first participant of the first group to speak was himself a genocide survivor. He spoke of the case of his sister whose suffering he did not witness but had been told about upon inquiring about her death. He began his sharing by taking a deep breath, his eyes turning red and acting very nervous. He then said that it is not easy and not even important to speak about the pain that his sister died of. He narrated that she was first forced to nudity by the youth in their neighbourhood who then resorted to not only mocking her but also beat her breasts until she became unconscious. When she regained her consciousness, she pleaded with her tormentors to give her water to drink. Instead, one of them took his nailed cabs (stick), inserted it in her vagina and as she bled, her tormentor and other *Interahamwe* present took a container, collected the blood from her vaginal bleeding and forced her to drink it. I remember him finishing by

---

58 The *interahamwe*, initially a youth movement formed early 1990's and linked to the then ruling party MRND, developed into a militia which became the motor behind de genocide.

questioning if there could be any justice for such "beasts". When he finished talking, the room was different; participants that initially seemed resistant or even laid back, looked tense and a number of them raising hands to share their cases.

The second trainee, a trauma counsellor, shared about her client who had been raped and then had broken bottles inserted into her sexual organs. This victim, according to the counsellor, identified herself as living with hell, and she had developed a distinct smell and could only afford to speak with a person who could sustain her smell.

Trainees revealed that male victims were also numerous although social stigma and cultural beliefs discourage them from revealing their ordeal. Many cases are known of young boys who were beaten into erection in order to make it possible to have sexual intercourse against their will. Examples include cases of boys as young as seven being forced into sexual intercourse with their mothers. In one case the *Interahamwe* intended to have the mother transmit HIV/AIDS to her seven year old son since she had just been raped by an HIV/AIDS positive *Interahamwe*. One of the torturous cases, though not unique in any one region, concerned mutilating the sexual organs of a man, often husband, and forcing their wives to use the mutilated organs to rape themselves. Some men were forced to have sexual intercourse with their children, parents, and enemies. They were mutilated, castrated, hanged by their sexual organs. Some middle aged men were in different places laid down nude and forced to have sex with dead animals like dogs and cats specifically killed for that purpose by the perpetrators, while the family members of the victims were forced to watch. Bestiality is unaccepted and even unimagined in Rwandan society. The genocide apparently allowed the perpetrators to humiliate their victims into doing anything unacceptable in the community. Such cases included both male and female *Interahamwe*.

6. EPILOGUE

Genocidal rape and sexual torture is extremely difficult to understand and to explain, different as it is from 'ordinary' sexual violence.

First of all, it is not too daring to say that rape and sexual torture were used as a means of genocide. An illustration of this is Mikaeli Muhimana, who, during his trial, expressed that when he mistakenly had raped a Hutu woman confusing her to be Tutsi, he apologized to the victim.[59] Further, sexual violence was not only committed against women but also against men, children and elderly persons. And although predominantly by men, sexual violence was perpetrated by children and women as well. In light of this, Nowrojee argues that "[t]he sexual violence that took place during the Tutsi genocide was not some sort of

---

[59] *Prosecutor v. Mikaeli Muhimana*, Case No ICTR-95–1B-T (April 28, 2005), p. 571.

random, opportunistic, unfortunate by-product of the genocide. This was a tactic of genocide".[60] It is important to reflect rape and sexual torture for what they represented in the Tutsi genocide, different from any other previously recorded wars.

It is also clear that rape and sexual torture was widespread and systematic at least. The stories narrated above are no mere incidents. Eyewitnesses of the genocide like Major Brent Beardsley and General Romeo Dallaire expressed that

Rape was one of the hardest things to deal with in Rwanda on our part. It deeply affected every one of us. (…) [T]he hardest thing that we had to deal with was not so much the bodies of people, the murder of people. I know that can sound bad, but that wasn't as bad to us as the rape and especially the systematic rape and gang rape of children. Massacres kill the body and rape kills the soul. And there was a lot of rape. It seemed that everywhere we went, from the period of 19th of April until the time we left, there was rape everywhere near these killing sites.[61]

And that:

When they killed women, it appeared that the blows that killed them were aimed at sexual organs, either breasts or vagina. They had been deliberately swiped or slashed in those areas. And secondly, there was a great deal of what we came to believe was rape, where the women's bodies or clothes would be ripped off their bodies. They would be lying back in a back position, their legs spread, especially in the case of very young girls. I'm talking girls as young as six, seven years of age. Their vaginas would be split and swollen from obviously multiple gang rape, and then, they would have been killed in that position. So they were lying in the position that they had been raped.[62]

Further, the Rwandan reality reveals that sexual torture or 'rape' during the genocide in many cases can by no means be compared with the rape that Askin referred to as a normal act in life – sexual intercourse – except for the non-consent or force used.[63] Of very few of the rape and sexual torture cases during the genocide as for instance described above one can say that the act as such – not taking into account the force or non-consent – is ordinary.

However, speaking of those extreme cases can easily elude into forgetting the number of abuses falling into the category of 'normal' sexual abuse, like what we

---

60   B. Nowrojee, *The Media and the Rwandan Genocide*, Symposium, 13 March 2004, www. rwandainitiative.ca/symposium/transcript/panel1/nowrojee.html (last visited: 25 February 2010).

61   *The Prosecutor v. Théoneste Bagosora et al.*, Transcripts, Case No. ICTR-98–41-T, 3 February 2004, pp. 51–52.

62   *Ibidem.* Binaifer Nowrojee on the expert testimony of General Romeo Dallaire and Major Brent Beardsley in the ICTR case against *Théoneste Bagosora*, (ICTR-96–7).

63   K. Askin, *The Presence of Sexual Violence in Conflicts: A Historic Perspective*, Presentation at the Interdisciplinary Colloquium: Sexual Violence as International Crime: Interdisciplinary Approaches to Evidence, The Hague, 17th June 2009.

term as classical rape (referring to sex without consent), forced marriage and sexual slavery. 'Ordinary' rape within the context of the genocide did not necessarily constitute a serious issue especially because of the nature of relations of families and neighbours in whose vicinity the crimes happened and the trials were to be held. Many of the neighbours understood that someone was forced into sexual or apparent marital relations just because of the genocide. Nevertheless, especially women and girls who suffered these seemingly more common 'agreeable' rapes were traumatised because they often feel guilty and are accused of apparently trading off their bodies for protection. Here, we particularly remember the testimony of a surviving victim speaking of being abused by a government soldier who kept her into his house and warned his soldiers and *Interahamwe* to never touch her. This woman, even though realising the abusiveness of this commander who never knew her before and violently had sex with her, telling her how many other Tutsi had been raped and killed, and threatening to release her into such violence if she persisted, regrettably seems to have appreciated the fact that her abuser at least saved her from much more violent abuses suffered by fellow Tutsi women. Her narration leaves a feeling of the common personal and social blame faced by such victims of sexual violence, who exchanged their bodies for their own protection. She struggles with the desire to express that she did not choose to stay with her abuser although seemingly it was a lesser evil. Often the coerciveness of this abuse is not as eminent as that of the most obvious cases described above, but the fact that her staying was instigated by the genocide makes it equally grave. This illustrates another issue that arose during the training, notably the absence of definitions in existing laws.

Lastly, eyewitnesses' testimonies, especially those expressed during the trainings, filled the missing gap of sexual torture against men (in some cases committed by women). This reality makes it clearly different from what is often put forward by feminist scholars, that rape and sexual violence is a weapon of male dominance against women (e.g. Jasinski 2001; see also MacKinnon 1991; Brownmiller 1975). Existing literature and decided cases do not reveal much on rape and sexual torture of men and boys. Nonetheless, this should not indicate the absence of those acts in the genocide; instead the even greater social stigma on the attack against their manhood (*ubugabo bwabo*) should be blamed for the silence. Research has mainly remained focused on women's victimisation in matters of rape and sexual violence, thus not revealing the extent to which men indeed suffered in this regard.

The impressions expressed above are hard to understand and difficult to place in a framework that could explain what happened. Many cases express that what is called rape and sexual violence during the genocide is totally different from 'ordinary' rape and sexual violence. Accordingly, the 'ordinary' explanations for rape and sexual violence seemingly do not suffice in the context of the genocide in Rwanda. Consequently, it seems no longer clear how to respond to genocidal sexual violence. One way to respond to it could be through establishing state responsibility for these violations. The *gacaca* in Rwanda is another example of how to respond to genocidal rape and sexual torture.

The new *gacaca* approach to rape and sexual torture during the genocide has created an innovative judicial approach that takes into consideration the complex reality of the victims of rape and sexual torture. It not only moves away from classical criminal justice that does not consider the impact of a judicial process to the victims of the crime, but also deviates from *gacaca* in ordinary genocide cases. These deviations from the ordinary *gacaca* in cases of genocide in general include professional secrecy, closed trial sessions, no obligation for the victim to reveal what she or he knows, and a decisive role for the victim regarding the question whether or not to lodge a claim. These deviations appeared to be crucial to satisfy the specific needs of the victims of rape and sexual torture during the genocide. The *gacaca* approach to rape and sexual torture may not be an all-encompassing solution without flaws, it is, however, a new approach to a complex problem without precedence.

XVI. THE ROLE OF CIVIL SOCIETY IN ADDRESSING PROBLEMS FACED BY VICTIMS IN POST-GENOCIDE RWANDA

Alphonse MULEEFU

1. INTRODUCTION

Writing about the role of 'civil society' in addressing problems faced by victims in post war and post genocide Rwanda is complex and challenging. The subject is too wide-ranging to be covered in one chapter and any attempt to do so would not do justice to the subject matter and the people it concerns. Such complexities exist for three main reasons.

Firstly, the definition of the civil society does not provide a border of clear bold lines and its composition is extremely vast. Civil society is understood as a complex of non-state / governmental organisations created for the promotion of a certain or some shared value(s) in society. It centres on a

> (...) collective action around shared interests, purposes and values. In theory, its institutional forms are distinct from those of the state, family and market, though in practice, the boundaries between state, civil society, family and market are often complex, blurred and negotiated. Civil society commonly embraces a diversity of spaces, actors and institutional forms, varying in their degree of formality, autonomy and power (...).[1]

Civil society is believed to be composed of

> registered charities, development non-governmental organisations, community groups, women's organisations, faith-based organisations, professional associations, trades unions, self-help groups, social movements, business associations, coalitions and advocacy group.[2]

---

[1] Definition adopted by the London School of Economics Centre for Civil Society's www.lse. ac.uk/collections/CCS/what_is_civil_society.htm, last updated: 1 March 2004.

[2] *Ibidem.*

Discussing the role of civil society in a country like Rwanda where every person from at least a young age, is encouraged to belong to a certain mutual benefit cooperative or association for purposes of community development and social cohesion,[3] is like being asked to tell a story about every Rwandan. Cooperatives which are coordinated by the Rwanda Cooperative Agency (RCA) bring together individuals in numerous professional categories, agriculturalists or farmers, small processing and marketing groups, workers/employees of different institutions, artisanal and handcrafts, fishery, consumers, youth and women.[4] Such different cooperatives add to the already existing Rwanda Private Sector Federation (RPSF), an umbrella of 9 professional chambers, that promotes business in Rwanda,[5] the *Centrale des Syndicats des Travailleurs du Rwanda* (CESTRAR), an umbrella of 21 workers unions,[6] *Pro-Femmes Twese Hamwe,* a coalition of about 27 women's associations which operates in different sectors including assisting victims of the 1994 genocide,[7] the *Ligue des Droits de la personne dans la région des Grands Lacs* (LDGL), a coalition of non-governmental organisations working in the Democratic Republic of Congo (DRC), Burundi and Rwanda (11 out of 27 member organisations are Rwandan local NGOs),[8] the *Conseil de Concertation des Organisations d'Appui aux Initiatives de Base* (CCOAIB), a coalition of Local NGOs that are mainly involved in developmental local initiatives, with 32 member organisations,[9] and the Legal Aid Forum (LAF), a coalition of about 33 local and international NGOs committed to legal aid services in Rwanda.

This list of civil society organisations is not exhaustive. Civil society also includes small different mutual benefit associations, students and youth groups, women and faith based groups, registered at local administrative authorities

---

3   Republic of Rwanda, Ministry of Trade and Industry, National Policy on Promotion of Cooperatives, (Unknown date of publication), pp.1–2, available at www.minicom.gov.rw/spip. php?article27 (last visited: 6 July 2010).

4   *Ibidem.*

5   Rwanda Private Sector Federation (RPSF), brings together the Chamber of Agriculture & Livestock, Chamber of Industry, Chamber of Commerce & Services, Chamber of Tourism, Chamber of Tourism, Chamber of Crafts, Artists & Artisans, Chamber of Liberal Professionals, Chamber of Women Entrepreneurs, Chamber of Young Entrepreneurs available at www.amis.minagri.gov.rw/content/rpsf-rwanda-private-sector-federation (last visited: 6 July 2010).

6   *Centrale des Syndicats des Travailleurs du Rwanda* (CESTRAR), created by MRND in 1985 by the then single ruling party. In 1991when Rwanda started multiparty politics, CESTRAR became independent from political parties and got its legal personality in 1992 and is currently composed of 21 workers' unions; see its history at www.cestrar.net/menu/menu1b. php?recordid=7 (last visited: 6 July 2010).

7   Website *Profemme Twese Hamwe,* www.profemme.org.rw/ (last visited: 13 July 2010).

8   *Ligue des Droits de la personne dans la région des Grands Lacs* (LDGL), *Qu'est-ce que la LDGL?* www.ldgl.org/spip.php?article1 (last visited: 11 July 2010).

9   See the list of 32 member organizations that make the coalition of CCOAIB on their website at, www.ccoaib.org.rw/index.php?option=com_content&view=article&id=69&Itemid=48 (last visited: 15 July 2010).

where their projects are based. Most of these local associations directly or indirectly contribute to the national reconciliation process and assist victims and survivors of the genocide. Having many civil society organisations is not new to Rwanda; it is believed that before the 1994 genocide, "[t]here was approximately one farmers' organization per 35 households, one cooperative per 350 households, and one development NGO per 3,500 households" (Kelly 1999, 59–60).

Second and probably linked to the first reason is that it is very hard to make a categorical distinction between the contribution of a certain local civil society organisation from another one, or to separate what is being done by local civil society organisations from international non-governmental organisations and coalitions that bring up local and international NGOs. The composition of these coalitions and their member organisations is in itself complex. One organisation can be a member of different coalitions, and a coalition itself can be a member of another coalition. AVEGA for example, the association of widows survivors of genocide, is a member of *Pro-Femmes Twese Hamwe*, IBUKA and LAF; at the same time *Pro-Femmes* and LDGL coalitions are members of the LAF. Such coalitions are mainly aimed at bringing together civil society efforts to realise shared values, but it sometimes makes it complicated to establish each organisation's contributions. Most projects are jointly implemented and or funded. Similarly, the most challenging of all is that such an intertwined coexistence extends to different government agencies and ministries. The Government provides funding to some projects of the civil society, and sometimes the Government jointly implements some projects together with the civil society.

The third reason why writing about the role of 'civil society' in addressing problems faced by victims in post war and post genocide Rwanda is complex and challenging is related to enormous problems victims and survivors face in a society where also ordinary citizens face extreme levels of vulnerability and poverty. It is extremely difficult to distinguish the role of civil society purposely aimed at assisting victims of genocide from initiatives that are designed to help vulnerable Rwandans in general. Thus, this paper does not attempt to define who the victim is, due to the conviction that it would be an oversimplification to distinguish victims in a society where the majority of the population were either direct or indirect victims of the war and the genocide. This does not mean that it should not be studied, but doing it in this short chapter risks drawing quick conclusions that would neither serve the purpose of civil society nor that of the victims and the society as a whole. Victims of the genocide can be placed in both categories, that is as vulnerable victims and as vulnerable Rwandans in general. The high level of poverty that existed shortly before the genocide combined with the aftermath of war and the 1994 genocide against the Tutsi left Rwanda in shambles. All sectors in the country were destroyed and more particularly, the lives of victims were shattered. In addition to the unspeakable killings and acts of torture, perpetrators had also targeted properties of victims. Due to pillage, looting and destruction of property and the effects of mental and physical disabilities, some victims are still trapped in extreme poverty. The most affected are children-orphans, widows, and the elderly. Destruction of houses during the genocide left a number of victims with no shelter; more than sixteen years after the genocide thousands of vulnerable survivors still have no proper homes. Some women and girls were gang raped, others intentionally infected with HIV/AIDS, different sorts of objects and fluids were put into victims' sexual organs resulting into different incurable vaginal infections and HIV/AIDS, which continue to claim the lives of victims across the country. Such problems are exacerbated sixteen years after the crimes due to increased sickness, trauma, depression, despair and grief. There is limited access to free anti-retroviral treatment; the health condition of those to whom treatment is provided is weakened by lack of a balanced diet required for effective treatment.

The purpose of this paper is to serve as a tribute to the work of NGOs but most importantly highlight the challenges they face and those faced by victims. But it is impossible to cover such a wide range of issues and actors in a thorough manner without conducting an in-depth research into the subject. I will therefore limit the scope of this chapter. It starts with a brief description of the role of some of the Rwandan organisations. In addition, the role of some international NGOs will be briefly mentioned. Then I will note a number of challenges faced by civil society in assisting victims.

2. SOME CIVIL SOCIETY ORGANISATIONS

After the 1994 genocide, a number of organisations focusing on specific needs and concerns of victims were created. Some were created by victims themselves while others were created by individuals who felt that there was a need to pay special attention to problems faced by victims and survivors of the genocide. These organisations have worked in collaboration with the Government, United Nations agencies together with other civil society organisations, local and international, in lobbying and advocating for the cause of victims of genocide and other crimes against humanity committed in Rwanda. Where possible direct support has been offered to some specific needs. Organisations discussed in this chapter are not the only ones involved in assisting victims; they serve as a mere illustration of the activities undertaken by many other members of the civil society in Rwanda.

A.E.R.G

L'association des Etudiants et Elèves des Rescapés du Génocide (A.E.R.G), is a non-profit making and non-governmental association that was formed in 1996 on an

initiative of about 20 students at the National University of Rwanda, after facing
the challenge of a high number of school drop-outs among survivor students. It
is currently represented in 12 institutions of higher learning in Rwanda and in
about 220 secondary schools with about 30,000 members. A.E.R.G was created
for the promotion of quality education to children survivors of genocide, to help
their fellow students in obtaining documents necessary for government
scholarships, collect information on students school drop-outs, provide a voice
to students survivors of genocide, provide housing, and deal with the high level
of trauma and extreme poverty affecting students.[10]

A.O.C.M

L'Association des Orphelines Chefs de Ménages (A.O.C.M), created on August 22,
2000, is a non-profit making association of children orphans of the 1994
genocide/heads of households.[11] Formed to deal with a lot of shared challenges
orphans heads of households faced, decided to put together their meagre efforts
through this association by focusing on education, health, housing and justice.[12]

A.R.C.T. – Ruhuka

L'Association Rwandaise des Conseillers en Traumatisme (A.R.C.T.) – *RUHUKA*,
was created in April 1998, on the initiative of 13 Professional Trauma
Counsellors. It is a non-profit making and non-governmental association. In
1995, these trauma counsellors received training on handling traumatic
challenges in Rwanda by TROCAIRE International. A.R.C.T members have been
using the acquired expertise through their program of trauma healing, awareness
and group healing, to help students in various schools deal with trauma.[13]

A.S.R.G. – Mpore

L'Association de Soutiens aux Rescapés du génocide (A.S.R.G.) – *MPORE*, the
association for support of survivors of the genocide was created on February 1,
1995. A.S.R.G. – Mpore has the mission of contributing to the reduction of the
physical and moral impact of the genocide and abuse of power, defending and

---

[10]   A.E.R.G website www.aerg.org.rw/index.php?&aboutus (last visited: 7 July 2010). See also
       One Dollar Campaign, Project 1, Feasibility study for an AERG project proposal to develop a
       hostel and training centre for AERG members, available at www.1dollarcampaign.org/project.
       html (last visited: 10 July 2010).
[11]   SURF, AOCM (Partner of SURF), available at www.survivors-fund.org.uk/projects/partners.
       php (last visited: 10 July 2010), see also Rwanda Development Gateway, of August 9, 2005,
       'Premier congrès national des enfants orphelins chefs de Ménage,' available at www.
       rwandagateway.org/article.php3?id_article=864 (last visited: 10 July 2010).
[12]   Musila Cyril, *L'Association des Orphelines Chefs de Ménages* (AOCM), Paris, Février 2003,
       available at www.irenees.net/fr/fiches/acteurs/fiche-acteurs-72.html (last visited: 10 July
       2010).
[13]   Registered by ministerial decree number 97/11 of 28/07/2004. A.R.C.T Ruhuka, *Rapport Final
       du Projet "Trauma Awareness, Healing and Group Counselling"*, available at www.
       businessdaily.rw/tmp.html (last visited: 10 July 2010).

promoting victims' rights, encouraging collective memory of the genocide and educating people of Rwanda on mutual understanding, tolerance and peaceful co-existence.[14]

AVEGA – Agahozo

L'association des Veuves du Génocide Agahozo-AVEGA, is a non-profit making and non-governmental organisation created in 1995 on the initiative of 50 widows survivors of the 1994 genocide, currently composed of over 25,000 widows of the genocide and thousands of orphans.[15] In addition to two decentralised regional offices, AVEGA has four main departments: (a) the *Program Psycho-Socio-Medical (P.P.S.M.)*, that offers trauma counselling, operates a medical support unit and offers financial support and treatment to members that were infected with HIV/AIDS during the genocide; (b) the department of Social and Economic empowerment, which department helps in elaborating micro-credit projects for AVEGA members and in obtaining financial support for income generating projects of members; (c) the department of Advocacy, Justice and Information, which deals with the collection of information and dissemination, defending/protection and promotion of orphans and widows' rights, and carries out lobby and advocacy for the benefit of AVEGA members; (d) the department of Capacity Building and Finance, which is responsible for the administration, financial management, fundraising, drafting of annual and financial reports.[16]

IBUKA

IBUKA, formed in 1995, is a non-profit making organisation that brings together all individual victims and about 15 different associations of survivors of the 1994 genocide committed against the Tutsi.[17] IBUKA, which means '*remember*', was created to address issues related to justice, to keep the memory, commemorations and documentation of the 1994 genocide, to fight genocide denial and revisionism, to advocate for social and economic support for victims and to coordinate related initiatives.[18]

---

[14] Musila Cyril, ASRG- *Mpore, L'Association de Soutiens aux Rescapes du génocide,* Paris, Fevrier 2003, available at www.irenees.net/fr/fiches/acteurs/fiche-acteurs-71.html (last visited: 10 July 2010).

[15] Approved by Ministerial decree n°156/05 on 30th October 1995. AVEGA, *Information Générales sur l'association AVEGA* (obtained from Uwase Sabine, AVEGA department of Advocacy and Justice, 01/04/2009), see also www.avega.org.rw/historique.html (last visited: 10 July 2010).

[16] *Ibidem.*

[17] Registered by Ministerial Decree number 029/17 of 11 October 2001. Republic of Rwanda, Ministry of Justice, (February, 2003) Seventh Periodic Report of Rwanda to the African Human and People's Rights 1999–2002, DOC/OS/(XXXVI)373b, pp.22–23.

[18] *Op. cit*, see also the mission of IBUKA available at www.ibuka.net/pres.html (last visited: 10 July 2010), see also www.neveragaininternational.org/news/ibuka.html (last visited: 10 July 2010).

Rwanda Partners

This is a Christian based organisation that promotes reconciliation and healing
in Rwanda. It is mainly working with 'Widows and Victims of Rape, Orphans
and Child-Headed Households, Rural Poor Women, Impoverished Rural
Families, Genocide Survivors and Street Children' through reconciliation and
healing programmes and income generating projects. It also started the Centre
for Champions Street Kids, that takes care of street children, first founded by the
Presbyterian Church of Bellevue (a US-based church), operated by African
Evangelistic Enterprises/Rwanda (AEE), a Rwandan non-governmental Christian
interdenominational, multicultural ministry of evangelism, reconciliation,
leadership development training, relief and community development.[19]

Solace Ministries – Rwanda

Solace ministries was established in 1995 with the aim of comforting widows
and orphans through counselling and trauma healing, income generating
activities, education and community based development.[20] Created on the
initiative of Jean Gakwandi, Solace Ministries has expanded into other partner
Solace Ministries in UK,[21] Australia,[22] USA,[23] and Germany.[24] Solace Ministries
Rwanda is also a partner organisation to MUKOMEZE, a Dutch non-
governmental organisation started by Anne-Marie de Brouwer and Freek
Dekkers to support female survivors of sexual violence during the 1994
genocide.[25]

Together against Impunity in the Great Lakes Region (TAI/GLR)

Together against Impunity in the Great Lakes Region (TAI/GLR) is a non-profit
making and non-governmental organisation that was established in 2005,[26] for
the promotion of victims' rights according to the 1985 United Nations
Declaration of Basic Principles of Justice for Victims of Crime and Abuse of
Power. TAI/GLR's mission is not limited to victims of genocide, but since they
form the biggest part of the crime victims in Rwanda, special concern for victims
of the genocide is central to the organisation's mission. It focuses on influencing
prosecution policy changes to ensure that criminal justice administration is

---

[19]   Rwanda Partners website, www.rwandapartners.org/ourpartners.php (last visited: 10 July
2010).

[20]   Solace Ministries website www.solacem.org/ (last visited: 10 July 2010).

[21]   See website Solace Ministries UK, www.solaceministriesuk.com/ (last visited: 11 July 2010).

[22]   See website Solace Ministries Australia, www.solaceministriesaustralia.com/solace/
about%20us.htm (last visited: 11 July 2010).

[23]   See website, Solace Ministries USA, www.solaceusa.org/ (last visited: 10 July 2010).

[24]   See website Solace Ministries Germany, www.solace-ministries.de/ (last visited: 11 July 2010).

[25]   Mukomeze website, www.mukomeze.nl/eng/pagina18.html (last visited: 10 July 2010).

[26]   TAI/GLR is registered by Ministerial Decree N°. 69/11 of 12 April 2006, Official Gazette N°10
of 15 May 2007.

sensitive to victims' issues and at the same time helping victims and the entire population to understand victims' rights for effective implementation.

UYISENGA N'IMANZI
UYISENGA N'IMANZI, established in 2002 as a local non profit making and non-governmental organisation aimed at addressing needs of orphans of genocide and AIDS. In addition to perpetuating the memory of 1994 genocide and promotion of justice and peace, it ensures that children orphans are involved in national recovery and reconstruction programs, it focuses on social economic empowerment of children orphans, medical assistance, counselling, education and training.[27]

3. CIVIL SOCIETY INTERVENTIONAL ROLE

The role of the civil society organisations can be placed in one of three main categories:

(a) An intermediary role, where civil society has acted as an interlocutor between victims and the Government. Civil society helps in identifying the categories of the most vulnerable victims and contributes in choosing the kind of priority assistance victims need.
(b) Civil society has been influencing the state to meet its obligations towards the victims. This has been through reports on the situation of victims, conferences and meetings with state institutions concerned.
(c) Civil society in some situations has offered direct assistance to victims, thus reducing the gap left by the assistance provided by the Government. This has been through projects funded by either international organisations, grants/ donations from foreign government and or individuals.

As briefly introduced, the needs of victims of the 1994 genocide are enormous. Throughout these three main categories, the contribution of civil society relates to these needs, to be distinguished into poor health conditions, extreme poverty, education and training, poor housing, search for justice and reparations and persistence of genocide ideology and insecurity. This section will show what has been the role of the civil society in finding solutions with regard to these issues.

---

[27] Registered by Ministerial decree no 70/11 of 10th August 2005. UYISENGA N'IMANZI website http://uyisenganmanzi.org/index.html (last visited: 10 July 2010).

3.1. HOUSING, POVERTY AND EDUCATION

Rwanda was one of the poorest countries shortly before 1990. The civil war between 1 October 1990 and the genocide that started in April 1994 left a number of Rwandans in extreme poverty.[28] It has been claimed that any conflict that results into killing of people, destruction of properties, displacements (internal or external), and a breakdown of social cohesion and institutions, pushes households into poverty, even those that were not originally poor (Justino & Verwimp 2008, 3). The fact that perpetrators targeted properties of Tutsi and destroyed houses and cattle, together with the huge number of children orphans and widows, and a high level of physical and psychological impact of the genocide, affected the socio-economic situation of victims and their housing conditions in particular (Verpoorten & Berlage 2007; Mutebi, Stone & Thin 2003). The problem of poverty is the mother of many other problems victims face. Poverty exacerbates other needs, like health, education, housing, reconciliation and safety.

Housing is a huge problem. AVEGA for instance claims that a big number of their members need housing.[29] That requires a lot of funding that most associations are not able to raise, therefore most of their work has focused on advocacy and lobbying to ensure that there is something concrete done to get housing for thousands of homeless victims. Most of housing activities are mainly funded by the FARG.[30] FARG is a Government Fund that was created in 1998 to assist vulnerable victims of genocide and other crimes against humanity committed from October 01, 1990 to December 31, 1994.[31] FARG has been a strong partner of civil society in assisting victims in different sectors including poverty reduction and housing projects. FARG has the responsibility of providing the following assistance to various categories of victims:

(a) Building houses to the elderly people who survived with no a single child or who are needy, widows, widowers, orphans and disabled.

---

[28] See Koster M., 'Linking Poverty and Household Headship in Post-Genocide Rwanda', Paper selected for presentation at the HiCN's Fourth Annual Workshop, Yale University, New Haven, USA (5/6 December 2008), available at www.hicn.org/FourthAnnualWorkshop_Koster.pdf (last visited: 13 July 2010); see also The International Development Association (IDA), Report, *Rwanda: From Post-Conflict Reconstruction to Development*, August 2009, p.1, available at http://web.worldbank.org/WBSITE/EXTERNAL/EXTABOUTUS/IDA/0,,contentMDK:21358166~pagePK:51236175~piPK:437394~theSitePK:73154,00.html (last visited: 13 July 2010).

[29] AVEGA, Informations Générales sur l'Association, (unpublished, obtained from Sabine Uwase on 01/04/2008, Department of Justice and Advocacy), p. 4.

[30] A variety of government ministries, institutions and agencies, are working with or supporting the civil society in assisting victims in different ways.

[31] Law n° 02/1998 of 22/01/1998 creating the national fund for assistance to victims of genocide and massacres perpetrated in Rwanda from 01 October 1990 to 31 December 1994, (Official Gazette n° 3 of 01/02/1998).

(b) Paying school fees for the needy orphans at least until the completion of the second level of higher education (similar to a Bachelor's degree).

(c) Providing medical treatment to the needy and handicapped victims and to those infected with incurable diseases through rape and sexual violence.

(d) Determining permanent financial assistance to the elderly and incapacitated victims.

(e) Provide support to income generating projects to improve social economic conditions of victims.[32]

The Fund collaborates with civil society and local authority administration to identify the needy beneficiaries. 6% of the annual domestic income of the State Ordinary Budget is allocated to FARG, and it gets grants from individuals, associations, (inter)national organisations and foreign countries, profits from activities carried out by genocide convicts in the community service as an alternative sentence to imprisonment, interest from deposits and investments of the fund, legacies and donations and other means.[33] From the year 1998 up to 2007, houses that had been occupied were 11,352 out of 14,000 houses that were needed according to the needs assessment that was carried out in 1998. In 2008, the activity to provide shelter to genocide survivors was reinforced and the Government undertook to continue in the pursuit of solving this problem although the number of beneficiaries that needed houses continued to increase as it was shown by reports from Districts. At the beginning of the year 2008, out of 15,122 houses that were needed by Districts to solve the shelter problem, 8,802 houses were erected. Out of these houses, 2,990 were completed, 4,263 are in the process of being finished whereas 1,014 houses are at the level of roofing.[34] Until July 2010 the Fund has provided 13.3 billion RWF (appr. € 15 million) for housing in which 38,657 houses have been constructed, but still about 173,663 genocide survivors need proper housing.[35]

Although there is a recognized success in what the Fund is doing,[36] a report from an auditing team revealed in 2010 serious cases of misuse, corruption and

---

[32] Article 4 (4°-8°), Law N° 69/2008 of 30/12/2008 relating to the Establishment of the Fund for the Support and Assistance to the Survivors of the Genocide Against the Tutsi and other Crimes Against Humanity Committed between 1st October 1990 and 31st December 1994 and Determining its organization, Competence and Functioning (Official Gazette n° Special of 15/04/2009).

[33] As it might be determined by the Minister in Charge of supervising the Fund. Article 22, Law N° 69/2008 of 30/12/2008.

[34] The Ministry of Local Government and the Ministry of Finance and economic Planning, Strategies to improve the performance of the genocide survivors' assistance fund (FARG), Study released in January 2009, p. 6.

[35] The New Times, (Edwin Musoni) 'Rwf 13bn spent on Genocide survivors' houses –FARG', Kigali, 13th July 2010, available at www.newtimes.co.rw/index.php?issue=14320&article=31286 (last visited: 13 July 2010).

[36] *Recommending* of the Preamble, United Nations General Assembly Resolution, 'Assistance to survivors of the 1994 genocide in Rwanda, particularly orphans, widows and victims of sexual

embezzlement of funds blamed on top and lower officials of the government, civil society and beneficiaries.[37] FARG is also blamed for contracting with some private constructors who left a number of houses unfinished and some beneficiary victims were unable to raise money themselves to complete the construction; most of these houses were later destroyed by rain.[38]

Civil society has tried to tackle the problem of housing faced by vulnerable victims and or survivors of genocide whose houses were destroyed during the genocide, by joining the government program of construction of so called *Imidugudu*, small agglomerations, and reconstruction of damaged houses, but their contribution still remains insignificant.

The One Dollar campaign, an initiative of the Rwandan community in Diaspora with the support of the Ministry of Foreign Affairs, started a campaign for the construction of houses for the vulnerable orphaned children students without shelter and without homes to go to during holidays. In 2010 it was revealed that the campaign has received about 885 Millions RWF (appr. € 1 million) of 1.4 billion pledges for the project that will cost about 4 billion. It was also reported that some construction materials were pledged in kind. If this project is successfully finished it will house about 800 students out of about 4000 students that are in similar situation.[39]

Poverty too is being dealt with by both FARG and civil society. Small income generating and self-help projects have been started and grants or credits have been found to increase the economic status of victims.[40] Groups of widows have been facilitated through different associations and cooperatives to receive micro-loans through banks to start income-generating activities to enable them to escape poverty. The same activities are supported through the Multi-sectoral AIDS Program (MAP) funding. At the headquarters of each AVEGA decentralised office, sales shops were opened where various items produced by its members are sold. These include items like baskets, tablecloths, juices and wines of bananas or pineapples, bead necklaces and knitted items. In 2003, with

---

violence' (A/RES/64/226), adopted in the 67th plenary meeting of 22 December 2009 distributed 2 March 2010.

[37] The Republic of Rwanda, the Senate, *Sena yafashe imyanzuro kuri raporo ya FARG*, available at www.parliament.gov.rw/re/index.php?option=com_content&task=view&id=549&Itemid= 259 (last visited: 13 July 2010).

[38] Rombouts H., *Women and Reparations in Rwanda, A Long Path to Travel*, available online at www.ictj.org/en/research/projects/gender/country-cases/1823.html (last visited: 16 July 2010).

[39] See the website of One Dollar Campaign, www.1dollarcampaign.org/index.html, also report ORINFOR, (by Mutesi Théopiste), '15th July Set for the Launch of the One Dollar Complex,' www.orinfor.gov.rw/printmedia/topstory.php?id=875, see also The New Times of May 18, 2010, 'RDRC Donates to One Dollar Campaign', (by Bosco R. Asiimwe) www.newtimes.co. rw/pdf.php?issue=14315&article=29265.

[40] IBUKA, *Raporo y'Ibyagezweho* 2007 – power point presentation, p. 13.

financial support from the Survivors Fund (SURF),[41] AVEGA undertook the construction of an administrative block, a clinic and a hall, to be rented for meetings and trainings. This centre is an income generating project to meet the urgent needs of vulnerable members. AVEGA also grouped widows into three types of livestock activities; cattle, goats and pigs keeping.

Msaada, (a Swahili word meaning 'help') has been offering support to survivors of Genocide through AVEGA and through the Survivors Fund.[42] Msaada provides bursaries to about 70 children at Excel Bilingual School, a parent funded school that teaches in English and French, and is assisting about 100 students in Rwanda to attend primary and secondary education. It has donated a science library to Rwamagana Secondary School.[43] Msaada also supports a honeybee project in Nyarubuye Sector, Eastern Province that is helping about 200 families generate income. It supported AVEGA to reconstruct destroyed houses.[44]

The education of children survivors of the genocide is mainly provided by the government through FARG. Depending on the availability of funding, FARG sets grades on which it will sponsor students and those who are not taken are the ones who are largely taken up by the civil society. But still not all can be funded to the level of university – civil society has helped some of them get vocational trainings like tailoring and carpentry and few have been offered sponsorship to higher institutions of learning. To those in primary and secondary schools, different members of civil society have provided scholastic materials and created social and leisure opportunities to reduce children's isolation.

It is estimated that about 20,000 children were born out of rape.[45] It has been unclear[46] and sometimes wrongly implied from Article 27 of the FARG law, which prohibits persons who participated in the genocide and other crimes against humanity to benefit from the fund, to exclude children born out of rape with an obvious assumption that their fathers are perpetrators of genocide. Foundation Rwanda started in February 2007 assisting those children by

---

[41]   Survivors Fund Supporting survivors of Rwanda genocide, www.survivors-fund.org.uk/, see also Msaada, Infrastructure, at www.msaada.org/Msaada/Infrastructure.html (last visited: 15 July 2010).

[42]   Msaada is a UK based development agency established in 2005 on the initiative of Fergal Keane, a journalist and writer who was a reporting on the killings in the Eastern Province during the 1994 genocide is involved in helping survivors especially from that province. See the History of Msaada at www.msaada.org/Msaada/History.html (last visited: 15 July 2010).

[43]   Msaada, 'Education', available at www.msaada.org/Msaada/Education.html (last visited: 15 July 2010).

[44]   Msaada, 'Livestock' at www.msaada.org/Msaada/Livestock.html, see also Msaada, 'Humanitarian' at www.msaada.org/Msaada/Humanitarian.html (last visited: 15 July 2010).

[45]   BBC, *Rwanda's children of rape*, available at http://news.bbc.co.uk/2/hi/programmes/newsnight/8768943.stm (last visited: 16 July 2010).

[46]   Rombouts H., *Women and Reparations in Rwanda, A Long Path to Travel* (2006), available at www.ictj.org/en/research/projects/gender/country-cases/1823.html (last visited: 16 July 2010).

providing school fees, help them and their mothers to psychological and medical health services and raise awareness on the consequences of sexual violence and rape through media and photography.[47] SURF Rwanda, through KANYARWANDA, a non-profit making association created for the promotion of unity through social justice, gave bursaries to 60 children born out of rape in Kamonyi district, Southern province to attend secondary education.[48] SEVOTA, created to rebuild broken social fabric, is also focusing on needs of widows and orphans. It promotes different initiatives for development and self-sufficiency to improve livelihoods of its beneficiaries, in particular children born out of rape.[49]

The association of orphans heads of households, AOCM, reported in 2008 that they were able to support 30 students to study as private candidates in secondary schools. SURF Rwanda and the Donald & Lorna Miller family, a California group,[50] helped AOCM to continue paying tuition fees in private universities for 90 orphan heads of households who were unable to get support through the government fund. In 2008, AOCM had a budget proposal of 26,035,200 RWF (appr. €30,000) for ending year parties for children to be celebrated in 13 districts.[51] Similarly, AERG, the association for child survivors (now students), seeks financial support through different grant foundations like SURF RWANDA for their colleagues who completed secondary education but never got a chance to attend higher education through the government fund to study in private universities. ASRG–MPORE has been teaching how to read and write in Ngoma district. Fifty orphans heads of households have been taught how to make fertilizers and pesticides to use in their gardens. Additionally, ASRG–MPORE has a dormitory in Gacuriro, a suburb in Kigali City, for homeless genocide orphans attending vocational trainings in CFJ/GACURIRO, a youth vocational training centre.[52]

---

[47] Founded on the initiative of Jonathan Torgovnik, a photojournalist. Foundation Rwanda, 'History and Mission' available at www.foundationrwanda.org/ (last visited: 16 July 2010).

[48] Association Pour la Promotion de l'Union par la Justice Sociale, Kanyarwanda, '*Raporo y'Igenzura Ry'umutungo n'Ibikorwa Kanyarwanda*', (October 2009), pp. 8–9, available at www. kanyarwanda.org/docs/rapport_controle_2009.doc (last visited: 15 July 2010).

[49] An association created on 28 December 1994 in Taba-Gitarama, Southern Province. SEVOTA website, www.sevota.org/ (last visited: 17 July 2010).

[50] Donald E. Miller is Professor of Religion at the University of Southern California and Lorna Touryan Miller is Director of the Office for the Creative Connections at all saints Episcopal Church in Pasadena, California. Her parents survived the Armenian genocide. Both co-authors of Survivors, An Oral History of the Armenian genocide. they have been supporting AOCM for a long time, see also, A bond born of genocide http://articles. chicagotribune.com/2007–04–15/news/0704140068_1_hutu-extremists-rwandans-armenian-genocide.

[51] AOCM asbl, *Fêtes de Fin d'année 2008 pour les orphelins chefs de menages, Octobre*, 2008 as signed on 22/10/2008 by Rwamasirabo Roger, President of the association.

[52] ASRG – MPORE asbl, *Incamake ya raporo y'ibikorwa na Gahunda y'Umuryango* ASRG – MPORE (1995–2010), *Nyakanga*, 2008. See also, Press release (No.: RWoDA/013/08) of August

Different foreign agencies are involved in grass-root cross-cutting projects aimed at socio-economic empowerment of victims. Norwegian People's Aid (NPA) is focusing on women and youth rights, justice, democratisation, reconciliation and land issues in Rwanda. NPA is a partner organisation to more than 14 local organisations including some that are supporting victims of the 1994 genocide like *l'Association pour la promotion de la femme et de l'enfant* (APROFER), a local organisation with focus on genocide widows and orphans; *Tubibe Amahoro*, a local organisation focusing on conflict resolution and peace building; and *Never Again Rwanda Chapter*, a youth organisation for genocide prevention.[53] The European Union has been helping some local organisations involved in assisting victims of the 1994 genocide.[54] Friends of Rwanda (FORA), a non-governmental organisation based in the US working with rural community organisations of genocide survivors, together with the Association of Family and Friends of genocide Victims (PAGE)-Rwanda (an organisation based in Canada founded by Canadians of Rwandan origin and their friends) and the International Red Cross-Rwanda are currently assisting the Association for support of orphans of genocide of Mayaga in school fees and income generating projects.[55]

3.2. HEALTH CONDITIONS

The health conditions of victims of the 1994 genocide against the Tutsi has been deplorable. It is estimated that approximately more than 350,000 women and girls were victims of rape and sexual violence (Bijleveld *et al.* 2009, 219; see also De Brouwer 2005, 11; Obote-Odora 2009, 175; Kaitesi & Haveman, this volume). Different forms of sexual violence and torture were used during the genocide, objects and fluids were put into victims' sexual organs resulting into different incurable vaginal infections (Blizzard 2006, 20). According to the study carried out by AVEGA Agahozo in 1999, it is suggested that most of the women contracted AIDS during rape; about 66% of victims of rape tested were found to be HIV positive.[56] Moreover, the genocide left a number of victims physically

---

22, 2008, Murekezi announces major reforms in vocational training, available at www.wda. gov.rw/Press%20releases/2.doc (last visited: 15 July 2010).

53   NPA in Rwanda, available at www.folkehjelp.no/www_-_English/Where_we_work/Africa/ Rwanda/ (last visited: 11 July 2010).

54   EU Website, www.delrwa.ec.europa.eu/en/eu_and_rwanda/civil_society.htm (last visited: 10 July 2010).

55   FORA website, www.friends-of-rwanda.org/partners.html (last visited: 10 July 2010).

56   National Unity and Reconciliation Commission (NURC), The Role of Women in Reconciliation and Peace Building in Rwanda: Ten Years After the Genocide 1994–2004, Contributions, Challenges and Way forward, a Study carried out by John Mutamba and Jeanne Izabiliza, Kigali, (May 2005), pp.16–17, available online at www.nurc.gov.rw/index. php?option=com_content&view=article&id=61%3Athe-role-of-women-in-reconciliation-and-peace-building-in-rwanda&Itemid=40 (last visited: 13 July 2010).

incapacitated and psychologically traumatised or mentally disabled (Thomas 2005, 17–18). FARG estimates that about 300,000 survivors were disabled in some way and about 26,000 of them at least lost a limb during the genocide (Thomas 2005, 17–18).

The poor health conditions appeared out of control and many international and local NGOs swiftly intervened to provide physical and psycho-trauma treatment. The Government through FARG concentrated in providing basic health care and financial support to some individuals who need specialised treatment.[57] The civil society has been offering substantial supplementary assistance to victims. International organisations, foreign government agencies, individual contributions and donations have financially supported different initiatives of the local civil society,[58] such as Oxfam-NOVIB, a Dutch apolitical and non-religious development organisation,[59] that provided financial support to health initiatives,[60] and ICAP/Columbia University, the International Center for AIDS care and Treatment Programs.[61] The United Nations Development Fund for Women (UNIFEM) has contributed to efforts that are aimed at fighting gender based violence, and has provided assistance to women associations affected with HIV/AIDS especially to women and girls, victims of rape and sexual violence during the 1994 genocide.[62] Christian Aid, originating from an initiative of British and Irish church leaders,[63] collaborates with local partners to monitor people's rights, improve agriculture, raise awareness on HIV/AIDS and provides care to communities.[64]

Since 1996 AVEGA has established a department of psychological care offering psycho-socio-medical support. It provides medical, social and trauma counselling to many members and beneficiaries of AVEGA which is decentralised to all parts of the country.[65] AVEGA also established a specific medical support unit in 1997 with a team of doctors, nurses, laboratory technicians and social

---

[57]　The Ministry of Local Government and the Ministry of Finance and economic Planning, Strategies to improve the performance of the genocide survivors assistance fund (FARG), Study released in January 2009, p. 3.

[58]　Some of the mentioned organisations are also part of the civil society, but their role has been mainly of supporting other civil society initiatives.

[59]　History of Novib available at, www.oxfamnovib.nl/history.html (last visited: 10 July 2010); see also AVEGA Report of 2006, p. 25.

[60]　AVEGA, *Programme Psycho-Socio-Medical (P.P.S.M.)* available at www.avega.org.rw/ppsm. htm (last visited: 10 July 2010); see also AVEGA Report of 2006, p. 25.

[61]　ICAP/Columbia University website, www.columbia-icap.org/wherewework/rwanda/index. html (last visited: 10 July 2010).

[62]　UNIFEM, UN Secretary-General Visits Rwanda: UNIFEM-Supported Projects Showcased, Kigali, 4 February 2008, available at www.unifem.org/news_events/story_detail.php?-StoryID=653 (last visited: 10 July 2010).

[63]　See the history of Christian Aid at www.christianaid.org.uk/aboutus/who/history/index.aspx (last visited: 10 July 2010).

[64]　See Christian Aid website on Rwanda, at www.christianaid.org.uk/whatwedo/africa/rwanda. aspx (last visited: 10 July 2010); see also AVEGA report of 2006.

[65]　See AVEGA website, www.avega.org.rw/historique.html (last visited: 17 July 2010).

workers regularly taking care of the sick.[66] In 2001, AVEGA created a specific project for the care of victims of sexual violence infected with AIDS during the genocide, 'PAPI',[67] which provides specific medical, social and trauma-counselling assistance. Support has been provided by different donors including the Multisectorial AIDS Project (MAP), a World Bank project that focuses on HIV/AIDS through initiatives that support government institutions, communities, civil society, faith-based organizations, and the private sector.[68]

The 'Care and Treatment of Genocide Survivors Infected by HIV/AIDS Project' (CTP), is another crucial achievement of the civil society. The project received support from the British Department for International Development (DFID), and includes shelter, food, income, education and medicine to individual victims of sexual violence and rape.[69] CTP which is part of Imbuto Foundation, works with local civil society organisations like IBUKA, Solace Ministries, Rwanda Women's Network and AVEGA Agahozo. Other CTP partner organisations include SURF, Survivor's Fund – an organisation committed to supporting victims of the 1994 genocide focusing on HIV/AIDS, Psychosocial Support, Education/Vocational Training, Income Generating Activities, Shelter, and legal assistance/advocacy[70] – the National Aids Control Commission (CNLS), Rwanda Treatment and Research AIDS Centre (TRAC), World Vision, Compassion International, World Food Program (WFP), The Central Purchasing Drugs, Consumables, Medical Equipment in Rwanda (CAMERWA) and The National Reference Laboratory (NRL).[71] CTP is part of a five year programme launched on 07 December 2005 by the First Lady to be coordinated with SURF and PACFA, a project for the Protection and Care of Families against HIV/Aids under the First Lady's Office.[72]

TROCAIRE International, an Irish Catholic development overseas charity agency, working to contribute to positive change in the poorest places, works

[66] See AVEGA website, www.avega.org.rw/ppsm.htm (last visited: 15 July 2010).

[67] PAPI, French acronym for *"Projet d'Appui aux Personnes Infectées"*.

[68] For details see the mission and the working approach of the Multisectorial Aids project (MAP), available at http://web.worldbank.org/WBSITE/EXTERNAL/COUNTRIES/AFRICAEXT/EXTAFRHEANUTPOP/EXTAFRREGTOPHIVAIDS/0,,contentMDK:20415735~menuPK:1001234~pagePK:34004173~piPK:34003707~theSitePK:717148,00.html (last visited: 10 July 2010); see also MAP's support to Kacyiru Police Health Center and their mission at http://siteresources.worldbank.org/EXTAFRREGTOPHIVAIDS/Resources/717147-1181218501159/KACYIRU_HC_flyer.pdf (last visited: 10 July 2010).

[69] DFID, The Rwandan genocide: Fifteen years on, (01/04/2009), available at http://webarchive.nationalarchives.gov.uk/+/www.dfid.gov.uk/Media-Room/Case-Studies/2009/The-Rwandan-genocide---Hope-beyond-HIV/ (last visited: 11 July 2010).

[70] SURF, 2009 Annual report, available online at http://survivors-fund.org.uk/blog/surf-annual-report/ (last visited: 11 July 2010).

[71] Imbuto Foundation, Care and Treatment of Women Genocide Survivors Project, available at www.imbutofoundation.org/spip.php?article7 (last visited: 10 July 2010).

[72] SURF, First Lady Launches DFID Sponsored Antiretroviral Programme for women survivors, available at www.survivors-fund.org.uk/assets/docs/pr/dfid-programme-launch.pdf (last visited: 10 July 2010).

through partnerships with local organisations.[73] It assisted in the creation of ARCT-Ruhuka and offered its members training in trauma counselling which has benefited a number of students survivors of the genocide.[74] CAFOD, a Catholic aid agency for England and Wales, supports a psycho-social programme through different organisations that provide counselling.[75]

The One Percent Scheme, a project started by a group of friends at Nottingham University, in 2003 provided support to the Rwanda Development Trust (RDT) to assist victims who were maimed or disabled during the 1994 genocide through their local association in Rwanda.[76] The NGO Mulindi Japan One Love Project was set up to assist the handicap society of Rwanda.[77] Mulindi estimates that Rwanda has "over 800,000 disabled people due to genocide, landmines, accidents, birth defects and medical malpractice," the project has been able to supply about 5,000 artificial limbs, sticks, wheel chairs and other materials at no cost to disabled people irrespective of their family or the cause of the disability.[78] Handicap International, an international independent aid organisation, started assisting the government of Rwanda and civil society immediately after the genocide, contributing in reconstruction and development of the country, "ensuring that vulnerable groups, in particular people with disabilities, are not forgotten".[79]

3.3. PROSECUTION OF PERPETRATORS

Civil society supports victims to receive justice and ensure that their voice is heard as crucial witnesses in *gacaca* courts. For example, IBUKA and AVEGA have been providing paralegals in different parts of the country that help victims understand intricacies of criminal justice in general and *gacaca* in particular. AVEGA has been providing transportation fees to its members, who were relocated to other places, to attend *gacaca* hearings in their villages of origin.

---

[73] See the website of Trocaire International, www.trocaire.org/ (last visited: 10 July 2010).

[74] ARCT Ruhuka report at www.businessdaily.rw/main.pl?feature=article&action=article & ID=1094825730 (last visited: 10 July 2010).

[75] See CAFOD website, www.cafod.org.uk/about-us/where-we-work/rwanda-burundi (last visited: 11 July 2010).

[76] One Percent Scheme charities, *The Rwanda Development Trust: The Association of Disabled People in Rwanda*, available at www.onepercentscheme.org/public/Rwanda%20 Development%20Trust.htm (last visited: 10 July 2010).

[77] Established in Kigali, in 1997 by Mr. Gatera Rudasingwa, a Rwandan, and Ms. Mami Yoshida Rudasingwa, a Japanese. Website, Mulindi Japan One Love Project, www.onelove-project. info/oneloveproject.org/index.htm (last visited: 13 July 2010).

[78] Website, Mulindi Japan One Love Project, www.onelove-project.info/oneloveproject.org/ index.htm (last visited: 13 July 2010).

[79] Handicap International website, Rwanda, *Ensuring people with disabilities are not forgotten*, www.handicap-international.org.uk/where_we_work/africa/Rwanda (last visited: 13 July 2010).

Different religious leaders participated in educating perpetrators of genocide to confess and to remorsefully ask for forgiveness; to some extent, where genuine confessions took place reduced the burden of proof on the side of victims. *Avocats Sans Frontières* and the Danish Centre for Human Rights with the *Corps des Défendeurs Judiciaire* also provided legal assistance during trials in ordinary courts in cases related to civil damages arising from genocide cases (see Ndahinda, this volume).

NGOs, especially women associations, contributed to the possible prosecution of rape cases before the ICTR. In the Akayesu case, human rights organisations and women activists, especially the international NGO Coalition for Women's Human Rights in Conflict Situations,[80] filed for *amicus curiae* on sexual violence as it was not among the charges filed by the prosecutor. It is believed that this filing contributed to the amendment of the indictment against Akayesu. On June 17, 1997, Deputy Prosecutor Bernard Muna, responding to worldwide criticism from feminists and human rights groups, added three more counts of genocide and crimes against humanity (Ball 1999, 28). Victims and women associations in Rwanda have keenly stressed the seriousness of the crime of rape and sexual violence committed during the genocide and insisted that the crime of rape be given special attention and considered as part of the first category crimes, the most severe category of genocide related crimes in Rwanda. With the introduction of some 7,000 rape cases in *gacaca* courts AVEGA and IBUKA provided trauma counsellors to accompany all victims of rape in *in camera* trials (see Kaitesi & Haveman, this volume).

Some international organisations have been at loggerheads with countries especially in Europe to end safe havens for perpetrators of genocide. The fact that Rwanda has no extradition agreements with most countries, African Rights and Redress are tracking down individuals suspected of having committed genocide and other crimes still at large in different countries by documenting testimonies and identifying their locations.[81] In 2008, the two organisations organized a conference that brought participants from different countries in Europe to consider issues and challenges related to the extradition of Rwandese genocide suspects to Rwanda.[82] In 2007, The International Federation for Human Rights (FIDH), the French *Ligue des Droits de l'Homme*-LDH, *Survie* and the *Collectif des Parties Civiles pour le Rwanda* (CPCR) requested the government of France

---

[80] Gaëlle Breton-le Goff and Anne Saris, *Amicus Curiae before ICTR two schools of thought, one document, one imperfect* available at www.ichrdd.ca/english/commdoc/publications/women/ bulletin/vol4no1/amicusLeGoffSaris.html, Volume 4, number 1, fall 2001.

[81] Redress and African Rights, 'Major Pierre Claver Karangwa, Accused of Genocide in Rwanda, Today Living in The Netherlands', (April 2010), available at www.redress.org/downloads/ publications/Pierre%20Claver%20Karangwa_%20Accused%20of%20Genocide-%20 Living%20in%20The%20Netherlands.pdf (last visited: 10 May 2010).

[82] Redress and Africa Rights, *Extraditing Genocide Suspects From Europe to Rwanda, Issues and Challenges*, Report of a Conference Organised by Redress and African Rights at the Belgian Parliament, 1 July 2008, p.3 available online: www.redress.org.

to arrest Father Wenceslas Munyeshyaka, Laurent Bucyibaruta and Dominique Ntawukuriryayo. This call followed the request made by Hassan Jallow, the Prosecutor of the ICTR, asking the French government to seek arrest and keep them under detention until the ICTR consents to the request to transfer their cases to France, within the framework of the completion strategy of the ICTR mandate. This was similarly rebuked by the European Court of Human Rights (ECHR) in France's failure to deal swiftly with cases against Munyeshyaka first lodged in 1995.[83] The CPCR and other organisation's role in pursuing justice for victims of the 1994 genocide against the Tutsi is well tabulated on their website.[84]

Other similar lobby and advocacy campaigns or forums continue to be organised to ensure that perpetrators of genocide are held accountable. In 2007 FIDH and Redress organised a conference in Brussels on how to hold Rwandese genocide suspects accountable in Europe. "13 Years after the Rwandan genocide, it is unacceptable that perpetrators continue to live freely in Europe", said FIDH and Redress. "Governments were reminded of their obligation to investigate these allegations and where sufficient evidence exists, to bring these persons to justice". These organisations stressed that "[i]mpunity for genocide is unacceptable in the 21st century".[85]

3.4. REPARATION

Reparation is an issue much developed in theory without practical/concrete response in terms of implementation. Adopting a viable approach for reparation of gross human rights violations is a complicated phenomenon especially in a country like Rwanda, with little resources, a huge number of victims with enormous continuing challenges. However, in most cases lack of commitment from the government to do the least possible in the available means can also be a hindrance.

Various members of civil society have been advocating for the respect of victims' right to compensation to the victims of the 1994 genocide, but due to the continued hesitation to adopt the possible compensation fund law, most of these activists are tired or discouraged to continue pushing harder. In the early stages of genocide-trials through ordinary courts, victims were awarded compensation according to the law[86] and sums of compensation were awarded to victims in

---

83   FIDH Press release of July 2007, Rwanda/France; *France should arrest Wenceslas Munyeshyaka, Laurent Bucyibaruta and Dominique Ntawukuriryayo immediately!*.
84   Www.collectifpartiescivilesrwanda.fr/affairesjudiciaire.html.
85   FIDH Press release, *Call to end European safe havens for Rwandan Perpetrators*, 3 April 2007.
86   Article 29 of Organic law n° 08/96 of August 30, 1996 organizing proceedings for offences constituting the crime of genocide and crimes against humanity committed from October 1, 1990.

different judgments to be paid by perpetrators together with the state. Enforcement of these Court decisions concerning civil damages has not been successful; this is due to exorbitant damages awarded in relation to the financial capacity of the convicted perpetrators. A report of Redress and African Rights clearly states that:

> In many cases, the State was held jointly liable, given that the convicted perpetrators were state agents and/or because the state failed in its duty to end the killings. (...) Virtually no claimants had actually received compensation even when it was awarded, since perpetrators were unwilling, insolvent or otherwise unable to pay, and no judgments against the state had been enforced when it has been held civilly responsible. This discouraged victims.[87]

The continued shift of the government's initial commitment to respect victims' right to compensation is visible in the legislator's intention where different successive legislations are noticeably changing the language used. The state's failure to execute Court decisions rendered in first trials was followed by the adoption of the 2001 Gacaca law which stipulated in Article 90:

> Ordinary and 'Gacaca [Courts]' forward to the Compensation Fund for Victims of the Genocide and Crimes against humanity copies of rulings and judgments they have passed, which shall indicate the following:
>
> – the identity of persons who have suffered material losses and the inventory of damages to their property;
> – the list of victims and the inventory of suffered body damages;
> – as well as related damages fixed in conformity with the scale provided for by law.
>
> The Fund, based on the damages fixed by [courts], fixes the modalities for granting compensation.[88]

The 2004 Gacaca law that abrogated its predecessor laws stipulates, in just one sentence, that "any other form of compensation to victims shall be determined by a particular law",[89] thus putting everything concerning compensation pending.

---

[87] Avocats sans Frontières, *L'état de la jurisprudence sur l'indemnisation liée au contentieux du génocide. Exposé donné lors du " Séminaire sur l'indemnisation des victimes du génocide", organisé par le Ministère de la Justice du 3 au 4 avril 2000* as cited by African Rights and Redress, *Survivors and Post-Genocide Justice in Rwanda, Their Experiences, Perspectives and Hopes*, November 2008, 100.

[88] Organic law n° 40/2000 of 26/01/2001 Setting up "Gacaca Jurisdictions" and Organizing Prosecutions for Offences Constituting the Crime of Genocide or Crimes Against Humanity committed between October 1, 1990 and December 31, 1994.

[89] Article 96, Organic law n°16/2004 of 19/6/2004 Establishing the Organisation, Competence and Functioning of Gacaca Courts Charged with Prosecuting and Trying the Perpetrators of

The Justice Minister, Tharcisse Karugarama, clearly stated that the Government has not abandoned its plan to establish the Fund.[90] According to Benoit Kaboyi, then Executive Secretary of IBUKA, there is little hope to have the compensation law passed soon: "it seemed that there is little happening on this law in Parliament at the moment". Kaboyi emphasises IBUKA's position to see victims' right to compensation respected. He finds the compensation of victims of the genocide a crucial but forgotten element of justice. He contends that while the law provides for compensation for most other forms of victimisation, there is no provision in Rwanda that provides for compensation for the victims of the genocide. Asked on what should be done, he said it is the responsibility of our legislators to put in place such provisions in order to respect the victims' constitutional rights.[91] The only remaining possibility to claim compensation on perpetrators for the harm caused is provided by the FARG law. It is the Fund that can file a civil action on behalf of all victims and to only those suspects in the first category.[92]

The civil society has raised the issue of compensation to the level of the United Nations through a letter of IBUKA and AVEGA to the Secretary General in 2007.[93] The international community was reminded that the genocide was committed in the presence of the UN Armed Forces and for several reasons the victims of genocide have suffered the inaction of the international community. The civil society called on the international community to stand on the side of the Rwandan government in making available compensation for the wrongs done to the 1994 genocide survivors. However, until now the impact of that communication has remained a mystery.

---

the Crime of Genocide and other crimes against Humanity committed between 1 October 1990 and December 31, 1994.

[90] African Rights and Redress, *Survivors and post-genocide justice in Rwanda, Their Experiences, Perspectives and Hopes*, November 2008, 101.

[91] Together Against Impunity in the Great Lakes Region, Radio Show entitled "Tumenye Uburenganzira bw'Uwahohotewe" (meaning lets know victims' rights), aired on Radio Rwanda on 17/11/2007, report available online: www.against-impunity.org/IMG/pdf/Radio_Report.pdf.

[92] Articles 20 and 21, Law N° 69/2008 of 30/12/2008, relating to the establishment of fund for the support and assistance to victims and survivors of genocide committed against the Tutsi and other crimes against humanity committed in Rwanda from 01 October 1990 to 31 December 1994, OG.n° Special of 15/04/2009.

[93] Hirondelle News Agency – Arusha, 10 July 2007, '*TPIR/GREFFE – Environ 250.000 Femmes Violées pendant le Génocide, Selon le TPIR*'. See also Rwanda News Agency, 26 June 2007, 'Ibuka Intensifies Demands for ICTR Archives', and 'ICTR denies existence of Genocide Fund', July 16, 2007.

3.5. PROTECTION OF VICTIMS AND WITNESSES

From 1995 until 2002, Rwanda was in a period of pondering ways of challenging impunity. On the other hand, efforts to reach justice of any form were much challenged by different threats of reprisal, intimidation, and harassment aimed at stopping victims and witnesses from cooperating with the justice system in general (ICTR, ordinary courts and *gacaca* courts). At the worst, from 2003 to 2006, the number of killings targeting witnesses and victims of the 1994 genocide had sharply increased.[94] This unfortunate milestone strengthened the civil society's idea to advocate for the protection of victims and witnesses and somehow made it easy to bring policy makers to understand that in such a situation it is fundamental to put the security and safety of victims at the centre of the prosecution mandate.

In the beginning of 2005, immediately after the creation of TAI/GLR, security of victims and witnesses was an eminent problem, becoming the number one priority issue of TAI/GLR's concern. Efforts to achieve changes in law enforcement and justice administration towards a victims' rights sensitive system concentrated at the Ministry of Justice, the Supreme Court and at the NPPA. The intention of this focus was to make sure that officials directly concerned with criminal justice politics became aware of ways in which victims are ignored and mistreated, and at worst killed through their cooperation with law enforcement institutions.

Out of these meetings with officials of different institutions, Prof. Samuel Rugege, Vice President of the Supreme Court, supported TAI/GLR's cause to call for protection of victims and accepted that this was a national issue that required special attention. In his note to TAI/GLR, Justice Prof. Rugege, recognised that "TAI/GLR has very positive and crucial objectives in today's Rwanda. [That] Concern for the protection of witnesses is a national concern but existing institutions are overstretched and need the support of civil society".[95] Subsequent to this note, on 8 November 2005, the NPPA organised a conference on security of victims and witnesses. TAI/GLR was invited to this conference and participated in drafting recommendations for the establishment of the protection unit at the prosecution. In doing so, TAI/GLR with other organisations, especially IBUKA which regularly communicated the number of victims killed country-wide, contributed to the creation of the Victims and Witnesses Protection Unit in the National Public Prosecution Authority (NPPA).

Since the creation of the victims and witnesses protection unit in the NPPA, TAI/GLR, in collaboration with the International Organisation for Victims

---

94 Report of the Prosecutor General to the Prime Minister on the killings targeting survivors of genocide and witnesses, from 1995 to 2008, Kigali, 2008, p. 17.

95 Www.against-impunity.org/IMG/jpg/Support_note.jpg.

Assistance (IOVA) and the Charity Committee of the International English Speaking Roman Catholic Church of the Hague, has been providing trainings to the staff of the prosecution, local administration and police on crisis response, treatment of victims, security threats, risk assessment and management through community based approaches for protection of victims and witnesses.

3.6. RAISING AWARENESS ON VICTIM'S RIGHTS

To ensure that victims' rights are widely known to the entire population, and to ensure a similar knowledge amongst victims' service providers, TAI/GLR organised radio forums on victims' rights. In these shows, the invitees included the Ministry of Justice, the NPPA, HAGURUKA (an association for promotion of women and children's rights), IBUKA, FACT Rwanda (association against torture) and the National Police and interviews with the general public. The program was divided into two; one was an English live show aired on October 14, 2007 on Contact FM (a private owned Radio station) with the theme *Ijambo n'iryawe* meaning *the word/floor is yours*; the other was an educative presentation in Kinyarwanda on Radio Rwanda. A radio program on radio Rwanda was a serial show called *Tumenye Uburenganzira bw'Uwahohotewe* meaning 'let's understand victims' rights' that ran 6 times during November and December 2007.[96]

In addition to these radio programs, TAI/GLR has put together all victims' rights related provisions found in different Rwandan laws on its website and a toll free phone line (**3935**), which is used by the victims and witnesses protection unit.[97] To emphasise the crucial need to understand the victims' rights, TAI/GLR has used posters to educate the general public on victims' rights. On these posters most of referral contacts are listed and 2000 copies were distributed to all local leaders, to different ministries, Police offices, Prosecution Offices, the Supreme Court and other prominent places.

On September 14, 2007, TAI/GLR organized a one-day conference in Kigali with the theme, 'Understanding International Criminal Justice and the International Criminal Court'.[98] This event was in the framework of promoting International Criminal Law and International Humanitarian Law combined with a belief that government's commitment to ensure victims of gross human rights violations and the general population that such crimes will never happen again, should adhere to international mechanisms available for repression of these crimes. The main goal of this conference was to spread knowledge on the benefits of the Rome Statute and the ICC in the crusade against impunity.

---

[96]   Www.against-impunity.org/IMG/pdf/Radio_Report.pdf.
[97]   Www.against-impunity.org.
[98]   Conference report available online, www.against-impunity.org/?rubrique3.

TAI/GLR in collaboration with the NPPA and United Nations Office on Drugs and Crime (UNODC) through the programme Data for Africa, which was developed by the UNODC through the Project "Collection and analysis of data on drugs, crime and victimisation in Africa",[99] in July and August 2008, among other issues TAI/GLR carried out a national crime victim survey to understand the crime rate, the socio-economic impact of crime and the perception of victims on the work of police and law enforcing agents.[100]

Inspired by the South African victims' rights charter,[101] TAI/GLR since its creation has been advocating for the adoption of a victims' rights law. At present there is a promising step in having a law on rights of victims of international offences. The preliminary draft has been developed by the consultant of the NPPA for the Victims and Witnesses Protection Unit. The draft law focuses on victims and witnesses of international crime. It deals with issues of protection of victims and witness and compensation to victims. The progress on its adoption seems to be taking longer, it has been kept at the level of the Ministry of Justice, which has to table it to the Cabinet before it can be sent to the Parliament for discussion and possible adoption.

4. CHALLENGES IN ADDRESSING PROBLEMS OF VICTIMS

The role of civil society in addressing problems faced by victims of the 1994 genocide is being limited by a huge number of problems to be dealt with combined with limited resources. Given the fact that the 1994 genocide was committed on the entire territory of Rwanda leaving multiple and complex problems, meeting an enormity of various needs faced by victims in such a wide context is too huge to be viably achieved. Problems faced with victims bypass the capacity of civil society organisations.

There is a shift of interest on the donors' side from victims' needs to general developmental initiatives. It is to some civil society members' observation that donors think that 16 years is enough for victims to take on their lives and start living normally like any other citizen. This kind of shift in support of victims is very unfortunate and short-sighted – it is being insensitive to multiple socio-economic impacts of the genocide that keeps many victims in more vulnerable situations than any other citizen. Let me give an example. Someone who was 50

---

[99]   UNODC, approved by UN General Assembly resolution 60/247 A of 23 December 2005, from the Special Account for Supplementary Development Activities (RO) of the Development Account.

[100] Executive Summary of the Rwanda National crime victim survey report is available on the UNODC website; www.unodc.org/unodc/en/data-and-analysis/Data-for-Africa-publications. html.

[101] South Africa, Victims' rights charter website, www.doj.gov.za/VC/VCmain.htm.

years during the 1994 genocide and survived after maybe being crippled or without any relative – after 16 years is now 66 years old, no child left to take care of him or her, no any sort of pension allocation available. This person needs more assistance today than 16 years ago. A child who was 5 years or younger in 1994 is now 21. At this time she or he is questioning her or himself about what happened, there is much more expectation of increased trauma among the youth survivors of genocide today than 16 years ago.[102] A third example: those infected with HIV/AIDS and other incurable diseases and cancer resulting from machete wounds etcetera see their lives significantly weakening. These victims need us today even much more than 16 years ago. And those victims who have been strong and tough in getting themselves together will still need a civil society on their side because we cannot easily predict what might come-out of that resilience in the near future.

On a practical note, with no distinction whatsoever but at different levels, each civil society member organisation has logistical problems and limited human resources to effectively provide reasonable assistance. Issues of staff salaries, office rent, office equipment, transportation to their beneficiaries outside Kigali city etcetera are recurrent.

5. CONCLUSION

After the war and 1994 genocide against the Tutsi, Rwanda was confronted with many serious problems including a huge number of victims of the genocide, extreme high levels of poverty, health, destroyed infrastructure, security and justice, social mistrust and divisions. In the process of dealing with these challenges the Government of Rwanda has been facilitated and sometimes complemented by the work of civil society (local and international). In this chapter I discussed some of the initiatives and actions undertaken by the civil society independently or jointly with the Government and showed challenges that face both the civil society and their beneficiaries (victims). It is in this context that a conclusive remark is made. The civil society in Rwanda has played a significant role in the reconstruction of Rwanda and in helping victims and survivors of genocide. Their impact is seen in all crucial sectors of the country and at all levels, but most importantly their role is felt at the lowest levels within local communities where local organisations are based. Thus, helping in re-establishing hope and individual human dignity. But as we have seen, their

---

[102]   "Many were too young to understand why genocide occurred; they still don't know the facts. With no questions asked because no one is there to listen, these children are growing up to be angry, frustrated and resentful adults. (…) There is a very high level of trauma among these young survivors". See Blewitt M.K., *Trauma in Young Survivors of the Rwanda Genocide*, (2009), Research Center for Leadership in Action.

contribution is faced with a number of difficulties and challenges, which are related to human resource capacity, lack of coordination and unsustainable projects due to limited financial resources. There is a need to form a national coordination of all available resources and efforts to the benefit of all victims, to avoid over-concentration in some few places like Kigali or to some victims who are capable of reaching to offices of these organisations.

PART IV
INTERNATIONAL AND NATIONAL
LEGAL AND POLICY APPROACHES

XVII. UNIVERSAL JUSTICE?

The Practice and Politics of Universal Jurisdiction Cases Relating to Crimes Committed in Africa

Carla FERSTMAN and Jürgen SCHURR

1. INTRODUCTION

Jurisdiction is the basis upon which courts derive their authority – the limits or contours of their competence to take up a particular matter. Usually, courts will have the jurisdiction to deal with events which occurred within their State's territory, with nationals of that State or with crimes which have had an impact on the interests of that State even if committed by non-nationals.

Universal jurisdiction is an additional basis for jurisdiction which recognises that the most serious crimes under international law are crimes which offend the sensibilities of the international community as a whole. As such, all States have the ability, and at times the obligation, to ensure that justice is done by investigating, with a view to prosecuting, individuals accused of certain crimes recognised as the most serious, regardless of where the offence took place and irrespective of the nationality of the accused person or the victim.

The principle of universal jurisdiction is recognised in a number of treaties including the 1949 Geneva Conventions, which require each of the High Contracting Parties to "seek out and prosecute" persons alleged to have committed, or to have ordered to be committed, such grave breaches of the Conventions, and "shall bring such persons, regardless of their nationality, before its own courts".[1] The related 'prosecute or extradite' requirement is recognised

---

[1] Convention for the Amelioration of the Condition of the Wounded and Sick in Armed Forces in the Field, 12 August 1949 (hereinafter 'First Geneva Convention'), Article 49(2); Convention for the Amelioration of the Condition of Wounded, Sick and Shipwrecked Members of Armed Forces at Sea, 12 August 1949 (hereinafter 'Second Geneva Convention'), Article 50(2); Convention relative to the Treatment of Prisoners of War, 12 August 1949 (hereinafter 'Third Geneva Convention'), Article 129(2); Convention relative to the Protection of Civilian Persons in Time of War, 12 August 1949 (hereinafter 'Fourth Geneva Convention'), Article 146(2).

in the UN Convention Against Torture, which requires States to investigate with a view to prosecuting suspects of torture where there is no extradition request from another country,[2] and this requirement is replicated in approximately 61 multilateral conventions at the universal and regional level including the European Convention on the Suppression of Terrorism, the International Convention against the Taking of Hostages and the International Convention for the Protection of All Persons from Enforced Disappearance, and has further been recognised by some scholars as a general duty of customary international law, at least as it concerns certain categories of crimes.[3] Other crimes over which universal jurisdiction and/or the related 'prosecute or extradite' jurisdiction can be exercised include: genocide, crimes against humanity, enforced disappearances, slavery, and terrorist offences.

In our modern world of travel and migration, victims and alleged perpetrators alike, may end up in other countries or continents, particularly at the end of a period of conflict. Yet, extradition back to the territorial State will not always be an option. Sometimes, the territorial State will not be interested in undertaking a prosecution and will not seek extradition. Even when they do seek extradition, there may be difficulties for the requested States to honour extradition requests in cases where the legal frameworks for extradition have not been agreed between the two countries or where there are serious fair trial concerns.[4] The ICC does not provide a real alternative, given that it is a treaty-based court with a mandate only over crimes committed after 1st July 2002 mainly by or against individuals who are nationals of States parties or on the territory of States parties. Furthermore, the ICC is focussing on those most responsible for genocide, crimes against humanity or war crimes, and does not have sufficient resources to investigate and prosecute all alleged perpetrators. Indeed, the Office of the Prosecutor of the ICC indicated a "risk of an impunity gap unless national authorities, the international community and the ICC work together to ensure that all appropriate means for bringing other perpetrators to justice are used".[5] Given the limited mandate of the ICC, it will only be capable of pursuing a handful of cases. The exercise by States of universal jurisdiction is therefore

---

[2]   Convention against Torture and Other Cruel, Inhuman or Degrading Treatment or Punishment, 1984, entered into force 26 June 1987, Article 5.

[3]   International Law Commission, *Preliminary Report on the Obligation to Extradite or Prosecute ("Aut Dedere, Aut Judicare")*, by Mr. Zdzislaw Galicki, Special Rapporteur, UN Doc. A/CN.4/571, 7 June 2006, 40.

[4]   See, in relation to the challenges of extraditing Rwandan genocide suspects to Rwanda, Redress & African Rights, *Extraditing Genocide Suspects from Europe to Rwanda, Issues and Challenges*, Report of a Conference Organised by Redress and African Rights at the Belgian Parliament on 1 July 2008.

[5]   Paper on some policy issues before the Office of the Prosecutor, September 2003, at www.icc-cpi.int/NR/rdonlyres/1FA7C4C6-DE5F-42B7-8B25-60AA962ED8B6/143594/030905_Policy_Paper.pdf.

important in promoting accountability for the worst crimes, and ensuring that there are no 'safe havens'.

2. THE CHALLENGES ASSOCIATED WITH THE EXERCISE OF UNIVERSAL JURISDICTION

There are a number of challenges associated with the exercise of universal jurisdiction. These challenges relate mainly to the fact that the investigations and prosecutions take place far away from where the crime took place, which can pose a number of difficulties. While universal jurisdiction prosecutions may contribute to the goals of specific and general deterrence and the public assignation of responsibility by an official body, such 'distant' prosecutions arguably contribute less to the restoration of the rule of law in the countries where the crimes occurred, though they can serve as a catalyst for future domestic prosecutions, as for example has been the case in Chile, where, after Pinochet's arrest in the United Kingdom and his return to Chile in 2000, Chilean courts rendered several decisions that lifted the former president's immunity from prosecution.[6] The distance from the crimes can mean that it will be difficult for foreign authorities to comprehend the local context of the crimes, to locate witnesses and to ensure effective witness protection. Also, it can be difficult for such officials to obtain the cooperation of the territorial State to conduct investigations in the country. Foreign judges and jurors may also have difficulty assessing foreign witnesses and appreciating the evidence.

The exercise by States of universal jurisdiction in order to undertake investigations and prosecutions remains the exception rather than the rule, despite the presence of known suspects of serious crimes under international law in a range of countries worldwide. Often, States will have failed to include in their domestic laws a sufficient legal basis for the exercise of universal jurisdiction. This can be particularly problematic in States which have a dualist legal tradition in which it is required that treaties be translated into domestic law before they can be applied. At times, States will lack the specialised investigative, prosecutorial and judicial capacity to undertake universal jurisdiction prosecutions, given the complexity of the evidence and the special nature of the crimes. The costs of such prosecutions have also played a part in the decisions of some countries not to pursue suspects or limiting the number of investigations or prosecutions undertaken by any particular State. Also, certain States impose additional procedural requirements upon an exercise of universal jurisdiction, at

---

[6] Commission on Human Rights, *Independent Study on Best Practices, Including Recommendations, to Assist States in Strengthening their Domestic Capacity to Combat all Aspects of Impunity*, by Professor Diane Orentlicher, UN Doc. E/CN.4/2004/88, 27 February 2004, 49–53.

times incorporating such requirements into their domestic legislation. Examples of such requirements that have been set by certain States include, the need for a connection (typically some form of presence) between the suspect and the State considering to exercise jurisdiction and, the impossibility of a domestic (territorial) prosecution, sometimes referred to as a principle of 'subsidiarity'. Additionally, certain States have taken an extremely expansive view of the legality principle to deny retroactive universal jurisdiction prosecutions of crimes under international law, even where the crimes in questions were recognised as crimes under customary international law at the time of their commission. For instance, the prosecution of Michel Bagaragaza, who was transferred from the International Criminal Tribunal for Rwanda (ICTR) to Norway and The Netherlands respectively failed in both countries as neither country provided for universal jurisdiction over genocide committed in 1994. As a result, Norway subsequently changed its domestic legislation and today provides for retroactive universal jurisdiction over genocide. Similar changes were under way in The Netherlands at the time of writing. Immunities have also shielded certain suspects from prosecution as has a lack of prospect of cooperation from the State where the crimes were committed.

3. THE PRACTICE OF UNIVERSAL JURISDICTION

A range of universal jurisdiction proceedings have been initiated in recent years, with a number of cases proceeding to trial and several convictions entered. Many cases have been lodged in European countries (including The United Kingdom, France, Belgium, Spain, The Netherlands, Germany, Denmark, Finland, Norway, Switzerland and Sweden). Cases have also been lodged in Argentina, Australia, Canada, Israel and the United States of America. In Africa, as will be elaborated in greater detail in the following sections, it has been stated that 'no African State is known to have exercised universal jurisdiction effectively'.[7] There is an ongoing investigation in Senegal and there have been several complaints filed in South Africa.

Most of the initiated universal jurisdiction cases relate to crimes committed during conflict, in particular, crimes linked to the genocide in Rwanda or the war in the former Yugoslavia, or torture perpetrated in or outside of conflict. Universal jurisdiction cases that have been investigated or have led to trials have concerned crimes committed in a wide array of countries and continents, including:

---

[7] African Union – European Union Technical Ad hoc Expert Group on the Principle of Universal Jurisdiction, *Report on the Principle of Universal Jurisdiction*, 16 April 2009, 8672/1/09 REV 1, Annex, para. 19.

- In Europe: Bosnia-Herzegovina, Croatia, Serbia, Germany (and related World War II cases);
- Middle East: Israel;
- In Asia: Afghanistan, Bahrain, Burma/Myanmar, Cambodia, China, India, Iran, Iraq, Sri Lanka;
- In Africa: Chad, Congo (Brazzaville), Democratic Republic of the Congo, Liberia, Mauritania, Morocco, Rwanda, Sierra Leone, Sudan, Tunisia;
- In the Americas: Argentina, Chile, Cuba, Guatemala, Peru, United States of America.

Universal jurisdiction trials have led to convictions in relation to crimes perpetrated in Afghanistan, Argentina, Democratic Republic of Congo, Germany (WWII-era), Iraq, Mauritania, Rwanda, Sierra Leone, Tunisia and the former Yugoslavia. For example, Heshamuddin Hesham and Habibullah Jalalzoy were convicted in the Netherlands for war crimes and torture perpetrated in Afghanistan and Faryadi Zardad, a former Afghani warlord, was convicted of torture and hostage-taking in the United Kingdom. Adolfo Scilingo was convicted in Spain and given a 640 year term of imprisonment for crimes against humanity committed in Argentina. Sebastien Nzapali, or the 'King of the Beasts' as he was known, a former army officer from the Democratic Republic of the Congo (then Zaire) was convicted of torture by a Dutch court in April 2004. One Mauritanian, Ely Ould Dah, was convicted of torture in absentia in France. One Rwandan, Joseph Mpambara, was convicted in the Netherlands for his role in the 1994 genocide. Four Rwandans known as 'the Butare Four' who included two nuns as well as Etienne Nzabonimana and Samuel Ndashykirwa; and Bernard Ntuhayaga and Ephrem Nkezabera were convicted in Belgium for crimes associated with the genocide in Rwanda. Another Rwandan, Fulgence Niyonteze, was convicted in Switzerland and another, Desire Munyaneza, was convicted in Canada. Chucky Taylor, the son of Charles Taylor, was convicted by US courts for crimes committed in Sierra Leone (under the active personality principle as he has dual citizenship). Refik Saric was convicted in Denmark for crimes committed in Bosnia, and Novislav Djajic, Maksim Sokolovic, Djuradj Kusljic and Nikola Jorgic were convicted in Germany for crimes committed in the former Yugoslavia.[8]

Universal jurisdiction cases have generally been lodged in one of three ways:

---

[8]   See below for further details in some of these cases. For an overview of prosecutions based on universal and extraterritorial jurisdiction see, *inter alia*, Rikhof 2008; FIDH & Redress, *EU Update on Serious International Crimes*, All Four Editions, June 2006 to July 2008; Human Rights Watch, *Universal Jurisdiction in Europe: The State of the Art*, 2006; FIDH & Redress, *Legal Remedies for Victims of "International Crimes". Fostering an EU Approach to Extraterritorial Jurisdiction*, 2004; Redress, *Universal Jurisdiction in Europe, Criminal Prosecutions in Europe Since 1990 for War Crimes, Crimes against Humanity, Torture and Genocide*, 1999.

(i)   A dossier of evidence is provided by third parties (victims, NGOs, investigative journalists) to police or prosecution services;
(ii) A criminal action is initiated directly by victims; or
(iii) Police or prosecution services initiate investigations and prosecutions themselves.

The first route has been used primarily in common law countries where there is less ability for victims to initiate criminal proceedings on their own and/or in both common law and civil law countries when national authorities have not acted on their own. Success is predicated on strong evidence and therefore it will be important for civil society groups and lawyers working with victims to work closely with the police and prosecution services from the outset, to assist in the transmission of evidence, provide background factual information and liaise with victims and where appropriate, assist prosecutors to be in contact with victims. Cases rarely succeed without such an international network of support.[9] The second route is used primarily in certain civil law countries in particular Spain and France where it is possible to initiate a criminal action directly, which then necessitates that the competent investigating judge evaluates the evidence. It has also been used in certain common law countries such as the United Kingdom where it is possible for victims' lawyers to make an application to a magistrate's court for the issuance of an arrest warrant. The third route is increasingly used in countries where there is a unit within the investigation and/or prosecution services specialised in investigating and prosecuting serious international crimes, such as the units established in Canada, Belgium, Denmark, Germany, Norway and The Netherlands.

4. EXTRATERRITORIAL JURISDICTION CASES RELATING TO AFRICA

About half or slightly more of recent universal jurisdiction investigations and prosecutions to date relate to crimes committed in Africa. Many of these cases relate to Rwanda (see Ndahinda, this volume), though cases have also related to a range of other countries in Africa. There are several reasons for the high numbers of African cases.

Firstly, there have been many conflicts in Africa involving mass crimes with many victims and perpetrators fleeing to other countries and continents. In some cases, networks of perpetrators have regrouped in these new locations, directing criminal operations from abroad, intimidating victims and thereby

---

9   See for instance, *Universal Jurisdiction: Meeting the Challenge through NGO Cooperation*, Report of a conference organized by the Lawyers Committee for Human Rights, at www. humanrightsfirst.org/international_justice/w_context/meeting_challenge310502.pdf.

raising security concerns for host States.[10] Secondly, with some exceptions, there has been only limited success with territorial prosecutions of such crimes in Africa, leading victims to seek alternative avenues for justice.

4.1. A REVIEW OF KEY TERRITORIAL PROSECUTIONS IN AFRICA

Territorial prosecutions – i.e. prosecutions in the country where the crime was committed – for serious crimes under international law perpetrated in Africa have had only limited success. The reasons for this are complex and range from a lack of capacity to adequately respond to the level and nature of criminality, inability to obtain custody over perpetrators, and in some cases a lack of will.

In Rwanda, there was great will to try genocide suspects but insufficient capacity in light of the sheer volume of the individuals suspected of being involved in the perpetration of genocide. There have been extensive attempts over many years to prosecute genocide suspects, though the vast number of cases and insurmountable backlogs led the Government to abandon the trials of mid- and lower level suspects in favour of village community courts (*gacaca*) (Ndahinda and Kaitesi & Haveman, this volume). In addition, there are estimated to be thousands of Rwandan genocide suspects outside of the country but efforts to have them returned to face trial have been difficult. The Rwandan government has indicated that it would hold criminal trials conforming to international standards for the suspects if returned and it has for instance abolished the death penalty to encourage the extradition of suspects though arguably it does not yet have the track record to instil confidence that domestic trials would conform to international standards of fair trial, and this has frustrated extradition attempts. In particular, concerns have been voiced by the ICTR as well as national courts in France, the United Kingdom, Germany and Finland (to some extent relying on the ICTR's decisions in 2008 not to transfer any cases to Rwanda) that the witness protection programme in Rwanda could not provide adequate protection for defence witnesses to testify in Rwanda in support of the accused. Other concerns were raised in respect of the independence of the judiciary and ambiguous legislation providing for the solitary confinement of prisoners. The Rwandan government has undertaken efforts to address the concerns voiced by the ICTR and national courts and introduced changes to its domestic legislation, ensuring for instance that the imprisonment of potential perpetrators in Rwanda would not contravene human rights standards. New prisons were built and

---

[10]   For example, the United Nations Security Council has referred to the continued presence of the *Forces Démocratiques de Libération du Rwanda* (FDLR) and others in the eastern Democratic Republic of Congo as a situation which continues to "pose a serious threat to the peace and security of the entire Great Lakes region". Resolution 1804 (2008), adopted by the Security Council in its 5852nd meeting, on 13 March 2008.

changes to its witness protection programme were introduced designed to make it more independent and the possibility for international judges to sit in genocide cases together with their Rwandan counterparts may further counter concerns of a lack of independence (Oosthuizen 2010). So far, however, the ICTR has refused to transfer to Rwanda some of its extra caseload and to date, no country aside from Sweden has authorised the extradition of suspects to Rwanda, and, even in the case of Sweden, the extradition is held up in review proceedings at the European Court of Human Rights.[11]

In Ethiopia, efforts to account for the crimes committed during the 'Red Terror' of 1977–78 led to trials of more than 100 Derg officials. However, many, including Mengistu Haile Mariam, were convicted in absentia and efforts to secure their return to Ethiopia have not been successful. Mengistu is living in Zimbabwe under that Government's protection. Zimbabwe has thus far ignored Ethiopia's extradition requests. When Mengistu travelled to South Africa a complaint was filed with South African police to initiate an investigation, however the police were too slow to move.

In Sierra Leone, the Lomé accords provided for an amnesty to shield suspects from justice. Yet, this did not prevent the Government of Sierra Leone and the United Nations to jointly establish the internationalised Special Court for Sierra Leone with a mandate to investigate and prosecute those "who bear the greatest responsibility for serious violations of international humanitarian law and Sierra Leonean law committed in the territory of Sierra Leone since 30 November 1996".[12] The Special Court has successfully prosecuted several suspects, including Charles Taylor, former President of Liberia, whose trial was ongoing at the time of writing. Nonetheless, the number of persons prosecuted was very limited when compared with the many persons suspected of participating in the commission of atrocities.

In Congo (Brazzaville), a domestic criminal trial was held in the 'Disappeared of the Beach' case (relating to the disappearance of 350 returning refugees from Brazzaville Beach), in which all accused persons were acquitted. The International Federation for Human Rights, which is involved together with local counterparts in Congo in the initiation of a criminal action on the basis of universal jurisdiction in France, noted, in respect of the Congolese proceedings that the investigation had been faulty and incomplete, the trial took place in an atmosphere of intimidation and insecurity for victims and the process as a whole was a 'masquerade'.[13]

---

[11] Redress & African Rights, *Extraditing Genocide Suspects from Europe to Rwanda, Issues and Challenges*, Report of a Conference Organised by Redress and African Rights at the Belgian Parliament on 1 July 2008.

[12] Agreement between the United Nations and the Government of Sierra Leone on the Establishment of the Special Court for Sierra Leone, signed on 16 January 2002, Article 1.

[13] Fédération Internationale des ligues des Droits de l'Homme (FIDH), *Rapport d'une Mission FIDH d'Observation Judiciaire au Procès des "Disparus du Beach" Brazzaville, Été 2005,*

In recent years, military courts in the eastern part of the Democratic Republic of the Congo have begun to prosecute members of armed groups for their role in perpetrating mass atrocities. However, to date, these efforts have been piece-meal and the majority of alleged perpetrators still remain at large.[14]

In other African countries also impacted by ICC proceedings, there have been some efforts to establish domestic criminal courts to try individuals accused of genocide, crimes against humanity and war crimes. In Uganda, a War Crimes Division of the High Court is in the process of being established, and it will have jurisdiction over genocide, crimes against humanity, and war crimes, and underlying offenses specified under Ugandan law.[15] Whilst this is an important initiative, victims' groups in Uganda have indicated that the country lacks sufficient competently trained personnel in delivering justice such as investigators, judges and prosecutors, and that the different timeframes being identified for the operation of the War Crimes Division may not cover all the mass crimes committed in Uganda's history.[16] The Government of Sudan has established several Special Courts, Commissions, Committees and other bodies to investigate and prosecute crimes in Darfur. However, these bodies and courts have to date not brought meaningful criminal justice because of, *inter alia*, the limitations of Sudanese criminals laws which do not recognise the international crimes of genocide, crimes against humanity and war crimes and the existence of immunities from prosecution.[17]

4.2. A REVIEW OF KEY UNIVERSAL JURISDICTION CASES REGARDING CRIMES ALLEGEDLY COMMITTED IN AFRICAN STATES

4.2.1. Genocide cases relating to Rwanda

After the 1994 genocide in Rwanda, many suspects fled the country. Some went to neighbouring countries in Africa, including the Democratic Republic of the Congo, Kenya, Tanzania, Burundi, Zambia and other southern African States. Others went further afield to countries in Europe, to Canada and the United

---

Report no. 435, 2005.

[14] See e.g. Avocats Sans Frontières, *Case Study: The Application of the Rome Statute of the International Criminal Court by the Courts of the Democratic Republic of Congo,* 2009, available at www.asf.be/publications/ASF_CaseStudy_RomeStatute_Light_PagePerPage.pdf.

[15] Government of Uganda, The International Crimes Bill of 2009, Article 18*bis*, on file with the authors.

[16] Uganda Victims' Foundation, *Statement on the International Crimes Bill,* 4 November 2009, available at www.vrwg.org/Publications/02/UVF%20Position%20Paper%20International%20Crimes%20Bill%20of%202009.pdf.

[17] Redress, *Accountability and Justice for International Crimes in Sudan: A Guide on the Role of the International Criminal Court,* 2007, 17–18.

States, Australia and New Zealand, amongst other destinations. In the melee which immediately followed the genocide, there was not much consideration by States of Article 1F(a) of the 1951 Convention Relating to the Status of Refugees, the exclusion clause which bars those suspected, for serious reasons, of committing crimes against peace, war crimes or crimes against humanity, from being recognised as refugees. Consequently, many Rwandans gained access to foreign jurisdictions, some gaining refugee status and even citizenship, despite their suspected links to the perpetration of genocide.

There have been efforts to track down these genocide suspects. In 2005, the Rwandan Office of the Prosecutor General had released a preliminary list of 93 genocide suspects living abroad. The Government also established a Genocide Fugitives Tracking Unit (GFTU), specifically mandated to track down fugitives around the world. The international police agency Interpol has established a Rwandan Genocide Fugitives Project to facilitate arrests through coordination of the activities of Rwandan authorities and the national investigative authorities of countries where genocide suspects are living.

Increasingly, the Government of Rwanda has been issuing extradition requests for the return of genocide suspects located abroad. At the time of writing, all of these requests, aside from a recent request to Sweden for the extradition of Sylvere Ahorugeze (which itself is now the subject of a petition to the European Court of Human Rights), had been denied. The reasons for the denials range from technical grounds associated with the lack of bilateral extradition treaties between the requested and requesting States, in some cases the lack of factual detail to substantiate the requests as well as concerns linked to fair trial as outlined further above. Similarly, Rwanda's requests to the ICTR for the transfer of suspects to Rwanda as part of the Tribunal's efforts to reduce some of its caseload have also been denied largely on fair trial grounds. It remains to be seen how the steps taken by the Rwandan Government to address the concerns of national courts and the ICTR as outlined above will impact on future extradition and transfer requests.

At last count, aside from the ICTR, there have been eleven Rwandans convicted of crimes relating to the genocide mainly in European countries (Switzerland, Belgium, The Netherlands, Finland) with one conviction in Canada (also Ndahinda, this volume). In addition, there are many further investigations and prosecutions underway. Whilst this number represents the highest rate of extraterritorial convictions for international crimes aside from those relating to World War II, the figure still pales when compared with the estimated number of suspects that remain at large. The reasons for the relatively limited number of investigations and prosecutions of Rwandan genocide suspects mirror the challenges inherent to universal jurisdiction cases more broadly: the inadequacy of legislation enabling universal jurisdiction prosecutions over genocide, the challenges associated with finding witnesses and collecting sufficient evidence of the crime, limited budgets and personnel resources made available for universal jurisdiction cases. Often, national police and prosecution authorities do not even know about the presence of suspects in their country, or about the possibility to investigate and prosecute these suspects, as even where domestic criminal codes provide for such prosecutions, that legislation may have never been applied before. Some countries have been better (or worse) than others. France, for instance, where numerous genocide suspects are said to reside, only very recently began serious efforts to institute proceedings. In 2004, the European Court of Human Rights had gone so far as to condemn France for its failure to investigate complaints that had been filed by genocide survivors against one suspect almost nine years earlier.[18]

More recently, in what can be seen as a significant shift, the French Government accepted to receive two transfer cases from the ICTR in 2007 and as a direct result of the many other cases involving Rwandan genocide suspects living in France and that are pending before French courts, announced in January 2010 plans to set up a specialised unit within the Paris High Court to try cases of genocide and crimes against humanity.[19]

Until such time as extradition to Rwanda is possible (and it remains to be seen what the view is with pending cases), universal jurisdiction prosecutions are the only way in which genocide fugitives can be held accountable. The Rwandan Government had not challenged the respective countries' universal jurisdiction under international law to bring genocide suspects to justice before their own courts. To the contrary, the Rwandan government has been (and still is) supportive of and cooperative with national authorities of third countries who are investigating alleged *génocidaires* residing abroad, as it supports efforts to hold perpetrators of the 1994 genocide accountable, while at the same time taking steps to build its justice system with a view to facilitate extraditions from third countries and transfers from the ICTR. The same extent of cooperation has not yet been rendered in relation to investigations by national authorities and by the ICTR pertaining to suspects who are officials of the Rwandan army or government.[20]

---

18   Complaints were filed against Father Wenceslas Munyeshyaka as early as July 1995. See, the decision of the European Court of Human Rights in Mutimura v. France (Application No. 46621/99), 8 June 2004.

19   RFI, *Paris Courts set up Genocide, War Crimes Unit*, 6 January 2010.

20   When the ICTR announced in 2002 that it would investigate crimes allegedly committed by the Rwandan Patriotic Front (RPF), Rwandan officials prevented witnesses from travelling to the Tribunal and thereby forced the suspension of trials for several months. To date, no RPF official has been indicted by the ICTR. See www.hrw.org/en/news/2009/05/26/letter-prosecutor-international-criminal-tribunal-rwanda-regarding-prosecution-rpf-c.

4.2.2. Senegal and the Hissène Habré case

Hissène Habré, former President of Chad, has resided in Senegal ever since he was ousted from power in 1990. Criminal proceedings were lodged by Chadian victims in collaboration with human rights NGOs in both Senegal and Belgium in 2000. The proceedings were initially dismissed in Senegal on the basis that Senegal did not have jurisdiction to entertain a prosecution. In 2005, Belgium requested Habré's extradition from Senegal.

The United Nations Committee Against Torture later determined that Senegal violated the United Nations Convention Against Torture by failing to either prosecute or extradite Habré,[21] noting that

> [t]he Committee considers that the State party cannot invoke the complexity of its judicial proceedings or other reasons stemming from domestic law to justify its failure to comply with these obligations under the Convention. It is of the opinion that the State party was obliged to prosecute Hissène Habré for alleged acts of torture unless it could show that there was not sufficient evidence to prosecute, at least at the time when the complainants submitted their complaint in January 2000.[22]

Thereafter, the African Union set up a Committee of Eminent African Jurists to consider all aspects and implications of the Hissène Habré case as well as the options available for his trial.[23]

In February 2007, Senegal amended its laws to allow for extraterritorial prosecutions for genocide, crimes against humanity, war crimes and torture, paving the way for it to exercise jurisdiction in the Habré case. To date, the case has not progressed, ostensibly as a result of insufficient funds. Belgium in 2009 lodged a complaint against Senegal before the International Court of Justice (ICJ) as a result of the failure to comply with its obligations to prosecute Habré (having already failed to extradite him to Belgium). Whilst the case is still pending, Belgium's request to the Court for the indication of provisional measures requiring Senegal to take all the steps within its power to keep Mr. Habré under the control and surveillance of the judicial authorities of Senegal pending the final outcome of the case, was denied on the basis that Senegal had provided sufficient assurances.[24]

---

[21]   UN Committee Against Torture, Decisions of the Committee Against Torture under Article 22 of the Convention against Torture and Other Cruel, Inhuman or Degrading Treatment or Punishment, Communication No. 181/2001, CAT/C/36/D/181/2001 of 19 May 2006.

[22]   *Idem*, para. 9.8.

[23]   African Union, Decision on the Hissene Habre Case and the African Union (Doc.Assembly/ AU/8 (VI)) Add. 9.

[24]   International Court of Justice, Case Concerning Questions Relating to the Obligation to Prosecute or Extradite (Belgium v. Senegal), Request for the Indication of Provisional Measures, Order dated 28 May 2009.

4.2.3. Liberia and the case of Chuckie Taylor in the United States

On 30 October 2008, a US jury found Charles "Chuckie" Taylor Jr. guilty of torture committed in Liberia between 1997 and 2003 during the time in which he headed the Anti-Terrorist Unit in Liberia during his father's presidency. He was subsequently sentenced to 97 years imprisonment. It was the first case where a suspect was convicted by a US court for torture committed elsewhere. While not a pure universal jurisdiction case – he had Liberian and US citizenship – the case was also significant as it was the first time that an individual was tried for the atrocities committed during Liberia's brutal civil war. Liberian authorities have yet to hold anyone accountable for the crimes during that period and no international tribunal was established to prosecute these crimes in Liberia, and therefore this universal jurisdiction prosecution was particularly important.[25]

4.2.4. Congo Brazzaville and the 'Disappeared of the Beach' case in France

In December 2001, several French and Congolese human rights organizations filed a civil complaint before French courts to initiate an investigation into the disappearance of up to 350 Congolese returning refugees on a beach at Brazzaville in May 1999. Due to the inaction of the Congolese authorities at the time, the complaint was brought before French courts on the basis of universal jurisdiction. On 1 April 2004, a French judge ordered the arrest of Jean Francois Ndengue, then Director of the National Police and in 1999 in charge of security at the Beach river port from where the refugees disappeared. He was duly arrested upon his arrival in Paris that same day. However, due to immense political pressure exercised by Congolese authorities on their French counterparts, he was subsequently released on 4 April 2004 and enabled to leave France.

As a result of the proceedings in France, Congo (Brazzaville), in 2005, initiated its own criminal trial in Brazzaville, however, as has already been indicated, concerns had been expressed about the lack of impartiality of the proceedings. The Congolese court acquitted all of the 15 accused, yet held that the State as such was responsible for the disappearance and ordered the payment of 10 million Congolese Francs to the families of the victims. According to NGOs involved the case, most families rejected the idea of compensation payments, arguing that the case required a finding of criminal liability. Irrespective of the Congolese court's decision, proceedings in France are still ongoing, with a French investigative court currently in charge of investigations. The French Supreme court in a decision in January 2007 did not consider the proceedings

---

25   See Human Rights Watch, *First Verdict for Overseas Torture*, 30 October 2008.

before Congolese courts to bar investigations in France under the principle of *ne bis in idem*.[26]

4.2.5. Mauritania and the Ely Ould Dah case in France

On 25 July 2005, the French *Cour d'Assises* of Nimes convicted Ely Ould Dah, a captain of the Mauritanian army, to 10 years imprisonment for torturing black African members of the military in 1990 and 1991 in Mauritania. He was protected from investigations in Mauritania by an amnesty law which was passed in 1993. However, when he arrived in France in August 1998, a criminal complaint was lodged against him by Mauritanian victims and several human rights organizations, alleging his involvement in torture.

The complainants based their case on the UN Convention against Torture and relevant universal jurisdiction provisions in the French criminal code. The case is remarkable in several respects. First, it underscored that universal jurisdiction could be a useful alternative to the exercise of territorial jurisdiction. Second, the French Supreme Court confirmed that the amnesty laws passed in Mauritania would not have any effect in France, as to apply them in France would render the French universal jurisdiction provisions over torture meaningless; this decision to ignore territorial amnesty legislation was an important signal that amnesty legislation may not shield perpetrators of the worst crimes from accountability and as such the decision will have an impact in future cases where States seek to protect their officials by invoking an amnesty legislation. Third, the decision of the French Court was confirmed by the European Court of Human Rights, which, in March 2009, not only recognised universal jurisdiction over torture, but furthermore held that an amnesty law is generally incompatible with the duty on States "to investigate acts of torture or barbarity".[27]

The trial of Ely Ould Dah was held in absentia, as he managed to escape from France in April 2000, when he was released from prison and put under house arrest. Throughout the trial in France, he was represented by a lawyer, who, at a later stage, appealed the judgment of the French Court to the European Court of Human Rights. Despite an extradition request issued by the French Court, Ely Ould Dah is currently living in Mauritania, with the Mauritanian government refusing to extradite him to France.

---

[26] See FIDH, *An Important Victory for Victims*, 10 January 2007.

[27] European Court of Human Rights, *Ould Dah v. France* (Application No. 13113/03), 17 March 2009.

4.2.6. *Tunisia and the case of Khaled Ben Said in France*

In May 2001, a Tunisian victim living in France in collaboration with Tunisian and French human rights organizations lodged a complaint before French courts against Khaled Ben Said, who in 1996 was the chief of the Jendouba police station, where the victim was tortured under his orders in October 1996. After French authorities initiated an investigation against him, Khaled Ben Said, who in 2001 lived in France as a Tunisian diplomat, fled to Tunisia. He currently works there for the Home Office. Ben Said's escape to Tunisia did not, however, stop French investigations into the complaint. French law provides for in absentia investigations and prosecutions and an international arrest warrant was issued by a French investigative judge in 2002. After more than seven years of investigations and proceedings, a delay caused mainly by the lack of cooperation from Tunisian authorities, a French court on 15 December 2008 convicted Ben Said in absentia to eight years imprisonment for instructions to commit torture.[28]

As in the Ely Ould Dah case, universal jurisdiction provided the only alternative to Tunisian victims to obtain a measure of justice in the sense that the crimes that were committed against them were acknowledged in an open court. At the same time, both cases serve as an example of how difficult and, at times, symbolic these trials can be if the territorial State or the State where the perpetrator is residing does not cooperate with the investigation or the implementation of the sentence or the execution of the international arrest warrant. Nevertheless, even in the absence of an arrest or the serving out of the actual sentence, the trial was considered significant as it pointed out a State practice of torture and sent an important signal that these crimes can no longer be committed without consequence.

4.2.7. *Rwanda and the RPF cases in France and Spain*

On 17 November 2006, French investigative judge Jean-Louis Bruguière requested international arrest warrants to be issued against nine Rwandan officials and suggested that the sitting Rwandan President, Paul Kagame, as a Head of State, should be tried by the ICTR. Bruguière alleged that the officials were all complicit in the shooting down of the plane carrying the former Rwandan President Habyarimana on 6 April 1994, an event widely believed to have triggered the 1994 genocide in Rwanda (Thalmann 2008).[29]

---

[28] See FIDH, *Khaled Ben Said, former Tunisian Vice-Consul in France, Condemned for Torture by the Criminal Court in Strasbourg*, 16 December 2008.

[29] See also the 'Bruguière Report' at www.taylor-report.com/Documents/BrugiereReport-English.pdf.

Judge Bruguière acted on a complaint filed on 31 August 1997 by family members of the French crew of the airplane that was shot down on 6 April 1994. As such, it was not a case of universal jurisdiction, but rather passive personality jurisdiction. However, the ramifications of the case render it important if one is to understand most recent developments and reactions by Rwanda and other African States to international criminal justice as a whole and universal jurisdiction in particular.

The Rwandan government was enraged by the decision. One day after the issuance of the arrest warrants, it cut all diplomatic ties with France, ordered the French Ambassador to Rwanda to leave the country, closed down France's cultural centre in Rwanda and attempted to initiate proceedings against France before the ICJ, arguing that France had violated Rwandan sovereignty. The Court, however, could not register the complaint as France refused to accept the ICJ's jurisdiction over the matter.

The French case culminated in the arrest of Rose Kabuye in Germany in November 2008. Kabuye, Kagame's chief of protocol and a former officer in the Rwandan Patriotic Army (RPA), was one of the nine officers accused by Bruguière and was accused of complicity in terrorism. She was subsequently extradited from Germany to France. While the arrest sparked outrage in Rwanda – the German Ambassador was also expelled from Rwanda – it has been suggested that it could have been a deliberate move by Rwanda to expose the weakness of Bruguière's dossier and to point to France's lack of commitment in initiating investigations against the 'real culprits' – the many alleged *génocidaires* who have found a safe haven in France. Apparently, Kabuye was warned by German authorities prior to her trip that they would have to arrest her if she was to travel to Germany. Her first hearing took place in December 2008 and she was allowed to leave France for Rwanda while her trial was still ongoing. On 26 September 2009, the French court lifted all judicial restrictions against Kabuye.[30] Recently all diplomatic relations have been restored.

The negative perception of international criminal justice within Rwanda and other African countries – partly as a result of dissatisfaction with the work of the ICTR[31] and the 'French RPF case' – worsened on 8 February 2008 when a Spanish investigative judge issued a 180 page indictment, issuing arrest warrants against 40 current or former high ranking Rwandan military officials of the Rwanda Patriotic Army (RPA)/Rwandan Patriotic Front (RPF) and allied military groups with genocide, crimes against humanity, war crimes and terrorism. The indictment alleges that all these crimes had been perpetrated against civilians, in particular against Hutu, over a 12 year period, from 1990 to 2002, in Rwanda as well as in the neighbouring Democratic Republic of the

---

[30] The New Times, *Judicial Restrictions on Rose Kabuye Lifted*, 26 September 2009.
[31] E.g Redress & African Rights, *Survivors and Post-Genocide Justice in Rwanda: Their Experiences, Perspectives and Hopes*, Report, November 2008, 55–72.

Congo. The complaint was brought by families of Spanish victims as well as relatives of victims of Rwandan and Congolese nationality, therefore based on passive personality as well as universal jurisdiction.

The indictment accuses some prominent Rwandans of being responsible for the killing of hundreds of thousands of civilians.[32] Among the accused is the Rwandan Ambassador to India and the Deputy Force Commander of the United Nations-African Union Mission in Darfur. The indictment does not refer to possible trials held against any of the accused by a Rwandan court. Indeed, one case has been reported in which the Military Court in Kigali rendered a judgment against one of the accused in the Spanish case, Wilson Gumisiriza, acquitting him of all the charges included in the Spanish indictment.[33]

The Spanish legal system – as opposed to the French legal system – does not provide for trials in absentia, and therefore the case has not progressed due to the lack of presence of the accused persons. While the Spanish case has not (yet) resulted in an arrest of the 40 officials accused, it has nonetheless had a profound political impact in Rwanda and throughout Europe, given the simplified extradition procedures set out under the European Arrest Warrant. For instance, the Rwandan Foreign Minister cancelled her visit to Belgium in May 2008 after she was notified that one member of her delegation, Joseph Nzabamwita, one of the 40 accused in Spain, would not receive a visa as he was wanted by the Spanish judiciary. The Belgian authorities made it clear that they would enforce the arrest warrants issued by the Spanish judge where they do not refer to people benefiting from immunity.[34] Similarly, Col. Gacinya, also one of the accused, who at the time of the indictment was a military attaché at the Rwandan embassy in Washington, was recalled to Rwanda soon after the arrest warrants were issued to avoid diplomatic complications.[35]

By far the strongest reaction to the indictment was, unsurprisingly, from Rwanda itself. The Rwandan government called on other governments to ignore the arrest warrants and initiated a process to address the 'Abuse of the Principle of Universal Jurisdiction' before the African Union (AU), the European Union (EU) and the United Nations (UN). Shortly after the indictment was issued, the Rwandan Minister of Justice and Attorney General, Tharcisse Karugarama on 18 April 2008 addressed a meeting of AU Ministers of Justice and Attorney Generals on the issue of universal jurisdiction, a concept under which he argued that foreign judges seek to recolonize Africa through a form of 'Judicial Coup d'Etat' under the guise of 'Judicial Independence' and 'Universal Jurisdiction.'

---

[32]   For an English summary of the Indictment see www.veritasrwandaforum.org/material/press_release_080208_eng.pdf.

[33]   Hirondelle News Agency, *Meurtres d'Evêques: Deux Acquittements et Deux Condamnations*, 24 October 2008.

[34]   Hirondelle News Agency, *Belgium Prosecutor: Brussels can Effect Arrest Warrants against RPF*, 18 July 2008.

[35]   Human Rights Watch, *Law and Reality- Progress in Judicial Reform in Rwanda*, 2008, 99.

He called on all African States to resist foreign domination through neo-colonial Judicial Coup d'Etat and to condemn 'those hostile manoeuvres.'[36]

Through its application in practice, universal jurisdiction had once again reached a stage of intense politicisation, this time being labelled a neo-colonial tool used by the North against the South.

5. THE POLITICS OF UNIVERSAL JURISDICTION

The politics relating to the investigation of 'sensitive' cases have made them practically difficult to pursue. In some cases, the territorial State has simply refused to cooperate making it difficult to locate and access the evidence. In other cases, diplomatic pressure has been exerted to avoid cases getting to the trial stage. This has, in some cases, resulted in politically strong countries managing to avoid universal jurisdiction prosecutions relating to their officials, contributing to the perception that universal jurisdiction is not truly universal, and is a mere political tool used by strong States against weaker ones. For instance, while universal jurisdiction complaints had been filed against leaders and officials of 'Western countries', such as George Bush senior and Donald Rumsfeld, these were dismissed at an early stage.

Cases have not always moved forward on predictable or transparent grounds. The perception of lack of predictability and transparency in decision-making was underscored when Germany, having just arrested Rose Kabuye, one week later released from extradition detention Callixte Mbarushimana, a genocide suspect and Secretary General of the FDLR – the *Forces Démocratiques de Libération du Rwanda*, an armed group with links to those who orchestrated the genocide – despite a pending extradition request from Rwanda and despite ongoing proceedings against Mbarushimana before French courts. German authorities did not see a prospect for Mbarushimana's extradition to Rwanda to succeed in light of the ICTR's refusal to transfer cases to Rwanda and the Court ordered his release from extradition detention. Since German authorities did not initiate investigations themselves and as France did not ask for Mbarushimana's extradition to France, he was released and could return to France.

However, it was not only universal jurisdiction cases or the French and Spanish RPF cases that helped those interested to sully the reputation of international criminal justice in recent years. The ICC's principle focus on suspects from African countries, with cases from the Democratic Republic of the Congo, Uganda, Sudan, the Central African Republic and Kenya was seen in the same light as an attack on Africa, with all issues remotely connected to international criminal justice lumped haphazardly together. The fact that these

---

[36] Statement of Rwanda to the meeting of Ministers of Justice and Attorneys General on legal matters, Addis Ababa, Ethiopia, 18 April 2008; copy on file with the authors.

cases are ostensibly against individuals on the basis of individual criminal responsibility and not against States has not helped. In a climate heavily influenced by such developments, a debate on universal jurisdiction ensued at various international levels, leading to a mischaracterisation of the legal basis for universal jurisdiction and the conditions for its exercise in practice. What was often discussed in political debates had little to do with universal jurisdiction as such, but rather was a discussion influenced by the (negative) perception of international criminal justice as a whole. A small number of countries demanded the solidarity of all African States against the use of universal jurisdiction, when what was principally under discussion was the prosecutions policy of the Office of the Prosecutor of the ICC or passive and active personality jurisdiction. This climate and these perceptions formed the background for discussions on universal jurisdiction at the African Union, and to some extent at the European Union and United Nations.

Since the first submission by Rwanda on universal jurisdiction in 2008, the AU adopted five decisions on the 'Abuse of the principle of Universal Jurisdiction' at each of its summits.

The main objectives of the five decisions can be summarised as follows:

1) To denounce a 'blatant' abuse of universal jurisdiction in some non-African States against African officials;
2) To call for immediate termination of all pending indictments;
3) To establish an international regulatory body with competence to handle universal jurisdiction complaints.

The AU decided to engage in a dialogue with the EU in respect of point 2, as most of the indictments and arrest warrants of concern to African States were issued in European countries and to raise the issue of universal jurisdiction with the United Nations in order to discuss point 3.

On 22 November 2008, at the 11th AU-EU Ministerial Troika, the Ministers decided to establish a technical ad hoc expert group to clarify the respective understanding on the African and European side on the principle of universal jurisdiction. The group, composed of three experts from the AU and the EU, submitted its report on the Principle of Universal Jurisdiction on 16 April 2009. While the report included a number of recommendations that seemed to have been heavily influenced by the need to come to a respective understanding between the two 'sides', it also underlined that the principle of universal jurisdiction is a "vital element in the fight against impunity", and recognises that both, customary international law and international treaty law permits, and at times obliges States to exercise universal jurisdiction.[37] The report underlined

---

[37] See the letter sent by Redress and FIDH to the EU Council Africa Working Group, 22 April 2009, www.redress.org/downloads/publications/FIDH_REDRESS_Letter_on_Universal_

that there is more or less a general consensus when it comes to the legal basis for universal jurisdiction, yet that there is a real difference between AU and EU Member States in relation to its exercise in practice. When pressed to withdraw the arrest warrants issued by judges of EU member States against African officials, the EU officials refused, arguing that the exercise of universal jurisdiction is a matter exclusively of States' national competence, which falls outside EU competence.

A report of the African Commission on 'the Abuse of the Principle of Universal Jurisdiction' presented at its 16th Session on 25–29 January 2010 recognises that despite considerable action taken in respect of the European Union, "it will be difficult to find a durable solution in further discussions on this matter with the EU side".[38]

The EU appears to have hoped that the 'issue of universal jurisdiction' would go away with the publication of the Expert Report, and that business could continue as usual at subsequent AU-EU Troika meetings. This, however, does not yet seem to have happened. At its 15th Ordinary Session held on 27 July 2010, the AU adopted yet another decision (its fifth, see above) on the abuse of the principle of universal jurisdiction, urging the EU and its Member States "to extend the necessary cooperation to the AU to facilitate the search for a durable solution to the abuse of the Principle of Universal Jurisdiction".[39] Furthermore, the AU's submission to the United Nations to deal with the principle of universal jurisdiction [see below] will require the respective Presidency of the EU to take a formal position in respect of universal jurisdiction on behalf of the EU. Furthermore, it remains to be seen what action the AU might take if further arrest warrants are issued and if the EU ignores that this presents a problem to some African countries.

Since for the time being, relatively little has been achieved to convince the EU to formulate a joint position on the principle of universal jurisdiction, current African Union efforts seem to focus on the United Nations.

At its 64th session, on 14 September 2009, the United Nations General Assembly (UNGA) decided, after 'intense efforts by the African Group',[40] that the UN's Sixth Committee (legal committee) should consider item 84, namely the 'The Scope and Application of the Principle of Universal Jurisdiction'. The Sixth Committee issued a draft resolution for consideration of the General Assembly, which adopted a resolution on 16 December 2009. The resolution requests Member States to submit relevant information on national legislation

---

Jurisdiction_22_April_2009.pdf.

[38] African Union, Progress Report of the Commission on the Abuse of the Principle of Universal Jurisdiction, 25–29 January 2010, EX.CL/540 (XVI).

[39] Decision on the Abuse of the Principle of Universal Jurisdiction, Doc.Ex.CL/606 (XVII).

[40] African Union, Progress Report of the Commission on the Abuse of the Principle of Universal Jurisdiction, 25–29 January 2010, EX.CL/540 (XVI), p. 4.

and practice to the Committee and requires the Sixth Committee to continue to consider the issue and to include item 84 at its 65th session.[41]

The African Union reacted to the developments by sending a representative of the Commission to the African Group's legal experts in order to devise an 'African strategy' for engagement in the process. The Strategy includes pushing forward the initial proposal for the establishment of an international regulatory mechanism with a competence "to review and/or handle complaints or appeals arising out of the abuse of the Principle of Universal Jurisdiction by individual States".[42]

6. PROSPECTS AND TRENDS OF UNIVERSAL JURISDICTION

Despite the important developments in relation to the application of the principle of universal jurisdiction, much 'confusion' remains as to what the principle means in practice and in law. Much of this 'confusion' had been influenced by the politics and indeed by the statements made by African States at AU summits, as well as by other States before the GA and the 6th Committee, which seem to deliberately downplay the principle or paint it as a hegemonic tool of Western States. Such statements are particularly made by those States whose officials have in the past been targeted by universal jurisdiction investigations, such as China, Rwanda or Israel, or States that do not have a very convincing track record in international justice more generally, such as Libya.

Efforts to clarify the principle on an international level are welcome and perhaps overdue. However, such discussion must take place in an informed and transparent arena, not solely a political one. Such an informed discussion requires the consultation of experienced practitioners as well as experts in public international and international criminal law. Opportunities for States as well as civil society to provide relevant information must be guaranteed. It must be recalled that the principle is derived in part from international treaties to which States have already agreed to be bound and from customary international law. It is therefore not appropriate or feasible to re-negotiate or re-write legal obligations simply because the politics relating to their application have changed or become out of fashion. This denigrates the strength of law as a whole.

---

41   UNGA Resolution on the Scope and Application of the Principle of Universal Jurisdiction, 15 January 2010, A/RES/64/117.

42   See Decision on the Abuse of the Principle of Universal Jurisdiction, Doc.Ex.CL/606 (XVII), point 4.

7. CONCLUSION

Universal jurisdiction should not replace or reduce the emphasis on States' obligations to carry out investigations and prosecutions into the most serious crimes under international law allegedly committed on their territory. As such, it will be important to assist territorial States to carry out such legally and procedurally complex and often time-consuming investigations. Training, building capacity and professional exchanges of best practice and experience are vital to help ensure that a country's justice system, in particular in a post-conflict situation, will be able to undertake such investigations and prosecutions. Universal jurisdiction can contribute to end the culture of impunity, but it is no panacea to impunity itself. That is the prerogative of territorial jurisdictions. The ICC, as well as the experienced staff of *ad hoc* or specialised criminal tribunals have an important role to play to ensure that expertise is shared with national judicial authorities. In the present debate, it is often overlooked that countries do not actually want to exercise universal jurisdiction; in the experience of the authors it is more typically a jurisdiction that authorities actively seek to avoid and it is only exercised as a jurisdiction of last resort, where no other viable alternative to accountability and justice exists. Universal jurisdiction investigations and prosecutions are difficult, time-consuming and expensive and the far-away factual contexts do not resonate easily with investigators and other judicial officials caught up in more immediate, closer concerns. Support and assistance to the territorial State is therefore the only long term viable option to ensure accountability and justice on a broad scale.

While the emphasis should therefore be on the territorial State, it is also obvious that universal jurisdiction must expand to become truly universal. At the moment, it is only a few States, mainly European, that effectively exercise universal jurisdiction. A prominent example is the 1994 genocide in Rwanda: while some universal jurisdiction proceedings are ongoing in Europe against suspects living in European countries, far more alleged perpetrators fled to African countries. Yet despite the presence of such suspects on their territories, no investigation and prosecution was carried out against any of these suspects in any African country. Nor, for that matter, have such suspects been extradited to Rwanda. Legal and practical problems may impede such proceedings, yet these barriers can be overcome as they have been in other countries and regions. However, this requires a degree of political willingness to exercise universal jurisdiction.

The debate on universal jurisdiction not only takes place in a much politicised environment, but also invokes the most controversial cases to limit the practical implementation of universal jurisdiction or to even dismiss the whole concept as such. However, the politicised debates rarely consider the many instances in which universal jurisdiction was applied successfully and in a non-political way.

The debate does not acknowledge that over the recent years it has been applied to hold accountable those that would otherwise slip through the net of impunity. Several countries have begun to establish specialised war crimes units within their police and prosecution services, designed to ensure that perpetrators of serious international crimes such as war crimes, genocide, crimes against humanity and torture no longer go unpunished. Real practical expertise has developed in recent years at the national level. The starting point for a discussion on universal jurisdiction should therefore not be the attempt to limit its application in practice or focus on its abuse, but rather how to build on what has been achieved so far, how to expand the concept and enable more countries, in particular African countries, to effectively exercise universal jurisdiction for the worst crimes. This is especially true, as it was African countries that have played such an important role in supporting the development of international criminal justice, resulting not only in the establishment of the ICC, but also in important steps made by those countries to enhance their domestic capacity to respond to international crimes.

XVIII. SURVIVORS OF THE RWANDAN GENOCIDE UNDER DOMESTIC AND INTERNATIONAL LEGAL PROCEDURES

Felix Ndahinda

1. INTRODUCTION

The notion of 'victim' in relation to the genocide perpetrated against the Tutsi population of Rwanda is not easily translatable in *Kinyarwanda*, the national language of Rwanda. Generally, the concept of victimhood encompasses those who were killed and those who survived the atrocities.[1] However, *Kinyarwanda* generally uses 'victims' to refer to persons who were killed while other victimized individuals who were not killed during the atrocities are generally referred to as survivors.[2] Most survivors lost nearly all they had or cared for during the genocide or the civil war that preceded and accompanied it. They are the first to acknowledge that nothing can be done to give them back what they lost. This does not prevent the resolute action by individual survivors or their organisations to participate in endeavours aimed at ensuring accountability for perpetrators of the genocide. The quest for retribution and reparation only represents partial remedies as they can only provide minimal satisfaction to survivors who have endured tremendous pain and suffering.

---

[1]   Hence, *abazize itsembabwoko* literally refers to dead and surviving victims of the genocide of the Tutsi population of Rwanda. It should be noted that since the genocide in 1994, there have been numerous terminological uses in reference to the acts committed. Initially *itsembabwoko* (the adopted *Kinyarwanda* translation for 'genocide') was always paired with *itsembatsemba* (massacres) so as to clarify that the killings also targeted Hutu opposed to the Habyarimana regime or extremists agenda (commonly referred to in Rwanda as 'moderate Hutu'). However, as the negationist/revisionist movement took hold – mainly in the Western world since the mid-2000s – survivors and the Rwandan government started using more *itsembabwoko ryakorewe Abatusi* (genocide against the Tutsi), without downplaying the victimization of moderate Hutu.

[2]   *Abazize itsembabwoko* (or *abishwe mu itsembabwoko*) and *abacitse ku icumu/abarokotse Itsembabwoko* respectively. The commonly used terminology for survivors, *abacitse ku icumu*, literally translates 'those who escaped [death by] the spear'; the spear being the ultimate weapon used in pre-colonial battles. For that reason, the present analysis mostly uses the term survivors instead of victims. However, where required, they will be referred to as 'victims' (especially in relation to specific legislations) or as 'surviving victims'.

The present analysis looks at how the needs and interests of the survivors of the 1994 genocide either have or have not been accommodated under various judicial procedures dealing with the genocide legacy. The chapter dwells on procedures in Rwanda as the scene of the crimes but also as the forum where the overwhelming number of cases were handled. However, it also touches upon the position of survivors in other proceedings – the ICTR and foreign domestic jurisdictions – dealing with the Rwandan genocide. The chapter is generally concerned with the various forms of involvement of survivors in legal proceedings, from the time of instigation of proceedings to the trial phase and the aftermath or procedures of extradition. Analytical focus on survivors of the genocide is not intended to downplay any other form of victimization before, during and after the 1994 genocide. A number of authors have explored the fact from the end 1950s – with the country's transition towards independence from Belgium – until the 1990 civil war and the 1994 genocide, violent repression was part of the country's strategy of governance (Prunier 1995; Mamdani 2001; De Feyter *et al.* 2005). Persons other than genocide survivors were victimized throughout the troubled history of Rwanda before and during the 1990 civil war, the genocide and the regionalisation of the Rwandan conflict in the aftermath of the genocide (Mamdani 2001; Prunier 2008; Turner 2007). Every tragic loss of a human life at the hand of other human beings should be given the importance it deserves. However, the special intent and modes of perpetration of a crime whose aim is to erase an entire group of human beings sets Tutsi survivors of genocide apart.

2. LIVING AFTER DEATH: THE REALITIES OF SURVIVORS AFTER THE GENOCIDE

2.1. LIVING IN THE AFTERMATH OF THE GENOCIDE

Numerous publications have documented how, and tentatively why, a genocide was perpetrated against the Tutsi population of Rwanda between April and July 1994 (Mamdani 2001; Prunier 1995; Des Forges 1999; Eltingham 2006; Ruvebana, this volume). It is necessary to mention that the killings further targeted Hutu opposed to the genocide agenda. The genocide took place following nearly four years of a civil war between the rebels of the Rwandan Patriotic Front (RPF) and its army the Rwandan Patriotic Army (RPA) and the governmental Rwandan Armed Forces (FAR in French). The macabre plan to wipe out the entire Tutsi population of Rwanda did not materialise as it was halted with the military victory of the RPF/RPA. From the start of the civil war in October 1990 to RPF victory in July 1994, around one million mothers and fathers, children and parents, grandparents, brothers and sisters, uncles and aunts, friends and acquaintances, neighbours or simply: human beings, were slaughtered.

Numerous survivors witnessed the atrocities perpetrated against their loved ones as many of them were themselves powerlessly victimized. Many of them bear the scars of rape, and other forms of sexual, physical and psychological violence that they suffered.

The destruction and desolation were indescribable in the immediate aftermath of the genocide. The chaos reached proportions that made it hard to imagine that there would be life in Rwanda and in particular for survivors after the genocide. It is not surprising to note that since the aftermath of the genocide, Rwanda features in thousands of academic or other publications and is a favourite topic or destination for social scientists eager to test their ideas on people, societies and polities in (post) crisis. More than seventeen years after the tragedy, the scars of the genocide are still visible and the wounds far from healed. In the early post-genocide era, the lasting (mental) trauma – or *guhahamuka* as it is widely known in Rwanda – was, and still is, an omnipresent phenomenon within Rwandan society. But more than others, genocide survivors suffered various levels of trauma. Their multiple needs and demands have not often been met. Survivors remain inconsolable as things can never be the same again for people who witness such atrocities and suffered losses as they did. Yet, most of them have beaten the odds by carrying on with their lives and facing life challenges with a semblance of normalcy.

2.2. NEGOTIATING POST-GENOCIDE SOCIAL HARMONY: JUSTICE AND SACRIFICES

The post-genocide administration headed by the RPF faced numerous challenges in their efforts to govern a country in ruins. Those challenges dictated pragmatic approaches to solutions to the various compelling problems the administration had to tackle. Some of those challenges had to do with finding the right balance between justice and reconciliation imperatives. Depicted by the previous regime as an essentially Tutsi political organization whose sole purpose was to capture power in order to subjugate the Hutu, the RPF had to overcome the ambient hostility of a pre-genocide indoctrinated population in efforts to govern the country. For that reason, RPF authorities experimented numerous forms of political arrangements and social policies aimed at gaining the confidence of the population. In spite of a military victory that enabled them to determine how to govern the country, the authorities engaged in coalition governments (that were not always successful), initiated reconciliation campaigns[3] and adopted social

---

[3] It was generally not easy to get a clear answer to such a simple question as to who should be reconciled with whom? All Tutsi with all Hutu (and what about the Twas)? Or just the perpetrators and their surviving victims? And should reconciliation be effected at the individual level or in a collective manner?

policies that tried to be inclusive. In the meantime, the defeated regime and militia regrouped (mostly in DR-Congo) and launched attacks and series of killings aimed at recapturing power or destabilising the new government.[4] The prevailing insecurity that followed the genocide was met by numerous military campaigns conducted by the new Rwandan army within and beyond national boundaries (Mamdani 2001; Prunier 2008).

Millions of refugees that had followed the former Rwandan regime into exile returned to the country. In a context whereby the habitat is such that the survivors and perpetrators have lived together on the same hills, in the same villages or neighbourhoods for ages, many returnees went back to their homes to resume their life alongside surviving victims. Upon denunciations, more than one hundred thousand people suspected of having played a role in the atrocities were incarcerated in the most precarious conditions – at least during the first post-genocide years (Schabas 1996 and 2005; Fierens 2005). Subsequently, a Presidential Communiqué issued on 1 January 2003 allowed for the release of some 22,000 people comprising some who had confessed to the killings and others who were seriously sick, elderly or minors at the time of the commission of the offense.[5] Around 36,000 and 8,000 other suspects were released in 2005 and 2007 respectively.[6]

Ingelaere (2009b, 508) contends that in the years that followed the 1994 genocide, "retributive justice and reconciliation were seen as mutually exclusive objectives by the Rwanda[n] Government". This unsubstantiated statement somewhat ignores the fact that the first legal text organizing prosecutions of genocide suspects – Organic Law No. 08/96 of August 30, 1996[7] – but also the power-sharing process that led to the establishment of post-genocide political institutions[8] clearly translated reconciliation aspirations. Concrete steps were taken since 1998, culminating in the establishment in 1999 of a National Unity and Reconciliation Commission.[9] As evident in the preamble of the 1996

---

4   Section 4.1.1 further elaborates on the armed insurgency and insecurity that followed the defeat of the former Rwandan government.

5   Penal Reform International (PRI), *From Camp to Hill, the Reintegration of Released Prisoners*, Gacaca Research Report No. 6, 2004, 2.

6   Penal Reform International (PRI), *Eight Years on: A Record of* Gacaca *Monitoring in Rwanda*, 2010, 9.

7   Organic Law No. 08/96 of 30 August 1996 on the Organization of Prosecutions for Offences constituting the Crime of Genocide or Crimes against Humanity committed since October 1, 1990, Official Gazette, Year 35, No 17, September 1996, at 14 (hereinafter the 1996 Genocide law). The last paragraph of the preamble read "in order to achieve reconciliation and justice in Rwanda, it is essential that the culture of impunity be eradicated forever".

8   As mentioned above, institutions were established through a power-sharing between the RPF and other political parties.

9   See: Law N° 03/99 of 12 March 1999 Establishing the National Unity and Reconciliation Commission, Official Gazette, N° 6 of 15 March 1999. See also: Institute for Justice and Reconciliation (IJR), *Evaluation and Impact Assessment of the National Unity and Reconciliation Commission (NURC)*, Final Report, December 2005.

Genocide law, Rwandan authorities only insisted that the pursued policy of reconciliation would not trump the search for justice. Against all odds, they expressed their determination to hold accountable those responsible for the genocide (Schabas 1996).[10] For a country whose reconstruction was heavily reliant on mobilisation of funds from abroad, mainly from Western donor countries, there was some kind of stubborn determination to ignore the prescriptions of many foreign partners sceptical about the success of systematic prosecutions in Rwanda. Schabas – a scholar who closely followed the evolution – refers to an "intransigent course" and "a stubborn resistance to compromise" in reference to the determination by Rwandan authorities to hold genocide perpetrators accountable (in Clark & Kaufman 2009, 207). Proposals for the establishment of truth and reconciliation commissions inspired by the South African and other experiences were clearly excluded as the sole way of dealing with the legacy of the genocide. Through trials and errors, the Rwandan government went through several paths in efforts aimed at holding those responsible for the genocide accountable. The judicial proceedings put in motion since 1996 encouraged those who participated in the genocide to confess their crimes, denounce co-perpetrators and ask for forgiveness; the reward being a substantial reduction of applicable sentences. But the imperatives of bringing back stability and the determination to hold the perpetrators individually accountable could not always be served to the satisfaction of all. For subjective reasons, it would be unreasonable to expect that most relatives of the dozens of thousands of incarcerated genocide suspects were in favour of prosecutions. At the same time, survivors had to come to terms with the fact that some perpetrators of the most horrendous crime were set free while most of them incurred lower punishment than perpetrators of comparable ordinary crimes. Accordingly, it is not surprising that post-genocide authorities have been accused by some survivors of being lenient on the perpetrators while others claim that they are victimizing the entire Hutu population under the (*Gacaca*) judicial process (as in Corey & Joireman 2004).

2.3. THE VOICE OF SURVIVORS IN THE AFTERMATH OF THE 1994 GENOCIDE

In the wake of the 1994 genocide in Rwanda, aggrieved survivors were quick to establish organizations aimed at bringing them together in keeping the memory of the dead and caring for those who survived the atrocities. Such organizations include AVEGA-AGAHOZO (*Association des Veuves du Génocide* or Association

---

[10]   Since 1994, in songs, political speeches or conversations the recurrent pledge relating to perpetrators of the genocide was: *Abakoze ayo marorerwa bagomba guhanwa by'intagarugero*: those who committed the atrocities should be exemplary held accountable.

of the Widows of the Genocide), AERG (*Association des Etudiants Rescapés du Génocide* or Association of Student Survivors of the Genocide) and IBUKA (*Kinyarwanda* for 'Remember') (see Muleefu, this volume). IBUKA fulfils a federative role as an umbrella organization regrouping several survivors' organizations, including AVEGA-AGAHOZO.[11] The organization is active in Rwanda but has also opened branches in foreign countries such as France and Belgium. Nationally and internationally, IBUKA has been particularly active as the memory of the dead and the voice of the survivors of the genocide. It acts as the main partner with all actors involved in addressing problems of political, socio-economic, psychological and legal nature that are part of the genocide legacy. IBUKA further undertakes an activist role vis-à-vis the Rwandan government but also other national and international actors in matters of interest to survivors of the genocide. In this particular role, the organization has sometimes clashed with other actors involved in dealing with the aftermath of the genocide including the Rwandan government (on the processes of releasing suspects), the International Criminal Tribunal for Rwanda (ICTR), or foreign countries harbouring genocide suspects.[12]

3. LEGAL PROCEDURES IN RWANDA AND THE POSITION OF GENOCIDE SURVIVORS

3.1. POST-1994 JUDICIAL LANDSCAPE

The Rwandan judiciary, like nearly every other sector, was in ruins in the wake of the genocide. Following the killing or the exile of the still limited number of pre-genocide legal practitioners and the destruction of existing infrastructure, nearly everything needed to be rebuilt from scratch. It took some two years for national authorities to put in motion legal mechanisms of accountability for the genocide (Schabas 2003 and 2005). In August 1996, the Transitional National Assembly adopted the 1996 Genocide law laying the ground for prosecution of genocide suspects. This law introduced a system of categorisation of genocide suspects into four main categories (Article 2), and a procedure of confession and guilty plea which, if declared valid, was accompanied by a substantial reduction of the sentence that the suspect should otherwise have incurred (Articles 4–13 and 15–16) (see Kaitesi & Haveman, this volume). The said law further established specialized chambers within existing Tribunals of First Instance to specifically

---

[11]   For more, see: www.ibuka.net/pres.html (last visited: 15 July 2010).

[12]   Redress & African Rights, *Survivors and Post-Genocide Justice in Rwanda: Their Experiences, Perspectives and Hopes*, Report, 2008, 4 *et seq.* In early 2003 the present author participated on an IBUKA project of examining the regularity of the release of those concerned by the Presidential Communiqué of 1 January 2003. For disagreements with the ICTR, see section 4.1.3.

deal with genocide cases (Articles 19–21). In spite of its innovative features, the mechanism of accountability established under the 1996 genocide law faced serious challenges of being inadequate in handling all the cases of an ever-growing number of suspects within a reasonable timeframe. Upon realization of the shortcomings of the proceedings before the Specialized Chambers, the government embarked on the path that led to the establishment of the *gacaca* courts inspired by Rwandan traditional forms of justice.[13] Initially, 12,103 community-based *Gacaca* Jurisdictions were established throughout the country to hear cases relating to the genocide.[14] In establishing the *gacaca* courts, the Rwandan government defied the scepticism – characterising most international partners, namely foreign (western) governments and leading human rights organizations – over a process perceived as not conforming to internationally acceptable due process guarantees (Fierens 2005; Oomen 2005).

According to Rwandan authorities, the creation of the *gacaca* courts aimed at fulfilling the following objectives: revealing the truth about what happened during the genocide; speeding up genocide trials; eradicating the culture of impunity; reconciling Rwandans and reinforcing their unity and; proving to the rest of the world that the Rwandan society has the capacity to settle its own problems through a system of justice based on the Rwandan custom.[15] The *gacaca* process kept the categorization as well as the confession and guilt plea features introduced by the 1996 Genocide law. The 2001 *gacaca* law provided that people living on the 'hills' where crimes were committed should draw the lists of victims, perpetrators and damaged property (Articles 33–34). The population was encouraged to participate in the *gacaca* process, acting as witnesses, prosecution and defence. The information gathering and subsequent trial phase took place before a bench composed of "persons of integrity" elected from and by the population of the place where a *gacaca* court should operate (Articles 5 19) (see Kaitesi & Haveman, this volume).

The experimental nature of this new form of justice has led to several modifications of the law establishing the *gacaca* courts. Hence, the 2001 *gacaca* law was amended in 2004.[16] The latter law has also been modified and

---

13 Organic Law N° 40/2000 of 26 January 2001 setting up 'Gacaca Jurisdictions' and Organizing Prosecutions for Offences Constituting the Crime of Genocide or Crimes against Humanity Committed between October 1, 1990 and December 31, 1994, Official Gazette, No. 6 of 15 March 2000 (hereinafter the 2001 *Gacaca* law).

14 Www.inkiko-gacaca.gov.rw/Fr/Composition.htm (last visited: 10 July 2010). Following administrative restructuring of the country, the number of *Gacaca* courts was scaled down.

15 See: www.inkiko-gacaca.gov.rw/En/EnObjectives.htm (last visited: 25 January 2010). See also the preamble of the 2001 *Gacaca* law.

16 Organic Law N° 16/2004 of 16 June 2004 establishing the Organisation, Competence and Functioning of Gacaca Courts Charged with Prosecuting and Trying the Perpetrators of the Crime of Genocide and other Crimes against Humanity, Committed between October 1, 1990 and December 31, 1994, Official Gazette, No. Special of 19 June 2004 (hereinafter the 2004 *Gacaca* law).

complemented on more than one occasion.[17] Administrative remapping of the country but also the need to make the system more efficient through a revision of the categorisation system, the composition of the Seat and of the General Assembly of a *gacaca* court, were among the reasons for the frequent modifications of the *gacaca* laws. In spite of the many criticisms of the system – mostly relating to the perceived shortcomings in terms of the right to defence and other due process guarantees, and non-coverage of alleged RPF crimes (Fierens 2005; Corey & Joireman 2004; responding to criticism, see: Haveman 2008; Haveman & Muleefu 2010) – the *gacaca* process has registered many successes in gathering information about the way in which the genocide was perpetrated. More relevant for survivors, many of them came to know more about the fate of their loved ones killed during the genocide and where their remains were thrown. As a result of (at least part of) the truth from *gacaca* sessions, new (mass) graves were identified, slain victims unearthed and re-buried in dignity.[18] Furthermore, one of the benefits of the confession and guilty plea procedure but also of the whole *gacaca* process is that many survivors came to know how their relatives and friends were killed and by whom.

3.2. THE STATUS OF SURVIVORS UNDER RELEVANT POST-GENOCIDE LEGISLATION

The United Nations *Declaration of Basic Principles of Justice for Victims of Crime and Abuse of Power*[19] prescribes that victims of crime should have access to justice, be treated fairly, be entitled to restitution, compensation and to "material, medical, psychological and social assistance" (para. 14). Similar entitlements are recognized in the *Basic Principles and Guidelines on the Right to a Remedy and Reparation for Victims of Gross Violations of International Human Rights Law and Serious Violations of International Humanitarian Law* (UN G.A. Res. 60/147).[20] The International Criminal Tribunal for Rwanda has characterized the

---

[17] Modifications and complements can be found in: Organic Law N° 28/2006 of 27 June 2006, Official Gazette, No. Special of 12 July 2006; Organic Law N° 10/2007 of 1 March 2007, Official Gazette, N° 5 of 1 March 2007 and Organic Law N° 13/2008 of 19 May 2008, Official Gazette, N° 11 of 1 June 2008 (hereafter the 2006, 2007 and 2008 *Gacaca* laws).

[18] Redress & African Rights, *Survivors and Post-Genocide Justice in Rwanda: Their Experiences, Perspectives and Hopes*, Report, 2008, 5 *et seq.*

[19] Declaration of Basic Principles of Justice for Victims of Crime and Abuse of Power, UN General Assembly Resolution 40/34 of 29 November 1985 (hereinafter UN Declaration of Basic Principles of Justice for Victims).

[20] Basic Principles and Guidelines on the Right to a Remedy and Reparation for Victims of Gross Violations of International Human Rights Law and Serious Violations of International Humanitarian Law (hereinafter Basic Principles and Guidelines on Victims), UN General Assembly Resolution 60/147 of 16 December 2005. In addition to access to justice and fair treatment, the Basic Principles and Guidelines on Victims refer to a right to "full and effective

committed crime of genocide as "the crime of crimes".[21] Accordingly, it is more
than legitimate to reflect on how victims of that most heinous crime are
accommodated or not in relevant legal proceedings. The present analysis focuses
on legal (non-)recognition of survivors beyond the usual mode of participation
as witnesses in criminal proceedings.

3.2.1. Survivors rights under the Organic Law No. 08/96

In comparison with subsequent laws, the regime established under the 1996
Genocide law was, normatively, relatively rich in terms of legal entitlements of
persons victimized during the genocide. Relevant provisions were inspired by
generally applicable norms on rights of victims of crimes under Rwandan law.[22]
The said 1996 law only provided for participation rights of victims in legal
proceedings and their right to claim damages. It did not elaborate on how other
needs of genocide survivors – be they psychological, material and social – should
be met. Articles 27–32 codified the entitlement of, and procedures to be followed
by, victims intending to initiate criminal proceedings, to participate in
proceeding as civil parties and/or to claim damages. The 1996 law provided that
"ordinary rules governing denunciations, complaints and civil actions are
applicable to cases before the specialized chambers" (Article 29 (1)). In terms of
claiming and paying damages, Article 30 reads:

> *Convicted persons whose acts place them within Category 1 under Article 2 shall be
> held jointly and severally liable for all damages caused in the country by their acts of
> criminal participation, regardless of where the offences were committed.*
>
> *Persons whose acts place them within Categories 2, 3, or 4 shall be held liable for
> damages for the criminal acts they have committed.*
>
> *Without prejudice to the rights of civil parties present or represented at trial, and at the
> request of the Public Prosecution Department, the court shall award damages to victims
> not yet identified.*

---

reparation (…) which include (…) restitution, compensation, rehabilitation, satisfaction and
guarantees of non-repetition" (see paras. 18–23).

21   *Prosecutor v. Jean Kambanda*, Case no.: ICTR 97-23-S, Judgement, 4 September 1998, para.
16.

22   See for instance Articles 258–262 of décret du 30 Juillet 1888, Code Civil – [Livre 1er:] Des
Contrats ou des Obligations Conventionnelles, (B.O., 1888, P. 109), as modified; Articles 9–17
of Law N° 13/2004 of 17 May 2004 relating to the Code of Criminal Procedure, Official
Gazette, No. Special of 30 July 2004 (this currently applicable law replaced the then applicable
law of February 23, 1963 relating to Criminal Procedure as amended). Articles 160–165 of
Organic Law N° 51/2008 of 09 September 2008 Determining the Organisation, Functioning
and Jurisdiction of Courts (replacing previously applicable laws, including then applicable
Law Decree n° 9/80 of 7th July 1980 as modified and complemented).

It is clear from the reading of relevant provisions that the rights of victims were not necessarily conditioned to the outcome of the criminal action against the accused responsible for the harm caused to the victim (for instance Article 31). Under Article 32 damages could even be awarded to victims who had not yet been identified. The same provision referred to the establishment of a 'Victims Compensation Fund' whose creation and operation were to be determined by a separate law. Research (De Feyter *et al.* 2005) has shown that judgments passed under the 1996 Genocide law regime awarded compensation to survivors, even if a 2005 assessment found that awarded compensation was not actually paid.

Instead of creating a 'Victims Compensation Fund' as spelt out in the 1996 law, the Rwandan government established in 1998 a 'National Fund for Assistance to Victims of Genocide and Massacres Perpetrated in Rwanda from 01 October 1990 to 31 December 1994', commonly known as FARG.[23] As its very name suggests, the created FARG could obviously not be expected to perform the functions of the contemplated Compensation Fund. The mere fact that is was managed by the Rwandan Ministry of Social Affairs coupled with provisions on the sources of the Fund's assets make it clear that it was established as a means of trying to attend to the most urgent – material and other social – needs of genocide survivors.[24] The state undertook to dedicate five percent (5%) of its own revenue to the Fund,[25] to be supplemented by funds from other multiple sources (Article 12).

In force for more than a decade, the 1998 FARG law was abolished and replaced by a new law creating a 'Fund for the *Support and Assistance* to the Survivors of the Genocide against the Tutsi and Other Crimes against Humanity'.[26] The law establishing this new fund was adopted at a time when the activities of *Gacaca* Courts were in the process of winding up. For that reason, relevant provisions on entitlements of survivors of the genocide are examined

---

[23] Law N° 02/1998 of 22 January 1998 Creating the National Fund for Assistance to Victims of Genocide and Massacres Perpetrated in Rwanda from 1 October 1990 to 31 December 1994 (FARG stands for: *Fonds National pour l'Assistance aux Rescapés du Génocide*), Official Gazette No. 3 of 1 February 1998.

[24] The French title of the law referred to a fund charged with assisting the neediest victims of the genocide (Loi No. 2/1998 du 22 janvier 1998 portant création du fonds national pour l'assistance aux *victimes les plus nécessiteuses du génocide* et des massacres perpétrés au Rwanda entre le 1 octobre 1990 et le 31 décembre 1994). The social dimension is also clear in Article 14 on the beneficiaries of the Fund (prioritizing orphans, widows and the disabled).

[25] Article 1 (2) of: Loi No. 11/1998 du 2 novembre 1998 modifiant et complétant la loi No. 2/1998 du 22 janvier 1998 portant création du fonds national pour l'assistance aux victimes les plus nécessiteuses du génocide et des massacres perpétrés au Rwanda entre le 1 octobre 1990 et le 31 décembre 1994, Official Gazette, No. Special of 2 November 1998.

[26] Law N° 69/2008 of 30/12/2008 Relating of the Establishment of the Fund for the Support and Assistance to the Survivors of the Genocide against the Tutsi and Other Crimes against Humanity Committed between 1st October 1990 And 31st December 1994, and Determining its Organisation, Competence and Functioning, No. Special of 15 April 2009 (hereafter 2008 FARG law). Emphasis added. The law is hereafter referred to as the '2008 FARG law' in spite of the fact that 'FARG' is no longer its exact title.

subsequently to an inquiry into the legal entitlements of survivors under the various *Gacaca* laws.

3.2.2. Survivors under the Gacaca system

Throughout the amendments and revisions of the initial *gacaca* law, it is evident that the philosophy on entitlements of surviving victims, mainly in terms of claiming damages in their own capacity, shifted progressively towards restricted forms of participation. The initial, 2001, *gacaca* law contained a set of provisions of specific relevance to survivors of the genocide (for instance: Articles 33, 34, 54, 64–71, 90 and 91). During the information-gathering phase, the General Assembly of the *gacaca* jurisdiction of the Cell was tasked, among others, to preparing lists of persons who lived in the Cell before the genocide and massacres, of victims and of the perpetrators (Article 33(a)). Furthermore, in addition to providing details relating to the commission of the crimes, the names of accomplices and witnesses, the validity of a confession procedure and guilty plea was conditioned to a listing of victims and their damaged assets (Article 54(a) and (b)). During the trial and judgment phase, the Seat of the *gacaca* jurisdiction had to establish "the identity of persons having suffered material damages and the inventory of damages caused to their assets as well as the list of victims and the inventory of suffered body damages" (Article 64(9), and similarly, Articles 65(13), 66(9) and 67(9)). Under the 2001 *gacaca* law, the Specialized Chambers established in ordinary courts subsisted, for purposes of winding up initiated cases (Article 96). Moreover, persons put in the first category were to be tried by ordinary courts, applying the ordinary penal norms and procedure, subject to few exceptions laid down in the 2001 *gacaca* law (Article 2). According to Article 90:

> *Ordinary jurisdictions and 'Gacaca Jurisdictions' forward to the Compensation Fund for Victims of the Genocide and Crimes against humanity copies of rulings and judgements they have passed, which shall indicate the following:*

> – *the identity of persons who have suffered material losses and the inventory of damages to their property;*
> – *the list of victims and the inventory of suffered body damages;*
> – *as well as related damages fixed in conformity with the scale provided for by law.*

> *The Fund, based on the damages fixed by jurisdictions, fixes the modalities for granting compensation.*

Despite the minor differences – the 1996 law refers to a 'Victims Compensation Fund' while the 2001 *gacaca* law refers to a 'Compensation Fund for Victims of the Genocide and Crimes against humanity' – the initial *gacaca* law, like the 1996 Genocide law, contemplated the establishment of a body to specifically deal with compensation. However, the first *gacaca* law clearly displayed some form of ambiguity, if not confusion, between the principle (or policy) of assistance to survivors of the genocide – as evidenced by the creation of a fund for that purpose – and survivors' legal entitlement to compensation. The 2001 *gacaca* law provided for the inadmissibility of any civil action against the State before the ordinary *gacaca* jurisdictions using the argument that the country had "acknowledged its role in the genocide and that in compensation it pays each year a percentage of its annual budget to the Compensation Fund" (Article 91 (3)). Since that Compensation Fund has never been established, it is not clear whether this provision referred to the government's contribution to the Assistance Fund established under the 1998 FARG law as modified and complemented.

In 2004, the 2001 *gacaca* law was replaced by Organic Law No. 16/2004 of 19/6/2004 (the 2004 *gacaca* law).[27] Unlike its predecessors, which remained silent on the matter, the 2004 law defined the victim as

> *anybody killed, hunted to be killed but survived, suffered acts of torture against his or her sexual parts, suffered rape, injured or victim of any other form of harassment, plundered, and whose house and property were destroyed because of his or her ethnic background or opinion against the genocide ideology.* (Article 34)[28]

Owing to the sensitivity and societal stigmatization of victims of rape and other forms of sexual violence, Article 38 of the 2004 *gacaca* law, as amended by Article 6 of the 2008 *gacaca* law, introduced confidentiality measures and special proceedings in camera for prosecutions of such crimes (Kaitesi & Haveman, this volume).

Cases relating to damaged property were to be submitted to the *gacaca* court of the Cell or other courts before which the defendants had to appear, without a possibility of appeal (Article 94). Under Article 95, forms of reparation – under modalities to be determined by the court and enforced by public authority – include: 1° restitution of the property looted whenever possible; 2° repayment of the ransacked property or carrying out the work worth the property to be repaired. Unlike preceding laws, the 2004 *gacaca* law, as amended, did not specifically provide for the establishment of a Compensation Fund for victims. It simply stated that other forms of compensation the victims receive "shall be determined by a particular law" (Article 96). The subsequently adopted law did

---

[27]　Among other features of the new law were: 1) a reorganization of levels of *Gacaca* Courts (*Gacaca* Courts of Cell, Sector and Appeal instead of the *Gacaca* Courts of Cell, Sector, District and Province in the 2001 *Gacaca* law), 2) a review of the categorisation of system (from four to three categories of genocide suspects), 3) a simplification of procedures and requirements for the functioning of the various *Gacaca* Courts, and 4) confidentiality procedures for prosecutions of the crime of rape and other acts of sexual violence.

[28]　Articles 33(f) and 34(f) 51, 54, 64(9), 65(f), 66(g), 67(9), 68(2) and (11), and 69(8) also refer to victims.

not establish a compensation fund but rather a fund for the support and assistance to survivors as discussed in the next section.

3.2.3. *The Fund for the support and assistance to the survivors of the genocide against the Tutsi and other crimes against humanity*

Somehow moving away from the strict philosophy of compensation,[29] the Rwandan parliament passed a law establishing a Fund for the *support* and *assistance* to the survivors of the Tutsi genocide and other crimes against humanity.[30] The preamble of this law makes express reference to Article 96 of the 2004 *gacaca* law promising the adoption of a "particular law" on compensation to victims; thereby suggesting that the established fund is meant to fulfil this purpose. The same preamble and Article 22(7) specifically provide that the fund created under the 2008 FARG law replaces the 1998 FARG law. The restructured fund under the 2008 FARG law is "responsible for the monitoring, collection and distribution of contributions for the survivors of the Genocide against the Tutsi and other crimes against humanity, starting with the needy" (Article 4).

In addition to a list of tasks the fund shall perform to ensure the welfare of survivors, it is also charged with the mission of taking action, seeking and collecting "indemnity against persons convicted of the Genocide against the Tutsi and other crimes against humanity that categorise them in the first category" (Article 4(2)(3)). Under Article 20, the created fund is given exclusive authority to initiate civil action against persons convicted of crimes classifying them in the first category. The action is undertaken by the fund on behalf of survivors (victims in the law) of the genocide and other crimes against humanity. Survivors can only "assist" the fund throughout legal proceedings, without a guarantee of directly recovering damages from the process (Article 21). Resources mobilised by the fund are allocated on the basis of the pressing needs of the surviving beneficiaries (Article 26). It is important to note that the authoritative Kinyarwanda text of the law and the French translation of Article 3(2) on "definition of terms" provide that the Fund is intended to support survivors of the genocide perpetrated against the Tutsi and other crimes against humanity. This reading seems to go in line with the practice on the ground whereby some Hutu (for instance widows whose Tutsi husbands were killed or some 'moderate Hutu') are part of survivors' associative initiatives such as IBUKA, AERG and AVEGA, and thus (potential) beneficiaries of survivors' assistance (Rombouts

---

29   Penal Reform International (PRI), *Trials of Offences against Property Committed during the Genocide: A Conflict between the Theory of Reparation and the Social and Economic Reality in Rwanda*, Monitoring and Research Report on the Gacaca, 2007, 3.

30   Law N° 69/2008 of 30 December 2008; *supra* note 26. Emphasis added.

2004). The English translation is somehow misleading as it seems to suggest that only Tutsi can be assisted by the Fund.[31]

3.3. ASSESSING THE POSITION OF VICTIMS IN POST-GENOCIDE RWANDA

From the above legislative overview, it is clear that the role and entitlements of genocide survivors have fluctuated under the various laws enacted by post-genocide Rwandan authorities. In proceedings initially before the Specialized Chambers in ordinary courts and later before the *gacaca* courts, survivors played the traditional role as witness in criminal proceedings against genocide suspects. Beyond that role, the normative, procedural and institutional dynamism characterizing Rwandan criminal prosecutions of the genocide and related crimes is also evident in the position of surviving victims. Among other noticeable changes in the role and entitlement of survivors, the most important changes are: (1) the right of survivors to trigger criminal proceedings; (2) the subrogation of the Assistance Fund in the victims' right to initiate civil action and seek compensation and; (3) the admissibility requirements for a confession and guilt plea procedure.

Under the 1996 genocide law, victims could, acting individually or collectively, trigger criminal proceeding against suspects, and file claims (civil action) for damages (Article 29). The unique mode of participation of the (local) population as prosecution, defence and witness in the *gacaca* process somehow nullified the very *raison d'être* of this prerogative. During the information-gathering but also during the trial phase, the law entitles not only survivors but also any member of the community to press charges against anyone for participation in the genocide or speak in defence of an accused person. In proceedings whose main objective is to unearth the truth about what happened during the genocide, false denunciations or testimonies are punishable under the law.[32]

Early in the judicial process, Rwandan authorities projected that proceedings would involve over 800,000 suspects (Schabas 2005). The *gacaca* process was revived and remodelled as a solution that would, among other objectives, expedite genocide trials. However, the exceptionally high number of suspects, the limited solvability of most of them and the complexity of designing a suitable system of active participation and reparation for all surviving victims, arguably, led to the progressive suppression of their individual right to seek compensation,

---

[31] The English translation reads: "Fund": Fund for the support and assistance to the Tutsi survivors of the genocide and other crimes against humanity committed between 1st October 1990 and 31st December 1994.

[32] Article 29 of the 2004 *Gacaca* law.

although still entitled to claim restitution or compensation for the material
damages suffered during the genocide (initially category four, then three, on
property crimes). Somehow incoherently, "other forms of compensation" were
replaced by a policy of support and assistance to survivors through a reshaped
ad hoc fund. Under the general theory of victims' rights, the somehow automatic
subrogation of the victims by the Fund contravenes with their entitlement to full
and effective reparation (UN G.A. Res. 60/147: paras. 18–23). In practice, one
may question whether it is possible at all to fully comply with these guidelines in
light of the magnitude of the task at hand and the needed resources for effective
redress to victims of crimes such as those committed in Rwanda.

The Confession and Guilty Plea Procedure is one of the major pillars of
criminal proceedings against suspects in the Rwandan post-genocide judicial
landscape. Accompanied by a substantial reduction of sentences when it fulfils
all the legal requirements, the procedure was intended to serve the main
objectives pursued by criminal prosecutions against genocide suspects. It was
based on the assumption that confessions and guilt pleas would deliver more
facts (relevant provisions refer to revealing the 'truth') about the genocide, lead
to expeditious trials and the spirit of repentance supposed to characterise
confessions would foster national reconciliation. Initially, relevant provisions on
the Confession and Guilty Plea Procedure in the 1996 Genocide law and in the
2001 *gacaca* law simply listed the formal requirements for an admissible
confession. The subject had to provide all the necessary details on the committed
crime; denounce the accomplices and offer apologies. The 2004 *gacaca* law added
the requirement that a person confessing and pleading guilty had to publicly
apologise "to the victims in case they are still alive and to the Rwandan
Society".[33] For obvious reasons, the law does not expressly require the victims to
forgive. More than one analysis of the process has discoursed over the contested
truthiness of the confessions, the genuineness of the repentance and forgiveness
by genocide survivors (Ingelaere 2009b; Fierens 2005; Clark & Kaufman 2009;
Sosnov 2008). Given the magnitude of the committed crime, it is indeed very
difficult to imagine that many survivors would be keen to truly forgive those
who committed the most barbaric acts against them (such as rapes) or deprived
them with their loved ones. At the same time, the existence of practices such as
kugura umusozi – arrangements between some genocide suspects whereby one
of them accepts to take responsibility for the crimes committed by others in
exchange for their protection for him/her and his/her family[34] – illustrate the
limitations of the Confession and Guilty Plea Procedure. Yet, notwithstanding
the legitimacy of some of the criticisms over confessions, truth, repentance and

---

33   Article 54 of the 2004 *Gacaca* law.
34   Penal Reform International (PRI), *The Settlement of Property Offence Cases Committed
      During the Genocide: Update on the Execution of Agreements and Restoration Condemnations*,
      Monitoring and Research Report on the *Gacaca*, August 2009.

forgiveness, it is an undeniable fact that very significant information was collected from testimonies of several dozens of thousands people who confessed their participation in the genocide (Meyerstein 2007).

4. JUSTICE FOR SURVIVORS OUTSIDE RWANDA

A growing literature has explored the repercussions of the civil war and genocide in Rwanda beyond national boundaries (Mamdani 2001; Prunier 2008; Turner 2007). An exhaustive analysis of political, economic, social and security-related repercussions of the genocide in Rwanda on the wider region goes beyond this chapter. The focus of the present section is on the resulting legal challenges beyond Rwanda. Millions of Rwandans followed the defeated government into exile as the RPF took control of the country in the wake of the genocide. Since the immediate aftermath of the genocide, the great majority of Rwandan refugees have eventually returned to Rwanda. However, the UNCHR estimated in 2009 that there were still some 72,530 Rwanda refugees scattered across the globe.[35] Absent relevant data thereon, it is possible to assume that the causes of their refugee status are not all directly linked to the 1994 genocide. After all, the Rwandan refugee problem predates the genocide – thousands of Rwandans, mainly Tutsi, fled the country since the pogroms of 1959 – and their repatriation was one of the major causes of the civil war that preceded it (Prunier 1995). Nonetheless, among these refugees are people who are suspected of having played an active role in the genocide. Their dispersion throughout the world has raised legal challenges in, at least some, host countries. The most prominent suspects have been indicted by, and some surrendered to, the UN created ICTR. Others are left to national authorities of their host countries to decide on their fate. Some are hardly disturbed while others have faced justice in host countries or are still facing protracted processes of either domestic adjudication or extradition to Rwanda. At variance, survivors have participated or tried hard to have their voice heard in any of these proceedings. Their organisations, mainly IBUKA and AVEGA, have also unrelentingly called for prosecution or extradition to Rwanda of genocide suspects who have so far remained undisturbed. The analysis below precisely looks at that involvement of survivors in legal proceedings at the ICTR and in foreign domestic proceedings.

---

[35]   *UNHCR Country Operations Profile – Rwanda*, www.unhcr.org/cgi-bin/texis/vtx/page?page=49e45c576 (last visited: 26 February 2010).

4.1. SURVIVORS AND THE INTERNATIONAL CRIMINAL TRIBUNAL FOR RWANDA (ICTR)

4.1.1. Accountability, deterrence, reconciliation and pacification

Created by UN Security Council Res. 955 (1994), the ICTR was mandated to "prosecute persons responsible for serious violations of international humanitarian law committed in the territory of Rwanda and Rwandan citizens responsible for such violations committed in the territory of neighbouring States, between 1 January 1994 and 31 December 1994" (Article 1). This mission was pursued under the assumption that through criminal prosecutions, the ICTR would "contribute to the process of national reconciliation and to the restoration and maintenance of peace".[36] In prosecutor Jallow's words, the tribunal was entrusted with a dual mandate: "first, accountability and deterrence and, second, reconciliation and peace" (Clark & Kaufman 2009, 263). It is an established fact that criminal prosecutions of several dozens of former Rwandan dignitaries by the ICTR represent a positive and somehow relieving dynamic for survivors. This is evidenced by the fact that they, individually or through their organisations, have actively cooperated with the tribunal mainly as witnesses. It can realistically be assumed that survivors' cooperation embodies their concurrence with the ICTR founding texts on the need for the suspects of crimes under the court's jurisdiction to account for their acts or omissions. However, the real impact of ICTR prosecutions in acting as a deterrent, fostering reconciliation and contributing to the pacification of the country and the wider region is yet to be determined. While such determination does not fall within the scope of the present analysis, it is worth noting that the role of the ICTR as a tool for deterrence, reconciliation and pacification should not be overestimated. Despite recent efforts under the outreach programme to bring its activities to the Rwandans, the latter have overwhelmingly remained ignorant of, and indifferent towards, the activities of the tribunal (Peskin 2005; Møse 2005).

Furthermore, Ndahiro and the International Crisis Group (ICG) have documented how, since the end of the genocide, different armed groups with ties to the Rwandan pre-genocide establishment have continuously attempted to make a forceful comeback in Rwanda or have been instrumental in the destabilization of neighbouring D.R Congo (Ndahiro 2009).[37] Between 1997 and 1998, members of the defeated Rwandan army and militia launched an insurgency war – they were known as *abacengezi*, the infiltrators – with the dual purpose of destabilising the RPF-led government and killing survivors (Ingelaere

---

[36]   Preamble of SC Res. 955 (1994).
[37]   International Crisis Group, *The Congo: Solving the FDLR Problem Once and for All*, ICG Report Congo Africa Briefing N° 25, 12 May 2005.

2009a).[38] The government responded with a very robust military action in the most affected area, mainly northern Rwanda (Jackson 2004). It should be noted that the insurgency war occurred subsequently to the Rwandan intervention in DR-Congo (then Zaire) in order to dismantle the refugee camps in the eastern part of the country some of which served as operational bases for the training for and the launching of the insurgency war. Some sixteen years after the genocide, a number of armed groups including the Democratic Forces for the Liberation of Rwanda (known by the French acronym FDLR, for *Forces Démocratiques de la Libération du Rwanda*) still represent real threats to peace and security in the region. Most of them are based in DR-Congo but have ramifications around the world, including in a number of African and European countries (Ndahiro 2009).[39] Hence, without nullifying the role of the ICTR in bringing about peace, reconciliation and deterrence, the point made here is that other domestic and regional legal and socio-political dynamics have comparatively played a far more significant role in taking steps towards peace and reconciliation.

Keeping that in mind, it is important to acknowledge that the arrest of major figures suspected of having played a central role in the preparation and execution of the genocide subtracted them from individually engaging into destabilizing activities in a troubled African Great Lakes region. Arguably, next to the ascertainment of the reality that a genocide took place in Rwanda (Nsanzuwera 2005), the greatest achievement of the ICTR from the survivors' perspective is that the tribunal succeeded in triggering the arrest and surrender of some of the major figures suspected of being the master minders of the genocide (Rombouts 2004; Møse 2005). Being a UN Charter Chapter VII creation, the ICTR enjoys a relatively high level of cooperation from various states hosting the suspects in a way that no country, certainly not Rwanda, can match. For various reasons, including concerns over due process guarantees, the prospect of applying death penalty before it was abolished in 2007, or political considerations, post-genocide Rwandan authorities have not succeeded in securing the extradition of some genocide suspects – mostly based in Western countries – to Rwanda (Boctor 2009).[40] By February 2010, some 81 had been arrested following ICTR indictments.[41] The status of cases before the ICTR shows that in addition to the

---

38 African Rights, *Rwanda Killing the Evidence: Murder, Attacks, Arrests and Intimidation of Survivors and Witnesses*, 1996.

39 Omaar, R., The Leadership of Rwandan Armed Groups Abroad with a Focus on the FDLR and RUD/URUNANA, 2008; www.rdrc.org.rw/Documentation/The%20Leadership%20 of%20Rwandan%20Armed%20Groups%20abroad%20with%20a%20focus%20on%20the%20 FDLR%20and%20RUD%20Urunana.pdf (last visited: 9 March 2010).

40 Redress & African Rights, *Extraditing Genocide Suspects from Europe to Rwanda, Issues and Challenges*, Report of a Conference Organised by Redress and African Rights at the Belgian Parliament on 1 July 2008.

41 See ICTR status of the Detainees at www.ictr.org/default.htm (last visited: 2 March 2010). There are still some challenges as in the case of Félicien Kabuga thought to be the financier of the genocide and believed to be hiding and protected by some officials in Kenya (see: *Alleged*

many cases still on trial, many accused have been convicted, some acquitted, few released due to lack of prosecutorial evidence and others had their files transferred to domestic courts.[42] Thus, it is possible to fairly commend the work of the tribunal in securing the arrest, detention and trial of high-profile genocide suspects – the so-called "big fish" – and at the same time argue that it plays a very limited, if any, role on the reconciliation process between Rwandans.

4.1.2. The survivors before the ICTR

Numerous publications have commented on the lack of a statutory right to reparation for surviving victims of the genocide in proceedings before the ICTR (Paradelle *et al.* 2005; Feyter *et al.* 2005; Rombouts 2004; De Brouwer 2005 and 2007).[43] Besides provisions for protection of victims and witnesses, the statutes of the International Criminal Tribunals for the former Yugoslavia (ICTY-Article 22) and Rwanda (ICTR-Article 21) do not expressly address the issue of compensation for victims of crimes under their jurisdiction. Article 23(3) of the ICTR statute provides for a possibility for a Trial Chamber to "order the return of any property and proceeds acquired by criminal conduct, including by means of duress, to their rightful owners". This provision on restitution is of limited relevance since the tribunal deals much more with master minders of the genocide than with executioners who were also involved in the commission of property crimes.

Rule 106 common to ICTY and ICTR Rules of Procedure and Evidence provides for a possibility for victims to introduce actions before national courts or other competent bodies to obtain compensation.[44] Such actions are only possible if they are provided for and in conformity with national legislations. Thus, even for those survivors somehow involved in criminal proceedings before the two tribunals, the ICTY and ICTR were not statutorily empowered to award damages or other forms of reparation. The ICTR eventually adopted limited measures of assistance to survivors, such as the programme of medical assistance to victims – including anti-retroviral treatment for victims of rape (De Brouwer 2007). Even these measures were somewhat a response to complaints from Rwandan survivors and authorities who lamented the fact that the ICTR accorded better treatment and services to genocide suspects than to surviving victims (Pillay 2008). Absent a right to trigger criminal proceedings or file a civil

---

Rwandan Genocide Financier still in Kenya: US, at www.google.com/hostednews/afp/article/ ALeqM5izu-hVhL0SlLNbl8RIqxuqjuWbMg (last visited: 2 March 2010).

42 See www.ictr.org/default.htm (last visited: 4 March 2010). As of February 2010, two cases were transferred to France.

43 Redress & African Rights, *Survivors and Post-Genocide Justice in Rwanda: Their Experiences, Perspectives and Hopes*, Report, 2008.

44 ICTR, Rules of Procedure and Evidence, 14 March 2008; ICTY, Rules of Procedure and Evidence, 10 December 2009, IT/32/Rev. 44.

action before the ICTR, it would be fair to state that survivors have a far limited standing before the ICTR in comparison with proceedings in Rwanda examined above. Efforts by ICTR officials to include a compensation scheme for victims were unfruitful (Rauschenbach & Scalia 2008; de Feyter *et al.* 2005).

The lack of a legal entitlement to claim reparation before the ICTR has not prevented survivors, mainly their organisations, to constantly try to ensure that their voices are heard and their interests served by the institution. Participation of survivors as witnesses remains central to ICTR prosecutions. Proceedings are overwhelmingly reliant on testimonial evidence. African Rights and Redress have documented how dangerous, painful, and traumatizing it can be for a survivor to testify before both domestic and international courts.[45] Arguably, socio-cultural considerations might make it even harder for most Rwandan survivors to testify before such a relatively removed institution as the ICTR than it might be the case in Rwandan legal proceedings (ordinary or *gacaca* courts). Since many of the surviving witnesses are rural-dwellers with limited, if any, education, the mere fact of appearing before non-*Kinyarwanda* speaking international prosecutors, lawyers and judges can be intimidating. In some instances – such as the "laughing judges" incident examined in the section below – insensitivity to cultural taboos has resulted into a secondary victimization of surviving victims testifying before the ICTR (Nowrojee 2005b).

It is generally expected and believed that an international institution such as the ICTR comparatively offers more due process guarantees than domestic proceedings in Rwanda (Sarkin 2001; Apuuli 2009; Meyerstein 2007; Møse 2005). However, the cultural disconnection or removed attitude of (some international) lawyers does not always leave room for accommodation of sensitivities of Rwandan witnesses. A number of incidents opposing the ICTR and survivors' organisations have displayed the challenges faced by efforts to strike the right balance between compliance with due process guarantees for the accused and victims' sensitivities in their quest for justice and accountability, as discussed in the next section.

4.1.3. *Cooperation or condemnation?*

The ICTR has always had an uneasy relationship with survivors' organisations in Rwanda. While some relevant academic literature has a tendency to reduce survivors' grievances to instrumentalisation by the Rwandan government (Peskin 2005), there are numerous examples whereby they expressed dissatisfaction with the work of the tribunal related to matters that specifically affect them. For instance, the facts of the matter and the nature of cross-examination in the "laughing judges" incident – when judges started laughing as

---

[45]   Redress & African Rights, *Survivors and Post-Genocide Justice in Rwanda: Their Experiences, Perspectives and Hopes*, Report, 2008.

a survivor of rape was testifying – displayed how particular survivors might subjectively feel once more "violated" or re-victimized through their participation in criminal proceedings (Nowrojee 2005b, 23; Burnett 2005, 768). In this and similar cases, the formulation of questions put to victims of sexual violence has displayed either a complete ignorance, or a disregard, for witnesses' cultural background whereby talking about sexual matters plainly and in public is generally a societal taboo. Without challenging the *raison d'être* of due process guarantees for the defence, including the right to cross-examine prosecution witnesses, a victim of rape who has to answer some 1,194 questions, many of them very explicit, from the defence (Nowrojee 2005b) would possibly reconsider her willingness to participate in the process, had she known beforehand (Paradelle *et al.* 2005).

In 1999, the ICTR Appeals Chamber ruled that Jean-Bosco Barayagwiza, one of the founders and a prominent leader of the openly extremist Coalition for the Defence of Democracy (CDR), should be released on the ground that a prolonged detention of the accused by the ICTR had resulted into violations of fundamental rights of the accused to the extent that proceeding with his trial would cause "irreparable damage to the integrity of the judicial process".[46] The decision angered survivors' organisations and the Rwandan government, which responded by announcing the suspension of cooperation with the tribunal. From the survivors' and government's viewpoint, legal technicalities were not valid enough reasons to trump the imperative of holding a key player in the genocide enterprise such as Jean-Bosco Barayagwiza accountable for his acts (Bertodano 2002). Upon their radical reaction, the judgment was eventually revised in 2000 – on dubious grounds of new facts – opening a way for Barayagwiza to stand trial and eventually be sentenced to life imprisonment, commuted into a 35 years of imprisonment as a form of redress for his initially violated rights.[47]

These are only some among other early instances whereby genocide survivors clashed with the tribunal over some of its decisions and practices. In spite of not being offered an independent standing in ICTR proceedings, survivors' organisations, mainly IBUKA and AVEGA, have generally forced their way to ensure that their voice is heard by the tribunal's authorities. Oftentimes, they have denounced the ICTR for alleged mismanagement, corrupt practises, harassment of witnesses or institutional collaboration with a rather considerable number of genocide suspects (Husketh 2005; Haskell 2009, 73).[48] In the latter case, two notorious examples are the cases of Siméon Nchamihigo and Joseph Nzabirinda. The first – Siméon Nchamihigo – was on ICTR defence payroll since

---

[46] *Jean-Bosco Barayagwiza v. The Prosecutor*, Appeals Chamber, Decision, Case No.ICTR-97–19-AR72, 3 November 1999, par. 108.

[47] *The Prosecutor v. Ferdinand Nahimana, Jean-Bosco Barayagwiza Hassan Ngeze*, Judgment and Sentence, 3 December 2003, Case No. ICTR-99–52- T, paras. 1106–1107.

[48] Also Redress & African Rights, *Survivors and Post-Genocide Justice in Rwanda: Their Experiences, Perspectives and Hopes*, Report, 2008.

July 1998 for Samuel Imanishimwe as an investigator until he was arrested by the tribunal on 19 May 2001.[49] He was eventually found guilty of genocide and of murder, extermination and other inhumane acts as crimes against humanity and sentenced to forty years of imprisonment.[50] Similarly, Joseph Nzabirinda worked for the defence team of Sylvain Nsabimana before he was arrested on 21 December 2001 and sentenced to seven years of imprisonment after pleading guilty to murder, as a crime against humanity.[51] Not only the Rwandan government but also survivors' organisations were instrumental in triggering the arrest and detention of these suspects employed by ICTR defence councils.[52]

Relatively recent attempts by survivors' organisations to have their voices heard before the ICTR relate to discussions over the transfer of ICTR cases to Rwanda and some ICTR acquittals, including of Mr. Protais Zigiranyirazo. Since 2003, the UN Security Council has instructed the ICTR and the ICTY to design what is known as completion strategies.[53] Among other measures to achieve this goal, the tribunals were urged to consider the possibility of transferring cases to competent national jurisdictions, including to Rwanda in the case of the ICTR (Møse 2008; Marong, Jalloh & Kinnecome 2007). As the latter sources indicate, in efforts to comply with Security Council recommendations, the ICTR Office of the Prosecutor established a distinction between the transfer of cases concerning indictees and the transfer of files of suspects. Some sixty files were transferred to Rwandan judicial authorities and one to Belgium by June 2010 (Møse 2008).[54] The transfer of cases of persons indicted by the ICTR became a more intricate matter as it requires a judicial decision (Møse 2008). Rwandan authorities have always expressed their willingness to receive cases from the ICTR. The country took serious steps to correct the most salient impediments to the transfer, namely though the suppression of the death penalty in 2007,[55] the adoption of a law subjecting transferred cases to a special legal regime[56] and the

---

[49]   See   www.trial-ch.org/en/trial-watch/profile/db/facts/simeon_nchamihigo_357.html   (last visited: 19 March 2010).

[50]   *Siméon Nchamihigo v. The Prosecutor*, Appeals Chamber, Judgment, Case No. ICTR-2001–63-A, 18 March 2010, para. 405.

[51]   *The Prosecutor v. Joseph Nzabirinda*, Judgement, Trial Chamber II, Case No. ICTR-2001–77-T, 23 February 2007. See also: www.trial-ch.org/en/trial-watch/profile/db/facts/joseph_nzabirinda_595.html (last visited: 19 March 2010).

[52]   See www.unwatch.com/ICTRnewsApr02.htm (last visited: 19 March 2010).

[53]   UN S.C. Resolution 1503 (2003).

[54]   Thirty-five files were transferred before July 2005 while twenty-five others were handed over to Rwandan authorities in June 2010 as reported on: www.hirondellenews.com/content/view/13529/1166/ (last visited: 23 August 2010).

[55]   Organic Law n° 31/2007 of 25 July 2007 relating to the Abolition of the Death Penalty, Official Gazette, Special Issue of 25 July 2007.

[56]   Organic Law N° 11/2007 of 16 March 2007 concerning the Transfer of Cases to the Republic of Rwanda from the International Criminal Tribunal for Rwanda and from other States, Official Gazette, Year 46, Special Issue of 19 March 2007. This raises a question beyond the scope of the present analysis as to the legality and legitimacy of the institution of a favourable

creation of more adequate prison facilities (Mpanga prison in the Southern province and special cells in the Kigali Central Prison (Boctor 2009).[57]

During the 2008 judicial debates over the eventually unsuccessful transfer of four cases to Rwanda, survivors' organizations IBUKA and AVEGA filed applications – under Rule 74 of ICTR Rules of Procedure and Evidence – for leave to appear as *amicus curiae* in support of the referral request by the prosecutor.[58] In all the four cases, their applications were rejected on the grounds that the organizations could not prove their expertise or ability to assist the Chambers in deciding on the readiness of Rwanda to receive the cases. As illustrated by the reasoning in the *Fulgence Kayshema* case, ICTR Trial Chamber III took the view that the case made by IBUKA and AVEGA could not be different from the one made by the Republic of Rwanda or be of further assistance than *amicus curiae* briefs by Rwanda, Human Rights Watch and the International Criminal Defence Attorney's Association. However compelling the reasons of the court might be, the dismissal of arguments likely to be made by survivors' organizations – while allowing the actors mentioned above to appear – is clearly telling about the Chamber's position of the victims need for their voice to be heard.

Regarding controversial ICTR acquittals, on 16 November 2009, the ICTR Appeals Chamber rendered a judgment ordering the release of Protais Zigiranyirazo, initially sentenced by Trial Chamber III to serve 20 years of imprisonment for genocide, aiding and abetting genocide and extermination as a crime against humanity. His conviction was overturned by the Appeals Chamber on the ground that the Trial Chamber erred in fact and in law "in its assessment of the alibi evidence, by misapprehending the applicable legal principles, failing to consider or provide a reasoned opinion with respect to relevant evidence, and misconstruing key evidence which further bolstered Zigiranyirazo's alibi".[59] One of the three influential brothers of first-lady Agathe Kanziga Habyarimana, the accused is popularly believed to be a member of the inner cycle – the *Akazu* – the clique of northerners who effectively controlled president Habyarimana's regime in the lead up to the genocide (Prunier 1994;

---

legal regime for the treatment of transferred cases vis-à-vis all other cases adjudicated in Rwanda.

[57] Also Redress & African Rights, *Survivors and Post-Genocide Justice in Rwanda: Their Experiences, Perspectives and Hopes*, Report, 2008.

[58] *The Prosecutor v. Gaspard Kanyarukiga*, Decision on Amicus Curiae Request by IBUKA and AVEGA, Case No. ICTR-2002-78-I, 22 February 2008; *The Prosecutor v. Ildephonse Hategekimana*, Decision on Amicus Requests and Pending Defence Motions and Order for Further Submissions, Case No. ICTR-00-55B-R11bis, 20 March 2008; *The Prosecutor v. Jean-Baptiste Gatete*, Decision on *Amicus Curiae* Requests (IBUKA, AVEGA and ICDAA), Case No. ICTR-2001-61-Ilbis, 30 June2008; *The Prosecutor v. Fulgence Kayishema*, Decision on the Request by IBUKA & AVEGA for Leave to Appear and Make Submissions as *Amicus*, Case No. ICTR-2001-67-I, 1 July 2008.

[59] *Protais Zigiranyirazo v. The Prosecutor*, Appeals Chamber, Judgment, *Case No. ICTR-01-73-A*, 16 November 2009, para. 51, and, similarly, para. 73.

Melvern 2004). The acquittal of Zigiranyirazo based on Trial Chamber errors in the treatment of the evidence irked survivor groups, including IBUKA, which, once more, threatened to cut their ties with a tribunal they perceived as not acting in their interests.[60] Their anger was reinforced by the fact that just one day after the acquittal of Zigiranyirazo, the ICTR also acquitted – even though less contentiously – catholic priest Hormisdas Nsengimana.[61] In the particular case of Mr Zigiranyirazo, the reversal of the burden of proof in examining the alibi of the accused indeed justifies the decision by the Appeals Chamber to acquit the suspect. However, survivors dissatisfaction with the judgment relate to the fact that the accused was not, strictly, absolved from wrongdoing but simple given the benefit of the doubt under a proper application of evidentiary rules. An acquittal on the ground of prior judgment's misapprehension of applicable legal principles left the impression that a different outcome could have been reached if the available evidence had rightly been handled during the Trial Chamber phase.

Despite the numerous criticisms of the ICTR by survivors, Rwandans in general or the Rwandan government, the tribunal's *raison d'être* or usefulness are hardly questioned. Persistent disagreements and misunderstandings are based on domestic perceptions informed by documented shortcomings in the working of the tribunal. Survivors have frequently expressed their disappointment over an institution that they consider as not acting professionally and competently enough in efforts to establish the responsibility of suspects; document the reality of the genocide and appropriately accommodate survivors in their pain and suffering.

4.2. SURVIVORS' INVOLVEMENT IN FOREIGN JUDICIAL PROCEEDINGS

Following the 1994 genocide, a number of countries around the world have faced legal challenges of either adjudicating on cases of genocide suspects from Rwanda or extraditing them to places where they can face justice (also Ferstman & Schurr, this volume). Many factors might explain the relative action or inaction by different states in dealing with this legacy of the genocide in Rwanda. Some of those factors are legal while others are more political. In some countries, genocide and related crimes were not, strictly defined, offences punishable under

---

[60] See www.bbc.co.uk/worldservice/africa/2009/11/091120_rwaictr.shtml (last visited: 19 March 2010).

[61] *The Prosecutor v. Hormisdas Nsengimana*, Trial Chamber I, Judgment, Case No. ICTR-01–69-T, 17 November 2009. See also: www.fairtrialsforrwanda.org/kinyarwanda/ (last visited: 31 March 2010).

municipal law at the time the Rwandan genocide was committed.[62] In these and similar instances, domestic legal systems are not in the position to exercise universal jurisdiction over genocide, and, in some cases, crimes against humanity and war crimes committed in Rwanda in 1994. Unless they extradite suspects to countries where they might face trial, including Rwanda, they have no other choice than either remain passive – thereby standing a chance of being accused of condoning impunity – or undertake criminal prosecution under a requalification of the acts. A typical example in the latter instance is the first trial in Europe of a Rwandan suspect – Fulgence Niyonteze – by a Swiss court. Since the suspect, arrested in 1996, could not be tried for genocide – a crime introduced in the Swiss Penal Code in December 2000 – he stood trial for murder, incitement to murder and serious violations of the laws of war and was convicted to 14 years of imprisonment for the latter count (Arnold 2005).

Similarly, Joseph Mpambara was arrested in 2006, tried and sentenced by the Hague District Court (the Netherlands) in March 2009 to 20 years in custody for torture (van den Herik 2009). The trial of Joseph Mpambara in the Netherlands was procedurally simplified by the fact that the ICTR declined to use its jurisdictional primacy over Dutch domestic courts (van den Herik, 2009). Paradoxically, a prior attempt to transfer Michel Bagaragaza to Norway and, later, to the Netherlands under the tribunal's completion strategy failed on jurisdictional grounds before he pleaded guilty to complicity in genocide, and he was convicted by the ICTR to eight years of imprisonment (Canter 2009).[63]

African Rights, *Survie*, Redress and Human Rights Watch are among many other actors that have regularly documented the whereabouts of Rwandan genocide suspects. Some of these organisations have equally documented the challenges involved in either extraditing them to Rwanda or instituting criminal proceedings against them in foreign jurisdictions.[64] There are suspects whose whereabouts are not known as many are still in hiding or using false identities to escape accountability. However, a considerable number of others have been located. Most European countries hosting genocide suspects have been much more eager to co-operate with the ICTR than with Rwanda. The ICTR is, however, under Security Council pressure to wind up its activities and has structural limitations in terms of the workload it can handle. For that reason and in spite of its prerogative of primacy over domestic courts, the institution is

---

[62] As in the House of Lords-House of Commons Joint Committee on Human Rights (HL-HC), *Closing the Impunity Gap: UK Law on Genocide (and Related Crimes) and Redress for Torture Victims*, Twenty–Fourth Report of Session 2008–09, HL Paper 153-HC 553, 11 August 2009.

[63] *The Prosecutor v. Michel Bagaragaza*, Trial Chamber III, Judgment, *Case No. ICTR-05–86-S*, 17 November 2009.

[64] Redress & African Rights, *Extraditing Genocide Suspects from Europe to Rwanda, Issues and Challenges*, Report of a Conference Organised by Redress and African Rights at the Belgian Parliament on 1 July 2008. See also: www.collectifpartiescivilesrwanda.fr/affairesjudiciaire. html and www.survie-alsace.org (last visited: 14 April 2010).

simply unable to investigate and prosecute all cases of Rwandan genocide suspects living outside Rwanda. Various dynamics have taken place particularly in North America and Europe examining the possibility of domestic adjudication or extradition of suspects to Rwanda. In many cases, survivors and organizations acting on their behalf such as the *Collectif des Parties Civiles* in Belgium and France played a key role in triggering the said-dynamics.[65]

Belgium applied for the first time its law on universal jurisdiction in the trial of Rwandan genocide suspects Vincent Ntezimana, Alphonse Higaniro, sisters Consolata Mukangango and Julienne Mukabutera (*the Butare Four*) in a 2001 trial that saw the participation of more than 100 civil parties, including genocide survivors (Reydams 2003). Subsequently, Belgium held trials of Etienne Nzabonimana and Samuel Ndashyikirwa (2005), Bernard Ntuyahaga (2007) and Ephrem Nkezabera (2009) in which several Rwandan aggrieved parties were allowed to participate as civil parties.[66] The 2001 trial did not address the issue of reparation for participating civil parties. However, some 15 victims out of 63 represented in the proceedings were awarded a total amount of 570,000 Euros during the 2005 trial while the court awarded 575,070 Euros in reparation to 21 Rwandan civil parties out of nearly 150 represented in the 2007 trial.[67] Granted in conformity with applicable Rwandan law, the reparation amounts remain somewhat symbolic as arguments have been made that they should be paid by the country where crimes took place rather than Belgium, the forum of criminal proceedings.[68] The presence of other genocide suspects in Belgium – such as Emmanuel Bagambiki acquitted by the ICTR but sought in Rwanda for counts not covered by the tribunal – and the continued activism for action against genocide fugitives are indications that the prosecution-extradition chapter of Rwandans in Belgium is far from closed.

For more than a decade and a half after the genocide, France was at odds with Rwandan authorities, the latter accusing France of having played both a direct and an indirect role in the genocide. Not surprisingly, the country's judicial and political authorities have uncomfortably wrestled genocide-related cases choosing rather to give priority to indicting high-ranking Rwandan officials in the downing of former president Habyarimana's plane that, according to that particular narrative, is a determinant factor for the commission of the genocide. Survivors and organizations speaking on their behalf have been

---

[65] Redress & African Rights, *Survivors and Post-Genocide Justice in Rwanda: Their Experiences, Perspectives and Hopes*, Report, 2008.

[66] See www.trial-ch.org/en/trial-watch/search.html (last visited: 12 April 2010). Ephrem Nkezabera was sentenced *in absentia* to 30 years of imprisonment in December 2009; the Assize Court of Brussels ordered his retrial on 1 March 2010, but he died in May 2010 before the retrial, http://fr.hirondellenews.com/content/view/15352/325/ (last visited: 25 June 2010).

[67] See www.hirondellenews.com/content/view/4958/26/ and www.rnw.nl/international-justice/article/large-compensation-awards-never-paid (last visited: 13 April 2010).

[68] See www.hirondellenews.com/content/view/9907/274/ (last visited: 12 April 2010).

particularly active in pushing for action in establishing responsibilities but also accountability for suspects of the genocide on French soil. Challenges pertaining to prosecuting genocide suspects in France are epitomized by the Wenceslas Munyeshyaka case initiated by genocide survivors and their backers in 1995 but still pending by March 2010. In *Mutimura v. France*, the European Court of Human Rights held that France violated the right of the Applicant to have a trial in a reasonable time due to procedural delays in the Munyeshyaka case and awarded her damages.[69] The suspect's file was eventually deferred to France by the ICTR in November 2007 together with the case against Laurent Bucyibaruta.[70] Acting as civil parties, victims and their advocates have documented a dozen of suspects whose cases have been submitted to French authorities for prosecution or extradition to Rwanda.[71] Victims have also submitted applications to the French judiciary (*plaintes contre X devant le Tribunal aux armées de Paris*) aimed at establishing alleged responsibilities of some French soldiers in Rwanda during the civil war and the genocide.[72] Following a thaw in Rwanda-France relations under French President Sarkozy, there seems to be hope that genocide cases against Rwandan suspects living in France are increasingly receiving a more serious consideration, whether this concerns domestic adjudication or extradition to Rwanda.[73]

A number of other countries hosting Rwandan genocide suspects are still struggling to find suitable outcomes.[74] After a United Kingdom High Court

---

69   *Mutimura v. France* (application No. 46621/99), Judgement of 8 June 2004.

70   *The Prosecutor v. Wenceslas Munyeshyaka*, Decision on the Prosecutor's Request for the Referral of Wenceslas Munyeshyaka's Indictment to France: *Rule 11 bis of the Rules of Procedure and Evidence,* Case No. ICTR-2005–87-I, 20 November 2007; and *The Prosecutor v. Laurent Bucyibaruta*, Decision on Prosecutor's Request for Referral of Laurent Bucyibaruta's Indictment to France: Rule 11 bis of the Rules of Procedure and Evidence, Case No. ICTR-2005–85- I, 20 November 2007.

71   They are: Cyprien Kayumba, Laurent Serubuga, Sosthène Munyemana, Eugène Rwamucyo, Dominique Ntawukuriryayo, Callixte Mbarushimana, Fabien Neretse (Nsabimana), Stanislas Mbonampe, Isaac Kakamali, Claver Kamana, Marcel Bivugabagabo, Pascal Simbikangwa, Agathe Kanziga Habyarimana, Charles Twagira, Pierre Tegera. See: www.collectifparties civilesrwanda.fr/affairesjudiciaire.html and www.survie-alsace.org (last visited: 14 April 2010). A number of extradition requests have been rejected.

72   See www.survie-alsace.org/ (last visited: 14 April 2010).

73   See www.survie-alsace.org (last visited: 14 April 2010) for details on political and legal dynamics.

74   Redress & African Rights, *Extraditing Genocide Suspects from Europe to Rwanda, Issues and Challenges*, Report of a Conference Organised by Redress and African Rights at the Belgian Parliament on 1 July 2008. In addition to countries already mentioned, some suspects who are (or believed to be) in different other countries such as D.R Congo, South Africa, Malawi, Mozambique, Zambia, US, Sweden, Finland – among many others – are facing proceedings of arrest, trial or extradition; even if most western countries are so far reluctant to send them back to Rwanda (safe for the case of Enos Kagaba sent back from the US in 2005). *Mushikiwabo v. Barayagwiza*, 1996 U.S. Dist. LEXIS 4409 (S.D.N.Y. 1996) is another interesting case in which victims were awarded over US$ 103 million. The sum was not actually paid (by whom being the big question).

reversed a Magistrates Court's favourable decision to extradite Vincent (Bajinya) Brown, Charles Munyaneza (Muneza), Emmanuel Nteziryayo, Célestin Ugirashebuja to Rwanda,[75] the country faces an uphill battle in efforts to amend its existing laws in order to try these genocide suspects domestically (Drumbl 2010).[76] In Canada, Désiré Munyaneza was sentenced in first instance to life in prison for "seven counts of genocide, crimes against humanity and war crimes for acts of murder, sexual violence and pillage" (Lafontaine 2010, 269). The country has embarked on a second trial of a Rwandan genocide suspect, Jacques Mungwarere.[77] Efforts to expel Léon Mugesera – for his alleged criminal responsibility arising from, among others, a hate speech he made in 1992 – have so far proven unsuccessful (Rikhof 2005). Canadian immigration authorities initiated deportation procedures since 1995. A favourable decision for the deportation issued by competent immigration adjudicatory authorities (1996 and 1998) was confirmed through a judicial review by the Federal Court, Trial Division,[78] overturned by the Federal Court of Appeal,[79] before being reconfirmed by the Supreme Court of Canada (Rikhof 2005).[80] The implementation of the 2005 judgment of the Canadian Supreme Court allowing for the deportation of Léon Mugesera is still pending as authorities still examining whether he could receive a fair trial, if sent back to Rwanda.[81] In nearly all past and pending cases before domestic judicial or other authorities in various countries, survivors or persons mobilized for their cause play(ed) a key role in setting in motions proceedings for accountability.

---

[75] For the judgments by the Westminster Magistrates Court and by the High Court of Justice, see: *The Government of the Republic of Rwanda v. Vincent Bajinya, Charles Munyaneza, Emmanuel Nteziryayo and Celestin Ugirashebuja*, City of Westminster Magistrates Court, 6 June 2008; *Brown, Munyaneza, Nteziryayo, and Ugirashebuja v. The Government of Rwanda and the Secretary of State for the Home Department*, Case No. CO/8862/2008, [2009] EWHC 770 (Admin), 8 April 2009.

[76] See also the House of Lords-House of Commons Joint Committee on Human Rights (HL-HC), *Closing the Impunity Gap: UK Law on Genocide (and related crimes) and Redress for Torture Victims*, Twenty–Fourth Report of Session 2008–09, HL Paper 153-HC 553, 11 August 2009.

[77] See www.hirondellenews.com/content/view/13007/26/ (last visited: 13 April 2010).

[78] See: *Mugesera v. Canada (Minister of Citizenship and Immigration)*, Federal Court, Trial Division, 4 F.C. 421, IMM-5946-98, 10 May 2001, reproduced at www.haguejusticeportal.net/ Docs/NLP/Canada/Mugesera_Federal_Court_Reasons_for_Order_10-5-2001.pdf (last visited: 15 July 2010).

[79] *Mugesera v. Canada* (Minister of Citizenship and Immigration), Federal Court of Appeal, A-316-01, 8 September 2003, reproduced at www.haguejusticeportal.net/Docs/NLP/Canada/ Mugesera_Court_Appeal_Judgement_8-9-2003.pdf (last visited: 14 July 2010).

[80] *Mugesera v. Canada* (Minister of Citizenship and Immigration), [2005] 2 S.C.R. 100, 2005 SCC 40, 28 June 2005, reproduced at www.haguejusticeportal.net/Docs/NLP/Canada/ Mugesera_Cour_Supreme_Decision_28-6-2005.pdf (last visited: 15 July 2010).

[81] See: Rwanda presses for deportation, at www.montrealgazette.com/news/Rwanda+presses+d eportation/3317520/story.htm (last visited: 2 August 2010).

5. CONCLUSION

More than seventeen years after Rwanda experienced one of the most horrendous atrocities of the twentieth century, legal dynamics in response to the tragedy are still an unfinished matter. Experimental and challenging, criminal proceedings against a massive number of suspect in Rwanda are nearly winding up while prosecutions against suspected fugitives not indicted by the ICTR are still a protracted process. A clear assessment of the position of surviving victims in the various dynamics can therefore only be partial at this junction. During judicial proceedings against genocide suspects in Rwanda or before the ICTR and foreign jurisdiction, survivors have mainly played the traditional role as witnesses. Their entitlement to "full and effective reparation" in accordance with relevant international guidelines has mostly not been served.

Postponed on several occasions, the closure of *gacaca* proceedings that have dealt with an overwhelming number of cases of genocide suspects took place in 2010/2011. Like other Rwandans, survivors actively participated in as initiators of, or witnesses in, criminal proceedings of genocide cases before ordinary courts. They also played a role in the process of the establishment and in the functioning of the *gacaca* courts. In terms of compensation to genocide survivors, the successive amendments of Rwandan laws on prosecution of genocide suspects progressively watered down the principle. Eventually, the idea of compensation and assistance to survivors of the genocide were somehow conflated under Law No. 69/2008 of 30 December 2008 establishing a Fund for the *support* and *assistance* to the survivors of the Tutsi genocide and other crimes against humanity. The policy of assistance to genocide survivors adopted since the establishment of the FARG in 1998 was very beneficial in helping many survivors to somehow restart their lives. Yet, actions undertaken in implantation of this policy cannot fully substitute the whole idea of full reparation. The fact that the fund established under Law No. 69/2008 subrogates survivors in their right to claim damages against genocide suspects only suggests that the principle of direct reparation is somehow abandoned. The prevailing insolvency of many actors of the genocide might explain the move. However, the Rwandan legislator should have done a better job in avoiding the ambiguous conflation of the principles of compensation on the one hand and implementing the adopted policy of support and assistance to genocide survivors on the other hand.

Some survivors equally participated in proceedings before the ICTR and foreign domestic courts. But beyond retribution for some of the prosecuted suspects, the various processes have hardly accommodated their other needs and demands. The idea of reparation to genocide survivors has always proved to be problematic in Rwanda as well as in other proceedings outside of the country. Absent a statutory possibility to accommodate victims' rights, the ICTR has generally exercised discretion in dealing with victims while foreign domestic proceedings against genocide suspects are conducted in accordance with differing national laws but share in common the fact that they are all limited in accommodating victims' right to compensation either on the statutory or on the practical level.

XIX. UNDERSTANDING LIMITATIONS
Victim Participation and the International Criminal Court

Brianne McGonigle Leyh

The ICC, at least on paper, is a 'victim's court'.
Only time will tell if this proves to be a blessing or a curse.
(Stover 2005, 148)

1. INTRODUCTION

There is little argument that the primary function of international criminal tribunals is to investigate, prosecute and punish those believed to be responsible for the most serious crimes of concern to the international community, namely war crimes, crimes against humanity and genocide. International criminal courts, from the time of the Nuremberg trials to today, have steadfastly attempted to carry out their respective functions through condemnation of the criminal acts in question and of the perpetrators found guilty. In line with traditional theories of criminal justice, the focus of international criminal courts has unquestioningly been on the seriousness of the crime committed and the role of the offender. Thus, the spotlight of international criminal trials has almost exclusively centred on the crime committed rather than on the harm suffered. For example, at the *ad hoc* International Criminal Tribunals for former Yugoslavia (ICTY) and for Rwanda (ICTR) or the Special Court for Sierra Leone (SCSL), if the victims played a part in the trial process it was solely as witnesses called by the parties or by the court but never participating in his or her own right as a victim. When preparing the Statute for the ICTY a proposal for allowing the appointment of separate counsel for victims was rejected (Morris & Scharf 1995). The rejection, mainly by delegates from the United States but also from other states, was out of fear that third-party participation would lead to conflicts with the prosecution's case (Tochilovsky 1999).

The exclusion of the victim from any role other than a witness at the international level, however, has met with strong criticism. In almost all domestic legal systems victims are permitted to play a broader role in the process. In general, common law countries tend to allow victims the opportunity to present their views and concerns to the court at the sentencing stage of a criminal process through either oral or written victim-impact statements. In civil law countries victims are usually allowed to participate either as civil parties, in which case they attach their reparation claim to the criminal process, or as private or subsidiary prosecutors, in which they may have the opportunity to initiate prosecutions (Brienen & Hoegen 2000). And although the primary focus of international courts is unlikely to change (nor should it necessarily change), a shift in thinking has occurred. The idea of justice for victims, to a large extent, now implies that international courts should afford victims a greater role in the criminal process.

To this end, international criminal courts are increasingly broadening their mandates in an attempt to better address the needs and concerns of the victims of the crimes under their respective jurisdictions. In addition to their primary task, courts have taken on additional functions related to the notions of reconciliation, restoration and victim empowerment. These ideals are, in many ways, addressed through greater rights concerning protection, reparation and participation. Accordingly, the procedural position of victims in international criminal proceedings has been significantly advanced. As mentioned above, whereas proceedings before the ICTY, the ICTR and the SCSL only allowed victims to participate as witnesses, victims now have a limited opportunity to participate in their own right – as victims – before a handful of international, internationalized and UN administered courts, including, for example, the UNMIK/EULEX war crimes panels in Kosovo, the Special Panels for Serious Crimes in East Timor, and the Extraordinary Chambers in the Courts of Cambodia.[1] Foremost among those courts allowing victim participation is the International Criminal Court (ICC or Court).

The Preamble of the Rome Statute of the ICC acknowledges the suffering of millions of victims of human rights and humanitarian law violations, and that such violations are contrary to the values and conscience of the world community. In furtherance of this recognition, the Rome Statute and ICC Rules of Procedure and Evidence (Rules) provide victims with general and specific rights to participate in the criminal process regardless of whether or not they testify as witnesses. In this regard, they may be represented by legal counsel and present their views and concerns at appropriate stages of the proceedings so long as this participation is not prejudicial or inconsistent with the rights of the accused and a fair trial. Moreover, they may also claim reparations for their harm suffered regardless of whether or not they testify as witnesses or participate with victim

---

[1] See Article 80 of the Provision Criminal Procedural Code of Kosovo, available at: www.unmikonline.org/regulations/2003/RE2003–26.pdf; UNTAET Regulation 2000/30 on Transitional Rules of Criminal Procedure, as amended by UNTAET Regulation 2001/25 of 14 September, Section 12(3); and ECCC, Internal Rules, as revised 9 February 2010, Rule 23. See also McGonigle 2009.

status. These procedural rights have been heralded as innovative and praised by many (Cassese 1999; Fernandez de Gurmendi 2001a; Jorda & De Hemptinne 2002; Haslam 2004). But, has the Court provided for meaningful participation with clearly defined rights and procedures? Regrettably, case law indicates that the Court is still struggling to find the most appropriate way to afford victims' their participatory rights in proceedings without affecting its primary goals of investigation, prosecution and punishment.

Thus, although the victim scheme at the ICC was a well-intentioned attempt to address the shortcomings of previous tribunals that for one reason or other failed to properly address victims' concerns, its effective and efficient implementation has nonetheless proven problematic. There are a numerous concerns surrounding the fragmented and inconsistent case law, the allocation of resources, ensuring effective Legal Representatives for victims, managing victim expectations, and the selectivity of victims. Understanding these limitations is crucial to understanding the limitations of international criminal justice generally. Unable to address all of these issues, this chapter will focus its attention on the Court's case law concerning victims' participatory rights and how the case law continues to be in a constant state of fluctuation, which neither benefits victims nor contributes substantively to the criminal process.

The aim of this chapter, therefore, is to critically examine the scope and content of victim participation at the ICC. It will first explore what the Rome Statute and Rules provide with regard to participatory rights. Next, it will examine the potential of victim participation and touch upon ways in which victims have sought to have a substantive impact on proceedings, focusing on their desire to broaden the charges against one of the accused and their support of *in situ* proceedings. The chapter will then focus on two specific developments at the Court which shed light on the fragmented and inconsistent approach hitherto taken by the Court, namely (i) the systematic versus piecemeal approach taken by different Chambers with regard to the manner and scope of participation and (ii) the divergent opinions on anonymous and non-anonymous victim participation at the pre-trial stage. Finally, the chapter will examine the need for further improvements and detail how the various Chambers are attempting to provide more clarity.

This chapter will conclude that victim participation at the Court has not been wholly appreciated and that it remains in a state of continued fluctuation, which neither benefits victims nor contributes substantively to the criminal process. Due, in part, to the fact that the Court (as a whole) has little conceptual understanding of and agreement on how to approach victim participation in international criminal proceedings, the various Chambers continue to struggle with harmonizing opinions and clarifying important issues affecting victims and other Court actors. An important obstacle to a coherent victim participation approach is the setup of the Court itself, which allows for the re-litigation of procedural issues in each case and the fact that very few procedural decisions have been allowed to reach the Appeals Chamber. Thankfully, the Trial Chambers and Appeals Chamber appear to be attempting to provide greater clarity and harmonize decisions, which is a welcome improvement to current ICC practice. Nevertheless, without the ability to easily revise or amend the Rules of Procedure and Evidence, the Court will continue to litigate over the procedural rights of victims in proceedings, leaving parties and participants uncertain about how any given Chamber will approach the issue. It would undoubtedly be desirable if greater clarity and certainty could be agreed upon concerning the appropriate role to be played by victims in proceedings. Until such a time, understanding the current limitations of the participation regime is a necessity.

2. PROCEDURAL FRAMEWORK OF THE COURT IN RELATION TO VICTIMS

In 1985 the General Assembly of the United Nations adopted by consensus the Declaration of Basic Principles of Justice for Victims of Crime and Abuse of Power (Victims' Declaration), which endorsed victim participation in domestic criminal proceedings at appropriate stages of the criminal process.[2] The wide support amongst states for the Victims' Declaration is due, in part, to the fact that the phrasing in support of victim participation is worded so broadly that governments from a wide-variety of legal traditions could come to an agreement. In other words, countries that only allow victims to participate after the establishment of the guilt of the accused as well as countries that allow private prosecutions were able to agree that within their respective systems victims should be afforded the right to present their views and concerns at appropriate stages of proceedings. The critical element being that each national jurisdiction has its own conceptual understanding of when participation is most appropriate and in what way participation is most appropriate.

Therefore, the idea that victims should have some form of participatory rights in the criminal process was, at least at the national level, broadly accepted by July of 1998 when the UN Conference of Plenipotentiaries on the Establishment of an International Criminal Court met in Rome, Italy. At the Rome Conference, which it came to be called, one hundred-sixty states and many international organizations participated in the drafting of the Rome Statute. The complexity of this undertaking is highlighted by the original draft Statute submitted to the Conference which had numerous options with over 1400 brackets indicating

---

[2]   The Declaration of Basic Principles of Justice for Victims of Crime and Abuse of Power, G.A. Res. 40/34, adopted 29 Nov. 1985, U.N. GAOR, 40th Sess., Annex, U.N. Doc. A/Res/40/34/ Annex (1985) (hereinafter Victims' Declaration).

disagreement among the delegates. Five weeks of intense negotiations followed, and through working groups, negotiations, and heated debates a delicately balanced text was created. This text included a number of references to victim participation in the proceedings, which certainly would not have been achievable without the important role played by NGOs and civil society throughout the negotiations.[3]

Throughout the negotiations on the Rome Statute, and later on the Rules, delegates presented different, and at times competing, ideas concerning victim participation (Bitti & Friman 2001). Fernández de Gurmendi, then a member of the Working Group for the Rules of Procedure and Evidence relating to Part 4: Composition and Administration of the Court, and now a newly elected Judge to the Court, has noted that "the crafting of the regime on victims was probably the most challenging task undertaken by the Preparatory Commission", due to the fact that delegates came from different legal traditions where victims have a wide-range of participatory rights (Fernández de Gurmendi 2001b, 256). Despite the differences, after numerous talks and compromises delegates reached agreements. Both the Statute and Rules provided for victim participation with the understanding that participation was never meant to detract from the primary purposes of the Court, namely investigation, prosecution and punishment (Chung 2008).

In reaching agreement, however, many of the provisions remained vague and unclear. For example, it was unclear whether the ability to participate also included the opportunity to present evidence at trial, whether victims would be allowed to participate at the confirmation of charges hearing since the general Article on participation falls under the Part 6 of the Statute dealing with trial, whether victims would be able to represent themselves, or whether extended family members could qualify as victims. These and many other questions aside, drafters were grateful that agreements were reached and left it to the future Judges of the Court to work out the uncertainties.

To be sure, the Statute and Rules provide for a variety of ways in which victims may participate other than as witnesses. The first opportunity for victims to participate is by submitting a communication to the Court complaining about an offense and requesting a preliminary examination into alleged crimes.[4] However, the opportunity to submit information to the Court is non-exclusive because it exists for all individuals whether victims of a crime or not. Moreover, neither victims nor any other individual or group submitting information can force the initiation of an investigation into alleged crimes as is the case in some national jurisdictions (Dadomo & Ferran 1993). Thus, while the ability to submit

---

3   Rome Statute of the International Criminal Court, Articles 15, 19, 68, 75, and 82, adopted 17 July 1998 by the U.N. Diplomatic Conference of Plenipotentiaries on the Establishment of an International Criminal Court, entered into force, 1 July 2002, U.N. Doc. A/CONF.183/9 (hereinafter Rome Statute).
4   *Idem*, Article 15.

information about a crime to the Court is important, the limitations of the complaint procedure as well as its non-exclusiveness do not necessarily make the process a significant advancement for the active participatory rights of victims.

Another opportunity to participate in the judicial process is by submitting a claim for reparations.[5] The opportunity to submit a claim for reparations is considered a significant achievement in the push for greater victim rights (see e.g. Bassiouni 2003). Notably, and in contrast with many national systems, victims may claim reparations regardless of whether or not they participate at trial. Moreover, a Trust Fund was established so that victims would have the possibility of receiving reparations even if the convicted individual was found to be indigent. Submitting a claim for reparations does not necessarily mean that a victim wishes to participate in trial proceedings. For this reason, it is viewed as a separate means of participation.

Finally, victims may participate as victim-participants directly in proceedings, usually through legal counsel. At the ICC, participation entails the right of victims to present their views and concerns to the Court so long as their participation does not infringe upon the rights of the accused and a fair and impartial trial. In practice, the Legal Representatives of victims may (depending upon the Chamber) have, amongst other rights, the opportunity to make opening and closing statements, to make submissions on fact and law, and to lead and challenge evidence. Again, although victim-participants may wish to claim reparations there is no obligation to do so, meaning that participation is not necessarily linked to their right to claim damages and is in fact a distinct right of victims in the criminal process. The below sections will focus on the right to direct participation in the proceedings.

3. THE PARTICIPATORY REGIME

The potential impact that the right to direct participation in the criminal process at the international level has is great – for victims and for the Court. For many victims, participation in the process provides a chance for the Court to recognize their suffering. For the Court, victim participation often legitimizes the role of the Court in affected communities. Many commentators, however, have, perhaps too optimistically, referred to the ICC's participatory regime as a form of restorative justice (Schabas 2004; Friman 2009). Despite the fact that the notion of restorative justice has no clear definition (Walgrave 2008; Dignan 2005), it is generally used to describe a process whereby the offender, victim and potentially the wider community begin to attempt to repair the harm suffered by the victim (Rauschenbach 2008). This process usually takes place outside of the traditional justice system and "is a process whereby parties with a stake in a specific offence

---

5   *Idem*, Article 75.

collectively resolve how to deal with the aftermath of that offence and its implications for the future" (Marshall 1999, 5). While autonomous participation in proceedings may offer a tangible avenue for expressing emotional suffering and therefore the Court can see a broader extent of a victims' harm, it is important to "take care to distinguish between procedural rights for victims [within criminal trials] and systems of restorative justice" (Ashworth 2000, 192). Although procedural rights and restorative justice principles may coincide it is equally possible that they may not. In other words, it is possible to grant extensive procedural rights to victims within the framework of a classical punitive system without necessarily converting that system into a restorative one (Ashworth 2000). For this reason, this chapter takes the view that it is better to perceive victim participation at the ICC as an important component of victim-oriented or victim-focused reforms. To state that the participatory regime converts the proceedings into a restorative process is misleading and potentially harmful with regard to victim expectations. Although the aim may well be to achieve restorative goals, the process is not necessarily restorative. Understanding this limitation of the potential impact of participation is important, particularly when evaluating jurisprudence to date.

3.1. DEFINITION OF VICTIMS

Rule 85 defines victims as "natural persons who have suffered harm as a result of the commission of any crime within the jurisdiction of the Court".[6] It further states that "victims may include organizations or institutions that have sustained direct harm to any of their property" so long as that property is dedicated to "religion, education, art or science or charitable purposes", historic monuments, hospitals and other places and objects that deal with humanitarian purposes.[7] This definition is remarkable for a number of reasons.

First, the drafters opted not to adopt the definition for victims found in Rule 2 of both the ICTY and ICTR Rules of Procedure and Evidence, which defines a victim as "a person against whom a crime over which the Tribunal has jurisdiction has allegedly been committed". During drafting negotiations, it had been argued by victims' rights groups and others that the ICTY/ICTR definition was too limited in that it is worded in the singular and it does not include family members or institutions (Fernández de Gurmendi 2001a). Also notable is the decision not to adopt the wording "allegedly been committed". Arguably the wording "allegedly been committed" promotes the presumption of innocence for the accused; however, it was problematic because it linked the status of victim

---

6   International Criminal Court Rules of Procedure and Evidence, Rule 85(a), adopted
     September 9, 2002, ICC-ASP/1/3 (hereinafter ICC RPE).
7   *Idem,* Rule 85(b).

with specific actions of an accused. Instead, Rule 85 links the status of victims to the commission of a crime within the Court's jurisdiction rather than defining victims in relation to proceedings against a specific individual in respect to specific conduct (Stahn, Olásolo & Gibson 2006). The ICTY and ICTR definition was also problematic for the drafters of the ICC Rules in that it was not in agreement with the unanimously adopted Victims' Declaration.[8] The definition of victims found in the Victims' Declaration was referred to by the drafters of the Rome Statute and was originally proposed as the definition for the Rules. However, despite NGO lobbying efforts for acceptance of a definition mirrored on the Victims' Declaration (Fernández de Gurmendi 2001a), the ICC definition is not a replica of the Declarations' definition, although it does closely resemble it (Donat-Cattin 1999).[9] A definition emulating the Victims' Declaration proved too difficult to build a consensus around; in particular, delegations expressed concern over terms such as "collectively" and "emotional suffering". Instead a similar but slightly different definition surfaced (Fernández de Gurmendi 2001a). Nonetheless, both the Victims' Declaration and the ICC definition provide victim status to those who suffered harm falling under the jurisdiction of the Court regardless of the actions of the accused. Second, the definition does not define the term "harm", leaving it instead to the discretion of the Court to define this term.[10] As a result, early in the Court's case law, Pre-Trial Chamber found that emotional suffering constitutes harm under the Statute and Rules.[11] Third, the ICC definition does not limit victim status to direct victims. Family members of direct victims, who have suffered emotional harm, can also qualify as victims before the Court.[12] With regard to the practical operations of the Court, the

---

[8]   The Declaration of Basic Principles of Justice for Victims of Crime and Abuse of Power, G.A. Res. 40/34, adopted 29 Nov. 1985, U.N. GAOR, 40th Sess., Annex, U.N. Doc. A/Res/40/34/ Annex (1985) (hereinafter Victims' Declaration).

[9]   The Victims' Declaration definition reads in part: (1) "Victims" means persons who, individually or collectively, have suffered harm, including physical or mental injury, emotional suffering, economic loss or substantial impairment of their fundamental rights, through acts or omissions that are in violation of criminal laws operative within Member States, including those laws proscribing criminal abuse of power. (2) A person may be considered a victim, under this Declaration, regardless of whether the perpetrator is identified, apprehended, prosecuted or convicted and regardless of the familial relationship between the perpetrator and the victim. The term "victim" also includes, where appropriate, the immediate family or dependants of the direct victim and persons who have suffered harm in intervening to assist victims in distress or to prevent victimization.

[10]   Cf. ECCC Internal Rules, at Rule 23.

[11]   Situation in Democratic Republic of the Congo, Decision on the Applications for Participation in the Proceedings of VPRS 1, VPRS 2, VPRS 3, VPRS 4, VPRS 5 and VPRS 6, Pre-Trial Chamber I, 17 January 2006, para. 116.

[12]   Prosecutor v. Joseph Kony et al., Appeals Chamber, Judgment on the appeals of the Defence against the decisions entitled "Decision on victims' applications for participation a/0010/06, a/0064/06 to a/0070/06, a/0081/06, a/0082/06, a/0084/06 to a/0089/06, a/0091/06 to a/0097/06, a/0099/06, a/0100/06, a/0102/06 to a/0104/06, a/0111/06, a/0113/06 to a/0117/06, a/0120/06, a/0121/06 and a/0123/06 to a/0127/06" of Pre-Trial Chamber II, 23 February 2009; See Situation in Uganda, Appeals Chamber, Judgment on the appeals of the Defence against the

broad definition allows for a greater number of victims to potentially participate in proceedings. Although manageable at the present moment due to the relatively low number of victims who have applied to participate to date (the Court has received approximately 2500 applications), in the future the potentially high number of victims may prove unworkable for the Court because of the work necessary to process applications, facilitate communication and in many cases provide protection. In order to manage the high number of potential victims the Court may, at its discretion, group victims together under common Legal Representatives.[13] In fact, the Court has already taken advantage of its ability to consolidate victim representation; in one of its cases it downsized from eight victims' Legal Representatives to two legal teams.[14]

3.2. VICTIMS OF A 'SITUATION' AND VICTIMS OF A 'CASE'

Unlike previous international criminal tribunals, the ICC divides its work into *situations* and *cases*. Situations are "generally defined in terms of temporal, territorial and in some cases personal parameters", and are investigated to see whether specific criminal investigations should arise and whether individuals should be charged with a criminal offense under the jurisdiction of the Court.[15] Cases, on the other hand, are comprised of specific incidents falling under the jurisdiction of the Court and include proceedings that follow the issuance of an arrest warrant or a summons to appear. The Court may deal with a number of situations at any given time and within these situations may try a number of cases and accused. Dividing its work into situations and cases arguably allows for greater transparency during the formal investigation stage by providing an opportunity for the Pre-Trial Chamber, the victims and others to be made aware of how the Prosecution intends to shape investigations and which suspects may or may not face charges.

Victims may apply to have victim status in both the situation and case; although the status as a victim is the same whether granted in a situation or a case, the exercisable rights are far greater at the case stage of proceedings because it is at this stage (after an individual has been named as a suspect/accused) where the actual trial proceeds. At the time of writing there are five situations: (1) Democratic Republic of Congo, (2) Uganda; (3) Central African Republic; (4)

---

decisions entitled "Decision on victims' applications for participation a/0010/06, a/0064/06 to a/0070/06, a/0081/06, a/0082/06, a/0084/06 to a/0089/06, a/0091/06 to a/0097/06, a/0099/06, a/0100/06, a/0102/06 to a/0104/06, a/0111/06, a/0113/06 to a/0117/06, a/0120/06, a/0121/06 and a/0123/06 to a/0127/06" of Pre-Trial Chamber II, 23 February 2009, paras. 35–36.

[13] ICC RPE, Rule 90(2).

[14] See *Prosecutor v. Germain Katanga and Mathieu Ngudjolo Chui*, Order on the Organisation of Common Legal Representation of Victims, Trial Chamber II, 22 July 2009.

[15] Decision on the Applications for Participation in the Proceedings of VPRS 1, VPRS 2, VPRS 3, VPRS 4, VPRS 5 and VPRS 6, *supra* note 11, at para. 65.

Darfur, Sudan; and (5) Kenya. Within the situation in DR-Congo there is a case against Thomas Lubanga Dyilo, Bosco Ntaganda, Germain Katanga and Mathieu Ngudjolo Chui; within the situation in Uganda the Court has issued arrest warrants for Joseph Kony, Vincent Otti, Okot Odhiambo and Dominic Ongwen; within the situation in Darfur, Sudan the Court has initiated cases against Ahmad Muhammad Harun, Ali Muhammad Ali Abd-Al-Rahman, Omar Hassan Ahmad Al Bashir, and Bahr Idriss Abu Garda; and within the situation in the Central African Republic the Court has a case against Jean-Pierre Bemba Gombo. To date, there are no cases within the investigation into the situation in Kenya. As of June 2010, over 2500 victims have applied to participate and 770 victims have been granted victim status in the various situations and cases before the Court.[16]

3.3. COMPLEX MAZE OF PARTICIPATORY PROVISIONS

In regards to the direct participation of victims in the proceedings, the negotiation processes culminating in the Rome Statute and Rules established an unnecessarily complex system. First, pursuant to Article 15(3) of the Rome Statute, victims may make representations to the Pre-Trial Chamber when the Prosecutor, acting pursuant to his *proprio motu* powers, requests an authorization of an investigation from the Pre-Trial Chamber. Rules 50 further clarifies the procedure for participation by providing that victims shall be informed that the Prosecution is seeking authorization and they may submit written representations. The rationale for involvement at this stage, i.e. before the naming of a suspect, is that victims are well positioned to provide information to the Court about alleged crimes (Stahn, Olásolo & Gibson 2006). Second, in accordance with Article 19(3), victims may submit observations to the Court when a challenge to the jurisdiction of the Court or the admissibility of a case arises. This participatory right arises after the naming of a suspect and allows victims to comment on whether a case should move forward. Third, Article 75 provides for the participation of victims in reparation hearings. As mentioned above, victims submitting reparations claims do not need to participate in trial proceedings because a reparations hearing may be bifurcated from the trial. However, victims who directly participate in trial may also claim reparations and raise relevant issues at trial. For this reason, the right to claim reparations can also be viewed together with the right to participate directly in trial, although in many situations this may not be the case. The ICC aims to properly address this right even allowing victims to appeal reparation orders pursuant to Article 82(4). Fourth, the Court has the power, in accordance with Rule 93, to seek the

---

[16] ICC Review Conference, Stocktaking Panel-Impact of the Court on Victims and Affected Communities, Remarks by ICC Registrar Silvana Arbia, Kampala, Uganda, 2 June 2010.

views of victims and their Legal Representatives on any issue. And, finally, under its most far reaching provision concerning victims' participatory rights, pursuant to Article 68(3), the Court shall permit victims to express their views and concerns in appropriate proceedings so long as this participation does not infringe upon the rights of the accused and a fair and impartial trial.[17]

Article 68(3) reproduces text found in Article 6(b) of the Victims' Declaration,[18] and is an attempt to move from a court that merely punishes individual perpetrators to a court with a more victim-centred approach (Donat-Cattin 1999). However, its vague wording has caused the Prosecution, Defence teams, and victims to spend considerable time and resources arguing for how the provision should be interpreted, and has required the various Chambers to spend a considerable amount of time and resources on how best to interpret its provisions (Vasiliev 2009). Indeed, as noted above, the wording was originally conceived as a way to encourage states to incorporate victim-oriented measures in their respective domestic systems and was formulated in such a way that it could apply in a wide-range of legal systems. Its interpretation at the ICC has unsurprisingly been problematic as Judges from a wide-variety of legal traditions must decide upon core participation issues. The following non-exhaustive list of issues pertaining to Article 68(3) has all fallen to the discretion of the Judges:

- whether the Article is applicable during all stages of proceedings, including proceedings that take place prior to the naming of a suspect;
- whether "shall permit their views and concerns to be presented" entails the right of victims to directly post questions to witnesses or lead and challenge evidence;
- whether a determination of "appropriate" stages of proceedings should be done broadly or narrowly; and
- how the Court should interpret "personal interests".

Confounding the issue of interpretation is the fact that Article 68(3) can apply equally to narrow and broad forms of participation, which is evidence of the fact that the vague language is widely accepted by national legal systems.

For the sake of efficiency individuals wishing to participate need to apply to the Court pursuant to Rules 89 to 91. These individuals must submit a written request indicating their harm suffered and whether they would like to participate in a situation, case or both. After the Registrar's Victim Participation and Reparation Section (VPRS) processes the applications they are then sent to the

---

[17] Rome Statute, Article 68(3).

[18] Article 6(b) of the Victims' Declaration reads: "The responsiveness of judicial and administrative processes to the needs of victims should be facilitated by: Allowing the views and concerns of victims to be presented and considered at appropriate stages of the proceedings where their personal interests are affected, without prejudice to the accused and consistent with the relevant national criminal justice system".

relevant Chamber for an initial assessment determining whether or not to grant the victim-applicant victim status. In determining victim status, Pre-Trial Chamber I, in an early decision, used criteria found in the definition of victims provided for in Rule 85 together with Article 68(3).[19] This approach was essentially followed by other Chambers.[20] As a result, Judges determining victim status at the ICC ask (i) whether the identity of the applicant as a natural person appears duly established; (ii) whether the events described by each applicant constitute a crime within the jurisdiction of the Court; (iii) whether the applicant claims to have suffered harm; and (iv) whether such harm appears to have arisen "as a result" of the event constituting a crime within the jurisdiction of the Court for situations or "as a result" of the crimes brought against an accused for participation in particular cases.[21]

As with determinations of whether Article 68(3) is satisfied, this initial determination of whether a victim-applicant meets the criteria outlined in Rule 85, however, is not as simple and clear as it may appear. For instance, there was a great deal of litigation over proof of identity issues both at the pre-trial and trial stage.[22] Another example was the time spent arguing over whether it is necessary

---

[19]   See Decision on the Applications for Participation in the Proceedings of VPRS 1, VPRS 2, VPRS 3, VPRS 4, VPRS 5 and VPRS 6, *supra* note 11.

[20]   *Situation in Uganda*, Decision on victims' applications for participation a/0010/06, a/0064/06 to a/0070/06, a/0081/06 to a/0104/06 and a/0111/06 to a/0127/06, Pre-Trial Chamber II (Single Judge), 10 August 2007, para. 12; *Prosecutor v. Thomas Lubanga Dyilo*, Decision on victims' participation, Trial Chamber I, 18 January 2008, paras. 84–86 (hereinafter Lubanga Decision on victims' participation).

[21]   See Decision on the Applications for Participation in the Proceedings of VPRS 1, VPRS 2, VPRS 3, VPRS 4, VPRS 5 and VPRS 6, *supra* note 11; Decision on victims' applications for participation a/0010/06, a/0064/06 to a/0070/06, a/0081/06 to a/0104/06 and a/0111/06 to a/0127/06, *supra* note 20; Lubanga Decision on victims' participation, *supra* note 20.

[22]   Leaving the pleadings aside, see for example some of the various decisions relating to proof of identity issues: Decision on victims' applications for participation a/0010/06, a/0064/06 to a/0070/06, a/0081/06 to a/0104/06 and a/0111/06 to a/0127/06, *supra* note 20, paras. 16–21; *Situation in Democratic Republic of Congo*, Decision on the Requests of the Legal Representative of Applicants on application process for victims' participation and legal representation, Pre-Trial Chamber I, 17 August 2007, paras. 13–15; *Situation in Democratic Republic of Congo*, Corrigendum à la "Décision sur les demandes de participation à la procédure déposées dans le cadre de l'enquête en République démocratique du Congo par a/0004/06 à a/0009/06, a/0016/06 à a/0063/06, a/0071/06 à a/0080/06 et a/0105/06 à a/0110/06, a/0188/06, a/0128/06 à a/0162/06, a/0199/06, a/0203/06, a/0209/06, a/0214/06, a/0220/06 à a/0222/06, a/0224/06, a/0227/06 à a/0230/06, a/0234/06 à a/0236/06, a/0240/06, a/0225/06, a/0226/06, a/0231/06 à a/0233/06, a/0237/06 à a/0239/06 et a/0241/06 à a/0250/06, Pre-Trial Chamber I (Single Judge), 31 January 2008, paras. 15 and 27; *Prosecutor v. Joseph Kony, et al.*, Decision on victim's application for participation a/0010/06, a/0064/06 to a/0/0070/06, a/0081/06, a/0082/06, a/0084/06 to a/0089/06, a/0091/06 to a/0097/06, a/0099/06, a/0101/06, a/0102/06 to a/0104/06, a/0111/06, a/0113/06 to a/0117/06, a/0120/06, a/0121/06 and a/0123/06 to a/0127/06, Pre-Trial Chamber II (Single Judge), 14 March 2008, para. 6; *Prosecutor v. Germain Katanga and Mathieu Ngudjolo Chui*, Decision on the provisional separation of Legal Representative of Victims a/0015/08, a/0022/08, a/0024/08, a/0025/08, a/0027/08, a/0028/08, a/0029/08, a/0032/08, a/0033/08, a/0034/08 and a/0035/08, Pre-Trial Chamber I, 3 July 2008, paras. 20–21; *Prosecutor v. Joseph Kony, et al.*, Appeals Chamber, Judgment on the

to show a nexus between the harm suffered and the crimes brought against an accused.[23] It took years for the Court to work out even seemingly simple determinations concerning participation. The role of the Appeals Chamber in this regard cannot be emphasized enough but it was some time before the various Chambers began granting leave to appeal participation issues. Moreover, problems arise because Appeals Chamber decisions are only binding upon the specific case in which they are rendered. Therefore, although it can be expected that the various Chambers would want to harmonize their procedural decisions, this has not always been the case. In fact, the parties and participants very often have re-litigated on the same issue before multiple Chambers, having some Chambers adopt their positions and others not. These different approaches have a direct effect on the manner and scope of participation for victims in proceedings. Moreover, the divergent approaches have created legal uncertainty for victims, their Legal Representatives and other Court actors.

4. SEEKING TO MAKE AN IMPACT

Despite the structural and procedural challenges encountered throughout participation, victims' Legal Representatives continue to seek to make a substantial impact in the proceedings. Many times this impact is subtle, for instance, when victims' Legal Representatives are able to add points of fact to the Prosecution's case to further clarify specific issues. For instance, the Legal Representatives for victims in the *Lubanga* trial played an important role in clarifying the use of first and second names in the DRC and requested the Court

---

appeals of the Defense against the decisions entitled 'Decision on victims' applications for participation a/0010/06, a/0064/06 to a/0070/06, a/0081/06, a/0082/06, a/0084/06 to a/0089/06, a/0091/06 to a/0097/06, a/0099/06, a/0100/06, a/0102/06 to a/0104/06, a/0111/06, a/0113/06 to a/0117/06, a/0120/06, a/0121/06 and a/0123/06 to a/0127/06' of Pre-Trial Chamber II, 23 February 2009, para. 1; Lubanga Decision on victims' participation, *supra* note 20, paras. 87–89.

23   See e.g. *Prosecutor v. Thomas Lubanga Dyilo*, Decision on the Applications for Participation in the Proceedings Submitted by VPRS 1 to VPRS 6 in the Case the Prosecutor v. Thomas Lubanga Dyilo, Pre-Trial Chamber I, 29 June 2006, pp. 6–8; Decision on victims' application for participation a/0010/06, a/0064/06 to a/0070/06, a/0081/06 to a/0104/06 and a/0111/06 to a/127/06, *supra* note 764, paras. 14–15, Lubanga Decision on victims' participation, *supra* note 20, paras. 93–94; *Situation in Democratic Republic of Congo*, Corrigendum à la "Décision sur les demandes de participation à la procédure déposées dans le cadre de l'enquête en République démocratique du Congo par a/0004/06 à a/0009/06, a/0016/06 à a/0063/06, a/0071/06 à a/0080/06 et a/0105/06 à a/0110/06, a/0188/06, a/0128/06 à a/0162/06, a/0199/06, a/0203/06, a/0209/06, a/0214/06, a/0220/06 à a/0222/06, a/0224/06, a/0227/06 à a/0230/06, a/0234/06 à a/0236/06, a/0240/06, a/0225/06, a/0226/06, a/0231/06 à a/0233/06, a/0237/06 à a/0239/06 et a/0241/06 à a/0250/06, Pre-Trial Chamber I (Single Judge), 31 January 2008, para. 38; *Prosecutor v. Thomas Lubanga Dyilo*, Judgment on the Appeals of The Prosecutor and The Defence against Trial Chamber I's Decision on Victims' Participation of 18 January 2008, Appeals Chamber, 11 July 2008, paras. 2 and 64.

to appoint an expert on this matter.[24] Although this participation may appear minor in comparison to broader issues brought out at trial, other times, the impact of their role in proceedings is far more noticeable and potentially more significant. One situation in which their impact has been most evident is in the *Lubanga* trial where victims' Legal Representatives, including the vital role played by the Office of Public Counsel for Victims (OPCV), pushed to have the facts in the *Lubanga* case re-characterized in an attempt to better reflect the harm suffered by victims, namely harm suffered from sexual crimes (Mesters & Adeboyejo, this volume). In addition, it is the victims in the *Bemba* case who have played an important role with the continued push for *in situ* proceedings. Unlike the situation in the *Lubanga* case, where the victims' desire to re-characterize the facts were at odds with the wishes of the Prosecution, in the *Bemba* case both the Prosecution and victims have submitted arguments for why *in situ* proceedings are beneficial. Importantly, these examples highlight the unique role of victims – at times arguing against the position of the Prosecution and at times arguing with the position of the Prosecution.

4.1. NEW CHARGES AGAINST THE ACCUSED

Thomas Lubanga Dyilo is charged with offenses falling under Articles 8(2)(b) (xxvi) and 8(2)(e)(vii) of the Rome Statute related to the conscription and enlistment of child soldiers. Victims' advocates both inside and outside the Court have lamented over these narrow charges.[25] Nevertheless, in spite of the narrow charges, many of the Prosecution witnesses testified about repeated rapes and other sexual offenses carried out by army commanders.[26] On 22 May 2009,

---

[24]   *Prosecutor v. Thomas Lubanga Dyilo*, Analyse relative à l'attribution et aux composantes du nom en République démocratique du Congo, Submission of Legal Representatives for Victims to Trial Chamber I, 20 March 2009.

[25]   See, e.g., DR Congo: ICC Charges Raise Concern, Joint Letter to the Chief Prosecutor of the ICC, Avocats Sans Frontières, Center for Justice and Reconciliation, Coalition Nationale pour la Cour Pénale Internationale – RCD, Fédération Internationale des Ligues des Droits de l'Homme, Human Rights Watch, International Center for Transitional Justice, Redress, Women's Initiatives for Gender Justice, 31 July 2006, available at: www.hrw.org/en/news/2006/07/31/dr-congo-icc-charges-raise-concern; Sheila Vélez, Victims raise their voice in the Lubanga case, Aegis Trust, 2009, available at: www.aegistrust.org/Lubanga-Chronicles/victims-raise-their-voice-in-the-lubanga-case.html, citing OPCV Principal Counsel, Paolina Massida as saying "The majority of Victims if not all of female victims, represented by the Legal representatives were actually recruited to became sexual slaves or forced wives to commanders. (...) This was an essential component of the recruitment. And it is important for victims that their story is told in the way it happened. They want that the truth and the facts are qualified as they were in the context of the charges." See also, *Prosecutor v. Thomas Lubanga Dyilo*, Joint Application of the Legal Representatives of the Victims for the Implementation of the Procedure under Regulation 55 of the Regulations of the Court Trial Chamber I, 22 May 2009.

[26]   *Idem*, paras. 32–36.

victims' Legal Representatives in the case filed a joint motion requesting the Trial Chamber to consider adding the charges of sexual slavery as a crime against humanity and war crime and cruel and/or inhuman treatment as a war crime pursuant to Regulation 55 of the Regulations of the Court.[27] Regulation 55 provides, in part, that, the Chamber has the power to change the legal characterization of facts to fit with new charges "without exceeding the facts and circumstances described in the charges and any amendments to the charges".[28] Regulation 55(2) allows the Chamber to change the legal characterization of the facts at any time during trial and Regulation 55(3) obliges the Court to ensure that the Defence has adequate time and facilities to prepare a defence, including, if necessary, to re-examine witnesses.

The victims' Legal Representatives argued that facts alleged in the charging document could constitute new crimes against the accused, including inhuman treatment and sexual slavery. In turn, the Defence argued not only that the request by victims' Legal Representatives exceeds the facts as laid out in the indictment, but also that any re-characterizing of facts at this stage of the proceedings would infringe upon the rights of the accused to a trial without undue delay. Just as the Prosecution finished presenting its evidence in mid-July 2009, a majority of the Trial Chamber found that it, in fact, would consider adding the new charges as requested by the victims' Legal Representatives.[29] This decision seemed to hold that the Court may even add new charges based on facts that came to light during trail but that are not explicitly mentioned in the charging document. However, later the Trial Chamber clarified that facts coming to light at trial must still be connected with those described in the charging document.[30]

This decision is significant for many reasons, not least because of the role played by victims' legal counsel in potentially having the charges against the accused broadened so that they better reflect the harms suffered by victims. Both the Prosecution and Defence sought leave to appeal the decision and on 3 September 2009 the Appeals Chamber granted leave to appeal. The trial was postponed, for yet another time, until the Appeals Chamber, on 8 December 2009, unanimously reversed the Trial Chamber's decision. The Appeals Chamber found that Trial Chamber I erred in law when it found that Regulation 55 has two separate procedures, which in essence, allowed the Court under Regulation

---

27   *Ibidem.*
28   International Criminal Court, Regulations of the Court, Regulation 55(1), adopted 26 May 2004, ICC-BD/01-01-04.
29   See *Prosecutor v. Thomas Lubanga Dyilo*, Decision giving notice to the parties and participants that the legal characterisation of the facts may be subject to change in accordance with Regulation 55(2) of the Regulations of the Court, Trial Chamber I, 14 July 2009.
30   See *Prosecutor v. Thomas Lubanga Dyilo*, Clarification and further guidance to parties and participants in relation to the "Decision giving notice to the parties and participants that the legal characterisation of the facts may be subject to change in accordance with Regulation 55(2) of the Regulations of the Court", Trial Chamber I, 27 August 2009.

55(2) and (3) to include additional facts and circumstances not described in the charging document.[31]

Despite this unanimous decision, on 15 December 2009, the victims' Legal Representatives filed observations on the Appeals Chamber judgment. These observations requested the Trial Chamber to interpret the Appeals Chamber judgment as not preventing a new legal characterization of the facts as described in the charges.[32] Essentially, they were again asking the Trial Chamber to use its powers under Regulation 55 to modify the legal characterization of facts (found only in the charging document) in order to include additional charges pertaining to sexual crimes. The Defence has responded, arguing that the Appeals Chamber judgment ends any attempts to re-characterize the facts and modify the charges.[33] As of June 2010 the Trial Chamber has not yet responded but there is a possibility that facts of sexual violence will be recognized in the judgment and could be seen as an aggravating factor for sentencing should the accused be convicted. Out of all of this litigation, one thing is certain: the impact of victims upon the proceedings cannot be ignored.

4.2. IN SITU PROCEEDINGS

Commentators have long criticized the ICTY and the ICTR for not fully addressing the needs and concerns of the victims and communities affected by the crimes covered by the tribunal (Donat-Cattin 1999).[34] One reason for this failing is due to the fact that the courts are located far from the victim communities. Without robust outreach programs, the distance makes it difficult for the affected populations to closely follow and understand the often lengthy and complex proceedings. When located in the proximity of where the crimes occurred or near affected communities, courts are usually in a position to better explain the process of the proceedings and the rule of law with regard to international criminal law and victims will have greater access to watch proceedings. Moreover, if victims and their local communities are meant to be

---

31   See *Prosecutor v. Thomas Lubanga Dyilo*, Judgment on the appeals of Mr Lubanga Dyilo and the Prosecutor against the Decision of Trial Chamber I of 14 July 2009 entitled "Decision giving notice to the parties and participants that the legal characterisation of the facts may be subject to change in accordance with Regulation 55(2) of the Regulations of the Court," Appeals Chamber, 8 December 2009.

32   See *Prosecutor v. Thomas Lubanga Dyilo*, Observations conjointes des Représentants Légaux des Victimes quant aux conséquences de l'arrêt de la Chambre d' appel du 8 décembre 2009, Trial Chamber I, 15 December 2009.

33   See *Prosecutor v. Thomas Lubanga Dyilo*, Réponse de la Défense aux "Observations conjointes des Représentants Légaux des Victimes quant aux conséquences de l'arrêt de la Chambre d' appel du 8 décembre 2009", datées du 15 décembre 2009, Trial Chamber I, 18 December 2009.

34   Glasius, M., How Activists Shaped the Court, The International Criminal Court: An End to Impunity? (Crimes of War Project), 2003; available at www.crimesofwar.org/icc_magazine/icc-glasius.html.

the beneficiaries of international justice then having trials held locally, where possible, may lend legitimacy to the criminal process (Kermani Mendez 2009). Therefore, proceedings held in or near to affected communities are often viewed largely desirable.[35]

Article 3(3) of the Rome Statute states that "[t]he Court may sit elsewhere, whenever it considers it desirable (…)". This provision allows that proceedings of the Court be held *in situ*, or on-site, meaning that proceedings may be held in the territory of the countries affected by a particular case. At the first status hearing in the *Bemba* case before Trial Chamber III, the Court asked the Prosecutor to submit observations on whether part of the trial should, in fact, be conducted *in situ*.[36] This request is in line with a commitment of the Court to examine the feasibility of such a trial – which would be a first for the Court. The Prosecution submitted its observations on 12 October 2009 and proposed to carry out parts of the trial in the CAR, citing the need to reach out to affected communities and to provide maximum access to the trial process for victims and the wider public.[37] To this end, the Prosecution submitted that opening statements, the examination of victims and crime-based witnesses and the delivery of the final judgment could all take place *in situ*.

Importantly, the Legal Representatives for victims were also able to comment upon the issue. On 3 November 2009, the Legal Representatives for victims responded in full support of *in situ* proceedings, arguing that they are beneficial to affected communities and allow for broader victim access to the court.[38] Nevertheless, for security purposes, the victims' Legal Representatives warned against having *in situ* hearings during the election period scheduled for early 2010. Indeed, they stressed the importance of protective measures should these hearings take place. In this role, the victims' Legal Representatives were, on the one hand, able to support the Prosecution, and on the other hand, provide additional insight into the issue from the unique position of victims.

The two above examples, pertaining to the request for a re-characterization of the facts and the request for *in situ* hearings, highlight the unique role victims have thus far played in proceedings before the ICC. At times the victims are arguing a position not held by the Prosecution and at other times are bolstering positions supported by the Prosecution. The position of victims in the proceedings has nonetheless proven challenging for the Court and despite the

---

35 See Prof. J.A. Ayua, Solicitor General of the Federal Republic of Nigeria and Permanent Secretary, "Nigeria Statement on behalf of the African States Parties to the Rome Statute of the ICC," Fourth Session of the ASP, The Hague, The Netherlands, 3 December 2005.

36 See *Prosecutor v. Jean-Pierre Bemba Gombo*, Transcripts: First status conference, 7 October 2009, ICC-01/05–01/08-T-14.ENG.

37 *Prosecutor v. Jean-Pierre Bemba Gombo*, Prosecution's Submission to Conduct Part of the Trial *In Situ*, Trial Chamber III, 12 October 2009, para. 2.

38 See *Prosecutor v. Jean-Pierre Bemba Gombo*, Réponse conjointe des représentants légaux des victimes aux observations du Bureau du Procureur concernant la tenue de certaines audiences du procès en République centrafricaine, Trial Chamber III, 3 November 2009.

impact victims have had on proceedings, which admittedly is difficult to measure at this stage, the Court has struggled with the concept of victim participation. The following section will shed light on the fragmented and inconsistent approach towards victim participation.

5. FRAGMENTATION AND INCONSISTENCY

Regrettably for the parties and participants, the Court as a whole has failed to take a clear approach to victim participation. Its jurisprudence to date has been fragmented and inconsistent. Two examples of this scattered approach stand out.[39] The first has to do with how the different chambers carry out their Article 68(3) evaluations, concerning whether or not victims will be permitted to present their views and concerns in proceedings. The second concerns how the different chambers treat anonymous and non-anonymous victims.

5.1. ARTICLE 68(3) AND THE MODALITIES OF PARTICIPATION

Due to the fact that the Rome Statute and Rules provide for only a handful of specific procedural rights in regards to the modalities of participation, including for instance the general right to file requests with the Court, the Judges have broad discretion in shaping the manner and scope of participation. However, it is only after the Court has determined that the victim-applicant qualifies for victim status pursuant to Rule 85 and meets the additional criteria found in Article 68(3) that the Judges can then lay out the parameters of participatory rights. Regrettably for the victims and their Legal Representatives, the various Chambers of the Court have adopted inconsistent approaches on how they carry out an Article 68(3) analysis, which in turn shapes the manner and scope of participation.

Notably, the Pre-Trial Chamber in the *Katanga/Ngudjolo* case, as well as other subsequent cases, adopted a systematic approach whereby the Judges view the proceedings in a broad context, as will be further elaborated upon in the

---

[39]   Another example of the Court's fragmented and inconsistent approach to victim participation has to do with their approach to child-victims participating before the Court and those acting on their behalf. See *Situation in the Democratic Republic of Congo*, Decision on the Requests of the Legal Representatives of Applicants on application process for victims' participation and legal representation, Pre-Trial Chamber I, 17 August 2007, para. 12 (requiring that those persons acting on behalf of child-victims provide proof of kinship or legal guardianship); Cf. *Prosecutor v. Thomas Lubanga Dyilo*, Decision on the applications by victims to participate in the proceedings, Trial Chamber I, 15 December 2008, paras. 66–72 (finding nothing in the Statute or Rules that requires proof of kinship or legal guardianship for those persons acting on behalf of child-victims).

following section.[40] In contrast, the Trial Chamber in *Lubanga*, as well as various other Appeals Chamber judgments, has adopted a piecemeal, or casuistic, approach whereby the notion of proceedings is viewed in a narrow context.[41] Both approaches have their advantages and disadvantages and there is no lack of commentaries advocating one approach over another. However, it is the fact that both approaches still operate at the Court that is so troubling; essentially creating a legal maze for victims' Legal Representatives to navigate.

5.1.1. Systematic approach

At the pre-trial stage of a case leading up to and including the confirmation of charges hearing, the Single Judge in *Katanga/Ngudjolo* provided a fairly clear, systematic system of rights for those granted victim status. In effect, she divided the analysis of Article 68(3) in two. First, she determined that those individuals who meet the criteria of Rule 85 and who are granted victim status in the case will have a personal interest in participating in pre-trial proceedings leading up to and including the confirmation of charges hearing. In other words, the determinations of whether a victim's personal interests are affected, pursuant to Article 68(3), may be carried out with respect to all victims rather than on an individual basis. And this assessment is to be carried out in relation to the stage of proceedings rather than in relation to specific proceedings or specific pieces of evidence. To this end, certain stages of proceedings, such as the confirmation of charges hearing, can automatically be considered appropriate for the views and concerns of victims to be shared. Viewing the pre-trial proceedings in a broad context, the Single Judge then laid out the appropriate manner and scope of participation.

In this regard, in *Katanga/Ngudjolo* all non-anonymous victims were given the same set of procedural, participatory rights. The modalities of participation included: notification rights,[42] access to transcripts and documents in the case in the form they are made available to the non-proposing party;[43] the right to

---

[40]   See *Prosecutor v. Germain Katanga and Mathieu Ngudjolo Chui*, Decision on the Set of Procedural Rules Attached to Procedural Status of Victim at the Pre-Trial Stage of the Case, Pre-Trial Chamber I (Single Judge), 13 May 2008.

[41]   See Lubanga Decision on victims' participation, *supra* note 20, and Judgment on the Appeals of the Prosecutor and The Defence against Trial Chamber I's Decision on Victims' Participation of 18 January 2008, *supra* note 23.

[42]   Decision on the Set of Procedural Rules Attached to Procedural Status of Victim at the Pre-Trial Stage of the Case, *supra* note 40, para. 129; Anonymous victims, however, will only receive notification of the public documents contained in the record of the case and public sessions of the hearing in order to avoid violating the principle of prohibiting anonymous accusations; See also *Prosecutor v. Thomas Lubanga Dyilo*, Decision on the Arrangements for Participation of Victims a/0001/06, a/0002/06 and a/0003/06 at the Confirmation Hearing, Pre-Trial Chamber I, 22 September 2006, pp. 7–8.

[43]   Decision on the Set of Procedural Rules Attached to Procedural Status of Victim at the Pre-Trial Stage of the Case, *supra* note 40, at paras. 130, 132–133.

examine and make submissions on the admissibility and value of evidence on which the Prosecution and Defence intend to rely at the confirmation hearing;[44] attend hearings;[45] make oral motions, responses and submissions;[46] and file written motions, responses and replies.[47] Importantly, the Court retained the right to limit the set of procedural rights outlined by the Single Judge *proprio motu* or at the request of the parties, the Registry or any other participant if it is shown that the relevant limitation is necessary to safeguard another competing interest protected by the Statute or Rules. These other interests may include national security, the physical or psychological well-being of victims and witnesses, or the Prosecution's investigations.[48] Therefore, the Single Judge left room for the Court to carry out the final part of the analysis under Article 68(3) relating to the rights of the accused and fair trial principles.

In addition to these participatory rights outlined above, at the confirmation of charges hearing, non-anonymous victims had the right to make opening and closing statements and examine any witness called by the Prosecution or Defence.[49] The Court determined that victims exercising their right to examine witnesses will do so after the Prosecution but before the Defence and within the time allocated by the Chamber. Victims were not required to file the list of questions they intended to pose prior to the examination of the witness.[50] The victim's right to participate did not, however, include the right to extend the factual basis contained in the Prosecution charging document.[51] Instead, victims could attempt to extend the legal characterization of the facts contained in the charging document with the intention of encouraging the Court to ask the Prosecution to consider amending the charges to include a different crime.

The approach adopted by the Single Judge in the *Katanga/Ngudjolo* case builds upon and refines earlier case law from the pre-trial stage of the *Lubanga* case,[52] and attempts to provide an 'easy-to-apply' set of procedural rights for victims. This broad approach has also been followed in the *Bemba* pre-trial

---

44   *Idem*, para. 134.
45   *Idem*, para. 140.
46   *Idem*, para. 141.
47   *Idem*, paras. 141–144; This group of rights does not include the right to make challenges to, or raise issues relating to, the jurisdiction of the Court or the admissibility of a case pursuant to Article 19(2) and (3) of the Rome Statute and Rule 122(2) of the ICC RPE.
48   *Idem*, paras. 147–148.
49   *Idem*, paras. 135 and 137–138, finding that at the confirmation of charges hearing, non-anonymous victims will have the right to examine any witness called by the Prosecution or Defense.
50   *Ibidem*.
51   *Idem*, paras. 122–123.
52   Decision on the Applications for Participation in the Proceedings of VPRS 1, VPRS 2, VPRS 3, VPRS 4, VPRS 5 and VPRS 6, *supra* note 11; Decision on the Applications for Participation in Proceedings of a/0001/06, a/0002/06 and a/0003/06 in the case against the Prosecutor v. Thomas Lubanga Dyilo and of the Investigations in the Democratic Republic of Congo, Pre-Trial Chamber I, 28 July 2006.

stage[53] and *Katanga/Ngudjolo* trial stage.[54] The benefit of such an approach is that Legal Representatives of victims know in advance what their rights are and can prepare better for hearings. This benefit also applies to the other parties who will know in advance when and how victims' Legal Representatives and victims themselves (if permitted) will be able to participate and to what extent. The drawback of this approach is that in a case where every Legal Representative for victims has the right to participate, even on issues that may not directly affect their personal interests, essentially nullifies the personal interest pre-condition found in Article 68(3) and could potentially increase repetitive questions and interjections (Thomas & Chy 2009).

5.1.2. *Piecemeal approach*

In contrast to the systematic approach adopted by the Single Judge in *Katanga/Ngudjolo*, the Trial Chamber in the *Lubanga* case has adopted a piecemeal, or casuistic, approach to determining the manner and scope of participation. This approach has, in turn, largely been endorsed by the Appeals Chamber. Although Trial Chamber I in *Lubanga* recognized that victims share several general interests, it nonetheless found that an Article 68(3) analysis requires a determination of the specific personal interests of individual victims. Therefore, once granted victim status in the case, in order to exercise their participatory rights, the Trial Chamber determined that victims must: (i) file a discrete written application to the Chamber; (ii) give notice to the parties; (iii) demonstrate how their personal interests are affected by the *specific* proceedings; and (iv) comply with disclosure obligations and protection orders.[55] In other words, victims' Legal Representatives will need to show how their clients' personal interests are affected by specific proceedings at trial rather than at trial generally as was the case in the pre-trial stage both in *Lubanga* and *Katanta / Ngudjolo*. This means that a victims' Legal Representative will need to show how the testimony of witness X or the admission of evidence Y affects the personal interests of one of their clients before they are granted an exercisable right to participation. The Chamber believed that this piecemeal approach would best determine the appropriateness of participation so that the participation is consistent with Article 68(3) and the rights of the accused and a fair trial.[56]

Once the victim can show how his or her personal interests are affected by a specific matter, the modalities of participation may include: notification rights,

---

[53]   See *Prosecutor v. Jean-Pierre Bemba Gombo*, Fourth Decision on Victims' Participation, Pre-Trial Chamber III, 12 December 2008.
[54]   See *Prosecutor v. German Katanga and Mathieu Ngudjolo Chui*, Decision on the Modalities of Victims Participation at Trial, Trial Chamber II, 22 January 2010.
[55]   Judgment on the Appeals of The Prosecutor and The Defence against Trial Chamber I's Decision on Victims' Participation of 18 January 2008, *supra* note 23, para. 4.
[56]   *Ibidem.*

513

access to documents,[57] ability to make submissions on matters of admissibility and relevance of evidence,[58] questioning witnesses, including experts and accused,[59] attending closed and *ex parte* hearings,[60] orally participating, including making opening and closing statements at trial,[61] filing written motions,[62] and leading and challenging evidence.[63] However, one thing is certainly clear, victims do not have an unfettered right to participate in all manners available to the Prosecution and Defence. Although Article 68(3) provides that victims have the right to participate, victims are nonetheless not full parties to the proceedings. Instead, they are afforded a number of party-like rights that are neither automatic nor unconditional.

In its 11 July 2008 decision the Appeals Chamber appears to support the Trial Chamber's approach when it states that the Trial Chamber correctly identified the procedure for determining victim participation under Article 68(3).[64] The fact that the Appeals Chamber appears to have endorsed the piecemeal approach over a more systematic approach like that in place during pre-trial proceedings suggests that many Judges at the Court are uneasy with affording broad, easy-to-apply participatory rights – regardless of whether or not Judges could limit such rights on a case-by-case basis. The requirement for victims' Legal Representatives to file discrete written applications pertaining to specific proceedings at trial, such as the testimony of a specific witness or a hearing on a specific piece of evidence, is burdensome on both victims and the Court. Nevertheless, arguably such a procedure is consistent with the requirements of Article 68(3) and the need to ensure a fair trial. Moreover, the benefit of such a procedure is that those victims who can show how their personal interests are affected by a specific proceeding may have greater opportunities to participate. For instance, the Judges may grant them greater latitude when questioning a witness or be more open to the leading of evidence. Whether this is the case or not is yet to be determined.

---

[57] Lubanga Decision on victims' participation, *supra* note 20, paras. 105, 106 and 111, also finding that contrary to the Pre-Trial Chamber decision of 13 May 2008, *supra* note 40, legal representatives of victims at the trial stage will be able to access public filings only if they can show that confidential filings are of material relevance to their client's personal interests and will not breach existing protective measures.

[58] *Idem*, para. 109.

[59] *Idem*, para. 108.

[60] *Idem*, para. 113.

[61] *Idem*, para. 117.

[62] *Idem*, paras. 114 and 118.

[63] *Idem*, para. 108.

[64] Judgment on the Appeals of the Prosecution and the Defense against Trial Chamber I's Decision on Victim Participation of 18 January 2008, *supra* note 23, at para. 104.

5.2. ANONYMOUS AND NON-ANONYMOUS VICTIMS

Another important instance of the Court's fragmented and inconsistent approach on victim participation has to do with a split amongst Pre-Trial Chambers concerning the rights of anonymous victim participants.

5.2.1. Drawing a distinction

In an early decision by the Court, Pre-Trial Chamber I in the *Lubanga* case differentiated between the modalities of participation granted to non-anonymous victims and anonymous victims participating in the first ever confirmation of charges hearing.[65] The Pre-Trial Chamber found that, at this stage of the proceedings, the anonymous participation of the said victims, should, in principle, "be limited to: i) access to the public documents only; and ii) presence at the public hearings only; but that the Chamber retains the option to make an exception to this principle in the event of exceptional circumstances".[66] In addition, the anonymous victims were permitted to make opening and closing statements and request leave to intervene during public sessions. However the Court emphasized that "the fundamental principle prohibiting anonymous accusations would be violated if [the said victims] were permitted to add any point of fact or any evidence at all to the Prosecution's case-file"; nor would they be permitted to question the witnesses.[67]

The Prosecutor in the *Katanga/Ngudjolo* case agreed with this Chamber's evaluation of the principle prohibiting anonymous accusations and in its 14 April 2008 filing noted that participatory rights granted at the pre-trial stage should not be granted irrespective of a victim's anonymity. Pre-Trial Chamber I in *Katanga/Ngudjolo* agreed, granting different rights based on whether a victim participant was anonymous or not.[68] Similar to the Pre-Trial Chamber's decision in *Lubanga*, the Single Judge at the Pre-Trial stage in *Katanga/Ngudjolo* prohibited anonymous victims from adding any point of fact or evidence and from questioning witnesses in accordance with Rule 91(3).[69] Anonymous victims were, however, granted notification rights, attendance at public hearings and conferences, the right to make opening and closing statements and the right to request leave to intervene at public sessions.[70] Similar to the approach taken by the Pre-Trial Chambers in *Lubanga* and *Katanga/Ngudjolo*, the Trial Chamber

---

[65] Decision on the Arrangements for Participation of Victims a/0001/06, a/0002/06 and a/0003/06 at the Confirmation Hearing, *supra* note 42, p. 6.

[66] *Ibidem.*

[67] *Idem*, p. 7.

[68] Decision on the Set of Procedural Rights Attached to Procedural Status of Victim at the Pre-Trial Stage of the Case, *supra* note 40.

[69] *Idem*, p. 182.

[70] *Ibidem.*

in *Lubanga* has also held that extreme care must be used before permitting the use of anonymous victim participation and noted that "the greater the extent and the significance of the proposed participation, the more likely it will be that the Chamber will require the victim to identify himself or herself".[71] While taking note of the safety and security of victims, the Court emphasized that the participation of anonymous victims "in the proceedings cannot be allowed to undermine the fundamental guarantee of a fair trial".[72] Likewise, with regard to oral testimony, the Trial Chamber in *Katanga/Ngudjolo* found that under no circumstances will the Chamber allow victims to testify anonymously.[73]

All of the above mentioned decisions are in line with the argument that the prohibition against anonymous accusations protects the fair trial rights of the accused. However, the practice of anonymous witness testimony in international criminal law is not clear cut. The granting of full anonymity, i.e. concealing a witness' identity from the public as well as the Defence, to a witness is certainly controversial as it arguably constitutes a violation of the right of an accused to a fair trial. At the ICTY, the court granted full anonymity to two witnesses in the *Tadić* case, laying out various criteria that had to be met in order for such an extreme measure to be granted, including a real fear for the victim's safety, the relevance of the testimony to the case of the Prosecutor, and the absence of other possible protective measures.[74] However, the ICTY has been severely criticized for this decision, and as a result full anonymity has yet to be granted in subsequent cases (De Brouwer 2005). Anonymity is not specifically discussed in the Rome Statue or Rules although the duty of the Court to provide for protective measures is discussed. Article 64(6)(e) stipulates that the trial chamber may provide protection for victims and witnesses.[75] Similarly, Article 68(1) provides that the Court shall "take appropriate measures to protect the safety, physical and psychological well-being, dignity and privacy of victims and witnesses".[76] This Article further states, however, that "these measures shall not be prejudicial to or inconsistent with the rights of the accused and a fair trial and impartial trial".[77] Therefore, the Court must carry out a balancing test similar to that carried out at other international criminal courts and it appears clear that Article 68 does not prohibit the possibility of anonymous victim participation.

---

[71]   Lubanga Decision on Victims' Participation, *supra* note 20, para. 131.

[72]   *Ibidem.*

[73]   *Prosecutor v. Germain Katanga and Mathieu Ngudjolo Chui,* Directions for the conduct of the proceedings and testimony in accordance with Rule 140, Trial Chamber II (Single Judge), 20 November 2009, para. 22.

[74]   ICTY, *Prosecutor v. Duško Tadić,* Decision on the Prosecutor's motion requesting protective measures for victims and witnesses, Case No. IT-94-1, 10 August 1005, paras. 62–66.

[75]   ICC RPE, Rule 64(6)(e).

[76]   *Idem,* Rule 68(1).

[77]   *Idem.*

5.2.2. Drawing no distinction

In the 12 December 2008 Pre-Trial Chamber II decision in the *Bemba* case, the Court has gone in a new direction than that previously taken by the various Chambers, holding that no differentiation should be "made between victims whose identity is known to the Defence and those for whom anonymity has been granted by the Chamber".[78] The Court reasoned that an anonymous victim should not face "detriment[al]" treatment due to their request for protective measures. In addition, the Court reasoned that since victims are not parties to the proceedings they do not assume the role of accuser. As a result, in *Bemba*, all victims, regardless of their anonymity, were entitled to attend public sessions, have access to public documents, transcripts and evidence, make opening and closing statements, have notification rights, make oral submissions on issues of law and fact during the confirmation hearing, and make written submissions on law and fact. Therefore, in general it appears that the rights of non-anonymous victims in the *Bemba* pre-trial stage were somewhat curtailed in that they would no longer have access to confidential filings and closed hearings which non-anonymous victims in previous pre-trial proceedings in *Lubanga* and *Katanga/ Ngudjolo* enjoyed. In contrast, anonymous victims now had a right to make submissions on both law and fact, which did not exist previously. Thus, while anonymous victims seemed to gain rights, non-anonymous victims lost rights exercised by non-anonymous victims in other cases. Unfortunately, it is still unclear whether anonymous victims would have been permitted to question witnesses since this issue was not dealt with by the Court due to the fact that no witnesses were called.

The reasoning employed by the Court, finding that there should be no difference between anonymous and non-anonymous participants, is inconsistent with previous Court practice as well as general practice in international criminal law. Prior Court practice limited the rights of anonymous victims in comparison with non-anonymous victims. In addition, the Chamber failed to rely on earlier decisions of Pre-Trial Chamber I which found that the identification, prosecution and punishment of those responsible for crimes under the Court's jurisdiction "are at the root of the well-established right to justice for victims of serious violations of human rights, which international human rights bodies have differentiated from the victims' right to reparations".[79] Had they done so, they likely would have found that victims' participatory rights appear to extend to rights that reflect the role of an accuser, whether they are full parties to the proceedings or not. This is particularly true when victims are able to challenge witnesses and talk on points connected to both law and fact that go towards the

---

[78]   Fourth Decision on Victims' Participation, *supra* note 53, para. 99.
[79]   Decision on the Set of Procedural Rules Attached to Procedural Status of Victim at the Pre-Trial Stage of the Case, *supra* note 40, paras. 38–39.

guilt of the accused. Indeed, the 12 December 2008 decision is remarkable because it erodes the distinction between anonymity and non-anonymity, based in part on novel and inconsistent reasoning. The repercussions of this decision may in turn have an impact on the trial proceedings and the expansion of the exception to the principle against anonymous accusations. Many would argue that the fair trial rights of an accused demand that anonymous accusations, through victim participation, be limited in use or prohibited at trial (Zappalà 2010).

6. ADDRESSING THE NEED FOR IMPROVEMENTS

Essentially, there are two factors that contribute to the continued problems surrounding victim participation. The first is the fact that institutionally there is little conceptual understanding of and agreement over victim participation. The Judges come from all over the world and victim participation is different in almost every domestic jurisdiction. Even in countries that share similar victim participation laws, in practice, the difference is often great (Brienen & Hoegen 2000). Secondly, there is little guidance or conceptual clarity that can be found in the Statute or Rules. During the drafting process the drafters purposefully adopted broad language that could apply to both a restrictive and non-restrictive participatory regime so that a consensus could be reached during negotiations. Leaving final interpretation of major points to the Judges' discretion was likely the only way of getting victim participation provisions approved. For these reasons, the various Chambers must begin to look at victim participation more holistically and from the standpoint of the *sui generis* system of the ICC. The Chambers should begin to harmonize their opinions and lower Chambers should be encouraged to allow procedural issues pertaining to victims to be heard on appeal.

6.1. GREATER CLARITY: APPEALS CHAMBER ROLE

The two above examples, concerning the piecemeal versus systemic approach to Article 68(3) evaluations and the divergence of Court opinion on how to treat anonymous victims, highlight that four years following the first major decision on victim participation the Court is still grappling with finding the most suitable way in which victims can participate in appropriate stages of the proceedings. Nevertheless, improvements have occurred. The Appeals Chamber is finally playing a larger role in providing clarity. Two instances, in particular, stand out. The first concerns the 12 July 2008 judgment clarifying (to some extent) victim participation at trial in the *Lubanga* case. The second concerns the 19 December

2008 judgment disallowing a general right of participation during the investigation stage of a situation.

The *Lubanga* Trial Chamber majority decision on victim participation was remarkable for a number of reasons but most certainly because it went against previous Pre-Trial Chamber practice by concluding that the harm alleged by victims and the concept of personal interests do not need to be linked to the charges against the accused in order for victims to be granted victim status at trial. Both the Prosecution and Defence sought leave to appeal and the Appeals Chamber reversed the Trial Chamber decision on this point, finding that indeed the harm alleged and personal interests of the victim must relate to the charges against the accused.[80] This part of the judgment was welcomed by many not least because it was consistent with previous holdings of the Pre-Trial Chamber but also because it could make participation manageable for the Trial Chamber (Zappalà 2010).

Another welcome judgment from the Appeals Chamber concerned one of the most contentious decisions handed down by the Court which occurred early in its jurisprudence. In its 17 January 2006 decision on victim participation in pre-trial proceedings, Trial Chamber I determined that

> the personal interests of victims are affected in general at the investigation stage, since the participation of victims at this stage can serve to clarify the facts, to punish the perpetrators of crimes and to request reparations for the harm suffered,"[81] and that "during the stage of investigation of a situation, the status of victim will be accorded to applicants who seem to meet the definition of victims set out in rule 85 of the Rules of Procedure and Evidence in relation to the situation in question.[82]

The Chamber further found that

> [t]he right to present their views and concerns and to file material pertaining to the ongoing investigation stems from the fact that the victims' personal interests are affected because it is at this stage that the persons allegedly responsible for the crimes from which they suffered must be identified as a first step towards their indictment.[83]

The Prosecution was not granted leave to appeal this decision based on the reasoning that the decision did not significantly affect the fair conduct of the proceedings or outcome of the trial,[84] leading both parties, in other cases and

---

[80]   Judgment on the Appeals of The Prosecutor and The Defence against Trial Chamber I's Decision on Victims' Participation of 18 January 2008, *supra* note 23, paras. 2 and 64.

[81]   Decision on the Applications for Participation in the Proceedings of VPRS 1, VPRS 2, VPRS 3, VPRS 4, VPRS 5 and VPRS 6, *supra* note 11, para. 63.

[82]   *Idem*, para. 66.

[83]   *Idem*, para. 72.

[84]   *Situation in the Democratic Republic of Congo*, Decision on the Prosecution's Application for leave to appeal the Chamber's decision of 17 January 2006 on the applications for participation

situations, to continuously argue against such broad participation rights at the investigative stage.

Later, decisions in the situation in the DR-Congo and Darfur (Sudan) followed the reasoning of the 17 January 2006 decision. The Pre-Trial Chambers essentially found that individuals who were determined to meet the criteria for victim status would be permitted, notwithstanding any specific proceedings being conducted in the framework of such an investigation, to be heard by the Chamber and to file documents pertaining to the current investigation of a situation. In both situations the Prosecution and Defence requested leave to appeal.

Not until late 2008, almost three years after the first decision allowing victims to participate in the investigative stage of proceedings, did the Appeals Chamber reverse previous Court practice by disallowing general victim participation during the investigative stage outside of specific proceedings.[85] The Appeals Chamber found that "[t]he article of the Statute that confers power upon a victim to participate in any proceedings is article 68 (3)", adding that "participation can take place only within the context of judicial proceedings" which stands in contrast to investigations.[86] Investigations, it found, are not judicial proceedings but inquiries conducted by the Prosecutor into the commission of crimes with a view to bringing to justice those deemed responsible.[87] The Appeals Chamber went on to distinguish the provisions in the Rome Statute and Rules which provide for specific references authorizing victims to participate under Article 68(3).[88] The Appeals Chamber stressed that pursuant to Article 42 of the Statute, the "authority for the conduct of investigations vests in the Prosecutor" and that "[a]cknowledgment by the Pre-Trial Chamber of a right to victims to participate in the investigation would necessarily contravene the Statute by reading into it a power outside its ambit and remit".[89]

---

in the proceedings of VPRS 1, VPRS 2, VPRS 3, VPRS 4, VPRS 5 and VPRS 6, Pre-Trial Chamber I, 31 March 2006, par. 61.

[85] In its 19 December 2008 Judgment on victim participation, the Appeals Chamber reversed the decision of Pre-Trial Chamber I of 7 December 2007 and the decision of Pre-Trial Chamber I of 24 December 2007. The common issue dealt with under the appeal was whether it was possible to acknowledge a victim's general participatory right in the investigation stage of a situation. See *Situation in Democratic Republic of Congo*, Judgment on victim participation in the investigation stage of the proceedings in the appeal of the OPCD against the decision of the Pre-Trial Chamber I of 7 December 2007 and in the appeals of the OPCD and the Prosecutor against the decision of Pre-Trial Chamber I of 24 December 2007, Appeals Chamber, 19 December 2008, paras. 1–2; See also *Situation in Darfur*, Judgment on victim participation in the investigation stage of the proceedings in the appeal of the OPCD against the decision of Pre-Trial Chamber I of 3 December 2007 and in the appeals of the OPCD and the Prosecutor against the decision of Pre-Trial Chamber I of 6 December 2007, Appeals Chamber, 2 February 2009.

[86] *Idem*, para. 45.

[87] *Ibidem*.

[88] *Idem*, paras. 46–48 and 50.

[89] *Idem*, para. 52.

This decision came as a blow to victim advocates who argue that victims can provide positive contributions to early stages of the proceedings, for example, by influencing the charges brought against a suspect which better reflect the harms suffered by victims. However, the Appeals Chamber noted that there is nothing stopping victims from informing the Prosecutor (outside of Court) of their harms suffered and requests for investigation. Moreover, because these decisions are not binding in other cases, they can continue to seek participation in those cases.

In addition to these two examples of the important role played by the Appeals Chamber in providing clarity about the role of victims in the proceedings, the Trial Chamber in *Katanga/Ngudjolo* granted the Defence leave to appeal three of the five issues raised from the 22 January 2010 decision on the modalities of victim participation. The three grounds for appeal include: whether it is possible for the Legal Representatives of victims to lead evidence and to call victims to testify on the crimes against the accused, in a manner which includes incriminating evidence and testimony, without disclosing it to the Defence prior to trial; whether it is possible for the Legal Representatives of Victims to call victims to testify on matters including the role of the accused in crimes charged against them; and whether every item of evidence in possession of the Legal Representatives of victims, be it incriminating or exculpatory, must be communicated to the parties. While it will be interesting to see how the Appeals Chamber decides to approach these serious issues, it is notable that the Appeals Chamber will not have the opportunity to rule on the part of the *Katanga/Ngudjolo* which diverts from the practice of *Lubanga*, namely the setting aside of the requirement for victims to establish their personal interests with respect to specific procedural actions.

6.2. GREATER CLARITY: TRIAL CHAMBER ROLE

Together with a greater role played by the Appeals Chamber it is becoming increasingly clear that the various Trial Chambers must also provide clarity to the parties and participants about the role of victims in the proceedings. This need for greater certainty is particularly evident after the decisions in the *Lubanga* trial raised additional questions. Thus, the Trial Chambers in *Katanga/Ngudjolo* and *Bemba* have attempted to provide greater clarity about the role of victims in the trial proceedings. However, in *Katanga/Ngudjolo* the Trial Chamber expressly acknowledges and appears to embrace the fact that victim participation may vary from case to case, thereby leading to the different treatment of victims in different cases.[90]

---

[90]   Decision on the Modalities of Victims Participation at Trial, *supra* note 54, para. 54.

Just before the start of trial, "[i]n order to avoid any ambiguity and to provide clear guidance" the Chamber in the *Katanga/Ngudjolo* case decided to issue detailed directions for the conduct of the trial proceedings.[91] A few points aside, the parties and participants were largely in agreement about how the trial should be conducted.[92] The directions included specific instructions on the different ways in which victims would be entitled to intervene. The directions divide the trial proceedings into phases. The first phase is the *'Prosecution case'* and the second phase is the *'Case for the Defence'*. Following the Defence case, the Chamber may call its own witnesses.

During the different phases, if the victims' Legal Representatives want to ask questions of a particular witness they may seek the permission of the Court to do so and if permitted will do so after the Prosecution has finished with their questions. When the victims' Legal Representative knows in advance that they have specific questions they would like posed to a witness, they should notify the Chamber and Prosecution at least seven days before the appearance of the witness and the application seeking participation should explain how the questions relate to the interests of the victims represented. For unanticipated questions, the Legal Representatives may submit the question to the Chamber. In principle, the directions provide that the scope of questioning should be "limited to questions that have as their purpose to clarify or complement previous evidence given by the witness".[93] However, the directions also provide that questions may be asked that go beyond matters raised during examination-in-chief, but that such questions should not be repetitive, must be limited to issues that are in controversy, and are relevant to the interests of victims represented. In general, victims may not ask questions pertaining to credibility of a witness' testimony (unless specifically permitted to do so) and they may not ask questions pertaining to potential reparations for specific individuals or groups of individuals.

Victims wishing to testify in person must petition the Court for permission to do so at the beginning of trial. The Court will only grant applications if it can be shown that their testimony will make a genuine contribution to the ascertainment of the truth. Moreover, the Chamber will prohibit testimony that infringes upon the rights of the accused, will not allow victims to become auxiliary prosecutors and under no circumstances will they allow anonymous

---

[91] *Prosecutor v. Germain Katanga and Mathieu Ngudjolo Chui*, Directions for the conduct of the proceedings and testimony in accordance with Rule 140, Trial Chamber II (Single Judge), 20 November 2009.

[92] *Idem*, para. 3.

[93] *Idem*, para. 90, citing *Prosecutor v. Thomas Lubanga Dyilo*, Decision on the Manner of Questioning Witnesses by the Legal Representatives of Victims, Trial Chamber I, 16 September 2009, para. 26.

victims to oral speak before the Court.[94] Although victims' Legal Representatives are, as a matter of principle, not able to call witnesses other than their own clients, they may suggest witnesses for the Court to call.

Although the directions issued by the Court are specific on a number of important procedures they do not fully detail the modalities of victim participation. Accordingly, the decision noted that a later decision, detailing the modalities of participation for the Legal Representatives of the victims, would be issued. The decision on modalities of participation was issued on 22 January 2010 and allows victims to make opening and closing statements, attend and participate in public and closed hearings, have access to public and confidential documents, question witnesses with the leave of the Chamber, call victims or witnesses with leave of the Chamber, tender evidence with leave of the Chamber, and make submissions on the admissibility and relevance of evidence.[95] The decision is remarkable for the fact that unlike in *Lubanga* the Chamber decided that victims do not need to show how their personal interests are affected by each piece of evidence or new issue to arise. Instead, the Chamber found that once granted the right to participate the Chamber recognizes that their personal interests are affected, thus adopting the systemic approach rather than the piecemeal approach.[96] The decision itself is detailed and attempts to provide the parties and participants more guidance, but divergence on key issues from prior court case law is clear. Thus, victims in future cases must again guess how the specific Chamber handling their respective cases will approach Article 68(3) evaluations and their modalities of participation.

In the *Bemba* case Trial Chamber III is also trying to provide greater clarity to the parties and participants before the trial lifts off the ground. On 7 October 2009 it requested that the Prosecution, Defence and victims review existing Court case law and submit their observations on whether or not it should adhere to or depart from this jurisprudence.[97] The Prosecution responded by arguing that adherence to existing jurisprudence is appropriate with regard to the requirements of victim participation, including the timing, modalities, mechanisms for exchange of information between the Prosecution and victims' legal teams and the treatment of victims authorized to participate in the proceedings.[98] However, it argued that departure from existing case law is appropriate with regard to how the Prosecution is allowed to contact victims that have a dual status as witnesses. Currently, the Prosecution must go through the

---

[94]   Directions for the conduct of the proceedings and testimony in accordance with Rule 140, *supra* note 73, para. 22.

[95]   Decision on the Modalities of Victim Participation at Trial, *supra* note 54.

[96]   *Idem*, para. 61.

[97]   Transcripts: First status conference, *supra* note 36.

[98]   See *Prosecutor v. Jean-Pierre Bemba Gombo*, Prosecution's Submission on whether the Chamber should adopt or depart from the existing jurisprudence on victim's participation at trial, Trial Chamber III, 4 November 2009.

Victims and Witnesses Unit (VWU).[99] It further argued that victims should only have access to confidential records in highly exceptional situations. The Defence requested a departure from jurisprudence that allowed the participation of anonymous victims and suggested that victims with dual witness status may need to disclose their applications for participation as documents qualifying as preliminary declarations.[100]

In response to the Prosecution, victims submitted that the VWU was the most suitable contact for victims holding dual status and argued that victims should have access to confidential filings.[101] To be otherwise, they argued, would affect their ability to participate effectively in the trial. In response to the Defence, victims argued that victims' applications could not be considered as preliminary declarations.[102] More importantly, however the victims also responded to an argument put forward by the Defence, on more than one occasion, that victims must re-submit his or her application for participation in order to participate during the trial stage. For obvious reasons, the victims rely on previous Court practice finding the re-filing of applications unnecessary.

It is hoped that the Trial Chamber in *Bemba* will harmonize its opinions as much as possible with previous Court practice, but given the divergence on key issues this may prove difficult. The idea that every single Trial Chamber must go through the exercise of determining how victims will be able to participate in the proceedings seems a waste of time. However, each opportunity allows the parties and participants to re-argue their case for how the Chambers should interpret Article 68(3) requirements and why victims should or should not have greater participatory powers.

7. CONCLUSION

At the ICC victim participation is neither automatic nor unconditional. Instead, participation is guided by the provisions of the Statute and the Rules, which in turn, assign the Chambers with wide discretionary powers to interpret the proper role of victims in the proceedings. Due, in part, to the fact that the Court has little conceptual clarity on how to approach victim participation, the various Chambers continue to struggle with harmonizing opinions and clarifying

---

[99] *Ibidem.*

[100] *Prosecutor v. Jean-Pierre Bemba Gombo*, Observations de la Défense relatives à la jurisprudence de l'Affaire Lubanga sur les questions procédurales se rapportant aux droits de la Défense, Trial Chamber III, 26 November 2009 and Corringendum Observations de la Défense relatives à la jurisprudence de l'Affaire Lubanga sur les questions procédurales se rapportant aux droits de la Défense, Trial Chamber III, 26 November 2009.

[101] *Ibidem.*

[102] *Prosecutor v. Jean-Pierre Bemba Gombo*, Réponse conjointe des représentants légaux des victimes aux Observations de la Défense relatives a la jurisprudence de l'Affaire Lubanga, Trial Chamber III, 18 December 2009.

important issues affecting victims. The various Chambers carry out divergent Article 68(3) evaluations pertaining to the personal interests of victims, with the Pre-Trial Chambers carrying out broad, systematic evaluations and the Trial Chambers largely carrying out narrow, piecemeal evaluations. In addition, the various Pre-Trial Chambers treat anonymous and non-anonymous victims differently. This difference in treatment has a direct effect on the participatory rights of victims. These are but two examples of the divergent approaches taken by the Chambers. These fragmented and divergent approaches have a negative effect on the clarity and certainty of proceedings. And time and again the same procedural issues are re-litigated, wasting valuable Court time and resources. In attempts to address the delays related to victims' participation some Chambers have opted to essentially bypass the personal interest requirement of Article 68(3) so as to help streamline proceedings. However, the question must then be asked whether such an approach is consistent with the Statute and agreements made during the drafting process.

One of the main concerns is the fact that victims of one case are treated differently than victims in another case (this also affects how the Defence and Prosecution must respond to victim participation). It would certainly be desirable for a clear set of procedural rules to apply to all cases, leaving little doubt about the procedural rights afforded to victims but also leaving some discretion to Judges to shape participation. An important obstacle to a coherent victim participation approach is the setup of the Court itself. It would be advantageous if the Rules could be amended to make specific clarifications, for example on how the Chambers should approach the personal interest requirement of Article 68(3) or expressly stating the procedural rights of anonymous victims in proceedings. Nevertheless, without the ability to easily revise or amend the Rules, which requires an affirmative vote by two-thirds of the members of the Assembly of States Parties, the Court will continue to litigate over the procedural rights of victims in proceedings, leaving parties and participants uncertain about how any given Chamber will approach the issue. Accordingly, the next best option is to have issues that split Chambers addressed by the Appeals Chamber.

Despite these issues, however, victims' legal teams continue to try to make a substantive impact in the proceedings. They have clearly shown how their interests are at times the same and at times different from the Prosecution. Undoubtedly, their participation adds a new dimension to the proceedings and understanding the limitations of what victim participation offers at the ICC is crucial to understanding the limitations of international criminal justice generally. But, more importantly, understanding the current limitations of the participation regime will be the first step in addressing problems and finding solutions to better serve the interests of victims specifically and the Court generally.

XX. SURVIVORS OF SEXUAL VIOLENCE IN CONFLICT

Challenges in Prevention and International Criminal Prosecution

Sandra Ka Hon CHU, Anne-Marie DE BROUWER
and Renée RÖMKENS

Testimonial of Marie Louise Niyobuhungiro[1]:

People think I am crazy because I am always crying, and I do not blame them for thinking so. I am always angry, and I do not sleep at night. I hoped secretly that I would die during the genocide, but being among other survivors within a survivors' organization has brought me comfort and hope. I feel like I have a family now, and I am very grateful for that. (…)

On April 6, 1994, when President Habyarimana died, the local authorities ordered my family to go back to our house. We had been walking outside. But we did not feel secure in our house, and we went to pass the night on our cassava plantation instead. The next morning, we went to our uncle's house, which was about a thirty-minute walk from our house. The Interahamwe [Hutu-militia] surrounded my uncle's house a few hours later. As the killings hadn't started yet, the militia were just trying to frighten us. When the Interahamwe got tired of this and left, we ran to the Catholic church of Mboza, which was about fifteen minutes' walking distance from my uncle's house. Almost three hundred Tutsi had found refuge in the church.

We arrived at the church at about ten in the morning, and a few minutes later the Interahamwe and FAR soldiers [Forces Armées Rwandaises/government soldiers] started shooting. They had guns and shot all the men, including my uncle. I fell, and some dead bodies fell on top of me. I was all covered with blood. I heard screams and babies crying, but I was unconscious for most of the time the attack was continuing.

---

[1]   Marie Louise Niyobuhungiro was born in 1975 (day and month unknown) in Shyorongi, just outside Kigali, the capital of Rwanda. Niyobuhungiro's testimonial was taken from: De Brouwer & Chu 2009, 28–33.

The next day, they came back to kill those who were not yet dead. There was blood all over me, and the killers thought that I was dead, too, so they left me there, lying among those dead bodies. Once I had regained consciousness, all I could see were a lot of bodies lying around the church. The stench of blood was thick in the air. Except for one of my sisters, all my other relatives died during this attack at the church. Out of three hundred people in the church, only five had survived. I felt completely empty. I had no thoughts and felt nothing, nothing at all.

(…) I spent three days hiding in the bushes. On the fourth day, I went to the house of another uncle, who had not yet had an opportunity to flee, because his wife had just given birth. He and his wife had already been warned by their neighbour, an Interahamwe, to leave their house immediately; they would not have much longer to live otherwise. Together with my uncle's relatives, I left his house that night. But, at the gate in front of his house, we ran into a group of Interahamwe militia. They took the girls among us and brought us to a nearby roadblock in order to kill us.

At some point, a FAR soldier picked me out of the group and took me to a nearby bush. I don't know what happened to the other girls I was with. This soldier raped me. After he was done with me, he took me to a house and told the owners of the house to keep me safe, so that he could rape me every time he came. He told them if anything happened to me he would kill them. Every time he came to the house after that, he took me to the forest to rape me. Over five days, I was raped five times a day. The rapist didn't say anything to me. In the forest, the local people often saw me being raped by this man. The local people, an Interahamwe militiaman and other Hutu would watch the soldier rape me and did not even raise their little finger to stop it. They didn't care, because I was Tutsi. They were silent. The FAR soldier who did this to me was so old – about forty – and so savage. It was the very first time I saw what a man was capable of doing.

(…) I managed to escape, and I walked all the way to Ruhengeri, which was already under the control of the RPF [Rwandan Patriotic Front, a political and military group composed of Tutsi refugees based in Uganda]. For two weeks, I hid myself during the day and walked during the night. I ate nothing and hid in the bushes. When the RPF went to Kigali, I followed them. I walked just behind them, back to my place of birth. I occupied a house that belonged to owners who had fled the country, because my family house had been destroyed during the genocide. To make a living, I dug the fields for a farmer. Later, a fund for survivors was established, which provided me with a bit of support.

I lost four brothers and sisters during the genocide, and one sister died of kidney failure right afterwards. Before the genocide, I had never been intimate with a man, and yet now I have gotten to know many without my consent. Even after the genocide, in 2000, a neighbour came to my house, forced my door open and raped me. There was no use screaming, because no one lived close by. I became pregnant as a result of this rape, and the child died immediately upon birth. The doctors then pressured me to take an HIV test, and I discovered I am HIV positive.

I live in very bad conditions because I didn't go to school. I have no job and am too weak now to dig the fields. I get food from an organization that helps me to survive. I have had four children since the genocide, all from different fathers. The father of one of my children is a neighbour, and the others have jobs in the neighbourhood. I never see them. I only had sex with each of them once. Luckily, my oldest three children are not HIV positive, but my youngest child has not been tested yet. I wish I could give my children some more support, including buying them school materials and clothes. I am always sick, sometimes because of HIV and other times because of the beatings I endured during the genocide. I was hit on my knees and head with a club and I suffer from severe headaches now. I don't think I can forgive the FAR soldiers or the Interahamwe. I don't want to hear about reconciliation. I accused them in the gacaca courts, including the one who raped me, those who participated in the killings in the church and those I saw at the roadblock, but now they are being released. Gacaca courts do not bring justice. I think the best punishment those men could get is the death penalty, because they killed others, too. We need justice. The génocidaires should not be released. I shared my testimony in order to help establish justice, and I hope it will do that.

1. INTRODUCTION

Shocking as Marie Louise Niyobuhungiro's experiences of rape and sexual slavery during and after the 1994 genocide in Rwanda are, they are representative of what many women, and increasingly men, suffer during times of conflict. In this chapter, we will tackle the question of how sexual violence in conflict situations is dealt with in international settings. In particular, we consider to what extent the international community succeeds in its efforts to protect women from abuse by preventing sexual violence in conflict situations, as agreed in United Nations Security Council (UNSC) Resolutions 1325 (2000)[2] and more specifically in UNSC Resolutions 1820 (2008) and 1888 (2009).[3] And where sexual violence does occur, do international tribunals such as the International Criminal Court (ICC)[4] enable victims to effectively take part in court proceedings, without fear of retribution or retraumatization?[5]

In section 2, we address various aspects of sexual violence and its aftermath. We provide a brief overview of data on the prevalence and nature of sexual violence in conflict situations and during 'peace time', focusing on the underlying

---

[2]   UN SC, *Security Council Resolution 1325*, 31 October 2000, S/RES/1325 (2000).

[3]   UN SC, *Security Council Resolution 1820 (2008) [on Acts of Sexual Violence Against Civilians in Armed Conflicts]*, 19 June 2008, S/RES/1820 (2008); UN SC, *Security Council Resolution 1888 (2009) [on Acts of Sexual Violence Against Civilians in Armed Conflicts]*, 30 September 2009, S/RES/1888 (2009).

[4]   The basic legal texts for the ICC include the Rome Statute (A/CONF.183/9), the Rules of Procedure and Evidence (ICC-ASP/1/3 (Part II-A)), and the Elements of Crimes (ICC-ASP/1/3(Part II-B)).

[5]   In this article, we will be using the terms 'victim' and 'survivor' interchangeably, in recognition of these mutual facets of individual experiences after sexual assault.

societal and cultural dynamics that contribute to the silencing and the normalization of sexual violence in both contexts. We conclude this section by discussing the effects of mass sexual victimization and what they imply for the immediate needs of victims.

In section 3, we consider current legal and policy responses of the international community that were developed to bring justice to victims of conflict-related crimes of sexual violence. We also reflect on the questions of whether and how preventive measures have been successfully implemented as well as whether the international criminal prosecution of sexual violence has succeeded in bringing justice to victims of sexual violence. Have these mechanisms been able to take into account the complexity of victims' experiences and their immediate needs?

2. SEXUAL VIOLENCE IN TIMES OF CONFLICT AND PEACE: PREVALENCE, NATURE, SOCIETAL ATTITUDES AND IMPACT

2.1. PREVALENCE AND NATURE OF SEXUAL VIOLENCE IN TIMES OF CONFLICT

During almost every recorded conflict in the world, sexual violence has been perpetrated against women in various ways, often with complete impunity. Reported instances include conflicts that have taken place in Europe involving armies of all sides during World War I (1914–1918); in Asia and Europe during WWII (1939–1945); Bangladesh (1971); Cambodia (1975–1979); Uganda (1987-today); Sierra Leone (1991–2001); Bosnia-Herzegovina (1992–1995); Kosovo (1998–1999); Democratic Republic of the Congo (DRC) (1998-today); Timor-Leste (1999); Liberia (1999–2003); Central African Republic (2002–2003); Darfur in Sudan (2003-today) and Burundi (2004–2007) (examples cited in De Brouwer & Chu 2009). The magnitude of sexual violence in conflict situations will never be fully known, since stigma associated with being a victim of sexual violence often discourages women and girls from reporting such crimes and many victims are killed following rape. Although no accurate data is available, the figures in relation to the number of victims of sexual violence run in the thousands (as was the case in Kosovo) to – more often – tens to hundreds of thousands of women (as were the cases in Asia and Europe during WWII and in Bangladesh, Cambodia, DRC and Rwanda). In light of the usual underreporting of these crimes for the reasons mentioned above, the prevalence of sexual violence is alarming. Only in exceptional cases is sexual violence not perpetrated in conflict or very rare (Wood 2009). According to Wood (2009, 152), this is the situation "where the organization prohibits sexual violence and effectively enforces that decision through a tightly controlled military hierarchy in which punishment is swift and severe," which was the case with the Liberation Tigers of Tamil Eelam of Sri Lanka. Wood (2009) argues that sexual violence is thus not an inevitable product of conflict and can be prevented.

It is now widely acknowledged that rape and other forms of sexual violence are not simply the by-products or spoils of war but tools of war and part of a planned and targeted policy to shatter families and societies.[6] Often, this involves subjecting women and girls, regardless of their age or whether they are pregnant, to the full range of sexual atrocities, which may include rape, gang rape, sexual slavery, forced incest, forced marriage, the mutilation of victims' breasts, pregnant bellies and vaginas, and killing of the foetus. The incomprehensible cruelty that is often exhibited by perpetrators of sexual violence has taken numerous forms beyond imagination.

Men too fall victim to sexual violence, which may include rape, forced sterilization, forced nudity, forced masturbation and genital mutilation (Carlson 2005; Carpenter 2006; Sivakumaran 2007; Zawati 2007; Johnson *et al.* 2008; De Brouwer & Chu 2009; Sivakumaran 2010; Johnson *et al.* 2010). Although sexual violence against men also has a long history, attention to and recognition of this phenomenon is fairly recent (Sivakumaran 2010).[7] Fear of stigma is considered a major cause for the silence surrounding these crimes; perceived homosexuality (and in some countries where homosexuality is still criminalized, the concomitant fear of prosecution) and concerns about demasculinazation play a role (Sivakumaran 2010). Underreporting of this crime by its male victims is thus very likely. Women have also been identified as primary perpetrators of sexual violence (Totten 2009; De Brouwer & Chu 2009; Hogg 2010; Durham & O'Byrne 2010)[8] or inflict sexual violence on others by acting as co-perpetrators (for example, by restraining women victims for men to rape) or ordering rape.[9]

Unlike the initial conceptualisation of sexual violence during times of war as inherently masculine (Brownmiller 1975), current research reveals a more complex picture severing the essentialist notion that victims of sexual violence during conflict are always women and perpetrators are always men. As argued by Durham and O'Byrne (2010, 22):

---

6   UN SC, *Security Council Resolution 1820 (2008) [on Acts of Sexual Violence Against Civilians in Armed Conflicts]*, 19 June 2008, S/RES/1820 (2008).

7   UNOCHA, Policy Development and Studies Branch, *Use of Sexual Violence in Conflict: Identifying Research Priorities to Inform More Effective Interventions*, Meeting Report, New York, 26 June 2008. The New York Times, *Symbol of Unhealed Congo: Male Rape Victims*, by Jeffrey Gettleman, 4 August 2009.

8   Also African Rights, *Rwanda – Not So Innocent: When Women Become Killers*, Kigali, 1995.

9   This is the case with Pauline Nyiramasuhuko, the former Minister of Family and Women's Development, who was convicted for, among other crimes, this crime, before an ICTR Trial Chamber on 24 June 2011.

A gender perspective on IHL [international humanitarian law] provides the capacity to consider different experiences of both women and men in order to break down stereotypes about how men and women 'should' operate, and the complex ways in which conflict impacts upon them. This advances the whole cause of gender justice, because it rejects perceptions of women and men that derive from dangerous and sexist assumptions, and are often the root of discrimination, sexual violence and torture.

Nevertheless, while sexual violence in times of conflict can be directed against both men and women, women and girls remain particularly susceptible to such violence and constitute the majority of victims. Women and girls also plainly experience sexual violence distinctly from men and boys (e.g. suffering permanent injuries to women's reproductive systems and unwanted pregnancies). When exacerbated by poverty, trauma and isolation, the experience of sexual violence can have a life-long effect on women (Totten 2009). In this chapter, we focus on female victims.

2.2. SEXUAL VIOLENCE IN 'PEACE TIME': PREVALENCE AND GENDERED ATTITUDES

In order to understand sexual violence during conflict, we must consider the larger cultural and social context in which sexual violence, notably against women, is condoned or minimized (Buchwald *et al.* 2005). Awareness of the widespread prevalence of rape and violence against women, both in and out of conflict, surfaced in the 1970s when feminists put women's physical and sexual victimization on the agenda as a widespread social problem and political concern (Brownmiller 1975). Research on sexual violence and rape since then has illustrated how sexual violence is part and parcel of dominant cultures worldwide.

Rape and sexual violence constitute a common part of social life in most societies, due to the legacy of what has been described as a "rape culture" in which physical and emotional violence against women is condoned by many and accepted as an inevitable fact of life (Buchwald *et al.* 2005, XI). The precise prevalence of rape in peace time is difficult to discern since research yields very different results due to a host of methodological challenges, such as differing definitions, differences in data measurement, and complications in comparing prevalence data. Focusing on conservative estimates, available research indicates an average *minimum* prevalence rate of 15 percent[10] among women. These figures predominantly involve male perpetrators, reflecting the gender-based nature of

---

[10]   These prevalence estimates are predominantly based on studies from the USA, Canada, Australia and Europe. Research in South Africa has indicated that one in four male respondents admitted having raped a woman at least once (Jewkes *et al.* 2009).

the crime[11] (Tjaden & Thoennes 2000; Rozee & Koss 2001; Campbell & Wasco 2005; Marx 2005). The estimated 15 percent of women reporting rape is conservative since persisting shame and guilt inevitably lead to underreporting.[12]

Attitudes towards rape and sexual victimization of women are profoundly influenced by *rape myths*: "attitudes and generally false beliefs about rape that are widely and persistently held, and that serve to deny and justify male aggression against women" (Lonsway & Fitzgerald 1994, 133; see also Bohner *et al.* 2009). Rape myths are deeply gendered. The most common recurring responses to rape include attributing responsibility or blame for rape on the victims ('she provoked him', 'she must have done something'), disbelief ('it wasn't really rape', 'she exaggerates', 'you cannot rape a woman if she doesn't want it'), and minimizing the severity of the rape or its impact (Lonsway & Fitzgerald 1994; also Newcombe *et al.* 2008; Gerber & Cherneski 2006; Bourke 2007). The persistence of rape myths not only marginalizes the suffering of rape victims, but also demonstrates what Bourke aptly describes as "the immense cultural sympathy for the sexual abuser" (Bourke 2007, 48). Rape myths underscore the reality that sexual violence against women is to a large extent condoned, normalized, denied and recast as acceptable, resting on the assumption that women's sexuality is available, particularly when the victim and perpetrator know each other. The net result is the social and cultural stereotyping, marginalization and silencing of rape victims (Horvath & Brown 2009). The fact that the concept of 'date rape' was only introduced in the early 1990s illustrates how pervasive the myth is that only rape committed by a stranger counts as 'real rape' (Estrich 1987; Bohner *et al.* 2009; Kitzinger 2009). Moreover, in a number of countries, there is no legal recognition of marital rape as men are understood to have unrestricted sexual access to their wives (Pearshouse & Symington 2009). However, the majority of cases of sexual assault involve a known perpetrator (partner, ex-partner, date or acquaintance), which go mostly unreported, adding to the invisibility of rape in partner relationships as a legal concern (Mouzos & Makkai 2004). When sexual assault is perpetrated by someone known to the victim, and there are no witnesses, the victim's lack of consent is, from an evidentiary perspective, difficult to prove. This is one of the factors contributing to the high rate of rape attrition in a legal context (Daly & Bouhours 2010), notably in jurisdictions where the legal definition of rape is based on 'force' (as is most often the case) and when the suspect claims (as is often the case) that consent was given (Hagemann-White *et al.* 2010).

Men and women tend to differ in their perception of the prevalence and severity of sexual assault (notably date rape) and in their assignment of

---

[11]   Although men and boys can be victims of sexual violence, as mentioned, we focus in this chapter on the sexual victimization of women and girls.

[12]   UNODC, *Manual on Victimization Surveys*, Geneva, 2010.

responsibility. Research reveals that more men than women systematically hold the female victim responsible and blameworthy for the assault (Newcombe *et al.* 2008; Gerber & Cherneski 2006; Black & Gold 2008). A recent European survey on attitudes towards domestic violence revealed that, depending on the country, between 10 and 20 percent of respondents still consider sexual violence to be only "fairly serious" as opposed to "very serious". More men than women are lenient in their judgment of severity.[13] Correspondingly, studies of rape victims indicate that negative reactions to the disclosure of victims' rape experiences are still common. These reactions include blaming, questioning the victim about her clothing at the time of the assault or about her sexual history, expressing doubt, detachment, and general lack of support (Ahrens *et al.* 2007: 39 percent of victims reported negative responses; see also Campbell & Raja 1999; Filipas & Ullmann 2001). Negative social reactions are even more common among those involved in formal support structures where victims turn to for professional support (Starzynski *et al.* 2005). Effective treatment of symptoms of rape trauma requires a supportive, non-judgmental response that enables the victim to be validated in her experiences. This is as an essential step toward integrating and accepting the 'unacceptable' experience. Negative reactions, notably disbelief or questioning the victim's responsibility, obviously obstruct this process and lead to self-blame. These dynamics have a profoundly deleterious effect on victims' recovery and make them reluctant to disclose the experience of sexual assault (Ahrens 2006). The ultimate consequence is a further silencing of victims.

The ongoing silencing of victims through attitudes that ambiguously condemn and condone sexual violence is most evident within the military. One of the essential characteristics of military training is the positioning of male bravery and comradeship in opposition to female weakness, lending itself in some cases to outright misogyny. The use of metaphors simultaneously denigrating and sexualizing women are fairly common in military training (Bourke 2007). Only during the past decade have sexual harassment and violence been slowly recognized as a problem that needs to be addressed from within the military. It comes then as no surprise that studies of US military found prevalence estimates for rape of female personnel ranging from 7 to 28 percent (Lipari *et al.* 2008; Sadler *et al.* 2003; Skinner *et al.* 2000), though most cases of sexual coercion went unreported (Lipari *et al.* 2008).[14] Although sexual transgressions within the military are officially met with strong apprehension and condemnation, rape stories in practice are contextualized in a military discourse

---

13   Report, *Domestic Violence against Women*, Special Eurobarometer 344 / Wave 73.2, Brussels: TNS Opinion & Social, 2010.

14   The culture of male-dominated comradeship and loyalty in the military makes it harder for servicewomen to bring charges of sexual abuse by positioning the accuser as disloyal for 'ratting' on her fellow soldier(s). Moreover, reporting sexual assault within the military realistically defeats any professional future within that (and potentially any other) army unit (Bourke 2007).

on the 'natural' aspects of wartime sexuality, where a certain level of sexual violence reflects 'normalcy' in abnormal conditions (Bourke 2007). Wood (2009), however, convincingly argues that sexual violence is not an inevitable product of conflict if military authorities exert effective control by conveying the message that sexual violence is prohibited and will be punished. Nevertheless, this is a challenge where there is an absence of pre-existing social norms against sexual violence within the military and in society at large, where gender inequality persists and enables violence against women. Sexual violence is thus intimately linked to the denigration of women and femininity in peacetime culture (Henry *et al.* 2004).

2.3. SILENCING OF SURVIVORS OF SEXUAL VIOLENCE: THE DOUBLE ASSAULT

The silencing of victims' experiences of sexual violence, in and outside of conflict, is one of the most profound obstacles to effectively and explicitly addressing rape in general. Minimizing the severity of rape and the humiliating brutalities of sexual violence evoke in survivors a sense of profound shame, guilt, fear of being stigmatized by the community (see below) and fear of disbelief. For some survivors, remaining silent is a deliberately-chosen coping strategy to avoid even more pain after sexual assault (Tankink & Richters 2007). The net result is a "solidified silence", and further traumatization of the victims (see Danieli, this volume). Just as damaging, such silencing facilitates the perpetuation of sexual violence both during, and after, conflict.

Primo Levi (1947; 1958) captured the paradox of the need to give voice to unspeakable cruelties in his autobiographical account of the atrocities he endured in Auschwitz. Levi referred to the "urgent impulse" to tell and share the story that motivated him to write a lucid analysis of human cruelty and depravation. Yet it mostly fell on deaf ears upon its initial publication in 1947 in Italy. Only in the early 1970s was the book widely distributed in Italy.[15] Presumably, there was a strong will to forget the most severe war time cruelties, fuelled by the limited ability of most people to accept feelings of powerlessness that are inevitably elicited by reading reports of incredibly brutal violence humans inflict upon each other.

A similar response of avoidance and outright denial was observed upon the release of a 1954 autobiographical account of rape of women in Berlin at the hands of Russian military forces during the final months of WWII (Anonyma 1954). The book was not only met with disapproval ('how could the Germans make any claim to victimization?'), but the author was blamed for her own

---

[15]   It took more than ten years before it was translated into German and English in the late 1950s.

victimization. She had succeeded in shielding herself from worse attacks by sexually submitting to a highly-ranked officer from the occupying forces. Because the author, like most women in Berlin, had managed to cope with her ordeal, she was met with suspicion and not considered a 'real' victim. Confronted with such responses to her book, the author vowed to remain anonymous (which the publisher respected), a decision that reflected a context marred by shame, blame and anger. It took almost fifty years, and the growing recognition of the widespread nature of gender-based violence in conflict, before the book was republished in 2003,[16] an event that the author did not live to witness.

This public response, involving both silencing and blaming the victim, vividly underscores the persistent dichotomy between victimization and agency with respect to women's victimization generally (Schneider 1993; Mahoney 1994) and reflects the stereotypical image of 'real' victims as being only weak and helpless (Römkens 1996; Van Dijk 2009). Exceptionally strong and resilient survivors of sexual violence often elicit ambiguous if not angry reactions, as if they are somehow responsible for their sexual assault. This was reflected, for example, in some of the public reactions to Mukhtar Mai, a woman in Pakistan who refused to obey her village council's order to commit suicide after she had been gang raped, and Natascha Kampusch in Austria, who refused to be categorized as a helpless victim, in spite of having been abducted and sexually enslaved for eight years as a child. In both cases, some commentators responded by blaming the victims and questioning the severity of the sexual violence (Mai & Cuny 2007; Kampusch 2010). A victim/survivor who in the aftermath of sexual assault does not behave helplessly is regularly considered a contradiction in terms. Apparently, a victim's resilience causes doubts about the severity of the violence and/or the victim's role in it, even leading to victim-blaming. The case of Libyan Iman al Obeidi is a tragic illustration of how a victim of rape in conflict is silenced and denounced: when Al Obeidi cried out in front of journalists on March 26, 2011 that she had been gang raped by Khadaffi troops, she was abducted, incarcerated, accused of being a prostitute with mental health problems and eventually criminally charged by some of the militiamen she had accused of rape. According to a government spokesman, "The boys she accused of rape are making a case against her because it's a grave offence to accuse someone of a sexual crime".[17] These cases reflect a deeply-rooted cultural discourse of blame and responsibility in which victims, notably women victims of sexual violence, are conveniently seen as complicit in their victimization (Thapar-Björkert & Morgan 2010).

---

[16] The movie *Anonyma: A woman in Berlin*, based on the book, was released in 2008 (Dir. Max Farberböck).
[17] The Guardian, *Iman al-Obeidi Faces Criminal Charges over Libya Rape Claim*, 29 March 2011.

As a result, first-hand narratives of sexual war crimes have been historically silenced and giving voice to unspeakable atrocities is rare (Walker 2009; De Brouwer & Chu, 2009). Understandably, some victims may remain silent as a result of their trauma and concomitant shame and fear. This response may be compounded by countertransference dynamics describing situations in which bystanders cannot bear to hear accounts that evoke a sense of powerlessness and pain. However, there is an emerging shift marked by victims of sexual violence who increasingly speak out against the atrocities committed against them.[18] In turn, the public is gradually beginning to comprehend the significance of hearing these stories in order to effectively respond to widespread sexual violence, no matter how graphic these stories may be (Ducey 2010; see furthermore Erez & Meroz-Aharoni, this volume).

2.4. IMPACT OF MASS SEXUAL VIOLENCE

If there can be any generality drawn about the impact of mass sexual violence on survivors, it is that the devastating consequences of such crimes continue long after hostilities have ended (also Ruvebana, this volume). Not only must survivors cope with the physical impact of sexual assault and other crimes of sexual violence, but with long-term psychological trauma. Where survivors of rape during conflict have experienced other crimes committed in the course of conflict, they are exposed to multiple traumas that can render healing a seemingly insurmountable challenge.

2.4.1. Physical and mental health problems

Sexual violence often has severe physical consequences for women, ranging from genital injuries to unwanted pregnancies to stomachaches, headaches, and back problems to gynaecological complications, such as bleeding, infection, chronic pelvic pain, pelvic inflammatory disease, and urinary tract infections (Heise *et al* 1999).[19] It also has a serious impact on women's mental health (Joffe 2010). Experiences of post-traumatic stress disorder (PTSD) or 'rape trauma syndrome' have been well-documented (Hanson 1990; Kramer & Green 1991; Heise *et al.* 1999)[20] Survivors' responses can include feelings of hopelessness, loss of control,

---

[18] See, *inter alia,* Betsy Kawamura's story in: Nobel Women's Initiative, *Not the Only Survivor in the Village,* 25 May 2011, available at www.nobelwomensinitiative.org/blogs/newsecurity/post/betsy-kwamara (last visited: 16 June 2011).

[19] UNPF, *State of the World Population 2000: Lives Together, Worlds Apart: Men and Women in a Time of Change,* 2000. See also World Health Organization, *First World Report on Violence and Health,* 2002.

[20] Orsillo, S., *Sexual Assault Against Females,* National Center for PTSD, 2003, available at www.ptsd.va.gov/public/pages/sexual-assault-females.asp.

anger and guilt, recurrent nightmares or intrusive memories of the event, social withdrawal, anxiety and feelings of numbness, as well as phobias, depression, sexual difficulties, failure to resume previous social or sexual relationships, failure to return to work, substance abuse and suicidal ideation (Greenberg *et al.* 2007; Danieli, this volume; Bacik *et al.* 1998). Survivors, particularly those living in close-knit rural communities with traditional gender patterns, may experience radical changes in their self-image and in their relations with others, who may view them as unfaithful or promiscuous. In some cases, this has led to survivors' alienation and rejection by their families and communities (Joffe 2010).

The impact of mass victimization can be long-lasting and is often cumulative[21] (Kuwert *et al.* 2007; Westermeyer & Williams 1998), since many victims must cope with multiple trauma (Shaw 2001). Survivors of sexual violence during a period of conflict may, for example, experience multiple incidents of rape, but may also witness the death and torture of family members and experience loss of housing, land and other possessions. Rape and other acts of violence also exacerbate women's vulnerability to sexually transmitted infections. In Rwanda as well as in the DRC, the systematic raping of women caused an outbreak of HIV and other sexually transmitted infections (Csete & Kippenberg 2002).[22]

2.4.2. Social isolation, stigma and ongoing victimization

In the aftermath of conflict, survivors of sexual violence may be coping in isolation, with little social support or infrastructure to address their immediate needs. Kept on the outskirts of society, survivors may be easy prey for retaliation by perpetrators. Post-conflict, women's ability to care and protect themselves and their families is often impeded. Insecure living circumstances, including unprotected housing, may expose women to continued victimization through unwanted sexual advances from neighbours and passers-by. In many cases, the grief and trauma afflicting these embattled women are further compounded by the burden of caring for the injured and the orphaned. Some women may also bear children conceived as a result of rape. In Rwanda, an estimated two thousand to twenty thousand *enfants mauvais souvenir* ('children of bad memories') were born after the genocide.[23] Poorly resourced health systems with

---

[21]   For example, research with victims of war crimes has demonstrated that children who have witnessed the atrocities of war and are displaced and living in refugee camps are more likely to suffer PTSD than children who have similarly witnessed war but continue to live at home in villages and cities (Thabet & Vostanis 1999).

[22]   African Rights, *Rwanda, Death, Despair and Defiance*, 1994 (revised 1995).

[23]   The lower figure is based on an estimate by the UN. See UN Commission of Human Rights, *Question of the Violation of Human Rights and Fundamental Freedoms in Any Part of the World, with Particular Reference to Colonial and Other Dependent Countries and Territories: Report on the Situation of Human Rights in Rwanda*, E/CN.4/1996/68, 1996, para. 16, available at   www.unhchr.ch/Huridocda/Huridoca.nsf/0/aee2ff8ad005e2f6802566f30040a95a?Opendo

an absence of specialist health care providers undoubtedly affect rape victims since they compound the inaccessibility of post-exposure prophylaxis (PEP) during conflict. Even where PEP is made available to sexual assault victims, adherence to treatment is a challenge. Many survivors are unable to adhere to the medication adequately since rape stigma, social isolation and fear of HIV play very powerful roles in debilitating women's ability to consistently take preventive medication (Abrahams & Jewkes 2010).

2.4.3. Poverty and economic damage

For women living in refugee camps, sexual assault and the threat of sexual assault not only affect their physical and emotional health, but also their ability to provide for their children and family. When camp conditions do not provide for women's safety when they venture to gather firewood or water, women may restrict their participation in such activities. This may impede women's ability to provide for their, and their children's, nutritional needs (Heise *et al.* 1999). In Rwanda, the physical and psychological trauma women experienced during the genocide meant many were no longer able to work. Survivors who have been widowed are often left without family income. The additional responsibility created by other family members who are unable to work plunges those households into extreme poverty.[24] Even when survivors are capable of working, their HIV status can lead to stigma and discrimination, loss of employment, difficulty in asserting property rights and other human rights violations.[25] The scarcity of basic needs and the lack of economic opportunities for women render women and girls more likely to engage in sex in exchange for food, shelter or services, further increasing their risk of sexual abuse, violence and contracting sexually transmitted infections.

2.5. NEEDS OF SURVIVORS OF MASS SEXUAL VIOLENCE

Not surprisingly, a high-level panel convened by the UN High Commissioner for Human Rights to hear directly from victims of sexual violence in the DRC in

---

cument (last visited: 2 February 2011); and UN Population Division, *Abortion Policies: A Global Review*, New York, June 2002. Save the Children, an international children's rights organization, estimates the number of women impregnated as a result of rape during the genocide to be much higher: 15,000 (Lawday 2002, 5, citing Esther Mujawayo & Mary Kayitesi Blewitt, "Sexual violence against women: Experiences from AVEGA's work in Kigali", 1999). According to "Intended Consequences", approximately 20,000 children were born as a result of rape. See http://mediastorm.com/publication/intended-consequences# (last visited: 2 February 2011).

24 African Rights, *Rwanda, Death, Despair and Defiance*, 1994 (revised 1995).

25 Amnesty International, *Rwanda: "Marked for Death", Rape Survivors Living with HIV/AIDS in Rwanda*, London: Amnesty International, 2004.

2010 found that their needs are largely unmet, particularly in remote areas where there is so little infrastructure that access to any form of assistance or reparation is virtually non-existent. As the panel observed, "The lives they knew have been largely destroyed, and they are suffering greatly – physically, psychologically, and materially".[26]

In order to address survivors' needs, long-term initiatives must be taken in recognition of the long-term impact of sexual violence. In addition to immediate medical attention, survivors require long-term health care, treatment and support (which includes emotional and psychological support and treatment), physical security, financial support and security, and recognition and respect within the criminal justice system. While these broad needs are obviously not exhaustive, States' obligations to address these needs have been codified in international law and form the basis of the United Nations *Declaration of Basic Principles of Justice for Victims of Crime and Abuse of Power.*[27] Moreover, the UN Special Rapporteur on Violence Against Women recently pointed to States' obligation to establish effective protection, support and rehabilitation services for survivors of gender-based violence.[28] Against the backdrop of the recent Resolutions 1820 (2008) and 1888 (2009) which specifically address the needs of victims of sexual violence in times of conflict, UN intervention missions are developing a multisectoral approach with four pillars of assistance – medical care, psychosocial support, legal assistance and support for socio-economic integration – though insufficient level of funding available for UN humanitarian programmes remains a major concern.[29]

2.5.1. Physical and mental health support

In many cases, survivors of sexual violence will require immediate medical attention. This will likely be a challenge during or post-conflict if health systems have deteriorated. Nevertheless, health services should seek to actively identify women (including those living in rural areas) who have experienced sexual violence and provide medical services in a respectful manner. Such medical services should include treatment for physical injuries, emergency contraception, testing and treatment for sexually transmitted infections including HIV, and psycho-social support. Under international law, health care providers should be

---

[26] UNOHCHR, *Report of the Panel on Remedies and Reparations for Victims of Sexual Violence in the Democratic Republic of Congo to the High Commissioner for Human Rights*, March 2011, 3.

[27] UNGA, Declaration of Basic Principles of Justice for Victims of Crime and Abuse of Power, A/RES/40/34, 29 November 1985 (hereafter: UN Declaration on Justice for Victims, 1985).

[28] UNHRC, Special Rapporteur on Violence Against Women, *Promotion and Protection of All Human Rights, Civil, Political, Economic, Social and Cultural Rights, Including the Right to Development*, A/HRC/14/22, 19 April 2010, paras. 33–66.

[29] UN SC, *Report of the Secretary-General Pursuant to Security Council Resolution 1820*, S/2009/362, 15 July 2009, 20.

adequately trained in order to document injuries and refer victims of sexual violence to legal assistance and psycho-social support services.[30] While in many cases, survivors may find the support they need in their informal or community-based networks (Denkers 1996), this does not negate the need for professional psychological support, especially for individuals who have experienced multiple trauma.

2.5.2. Physical security

The needs of survivors of sexual violence will not be adequately addressed where their physical security continues to be threatened. Attacks against a particular social group can rob people of their real or experienced security, resulting in greater vulnerability and fear of violence. This fear is evident in post-conflict societies in which victims and perpetrators must continue to live together after conflict, as are the cases in Rwanda and the former Yugoslavia, where some victims are forced to live daily with the threat of violence (de Brouwer & Chu 2009). In these conflict areas, many victims fled their homes, even after hostilities subsided (Parmentier & Weitekamp 2007). The fact that UN peacekeepers have also regularly engaged in sexual abuse towards female refugees further hampers the protection of survivors' security (Defeis 2008). Security and support for survivors of sexual violence is thus paramount, and the inclusion of safe spaces for women to live post-conflict must be a key security consideration given the prevalence of persisting gender-based violence, notably rape, in situations of crisis.

Individuals who act as witnesses in court may face further retaliatory risks to themselves and their families (De Brouwer 2005). Protective measures for witnesses, meant to shield the identity of the victim, are thus necessary and available in many jurisdictions as well as at the ICC.[31] However, the experiences of victims and witnesses who have testified before the *ad hoc* international tribunals reveal that such measures are not foolproof and that victims may continue to have real concerns about their safety (Stover 2005; De Brouwer 2005). Similar concerns exist at the national level. In Rwanda, for example, witnesses, judges and members of the domestic *gacaca* courts have been targeted with threats of retaliation and many survivors have expressed fear of attending *gacaca* because of the threats of intimidation and/or death at the hands of those related to the accused *génocidaires* (De Brouwer & Chu 2009).

---

[30] See UN Declaration on Justice for Victims, 1985, Articles 16 and 17.

[31] For example, individuals can testify behind a screen or via closed-circuit television in order to avoid being seen by the accused. Publication bans are also available to prohibit the identification of a witness in the media and are meant to protect his or her privacy. The risks for witnesses are significant and the International Criminal Court offers a witness protection program, which, as a measure of last resort, bestows a witness and his or her family with a new identity in a new country.

Ensuring the physical security of survivors of conflict should thus be a priority. The cessation of hostilities does not imply safety. All too often, continuing violence, notably gender-based violence is overlooked, or its significance is diminished, by police, judges, community and religious leaders, and other authority figures. Accordingly, longer-term measures to support victims should include the implementation of public education campaigns on violence against women and specific crime prevention policies to reduce gender-based violence.

2.5.3. Financial support and compensation

Survivors' physical, emotional and psychological healing will be difficult, if not impossible, to realize without financial security. Recognizing the need for compensation, the UN Declaration on Justice for Victims stipulates restitution and compensation for victims of crimes and their families, which may include the return of property or payment for the harm or loss suffered, whether the perpetrator is another individual or the State.[32] Where criminal courts are involved, the UN Declaration encourages governments to "review their practices, regulations and laws to consider restitution as an available sentencing option in criminal cases, in addition to other criminal sanctions" (Article 9). In 2010 the UN Special Rapporteur on Violence Against Women underlined that although legal procedures for compensation have been firmly codified in international and humanitarian law, they are often costly, painful, complicated and ultimately ineffective, especially for victims of sexual violence. In Rwanda and DRC, for example, national courts have awarded monetary claims to victims, but those without the financial means to pay their victims have simply avoided payment.[33] The Rapporteur thus concluded that gender-responsive administrative measures instead of legal reparations schemes can obviate some of the difficulties and costs

---

[32] See UN Declaration on Justice for Victims, 1985, Annex, Articles 8 and 11.

[33] Although Articles 27–32 of the 1996 genocide law, Organic Law on the Organisation of Prosecutions for Offences constituting the Crime of Genocide or Crimes against Humanity committed since 1 October 1990, recognized a victim's right to compensation, that law is no longer in force. The current genocide law does not include provisions for victims' compensation because those who were convicted pursuant to the 1996 genocide law were too poor to pay damages to victims and decisions were rendered that could not be executed. According to a report by the International Crisis Group, close to USD $100 million had been awarded after only 4000 people had been tried, but not a single penny has been paid out, because the defendants are all indigent. See International Crisis Group, *International Criminal Tribunal for Rwanda: Justice Delayed*, Africa Report No. 30 (Nairobi/Arusha/Brussels, 2001), p. 33. See also Ndahinda 2011, in this volume. In the case of the DRC, see UNOHCHR, *Report of the Panel on Remedies and Reparations for Victims of Sexual Violence in the Democratic Republic of Congo to the High Commissioner for Human Rights*, March 2011, 4.

associated with litigation.[34] Correspondingly, a UN-convened panel studying reparation for victims of sexual violence has recommended that the design of a reparations fund should be formulated in close consultation with victims of sexual violence, as well as civil society.[35]

2.5.4. Justice and the need for recognition and validation

A key need of survivors of conflict is the recognition and validation of their experiences (Shapland *et al.* 1985; Kirchhoff 1994; Herman 2003). Depending on the circumstances, this may involve fact-finding missions in which survivors' experiences are documented and disseminated, the establishment of truth and reconciliation commissions, and/or bringing perpetrators of the conflict to justice through informal or formal mechanisms, including criminal courts. All too often, these responses are not realized in the immediate months or years following a conflict, if at all. The Annex to the UN Declaration on Justice for Victims stipulates that, "[victims] are entitled to access to the mechanisms of justice and to prompt redress, as provided for by national legislation, for the harm that they have suffered" (Article 4). To make this feasible, "[j]udicial and administrative mechanisms should be established and strengthened where necessary to enable victims to obtain redress through formal or informal procedures that are expeditious, fair, inexpensive and accessible" (Article 5).

In a context where violence against women is not seen as a crime, documenting, investigating and prosecuting crimes of sexual violence has been a challenge. The Special UN Rapporteur on Violence against Women reported in 2010 that historically women and girls as victims of violence have been neglected, including in conflict areas. Although there have been efforts made to correct this both in national and international settings, the implementation of measures to counter the legacy of impunity regularly fails. In particular, where sexual violence is waged as a weapon of war by state actors, governments may deliberately refuse to hold perpetrators accountable. In Zimbabwe, for example, following the 2008 elections, members and supporters of the political opposition were subject to widespread, systematic rape, yet the police consistently refused to investigate and refer these cases for prosecution.[36]

In searching for recognition and validation, survivors wish to be included in the criminal justice process. In cases of mass victimization, survivors not only

---

34   UNHRC, Special Rapporteur on Violence Against Women, *Promotion and Protection of All Human Rights, Civil, Political, Economic, Social and Cultural Rights, Including the Right to Development*, A/HRC/14/22, 19 April 2010, para. 84.

35   UNOHCHR, *Report of the Panel on Remedies and Reparations for Victims of Sexual Violence in the Democratic Republic of Congo to the High Commissioner for Human Rights*, March 2011, 5. Available at: www.unhcr.org/refworld/docid/4d708ae32.html (last visited: 30 March 2011).

36   *Zimbabwe's 2008 Elections Featured Systematic Rape*, AIDS-Free World Press Release, 10 December 2009.

strive for recognition of the effects of a crime on them personally, but want recognition of the impact of such crimes on their community as a whole. This may be observed in a desire to discuss the impact of certain events on the group as well as on individuals personally, and in the desire to obtain validation and reparation for the group (Stover 2005).

3. RESPONSES OF THE INTERNATIONAL COMMUNITY: POTENTIAL AND LIMITS OF PREVENTIVE POLICIES AND CRIMINAL PROSECUTION

In light of the preceding discussion of the nature of sexual violence and its impact on victims, the question we now pose is: to what extent have international efforts succeeded to meet the needs of victims of sexual violence? Section 3.1 discusses international strategies to prevent sexual violence and enhance protection of women in conflict areas. Section 3.2 focuses on the international criminal prosecution of sexual violence as a war crime, crime against humanity and genocide, with a focus on the ICC.

3.1. INTERNATIONAL RESPONSES: PREVENTION

In the past two decades, the UN has increasingly recognized that women are a vulnerable group during armed conflicts who deserve more attention. The Beijing Declaration and Platform for Action,[37] which resulted from the UN World Conference on Women (1995), was one of the first consensus documents at the UN level to feature an entire chapter on women in armed conflicts. Since then, increasing media attention on the systematic and widespread nature of ongoing sexual violence in various active conflict areas[38] has put the magnitude of the problem squarely in the face of the international community. In particular, NGOs and women's organizations have often been the first to respond, provide support and relentlessly lobby governments into debate and action. Their work is explicitly recognized in many UN documents and reports, which reference NGOs and local women's organizations as an indispensable source of expertise that UN bodies should actively engage with to be effective in their interventions.[39]

---

[37] See www.un.org/womenwatch/daw/beijing/pdf/BDPfA%20E.pdf (last visited: 15 March 2011).
[38] See, *inter alia*, in Sudan, Chad, DRC, Liberia, Darfur, and Guatemala.
[39] See, for example, UNGA, *Report of the Secretary-General on the Implementation of Security Council Resolutions 1820 (2008) and 1888 (2009)*, 24 November 2010, A/65/592–S/2010/604, para. 46/i.

During the past decade, the UN has addressed the need to prevent sexual violence in various ways. UN Resolution 1325 (2000), for example, mandates the representation of women at all decision-making levels relating to peace and security issues, and the Resolution was the first to point to the specific vulnerabilities of women and children in conflict "as refugees and internally displaced persons, and increasingly targeted by combatants and armed elements". It calls on parties to armed conflict "to take special measures to protect women and girls from gender-based violence, particularly rape and other forms of sexual abuse".[40]

Security Council Resolutions 1820 (2008) and 1888 (2009)[41] have further specified what these measures should entail. The establishment of *UN Action Against Sexual Violence in Conflict*, which unites the work of twelve UN bodies to develop coordinated action to end sexual violence in conflict; the launch in 2008 of the UN Secretary-General's *UNiTE to End Violence against Women* campaign; and the recent appointment of a Special Rapporteur on Sexual Violence in Conflict, all reflect the historic momentum and an increasing willingness to actively combat sexual violence.

UN Resolution 1820 (2008) is the first Resolution specifically dedicated to addressing sexual violence against civilians in armed conflict, and marks a historic shift towards public recognition of the problem. Paragraph 3 of the Resolution demands that States

> *immediately take appropriate measures to protect civilians, including women and girls, from all forms of sexual violence, which could include, inter alia, enforcing appropriate military disciplinary measures and upholding the principle of command responsibility, training troops on the categorical prohibition of all forms of sexual violence against civilians, debunking myths that fuel sexual violence, vetting armed and security forces to take into account past actions of rape and other forms of sexual violence, and evacuation of women and children under imminent threat of sexual violence to safety.*

Protective and preventive measures are substantively addressed in the Resolution in very strong terms, including benchmarks to measure progress in preventing and responding to sexual violence. The Resolution demands a report after one year that contains an "analysis of the prevalence and trends of sexual violence in situations of armed conflict; proposals for strategies to minimize the susceptibility of women and girls to such violence; benchmarks for measuring progress in preventing and addressing sexual violence".[42]

---

40   UN SC, *Security Council Resolution 1325*, 31 October 2000, S/RES/1325 (2000).
41   UN SC, *Security Council Resolution 1820 (2008) [on Acts of Sexual Violence Against Civilians in Armed Conflicts]*, 19 June 2008, S/RES/1820 (2008); UN SC, *Security Council Resolution 1888 (2009) [on Acts of Sexual Violence Against Civilians in Armed Conflicts]*, 30 September 2009, S/RES/1888 (2009).
42   UN SC, *Security Council Resolution 1820 (2008) [on Acts of Sexual Violence Against Civilians in Armed Conflicts]*, 19 June 2008, S/RES/1820 (2008), para. 15.

The resulting 2009 report, however, addressed the issue of prevention only to a limited extent and in a general manner. States are urged to comply with existing obligations under international humanitarian, human rights and criminal law, including the CEDAW. The report acknowledges that prevention of sexual violence requires a profound change in social and cultural attitudes that actually condone sexual violence, even within organizations that are supposed to protect victims, including the UN, where many cases of sexual abuse of girls and young women by UN military and/or staff have been documented (Defeis 2008).[43] Accordingly, prevention and protection requires rigorous implementation of a zero tolerance policy on sexual exploitation and abuse by UN staff and related personnel. In spite of such acknowledgements, and binding obligations under international law, little progress had been made in curbing sexual violence during conflict one year after the introduction of Resolution 1820. Therefore, SC Resolution 1888 not only reiterates all the commitments and concerns of 1820 but further calls for more coherent and strategic leadership to address, at both UN headquarters and on a country level, sexual violence in armed conflict, and to promote cooperation and coordination of efforts among all relevant stakeholders.

This led to the appointment by the UN Secretary-General (SG) of the first Special Representative on Sexual Violence in Conflict (SR/SVC). Margot Wallström commenced office in April 2010. She presented her first report on the implementation of Resolutions 1820 and 1888 in November 2010.[44] The report includes a number of concrete measures that have been taken to combat sexual violence in conflict, notably the establishment of a team of experts in line with Resolution 1888 who are to be dispatched to countries with their consent in order to "assist national authorities in strengthening the rule of law".[45] Significantly, the SR/SVC emphasized the urgent need to actively involve women's protection advisers, while recognizing that preventing violence against women requires the active involvement of women in peace processes to effectively counteract the persisting tendency to marginalize the problem of sexual violence and silence victims. The SR/SVC cited a UNIFEM report which revealed that of 300 peace agreements reached in relation to 45 conflict situations since the end of the Cold War, only eighteen (six per cent) have addressed sexual violence. As the report stressed, "[i]f women do not participate, and if sexual violence is not addressed, it sets the stage for continued discrimination and the 'normalization' of violence".[46] In order to strengthen the prevention of sexual violence in conflict zones, the SR/SVC listed a range of measures to enhance the participation of women's police officers, and

---

[43] UN GA, *A Comprehensive Strategy to Eliminate Future Sexual Exploitation and Abuse in United Nations Peacekeeping Operations*, U.N.Doc. A/59/710, 2005.

[44] UN GA, *Report of the Secretary-General on the Implementation of Security Council Resolutions 1820 (2008) and 1888 (2009)*, 24 November 2010, A/65/592–S/2010/604 (hereafter: UN GA 1820/1888 Report 2010).

[45] UN GA 1820/1888 Report 2010, para. 26.

[46] *Idem*, para. 35.

recommended various training to enhance respect for the prohibition of sexual violence. Under the auspices of *UN Action*, a mobile support team on sexual violence has been set up to provide training to troop-contributing countries.[47] Moreover, the SG/SVC pointed to the need for increased gender awareness within the UN, citing UN findings that of more than 700 humanitarian projects (not necessarily in conflict zones), nearly half make no reference at all to gender-based violence. In response, the "roll-out of the gender marker system in humanitarian financing schemes in 2011 should strengthen project design in this regard".[48]

These proposed measures represent a shift in the UN towards recognizing sexual violence as a "peace and security deficit".[49] Correspondingly, the SG has underlined that combating sexual violence in times of conflict requires a comprehensive strategy that addresses gender and discrimination against women more broadly. The 2010 report of the SR/SVC thus concluded with a list of recommendations to develop a strong evaluation and monitoring system, which builds on research data as a crucial instrument to ultimately end impunity of, apply sanctions to, and enhance prosecution of sexual violence. As the SR/SVC recognized:

> *Sexual violence calls for sustained attention, action and cooperation commensurate with the scale of the challenge. Its enduring and ruinous consequences run counter to the aims of the United Nations system. Peace, justice and security are interdependent: there can be no peace without the peace of mind that enables women to undertake their daily tasks, no justice without a national capacity to deliver justice, and no security without women's security.[50]*

Based on this November 2010 Report, the UN Security Council adopted Resolution 1960 requesting the SG to establish "monitoring, analysis and reporting arrangements on conflict-related sexual violence, including rape in situations of armed conflict and post-conflict and other situations relevant to the implementation of Resolution 1888 (2009)".[51] Furthermore, the SG was requested to submit a detailed report by December 2011 on the implementation of Resolutions 1820 (2008), 1888 (2009) and 1960 (2010), which is to include information on a detailed coordination and strategy plan on data collection and on the progress made in monitoring, analysis and reporting.

Although these developments before the UN unequivocally reflect a growing dedication to address sexual violence against women during conflicts, it is too early to assess the effectiveness of such measures in practice and there are ample

---

[47] *Idem*, paras. 43–45.
[48] *Idem*, para. 41.
[49] *Idem*, para. 46.
[50] *Idem*, para. 47.
[51] UN SC, *Security Council Resolution 1960*, S/Res/1960 (2010), 16 December 2010 (hereafter UN SC 1960).

reasons to remain concerned over the slow progress of the implementation of proposed measures so far. The *Civil Society Advisory Group* to the SG on Sexual violence against women displaced by conflict has concluded that despite the existence of a "plethora of legal and policy documents", the problem of sexual violence in conflict "is widespread and growing" (Steinberg 2010, 3). They point to an ongoing lack of political will as well as a lack of knowledge among many stakeholders, and emphasize the need for training of governments, NGOs, peacekeeping forces, women and implementing UN agencies on existing guidelines to address gender-based violence. There also remains an urgent need to transform the underlying discourse regarding affected women, who are still regarded as victims in need of rescue rather than "vital resources for the design and implementation of programs" (Steinberg 2010, 3). The fact that international peacekeeping missions operating under the UN continue to commit sexual abuse of women and girls sadly underlines how deeply rooted the practice of gender-based violence is, and how profound the required transformation of attitudes towards women is, including within UN agencies.

In light of all these developments, one provisional conclusion can be drawn: the prevention of sexual violence during times of conflict is an exceedingly difficult goal to achieve, but not impossible. It requires challenging interventions directed at perpetrators, State governments and military authorities who are responsible for such atrocities. Wood's research (2009) suggests that the role of the military to prevent perpetration should not be underestimated. A firm 'top-down' prohibition of any sexual violence within the (Tamil) military, coupled with tightly-controlled swift and severe military punishment, was an effective way of preventing soldiers from engaging in sexual violence during the Sri Lankan conflict. Based on Wood's work, it remains an open question as to what extent the existence of prohibitive norms in wider society against sexual violence was a necessary factor in accounting for the rarity of sexual violence against civilians.

Nevertheless, ongoing attitudes condoning sexual violence in both peace and war time underlines the need for continuing campaigns to prevent sexual violence, including the educational work of both the UN and NGOs that operate locally. Support and protection interventions for victims can help to build a basis on which to extend educational efforts directed at the larger community. Only when supported by community-based structures is it feasible to re-establish social values and norms about respect for women and their rights, including the right to be free from violence and respect for their sexual integrity. The successful development of social norms condemning violence against women is a crucial condition to provide social and cultural legitimacy to legal norms (Römkens 2005).

3.2. INTERNATIONAL RESPONSES: PROSECUTION

The recognition, investigation and prosecution of crimes of sexual violence by international courts have significantly increased in the past two decades. Compared to the International Criminal Tribunals for the former Yugoslavia (ICTY) and that for Rwanda (ICTR), the first international criminal tribunals that recognized rape explicitly as a crime against humanity,[52] the ICC is mandated to investigate and prosecute an even wider range of sexual violence. In addition to rape, sexual slavery, enforced prostitution, forced pregnancy, enforced sterilization and any other form of sexual violence are defined as crimes against humanity and war crimes (Articles 7 and 8 Rome Statute). In addition, the Elements of Crimes recognize that rape and other forms of sexual violence can amount to the crime of genocide (Article 6(b), element 1, footnote 3 Elements of Crimes). These are major steps forward in the recognition of sexual violence and its different forms as self-standing crimes in international criminal law. Although tribunals such as the ICTY and the ICTR have been applauded for several breakthroughs in international criminal law and procedure (e.g. Askin 2005; Møse 2005),[53] they have also been criticized for their inadequate and incoherent investigation and prosecution policies, related to no or not enough charges of sexual violence being included in an indictment against an accused, charges of sexual violence being dropped over the course of proceedings, or charges not being representative of the sexual violence committed (Dembour & Haslam 2004; Nowrojee 2005b; Beltz 2008; Buss 2009; Mibenge 2011; Zawati 2011).

---

[52] The ICTR also recognized rape and enforced prostitution as the war crime of 'outrages upon personal dignity'.

[53] With regard to substantive international criminal law, the most notable achievements are the acknowledgements that rape and sexual violence can amount to genocide and that the definition of rape does not need to include lack of consent as an element of the crime. There seems to be no consensus on this definition yet as ICTY and ICTR Chambers have come up with different definitions of the crime, sometimes including lack of consent as an element. The non-binding Elements of Crimes of the ICC, however, assume that lack of consent is not an element of the crime (Viseur Sellers 2007). With regard to international criminal procedural law, of particular importance to victims/survivors of sexual violence are several evidentiary rules of the ICC, in particular the rules specifying that, as for any testimony, the testimony of a victim/survivor of sexual violence does not need to be corroborated, that consent cannot be inferred from words or conduct undermined by coercive circumstances, and that evidence on prior or later sexual conduct is not admitted (Rules 63(4), 70–72 RPE). While these rules are essentially concerned with the presentation of evidence, they also offer certain protective measures to victims/survivors of sexual violence when testifying. These rules, for the first time laid down in international criminal procedure of the ICTY and the ICTR (for both Tribunals in Rule 96 RPE), are a major achievement, particularly when compared with a number of national jurisdictions which use definitions of rape which allow defense counsel to introduce suggested consent of the victim as a defense strategy, even in a context of force. This discriminates against victims of sexual violence (who are mostly women) by allowing their credibility to be challenged, thus impeding them from participating in the legal process (Bohner *et al.* 2009; Krahé and Temkin 2009).

To a large extent because of lessons learned from the ICTY and ICTR, the ICC adheres to a more inquisitorial framework as far as victims' issues are concerned. This is due in part to a series of international legal and political developments over the past two decades in which a growing sensitization of the needs and rights of victims in legal proceedings went hand in hand with growing attention paid to the widespread prevalence of violence against women in general and in war time in particular, and the need to address this in international law (Bunch 1990; Chinkin 1994). The new prominence of victims within the framework of international criminal procedure is inspired by the 1985 UN Declaration on Justice for Victims and the 1985 Council of Europe Recommendation on the Position of the Victim in the Framework of Criminal Law and Procedure (Groenhuijsen & Letschert 2007; Groenhuijsen 2008). For the first time in history, victims are allowed to participate in the ICC not only as witnesses, but also as victim participants and are able to request and receive reparation.[54] Yet, the question remains as to whether victims can genuinely express their views and concerns during these proceedings, especially in light of the large number of victim applications the Court receives. Additionally, how can the reparation regime benefit many victims of sexual violence and in what forms? These questions cannot be addressed without also considering issues such as protection, outreach and institutional structures, including the issue of gender balance and expertise on sexual violence in conflict. In the following subsections an overview of the achievements of the ICC will be provided as well as the challenges ahead (see also McGonigle Leyh, this volume).

3.2.1. Victim participation and reparation

A development of great significance to victims, including victims/survivors of sexual violence, is victim participation and reparation. For the first time, victims can participate in international criminal proceedings by, for example, expressing their views and concerns (Article 68(3) Rome Statute and Rule 16 RPE) and they can request and be awarded reparation by the Court (Article 75 Rome Statute; Rules 94–99 RPE). Several institutional structures also provide new opportunities for victims wishing to participate. The Victims Participation and Reparation Section (VPRS) and the Office of Public Counsel for Victims (OPCV) are instrumental to the smooth operation of victim participation and/or reparation. The VPRS is, among other things, responsible for providing outreach to victims falling within the jurisdiction of the Court on reparation and participation possibilities. Correspondingly, the OPCV is responsible for representing victim

---

[54] Despite provisions on restitution of property and compensation, the issue of reparation to victims has rarely been dealt with by the ICTY and ICTR Tribunals. See Articles 24(3) of the ICTY Statute and 23(3) of the ICTR Statute (on restitution); and Rule 106 of both the ICTY and ICTR RPE (on compensation).

applicants wishing to participate in situations when they are without legal representation. In addition, a Trust Fund for Victims and their Families has been set up, which is authorized to provide assistance to victims and their families in an early phase of the proceedings (Article 79 Rome Statute).

As of April 2010, 760 victim applicants (out of 2035 applications received since 2005) had been accepted to participate in the various situations and cases before the ICC,[55] meaning many victims who applied to participate in ICC proceedings (63% of applicants received) were or are still awaiting a decision about their participation. To date, all victims participating in proceedings have been represented by a lawyer, and all victims in need of it have benefited from legal aid.[56] Although the rules allow for personal victim participation without legal representation, the practice before the Court has been that of victims presenting their views and concerns before the Court through their legal representative(s). For example, in the *Katanga and Chui* case, the Court consolidated victim representation by merging legal representation from eight victims' legal representatives into two legal teams.[57] Each legal representative is responsible for representing the common interests of the group assigned to him or her and for acting on behalf of specific victims when their individual interests are at stake.[58] It is not clear how many of the recognized applicants are victims of sexual violence, and the number is largely dependent on whether the accused is charged with sexual violence (in order to participate as a victim, the Court has ruled that there must be a link between the crimes suffered by the victim and the charges against the accused)[59] Given the diversity of experiences of survivors of sexual violence, it may be difficult for legal representatives to represent the unique interests of victims of sexual violence in addition to the interests of other victims (on this, see Mesters & Adeboyejo, this volume).

The distinct interests of survivors of sexual violence also requires relevant qualifications from common legal representative(s) (Rule 90(4) RPE and Article 68(1) Rome Statute). In cases involving sexual violence, legal representatives are

---

[55] International Criminal Court, *Registry and Trust Fund for Victims Fact Sheet*, 26 April 2010, p. 1.

[56] *Ibidem* (according to the Fact Sheet, "VPRS facilitated the appointment of a legal representative (including OPCV) by the Court for 967 victims").

[57] *Prosecutor v. Katanga and Chui, Situation in the DRC*, Order on the Organisation of Common Legal Representation of Victims, ICC-01/04–01/07–1328, Trial Chamber II, ICC, 22 July 2009.

[58] *Prosecutor v. Katanga and Chui, Situation in the DRC*, Order on the Organisation of Common Legal Representation of Victims, ICC-01/04–01/07–1328, Trial Chamber II, ICC, 22 July 2009, para. 13.

[59] See, for example, *Prosecutor v. Lubanga, Situation in the DRC*, Decision on the Applications for Participation in the Proceedings of VPRS 1, VPRS 2, VPRS 3, VPRS 4, VPRS 5 and VPRS 6, ICC-01/04–1 01-tEN-Corr, Pre-Trial Chamber I, ICC, 17 January 2006, paras. 77–101; and *Prosecutor v. Lubanga*, Judgment on the Appeals of The Prosecutor and The Defence against Trial Chamber I's Decision on Victims' Participation of 18 January 2008, ICC-01/04–01/06 OA 9 OA 10, Appeals Chamber, ICC, 11 July 2008.

required to have, *inter alia*, expertise dealing with victims of sexual violence, may need to come from the same region as the victims and speak their language and for some victims, the gender of their legal counsel may be a relevant factor. However, the accredited list of legal counsel does not to date include a significant number of legal counsel with expertise in sexual violence and very few women are on the list (18% or 63 out of 342 persons). Of those, only six are women from the situations under consideration by the Court (three from DRC; one from the Central African Republic (CAR); and two from Kenya).[60]

In terms of reparation, awards are provided by the Court only after an accused has been found guilty, despite the possibility (and likelihood) that victims of sexual violence may need physical, psychological and medical support much earlier. Since the ICC became operational in 2003, not one single trial has been concluded as of spring 2011. Fortunately, assistance is to be offered by the Trust Fund in an earlier phase, allowing for a broader system of reparation accessible at any stage of proceedings. The Trust Fund has, therefore, a double mandate: it will not only implement reparation awards from the Court, but may also implement programmes that will assist victims of mass crimes in terms of physical and psychological rehabilitation as well as material support (Rule 98 of the RPE; Regulation 50 of the Regulations of the Trust Fund for Victims[61]). Because the Trust Fund can assist victims in an early stage of proceedings (even those whose cases may not have been taken up by the Prosecutor), it has the potential to benefit many more victims and assist them to meet their immediate needs.

The Trust Fund for Victims and their Families has begun to implement several activities in Uganda and the DRC, which are expected to benefit 224,300 direct and indirect victims.[62] The projects implemented in these countries include specific activities that support survivors of sexual violence.[63] The Trust Fund opted for an approach in which it both targets victims of gender-based violence specifically and mainstreams a gender-based perspective throughout its

---

[60]   List of Legal Counsel, 19 October 2010, available on the ICC website (www.icc-cpi.int). The ICC recognized the lack of female counsel from the situations under consideration and started a campaign to increase the number of African female counsel. According to an ICC press release, the first phase of the campaign was a success – "more than 1,000 lawyers were engaged in the course of 17 events held in 16 countries" – but an actual increase in African female counsel has yet to happen. See ICC Press Release, *First Phase of the ICC's "Calling African Female Counsel Campaign" a Success*, 26 November 2010.

[61]   Regulations of the Trust Fund for Victims, ICC-ASP/4/Res.3, 3 December 2005.

[62]   See *Report of the Court on the Activities and Projects of the Board of Directors of the Trust Fund for Victims for the Period 1 July 2008 to 30 June 2009*, ICC-ASP/8/18, 29 July 2009, p. 2; The Trust Fund for Victims website (www.trustfundforvictims.org), under "projects" (last visited: 29 November 2010).

[63]   See *Report to the Assembly of States Parties on the Activities and Projects of the Board of Directors of the Trust Fund for Victims for the Period 1 July 2009 to 30 June 2010*, ICC-ASP/9/2, 28 July 2010, p. 1.

programming.[64] Some illustrative activities include, *inter alia*, fistula repair, trauma counselling, the provision of sanitary supplies and referrals to HIV and reproductive health services; screening and intake centres; job training programmes for victims; community awareness of sexual violence to address stigma and discrimination; special initiatives for children born out of rape; education, safe shelter, and the reintegration into communities of men and boys who have raped.[65] In Uganda, three of the eighteen projects (16.6 per cent) are specifically focused on survivors of sexual violence; in the DRC, eight of the 16 projects (50 per cent) are for programmes focused on survivors of sexual violence.[66] While the attention paid by the Trust Fund for Victims to survivors of sexual violence is promising, the Secretariat and the Board of the Trust Fund need to continue to actively fundraise as the monies in the Fund are arguably insufficient, especially from a long-term perspective (a mere € 4.5 million as of November 2009).[67]

On a final note, the role that victims may have before the ICC will only be fully realized if adequate outreach strategies by the Court are undertaken. Outreach is essential to ensure that affected communities in situations subject to investigation or proceedings can understand and follow the work of the Court through the different phases of its activities. Yet, despite an increase in outreach activities since the Court became operational, many victims in the situations concerned are still unaware of what the Court is about and how they can play a role in its proceedings.[68] In the DRC, only 27% had heard about the Court, 28% had heard of proceedings against the accused, Lubanga, and 12% knew how to access Court proceedings.[69] In the CAR, outreach has typically extended to wealthy and educated men, though the Bemba Gombo case primarily relates to

---

[64] See *Report to the Assembly of States Parties on the Activities and Projects of the Board of Directors of the Trust Fund for Victims for the Period 1 July 2009 to 30 June 2010*, ICC-ASP/9/2, 28 July 2010, pp. 2–3; The Trust Fund for Victims, *Recognizing Victims & Building Capacity in Transitional Societies*, Spring 2010 Programme Progress Report, pp. 10–13.

[65] ICC Press Release, *Global Appeal for € 10 Million to Assist 1.7 Million Victims of Sexual Violence Launched*, 10 September 2008; The Trust Fund for Victims website (www.trustfundforvictims.org), under "projects" (last visited: 29 November 2010).

[66] See annex II to the Report to the Assembly of States Parties on the activities and projects of the Board of Directors of the Trust Fund for Victims for the period 1 July 2008 to 30 June 2009, ICC-ASP/8/18*, 18 September 2009. A total of 3,100 victims of sexual and/or gender-based violence, including victims of rape and children who were born in captivity, were assisted by the Trust Fund for Victims in northern Uganda and the DRC. See The Trust Fund for Victims, *Recognizing Victims & Building Capacity in Transitional Societies*, Spring 2010 Programme Progress Report, p. 8.

[67] The Trust Fund for Victims website (www.trustfundforvictims.org), under 'about us' (last visited: 29 November 2010).

[68] See *Report of the Bureau on the Impact of the Rome Statute System on Victims and Affected Communities*, ICC-ASP/9/25, 22 November 2010, pp. 7, 10–11.

[69] Human Rights Center, Payson Center for International Development & International Center for Transitional Justice, *Living With Fear: A Population-based Survey on Attitudes about Peace, Justice, and Social Reconstruction in Eastern Democratic Republic of Congo*, 2008.

charges involving sexual violence.[70] Only a few outreach activities have been conducted which included specific strategies to reach victims/survivors of sexual violence in the conflict situations concerned.[71] Because they are so often stigmatized in their communities, the under-representation of female survivors of sexual violence in court will likely persist if the ICC does not pay specific attention to them in its outreach activities on participation and reparation.

3.2.2. Protective and support measures

A positive aspect of the ICC's institutional structure is the availability of protective and support measures for victims and witnesses (Articles 68 and 69(2) Rome Statute; Rules 87–88 RPE). The Court is required to take appropriate measures – including proceedings *in camera* (which in the case of victims/ survivors of sexual violence would in principle be ordered automatically) or allowing the presentation of evidence by electronic means – to protect the safety, physical and psychological well-being, dignity and privacy of victims and witnesses, taking into account such factors as age, gender, health and the nature of the crime, particularly where the crime involves sexual or gender-based violence. The Victim and Witness Unit (VWU), in consultation with the Office of the Prosecutor, is mandated to provide protective measures, security arrangements, counselling and other appropriate assistance to witnesses, victims and others at risk on account of their testimony. As the Court is very much dependent on the testimonies of witnesses, protection of witnesses is not to be taken lightly. In the course of the proceedings before the ICC, witnesses have already been threatened, as well as intermediaries and legal representatives for victims.[72] Before the ICTY and the ICTR, victims of sexual violence who testified in the trial proceedings were similarly intimidated, threatened or even rejected by family members or the community they lived in once they found out about their testimony and status as survivors of sexual violence (Nowrojee 2005b; De Brouwer 2005). As an additional measure, the ICC VWU must include staff with expertise in trauma, including trauma related to crimes of sexual violence, and also train the other organs of the Court on these aspects (Article 43(6) Rome Statute; Rules 17 and 19 RPE).

---

[70] See *Report of the Bureau on the Impact of the Rome Statute System on Victims and Affected Communities*, ICC-ASP/9/25, 22 November 2010, p. 10.

[71] See, for example, ICC Press Release, *The ICC Organises Open Discussions in Bunia (Ituri) and Béni (North Kivu)*, 10 March 2008; ICC Press Release, *ICC Involves Women in the Acholi and Lango Sub-regions of Northern Uganda in Discussion about the Court*, 14 July 2008; ICC Press Release, *ICC Extends Outreach Activities to Female Victims of Sexual Violence in Iga Barrière (Ituri, DRC)*, 15 September 2008.

[72] Institute for War & Peace Reporting, *Lubanga Trial a Landmark Case*, 23 January 2009; *Report of the Bureau on the Impact of the Rome Statute System on Victims and Affected Communities*, ICC-ASP/9/25, 22 November 2010, p. 7; Human Rights Watch, *Courting History: The Landmark International Criminal Court's First Years*, July 2008.

Codes of professional conduct also govern the treatment of victims-witnesses of sexual violence in court. Article 29 of the Code of Professional Conduct for Counsel[73] specifies that counsel shall refrain from intimidating, harassing or humiliating witnesses or victims or from subjecting them to disproportionate or unnecessary pressure and that particular consideration is given to victims of sexual violence. Article 8 of the Code of Judicial Ethics[74] requires judges to exercise vigilance in controlling the manner of questioning of witnesses or victims and to avoid conduct or comments which are racist, sexist or otherwise degrading. These rules are innovative in international criminal procedure, but imperative in order to facilitate the testimonies of survivors of sexual violence and ensure that the crimes that have been committed against them are reflected in the record (De Brouwer 2005).

As mentioned, the international criminal tribunals are principally concerned with establishing the liability of the accused for the crimes charged. Victims who appear before these Tribunals do this in their capacity as witnesses and are assumed to substantiate parties' arguments. There is little room to tell their stories. Tension thus exists between the requirements of the legal proceedings and victims' interests. According to Stover (2005, 106): "Judges can – and often do – admonish witnesses who stray from the facts, which in turn can frustrate victims who have waited years to tell their story publicly". Research on evaluating experiences of victims in international criminal tribunals is limited but generally not always very positive (Nowrojee 2005b; Dembour & Haslam 2004). Mertus (2004, 112), who studied the ICTY *Foča* case, which dealt primarily with sexual violence, concluded that the international trial proceedings had by and large disillusioned survivors: almost all experienced the trial as "dehumanizing and re-traumatizing". Conversely, Henry (2009, 114), who also focused on this case, concluded that "due to the sheer diversity and heterogeneity of wartime rape victims, the experience of giving testimony is likely to be mixed: while some victims may suffer under the constraints of legal process, under the right circumstances, war crimes trials may help others to make sense of their suffering" (see also O'Connell 2005).

3.2.3. Gender balance and expertise as structural characteristics of the institution

The Rome Statute mandates that a "fair representation of female and male judges" be taken into account in the selection process, a fair representation of women and men in the selection of staff in the Office of the Prosecutor and in all other organs of the Court (Articles 36 and 44 Rome Statute), and gender equity

---

[73]   ICC-ASP/4/Res.1, 2 December 2005.
[74]   ICC-BD/02–01–05, 9 March 2005.

among members of the Board of Directors of the Trust Fund.[75] Furthermore, the Prosecutor is required to appoint advisers with legal expertise in specific issues including sexual and gender violence (Article 42(9) Rome Statute).

The requirement to have gender balance and expertise on issues concerning violence against women is unique to the ICC. This requirement recognizes the specificity of gender-based violence and the need for specific legal expertise to effectively address these needs. In this respect, the Rome Statute extends well beyond most laws in national jurisdictions. Without the existence of these provisions, which enable the provision of key services to victims, victims' rights only remain valid on paper (Groenhuijsen 1998). Yet, after more than eight years of operation, there persists an overall under-representation of women in senior professional positions (especially within the Office of the Prosecutor (OTP)) where decisions are made and very few (female) legal counsel on the list of legal counsel who may be able and qualified to represent victims/survivors of sexual violence.[76] In November 2008, a Special Advisor on Gender Crimes was appointed by the Prosecutor, who will be able to provide a gender analysis to investigation and prosecution strategies, a role that proved effective in the Yugoslav Tribunal. The appointment of the Special Advisor on Gender Crimes was long awaited and is an important addition to the OTP focal point for gender issues, the Prosecutor and Deputy Prosecutor, and the OTP Gender and Children Unit – the specialized unit working on gender issues across all of the OTP's cases. However, the Special Advisor on Gender Crimes is only a part-time position based outside The Hague, which will undoubtedly impact on the work that needs to be done. A full time Hague-based Special Advisor is therefore still needed[77], as there is a strong need for gender and sexual violence expertise among the Court's staff (Sharratt 2011 and 2012).

The ICC faces real challenges in addressing crimes of sexual violence, given that its institutional structure does not currently reflect an equitable gender and geographic balance and there is insufficient expertise on gender-based and sexual violence among its staff. This is sadly reflected in the charging of sexual violence in the situations and cases currently before the Court.

3.2.4. Charges of sexual violence

Out of five conflict zones, nine cases have emerged to date, with a total of sixteen persons facing charges (one of whom has since passed away). Eight of those individuals (50%) have not been charged with crimes of sexual violence, despite the suspects' positions of leadership and available evidence of widespread sexual

---

[75]   Resolution ICC-ASP/1/Res.6, 9 September 2002.
[76]   Women's Initiatives for Gender Justice, *Gender Report Card 2009 on the International Criminal Court*, 2009, available at www.iccwomen.org/news/docs/GRC09_web-2–10.pdf (last visited: 29 November 2010).
[77]   *Ibidem.*

violence in the conflicts concerned. The remaining eight suspects[78] have been charged with various forms of sexual violence. However, the charges laid are narrow in light of the senior positions held by the accused and the documented magnitude and range of crimes of sexual violence committed in the situations concerned. Irrespective of the need to ensure the security of victims of sexual violence and for compelling evidence to secure a conviction in deciding whether to proceed to trial, the narrow charging of sexual violence is disturbing. This development suggests an inadequate understanding by the OTP of the seriousness of sexual violence and of the need for investigation and prosecution of a range of crimes of sexual violence representative of the experiences of victims/survivors. Former court investigators indicated that a lack of planning prior to investigations and a narrow investigative focus have resulted in many crimes of sexual violence being overlooked.[79] Gathering evidence of sexual violence crimes does, however, not pose any additional legal burden than any other crime and need not pose any additional investigative challenge. As mentioned by Marcus (2012): "The aim is to include it from the beginning, proceed in an informed and respectful manner, filling gaps as the investigation proceeds, with patient persistence and cautious determination" (on (methods of) investigating sexual violence in conflict, see also Agirre Aranburu 2010; Reis 2012; Lawry *et al.* 2012; Hagan *et al.* 2012). This development at the investigation phase has furthermore been exacerbated by the absence of full-time Hague-based gender legal advisors within the OTP.

The limited and narrow charging of crimes of sexual violence reflects poorly on the ICC's OTP, especially in those cases where no charges of sexual violence have been made despite documented reports of sexual violence. The purported aim of the ICC to deter perpetrators from the commission of serious crimes is undermined for those involving sexual violence, especially in light of the reality that such crimes have historically been overlooked and under-prosecuted in every corner of the world.

In spite of its intentions, the ICC is not setting an example for prosecutions of sexual violence at the national level, especially in the situations under consideration at the Court. This is troubling in the face of reports that the perpetration of sexual violence has persisted beyond the conflict and become normalized behaviour.[80] Moreover, narrowly prosecuting sexual violence is not representative of the totality of sexual violence that has been committed in the

---

[78] Germain Katanga and Mathieu Ngudjolo Chui (DRC), Ahmad Muhammad Harun, Ali Muhammad Ali Abd-Al-Rahman and Omar Hassan Ahmad Al Bashir (Darfur/Sudan), Joseph Kony and Vincent Otti (Uganda) and Jean-Pierre Bemba Gombo (CAR).

[79] Institute for War & Peace Reporting, *ICC Investigative Strategy Under Fire*, by Katy Glassborow, 2008, pp. 8–14, in: Institute for War & Peace Reporting, *Special Report: Sexual Violence in the Democratic Republic of Congo*, October 2008.

[80] Institute for War & Peace Reporting, *Press Release: CAR Case to Focus on Sexual Slavery*, 24 May 2007.

conflict and denies the extent of suffering by victims/survivors of sexual violence. This may ultimately dissuade victims/survivors of sexual violence from participating in the ICC, and more so if they are only able to participate in proceedings and request reparation from the Court in relation to specific (and limited) charges against an accused.

4. FINAL REMARKS: ONE SIZE DOES NOT FIT ALL

For too long, sexual violence in conflict was the long-forgotten crime. Increasingly, however, the severity of sexual violence and its impact on survivors is being recognized by the international community. We can no longer pretend that we are ignorant on this issue and we no longer have a reason not to act. In the context of international policy and law, concerted efforts have been made to prevent and bring justice to victims, with varying degrees of success. In light of the complexity and diversity of victims' needs, there is no singular strategy or response that can encompass all aspects of the problem. At minimum, what is necessary is a broad range of initiatives to address the multiplicity of victims' needs, actions taken for the primary prevention of sexual violence and appropriate and effective punishment of perpetrators. Moreover, in the face of an ongoing tendency to minimize sexual violence in war time, we must identify ways to memorialize it as a way to give voice to victims and raise awareness of violence against women.

As discussed above, international responses which focus on preventing sexual violence and providing victim support have only recently emerged, though they are promising. The appointment of a UN Special Rapporteur on Sexual Violence in Conflicts provides a champion and focal point to develop these preventive and support efforts more coherently. Governments have also increasingly made a commitment to speak out and take action against sexual violence, including by actively training military to prevent it. Nevertheless, the development of training and educational interventions directed at strict prohibition of sexual violence is still in its infancy. This is particularly complicated in light of the legacy of sexual objectification and denigration of women within the military. Much work remains to be done, and given this legacy active monitoring, reporting and sanctioning structures within the UN system are vital. NGOs are also crucial as independent watchdogs to help realize victims' rights and encourage a shift in attitudes towards unacceptability of sexual violence in war and peace time.

With regard to the international responses that focus on prosecution, we focused in this article on the ICC. This court has adopted a number of positive measures concerning the prosecution of crimes of sexual violence, such as prohibiting a broad range of sexual violence as well as including several strong procedural rules that make it easier for victims of sexual violence to take part in the proceedings as witnesses and/or participants. At the same time, many challenges persist in the implementation. Identifying legal counsel who are qualified to adequately represent the interests of victims of sexual violence is one such challenge, as is the fulfilment of the reparation mandate of the ICC and Trust Fund for Victims to address the needs of victims of sexual violence. In order for survivors of sexual violence to be informed of the possibilities of participation before the ICC, the court must make a greater effort at outreach towards those survivors, especially in remote areas. Where victims of sexual violence testify or participate before the ICC, attention must be paid so that they are not re-victimized by the way they are questioned and are not threatened or intimidated upon their return home because of their appearance in court. While participating and testifying in court can be an empowering experience, this is very much dependent on the way victims of sexual violence are treated there. Other innovative ways of dealing with witness testimony can also be considered, such as minimizing the number of victims to establish certain facts (Dembour & Haslam 2004) and using more written statements in lieu of oral testimony.[81] The rules of the Court also make it possible to appoint a gender-balanced court with personnel competent in the charging of gender-based crimes which may in turn lead to representative charging of crimes of sexual violence.

Significantly, international criminal legal responses are not the only means available for victims of sexual violence and national and local courts, Truth and Reconciliation Commissions, community based victims' groups, symbolic reparations (e.g. commemoration memorials), cultural forms of recognition (e.g. theatre), media (e.g. documentaries, movies), Victims' Tribunals (in a similar vein to the 2000 Women's Tribunal in Tokyo created to address the crimes committed against women who were held as sexual slaves by the Japanese during WWII) and education (e.g. schools, museums, books) are some other measures through which victims of sexual violence could obtain some form of justice and reconciliation (see also Mertus 2004; O'Connell 2005; Dembour & Haslam 2004). As underscored throughout this chapter, the diversity of victimization requires similarly diverse and multi-faceted responses and more research on the appropriate measures and how current mechanisms can be improved is needed (see for some research on this for ICTR, the Best Practices Manual 2008[82]; for the ICTY, Stover 2005 and Sharratt 2011 and 2012; for the Special Court for

---

[81] L. Bianchi, *The Investigation and Presentation of Evidence Relating to Sexual Violence*, presentation held during the Roundtable on Cooperation between the International Criminal Tribunals and National Prosecuting Authorities, Arusha, 26th-28th November 2008, available at www.unictr.org/Portals/0/English/News/events/Nov2008/EN/sexual-violence.pdf/ (last visited: 29 November 2010).

[82] ICTR, *Best Practices Manual for the Investigation and Prosecution of Sexual Violence Crimes in Situations of Armed Conflict: Lessons from the International Criminal Tribunal for Rwanda*, 2008, available at http://69.94.11.53/ENGLISH/international_cooperation/papers_presented/Best-Practices-Manual-Sexual-Violence.pdf (last visited: 29 November 2010).

Sierra Leone, Horn *et al.* 2010; on transitional justice mechanisms for sexual violence generally, see Zinsstag 2012). The international recognition of sexual violence is but a first step towards justice for survivors of sexual violence, and it is vital that the next steps involve their consultation. If they are no longer to be silenced, their participation in preventive strategies, justice and reconciliation efforts will be imperative to any meaningful form of such initiatives.

XXI. VICTIMS OF SEXUAL VIOLENCE IN THE INTERNATIONAL CRIMINAL COURT

Challenges Related to Legal Representation and Protection

Gabbi MESTERS and Adesola ADEBOYEJO

1. GENERAL INTRODUCTION

Over the centuries, rape has been a by-product of many wars and armed conflicts and its scale in some conflicts has led to its description as a weapon of war. Although there are no comprehensive statistics on the occurrence of rape during conflicts, 14,200 registered rape cases in South Kivu province of the Democratic Republic of the Congo (DRC) between 2005 and 2007, may suggest how high and common the incidence of rape in times of war is.[1]

The Rome Statute of the International Criminal Court (ICC or Court) has made very significant progress in recognizing several gender-based crimes, including rape, as genocide as well as crimes against humanity and war crimes. This focus has also led to significant strides in the description of the offence, its elements and profile. This is in contrast to the Statutes of the *ad hoc* International Criminal Tribunals for the former Yugoslavia (ICTY) and Rwanda (ICTR) where the definitions of the offences are given in general terms.[2] In recognising the mere fact that both sexes suffer sexual violence in times of armed conflicts, the boundaries of justice are expanded to the inclusion of assistance to both female and male victims/survivors (OCHA 2008).[3] The Rome Statute and the practice

---

[1] Stop Rape Now, *UN Actions Against Sexual Violence in Conflict*, Strategic Framework 2009–2010.

[2] Article 5(g) of the ICTY Statute: The International Tribunal shall have the power to prosecute persons responsible for the following crimes when committed in armed conflict, whether international or internal in character, and directed against any civilian population: rape; and Article 3(g) of the ICTR Statute, further discussed below.

[3] UNOCHA, *Use of Sexual Violence in Conflict: Identifying Research Priorities to Inform More Effective Interventions*, UNOCHA, Policy Development and Studies Branch, Meeting Report, New York, 26 June 2008.

of the ICC envisage and include support to victims, which is effected by the establishment of the Victims and Witnesses Unit (VWU), the Victims Participation and Reparations Section (VPRS), and the Office of Public Counsel for Victims (OPCV).

In this manner the ICC recognizes the right of every individual to his or her physical integrity and self-worth and for the first time, victims/survivors of sexual violence are empowered to fight such breaches of their physical integrity, through actively participating as victims in the criminal proceedings before the ICC. Where the personal interests of the victims are affected, the Court permits their views and concerns to be presented and considered at different stages of the proceedings,[4] thus departing from the *ad hoc* Tribunals practice of considering the victims as witnesses only.

This chapter will not attempt to exhaust each and every aspect of the forms of assistance rendered to victims of sexual violence either in the contextual framework of the texts of the ICC or even in the actual implementation as this would be beyond the scope of the focus of the chapter. This is also why the issue of reparation will not be addressed. Instead this chapter will highlight some of the aspects that have been particularly challenging in implementation. To start with the historical background of the definition of rape and sexual violence under international law will be addressed. In addition the specific charges of gender based crimes in the cases and situations before the ICC will be described and an overview provided of who is in custody and who is still at large. Subsequently, the various forms of assistance to victims under the legal text of the Court will be further discussed: victim participation, notification, protection measures and the choosing of common legal representatives. Finally some practical challenges for legal representatives of victims/survivors of sexual violence will be brought to the surface. What sort of legal qualification do they require in order to practice before the ICC? Which general challenges do they face and what specific challenges occur when representing single status witnesses or witnesses that double as both a witness and a victim; the so called dual status witnesses. To conclude, possible solutions will be proposed that could be the subject of further debate. Hopefully this chapter will aid in assuring that victim's rights are respected and that victims and their legal representatives have a clearer idea of what they can expect from the Court.

---

4   Article 68(3) of the Rome Statute: "Where the personal interests of the victims are affected, the Court shall permit their views and concerns to be presented and considered at stages of the proceedings determined to be appropriate by the Court and in a manner which is not prejudicial to or inconsistent with the rights of the accused and a fair and impartial trial. Such views and concerns may be presented by the legal representatives of the victims where the Court considers it appropriate, in accordance with the Rules of Procedure and Evidence."

2. GENDER-BASED CRIMES: DEFINITION AND CHARGES

2.1. INTRODUCTION

There have been various judicial efforts to give meaning to the notion of sexual violence in international law. A classic definition was elucidated by Chamber I of the ICTR in *The Prosecutor v. Jean-Paul Akayesu*.[5] In that case, the tribunal emphasized that rape as "non-consensual sexual intercourse", as traditionally defined under domestic jurisdictions, was too narrow a definition. Instead, the ICTR defined rape as "a physical invasion of a sexual nature, committed on a person under circumstances which are coercive". It went on to define sexual violence, which is broader than rape, as "any act of a sexual nature which is committed on a person under circumstances which are coercive. Sexual violence is not limited to physical invasion of a human body and may also consist of acts that do not include penetration or even physical contact".[6] In interpreting Article 3 of its Statute, the ICTR added that to constitute a crime against humanity, this act must be committed as part of a widespread or systematic attack on a civilian population on certain catalogued discriminatory grounds; namely national, ethnic, political, racial, or religious grounds.[7] The 1998 *Akayesu* description of sexual violence was a crucial expansion of the restrictive traditional ambits of the offence in several national jurisdictions.

The *Akayesu* definition of sexual violence was further elaborated upon in jurisprudence like *Furundzija*.[8] The Trial Chamber defended the view that international criminal rules punish any serious sexual assault short of actual penetration, with the observation that the prohibition of sexual violence in international law embraces all serious abuses of a sexual nature inflicted upon the physical and moral integrity of a person by means of coercion, threat of force or intimidation in a way that is degrading and humiliating for the victim's dignity.[9] In this particular case, the sexual assaults were committed in front of on looking soldiers who laughed at what was going on. The Tribunal found these events to be outrages of the personal dignity and sexual integrity of the victim.[10] *Furundzija* also illustrates that rape of a single person can constitute an international crime if it is committed on a person under circumstances which are coercive.

---

5   *The Prosecutor v. Jean-Paul Akayesu*, Judgment, Case No. ICTR-96–4-T, 2 September 1998.
6   *Idem*, para. 598.
7   *Idem*, para. 598.
8   *The Prosecutor v. Anto Furundzija*, Judgment, Case No. IT-95–17/1-T, 10 December 1998.
9   *Idem*, para. 186.
10   *Idem*, para. 272.

In 2002, there were attempts to reinforce in international law the application of the traditional consent based definition of rape as used in many national laws by the Trial Chamber of the ICTY, with affirmation by the Appeals Chamber in the case of *Kunarac et al.*[11] These were however neutralized by the finding of the Appeals Chamber of the ICTR in the case of *Gacumbitsi* in 2006, that the definition of rape is not limited to acts of penetration of the victim's vagina by the perpetrator with his genitals or with any other object.[12] This could be interpreted as including any other acts of a sexual nature hence reinstating the *Akayesu* holding. As well as addressing the role of consent in defining and proving rape at trial, the Appeals Chamber in *Gacumbitsi* also considered appeals of fact on specific allegations of rape, providing guidance on establishing crime base and linkage evidence to hold superiors responsible for rape under individual and command responsibility theory (Cole 2008). For purposes of the Rome Statute, sexual violence, when committed as part of a wide spread or systematic attack directed against any civilian population constitutes a crime against humanity.[13] Likewise, it would be a war crime; if it took place in the context of and was associated with an international or non-international armed conflict.[14] Forms of sexual violence under the Statute include rape, sexual slavery, enforced prostitution, forced pregnancy, enforced sterilization, or any other form of sexual violence of comparable gravity.[15] It is important to note that unlike under the Statute of the ICTR, proof of discriminatory grounds is not necessary for sexual violence to constitute a crime against humanity under the Rome Statute.[16] Article 7 of the Rome Statute however introduces an element of 'with knowledge of the attack'; it therefore requires that the perpetrator must commit the acts with knowledge of the broader widespread or systematic attack on the civilian population.[17]

---

[11]   *The Prosecutor v. Kunarac et al.*, Appeals Judgment, Case No. IT-96–23, 12 June 2002, paras. 127 and 128. The Appeals Chamber reaffirmed the Trial Chamber's conclusion that the *actus reus* of the crime of rape in international law is constituted by the sexual penetration, however slight of the vagina or anus of the victim by the penis of the perpetrator or any other object used by the perpetrator, where such penetration occurs without the consent of the victim.

[12]   *The Prosecutor v. Sylvestre Gacumbitsi*, Appeals Judgment, Case No. ICTR-2001–64-A, 7 July 2006.

[13]   Article 7(1) Rome Statute.

[14]   See Article 8(2)(b)(xxii) Rome Statute, Article 4 (2)(e) of Additional Protocol II to the Geneva Conventions of 1977 and Article 8(2)(a) Rome Statute.

[15]   See Article 7(1)(g) Rome Statute and the provisions on war crimes.

[16]   Article 3(g) of the ICTR Statute reads as follows: "The International Tribunal for Rwanda shall have the power to prosecute persons responsible for the following crimes when committed as part of a widespread or systematic attack against any civilian population on national, political, ethnic, racial or religious grounds: rape".

[17]   As was held in *The Prosecutor v. Tadic*, Opinion and Judgment, Case No. IT-94–1-T, 7 May 1997, para. 656.

For the first time in history, the crimes of sexual slavery, forced pregnancy, and gender-based persecution have been specifically codified in an international treaty. The inclusion of these crimes in the jurisdictional section of the Statute represents a historic development against the backdrop of the international community's inadequate treatment of crimes of sexual violence under international law. (Lee 1999, 364)

2.2. CHARGES FOR GENDER-BASED CRIMES IN THE CASES BEFORE THE ICC

The Court has currently five situations under review: Uganda, Darfur (Sudan), DRC, The Central African Republic (CAR) and Kenya. Besides these situations there are a total of ten cases pending. Four of the cases stem from Darfur. Three of the six suspects in the Darfur cases are charged with sexual violence: Mr. Harun, Mr. Kushayb and the President of Sudan, Omar Hassan Ahmad Al Bashir. All of them are still at large. The three other Darfurian suspects have voluntarily responded to summons to appear before the Court.

One case stems from the CAR: the case against Jean-Pierre Bemba Gombo who is charged with crimes of sexual violence and is currently detained in The Hague.

Four cases are originating from the DRC with a total of five suspects of whom three are charged with crimes of sexual violence: Mr. Katanga, Mr. Ngudjolo Chui and Mr. Mbarushimana. All three are detained in The Hague. The fourth, Mr. Lubanga Dyilo, is also detained in The Hague, but not charged with sexual violence.[18] The fifth, non-sexual violence, suspect is still at large.

The last case originates from Northern Uganda: the case against Joseph Kony *et al.* In this case the Court has issued five outstanding arrest warrants for leaders of the rebel group the *Lord's Resistance Army* (LRA), but only two suspects have been charged with rape: Mr. Kony and Mr. Otti.

In the following subsections the focus will be on situations and cases in which crimes of sexual violence were either part of the indictment, or the subject of an application by third parties requesting the Trial Chamber to change the legal characterization of the facts and supplement the charges accordingly.

2.2.1. *Prosecutor v. Lubanga*

At the ICC, Pre-Trial Chamber I made a decision on the Prosecutor's application for a warrant of arrest against Thomas Lubanga Dyilo in which it agreed to issue a sealed arrest warrant against Lubanga for alleged war crimes committed by

---

[18]   During the course of trial, the Prosecution though not charging the accused with sexual violence, has argued that acts of sexual violence were perpetrated through girl soldiers.

Lubanga's *Union des Patriotes Congolais* (UPC) in the Ituri region of the DRC.[19] The Prosecution alleged that the Military wing of UPC, the *Forces Patriotiques pour la Libération du Congo* (FPLC), conscripted and enlisted children under the age of fifteen and used them to participate actively in hostilities, during which time Lubanga was the head of the UPC and the commander-in-chief of the FPLC. These actions, the Prosecution alleged, constitute war crimes under Article 8(2)(b)(xxvi)[20] or Article 8(2)(e)(vii)[21] of the Rome Statute.

In its decision on the Confirmation of Charges of 29 January 2007[22], the Pre-Trial Chamber found *inter alia* that there was sufficient evidence to establish substantial grounds to believe that Lubanga is responsible as a co-perpetrator for the charges of enlisting and conscripting children under the age of 15 years into the FPLC and using them actively to participate in hostilities within the meaning of Articles 8(2)(b)xxvi and 25(3)(a)[23] of the Rome Statue between early September 2002 and 2 June 2003; and that there was sufficient evidence to establish substantial grounds to believe that Lubanga is responsible as a co-perpetrator for the charges of enlisting and conscripting children under the age of 15 years into the FPLC and using them actively to participate in hostilities within the meaning of Articles 8(2)(e)(vii) and 25(3)(a) of the Rome Statute between early September 2002 and 13 August 2003.

The Prosecutor however emphasized that his decision does not exclude that he may continue his investigation into crimes allegedly committed by Thomas Lubanga after the close of the present proceedings. In the event that additional investigations establish reasonable grounds to believe that Lubanga is criminally responsible for additional crimes, the Prosecutor retains the right to apply to the

---

19   See *The Prosecutor v. Lubanga*, Decision on the Prosecutor's Application for a Warrant of Arrest, Pre-Trial Chamber, Case No. ICC-01/04–01/06, 10 February 2006; See also *The Prosecutor v. Lubanga*, Decision Concerning Pre-Trial Chamber I's Decision of 10 February 2006, Pre-Trial Chamber, ICC-01/04–01/06-8-Corr, 24 February 2006; and *The Prosecutor v. Lubanga*, Decision to Unseal the Warrant of Arrest, Pre-Trial Chamber, ICC-01/04–01/06–37, 17 March 2006.

20   The Article reads: "Conscripting or enlisting children under the age of fifteen years into the national armed forces or using them to participate actively in hostilities". The crime is categorized as a serious violation of the laws and customs applicable in international armed conflict, within the established framework of international law.

21   The Article reads: "Conscripting or enlisting children under the age of fifteen years into the armed forces or groups or using them to participate actively in hostilities". The crime is categorized as a serious violation of the laws and customs applicable in non-international armed conflict, within the established framework of international law.

22   *The Prosecutor v. Lubanga*, Decision on the Confirmation of Charges, Pre-Trial Chamber I, Case No. ICC-01/04–10/06–803, 29 January 2007.

23   The Article reads: "In accordance with this Statute, a person shall be criminally responsible and liable for punishment for a crime within the jurisdiction of the Court if that person: (a) commits such a crime, whether as an individual, jointly with another or through another person, regardless of whether that other person is criminally responsible (…)".

Pre-Trial Chamber for a new warrant of arrest or to submit further documents containing the charges for confirmation by the Pre-Trial Chamber.[24]

Nevertheless, the restrictive nature of the charges brought by the Prosecution and the consequent confirmation decision was met with criticism by international and local NGOs and human rights organizations.[25] One of the primary reasons being that the widespread acts of sexual violence perpetrated during the conflict within the time frame referred to in the confirmation decision, was not reflected in the charges against the accused and this constituted a particular challenge to victims of sexual violence. However the Prosecutor did make a reference to these acts in his opening statement on January 26, 2009.[26] Stating "Lubanga's group recruited, trained and used hundreds of children to kill, pillage and rape". In doing so he fuelled victims' hopes unnecessarily. As it turned out, the charges remained restricted to recruiting and deploying child soldiers (Flint & De Waal 2009).

During the course of the trial, the Legal Representatives of victims and indeed one of the Judges of the trial, actively questioned the witnesses on cruel and inhumane acts to which they were subjected as well as acts of sexual violence and slavery perpetrated against the victims who were child soldiers. The accumulation of the evidence from the former child soldiers led the Legal Representatives of victims to file a joint application requesting the Trial Chamber to change the legal characterization of the facts and supplement the charges against Lubanga to include inhumane treatment and sexual slavery.[27] They referred to UN reports that showed that FPLC child soldiers were exposed to hard labour, food rations, gruelling punishment and that girls in particular were recruited by the militia as sex slaves (Senier 2010).[28]

Under Regulation 55, the Chamber has the power and authority to change the legal characterization of facts to accord with crimes under Articles 6, 7 and 8 of the Rome Statute or to accord with the form of participation of the accused in the said crimes under Articles 25 and 28 of the Rome Statute without exceeding the facts and circumstances described in the charges and any amendments to the charges. While sub regulation (2) allows a Chamber to change the legal

---

24 See *The Prosecutor v. Lubanga,* Prosecutor's Further Investigation, Pre-Trial Chamber I, ICC-01/04–01/06–170, 28 June 2006, para. 10.

25 Katy Glassborrow, Institute for War & Peace Reporting, *Call for Lubanga Charges to Cover Rape,* 12 May 2008.

26 *The Prosecutor v. Lubanga,* Opening Statement of the Prosecutor, Case No. ICC-01/04–01/06, 26 January 2009.

27 *The Prosecutor v. Lubanga,* Joint Application of the Legal Representatives of the Victims for the Implementation of the Procedure under Regulation 55 of the Regulations of the Court, Pre-Trial Chamber I, Case No. ICC-01/04–01/06–1891, 22 May 2009.

28 *Idem,* para. 23 (quoting Special Report on the Events in Ituri, January 2002 – December 2003, UN Doc S/2004/573, 16 July 2004, para. 147) and para. 29 (quoting "Written Submissions of the United Nations Special Representative of the Secretary General on Children and Armed Conflict Submitted in application of Rule 103 of the Rules of Procedure and Evidence," 18 March 2008, para. 26).

characterization "at any time during the trial", sub regulation (3) only requires that for such purposes, the defence be granted adequate "time and facilities for (…) effective preparation".

The majority in the Trial Chamber of the *Lubanga* Case gave notice to the parties and participants in the proceedings that the legal characterization of the facts may be subject to change.[29] In their view, Regulation 55(1) allowed for legal re-characterizations of facts at the decision stage, provided that the factual basis for such re-characterizations does not extend beyond the facts set forth in the charges. However, since sub-regulation (2) does not provide any definitive limitation to the legal characterization of facts and circumstances described in the charges, such re-characterization under Regulation 55(2) can exceed the factual scope of the charges. The minority opinion by Judge Adrian Fulford opposed this decision and ruled instead that the majority's decision rests upon facts beyond the scope for the charges which was as a result contrary to the intent and express language of Article 74(2) of the Rome Statute.[30] He further found that the changes proposed by the victims were predicated upon new crimes as well as new modes of liability which will deprive the accused of adequate notice to prepare his defence and which will impinge on his rights enshrined under international human rights instruments (Senier 2010).[31]

Both the Prosecution and Defence appealed the decision. In its decision reversing the Trial Chamber, the Appeals Chamber ruled that Regulations 55(2) and (3) set out measures protecting the rights of the accused in order to ensure that final judgments were not entered based on facts which were introduced into the trial through legal re-characterization without being included in the charges. It ruled that such a travesty of justice will run against the spirit and intent of Article 74(2) of the Rome Statute. The Appeals Chamber further found that the Trial Chamber's reading of Regulation 55 was also contrary to Article 61(9)[32] of the Rome Statute. In its opinion, new charges may only be added pursuant to a new confirmation hearing and the introduction of such new facts and

---

29   *The Prosecutor v. Lubanga*, Decision Giving Notice to the Parties and Participants that the Legal Characterisation of the Facts may be Subject to Change in Accordance with Regulation 55(2) of the Regulations of the Court, Trial Chamber I, Case No. ICC-01/04–01/06–2049, 14 July 2009.

30   Article 74(2) Rome Statute states: "The decision shall not exceed the facts and circumstances described in the charges and any amendments to the charges."

31   *The Prosecutor v. Lubanga*, Minority Opinion on the Decision Giving Notice to the Parties and Participants that the Legal Characterisation of the Facts may be Subject to Change in Accordance with Regulation 55(2) of the Regulations of the Court, Trial Chamber I, Case No. ICC-01/04–01/06–2049, 17 July 2009.

32   This Article reads: "After the charges are confirmed and before the trial has begun, the prosecutor may, with the permission of the Pre-Trial Chamber and after notice to the accused, amend the charges. If the Prosecutor seeks to add additional charges or to substitute more serious charges, a hearing under this article to confirm those charges must be held. After commencement of the trial, the Prosecutor may, with the permission of the Trial Chamber withdraw the charges."

circumstances during a process of legal re-characterization would empower a trial chamber to extend the trial beyond the facts alleged by the Prosecutor. This, the Appeals Chamber ruled, would be "contrary to the distribution of powers under the Statute".[33] The Appeals Chamber discountenanced the Trial Chamber's attempt at clarifying the scope of facts it would consider during re-characterization, finding such clarifications to be of "questionable legality".[34] Although, it was eventually thrown out, this attempt by the victims presents a definitive attempt to further introduce a stronger gender perspective to the issue of charging practise before the Court.

2.2.2. Prosecutor v. Katanga et al.

Contrary to the Lubanga case, the Prosecution in the Katanga/Ngudjolo case has charged Mr. Germaine Katanga and Mr. Ngudjolo Chui, with nine counts of war crimes (comprising sexual slavery and rape) and four counts of crimes against humanity (comprising sexual slavery and rape). They are both members of the *Force de Résistance Patriotique en Ituri* (FRPI) militia, a Beni based armed militia and political party in the Ituri province of North-eastern DRC. The FRPI was established in November 2002 from Ngiti ethnic group as an ally to the Lendu Nationalist and Integration Front (FNI). On 26 September 2008, Pre-Trial Chamber I confirmed all counts of gender-based crimes both as a crime against humanity and a war crime. In its ruling, the majority of the Pre-Trial Chamber confirmed that there is sufficient evidence to establish substantial grounds to believe that Katanga and Ngudjolo Chui, during and after the 24 February 2003 attack on Bogoro, jointly committed through other persons, within the meaning of Article 25(3)(a) of the Statute, the war crimes of sexual slavery and rape under Article 8(2)(b)(xxii) of the Statute. The majority of the Chamber further confirmed that there was sufficient evidence to establish substantial grounds to believe that the accused persons jointly committed through other persons, within the meaning of Article 25(3)(a) of the Statute, the crimes against humanity of rape and sexual slavery under Article 7(1)(g) of the Statute, as part of a widespread and systematic attack against the civilian population in the Ituri region.[35]

---

[33] *The Prosecutor v. Lubanga*, Appeals Chamber Judgment on the Legal Characterisation of the Facts, Appeals Chamber, Case No. ICC-01/04–01/06–2093, 7 December 2009, para. 94.

[34] *Idem*, para. 92.

[35] See *The Prosecutor v. Germain Katanga and Mathieu Ngudjolo Chui*, Decision on the Confirmation of Charges, Pre-Trial Chamber I, Case No. ICC-01/04–01/07–717, 30 September 2009.

2.2.3. Prosecutor v. Mbarushimana

Mr. Callixte Mbarushimana, alleged Executive Secretary of the *Forces Démocratiques pour la Libération du Rwanda – Forces Combattantes Abacunguzi* (FDLR-FCA) since July 2007, is held criminally responsible, under Article 25(3)(d) of the Rome Statute, for five counts of crimes against humanity (comprising rape) and six counts of war crimes (comprising rape).[36] Mbarushimana was arrested on 11 October 2010 in France after the ICC unsealed a warrant for his arrest issued in September of the same year. On 3 November 2010, a Paris Court approved Mbarushimana's extradition to the custody of the Court.[37]

2.2.4. Prosecutor v. Jean-Pierre Bemba Gombo

In the case against *Jean-Pierre Bemba Gombo* in the CAR, Pre-Trial Chamber I issued a warrant of arrest[38] holding him criminally responsible, jointly with another person or through other persons under Article 25(3)(a) of the Statute, for rape as a crime against humanity, punishable under Article 7(1)(g) of the Statute and rape as a war crime, punishable under Article 8(2)(e)(vi) of the Statute. At the confirmation hearings held from 12 to 15 January 2009, Prosecution led evidence to show the nexus between the acts of rape and the attack in order to show that acts of rape were committed by the *Movement for the Liberation of the Congo* (MLC) troops as part of a widespread or systematic attack directed against the CAR civilian population. The MLC used to be a rebel group that fought the government throughout the Second Congo War. It subsequently took part in the transitional government and is now the main opposition party.

In the confirmation decision,[39] the Pre-Trial Chamber having reviewed the disclosed evidence, and in particular, the statements of direct witnesses found that there is sufficient evidence to establish that multiple acts of rape were carried out by MLC soldiers in the context of war crimes and crimes against humanity. The Chamber ruled that it had substantial grounds to believe that Bemba is criminally responsible as a person effectively acting as military commander within the meaning of Article 28(a) of the Statute and charged him, besides rape,

---

[36] ICC Press Release, *Callixte Mbarushimana Arrested in France for Crimes Against Humanity and War Crimes Allegedly Committed in the Kivus (Democratic Republic of the Congo)*, Doc. No ICC-CPI-20101011-PR581, 11 October 2010.

[37] The Hague Justice Portal, *ICC War Crimes Suspect Arrested in Paris: FDLR Leader Callixte Mbarushimana has been Arrested by French Authorities*, 11 October 2010; The Hague Justice Portal, *French Court Approves Mbarushimana Extradition: A Paris Appeals Court has Approved the Extradition of an Accused Rwandan Rebel Leader to the ICC*, 3 November 2010.

[38] *The Prosecutor v. Germain Katanga and Mathieu Ngudjolo Chui*, Warrant of Arrest for Germain Katanga, Pre-Trial Chamber I, Case No. ICC-01/04–01/07–1, 2 July 2007.

[39] See *The Prosecutor v. Jean Pierre Bemba Gombo*, Decision on the Confirmation of Charges, Pre-Trial Chamber II, Case No. ICC-01/05–01/08–424, 15 June 2009.

with 1) count of crimes against humanity (murder) and 2) counts of war crimes (murder and pillaging).

Pre-Trial Chamber II further determined that there was insufficient evidence to establish substantial grounds to believe that Bemba had the necessary criminal intent within the meaning of Article 30 of the Statute to be individually criminally responsible as a co-perpetrator for crimes against humanity and war crimes as referred to in the Prosecutor's amended Document Containing the Charges, which he allegedly committed jointly with the former President of the CAR (1993–2003) Ange-Félix Patassé using MLC troops. Pre-Trial Chamber II also declined to confirm charges of torture as a war crime and torture as a crime against humanity as well as outrages against personal dignity. With respect to rape and sexual violence committed by Bemba's troops against the CAR civilian population, the Prosecution laid multiple, different, charges for what were in most instances the same underlying acts. Thus certain acts of rape were charged as rape, torture (both as a war crime and a crime against humanity), and outrages on personal dignity (as a war crime). The rationale behind such an approach is that it serves to recognize the full breadth of the harm caused by rape.

The Women's Initiative for Gender Justice (WIGJ) submitted its own observations in a *Amicus Curiae* in which it stated that the rights of the accused are not violated when crimes alleged are properly deemed cumulative, meaning within the prescriptions of the test as provided by the *Delalic*[40] case in the ICTY. WIGJ proceeded by arguing that in national courts, as long as a charge has a sufficient evidentiary basis, the determination of whether charges are cumulative can occur at the end of trial, after the judge's deliberation results in a conviction. In such proceedings it is not inimical to the due process rights of the accused, which remain safeguarded throughout the trial. Upon a finding of guilt, cumulative convictions are impermissible, but at the charging stage, whether charges are cumulative or not, their inclusion in the indictment does not violate fair trial practices.[41]

The Chamber, however, felt that in some instances, the Prosecution's approach constituted impermissible cumulative charging, and in other instances that the Prosecution didn't provide enough facts in its Amended Document Containing the Charges to put the Defence on notice. As a result, they confirmed the rape

---

[40]   *The Prosecutor v Delalic et al.*, Appeals Judgment, Case No. IT-96-21-A, 20 February 2001, para. 412.

[41]   *The Prosecutor v. Bemba*, Amicus Curiae Observations of the Women Initiatives for Gender Justice pursuant to Rule 103 of the Rules of Procedure and Evidence, Pre-Trial Chamber II, Case No. ICC-01/05-01/08-466, 31 July 2009, paras. 21 and 22.

charges, but refused to confirm the torture charges and the charge of outrages upon personal dignity.[42] In its 18 September 2009 decision[43]

> the Pre-Trial Chamber confirms its reasoning in its 15 June 2009 confirmation of charges decision, explaining that the 'essence' of the charges of torture and outrages upon personal dignity are fully subsumed by the charge of rape. The Chamber had decided not to confirm the two charges because, it reasoned, these counts did not possess a distinct legal element to the crime of rape, and because the Prosecutor relied on the same evidence pertaining to acts of rape to support all of the charges. The Chamber saw these charges as therefore 'cumulative' to the charge of rape, and prejudicial to the rights of the accused.[44]

2.2.5. Prosecutor v. Harun and Kushayb

In the Darfur situation, the Pre-Trial Chamber issued a warrant of arrest against both Ahmad Muhammad Harun, State Minister for Humanitarian Affairs for Sudan, and Ali Kushayb, alleged Janjaweed leader, charging them with, *inter alia*, two counts of rape as a crime against humanity and two counts of rape as a war crime. According to the Chamber, there are reasonable grounds to believe that the *Sudanese Armed Forces* (SAF) and the Militia/Janjaweed, acting together as part of the counter-insurgency campaign, carried out several attacks on the towns of Kodoom, Bindisi, Mukjar, Arawala and surrounding areas over an extensive period of time running at least between 2003 and 2004. During these attacks the SAF and Janjaweed committed murders, rapes and outrages upon the personal dignity of women and girls.[45] The arrest warrants for both Ahmad Harun and Ali Kushayb are still outstanding.

2.2.6. Prosecutor v. Omar Al Bashir

The Prosecutor on 14 July 2008 submitted to Pre-Trial Chamber I an application for a warrant of arrest against the President of Sudan, Omar Hassan Ahmad Al Bashir ('Al Bashir'), in his personal capacity under Article 25(3)(a) for

---

[42] *The Prosecutor v. Bemba*, Decision Confirming the Charges, Pre-Trial Chamber II, Case No. ICC-01/05–01/08–424, 15 June 2009, paras. 185, 190, 302.

[43] *The Prosecutor v. Bemba*, Application for Leave to Appeal the "Decision Pursuant to Article 61(7)(a) and (b) of the Rome Statute on the Charges of the Prosecutor Against Jean-Pierre Bemba Gombo", Pre-Trial Chamber II, Case No. ICC-01/05–01/08–532, 18 September 2009.

[44] Women's Initiatives for Gender Justice, *Making a Statement: A Review of Charges and Prosecutions for Gender-based Crimes before the International Criminal Court*, 2nd edition, February 2010, p. 1, available at www.iccwomen.org/publications/articles/docs/MaS22–10web.pdf.

[45] *The Prosecutor v. Harun and Kushayb*, Decision on the Prosecution's Application for a Warrant of Arrest against Ahmad Muhammad Harun and Ali Muhammad Ali Abd-Al-Rahman, Pre-Trial Chamber I, Case No. ICC-02/05–01/07–3, 27 April 2007.

commission of crimes through members of the state apparatus, the army and the Militia/Janjaweed. The arrest warrant under Article 58 contains among others, the following counts:

- Count 2 for Genocide against the Fur, Masalit and Zaghawa ethnic groups by using the state apparatus, the Armed Forces and Militia/Janjaweed, to cause serious bodily or mental harm through acts of rape, other forms of sexual violence, torture and forcible displacement, with intent to destroy the groups.
- Count 8 for Crime Against Humanity for rape of women and girls including but not limited to women and girls in Bindisi, Arawala, Shataya, Kailek, Silea, and Sirba and IDP camps.

The Prosecution alleged that the manner in which the attacks were carried out undermined the capacity of the protected group in Darfur to survive. The attacks on the women and girls often had the impact of making them outcasts in their own society, and of making marriage almost impossible. Furthermore, bearing the children of their attackers resulted in the dilution of their ethnicity and the potential of those children growing up to be outcasts. The pervasive rape and sexual violence against young girls and women wrought physical and psychological damage on the victims and ravaged family and community bonds, with devastating social consequences.[46]

On 4 March 2009 the Pre-Trial Chamber granted the application of the Prosecution for the issuance of a warrant of arrest against the suspect but without granting the charge of genocide.[47] Pursuant to the appeal by the Prosecutor, the Appeals Chamber ruled that the Pre-Trial Chamber had applied an incorrect standard of proof when disposing of the Prosecutor's application for an arrest warrant. The Appeals Chamber found that demanding that the existence of genocidal intent must be the only reasonable conclusion amounts to requiring the Prosecutor to disprove any other reasonable conclusions and to eliminate any reasonable doubt.[48] The Appeals Chamber found this standard of proof to be too demanding at the arrest warrant stage, which is governed by Article 58 of the Rome Statute which amounted to an error of law.

On 12 July 2010, the Pre-Trial Chamber issued a second warrant of arrest against Al Bashir, considering that there are reasonable grounds to believe he is responsible for three counts of genocide, that include: genocide by killing, genocide by causing serious bodily or mental harm and genocide by deliberately

---

[46] *The Prosecutor v. Omar Hassan Ahmad Al Bashir*, Decision on the Prosecution's Application for a Warrant of Arrest against Omar Hassan Ahmad Al Bashir, Pre-Trial Chamber I, Case No. ICC-02/05–01/09–3, 4 March 2009, para. 106.

[47] *Ibidem.*

[48] *The Prosecutor v. Omar Hassan Ahmad Al Bashir*, Judgement on the Appeal of the Prosecutor against the "Decision on the Prosecution's Application for a Warrant of Arrest against Omar Hassan Ahmad Al Bashir", Appeals Chamber, Case No. ICC-02/05–01/09, 3 February 2010.

inflicting on each target group conditions of life calculated to bring about the group's physical destruction.[49] In effect, the warrant of arrest against Al Bashir charges him with gender-based crimes for which he will be answerable when the arrest warrant is eventually executed.

The warrant of arrest against Al Bashir, including counts of genocide, demonstrates a clearer charging strategy (De Brouwer 2009). The document states that attacks aimed at civilians are exemplified "by the systematic raping of women".

> *Rape and gang rape are allegedly used as a weapon of destruction and thousands of women and girls belonging to the target groups were raped in all three States of Darfur (...) since 2003. Girls, as young as 5, have been raped. A third of the victims of rape are children.*

The charging document also has a specific section on "Massive rapes causing serious bodily and mental harm" where the rape and sexual violence experienced by women and children and their impact on their lives and on their communities is detailed. The section asserts that "Rape is an integral part of the pattern of destruction" and quotes from the ICTR in the *Akayesu* case, that rape is used to "kill the will, the spirit, and life itself". In establishing genocide, the filing states, "the magnitude of the rapes and sexual assaults (...) indicates an intent to destroy the target groups (...)". It also quotes the denials of rape by Al Bashir and states that imposing conditions "calculated to bring about the physical destruction of the target groups, if combined with a studied misinformation campaign, was an efficient strategy to achieve complete destruction".[50]

2.2.7. Prosecutor v. Joseph Kony et al.

In the Uganda situation, in the case against *Joseph Kony et al.*, the Court has issued five arrest warrants for leaders of the rebel group the Lord's Resistance Army, but only two have been charged with rape. Joseph Kony is charged with thirty-three counts (on the basis of his individual criminal responsibility under Articles 25(3)(a) and 25(3)(b) of the Statute) including:

- Twelve counts of crimes against humanity including Article 7(1)(g): sexual enslavement; Article 7(1)(g): rape; Article 7(1)(k): inhumane acts of inflicting serious bodily injury and suffering, and;
- Twenty-one counts of war crimes including Article 8(2)(e)(v): inducing rape; and Article 8(2)(e)(vi): forced enlistment of children.

---

[49]   *The Prosecutor v. Omar Hassan Ahmad Al Bashir*, Second Warrant of Arrest for Omar Hassan Ahmad Al Bashir, Pre-Trial Chamber I, Case No. ICC-02/05–01/09–95, 12 July 2010.

[50]   Women's Initiatives for Gender Justice, *Eye on the ICC*, 3rd edition, 17 June 2008, p. 4.

Similarly in the same case, Vincent Otti is charged with thirty-two counts on the basis of his individual criminal responsibility (Article 25(3)(b) of the Statute) including:

– Eleven counts of crimes against humanity including sexual enslavement (Article 7(1)(g)) and;
– Twenty-one counts of war crimes including inducing rape (Article 8(2)(e) (vi)).

To date, none of the named suspects have been arrested and brought before the Court and therefore proceedings have not advanced beyond the pre-trial phase.

2.3. FINAL REMARKS

Overall, gender-based crimes have been charged in the Sudan, CAR, Uganda and DRC situations, and the recent charging strategy appeared to be bolder than the previous charging pattern by the Prosecution.[51] Recent attempts of the Prosecution to lay different charges in respect of rape and sexual violence in *Bemba*, served as recognition of the harm caused by rape. However women's rights organisations expected a wider range of charging than finally allowed by the judges in the *Bemba* case, "to reflect the purpose and impact of sexualised violence including, but not limited to rape".[52] In order to determine whether more in-depth progress in the field of international criminal law and gender justice will be accomplished, the outcome of the ongoing cases needs to be awaited.

---

[51] Women's Initiatives for Gender Justice, *Gender Report Card 2009 on the International Criminal Court*, 2009, p. 52, available at www.iccwomen.org/news/docs/GRC09_web-2-10. pdf.

[52] Women's Initiatives for Gender Justice, *Making a Statement: A Review of Charges and Prosecutions for Gender-based Crimes before the International Criminal Court*, 2nd edition, February 2010, p. 38 (available at www.iccwomen.org/publications/articles/docs/MaS22– 10web.pdf): "The legal rights of women in CAR are limited and convictions for rape are few. While we hope the decision by the ICC to prosecute rape may assist in the future prosecution of non-conflict related rape by the national judiciary, as an international institution with significant resources at its disposal, we expected a wider range of charging by the ICC to reflect the purpose and impact of sexualised violence including, but not limited to, rape."

3. THE VARIOUS FORMS OF ASSISTANCE TO VICTIMS UNDER THE LEGAL TEXT OF THE COURT AND RELATED CHALLENGES

3.1. INTRODUCTION

The legal text of the Court provides for various forms of assistance to victims without necessarily differentiating between the two types: victims who have been granted the procedural status as victim in a case and those who are merely victims in the broader context of the crimes committed in a specific situation which is under the jurisdiction of the Court. The modalities of victim participation can take different forms and are still in the process of development. At the earliest stages within a situation the Statute and Rules of Procedure and Evidence (RPE) enable victims to pass information on crimes to the Prosecutor and to make representations to the Prosecutor and the Court bearing on their interests. In the DRC Situation Pre-Trial Chamber I allowed six victims to participate in the investigation stage of the DRC by "presenting their views and concerns", "file documents" and "request the Pre-Trial Chamber to order specific measures".[53] In the *Lubanga* case the Pre-Trial Chamber I further defined the modalities of victim participation.[54]

> *The Chamber held that for this stage of proceedings, the pre-trial phase, non-communication of the three victims' identities to the Defence was the only protective measure available to protect the victims, but also warned against anonymous accusations. As such victims could participate anonymously, but without introducing new facts or evidence or questioning witnesses. In particular, Pre-Trial Chamber I decided that legal representatives would have access to public documents and to status conferences and parts of the confirmation hearings which are held in public. Victims' representatives were, furthermore, to make opening and closing statements and request leave to intervene, to be decided on a case-by-case basis.* (Groenhuijsen & De Brouwer 2010, 278)

In order to assist the victims in acting out these various modalities of participation, the Court provides victims support that varies from assistance with the application for participation to the formal notification rights for victims having communicated with the Court, as well as providing information in general to the victims. The Court also renders assistance in the protection and

---

[53] *Situation in the DRC*, Decision on the Applications for Participation in the Proceedings of VPRS 1, VPRS 2, VPRS 3, VPRS 4, VPRS 5, VPRS 6, Pre-Trial Chamber I, Case No. ICC-01/04–101-tEN-Corr, 17 January 2006, p. 42.

[54] See *The Prosecutor v. Lubanga*, Decision on the Arrangements for the Participation of Victims, Pre-Trial Chamber I, Case No. ICC-01/04–01/06, 22 September 2006, p. 6.

security measures provided for victims as well as in the choosing of common legal representatives for the victims.

In the following subsections, the various forms of assistance to victims under the legal text of the Court will be further discussed: victim participation, notification, protection measures and the choosing of common legal representatives.

3.2. VICTIM PARTICIPATION

For the application to participate in the proceedings, the Court provides a set of guidelines the victim has to satisfy when making the application in writing.[55] These same guidelines are applicable for the reparations procedure.[56] The Court ensures, through the VPRS and the Public Information and Documentation Section (PIDS) that the application forms are available to the victims on the field along with a booklet explaining the contents of the form and how it is to be filled. VPRS has also been alive to its responsibility in ensuring that the forms are filled correctly by the victims to avoid the applications been rejected or deferred by the Judges.[57]

By the end of 2009, the Court had received a total of 1814 applications from victims seeking to participate in its proceedings of whom only 771 victims have been recognized by the ICC to participate (De Brouwer & Groenhuijsen 2009). As recently as October 2009, the considerable length of the form (17 pages) and the amount of details needed in order to complete the application form was problematic for many victims.[58] Especially since the majority of them are poor, illiterate and living in camps or conditions where access to information about the Court is often limited or non-existent. Furthermore, victims are hampered by a lack of knowledge of the justice system or even the capacity to make any informed choice on the available justice mechanism.

Nothing in the form for participation exclusively distinguishes the victims of sexual violence except the content of the application when describing the incident that occurred to the victim and the person most responsible for the harm suffered. In addition, according to the 2009 Gender Report Card on the ICC, only one third of the 1814 victims are women.[59] Statistics, which confirm that women still need to be further, sensitised on their role before the Court (Kielburger, Craig & Kielburger 2009). A possible reason for this pressing necessity might be that the stigma of sexual violence can be a huge burden for

---

[55]   See Regulation 86 of the Regulations of the Court.
[56]   See Regulation 88 of the Regulations of the Court.
[57]   See Regulations 106 and 107 of the Regulations of the Registry.
[58]   Rule 59(1–2) RPE.
[59]   Women's Initiatives for Gender Justice, *Gender Report Card 2009 on the International Criminal Court*, 2009, available at www.iccwomen.org/news/docs/GRC09_web-2-10.pdf.

women in many communities, forcing them to remain silent. The majority of female victims also come from backgrounds where women are regarded as second-class citizens, meaning they are given few chances to step forward even if they wanted to.

In trying to overcome these cultural, socio-economic, judicial and even linguistic barriers, the Court has tried to engage with NGOs and intermediaries who can assist the victims in filling in the application forms as well as promoting a wider outreach to inform the population on the available opportunities to participate in the Court's processes. However, even the assistance provided by the NGOs and intermediaries, though valuable, still has shortcomings. This is clearly shown by the fact that only four victim applicants participated in the *Lubanga* confirmation of charges hearing (De Brouwer & Groenhuijsen 2009).

The Court has now been working to change the major challenge the form constitutes. A present condensed draft of seven pages, which encompasses both the participation and reparation information (a joint form), is being circulated to the necessary stakeholders to comment on its workability. It is also circulated for testing on the field, and in particular in the recent Kenya situation, before it will be adopted.

At the same time it has also been a challenge to obtain the necessary identification documents to satisfy the identification requirements set by the Court as part of the condition of determining who is a victim pursuant to rule 85(a) Rules of Procedure and Evidence. Providing documentation is a huge challenge for victims, including victims of sexual violence, in view of the fact that these are mainly areas of ongoing conflict where communication and travelling is difficult and requests for such documents from persons in such living conditions are onerous to fulfil.

Furthermore the standards used by the Pre-Trial Chamber to determine the causality link between the harm to the victim and the crimes within the jurisdiction of the court have been a generally lower threshold encompassing such grounds as "grounds to believe". However, during the reparations phase, victims will take on the full status of parties in the proceedings and in view of the material consequences which may arise as a result of such status, the standard of proof to be adopted by the court to prove identification and the substance of the claim may become much higher and prove challenging for the victims.

3.3. NOTIFICATION

Another major area of assistance to victims is in the area of notification rights of the victim in the legal texts of the Court. The rules make a distinction between the notification to be provided by the Prosecutor in the context of Article 15(6)[60] and that, which is to be provided by the Registrar within the framework of Article 19(3).[61] Rule 49 RPE mandates the Prosecutor to "promptly ensure that notice is provided". However notice requirements that request the Court to inform the victims in order to allow them to apply to participate in the proceedings pursuant to Rule 92 as well as those required to be carried out by the Prosecutor, are in reality all undertaken by the Registry. Regulation 102 of the Regulations of the Registry in particular, allows the Registry to assist the Prosecutor in providing information to victims where it intends to initiate proceedings pursuant to Article 15(3) and (6). Notification rights extend to notifying the victims when the Chamber takes decisions relevant to their interest or when a status conference is to be undertaken or trial dates are to be decided.

3.4. PROTECTION MEASURES

It is virtually impossible to conduct a case without witnesses who are in most cases also victims. This section deals with the measures that have been put in place, in order to assist a witness/victim to come forward and either apply for victim's participation or become a witness for the Prosecution (or both).

The fact that victims of gender-based crimes are still too afraid or unaware to apply for victim's status, as shown by the small number of women amongst the victims that have done so, is an indication that still a lot remains to be done in terms of outreach. All the reports of the UN Special representatives and NGOs clearly state that during wartime women are being raped on a massive scale; but few come forward. It is no surprise that one of the conclusions reached in the stocktaking on victims and affected communities during the Review Conference held in May-June 2010 in Kampala, Uganda, is that the Court's field presence and outreach activities need to be optimised to enhance the ICC's impact. The development of more effective tools and strategies to reach women, children and other vulnerable populations was stressed in particular.[62]

Under the Rome Statute protective[63] and special measures[64] are provided to victims of gender-based crimes to amongst others avoid a direct confrontation with their aggressor. The VWU in consultation with the Office of the Prosecutor (OTP) are able to provide protective measures, security arrangements,

---

60   Article 15(6) Rome Statute provides: "If, after the preliminary examination referred to in paragraphs 1 and 2, the Prosecutor concludes that the information provided does not constitute a reasonable basis for an investigation; he or she shall inform those who provided the information. This shall not preclude the Prosecutor from considering further information submitted to him or her regarding the same situation in the light of new facts or evidence."

61   Rule 59(1–2) RPE.

62   Report of the Credentials Committee, RC-11-E-011110, 16 December 2010, p. 101.

63   Rule 87(3)(c) RPE.

64   Rule 88 RPE.

counselling and other appropriate assistance for witnesses, victims and others at risk on account of their testimony. The Court takes special measure to ensure that victims of sexual violence should not suffer secondary victimization as a result of testifying. Indeed it is especially important for this type of victims, since they may find it very painful to recount the terrible details of their ordeal. In order not to increase their trauma, the Chambers of the Court allow certain protective and special measures that avoid a face-to-face confrontation with the accused in the court; restrict questioning by the parties of the victim as well as the manner of questioning of the victim in order to spare a victim from repeated questioning.

Standards of protection vary during the course of the proceedings depending on the various stages of the proceedings because of the need to balance the rights of the accused and the needs of the victims. In balancing the rights of the accused, the accused is entitled to full disclosure of materials and elements that are supporting the case or which will assist in the preparation of the defence.

As a consequence, the Chambers allow anonymity during the preliminary stage as well as the use of summaries at the confirmation of hearing stage; but afterwards the right of the accused to an equitable trial must take precedence and require that the veil of anonymity be lifted in his favour, even if the veil must continue to obstruct the view of the public and the media.[65] Victims/witnesses of sexual violence require appropriate measures for their protection because of the risks for their security and danger to which witnesses could be exposed if their identity is disclosed. Victims of sexual violence are also under the risk of re-traumatisation and rejection by the victim's family and community and the possibility to recognise the voice of the witness.[66] In both the *Lubanga* and *Katanga* cases, the Chamber has ruled that the disclosure of the witnesses' case be made at a reasonable time before the start of the trial.[67]

Similarly, because the standard of proof is lower at the stage of confirmation, the Prosecution is not obliged to produce witnesses and this serves as a measure of further protection for the witnesses, which protection is removed once the disclosure obligations are adhered to, before the commencement of the trial. Anonymity has been allowed once, in the *Tadic* decision at the ICTY, but as a rule the Tribunals have not allowed anonymous witnesses to testify before the Chambers since this might infringe with the rights of the defendant, especially

---

[65] *The Prosecutor v. Blaškic*, Decision on the Application of the Prosecutor Dated 17 October 1996 Requesting Protective Measures for Victims And Witnesses, Trial Chamber I, Case No. IT–95–14–T, 5 November 1996, para. 24.

[66] *The Prosecutor v. Sesay et al.*, Decision on Prosecution Motion for Modification of Protective Measures for Witnesses, Trial Chamber I, Case No. SCSL–04–15–T, 5 July 2004, para. 33.

[67] *The Prosecutor v. Katanga et al.*, Decision on the Request of the Legal Representative of Victim a/0333/07 for Leave to Reply the Prosecution and the Defence's Observations on the Anonymity and Modalities of Participation in the Proceedings, Pre-Trial Chamber I, Case No. ICC-01/04–01/07–434, 23 April 2008.

in view of the fact that the anonymous witness in the *Tadic* case turned out to be unreliable. In *Blaskic*, the ICTY concluded that nothing in the rules supported anonymity of witnesses at the expense of the fairness of the trial.[68] The ICC has toed the general line of international criminal justice by, so far, not allowing anonymous witnesses to testify even though the Statute and the Rules may be open to interpretation suggesting the possibility for witnesses to testify anonymously.[69]

The Trial Chamber is usually seized of the application by the Prosecution for protective measures pursuant to rule 87 once it has received all the relevant materials for the trial from the investigators and decided on its list of witnesses. The request is open to be made by any of the parties including the victims' legal representatives, and the Chamber can seek the consent of the witness in respect of which the protective measure is sought. As a rule, such requests for protective measures are made after consultations with the VWU. The measures of confidentiality to the public are an exception to Article 64(7) that provides for the trial to be conducted in public. In this regard, the Prosecution submits to the Chamber a request for protective measures that could encompass pseudonyms, redactions, voice distortion, face distortion, audio/video link as well as putting the witness in a private room to testify.[70]

Additionally the rules allow the court to provide special measures for witnesses to facilitate the testimony of a traumatized victim or witness, a child, an elderly person or victim of sexual violence pursuant to Article 68(1) and (2).[71] These special measures include the provision of psychological support for the witness like the presence of a psychologist to sit with the victim/witness as his or she testifies. The Chamber has a general duty under this rule to also ensure the witness/victim is protected, by controlling the manner of questioning so as to avoid any harassment or intimidation. This includes asking victims and witnesses of sexual violence questions that allude to their prior or subsequent sexual conduct. The Chamber also protects the witness from having visual contact with the accused as well as taking measures to ensure members of the public do not see them when they go in or out of the courtroom.

Even during the court session, the court protects any feature of the victim/witness from being visible and may enter into closed session or private session where details that may identify the witness could be elucidated whilst giving testimony.

One of the greatest challenges of protection in the cases before the ICC as well as in the International Criminal Tribunals, was the fact that in most of these

---

[68] *The Prosecutor v. Blaškic*, Decision on the Application of the Prosecutor Dated 17 October 1996 Requesting Protective Measures for Victims and Witnesses, Trial Chamber I, Case No. IT–95–14–T, 5 November 1996, paras. 39 and 40.
[69] Rules 76, 81 and 82 RPE.
[70] Rule 67 RPE.
[71] Rules 88(5) and 140(2) RPE.

areas of conflict the victims are well known to the local population such that it is possible for the victim to be targeted by the relatives, friends and supporters of the accused since her/his identity is now known to the accused and his counsel. It is possible to argue that the accused is incarcerated and so unable to access the victims/witnesses; however it is possible for the defence team investigators to instigate such information. In any case, the fact that the accused themselves are allowed to communicate and such communication is privileged makes it difficult to ascertain that the witnesses have not been ordered to be tampered with.

It can be imagined that where witnesses are in the ICC Protection Program, and defence is entitled to disclosure of their identities in order to conduct their own investigations on the witnesses, the Chamber has to make a decision on how and in what manner disclosure can be made without violating the disclosure obligations to such witnesses.

The intermediaries also constitute a challenge in ensuring the confidentiality of the identities of witnesses/victims. In particular, intermediaries do not constitute staff or personnel of the Court and are not under the same obligations nor does there exist an ICC policy on intermediaries. Usually these intermediaries are non-professional and could be subject to financial pressures or influence the testimony of the witness in an adverse manner. The intermediaries are also not subject to the same level of confidentiality as staff members of the court since they act as independent actors. In the case of victims' intermediaries for instance, it is difficult to control the information they possess about the victims. Most of these victims become prosecution witnesses and so a degree of risk occurs by engaging these intermediaries. Unfortunately it is not possible to execute most of the work of the court without the assistance of these intermediaries.

At the NGO-ICC biannual meeting at The Hague in October 2010,[72] the Court released draft guidelines for discussion governing relations between the Court and intermediaries. NGO's welcomed this development as an important step in the right direction. The guidelines "provide a useful basis upon which to establish clear mutual responsibilities and entitlements between the Court and the intermediaries".[73]

In the international criminal tribunals and even in the ICC, the defence has resource persons and investigators who go to the field and are often engaged in

---

[72]   The document is available at www.bpi-icb.com/pdf/ICCNGObiannualMeeting_Oct2010_ Outreach.pdf. The guidelines included information on how persons were selected in DRC, Kenya and Sudan. E.g. in DRC, more information was needed on the selection criteria for those who participate in outreach activities, including certain 'invitation only' events. This information should be provided directly to victims. In Kenya, persons or organizations who participate in activities are selected mostly by referrals from local organizations whilst others are selected because they have been elected as victim group leaders. In Sudan, participants are selected through the community itself, as most people will only talk to other community members.

[73]   Coalition for the International Criminal Court, *Developing an ICC Policy on Intermediaries*, p. 9–11, in: *The Monitor*, No. 41, November 2010 – April 2011.

witness tampering. This problem has been addressed by bringing disciplinary measures and in extreme cases, such investigators are fined and relieved of their position.[74]

3.5. COMMON LEGAL REPRESENTATIVES

The court is mandated to assist the victim in the choosing of Legal Representatives and in the grouping of victims according to their common interest so that they are served by common legal representation. It does this in practice when VPRS receives the applications, reviews them to determine whether they are complete or not and then forwards them to the Chambers, which then determines whether the application form meets the criteria set out in Rule 85 RPE. The Registry provides the victims with the list of counsel provided for in regulation 122 and information regarding counsel or assistants are provided in accordance with its mandate to "take(s) measures to ensure that the victim understand(s) such information". In view of the difficulties encountered by the victims in understanding the legal requirement and the technicalities of the legal process, the Court has taken concrete steps to ensure that the Registry's field officers are able to properly inform the victims on the choice of legal representation.

4. SOME PRACTICAL CHALLENGES WHEN ASSISTING VICTIMS/SURVIVORS OF SEXUAL VIOLENCE BEFORE THE COURT

4.1. LEGAL QUALIFICATION FOR VICTIMS' REPRESENTATIVE UNDER THE LEGAL TEXTS OF THE COURT

Within the RPE, Rules 20 to 22 cover the topic of legal qualification for Counsel under the chapeau of 'Counsel for the Defence'. This title may be without mentioning counsel of the victim indicative of the limited role victims and their counsel play within the ICC proceedings. Both defence and victim's counsel need to fill in the same form if they want to be included on the ICC's List of Counsel that is held by the Registry. In order to be registered before the Court, they have to establish 10 years competence in international or criminal law and procedure and possess the requisite relevant experience. In addition they need to be fluent in one of the working languages of the Court (French, English).

---

[74]   Article 70 Rome Statute; Rule 46 ICTR and ICTY RPE.

Furthermore, to qualify as Legal Assistant to Counsel, 5 years of relevant experience in criminal proceedings is the minimum required qualification. The Registry publishes the following data on the list with regard to the Counsel:

– name;
– place and country of the BAR organization to which the counsel is affiliated;
– the languages spoken by the counsel;
– whether counsel represents accused, victims or both.

In contrast to the Court's gender responsibilities and special measures with regard to victims of sexual violence, experience in representing victims of gender-based crimes is not a criterion for being appointed to the list, nor does the ICC enquire about this expertise at any stage during the application process. Therefore the list of legal Counsel does not seem to contain enough information for a victim of gender-based crimes to make an informed decision. It would be highly advisable for the Registry to gain and publish information about the specific legal expertise held by the various Counsels on the list.

4.2. GENDER- AND GEOGRAPHICAL IMBALANCE IN ICC'S LIST OF COUNSEL

Women lawyers with expertise in gender-based violence can help to ensure effective representation of victims of sexual crimes. Therefore they are integral to the effective functioning of the ICC. However in November 2005 the Women's Initiatives for Gender Justice drew attention to the alarming fact that in the appointments to the ICC List of Legal only 17 of 109 appointees were women and almost 70% of those on the list came from one region: Western European and Others Group (WEOG) consisting of Western Europe, USA, Canada, Australia and New Zealand. These numbers were especially disturbing because victims/survivors of sexual violence might prefer a female lawyer from their own region that speaks their language and shares their cultural background when making a choice of counsel. Nonetheless, 4 years later little had changed. As before, very few women occurred on the list (19% or 57 out of 302 persons only). In addition still very few counsel came from the situations under consideration before the Court (13% or 39 out of 302 persons only, of whom only four (three from the DRC and one from the CAR) were women (De Brouwer 2009, 14).

In order to address this situation, the Registrar of the Court launched an initiative in 2010 to actively encourage African Female Lawyers to apply to join the List of Counsel before the Court.[75] This campaign has recorded some

---

[75] ICC Press Release, *ICC and IBA Launch National "Calling African Female Lawyers" Campaign in Uganda*, ICC-CPI-20100604-PR-539, 4 June 2010.

success in view of the marked increase in the number of female African lawyers applying on the Court's List of Counsel.

Currently, a number of African women lawyers are representing victims before the ICC. For example, Carine Bapita represents victims in the case against Thomas Lubanga Dyilo, Marie Edith Douzima-Lawson appears for victims in the case against Jean-Pierre Bemba and Hélène Cissé represented victims in the case against Mr Bahr Idriss Abu Garda.

4.3. GENERAL CHALLENGES

In general, in view of the unfolding nature of the Court's development, a lot is left to be discovered about just how extensive and in-depth the role of the legal representative of victims can be. An underlying complicating factor in this regard is the fact that within the ICC's basic legal texts, it is not specified how legal representatives of victims can participate in proceedings. As indicated in Rule 91(2) he/she is entitled to attend and participate in proceedings but only in accordance with the terms of ruling of the Chamber. They will decide on a case-by-case basis just how far the mandate of the legal representative stretches and shape the various modalities of victim participation.

To engage victims/survivors of gender-based crimes in court involves sensitivity to their culture, origin as well as knowledge of the marginalization sexually abused people are confronted with in most parts of the world. This may be a difficult balance to strike especially since, as discussed in the previous section, the majority of the legal counsels on the list of counsel are men who originate from one region – Western European and Others Group – with their attendant limited contextual information. Parachuting them into the remote areas where the victims live could be a potential disaster and likewise their explaining Court procedures to victim's living in remote parts of conflict societies that do not work by courts and rules is very difficult. In all of this, in cases where sexual violence is at stake with the moral censure attending such acts, it is very unlikely that clients of such a counsel will easily step forward; particularly since they risk being stigmatized if they do so.

Victims/survivors of sexual violence have experienced a feeling of unworthiness and abandonment on many occasions before they come in contact with the ICC. This fragile trust must be handled with care by their legal representative. If a victim's expectation of what the Court can contribute is unrealistic, disappointment is likely to set in. Over time a new feeling of abandonment, this time by the ICC, and resentment towards the legal representative and the legal process may emerge. Here lies another challenging task for the legal representative: to keep the client on board and prevent her/him from re-traumatisation. This can be done by keeping the client well informed about Court proceedings and what realistically can be expected from the Court in their specific case.

At the same time there is a pressing need to provide for high-level legal assistance during the filling of the very complicated participation forms. Presently, victims receive assistance from non-legal intermediaries and NGO workers, which may lead to the forms being improperly filled in, and the attendant rejection by the Chamber may result in re-traumatisation for the victims. It would be highly advisable if law clinics could be set up in which supervised law students could assist victims with filling in the forms since they are likely to possess the necessary legal knowledge and therefore will enhance the number of accepted victim's applications.

Another challenging factor is the impact of the psycho-sociological aspects on the victim. Very often victims of sexual violence develop severe mental disorders, eg. dissociative disorders which in some cases might disable them from giving trustworthy testimonies. To get a better insight in the victim's psychological situation and assess the risks that the victim might recall events incorrectly, a Legal Representative should ideally ask a psychiatrist to carry out a classification based on the *Diagnostic and Statistical Manual of Mental Disorders, Fourth Edition* (DSM IV) of the American Psychiatric Association. This manual covers all mental health disorders and is used by health professionals all over the world to better understand their patients' illness. This way it provides for an international standard. If it turns out on the basis of a DSM IV classification that a victim for example has developed a multiple personality disorder, the question remains whether it would be advisable for such a witness to stand trial. Especially in view of the fact that such a testimony could adversely affect the outcome of the case and at the same time cause severe re-traumatisation for the victim.

In addition, ICC's resource limitations on legal aid could be a major limiting factor in providing such support. Legal aid, in the modality of free assistance by a legal representative from the List of Counsel, is only supplied once the Chamber has granted the victim procedural status where he/she has fulfilled the criteria for participation. This means that the Legal Representative's role is cut down both in time and in resources. He or she is not present in the vital early stages when the participation form is filled in and when the dual status victims are being interviewed by the OTP.

In addition legal aid is limited and will only be granted for specific legal tasks. These limitations in resources also have an impact on counsel's ability and time to have meetings with the client. The legal representative usually lives thousands of kilometres away from the victim. The Court could consider it very costly to fly out and have face to face meetings with clients in remote parts of Africa and so deprive both the legal representative and their client of an opportunity for consultation. In reality discussing confidential matters of sexual violence over the phone doesn't work. In fact listening to the victim is very important. When there is no time for that, a victim will hardly come forward. To overcome this challenge it might be advisable to work together with a local legal Counsel that functions as an Assistant within the legal team.

Yet, another challenging factor is provided by the gender and cultural imbalance amongst ICC personnel. The conservative mind-set of the OTP and the Judges is subject to criticism. It should be noted though that history has shown that women have been at the forefront in addressing sexual violence in International Tribunals.[76] Not only are there within the OTP few women that occupy high level positions, a delay of almost six years ensued after the ICC's establishment, before the appointment of the Special Adviser on Gender Crimes. The fact that it took so long to appoint her, may indicate an initial resistance and hesitation with regard to the importance, status and need for legal expertise on gender issues. Furthermore, it turns out that Prof. MacKinnon is carrying out her duties on a part-time basis and outside of the Hague Office. This circumstance will undoubtedly have a negative impact on the work that needs to be done.

As stated by Brigid Inder, Executive Director of the Women's Initiatives for Gender Justice: "Experience tells us that in the absence of a senior decision-making position clearly mandated with this role, sexual violence and gender-based crimes are marginalized, overlooked, and under-investigated".[77] Several reports of the UN and NGOs indicate that rape and other forms of sexual violence have been committed on a wide scale in all the situations currently pending before the ICC. On the contrary, not in all of the cases emanating from the situations, rape and other forms of sexual violence have been charged against the suspect or accused, or if it has, the charges are limited (De Brouwer 2009). Therefore there is a strong need of gender and sexual violence expertise among the Court's staff, female and male, to further sensitize the legal apparatus on the subject of gender based violence.

4.4. SPECIFIC CHALLENGES WHEN ASSISTING DUAL STATUS WITNESSES

The time lapse between the initial interview and the beginning of the trial is a disadvantage to the dual status witness who doubles as both a victim wanting to participate and a witness for the prosecution. Very often witnesses are unable to remember what they said exactly about the incident a few years earlier when they were first interviewed by the OTP in the absence of a legal representative. This is

---

[76] Leslie Bennetts, *Vanity Fair Nominations: Women Groundbreakers in International Justice – In a Justice League of their Own*, Vanity Fair, November 2007.

[77] Association for Women's Rights in Development, *An interview with Brigid Inder*, 12 February 2008, available at: www.awid.org/eng/Issues-and-Analysis/Library/An-Interview-with-Brigid-Inder.

a perfectly normal human condition, however in Court the defence can and will use it against the victim.

In many civil law countries, a victim is entitled to deliver an equivalent of a *will-say statement*. A possibility like this is absent under the Rome Statute, which does not provide the possibility for the legal representative to file a submission stating relevant facts that came up after the interviews by the OTP. Experience with the ICTR shows that such a provision is essential after proofing of witnesses and was, later in the existence of the Court, included as Rule 73(B) RPE.

Furthermore, the legal representative of a dual status victim doesn't possess a transcript of the initial interview nor any of the other documents relating to the introduction of the victim to the OTP and their research material on the victim. In the majority of cases they are not allowed access or disclosure of such materials. As a result the legal representative is unable to provide the victims with the full benefits of having legal representation as obliged by the Code of Professional Conduct for Counsel.[78]

4.5. SPECIFIC CHALLENGES FOR COMMON LEGAL REPRESENTATIVES

Single status victims are victims who wish to participate in proceedings but are no witnesses for the Prosecution. Given the crimes that are being prosecuted by the ICC and the large number of single status victims involved, the use of common legal representatives is inevitable. However, presenting the view and concerns of a group of victims as a common legal representative on the basis of Rule 90 and regulation 79 of the Regulations of the Court brings with it several challenges for the legal representative. Especially for legal representatives stemming from a civil law country who, in general, hardly have any experience with group actions.[79]

> In addition, Judges have explained in the Katanga/Ngudjolo case that if any disagreements should arise between victims during the proceedings, the counsel would have to represent the divergent positions in an equitable fashion, but in the case where a conflict of interest develops, the Chamber shall take appropriate measures. Specifically, the Chamber could appoint the Office of Public Counsel for Victims (OPCV) to represent one of the conflicting groups of victims. Finally, the Registrar has received the order to propose a structure of assistance, in coordination with the common

---

[78] *Prosecutor v. Lubanga*, Decision on Certain Practicalities Regarding Individuals who have the Dual Status of Witness and Victim, Trial Chamber I, Case No. ICC-01/04–01/06–1379, 5 June 2008.

[79] A famous exception to this rule is the *Barbie* case in France, where indeed a group action was allowed in a civil law country: Case No. 77, Fn 908 KsD Lyon IV-B (gez. Ostubaf. Barbie) and BdS, Paris IV-B, 6 April 1944, RF-1235. Goni, Uki (2002).

legal representation, so that he can effectively accomplish his duties. This type of common legal representation is different from the one set out in the Thomas Lubanga case. The facts and the situations of the victims in both cases are different; it is thus understandable that the Judges have not reproduced the same legal representation system as in the Lubanga case. However the system adopted by the Judges is very restrictive and practical problems could arise during its implementation. One can only hope that certain aspects of the chosen solution – which is adapted to the specific characteristics of this case and could generate certain concerns – will not be interpreted as being a general precedent.[80]

When starting to represent a group of victims it is necessary for the Common Legal Representative to make an analysis of the common views and concerns of this sometimes quite large and divergent group. As correctly indicated by Anne-Marie de Brouwer and Marc Groenhuijsen:

Groups of victims that may seem homogenous at first sight may in reality be not so homogenous. A group of victims of sexual violence may come from different regions and may have been sexually violated by perpetrators of different ethnicity. (...) Although the appointment of Common Legal Representatives may be an outcome for streamlining the proceedings, the question of how many such representatives can be appointed without endangering the interest of the victims as well as the effectiveness and fairness of the trial remains. (De Brouwer & Groenhuijsen 2009, 22–23)

In this regard the logistical impact of representing a large number of clients at the same time must be taken into account as well. Is it possible for one legal representative and his/her assistants to handle so much and so many interests correctly?

In case the common legal representative receives conflicting instructions from one or more groups of victims, he or she shall endeavor to represent both positions fairly and equally before the Chamber. In case the conflicting instructions are irreconcilable with representation by one common legal representative, and thus amount to a conflict of interest, the common legal representative shall inform the Chamber immediately, who will take appropriate measures and may, for example, appoint the Office of Public Counsel for the Victims to represent one group of victims with regard to the specific issue which gives rise to the conflict of interest.[81]

The work of the common legal representative is additionally challenged by the fact that different legal representatives have been working on the victim's files

---

[80] De Vries, G., *ICC: A Few Remarks on the Common Legal Representation of Victims in the Katanga/Ngudjolo Case*, available at www.coalitionfortheicc.org/blog/?cat=20&langswitch_lang=en (last visited: 11 August 2009).

[81] ICC-Office of Public Counsel for Victims, *Representing Victims before the International Criminal Court. A Manual for Legal Representatives*, 2010, 108; www.icc-cpi.int/iccdocs/PIDS/tmp/Representing%20Victims%20before%20ICC.PDF.

until a common legal representative is appointed and files are transferred to the latter. Another challenge for Legal Representatives of victims lies in the fact that they are appointed to act as Counsel at a fairly advanced stage in the legal process when the victim has most likely developed a relationship of trust with the NGO or intermediary, who assisted in the victim's application. To this end, the Legal Representatives' independence and impartiality is challenged by a situation where the victims has more confidence in and a better working relationship with such an intermediary, than in the court appointed Counsel. "From a practical perspective, it will be a long and difficult process for the single counsel and his assistant to have a good understanding of the files (...), adding to this the fact hundreds of victims will participate".[82]

> Furthermore, the possibility that the counsel may have to represent divergent instructions of victims will pose additional constraints. In conclusion, one can only hope that the Court will envisage the structure of assistance to be created for the Common Legal Representative in a flexible fashion and that this structure will include a sufficient number of lawyers to be able to provide effective support to the Common Legal Representative and his assistant.[83]

On 22 July 2009, Trial Chamber II defined the modalities of the common legal representation of victims in the *Katanga/Ngudjolo* case.[84] The Chamber has divided victims into two groups: the first group includes all victims except for child soldiers, and the second group includes the latter. Judges have decided that the victims will be represented by one common legal representative (who will choose an assistant) except for the child soldiers, who will appoint a separate counsel.

5. CONCLUSION

In view of the analysis of procedures and mechanisms available to the victims of sexual violence in the International Criminal Court, the question is being justifiably asked: how far has the Rome Statute gone to ensure provision of adequate assistance to the victims of sexual violence? Since no trial has come to an end and participation is still a developing issue, an assessment to its fullest is not possible. The ICC however represents a historic opportunity to address the

---

[82] De Vries, G., *ICC: A Few Remarks on the Common Legal Representation of Victims in the Katanga/Ngudjolo Case*, available at www.coalitionfortheicc.org/blog/?cat=20&langswitch_lang=en (last visited: 11 August 2009).

[83] *Idem.*

[84] See *The Prosecutor v. Germain Katanga and Mathieu Ngudjolo Chui*, Order on the Organisation of Victims, Trial Chamber II, Case No. ICC-01/04–01/07, 22 July 2009, para. 16.

shortcomings of the *ad hoc* tribunals ICTR and ICTY with regards to investigating and prosecuting gender-based crimes.

The Rome Statute for the first time has recognized distinct characteristics of gender-based crimes including: rape, forced pregnancy, sexual slavery and gender-based persecution in contrast to the ICTR and ICTY Statutes. It has also described the offence and its elements. Moreover, the ICC introduced new forms of assistance to victims by establishing several victim-oriented units within the Court, thus aiming at guaranteeing their rights are enforced.

However, even these broad range of legal instruments, which may appear effective at first sight, will become ineffective when improperly implemented. In this regard one of the most important areas the Court needs to pay particular attention to is the appointment of Legal Representatives for victims. The gender balance and fair representation of Representatives from the situation countries should be respected in addition to ensuring that the distinct interests of victims of sexual violence of the particular situation are represented. It is hoped that the recent initiative by the Registry to attract more African female lawyers will assist in ameliorating this issue. However, so far no expertise in sexual violence is required. It would be advisable if this specialisation would be explicitly marked on the list of Counsel held by the Registry.

The International Criminal Court, and the OTP in particular, seems to have learnt the lesson of the *Lubanga* case where sexual violence was not charged, and seems to display a more unwavering commitment to investigate, charge and prosecute gender-based crimes in every Situation. This commitment must entail comprehensive and sustainable charges brought against suspects, and thereby eliminating the consequence of gender-based crimes being omitted from prosecutions before the Court.

XXII. RESPONDING TO THE MOST VULNERABLE

Child Victims of International Crimes[*]

Michelle G. Grossman

In the last decade, more than 2 million children have died
as a direct result of armed conflict, and more than three times
that number have been permanently disabled or seriously injured.
An estimated 20 million children have been forced to flee their homes,
and more than 1 million have been orphaned or separated from their families.
Some 300,000 child soldiers – boys and girls under the age of 18 –
are involved in more than 30 conflicts worldwide.[1]

1. INTRODUCTION

It is widely acknowledged that the latter part of the 20th century and the early years of the 21st century witnessed a shift in both the tactics and targets of modern warfare. Whereas armies of one nation once confronted those of another, during this period most wars were waged and fought between factions within the same nation. A shift in targets from trained and uniformed soldiers to unprotected, innocent civilians also occurred. The international justice community recognized the plight of the victims of such armed conflicts which, in many cases, included entire communities of people. In efforts to ensure an appropriate criminal justice response to international crimes (including war crimes, crimes against humanity and genocide) committed either in international or internal armed conflict settings, several international criminal tribunals and courts were created.[2] The establishment of these criminal justice mechanisms

---

[*]   This chapter (with modifications), is part of a larger in-progress project regarding child victims and international criminal justice (forthcoming unpublished DPhil thesis, Michelle G. Grossman, University of Oxford).

[1]   UNICEF, *Humanitarian Action Report*, 2005, www.unicef.org/emerg/HAR.html (last visited: December 2009).

[2]   Included amongst these were the 1993 International Criminal Tribunal for the Former Yugoslavia (ICTY), the 1994 International Criminal Tribunal for Rwanda (ICTR), the 2002 International Criminal Court (ICC) (the Rome Statute, the ICC's guiding Statute was adopted

served to increase attention to victims of international crimes in general and also to particularly vulnerable victims. In this regard, while victims of gender and sexual violence[3] have attracted attention,[4] child victims of international crimes – perhaps the most vulnerable of all victims due to a combination of physical, psychological, economic and political factors – are the focus of this chapter.[5]

In the years since the above statistics appeared in UNICEF's 2005 Humanitarian Action Report, they have been routinely quoted in numerous publications relating to children and armed conflict. This fact has signalled a critical need to respond to this particular group of victims.[6] Child victims of

---

      in 1998 and the ICC itself came into force in 2002), and the 2002 Special Court for Sierra Leone (SCSL).

[3]   Here both the terms 'gender' and 'sexual' violence are employed. The term 'gender violence' is used in reference to crimes that are committed specifically because of the gender of the victim even though such crimes are not always of a sexual nature (see Carpenter 2006 for a discussion of gender-based violence against males in conflict situations). As De Brouwer (2005, 26–27) explains, "*Gender violence is violence that is targeted at women or men because of their sex and/or their socially constructed gender roles. Gender violence may be sexual in nature, but also non-sexual.*" Crimes of 'sexual violence' however, are understood as those offences perpetrated with a sexual intent recognizing that such crimes are committed against both males and females (see De Brouwer 2005, 26, for a further discussion of the definition of sexual violence).

[4]   While victims of gender and/or sexual violence are undeniably worthy of specific attention and have indeed been the focus of a number of studies and initiatives, this chapter will not be addressing this particular group of victims. It should be noted, however, that during armed conflicts, girls are particularly at risk of "sexual violence, including rape, sexual mutilation, sexual humiliation, forced prostitution, and forced pregnancy" (Narayan 2002, 2). The ramifications of such abuse may be long-lasting not only in terms of physical and psychological symptoms but also by the fact that girls (many of whom become pregnant and subsequently bear children as a result of these assaults) are frequently stigmatized and ostracized by their communities even after the conflicts have subsided because of the sexual nature of the assaults (Arts 2006, 15).

[5]   Within the literature regarding children and armed conflict the issue of children's vulnerability is frequently noted (see for example: Barenbaum, Ruchkin & Schwab-Stone 2004, 42; Hart & Tyrer 2006, 9–10; Jamison 2008, 139; Narayan 2002, 2; UNICEF, *Children Affected by Armed Conflict: UNICEF Actions*, 2002, 3). Kuper (1997) provides a helpful reference to this issue when she notes that: "The issue of children's vulnerability was usefully analysed in a draft document prepared for submission to the UN Committee on the Rights of the Child. This stated bluntly that '[c]hildren are vulnerable', and categorized this vulnerability in two ways. First, as an 'inherent vulnerability', based on their physical weakness and lack of knowledge and experience; and secondly, as 'structural vulnerability', based on their lack of political and economic power and of civil rights in society: Children's Rights Development Unit, Civil and Political Liberties: Consultation Document (London, May 1993), 3." (Kuper, 15).

[6]   Several of the statistics noted in the UNICEF 2005 Humanitarian Action Report (*supra* note 1) actually appeared even earlier in the 1996 seminal report by Graça Machel on the Impact of Armed Conflict on Children and also in her 2001 book on The Impact of War on Children. Thus, when the 2005 UNICEF Humanitarian Action Report was published, some of these statistics were already nearly a decade old and at the time of the writing of this chapter, these statistics continued to be the primary ones routinely quoted. The fact that more current statistics regarding child victims of armed conflict seem to be unavailable (or at least not readily available) may speak to the difficulty of obtaining statistics in such a sensitive and

international crimes represent a priority for the international community as the needs[7] of arguably the most vulnerable victims of the most heinous crimes known to humankind must be addressed. Children are a distinct group of victims with their own needs, and should not merely be aggregated within the more broadly defined category of 'victims'. To integrate children into the larger group of 'victims' is to overlook the impact of international crimes not only on a generation of young people but on future societies as well.

This chapter draws attention to the needs of child victims of international crimes and notes the significance of children as the next generation. The essay highlights the importance of recognizing the existence of this specific victim population. As well, several international legal instruments which address child victims in the context and aftermath of international crimes are identified and discussed. The chapter reflects upon how the Rome Statute of the International Criminal Court (ICC) – the first permanent, international, treaty-based, independent criminal court has considered this particularly vulnerable victim population. This contribution provides an overview of the more salient issues concerning child victims of international crimes, but does not claim to provide a comprehensive evaluation of either the legal or the humanitarian actions undertaken or neglected with respect to these victims. Finally, the need to improve the effectiveness of the response to child victims of international crimes is emphasized.

2. KEY TERMS

It is important that clarity be provided regarding how key terms are to be understood in a specific context. For this reason, the terms child, victim and

---

challenging area. Regardless of the precise statistics regarding children affected by armed conflict (which may in fact never be exactly known), the fact remains that the numbers are concerningly high. As Elbedour, Ten Bensel, & Bastien suggest, *"No statistics can accurately reflect the extent to which the "collaterally damaged" children who are still alive have been victimized or continue to be victimized by war."* (1993, 806).

7   A distinction is frequently made between the use of the terms 'needs' and 'rights'. Many UN and humanitarian agencies and Non-Governmental Organizations (NGOs) prefer to employ a 'rights-based' versus a 'needs-based' discourse in their programming approaches. In doing so, the legal basis of an individual's human rights as set out in international treaties or declarations such as the Universal Declaration of Human Rights and the UN Convention on the Rights of the Child are emphasized. However, while recognizing that adherence to and enforcement of the legal rights of child victims is essential, this chapter opts to use the term 'needs' to focus on the more psycho/social/physical impacts of international crimes on young people. In this sense, the term 'needs' is used to focus on those most fundamental requirements essential for the fulfillment of a healthy, safe and productive subsistence. This choice of term is in no way meant to dismiss the significance of the term 'rights-based approach' when focusing on the rights of a child within more legislative processes and publications.

international crimes are discussed relative to their respective meanings employed throughout this chapter.

2.1. CHILD

When considering the meaning of the word 'child', several questions arise. 'Child' – is this someone of a specific chronological age? Is this a person with a certain physical stature or cognitive ability? Is this someone who exhibits particular mental or emotional behaviours? Or perhaps it is a person who has fulfilled a culture-specific goal? Is a child someone who has not yet achieved a defining life milestone? Is the definition of 'child' gender dependent? Does such a definition require evidence of certain biological or physiological characteristics? Such questions suggest that definitions of 'child' may differ depending on those doing the defining, and such definitions may be particularly dependent upon the culture to which the 'child' belongs. How, for instance, does one define a child by chronological age if, as in some cultures, age is never recorded? And if by virtue of the fact that a young person has offspring, does this person, regardless of his or her chronological or biological age cease to be a child him or herself? In considering these questions one must acknowledge that the notion of 'childhood' – the time when one is deemed to be a 'child' – is as much a developmental and chronological as a social construction.[8]

International criminal law, "a relatively new branch of international law" (Cassese 2008, 4), deals with international crimes including, *inter alia*, war crimes, crimes against humanity and crimes of genocide. Although 'war crimes' existed in the late nineteenth century, modern concepts of this international crime as well as crimes against humanity and crimes of genocide developed primarily since the 1945 International Military Tribunal at Nuremberg (IMT), the 1946 International Military Tribunal for the Far East (IMTFE), and the 1948 United Nations Convention on the Prevention and Punishment of the Crime of Genocide (*ibidem*). Since the IMT and the IMTFE are often considered the creation of what might be thought of as the 'political West' it might be argued that the international crimes evolving out of these proceedings might also be viewed as Western creations. Consequently, it may not be surprising that the definitions of 'child' included in the statutes of subsequent international criminal mechanisms (i.e., the ICC) reflect a Western bias. Western understandings of 'child' are primarily age based – usually under the age of 18 (Schafer 2004, 87) – whereas, in non-Western societies, this age distinction may be absent (*supra* note 1019).

---

[8] For discussions on the definition and/or meaning of a child or childhood, refer to: Cohn & Goodwin Gill 1997, 6–7; Freeland 2008, 28–29; Hart & Tyrer 2006, 6; Honwana 2001, 133–134; Kuper 1997, 13 & 16–17.

Since it is international criminal law that provides the framework within which crimes such as war crimes, crimes against humanity and genocide are dealt, the definition of 'child' employed within this chapter will be that set out in the key UN instrument guiding the treatment of children, that being the United Nations Convention on the Rights of the Child (UNCRC). The UNCRC is the most widely-ratified UN treaty to date, with only Somalia and the United States of America remaining as countries yet to ratify, and thus the definition of 'child' in this instrument has near universal acceptance. Part I, Article I of the UNCRC states that: "For the purposes of the present Convention, a child means every human being below the age of eighteen years unless, under the law applicable to the child, majority is attained earlier".[9]

2.2. VICTIM

In this chapter, 'victim' refers to a person who has been harmed intentionally or negligently by the culpable actions of others. This definition applies both to the understanding of a primary victim (a person who herself or himself has been harmed directly), and to that of a secondary victim (a person who has been harmed indirectly as the result of harm committed against others). The Rules of Procedure and Evidence (RPE) of the ICC set out a definition of victim which is adopted in this chapter. As per Rule 85(a), "'Victims' means natural persons who have suffered harm as a result of the commission of any crime within the jurisdiction of the Court".[10] Regardless of the definition employed it is necessary to recognize that 'victims' do not constitute a homogeneous group; individual victims vary considerably with respect to personal characteristics, individual experiences, and importantly, needs following victimization (Elbedour *et al.* 1993, 808–809; Goodey 2005, 121–124; Hart & Tyrer 2006, 10; Walklate 2007, 105). The impact of crime may be quite different on individuals depending upon a number of factors, not the least of which is a victim's age and vulnerability.

---

[9] While a definition of 'child' does not explicitly exist within the Rome Statute nor within the related ICC legal documentation (e.g., the Rules of Procedure and Evidence, Elements of Crimes, etc.), it can be assumed that the Rome Statute conforms to the UNCRC's definition of a child as Article 26 of the Rome Statute states that: *"The Court shall have no jurisdiction over any person who was under the age of 18 at the time of the alleged commission of a crime".* This exclusion of jurisdiction over persons under the age of eighteen would seem to indicate that for the purposes of the Rome Statute and the procedures of the ICC, 'child' would be defined as a person under the age of eighteen.

[10] The crimes currently within the jurisdiction of the ICC include crimes against humanity, war crimes, genocide and the crime of aggression. Although part (b) of Rule 85 states that: *"Victims may include organizations or institutions that have sustained direct harm to any of their property which is dedicated to religion, education, art or science or charitable purposes, and to their historic monuments, hospitals and other places and objects for humanitarian purposes"* this chapter will focus on 'natural' persons (specifically children) and not on organizations or institutions.

2.3. INTERNATIONAL CRIMES

International crimes are often associated with broader discussions of two distinct bodies of law, International Humanitarian Law (IHL) and Human Rights Law (HRL). IHL applies during international and internal armed conflicts and seeks to protect persons either not involved or no longer involved in the hostilities. HRL applies at any time and seeks to protect human rights as provided for in several key international human rights instruments such as, but not limited to, the Universal Declaration of Human Rights.[11] International crimes include those whose nature and consequences are deemed so serious as to be of concern not only to individual states but also to the international community. In defining international crimes this way, no distinction is made between offences that are committed between states and those committed within states. Thus, the term can be applied both to internal and international armed conflicts. What constitutes international crimes for use in this chapter rests primarily on the gravity of the offences, their duration, and the context within which they are committed. As previously noted, the crimes included within the Rome Statute are: genocide, crimes against humanity, war crimes, and the crime of aggression. Articles 6, 7, and 8 of the Rome Statute provide detailed definitions for all but the crime of aggression and these are the definitions that are employed in this chapter.[12]

3. CONSIDERATION OF CHILD VICTIMS OF INTERNATIONAL CRIMES OVER TIME

Prior to the Second World War, child victims of armed conflict received little attention in the academic or scholarly literature. In fact, Elbedour *et al.* (1993, 806) note that, "up until the mid-20th century, little attention was paid to women or children in the literature of war at all". Similarly, Myers-Walls (2004, 42) suggests that "[a]lthough countless volumes have been written addressing political violence, children have been almost invisible in that literature until recently". Dwork (1991, 253), author of *Children with a Star* – a book about children and the Holocaust – writes, regarding the written histories of the Holocaust, that although the literature regarding adults during this period of history is rich, "[c]hildren are conspicuously, glaringly, and screamingly silently

---

[11] See Cassese (2008, 99) for discussions of both bodies of law and their relationship to international crimes.

[12] See the Rome Statute and the specific definitions provided for Genocide, Crimes against Humanity and War Crimes within the Statute at: www.icc-cpi.int/NR/rdonlyres/EA9AEFF7–5752–4F84-BE94–0A655EB30E16/0/Rome_Statute_English.pdf (last visited: March 2010). Cassese (2008) also provides helpful discussions on these international crimes.

absent." These comments do not imply that children were not victims of armed conflicts prior to or during that time, only perhaps that compared with adults, children were seen as a peripheral concern (*ibid*, 254). In addition, as previously noted, traditional warfare was primarily conducted between trained armed forces and did not typically involve the direct participation of children. The shift from incidental to intended target may explain why it is only relatively recently that children victimized during armed conflicts have become a focus of attention.

The impact of war on young British children was studied during WWII by Anna Freud and Dorothy Burlingham (1943). These researchers examined the effects of air raids and family separation on the children. Of course the children observed in the Freud and Burlingham research were not the only child victims during WWII; many children were victims of horrific crimes under the Nazi regime. Children suffered greatly both within and outside of concentration camps and most egregiously as victims of the horrendous Nazi medical experiments. Despite this, academic and scholarly attention to the impact of these atrocities on the child victims was extremely limited.[13] While there is now a proliferation of personal stories, accounts and memoirs written by and/or about adults who experienced the Holocaust as children, it is interesting that, as Elbedour *et al.* (1993, 806) note, the most well-known source of information on the impact of armed conflict on a young person from that period came from the posthumously published diary of a particularly articulate young victim, Anne Frank.[14]

Modern armed conflicts – where children are now much more likely than in the past to be targeted as victims and recruited as combatants – have consequences which require specific attention from the international community. Evidence of the attention that these young victims have received in this regard appears in the progressive efforts of the ICC and the SCSL. Both courts have made provisions for the support and protection of children participating in their respective proceedings. Additionally, there has been an increase in the research literature regarding, and in the efforts of humanitarian organizations towards the plight of children who have participated as combatants in armed conflicts. Whether deemed 'voluntary' combatants (a term which many would suggest is

---

13 Danieli (2006b) refers to the "conspiracy of silence" (1634) where after WWII the stories of Holocaust survivors were not welcomed by society in general. This may account, to some extent, for why so little was written about the experiences of the survivors, as both adults and children, in the years immediately following the war. See also Fogelman (1988, 619–620).

14 Anne Frank's diary was first published in Dutch in 1947 under the title *Het Achterhuis: Dagboekbrieven van 12 juni 1942 – 1 augustus 1944* (translation: 'The Secret Annex: Diary Notes from 12 June 1942 – 1 August 1944') by Contact Publishing, Amsterdam. In 1952, the English translation, *Anne Frank: The Diary of a Young Girl* was published by Doubleday in the USA and by Vallantine, Mitchell & Co. in the UK.

problematic),[15] or forcibly recruited participants, the results of such direct involvement in armed conflicts have traumatic effects on young persons. It is encouraging that this area has received increasing attention through various international criminal justice mechanisms and through certain UN Security Council resolutions (in particular, UN Security Council Resolution 1612 which will be discussed below). However, attention must also focus on children who may not have participated as combatants but who have nevertheless suffered the extreme and traumatic consequences of armed conflict.

4. CHILDREN – A DISTINCT GROUP OF VULNERABLE VICTIMS

From a number of perspectives child victims represent a highly vulnerable group. Children are vulnerable by virtue of their age, their immature physical and mental development, their lack of political power or voice, as well as their economic and emotional dependency on adults. In short, child victims may well represent the most vulnerable of all crime victims.[16] Nowhere is this more evident than with respect to victims of the most serious forms of violence – international crimes. The distinctiveness of child victims rests upon two grounds: i) their inherent vulnerability – reflected in the international legal instruments which have been created and employed to protect their needs and rights, and ii) their status as a society's next generation (see Kuper 1997, 15).

4.1. CHILD VICTIMS AS A VULNERABLE POPULATION/ OBLIGATION TO PROTECT

Children, as Garbarino and Kostelny (1996, 34) have noted, "are not simply short adults", they differ in many ways from adults. The international community has an obligation to ensure that children are protected during armed conflicts and that they are not further harmed or victimized in the aftermath of such hostilities. Evidence of this obligation can be found in several international legal instruments, some of which are highlighted here.

---

[15] Some would argue that a child can never truly 'volunteer' for participation in hostilities during times of armed conflict. While it may appear as though a child has genuinely 'volunteered', cultural, economic, social or political pressures and/or threats can affect a child's 'free choice' in this regard. The decision of a child to 'volunteer' to join armed groups during an armed conflict can be influenced also by the need to survive and provide for others in the family particularly if the death of caregivers has left a child and his or her siblings orphaned. (See, for example, Barenbaum *et al.* 2004, 47; Jamison 2008, 139).

[16] *Supra* note 5.

United Nations Convention on the Rights of the Child and its two Optional Protocols

The 1989 UN Convention on the Rights of the Child (and its two Optional Protocols: one addressing the involvement of children in armed conflict and the other addressing the sale of children, child prostitution and child pornography) is the seminal treaty documenting the obligations of the States Parties and by extension, the international community, to children. While it was neither the first international instrument to consider the protection and needs of children, nor was it created specifically to address the impacts of armed conflict, it (and its two Optional Protocols) is one of the most significant international Conventions to focus exclusively on children. Article 38 outlines State Parties' obligations for the protection and care of children during armed conflicts in accordance with the rules of international humanitarian law (here, consideration of how the 1949 Geneva Conventions apply to children should be considered and will be addressed below). Despite the overarching definition in Article 1 of a child being a person under the age of 18, Article 38 specifies a minimum age of 15 for participation in either armed forces or hostilities. In an effort to strengthen the protection of children, the 2000 Optional Protocol on the involvement of children in armed conflict advances requirements to increase the age to 18 wherever feasible.

It is disturbing that children are increasingly involved as combatants in armed conflicts; however, in the face of this reality it is important that Article 40 of the UNCRC offers protection to children alleged to have infringed the penal law. In this regard, Article 40(1) states:

> *States Parties recognize the right of every child alleged as, accused of, or recognized as having infringed the penal law to be treated in a manner consistent with the promotion of the child's sense of dignity and worth, which reinforces the child's respect for the human rights and fundamental freedoms of others and which takes into account the child's age and the desirability of promoting the child's reintegration and the child's assuming a constructive role in society.*

Article 39 of the Convention is the only one which refers specifically to the recovery of children as a result of an armed conflict. The Article states that:

> *State Parties shall take all appropriate measures to promote physical and psychological recovery and social re-integration of a child victim of: any form of neglect, exploitation, or abuse; torture or any form of cruel, inhuman or degrading treatment or punishment; or armed conflicts. Such recovery and re-integration shall take place in an environment which fosters the health, self-respect and dignity of the child.*

Notwithstanding the landmark elements of the UNCRC, it has been argued by Hamilton (2006, 273) that, due to its vague provisions, its lack of "judicial function by which individual or group complaints can be heard" and its inability to respond to situations of emergencies, it "is not a particularly useful instrument in times of armed conflict". Nevertheless, the global attention that this instrument draws to the need to protect children not only in times of peace but importantly during times of armed conflict cannot be understated.

Geneva Conventions of 1949 and their two Additional Protocols of 1977
Article 38 of the UNCRC refers to the rules of international humanitarian law as they relate to child victims. As such, it is helpful to identify the international legal instruments which document such rules. In this regard, attention is drawn to the 1949 Geneva Conventions and their two Additional Protocols of 1977. Despite their status as "[t]he most significant humanitarian law instruments that apply to warfare today" (Hamilton 2006, 270), only the fourth Geneva Convention (GC IV) 'relative to the Protection of Civilian Persons in Time of War'[17] includes specific protections for children during situations of armed conflict. While GC IV does not provide a specific definition for a child, it does, in a number of its Articles (e.g. Articles 14, 23, 24, 38, 50 and 89) specify "children under the age of 15" suggesting that a child is defined as someone below the age of 15 (Happold 2008, 63). Common Article 3 (the Article contained in all four of the Geneva Conventions and applicable to "conflicts not of an international character") provides for basic protection to "[p]ersons taking no active part in the hostilities, including members of armed forces who have laid down their arms and those placed 'hors de combat' by sickness, wounds, detention, or any other cause" (Article 3(1)). Children who have previously engaged in hostilities but who have ceased such engagement are protected under Common Article 3 (Cohn & Goodwin-Gill 1997). The Article does not, however, mention child soldiers specifically. Hamilton argues that the Geneva Conventions are weak in their protection of children in situations of armed conflict. She bases her argument on the fact that the Conventions apply only to international armed conflicts and not to ones that are internal (with the exception of Common Article 3), and she notes that the majority of the armed conflicts today are internal (Hamilton 2006, 270–272). This weakness is rectified somewhat through the 1977 Additional Protocol II to the Geneva Conventions. This Protocol specifically includes protection provisions to child victims in non-international armed conflicts. Although both Additional Protocol I and Additional Protocol II provide protection to children under the age of 15 involved in armed forces, Hamilton argues that together, the Geneva Conventions and their two Additional Protocols do not provide an adequate protective framework for children in situations of internal armed conflict (*idem* 272).

---

[17] See website: www.icrc.org/ihl.nsf/CONVPRES?OpenView for full text of the 1949 Geneva Conventions and Additional Protocols (last visited: July 2010).

United Nations Security Council Resolutions 1612 and 1882

With respect to children involved as combatants in armed conflicts, several international bodies have taken action to provide for their protection. In terms of international courts, both the Statutes of the ICC and the SCSL include provisions for the protection of child combatants. They do this by defining the conscription, enlistment or use of children under the age of 15 as war crimes or serious violations of International Humanitarian Law.[18] The UN Security Council has also taken steps to address the issue of child combatants by adopting significant Resolutions that deal specifically with children affected by armed conflict. Security Council Resolution 1612 adopted in July 2005 is particularly relevant in this regard and has been described as a "landmark Resolution" that "established a monitoring and reporting mechanism to collect information on child soldiers with the aim of stopping this exploitative criminal practice" (Popovski 2006, 37–38). Resolution 1612 established a Working Group on Children and Armed Conflict whose purpose it is to monitor, document and report on six categories of grave violations against children. The six categories include: killing or maiming of children; recruiting or using child soldiers; attacks against schools or hospitals; rape and other grave sexual violence against children; abduction of children; and denial of humanitarian access for children (Kuper 2008).[19] The formal, structured monitoring and reporting mechanism is co-ordinated by UNICEF and works in cooperation with the Office of the Special Representative of the Secretary-General for Children and Armed Conflict and both national and international NGOs to provide reports and recommendations to the Security Council regarding parties carrying out violations against children in these 6 specified areas.[20] In August 2009, the Security Council unanimously adopted Resolution 1882 which expands upon Resolution 1612 in terms of the triggers for implementation of the Resolution 1612 monitoring and reporting mechanism.[21] Although a more detailed exploration of these two SC Resolutions is beyond the scope of this chapter they are clear testaments to the efforts of the

---

[18]   In defining what, for the purpose of its Statute, a war crime means, Article 8(2)(b) (xxvi) of the Rome Statute states, 'Conscripting or enlisting children under the age of fifteen years into the national armed forces or using them to participate actively in hostilities.'. The 'Other Serious Violations of International Humanitarian Law' section of the Statute of the SCSL Article 4(c) includes: 'Conscripting or enlisting children under the age of 15 years into armed forces or groups or using them to participate actively in hostilities'.

[19]   Office of the Special Representative of the Secretary General for Children and Armed Conflict, *Working Paper No. 1, the Six Grave Violations against Children During Armed Conflict: The Legal Foundation*, 2009, 3.

[20]   For additional information regarding SC Res. 1612 and its operations, see the following websites: Foreign Affairs and International Trade Canada at: www.international.gc.ca/cip-pic/features-manchettes/children_war-enfant_guerre/resolution1612.aspx?lang=eng and UNICEF at: www.unicef.org/protection/index_35071.html (last visited: July 2010).

[21]   UNICEF News Note, 2009, www.unicef.org/media/media_50685.html (last visited: July 2010).

Security Council towards providing protection for children involved in armed conflicts.

Paris Commitments and Principles

In February 2007, in Paris, France, representatives of 58 countries met and endorsed the Paris Commitments and Principles. These Commitments and Principles complement the efforts of the UN Security Council and other international mechanisms (e.g., the ICC) in protecting children from recruitment into, and provide assistance to those already involved with armed groups. According to the International Committee of the Red Cross (ICRC), the aim of the Paris Commitments and Principles is "to combat the unlawful recruitment or use of children by armed forces or armed groups" and "[t]heir specific objective is to prevent the occurrence of this phenomenon, to secure the release of children concerned, to support their social reintegration and to ensure that they are afforded the greatest protection possible".[22]

The Commitments and Principles exist as two formal documents which represent respectively the commitments of the participating countries to combat the unlawful recruitment and use of children in armed conflict and the detailed guidelines for the implementation of the commitments.

4.2. CHILD VICTIMS AS THE NEXT GENERATION

The main premise behind the 'next generation' position concerns recognition of the importance to 'get things right' for the children who have been victimized. This supposition can be viewed in two different but related ways. First, children are the 'building blocks' of future generations. From this perspective, the devastating effects of international crimes on children including everything from disrupted education, health and economic welfare to physical, social and emotional consequences may all have far reaching implications for future societies.[23]

The second element of the next generation perspective reveals the need to consider the potentially destructive emotional impact of being targeted

---

[22] International Committee of the Red Cross, *Paris Principles and Paris Commitments to Protect Children*, 2007; www.icrc.org/Web/Eng/siteeng0.nsf/html/paris-principles-commitments-300107 (last visited: July 2010).

[23] Studies of adults who were children during the Holocaust suggest that such victims continue to experience the impacts of the crimes committed against them in childhood well into their adult years. Additionally, similar studies have examined the transgenerational impact that the crimes of the Holocaust have not only on the now adult survivors, but on their children as well (Danieli 1985, 305; Nadler & Ben Shushan 1989, 293). Furthermore, Elbedour *et al.* (1993, 808) suggest that: "Often, the symptoms of war are delayed and may not manifest themselves for years".

specifically because *they are* the next generation (Kuper 1997, 217).[24] As Seymour (1999, 83) observes, sometimes children are "specifically targeted as a way of terrorizing their community". In this regard, it may be understood that "[y]oung people as the up-coming generation, may even be targeted to reduce the numbers of the future 'enemy' ".[25] The 1994 Rwandan public radio broadcasts where Hutu militia were incited to target Tutsi children as "[t]o destroy the big rats, you must kill the little rats" provides a striking example of the specific targeting of children.[26]

In order to respond appropriately to the needs of child victims of international crimes, it is important to be aware of the specific needs of this victim population. A number of these needs are thus highlighted below.

5. THE NEEDS OF CHILD VICTIMS OF CRIME

5.1. FUNDAMENTAL NEEDS OF CHILD CRIME VICTIMS

In discussing victims' needs and rights, Walklate (2007) notes that the needs of child crime victims may be quite different to those of adults. She states that the impact of crime will likely be greater on a child due to a child's vulnerability as associated with his or her age, level of maturity and cognitive ability. This is true for both victims of domestic and of international crimes. When considering the needs of child crime victims it is often useful to do so "in accordance with Maslow's hierarchy of needs" (Hamilton 2006, 301) which suggests that a person's most basic needs must be met before more complex needs can be addressed. Maslow's hierarchy is represented by a five level 'need pyramid' with basic needs such as food, water, and sleep (physiological needs) and security, safety and protection (safety needs) on the lower-most levels of the pyramid. Needs related to feelings of being loved and belonging, self-esteem and finally the ability to develop self-potential appear progressively higher on the pyramid (Harper, Harper & Stills 2003). What this suggests in terms of providing assistance to child crime victims is the importance of recognizing that in general, before a child will be able to cope with the demands of participating in the criminal justice system, his or her physiological needs and concerns regarding safety and security (or fear) must first be addressed.

When considering the needs of child victims, whether of domestic or international crimes, it is worth noting that while some children may be quite capable of identifying and expressing what they need, others may not. This

---

[24] No Peace Without Justice & UNICEF Innocenti Research Centre, *International Criminal Justice and Children*, Rome: XPress S.r.l., 2002, 30.

[25] Amnesty International (Ed.), *In the Firing Line: War and Children's Rights*, 1999, p. 17.

[26] *Idem*, p. 31.

inability to articulate one's needs may arise from developmental limitations, or equally from a victim's lack of knowledge of what is available in terms of assistance (Goodey 2005). While it is not always useful to tie a child's needs to his or her age or stage of development, it is worth recognizing that a very young child will almost certainly have different needs to that of an older child. It is also important to acknowledge that even with children of comparable ages at similar stages of development, the type of assistance needed will vary depending on the circumstances of the crime.

In a domestic study conducted on child victims in the early 1990s, Morgan and Zedner (1992) found that the predominant reaction of crime victims in general was one of psychological distress. With respect to child victims, however, they argued that a child's lack of understanding of the nature and meaning of the offence can lead to an intensification of this distress. Consequently, child victims of both domestic and international crimes will often need assistance in understanding the nature and meaning of the crimes committed against them. Crimes such as genocide and crimes against humanity are difficult even for adults to comprehend; thus, it is vital that child victims of these crimes be provided with developmentally-appropriate assistance to understand the nature and meaning of the atrocities committed against them.

5.2. NEEDS OF CHILD VICTIMS PARTICIPATING IN CRIMINAL JUSTICE PROCEEDINGS

Young (and vulnerable) victims will often require moral support in order to participate as witnesses in criminal justice proceedings. They may also need protection against secondary victimization by either the accused and his or her supporters, or by the criminal justice process itself (Harvey 2001, 73).[27] Recognition of the potentially traumatizing impact on children of appearing as victim-witnesses in criminal proceedings has now been well acknowledged, and specific protective testimonial provisions have become standard in numerous domestic courtrooms (Cordon, Goodman & Anderson, 2003).[28] Testimonial aids such as the use of one-way screens to shield the vulnerable child's view of the accused, testimony via closed circuit TV from a different location, or video-taped testimony are measures that are frequently used to minimize potentially traumatizing impacts on the child victim-witnesses. Furthermore, in efforts to address potential fear in the child victim-witness due to the trial procedure itself, judges in some jurisdictions may remove their wigs and their judicial robes, and may descend from the bench in order to sit closer to the child witness and thus

---

[27] Sas, L., *The Interaction between Children's Developmental Capabilities and the Courtroom Environment: The Impact on Testimonial Competency,* Canada: Department of Justice Canada, 2002, www.justice.gc.ca/eng/pi/rs/rep-rap/2002/rr02_6/rr02_6.pdf (last visited: July 2010).

[28] *Ibidem.*

appear less intimidating (Hoyle & Zedner 2007). Finally, in many jurisdictions, child victim-witnesses are permitted to use microphones, and as well, may be accompanied by a support person when testifying.

Testimonial aids may facilitate successful participation of young and vulnerable victims and as a result, reduce potential trauma to children required to testify. However, the reality is that given the nature of international crimes along with the numbers of potential child victims likely to exist, it is unlikely that a majority of these child victims will participate in the international trials of the alleged offenders. Nevertheless, for those child victims who will participate in international criminal justice proceedings, their need for these protections will undoubtedly be as critical as for their domestic counterparts and it is imperative that such provisions be available.

5.3. ADDRESSING THE NEEDS OF CHILD VICTIMS OF INTERNATIONAL CRIMES

Although their study involved domestic crimes, results from the Morgan/Zedner research (1992) can be helpful in understanding the needs of child victims of international crimes. Their results revealed that persistent physical problems – those which go on beyond the healing of the physical injuries – make it more difficult for children to recover emotionally or psychologically. Furthermore, their study found that two-thirds of the children in their sample suffered with some form of longer-term effects of the crimes. In addition, their results indicated that for the majority, emotional distress was the most persistent consequence, often persisting long after the crime. The level of violence associated with crimes suffered by child victims of mass atrocities will likely be significantly greater than that of the crimes suffered by the child victims in the Morgan/Zedner domestic study and as such, the implications of the need to address emotional distress with child victims of international crimes are clear.

"[C]hildren necessarily depend heavily on adults for their well-being; where the very presence of adults fails to prevent a crime or adults around fail to respond to stop a crime as it occurs, children are likely to be deeply shaken" (Morgan & Zedner 1992, 54). Although these authors were not specifically referring to child victims of international crimes, their observations are particularly relevant for such child victims. A key finding of their study was that along with the need for support from individuals outside of the family, one of the most important sources of both immediate and long-term emotional support for child victims is that provided by their families. Many child victims of international crimes will be at a loss for this significant source of emotional support as for many of these young victims, family support will be absent due to the death of family members. Significantly, in many domestic jurisdictions when the family is unable to help and support the child victim (due either to family breakdown or situations of abuse), the state in conjunction with social services will often step in and assume the caregiver role for those children in need. However, in situations of armed conflict where a child victim's family is unable to provide support, and the community and/or state cannot do so either due to widespread devastation, political corruption and/or criminal responsibility for the crimes causing the victimization, who then exists to fill the void and provide this support? In post-conflict situations where mass victimization has occurred, it may not be unusual to find many child-headed households. These children must struggle with the kind of family responsibilities unknown to most children in developed countries (Ogola 2010).

Providing assistance to crime victims (both adult and child) to address their needs has become routine in many domestic jurisdictions. Through government initiatives such as criminal injuries compensation schemes or victim support services, crime victims in many domestic jurisdictions are offered assistance of varying kinds. While it is certainly important and appropriate that child victims of national crimes receive assistance in this regard, the nature and gravity of international crimes serve to magnify the importance of the provision of assistance to and addressing the needs of these particular child victims.

Many child victims of international crimes will require assistance not only in the immediate term, but likely some time into the future as well. In referring to the effects of war on children, Goldson (1996) notes that the long-term impacts are likely to be more devastating than the immediate ones. This is significant when considering how best to address potential needs of children victimized by international crimes. In the immediate aftermath of international crimes (or in fact, even during the commission of the crimes), child victims will often need medical attention, food, shelter, protection and a sense of safety and support ideally provided by family members. Many child victims will require psychosocial interventions as well (Yule 2000). While these needs are perhaps not unlike those of adult victims of international crimes, they are likely to differ from what most child victims of conventional crimes in domestic jurisdictions might have. This is so due both to the magnitude of most international crimes and to the severity of the trauma likely experienced by the victims. In the mid-term, child victims of international crimes may also need financial and psychosocial assistance to cope with situations without the adult support that they may have previously had. Finally, the need for medical attention, psychosocial and financial assistance may persist into the long term.

Machel, in her study of the impact of war on children,[29] notes that age, stage of development, gender, level of violence involved in the crime, pre-existing

---

[29]   Machel, G., *Impact of Armed Conflict on Children, Report of the Expert of the Secretary-General, Ms. Graça Machel*, Submitted Pursuant to General Assembly Resolution 48/157 26th August 1996, www.unicef.org/graca/a51–306_en.pdf (last visited: March 2010).

personality characteristics, resilience, availability of social support, cultural, social and family background are all factors which influence the needs a child may have as a result of victimization. Regardless of how a child copes with the effects of crimes of mass atrocity, these crimes in particular will likely affect all aspects of a child's development including physical, emotional, intellectual, social and spiritual. The impact of violent international crimes on child victims will often be incredibly traumatic as their lives are altered by loss of home, family members, and in many cases, trust in adults and friends. Consequently, in the aftermath of crimes of this nature it is likely that common amongst the needs of these child victims will be the need for psychosocial support. Machel defines psychosocial as the "dynamic relationship between psychological and social effects, each of which continually influences the other".[30] She elaborates by noting that psychological effects include emotions, behaviour, thoughts, memory, learning ability, perceptions and understanding. Machel describes social effects as including those such as relationships between individuals or community (often, in these crime situations affected by death, separation or other losses), and damage or destruction to social values, customary practices, social facilities and services.[31]

It should also be noted that given the disturbing trend of child combatants, in some cases, a child might hold the dual status of both victim and perpetrator.[32] Such children will no doubt have specific needs which will differ from those of non-combatants. Thus, a former child soldier will likely have needs that differ from a same aged non-combatant despite the fact they both may have witnessed and/or experienced unimaginable atrocities (Ager 1996). With the goal of assisting and not further traumatizing child victims, sensitivity to cultural, developmental, and circumstantial factors must be a priority when providing assistance to child victims.

---

[30] *Idem*, p. 80.

[31] *Idem*, p. 81.

[32] Although many domestic legal systems specify the age at which a child can be deemed to be criminally responsible (with ages varying depending upon the jurisdiction), in international criminal law, no such age specification exists. In this regard, therefore, it is telling that the ICC does not have jurisdiction to prosecute any child below the age of 18 and while the jurisdictions of other criminal justice mechanisms such as the SCSL, the ICTY and the ICTR do not have the same age restriction within their respective mandates, none of these bodies have in fact prosecuted children. This might "be seen as recognition that in situations where children have been forced to commit crimes, they are first and foremost victims and should not be prosecuted by an international court" (No Peace Without Justice & UNICEF Innocenti Research Centre, *International Criminal Justice and Children*, Rome: XPress S.r.l., 2002, 56). As such, "[t]he recognition of child perpetrators as victims can establish that they are not the rational actors in a particular case and can thus mitigate their legal responsibility for the crimes they have allegedly committed." (*Ibidem*).

6. THE ROME STATUTE'S CONSIDERATION OF CHILD VICTIMS

Participation in criminal proceedings (and particularly within an adversarial model of justice) can be both intimidating and confusing to even the most confident adult participant. Nevertheless, child victims have increasingly become involved as witnesses in the proceedings of national criminal justice systems. The issue of child victim-witness participation in criminal justice proceedings at the domestic level has been the subject of much academic writing (e.g., Bala, Lindsay & McNamara 2001; Bottoms & Goodman 1996; Bull & Davies 1996; Cunningham & Hurley 2007; Dezwirek, Sas, Wolfe & Gowdey 1996; Flin, Kearney & Murray 1996; Garkawe 2005; Westcott, Davies & Bull 2002).[33] At the international level, however, the involvement of child victims in criminal justice proceedings has been less evident and in many cases, has been virtually non-existent. Certainly the pre-ICC history of international criminal tribunals and courts did not reflect such involvement.[34] The Special Court for Sierra Leone was exceptional in recognizing the importance of the participation of children in its proceedings. While most of the children who participated at the Special Court were former child combatants, their participation in the proceedings was as victims and not as offenders.[35]

When considering the lack of involvement of child victims in previous international criminal justice contexts, it is noteworthy that the ICC is the first permanent international criminal court to provide victims (including child victims) with the opportunity to participate in the proceedings beyond solely as witnesses.[36] Given the nature of the crimes within the ICC's jurisdiction – as well as the changing face of modern warfare – it is inevitable that children will account for many of the victims of the crimes to be prosecuted at the ICC. The

---

[33] Also: Sas, L., *The Interaction between Children's Developmental Capabilities and the Courtroom Environment: The Impact on Testimonial Competency*, Canada: Department of Justice Canada, 2002; www.justice.gc.ca/eng/pi/rs/rep-rap/2002/rr02_6/rr02_6.pdf (last visited: July 2010).

[34] In referring to pre-ICC participation in international criminal proceedings, Garkawe (2005, 73–74) noted that to his knowledge, "not one child victim has given evidence before any international criminal tribunal".

[35] Although the Statute of the SCSL allowed for the prosecution of children above the age of 15 at the time of the crime, it specified that only "persons who bear the greatest responsibility" (Statute of the SCSL Article 1(1)) will be prosecuted. Consequently, the Prosecutor of the SCSL "made an early policy decision not to prosecute any person below the age of 18, since children would not meet the Statute's personal jurisdiction requirement of 'those who bear the greatest responsibility' for crimes within the Court's jurisdiction". See UNICEF Innocenti Research Centre, *Transitional Justice and Children Concept Paper: Discussion 10–12 November 2005*, 3.

[36] Child victims who participate in ICC proceedings will benefit from the UN Economic and Social Council Guidelines on Justice in Matters involving Child Victims and Witnesses of Crime. These guidelines provide recommendations on how to assist child victims and witnesses in criminal justice systems.

Rome Statute acknowledges the impact of contemporary warfare on children by noting in its preamble that "during the twentieth century millions of children (...) have been victims of unimaginable atrocities that deeply shock the conscience of humanity". As noted earlier, the ICC's jurisdiction prohibits the prosecution of any person under the age of 18. This is relevant as many of the crimes that will result in prosecutions at the ICC will have involved former child combatants. This age restriction will ensure that former child combatants will be involved with the Court only in their role as victims or witnesses, not as alleged offenders.[37] It is interesting that the first case to be tried at the ICC, that of Thomas Lubanga Dyilo of the Democratic Republic of Congo, involved the war crimes charges of enlisting and conscripting children under the age of 15 and using them to participate actively in hostilities.[38]

The Rome Statute considers the special category of child victims in three ways: (1) by defining specific crimes against children; (2) by providing for the protection and support of child victims and witnesses and allowing them to express their views and concerns; and (3) by affirming the importance of employing specially-trained Court staff. Taken together, these constitute the most extensive consideration that child victims have been afforded in international criminal courts to date.[39]

Three crimes are defined under the jurisdiction of the ICC as having particular relevance to children. These include genocide by forcibly transferring

---

[37]   Sanin, K. & Stirnemann, A., *Child Witnesses at the Special Court for Sierra Leone,* University of California, Berkeley: War Crimes Studies Centre, 2006, 7; http://ist-socrates.berkeley.edu/~warcrime/documents/ChildWitnessReport.pdf (last visited: March 2006). The 2002 No Peace without Justice and UNICEF Innocenti Research Centre Report (p. 71) notes that "[t]he decision to exclude persons under 18 from the jurisdiction of the ICC recognizes that children are not likely to hold positions of leadership during armed conflict, and that other mechanisms – such as national courts or truth commissions – are more appropriate forums to address crimes allegedly committed by children."

[38]   See ICC Case Information Sheet (last visited: August 2010) at: www.icc-cpi.int/NR/rdonlyres/477CC240-07A5-4FAC-80AC-3A743C2CD649/282219/LubangaENG.pdf.

[39]   Referring to victims in general, Danieli (2006b) suggests that the sections in the Rome Statute and the RPE of the ICC relevant to victims were based theoretically on the UN Declaration of Basic Principles of Justice for Victims of Crime and Abuse of Power (or "the Magna Carta for victims" (Danieli's words, 1645)), and "practically upon both the positive as well as negative practical/operational experiences of the ad hoc Tribunals for the former Yugoslavia and Rwanda" (1647). She further contends that the ICC-related victim provisions "make for the most progressive provisions for victims in any international court, in fact, in international law." (*ibidem*). Funk (2010, 79) similarly notes that "[the most innovative feature] distinguishing the ICC from other predecessor tribunals and regional courts is that it formally, and comprehensively, enshrines the rights of victims to participate in proceedings, state their views and concerns, and claim reparations, including compensation, rehabilitation, and restitution." He continues by adding that "[t]he ICC's restorative system of victim rights, indeed, finds no equal in any other tribunal or regional court, with victim-related provisions distributed throughout the ICC's legal framework. Such rights did not exist in predecessor international criminal courts, including the ICTR, ICTY, or the Special Court for Sierra Leone" (*Ibidem*).

---

children from one national, ethnical, racial or religious group to another; crimes against humanity by trafficking children; and the war crimes of conscription, enlistment or use of children under the age of 15 into active hostilities. These crimes are defined respectively in Articles 6(e), 7(2)(c), 8(2)(b)(xxvi) and 8(2)(e) (vii) of the Rome Statute.

With respect to providing for the protection and support of child victims, children who appear as either victim-witnesses or victim-participants[40] at the court are protected under Article 68(1) which states that:

> *The Court shall take appropriate measures to protect the safety, physical and psychological well-being, dignity and privacy of victims and witnesses. In so doing, the Court shall have regard to all relevant factors, including age, gender as defined in article 7, paragraph 3, and health, and the nature of the crime, in particular, but not limited to, where the crime involves sexual or gender violence or violence against children. The Prosecutor shall take such measures particularly during the investigation and prosecution of such crimes. These measures shall not be prejudicial to or inconsistent with the rights of the accused and a fair and impartial trial.*

In addition to the protection provided by Article 68(1), Article 68(2) facilitates the testimony of child victim-witnesses. It does so by allowing (subject to certain criteria) for proceedings to be held *in camera*, and by allowing the presentation of evidence by electronic or other means.[41]

Regarding the importance of providing specially trained court staff, Articles 36(8)(b), 42(9), and 44(1) indicate the need for specialized expertise on violence against children respectively by judges, prosecutorial advisers and prosecutorial and registry staff. In addition, ICC Resolution ICC-ASP/4/Res.1 provides for a Code of Professional Conduct for Counsel. Articles 9 and 29 of this Code specifically mention that counsel should take into account the personal circumstances and specific needs of, and have particular consideration for, *inter alia*, children. Similarly, a Code of Judicial Ethics can be found at ICC-BD/02–01–05. Each of these Codes document appropriate conduct towards witnesses before the court (see Articles 7 and 29 of the former and Article 8 of the later). Article 43(6) of the Rome Statute provides for the creation of a Victims and Witnesses Unit (VWU) within the Registry of the Court. The VWU is staffed with persons who have expertise in trauma, including trauma related to crimes of sexual violence. The Unit provides protective measures and security arrangements, counselling and other appropriate assistance for witnesses and

---

[40] Note that 'victim-witnesses' are crime victims who testify before a court, whereas 'victim participants' are crime victims who participate in court proceedings by expressing their views and concerns. Victims can have a dual status both as witnesses and participants.

[41] According to No Peace Without Justice & UNICEF Innocenti Research Centre, *International Criminal Justice and Children*, Rome: XPress S.r.l., 2002, 16, 'other means' may include "(...) sight-screens between the victim and the accused, pre-recorded testimonies, video conferencing or closed-circuit television, and the use of pseudonyms.".

victims who appear before the Court and for others who are at risk on account of testimony given by such witnesses. While child victims are not specifically identified in Article 43(6), Rule 17(3) of the RPE, which addresses the functions of the Victims and Witnesses Unit, states that:

> [i]n performing its functions, the Unit shall give due regard to the particular needs of children, elderly persons and persons with disabilities. In order to facilitate the participation and protection of children as witnesses, the Unit may assign, as appropriate, and with the agreement of the parents or the legal guardian, a child-support person to assist a child through all stages of the proceedings.

Furthermore, with respect to the expertise in the Unit, Rule 19(f), states that the Unit may include, as appropriate, persons with expertise in children, in particular traumatized children.

Additional evidence of the Rome Statute's consideration of child victim-witnesses and participants can be found in the Regulations of the Office of the Prosecutor which specify that:

> [t]he Gender and Children Unit shall be comprised of staff with legal and other expertise on sexual and gender violence and violence against children in accordance with article 42, paragraph 9 [of the Rome Statute[42]]. The Unit shall be responsible for providing advice to the Prosecutor, ExCom and the Divisions in all areas related to sexual and gender violence and violence against children, and shall contribute to preliminary examinations and evaluations, investigations and prosecutions in those areas. (Regulation 12)

In addition, Article 79 of the Rome Statute also benefits child victims. This Article provided for the establishment of a 'Trust Fund for Victims' (TFV) by decision of the Assembly of States Parties. The TFV has two primary mandates, one which is linked directly to the Court and the other which allows for the provision of more independent general assistance. The mandate linked directly to the Court involves implementing reparation orders from the Court against convicted persons. The more independent mandate involves the discretionary use of voluntary funds from donors (subject to approval from the Court) to assist victims of crimes committed within the Court's jurisdiction but who may not be directly linked to a case before the Court. Assistance under this second mandate is provided in the form of physical rehabilitation, material support, and/or psychological rehabilitation.[43] It is from this second mandate of the TFV that many of the child victims of crimes within the jurisdiction of the Court are likely

---

42   Article 42(9) of the Rome Statute states that "The Prosecutor shall appoint advisers with legal expertise on specific issues, including, but not limited to, sexual and gender violence and violence against children.".

43   See 'The Two roles of the TFV' at: http://trustfundforvictims.org/two-roles-tfv (last visited: July 2010).

to benefit. The advantage of the second mandate is that it allows for the provision of immediate and urgent assistance to victims in need, subject to the conditions found in Regulation 50 of the Regulations of the TFV.[44] The provision of assistance and services need not wait until the conclusion of a trial when court-awarded reparations may be ordered. Examples of the Trust Fund for Victims' projects implemented under this mandate include, *inter alia*, counselling, vocational training and reintegration assistance for former child combatants, abductees, children orphaned by armed conflict and/or other vulnerable children; counselling and material support for family members caring for children who lost their parents during armed conflicts; reconstructive surgery; and peace and reconciliation activities for children abducted into armed forces, orphaned, or otherwise made vulnerable by war.[45]

7. THE ASSISTANCE/SERVICE PROVIDERS

Earlier in the chapter, the needs of child victims of international crimes were discussed. However, no specific mention has been made thus far of who might provide the assistance to address those needs. The reality is that the responsibility for the provision of assistance to child victims of international crimes does not, and reasonably cannot, fall on only one group or organization, be it local or international. Of course, where states are able to address the needs of, and provide assistance to the victims in their jurisdiction, this should be an obvious source of service provision. However, in a country whose infrastructure has been destroyed as a result of armed conflict, the state may be unable or ill-equipped to provide the necessary services. Furthermore, even if states do possess adequate resources to provide assistance (which, in many conflict-affected countries may be unlikely), they may not have the capacity or expertise required to deliver the specific kinds of services required (i.e., trauma counselling expertise). In addition, challenges in delivering services and providing assistance may exist where issues of trust or the lack thereof have played a significant role in the nature of the armed conflicts.

While local NGOs may be active on the ground in areas that are affected by armed conflict and thus may be best positioned to provide culturally appropriate assistance both quickly and efficiently (including, importantly, to more isolated or remote areas in the field), such organizations may not have the resources to provide the required services. International NGOs and UN Agencies may have

---

[44]   See Regulations of the Trust Fund for Victims at: www.icc-cpi.int/NR/rdonlyres/0CE5967F-EADC-44C9-8CCA-7A7E9AC89C30/140126/ICCASP432Res3_English.pdf (last visited: July 2010).

[45]   See Projects of the Trust Fund for Victims at: http://trustfundforvictims.org/projects#Assistance%20to%20children%20and%20youth (last visited: July 2010).

access to greater resources than smaller, local NGOs, however they do not necessarily have the advantages of the local NGOs with respect to experienced staff with culturally appropriate knowledge of both the people in need of assistance and the circumstances in the field. At a broader level, NGOs and UN agencies and organizations are guided by mandates and such mandates will unquestionably differ amongst the various organizations. Even in cases where organizations (national or international) have similar mandates, they will not necessarily agree on the types of services that ought to be provided, or on the manner in which the assistance can best be delivered. With a lack of agreement and coordination between service providers regarding service delivery and assistance, there is a risk that the differences in organizations' mandates will result in certain populations receiving no services or assistance, or perhaps duplication of services resulting in a waste of resources and ineffective service delivery.[46] What seems clear from this is the importance of working together. International and local NGOs, and UN agencies and organizations must work co-operatively with one other if the needs of child victims of international crimes are to be optimally addressed.

A potential approach to ensuring this kind of co-operation might be through the creation of an organizing body which could serve to co-ordinate and manage the activities of the organizations that would most likely provide services to child victims of international crimes. Some might suggest that such a body already exists in the form of UNICEF or even the Office of the Special Representative for Children.[47] However, evidence is not clear (perhaps due to constraints imposed by their respective mandates) that either of these bodies have undertaken such a role. Another suggestion in this regard might be the Trust Fund for Victims. However, events which resulted in the expulsion of 13 international NGOs and six local NGOs working in Sudan may suggest the need for further consideration of this option.[48]

---

[46] See Hamilton (2006, 299) for a discussion of what she terms "mandate drift" with respect to UN Agencies and NGOs.

[47] See the website of the Office of the Special Representative for Children and Armed Conflict at: www.un.org/children/conflict/english/index.html (last visited: July 2010). See also Hamilton (2006, 277 & 281–283) for a brief discussion of the aims and functions of both UNICEF and the Office of the Special Representative for Children. Dupuy & Peters (2010, 152–154) and Kuper (1997, 147–149) also provide descriptions of the roles of these organizations.

[48] This action occurred as a result of an arrest warrant issued by the ICC for President al-Bashir of Sudan. Following this, President al-Bashir expelled the NGOs working in the country in retaliation for what he perceived as their collusion with the ICC (see P.D. Bell, *International Relief and Development NGOs and the International Justice System*, p. 5, Discussion Paper Prepared for the Consultative Conference on International Criminal Justice, September 9–11, 2009, United Nations Headquarters, New York, at: www.internationalcriminaljustice.net/experience/papers/session6.pdf, last visited: July 2010). As the TFV is seen by many as one and the same as the ICC, the consequent result is that members of international and local NGOs and other potential TFV partners working on the ground may be reluctant to be seen as being associated in any way with the TFV for fear that they too will suffer a similar fate to the NGOs expelled by al-Bashir.

8. CONCLUSION – IMPROVING THE EFFECTIVENESS OF RESPONSE TO CHILD VICTIMS OF INTERNATIONAL CRIMES

This chapter has highlighted the vulnerability of child victims and has argued that they deserve special attention in efforts to address their needs arising from international crimes committed against them. Despite the bleak statistics cited at the outset of the chapter, there is evidence that the plight of child victims of international crimes has been recognized by the international community. However, while it is encouraging that some efforts have been made to assist the specific group of child victims who have participated as combatants in armed conflicts, it is equally important to address the needs of all child victims of international crimes. The protections provided by international criminal justice instruments (e.g. the Geneva Conventions and their Additional Protocols, the UNCRC and its Optional Protocols, and the Rome Statute) are important for children affected by armed conflicts, as are the efforts to address the needs of child victims who participate in criminal justice proceedings.

It has been recognized that the effects of crimes can persist long after the cessation of hostilities and the criminal justice proceedings that deal with them, and thus there is a need to focus attention on the recovery of all child victims. This need must be addressed jointly by all members of the international community, including that of the justice community. It is neither sufficient nor reasonable to expect that NGOs or UN organizations can or will assume the role in its entirety and it is clear that joint efforts are required. How can this be accomplished? Co-ordination and co-operation, training, education, information and knowledge dissemination and outreach are all important. Resources are essential. Tangible steps must be taken if not to eradicate the challenges faced by children affected by international crimes, then at least to improve their circumstances. Time is of the essence, as, childhood, no matter how it is defined, is time-limited. As time passes, young people develop and gradually become adult members of society. Future generations depend on the timely and progressive efforts of the international community to get things right for children affected by international crimes. The road ahead might require concentrated efforts to more vigorously implement salient Articles of the UNCRC – Article 39 for example which promotes the need for recovery. More comprehensive approaches need to be made in order to address all children affected by international crimes, not only select groups. This may seem ambitious, but it is necessary when the stakes are so high. As Graça Machel remarked, "When we speak of hundreds, thousands and millions of war-affected children, it is essential to remember that each number and each statistic represents a child's life – someone's son, daughter, sister or brother".[49]

Efforts are required to broaden or at a minimum co-ordinate, the mandates of those already offering assistance to child victims. Improved advocacy on behalf of all members of this particular group of victims is necessary. Better communication and co-ordination between those already working on behalf of child victims is essential so that the limitations of one organization may be addressed by the strengths of another. In times of fiscal constraints and priority setting, it is imperative that resources not be wasted on duplication of services and that the needs of child victims of international crimes be brought to the forefront of national and international political and social agendas. Perhaps the creation of an organizing body could serve to achieve these goals, and in this way, existing gaps can be filled resulting in comprehensive assistance being provided to all child victims. Certainly research into such a possibility merits consideration. The duty is upon all members of the international community to ensure that the trauma and devastation experienced by children as a result of their victimization by international crimes is addressed in a timely and effective way so that these young people can go on to live full and rewarding lives.

---

[49]   Machel, G., *Impact of Armed Conflict on Children, Report of the Expert of the Secretary-General, Ms. Graça Machel*, Submitted Pursuant to General Assembly Resolution 48/157, 26 August 1996, p. 6; www.unicef.org/graca/a51–306_en.pdf (last visited: March 2010).

PART V
VICTIMOLOGICAL APPROACHES
TO INTERNATIONAL CRIMES

XXIII. VICTIMOLOGICAL APPROACHES APPLIED TO INTERNATIONAL CRIMES
Concluding Remarks

Rianne LETSCHERT, Roelof HAVEMAN,
Anne-Marie DE BROUWER and Antony PEMBERTON

1. INTRODUCTION

In *Rwanda: Death, Despair and Defiance*, African Rights (1994) described the horrific cruelties against and killings of Tutsi and moderate Hutu by extremist Hutu over a period of a few months only (see also Ruvebana, this volume). In 1994, the beautiful country of Rwanda – also known as the country of one thousand hills – was engulfed by one of the most effective and most public genocides of all time. Within 100 days, from April 7 to July 18, about 800,000 Tutsi and moderate Hutu were brutally murdered by extremist Hutu, including their neighbours, friends and acquaintances. In those 100 days, an estimated 250,000 to 500,000 women and girls, but also men, were raped and experienced other forms of sexual violence. As a 1996 United Nations report observed, "rape was the rule and its absence the exception". For many survivors, rape and other forms of sexual violence, but also the resulting HIV infection, babies born from rape, and stigmatization and isolation by their family and community members, constitute the ultimate violation of their human rights. In addition, the genocide left hundreds of thousand children orphaned and a similar large number of survivors lost their husband, wife and/or child(ren). Many lost their houses and other possessions. The country's economy, its judicial institutions and social services were completely destroyed. Over 1 million people were involved in the genocide and survivors and perpetrators are now again living side by side. Slowly but with strong determination, the country is recovering from its horrific past. Programs of reparation and reconciliation, national and local, have been developed, and (tradition-inspired) justice mechanisms put in place.

Many instances of mass atrocities and in many ways similar carnage preceded and followed the period of the Rwandan genocide in different parts of the world.

In the 20th century alone, hundreds of millions fatalities occurred (Rummel 1994), and the scourge of international crimes – genocide, crimes against humanity and war crimes – remains a reality today. Attempting to do justice under the sceptre of such heinous cruelty and unspeakable suffering is a daunting task, with the enormity of evil blowing up the limits of normally held trials and convictions. What response fits the murder of hundreds of thousands of human beings? Is it possible to adequately distinguish perpetrators, bystanders and victims in the chaos following the collapse of the rule of law? How can we conceive of reparations for victims who lost everything – their families, their possessions, their livelihood – and have witnessed atrocities first-hand? And what, if anything, can and should the justice response to these atrocities contribute to the rebuilding of societies in which the seeds of new violence are already sown? Is justice possible for individual perpetrators, for individual victims, and for society as a whole? There are no easy answers to any of these questions.

The essays in this volume contribute to the further understanding of how to do justice in the aftermath of mass atrocities from a victimological perspective with a focus on conflicts that took place in the African region.[1] Following the widely touted example of the South African Truth and Reconciliation Commission, the importance of a wide range of approaches for dealing with atrocities (see Chouliaris, this volume) is acknowledged, and ways of interlinking truth commissions and amnesties (see Van Wijk, this volume; Haldemann, this volume; Roht-Arriaza 2006) with trials are explored. This volume contains various examples of such other approaches than the classical penal approach, which can be collected under the noun *transitional justice*. It clearly illustrates that the times that a criminal approach to mass atrocities was considered the one and only approach fitting each and every situation of mass atrocities is since long gone. Even the times that other approaches were seen as 'alternatives' to the criminal justice approach has passed.

In the – albeit short – history of international criminal justice, the victimological perspective has all too often been neglected. The trials of Nuremberg and Tokyo after WWII, as well as the International Criminal Tribunals for Rwanda (ICTR) and the former Yugoslavia (ICTY) and the Special Court for Sierra Leone (SCSL), solely involved victims as witnesses. In addition, the aforementioned trials evidenced a too strict adherence to the practice of criminal justice, in particular of an adversarial nature, in the domestic sphere (Drumbl 2007). If really necessary, amendments were made to the rules to avoid violation of core criminal justice principles, for instance *nullum crimen, nulla poena sine praevia lege poenali* (Bassiouni 1996) or *male captus, bene/male*

---

[1]　Future planned volumes will take examples from other regions of the world. In a final volume we aim to provide comparative reflections on possible regional, cultural or other differences in specific victimological approaches to international crimes.

detentus (Paulussen 2010). Less thought, however, was reserved for the extent to which trying some perpetrators, following European/American criminal justice procedure, can and should be expected to inculcate a sense of justice in victimized populations. The development of international criminal justice should, as Chouliaris in this volume contends "not be perceived and approached as an end itself, but as a means to deliver justice to those directly affected". More so than at the national level, justice after international crimes has an expressivist function (Feinberg 1970): justice is done, only when it is also seen to be done. Of course, advances have already been made. The Rome Statute of the International Criminal Court (ICC) is heralded as a victim-focused improvement, affording victims a participatory role. In the wake of the adoption of the 2005 Bassiouni/ Van Boven reparation principles, reparation regimes have flourished (see generally De Greiff 2009; and Correa and Letschert & Van Boven, this volume).

Nevertheless, the recognition that in the aftermath of international crimes the proof of the justice pudding is in the extent to which victimized populations are likely to eat or somehow digest it is still not sufficiently recognized. Debates concerning concrete examples of countries grappling with the aftermath of international crimes are fought on dogmatic grounds, in which assertions are trotted out as facts, predictions about the chances of success are made not on sound evidence, but on the apparent possession of a crystal ball (see Van Wijk, this volume, for many examples regarding amnesty) and the shortcomings of criminal justice in the domestic sphere (see Bach 2009, for a devastating account of the actual working of criminal justice in the United States) are swept aside in the transplant to the international sphere, although its procedures are less rather than more suited to these situations (Drumbl 2007; Fletcher & Weinstein 2002; Groenhuijsen & Pemberton, this volume).

In this concluding chapter we will present the main conclusions drawn from the various contributions in this volume and will reflect on the different components that deserve further attention in the development of a victimological perspective applied to international crimes (section 10). First, we will outline some of the features that distinguish international crimes from criminal behaviour in the domestic sphere, and reflect on these special features influencing the development of a victimological perspective (sections 2 and 3). Second, we will discuss different ways to provide reparative measures to victims of international crimes, discussing, among others, the need to find an adequate balance between individual and collective needs (sections 4 and 5). The activities of international criminal tribunals in providing justice to victims is extensively discussed in this volume. We will reflect upon the main complexities and challenges in general, and in relation to specific vulnerable groups. Also, the efforts of national jurisdictions are examined (sections 6 and 7). A separate section is devoted to preventive measures, specifically in relation to sexual violence crimes (section 8). Section 9 examines the different transitional justice measures discussed in this volume, and if and how a victimological perspective is incorporated in such initiatives.

2. INTERNATIONAL CRIMES: THE ULTIMATE PERVERSION OF THE RULE OF LAW

The first main characteristic of international crimes is that they are usually committed under the guise of state authority. In this volume, both Groenhuijsen and Pemberton as well as Chouliaris demonstrate that this amounts to the ultimate perversion of the rule of law, in that the same power established to protect citizens is employed to harm or kill those citizens instead. In the response to international crimes, rebuilding the rule of law has backward and forward-looking aspects (also Teitel 2002). It is backward looking in that it should incorporate a reaction to the atrocities already committed, and forward looking in that it should contribute to the perceived legitimacy of government and legal authorities, the rule of law in a material sense.

These functions are overlapping, but distinct, and part of the shortcomings of international criminal justice is that it presupposes a smooth link between these functions. It is often assumed that trials for previous atrocities will automatically contribute to rebuilding the rule of law. Norm-cascading (e.g. Sunstein 1997) is supposed to lead the ravaged societies to repeat the good example of international criminal justice in their own domestic sphere (Finnemore & Sikkink 1998). This is, however, not confirmed by evidence (Snyder & Vinjamuri 2004; Vinjamuri & Snyder 2004), and Groenhuijsen and Pemberton discuss in this volume in some depth why this is the case.

First of all, it remains to be seen whether international criminal justice can realistically provide an example worth repeating. Much of the features of international criminal procedures raise additional problems; the abundance of evidence of collective evil, but the lack of proof of individual wrongdoing; the complexities of establishing guilt for crimes committed as a collective; and the uncertain line between culpable and inculpable parties, of which the sometimes overlapping nature of victimization and perpetration is the most poignant example (see Smeulers, this volume). Similarly, classic functions of criminal law, its provision of deterrence and/or a means to provide just deserts, do not apply with equal force to the situation of international crimes (Aukerman 2002). In practice this is further exacerbated by the selective nature of international criminal justice; only a small minority of perpetrators will be tried (Goldstone 1996). This leads to a discrepancy between wrongdoing and punishment, which is not helped by the fact that the punishment meted out for international crimes is sometimes *lower* rather than higher than for ordinary crimes. Taken together, this suggests that international criminal justice – even more than domestic criminal justice – is *partial* justice at best (Roberts 2003) and the limits of criminal justice in these situations should be clearly delineated and acknowledged (Drumbl 2007; Groenhuijsen & Pemberton, this volume).

In the second place, the legitimacy of institutions providing international criminal justice should be problematized. Although the phrase 'international community' may have positive connotations for many commentators, in the experience of war-torn societies its actions are most often characterized succinctly as 'too little, too late' (e.g. Aukerman 2002), of which the role of the international community before, during and after the Rwandan genocide is a telling example. The demand of justice in the aftermath of international crimes would ring less hollow if actors within the international community had actively strived to prevent them from happening, or at least had refrained from complicity in their commission (see Power 2003). However, the structure of international criminal law and, in particular, its recurring emphasis on *independence* from domestic attempts to provide justice, from other, concurrent, attempts to rebuild state structures and from the historical, traditional and political realities of the societies in question suggests that legitimacy in the eyes of the victimized populations is neither a prime consideration, nor a realistic outcome (Chouliaris, this volume; Drumbl 2007; Groenhuijsen & Pemberton, this volume). Of course a neutral and independent administration of criminal justice is essential to its realization in individual cases; this does not and should not, however, provide cover for an institutional design that sees its abstraction and removal from the actual situation on the ground as a virtue rather than a vice. The extent to which justice is done should be measured by its actual contribution to rebuilding society rather than its adherence to the blueprint of European-Americanized criminal justice procedures.

3. MASS VICTIMIZATION AND 'THE SOCIAL DEATH OF VICTIMS'

As Chouliaris in this volume argues, the victimological concern should lie at the heart of the quest for justice in the aftermath of international crimes. In establishing a link between the backward and forward-looking aspects of re-establishing the rule of law, the second (the large number of victims) and third (the social and psychological processes that feature in the perpetration of these crimes) characteristics of victimization after international crimes are of great importance.[2] However, generalized facts about how international crime is committed and experienced cannot replace fully the necessity of reviewing the reality of a given international crime (Fletcher & Weinstein 2002; see also

---

[2]   The first characteristic concerns the complicity of government agencies in the commission of international crimes.

Ruvebana, this volume). As is evidenced by the contributions of Ruvebana and Van Wijk in this volume, historical and cultural aspects may give rise to different solutions, while Erez and Meroz-Aharoni in this volume show that the interplay between the crimes committed and the views of victimized populations may differentiate the reactions from one instance of victimization to another, *within* the same societies.

International crimes do not necessarily involve large numbers of victims, but as a rule they do, while most of the complexities solely arise in situations of mass rather than individual victimization (Groenhuijsen & Pemberton, this volume). The existence of thousands or even millions of victims outstretches the resources afforded of justice procedures and reparation programmes: hard choices are inevitable (Letschert & Van Boven; Correa, both this volume).

In making these choices international criminal justice could do worse than review the processes involved in what Waller (2007) calls 'the social death of victims', which adequately reflects the processes by which victims of international crimes become mere objects in the eyes of perpetrators, enticing ordinary people to commit atrocities, even against friends and neighbours. A severely escalated form of us-them thinking and xenophobia; moral justification of mass-murder; dehumanization of victims and euphemistic labelling of evil actions; which together lead to the view that the victims are beyond the scope of morality and finally blaming the victims for their suffering, maintaining the view that victims are perpetrators themselves, deserving their fate.

In this volume, Groenhuijsen and Pemberton contend that justice should strive to act as a countervailing force to these processes, *en passant* taking into account the dynamics of perpetration of international crimes, its severe consequences as well as the somewhat unnerving observation that these crimes are committed by ordinary people. Central stage should be afforded to the re-emphasizing of victims' membership of the moral sphere, at least by acknowledging their victimization. The mere act of conferring victim status may be a more important consideration than more far-reaching rights, for example participatory rights, in particular if implementation of these rights will entail the necessity of denying acknowledgement.

Acknowledging victimization may also go some way in relieving the feelings of self-blame victims often have, although expectations of the impact of justice procedures should not run too high. Indeed, any 'therapeutic' impact on victims' recovery will be extremely limited (Fletcher 2005). Justice procedures as a rule are not magical vessels of catharsis, and this is further compounded by the deeply traumatic experiences, the limited resources and the complexities in delivering justice after international crimes. This not only applies to criminal justice, but also to other approaches, such as truth commissions and tradition-inspired mechanisms. To be true, a major benefit of all these procedures for victims is its potential to contribute to re-humanizing victims, allowing them to voice their own perspective, in their own words, as individual humans. However, truth is not a panacea for all ills – particularly considering that the truth often shows that atrocities were committed by ordinary people, for no clear reason – nor is it a royal road to reconciliation, while there is increasing evidence of counterproductive effects on victims who participate (Allan *et al.* 2006; Mendeloff 2009, Brouneus 2010).

4. REPARATIVE JUSTICE

Coherence of measures through the notion of *reparative* justice is considered key to several authors in this volume. Reparative justice in the context of international crimes can be loosely defined as the total of initiatives and measures seeking to ensure that all persons victimized are offered an adequate level of protection under the law. A landmark in the promotion of reparative justice is the adoption of the 2005 'Basic Principles and Guidelines on the Right to a Remedy and Reparation for Victims of Gross Violations of International Human Rights Law and Serious Violations of International Humanitarian Law,' (Reparation Principles), preceded a few years before (in 1998) by the establishment of the ICC in The Hague. The growing attention for international criminal and humanitarian law and specifically for the procedural role of victims therein, has led to the inclusion of an elaborate set of procedural victims' rights in the Court's Statute and Rules of Procedure and Evidence.

As explained by Danieli in this volume,

> *reparative justice insists that every step throughout the justice experience – from the first moment of encounter of the Court with a potential witness through the follow up of witnesses after their return home to the aftermath of the completion of the case – presents an opportunity for redress and healing, a risk of missing or neglecting the opportunity for healing victims and reintegrating them into their communities and societies, or, worse, causing (re)victimization and (re)traumatization.*

She presents a set of necessary elements of healing in the wake of massive trauma, presented as goals and recommendations, focussing on different levels, namely the individual, societal, national, and international level. On the *individual* level, the reestablishment of the victims' equality of value, power, and esteem (dignity) is imperative. This can be accomplished by different measures, for instance, through compensation, both real and symbolic, restitution; rehabilitation; and commemorations. On the *societal* level it is important to relieve the victim's stigmatization and separation from society. Also here, commemorations play an important role, next to measures focusing on empowerment and education. Rebuilding justice structures in the wake of mass victimization in order to provide and maintain equal value under the law and the provisions of justice on the *national* level is another component in the process of healing according to Danieli's analysis. This is accomplished by prosecutions, apologies, securing public records, education and lastly creating national mechanisms for monitoring, conflict resolution and preventive interventions. Also on the *international* level, establishing justice and redress mechanisms combating impunity is considered important. Danieli refers to, among other things, the creation of *ad hoc* and permanent mechanisms for prosecution (e.g. *ad hoc* tribunals and the ICC) and creating international mechanisms for monitoring, conflict resolution and preventive interventions. It may be interesting to compare these elements and measures with what is being discussed within the framework of *transitional justice* mechanisms (see below). These different elements and measures are also included in the 2005 Reparation Principles. Providing guidelines on how to implement such a comprehensive reparative framework in post-conflict societies is a challenging if not impossible task. Societies trying to overcome a period of conflict show several profound shortcomings, both in the legal and social order that also affect possibilities to provide proper reparation afterwards (Tomuschat 2008; Letschert & Van Boven, this volume).

As follows from the different contributions in this volume, the need for contextualization of reparative justice processes is also increasingly acknowledged. Also Danieli underlines that this comprehensive framework "sets out necessary *cumulative complementary* elements, *all* of which are needed to be applied in different weights, in different situations, cultures and contexts". The view of victims themselves is of utmost importance in this regard. This also fits into the notion of reparation-as-process as described by Letschert and Van Boven in this volume, where concepts such as participation and empowerment of victims play a prominent role. The different studies assessing victims' perceptions on reparative justice also demonstrate the importance of including victims' voices in the design of reparative measures. Correa's analysis in this volume provides some concrete examples on how to define and implement reparations for victims, not relying on judicial decisions or standards, but on policy and administrative mechanisms aiming to address the most fundamental needs of victims. The examples demonstrate the advantages of comprehensive transitional justice policies, which include establishing the crimes committed and what made them possible to happen; making a serious effort to investigate and try the most severe crimes; and reforming institutions in order to avoid repetition of such crimes. According to Correa, "such an approach can both provide coherence to the reparations effort, and also demonstrates the sincerity of the state to implement them".

That being said, various studies reveal that it is still exceptional that transitional justice efforts, including reparative measures, are based on perceptions of future beneficiaries (Pham *et al.* 2009).[3] In addition, the impact

---

[3]   Also Redress, *Torture Survivors' Perceptions of Reparations; Preliminary Survey*, 2001.

of interventions, be it tradition-based (see Schotsmans, this volume) or internationally influenced, or mixtures of both, is hardly consistently evaluated. This makes it difficult to give far-fledged or evidence-based statements regarding the short or long term effects of such measures on individual or collective groups of victims or society at large.

5.   INDIVIDUAL VERSUS GROUP PERSPECTIVE

The importance of the individual and group perspective when analysing the concept of justice in the wake of mass victimization is generally accepted, and analysed by various authors in this volume. According to Wemmers (this volume), with regard to mass victimizations, especially those that target specific social groups, such as genocide, social identity is particularly salient as well as group perceptions of justice. Wemmers argues that when victims focus on the collective needs of their social group, they are less punitive than when they focus on their individual needs. When discussing the concept of procedural justice, she notes that both individual and group perceptions of fairness are important. She holds that when crimes have been committed against a social group, it is important that the victimized group is recognized through, for example, the participation of its members in justice procedures. If their group as such is not recognized, victims might become frustrated and it will potentially undermine their self-esteem as a member of the group. This in turn can fuel animosity between social groups. The importance of finding a proper balance between the individual and collective perspective in providing recognition and acknowledgement is also underlined by Haldemann in this volume:

> On the one hand, they have an inherently social and political dimension that is captured by the idea of collective recognition. On the other hand, these crimes are, first and foremost, planned and performed by individuals against individuals and thus remain rooted in perceptions of interpersonal meaning – that is why interpersonal recognition is important.

Also Letschert and Van Boven reflect in this volume on finding the right balance between the group and individual perspective. They refer to the difficulties in adapting the existing judicial right to an effective *individual* remedy to the context of mass victimization where it is often claimed that *collective* reparations might be better suited to provide reparative justice. While the judicial approach to reparation characterizes the Reparation Principles, non-judicial schemes and programmes offering redress and reparation (as described also by Correa, this volume) also contribute to reparative justice for the benefit of large number of victims. The Reparation Principles reflect this by combining individual measures intended to implement the right to reparation (restitution, compensation and rehabilitation) as well as a strong focus on collective measures of satisfaction and guarantees of non-repetition. To give a concrete example, the provision of material goods and services so as to restore decent living conditions, and to secure health and educational facilities may serve as a mode of collective reparation which will not only benefit victimized communities but also has the potential to benefit society at large (see also Ndahinda and Muleefu, both this volume). A lot of discussion takes place on including development goals in reparative justice measures. In societies that have been struck by gross and massive violations of human rights, collective reparations focusing also on development aid can be considered a possible and effective means to achieve a fair degree of reparative justice. Complex and agonizing issues of accountability are being avoided as well as troublesome classifications of people, as victims and as perpetrators. Such expeditious policy considerations therefore appear to be attractive. However, they fail to recognize the essential notion of reparation as constituting part of a process towards peace, justice and reconciliation. They also fail to acknowledge a victim-oriented perspective that keeps faith with the plight of victims and survivors (see in similar terms Groenhuijsen & Pemberton, this volume). Reparative measures focusing on society at large should therefore never stand alone. Also, various victimological studies reveal that denying specific acknowledgment and recognition of a person's individual victimization can have negative effects on victim's recovery.

What follows from the different contributions in this volume is that a further conceptualization of the notion of collective victimization is needed. The existing international (quasi) legal instruments refer both to individual and collective victims (see Articles 1 and 2 of the 1985 UN Victims Declaration, and Article V.8 of the Reparation Principles). Various scholars have referred to the complexities in and possible negative ramifications of categorizing victims into collective victim groups. For instance, within the course of the same conflict, groups and individuals may switch roles over time: a victim one day might turn perpetrator the next in a perceived struggle for survival (see also Smeulers, this volume). Also the notion of innocent bystander is considered controversial in situations of mass conflict (Fletcher & Weinstein 2002). Providing reparative justice in these contexts is therefore a difficult if not sometimes impossible task, especially if it entails categorizing individuals or groups in beneficiaries or victimized groups and perpetrator groups. Reparative measures in these contexts should therefore aim to be as inclusive as possible, thereby recognizing the tremendous harm suffered by different individuals and groups in society.

The typology discussed by Letschert and Van Boven, using the categorization of primary, secondary and tertiary victims and applying this within the reparation-as-right, as symbol or as process framework could be helpful in further conceptualizing this notion of inclusiveness. From a purely legal point of view it seems reasonable to include both primary and secondary victims under the reparation-as-right formula. Nevertheless, in situations of mass victimization this might be too ambitious and in the end raise false expectations by victims. When providing reparation-as-symbol, or as process, the entitlements and the needs of different communities affected by mass violence can be addressed, thereby including all three victim categories and depending on the form of reparation, also the community at large.

6.   THE ICC AND THE ICTR

Several contributions in this volume focus on the role of the ICC and the ICTR in providing justice to victims. By mid-2011, the ICC was looking into international crimes committed in several African countries, namely Uganda, the Democratic Republic of the Congo, Sudan (Darfur), Central African Republic, Kenya and Libya. Despite its relatively short existence, the ICC has already been instrumental in creating and expanding on victims' rights, such as the right to participate in trial proceedings and to request reparation. As pointed out by Ndahinda in this volume, these rights were largely ignored by previous international criminal tribunals, such as the ICTR, where victims only appeared in court in order to provide testimony. Furthermore, possibilities to receive reparation at the ICTR were minimal and the way victims were treated in court sometimes highly questionable, which lead at times to difficulties in the cooperation of the Rwandan government, NGOs and victims with the Tribunal. At the ICC, inspired partly due to the lack of such possibilities at the ICTR, a victim can participate as a victim, testify as a witness or both, and additionally request reparation from the Court and/or receive assistance from the Trust Fund for Victims. Furthermore, the Court has developed strong specific provisions for vulnerable groups of victims, such as survivors of sexual violence and children, to ameliorate their participation and/or testimony (see Grossman; Mesters & Adeboyejo; Chu, De Brouwer & Römkens, all this volume). For example, the testimony in court of a child victim or victim of sexual violence can take place in closed session in order to protect the person's safety, physical and psychological well-being, dignity and privacy. Furthermore, special rules have been developed which govern the treatment of victims-witnesses of sexual violence in court, including that counsel shall refrain from intimidating, harassing or humiliating questioning and that judges shall adequately control such questioning. The requirement included in the Rome Statute to hire specially trained court staff with expertise in dealing with victims of sexual violence and child victims, is another indication of the special attention given to these two categories.

The implementation of these victims' rights provisions in practice has been challenging if not sometimes problematic. For instance, how should the Court balance victims' right to participation with the right of the accused to a fair and expeditious trial? In other words, how to effectively organize the participation of hundreds of victims during the proceedings? Unfortunately, this task seems not easy. Developments pertaining to victim participation at the Court have shown that so far the Court has taken a rather fragmented and inconsistent approach, partly due to the fact that the provisions of the Statute and the Rules of Procedure and Evidence assign the Chambers with wide discretionary powers to interpret the proper role of victims in the proceedings (McGonigle Leyh, this volume). For instance, different Chambers apply diverse approaches to the manner and scope of participation (either a broad, systematic approach, whereby Legal Representatives have to show how their clients' personal interests are affected by the trial generally; or a narrow, piecemeal approach, whereby Legal Representatives need to show how their clients' personal interests are affected by specific proceedings at trial) and Pre-Trial Chambers have divergent opinions on anonymous and non-anonymous victim participation at the pre-trial stage. This difference in treatment has a direct effect on the participatory rights of victims. These fragmented and divergent approaches to victim participation have furthermore a negative effect on the clarity and certainty of proceedings. And time and again the same procedural issues are re-litigated, wasting valuable Court time and resources. One of the main concerns is the fact that victims of one case are treated differently than victims in another case. This does not only affect how the Defence and Prosecution must respond to victim participation, it also does not benefit victims, who might get disappointed with the whole international criminal justice process in case their expectations on victim participation are not met. Managing victim expectations is therefore important. For these reasons it would be desirable to have a clear set of procedural rules to apply to all cases, leaving little doubt about the procedural rights afforded to victims but also leaving some discretion to Judges to shape participation (McGonigle Leyh, this volume; see also De Brouwer & Groenhuijsen 2009). The question how this should be done – either by revising or amending the Court's provisions on victim participation, by drafting a separate document with regulations on victim participation, or by leaving it to the Appeals Chamber to decide or otherwise – is still a question mark, and requires further research, as is the question of the contents of such victim participation provisions.

It is difficult to measure the impact of the workings of the international criminal tribunals on the victims concerned. For example, apart from accountability for and deterrence of perpetrators of international crimes, the ICTR was also set up to contribute to reconciliation and restoration and maintenance of peace in Rwanda. However, the real impact of ICTR prosecutions in acting as a deterrent, fostering reconciliation and contributing to the pacification of the country and the wider region has yet to be determined. The role of the ICTR in this regard should not be overestimated (Ndahinda, this volume). Without nullifying the role of the ICTR in bringing about peace, reconciliation and deterrence, Ndahinda points out that other domestic and regional legal and socio-political dynamics have comparatively played a far more significant role in taking steps towards peace and reconciliation. In addition, despite some efforts under the ICTR outreach programme to bring its activities to the Rwandans, the latter have overwhelmingly remained ignorant of, and indifferent towards, the activities of the Tribunal (Peskin 2005; Møse 2005). Arguably, next to the ascertainment of the reality that a genocide took place in Rwanda (Nsanzuwera 2005), the greatest achievement of the ICTR from the survivors' perspective is that the tribunal succeeded in triggering the arrest and surrender of some of the major figures suspected of being the masterminds of the genocide (Ndahinda, this volume; see also Rombouts 2004; Møse 2005). The arrest and prosecution of these masterminds subsequently subtracted them from individually engaging into destabilizing activities in a troubled African Great Lakes region. More empirical research would be needed to answer the question to what extent international criminal tribunals have a role to play in achieving reconciliation and peace, and if so, how this could be done best.

6.1. VICTIMS OF SEXUAL VIOLENCE

Another closely related question concerns the participation and protection of victims of sexual violence in court proceedings, a group which has historically been overlooked in terms of having the crimes committed against them investigated and prosecuted. In this volume some of the challenges involved for victims of sexual violence and the Court were outlined (Mesters & Adeboyejo; Chu, De Brouwer & Römkens) and possible answers to deal with these challenges were given. For example, based on a survey of the situations and cases currently before the ICC, it was noted that there is only a small number of female applicants – those most often targeted for sexual violence – participating in the proceedings. It was suggested that this could be partly ameliorated by increasing outreach activities, especially in remote areas, directly targeting women in the situations concerned by the Court and through intermediaries in direct contact with these women. Yet, the primary and final responsibility to contact possible participating victims lies with the Court and better avenues to address this issue should be developed. Another challenge concerns the low number on the List of Legal Counsel of female legal counsel, counsel with expertise on sexual violence, and counsel from the situations concerned, while such background and/or expertise can be critical to adequately represent survivors of sexual violence. In order to address this, the Court, in 2010, actively campaigned and encouraged female African legal counsel to apply to the list of Legal Counsel, which outcome still needs to be awaited. It was furthermore suggested that the Court marks expertise in sexual violence as an explicit specialization on the List of Legal Counsel. A third challenge concerns the organization of common legal representatives, as victims of sexual violence may come from different regions, may have been sexually violated by perpetrators of different ethnicity, or may be grouped together with victims of other crimes and therefore have different interests to be represented. The current approach of the Court is that in case of irreconcilable interests, the common legal representative shall inform the Chamber immediately, which will then take appropriate measures by, for example, appointing the Office of Public Counsel for the Victims (OPCV) to represent such a group of victims. Yet, to what extent is such a solution a good one in light of the potentially high number of victims participating and the conflicting interests they may have, and taking into account the right of the accused to a fair and expeditious trial? A challenge that continues to glimmer or persist with regard to the protection of victims of sexual violence testifying and/or participating in court is their re-victimization in court if questioning by counsel is done in an intimidating and harassing manner and judges do not adequately control such questioning. While participating and testifying in court can be an empowering experience, this is to a large part dependent on the way victims of sexual violence are treated here. Even after the victim has been at the Court, victims of sexual violence may experience re-victimization by community members who have found out about the victim's appearance in court. International criminal tribunals will need to think about more innovative ways of how to deal with the protection of sexual violence victims and victims generally, which may include minimizing the number of victims to establish certain facts and using more written statements in lieu of oral testimony.

Overall, gender-based and sexual violence crimes have been charged by the Prosecutor in all situations before the Court, although not in all cases and not always in a way that the charges are representative of the sexual violence committed in the particular case. The absence of sexual violence charges in approximately half of the cases before the Court is disturbing, especially in light of the widespread documentation by the UN and NGOs of sexual violence in all situations concerned and the high-level positions held by the accused. To include a representative range of sexual violence crimes in the indictments against the accused requires a good Prosecutor's strategy on sexual violence crimes prior to investigations into these crimes with a team of investigators experienced in dealing with interviewing victims of sexual violence. The question could be asked as to why investigators and prosecutors at times shy away from investigating crimes of sexual violence, even though these crimes have no greater evidentiary burden than any other non-sexual violence crimes? Bringing solid charges of sexual violence is primarily the task of the Office of the Prosecutor, and should not be constantly remedied when the trial is ongoing by interventions of Legal Representatives of Victims, expert-witnesses, NGOs or even Judges, as recent practices before the Court – for instance in the *Lubanga* case – have already shown. In addition, the development in the *Bemba* case, where despite the Prosecutor's attempt to lay different charges (torture, rape, outrages upon personal dignity) in respect of the same sexual violence conduct to recognize the different harms caused by sexual violence, but in which case the Judges did not allow for such cumulative charging, is troublesome. An amicus curiae submitted to the Court by an international women's rights NGO, holding that cumulative charging is a long established permissible practice before international tribunals as long as the elements of the crimes charged differ from each other, was rejected by the Court. Victims of sexual violence may not only need to see that their case is on trial, but also that the accused is facing charges for all the sexual violent conduct the accused has been implicated in; as this proposition has not yet been tested empirically, this may at the very least require further empirical research. Needless to say, when sexual violence is not or not adequately charged, this has repercussions on the participation of victims of sexual violence in court as they cannot be linked to the particular charges against the accused.

6.2. CHILD VICTIMS

Another vulnerable group of victims of international crimes concern children. Children are especially vulnerable because of their age, their immature physical and mental development, their lack of political power or voice, as well as their economic and emotional dependency on adults. Therefore, child victims may well represent the most vulnerable of all crime victims. In this volume, Grossman argues that the distinctiveness of child victims rests upon two grounds, namely their inherent vulnerability reflected in the international legal instruments (such as the United Nations Convention on the Rights of the Child and its two Optional Protocols, which have been created and employed to protect their needs and rights) and their status as a society's next generation. Just as for survivors of sexual violence, the needs of children during and after conflict are immense and may include physiological (housing, water, food, medical attention), safety and justice needs. While local NGOs may be active on the ground in areas that are affected by conflict and thus may be best positioned to provide culturally appropriate assistance both quickly and efficiently, such organizations may not have the resources to provide the required services. International NGOs and UN Agencies may have access to greater resources than smaller, local NGOs, however, they do not necessarily have the advantages of the local NGOs with respect to experienced staff with culturally appropriate knowledge of both the people in need of assistance and the circumstances in the field. At a broader level, NGOs and UN agencies and organizations are guided by mandates and such mandates will unquestionably differ amongst various organizations. Even in cases where organizations (national or international) have similar mandates, they will not necessarily agree on the types of services that ought to be provided, or on the manner in which the assistance can best be delivered. With a lack of agreement and co-operation between service providers regarding service delivery and assistance, there is a risk that gaps in the mandates of different organizations will result in certain populations receiving no services or assistance, or perhaps duplication of services resulting in a waste of resources and ineffective service delivery. International and local NGOs, and UN agencies and organizations must therefore work together if the needs of child victims of international crimes are to be optimally addressed. A possible solution to ensuring this kind of co-operation might be through the creation of an organizing body which could serve to co-ordinate and manage the activities of the organizations that would most likely provide services to child victims of international crimes. Such an organization does not presently exist and more research will be needed to see what such an organization could look like. In addition, would such an organization also be needed for survivors of sexual violence, who such as children, are considered a vulnerable group with certain specific needs? Or would such an organisation need to be all-inclusive of all survivor groups?

On the international criminal level, the tribunals have only slowly recognized the importance of child participation and testimony in trial proceedings, despite the large-scale impact conflict has had on children. Children have testified at the SCSL and are now participating and testifying in the proceedings before the ICC. What is significant to underline is that the ICC does not allow for the prosecution of persons under the age of eighteen. This age restriction ensures that former child soldiers will not be prosecuted themselves for the crimes they may have committed before the ICC, which focuses on the most senior responsible. Also before other Tribunals, such as the SCSL, no children have ever been prosecuted. In the case of the SCSL the Prosecutor made the policy decision not to prosecute any person below the age of eighteen (even though the SCSL Statute allowed the prosecution of children above the age of fifteen), since children are not considered to bear the greatest responsibility for international crimes. It could be questioned whether some children would indeed need to be prosecuted and through which fora.

The Rome Statute of the ICC gives specific attention to child victims: (1) by defining specific crimes against children, such as the war crime of conscription, enlistment or use of children under the age of 15 into active hostilities; (2) by providing for the protection and support of child victims and witnesses and allowing them to express their views and concerns; and (3) by affirming the importance of employing specially-trained Court staff. Taken together, these constitute the most extensive consideration that child victims have been afforded in international criminal courts to date. Similar as to the prosecution of sexual violence, in the case of the prosecution of international crimes against children, much is dependent on good investigation and prosecution strategies, outreach, the way children are treated in court, and the availability of court personnel experienced in dealing with violence against children. Especially considering the fact that hardly any experience on the international criminal level exists with regard to the prosecution of crimes against children, it is important that best practices are developed in order to assure they are not re-victimized by taking part in the court proceedings.

7. NATIONAL PROCEDURES

7.1. UNIVERSAL JURISDICTION

Given the limited mandate of international criminal tribunals such as the ICTR, ICTY, SCSL and the ICC, these courts will only be capable of pursuing a handful of cases, with a focus on those most responsible. As argued by Ferstman and Schurr in this volume, the exercise by national states of universal jurisdiction is therefore important in establishing accountability for international crimes, and ensuring that there are no 'safe havens'. While the primary responsibility to prosecute international crimes rests with the territorial state, universal jurisdiction can contribute to end the culture of impunity for committing genocide, crimes against humanity or war crimes, especially where the state is not able to prosecute on the basis of territorial jurisdiction. To date, no African state is known to have exercised universal jurisdiction effectively, with most universal jurisdiction cases taking place in European countries. This is an interesting fact since about half of recent universal jurisdiction investigations and prosecutions relate to crimes committed in Africa, with most cases resulting from the crimes committed during the Rwandan genocide of 1994. The reasons for the relatively limited number of investigations and prosecutions of international crimes suspects mirror the challenges inherent to universal jurisdiction cases, including the inadequacy of legislation enabling universal jurisdiction prosecutions over such crimes, the challenges associated with finding witnesses and collecting sufficient evidence of the crime, and limited budgets and human resources made available for universal jurisdiction cases. Often, national police and prosecution authorities do not even know about the presence of suspects in their country, or about the possibility to investigate and prosecute these suspects, and even where domestic criminal codes provide for such prosecutions, that legislation may have never been applied before. In light of these challenges, it should be recognized that countries do not really wish to exercise universal jurisdiction over international crimes; on the contrary, authorities generally actively seek to avoid the exercise of universal jurisdiction and only take recourse to it as a jurisdiction of last resort, where no other viable alternative to accountability and justice exists (Ferstmann & Schurr, this volume). According to Ferstmann & Schurr, support and assistance to the territorial state seems therefore the only long term viable option to ensure accountability and justice on a broad scale. The ICC, as well as the experienced staff of international criminal tribunals, has an important role to play to ensure that expertise is shared with national judicial authorities.

Some positive trends can also be observed. Several countries have begun to establish specialized war crimes units within their police and prosecution services, designed to ensure that perpetrators of serious international crimes no longer go unpunished. Real practical expertise has developed in recent years at the national level. The starting point for a discussion on universal jurisdiction should therefore not be the attempt to limit its application in practice or focus on its abuse, but rather how to build on what has been achieved so far, how to expand the concept and enable more countries, in particular African countries, to effectively exercise universal jurisdiction for the worst crimes.

7.2. TERRITORIAL JURISDICTION

Despite the possibility the universal jurisdiction principle offers to prosecute and try cases in third countries, the territorial state should still be the primary state responsible for prosecuting international crimes (Ferstman & Schurr, this volume). An interesting example concerns the case of Rwanda. The way the government of Rwanda tried to deal with the perpetrators of the genocide has been heavily discussed in debates by both academics and practitioners. After the genocide, the new government struggled with developing just means for the humane detention and prosecution of the more than – at that time identified – 120,000 people accused of genocide and related crimes against humanity. By 2000, most of these people were still held in Rwanda's prisons awaiting trial. The ordinary courts would never have managed to try all these perpetrators in due time. Therefore, the government, urged also by local leaders, decided to re-implement the *gacaca* court system, a 'modernized' version of an indigenous form of dispute settlement developed and applied in the aftermath of the 1994 genocide (Haveman 2011). From 2001 to 2011, the *gacaca* courts – involving the whole community – have prosecuted some 1,4 million cases of genocidal acts during the Rwandan genocide, with sentences ranging from five to thirty years, life imprisonment (5–8% of the verdicts) and acquittals (20–30% of the verdicts), but also community work, replacing detention.[4] In spite of the many criticisms of the system from the North – mostly relating to the perceived shortcomings in terms of the right to defence and other due process guarantees, and non-coverage of alleged RPF crimes (Ndahinda, this volume; see also Haveman 2008; Haveman & Muleefu 2010 for a discussion of the criticism on *gacaca*) – the gacaca process has registered many successes in gathering information about the way in which

---

4   Hirondelle News Agency, *Official Closure of Gacaca Courts Set for December, Says Justice Minister*, 20 May 2011.

the genocide was perpetrated, by whom and why. More relevant for survivors, many of them came to know more about the fate of their loved ones killed during the genocide and where their remains were thrown. According to the Rwandan Minister of Justice Karugarama: "All in all we are happy that we have a unique system that caters to our people needs, it may not be perfect for other nations but it serves us very well."[5] Although the gacaca courts may indeed have been an outcome for dealing with the atrocities that took place in Rwanda on the level of society as a whole, this may not always have been the case on the level of the individual, as several victims feared testifying at these courts or felt that justice was not done through these courts (e.g. De Brouwer & Chu 2009).[6] Despite everything that has been said on *gacaca*, what is clear is that Rwanda took its responsibility in pursuing criminal prosecutions of *génocidaires* before national courts and *gacaca* (see also Schotsmans; Kaitesi & Haveman, both this volume).

8. PREVENTIVE MEASURES

Another issue that needs to receive more scholarly attention is the question of how to prevent international crimes from taking place. This topic has only been shortly touched upon in this volume by Chu, De Brouwer and Römkens with regard to the question of how to prevent sexual violence in conflict situations. Sexual violence in conflict is increasingly used as a very effective tool of warfare; much cheaper than bullets, with the effect of shattering whole families, communities and countries. The brutality with which sexual violence is taking place – against both women and men – as well as the scale on which it is perpetrated are beyond imagination (see also Kaitesi & Haveman, this volume). The shame and stigma surrounding this crime has for a long time prevented – and still is preventing – women, but also men, from speaking out. At the same time, society seems not always capable of hearing these stories, which also contributes to silencing this crime. Although the severity of sexual violence and its impact on survivors is increasingly being recognized by the international community, the first concrete steps to prevent sexual violence in conflict are of recent date. The appointment of a UN Special Rapporteur on Sexual Violence in Conflicts provides an opportunity to develop these preventive and support efforts more coherently. In addition, governments have also increasingly made a commitment to speak out and take action against sexual violence, including by actively training military to prevent it. Previous studies have shown that where the military organization prohibits sexual violence and effectively enforces that decision by punishment when such violence occurs, sexual violence can be

---

5   *Ibidem.*
6   See also Human Rights Watch, *Justice Comprised: The Legacy of Rwanda's Community-Based Gacaca Courts,* 31 May 2011.

prevented (Wood 2009). Nevertheless, the development of training and educational interventions directed at strict prohibition of sexual violence is still in their infancy. This is particularly complicated in light of the legacy of sexual objectification and denigration of women within the military. Much work remains to be done, and given this legacy active monitoring, reporting and sanctioning structures within the UN system are vital.

NGOs are also crucial as independent watchdogs to help realize victims' rights and encourage a shift in attitudes towards unacceptability of sexual violence in conflict. The international recognition of sexual violence is a first step towards prevention and justice for victims, and it seems vital that the next steps involve their consultation. If they are no longer to be silenced, their participation in preventive strategies, but also in justice and reconciliation efforts will be imperative to any meaningful form of such initiatives, but in this area much more research needs to be conducted in order to identify the best legal and policy approaches to prevent sexual violence crimes from taking place in conflict. The same applies to the prevention of other international crimes.

9. TRUTH, RECONCILIATION, AMNESTY AND TRADITION

As discussed above, the times that a criminal justice approach to mass atrocities was considered the one and only approach fitting each and every situation of mass atrocities is since long gone. No one can ignore any longer the existence of other approaches. One has to acknowledge their advantages, and of course disadvantages. Whereas a criminal justice approach for centuries seemed untouchable and its efficacy beyond proof, a growing number of scholars have challenged over time this prominent position. This has created ample space for Truth Commissions, Reconciliation Commissions and tradition-inspired approaches; even amnesty is on the agenda again.

This change of views seems not the least due to a growing attention for victims. The nature of mass atrocities may be an important reason to consider these acts as crimes against humanity and the multitude of perpetrators as *hostes humani generis*, enemies of all humankind, and therefore in the focus of attention.[7] However, considering the even larger number of victims involved – depending on the definition one has to think of many millions of persons including direct victims (e.g. in the DR-Congo wars more than 3 million persons) plus the indirect victims (a tenfold perhaps of the number of direct victims) – it has become impossible to neglect their cause. As mentioned before, victims' needs have for long been denied. We agree with Haldemann (this volume) that

---

[7] See about the denial by states: Cohen 1996 and 2000. Although nowadays recognised by criminal law, neglected until recently by criminology, see e.g. Smeulers & Haveman 2008.

this denial "is immoral, because it involves treating the victims of those wrongs as if they simply did not matter, as if they were politically and morally negligible – an attitude that is disrespectful in its very essence". He therefore proposes "to construe transitional justice as a moral, political and legal project of overcoming 'denial' that puts victims and their legitimate feelings of indignation and resentment at its centre".

Transitional justice or *post-conflict justice* can be seen as the collective noun for all approaches possible in a period of transition after a conflict or undemocratic regime. It is clear that one particular approach cannot serve all needs of all victims after a period of atrocities. Five strategies are distinguished, with accompanying interventions, which together could give an effective answer to addressing victims' needs:

- individual accountability, with criminal prosecution, in particular but not exclusively, as intervention tool;
- truth, for example with the help of a truth finding commission;
  reparations, by individual compensation, educational support or pensions, but also by erecting monuments;
- institutional reformation, of political and legal powers for example, but equally within companies or other 'powerful' players in the 'old' situation;
- reconciliation, where reconciliation commissions and 'peace education' are interesting examples.

These five strategies should be adjusted to each situation, next to a large range of other contextually decided specific measures.

Some possible measures have already been discussed in section 4, in particular measures relating to providing reparation. Adding to this the important role of civil society, either or not in concert with governmental activities, one realizes the vastness of the number of possible approaches, instruments and mechanisms in a period of transition (see Muleefu, this volume, illustrating the role of civil society for the Rwandan post-genocide situation). It even more shows that a criminal justice approach forms only one of many responses, serving only one of many goals to be achieved.

Part IV of this volume focused on non-penal approaches, including truth and reconciliation commissions and tradition-inspired instruments. The South African Truth and Reconciliation Commission is the most famous amongst those instruments, although certainly not the only one. Apartheid sought to dehumanize South Africans, and the Truth and Reconciliation Commission (TRC) forced the country to redefine itself through the accounts of its victims and perpetrators. An interesting aspect of the South African TRC is that it is founded in the ancient African philosophy of *Ubuntu*, which can be described as "emphasising communality and interdependence where the life and dignity of another is considered as valuable as one's own" (see Peacock, this volume). Stressing Ubuntu as the underlying philosophy marks an interesting development in transitional justice that can no longer be ignored, which is that the importance of 'tradition' is to a growing extent recognized with regard to approaches to atrocities.

Prompted by the Rwandan experiment with *gacaca*, international attention to the potential role of traditional or tradition-inspired mechanisms in transitional justice strategies has increased. In this volume, Schotsmans addressed the potential role of such tradition-inspired mechanisms, more in particular the *Fambul Tok* in Sierra Leone, the *Mato Oput* in Uganda and the *Gacaca* in Rwanda. Common to these three countries is that they have experienced mass violence against the civilian population, and that society has to be reconstructed with victims and perpetrators living closely together:

> *Looking for inspiration in the community's (former) traditional practices can have the advantage of calling upon an existing normative framework. In such cases, tradition-based hybrid mechanisms may have better chances for popular ownership and support than international courts or tribunals, which are alien to the society concerned.* (Schotsmans, this volume)

Whether these mechanisms are a success, in itself and compared to the classical state penal systems, is an extremely difficult question to answer, as Schotsmans' 'preliminary assessment' shows, and deserves more scholarly attention.

One of the factors determining the success of transitional justice mechanisms is related to the concept of 'truth'. Truth and reconciliation are considered to be closely linked: no reconciliation without truth is often heard. Although the truthfulness of testimonies before the South African TRC is criticized by various researchers, it may be considered as having been "crucial in breaking the tyranny of silence" (Peacock, this volume). The same criticism regarding the truth is expressed with regard to the Rwandan *gacaca* (see e.g. Ingelaere 2008; 2009a, b & c). However, also in that case one could argue at the same time that the *gacaca* were a platform to tell (at least part of) the truth, which led, as mentioned above, to the discovery of corpses of killed persons.

Different from the South African TRC that covered a broad spectre of society – including media, business and politics, apart from individual victims – the *gacaca* focused on individual cases – about 1,4 million cases were tried – leaving the political and military structures behind the genocide to the ICTR.

One specific group of atrocities that gained considerable attention at the *gacaca* is sexual violence against women and men. Significantly, international criminal legal responses, as discussed above, are not the only means available for victims of sexual violence. National and local courts, Truth and Reconciliation Commissions, community based victims' groups, symbolic reparations (e.g. commemoration memorials), cultural forms of recognition (e.g. theatre), media (e.g. documentaries, movies), Victims' Tribunals (in a similar vein to the 2000 Women's Tribunal in Tokyo created to address the crimes committed against women who were held as sexual slaves by the Japanese during WWII) and education (e.g. schools, museums, books on expressing trauma through literature, see Erez & Meroz-Aharoni, this volume) are some other measures through which victims of sexual violence could obtain a form of acknowledgement (see also Mertus 2004; O'Connell 2005; Dembour & Haslam 2004). The diversity of victimization requires similarly diverse and multi-faceted responses and more research on the appropriate measures and how current mechanisms can be improved is needed (Chu, De Brouwer & Römkens, this volume; for some research on this for the ICTR, see the ICTR Best Practices Manual of 2008; for the ICTY, Stover 2005 and Sharratt 2011a and b; for the Special Court for Sierra Leone, Horn *et al.* 2010; on transitional justice mechanisms for sexual violence generally, Zinsstag 2011).

In Rwanda, sexual violence and sexual torture committed during the 1994 genocide were also dealt with by the *gacaca* (Kaitesi & Haveman, this volume). The *gacaca* tribunals tried approximately 7,000 cases. The trials and the preceding training of the 'judges' showed that these cases were different from 'ordinary' sexual violence in various aspects, one of which is the extreme cruelty of the acts, to which for instance the ordinary legal definitions did not apply. The flexible nature of the *gacaca* made it possible to adapt to these differences and to take into consideration the complex reality of the victims of sexual violence and sexual torture, both with regard to the formal state penal system as to the way other genocidal acts had been tried by the *gacaca* tribunals. The *gacaca* option for rape and sexual torture may not be an all-encompassing solution without flaws; it is, however, an approach to a complex problem without precedent.

Last but not least, amnesty keeps playing an intriguing part in the transitional justice discussion. As Freeman (2010, 5) notes, "up until the 1990s, the practice of turning the page appears to have dominated state practice through history, especially in contexts in which there was neither a clear winner nor a clear loser". Due to a strong human rights lobby, the granting of amnesties to perpetrators of international crimes has attracted more and more opposition, leading to a dogmatic rejection of amnesties, where even the word itself was sufficient to arouse intense emotions during fierce debates. Academia, however, is the forum to challenge these kinds of dogmas. With regards to amnesty various arguments against at least a blanket amnesty are raised: dogmatic/normative – a perceived international community's moral obligation; victim's rights – and a series of pragmatic arguments: amnesty leads to impunity; creates a culture of impunity; denies victims' wishes; increases victim traumatization; hinders truth seeking; and obstructs peace. At least the said pragmatic arguments seem to lack any empirical basis (Van Wijk, this volume). An analysis of amnesties granted in

Mozambique, Angola and Uganda leads to the conclusion that no negative effects as raised by opponents of amnesties can be observed (Van Wijk, this volume). "[T]he pragmatic arguments (...) are therefore not more than theoretical assumptions (...) [and] alone do not suffice to under all circumstances repudiate the option to grant blanket amnesties", Van Wijk concludes. A similar conclusion can be drawn with regard to the dogmatic/normative arguments:

> [T]he fundamental question we need to answer is if this dogmatic line of argumentation is sufficient to take the inflexible and rigid position that perpetrators of international crimes should never be granted amnesty? Is this argumentation sufficient, even if the most directly affected victims might want to make use of the slightest chance that amnesty may help to end the conflict? To make it concrete: is it sufficient to explain to Sudanese and Congolese villagers who currently fall prey to the attacks of Kony's LRA that Kony should never be granted amnesty, only because the 'international community' is shocked?

On the other hand, amnesty may imply high moral costs for the survivors of the atrocities that are amnestied (Haldemann, this volume). Those moral costs should at least be acknowledged: "Social institutions, policy strategies and even a new language should be visibly in place to validate the victims' related emotions or attitudes – outrage, anger, consternation, horror, fear, distrust, shame, and the like," in order to avoid that an amnesty policy is considered an easy way of continued impunity for perpetrators and continued denial of victims. Similarly, in the South African truth and reconciliation process it was not necessary to express remorse or ask for forgiveness in order to receive amnesty: "[s]uch negation of acknowledgement, repentance and inter-communal understanding certainly distracts from the healing potential of the spirit of *Ubuntu*, and therefore, also on achieving reconciliation at inter-personal level"(Peacock, this volume).

Regarding transitional justice we may conclude that practice has overruled theory. Whereas lawyers for years seemed to consider a classical criminal justice approach – on a domestic level as well as international and internationalized systems – as the only acceptable approach, the reality on the ground has proven that there is a great variety of instruments that – in itself and combined with each other, including the criminal justice approach – together could respond to a situation of large-scale atrocities. An important pushing factor in this process has been the increasing acknowledgement of the needs of victims of these atrocities.

10. FINAL REMARKS: CENTRAL FEATURES OF A VICTIMOLOGICAL PERSPECTIVE ON INTERNATIONAL CRIMES

Several contributors have reflected upon the various possibilities of victims of international crimes to achieve acknowledgement of their victimhood and getting access to reparative measures (in the form of either compensation or symbolic means) through the criminal justice system (either national or international). In addition, other ways in finding justice and providing reparation, either through mechanisms aiming to contribute to truth and reconciliation processes or tradition-inspired mechanisms, were extensively discussed. The complexities of doing justice and providing reparation in situations of mass victimization have been clearly shown. With regard to all the different mechanisms and forms discussed in this volume, the position of victims should be offered central stage.

The framework for doing so rests on three main principles, which are mainly derived from the contribution by Groenhuijsen and Pemberton in this volume. *In the first place*, the limits of justice responses should be acknowledged. The impact of trials on goals such as deterrence, just deserts and victim recovery is likely to be very slight, if measurable at all. This applies to criminal justice, but also to truth commissions, reparations programmes and indigenous justice processes. Behind the glowing image of the South-African TRC, the jubilant headlines of the capture and trial of former war-criminals and the accompanying rhetoric of redress and repair lies a complex and often disheartening reality, in which the only stable factor is the recognition that small steps forward will always be accompanied by, hopefully smaller, steps back. Meeting collective needs may stand in the way of acknowledging individual victimization. The challenge of trying hundreds of thousands of perpetrators may entail short-cuts around due process and, as was the case in Rwanda, task victims to testify under less than ideal circumstances.

Achieving justice for victims of international crime involves a connection to and cooperation with other initiatives with similar goals, seeking to achieve redress and reparation for victimized populations. Justice in the aftermath of mass victimization is often delivered by non-judicial means, more suited to the rebuilding of ravaged societies. Acknowledging the limits of justice responses therefore necessitates forging alliances with these other approaches.

In the second place, any reaction should be adapted to the victimized population. Both vertical integration (connecting the international and domestic legal reactions) and horizontal integration (connecting the legal reaction with quasi-legal and non-legal reactions) are necessary. In addition, the historical, cultural and current political realities should be taken into account; in a sense the reaction should be ecologically appropriate (see Fletcher & Weinstein 2002).[8] Tradition may be a worthwhile resource to build upon in certain situations, while in others tradition itself may be a part of the problem.

More generally, what works in one situation may not apply to another. Sound bite solutions are not helpful in the aftermath of international crimes. Outright and dogmatic condemnation of the way that societies muddle through in the aftermath of mass victimisation is an easy way for the international community to make peace with its own troubled conscience, but often does not contribute to the plight of the victimized populations of said societies. True enough: some amnesties of perpetrators of atrocities should be condemned as horrendous miscarriages of justice, but the cause of justice, however important, holds no trump-value. This is particularly true if the conception of justice is narrowed to the extent that it solely relates to the punishment of a small minority of the offenders who perpetrated the crimes in question.

In the third place, the structure of victim-oriented measures needs to be internally coherent, complemented by adequate implementation with effects being felt in reality, not solely asserted on paper. This victimological truth is a particularly acute consideration in the situation of international crimes, given the fact that resources for these measures are spectacularly inadequate for the task they are supposed to achieve. Even in the most advanced – in terms of resources for victims of crime – nations, victim assistance and support is delivered with shoe-string budgets, which does not bode well for the match between resources and needs in situations of mass victimisation. The focus should therefore not be on the unrealistic rhetoric such as victims 'healing' through participation in transitional justice, which will lead to the squandering of the extremely limited resources in the search of this cathartic *fata morgana*, but rather, for example, on the superficially more mundane, but equally more realistic, notion of acknowledgement of victimization.

This latter point may appear to be disconcertingly modest, but seeing the fact that denying this lies at the heart of the evil inherent to genocide, crimes against humanity and war crimes, acknowledgement of victimization may prove to be an important commodity for victims of international crimes; one of the most important commodities that justice may hope to provide.

---

[8]   Fletcher and Weinstein (2002, 581) propose "an ecological model of social reconstruction that considers a spectrum of interventions that includes, but is broader than, criminal trials. This approach, grounded in empirical studies of the actions of individuals in group contexts as well as some current perceptions of the contribution of criminal trials to social reconstruction, contributes to a fuller understanding of the complex processes that underlie the rebuilding of fragmented societies." The 'ecological paradigm' was developed by community psychology scholars, see, among others, James Kelly *et al.* 2000).

THE AUTHORS

Adesola Adeboyejo is a Trial Lawyer at the Office of the Prosecutor at the International Criminal Court. She had also worked with the Victims Participation and Reparations Section of the Registry of the Court. Prior to joining the Court, she worked as Prosecution Counsel in the Office of the Prosecutor at the International Criminal Tribunal for Rwanda (ICTR) from 2001 to 2007, and as a Legal Adviser in the Investigations Division from 1999 to 2001. Mrs. Adeboyejo served as Prosecution Counsel in several cases at the ICTR. Prior to this she was the Legal Secretary to African Concern, an international NGO (1998) and ran her own law firm out of Lagos, Nigeria (1995–1998). Mrs. Adeboyejo lectures regularly, and has been both a panel presenter and trainer at the annual ICC Seminar and Training for Counsel. She has also participated in training investigators, prosecutors and judges in national jurisdictions. Mrs. Adeboyejo is a 1989 graduate of the Nigerian Law School.

Prof. Theo van Boven is Professor emeritus of international law at Maastricht University and a co-founder of the Maastricht Centre for Human Rights. He served in various United Nations capacities in the field of human rights. He was the Netherlands representative to the United Nations Commission on Human Rights (1970–1975). Further, he was the Director of the United Nations Division of Human Rights (1977–1982). As an independent expert he was a member of the UN Sub-Commission on Human Rights and in that capacity the Sub-Commission's Special Rapporteur on the Right of Victims of Gross Violations of Human Rights to Reparation (1989–1993) and the author of the first version of the UN Basic Principles and Guidelines on the subject matter, later adopted by the UN General Assembly (2005). Theo van Boven also served as a member of the UN Committee on the Elimination of Racial Discrimination (1991–1999) and he was the UN Special Rapporteur on Torture (2001–2004). Theo van Boven has been actively involved in the work of a number of civil society organisations and institutions. Thus, he was a Vice-President and a member of the Executive Committee of the International Commission of Jurists. He holds honorary doctorates from the Université Catholique de Louvain, Erasmus University of Rotterdam, New York University at Buffalo and Universidad de Buenos Aires.

Dr. Anne-Marie de Brouwer is an Associate Professor in international criminal law at the Department of Criminal Law, and a research fellow with the

International Victimology Institute Tilburg (INTERVICT), at Tilburg University, the Netherlands. Previously, she was an associate legal officer at the Women's Initiatives for Gender Justice in The Hague. She is the author of the book "Supranational Criminal Prosecution of Sexual Violence: The ICC and the Practice of the ICTY and the ICTR (Oxford – Antwerp: Intersentia, 2005)", for which she received the Max van der Stoel Human Rights Award 2006. She also co-edited the book "The Men Who Killed Me: Rwandan Survivors of Sexual Violence (Douglas & McIntyre, 2009; Wolf Legal Publishers, 2011 (Dutch edition))", which features seventeen testimonials of survivors of sexual violence. She has published various articles in the field of international criminal law and procedure, with a focus on victims' rights. She is the co-founder and chair of the Mukomeze Foundation, which aims to improve the lives of women and girls who survived sexual violence during the Rwandan genocide. Mrs. de Brouwer studied Dutch law, human rights law and international law at Tilburg University, La Sapienza and the University of Essex.

Dr. Athanasios Chouliaras is an Attorney at Law in Greece. After completing his graduate studies in law (University of Thrace, Greece) he studied at post-graduate level criminology (University of Barcelona, Spain), philosophy and sociology of law (both at National and Kapodistrian University of Athens, Greece). He has recently concluded his PhD thesis on the formation of an international criminal justice system, combining both criminological and criminal law approaches (University of Thrace, Greece), for which he was awarded a research grant from Alexander S. Onassis Public Benefit Foundation. He has published various articles in Greek and English on human rights protection, criminology and international criminal law.

Sandra Ka Hon Chu is a Senior Policy Analyst with the Canadian HIV/AIDS Legal Network, where she works to promote the rights of people living with and vulnerable to HIV, in Canada and internationally, focusing on women, incarcerated people, sex workers and immigrant communities. She is the co-editor of "The Men Who Killed Me: Rwandan Survivors of Sexual Violence" (Douglas & McIntyre, 2009). Previously, she worked at the Women's Initiatives for Gender Justice, an international women's human rights organization advocating for gender-inclusive justice before the International Criminal Court. Her broad international experience has also included assignments in Libya for Adam Smith International, in Timor-Leste for UNICEF, and in Hong Kong for the Asian Migrant Centre. Mrs. Chu holds a BA in Sociology from the University of British Columbia, an LL.B. from the University of Toronto, and an LL.M. from the Osgoode Hall Law School of York University. She was called to the bar of British Columbia in 2003.

Cristián Correa is a Senior Associate with the Reparative Justice Program at the International Center for Transitional Justice. As such he assists victims' groups, civil society organizations and governments in defining and implementing reparations policies in a diversity of settings, including Peru, East Timor, Colombia, Nepal, the former Yugoslavia, Sierra Leone, and Liberia. Previously, he was Legal Advisor to the Commission for Human Rights Policies of the Presidency of the Republic of Chile. He was also the Secretary of the Presidential Commission for Political Imprisonment and Torture (known as the Valech Commission), and later he coordinated the implementation of reparation policies for the victims identified by it. Mr. Correa holds a law degree from the Pontificate Catholic University of Chile and a M.A. in International Peace Studies from the University of Notre Dame.

Dr. Yael Danieli is a Clinical Psychologist and Traumatologist in private practice in New York City. She is also the co-founder and Director of the Group Project for Holocaust Survivors and their Children; Founding President, International Network for Holocaust and Genocide Survivors and their Friends; and Co-founder, past-President, Senior United Nations Representative, International Society for Traumatic Stress Studies (ISTSS). She is Chair of the NGO Alliance on Crime Prevention and Criminal Justice. Dr. Danieli integrates treatment, worldwide study, teaching/training, publishing, expert advocacy, and consulting to numerous governments, news, international and national organizations and institutions on victims' rights and optimal care, including for their protectors and providers. She received the ISTSS Lifetime Achievement Award. Her books include "International Responses to Traumatic Stress"; "The Universal Declaration of Human Rights: Fifty Years and Beyond"; "Sharing the Front Line and the Back Hills" (Baywood) (all published for and on behalf of the United Nations); "International Handbook of Multigenerational Legacies of Trauma" (Kluwer/Plenum); and "The Trauma of Terrorism: Sharing Knowledge and Shared Care: an International Handbook"; and "On the Ground after September 11: Mental Health Responses and Practical Knowledge Gained" (Haworth Press, 2005).

Prof. Edna Erez is Professor in the Department of Criminology, Crime, and Justice at the University of Illinois at Chicago. She has a Law degree (LL.B) from the Hebrew University of Jerusalem, and M.A. in Criminology and Ph.D. in Sociology from the University of Pennsylvania. Her research interests include comparative justice, victims in the justice system, violence against women and the criminal justice system response to it, victimization in the context of transnational crime and terrorism, and women in terrorism. Prof. Erez received close to two million dollar in grants from state and federal grants in the US and overseas. She has published extensively articles, book chapters and reports (altogether over 100 publications and two edited books). She is a co-editor of *International Review of Victimology,* Associate Editor of *Violence and Victim,* and she also serves on the editorial board of several major professional journals in criminology, criminal justice and legal studies. Prof. Erez was Visiting Professor at Warsaw University, University of Melbourne and Haifa University. She was also a resident scholar at the Max Planck Institute for International and Comparative Criminal Law in Freiburg, Germany, and the Australian Institute of Criminology in Canberra, Australia. Her recently funded research projects include a national study on violence against immigrant women and systemic responses, evaluation of the electronic monitoring of batterers, policing domestic violence in the Arab/Palestinian community in Israel, women in terrorism and suicide terrorism, and the connection between Jihad, crime and the internet.

Carla Ferstman is the Director of REDRESS, which she joined in 2001. She was called to the Bar in British Columbia, Canada, where she practiced as a criminal law barrister. She has also worked with the UN High Commissioner for Human Rights on legal reform and capacity building in post-genocide Rwanda, with Amnesty International's International Secretariat as a legal researcher on trials in Central Africa and as Executive Legal Advisor to Bosnia and Herzegovina's Commission for Real Property Claims of Displaced Persons and Refugees (CRPC). She has an LL.B. from the University of British Columbia, an LL.M. from New York University and is a doctoral candidate at the University of Oxford. Ms. Ferstman has published and is a regular commentator on victims' rights, the International Criminal Court and the prohibition against torture.

Prof. Marc Groenhuijsen is Professor of criminal law, criminal procedure and victimology at Tilburg University in the Netherlands. In 2005, he became the founding director of INTERVICT, the International Victimology Institute Tilburg. He has published widely on various victims' issues. He is president of the World Society of Victimology, member of the Board of Directors of the International Organization for Victim Assistance, and member of the Board of Directors of the International Society for Criminology. He also serves as a part-time judge in the Court of Appeal in Arnhem.

Michelle G. Grossman has graduate degrees in Criminology and Social Work from the University of Toronto, Canada. She has held clinical and research/policy positions focusing on both adult and child victims of crime. As a Manager for a non-profit organization in Toronto, Michelle supervised clinical programs for child victims of sexual assault and also for adult male sex offenders. She has worked for the Government of Canada at the Department of Justice, Research and Statistic Division where she was Senior Research Officer for the Policy Centre for Victim Issues. She also held the position of Policy Officer at the Department of Public Safety Canada (formerly the Solicitor General Canada).

Currently Mrs. Grossman is undertaking a Doctorate in the Faculty of Law, University of Oxford.

Dr. Frank Haldemann is Assistant Professor at the Law Faculty of the University of Geneva and teaches Transitional Justice at the Geneva Academy for International Humanitarian Law and Human Rights. Prior to joining the University of Geneva, he was a post-doctoral fellow at the New York University School of Law, the University of Leiden and the University of Pretoria. He holds a law degree from the University of Fribourg, an LL.M. from the London School of Economics and Political Science and a doctorate in Law from the University of Zurich. His publications include: "Gustav Radbruch v. Hans Kelsen: A Debate on Nazi Law" in *Ratio Juris* (2005) and "Another Kind of Justice: Transitional Justice as Recognition" in *Cornell International Law Journal* (2008).

Dr. Roelof H. Haveman (LL.M. Erasmus University Rotterdam, 1983; PhD Utrecht University, 1998) works as free-lance Rule of Law Consultant. From June 2010 until March 2011 he worked as a Field Programme Manager for IDLO/International Law Development Organization in Juba, South Sudan, supporting the judiciary and the Ministry of Legal Affairs. Since its start early 2008 until May 2010 he was the Vice Rector in charge of Academic Affairs and Research of the ILPD/Institute of Legal Practice and Development in Rwanda. As from 2005 he worked for the Dutch Center for International Legal Cooperation (CILC), supporting the law faculties of the Université Nationale du Rwanda (UNR, Butare) and the Université Libre de Kigali (ULK, Kigali) in strengthening their academic and managerial capacity and quality. Since its establishment in 2002 and until 2005, Roelof Haveman was the programme-director of the Grotius Centre for International Legal Studies at Leiden University's Campus in The Hague. Until the summer of 2005 he has been an associate professor of (international) criminal law and criminal procedure at Leiden University. Over the past 20 years he published many articles and a number of books on e.g. gender-related crimes, trafficking in persons and prostitution, *adat* criminal law in modern Indonesia, Rwandan *gacaca*, supranational criminology and comparative criminal law.

Usta Kaitesi is a Vice Dean for postgraduate and research and a Lecturer at the Faculty of Law of the National University of Rwanda (NUR), where she teaches International Criminal Law, Criminal Procedure and Gender and Law. She is writing her Ph.D. thesis on "Combating Impunity for Genocidal Sexual Violence: The Legacy of the ICTR, Rwandan Ordinary Courts and the Gacaca Jurisdictions" at the Netherlands Institute of Human Rights, Utrecht University. She is also a member of the Kigali Bar Association and the East African Law Society. She holds a bachelors Law degree from the National University of Rwanda and an LL.M. from the University of Ottawa (Canada).

Prof. Rianne Letschert is Professor in international law and victimology, and Deputy Director of INTERVICT. She works on issues such as victims' rights and human security, more particular on international lawmaking in the field of victims' rights and victims of international crimes, in particular reparations. As Deputy Director she is, amongst others, responsible for the execution and coordination of the research programme of the Institute. In 2010, she was visiting researcher at the Lauterpacht Centre for International Law of Cambridge University (UK). She recently published the book "The New Faces of Victimhood" (with Jan Van Dijk, Springer Press). For a detailed overview of her work, see www.tilburguniversity.edu/webwijs/show/?uid=r.m.letschert.

Dr. Brianne McGonigle Leyh is an Attorney specializing in international criminal law and procedure, human rights, victims' rights and transitional justice. She received her Bachelors degree (BA) from Boston University, graduating magna cum laude with a self-crafted major in the study of international law and human rights, her Law degree (JD) from American University's Washington College of Law, graduating cum laude, and her Masters (MA) in International Affairs from American University's School of International Service. In 2011 she obtained her Ph.D. from Utrecht University's Netherlands Institute of Human Rights where she wrote her dissertation on victim participation in international criminal proceedings. Currently, she holds a research position with this same institute. In addition to her academic work she co-Directs the Netherlands Office of the Public International Law & Policy Group. Previously, she has worked as co-Counsel on a legal team representing civil parties before the Extraordinary Chambers in the Courts of Cambodia.

Prof. Tikva Meroz Aharoni is a Professor of Comparative and Hebrew Literature in Ashkelon Academic College, an extension of Bar-Ilan University. She got her Ph.D. magna cum laude from Colombia University, New York. She taught at Columbia University. She was head and coordinator of Hebrew Studies at University of Pen., Philadelphia. Taught at Ben Gurion University in the Negev and in the University of Judaism, California, before moving back to Israel. She published articles and chapters in books related to Israeli poetry, prose related to political ideas. Currently she is writing about literature of immigration around the world. She won the first prize for a short story, and her first novel will be published in 2011–12.

Gabbi Mesters is a Barrister specializing in sexual violence cases and writing her Ph.D. research at Tilburg University on the subject of "Sexual Violence Against Men in Times of Violent Conflict". She received her LL.M. with a thesis on Women's Rights from the University of Amsterdam and was admitted to the Dutch Bar Association in 2002. Ever since, she worked for various Women's Rights law firms and is co-author of the book "In her Right. A practical Legal

Guide on Women's Rights Issues". She was a visiting professional at the ICC's Office of Public Counsel for Victims, worked as a civil servant for the Human Rights section of the Dutch Permanent Representation to the U.N. in Geneva (Switzerland) as well as for the Freedom of Xpression Institute in Johannesburg (South Africa). She also holds a Master of Arts (Theatre Science) and a First Year Examination in Political Science. Currently, she is working as a barrister and legal counsel for the Cultural Participation Fund.

Dr. Felix Mukwiza Ndahinda is an Assistant Professor at the International Victimology Institute of Tilburg University, the Netherlands. In 2009, he completed a Ph.D. entitled "Indigenousness in Africa: A contested Legal Framework for Empowerment of Marginalised Communities" (Asser Press). He holds a law degree from the National University of Rwanda and an LL.M. at the Raoul Wallenberg Institute of Human Rights (Sweden). He worked for the Office of the Auditor General for State Finances in Rwanda and for the International Criminal Tribunal for Rwanda in Arusha, Tanzania.

Alphonse Muleefu is a Ph.D. Researcher at Tilburg University based in INTERVICT. His research topic is "Victims of War Situations: The Quest for Reparation to Collateral Damage". Mr. Muleefu is a holder of a LL.B. (Law Degree) from the National University of Rwanda and LL.M. in International and European Public Law from the University of Tilburg, the Netherlands. He has participated in short courses on Transitional Justice, International Criminal law and International Criminal Investigations. He worked as a research student and legal researcher at the International Criminal Tribunal for Rwanda and as a legal intern at the International Criminal Court (ICC). In Rwanda he worked as a Legal Officer in the National Service of Gacaca Courts and is a Founder of Together Against Impunity in the Great Lakes Region (TAI/GLR). His research interest is in *Gacaca* Courts and Transitional Justice in general, International Criminal Law, International Humanitarian Law and victims' rights.

Prof. Stephan Parmentier studied law and sociology at the K.U. Leuven (Belgium) and sociology and conflict resolution at the Humphrey Institute for Public Affairs, University of Minnesota-Twin Cities (U.S.A.). He currently teaches sociology of crime, law, and human rights at the Faculty of Law of the K.U. Leuven, and has served as head of the Department of Criminal Law and Criminology (2005–2009). In July 2010 he was appointed Secretary-General of the International Society of Criminology and he also serves as a Board member of the Oxford Centre for Criminology and the International Institute for Sociology of Law (Oñati, Spain). He has been a visiting professor at the International Institute for Sociology of Law in Oñati (Spain), and the universities for Peace (San José, Costa Rica), New South Wales (Sydney, Australia) and Tilburg (the Netherlands), and a visiting scholar at the universities of Stellenbosch

(South Africa), Oxford (U.K.) and New South Wales (Sydney, Australia). Stephan Parmentier was the editor-in-chief of the Flemish Yearbook on Human Rights and is currently the co-general editor of the new international book Series on Transitional Justice.

Prof. Robert Peacock is the Head of the Criminology and Criminal Justice Department on the South African campus of Monash University (Melbourne). He has obtained graduate degrees in psychology and criminology (with honours) from the University of Pretoria as well as a Masters degree (cum laude) and Ph.D. (cum laude) in Criminology. Since the apartheid years in South Africa he has been conducting research on structural and institutional victimisation. Within a victimological and human rights framework his exploratory research focused on the phenomenon of street/community children as symptom-bearers of prejudice, discrimination and conflict. Additional critical analyses of child justice refer to descriptive and explanatory (quantitative) accounts of the phenomenon of children deprived of their liberty with a particular focus on adolescent identity, social justice, redress and harm reduction. Mr. Peacock continues with his work on transitional justice with institutional victimization as a particular focus area.

Dr. Antony Pemberton is a Political Scientist, Senior Researcher and Research Coordinator at INTERVICT. He is involved in the management and undertaking of a number of research projects concerning victims. He was project leader of the Justice Department projects concerning the oral victim impact statement, qualifying victims and the development of a quality monitor for victim assistance, and developed and participated in the EU-funded projects into Victims of Terrorism (DESVICT) and Victims and Restorative Justice as well as coordinated the legal part of the Evaluation of the EU Framework Decision on victims of crime (VINE). He was expert adviser in the Impact Assessment of the Framework Decision. For a detailed overview of his work, see www.tilburguniversity.edu/webwijs/show/?uid=a.pemberton.

Prof. Renée Römkens is Professor of Victimology and holds the Chair on Interpersonal Violence, in particular Violence in Intimate Relationships, at the International Victimology Institute Tilburg (INTERVICT). Her research focuses on the impact of Dutch as well as European legislation and regulation in the area of gender based violence. She is particularly interested in the cooperation between the police/judicial authorities and social support services for victims, as well as unintended gender specific consequences of legal regulation. She is frequently asked to act as consultant on these topics at different fora, such as the Council of Europe, United Nations and European Union.

Etienne Ruvebana is a Ph.D. researcher at the University of Groningen, the Netherlands, where he conducts research on the legal obligation to prevent genocide under international law and the legal consequences of its breach by states and the UN vis-a-vis the victims. He is also a lecturer at the Kigali Independent University in Rwanda. Before starting his Ph.D. in September 2009, he served as the head of the Department of Law and Acting Dean of the Faculty of Law of Kigali Independent University. Ruvebana authored a book on the responsibility of states and international organisations for the omission to prevent and suppress the genocide of Tutsi, published in *Les Editions Rwandaises* (2008) and an article on the protection of the environment during armed conflicts in the *Revue Scientifique* of the Kigali Independent University (2008). He holds a LL.B. degree in law from the National University of Rwanda (2004) and a LL.M. degree in international law and the law of international organisations from the University of Groningen (2007).

Martien Schotsmans holds a Master in Law and a Master in Criminology. After having worked as a private practice lawyer in Belgium for over ten years, she worked in Rwanda on domestic genocide trials with the Belgian NGO Avocats sans Frontières and did field research on victims' perceptions with GTZ. In Chad, she worked with victims and conducted investigations in the case against Hissène Habré, working with FIDH and HRW, and in Sierra Leone she acted as the Head of the Legal and Reconciliation Unit at the Truth and Reconciliation Commission. In addition, she acted as a consultant on justice sector reform and transitional justice in Rwanda, Benin, the DRC and Morocco. In Belgium, she continued working with Avocats Sans Frontières on the legal representation of Congolese victims at the ICC and on other issues of international and transitional justice. Since April 2008, she is a researcher at the University of Ghent, looking into the role of international actors regarding the use of tradition in the framework of transitional justice in post-conflict Africa. She is currently writing her Ph.D.

Jürgen Schurr is a Legal Adviser with REDRESS, which he joined as Project Coordinator of a joint project with the International Federation for Human Rights on Universal Jurisdiction in 2006. He also worked as Project Coordinator on a joint project on genocide justice with African Rights, as legal consultant with Human Rights Watch and as an Associate Legal Officer at the International Criminal Tribunal for Rwanda. He obtained his law degree from the University of East Anglia and a LL.M. from the University of Trier.

Prof. Alette Smeulers is Director of the Amsterdam Centre of Interdisciplinary Research on International Crimes and Security (ACIC, www.rechten.vu.nl/ACIC) and Director of the master programme International Crimes and Criminology (www.vu.nl/ICC) at VU University Amsterdam where she works since December 2006. Since September 2011, she is also a Professor in international criminology at the Department of Criminal Law of Tilburg

University. She studied political science at the Free University in Brussels and received her Ph.D. in international criminal law at Maastricht University. Ever since her studies she specialized in international crimes and causes of gross human rights violations to which she takes an interdisciplinary approach. Her main focus is on the perpetrators of international crimes.

Dr. Pietro Sullo is an Adjunct Professor in History of Justice at the Faculty of Law of the Ateneo Federico II in Naples, Italy, and a Research Fellow at the Max Planck Institute for Comparative Public Law and International Law in Heidelberg, Germany. He holds a Ph.D. from the Sant'Anna School of Advanced Studies in Pisa, Italy, where he has defended a thesis entitled "Genocide and Transitional Justice in Rwanda: Gacaca Courts and the Search for Truth, Justice and Reconciliation". Mr. Sullo's main research areas include international human rights and criminal law, transitional justice and contemporary legal history. Within the Africa Project of the Max Planck Institute he is currently involved in Khartoum and Juba in a capacity-building programme aimed at providing Sudanese lawyers with legal training.

Prof. Jo-Anne Wemmers obtained her Ph.D. from the University of Leiden, the Netherlands. Presently, she is a Professor at the School of Criminology of the Université de Montréal (Canada) as well as Head of the Research Group Victimology and Restorative Justice at the International Centre for Comparative Criminology. Professor Wemmers has published many articles and books in the area of victimology, including "Therapeutic Jurisprudence and Victim Participation in Justice: International Perspectives" (Carolina Academic Press), "Introduction à la Victimologie" (Les Presses de l'Université de Montréal) and "Victims in the Criminal Justice System" (Kugler Publications). Former Secretary General of the World Society of Victimology, she is currently Editor of the International Review of Victimology as well the Journal international de victimology.

Dr. Joris van Wijk works as an Assistant Professor in Criminology at VU University Amsterdam. He finished his Ph.D. research on irregular (asylum) migration from Angola to the Netherlands in 2007. In 2008 the European Society of Criminology granted him the Young European Criminologist Award for an article published in the journal *International Migration*. He briefly worked as a coordinator and researcher at the International Organization for Migration (IOM) and continues to work as a freelance consultant in migration affairs. At this moment he teaches the course "Victimology of International Crimes" in the selective Master International Crimes and Criminology at VU University. His current academic research project "Escaping Justice" focuses on the granting of amnesty after large scale conflicts and the application of exclusion clause 1F of the Refugee Convention.

BIBLIOGRAPHY

Aarts, P.G.H. (1998).
Intergenerational Effects in Families of World War II Survivors from the Dutch East Indies: Aftermath of another Dutch War, in: Danieli, Y. (ed.), *International Handbook of Multigenerational Legacies of Trauma*, New York: Plenum Press, 175–190.

Abrahams, N. & Jewkes, R. (2010).
Barriers to Post Exposure Prophylaxis (PEP) Completion after Rape: A South African Qualitative Study, *Culture, Health, and Sexuality* 12(5), 471–484.

Abrams, J.S. & Hayner, P. (2002).
Documenting, Acknowledging and Publicizing the Truth, in: Bassiouni, M.C. (ed.), *Post-Conflict Justice*, New York: Transnational Publishers, 283–293.

Adams, J.S. (1965).
Inequity in Social Exchange, in: Berkowitz, L. (ed.), *Advances in Social Psychology, vol. 2*, New York: Academic Press, 267–299.

Adelman, M. (2003).
The Military, Militarism, and the Militarization of Domestic Violence, *Violence Against Women* 9, 1118–1152.

Aertsen, I. (2008).
Racak, Mahane Yehuda & Nyabyondo: Restorative Justice between the Formal and the Informal, in: Aertsen, I., Arsovskla, J., Rohne, H.-C., Valinas, M., & Vanspauwen, K. (eds.), *Restoring Justice after Large-Scale Violent Conflicts. Kosovo, DR Congo and the Israeli-Palestinian Case*, Cullompton, Devon: Willan Publishing, 413–443.

Aertsen, I., Arsovska, J., Rohne, H.-C., Valiñas, M., & Vanspauwen, K. (eds.) (2008).
Restoring Justice after Large-Scale Violent Conflicts. Kosovo, DR Congo and Israeli-Palestinian Case, Cullompton, Devon: Willan Publishing.

Ager, A. (1996).
Children, War, and Psychological Intervention, in: Carr, S.C. & Schumaker, J.F. (eds.), *Psychology and the Developing World*, Westport, Connecticut: Praeger Publishers, 162–172.

Agirre Aranburu, X. (2010).
Sexual Violence beyond Reasonable Doubt: Using Pattern Evidence and Analysis for International Cases, *Leiden Journal of International Law* 23, 609–627.

Ahrens, C.E. (2006).
Being Silenced: The Impact of Negative Social Reactions on the Disclosure of Rape, *American Journal of Community Psychology* 38(3), 263–274.

Ahrens, C.E., Campbell, R., Ternier-Thames, N.K., Wasco, S.M., & Sefl, T. (2007).
Deciding Whom to Tell: Expectations and Outcomes of Rape Survivors' First Disclosure, *Psychology of Women Quarterly* 31(1), 38–49.

Aitcheson, A. (2011).
Making the Transition: International Intervention, State-Building and Criminal Justice Reform in Bosnia and Herzegovina, Volume 3 Series on Transitional Justice, Antwerp/Cambridge: Intersentia Publishers.

Akhavan, P. (2001).
Beyond Impunity: Can International Criminal Justice Prevent Atrocities?, *American Journal of International Law* 95(1), 7–31.

Al-Haj, M. & Ben Eliezer, U. (2003).
In the Name of Security: Sociology of Peace and War in Israel in Changing Times, Haifa: Haifa University Press (in Hebrew).

Albrecht, H.J. (2002).
Preliminary Remarks, *European Journal of Crime, Criminal Law and Criminal Justice* 2–3, 87–89.

Aldana-Pindell, R. (2002).
In Vindication of Justiciable Victims' Rights to Truth and Justice for State-Sponsored Crimes, *Vanderbilt Journal of Transnational Law* 35, 1399–1501.

Aldana-Pindell, R. (2004).
An Emerging Universality of Justifiable Victims' Rights in the Criminal Process to Curtail Impunity for State-Sponsored Crimes, *Human Rights Quarterly* 26, 605–686.

Ali, T.M., Matthews, R.O., & Spears, I. (2004).
Failures in Peace Building: Sudan (1972–1983) and Angola (1991–1998), in: Ali, T.M. & Matthews, R.O. (eds.), *Durable Peace; Challenges for Peace Building in Africa*, Toronto: University of Toronto Press, 282–311.

Alie, J.A.D. (1990).
A New History of Sierra Leone, London: McMillan Publishers.

Alie, J.A.D. (2008).
Reconciliation and Traditional Justice: Tradition-Based Practices of the Kpaa Mende, in: Huyse, L. & Salter, M. (eds.), *Traditional Justice after Violent Conflict. Learning from African Experiences*, Stockholm: IDEA, 123–146.

Alison, L. (2005).
The Forensic Psychologist's Casebook, Cullompton, Devon: Willan Publishing.

Allen, J. (1999).
Balancing Justice and Social Unity: Political Theory and the Idea of a Truth and Reconciliation Commission, *The University of Toronto Law Journal* 49, 315–353.

Allen, T. (2006).
Trial Justice; The International Criminal Court and the Lord's Resistance Army, London: Zed Books.

Alvarez, A. (2008).
Destructive Beliefs: Genocide and the Role of Ideology, in: Smeulers, A. & Haveman, R. (eds.), *Supranational Criminology: Towards a Criminology of International Crimes*, Antwerp: Intersentia, 213–231.

Ambos, K., Large, J., & Wierda, M. (eds.) (2009).
> *Building a Future on Peace and Justice. Studies on Transitional Justice, Peace and Development*, Berlin: Springer.

Anonyma (2008).
> *Eine Frau in Berlin. Tagebuch-Aufzeichnungen vom 20. April bis 22. Juni 1945*, München: btb Verlag-Random House.

Apuuli, K.P. (2009).
> Procedural Due Process and the Prosecution of Genocide Suspects in Rwanda, *Journal of Genocide Research* 11, 11–30.

Arendt, H. (1964).
> *Eichmann in Jerusalem – A Report on the Banality of Evil*, New York: Penguin.

Arendt, H. (1970).
> *On Violence*, London: Penguin Press.

Armour, M. (2007).
> Violent Death, *Journal of Human Behavior in the Social Environment* 14(4), 53–90.

Arnold, R. (2005).
> Military Criminal Procedures and Judicial Guarantees: The Example of Switzerland, *Journal of International Criminal Justice* 3, 749–777.

Arts, K. (2006).
> International Law, Criminal Accountability and the Rights of the Child, in: Arts, K. & Popovski, V. (eds.), *International Criminal Accountability and the Rights of Children*, The Hague: Hague Academic Press, 1–17.

Ashworth, A. (1993).
> Victim Impact Statements and Sentencing, *Criminal Law Review*, 498–509.

Ashworth, A. (2000).
> Victims' Rights, Defendants' Rights and Criminal Procedure, in: Crawford, A. & Goodey, J. (eds.), *Integrating a Victim Perspective within Criminal Justice*, Aldershot: Darmouth Publishing, 185–206.

Ashworth, A. & Von Hirsch, A. (1998).
> Desert and the Three R's, in: Von Hirsch, A. & Ashworth, A. (eds.), *Principled Sentencing: Readings on Theory and Policy*, 2nd edition, Oxford: Hart Publishing, 331–335.

Askin, K.D. (2004).
> A Decade of the Development of Gender Crimes in International Courts and Tribunals: 1993 to 2003, *Human Rights Brief* 11(3), 16–19.

Askin, K.D. (2005).
> Gender Crimes Jurisprudence in the ICTR: Positive Developments, *Journal of International Criminal Justice* 3(4), 1007–1018.

Askin, K.D. (2008).
> Gender Justice: The Work of the International Criminal Tribunal for Rwanda (ICTR), *Africa Legal Aid Quarterly*, Fall 2008.

Auerhahn, N.C. & Laub, D. (1998).
> Intergenerational Memory of the Holocaust, in: Danieli, Y. (ed.), *International Handbook of Multigenerational Legacies of Trauma*, New York: Plenum Press, 21–42.

Aukerman, M.J. (2002).
Extraordinary Evil, Ordinary Crime: A Framework for Understanding Transitional Justice, *Harvard Human Rights Journal* 15, 39–98.

Austin, W. & Tobiason, J.M. (1984).
Legal Justice and the Psychology of Conflict Resolution, in: Folger, R. (ed.), *The Sense of Injustice: Social Psychological Perspectives*, New York: Plenum Press, 227–274.

Babbie, E. (1990).
Survey Research Methods, 2nd edition, Belmont: Wadsworth.

Bacik, I., Maunsell, C., & Gogan, S. (1998).
The Legal Process and Victims of Rape, Dublin: Cahill Printers.

Baines, E.K. (2007).
The Haunting of Alice: Local Approaches to Justice and Reconciliation in Northern Uganda, *The International Journal of Transitional Justice* 1, 91–114.

Baines, E.K. (2009).
Complex Political Perpetrators: Reflections on Domenic Ongwen, *The Journal of Modern African Studies* 47, 163–191.

Bala, N., Lindsay, R.C.L., & McNamara, E. (2001).
Testimonial Aids for Children: The Canadian Experience with Closed Circuit TV, Screens, and Videotapes, *Criminal Law Quarter* 4, 461–489.

Ball, H. (1999).
Prosecuting War Crimes and Genocide, Kansas: University Press of Kansas.

Bandura, A. (1999).
Moral Disengagement in the Perpetration of Inhumanities, *Personality and Social Psychology Review* 3, 193–209.

Barenbaum, J., Ruchkin, V., & Schwab-Stone, M. (2004).
The Psychosocial Aspects of Children Exposed to War: Practice and Policy Initiatives, *Journal of Child Psychology and Psychiatry* 45(1), 41–62.

Baril, M. (1984).
L'inverse du crime, Centre International de Criminologie Comparée, cahier no. 2, Université de Montréal, Montréal.

Baristain, C.M. (2009).
Diálogos Sobre la Reparación: qué Repara en los Casos de Violaciones a los Derechos Humanos, Quito, Ecuador: Ministerio de Justicia y Derechos Humanos.

Barkan, S.E. & Snowden, L.L. (2001).
Collective Violence, Boston: Allyn and Bacon.

Barnett, R.E. (1977).
Restitution: A New Paradigm of Criminal Justice, *Ethics* 87(4), 279–301.

Bartol, C.R. & Bartol, A.M. (2005).
Criminal Behavior: A Psychosocial Approach, New Jersey: Prentice-Hall.

Bassiouni, M.C. (1988a).
The Protection of Collective Victims in International Law, in: Bassiouni, M.C. (ed.), *International Protection of Victims*, Toulouse: Erès, 181–198.

Bassiouni, M.C. (1988b).
> Introduction to the U.N. Resolution and Declaration of Basic Principles of Justice for Victims of Crime and Abuse of Power, in: Bassiouni, M.C. (ed.), *International Protection of Victims*, Toulouse: Erès, 17–24.

Bassiouni, M.C. (1992).
> *Crimes against Humanity and International Law*, Dordrecht: Martinus Nijhoff.

Bassiouni, M.C. (1996a).
> International Crimes: *Jus Cogens* and *Obligatio Erga Omnes, Law and Contemporary Problems* 59, 63–74.

Bassiouni, M.C. (1996b).
> Searching for Peace and Achieving Justice: The Need for Accountability, *Law and Contemporary Problems* 59, 9–28.

Bassiouni, M.C. (2001).
> Universal Jurisdiction for International Crimes. Historical Perspectives and Current Practice, *Virginia Journal of International Law* 42, 81–162.

Bassiouni, M.C. (2002).
> The Universal Model: The International Criminal Court, in: Bassiouni, M.C. (ed.), *Post-Conflict Justice*, New York: Transnational Publishers, 813–825.

Bassiouni, M.C. (2002).
> Accountability for Violations of International Humanitarian Law and Other Serious Violations of Human Rights, in: Bassiouni, M.C. (ed.), *Post-conflict Justice*, Ardsley, New York: Transnational Publishers.

Bassiouni, M.C. (2003).
> *Introduction to International Criminal Law*, New York: Transnational Publishers.

Bassiouni, M.C. (2006).
> International Recognition of Victims' Rights, *Human Rights Law Review* 6, 203–279.

Bassiouni, M.C. (2008).
> The Duty to Prosecute and/or Extradite: Aut Dedere Aut Judicare, in: Bassiouni, M.C. (ed.), *International Criminal Law, Vol. II: Multilateral and Bilateral Enforcement Mechanisms*, Leiden: Martinus Nijhoff Publishers, 35–45.

Baumeister, R.F. (1997/1999).
> *Evil. Inside Human Violence and Cruelty*, New York: Henry Holt and Company.

Baumeister, R.F. (2005).
> *The Cultural Animal. Human Nature, Meaning and Social Life*, Oxford: Oxford University Press.

Beah, I. (2007).
> *A Long Way Gone – Memoires of a Boy Soldier*, New York: Farrar, Straus and Giroux.

Becker, D., Lira, E., Castillo, M.I., Gomez, E., & Kovalskys, J. (1990).
> Therapy with Victims of Political Repression in Chile: The Challenge of Social Reparation, *Journal of Social Issues* 40(3), 133–149.

Becker, H. (1963).
> *Outsiders: Studies in the Sociology of Deviance*, New York: Free Press.

Beilin, Y. (1992).
> *Israel: A Concise History*, New York: St. Martin's Press.

Beke, D. (2004).
Legislation and Decentralisation in Uganda: From Resistance Councils to Elected Local Councils with Guaranteed Representation, in: Foblets, M.-C. & Von Trotha, T. (eds.), *Healing the Wounds. Essays on the Reconstruction of Societies after War*, Oxford/Portland: Hart Publishing.

Bell, T. & Ntsebeza, D.B. (2003).
Unfinished Business. South Africa, Apartheid and Truth, London: Verso.

Beltz, A. (2008).
Prosecuting Rape in International Criminal Tribunals: The Need to Balance Victim's Rights with the Due Process Rights of the Accused, *Saint John's Journal of Legal Commentary* 23(1), 167–209.

Bennett, Ch. (2006).
Taking the Sincerity Out of Saying Sorry: Restorative Justice as Ritual, *Journal of Applied Philosophy* 23, 127–143.

Bergsmo, M. & Triffterer, O. (2008).
Preamble, in: Triffterer, O. (ed.), *Commentary on the Rome Statute of the International Criminal Court: Observers' Notes, Article by Article*, 2nd edition, Munchen: Beck-Hart-Nomos, 1–14.

Bernstein, M.M. (1998).
Conflicts in Adjustment: World War II Prisoners of War and Their Families, in: Danieli, Y. (ed.), *International Handbook of Multigenerational Legacies of Trauma*, New York: Plenum Press, 119–124.

Bertodano, S. (2002).
Judicial Independence in the International Criminal Court, *Leiden Journal of International Law* 15(2), 409–430.

Bettelheim, B. (1984).
Afterword, in: Vegh, C., *I Didn't Say Goodbye*, New York: E.P. Dutton (Translated by R. Schwarz).

Bhargava, R. (2000).
Restoring Decency to Barbaric Societies, in: Rotberg, R.I. & Thompson, D. (eds.), *Truth v. Justice*, Princeton: Princeton University Press, 45–67.

Birkbeck, C. (1983).
"Victimology Is What Victimologists Do" But What Should They Do?, *Victimology* 8, 270–275.

Bijleveld, C. (2008).
Missing Pieces. Some Thoughts on the Methodology of the Empirical Study of International Crimes and Other Gross Human Rights Violations, in: Smeulers, A. & Haveman, R. (eds.), *Supranational Criminology: Towards a Criminology of International Crimes*, Antwerp: Intersentia, 77–97.

Bijleveld, C., Morssinkhof, A., & Smeulers, A. (2009).
Counting the Countless: Rape Victimization During the Rwandan Genocide, *International Criminal Justice Review* 19(2), 208–244.

Biko, N. (2000).
Amnesty and Denial, in: Villa-Vicencio, Ch. & Verwoerd, W. (eds.), *Looking Back Reaching Forward*, Cape Town: University of Cape Town, 193–198.

Bitti, G. & Friman, H. (2001).
Participation of Victims in the Proceedings, *The Elements of Crimes and Rules of Procedure and Evidence of the International Criminal Court*, New York: Transnational Publisher, 456–474.

Black, K.A. & Gold, D.J. (2008).
Gender Differences and Socioeconomic Status Biases in Judgments about Blame in Date Rape Scenarios, *Violence and Victims* 23(1), 115–128.

Blader, S. & Tyler, T. (2003).
A Four-Component Model of Procedural Justice: Defining the Meaning of a "Fair" Process, *Personality and Social Psychology Bulletin* 29(6), 747–758.

Bleich, A., Gelkopf, M., & Solomon, Z. (2003).
Exposure to Terrorism, Stress-Related Mental Health Symptoms, and Coping Behaviors among a Nationally Representative Sample in Israel, *Journal of the American Medical Association* 290(5), 612–620.

Bless, C. & Higson-Smith, C. (1995).
Fundamentals of Social research: An African Perspective, Cape Town: Juta.

Blewitt, M.K. (2010).
You Alone May Live. One Woman's Journey through the Aftermath of the Rwandan Genocide, Colorado Springs: Dialogue.

Blizzard, S.M. (2006).
Women's Roles in the 1994 Rwanda Genocide and the Empowerment of Women in the Aftermath, Master's Thesis, Georgia Institute of Technology.

Bloomfield, D. (2003).
The Process of Reconciliation, in: Bloomfield, D., Barnes, T., & Huyse, L. (eds.), *Reconciliation After Violent Conflict. A Handbook*, Stockholm: International Idea, 1–18.

Bloomfield, D. (2006).
On Good Terms: Clarifying Reconciliation, Berghof Report No. 14, Berlin: Berghof Research Center for Constructive Conflict Management.

Boctor, A. (2009).
The Abolition of the Death Penalty in Rwanda, *Human Rights Review* 10, 99–118.

Bodansky, D. & Crook, J.R. (2002).
The ILC State Responsibility Articles Introduction and Overview, *The American Journal of International Law* 96, 773–791.

Bodelier, R. (2011).
Human Security and the Emergence of a Global Conscience, in: Letschert, R.M. & Van Dijk, J.J.M. (eds.), *The New Faces of Victimhood*, Dordrecht: Springer, 41–70.

Boersch-Supan, J. (2009).
The Communities: The Crossroads between Reintegration and Reconciliation. What Can Be Learned from the Sierra Leonean Experience?, Crise Working Paper no. 63.

Bohler-Muller, N. (2008).
Against Forgetting: Reconciliation and Reparations after the Truth and Reconciliation Commission, *Stellenbosch Law Review* 3, 466–482.

Bohner, G., Eyssel, F., Pina, A., Siebler, F., & Tendayi Viki, G. (2009).
Rape Myth Acceptance: Cognitive, Affective and Behavioural Effects of Beliefs That Blame the Victim and Exonerate the Perpetrator, in: Horvath, M. & Brown,

J.M. (eds.), *Rape. Challenging Contemporary Thinking*, Cullompton, Devon: Willan Publishing, 17–45.

Boot, M. (2001).
Nullem Crimen Sine Lege and the Subject Matter Jurisdiction of the International Criminal Court, Antwerp/Oxford: Intersentia.

Boraine, A. (2000a).
A Country Unmasked: Inside South Africa's Truth and Reconciliation Commission, Oxford: Oxford University Press.

Boraine, A. (2000b).
Truth and Reconciliation in South Africa: The Third Way, in: Rotberg, R.I. & Thompson, D. (eds.), *Truth v. Justice. The Morality of Truth Commissions*, Princeton/ Oxford: Princeton University Press, 141–157.

Boraine, A., Levy, J., & Scheffer, R. (1994).
Dealing with the Past: Truth and Reconciliation in South Africa, Cape Town: Idasa.

Borneman, J. (1997).
Settling Accounts: Violence, Justice and Accountability in Postsocialist Europe, Princeton: Princeton University Press.

Bottoms, B.L. & Goodman, G.S. (eds.) (1996).
International Perspectives on Child Abuse and Children's Testimony: Psychological Research and Law, Thousand Oaks, California: Sage Publications.

Bourke, J. (2007).
Rape: Sex, Violence, History, Emeryville: Shoemaker & Hoard.

Braeckman, C. (1994).
Rwanda: Histoire d'un Génocide, Paris: Fayard.

Brahm, E. (2007).
Uncovering the Truth: Examining the Truth Commission Success and Impact, *International Studies Perspectives* 8(1), 16–35.

Brienen, M.E.I. & Hoegen, E.H. (2000).
Victims of Crime in 22 European Criminal Justice Systems, Nijmegen: Wolf Legal Publishers.

Brocklehurst, H., Stott, N., & Hamber, B. (2000).
Lesson Drawing from Negotiated Transitions in Northern Ireland and South Africa, Paper Presented at the Annual Meeting of the American Political Science Association, Marriot Warden Park, 31st August-3rd September.

Broomhall, B. (2003).
International Justice and International Criminal Court: Between Sovereignty and the Rule of Law, Oxford: Oxford University Press.

Brounéus, K. (2008).
Truth Telling as Talking Cure? Insecurity and Retraumatization in the Rwandan Gacaca Courts, *Security Dialogue* 39(1), 55–76.

Brounéus, K. (2010).
The Trauma of Truth Telling: Effects of Witnessing in the Rwandan Gacaca Courts on Psychological Health, *Journal of Conflict Resolution* 54, 408–437.

Brownmiller, S. (1975).
Against Our Will: Men, Women and Rape, New York: Simon & Schuster.

Brudholm, T. (2008).

Resentment's Virtue: Jean Améry and the Refusal to Forgive, Philadelphia: Temple University Press.

Brudholm, T. & Rosoux, V. (2009).

The Unforgiving Reflections on the Resistance to Forgiveness after Atrocity, *Law and Contemporary Problems* 72(33), 33–49.

Bryman, A. (2008).

Social Research Methods, Oxford: Oxford University Press.

Buchwald, E., Fletcher, P., & Roth, M. (2005).

Transforming a Rape Culture, Minneapolis: Milkweed Editions.

Buckley-Zistel, S. (2008).

We Are Pretending Peace: Local Memory and the Absence of Social Transformation and Reconciliation in Rwanda, in: Clark, P. & Kaufman, Z.D. (eds.), *After Genocide: Transitional Justice, Post-Conflict Reconstruction and Reconciliation in Rwanda and Beyond*, London: Hurst & Company, 125–143.

Bull, R. & Davies, G. (1996).

The Effect of Child Witness Research on Legislation in Great Britain, in: Bottoms, B.L. & Goodman, G.S. (eds.), *International Perspectives on Child Abuse and Children's Testimony: Psychological Research and Law*, Thousand Oaks, California: Sage Publications, 96–113.

Bunch, C. (1990).

Women's Rights as Human Rights: Towards a Revision of Human Rights, *Human Rights Quarterly* 12, 486–498.

Burnett, M.J. (2005).

Remembering Justice in Rwanda: Locating Gender in the Judicial Construction of Memory, *Seattle Journal for Social Justice* 3, 757–784.

Burt, M.R. (1983).

A Conceptual Framework for Victimological Research, *Victimology* 8, 261–269.

Buss, D.E. (2009).

Rethinking 'Rape as a Weapon of War', *Feminist Legal Studies* 17, 145–163.

Campbell, R. & Raja, S. (1999).

Secondary Victimization of Rape Victims: Insights from Mental Health Professionals Who Treat Survivors of Violence, *Violence and Victims* 14(3), 261–275.

Campbell, R. & Wasco, S.M. (2005).

Understanding Rape and Sexual Assault: 20 Years of Progress and Future Directions, *Journal of Interpersonal Violence* 20(1), 127–131.

Canter, A.S. (2009).

For These Reasons, the Chamber: Denies the Prosecutor's Request for Referral: The False Hope of Rule 11 bis, *Fordham International Law Journal* 32, 1614–1656.

Caranza, R. (2008).

Plunder and Plain: Should Transitional Justice Engage with Corruption and Economic Crimes?, *International Journal of Transitional Justice* 2(3), 310–330.

Carlson, E.S. (2005).

The Hidden Prevalence of Male Sexual Assault during War, *British Journal of Criminology* 46(1), 16–25.

Carpenter, R.C. (2006).
Recognizing Gender-Based Violence against Civilian Men and Boys in Conflict Situations, *Security Dialogue* 37(1), 83–103.

Cassese, A. (1999).
The Statute of the International Criminal Court: Some Preliminary Reflections, *European Journal of International Law* 10, 144–171.

Cassese, A. (2003).
International Criminal Law, Oxford: Oxford University Press.

Cassese, A. (2008).
International Criminal Law, New York: Oxford University Press.

Ceretti, A. (2009).
Collective Violence and International Crimes, in: Cassese, A. (ed.), *The Oxford Companion to International Criminal Justice*, Oxford: Oxford University Press, 5–15.

Chambliss, W.J. (1993).
The Creation of Criminal Law and Crime Control in Britain and America, in: Chambliss, W.J. & Zatz, M.J. (eds.), *Making Law. The State, the Law, and Structural Contradictions*, Bloomington, Indianapolis: Indiana University Press, 36–64.

Chesterman, J. (2001).
Civilians in Wars, Boulder: Riener.

Chinkin, C. (1994).
Rape and Sexual Abuse of Women in International Law, *European Journal of International law* 5, 326–341.

Chirot, D. & McCauley, C. (2006).
Why Not Kill Them All? The Logic and Prevention of Mass Political Murder, Princeton: Princeton University Press.

Chouliaras, A. (2010a).
State Crime and Individual Criminal Responsibility: Theoretical Inquiries and Practical Consequences, in: Burchard, C., Triffterer, O., & Vogel, J. (eds.), *The Review Conference and the Future of the ICC. Proceedings of the First AIDP Symposium for Young Penalists in Tübingen, Germany*, The Netherlands: Kluwer Law International, 191–214.

Chouliaras, A. (2010b).
The Reason of State: Theoretical Inquires and Consequences for the Criminology of State Crime, in: Chambliss, W., Michalowski, R., & Kramer, R. (eds.), *State Crime in the Global Age*, Cullompton, Devon: Willan Publishing, 232–246.

Chouliaras, A. (2010c).
Discourses on International Criminality, in: Smeulers, A. (ed.), *Collective Violence and International Criminal Justice – An Interdisciplinary Approach*, Antwerp/Oxford/Portland: Intersentia, 63–101.

Christie, N. (1986a).
The Ideal Victim, in: Fattah, E.A. (ed.), *From Crime Policy to Victim Policy*, New York: St. Martin's Press, 17–30.

Christie, N. (1986b).

Suitable Enemies, in: Bianchi, H. & Van Swaaningen, R. (eds.), *Abolitionism. Towards a Non-Repressive Approach to Crime*, Amsterdam: Free University Press, 42–54.

Christie, N. (2001).

Answers to Atrocities. Restorative Justice as an Answer to Extreme Situations, in: Fattah, E. & Parmentier, S. (eds.), *Victim Policies and Criminal Justice on the Road to Restorative Justice. A Collection of Essays in Honour of Tony Peters*, Leuven: Leuven University Press, 379–392.

Christie, N. (2007).

Restorative Justice – Answers to Deficits in Modernity?, in: Downes, D., Rock, P., Chinkin, C., & Gaerty, C. (eds.), *Crime, Social Control and Human Rights. From Moral Panics to States of Denials. Essays in Honour of Stanley Cohen*, Cullompton, Devon: Willan Publishing, 368–378.

Christie, R. (2010).

Critical Voices and Human Security: To Endure, to Engage or to Critique?, *Security Dialogue* 41(2), 169–190.

Chung, C.H. (2008).

Victim Participation at the International Criminal Court: Are Concessions of the Court Clouding the Promise?, *Northwestern Journal of International Human Rights* 6, 459–545.

Clark, P. (2007).

Hybridity, Holism and "Traditional Justice": The Case of the Gacaca Courts in Post-Genocide Rwanda, *George Washington International Law Review* 39(4), 765–832.

Clark, P. (2010).

The Gacaca Courts, Post-Genocide Justice and Reconciliation in Rwanda. Justice without Lawyers, Cambridge: Cambridge University Press.

Clark, P. & Kaufman, Z.D. (eds.) (2009).

After Genocide: Transitional Justice, Post-Conflict Reconstruction and Reconciliation in Rwanda and Beyond, New York: Columbia University Press.

Clayton, S. & Opotow, S. (2003).

Justice and Identity: Changing Perceptions of What is Fair, *Personality and Social Psychology Review* 7, 298–310.

Cobban, H. (2007).

Amnesty after Atrocity? Healing Nations after Genocide and War Crimes, London: Paradigm Publishers.

Cockayne, J. (2009).

Truth and Reconciliation Commissions (General), in: Cassese, A. (ed.), *The Oxford Companion to International Criminal Justice*, Oxford: Oxford University Press, 543–545.

Coelho, J.P.B. (2003).

Antigos Soldados, Novos Cidadãos; uma Avaliação da Reintegração dos Ex-Combatentes de Maputo in: Santos, B. & Trindade, J.C. (eds.), *Conflito e Transformação Social; uma Paisagem das Justiças em Moçambique*, Santa Maria da Feira: Rainho & Neves, 195–228.

Cohen, M.H., Fabri, M., Cai, X., Shi, Q., Hoover, D.R., Binagwaho, A., Culhane, M.A., Mukanyonga, H., Ksahaka Karegeya, D., & Anastos, K. (2009).
> Prevalence and Predictors of Posttraumatic Stress Disorder and Depression in HIV-Infected and At-Risk Rwandan Women, *Journal of Women's Health* 18(11), 1783–1791.

Cohen, S. (1995).
> State Crimes of Previous Regimes: Knowledge, Accountability, and the Policing of the Past, *Law and Social Inquiry* 20, 7–50.

Cohen, S. (1996).
> Government Responses to Human Rights Reports: Claims, Denials, and Counterclaims, *Human Rights Quarterly* 18, 517–543.

Cohen, S. (2001).
> *States of Denial. Knowing about Atrocities and Suffering*, Cambridge: Polity Press.

Cohen-Jonathan, G. (2003).
> Universalité et Singularité des Droits de L'Homme, *Revue Trimestrielle des Droits de l'Homme* 53, 1–13.

Cohn, I. (2001).
> The Protection of Children and the Quest for Truth and Justice in Sierra Leone, *International Law Affairs* 55(1), 1–34.

Cohn, I. & Goodwin-Gill, G.S. (1997).
> *Child Soldiers: The Role of Children in Armed Conflicts*, New York: Oxford University Press.

Cole, A. (2008).
> Prosecutor v. Gacumbitsi: The New Definition for Prosecuting Rape Under International Law, *International Criminal Law Review* 8(1–2), 55–85.

Coleridge, L. (2000).
> The Amnesty Process of the Truth and Reconciliation Commission (TRC) with Specific Reference to Female Amnesty Applicants, *South African Journal of Psychology* 30(1), 56–58.

Colonomos, A. & Armstrong, A. (2006).
> German Reparations to the Jews after World War II: A Turning Point in the History of Reparations, in: De Greiff, P. (ed.), *The Handbook of Reparations*, Oxford: Oxford University Press, 390–420.

Colquitt, J.A. (2001).
> On the Dimensionality of Organization Justice: A Construct Validation of a Measure, *Journal of Applied Psychology* 86(1), 386–400.

Colvin, C.J. (2006).
> Reparations Program in South Africa, in: De Greiff, P. (ed.), *The Handbook of Reparations*, Oxford: Oxford University Press, 176–214.

Comerford, M.G. (2005).
> *The Peaceful Face of Angola: Biography of a Peace Process (1991–2002)*, Windhoek: John Meinert Printing.

Cordon, I., Goodman, G., & Anderson, S. (2003).
> Children in Court, in: Van Koppen, P.J. & Penrod, S.D. (eds.), *Adversarial versus Inquisitorial Justice: Psychological Perspectives on Criminal Justice Systems*, New York: Kluwer Academic, 167–189.

Corey, A. & Joireman, S.F. (2004).
   Retributive Justice: The *Gacaca* Courts in Rwanda, *African Affairs* 103, 73–89.
Corradi, G. (2010).
   Human Rights Promotion in Post Conflict Sierra Leone: Coming to Grips with Plurality in Customary Justice, *Journal of Legal Pluralism and Unofficial Law* 60, 73–103.
Correa, C., Guillerot, J., & Magarrell, L. (2009).
   Reparations and Victim Participation: A Look at the Truth Commission Experience, in: Ferstman, C., Goetz, M., & Stephens, A. (eds.), *Reparations for Victims of Genocide, War Crimes and Crimes against Humanity. Systems in Place and Systems in Making*, Leiden/Boston: Martinus Nijhoff Publishers, 385–414.
Courtemanche, G. (2003).
   A Sunday at the Pool in Kigali, Edinburgh: Canongate Books (Translated by Patricia Claxton).
Crawford, J. (2002).
   The International Law Commission's Articles on State Responsibility. Introduction, Text and Commentaries, Cambridge: Cambridge University Press.
Crocker, D.A. (1998).
   Transitional Justice and International Civil Society: Toward a Normative Framework, *Constellations* 5(4), 492–517.
Crocker, D.A. (1999).
   Reckoning with Past Wrongs: A Normative Framework, *Ethics and International Affairs* 13, 43–64.
Crocker, D.A. (2003).
   Reckoning with Past Wrongs: A Normative Framework, in: Prager, C.A.L. & Govier, T. (eds.), *Dilemmas of Reconciliation*, Waterloo: Wilfrid Laurier University Press, 39–63.
Cross jr., W.G. (1998).
   Black Psychological Functioning and the Legacy of Slavery: Myths and Realities, in: Danieli, Y. (ed.), *International Handbook of Multigenerational Legacies of Trauma*, New York: Plenum Press, 387–402.
Csete, J. & Kippenberg, J. (2002).
   Sexual Crimes Increase in Climate of Impunity and Culture of Violence, New York: Human Rights Watch.
Cunningham, A. & Hurley, P. (2007).
   A Full and Candid Account: Using Special Accommodations and Testimonial Aids to Facilitate the Testimony of Children, Centre for Children and Families in the Justice System, London Family Court Clinic, London, Ontario.
Czarnota, A. (2007).
   Sacrum, Profanum and Social Time: Quasi-theological Reflections on Time and Reconciliation, in: Veitch, S. (ed.), *Law and the Politics of Reconciliation*, Aldershot: Ashgate.
Dadomo, C. & Ferran, S. (1993).
   The French Legal System, 2nd edition, London: Sweet & Maxwell.

Dadrian, V.N. (1974).
> The Structural-Functional Components of Genocide: A Victimological Approach to the Armenian Case, in: Drapkin, I. & Viano, E. (eds.), *Victimology*, Massachusetts/Toronto/London: Lexington Books, 123–136.

Dallaire, R. (2004).
> *Shake Hands with the Devil. The Failure of Humanity in Rwanda*, Jackson: De Capo Press.

Daly, E. & Sarkin, J. (2007).
> *Reconciliation in Divided Societies. Finding Common Ground*, Philadelphia: University of Pennsylvania Press.

Daly, K. & Bouhours, B. (2010).
> Rape and Attrition in the Legal Process: A Comparative Analysis of Five Countries, *Crime and Justice: A Review of Research* 39, 565–650.

Damgaard, C. (2008).
> *Individual Criminal Responsibility for Core International Crimes. Selected Pertinent Issues*, Heidelberg: Springer.

Danieli, Y. (1981a).
> On the Achievement of Integration in Aging Survivors of the Nazi Holocaust, *Journal of Geriatric Psychiatry* 14(2), 191–210.

Danieli, Y. (1981b).
> Exploring the Factors in Jewish Identity Formation (in Children of Survivors), in: Rosen, G., *Consultation on the Psycho-Dynamics of Jewish Identity: Summary of Proceedings*, New York: American Jewish Committee and the Central Conference of American Rabbis, 22–25.

Danieli, Y. (1982).
> Therapists' Difficulties in Treating Survivors of the Nazi Holocaust and Their Children, *Dissertation Abstracts International*, 42(12-B, Pt 1), 4927 (UMI No. 949–904).

Danieli, Y. (1984).
> Psychotherapists' Participation in the Conspiracy of Silence about the Holocaust, *Psychoanalytic Psychology* 1(1), 23–42.

Danieli, Y. (1985).
> The Treatment and Prevention of Long-Term Effects and Intergenerational Transmission of Victimization: A Lesson from Holocauset Survivors and Their Children, in: Figley, C.R. (ed.), *Trauma and Its Wake: The Study and Treatment of Post-Traumatic Stress Disorder*, New York: Brunner/Mazel, 295–313.

Danieli, Y. (1988).
> Treating Survivors and Children of Survivors of the Nazi Holocaust, in: Ochberg, F.M. (ed.), *Post-Traumatic Therapy and Victims of Violence*, New York: Brunner/Mazel, 278–294.

Danieli, Y. (1992).
> Preliminary Reflections from a Psychological Perspective, in: Van Boven, T.C., Flinterman, C., Grunfeld, F., & Westendorp, I. (eds.), *The Right to Restitution, Compensation and Rehabilitation for Victims of Gross Violations of Human Rights and Fundamental Freedoms*, Special issue No. 12, Utrecht: Studie- en Informatiecentrum Mensenrechten, 196–213.

Danieli, Y. (1994a).
> Resilience and Hope, in: Lejuene, G. (ed.), *Children Worldwide*, Geneva: International Catholic Child Bureau, 47–49.

Danieli, Y. (1994b).
> Countertransference, Trauma and Training, in: Wilson, J.P. & Lindy, J. (eds.), *Countertransference in the Treatment of Post-Traumatic Stress Disorder*, New York: Guilford Press, 368–388.

Danieli, Y. (1995).
> Preliminary Reflections from a Psychological Perspective, in: Kritz, N.J. (ed.), *Transitional Justice: How Emerging Democracies Reckon with Former Regimes. Volume I: General Considerations*, Washington D.C.: United States Institute of Peace, 572–582.

Danieli, Y. (ed.) (1998).
> *International Handbook of Multigenerational Legacies of Trauma*, New York: Plenum Press.

Danieli, Y. (ed.) (2002).
> *Sharing the Front Line and the Back Hills*, New York: Baywood Publishing Company.

Danieli, Y. (2006a).
> Essential Elements of Healing after Massive Trauma: Complex Needs Voiced by Victims/Survivors, in: Sullivan, D. & Tifft, L. (eds.), *Handbook of Restorative Justice. A Global Perspective*, London/New York: Routledge, 343–354.

Danieli, Y. (2006b).
> Reappraising the Nuremberg Trials and Their Legacy: The Role of Victims in International Law, *Cardozo Law Review* 27, 1633–1649.

Danieli, Y. (2009a).
> Massive Trauma and the Healing Role of Reparative Justice, *Journal of Traumatic Stress* 22(5), 351–357.

Danieli, Y. (2009b).
> Massive Trauma and the Healing Role of Reparative Justice, in: Ferstman, C., Goetz, M., & Stephens, A. (eds.), *Reparations for Victims of Genocide, War Crimes and Crimes against Humanity. Systems in Place and Systems in Making*, Leiden/Boston: Martinus Nijhoff Publishers, 41–78.

Danner, A.M. & Martinez, J.S. (2005).
> Guilty Associations: Joint Criminal Enterprise, Command Responsibility, and the Development of International Criminal Law, *California Law Review* 93, 75–169.

Darley, J.M. (1992).
> Social Organization for the Production of Evil, *Psychological Inquiry* 3, 199–218.

Davis, L. & Snyman, R. (2005).
> *Victimology in South Africa*, Pretoria: Van Schaik.

De Beer, A.S. & Fouche, J.H. (2000).
> In Search of the Truth: The TRC and the South African Press – a Case Study, *Ecquid Novi* 21(2), 194–206.

De Brouwer, A.L.M. (2005).
> *Supranational Criminal Prosecution of Sexual Violence: The ICC and the Practice of the ICTY and the ICTR*, Antwerp/Oxford: Intersentia.

De Brouwer, A. (2007).

Reparation to Victims of Sexual Violence: Possibilities at the International Criminal Court and at the Trust Fund for Victims and Their Families, *Leiden Journal of International Law* 20, 207–237.

De Brouwer, A. (2009).

What the International Court has Achieved and Can Achieve for Victims/Survivors of Sexual Violence, *International Review on Victimology* 16, 183–209.

De Brouwer, A. & Chu, S.K.H. (2009).

The Men Who Killed Me: Rwandan Survivors of Sexual Violence, Vancouver/Toronto/Berkeley: Douglas & McIntyre.

De Brouwer, A. & Groenhuijsen, M. (2009).

The Role of Victims in International Criminal Proceedings, in: Sluiter, G. & Vasiliev, S. (eds.), *International Criminal Procedure: Towards a Coherent Body of Law,* London: CMP Publishing, 22–23.

De Brouwer, A. & Heikkilä, M. (2012) [forthcoming].

The Victims' Role in International Criminal Proceedings: Participation, Protection, Reparation and Assistance, in: Sluiter, G. *et al., International Criminal Procedure: Towards the Codification of General Rules and Principles,* Oxford: Oxford University Press.

De Cataldo Neuburger, L. (1985).

An Appraisal of Victimological Perspectives in International Law, *Victimology* 10, 700–709.

De Feyter, K., Parmenier, S., Bossuyt, M., & Lemmens, P. (eds.) (2005).

Out of the Ashes: Reparation for Victims of Gross Human Rights Violations, Antwerp/Oxford: Intersentia.

De Greiff, P. (2006a).

The Handbook of Reparations, Oxford: Oxford University Press.

De Greiff, P. (2006b).

Introduction, in: De Greiff, P. (ed.), *The Handbook of Reparations,* Oxford: Oxford University Press, 1–18.

De Greiff, P. (2006c).

Justice and Reparations, in: De Greiff, P. (ed.), *The Handbook of Reparations,* Oxford: Oxford University Press, 451–477.

De Greiff, P. & Duthie, R. (2009).

Transitional Justice and Development: Making Connections, Advancing Transitional Justice Series, New York: Social Science Research Council.

De Jong, K., Mulhern, M., Ford, N., Van der Kam, S., & Kleber, R. (2000).

Health and Human Rights; the Trauma of War in Sierra Leone, *The Lancet* 335, 2067–2068.

Defeis, E. (2008).

U.N. Peacekeepers and Sexual Abuse and Exploitation: An End to Impunity, *Global Studies Law Review* 7(2), 185–214.

Dekel, R. (2004).

Motherhood in Times of Terror: Subjective Experiences and Responses of Israeli Mothers, *Affilia* 19(1), 24–38.

Del Ponte, C. (2008).
Madame Prosecutor: Confrontations with Humanity's Worst Criminals and the Culture of Impunity, Pittsfield: Other Press.

Delmas-Marty, M. (2009).
Violence and Massacres – Towards a Criminal Law of Inhumanity?, *Journal of International Criminal Justice* 7, 5–16.

Dembour, M.-B. & Haslam, E. (2004).
Silencing Hearings? Victim-Witnesses at War Crimes Trials, *European Journal of International Law* 15(1), 151–177.

Denkers, A.J.M. (1996).
Psychological Reactions of Victims of Crime: The Influence of Pre-Crime, Crime and Post-Crime Factors, Doctoral dissertation, Amsterdam: Vrije Universiteit Amsterdam.

Denov, M. (2006).
Wartime Sexual Violence: Assessing a Human Security Response to War-Affected Girls in Sierra Leone, *Security Dialogue* 37(3), 319–342.

Des Forges, A. (1999).
Leave None to Tell the Story: Genocide in Rwanda, New York/Paris: Human Rights Watch and International Federation of Human Rights.

Des Forges, A. (ed.) (1999).
Aucun Témoin Ne Doit Survivre. Le Génocide au Rwanda, Paris: Karthala.

Des Forges, A. & Longman, T. (2004).
Legal Responses to Genocide in Rwanda, in: Stover, E. & Weinstein, H.M. (eds.), *My neighbor, my Enemy. Justice and Community in the Aftermath of Mass Atrocity*, Cambridge: Cambridge University Press.

Deutsch, M. (1975).
Equity, Equality, and Need: What Determines which Value Will Be Used as the Basis for Distributive Justice?, *Journal of Social Issues* 31, 137–149.

Dezwirek Sas, L., Wolfe, D., & Gowdey, K. (1996).
Children and the Courts in Canada, in: Bottoms, B.L. & Goodman, G.S. (eds.), *International Perspectives on Child Abuse and Children's Testimony: Psychological Research and Law*, Thousand Oaks, California: Sage Publications, 77–95.

Díaz, C. & Sánchez, N.C. (2009).
El Diseño Institucional de Reparaciones en la Ley de Justicia y Paz: Una Evaluación Preliminar, in: Díaz, C., Sánchez, N.C., & Umprimny, R. (eds.), *Reparar en Colombia: Los Dilemas en Contextos de Conflicto, Pobreza y Exclusión*, Bogota: Centro Internacional para la Justicia Transicional & Centro de Estudios de Derecho, Justicia y Sociedad – DeJuSticia, 581–621.

Dieng, A. (2009).
Bridging the Divide between Reconciliation and Justice, *African Prospect*, 23–26.

Digeser, P.E. (2001).
Political Forgiveness, Ithaca: Cornell University Press.

Dignan, J. (2005).
Understanding Victims and Restorative Justice, Berkshire: Open University Press.

Doak, J. (2011).

The Therapeutic Dimension of Transitional Justice: Emotional Repair and Victim Satisfaction in International Trials and Truth Commissions, *International Criminal Law Review* 11, 263–298.

Dolan, Ch. (2009).

Social Torture; the Case of Northern Uganda 1986–2006, Oxford: Berghahn Books.

Donat-Cattin, D. (1999).

Article 68 Protection of Victims and Witnesses and Their Participation in the Proceedings, in: Triffterer, O. (ed.), *Commentary on the Rome Statute of the International Criminal Court: Observers' Notes Article by Article*, Baden-Baden: Nomos, 869–888.

Dougherty, B.K. (2004a).

Right-Sizing International Criminal Justice: The Hybrid Experiment at the Special Court for Sierra Leone, *International Affairs* 80(2), 311–328.

Dougherty, B.K. (2004b).

Searching for Answers: Sierra Leone's Truth & Reconciliation Commission, *Africa Studies Quarterly* 8(1).

Drumbl, M.A. (2000).

Punishment, Postgenocide: From Guilt to Shame to *Civis* in Rwanda, *New York University Law Review* 75, 1221–1326.

Drumbl, M.A. (2005).

Collective Violence and Individual Punishment: The Criminality of Mass Atrocity, *Northwestern University Law Review* 99, 539–610.

Drumbl, M.A. (2007).

Atrocity, Punishment and International Law, Cambridge: Cambridge University Press.

Drumbl, M.A. (2010a).

Prosecution of Genocide v. the Fair Trial Principle: Comments on Brown and others v. The Government of Rwanda and the UK Secretary of State for the Home Department, *Journal of International Criminal Justice* 8, 289–309.

Drumbl, M.A. (2010b).

Child Soldiers: Agency, Enlistment and the Collectivization of Innocence, in: Smeulers, A. (ed.), *Collective Crimes and International Criminal Justice: An Interdisciplinary Approach*, Antwerp: Intersentia, 205–229.

Du Toit, A. (2000).

The Moral Foundations of the South African TRC: Truth as Acknowledgment and Justice as Recognition, in: Rotberg, R.I. & Thompson, D. (eds.), *Truth v. Justice. The Morality of Truth Commissions*, Princeton/Oxford: Princeton University Press, 122–140.

Dubinsky, P. (2004).

Justice for the Collective: The Limits of the Human Rights Class Action, *Michigan Law Review* 104, 1152.

Ducey, K.A. (2010).

Dilemmas of Teaching the "Greatest Silence": Rape-as-Genocide in Rwanda, Darfur, and Congo, *Genocide Studies and Prevention* 5(3), 310–322.

Duff, R.A. (2001).
Punishment, Communication, and Community, Oxford: Oxford University Press.

Dugard, J. (2002).
Possible Conflicts of Jurisdiction with Truth Commissions, in: Cassese, A., Gaeta, P., & Jones, J.R.W.D. (eds.), *The Rome Statute of the International Criminal Court: A Commentary, Vol. I*, Oxford: Oxford University Press, 693–704.

Dunn, P.C., Vail-Smith, K., & Knight, S.M. (1999).
What Date/Acquaintance Rape Victims Tell Others: A Study of College Student Recipients of Disclosure, *Journal of American College Health* 47(5), 213–219.

Dupaquier, J.F. (2010).
L'agenda de génocide. Le témoignage de Richard Mugenzi ex-espion Rwandais, Paris: Editions Karthala.

Dupuy, K.E. & Peters, K. (2010).
War and Children: A Reference Handbook, Santa Barbara, California: ABC-CLIO.

Duran, E., Duran, B., Yellow Horse Brave Heart, M., & Yellow Horse-Davis, M. (1998).
Healing the American Indian Soul Wound, in: Danieli, Y. (ed.), *International Handbook of Multigenerational Legacies of Trauma*, New York: Plenum Press, 341–354.

Durán, T., Bacic, R., & Pérez, P. (1998).
Muerte y Desaparición Forzada en la Araucanía: Una Aproximación Étnica, Temuco, Chile: Ediciones Universidad Católica de Temuco-LOM Ediciones.

Durham, H. & O'Byrne, K. (2010).
The Dialogue of Difference: Gender Perspectives on International Humanitarian Law, *International Review of the Red Cross* 92(877), 1–22.

Durkheim, E. (1893).
De la division du travail social, 8e édition, Paris: Les Presses Universitaires de France, http://classiques.uqac.ca/classiques/Durkheim_emile/division_du_travail/division_travail.html, last visited: October 2009.

Duthie, R. (2009).
Introduction to Transitional Justice and Development, in: De Greiff, P. & Duthie, R., *Transitional Justice and Development, Making Connections*, Advancing Transitional Justice Series, New York: Social Science Research Council, 17–28.

Dwork, D. (1991).
Children with a Star: Jewish Youth in Nazi Europe, New Haven: Yale University Press.

Edelman, L., Kordon, D., & Lagos, D. (1992).
Argentina: Physical Disease and Bereavement in a Social Context of Human Rights Violations and Impunity, in: Van Willigen, L.H.M. (chair), *The Limitations of Current Concepts of Post Traumatic Stress Disorders Regarding the Consequences of Organized Violence*, Session Presented at the World Conference of the International Society for Traumatic Stress Studies, Amsterdam.

Edelman, L., Kordon, D., & Lagos, D. (1998).
Transmission of Trauma: The Argentine Case, in: Danieli, Y. (ed.), *International Handbook of Multigenerational Legacies of Trauma*, New York: Plenum Press, 447–464.

Eichstaedt, P. (2009).

First Kill Your Family: Child Soldiers of Uganda and the Lord's Resistance Army, Chicago: Lawrence Hill Books.

Eitinger, L. (1980).

The Concentration Camp Syndrome and Its Late Sequelae, in: Dimsdale, J.E. (ed.), Survivors, Victims, and Perpetrators: Essays on the Nazi Holocaust, New York: Hemisphere.

Eitinger, L. & Krell, R. (eds.) (1985).

The Psychological and Medical Effects of Concentration Camps and Related Persecutions of Survivors of the Holocaust: A Research Bibliography, Vancouver: University of British Columbia Press.

Elbedour, S., Ten Bensel, R., & Bastien, D.T. (1993).

Ecological Integrated Model of Children of War: Individual and Social Psychology, Child Abuse & Neglect 17, 805–819.

Elias, R. (1985).

Transcending Our Social Reality of Victimization: Toward a New Victimology of Human Rights, Victimology 10, 6–25.

Elias, R. (1986).

The Politics of Victimization. Victims, Victimology and Human Rights, New York/ Oxford: Oxford University Press.

Ellian, A. (2003).

Een Onderzoek naar de Waarheids- en Verzoeningscommissie, Nijmegen: Wolf Legal Publishers.

Emmanuel, K. (2007).

Between Principle and Pragmatism in Transitional Justice: South Africa's TRC and Peace Building, Paper No. 156, November, Pretoria: Institute for Security Studies.

Engdahl, B., Jaranson, J., Kastrup, M., & Danieli, Y. (1999).

Traumatic Human Rights Violations: Their Psychological Impact and Treatment, in: Danieli, Y., Stamatapoulou, E.C., & Dias, C. (eds.), The Universal Declaration of Human Rights Fifty Years and Beyond, New York: Baywoord Publishing Company, 337–356.

Erez, E. (1999).

Who's Afraid of the Big Bad Victim? Victim Impact Statements as Victim Empowerment and Enhancement of Justice, Criminal Law Review, 545–556.

Erez, E. (2006).

Protracted War, Terrorism and Mass Victimization: Exploring Victimological/ Criminological Theories and Concepts in Addressing Terrorism in Israel, in: Ewald, U. & Turković, K. (eds.), Large-Scale Victimisation as a Potential Source of Terrorist Activities. Importance of Regaining Security in Post-Conflict Societies, Amsterdam: IOS Press, 89–102.

Espinoza, V., Ortiz, M.L., & Rojas, P. (2003).

Comisiones de Verdad: ¿Un Camino Incierto?, Santiago: CODEPU/LOM Ediciones.

Estrich, S. (1987).

Real Rape, Cambridge: Harvard University Press.

Ewald, U. (2008).
'Reason' and 'Truth' in International Criminal Justice – A Criminological Perspective on the Construction of Evidence in International Trials, in: Smeulers, A. & Haveman, R. (eds.), *Supranational Criminology: Towards a Criminology of International Crimes*, Antwerp: Intersentia, 398–432.

Fabri, M. (2007).
Responding to Trauma and HIV in Rwanda, Symposium conducted at the meeting of the International Society for Traumatic Stress Studies, Baltimore, United States.

Falandysz, L. (1982).
Victimology in the Radical Perspective, in: Schneider, H.J. (ed.), *The Victim in International Perspective*, Berlin/New York: Walter de Gruyter, 105–114.

Falk, R. (2006).
Reparations, International Law and Global Justice: A New Frontier, in: De Greiff, P. (ed.), *The Handbook of Reparations*, Oxford: Oxford University Press.

Fallon, R.H. (2005).
Legitimacy and the Constitution, *Harvard Law Review* 118(6), 1787–1853.

Fattah, E.A. (1991).
Understanding Criminal Victimization, Scarborough, Ontario: Prentice-Hall Canada.

Fattah, E.A. (ed.) (1992).
Towards a Critical Victimology, New York: St. Martin's Press.

Fattah, E.A. (1997).
Criminology: Past, Present and Future. A Critical Overview, London: Macmillan.

Fattah, E.A. (2006).
Is Punishment the Appropriate Response to Gross Human Rights Violations? Is a Non-Punitive Justice System Feasible?, Paper Presented at the Conference of the Politics of Restorative Justice in Post-Conflict South Africa and Beyond, Cape Town, 21st-22nd September.

Fattah, E.A. (2010).
The Evolution of a Young, Promising Discipline. Sixty Years of Victimology, a Retrospective and Prospective Look, in: Shoham, S.G., Knepper, P., & Kett, M. (eds.), *International Handbook of Victimology*, Boca Raton/London/New York: CRC Press, 43–94.

Fein, H. (1993).
Genocide: A Sociological Perspective, London: Sage Publications.

Feinberg, J. (1970).
The Expressive Function of Punishment, in: Feinberg, J. (ed.), *Doing and Deserving: Essays in the Theory of Responsibility*, Princeton: Princeton University Press.

Feinberg, J. (1984).
Harm to Others – The Moral Limits of the Criminal Law, Oxford: Oxford University Press.

Feinberg, J. (1988).
Harmless Wrongdoing – The Moral Limits of the Criminal Law, Oxford: Oxford University Press.

Feldthusen, B. (2000).

    Therapeutic Consequences of Civil Actions of Damages and Compensation Claims by Victims of Sexual Abuse, *Canadian Journal of Women and the Law* 12(1), 66–116.

Felman, S. (2002).

    The Juridical Unconscious: Trials and Traumas in the Twentieth Century, Cambridge: Harvard University Press.

Fernández de Gurmendi, S.A. (2001a).

    Definition of Victims and General Principles, in: Lee, R.S. (ed.), *The Elements of Crimes and Rules of Procedure and Evidence of the International Criminal Court,* New York: Transnational Publisher, 427–456.

Fernández de Gurmendi, S.A. (2001b).

    Elaboration of the Rules of Procedure and Evidence, in: Lee, R.S. (ed.), *The Elements of Crimes and Rules of Procedure and Evidence of the International Criminal Court,* New York: Transnational Publisher, 235–257.

Ferstman, C. (2005).

    The Role of Victims at the International Criminal Court: Key Prospects, in: Vetere, E. & David, P. (eds.), *Victims of Crime and Abuse of Power: Festschrift in Honour of Irene Melup,* 150–157, 11th Congress on Crime Prevention and Criminal Justice, Bangkok, April 2005.

Ferstman, C. & Goetz, M. (2009).

    Reparations before the International Criminal Court: The Early Jurisprudence on Victims Participation and Its Impact on Future Reparations Proceedings, in: Ferstman, C., Goetz, M., & Stephens, A. (eds.), *Reparations for Victims of Genocide, Crimes against Humanity and War Crimes: Systems in Place and Systems in the Making,* The Hague: Martinus Nijhoff, 313–350.

Festinger, L., Pepitone, A., & Newcomb, T. (1952).

    Some Consequences of Deindividuation in a Group, *Journal of Abnormal and Social Psychology* 47, 382–389.

Fielding, D. (2004).

    How Does Violent Conflict Affect Investment Location Decisions? Evidence from Israel during the Intifada, *Journal of Peace Research* 41(4), 465–484.

Fierens, J. (2005).

    Gacaca Courts: Between Fantasy and Reality, *Journal of International Criminal Justice* 3, 896–919.

Figley, C.R. (ed.) (1995).

    Compassion Fatigue: Coping with Secondary Traumatic Stress Disorder in Those Who Treat the Traumatized, New York: Brunner/Mazel.

Filipas, H.H. & Ullman, S.E. (2001).

    Social Reactions to Sexual Assault Victims from Various Support Sources, *Violence and Victims* 16(6), 673–692.

Findlay, M. (2009).

    Activating a Victim Constituency in International Criminal Justice, *The International Journal of Transitional Justice* 3, 183–206.

Findlay, M. & Henham, R. (2005).
> *Transforming International Criminal Justice. Retributive and Restorative Justice in the Trial Process*, Cullompton, Devon: Willan Publishing.

Findlay, M. & Henham, R. (2010).
> *Beyond Punishment: Achieving International Criminal Justice*, UK/USA: Palgrave Macmillan.

Finnemore, M. & Sikkink, K. (1998).
> International Norm Dynamics and Political Change, *International Organization* 52(4), 894–902.

Fletcher, L.E. (2005).
> From Indifference to Engagement. Bystanders and International Criminal Justice, *Michigan Journal of International Law* 26, 1013–1062.

Fletcher, L.E. & Weinstein, H. (2002).
> Violence and Social Repair: Rethinking the Contribution of Justice to Reconciliation, *Human Rights Quarterly* 24(3), 573–639.

Flin, R., Kearney, B., & Murray, K. (1996).
> Children's Evidence: Scottish Research and Law, in: Bottoms, B.L. & Goodman, G.S. (eds.), *International Perspectives on Child Abuse and Children's Testimony: Psychological Research and Law*, Thousand Oaks, California: Sage Publications, 114–131.

Flint, J. & De Waal, A. (2009).
> Case Closed: A Prosecutor without Borders, *World Affairs Journal*, Spring 2009.

Foa, E.B. & Rothbaum, B.O. (1998).
> *Treating the Trauma of Rape: Cognitive-Behavioral Therapy for PTSD*, New York: Guildford Press.

Fogelman, E. (1988).
> Intergenerational Group Therapy: Child Survivors of the Holocaust and Offspring of Survivors, *Psychoanalytic Review* 75(4), 619–640.

Folger, R. (1977).
> Distributive and Procedural Justice: Combined Impact of "Voice" and Improvement of Experienced Inequity, *Journal of Personality and Social Psychology* 35, 108–119.

Foster, D., Davis, D., & Sandler, D. (1987).
> *Detention and torture in South Africa*, Cape Town: David Philip.

Foster, D., Haupt, P., & De Beer, M. (2005).
> *The Theatre of Violence – Narratives of Protagonists in the South African Conflict*, Cape Town: Institute of Justice and Reconciliation.

Foucault, M. (2004a).
> *Sécurité, territoire, population. Cours au Collège de France, 1977–1978*, Paris: Gallimard-Seuil.

Foucault, M. (2004b).
> *Naissance de la biopolitique. Cours au Collège de France, 1978–1979*, Paris: Gallimard-Seuil.

Francis, D.J. (2000).
> Tortuous Path to Peace: The Lomé Accord and Postwar Peacebuilding in Sierra Leone, *Security Dialogue* 31(3), 357–373.

Frankfurt, H. (1997).
Equality and Respect, *Social Research* 64, 3–15.

Fraser, N. (2001).
Recognition without Ethics?, *Theory, Culture & Society* 18, 21–42.

Freeland, S. (2008).
Mere Children or Weapons of War – Child Soldiers and International Law, *University of La Verne Law Review* 29, 19–55.

Freeman, M. (2009).
Necessary Evils: Amnesties and the Search for Justice, Cambridge: Cambridge University Press.

Frei, N. (2002).
Adenauer's Germany and the Nazi Past: The Politics of Amnesty and Integration, New York: Columbia University Press (Translated by Joel Golb).

French, P. (1984).
Corporate and Collective Responsibility, New York: Columbia University Press.

Freud, A. & Burlingham, D.T. (1943).
War and Children, New York: Medical War Books.

Friedman, M.J., Charney, D.S., & Deutch, A.Y. (1995).
Neurobiological and Clinical Consequences of Stress: From Normal Adaptation to PTSD, Philadelphia: Lippincott Williams & Wilkins.

Friedrichs, D.O. (1983).
Victimology: A Consideration of the Radical Critique, *Crime & Delinquency* 29, 283–294.

Friedrichs, D. (2003).
Trusted criminals. White Collar Crime in Contemporary Society, 3rd edition, USA: Thomson Wadsworth.

Friman, H. (2009).
The International Criminal Court and Participation of Victims: A Third Party to the Proceedings?, *Leiden Journal of International Law* 22, 485–500.

Froestad, J. & Shearing, C. (2007).
Conflict Resolution in South Africa: A Case Study, in: Johnstone, G. & Van Ness, D.W. (eds.), *Handbook of Restorative Justice*, Cullompton, Devon: Willan Publishing, 534–555.

Fujii, L.A. (2009).
Killing Neighbors: Webs of Violence in Rwanda, Ithaca: Cornell University Press.

Fuller, L.F. (1958).
Positivism and Fidelity to Law. A Reply to Professor Hart, *Harvard Law Review* 71(4), 630–672.

Funk, T.M. (2010).
Victims' Rights and Advocacy at the International Criminal Court, New York: Oxford University Press.

Gagne, M.-A. (1998).
The Role of Dependency and Colonialism in Generating Trauma in First Nations Citizens: The James Bay Cree, in: Danieli, Y. (ed.), *International Handbook of Multigenerational Legacies of Trauma*, New York: Plenum Press, 355–372.

Galaway, B. & Hudson, J. (eds.) (1996).
   Restorative Justice: International Perspectives, Monsey, New York: Criminal Justice Press.

Galtung, J. (1969).
   Violence, Peace, and Peace Research, *Journal of Peace Research* 6(3), 167–191.

Galtung, J. (2001).
   After Violence, Reconstruction, Reconciliation and Resolution, in: M. Abu-Nimer (ed.), *Reconciliation, Justice and Coexistence: Theory and Practice*, Lanham, MD: Lexington Books, 3–23.

Garbarino, J. & Kostelny, K. (1996).
   What Do We Need to Know to Understand Children in War and Community Violence?, in: Apfel, R.J. & Bennet, S. (eds.), *Minefields in Their Hearts: The Mental Health of Children in War and Communal Violence*, Chelsea, Michigan: BookCrafters, 33–51.

Garfield, R.M. & Neugut, A. (1997).
   The Human Consequences of War, in: Levy, B.S. & Sider, V.W. (eds.), *War and Public Health*, Oxford: Oxford University Press, 27–38.

Garkawe, S. (2001).
   The Victim-Related Provisions of the Statute of the International Criminal Court: A Victimological Analysis, *International Review of Victimology* 8, 269–289.

Garkawe, S. (2003a).
   The South African Truth and Reconciliation Commission: A Suitable Model to Enhance the Role and Rights of the Victims of Gross Violations of Human Rights?, *Melbourne University Law Review* 27, 334–380.

Garkawe, S. (2003b).
   Victims and the International Criminal Court: Three Major Issues, *International Criminal Law Review* 3, 345–367.

Garkawe, S. (2005).
   Rights for Child Victims: An Australian Perspective, in: Joyal, R., Noel, J.-F., & Feliciati, C.C. (eds.), *Final Report of the Conference Held in Montreal on November 18 to 20, 2004 – Making Children's Rights Work: National and International Perspectives*, Quebec: Les Editions Yvon Blais, 73–77.

Garton Ash, T. (1998).
   The Truth About Dictatorship, *The New York Review of Books* 45(3), 35–40.

Gasibirege, S. (2002).
   Résultats Définitifs de l'Enquête Quantitative sur les Attitudes des Rwandais vis-à-vis des Juridictions Gacaca, *Cahiers du Centre de Gestion des Conflits, no. 6*, de la Paix à la Justice: Les Enjeux de la Réconciliation Nationale, Editions de l'Université Nationale du Rwanda, 38–92.

Gaudin, I. (1996).
   Les Crises Rwandaises depuis 1959 Vues à Travers La Croix, L'humanité et le monde, Mémoire de Maîtrise, Université Paris 1, Panthéon-Sorbonne, UFR d'histoire.

Georgiou, P. (1973).
   The Goal Paradigm and Notes towards a Counter Paradigm, *Administrative Science Quarterly* 18, 291–300.

Gerber, G. & Cherneski, L. (2006).

Sexual Aggression toward Women: Reducing the Prevalence, *Annals of the New York Academy of Sciences* 1087, 35–46.

Gibson, J.L. (2004a).
Overcoming Apartheid: Can Truth Reconcile a Divided Nation?, Cape Town: HSRC Press.

Gibson, J.L. (2004b).
Does Truth Lead to Reconciliation? Testing the Causal Assumptions of the South African Truth and Reconciliation Process, *American Journal of Political Science* 48(2), 201–217.

Gibson, J.T. & Haritos-Fatouras, M. (1986).
The Education of a Torturer, *Psychology Today*, 50–58.

Gidron, Y., Kaplan, Y., Velt, A., & Shalem, R. (2004).
Prevalence and Moderators of Terror-Related Post-Traumatic Stress Disorder Symptoms in Israeli Citizens, *Israel Medical Association Journal* 6(7), 387–391.

Glover, J. (2001).
Humanity. A Moral History of the Twentieth Century, London: Pimlico.

Goetz, M. (2006).
From Victims to Rights Holders: Women and Girls' Demands from Transitional Justice, London: Actionaid.

Goldson, E. (1996).
The Effect of War on Children, *Child Abuse & Neglect* 20(9), 809–819.

Goldstone, R.J. (1996).
Justice as a Tool for Peacemaking: Truth Commissions and International Criminal Tribunals, *New York University Journal of International Law and Politics* 28, 485–503.

González-Rey, F. (2007).
Atención Psicosocial de las Víctimas: Proyección para Nuevas Acciones que Permitan Superar las Omisiones, in: Programa Nacional de Resarcimiento (ed.), *La Vida No Tiene Precio: Acciones y Omisiones de Resarcimiento en Guatemala*, Ciudad de Guatemala, Guatemala: Programa Nacional de Resarcimiento, 95–105.

Goodey, J. (2005).
Victims and Victimology: Research, Policy and Practice, Harlow, England: Pearson Education.

Gourevitch, P. (1999).
We Wish to Inform You That Tomorrow We Will Be Killed with Our Families: Stories from Rwanda, New York: Picador.

Gouri, H. (2008).
On Poetry and Time: A Literary Autobiography, Jerusalem: Bialik Institute, Hakibbutz Hameuchad Publishing.

Gouteux, J.P. (2002).
La nuit rwandaise. L'implication française dans le dernier génocide du siècle, Paris: Esprit Frappeur.

Govier, T. (2003).
What is Acknowledgement and Why It is Important, in: Prager, C.A.L. & Govier, T. (eds.), *Dilemmas of Reconciliation*, Waterloo: Wilfrid Laurier University Press, 65–89.

Govier, T. (2006).

> Taking Wrongs Seriously: Acknowledgement, Reconciliation and the Politics of Sustainable Peace, New York: Humanity Books.

Green, P. & Ward, T. (2000).

> State Crime, Human Rights, and the Limits of Criminology, Social Justice 27(1), 101–115.

Green, P. & Ward, T. (2004).

> State Crime. Governments, Violence and Corruption, London: Pluto Press.

Greenawalt, K. (2000).

> Amnesty's Justice, in: Rotberg, R.I. & Thompson, D. (eds.), Truth v. Justice, Princeton: Princeton University Press, 189–210.

Grimshaw, A. (1970).

> Interpreting Collective Violence: An Argument for the Importance of Social Structure, Annals of the American Academy of Political and Social Science 391, 9–20.

Groen, K. (1994).

> Als Slachtoffers Daders Worden – de Zaak van de Joodse Verraadster Ans van Dijk, Baarn: Ambo.

Groenhuijsen, M.S. (1998).

> The Development of Victimology and Its Impact on Criminal Justice Policy in the Netherlands, in: Fattah, E. & Peters, T. (eds.), Support for Crime Victims in a Comparative Perspective, Leuven: Leuven University Press, 37–54.

Groenhuijsen, M.S. (1999).

> Victims' Rights in the Criminal Justice System: A Call for a More Comprehensive Implementation Theory, in: Van Dijk, J.J.M., Van Kaam, R.G.H., & Wemmers, J.-A. (eds.), Caring for Crime Victims. Selected Proceedings of the 9th International Symposium on Victimology, Monsey, New York: Criminal Justice Press.

Groenhuijsen, M.S. (2008).

> Victims' Rights and the International Criminal Court: the Model of the Rome Statute and Its Operation, in: Van Genugten, W., Scharf, M., & Radin, S. (eds.), Criminal Jurisdiction 100 Years after the 1907 Hague Peace Conference, The Hague: T.M.C. Asser Press, 300–309.

Groenhuijsen, M.S. & De Brouwer, A.L.M. (2010).

> Participation of Victims: Commentary, in: Klip, A. & Sluiter, G. (eds.), Annotated Leading Cases of International Criminal Tribunals: The International Criminal Court 2005-2007, vol. 23, Antwerp/Oxford/Portland: Intersentia, 273–280.

Groenhuijsen, M.S. & Kwakman, N.J. (2002).

> Het Slachtoffer in het Vooronderzoek, in: Groenhuijsen, M.S. & Knigge, G. (eds.), Dwangmiddelen en Rechtsmiddelen. Derde Interimrapport Strafvordering 2001, Deventer: Kluwer.

Groenhuijsen, M.S. & Letschert, R.M. (2007).

> Compilation of Victims' Rights, Nijmegen: Wolf Legal Publishers.

Groenhuijsen, M.S. & Pemberton, A. (2009).

> The EU Framework Decision on Victims. Does Hard Law Make a Difference?, European Journal on Crime, Criminal Law and Criminal Justice 17, 43–59.

Gross, E. (1980).
> Organizational Structure and Organizational Crime, in: Geis, G. & Stotland, E. (eds.), *White-Collar Crime: Theories and Research*, Beverly Hills: Sage, 52–76.

Guembe, M.J. (2006).
> Economic Reparations for Grave Human Rights Violations: The Argentinean Experience, in: De Greiff, P. (ed.), *The Handbook of Reparations*, Oxford: Oxford University Press, 21–54.

Guillerot, J. & Magarrell, L. (2006).
> *Reparaciones en la Transición Peruana: Memorias de un Proceso Inacabado*, Lima: Asociación Pro Derechos Humanos & International Center for Transitional Justice.

Gullota, G. (1985).
> Collective Victimization, *Victimology* 10, 710–723.

Gulu District NGO Forum and Liu Institute for Global Issues (2007).
> 'The Cooling of Hearts'. Community Truth-Telling in Acholi-land, Special report, Justice and reconciliation Project.

Hafer, C.L. & Begue, L. (2005).
> Experimental Research on Just-World Theory. Problems, Developments and Future Challenges, *Psychological Bulletin* 131(1), 128–167.

Hagan, J. & Richmond-Rymand, W. (2009).
> *Darfur and the Crime of Genocide*, Cambridge: Cambridge University Press.

Hagan, J., Brooks, R., Haugh, T.J. (2012) [forthcoming].
> "Reasonable Grounds" Evidence Involving Sexual Violence in Darfur, in: De Brouwer, A. *et al.* (eds.), *Sexual Violence as an International Crime: Interdisciplinary Approaches*, Antwerp: Intersentia.

Hagemann-White, C., Kelly, E., & Römkens, R. (2010).
> *Feasibility Study to Assess the Possibilities, Opportunities and Needs to Standardise National Legislation on Violence against Women, Violence against Children and Sexual Orientation Violence*, Brussels: European Union.

Haidt, J. (2007).
> The New Synthesis in Moral Psychology, *Science* 316, 998–1002.

Haldemann, F. (2008).
> Another Kind of Justice: Transitional Justice as Recognition, *Cornell International Law Journal* 41, 675–737.

Hamber, B. (2001).
> Does the Truth Heal? A Psychological Perspective on Political Strategies for Dealing with the Legacy of Political Violence, in: Biggar, N. (ed.), *Burying the Past. Making Peace and Doing Justice after Civil Conflict*, Washington D.C.: Georgetown University Press, 131–148.

Hamber, B. (2005).
> The Dilemmas of Reparations: In Search of a Process Driven Approach, in: De Feyter, K., Parmentier, S., Bossuyt, M., & Lemmens, P. (eds.), *Out of the Ashes: Reparations for Victims of Gross and Systematic Human Rights Violations*, Antwerp: Intersentia, 135–150.

Hamber, B. (2006).
> Narrowing the Micro and the Macro, in: De Greiff, P. (ed.), *The Handbook of Reparations*, Oxford: Oxford University Press, 560–588.

Hamber, B. (2009).
> *Transforming Societies after Political Violence*, Dordrecht: Springer.

Hamber, B., Nageng, D., & O'Malley, G. (2000).
> Telling It Like It is. Understanding the Truth and Reconciliation Commission from the Perspectives of Survivors, *Psychology in Society* 26, 18–42.

Hamber, B. & Rasmussen, K. (2000).
> Financing a Reparations Scheme for Victims of Political Violence, in: Hamber, B. & Mofokeng, T. (eds.), *From Rhetoric to Responsibility: Making Reparations to the Survivors of Post Political Violence in South Africa*, Johannesburg: Center for the Study of Violence and Reconciliation, 55–59.

Hamber, B. & Van der Merwe, H. (1998).
> What is This Thing Called Reconciliation?, *Reconciliation in Review* 1(1), 1–4.

Hamilton, C. (2006).
> Child Protection in Complex Emergencies, in: Greenbaum, C.W., Veerman, P., & Bacon-Shnoor, N. (eds.), *Protection of Children During Armed Political Conflict: A Multidisciplinary Perspective*, Antwerp: Intersentia, 269–302.

Hampton, J. (1988).
> The Retributive Idea, in: Murphy, J.G. & Hampton, J., *Forgiveness and Mercy*, Cambridge: Cambridge University Press, 111–161.

Hannaham, J. (1996).
> Holding History, *Public Access: the Program of The Joseph Papp Public Theater/New York Shakespeare Festival* 3(2), 22–26.

Hanson, R.K. (1990).
> The Psychological Impact of Sexual Assault on Women and Children: A Review, *Sexual Abuse: A Journal of Research and Treatment* 3(2), 187–232.

Happold, M. (2008).
> Child Soldiers: Victims or Perpetrators?, *University of La Verne Law Review* 29, 56–87.

Harff, B. (2003).
> No lessons Learned from the Holocaust? Assessing Risks of Genocide and Mass Murder Since 1955, *American Political Science Review* 97(1), 57–73.

Harff, B. & Gurr, T.R. (1989).
> Victims of the State: Genocides, Politicides and Group Repression Since 1945, *International Review of Victimology* 1, 23–41.

Haritos-Fatouras, M. (2003).
> *The Psychological Origins of Institutionalized Torture*, London: Routledge.

Harlacher, T., Xavier Okot, F., Aloyo Obonyo, C., Balthazard, M., & Atkinson, R. (2006).
> *Traditional Ways of Coping in Acholi: Cultural Provisions for Reconciliation and Healing from War*, Kampala: Thomas Harlacher and Caritas Gulu Archdiocese.

Harper, F.D., Harper, J.A., & Stills, A.B. (2003).
> Counseling Children in Crisis Based on Maslow's Hierarchy of Basic Needs, *International Journal for the Advancement of Counselling* 25(1), 11–25.

Harrell, M.C., Castaneda, L.W., Adelson, M., Gaillot, S., Lynch, C., & Pomeroy, A. (2010).
A Compendium of Sexual Assault Research, Santa Monica/Arlington/Pittsburgh: Rand National Defense Research Institute.

Hart, H.L.A. (1958).
Positivism and the Separation of Law and Morals, *Harvard Law Review* 71(4), 593–629.

Hart, H.L.A. (1961).
The Concept of Law, Oxford: Oxford University Press.

Hart, J. & Tyrer, B. (2006).
Research with Children Living in Situations of Armed Conflict: Concepts, Ethics & Methods, *University of Oxford Refugee Studies Centre, Working Paper Series, RSC Working Paper No. 30*, Oxford: Department of International Development, University of Oxford.

Haskell, J.D. (2009).
The Complicity and Limits of International Law in Armed Conflict Rape, *Boston College Third World Law Journal* 29, 35–84.

Haslam, E. (2004).
Victim Participation at the International Criminal Court: A Triumph of Hope Over Experience?, in: McGoldrick, D., Rowe, P., & Donnelly, E. (eds.), *The Permanent International Criminal Court. Legal and Policy Issues*, Oxford/Portland: Hart Publishing, 316–334.

Haslam, N. (2006).
Dehumanization: An Integrative Review, *Personality and Social Psychology Review* 10, 252–264.

Hatzfeld, J. (2007).
La Stratégie des Antilopes, Paris: Seuil.

Hatzfeld, J. (2010).
The Antelope's Strategy: Living in Rwanda after the Genocide, New York: Picador.

Havel, B.F. (2002).
Public Law and the Construction of Collective Memory, in: Bassiouni, M.C. (ed.), *Post-Conflict Justice*, New York: Transnational Publishers, 383–397.

Haveman, R. (2008).
Doing Justice to Gacaca, in: Smeulers, A. & Haveman, R. (eds.), *Supranational Criminology: Towards a Criminology of International Crimes*, Antwerp: Intersentia, 357–398.

Haveman, R. (2011) [forthcoming].
Gacaca in Rwanda: Customary Law in Case of Genocide, in: Fenrich, J., Galizzi, P., & Higgins, T. (eds.), *The Future of Customary Laws in Africa*, Cambridge: Cambridge University Press.

Haveman, R. & Muleefu, A. (2010).
Gacaca and Fair Trial, in: Rothe, D. (ed.), *State Crimes*, Rutgers University Press.

Haveman, R. & Olysanya, O. (eds.) (2008).
Sentencing and Sanctioning in Supranational Criminal Law, Antwerp: Intersentia.

Haveman, R. & Smeulers, A. (2008).
Criminology in a State of Denial – towards a Criminology of International Crimes: Supranational Criminology, in: Smeulers, A. & Haveman, R. (eds.), *Supranational*

Criminology: Towards a Criminology of International Crimes, Antwerp: Intersentia, 3–26.

Hayner, P.B. (1994).

Fifteen Truth Commissions – 1974 to 1994: A Comparative Study, *Human Rights Quarterly* 16, 597–655.

Hayner, P.B. (1996).

International Guidelines for the Creation and Operation of Truth Commissions: A Preliminary Proposal, *Law and Contemporary Problems* 59, 173–180.

Hayner, P.B. (2001).

Unspeakable Truths. Confronting State Terror and Atrocity, New York/London: Routledge.

Hayner, P.B. (2002).

Unspeakable Truths: Facing the Challenge of Truth Commissions, New York: Routledge.

Hayner, P. (2007).

Negotiating the Peace in Sierra Leone: Confronting the Justice Challenge, Center for Humanitarian Dialogue and International Center for Transitional Justice.

Hegtvedt, K.A. (2006).

Justice Frameworks, in: Burke, P. (ed.), *Contemporary Social Psychological Theories*, Stanford: Stanford University Press, 46–69.

Heidenrich, G.J. (2001).

How to Prevent Genocide: A Guide for Policymakers, Scholars, and Concerned Citizen, Westport, Connecticut: Praeger.

Heise, L., Ellsberg, M., & Gottemoeller, M. (1999).

Ending Violence against Women, *Population Reports* L(11), Baltimore: Population Information Program, Johns Hopkins University School of Public Health.

Helmreich, W.B. (1992).

Against All Odds: Holocaust Survivors and the Successful Lives They Made in America, New York: Simon & Schuster.

Henham, R. (2004).

Some Reflections on the Role of Victims in the International Criminal Trial Process, *International Review of Victimology* 11, 201–224.

Henry, N. (2009).

Witness to Rape: The Limits and Potential of International War Crimes Trials for Victims of Wartime Sexual Violence, *The International Journal of Transitional Justice* 3, 114–134.

Henry, N. (2010).

The Impossibility of Bearing Witness: Wartime Rape and the Promise of Justice, *Violence Against Women* 16, 1098–1119.

Henry, N., Ward, T., & Hirshberg, M. (2004).

A Multifactorial Model of Wartime Rape, *Aggression and Violent Behavior* 9, 535–562.

Herman, J. (1992).

Trauma and Recovery, New York: Basic Books.

Herman, J.L. (2003).
The Mental Health of Crime Victims: Impact of Legal Intervention, *Journal of Traumatic Stress* 16(2), 159–166.

Hertzfeld, S. (1994).
Inti Omri, Tel Aviv: Yedioth Achronot.

Heylen, B., Parmentier, S., Weitekamp, E. (2010).
The Emergence of Holistic Reconciliation: Lessons Learned from Victims and Offenders inside the South African Truth and Reconciliation Commission, *International Perspectives in Victimology* 5(1), 1–12.

Higonett, E.R. (2006).
Restructuring Hybrid Courts: Local Empowerment and National Criminal Justice Reform, *Arizona Journal of International and Comparative Law* 23(2), 347–435.

Hillyard, P., Pantazis, C., Tombs, S., & Gordon, D. (eds.) (2004).
Beyond Criminology. Taking Harm Seriously, London: Pluto Press.

Hillyard, P. & Tombs, S. (2004).
Beyond Criminology?, in: Hillyard, P., Pantazis, C., Tombs, S., & Gordon, D. (eds.), *Beyond Criminology. Taking Harm Seriously*, London: Pluto Press.

Hodges, T. (2001).
Angola, from Afro-Stalinism to Petro-dollar Capitalism, London: James Currey.

Hoffman, E. (2008).
Reconciliation in Sierra Leone. Local Processes Yield Global Lessons, *The Fletcher Forum of World Affairs* 32(2), 129–141.

Hofmann, R. (2010).
Reparations for Victims of Armed Conflicts, Report to the ILA Hague Conference 2010.

Hogg, M.A. (2006).
Social Identity Theory, in: Burke, P. (ed.), *Contemporary Social Psychological Theories*, Stanford: Stanford University Press, 112–136.

Hogg, N. (2010).
Women's Participation in the Rwandan Genocide: Mothers or Monsters?, *International Review of the Red Cross* 92(877), 69–102.

Holtzmann, H. & Kristjánsdóttir, E. (2007).
International Mass Claims Processes: Legal and Practical Perspectives, Oxford: Oxford University Press.

Homans, G.C. (1961).
Social Behaviour: Its Elementary Forms, London: Routledge and Kegan Paul.

Honneth, A. (2001).
Invisibility: On the Epistemology of Recognition, *The Aristotelian Society Supplementary* 75(1), 111–126.

Honwana, A. (2001).
Children of War: Understanding War and War Cleansing in Mozambique and Angola, in: Chesterman, S. (ed.), *Civilians in War*, Boulder, Colorado: Lynne Rienner Publishers, 123–142.

Honwana, A. (2005).
>   Healing and Social Reintegration in Mozambique and Angola, in: Skaar, E., Gloppen, S., & Suhrke, A. (eds.), *Roads to Reconciliation*, Oxford: Lexington Books, 83–100.

Horn, R. (2009).
>   Testifying in an International War Crimes Tribunal: The Experience of Witnesses in the Special Court for Sierra Leone, *International Journal of Transitional Justice*, March 2009.

Horn, R., Vahidy, S., & Charters, S. (2010).
>   Testifying in the Special Court for Sierra Leone: Witness Perceptions of Safety and Emotional Welfare, *Psychology, Crime & Law*, 1–21.

Horovitz, S. (2009).
>   *Sierra Leone: Interaction between International and National Responses to the Mass Atrocities*, Domac/3.

Horowitz, M.J. (1976).
>   *Stress Response Syndrome*, New York: Jason Aaronson.

Horvath, M. & Brown, J.M. (eds.) (2009).
>   *Rape, Challenging Contemporary Thinking*, Cullompton, Devon: Willan Publishing.

Hoyle, C. & Zedner, L. (2007).
>   Victims, Victimization and Criminal Justice, in: Maguire, M. & Reiner, R. (eds.), *The Oxford Handbook of Criminology Fourth Edition*, New York: Oxford University Press, 461–495.

Hulsman, L.H.C. (1986).
>   Critical Criminology and the Concept of Crime, *Contemporary Crises* 10, 63–80.

Hulsman, L. (1989).
>   The "Right of the Victim" not to be Subordinated to the Dynamics of Criminal Justice, in: Separovic, Z.P. (ed.), *Victimology. International Action and Study of Victims, Vol. II*, Zagreb: University of Zagreb, 25–33.

Hulsman, L. (1991).
>   The Abolitionist Case: Alternative Crime Policies, *Israel Law Review* 25, 681–709.

Humphreys, M. & Weinstein, J.M. (2007).
>   Demobilization and Reintegration, *Journal of Conflict Resolution* (51)4, 531–567.

Husketh, E. (2005).
>   Pole Pole: Hastening Justice at UNICTR, *Northwestern University Journal of International Human Rights* 3, 1–35.

Huyse, L. (1995).
>   Justice after Transition: On the Choices Successor Elites Make in Dealing with the Past, *Law and Social Inquiry* 20(1), 51–78.

Huyse, L. (2008).
>   Introduction: Tradition-Based Approaches in Peacemaking, Transitional Justice and Reconciliation Policies, in: Huyse, L. & Salter, M. (eds.), *Traditional Justice After Violent Conflict. Learning from African Experiences*, Stockholm: IDEA, 1–22.

Huyse, L. & Salter, M. (eds.) (2008).

Traditional Justice and Reconciliation after Violent Conflict: Learning from African Experiences, Stockholm: International Institute for Democracy and Electoral Assistance.

Igreja, V. (2007).

The Monkeys' Sworn Oath; Cultures of Engagement for Reconciliation and Healing in the Aftermath of the Civil War in Mozambique, Leiden: Leiden University.

Ilibagiza, I. (2007).

Left to Tell: Discovering God amidst the Rwandan Holocaust, New York: Hay House.

Ingelaere, B. (2008).

The Gacaca Courts in Rwanda, in: Huyse, L. & Salter, M. (eds.), *Traditional Justice after Violent Conflict. Learning from African Experiences*, Stockholm: IDEA, 25–59.

Ingelaere, B. (2009a).

Living the Transition: Inside Rwanda's Conflict Cycle at the Grassroots, *Journal of Eastern African Studies* 3, 438–463.

Ingelaere, B. (2009b).

Does the Truth Pass across the Fire without Burning? Locating the Short Circuit in Rwanda's Gacaca Courts, *The Journal of Modern African Studies* 47(4), 507–528.

Ingelaere, B. (2009c).

Mille Collines, Mille Gacaca, la Vie en Marge du Processus Gacaca, in: Marysse, S., Reyntjens, F., & Vandeginste, S., *L'Afrique des Grands Lacs, Annuaire 2008–2009*, Paris: L'Harmattan, 29–42.

Jackson, P. (2004).

Legacy of Bitterness: Insurgency in North West Rwanda, *Small Wars & Insurgencies* 15, 19–37.

Jamison, M.A. (2008).

The Sins of the Father: Punishing Children in the War on Terror, *University of La Verne Law Review* 29, 88–151.

Janoff-Bulman, R. (1979).

Characterological versus Behavioral Self-Blame: Inquiries into Depression and Rape, *Journal of Personality and Social Psychology* 37, 1798–1809.

Janoff-Bulman, R. & Werther, A. (2008).

The Social Psychology of Respect: Implications for Delegitimization and Reconciliation, in: Nadler, A., Malloy, T., & Fisher, J. (eds.), *The Social Psychology of Intergroup Reconciliation*, Oxford: Oxford University Press, 145–170.

Jasinski, J.L. (2001).

Theoretical Explanations for Violence against Women, in: Renzetti, C.M., Edleson, J.L., & Bergen, R.K. (eds.), *Sourcebook on Violence Against Women*, London: Sage publications, 5–22.

Jewkes, R., Sikweyiya, Y., Morrell, R., & Dunkle, K. (2009).

Understanding Men's Health and Use of Violence: Interface of Rape and HIV in South Africa, Pretoria: Medical Research Council Policy Brief.

John-Nambo, J. (2002).
Quelques Héritages de la Justice Coloniale en Afrique Noire, *Droit et Société* 51/52, 325–244.

Johnson, K., Scott, J., Rughita B., Kisielewski, M., Ong, R., Lawry, L. (2008).
Association of Combatant Status and Sexual Violence with Health and Mental Health Outcomes in Postconflict Liberia, *JAMA* 300(6), 676–690.

Johnson, K., Scott, J., Rughita B., Kisielewski, M., Ong, R., Lawry, L. (2010).
Association of Sexual Violence and Human Rights Violations with Physical and Mental Health in Territories of the Eastern Democratic Republic of the Congo, *JAMA* 304(5), 553–562.

Johnston, S.W. (1973).
Toward a Supra-National Criminology: The Right and Duty of Victims of National Government to Seek Defence through World Law, in: Drapkin, I. & Viano, E. (eds.), *Victimology: A New Focus, Vol. I: Theoretical Issues in Victimology*, Massachusetts/Toronto/London. Lexington Books, 37–53.

Johnston, S.W. (1976).
Instituting Criminal Justice in the Global Village, in: Viano, E.C. (ed.), *Victims & Society*, Washington D.C.: Visage Press, 325–347.

Joinet, L. (ed.) (2002).
Lutter Contre l'Impunité, Paris: Éditions la Découverte.

Jorda, C. & De Hemptinne, J. (2002).
The Status and the Role of the Victim, in: Cassese, A., Gaeta, P., & Jones, J.R.W.D. (eds.), *The Rome Statute of the International Criminal Court: A Commentary, Vol. II*, Oxford/New York: Oxford University Press, 1387–1419.

Josse, E. (2010).
'They Came with Two Guns': The Consequences of Sexual Violence for the Mental Health of Women in Armed Conflicts, *International Review of the Red Cross* 92(877), 177–195.

Josse, E. & Dubois, V. (2009).
Interventions Humanitaires en Santé Mentale dans les Violences de Masse, Brussels: De Boeck.

Joyce, D. (2004).
The Historical Function of International Criminal Trials: Re-thinking International Criminal Law, *Nordic Journal of International Law* 73, 461–484.

Justino, P. & Verwimp, P. (2008).
Poverty Dynamics, Violent Conflict and Convergence in Rwanda, MICROCON Research Working Paper 4, Brighton: MICROCON.

Kagee, A. (2006).
The Relationship between Statement Giving at the South African Truth and Reconciliation Commission and Psychological Distress among Former Political Detainees, *South African Journal of Psychology* 36(1), 10–24.

Kahana, B., Harel, Z., & Kahana, E. (1989).
Clinical and Gerontological Issues Facing Survivors of the Nazi Holocaust, in: Marcus, P. & Rosenberg, A. (eds.), *Healing Their Wounds: Psychotherapy with Holocaust Survivors and Their Families*, New York: Praeger, 197–211.

Kaminer, D., Stein, D.J., Mbanga, I., & Zungu-Dirwayi, N. (2001).
The Truth and Reconciliation Commission in South Africa: Relation to Psychiatric Status and Forgiveness among Survivors of Human Rights Abuses, *British Journal of Psychiatry* 178, 373–377.

Kaminer, H. & Lavie, P. (1991).
Sleep and Dreaming in Holocaust Survivors: Dramatic Decrease in Dream Recall in Well-adjusted Survivors, *Journal of Nervous and Mental Disease* 179(11), 664–669.

Kampusch, N. (2010).
3096 Tage, Berlin: List Verlag.

Kant I. (1991).
The Metaphysics of Morals (1785), Cambridge: Cambridge University Press (Translated by Mary Gregor).

Kanyarwanda, Association Pour la Promotion de l'Union par la Justice Sociale (2010).
Raporo y'Igenzura Ry'umutungo n'Ibikorwa Kanyarwanda, October 2009.

Karekezi, U.A., Nshimiyimana, A., & Mutamba, B. (2004).
Localizing Justice: Gacaca Courts in Post-Genocide Rwanda, in: Stover, E. & Weinstein, H.M. (eds.), *My Neighbour, My Enemy. Justice and Community in the Aftermath of Mass Atrocity*, Cambridge: Cambridge University Press, 69–84.

Kato, J. (2009).
Rebel Scare Hits Masaka, *The New Vision*, 10th July.

Kauzlarich, D. (1995).
A Criminology of the Nuclear State, *Humanity & Society* 19, 37–57.

Kauzlarich, D. (2008).
Victimization and Supranational Criminology, in: Smeulers, A. & Haveman, R. (eds.), *Supranational Criminology: Towards a Criminology of International Crimes*, Antwerp: Intersentia, 435–453.

Kauzlarich, D. & Friedrichs, D.O. (2003).
Crimes of the State, in: Schwartz, M.D. & Hatty, S. (eds.), *Controversial Issues in Criminology: Critical Criminology*, Cincinnati: Anderson, 109–120.

Kauzlarich, D. & Kramer, R. (1998).
Crimes of the American Nuclear State. At Home and Abroad, Boston: Northeastern University Press.

Kauzlarich, D., Matthews, R.A., & Miller, W.J. (2001).
Toward a Victimology of State Crime, *Critical Criminology* 10, 173–194.

Keen, D. (2003).
Greedy Elites, Dwindling Resources, Alienated Youths. The Anatomy of Protracted Violence, *Internationale Politik und Gesellschaft* 2.

Keilson, H. (1992).
Sequential Traumatization in Children, Jerusalem: The Hebrew University Magnes Press.

Kelly, J.G., Ryan, A., Altman, B.E.; Stelzner, S.P. (2000).
Understanding and Changing Social Systems: An Ecological View, in: Rappaport, J. & Seidman, E. (eds.), *Handbook of Community Psychology*, Dordrecht: Kluwer Academic Publishers, 133–159.

Kelly, K. (1999).
> Development for Social Change: The Challenge of Building Civil Society in Rwanda, *Trocaire Development Review*, 57–80.

Kelman, H.C. & Hamilton, V.L. (1989).
> *Crimes of Obedience. Toward a Social Psychology of Authority and Responsibility*, New Haven: Yale University Press.

Kelsall, T. (2005).
> Truth, Lies, Ritual: Preliminary Reflections on the Truth and Reconciliation Commission in Sierra Leone, *Human Rights Quarterly*, 383–384.

Kendall, S. & Staggs, M. (2005).
> Silencing Sexual Violence: Recent Developments in the CDF Case at the Special Court for Sierra Leone, U.C. Berkeley War Crimes Studies Center, 25th June 2005, http://socrates.berkeley.edu/~warcrime/Papers/Silencing_Sexual_Violence.pdf.

Kermani Mendez, P. (2009).
> The New Wave of Hybrid Tribunals: A Sophisticated Approach to Enforcing International Humanitarian Law or an Idealistic Solution with Empty Promises?, *Criminal Law Forum* 20, 53–95.

Kestenberg, M. (1982).
> Discriminatory Aspects of the German Indemnification Policy: A Continuation of Persecution, in: Bergman, M.S. & Jucovy, M. (eds.), *Generations of the Holocaust*, New York: Basic Books.

Kirchhoff, G.F. (1994).
> Victimology – History and Basic Concepts, in: Kirchhoff, G.F., Kosovski, E., & Schneider, H.J. (eds.), *International Debates of Victimology*, Mönchengladbach: WSV Publishing, 1–81.

Kirchhoff, G.F. (2005).
> What is Victimology?, Monograph Series No. 1, Tokiwa International Victimology Institute.

Kitzinger, J. (2009).
> Rape in the Media, in: Horvath, M. & Brown, J.M. (eds.), *Rape. Challenging Contemporary Thinking*, Cullompton, Devon: Willan Publishing, 74–98.

Kiza, E. (2006).
> Victimization in Wars – A Framework for Further Inquiry, in: Ewald, U. & Turković, K. (eds.), *Large-Scale Victimization as a Potential Source of Terrorist Activities*, Amsterdam: IOS Press, 73–88.

Kiza, E., Rathgeber, C., & Rohn, H.C. (2006).
> *Victims of War: An Empirical Study on War Victimization and Victims' Attitudes towards Addressing Atrocities*, Hamburger Online Edition.

Klain, E. (1998).
> Intergenerational Aspects of the Conflict in the Former Yugoslavia, in: Danieli, Y. (ed.), *International Handbook of Multigenerational Legacies of Trauma*, New York: Plenum Press, 279–296.

Klein, M.E. (1987).
> *Transmission of Trauma: the Defensive Styles of Children of Holocaust Survivors*, Doctoral dissertation, Berkeley: California School of Professional Psychology, University Microfilms International, no. 8802441.

Klein-Parker, F. (1988).

> Dominant Attitudes of Adult Children of Holocaust Survivors Toward Their Parents, in: Wilson, J.P., Harel, Z., & Kahana, B. (eds.), *Human Adaptation to Extreme Stress: From Holocaust to Vietnam*, New York: Plenum, 193–218.

Kolber, J. (1997).

> Ezra Pound – Comments on Literature and Politics, *Helicon: Magazine of Poetry*, 19–27.

Kordon, D., Edelman, L., Lagos, D., & Kersner, D. (1998).

> Argentina: Psychological and Clinical Consequences of Political Repression and Impunity, *Q.J. Rehab of Torture and Prevention of Torture* 8, 43–47.

Kordon, R.K., Edelman, L.I., Lagos, D.M., Nicoletti, E., & Bozzolo, R.C. (1988).

> *Psychological Effects of Political Repression*, Buenos Aires: Sudamericana Planeta.

Koster, M. (2008).

> *Linking Poverty and Household Headship in Post-Genocide Rwanda*, Paper Selected for Presentation at the HiCN's Fourth Annual Workshop, Yale University, 5th-6th December 2008.

Krahé, B. & Temkin, J. (2009).

> Addressing the Attitude Problem in Rape Trials: Some Proposals and Methodological Considerations, in: Horvath, M. & Brown, J.M. (eds.), *Rape. Challenging Contemporary Thinking*, Cullompton, Devon: Willan Publishing, 301–324.

Kramer, R. & Michalowski, R. (2005).

> War, Aggression and State Crime, A Criminological Analysis of the Invasion and Occupation of Iraq, *The British Journal of Criminology* 45(4), 446–469.

Kramer, R., Michalowski, R., & Rothe, D. (2005).

> The Supreme International Crime: How the U.S. War in Iraq Threatens the Rule of Law, *Social Justice* 32(2), 52–81.

Kramer, T. & Green, B. (1991).

> Posttraumatic Stress Disorder as an Early Response to Sexual Assault, *Journal of Interpersonal Violence* 6, 160–173.

Kritz, N.J. (ed.) (1995).

> *Transitional Justice: How Emerging Democracies Reckon with Former Regimes, vol. III*, Washington D.C.: United States Institute of Peace Press.

Kritz, N.J. (1996).

> Coming to Terms with Mass Atrocities: A Review of Accountability Mechanisms for Mass Violations of Human Rights, *Law and Contemporary Problems* 59(4), 127–152.

Kritz, N. (2002).

> Where We Are and How We Got Here: An Overview of Developments in the Search for Justice and Reconciliation, in: Henkin, A.H. (ed.), *The Legacy of Abuse: Confronting the Past, Facing the Future*, Washington D.C.: Aspen Institute.

Krog, A. (1999) (2nd edition 2002)

> *Country of My Skull: Guilt, Sorrow, and the Limits of Forgiveness in the New South Africa*, New York: Random House.

Kupelian, D., Kalayjian, A.S., & Kassabian, A. (1998).
The Turkish Genocide of the Armenians: Continuing Effects on Survivors and Their Families Eight Decades after Massive Trauma, in: Danieli, Y. (ed.), *International Handbook of Multigenerational Legacies of Trauma*, New York: Plenum Press, 191–210.

Kuper, J. (1997)
International Law Concerning Child Civilians in Armed Conflict, Oxford: Clarendon Press.

Kuper, J. (2008).
Child "Soldiers" and Civilians – Some Controversial Issues, *University of La Verne Law Review* 29, 12–18.

Kuwert, P., Spitzer, C., Träder, A., Freyberger, H., & Ermann, M. (2007).
Sixty Years Later: Post-Traumatic Stress Symptoms and Current Psychopathology in Former German Children of World War II, *International Psychogeriatrics* 19(5), 955–961.

Lafontaine, F. (2010).
Canada's Crimes against Humanity and War Crimes Act on Trial: An Analysis of the Munyaneza Case, *Journal of International Criminal Justice* 8, 269–288.

Lamborn, R.L. (1988).
The United Nations Declaration on Victims: The Scope of Coverage, in: Bassiouni, M.C. (ed.), *International Protection of Victims*, Toulouse: Erès, 105–116.

Lambourne, W. (2004).
Post-Conflict Peacebuilding: Meeting Human Needs for Justice and Reconciliation, *Peace, Conflict and Development* 4, 1–23.

Landsman, S. (1996).
Alternative Responses to Serious Human Rights Abuses: Of Prosecutions and Truth Commissions, *Law and Contemporary Problems* 59(4), 81–96.

Langa, P. (1987).
South African Security Laws versus the Child, Paper Presented at the International Conference on Children, Repression and the Law in Apartheid South Africa, Harare.

Latigo, J.O. (2008).
Northern Uganda: Tradition-Based Practices in the Acholi Region, in: Huyse, L. & Salter, M. (eds.), *Traditional Justice after Violent Conflict. Learning from African Experiences*, Stockholm: IDEA, 85–120.

Lawday, A. (2002).
HIV and Conflict: A Double Emergency, London: Save the Children.

Lawry, L., Johnson, K., & Asher, J. (2012) [forthcoming].
Evidence-Based Documentation of Gender-Based Violence, in: De Brouwer, A. *et al.* (eds.), *Sexual Violence as an International Crime: Interdisciplinary Approaches*, Antwerp: Intersentia.

Le Bon, G. (1895).
Psychologie des Foules, Paris: Édition Félix Alcan, 9e édition, 1905.

Lee, R.S. (1999).
The International Criminal Court, the Making of the Rome Statute, Issues, Negotiations, Results, The Hague: Kluwer Law International.

Leitner, I. & Leitner, I.A. (1985).

> *Saving the Fragments, From Auschwitz to New York*, New York: New American Library.

Lemkin, R. (1944).

> *Axis Rule in Occupied Europe*, Washington: Carnegie Endowment for International Peace.

Lemkin, R. (1947).

> Genocide as a Crime under International law, *The American Journal of International Law* 41(1), 145–151.

Lens, K.M.E., Pemberton, A., & Groenhuijsen, M.S. (2010).

> *Evaluatie Spreekrecht voor Slachtoffers*, Tilburg: Intervict (in Dutch with an English summary).

Lerche, C.O. (2000).

> Truth Commissions and National Reconciliation: The Construction of a Victim-Centred Approach in the South African Truth Commission, *Criminology* 33(1), 146–165.

Lerner, M.J. (1980).

> *The Belief in a Just World*, New York: Plenum.

Letschert, R.M. & Ammerlaan, V.C. (2010).

> Compensation and Reparation for Victims of Terrorism, in: Letschert, R.M., Staiger, I., & Pemberton, A. (eds.), *Assistance to Victims of Terrorism: Towards a European Standard of Justice*, Dordrecht: Springer.

Letschert, R.M., Staiger, I., & Pemberton, A. (eds.) (2009).

> *Assisting Victims of Terrorism: Towards a European Standard of Justice*, Dordrecht: Springer.

Letschert, R.M. & Van Dijk, J.J.M. (2011).

> *The New Faces of Victimhood, Globalization, Transnational Crimes and Victim Rights*, Dordrecht/Heidelberg/London/New York: Springer.

Levi, P. (1958).

> *If This is a Man*, London: Abacus, Sphere books.

Levi, B. & Sider, V. (1997).

> *War and Public Health*, New York: Oxford University Press.

Lévinas, E. (1969).

> *Totality and Infinity*, Pittsburgh: Duquesne University Press (Translated by Alphonso Lingis).

Levinson, D.J. (2003).

> Collective Sanctions, *Stanford Law Review* 56, 345–428.

Leyens, J.P., Paladino, P.M., Rodriguez, R.T., Vaes, J., Demoulin, S., & Rodriguez, A.P. et al. (2000).

> The Emotional Side of Prejudice: The Role of Secondary Emotions, *Personality and Social Psychology Review* 4, 186–197.

Licklider, R. (2008).

> Ethical Advice. Conflict Management versus Human Rights in Ending Civil Wars, *Journal of Human Rights* 7(4), 376–387.

Liebes, T. & Kamph, Z. (2005).
> Observing Terror from a Distance: The TV Presentation and National Strength, in: Somer, E. & Bleich, A. (eds.), *Mental Health in Terror's Shadow: The Israeli Experience*, Tel Aviv: Tel Aviv University Press, 479–499.

Lifton, R.J. (1979).
> *The Broken Connection*, New York: Simon & Schuster.

Lillie, C. & Janoff-Bulman, R. (2007).
> Macro versus Micro Justice and Perceived Fairness of Truth and Reconciliation Commissions, *Peace and Conflict: Journal of Peace Psychology* 13(2), 221–236.

Lind, E.A. & Tyler, T. (1989).
> *The Social Psychology of Procedural Justice*, New York: Plenum Press.

Lind, E.A. & Van den Bos, K. (2002).
> When Fairness Works: Toward a General Theory of Uncertainty Management, *Research in Organizational Behavior* 24, 181–223.

Lipari, R.N., Cook, P.J., Rock, L.M., & Matos, K. (2008).
> *2006 Gender Relations Survey of Active Duty Members*, Arlington: Defense Manpower Data Center.

Llewellyn, J. (2007).
> Truth Commissions and Restorative Justice, in: Johnstone, G. & Van Ness, D.W. (eds.), *Handbook of Restorative Justice*, Cullompton, Devon: Willan Publishing, 351–371.

Lodge, T. (2003).
> *Politics in South Africa: From Mandela to Mbeki*, 2nd edition, Indiana: Indiana University Press.

Longman, T., Pham, P., & Weinstein, H.M. (2004).
> Connecting Justice to Human Experience: Attitudes towards Accountability and Reconciliation in Rwanda, in: Stover, E. & Weinstein, H.M. (eds.), *My Neighbour, My Enemy. Justice and Community in the Aftermath of Mass Atrocity*, Cambridge: Cambridge University Press, 206–225.

Longman, T. & Rutagengwa, T. (2004).
> Memory, Identity and Community in Rwanda, in: Stover, E. & Weinstein, H.M. (eds.), *My Neighbour, My Enemy. Justice and Community in the Aftermath of Mass Atrocity*, Cambridge: Cambridge University Press, 162–182.

Lonsway, K.A. & Fitzgerald, L.F. (1994).
> Rape Myths: In Review, *Psychology of Women Quarterly* 18, 133–164.

Loomba, A. (2005).
> *Colonialism/Postcolonialism*, London: Routledge.

Louw, D.J. (2007).
> The African Concept of Ubuntu and Restorative Justice, in: Johnstone, G. & Van Ness, D.W. (eds.), *Handbook of Restorative Justice*, Cullompton, Devon: Willan Publishing.

Lugan, B. (1997).
> *Histoire du Rwanda. De la préhistoire à nos jours*, Paris: Bartillat.

Lugan, B. (2004).
> *Rwanda. Le Génocide, l'Eglise et la Démocratie*, Paris: Editions du Rocher.

Lukes, S. (1997).
  Humiliation and the Politics of Identity, *Social Research* 64(1), 36–51.
Lykes, M.B. & Mersky, M. (2006).
  Reparations and Mental Health: Psychosocial Interventions towards Healing, Human Agency, and Rethreading Social Realities, in: De Greiff, P. (ed.), *The Handbook of Reparations*, Oxford: Oxford University Press, 589–622.
Lynch, M. & Michalowski, R. (2006).
  Primer in Radical Criminology: Critical Perspectives on Crime, Power & Identity, 4th edition, Monsey, New York: Criminal Justice Press.
Machel, G. (2001).
  The Impact of War on Children, London: C. Hurst & Co Publishers.
Mackenzie, M. (2010).
  Securitizing Sex?, *International Feminist Journal of Politics* 12(2), 202–221.
MacKinnon, C.A. (1991).
  Reflections on Sex Equality under Law, *Yale Law Journal* 100(5), 1281–1328.
Mahoney, M.R. (1994).
  Victimization or Oppression? Women's Lives, Violence & Agency, in: Fineman, M. & Mykitiuk, R. (eds.), *The public Nature of Private Violence. The Discovery of Domestic Abuse*, New York: Routledge 59–92.
Mai, M. & Cuny, T. (2007).
  In the Name of Honour. A Memoir, Washington D.C.: Washington Square Press.
Maier, Ch.S. (2000).
  Doing History, Doing Justice: The Narrative of the Historian and of the Truth Commission, in: Rotberg, R.I. & Thompson, D. (eds.), *Truth v. Justice*, Princeton: Princeton University Press, 261–278.
Makhalemele, O. (2009).
  Still Not talking: The South African Government's Exclusive Reparations Policy and the Impact of the R30,000 Financial Reparations on Survivors, in: Ferstman, C., Goetz, M., & Stephens, A., (eds.), *Reparations for Victims of Genocide, War Crimes and Crimes against Humanity: Systems in Place and Systems in the Making*, Leiden: Koninklijke Brill, 541–566.
Malamud-Goti, J. (1990).
  Transitional Governments in the Breach: Why Punish State Criminals?, *Human Rights Quarterly* 12, 1–16.
Malamud Goti, J. (2002).
  Equality, Punishment, and Self-Respect, *Buffalo Criminal Law Review* 5, 504.
Malaquias, A. (2007).
  Rebels and Robbers; Violence in Post-Colonial Angola, Uppsala: The Nordic Africa Institute.
Mamdani, M. (2000).
  The Truth According to the TRC, in: Amadiume, I. & An-naim, A. (eds.), *The Politics of Memory*, London: Zed Books.
Mamdani, M. (2001).
  When Victims Become Killers: Colonialism, Nativism and Genocide in Rwanda, New Jersey: Princeton University Press.

Mangelsdorf, A.D. (1985).
> Lessons Learned and Forgotten: The Need for Prevention and Mental Health Interventions in Disaster Preparedness, *Journal of Community Psychology* 13, 239–257.

Mani, R. (2005a).
> Rebuilding an Inclusive Political Community after War, *Security Dialogue* 36(4), 511–526.

Mani, R. (2005b).
> Reparation as a Component of Transitional Justice: Pursuing 'Reparative Justice' in the Aftermath of Violent Conflict, in: De Feyter, K. & Parmentier, S. (eds.), *Out of the Ashes: Reparation for Victims of Gross and Systematic Human Rights Violations*, Antwerp/Oxford: Intersentia.

Mann, M. (2005).
> *The Dark Side of Democracy. Explaining Ethnic Cleansing*, Cambridge: Cambridge University Press.

Marcus, M. (2012) [forthcoming].
> Investigation of Crimes of Sexual and Gender-Based Violence under International Criminal Law, in: De Brouwer, A. *et al.* (eds.), *Sexual Violence as an International Crime: Interdisciplinary Approaches*, Antwerp: Intersentia.

Margalit, A. (1996).
> *The Decent Society*, Cambridge, Massachusetts: Harvard University Press (Translated by Naomi Goldblum).

Marong, A., Jalloh, C.C., & Kinnecome, D.M. (2007).
> Concurrent Jurisdiction at the ICTR: Should the Tribunal Refer Cases to Rwanda? in: Decaux, E., Dieng, A., & Sow, M., *From Human Rights to International Criminal Law: Studies in Honour of an African Jurist, the Late Judge Laïty Kama. (Des Droits de l'Homme au Droit International Pénal: Etudes en l'Honneur d'un Juriste Africain, Feu le Juge Laïty Kama)*, Leiden/Boston: Martinus Nijhoff Brill, 159–201.

Marshall, T.F. (1996).
> The Evolution of Restorative Justice in Britain, *European Journal of Criminal Policy and Research* 4, 21–43.

Marton, V. (2009).
> Transition as a Concept of European Human Rights Law, *European Human Rights Law Review* 2, 170–189.

Marx, B.P. (2005).
> Lessons Learned from the Last Twenty Years of Sexual Violence Research, *Journal of Interpersonal Violence* 20(2), 225–230.

Maslow, A. (1968).
> *Toward a Psychology of Being*, 2nd edition, New York: Van Nostrand Reinhold.

Matalon, R. (2000).
> *Sarah, Sarah*, Tel Aviv: Am Oved (English translation: New York: Metropolitan Books, 2003).

Mattarollo, R. (2002).
> Truth Commissions, in: Bassiouni, M.C. (ed.), *Post-Conflict Justice*, New York: Transnational Publishers, 295–324.

Matthews, R.A. & Kauzlarich, D. (2007).
State Crimes and State Harms: A Tale of Two Definitional Frameworks, *Crime, Law, and Social Change* 48, 43–55.

Mawby, R.I. & Walklate, S. (1994).
Critical Victimology. International Perspectives, London/Thousand Oaks/New Delhi: Sage.

Mazower, M. (2002).
Violence and the State in the 20th century, *The American Historical Review* 107(4), 1158–1178.

McAdams, A.J. (ed.) (1997).
Transitional Justice and the Rule of Law in New Democracies, Notre Dame: University of Notre Dame Press.

McDonald, A. (2006).
The Development of a Victim-Cantered Approach to International Criminal Justice for Serious Violations of International Humanitarian Law, in: Carey, J., Dunlap, W.V., & Pritchard, R.J. (eds.), *International Humanitarian Law: Origins, Challenges, Prospects*, New York: Transnational Publishers, 237–276.

McEvoy, K. & McGregor, L. (2008).
Transitional Justice from Below. Grassroots Activism and the Struggle for Change, Oxford: Hart Publishing.

McGonigle, B. (2009).
Apples and Oranges? Comparing the Victim Participation Approaches at the ICC and ECCC, in: Ryngeart, C. (ed.), *Effectiveness of International Criminal Tribunals*, Antwerp: Intersentia, 91–115.

McNamara, R.S. & Blight, J.G. (2001).
Wilson's Ghost. Reducing the Risk of Conflict, Killing and Catastrophe in the 21st Century, New York: Public Affairs.

McSherry, J.P. & Molina Mejía, R. (1992).
Confronting the Question of Justice in Guatemala, *Social Justice Research* 19(3), 1–28.

Meernik, J. (2005).
Justice and Peace? How the International Criminal Tribunal Affects Societal Peace in Bosnia, *Journal of Peace Research* 42(3), 271–289.

Melvern, L. (2000).
A People Betrayed: The Role of the West in Rwanda's Genocide, 2nd edition, London/ New York: Zed Books.

Melvern, L. (2004).
Conspiracy to Murder: The Rwandan Genocide, New York: Verso.

Mendeloff, D. (2004).
Truth-Seeking, Truth-Telling and Post-Conflict Peacebuilding: Curb the Enthusiasm?, *International Studies Review* 6(3), 355–380.

Mendeloff, D. (2009).
Trauma and Vengeance: Assessing the Psychological and Emotional Effects of Post-Conflict Justice, *Human Rights Quarterly* 31, 592–623.

Mendelsohn, B. (1974).
> The Origin of the Doctrine of Victimology, in: Drapkin, I. & Viano, E. (eds.), *Victimology*, Massachusetts/Toronto/London: Lexington Books, 3–11.

Meredith, M. (2005).
> *The State of Africa: A History of Fifty Years of Independence*, Johannesburg: Jonathan Ball Publishers.

Meron, T. (1993).
> The Case for War Crimes in Yugoslavia, *Foreign Affairs* 72(3), 122–135.

Mertus, J. (2004).
> Shouting from the Bottom of the Well: The Impact of International Trials for Wartime Rape on Women's Agency, *International Feminist Journal of Politics* 6(1), 110–128.

Messiant, Ch. (2004).
> Why Did Bicesse and Lusaka Fail? A Critical Analysis, in: Meijer, G. (ed.), *From Military Peace to Social Justice? The Angolan Peace Process*, Conciliation Resources Accord 15, 16–23.

Meyerstein, A. (2007).
> Between Law and Culture: Rwanda's *Gacaca* and Postcolonial Legality, *Law & Social Inquiry* 32, 467–508.

Mibenge, C. (2011) [forthcoming].
> *Show Me a Woman! Narratives of Gender and Violence in Human Rights Law and Processes of Transitional Justice*, Philadelphia: University of Pennsylvania Press.

Miers, D. (1989).
> Positivist Criminology: A Critique, *International Review of Victimology* 1, 3–22.

Miers, D. (1990).
> Positivist Criminology: A Critique. Part 2: Critical Criminology, *International Review of Victimology* 1, 219–230.

Miller, Z. (2008).
> Effects of Invisibility: In Search of the 'Economic' in Transitional Justice, *International Journal of Transitional Justice* 2(3), 266–291.

Minow, M. (1998).
> *Between Vengeance and Forgiveness. Facing History after Genocide and Mass Violence*, Boston: Beacon Press.

Minow, M. (2000).
> The Hope for Healing: What Can Truth Commissions Do?, in: Rotberg, R.I. & Thompson, D. (eds.), *Truth v. Justice. The Morality of Truth Commissions*, Princeton/Oxford: Princeton University Press, 235–260.

Mohor, L. (1972).
> The Concept of Organizational Goals, *American Political Science Review* 67, 470–481.

Molina, L.F. (1995).
> Can States Commit Crimes? The Limits of Formal International Law, in: Ross, J.I. (ed.), *Controlling State Crime. An Introduction*, New York/London: Garland Publishing, 349–388.

Mollica, R.F. (2006).
> *Healing Invisible Wounds*, New York: Harcourt.

Moore, M. (2009).
> The Moral Worth of Retribution, in: Von Hirsch, A., Ashworth, A., & Roberts, J. (eds.), *Principled Sentencing. Readings on Theory and Policy*, Oxford/Portland: Hart Publishing, 110–114.

Morgan, J. & Zedner, L. (1992).
> *Child Victims: Crime, Impact, and Criminal Justice*, Oxford: Oxford University Press.

Morris, V. & Scharf, M.P. (1995).
> *An Insider's Guide to the International Criminal Tribunal for the Former Yugoslavia: A Documentary History and Analysis*, New York: Transnational Publishers.

Møse, E. (2005).
> Main Achievements of the ICTR, *Journal of International Criminal Justice* 3, 920–943.

Møse, E. (2008).
> The ICTR's Completion Strategy – Challenges and Possible Solutions, *Journal of International Criminal Justice* 6, 667–679.

Mouton, J. & Marais, H.C. (1988).
> *Basic Concepts in the Methodology of the Social Sciences*, Pretoria: Human Sciences Research Council.

Mouzos, J. & Makkai, T. (2004).
> *Women's Experiences of Male Violence. Findings from the Australian Component of the International Violence against Women Survey*, Canberra: Australian Institute of Criminology.

Mueller, G. & Adler, F. (2005).
> Victimology; from Hans Ritter Von Hentig to Irene Mellup, in: Vetere, E. & David, P. (eds.), *Victims of Crime and Abuse of Power*, New York: United Nations.

Mukagasana, Y. (1997).
> *Le Mort Ne Veut Pas de Moi*, Paris: Edilionos Fixot.

Mullins, C. (2009a).
> We Are Going to Rape You and Taste Tutsi Women, *British Journal of Criminology* 49, 719–735.

Mullins, C. (2009b).
> He Would Kill me With His Penis: Genocidal Rape in Rwanda as a State Crime, *Critical Criminology* 17(1), 15–33.

Mullins, C. & Rothe, D. (2008).
> *Blood, Power, and Bedlam. Violations of International Criminal Law in Post-Colonial Africa*, New York: Peter Lang.

Murphy, J.G. (1988).
> Forgiveness and Resentment, in: Murphy, J.G. & Hampton, J., *Forgiveness and Mercy*, Cambridge: Cambridge University Press, 14–34.

Murphy, K. & Tyler, T.R. (2008).
> Procedural Justice and Compliance Behavior: The Mediating Role of Emotions, *European Journal of Social Psychology* 38, 652–668.

Mutamba, J. & Izabaliza, J. (2005).

> *The Role of Women in Reconciliation and Peace Building in Rwanda: Ten Years after the Genocide 1994-2004. Contributions, Challenges and Way Forward*, Kigali: National Unity and Reconciliation Commission (NURC).

Mutebi, F.G., Stone, S., & Thin, N. (2003).

> Rwanda, *Development Policy Review* 21(2), Oxford: Blackwell Publishing, 253-270.

Myers-Walls, J.A. (2004).

> Children as Victims of War and Terrorism, *Journal of Aggression, Maltreatment & Trauma* 8(1), 41-62.

Nabudere, D.W. (2002).

> Towards the Study of Post Traditional Systems of Justice in the Great-Lakes Region of Africa, *East-African Journal of Peace & Human Rights* 8(1), 1-40.

Nadler, A. & Ben Shushan, D. (1989).

> 40 years Later: Long Term Consequences of the Holocaust on Kibbutz and City Survivors, *Journal of Consulting and Clinical Psychology* 57, 287-294.

Nagata, D.K. (1998).

> Intergenerational Effects of the Japanese American Internment, in: Danieli, Y. (ed.), *International Handbook of Multigenerational Legacies of Trauma*, New York: Plenum Press, 125-140.

Nagel, T. (1979).

> War and Massacre, in: Nagel, T., *Mortal Questions*, Cambridge: Cambridge University Press, 53-74.

Narayan, G. (2002).

> *Children Affected by Armed Conflict: Programming Framework*, Hull, Quebec: Canadian International Development Agency (CIDA).

Nattrast, N. (1999).

> The Truth and Reconciliation Commission on Business and Apartheid. A Critical Evaluation, *African Affairs* 98, 373-391.

Ndahiro, T. (2009).

> Genocide-Laundering: Historical Revisionism, Genocide Denial and the Role of the Rassemblement Républicain Pour La Démocratie au Rwanda, in: Clark, P. & Kaufman, Z.D. (eds.), *After Genocide: Transitional Justice, Post-Conflict Reconstruction and Reconciliation in Rwanda and Beyond*, New York: Columbia University Press, 101-124.

Newcombe, P.A., Van Den Eynde, J., Hafner, D., Jolly, L. (2008).

> Attributions of Responsibility for Rape: Differences Across Familiarity of Situation, Gender, and Acceptance of Rape Myths, *Journal of Applied Social Psychology* 38(7), 1736-1754.

Niederland, W.G. (1964).

> Psychiatric Disorders among Persecution Victims: A Contribution to the Understanding of Concentration Camp Pathology and its Aftereffects, *Journal of Nervous and Mental Diseases* 139, 458-474.

Nikolic-Ristanovic, V. (2006).

> Truth and Reconciliation in Serbia, in: Sullivan, D. & Tifft, L. (eds.), *Handbook of Restorative Justice. A Global Perspective*, London/New York: Routledge, 369-386.

Nimanga, S. (2007).
An International *Conscience Collective*. A Durkheimian Analysis of International Criminal Law, *International Criminal Law Review* 7, 561–619.

Nino, C. (1991).
The Duty to Punish Past Abuses of Human Rights Put into Context: The Case of Argentina, *The Yale Law Journal* 100, 2619–2640.

Nomoyi, C. (2001).
Impact of the Dynamics of the Reparations and Rehabilitation Committee of the Truth and Reconciliation Commission on Female Victims, *Acta Criminologica* 14(1), 1–10.

Norris, F.H. (2002).
Psychological Consequences of Disasters, *PTSD Research Quarterly* 13(2), 1–7.

Nowrojee, B. (2005a).
Making the Invisible War Crime Visible: Post-Conflict Justice for Sierra Leone's Rape Victims, *Harvard Human Rights Journal* 18, 85–105.

Nowrojee, B. (2005b).
"Your Justice is Too Slow": Will the ICTR Fail Rwanda's Rape Victims?, United Nations Research Institute for Social Development, Occasional Paper 10, November 2005.

Nsanzuwera, F.-X. (2005).
The ICTR Contribution to National Reconciliation, *Journal of International Criminal Justice* 3, 944–949.

Ntaganda, F. (2003).
La Justice Participative (Gacaca) et la Justice Internationale; Opposition ou Complémentarité?, Mémoire DEA Université de Lyon, 2003.

Ntsebeza, D.B. (2000).
The Use of Truth Commissions: Lessons for the World, in: Rotberg, R.I. & Thompson, D. (eds.), *Truth v. Justice*, Princeton: Princeton University Press, 158–169.

Obote-Odora, A. (2009).
The Prosecution of Rape and other Sexual Violence, *Development Dialogue* 51, 175–191.

O'Connell, J. (2005).
Gambling with the Psyche: Does Prosecuting Human Rights Violators Console Their Victims?, *Harvard International Law Journal* 46(2), 295–345.

Oduro, F. (2008).
Reparations in Ghana: Implementing the National Reconciliation Commission (NRC) recommendations, International Center for Transitional Justice.

Olsen, T., Payne, L., & Reiter, A. (2007).
At What Cost? A Political Economy Approach to Transitional Justice, Paper Prepared for the Midwest Political Science Association Conference, Chicago, 14th April 2007.

Olysanya, O. (2006).
Granting Immunity to Child Combatants Supranationally, in: Haveman, R. & Olysanya, O. (eds.), *Sentencing and Sanctioning in Supranational Criminal Law*, Antwerp: Intersentia, 87–108.

Oomen, B. (2005a).

> *Chiefs in South Africa: Law, Power and Culture in the Post-Apartheid Area*, New York: Palgrave.

Oomen, B. (2005b).

> Donor-Driven Justice: The Case of Rwanda, *Development & Change* 36(5), 887–910.

Op den Velde, W. (1998).

> Children of Dutch War Sailors and Civilian Resistance Veterans, in: Danieli, Y. (ed.), *International Handbook of Multigenerational Legacies of Trauma*, New York: Plenum Press, 147–162.

Opotow, S. (2001).

> Reconciliation in Times of Impunity: Challenges for Social Justice, *Social Justice Research* 14, 149–170.

Orentlicher, D.F. (1991).

> Settling Accounts: The Duty to Prosecute Human Rights Violations of a Prior Regime, *The Yale Law Journal* 100(8), 2537–2615.

Orentlicher, D.F. (2007).

> 'Settling Accounts' Revisited: Reconciling Global Norms with Local Agency, *International Journal of Transitional Justice* 1(1), 10–22.

Organization of African Unity/African Union (2000).

> *Rwanda: The Preventable Genocide*, Report of the International Panel of Eminent Personalities to Investigate the 1994 Genocide in Rwanda and the Surrounding Events, 7th July 2000, Addis Ababa, Ethiopia: Organization of African Unity.

Orr, W. (2000).

> Reparation Delayed Is Healing Retarded, in: Villa-Vicencio, Ch. & Verwoerd, W. (eds.), *Looking Back Reaching Forward*, Cape Town: University of Cape Town, 239–249.

Orth, U. (2002).

> Secondary Victimization of Crime Victims by Criminal Proceedings, *Social Justice Research* 15(4), 313–325.

Orth, U. (2003).

> Punishment Goals of Crime Victims, *Law and Human Behavior* 27(2), 173–186.

Orth, U., Montada, L., & Maercker, A. (2006).

> Feelings of Revenge, Retaliation Motive, and Posttraumatic Stress Reactions in Crime Victims, *Journal of Interpersonal Violence* 21, 229–243.

Osiel, M. (1997).

> *Mass Atrocity, Collective Memory, and the Law*, New Brunswick: Transaction Publishers.

Osiel, M.J. (2000).

> Why Prosecute? Critics of Punishment for Mass Atrocity, *Human Rights Quarterly* 22(1), 118–147.

Osiel, M.J. (2005).

> The Banality of Good: Aligning Incentives against Mass Atrocity, *Columbia Law Review* 105, 1751–1861.

Othman, M. (2005).
> Justice and Reconciliation, in: Skaar, E., Gloppen, S., & Suhrke A. (eds.), *Roads to Reconciliation*, Lanham: Lexington Books, 249–270.

Pakes, F. & Pakes, S. (2009).
> *Criminal Psychology*, Cullompton, Devon: Willan Publishing.

Paradelle, M., Dumont, H., & Boisvert, A.-M. (2005).
> Quelle Justice pour Quelle Réconciliation? Le Tribunal Pénal International pour le Rwanda et le Jugement du Genocide, *McGill Law Journal* 50, 359–413.

Paris, R. (2001).
> Human Security, Paradigm Shift or Hot Air, *International Security* 26(2), 87–102.

Park, A.S.J. (2010).
> Community-Based Restorative Transitional Justice in Sierra Leone, *Contemporary Justice Review* 13(1), 95–119.

Parmentier, S. (2003).
> *Global Justice in the Aftermath of Mass Violence: The role of the International Criminal Court in Dealing with Political Crimes*, 41/1–2 International Annals of Criminology, 203–224.

Parmentier, S., Valiñas, M., & Weitekamp, E. (2009).
> How to Repair the Harm after Violent Conflict in Bosnia? Results from a Population-Based Survey, *Netherlands Quarterly of Human Rights* 27(1), 27–44.

Parmentier, S., Vanspauwen, K., & Weitekamp, E. (2008).
> Dealing with the Legacy of Mass Violence: Changing Lenses to Restorative Justice, in: Smeulers, A. & Haveman, R. (eds.), *Supranational Criminology: Towards a Criminology of International Crimes*, Antwerp: Intersentia, 335–356.

Parmentier, S. & Weitekamp, E. (2007).
> Political Crimes and Serious violations of Human Rights: Towards a Criminology of International Crimes, in: Parmentier, S. & Weitekamp, E. (eds.), *Crime and Human Rights. Sociology of Crime, Law and Deviance* 9, Amsterdam: Elsevier, 109–144.

Parmentier, S. & Weitekamp, E. (2011).
> Dealing with War Crimes in Bosnia: Retributive and Restorative Options through the Eyes of the Population, in: Crawford, A. (ed.), *International and Comparative Criminal Justice and Urban Governance. Convergence and Divergence in Global, National and Local Settings*, 140–167. Cambridge: Cambridge University Press.

Paulussen, C. (2010).
> *Male Captus, Bene Detentus? Surrendering Suspects to the International Criminal Court*, Antwerp/Oxford: Intersentia.

Pauw, J. (1991).
> *In the Heart of the Whore – the Story of Apartheid's Death Squads*, Halfway House: Southern Book Publishers.

Pauw, J. (1997).
> *Into the Heart of Darkness – Confessions of Apartheid's Assassins*, Johannesburg: Jonathan Ball Publishers.

Peacock, R. (1989).
> *Die Manlike Swart Straatkind: 'n Verkennende Psigokriminologiese Ondersoek*, Unpublished Masters degree dissertation, University of Pretoria.

Peacock, R. (1991).
> Situacion Socio-Politica y Sistema de Justicia Penal en Sudafrica: Especial Referencia Al Problema de los Ninos Negros en Prision, *Revista Juridica de Castilla la Manch* 3, 57–72.

Pearce, J. (2005).
> *An Outbreak of Peace: Angola's Situation of Confusion*, Cape Town: David Philip

Pearshouse, R. & Symington, A. (2009).
> *Respect, Protect and Fulfill: Legislating for Women's Rights in the Context of HIV/AIDS*, Toronto: Canadian HIV/AIDS Legal Network.

Pemberton, S. (2007).
> Social Harm Future(s): Exploring the Potential of the Social Harm Approach, *Crime, Law and Social Change* 48, 27–41.

Pemberton, A. (2009).
> Victim Movements: From Diversified Needs to Varying Criminal Justice Agenda's, *Acta Criminologica* 22(3), 1–23.

Pemberton, A. (2010a).
> The Needs of Victims of Terrorism, in: Letschert, R.M., Staiger, I., & Pemberton, A. (eds.), *Assistance to Victims of Terrorism: Towards a European Standard of Justice*, Dordrecht: Springer.

Pemberton, A. (2010b).
> Al Qaeda and Vicarious Victims. Some Victimological Insights in Terrorist Strategy, in: Letschert, R.M. & Van Dijk, J.J.M. (eds.), *The New Faces of Victimhood. Globalisation, Transnational Crimes and Victims' Rights*, Dordrecht: Springer.

Pemberton, A. (2010c).
> *The Cross-Over: An Interdisciplinary Approach to the Study of Victims of Crime*, Antwerp/Apeldoorn/Portland: Maklu Publishers.

Pennebaker, J.W., Barger, S.D., & Tiebout, J. (1989).
> Disclosure of Trauma and Health among Holocaust Survivors, *Psychosomatic Medicine* 51, 577–589.

Percival, V. & Homer-Dixon, Th. (1995).
> *Environmental Scarcity and Violent Conflict: The Case of Rwanda*, Occasional Paper on Project on Environment, Population and Security, Washington D.C.: American Association for Advancement of Science and the University of Toronto, June 1995.

Perrow, C. (1961).
> The Analysis of Goals in Complex Organizations, *American Sociological Review* 26, 854–866.

Peskin, V. (2005).
> Courting Rwanda. The Promises and Pitfalls of the ICTR Outreach Programme, *Journal of International Criminal Justice* 3, 950–961.

Pham, P. & Vinck, P. (2007).
> Empirical Research and the Development and Assessment of Transitional Justice Mechanisms, *International Journal of Transitional Justice* 1(2), 231–248.

Pham, P., Vinck, P., Hean, S., & Stover, E. (2009).
> *So We Will Never Forget: A Population-Based Survey on Attitudes about Social Reconstruction and the Extraordinary Chambers in the Courts of Cambodia*, Human Rights Center, University of California, Berkeley.

Pham, P., Vinck, P., Stover, E., Moss, A., Wierda, M., & Baily, R. (2007).
When the War Ends; a Population-Based Survey on Attitudes about Peace, Justice a Social Reconstruction in Northern Uganda, New York/Berkeley/New Orleans: Human Rights Center, University of California, Berkley; Payson Center, Tulane University & International Center for Transitional Justice, December 2007.

Pham, P., Vinck, P., Wierda, M., Stover, E., & di Giovanni, A. (2005).
Forgotten Voices: A Population-Based Survey on Attitudes about Peace and Justice in Northern Uganda, New York/Berkeley: International Centre for Transitional Justice/Human Rights Centre, University of California, Berkeley.

Pillay, N. (2008).
Equal Justice for Women: A Personal Journey, Arizona Law Review 50(3), 657–672.

Pizam, A. & Fleischer, A. (2002).
Severity versus Frequency of Acts of Terrorism: Which Has a Larger Impact on Tourism Demand?, Journal of Travel Research 40(3), 337–339.

Popovski, V. (2006).
Children in Armed Conflict: Law and Practice of the United Nations, in: Arts, K. & Popovski, V. (eds.), International Criminal Accountability and the Rights of Children, The Hague: Hague Academic Press, 37–52.

Posel, D. & Simpson, G. (2002).
Commissioning the Past: Understanding South Africa's Truth and Reconciliation Commission, Johannesburg: Witwatersrand University Press.

Power, S. (2003).
"A Problem from Hell". America and the Age of Genocide, London: Harper Perennial.

Pratt, A. (2005).
Practising Reconciliation? The Politics of Reconciliation in the Australian Parliament, 1991–2000, Canberra: Parliament of Australia.

Pratto, F. & Glasford, D.E. (2008).
How Needs Can Motivate Intergroup Reconciliation in the Face of Intergroup Conflict, in: Nadler, A., Malloy, T., & Fisher, J. (eds.), The Social Psychology of Intergroup Reconciliation, Oxford: Oxford University Press, 117–144.

Prigerson, H. & Jacobs, S.C. (2001).
Traumatic Grief as a Distinct Disorder: A Rationale, Consensus Criteria, and a Preliminary Empirical Test, in: Stroebe, M.S., Hanson, R.O., Stroebe, W., & Schut, H.A.W. (eds.), Handbook of Bereavement Research: Consequences, Coping, and Care, Washington D.C.: American Psychological Association, 613–645.

Pross, C. (1998).
Paying for the Past: The Struggle over Reparations for Surviving Victims of the Nazi Terror, London: The John Hopkins University Press.

Prunier, G. (1994).
La Crise Rwandaise: Structures et Déroulement, Refugee Survey Quarterly 13, 13–46.

Prunier, G. (1995).
The Rwandan Crisis: History of a Genocide, Kampala: Fountain Publishers.

Prunier, G. (2008).

Africa's World War: Congo, the Rwandan Genocide, and the Making of a Continental Catastrophe, Oxford: Oxford University Press.

Prunier, G. (2009).

From Genocide to Continental War. The 'Congolese' Conflict and the Crisis of Contemporary Africa, London: Hurst and Company.

Quinn, J.R. (2009).

What of Reconciliation? Traditional Mechanisms of Acknowledgment in Uganda, in: Quinn, J.R. (ed.), *Reconciliation(s). Transitional justice in Post-Conflict Societies*, Montréal: McGill-Queen's University Press, 174–206.

Quinney, R. (1972).

Who is the Victim?, *Criminology* 10, 314–323.

Quinney, R. (1974).

Critique of the Legal Order, Boston: Little, Brown & Co.

Quint, P.E. (2000).

The Border Guard Trials and the East German Past – Seven Arguments, *American Journal of Comparative Law* 48, 541–572.

Radin, M.J. (1989).

Reconsidering the Rule of Law, *Boston University Law Review* 69(4), 781–822.

Raphael, B., Swan, P., & Martinek, N. (1998).

Intergenerational Aspects of Trauma for Australian Aboriginal People, in: Danieli, Y. (ed.), *International Handbook of Multigenerational Legacies of Trauma*, New York: Plenum Press, 327–340.

Raquel, A. (2006).

A Victim-Centred Reflection on Truth Commissions and Prosecutions as a Response to Mass Atrocity, *Journal of Human Rights* 5, 107–126.

Rauschenbach, M. & Scalia, D. (2008).

Victims and International Criminal Justice: A Vexed Question, *International Review of the Red Cross* 90, 441–459.

Regan, N. (2004).

The Covenant, New York: St. Martin Press.

Reis, C. (2012) [forthcoming].

Ethical, Safety and Methodological Issues Related to Collection and Use of Data on Sexual Violence in Conflict, in: De Brouwer, A. *et al.* (eds.), *Sexual Violence as an International Crime: Interdisciplinary Approaches*, Antwerp: Intersentia.

Reyntjens, F. (1985).

Pouvoir et droit au Rwanda. Droit public et évolution politique, 1916–1973, Musée Royale de l'Afrique Centrale, Belgium.

Reyntjens, F. (1990).

Le Gacaca ou la Justice du Gazon au Rwanda, *Politique Africaine* 40, 31–41.

Rich, M.S. (1982).

Children of Holocaust Survivors: A Concurrent Validity Study of a Survivor Family Typology, Unpublished Doctoral Dissertation, Berkeley: California School of Professional Psychology.

Ricœur, P. (2000).
Memory, History, and Forgetting, Chicago: The University of Chicago Press (Translated by Kathleen Blamey and David Pellauer).

Rikhof, J. (2005).
Hate Speech and International Criminal Law: The *Mugesera* Decision by the Supreme Court of Canada, *Journal of International Criminal Justice* 3, 1121–1133.

Rikhof, J. (2008).
'Fewer Places to Hide? The Impact of Domestic War Crimes Prosecutions on International Impunity', Conference Paper 2008.

Roach, K. (1999).
Due Process and Victims' Rights, Toronto: University of Toronto Press.

Roberts, P. (2003).
Restoration and Retribution in International Criminal Justice: An Exploratory Analysis, in: Von Hirsch, A., Roberts, J.V., Bottoms, A.E., Roach, K., & Schiff, M. (eds.), *Restorative Justice and Criminal Justice. Competing or Reconcilable Paradigms?*, Oxford: Hart Publishing.

Robinson, P. & Darley, J.M. (2007).
Intuitions of Justice: Implications for Criminal Law and Justice Policy, *Southern California Law Review* 81, 1–67.

Rock, P. (1998).
After Homicide, Oxford: Clarendon Press.

Roht-Arriaza, N. (1990).
State Responsibility to Investigate and Prosecute Grave Human Rights Violations in International Law, *California Law Review* 78, 449–514.

Roht-Arriaza, N. (ed.) (1995).
Impunity and Human Rights in International Law and Practice, New York: Oxford University Press.

Roht-Arriaza, N. (2004a)
Reparations Decisions and Dilemmas, *Hastings International & Comparative Law Review* 27, 157–219.

Roht-Arriaza, N. (2004b).
Reparations in the Aftermath of Repression and Mass Violence, in: Stover, E. & Weinstein, H. (eds.), *My Neighbor, My Enemy: Justice and Community in the Aftermath of Mass Atrocity*, Cambridge: Cambridge University Press.

Roht-Arriaza, N. (2006).
The New Landscape of Transitional Justice, in: Roth-Arriaza, N. & Mariezcurrena, J. (eds.), *Transitional Justice in the Twenty-First Century. Beyond Truth versus Justice*, Cambridge: Cambridge University Press, 1–16.

Roht-Arriaza, N. & Mariezcurrena, J. (2006).
Transitional Justice in the Twenty-First Century, Beyond Truth versus Justice, Cambridge: Cambridge University Press.

Rombouts, H. (2004).
Victim Organisations and the Politics of Reparation: A Case Study on Rwanda, Antwerp/Oxford: Intersentia.

Rombouts, H. (2006).

> Women and Reparations in Rwanda. A Long Path to Travel, The International Center for Transitional Justice.

Rombouts, H., Sardaro, P., & Vandeginste, S. (2005).

> The Right to Reparation for Victims of Gross and Systematic Violations of Human Rights, in: De Feyter, K., Parmentier, S., Bossuyt, M., & Lemmens, P. (eds.), Out of the Ashes: Reparations for Victims of Gross and Systematic Human Rights Violations, Antwerp: Intersentia, 460–463.

Rombouts, H. & Vandeginste, S. (2005).

> Reparations for Victims in Rwanda: Caught Between Theory and Practice, in: De Feyter, K., Parmentier, S., Bossuyt, M., & Lemmens, P. (eds.), Out of the Ashes: Reparations for Victims of Gross and Systematic Human Rights Violations, Antwerp: Intersentia, 309–344.

Römkens, R. (1996).

> 'Zwei Seelen in einer Brust.' De Partnerdoodster als Slachtoffer en Dader, in: Römkens, R. & Dijkstra, S. (red.), Het Omstreden Slachtoffer. Geweld van Vrouwen en Mannen, Baarn: Ambo 77–100.

Römkens, R (2005).

> In the Shadow of No Law. Navigating Cultural Legitimacy and Legal Protection of Women against Violence in Afghanistan, in: Wolleswinkel, R. (ed.), Violence in the Domestic Sphere, Antwerp: Intersentia, 71–98.

Römkens, R. (2008).

> Law as a Trojan Horse. Unintended Consequences of Rights-Based Interventions to Support Battered Women, in: Freeman, M.D. (ed.), Domestic Violence, Aldershot: Ashgate Publishers.

Rosenfeld, F. (2010).

> Collective Reparations for Victims of Armed Conflict, International Review of the Red Cross 92(879), 731–746.

Rosenthal, G. & Volter, B. (1998).

> Three Generations within Jewish and Non-Jewish German Families after the Unification of Germany, in: Danieli, Y. (ed.), International Handbook of Multigenerational Legacies of Trauma, New York: Plenum Press, 297–314.

Rotberg, R.I. & Thompson, D. (eds.) (2000).

> Truth v. Justice. The Morality of Truth Commissions, Princeton/Oxford: Princeton University Press.

Rozee, P.D. & Koss, M.P. (2001).

> Rape: A Century of Resistance, Psychology of Women Quarterly 25(4), 295–311.

Rubio Marin, R. (2006).

> What Happened to the Women? Gender and Reparations for Human Rights Violations, New York: Social Science Research Council.

Rummel, R.J. (1994).

> Power, Genocide and Mass Murder, Journal of Peace Research 31(1), 1–10.

Sadat, L.N. (2007).

> The Effect of Amnesties before Domestic and International Tribunals: Morality, Law and Politics, in: Hughes, E., Schabas, W.A., & Thakur, R. (eds.), Atrocities and

International Accountability: Beyond Transitional Justice, United Nations University Press, 225–245.

Sadler, A.G., Booth, B.M., Cook, B.L., & Doebbeling, B.N. (2003).
Factors Associated with Women's Risk of Rape in the Military Environment, *American Journal of Industrial Medicine* 43(3), 262–273.

Sands, P. (2006).
Lawless World. The Whistle-Blowing Account of How Bush and Blair Are Taking the Law into Their Own Hands, London: Penguin Books.

Saris, A. & Lofts, K. (2009).
Reparation Programmes, in: Ferstman, C., Goetz, M., & Stephens, A., *Reparations for Victims of Genocide, War Crimes and Crimes against Humanity. Systems in Place and Systems in the Making*, Leiden: Martinus Nijhoff Publishers, 79–99.

Sarkin, J. (2001).
The Tension Between Justice and Reconciliation in Rwanda: Politics, Human Rights, Due Process and the Role of the *Gacaca* Courts in Dealing with the Genocide, *Journal of African Law* 45, 143–172.

Sawin, J.L. & Zehr, H. (2007).
The Ideas of Engagement and Empowerment, in: Johnstone, G. & Van Ness, D.W. (eds.), *Handbook of Restorative Justice*, Cullompton, Devon: Willan Publishing, 41–58.

Sawyer, E. & Kelsall, T. (2007).
Truth vs. Justice? Popular Views on the Truth and Reconciliation Commission and the Special Court for Sierra Leone, *The Online Journal of Peace and Conflict Resolution* 7(1), 36–68.

Schabas, W.A. (1996).
Justice, Democracy, and Impunity in Post-Genocide Rwanda: Searching for Solutions to Impossible Problems, *Criminal Law Forum* 7, 523–560.

Schabas, W.A. (2000).
Genocide in International Law. The Crime of Crimes, Cambridge: Cambridge University Press.

Schabas, W.A. (2003).
National Courts Finally Begin to Prosecute Genocide, the 'Crime of Crimes', *Journal of International Criminal Justice* 1, 39–63.

Schabas, W.A. (2004).
An Introduction to the International Criminal Court, Cambridge: Cambridge University Press.

Schabas, W. (2005).
Reparations Practices in Sierra Leone and the Truth and Reconciliation Commission, in: De Feyter, K., Parmentier, S., Bossuyt, M., & Lemmens, P. (eds.), *Out of the Ashes: Reparations for Victims of Gross and Systematic Human Rights Violations*, Antwerp: Intersentia, 289–308.

Schabas, W.A. (2005).
Genocide Trials and Gacaca Courts, *Journal of International Criminal Justice* 3, 879–895.

Schabas, W.A. (2008a).
  State Policy as an Element of International Crimes, *The Journal of Criminal Law and Criminology* 98, 953–982.
Schabas, W.A. (2008b).
  Post-Genocide Justice in Rwanda: A Spectrum of Options, in: Clark, P. & Kaufman, Z.D. (eds.), *After Genocide: Transitional Justice, Post-conflict Reconstruction and Reconciliation in Rwanda and Beyond*, London: Hurst & Company, 207–227.
Schabas, W.A. (2010).
  The International Criminal Court: A Commentary on the Rome Statute, Oxford: Oxford University Press.
Schafer, J. (2004).
  The Use of Patriarchal Imagery in the Civil War in Mozambique and its Implications for the Reintegration of Child Soldiers, in: Boyden, J. & De Berry, J. (eds.), *Children and Youth on the Front Line: Ethnography, Armed Conflict, and Displacement*, New York: Berghahn Books, 87–104.
Scharf, M.P. (1997).
  The Case for a Permanent Truth Commission, *Duke Journal of Comparative and International Law* 7, 375–410.
Scharf, M.P. (2007).
  Trading Justice for Peace: The Contemporary Law and Policy Debate, in: Hughes, E., Schabas, W.A., & Thakur, R. (eds.), *Atrocities and International Accountability: Beyond Transitional Justice*, United Nations University Press, 246–273.
Scharf, M.P. & Rodley, N. (2002).
  International Law Principles on Accountability, in: Bassiouni, M.C. (ed.), *Post Conflict Justice*, Ardsley, New York: Transnational Publishers, 89–96.
Schmid, A. (2003).
  Magnitudes and Focus of Terrorist Victimisation, in: Das, D.K. & Kratcoski, P.C. (eds.), *Meeting the Challenges of Global Terrorism: Prevention, Control and Recovery*, Lanham: Lexington Books, 33–74.
Schneider, E. (1993).
  Feminism and the False Dichotomy of Victimization and Agency, *New York University Law Review* 38, 387–399.
Schönsteiner, J. (2008).
  Dissuasive Measures and the 'Society as Whole': A Working Theory of Reparations in the Inter-American Court of Human Rights, *American University International Law Review* 23, 127–164.
Schotsmans, M. (2000).
  A l'Écoute de Rescapés. Recherche sur la Perception des Rescapés de Leur Situation Actuelle, Kigali: GTZ.
Schotsmans, M. (2005).
  Victims Expectations, Needs and Perspectives After Gross and Systematic Human Rights Violations, in: De Feyter, K., Parmentier, S., Bossuyt, M., & Lemmens, P. (eds.), *Out of the Ashes: Reparations for Victims of Gross and Systematic Human Rights Violations*, Antwerp: Intersentia, 105–134.

Schotsmans, M. (2010).
> Blow Your Mind and Cool Your Heart: Can Tradition-Based Justice Fill the Transitional Justice Gap in Sierra Leone?, in: Oxford Transitional Justice Research (eds.), *Tensions in Transitional Justice: A Critical Approach.*

Schwendinger, H. & Schwendinger, J. (1970).
> Defenders of Order or Guardians of Human Rights?, *Issues in Criminology* 5, 123–157.

Sebarenzi, J. (2009).
> *God Sleeps in Rwanda. A Journey of Transformation*, United Kingdom: Oneworld Publications.

Sebba, L. (2006).
> Formal and Informal Conflict Resolution in International Criminal Justice, in: Albrecht, H.-J., Simon, J.-M., Rezaei, H., Rohne, H.-C., & Kiza, E. (eds.), *Conflicts and Conflict Resolution in Middle Eastern Societies – Between Tradition and Modernity*, Berlin: Duncker & Humblot, 25–43.

Seibert-Fohr, A. (2003).
> The Relevance of the Rome Statute of the International Criminal Court for Amnesties and Truth Commissions, *Max Planck Yearbook of United Nations Law* 7, 553–590.

Seibert-Fohr, A. (2009).
> *Prosecuting Serious Human Rights Violations*, Oxford: Oxford University Press.

Sen, A. (2004).
> Elements of a Theory of Human Rights, *Philosophy and Public Affairs* 32, 315–356.

Senier, A. (2010).
> The ICC Appeals Chamber Judgment on the Legal, Characterisation of the Facts in Prosecutor V Lubanga, *ASIL Journal* 14(1), 8th January 2010.

Seymour, D. (1999).
> Children's Rights in Armed Conflict, in: Amnesty International (ed.), *In the Firing Line: War and Children's Rights,* London: Amnesty International, 83–94.

Separovic, P. (1985).
> Victimology: Studies of Victims, Croatia, Samobor.

Shaked, G. (1983).
> *Hebrew Narrative Fiction 1880–1980: In the Land of Israel and the Diaspora*, Jerusalem: Keter.

Shapland, J., Wilmore, J., & Duff, P. (1985).
> *Victims in the Criminal Justice System*, Aldershot: Gower Publishing.

Sharratt, S. (2011).
> *Gender, Shame and Sexual Violence: The Voices of Witnesses and Court Members at War Crimes Tribunals*, London: Ashgate.

Sharratt, S. (2012) [forthcoming].
> The Prosecution of Rape and Sexual Violence at the International Criminal Court for the Former Yugoslavia (ICTY) and Bosnian War Crimes Court (BIH): Voices of Court Members – A Phenomenological Journey, in: De Brouwer, A. *et al.* (eds.), *Sexual Violence as an International Crime: Interdisciplinary Approaches*, Antwerp: Intersentia.

Shaw, M. (1996).
> Crime, Political Transformation and Changing Forms of Policing Control: Policing the Transformation: New Issues in South Africa's Crime Debate, *IDP Monograph Series, No. 3*.

Shaw, M. (2001).
> Time Heals All Wounds?, in: Farrell, G. & Pease, K. (eds.), *Repeat Victimization: Crime Prevention Studies* 12, Monsey: Criminal Justice Press, 218–233.

Shaw, R. (2007).
> Memory Frictions: Localizing the Truth and Reconciliation Commission in Sierra Leone, *International Journal of Transitional Justice* 1, 183–207.

Shaw, R. & Waldorf, L. (2010).
> *Localizing Transitional Justice. Interventions and Priorities after Mass Violence*, Stanford: Stanford University Press.

Shear, K.M., Frank, E., Foa, E., Cherry, C., Reynolds, C.F., Vander Bilt, J., & Masters, S. (2001).
> Traumatic Grief Treatment: A Pilot Study, *American Journal of Psychiatry* 158, 1506–1508.

Shelton, D. (2005).
> The United Nations Principles and Guidelines on Reparations: Context and Contents, in: De Feyter, K., Parmentier, S., Bossuyt, M., & Lemmens, P. (eds.), *Out of the Ashes. Reparation for Victims of Gross and Systematic Human Rights Violations*, Antwerp/Oxford: Intersentia, 11–33.

Shelton, D. (2006).
> *Remedies in International Human Rights Law*, Oxford: Oxford University Press.

Shelton, D. (2008)
> The UN Principles and Guidelines on Reparations: Context and Contents, in: De Feyter, K., Parmentier, S., Bossuyt, M., & Lemmens, P. (eds.), *Out of the Ashes, Reparations for Victims of Gross and Systematic Human Rights Violations*, Antwerp: Intersentia.

Sherif, M., Harvey, O.J., White, B.J., Hood, W.R., & Sherif, C. (1954).
> *Experimental Study of Positive and Negative Intergroup Attitudes between Experimentally Produced Groups: Robber's Cave experiment*, Norman: University of Oklahoma.

Shilo, S. (2005).
> *No Gnomes Will Appear*, Tel Aviv: Am Oved.

Shipley, J.T. (1970).
> *Dictionary of World Literary Terms*, Boston: The Writer.

Shklar, J.N. (1964).
> *Legalism*, Cambridge: Harvard University Press.

Shriver Jr., D.W. (1995).
> *An Ethic for Enemies: Forgiveness in Politics*, New York: Oxford University Press.

Shuman, D.W. & McCall, S.A. (2000).
> *Justice and the Prosecution of Old crimes*, Washington D.C.: American Psychological Association.

Sidanius, J. & Pratto, F. (1999).

    Social Dominance: An Intergroup Theory of Social Hierarchy and Oppression, Cambridge: Cambridge University Press.

Siegel, R. (1998).

    Transitional Justice: A Decade of Debate and Experience, *Human Rights Quarterly* 20, 431–454.

Sigal, J.J. & Weinfeld, M. (1989).

    Trauma and Rebirth: Intergenerational Effects of the Holocaust, New York: Praeger.

Simpson, G. (1998).

    A Brief Evaluation of South Africa's Truth and Reconciliation Commission: Some Lessons for Societies in Transition, Paper written for the Centre for the Study of Violence and Reconciliation, Johannesburg.

Simpson, G. (2002).

    Tell No Lie, Claim No Easy Victories: A Brief Evaluation of South Africa's Truth and Reconciliation Commission, in: Posel, D. & Simpson, G. (eds.), *Commissioning the Past: Understanding South Africa's Truth and Reconciliation Commission*, Johannesburg: Witwatersrand University Press, 220–251.

Simpson, M.A. (1998).

    The Second Bullet: Transgenerational Impacts of the Trauma of Conflict within a South African and World Context, in: Danieli, Y. (ed.), *International Handbook of Multigenerational Legacies of Trauma*, New York: Plenum Press, 487–512.

Singer, P.A.D. (1981).

    The Expanding Circle. Ethics and Sociobiology, Oxford: Oxford University Press.

Singer, P. (ed.) (2000).

    A Companion to Ethics, Oxford: Blackwell Publishing.

Singer, P.W. (2006).

    Children at War, Berkeley: University of California Press.

Sivakumaran, S. (2007).

    Sexual Violence against Men in Armed Conflict, *The European Journal of International Law* 18(2), 253–276.

Sivakumaran, S. (2010).

    Lost in Translation: UN Responses to Sexual Violence against Men and Boys in Situations of Armed Conflict, *International Review of the Red Cross*, 92(877), 1–19.

Skinner, K.M., Kressin, N., Frayne, S., Tripp, T.J., Hankin, C.S., Miller, D.R., & Sullivan, L.M., (2000).

    The Prevalence of Military Sexual Assault among Female Veterans' Administration Outpatients, *Journal of Interpersonal Violence* 15(3), 291–310.

Slabbert, M. (1980).

    Repetitive Cycles: Analyses of Socialisation and Institutionalisation Patterns and Discussion on Crime Prevention, Intervention and Diversion Studies, Institute of Criminology, University of Cape Town.

Slone, M. (2000).

    Responses to Media Coverage of Terrorism, *Journal of Conflict Resolution* 44(4), 508–522.

Smart, C. (1989).

    Feminism and the Power of Law, London/New York: Routledge.

Smeulers, A. (2004).
> What Transforms Ordinary People into Gross Human Rights Violators, in: Carey, S.C. & Poe, S.C. (eds.), *Understanding Human Rights Violations: New Systematic Studies*, Aldershot: Ashgate Publishing, 239–256.

Smeulers, A. (ed.) (2010).
> *Collective Violence and International Criminal Justice – An Interdisciplinary Approach*, Antwerp/Oxford/Portland: Intersentia.

Smeulers, A. & Haveman, R. (eds.) (2008).
> *Supranational Criminology: Towards a Criminology of International Crimes*, Antwerp: Intersentia.

Smeulers, A. & Hoex, L. (2010).
> Studying the Micro-dynamics of the Rwandan genocide, *British Journal of Criminology* 50(3), 435–454.

Smith, D. (2004).
> *Towards a Strategic Framework for Peacebuilding: Getting Their Act Together. Overview Report of the Joint Utstein Study of Peacebuilding*, Oslo: Royal Norwegian Ministry of Foreign Affairs.

Smyth, M. & Robinson, G. (2001).
> *Researching Violently Divided Societies: Ethical and Methodological Issues*, Tokyo/London: United Nations University Press/Pluto Press.

Snyder, S. & Vinjamuri, R. (2004).
> Trials and Errors: Principle and Pragmatism in Strategies of International Justice, *International Security* 28(3), 5–44.

Solomon, Z. (1995).
> Oscillating between Denial and Recognition of PTSD: Why are Lessons Learned and Forgotten?, *Journal of Traumatic Stress* 8(2), 271–282.

Somer, E., Buchbinder, E., Peled-Avram, M., & Ben-Yizhack, Y. (2004).
> The Stress and Coping of Israeli Emergency Room Social Workers Following Terrorist Attacks, *Qualitative Health Research* 14, 1077–1093.

Somers, E. (2010).
> *Voorzitter van de Joodse Raad. De Herinneringen van David Cohen (1941–1943)*, Zutphen: Walburg Pers.

Sosnov, M. (2008).
> The Adjudication of Genocide: Gacaca and the Road to Reconciliation in Rwanda, *Denver Journal of International Law & Policy* 36, 125–153.

Sprang, G. (2001).
> Vicarious Stress: Patterns of Disturbance and Use of Mental Health Services by Those Indirectly Affected by the Oklahoma City Bombing, *Psychological Reports* 89(2), 331–338.

Stahn, C. (2005).
> Complementarity, Amnesties and Alternative Forms of Justice: Some Interpretative Guidelines for the ICC, *Journal of International Criminal Justice* 3, 695–720.

Stahn, C., Olasolo, H., & Gibson, K. (2006).
> Participation of Victims in the Pre-Trial Proceedings of the ICC, *Journal of International Criminal Justice* 4, 219–238.

Stark, L. (2006).

Cleansing the wounds of war: An Examination of Traditional Healing, Psychosocial Health and Reintegration in Sierra Leone, *Intervention* 4(3), 206–218.

Starzynski, L.L., Ullman, S.E., Filipas, H.H., & Townsend, S.M. (2005).

Correlates of Women's Sexual Assault Disclosure to Informal and Formal Support Sources, *Violence and Victims* 20(4), 417–432.

Staub, E. (1989).

The Roots of Evil – the Origins of Genocide and Other Group Violence, Cambridge: Cambridge University Press.

Staub, E. (1996).

Preventing Genocide: Activating Bystanders, Helping Victims, and Creation of Caring, *Peace and Conflict: Journal of Peace Psychology* 2, 189–200.

Staub, E. (2000).

Genocide and Mass Killing: Origins, Prevention, Healing, and Reconciliation, *Political Psychology* 21(2), 367–382.

Staub, E. (2006).

Reconciliation after Genocide, Mass Killing, or Intractable Conflict: Understanding the Roots of Violence, Psychological Recovery, and the Steps toward a General Theory, *Political Psychology* 27, 867–894.

Staub, E., Pearlman, L.A., Gubin, A., & Hagengimana, A. (2005).

Healing, Forgiveness and Reconciliation in Rwanda: Intervention and Experimental Evaluation, *Journal of Social and Clinical Psychology* 24(3), 297–334.

Steinberg, D. (2010).

Working Paper on Preventing and Responding to Sexual Violence against Women Displaced by Conflict, *Civil Society Advisory Group (to the UN SG) on Women, Peace, and Security (CSAG)*, Peace for Women.

Stovel, L. (2008).

There's No Bad Bush to Throw Away a Bad Child: 'Tradition'-Inspired Reintegration in Post-War Sierra Leone, *Journal of Modern African Studies* 46(2), 305–324.

Stovel, L. (2010).

Long Road Home. Building Reconciliation and Trust in Post-War Sierra Leone, Series on Transitional Justice, no. 2, Antwerp/Oxford/Portland: Intersentia.

Stover, E. (2005).

The Witnesses: War Crimes and the Promise of Justice in The Hague, Philadelphia: University of Pennsylvania Press.

Stover, E. & Weinstein, H.M. (2004).

Conclusion: A Common Objective, a Universe of Alternatives, in: Stover, E. & Weinstein, H.M. (eds.), *My Neighbour, My Enemy. Justice and Community in the Aftermath of Mass Atrocity*, Cambridge: Cambridge University Press, 323–342.

Stover, E. & Weinstein, H.M. (eds.) (2004).

My Neighbour, My Enemy. Justice and Community in the Aftermath of Mass Atrocity, Cambridge: Cambridge University Press.

Straus, S. (2006).

The Order of Genocide: Race, Power, and War in Rwanda, Ithaca, New York: Cornell University Press.

Strous, R.D. & Kotler, M. (2004).

The Ripple Effect of the Toll of Terror, *Israel Medical Association Journal* 6(7), 425–426.

Suma, M. & Correa, C. (2009).

Report and Proposals for the Implementation of the Reparations in Sierra Leone, International Center for Transitional Justice.

Summers, C. & Markusen E. (eds.) (1999).

Collective Violence. Harmful Behaviour in Groups and Governments, Lanhan/Boudler/New York/Oxford: Rowman & Littlefield Publishers.

Sunga, L.S. (2009).

Ten Principles for Reconciling Truth Commissions and Criminal Prosecutions, in: Doria, J., Gasser, H.-P., & Bassiouni, M.C. (eds.), *The Legal Regime of the International Criminal Court. Essays in Honour of Professor Igor Blishchenko*, Leiden/Boston: Martinus Nijhoff Publishers, 1071–1104.

Tajfel, H. & Turner, J.C. (1979).

An Integrative Theory of Intergroup Conflict, in: Austin, W.G. & Worchel, S. (eds.), *The Social Psychology of Intergroup Relation*, Monterey CA: Brooks/Cole, 33–47.

Tamuz, B. (1974).

Requiem to Naaman, Tel Aviv: Hakibbutz Hameuchad Publishing.

Tankink, M. & Richters, A. (2007).

Silence as a Coping Strategy: The case of Refugee Women in the Netherlands from South-Sudan Who Experienced Sexual Violence in the Context of War, in: Wilson, J.P. & Drozdek, B. (eds.), *Voices of Trauma: Treating Survivors Across Cultures*, New York: Springer, 191–210.

Tavuchis, N. (1991).

Mea Culpa: A Sociology of Apology and Reconciliation, Stanford: Stanford University Press.

Taylor, Ch. (1995).

The Politics of Recognition, in: Taylor, Ch., *Philosophical Arguments*, Cambridge, Massachusetts: Harvard University Press, 225–256.

Taylor, I., Walton P., & Young J. (eds.) (1975).

Critical Criminology, London/Boston: Routledge & Kegan Paul.

Tedeschi, R.G. & Calhoun, L.G. (1996).

The Post-Traumatic Growth Inventory: Measuring the Positive Legacy of Trauma, *Journal of Traumatic Stress* 9, 455–471.

Teitel, R.G. (2002).

Transitional Justice, Oxford: Oxford University Press.

Teitel, R.G. (2003).

Transitional Justice Genealogy, *Harvard Human Rights Journal* 16, 69–94.

Teitel, R. (2009).

Transitional Jurisprudence: The Role of Law in Political Transformation, *Yale Law Journal* 106(7), 2009–2080.

Thabet, A.A.M. & Vostanis, P. (1999).

Stress Reactions in Children of War, *Journal of Child Psychology and Psychiatry* 40(3) 385–391.

Thalmann, V. (2008).
  French Justice's Endeavours to Substitute for the ICTR, *Journal of International Criminal Justice* 6, 995–1002.
Thapar-Björkert, S. & Morgan, K. (2010).
  "But Sometimes I Think … They Put Themselves in the Situation": Exploring Blame and Responsibility in Interpersonal Violence, *Violence Against Women* 16(1), 32–59.
Thibaut, J. & Walker L. (1975).
  Procedural Justice: A Psychological Analysis, Hillsdale, New Jersey: Wiley.
Thomas, I.W. & Thomas, D. (1929).
  The Child in America, New York: Alfred A. Knopf.
Thomas, P. (2005).
  Mainstreaming Disability in Development: Country-level Research. Rwanda Country Report, Disability Knowledge and Research, April 2005.
Thomas, S. & Chy, T. (2009).
  Including the Survivors in the Tribunal Process, in: Ciorciari, J.D. & Heindel, A. (eds.), *On Trial: The Khmer Rouge Accountability Process*, Cambodia: Documentation Center of Cambodia, 214–293.
Thoms, O., Ron, J., & Paris, R. (2008).
  The Effects of Transitional Justice Mechanisms: A Summary of Empirical Research Findings and Implications for Analysts and Practitioners, Ottawa: Centre for International Policy Studies, University of Ottawa.
Tilly, C. (2003).
  The Politics of Collective Violence, Cambridge: Cambridge University Press.
Tjaden, P. & Thoennes, N. (2000).
  Extent, Nature, and Consequences of Rape Victimization: Findings from the National Violence Against Women Survey, Washington D.C.: National Institute of Justice, Office of Justice Programs, NCJ-210346.
Tochilovsky, V.N. (1999).
  Victims' Procedural Rights at Trial: Approach of Continental Europe and the International Tribunal for the Former Yugoslavia, in: Van Dijk, J.M., Van Kaam, R.G.H., & Wemmers, J. (eds.), *Caring for Victims: Selected Proceedings of the Ninth International Symposium on Victimology*, New York: Criminal Justice Press, 287–292.
Tomuschat, C. (1999).
  Individual Reparation Claims in Instances of Grave Human Rights Violations: The Position under General International Law, in: Randelzhofer, A. & Tomuschat, C. (eds.), *State Responsibility and the Individual. Reparation in Instances of Grave Violations of Human Rights*, The Hague/London/Boston: Martinus Nijhoff Publishers, 1–25.
Tomuschat, C. (2008).
  Human Rights, Between Idealism and Realism, Oxford: Oxford University Press.
Totten, S. (2009).
  The Plight and Fate of Females During and Following the 1994 Rwandan Genocide, in: Totten, S., *Plight and Fate of Women During and Following Genocide*, New Brunswick: Transaction Publishers, 107–135.

Triffterer, O. (2001).
> Genocide, Its Particular Intent to Destroy in Whole or in Part the Group as Such, *Leiden Journal of International Law* 14, 399–408.

Turk, A.T. (1972).
> *Criminality and Legal Order*, Chicago: Rand McNally & Company.

Turković, K. (2002).
> Overview of the Victimological Data Related to War in Croatia, *European Journal of Crime, Criminal Law and Criminal Justice* 10, 202–215.

Turner, T. (2007).
> *The Congo Wars: Conflict, Myth and Reality*, London/New York: Zed Books.

Tutu, D. (1999).
> *No Future without Forgiveness*, New York: Doubleday.

Tyler, T.R. (2003).
> Procedural Justice, Legitimacy and the Effective Rule of Law, in: Tonry, M. (ed.), *Crime and Justice: A Review of the Research* 30, Chicago: Chicago University Press, 283–358.

Tyler, T. & Lind E.A. (1992).
> A Relational Model of Authority in Groups, in: Zanna, M.P. (ed.), *Advances in Experimental Social Psychology*, Vol. 25, San Diego: Academic Press, 115–191.

Upadhyaya, P. (2005).
> Human Security, Humanitarian Intervention, and the Third World Concerns, *Denver Journal of International Law and Policy* 33, 71–91.

Valentino, B.A. (2004).
> *Final Solutions: Mass Killing and Genocide in the Twentieth Century*, Ithaca, New York: Cornell University Press.

Van Boven, T. (1995).
> Human Rights and Rights of Peoples, *European Journal of International Law* 6(1), 461–476.

Van Boven, T. (1999).
> The Perspective of the Victim, in: Danieli, Y., Stamatopoulou, E., & Dias, C.J. (eds.), *The Universal Declaration of Human Rights: 50 Years and Beyond*, New York: Baywood.

Van Boven, T. (2007).
> Reparative Justice – Focus on Victims, SIM lecture 2007, *Netherlands Quarterly of Human Rights* 25, 723–735.

Van Boven, T. (2008).
> Preface, in: De Feyter, K., Parmentier, S., Bossuyt, M., & Lemmens, P. (eds.), *Out of the Ashes, Reparations for Victims of Gross and Systematic Human Rights Violations*, Antwerp: Intersentia.

Van Boven, T. (2009).
> Victims' Rights to a Remedy and Reparation: The New United Nations Principles and Guidelines, in: Ferstman, C., Goetz, M., & Stephens, A., *Reparations for Victims of Genocide, War Crimes and Crimes against Humanity, Systems in Place and Systems in the Making*, Leiden: Martinus Nijhoff Publishers.

Van den Bergh, L. (2009).
> *Why Peace Worked; Mozambicans Look Back*, Amsterdam: AWEPA.

Van den Bos, K. (1996).
Procedural Justice and Conflict, Rijksuniversiteit Leiden, Doctoral Thesis.

Van den Bos, K. & Lind E.A. (2002).
Uncertainty Management by Means of Fairness Judgements, *Advances in Experimental Social Psychology* 34, 1–59.

Van den Herik, L. (2009).
A Quest for Jurisdiction and an Appropriate Definition of Crime: Mpambara before the Dutch Courts, *Journal of International Criminal Justice* 7, 1117–1132.

Van der Merwe, H. (2008).
What Survivors Say About Justice: An Analysis of the TRC Victim Hearings, in: Chapman, A. & Van der Merwe, H. (eds.), *Truth and Reconciliation in South Africa*, Philadelphia: University of Pennsylvania Press, 23–44.

Van der Wilt, H. & Nollkaemper, A. (eds.) (2009).
System Criminality in International Law, Cambridge: Cambridge University Press.

Van Dijk, J. (2009).
Free the Victim: A Critique of the Western Conception of Victimhood, *The International Review of Victimology* 16(1), 1–33.

Van Dijk, J.J.M., Groenhuijsen, M.S., & Winkel, F.W. (2007).
Victimologie. Voorgeschiedenis en Stand van Zaken, *Justitiële Verkenningen* 33(3), 9–29.

Van Liempt, A. (2002).
Kopgeld – Nederlands Premiejagers Op Zoek Naar Joden 1943, Amsterdam: Uitgeverij Balans.

Van Ness, D.W. (2002).
Creating Restorative Systems, in: Walgrave, L. (ed.), *Restorative Justice and the Law*, Cullompton, Devon: Willan Publishing, 130–149.

Van Sliedregt, E. (2003).
The Criminal Responsibility of Individuals for Violations of International Humanitarian Law, The Hague: TMC Asser Press.

Van Swaaningen, R. (1997).
Critical Criminology: Visions from Europe, London/Thousand Oaks/New Delhi: Sage Publications.

Vanspauwen, K. & Savage, T (2008).
Restorative Justice and Truth-Seeking in the DR Congo: Much Closing for Peace, Little Opening for Justice, in: Aertsen, I., Arsovskla, J., Rohne, H.-C., Valinas, M., & Vanspauwen, K. (eds.), *Restoring Justice after Large-Scale Violent Conflicts. Kosovo, DR Congo and the Israeli-Palestinian Case*, Cullompton, Devon: Willan Publishing, 392–411.

Vasiliev, S. (2009).
Article 68(3) and Personal Interests of Victims in the Emerging Practice of the ICC, in: Stahn, C. & Sluiter, G. (eds.), *The Emerging Practice of the International Criminal Court*, Leiden: Martinus Nijhoff Publishers, 635–690.

Vaughan, D. (2002).
Criminology and the Sociology of Organizations, *Crime, Law & Social Change* 37, 117–136.

Vaughan, D. (2007).
Beyond Macro- and Micro-Levels of Analysis, Organizations, and the Cultural Fix, in: Pontell, H.N. & Geis, G. (eds.), *International Handbook of White-Collar and Corporate Crime*, New York: Springer, 3–24.

Velásquez, L. (2007).
Maya Kem: Nuevo Paradigma de Integralidad en el Resarcimiento, in: Programa Nacional de Resarcimiento (ed.), *La Vida No Tiene Precio: Acciones y Omisiones de Resarcimiento en Guatemala*, Ciudad de Guatemala, Guatemala: Programa Nacional de Resarcimiento, 107–131.

Verpoorten, M. & Berlage, L. (2007).
Economic Mobility in Rural Rwanda: A Study of the Effects of War and Genocide at the Household Level, *Journal of African Economies* 16(3), 349–392.

Viano, E.C. (ed.) (1976).
Victims & Society, Washington D.C.: Visage Press.

Villa-Vicencio, C. (2000).
Why Perpetrators Should Not Always Be Prosecuted. Where the International Criminal Court and Truth Commissions Meet, *Emory Law Journal* 49, 205–222.

Villa-Vicencio, Ch. (2003).
Restorative Justice in Social Context: The South African Truth and Reconciliation Commission, in: Biggar, N. (ed.), *Burying the Past: Making Peace and Doing Justice After Civil Conflict*, Washington D.C.: Georgetown University Press, 235–250.

Villa-Vicencio, C. (2006).
Transitional Justice, Restoration, and Prosecution, in: Sullivan, D. & Tifft, L. (eds.), *Handbook of Restorative Justice. A Global Perspective*, London/New York: Routledge, 387–400.

Vinjamuri, R. & Snyder, C. (2004).
Advocacy and Scholarship in the Study of International War Crime Tribunals and Transitional Justice, *Annual Review of Political Science* 7, 345–362.

Viseur-Sellers, P. (2001).
Rule 89(C) and (D): At Odds or Overlapping with Rule 96 and Rule 95?, in: May, R., Tolbert, D., Hocking, J., Roberts, K., Jia, B.B., Mundis, D., & Oosthuizen, G. (eds.), *Essays on ICTY Procedure and Evidence: In Honour of Gabrielle Kirk McDonald*, The Hague/London/Boston: Kluwer Law International, 275–290.

Viseur-Sellers, P. (2007).
The 'Appeal' of Sexual Violence: Akayesu/Gacumbitsi Cases, in: Stefisyn, K. (ed.), *Gender-Based Violence in Africa*, Pretoria: University of Pretoria, 51–103.

Vold, G.B. (1958).
Theoretical Criminology, Oxford: Oxford University Press.

Von Hirsch, A. (1985).
Past or Future Crimes: Deservedness and Dangerousness in Sentencing Criminals, New Brunswick: Rutgers University Press.

Wald, P.M. (2002).
Dealing with Witnesses in War Crime Trials: Lessons from the Yugoslav Tribunal, *Yale Human Rights & Development Law Journal* 5, 217–239.

Waldorf, L. (2006).

Mass Justice for Mass Atrocity: Rethinking Local Justice as Transitional Justice, *Temple Law Review* 79(1), 1–87.

Walgrave, L. (2008).

Restorative Justice, Self-Interest and Responsible Citizenship, Cullompton, Devon: Willan Publishing, 11–43.

Walker, A. (2009).

Overcoming Speechlessness, New York: Seven Stories Press.

Walklate, S. (1990).

Researching Victims of Crime: Critical Criminology, *Social Justice* 17, 25–42.

Walklate, S. (1992).

Appreciating the Victim: Conventional, Realist or Critical Victimology?, in: Matthews, R. & Young, J. (eds.), *Issues in Realist Criminology*, London/Newbury Park/New Delhi: Sage, 102–118.

Walklate, S. (2007).

Imagining the Victim of Crime, Maidenhead, England: Open University Press.

Waller, J. (2007).

Becoming Evil. How Ordinary People Commit Genocide and Mass Killing, 2nd edition, Oxford: Oxford University Press.

Walster, E., Walster, G.W., & Berscheid, E. (1973).

New Directions in Equity Research, *Journal of Personality and Social Psychology*, 25(2), 151–176.

Ward, T. (2004).

State Harms, in: Hillyard, P., Pantazis, C., Tombs, S., & Gordon, D. (eds.), *Beyond Criminology. Taking Harm Seriously*, London: Pluto Press, 84–100.

Watson, D.R. (1976).

Some Conceptual Issues in the Social Identification of Victims and Offenders, in: Viano, E.C. (ed.), *Victims & Society*, Washington D.C.: Visage Press, 60–71.

Weber, M. (2002).

Economía y Sociedad, España: Fondo de Cultura Económica [*Wirtschaft und Gesellschaft. Grundriss der Verstehender Sociologie*, 1956] (Translated by Medina Echavarría).

Weitekamp, E.G.M., Parmentier, P., Vanspauwen, K., Valiñas, M., & Gerits, R. (2006).

How to Deal with Mass Victimization and Gross Human Rights Violations. A Restorative Justice Approach, in: Ewald, U. & Turković, K. (eds.), *Large-Scale Victimization as a Potential Source of Terrorist Activities*, Amsterdam: IOS Press, 217–241.

Wemmers, J.M. (1996).

Victims in the Criminal Justice System, Amsterdam: WODC/Kugler Publications.

Wemmers, J.M. (2003).

Introduction à la Victimologie, Montreal: Les Presses de l'Université de Montréal.

Wemmers, J. (2009).

Victims and the International Criminal Court: Evaluating the Success of the ICC with Respect to Victims, *International Review of Victimology* 16(2), 211–227.

Wemmers, J.M. & Canuto, M. (2002).

Victims' Experiences, Expectations, and Perceptions of Restorative Justice: A Critical Review of the Literature, Department of Justice Canada, Ottawa.

Wemmers, J. & Cyr, K. (2006).

What Fairness Means to Crime Victims: A Social Psychological Perspective on Victim-Offender Mediation, *Applied Psychology in Criminal Justice* 2(2), 102–128.

Wemmers, J. & De Brouwer, A.L.M. (2011).

Globalization and Victims' Rights at the International Criminal Court, in: Letschert, R.M. & Van Dijk, J.J.M., *The New Faces of Victimhood*, Dordrecht/ Heidelberg/London/New York: Springer.

Werle, G. (2009a).

Principles of International Criminal Law, 2nd edition, The Netherlands: T.M.C. Asser Press.

Werle, G. (2009b).

General Principles of International Criminal Law, in: Cassese, A. (ed.), *The Oxford Companion to International Criminal Justice*, Oxford: Oxford University Press, 54–62.

Weschler, I. (1990).

A Miracle, a Universe: Settling Accounts with Torturers, Chicago: The University of Chicago Press.

Wessels, M. (2006).

Child Soldiers – from Violence to Protection, Cambridge: Harvard University Press.

Westcott, H., Davies, G., & Bull, R. (eds.) (2002).

Children's Testimony: A Handbook of Psychological Research and Forensic Practice, Chichester: John Wiley & Sons.

Westermeyer, J. & Williams, M. (1998).

Three Categories of Victimization Among Refugees in a Psychiatric Clinic, in: Jaranason, J.M. & Popkin, M. (eds.), *Caring for Victims of Torture*, Washington D.C.: American Psychiatric Association, 61–87.

Wiesel, E. (1985).

Listen to the Wind, in: Abrahamson, I. (ed.), *Against Silence: The Voice and Vision of Elie Wiesel 1*, New York: Holocaust Library, 166–168.

Williams, J.J. (2000).

Truth and Reconciliation – Beyond the TRC Process and Findings, *Ecquid Novi* 21(2), 207–219.

Winkel, F.W. (2007).

Posttraumatic Anger. Missing Link in the Wheel of Misfortune, Inaugural Lecture at Tilburg University, Nijmegen: Wolf Legal Publishers.

Wise, E.M., Podgor, E.S., & Clark, R.S. (2004).

International Criminal Law: Cases and Materials, New York: Lexis Nexis.

Wood, E.J. (2009).

Armed Groups and Sexual Violence: When is Wartime Rape Rare?, *Politics & Society* 37(1), 131–161.

Yehoshua, A.B. (2006).

A Woman in Jerusalem, New York: Harcourt (Translated by Hillel Halkin).

Yule, W. (2000).
From Pogroms to "Ethnic Cleansing": Meeting the Needs of War Affected Children, *Journal of Child Psychology and Psychiatry* 41(6), 695–702.

Zack-Williams, T.B. (2006).
Child Soldiers in Sierra Leone and the Problems of Demobilisation, Rehabilitation and Reintegration into Society: Some Lessons for Social Workers in War-torn Societies, *Social Work Education* 25(2), 119–128.

Zalaquett, J. (1990).
Confronting Human Rights Violations Committed by Former Governments: Applicable Principles and Political Constrains, *Hamline Law Review* 13, 623–660.

Zappalà, S. (2010).
The Rights of Victims v. The Rights of the Accused, *Journal of International Criminal Justice* 8, 137–164.

Zawati, H.M. (2007).
Impunity or Immunity: Wartime Male Rape and Sexual Torture as a Crime against Humanity, *Torture Quarterly Journal on Rehabilitation of Torture Victims and Prevention of Torture* 17(1), 27–47.

Zawati, H.M. (2011) [forthcoming].
Symbolic Judgements or Judging Symbols: Fair Labelling and the Dilemma of Prosecuting Gender-Based Crimes under the Statutes of the International Criminal Tribunals, Philadelphia: University of Pennsylvania Press.

Zegveld, L. (2010).
Victims' Reparations Claims and International Criminal Courts, *Journal of International Criminal Justice* 8(1), 79–111.

Zehr, H. (2002).
The Little Book of Restorative Justice, Intercourse, Pennsylvania: Good Books.

Zimbardo, P. (2007).
The Lucifer Effect, New York: Random House.

Zinsstag, E. (2012) [forthcoming].
Sexual Violence against Women in Armed Conflicts: Towards a Transitional Justice Perspective, Antwerp/Oxford: Intersentia.

Zwi, A.B., Garfield, R., & Loretti, A. (2002).
Collective Violence, in: Krug, E.G., Dahlberg, L.L., Mercy, G.A., Zwi, A.B., & Lozano, R. (eds.), *World Report on Violence and Health*, Geneva: World Health Organization, 213–239.